PRINCIPLES OF PSYCHOLOGY

To the Student:

A Study Guide for the textbook is available through your college bookstore under the title *Study Guide to Accompany Principles of Psychology*, 6th edition, by Gregory A. Kimble, Norman Garmezy, and Edward Zigler. The Study Guide can help you with course material by acting as a tutorial, review, and study aid. If the Study Guide is not in stock, ask the bookstore manager to order a copy for you.

PRINCIPLES OF PSYCHOLOGY

SIXTH EDITION

GREGORY A. KIMBLE
Duke University

NORMAN GARMEZY
University of Minnesota

EDWARD ZIGLER
Yale University

JOHN WILEY & SONS
New York Chichester Brisbane
Toronto Singapore

Photo Researcher: Inge King
Photo Editor: Stella Kupferberg
Text and Cover Designer: Laura C. Ierardi
Cover Photographer: Geoff Gove/The Image Bank
Production Manager: Rose Mary Scarano
Development Editor: Priscilla Todd
Basic Book Coordinator: Edward Starr

Library of Congress Cataloging in Publication Data:

Kimble, Gregory A.
  Principles of psychology.

  Rev. ed. of: Principles of general psychology.
5th ed. c1980.
  Includes bibliographical references and indexes.
  1. Psychology. I. Garmezy, Norman. II. Zigler,
Edward Frank, 1930–   . III. Kimble, Gregory A.
Principles of general psychology. IV. Title.
BF121.K52 1984   150   83–21716
ISBN 0-471–86284–3
Printed in the United States
10 9 8 7 6 5 4 3 2 1

To Lucille, Edith, and Bernice

About the Authors

Gregory A. Kimble is at present professor of psychology at Duke University. He was formerly chairman of the Psychology Department and the director of undergraduate and graduate studies at this university. Earlier he taught at Brown and Yale universities and was professor and chairman of the Department of Psychology at the University of Colorado. Dr. Kimble frequently contributes to professional journals on topics pertaining to learning and memory. He edited the book *Foundations of Conditioning and Learning* and is the author of *Hilgard and Marquis' Conditioning and Learning, How to Use (and Misuse) Statistics,* and *The Departmental Chairmanship: A Survival Manual.* Dr. Kimble has served as chairman of the Experimental Psychological Research Review Committee, of the National Institute of Mental Health, and was a NATO fellow at Cambridge University. He is a member of the Society of Experimental Psychologists and is currently the chairman of the American Psychological Association's *Psychology Today* Advisory Committee.

Norman Garmezy is now professor of psychology at the University of Minnesota; earlier appointments were clinical professor of psychiatry at the School of Medicine, University of Rochester, and professor of psychology at Duke University. Dr. Garmezy was a visiting fellow at the Center for Advanced Study in the Behavioral Sciences, 1979–1980. He has been honored with the 1974 Distinguished Scientist Award, Section III (Experimental), Division of Clinical Psychology, American Psychological Association; with the Stanley Dean Award for basic research in schizophrenia; and with the Lifetime Research Career Award of the National Institute of Mental Health. He is a member of the APA's Board of Scientific Affairs, chairman of the MacArthur Foundation's Network on Research on Risk and Protective Factors in the Major Mental Disorders, and a member of the Scientific Advisory Committee to the Health Committee of the MacArthur Foundation. Dr. Garmezy is corresponding editor of the *Journal of Child Psychology and Psychiatry* and coeditor of the recently published *Stress, Coping, and Development in Children.* He has published widely on topics concerning personality, psychopathology, children at risk for mental retardation, and stress research.

The current appointments of Edward Zigler at Yale University are Sterling Professor of Psychology, head of the Psychology Section of the Yale Child Study Center, and Director of the Bush Center in Child Development and Social Policy. He was the first director of the Office of Child Development and headed the United States Children's Bureau, Department of Health, Education and Welfare, from 1970 through 1972. Dr. Zigler was one of the planners of this country's Head Start Program. He is coauthor of several books, including *Socialization and Personality Development* and *Mental Retardation: The Developmental-Difference Controversy.* He has won the Dale Richmond Memorial Award from the American Academy of Pediatrics, the Gunnar Dybwad Distinguished Scholar in the Behavioral and Social Sciences Award, bestowed by the National Association for Retarded Citizens, the G. Stanley Hall Award and the Award for Distinguished Contributions to Psychology in the Public Interest, both given by the American Psychological Association, and the Career Research Award of the American Academy on Mental Retardation. Dr. Zigler was named one of the honorary commissioners of the United States Commission for the International Year of the Child.

PREFACE

Our first aim in preparing this sixth edition of *Principles of Psychology* was to bring our coverage of the field up to date, but our more important aims were to achieve a better organization and a more even balance of subject matter. Thus about one-third of the references for this edition are new, ten percent having dates in the 1980s, and important adjustments have been made in the space devoted to particular psychological topics and in the sequence of chapters.

As with earlier editions of this book, our introductory chapter gives the student a general view of the field of psychology and its methods. Then we move to a series of chapters that cover the interactions between biological and environmental factors in the determination of behavior. The progression is from biological psychology to social psychology. We introduce the subjects of behavioral genetics and the evolution of behavior early in the book; later on cognitive development and social development are given in two successive chapters. We have tightened the presentation of psychopathology and increased the coverage of social psychology to two chapters, one on social cognition and one on social influence.

To look at the revision in somewhat closer detail, we have given more attention to the endocrine system, problem solving, sexuality, stress, moral development, cognitive assessment of personality, and cognitive therapy. Throughout the book there is a recognition of the fact that psychology has progressed to the point that it is ready to "give itself away," to contribute to the solutions to important human problems.

An important aspect of the book is our continuing effort to enhance its appeal to students. In the various stages of its development, the manuscript was reviewed by a great many people—students, their instructors, other colleagues, and our editor—all of whom provided reactions that influenced the style and content of the book.

SUPPLEMENTARY MATERIALS

This textbook is one of an extensive number of items available for use in planning an effective course in introductory psychology. The others are an *Instructor's Resource Manual*, prepared by Gregory Kimble and David Rubin; a *Student Study Guide*, developed by William F. Hodges and Richard Olson; a *Test File*, a set of 2000 test items, prepared by Ryan D. Tweney and Michael Doherty; and a series of 190 four-color slides with an accompanying *Instructor's Manual*, created by Richard A. Kasschau.

Although the chapters of the textbook are organized according to our preferred sequence, other arrangements are practicable, as are adjustments of the text material to fit courses with individual emphases. The *Instructor's Resource Manual* describes some of these possibilities. A set of "Lecture Modules" and materials for class demonstration make up the body of this manual.

The separate *Test File* consists of multiple-choice items with answers and references to the pages in the text where the subject covered by each item is discussed. The *Test File* is also available on computer tape and diskette for the convenience of adopters.

Hodges and Olson maintain in the *Student Study Guide* the same style that has won universal approval for earlier editions. The guide provides students with detailed guidance on how to study as well as giving them practice in taking objective examinations.

Richard Kasschau's series of four-color slides illuminate topics from every chapter in the book.

ACKNOWLEDGMENTS

Many people have made vital contributions to this revision, and we are grateful for the opportunity to acknowledge their assistance. First and foremost were the invaluable contributions of those who wrote three chapters for the book: Rosa Cascione, who revised Chapter 3, "Nervous and Endocrine Systems," and Edward E. Jones and Charles Lord, who wrote Chapter 18, "Social Cognition and Social Behavior," and Chapter 19, "Social Influence and Group Processes."

We also wish to thank our close colleagues who provided invaluable assistance: Winnie Berman, Yale University; David Rubin, Duke University; Victoria Seitz, Yale University; Sally Styfco, Yale University. Our reviewers guided us well with their many insightful suggestions: Patrick Campbell, Wright State University; Robert Emery, University of Virginia; Robert Fox, Vanderbilt University; Donald Heth, University of Alberta; William Hodos, University of Maryland; Neil MacMillan, Massachusetts Institute of Technology; Susan Mineka, University of Wisconsin; Sigfried Soli, University of Maryland; Dennis Turk, Yale University; Ryan Tweney, Bowling Green State University.

The following students at Duke University read most of the manuscript in its early drafts and made comments that have improved the appeal of the book to students: Frances Johnson, Lisa Kronfeld, and John Wiener.

Several persons contributed generously of their time in the preparation of the manuscript: Kathy Beck, Edna Bissette, Hazel Carpenter, Amby Peach, Verble Roberts, and Marge Williams, all of Duke University. We owe a very special note of thanks to Shari Alexander of Duke University, who brought her remarkable command of the intricacies of word processing to bear on the preparation of the manuscript.

Finally, we are much indebted to the staff of John Wiley and Sons for its strong support throughout the project—to Priscilla Todd for the care she brought to the editing of the manuscript; to Rose Mary Scarano for the efficient way in which she moved the manuscript through production; to Stella Kupferberg for her creativity in photographic research; to Laura Ierardi for her artistic design work on text and cover; and to Carol Luitjens for her sponsoring support and coordination of the project throughout.

Durham, North Carolina   *Gregory A. Kimble*
Minneapolis, Minnesota   *Norman Garmezy*
New Haven, Connecticut   *Edward Zigler*

CONTENTS

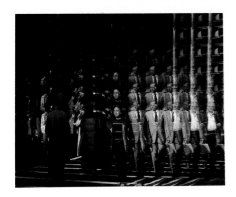
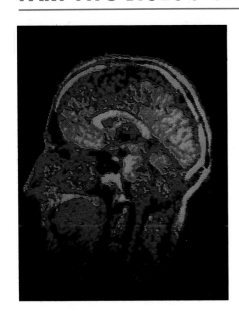

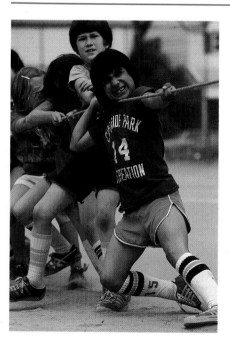

PART ONE INTRODUCTION

Picasso, Pablo. *Portrait of Jaqueline with Crossed Hands.*/Art Resource.

CHAPTER 1 THE SCIENCE AND PROFESSION OF PSYCHOLOGY

Psychology began its existence as a separate discipline a little over a hundred years ago. Many people set the beginning date as 1879, the year in which Wilhelm Wundt founded the first psychological laboratory at Leipzig University, in what is now the German Democratic Republic. In its earliest days psychology concentrated on the study of the sensory processes, perception, simple learning, and memory. Gradually, however, the field has expanded to the point that it now covers a range of topics broad enough to touch the lives of all of us. As this expansion took place, psychology developed along two parallel tracks to become both a science and a profession.

As a science psychology is usually defined in terms of its subject matter, sometimes as the science of behavior, sometimes as the science of mental activity. Fifty years ago the difference between these two definitions was a matter of bitter dispute. Some psychologists criticized the definition in terms of mental activity as too subjective. "How can there possibly be a science of anything as intangible as mental life?" these critics asked. Those who accepted the mentalistic definition responded that psychology must include these intangibles. Not to do so and to confine the science to behavior is to omit everything that is interesting and important in the field. Now most of the bitterness has disappeared. As the pages of this book will show, the science of psychology has important things to say on both topics, which no longer seem as different as they once did.

In 1875 Wilhelm Wundt (1832–1920) came to Leipzig. Four years later he began research that would be his first published in psychology. The year 1879 is usually given for the founding of his laboratory and of the discipline.

OVERVIEW

One of the most useful things a student can do as an aid to study is to obtain a general overview of the material to be learned. Even before you read on, it would be a good idea to spend half an hour leafing through the pages of this book, noting as you do the topics that are covered, and stopping now and then to read a paragraph or two on anything that looks interesting. Your first reaction as you make this survey is likely to be an impression of enormous heterogeneity because psychology ranges from what is almost biology to what is almost sociology. Your second reaction may be to ask, almost simultaneously, whether it is even conceivable that all these subjects are related. Can psychology possibly be a single discipline? The answer to this important question is yes, at least in the sense that we can begin with almost any important kind of behavior and show the relevance to it of many different kinds of psychological knowledge.

The Many Faces of Depression

To illustrate this last point, let us begin with the following case history taken from a contemporary textbook on abnormal psychology (Davison and Neal, 1982).

> Mr. J. was a fifty-one-year-old industrial engineer who, since the death of his wife five years earlier, had been suffering from continuing episodes of depression marked by extreme social withdrawal and occasional thoughts of suicide. His wife had died in an automobile accident during a shopping trip which he himself was to have made but had canceled because of professional responsibilities. His self-blame for her death, which became evident immediately after the funeral and was regarded by his friends and relatives as transitory, deepened as the months, and then years, passed by. He began to drink, sometimes heavily, and when thoroughly intoxicated would plead to his deceased wife for forgiveness. He lost all capacity for joy—his friends could not recall when they had seen him smile. His gait was typically slow and labored, his voice usually tearful, his posture stooped. Once a gourmet, he had lost all interest in food and good wine, and on those increasingly rare occasions when friends invited him for dinner, this previously witty, urbane man could barely manage to engage in small talk. As might be expected, his work record deteriorated markedly, along with his psychological condition. Appointments were missed and projects haphazardly started and then left unfinished. He was referred by his physician for psychotherapy after he had spent a week closeted in his home. Not long afterward, he seemed to emerge from his despair and began to feel his old self again (p. 231).

Mr. J.'s disorder was **depression.** Further description of this disorder appears in Chapter 16, and the forms of therapy available to such patients are discussed in Chapter 17. The more important point for examining the unity of psychology is that the literature on depression makes contact with many other aspects of psychology.

For example, many of the symptoms of depression are disorders of motivated behavior which is discussed in Chapter 9. The patient may have a poor appetite for food and lose weight or sometimes have a larger appetite and gain weight. Frequently there is a shift in activity level. Behavior may slow down and become lethargic or it may speed up and become agitated. The emotions of the patient are also disturbed (Chapter 10). A sad, depressed mood is typical. Often the individual loses interest in activities that had once brought great pleasure. A negative self-concept and feelings of worthlessness and guilt are common. The thought processes (Chapter 7) also suffer. The patient may find it difficult to concentrate on anything for very long. Reasoning may be illogical. For example, a depressed student might conclude that the low grade received on an exam is just another indication of the hopelessness of life.

As is common in psychopathology, Mr. J.'s symptoms differ from experiences that all of us have only in their severity. In fact, some of the most important research on depression was begun by testing (Chapter 13) the depressive tendencies of college students, who differ considerably in the extent to which they show these tendencies (Table 1.1). Some students experience a great deal more sadness, pessimism, and guilt than others. They dislike themselves and sometimes consider suicide. These depressed students seem particularly vulnerable to to the effects of punishment and to the loss of a source of rewards. Sigmund Freud (Chapter 15) developed a theory of depression that emphasized these vulnerabilities, but Freudian theory was somewhat vague. The learning theorists (Chapter 8), who also attempt to understand depression, have been more explicit. They have noted that much of our behavior continues only if it is rewarded; if rewards no longer follow, the individual ceases to act and, in a

Many different kinds of psychological knowledge contribute to our understanding of depression.

Table 1.1 Sample Items from a Depression Inventory

Attitudes	*	Depression Inventory
Sadness	0	I do not feel sad.
	1	I feel sad.
	2	I am sad all the time and I can't snap out of it.
	3	I am so sad or unhappy that I can't stand it.
Pessimism	0	I am not particularly discouraged about the future.
	1	I feel discouraged about the future.
	2	I feel I have nothing to look forward to.
	3	I feel that the future is hopeless and that things cannot improve.
Guilt	0	I don't feel particularly guilty.
	1	I feel guilty a good part of the time.
	2	I feel quite guilty most of the time.
	3	I feel guilty all of the time.
Self-dislike	0	I don't feel disappointed in myself.
	1	I am disappointed in myself.
	2	I am disgusted with myself.
	3	I hate myself.
Self-accusations	0	I don't feel I am worse than anybody else.
	1	I am critical of myself for my weaknesses or mistakes.
	2	I blame myself all the time for my faults.
	3	I blame myself for everything bad that happens.
Suicidal ideas	0	I don't have any thoughts of killing myself.
	1	I have thoughts of killing myself, but I would not carry them out.
	2	I would like to kill myself.
	3	I would kill myself if I had the chance.

* By checking 0, 1, 2, or 3 for each of these and other items, students indicate a degree of depression. The attitudes in the left column are not part of the inventory; they are listed to indicate what each group of items measures.

From Beck, 1978, as modified by Davison and Neale, 1982.

sense, gives up. According to this theory, in losing his wife, Mr. J. lost an important source of reward, and he gave up in resignation.

Of course, not everyone who suffers the loss of an important source of reward becomes depressed. People differ in their reactions to such happenings. It has been demonstrated that depressed students tend to remember their incorrect answers to questions better than they remember their correct answers.

One account of depression derived from learning theory treats the disorder as a form of **learned helplessness.** The original experiments on learned helplessness were done on dogs (see page 267). In these experiments animals that experienced painful electric shock over which they had no control behaved as thought they were helpless when control became possible. Later investigators interpreted the feelings of worthlessness of the depressed person as similar to this learned helplessness.

Studies with college students were soon to show that failure has the same consequences as uncontrollable physical punishment; it too causes learned helplessness. But new aspects of the depressive reaction also came to light. It was discovered that although failure contributes, the causes to which the individual attributes failure are important. Such thinking brings attribution theory, an idea from social psychology (Chapter 18), to bear on depression. Depressed individuals tend to blame their failures on personal faults, which they consider both persistent and pervasive. People who are not depressed tend to blame failure on external circumstances; they consider it to be of short duration and specific to the situation.

Studies of learned helplessness have also led to the discovery that physiological mechanisms are involved. The procedures that create learned helplessness in animals lead to the release of morphinelike substances (endorphins) in the brain (Chapter 3), reducing sensitivity to pain (Chapter 4). This discovery of a physiological aspect of a phenomenon related to depression inevitably leads to the notion that people may inherit a predisposition to develop a depressive disorder. The evidence for such causation has been growing. One very explicit hypothesis is that a dominant gene on the chromosome which determines sex is the culprit. The evidence for this theory is that female relatives of depressed patients are about twice as likely to be depressed themselves as male relatives are. These **concordance rates,** as they are called, are about 50 percent for patient-mother and patient-sister pairs. That is, about 50 percent of the mothers and sisters of depressed patients are also depressed. The concordance rates for patient-father and patient-brother pairs are about 25 percent.

Explanation in Psychology

The argument for the interconnectedness of the many subjects covered by psychology make an even more basic point. The causation of any significant psychological phenomenon will be complex. The individual's biological heritage and many conditions in the environment all contribute. Psychology is not a discipline in which explanations can be expected to be simple.

The question of what constitutes explanation in psychology leads in many directions and to some of the most fundamental issues in the history of the field. As basic as any of these is the fact that, when we speak of explanations of behavior, we imply that human behavior has causes that can be discovered, that behavior is **determined.** Most psychologists accept this deterministic assumption, even in its extreme version, which holds that all behavior, without exception, is determined. Such acceptance validates a search for the causes of creative genius, mother love, and the love of God and country, and for the reasons why people sometimes choose to die rather than violate ethical principles. Considered in these terms, the conception that behavior is determined is revolutionary in the history of ideas.

As with other revolutionary ideas, this one has not been easy for society to accept. For if human behavior is detemined, this means that the most personal and private aspects of our lives are potential matters for scientific understanding and even control. Many people would prefer to let such things remain in the realm of mystery. They cannot—perhaps should not—be explained scientifically.

The scientist's reaction to this attitude is that it is the business of science to explain away the mysteries of the world. The largest remaining mystery is human behavior. Nothing in the fact that the subject matter is behavior makes it immune to scientific understanding or, for moral reasons, beyond the scope of science. The extent of the mystery is an index of the importance of explaining it, not a reason for protecting behavior from study by the methods of science. The vigor with which the opposition advances its arguments makes it very important that we indicate clearly what we mean by explaining behavior.

Circular "Explanations." A set of all too common "explanations" tells us that behavior can be accounted for in terms of psychological states. Mr. J. has lost his interest in life *because* he suffers from depression. Little brother never will do as he is told *because* he is in a stage of negativism. The supervisor of people on a certain job browbeats his supervisees but knuckles under to his own supervisor *because* he has an authoritarian personality. A talented acquaintance refuses to enter her paintings in a juried show *because* of an inferiority complex. A professional associate always performs a little better than anyone else *because* he is strongly competitive. The valedictorian attained that honor *because* she was the most intelligent person in the graduating class.

The problem with these "explanations" is that they are circular. To say that little brother is in a negativistic stage says that he is in a stage in which he refuses to do as he is told. Saying that he refuses to do as he is told because he is in a negativistic stage, therefore, says that he refuses to do what he is told because he refuses to do what he is told. The behavior to be explained and the explanation turn out to be the same thing. The circular quality of the other "explanations" listed is equally apparent. More acceptable explanations of behavior will have to break such circles. This means that the behavior to be accounted for must be related to something other than itself. In psychology the chief candidates to serve as this something else are environmental circumstances and the inherited physical and physiological makeup of the individual.

Environmental and Biological Interactions. The extent to which behavior depends on environmental and biological factors is a question that we shall encounter frequently. It takes several different forms. In psychological development (Chapter 11 and 12) it is the question whether youngsters develop as a result of learning or through physical maturation. In interpretations of differences in intelligence (Chapter 2), personality (Chapter 15), and psychopathology (Chapter 16), it is the question whether traits are hereditary or acquired through experience. The study of perception (Chapter 5) raises the nature-nurture, or nativism-empiricism, issue. Are we born with the capacity to perceive the environment accurately or do we develop it through experience? In the case of motivation (Chapter 9), are we driven by inborn instincts or by learned motives?

As its understanding of behavior has grown, psychology has come to appreciate the contributions of both environmental and hereditary factors. Take, for example, the delinquent behavior which brings some young people repeatedly to the attention of the law. Several lines of evidence point to an inherited physiological basis for such behavior. Delinquent individuals tend to have parents who had similar problems themselves. Even as very young babies they were "difficult children," given to excessive crying and to temper tantrums when frustrated. Later on they tended to be somewhat limited in intelligence and to be aggressive and impulsive, traits which are in part inherited. Delinquents are also more frequently left-handed than nondelinquents (Gabrielli and Mednick, 1980), and handedness also depends substantially on heredity.

On the environmental side, delinquent youngsters tend to come from poor homes, in which alcoholism, crime, poverty, and family discord prevail. The parents give their children little attention and even less affection. They are unconcerned about their frequently unacceptable behavior at school, in the neighborhood, and elsewhere.

The thoughtful student will have noted that these biological and environmental factors are not purely biological or environmental; at best, they are more biological or more environmental. This observation serves only to emphasize an important point. The key question is not whether these two sets of factors contribute to the determination of behavior—they both clearly do—but rather how their joint contribution comes about. The fairly obvious answer to this question seems to be a correct one, at least as a first approximation. Biological factors provide the individual with a certain potential for accomplishment; environmental factors determine how much of this potential becomes actuality.

SUMMARY

In the century of its history, psychology has developed both as a science and as a profession. It has also acquired a great deal of information on a very heterogeneous set of subject matters. One of the important tasks facing psychology is to discover how all this varied information fits a general pattern. As a science psychology seeks an understanding of human behavior and mental activity. The broad range of topics studied by psychologists indicates that explanations in this field are sure to be complex. In general, however, explanation will come down to determining the contributions of hereditary and environmental factors.

THE SCIENCE OF PSYCHOLOGY

In its search for explanations of behavior, psychology applies the methods of science, recognizing that other ways of understanding are possible. Writers such as Dostoevski and Shakespeare, many philosophers, and the theologians have all offered their interpretations of human behavior and experience. The difference is one of emphasis. Psychology relies more on controlled observation and experiment; the others rely more on common knowledge and intuition. But the dividing line between the scientific approach to understanding behavior and the other approaches is not a sharp one. Particularly in the beginning stages of study in an area, psychologists, too, must resort to common knowledge.

To illustrate, case histories such as that of Mr. J. are not unlike the stories of characters created by authors of fiction. Case histories identify phenomena that cry for explanation. Why did Mr. J. become depressed? Was he somehow more vulnerable than people who do not break down in this way? Could his depression have been prevented? Was psychotherapy responsible for his recovery? By raising questions, case histories often provide the initial motivation for the study of a psychological subject. In and of themselves, however, case histories only raise such questions; answers require more powerful methods.

The various psychological methods to be discussed in this chapter vary in the extent to which the investigator is able to control and manipulate conditions. In a true experiment, the most important and powerful of these methods, a great deal of such control is possible. At the other extreme are the so-called correlational methods, in which no control at all is exercised. These methods sometimes deal with events as they occur in the real world. In between are the naturalistic experiments. In them some control is possible, but less than in a true experiment. For this reason some psychologists include them among the correlational methods. The following pages describe these procedures, beginning with the experimental method in which control is greatest and moving on to naturalistic experiments and correlational procedures in which the control becomes less and less.

Experimental Method

Let us begin with a straightforward experiment on an important subject. If our greatest resource is our children, there is reason to fear that we are squandering this resource, just as we have squandered the lesser ones represented by our forests, wildlife populations, and mineral reserves. In particular, our children are being short-changed by the educational system, emerging from it with less than minimal basic skills. The poor and otherwise disadvantaged suffer the most in this situation. The experimental work to be described suggests a possible way of helping children learn to read (Wallach and Wallach, 1976), perhaps alleviating to some extent an important educational problem of disadvantaged children.

The children in this study came from the first grades of two inner-city public schools on the south side of Chicago. They were predominantly from low-income families and black. The scores that these children had obtained on a test of reading readiness were so low that it was doubted that they would learn very much in the first grade. Two groups of thirty-six children each were matched child by child for sex, reading readiness, and the classroom from which they came.

After this had been accomplished, thirty-six of these children were assigned to a **control group** and thirty-six were placed in an **experimental group.** A control group is a reference group in an experiment. Usually the subjects in a control group do not receive any special treatment. The experimental group does receive this treatment. In this study the children in the experimental group were tutored in reading, according to a special program developed by Michael and Lise Wallach. This program emphasizes the skill of recognizing the sounds that letters stand for and of using them in words. The Wallachs believe that deficiencies in this skill are at the root of reading difficulties and must be corrected if a child is to learn to read. The children in the control group did not receive this tutoring.

The children in the experimental group were given their special tutoring and the others studied reading by the usual methods for a period of time. Then the reading ability of both groups of children was assessed in several ways. One measure was their score on a test requiring them to read twenty-five sentences correctly. Children in the experimental group had an average score of 16.08; those in the control group had an average score of 9.97.

Traditional Experimental Design

This study of reading with an experimental and a control group is the simplest type of experiment. It is useful to think of such experiments in terms of what happens in the three stages of the procedure (Figure 1.1).

Group		Stage of experiment		
		1 Equate groups	2 Experimental treatment	3 Evaluate outcome
	Experimental	Assess reading readiness	Special tutoring	Measure reading ability
	Control	Assess reading readiness	No special treatment	Measure reading ability

Figure 1.1
Two-group, three-stage experimental design. The entries indicate how this design applies to the Wallachs' (1976) experiment on reading.

Stage 1: Equating groups. When an experiment is begun, it is almost always with the belief that the special treatment employed will have an effect. Usually this comes down to the hope that groups initially the same will be different after the special treatment of one of them. The assumption of initial equality is crucial. In our sample experiment the outcome, better reading by the tutored group, could not have been attributed to the experimental treatment if the children in the control group were, for some reason, less gifted than those in the experimental group. To guard against this, the experimenters were careful to make the two groups as nearly equal as possible. The children in the control and experimental group were matched for age, sex, socioeconomic status, race, and, most importantly, reading readiness.

Stage 2: Experimental treatment. In the second stage of the study, the experimental group received special tutoring. We commonly refer to the special treatment in an experiment as an **independent variable.** A variable is any aspect or condition that can vary or any quantity that can change in value. It is called an independent variable if the experimenter can manipulate it in order to determine what effect this manipulation has on behavior, more specifically on another variable called the dependent variable, the ability to read in our example. In any simple experiment it is important to manipulate only one variable at a time. If more than one treatment were employed, it would be impossible to tell which was responsible for any differences that are evident at the end of the experiment. Because of this, experimenters go to great lengths to keep all conditions other than the manipulated one the same. The most important **controlled variables** in this experiment were the following. The control group and experimental groups were studied for the same period of time; the tests of reading ability for both groups were identical; the classroom environments were similar.

Stage 3: Evaluating outcomes. Attention is finally focused on the effects of the independent variable on the phenomenon of interest, scores on the reading test in this case. The "phenomenon of interest" just referred to is the **dependent variable** in an experiment. It is called dependent because it is affected by the manipulation of the independent variable and is, therefore, dependent on it. In psychology the dependent variable is usually a measure, direct or indirect, of the behavior of people in the experimental situation. In this case the measure is very direct, scores on the reading test, 9.97 for the control group and 16.08 for the experimental group. The difference of 6.11 points represents an improvement of about 52 percent in the tutored group. This outcome raises a question. Of what significance is this improvement of 52 percent? There are two answers to this important question.

The first of these two answers addresses the dependability of the result. No matter how carefully an experiment is done, accidents can happen. It is possible that most of the children in the experimental group accidentally happened to be children who learn to read easily, no matter how they are treated, and that the special tutoring contributed nothing. There are statistical methods of evaluating this possibility. These methods, the details of which will be given later (see page 653), provide an estimate of the probability that the result obtained was an accidental one that occurred "by chance" rather than being attributable to the special treatment given one group. In this experiment the probability was only 1 in 2000 that the experimental group scored better by chance rather than because they had been given special tutoring. Thus the investigators concluded that the result was **statistically significant,** that the result obtained is real in the sense of being reliable.

The second answer to the question of significance concerns the practical importance of the result. For this experiment the diminishing ability of the general population to read and write is one of the major crises facing the nation. Any procedure that promises to reverse that trend is significant.

Small-*N* Designs

In statistical notation the letter N stands for the number of participants in a study. In the experiment just described N was 72—thirty-six subjects in each of two groups. For many purposes it is desirable to have many subjects in a group. Other things being equal, the greater N is, the more dependable is the result; the more certain it is that the results apply generally. For certain purposes, however, it is useful to apply the experimental method to small groups of individuals or even to single individuals. These applications are called **small-*N* designs** and ***N*-of-1 designs** respectively.

ABAB Designs. Experiments with single or few subjects often have very practical applications. In one instance (Allen et al., 1964) two nursery school children had been a worry to their teacher because they played alone, refusing to interact, even with each other. Observation suggested that this isolated play was a device for getting attention from the teacher. An experiment to determine whether this hypothesis was true and also to correct the problem was devised. It consisted of four stages.

Stage 1: Observe baseline activity. Before they were given any special treatment, the children were observed for an hour on each of five days. During these periods the investigators made note of the percentage of their activities that was shared with other children. This was the dependent variable in the experiment. Stage 1, which is like stage 1 in the traditional experimental design, provided a measure of **baseline** activity to compare with activity produced by the introduction of an independent variable. In the **ABAB design** the letter A refers to the baseline condition.

Stage 2: Introduce independent variable. In stage 2 the teacher for six days paid attention to the children only when they interacted with other children. This procedure was the independent variable in the experiment, represented by the letter B. The children began to interact with other children when the teacher withheld attention unless they did so.

Stage 3: Return to baseline. In traditional experiments, whether the outcome is attributable to the experimental treatment or chance is dealt with by statistics. Although statistical analyses are usually possible in small-N studies, it is more common to answer this question by a **return to baseline,** that is, to withdraw the special treatment given in stage 2. If the behavior also returns to what it was originally, the change in behavior observed during stage 2 is attributed to the independent variable. So in this experiment the teacher stopped paying attention to the two children when they played with others. The two again isolated themselves in their play.

Stage 4: Reintroduce the independent variable. Finally, for another nine days, the teacher again paid attention to the children only when they interacted with other children, thus completing the ABAB design.

Results. Much of what is stated verbally in this book, and probably much of what your instructors present, will also be given in graphic form. Do not ignore or pass lightly over such presentations. They are important because they convey information very concisely.

Observing children at play.

The values of the independent variable in an experiment are represented on the horizontal axis of a graph, on its **x-axis** or **abscissa.** Values of the dependent variable are represented on the vertical axis, the **y-axis** or **ordinate.** Figure 1.2 makes a graphic presentation of the results of the experiment just described. The dependent variable, the percentge of activity shared with other children, is given on the ordinate of the graph. The abscissa corresponds to the twenty-five days of the experiment. The four panels in the graph lay out the ABAB design: baseline, independent variable, return to baseline, independent variable. You can see at a glance that more activities were shared with other children when the teacher paid attention to such behavior and fewer when she did not.

The line plotted in the last panel of Figure 1.2 suggests that the two youngsters now tended to spend more time with other children and had given up their isolated play. Follow-up observations over a period of weeks indicated that this was indeed the case. The fairly straightforward psychological treatment of rewarding social interactions had improved the behavior of the children.

SUMMARY

The wide-ranging interests of psychologists have led to the development of methods appropriate to studying them. The most powerful of these methods is the experimental method. In the simplest experiments one group of individuals, an experimental group, receives some special treatment and a control group

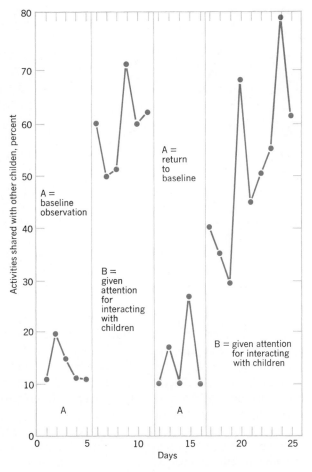

Figure 1.2
ABAB study of isolated behavior. The ordinate of the graph is the percentage of time that two children spent with other children. The abscissa is the series of 25 days over which the experiment was conducted. Section A, baseline observation, was a period when the children received no special treatment. In section B the independent variable was introduced. The teacher paid attention to the children when they played with other children. The third and fourth sections show what happened in a return to baseline (A) and in a reintroduction of the independent variable (B). (After Allen et al., 1964.)

does not. The treatment is considered an independent variable because the investigator manipulates it to determine its effect on some aspect of behavior called a dependent variable. Experiments proceed in three stages: equating groups, treating experimental and control groups differently, and assessing the effect on the behavior in which the psychologist is interested.

Although the traditional experiments study large groups of subjects, designs that can be applied to small groups of individuals or even single persons have been developed. In these small-N experiments the same subjects experience both the experimental and control conditions of the experiment. In the ABAB form of such experiments, the baseline observations of activity are made (A), experimental treatment is introduced (B), it is withdrawn and conditions are as they were at first (A), and then the experimental treatment is reintroduced (B).

In both types of experiments, the important question is whether the experimental treatment has a significant influence on behavior. In traditional experiments the assessment whether the effect is attributable to the treatment or could have occurred by chance is usually statistical. In small-N experiments the analysis is often graphic.

NATURALISTIC "EXPERIMENTS"

In the experiments described so far in this chapter, the investigator has taken an active hand in the procedures, creating the conditions whose effects were

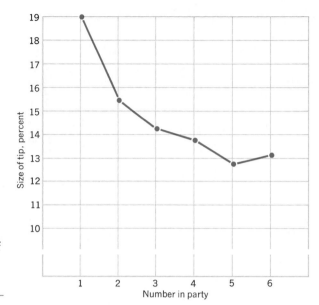

Figure 1.3
Cheaper by the bunch. As the number of people in a restaurant dinner party increases, the size of the tip goes down. (After Freeman et al., 1975.)

to be determined. In some situations it is possible to let nature handle the experimental manipulations.

If you have gone as a member of a large group to a good restaurant, you may have been infuriated to discover that an automatic 15 percent gratuity is added to the bill in some of these places. Restaurants have established this policy because the size of a customer's tip tends to vary inversely with the number of people in the party. The automatic gratuity forestalls dissatisfaction on the part of poorly tipped waiters. In one naturalistic experiment, which made the basic point, the investigator kept track of the tips left by parties of different sizes and plotted the percentage of the tip against the number of people in the party (Figure 1.3).

Obviously this study has most of the features of a true experiment. There is an independent variable, number of people in the party, and a dependent variable, size of the tip. The study was carried out in the same restaurants to control a number of other important variables. The chief difference between this and a true experiment was that the investigators could not manipulate the independent variable and had to accept, instead, the naturally occurring values of this variable, the number of people in the dinner party, as they happened.

The most important message of this study is not so much the results obtained as what everyone will recognize to be a more general implication. People alone or in small groups are identifiable, and if they leave a small tip the waiter will know it. Thus, under the waiter's eagle eye, they behave differently than they would in the relative anonymity of a dinner party of six or eight. More generally, this means that, when people know that their behavior is being observed, this fact alone influences their behavior. Recognition of this fact has altered methods of psychological experimentation and the look of experimental design.

Demand Characteristics of Experiments
Human participants in research treat the experience as though it places them under certain obligations, which may have nothing to do with the investigator's purposes. Their behavior may reflect these **demand characteristics** of the experiment rather than the hoped-for effect of the experimental treatment.

One experimenter's efforts to develop a set of tasks so meaningless or boring that college students would give up in disgust provide an amusing example. Martin Orne (1962) gave each of a group of students a stack of 2000 sheets of paper. Each sheet contained rows or random digits, which they were to add. The experimenter departed, and the students proceeded to tackle this Herculean project. Five and a half hours later, the students were still at the task! The experimenter surrendered.

Next he proceeded to make the task even more frustrating. The research participants were told that when they had finished adding the numbers of each sheet, they were to draw a card from a large pile, which would give them further instructions. Every card in the pile carried the same instruction.

> You are to tear up the sheet of paper which you have just completed into a minumum of thirty-two pieces and go on to the next sheet of paper an continue working as you did before; when you have completed this piece of paper, pick up the next card, which will instruct you further. Work as rapidly and accurately as possible (p. 777).

Certainly a meaningless task, but once again the students persisted.

A postexperimental inquiry explained this remarkable stamina; all the participants had perceived the task as a test of endurance. It is plain that research participants develop their own hypotheses about the experiments in which they serve, and these hypotheses may have little or no correspondence to the experimental intentions of the investigator.

The demand characteristics of a situation, as indicated in Orne's experiments, derive from cues that inform, and sometimes misinform, individuals of what is expected of them. Nowhere are such cues more important than in the doctor-patient relationship. The doctor's confident assertion that a proposed treatment will make the patient well can have more to do with recovery than the drugs prescribed or any other physical remedy the doctor may suggest. This is the **placebo effect.** Usually it operates in the direction of cure, for the doctor is by stereotype a healer.

The word *placebo* in Latin means, "I shall please," and a placebo has been defined as a medicine given "merely to humor the patient." It contains no active pharmacological substance but is administered for its psychological effect. A "sugar pill" is the well-known example. But the placebo effect applies to psychotherapies as well as to physical agents. Here, too, a cure may have nothing to do with the particular type of psychotherapy employed.

It is important to recognize that expectations other than the patient's may be involved. The clinical researcher usually has a heavy emotional investment in the worth of a particular therapy and may see more improvement in a treated patient than the objective facts warrant. The general term for this second effect is **experimenter bias.** Thus, in order to evaluate the success of any program of therapy, it is important to control for the overly optimistic evaluations of the therapist as well as for those of the patient.

In drug research, which will serve as an example, the usual method is a **double-blind procedure,** which exercises two types of control. (1) To control for effects on the patient of knowing that he or she is receiving a drug, experimenters give some patients placebos that are indistinguishable from the drug by sight, smell, and taste and have no pharmacological properties. Other patients receive the drug. (2) To control for effects on the investigators, judges who do not know which patients have received the drug and which the placebo rate their improvement.

Unobtrusive Measures

The message in all these studies, once again, is that scientific psychologists must always be alert to the possibility that obtained results may reflect their own biases or those of their research participants rather than the psychological process allegedly being studied. For a long time psychologists have also been aware of the danger that their results are at least contaminated by a sort of "guinea pig effect." If people know that they are being studied or tested, they may try to make a good impression, or sometimes a bad one. If the procedures suggest certain types of responses, people tend to comply or resist, depending on their perception of themselves and the situation. For these reasons many psychologists now propose that behavioral research rely to a greater extent on **unobtrusive measures.**

Unobtrusive measures make use of natural records, which participants need not know are being made (Webb and Campbell, 1981). They consist of evidence that accumulates in the course of everyday living and has a bearing on questions of psychological interest. The following are examples.

- Racial attitudes in college students were assessed by noting the degree of clustering of black and white students in lecture halls.
- The increasing fear of children being told a ghost story was measured in terms of the shrinking diameter of the circle of seated children.
- Rate of alcohol consumption in a "dry" town was determined by counting discarded liquor bottles in trashcans.
- One investigator studied the effects of television on library withdrawals by comparing them before and after television came to a community. Fiction withdrawals dropped off. Nonfiction was unaffected.
- Interest in a chick-hatching exhibit at the Chicago Museum of Science and Industry was evident from the fact that floor tiles in front of the exhibit lasted only six weeks, as compared to years before most other displays.
- Records of parking meter collections indicated the effect of a strike on business. There was a marked drop in revenue during the period of the strike.
- Measures of water pressure provided an index to patterns of television viewing. A marked periodicity of water pressure was linked to the beginning and end of programs, when people drew water for a drink or flushed the toilet.

Patterns of seating in the lunchroom may indicate that segregation exists in a supposedly integrated school.

- Even more dramatically, power blackouts in the United Kingdom coincided with the commercials on television. Apparently people simultaneously took that moment to plug in water heaters for making tea and overloaded the circuits of the national power system.
- In the world of baseball, studies of the histories of team managements have shown that many more former infielders and catchers, whose positions required considerable contact with fellow players, become managers than former pitchers and outfielders, whose positions required less.

SUMMARY

Many types of behavior are difficult or impossible to study by traditional experimental methods because both participants and experimenters may have needs and expectations that would affect the outcome of an experiment. Participants may evaluate the experimental situation in an unintended way and respond in terms of these demand characteristics of the experiment. Experimenters sometimes see experimental outcomes in terms of their hopes rather than in terms of the data. Naturalistic experiments can sometimes be carried out when a laboratory study seems likely to be biased by the operation of demand characteristics. These experiments often use unobtrusive measures, the information left behind by people in the normal course of living. The double-blind procedures used in medical research control for both of these sources of error. Subjects, being "blind" to the treatment they are in, are all influenced equally by placebo effects, a type of demand characteristic. Experimenters, being "blind" to the treatments received by individual subjects, are prevented from letting their biases influence their perceptions of outcomes.

CORRELATIONAL METHODS

In general terms, the aim of all the methods of psychology is to determine how behavior varies with different circumstances. In an experiment the investigator can manipulate an independent variable, control other possibly important variables, and observe the effect of the manipulation upon a dependent variable of interest. The so-called naturalistic experiments sacrifice some of this control, albeit for good reasons. In these naturalistic experiments the investigator cannot manipulate but can only select the values of the independent variable whose influences are to be studied. The **correlational methods,** to be described now, sacrifice further elements of control, again, however, for excellent reasons. Either the important variables cannot be manipulated or there are ethical reasons for not doing so.

Before we describe the methods themselves, it will be instructive to present several examples of the types of information that has been obtained with the correlational methods.

- Ratings of the quality of jug wines by expert tasters indicate that the judged quality and the price of these wines are closely related; the higher the price, the better the wine on the average.
- In a selection of districts in England, correlational methods revealed a strong relation between the amount of open park space in a district and the accident rate for children. The more park space, the lower the accident rate.
- In a selection of German communities, the percentage of babies who were breast-fed was found to be related to the mortality rate of these same infants; the higher the percentage of breast-fed babies, the lower the mortality rate of infants.

- The IQs of identical twins reared together are very similar, the higher or lower the IQ of one member of a pair of identical twins, the higher or lower the IQ of the other.

In addition to illustrating the type of information provided by the correlational method, these examples indicate the practical impossibility, ethical undesirability, or both of manipulating or controlling any aspect of such situations.

Direction and Degree of Relationship

In each of these examples, you will note that there is a relationship between two characteristics of the same thing: price and quality of jug wine, open spaces and children's accidents in English districts, breast feeding and mortality rates of babies in German communities, IQs of the two members of a pair of identical twins. In these examples the characteristics go together; they are co-related. The correlational methods search for such co-variation; **correlation coefficients** express the direction, positive or negative, and the degree or closeness of such relationships.

The first and last of the four examples just presented illustrate **positive correlations.** In the case of the jug wines, high price goes with good quality and low price with poor quality. In the case of IQs of pairs of identical twins, a high or low IQ in one twin tends to mean a similarly high or low IQ in the other. A positive correlation exists when high values on one measure go with high values of the other and low values of one measure go with low values on the other.

A **negative correlation** exists when high values on one measure go with low values of the other and vice versa. The second and third examples illustrate negative correlations. Large amounts of open space go with low accident rates for children; high percentages of breast feeding go with low infant mortality rates.

Whether positive or negative, the correlation between two measures can be anywhere from perfect to nonexistent. The closeness of the relationship is represented by a correlation coefficient, symbolized by r, which you may think of as standing for "relationship." Correlation coefficients always fall somewhere on a scale that goes from $r = -1.0$, perfect negative relationship; through 0, no relationship; to $r = +1.0$, perfect, positive relationship. The scale, of course, includes numbers in between these three values; for example, $r = +.95$, $r = +.47$, $r = -.36$, and $r = -.80$. It is important to understand that the absolute size of the correlation coefficient, *not* its sign, indicates the degree of relationship. Correlation coefficients of $+.65$ and $-.65$ represent equally strong relationships. Table 1.2 presents several correlation coefficients, including those for the examples we have been discussing. The two measures are numbered (1) and (2). The table will repay careful study.

How the Methods Are Applied

Whether there is a relation between speed of learning and memory for what was learned is a typical correlational question. It will serve to introduce the application of these methods. To answer this question, we would need first to teach a number of people something and to measure the amount of training they required to learn it. Then, after some standard length of time, these same people would be tested to find out how much they had remembered. The question, then, would be whether people who learn rapidly tend to forget quickly, as we sometimes hear, whether those who learn easily also retain things well, or whether, perhaps, the speed of learning and the amount retained are unrelated.

Table 1.2 Examples of Correlation Coefficients

Two Measures Obtained on the Same Thing	r
(1) Fahrenheit and (2) Celsius temperature for every day of 1983	+1.0
(1) IQ of twin A and (2) IQ of twin B for pairs of identical twins	+.90
(1) Price and (2) quality of jug wines	+.85
(1) IQ of father and (2) IQ of son for pairs of fathers and sons	+.65
(1) Open space and (2) accident rates for children in English districts	−.85
(1) Percentage of breast feeding and (2) mortality rate of infants in German communities	−.90
(1) Height and (2) distance from the top of the head to the ceiling for all children in the same classroom	−1.00

As an imaginary, but realistic, study of this question, let us suppose that the ten male subjects were required to learn a passage of poetry and that the measure of learning was the number of readings required to learn the passage. Let us assume, further, that after one month participants tried to recall the poem and that the measure of retention was the number of mistakes they made when reciting it. If these participants were typical, the results of this experiment might approximate those shown in Table 1.3. The middle column of the table gives the number of readings each individual required to learn the poem. The right-hand column indicates the number of mistakes made on the recall test. In general, the men who learned quickly tended to make few mistakes on the recall test. The results are opposite to those that would be expected were the popular idea true, that rapid learners soon forget what they have learned.

Scatter Plots. A graphic representation of these data will do much to clarify the meaning of the concept of correlation. Figure 1.4 is such a graph. The points on this graph, which is called a **scatter plot** or scatter diagram, represent the performances of the ten participants. The number near each point is that of the specific individual; you can identify each person's record in Table 1.3 and figure out how the plot was made.

The arrows leading to the point for participant 9 will help you to understand.

Table 1.3 Hypothetical Learning and Recall Data

Participant	Number of Readings Required To Learn Poem	Number of Mistakes Made on a Recall Trial One Month Later
1	12	3
2	14	7
3	15	6
4	17	12
5	18	8
6	21	12
7	23	14
8	25	13
9	28	17
10	31	22

Figure 1.4
Plotting a scatter diagram. This figure shows the relationship between learning and recall for each of ten subjects. Each point represents the score for one subject and is plotted at the spot where lines drawn from the subject's scores on the ordinate and on the abscissa would intersect. The method is illustrated for subject number 9, who took 28 readings to learn the material and made 17 mistakes in attempting to recall it.

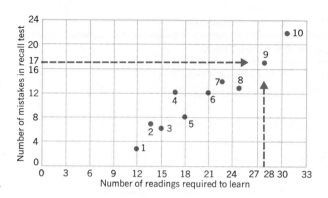

If you refer back to Table 1.3, you will see that he required twenty-eight readings to master the passage—hence the arrow from 28 on the abscissa. On the recall test he made seventeen mistakes, so another arrow is drawn from 17 on the ordinate. The point for this person appears at the spot where the paths of these arrows would cross. Each of the other points was plotted in the same way. As you can see, there is a close, positive relationship between the number of readings required to learn and the number of mistakes made on the recall test. By calculation, the correlation coefficient is $+.94$.

Figure 1.5 is a scatter plot showing the negative correlation of $-.86$ between the amount of open park space and the accident rate for children in eighteen districts in England. Figure 1.6 shows the positive correlation between quality and price of jug wines. This sample of scatter plots is probably sufficient to illustrate the general way in which they indicate the direction and degree of correlation. The points to be made are summarized in Figure 1.7. The scattering of points in a scatter plot forms a rough oval. If the oval extends from southwest to northeast, cartographically speaking, the correlation is positive; if it goes from northwest to southeast, the correlation is negative. The size of the correlation is reflected by the thinness of the oval; the thinner the oval, the higher the correlation. The scatter plot for a perfect correlation is a line, the limit reached as the oval becomes thinner and thinner. The scatter plot for a zero correlation is a circle, the limit reached as the oval becomes fatter and fatter.

Figure 1.5
Scatter plot showing the relation between open park space and accidents to children. The ordinate is actually the percentage of all accidents that are accidents to children. This figure controls for differential rates of accidents brought about by other factors. (Moroney, 1951.)

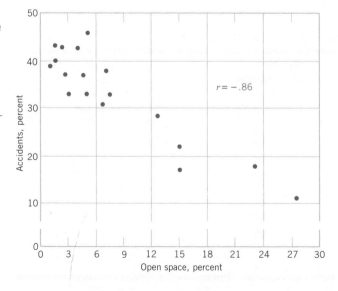

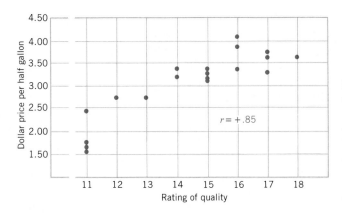

Figure 1.6
*Scatter plot showing a correlation of
+.85 between rated quality and price of
jug wines.* The judgment of quality is on
a commonly used scale in which 10 is
undrinkable and 20 is near perfection.
The data are from *Travel and Leisure*
(1976), a publication of the American
Express Company.

Correlation and Prediction.   The existence of a correlation between two measures tells us that the two measures are related. In more practical terms, it allows us to predict one of the two measures from the other. The higher the correlation, the more exact our prediction can be. A correlation coefficient of plus or minus 1.0 makes perfect prediction possible; a correlation coefficient of zero has no predictive value at all. Much of the value of correlational methods derives from their use in prediction. The most frequent application in psychology is the use of test scores to predict a person's success in various endeavors, and the most important of these are academic achievement and job performance.

Before you were admitted to college, it is quite likely that you took the Scholastic Aptitude Test (SAT) or some other test of college aptitude. When you apply for a job, you may be asked to take an aptitude test. In both cases the reason for using tests in the process of selecting candidates is that performance in the practical situation correlates with test scores. These ideas are developed much more fully in Chapter 13 of this book.

Correlation and Causation.   The existence of a correlation between two measures makes it very tempting to conclude that the relationship is causal. Although developments in correlational theory have led to methods that make causal thinking plausible in some cases, it is important to understand that a correlation between two measures does not usually imply causation. There are two principal points to be made here.

1. *If correlated measures are causally related, the direction of causality is ambiguous.* For example, there is reported to be a positive correlation, year by year, between the number of storks' nests and the number of babies born in northwestern Europe. This may be the origin of the folk legend that storks bring babies. In actuality, causation is in the other direction. As population and hence the number of buildings increase, there are more chimneys in which storks can build their nests. Similarly, there is a strong positive correlation between the

Figure 1.7
*Ellipses showing seven different patterns
of correlation.* The ovals sloping
downward represent negative
correlations. Those sloping upward to the
right represent positive correlations. The
"fatter" the ellipse, the nearer the
correlation is to zero. A circle represents a
zero correlation; a straight line represents
a perfect correlation.

Perfect
negative

High negative

Low negative

Zero

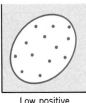

Low positive

High positive

Perfect
positive

number of fire engines in the several boroughs of New York City and the number of fires in these same boroughs. This almost certainly means that the number of fires is the causal factor, more fire engines being needed to control the greater numbers. Nothing in the correlation, however, rules out the theory that the crews of fire engines are responsible for setting the fires, that the more firemen, the greater the number of fires.

Finally, it has been claimed that a survey carried out in the state of Montana revealed a positive correlation between the number of churches and the number of saloons in a town; the more churches, the more saloons. Does this mean that the saloons exist as places where people go to wash away the guilt they feel after hearing the recitations of their sins in church; or does it mean the opposite, that the churches exist as places for people to go to atone for the sin of alcoholism? Actually, the answer is "neither," which brings us to the second point.

2. *A third factor may be responsible for both of the correlated measures.* In the example of the saloons and churches the third factor is town size. Numbers of saloons and churches both increase as the sizes of cities increase. The numbers of saloon and churches per thousand of poplulation are about the same, whether the city is large or small. Two additional related examples will makes the same point. There is a positive correlation between the lengths of boys' trousers and their mental ages, chronological age being responsible for both. There is a positive correlation between the sizes of boys' feet and the quality of their handwriting for the same reason.

Turning to less frivoulous examples, we find that some of the most controversial questions in psychology are correlational questions. Is skill in mathematics correlated with masculinity? Is superior intelligence correlated with membership in the Caucasian race? Is a tendency toward delinquency correlated with left-handedness? In connection with such questions, it is important to understand two points. First, the questions are questions of fact. The correlations may or may not exist. The truth of the matter must be decided with evidence. Second, and more important for our purposes here, even if the suggested correlations exist, this does not establish causal connections. Correlations are not explanations of behavior.

SUMMARY

The correlational methods are not experimental methods, because they examine naturally occurring relationships between variables. The degree and direction of such relationships are expressed by a correlation coefficient, ranging from -1.0 to $+1.0$. The absolute size of the correlation ranging from 0 to ± 1.0 indicates the closeness of the correlation. Correlations of $+.60$ and $-.60$ represent equally close relationships. The sign of the correlation, plus or minus, indicates the direction of the correlation.

Scatter plots are a graphic way of presenting correlational data. They contain one point for every individual whose data contribute to the correlation. These points indicate where the two measures being correlated fall for each individual. If these points form a narrow oval, the correlation is high. The wider the oval, the lower the correlation.

It is important to remember that correlation does not mean causation. Even if a causal relationship exists, the correlation does not reveal the direction of causality. Furthermore, a third factor may be responsible for the correspondence between the two correlated measures.

PROFESSIONS IN PSYCHOLOGY

Psychologists hold an almost endless variety of jobs. Many of them teach in colleges or universities. Some work in hospitals, some in school systems, some in penal systems. Some psychologists are employed in industry, where they may contribute to personnel selection, improving employer-employee relations, increasing production efficiency, or planning the physical layout of a factory. An increasing number of psychologists combine psychology with a knowledge of computers in many different contexts. The following statements give brief descriptions of the positions held by a few psychologists known to the authors of this book.

Professor A is a well-known clinical psychologist. He holds an appointment at a major university. He spends more time on research than teaching. He is trying to understand the factors that cause some children but not others to develop behavior disorders.

Dr. B was trained as an experimental psychologist but, with a colleague, he began to practice in applied psychology. He now owns a consulting firm that

Some of the work that psychologists do: observing animal behavior in nature, individual psychotherapy, psychological testing, laboratory experimentation with lower animals.

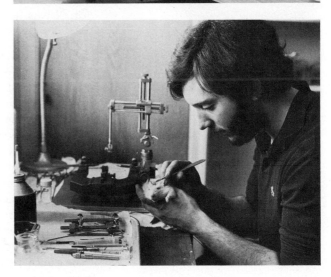

advises important corporations on matters related to advertising and corporate management.

Dr. C teaches at one of our major universities. Her research on visual perception is well-known. With some frequency she is consulted by industry on problems of vision.

Professor D is an expert on psychological testing, intelligence, and giftedness. He serves as an advisor to a commission in one of the Western states that is in the process of establishing a school for verbally, mathematically, and artistically gifted children.

Dr. E is in private clinical practice. She treats people who are in psychological trouble because of stress brought on by divorce, bereavement, and underemployment. She also offers group sessions, giving assertiveness training for women.

Dr. G is a comparative psychologist. He studies the mechanisms by which learning and genetic factors determine the songs that birds sing as adults.

Dr. H is a member of the department of psychiatry in a university hospital. She is trying to develop more effective ways of helping people to give up smoking.

Dr. J holds an administrative position in a university. She devotes most of her time to the management of one of the university's programs, but she teaches one psychology course a year, on the biological bases of behavior.

Dr. K is an authority on human memory. Lately he has become interested in the problems that older people have with memory. He is very much in demand as a speaker and gives many invited addresses at universities and at public meetings.

Dr. L is a statistician as well as a psychologist. He has developed a new statistical technique that permits the analysis of data in ways that had previously been impossible. He spends much of his time advising students and colleagues on how to design their experiments and how to evaluate their data.

Dr. M is an animal psychologist. He runs a kennel where he provides training for clients' pets. He specializes in retraining dogs that have developed undesirable habits.

Dr. N was trained both as a clinician and as a physiological psychologist. Now in private practice, she works with couples having sexual problems.

The list could go on but it should already have given some indication of the many professions that are available to psychologists. The work of some of the people in the list also raises a common question. Given the similarities in what they do, how can we distinguish between a clinical psychologist, a psychiatrist, and a psychoanalyst?

Clinical psychologists, psychiatrists, and psychoanalysts do similar work. They all study disturbed human behavior and concern themselves with the diagnosis and treatment of people with emotional problems. Their goal is to restore these individuals to psychological well-being. Because of these common interests, there is a fair amount of exchange of information and ideas among professional members of these disciplines. At the same time, there are important differences in these three professions, growing out of the training that these different types of clinicians have received.

The clinical psychologist usually has a Ph.D. degree in psychology. The Ph.D. degree is an academic one which requires a minimum of three years of study beyond the bachelor's degree at an accredited graduate school. As in other fields, the Ph.D. degree in psychology emphasizes training in research. In recent years some schools have begun to offer a Doctor of Psychology (Psy.D.) degree, for which less research and more training in therapy are required. The holder of a Ph.D. or Psy.D. in clinical psychology has ordinarily had an internship in some clinical setting prior to entering practice. The internship gives the clinician firsthand acquaintance with mental disorders and an opportunity to work with patients under expert supervision.

The psychiatrist holds a medical degree and has had, in addition, specialized training in the diagnosis and treatment of mental disorders. This specialized training is obtained by serving as a resident physician in a psychiatric hospital, usually for three years. As physicians, psychiatrists are able to prescribe drugs and use other medical procedures that are beyond the province of clinical psychology.

The relationship between the clinical psychologist and the psychiatrist varies considerably from one clinical setting to another. At one time a psychiatrist was usually in charge of a particular patient and the clinical psychologist administered and interpreted psychological tests. More recently psychologists have gained some autonomy in most clinical settings. Often in medical schools there is a Department of Medical Psychology, either as a separate department or as a subdivision of the Department of Psychiatry. Medical psychologists do diagnostic testing, provide psychotherapy, and quite commonly are active in research.

When clinical psychologists work outside institutions, in private practice, arrangements are more diverse. Some practice on their own; some accept referrals from medical doctors; some work in close contact with physicians. Many clinical psychologists maintain a practice, teach, and do research in colleges, universities, and medical schools.

Psychoanalysis is a branch of psychiatry. Most psychoanalysts, but not all, hold an M.D. degree. They differ from psychiatrists in the kind of training obtained beyond the medical degree. Psychoanalytic training consists of an intensive study of the theory and psychotherapeutic practices developed by Freud and his disciples. As a part of this training, the prospective analyst goes through a series of psychoanalytic sessions as a patient. Later on, the analyst in training performs a number of analyses under the close supervision of an accredited analyst. In recent years orthodox Freudian psychoanalysis has met with serious criticism and no longer holds a position of dominance in psychiatry.

Occasionally a psychoanalyst will have received his training in some field other than medicine. Such *lay analysts* may have degrees in sociology, religion, or psychology. They are a rarity, however, and anyone aspiring to a career as a psychoanalyst should plan to take an M.D. degree first.

HINTS ON HOW TO STUDY

In bringing this chapter to a close, we offer guidance which we hope will increase the value of your study of psychology. If you did not do so earlier, again we urge you to page through the rest of this book, in order to get an impression of its subject matter. Along the way read the pages at the end of Chapter 6 carefully. They present some practical hints on memory, which should be useful. Appendix B, on "Ethical Principles of Psychologists," examines their ethical obligations to others.

A major problem for us as authors and for many students is the topic of statistics. Our solution has been to present statistical materials as they are needed and to present them nonmathematically. You have already encountered most of these materials in this chapter. Although this nonmathematical coverage will make it possible for you to follow the psychological materials presented in this book, your understanding will be enriched by reading Appendix A. It will pay off if you do so early.

Each chapter in this book closes with two end notes. The first of these notes is always a list of the major concepts covered in the chapter. These concepts are listed in roughly the order in which they came up in the chapter. If you really know the contents of a chapter, you will be able to use these concepts as cues and reproduce its content. If you find that you cannot do so, although you feel that you understand the materials, the problem is likely to be with the standards that you are setting for yourself when you conclude that you have understood the chapter.

The second item suggests additional materials to study in this book and elsewhere. It will deepen your understanding of psychology if you do some of this extra study. We know, however, that your time is limited. Depending on your personal schedule, we suggest that you do as much as possible of the following, in this order. (1) Review recommended materials that you have already studied. This will be a very useful way to help pull things together. (2) Read ahead in this book when that is recommended. Sometimes you will be referred to materials that your instructors have not assigned. (3) At least browse through some of the other recommended readings. Particularly if you are going on in psychology, they will help you get an impression of what more advanced courses will be like. Our recommendations will frequently be the textbooks in these courses.

TO BE SURE YOU UNDERSTAND THIS CHAPTER

As we mentioned in the last section of this chapter, the major concepts will be listed in roughly the order in which they came up. In the text itself, these items almost always appear in boldface type. You should be able to define each concept. If your instructor uses objective tests, such definitions will go a long way toward preparing you for such tests. But your understanding of these concepts should go beyond the level of definition. You should be able to state the points that the text makes about each concept, in effect to reproduce the contents of the chapter. Here are the concepts for Chapter 1. Incidentally, most of these terms are defined in the glossary at the end of the book.

Depression	**Return to baseline**
Learned helplessness	**x-axis (abscissa)**
Concordance rate	**y-axis (ordinate)**
Determinism	**Naturalistic experiment**
Experimental method	**Demand characteristics**
Experimental group	**Placebo effect**
Control group	**Experimenter bias**
Independent variable	**Double-blind procedure**
Controlled variable	**Unobtrusive measures**
Dependent variable	**Correlational methods**
Statistical significance	**Correlation coefficient**
Small-N design	**Positive correlation**
N-of-1 design	**Negative correlation**
ABAB design	**Scatter plot**
Baseline	

Some materials do not lend themselves to recall with only the aid of concepts as cues. Examples from Chapter 1 are

Definition of psychology

Circular "explanations"

Stages in a typical experiment

Correlation and causation

The various professions of psychology

TO GO BEYOND THIS CHAPTER

In This Book. What might be included here has been covered in part in the final section of the text. If we have a single, strongest recommendation to make, it would be to read Appendix A. If you have time to do additional reading in this book, several sections of the chapter refer you to further discussion of topics brought up only briefly. Read anything that seems of interest.

Elsewhere. This paragraph directs you to other books that you might find useful. Usually we give just the title and author, listing complete references in the bibliography at the end of the book. This time we make some more general suggestions. Many journals and magazines, some of which will be available in the college library, include interesting treatments of the topics you will meet, possibly for the first time. As you gain expertise in psychology, you will discover that the technical journals in the field are sometimes within your understanding. Until then, and more frequently in any case, we can recommend a number of less technical treatments. Our nomination for best treatment, but of a limited number of topics in each issue, would go to *American Scientist,* the publication of the Society of the Sigma Xi. Another excellent journal of this type is *Scientific American,* although the articles are sometimes fairly technical. The review articles in *Science,* the publication of the American Association for the Advancement of Science, are sometimes on psychological topics. The *American Psychologist,* published by the American Psychological Association, has articles of general interest in each issue. Directed at the huge (60,000) and heterogeneous membership of the Association, these articles will almost always be ones that you can understand. Finally, the popular magazine *Psychology Today,* now published by the American Psychological Association, carries many useful stories in every issue.

PART TWO

BIOLOGICAL BASES OF BEHAVIOR

Tchelitchew, Pavel. *Mercure.* (1956). Sotheby Parke-Bernet/Art Resource.

CHAPTER 2 EVOLUTION AND GENETIC BASES OF BEHAVIOR

BASIC GENETIC MECHANISMS
Applications to Human Traits
Genotype versus Phenotype
Complex Traits and Multiple Genes
Chromosomes

NATURE VERSUS NURTURE
Inheritance of Behavioral Traits
Effects of Environment

INHERITANCE OF INTELLIGENCE
Heritability
Special Intellectual Abilities

PERSONALITY AND OTHER TRAITS
Inheritance of Personality
Similarities of Identical Twins Reared
  Apart

HUMAN EVOLUTION
Phylogenetic History
Cultural Evolution
Sociobiology

**RACE AND THE INHERITANCE
OF BEHAVIOR**
Evolution and Races
Race and Intelligence
Race Differences and Racism

**APPLICATION OF
GENETIC PRINCIPLES**
Eugenics
Medical Genetics
Genetic Engineering

Human beings are animals, unique and particularly complex ones, but animals nonetheless. Consequently, we share an evolutionary history with other animals and all living things. Examination of this common history gives us the perspective to see the similarities of the various forms of life, as well as the differences that have developed over time, and to recognize our place in the community of life's creatures. Human beings are programmed by their genes to become people, just as elephants are programmed by their genes to become elephants. So many of our human qualities are determined by this genetic template that a full understanding of human behavior is impossible without considering it.

The physical and behavioral differences that distinguish *species* are governed almost entirely by genetic factors. Variations in members of the same species, however, come from a combination of genetic differences and differences in environmental conditions. For example, no amount of training or effort would allow most of us to run a four-minute mile or become a piano virtuoso. People must be blessed with particular genetic predispositions to accomplish these feats. On the other hand, a predisposition does not in itself guarantee accomplishment. Individuals who are genetically able to develop the physical constitution required to run a four-minute mile will never realize this potential unless they receive adequate nourishment. By the same token, without musical training the potential virtuoso will never develop the finger dexterity required to perform difficult compositions and will appear in Carnegie Hall only as a paying customer.

To become an accomplished trumpet player requires the "ear" and finger dexterity provided by inheritance as well as long practice.

BASIC GENETIC MECHANISMS

The father of modern genetics was Gregor Mendel (1822–1884), who published in 1866 certain laws of inheritance that he had deduced from his years of study of the garden pea. This work went relatively unnoticed at the time and was not rediscovered until 1900. Most of our knowledge of genetics is the product of this century.

Mendel's laws were stated in terms of hypothetical "elements" of heredity, which were later called **genes.** In his experimental work Mendel crossed pure strains of peas that differed in single contrasting traits: purple versus white flowers, yellow versus green seeds, and smooth versus wrinkled seeds. In the first generation of offspring—the F_1 or **first filial generation**—the trait of one of the parents was usually present and the trait of the other parent did not

Gregor Johann Mendel, an Austrian monk educated in Vienna in mathematics and biology, bred his peas in the gardens of his order's monastery in Brünn.

appear. For example, when the purple-flowering plants were crossed with white-flowering plants, all the offspring had purple flowers. When the F_1 hybrids produced offspring (F_2), Mendel discovered that the dominant (purple) and recessive (white) grandparental traits reappeared in the F_2 progeny in a ratio of three dominants to one recessive. To summarize these findings, Mendel formulated his first law, the **law of segregation.** This law states that genes occur in pairs, and that one member of the pair is contributed by each parent (Figure 2.1). When a mature organism produces **germ cells**—cells for reproduction such as pollen, sperm, or ova—the paired genes segregate, and each germ cell receives only one member of the pair. When a sperm and ovum unite, a new gene pair is created and transmitted to the offspring.

We now know that genes can exist in two or more alternative states called **alleles.** In Mendel's peas, for example, the gene for flower color has two alleles, purple (A) and white (a). When the alleles inherited from each parent are the same (AA or aa), the offspring is **homozygous** with respect to the trait. When the alleles are different (Aa), the offspring is **heterozygous.** Many genes behave in a pattern of dominance and recessiveness. When two dominant genes or a **dominant gene** and a **recessive gene** for a particular trait are present, the dominant gene determines the trait. The trait governed by the recessive gene appears only when two recessive genes are present.

Further evidence of the way in which independent entities manage genetic transmission led Mendel to postulate his second law, the **law of independent assortment**. Mendel crossed some varieties of peas that differed in two traits, for example, yellow, smooth seeds versus green, wrinkled seeds. Since yellow is dominant over green and smooth over wrinkled, the F_1 generation seeds were all yellow and smooth. In the F_2 hybrids seed color was segregated in the ratio of three yellow (dominant) to one green (recessive). Similarly, the F_2 hybrid seeds segregated in a ratio of three smooth to one wrinkled.

The interesting question here was whether the yellow color was linked in

Figure 2.1
Mendel's law of segregation. Pure strains of purple-flowering and white-flowering peas are crossed, and the purple color is dominant in the first generation of hybrids (F_1). In the second generation (F_2) there is segregation of the purple and white colors. The allele for purple is represented by A and the allele for white by a. (After Dobzhansky, 1955.)

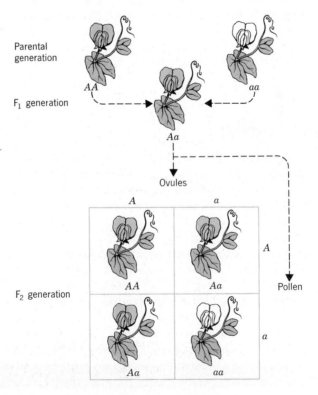

segregation with the smooth surface and the green with the wrinkled surface. This proved not to be the case. Mendel found that among the F_2 hybrids three-fourths of the smooth seeds were yellow, one-fourth green. Exactly the same proportions were found among the wrinkled seeds. This finding proved that separate genes affect separate traits, and that different genes undergo segregation independently of one another.

Applications to Human Traits

Mendelian laws of inheritance have now been established for many human traits, including *eye color, baldness, certain hereditary diseases,* and a condition called **albinism.** The albino individual is born with a virtually pigmentless skin, almost white hair, and eyes that usually have a pink retina. To illustrate the inheritance of this condition, we will let *N* represent the allele for normal pigmentation and *n* the allele for albinism. Albinism is known to be caused by a recessive gene, since albino children are usually born to parents who have the dominant, normal pigmentation but who are both heterozygous (*Nn*) for the albinism gene. In a union of two albinos, both of whom must be homozygous (*nn*) for this recessive gene, all the children will be albinos. As with many traits caused by recessive genes, albinism represents a weakness for the individual. The pigmentless skin makes albinos very sensitive to sunlight, and their vision is always poor.

Another human trait inherited according to Mendelian laws is the ability to taste the substance phenylthiocarbamide (PTC). To 70 percent of the population this substance has a very bitter taste, but 30 percent cannot taste it at all. The phenomenon of tasting or not tasting PTC is under the control of a gene pair in which one allele (*T*) is dominant, and imparts the ability to taste, and one allele (*t*) is recessive. Only individuals with two recessives (*tt*) are nontasters. From Mendel's principle of dominance, we know that nontasters can only be *tt*, but that tasters can be either *TT* or *Tt*. If the parents' genes for tasting PTC are known, we can apply the Mendelian principles just discussed to calculate the percentage of their offspring who will be either tasters or nontasters (Figure 2.2). Since there is a genetic basis for tasting or not tasting PTC, it seems possible that the taste of other substances might also vary as a result of genetic differences in people. For example, could it be that to people who hate them spinach and liver actually taste different from the way they taste to someone who likes them?

Genotype versus Phenotype

The material presented in Figure 2.2 helps to draw a distinction between a person's **genotype** and **phenotype**. The genotype refers to the genetic makeup the individual inherited from the parents. The phenotype refers to the observed characteristics of the individual. As we see in Figure 2.2, different genotypes, either *TT* or *Tt,* may bring about the same phenotype, in this example, the ability to taste PTC.

Up until now our examples, such as pea traits and tasting PTC, have concerned phenotypes that seem to be inexorable readouts of the underlying genotypes. For many physical characteristics and especially behavioral traits, however, the phenotype is influenced both by genotype and by the environment. Environment refers to all the external events to which the individual is subjected, including prenatal and neonatal conditions, nutrition, medical care, parents' child-rearing practices, cultural milieu, educational experiences, type and place of occupation, and even the climate of residence and epoch in which the person lives.

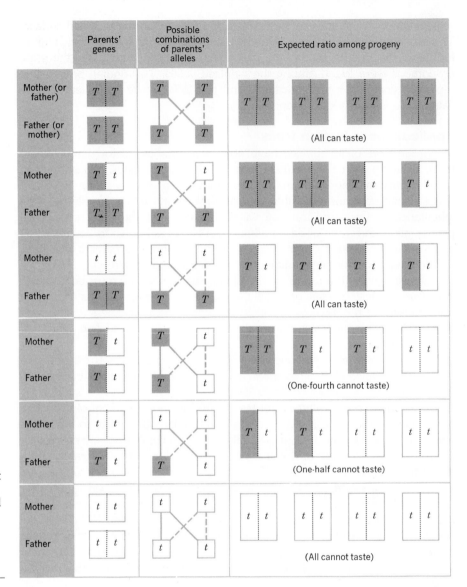

Figure 2.2
Inheritance of the ability to taste PTC.
There are six possible parental
combinations of the dominant gene for
tasting (*T*) and the recessive gene for not
tasting (*t*) PTC. Notice that the
combination of the parents' alleles would
be the same if the genes indicated in the
first column belonged to the opposite
parent. Each type of mating yields an
expected frequency of tasters and
nontasters among the progeny.

The importance of environment in determining even physical traits can be
seen in the coloring of Himalayan rabbits (Sinnott, Dunn, and Dobzhansky,
1958). When raised under natural conditions, these rabbits have a white body
with black extremities. When raised in a warm cage, however, they do not have
the black pigmentation. Thus rabbits with the same genetic makeup can have
different phenotypic appearances as a result of environmental factors.

For many human traits the phenotype is constantly changing, depending on
the nature of the interaction between the genotype and the environment. For
example, a man's physique is strongly determined by his genes, but nutrition,
an environmental influence, has an important effect on his shape and weight
at any given time. Similarly, a very intelligent person may through stress or lack
of rest experience a temporary inability to remember or reason abstractly. Figure
2.3 illustrates the notion that each genotype may be expressed in a number of
different phenotypes, depending on the person's environment. This variety,
however, is not infinite. A **norm of reaction** sets a limit to the range of
phenotypes that are possible for a single genotype. For example, a piano player

ENVIRONMENT (DIET)

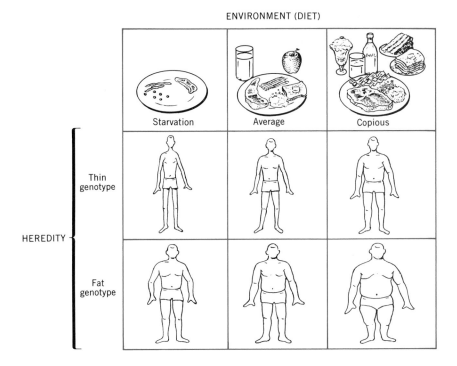

Figure 2.3
The norm of reaction. Although the environment is influential in determining the phenotype, heredity sets a limit to the range of possible phenotypes. In this illustration the two different genotypes for physique limit the effect of diet on actual appearance. (After Dobzhansky, 1964.)

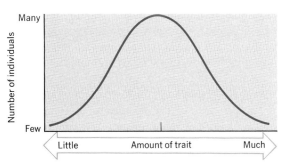

Figure 2.4
The normal curve. The typical distribution curve for human traits indicates that few individuals have either very little or very much of a trait. A larger number of individuals have amounts closer to the middle of the distribution. For later purposes, you should note that the wide distribution of human traits is reflected in measures of variance.

whose genotype does not include great finger dexterity and rhythm may benefit somewhat from musical training but will never have the phenotype of a musical virtuoso.

Complex Traits and Multiple Genes

Thus far we have discussed traits that can be classified into two distinct categories—for example, tasting and not tasting PTC. Many traits, such as human height or intelligence, do not fall into distinct categories but rather show a continuous variation. There are not two clear and separate classes of short people and tall people. Instead, the distribution is continuous, with relatively few very short and very tall people, and with most people having heights near the middle value of the distribution (Figure 2.4). This same **normal distribution** describes the frequencies of most psychological and biological traits.

The normal distribution of traits can be explained if we consider them to be determined by **polygenic inheritance** (poly-, many). When a trait is polygenically determined, each of a number of genes makes a small contribution to the phenotype, and these contributions add together to determine the trait. Individually, the genes contributing to polygenic inheritance are assumed to obey basic Mendelian laws.

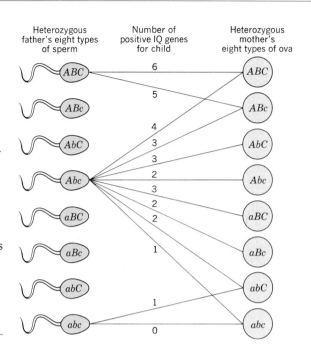

Figure 2.5
Possible results of matings between heterozygous persons. IQ is assumed to be controlled by three pairs of genes. For pictorial clarity, only a few of the possible unions of sperm and ova are shown. Lines may be drawn from any type of sperm to any type of ovum (a total of 8 × 8 = 64 possible lines). The total number of capital letters accrued by adding those of sperm and ovum denotes the genotypic value for the child. There are many ways (twenty) to produce a child with a genotypic value of 3, but only one of sixty-four combinations produces a child with a value of 0 or of 6.

Figure 2.6
The inheritance of IQ from matings of heterozygous parents. The bars indicate the frequencies of possible genotypic values when IQ is assumed to be controlled by three pairs of genes.

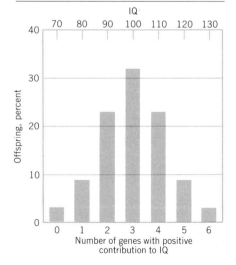

A model for polygenic inheritance was provided by Irving Gottesman (1963) for the trait of intelligence. For the sake of simplicity, we assume that the intelligence quotient (IQ) is determined by only three pairs of genes and that a person with the genotype *AaBbCc* has an average IQ, that is 100. We also assume that each gene represented by a capital letter increases IQ by 10 points, that the genes represented by a small letter have no influence, and that the effects of the genes are additive. The highest possible IQ in this model would be 130 for a person of genotype *AABBCC,* for this person has three more capital-letter genes than the average person. The lowest possible IQ would be 70 for a person of genotype *aabbcc,* since this person has three fewer capital-letter genes.

The completely heterozygous person (*AaBbCc*) could produce eight different types of gene combinations to be passed along to his or her children (Figure 2.5). If two such heterozygotes mate, there would be sixty-four (8 × 8) possible genotypes for their offspring, some of which are represented in Figure 2.5. The relative frequency of all possible genotypic values—the genotypic value is the number of capital letters—from such mating is shown in Figure 2.6. In this distribution each phenotype appears distinct and separable from the phenotype next to it, for we have assumed that only three pairs of genes determine IQ. If we had assumed instead that fifteen or more pairs determine IQ, the resulting distribution would be an excellent approximation of the normal curve. Such an assumption is not farfetched, since it has been estimated that there may be close to five million genes in a human cell (Cavalli-Sforza and Bodmer, 1971).

Many important traits are normally distributed in part because of the effects of environmental factors. Remember once again that the phenotype is not merely an expression of the underlying genotype. In Figure 2.6 several intermediate bars would have to be added to indicate the effects of these environmental influences. They would show that, depending on the environment, each genotype may emerge as a range of phenotypes (Figure 2.7).

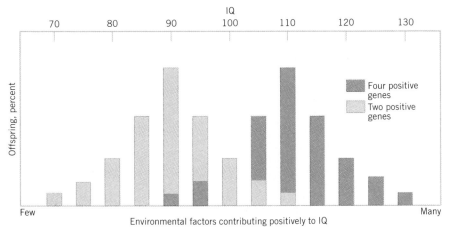

Figure 2.7
Hypothetical norms of reaction for two genotypes for IQ. The tallest black and white bars are from Figure 2.6. The added bars show how environmental factors might modify this potential. Notice that the genetic potential that most frequently produces an IQ of 110 may produce IQs from 90 to 130, and that the 90–IQ potential may be expressed in phenotypes ranging from 70 to 110.

Chromosomes

In the decades between Mendel's work and its rediscovery, scientists had sighted small, threadlike bodies located within the nucleus of cells and clearly visible under the microscope. These bodies, called **chromosomes,** were thought to be involved in genetic transmission. As the importance of Mendel's work was recognized, the connection was made between the laws of his "elements" of heredity and the function of chromosomes. Research has now shown that the thousands of physically much smaller genes, linearly arranged along each chromosome, are the basic units of inheritance.

Genes themselves are made up of chemical molecules of deoxyribonucleic acid, or **DNA,** which contains the "genetic code." The cracking of the genetic code by James Watson and Francis Crick, for which they received a Nobel prize, represents one of the greatest breakthroughs in the history of biology. As with so many great discoveries, the story of DNA is elegantly simple. This genetic material proved to have a surprisingly small number of components; minute variations in the way only four of the DNA elements are arranged provide the code and thus account for all the differences among genes.

Chromosomes and Cell Divisions. The entire genetic message of a human being resides in the single cell called the **zygote,** with which life begins. The zygote is formed when the male's sperm penetrates the egg or ovum of the female. The ovum and sperm, which are called the *germ cells,* each contain twenty-three chromosomes. When the zygote is formed, the chromosomes of the ovum and sperm combine. Thus the zygote contains twenty-three *pairs* of chromosomes—forty-six chromosomes in all—which become the normal complement of every cell in that person's body.

Twenty-two chromosomes from the sperm and twenty-two from the ovum are always pairs in that they determine the same traits. The chromosomes of the twenty-third pair are the sex chromosomes. The ovum always contributes an X chromosome, so called because of its distinct shape; the twenty-third chromosome in the sperm can be either an X or a Y chromosome. If the sex chromosome of the sperm is an X, the resulting XX combination guarantees that the zygote will develop into a female. If the sex chromosome of the sperm is a Y, the resulting XY combination guarantees that the zygote will be a male.

Chromosomes may be photographed through a microscope and then cut

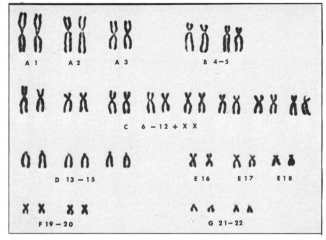

Figure 2.8
Karyotypes of the normal female (left)
and male (right). The sex chromosomes
of the female karyotype are in the second
line; the Y chromosome of the male
karyotype is the last one.

out of photographic enlargements and arranged into pairs according to their lengths. This arrangement is known as a **karyotype** (Figure 2.8). From a karyotype a trained examiner can observe gross abnormalities such as missing, broken, or additional chromosomes.

Sex Chromosome Abnormalities.   Ordinarily, formation of sperm and ova takes place smoothly and perfectly, and chromosomes are properly segregated and distributed. On rare occasions, however, sperm and ova do not have the normal number of sex chromosomes. Sometimes there is no sex chromosome, or there may be an extra one. When such an abnormal cell joins with a normal one (or with another abnormal one), the resulting zygote will have either too few or too many sex chromosomes. Although the individuals resulting from such zygotes may survive, they often have atypical physical and mental characteristics.

Females who are born with only one X chromosome (XO instead of XX) have a condition known as the **Turner syndrome.** These women are short, have incompletely developed breasts, and are sterile. Since doses of the hormone estrogen can induce the development of secondary sex characteristics such as pubic hair and breasts, estrogen therapy in adolescence can help women with the Turner syndrome to have a more normal appearance and to live relatively normal lives.

The abnormality of males who have an extra X chromosome is called the **Klinefelter syndrome.** These XXY men are tall, thin, and have long arms and legs; their testicles are small, and they are usually sterile. Psychologically, many have low IQs and show poor social adjustment. It is not known whether the individual's genetic makeup or the social consequences of the genetic abnormality are to blame for this poor adjustment.

A much-publicized abnormality is the extra Y chromosome found in some men. Early studies of **XYY males** suggested that there was a higher frequency of this chromosomal disorder among prison inmates and mentally retarded patients. These findings were widely reported by the press, and throughout the world an image emerged of the XYY male as a tall individual of low IQ, with strong tendencies toward aggression and violence. In nations as far apart as Australia and France, criminals with XYY karyotypes were defended on the premise that they were the helpless victims of their genetic inheritance and therefore could not be held accountable for their offenses. Many more recent studies have reported that the prevalence of XYY males among criminals is no higher than in the general population, and that most XYY men have no criminal tendencies. In the scientific community the current view of the XYY male is much more cautious. Some researchers still feel that there might be a slight criminal propensity in such men, but others do not.

SUMMARY

The first scientific work on heredity was Mendel's study of the garden pea. Mendel introduced the concept that discrete and independent entities are the true basis for hereditary transmission. His law of segregation postulated, in present-day terms, that genes exist in pairs of alleles within the organism, and that one allele of each pair is contributed by each parent. Mendel's law of independent assortment indicated that gene pairs for different traits segregate independently of one another. An individual may have two identical alleles for a trait—homozygosity; or have two different alleles—heterozygosity. In heterozygous organisms the effects of a dominant allele are expressed but not those of a recessive.

The environment may also affect the expressions of the trait, that is, its phenotype. The underlying genes, or genotype, may appear as a number of phenotypes, depending on the environment, but the extent of this variation is limited by a principle known as the norm of reaction.

Many human traits depend on a multiple system of genes, a form of inheritance called polygenic. Polygenic traits are continuously distributed, with individuals showing a wide range of phenotypes rather than falling into discrete classes or types.

Every ordinary human body cell contains twenty-three pairs of chromosomes, one of which is the pair of sex chromosomes. The specialized reproductive cells, the sperm and ova, contain only half the normal number of chromosomes. The successful fertilization of an ovum by a sperm unites two sets of unpaired chromosomes into a paired set to form a zygote.

NATURE VERSUS NURTURE

Is human behavior decided by nature, that is, by heredity, or by nurture, by the environment? This is one of the most fundamental questions that we can ask about the determination of our lives. Posed in this either-or manner, however, the question is meaningless. It is like asking whether the area of a rectangle is determined by its height or by its width. There could be no behavior at all without the contribution of both genetic and environmental factors.

The analogy to a rectangle can be pushed an important step further. The relative contributions of genetic and environmental factors differ from one behavioral trait to another. Just as a rectangle may be tall and not very wide, or vice versa, so a certain trait of an individual may be determined largely by heredity and not much by environment, or vice versa. Genes contribute more to intelligence than they do to personality but more to personality than to attitudes and prejudices. Although a tendency toward general aggressiveness may have a genetic base, an individual's hatred of others because of their skin color or political philosophy has much more to do with environment than with genes. Thus the real issue in understanding behavior is the question of how heredity and environment work together to produce differences in our psychological traits.

Inheritance of Behavioral Traits

Genetic studies of behavior are more often conducted on animals than on human beings for several reasons. The behavior of animals is not nearly as complex as that of human beings, and therefore the relation between genes and behavior can be more easily understood. The environments of animals can be kept more nearly the same than those of human beings, allowing genetic factors to reveal their influence. And, finally, animals breed and mature at a faster rate. A generation of lower mammals may grow to maturity within a few months instead of the twenty years or so taken by human beings. Although the results of studies on animals cannot be applied directly to people, they are important for demonstrating the different ways in which genetic inheritance may be expressed in various environmental circumstances.

Genes are primarily responsible for certain physical characteristics such as eye color in animals both high and low on the evolutionary scale. In lower forms of animals a good percentage of behavior is also very much dependent on the genotype. Even in these creatures, however, the environment plays a critical role by providing the stimulus that elicits particular behavior. For example, bees communicate by means of complex dances (see page 215), a system which appears to be completely genetically determined. Yet the environment provokes the dancing by providing the situation that calls for communication.

All members of a species low on the evolutionary scale may behave in highly stereotypic patterns. But individual animals of a species higher on the scale may be remarkably variable in their behavior. Whenever individuals of the same species differ in a particular trait, the heritability of that trait may be studied by means of **selective breeding,** in which animals that are similar in the degree to which the trait is manifested or not manifested are mated with each other.

For example, in a study to determine whether activity level is inherited, very active male rats would be mated with very active females, and very inactive males would be mated with very inactive females. In the next generation some of the progeny of the active animals would be very active and some of the progeny of the inactive animals would be very inactive. Only the most active offspring of active parents, and the most inactive offspring of inactive parents, would be further inbred. The procedure would continue for as many generations as necessary to determine whether there is or is not an inherited component for activity level. Selective-breeding methods have also been used to study the inheritance of emotionality and of learning ability and of the relation between these two important traits.

Emotionality.   When rats are put into a novel situation—for example, a large, brightly lit area—many of them become emotionally upset. They cower and "freeze," remain immobile in a fixed position, and are likely to defecate and urinate. To study the inheritance of these tendencies, Calvin Hall (1951) inbred the most and least emotional of 145 rats. His mating criterion of emotionality was whether or not the rats urinated and defecated during each of a series of twelve daily tests in an open field. The unselected parent generation showed such evidence of emotional upset on an average of slightly fewer than four days. In a series of successive generations, the strains gradually drew apart. At the end of the study, the emotional rats continued to be upset for ten or eleven days and the unemotional rats for only two days (Figure 2.9). Emotionality in rats thus appears to have a genetic base.

Maze Learning.   One of the classic experiments in behavior genetics is Robert Tryon's (1941) study of the maze learning of rats. Tryon initially selected 142

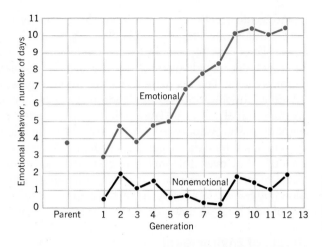

Figure 2.9
The inheritance of emotionality for twelve generations of rats. (Constructed from data in Hall, 1951.)

rats and gave them 19 trials in a complex maze. Some animals learned the maze very quickly, making few errors; others learned very slowly, making many errors. The frequency distribution of the errors—entrances into blind alleys—made by the original parent population is shown in Figure 2.10a.

The "bright" rats were then mated with one another, as were the "dull" rats, and both sets of offspring (F_1 generation) were tested in the maze. This process was repeated for eight generations. Figure 2.10b gives the error distributions for the F_1, F_3, and F_8 generations. By the eighth generation there was practically no overlap in the maze-learning abilities of the bright and dull rats.

Clearly, heredity and maze learning are related, and selective breeding can demonstrate that a genetic substrate is involved. But a caution is in order. What is inherited in these experiments is quite specific, as subsequent research by

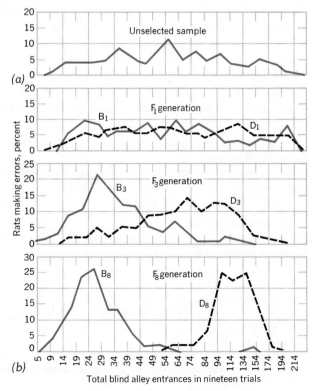

Figure 2.10
The maze performance of bright (B) and dull (D)rats. (a) The upper graph shows the distribution of errors for the parent population. (b) The lower graphs show the performances of first-, third-, and eighth-generation progeny. (From Tryon, 1942.)

Lloyd Searle (1949) showed. Bright rats were not bright on everything, nor were the dull rats altogether dull. Drawing from the twenty-second generation of the Tryon strains, Searle tested ten brights and ten dulls for some thirty different traits, including emotionality, activity level, discrimination learning, and performance in Tryon's maze as well as in other types of mazes.

Searle's bright and dull rats made roughly the same error and time scores on the original maze as Tryon's had, but on other mazes the differences in learning ability disappeared and differences in emotionality became apparent. In some tests the data suggested that the brights might be more emotional than the dulls, but even this trait was quite specific. In other tests the dulls were found to be more fearful. Table 2.1 summarizes some of the differences obtained by Searle. Obviously, the two groups of rats varied in many ways, almost any of which might have affected maze learning one way or another.

Effects of Environment

Many animal studies have examined how differences in environment interact with genotypic differences in determining behavior. For example, John Fuller (1967) studied the effects of early environment on the maze learning of two breeds of dog. Some pups of each breed were raised normally, others in isolation. Although the effects of isolated rearing varied with the breed, the learning ability of dogs reared in isolation was generally poorer. Fuller found that these dogs were hindered by emotionality rather than by any deficit in intelligence. When their emotionality was overcome, their maze performance improved.

Fuller's work is extremely important. Earlier studies of dogs raised in isolation had also shown them to be poor at learning a maze. Researchers had theorized that deprivation keeps animals from developing their full sensory and cognitive abilities. These notions were applied at the human level, fostering the claim that the low intelligence of children raised in impoverished circumstances could be blamed on their social deprivation. Fuller's work showing that isolated rearing did not necessarily affect the dogs' intelligence demonstrates the dangers of making analogies between canines and children.

In another study of environmental effects on maze learning, strains of bright and dull rats were reared in markedly different circumstances (Cooper and Zubek, 1958). Slides, tunnels, balls, and considerable sensory stimulation provided an *enriched environment*. The *restricted environment* consisted of cages

Table 2.1 Some Differences Between Bright and Dull Rats on a Number of Behavior Measures

Behavior	Brights	Dulls
Food drive	Above average	Below average
Escape from water drive	Inferior	Superior
Spontaneous activity	Relatively low	Relatively high
Emotional responsiveness	Fearful in "open-space" situations	Fearful of mechanical apparatus; emotionally reactive in maze
General intelligence	No evidence of a general superiority in capacity	No evidence of a general inferiority in capacity
Response to elevated structures	Greater timidity	Less timidity
Running speed	Above average	Below average

Adapted from Searle, 1949.

that faced a gray wall and contained only a food box and water pan. At sixty-five days of age, each group was tested for maze learning. The enriched early environment helped the dulls but not the brights; the restricted environment had no effect on the dulls but hurt the brights. Thus, in restricted conditions, even the rats with good genetic potential were prevented from developing it. Again we see that the phenotype is a result of the interaction between genotype and environment.

An important principle to emerge from genetic studies is that the same environment may have different effects on different genotypes. This is the principle of **nature-nurture interaction** or **gene-environment interaction.** J. B. S. Haldane (1946) illustrated this principle with some theoretical norms of reaction. In Figure 2.11*a* all individuals with genotype *A* always score higher than those with genotype *B,* but the scores of individuals with both genotypes improve markedly if they are exposed to environment *Y* rather than environment *X.* For example, better nutrition increases the height of both men and women, although on the average men remain taller.

In another possible gene-environment interaction (Figure 2.11*b*), genotype *A* is not superior to genotype *B,* nor is environment *X* superior to environment *Y.* Rather, the two genotypes react differently in different environments. An example is how the life expectancies of Europeans and blacks differ from one continent to another. In European cities Europeans outlive blacks partly because of their greater immunity to tuberculosis. But in many parts of Africa the blacks have the advantage, largely because of their resistance to yellow fever (Haldane, 1946).

In other situations environmental differences may have no effect on one genotype but dramatically affect another. A study of the effectiveness of two methods of teaching reading to eighteen pairs of twins (Naeslund, reported in Vandenberg, 1965) illustrates this type of interaction. Some of the twin pairs were of average intelligence and some were of superior intelligence. The twins of each pair were separated and assigned to different classrooms. Reading was taught by the phonics method in one room and the sight method in the second. Within each room, then, the same environmental treatment was given to children of two genotypes for intelligence, average and gifted. The average children learned to read better with the phonics method than with the sight method. The gifted children did equally well in both methods. Thus two different environments had the same effect on children of one genotype (gifted) but had different effects on children of another genotype (average).

An underlying assumption of all these studies is that the environment can act on the genotype, but that the genotype does not act on the environment. The genotype is considered to be full of potentialities but essentially passive. The environment, on the other hand, is the active agent which operates on the genotype and selects which phenotype will finally emerge. This assumption is not completely true, particularly in respect to the development of behavior. The

Figure 2.11
Norms of reaction between heredity and environment. (*a*) Genotype *A* scores higher than genotype *B* in environments *X* and *Y,* although environment *Y* improves the scores of both genotypes. (*b*) Genotype *A* scores higher in environment *X,* and genotype *B* scores higher in environment *Y.* Here the two environments have different effects on different genotypes.

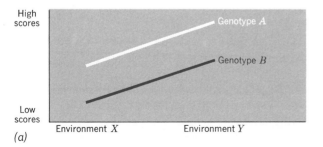

(*a*)

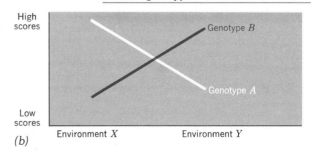

(*b*)

genotype of the individual does not react in simple reflex fashion to fixed environmental inputs. Rather, there is increasing evidence that the individual actively participates. Each person can manipulate and change the external world and thereby exert some control over the environment that he or she will experience.

An important way in which individuals act on the environment and contribute to their own development is by influencing the behavior of others toward them. Many cases of child abuse are unfortunate examples. It appears that children with certain inherited characteristics, such as sleeplessness or a tendency to cry a great deal, can irritate their parents so much that some parents may abuse them.

SUMMARY

Psychologists no longer ask whether human behavior is determined by a person's ancestry or by upbringing; they acknowledge both contributions. The questions of greater interest now concern the magnitude of genetic and environmental influences and how these influences interact in determining behavior.

An important task of the behavior geneticist is to answer these questions for particular traits. One method of study is selective breeding; animals that show extremes of some trait are mated. Such matings are carried through successive generations, always mating the animals that are the most similar behaviorally. Activity level, emotionality, and maze learning have all been investigated in the laboratory rat, and the gradual separation of the offspring into distinct strains after generations of interbreeding points to a genetic basis for such traits. Other studies, however, have shown that these behaviors are complexly determined. They depend on more than one trait, and it is difficult to infer exactly what traits are transmitted from parent to offspring. The role of environment in determining particular traits is also indefinite. Environmental factors have been found to affect the behavior of different animal strains in different ways.

The norm of reaction is a concept that indicates that each genotype has a range of expression. No amount of environmental impact can cause a trait to exceed the upper or lower limits of this range, but the environment can influence where the trait falls within the range. The operation of the norm of reaction is complicated, however, because the same environment may affect particular traits differently. There is, in short, a gene-environment or nature-nurture interaction.

INHERITANCE OF INTELLIGENCE

One of the most controversial topics in the field of psychology concerns the inheritance of intelligence. As often happens, the controversy is more an expression of different ideologies than it is a disagreement about facts. The extreme views that intelligence is fixed by heredity or that it is shaped by environment have been supported more by the proponents' philosophical, social, or political ideals than by any existing data.

Evidence gathered from many studies indicates that intelligence *is* influenced strongly by heredity, but that environment also plays an important role. Such evidence comes from numerous correlational studies that have examined the following proposition. If heredity influences intelligence, individuals who have more genes in common should be more similar in intelligence. This proposition has generally been supported (Erlenmeyer-Kimling and Jarvik, 1963; Bouchard and McGue, 1981). Similar IQ scores have been found for identical twins, who

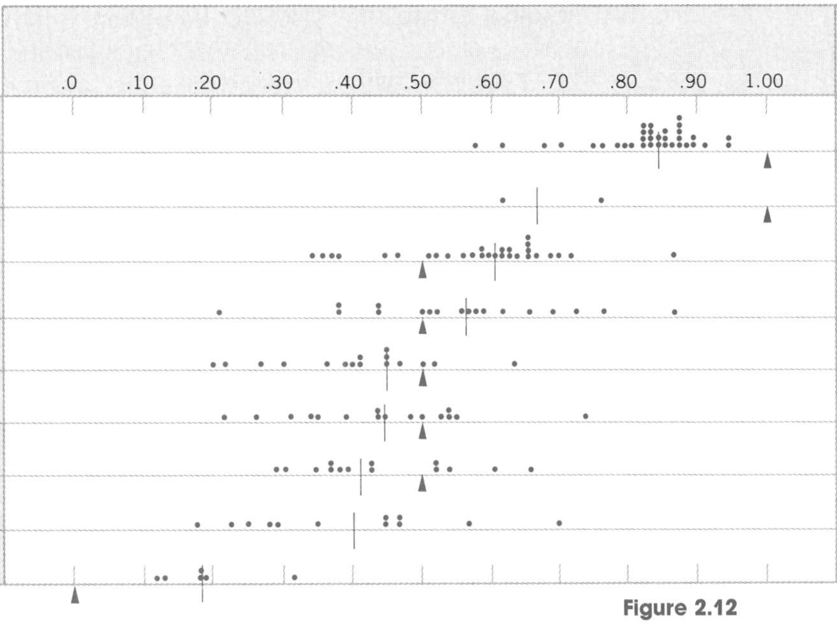

	.0 .10 .20 .30 .40 .50 .60 .70 .80 .90 1.00	Number of correlations	Number of pairings	Median correlation
Monozygotic twins reared together		34	4672	.85
Monozygotic twins reared apart		3	85	.67
Same-sex dizygotic twins		29	3.670	.61
Opposite-sex dizygotic twins		18	1592	.565
Same-sex sibling pairs		19	6098	.45
Opposite-sex sibling pairs		16	5127	.445
Same-sex parent—offspring pairings		14	4648	.41
Opposite-sex parent—offspring pairings		12	4476	.40
Adoptive parent—offspring		6	1397	.18

Figure 2.12
Familial correlations for IQ. The vertical bar in each distribution indicates the median correlation; the arrowhead indicates the correlation predicted by a simple polygenic model. (Adapted from Bouchard and McGue, 1981.)

develop from a single fertilized egg and thus have identical genes. Scores of siblings, fraternal twins, and parents and their children, all of whom have about 50 percent of their genes in common, show a moderate degree of similarity. There is a low correlation between the scores of adoptive parents and those of their children, who are genetically unrelated (Figure 2.12). As Thomas Bouchard and Mathew McGue (1981) have pointed out, however, the influence of environmental factors is demonstrated by the fact that the correlations are not exact in reflecting degree of relationship. The scores of identical twins reared apart are not as similar as those of identical twins reared together. Scores of fraternal twins are more alike than those of other siblings, and adoptive parents' scores do correlate to some extent with their adoptive children's.

Heritability

Let us now move beyond the position that heredity is important and begin addressing the question of how important. Central to this assessment is a statistical measure called a **heritability ratio.** This index provides a numerical estimate of the relative contributions of heredity and environment to the **variance (V)** of a given trait in a specific population. Variance refers to the differences in some trait that are found in individuals of the population. A crude index of variance is the range of values for the trait. For IQs this range is some 200 points, from nearly zero to over 200. In studies of heritability, variance is a statistical measure with a very useful property: it can be separated into additive components that reflect different causes. (The actual statistic is described in Appendix A, page 642).

In the case of intelligence, for example, it is possible to separate total or phenotypic variance into one component reflecting heredity and another reflecting environment. The two separate components are themselves both variances. Imagine a large number of individuals, all with identical inheritances but raised in different environments. Their IQs would vary as a result. The variance thus created would be **environmental variance**, symbolized by $V_{environmental}$. Now imagine another large group of individuals with many different genotypes who are reared in identical imaginary environments. They would have different IQs because of their genetic variation. This source of variance is **genetic**

variance, symbolized by $V_{genetic}$. In the real world variations in IQ are partly the result of genetic variance and partly the result of environmental variance. The total **phenotypic variance,** $V_{phenotypic}$, is the sum of these two components:

$$V_{phenotypic} = V_{genetic} + V_{environmental}$$

The heritability (H) of a trait is defined as the proportion of the total phenotypic variance that can be traced to genetic variance:

$$H = \frac{V_{genetic}}{V_{phenotypic}}$$

When genetic variation is more important than variations in environment in determining the trait variation, the heritability ratio will be large. When variations in the environments in which people live are more important than genetic variations, the heritability index will be small.

Twin Studies.   Most estimates of the heritability of human traits lean heavily upon comparisons of identical and same-sex fraternal twins. Identical twins are also know as **monozygotic twins** because they develop from a single fertilized egg; fraternal twins are known as **dizygotic twins** because they develop from two fertilized eggs. The logic behind the comparisons is as follows. Since identical twins have the same genes, they can show no genetic variation; any differences between the two must come from environment alone. Fraternal twins, on the average, are identical in only 50 percent of their genes. And, like identical twins, fraternal twins are assumed to have experiences that differ to some degree. Thus both hereditary and environmental factors contribute to the

The five-year-olds are identical twins and have exactly the same genes. The thirteen-year-old girls are fraternal twins. The genes of fraternal twins, like those of any siblings, average 50 percent the same; for individual pairs the percentage may be greater or less.

differences in fraternal twins. This means that the correlations between traits of identical twins should be higher than those for fraternal twins. The simplest of several formulas for calculating heritability ratios is based on these correlation coefficients. The formula is

$$H = 2\,(r_{MZ} - r_{DZ})$$

If these correlations are $+.85$ and $+.60$ (see Figure 2.12), the value of H is

$$H = 2\,(.85 - .60) = .50$$

Heritability ratios can range from a minimum of 0 to a maximum of 1.00. In general, when identical twins resemble each other in a trait much more than do same-sex fraternal twins, the heritability ratio is high. When differences between identical twins are the same as those between fraternal twins, heritability is zero. When similarities are modestly greater for identical twins than for fraternal, the heritability ratio is somewhere in between.

Table 2.2 lists heritability ratios for the trait of intelligence obtained from several studies comparing twins. As can be seen, the ratios vary from study to study. This happens for two reasons: (1) the index is very sensitive to the genetic and environmental variations in the population on which it is computed, and (2) the index varies when studies use different measures of a trait. It is clear, however, that for the populations studied and the tests used, variability in intelligence does have a substantial genetic component. The value of .50 computed in our example is on the low side of the range. There are several ways to estimate H, and our method gives conservative estimates.

Identical Twins Reared Apart. Comparisons of identical twins who by some quirk of fate have been separated early in life and who have had different upbringings provide a particularly powerful means of estimating heritability. If identical twins who are raised together are very similar in a trait, but those raised apart differ a great deal, this is strong evidence for the importance of environmental influences; the heritability ratio will be low. If identical twins who are raised apart nevertheless resemble each other almost as much as those

Table 2.2 Correlations and Heritability Ratios from Studies of Intelligence in Twins

Country	Year	Monozygotic (MZ) r	Dizygotic (DZ) r	H
England	1958	.97	.55	.93
U.S.A.	1932	.92	.61	.80
France	1960	.90	.60	.75
U.S.A.	1937	.90	.62	.74
Sweden	1953	.90	.70	.67
U.S.A.	1965	.87	.63	.65
U.S.A.	1968	.80	.48	.62
Sweden	1952	.89	.72	.61
England	1954	.76	.44	.57
England	1933	.84	.65	.54
Finland	1966	.69	.42	.51
England	1966	.83	.66	.50

Adapted from Vandenberg, 1971a.

Table 2.3 Correlations of IQ Scores for Identical Twins Raised Together and for Identical Twins Raised Apart

Country	Year	Raised Together	Raised Apart
U.S.A.	1937	.98	.77
England	1958	.92	.86
England	1962	.76	.77
Denmark	1965	—	.62

Adapted from Vandenberg, 1971b.

raised together, the evidence is strong that the trait is primarily influenced by genetic factors; the heritability ratio will be high. As can be seen in Figure 2.12 and Table 2.3, correlations of the IQ scores of identical twins reared apart remain quite high, thus providing further evidence of a hereditary influence on intelligence. At the same time, however, these correlations are usually lower than those for twins reared together. This difference reveals that environment does have an important influence.

Special Intellectual Abilities

In the studies discussed to this point, intelligence has been treated as a unitary trait which can be represented by a single score. Intelligence, however, is actually a collection of intellectual abilities. The typical IQ test measures these abilities separately, and the scores are combined to provide an overall intelligence score. Even if workers could agree on the value of the heritability ratio for such global scores, this value would not indicate how much each intellectual ability is influenced by hereditary factors. Louis L. Thurstone (1877–1955) found that seven intellectual abilities seemed to comprise intelligence, and he made them the focus of his Primary Mental Abilities Tests (1941). These abilities are verbal comprehension (vocabulary), word fluency, spatial perception, numerical ability, reasoning, memory, and perceptual speed.

Four twin studies have examined the heritability of six of these abilities (Table 2.4). As with the heritability ratios for total IQ scores, those for specific abilities often differ markedly from study to study. The data do suggest that verbal ability, word fluency, and spatial ability have relatively large genetic components. Evidence for a genetic influence on number ability, reasoning, and memory is less consistent.

SUMMARY

Populations show variability in a trait for both genetic and environmental reasons. One measure of the relative importance of these two factors is the heritability ratio, which is an estimate of the proportion of trait variance having genetic causes. A high heritability ratio indicates that the trait has a large genetic component; a low ratio indicates that environment is of greater importance.

Most ways of computing the heritability of a trait rely on comparisons of identical twins, who differ because of environment alone, with fraternal twins, who differ for both genetic and environmental reasons. In studies of intelligence, scores of identical twins reared apart provide evidence that this trait, although depending to a substantial degree on heredity, is also influenced by environ-

Table 2.4 Heritability Indices from Four Twin Studies for Six Primary Mental Ability Scores

Ability	Blewett (1954)	Thurstone (1955)	Vandenberg (1962)	Vandenberg (1966)
Verbal	.68	.64	.62	.43
Word fluency	.64	.59	.61	.55
Spatial	.51	.76	.59	.72
Number	.07	.34	.61	.56
Reasoning	.64	.26	.28	.09
Memory	—	.39	.20	—

Vandenberg, 1971a.

ment. No final consensus has been reached on the exact contributions to intelligence of heredity and of environment.

PERSONALITY AND OTHER TRAITS

Although intelligence appears to be inherited to a greater extent than other traits, genetic factors seem to be involved in many types of behavior. Stuttering, a trait commonly thought to have psychological origins, is an interesting example. Stuttering may begin gradually after a child first begins to talk, or it may be precipitated in a fluent child by shock or trauma. No stutterer will stutter all the time; there may be periods of fluency, but anxiety tends to exacerbate symptoms. The most frequent explanations of stuttering attribute the condition to upbringing. It has been suggested, for example, that a child imitates the speech of a stuttering parent or reacts to a parent's anxiety about the problem by further stuttering. Since most stutterers recover before adulthood, however, few children could have stuttering parents to imitate. The negative reaction of others remains a prime environmental suspect.

Because stuttering seems to run in families, another possible explanation is that susceptibility to stuttering is genetically transmitted. One study of 511 stutterers found that the risk of the disorder is significantly increased if at least one parent has ever stuttered (Kidd and Records, 1979). The fact that stuttering is four times more common in boys than girls (Scarr and Kidd, 1983) also suggests a physical and therefore a genetic link. Sandra Scarr and Kenneth Kidd have proposed an interaction in which genes predispose some individuals to stutter, and environments influence whether or not this potential materializes. This model would allow for both the occurrence of stuttering in families and the relation of the disorder to factors such as trauma and anxiety.

Inheritance of Personality

If genes can play a role in traits that appear to have psychological origins, what of our personalities in general? Are people who share more genes more alike in character, attitudes, interests? There are reasons to conclude that the answer to this question is "yes." Personality differences appear in early infancy as

The different emotional reactions of people to the same happening depend in part on inherited differences in personality.

different temperaments (see page 377). In their review of relevant literature, Scarr and Kidd (1983) pointed out that as infants identical twins tend to be more alike in temperament than fraternal twins. When they are adolescents and adults, identical twins indicate a moderate degree of similarity on measures of personality traits. Their scores on personality tests have correlations of about .50, compared with correlations for fraternal twins of about .25. In terms of specific traits, introversion–extroversion is often cited as the aspect of personality for which a genetic basis is clearest (Slater and Cowie, 1971, for example). Even in this case, however, heritability is less than for intelligence. Nonetheless, although the contribution may be relatively small, the findings do suggest that genes have some role in determining personality traits.

Similarities of Identical Twins Reared Apart

As with studies of intelligence, the most powerful data in research on the inheritance of personality come from studies of identical twins who have not been raised together. In the past few years researchers at the University of Minnesota have begun a major study of pairs of identical twins who were reared apart, assessing the twins' similarities and differences on a wide variety of physiological and psychological measures (Holden, 1980). Although the information collected has not yet been fully analyzed, what has been revealed is intriguing indeed.

Thomas Bouchard and his colleagues located and studied twenty-three pairs of identical twins from many parts of the world. All had been separated from an average age of six weeks. Some had been raised in similar environments, others in radically different ones. Most of the twins had had little contact with each other since infancy. Some met for the first time as adults at the Minneapolis airport.

Each pair of twins underwent eight days of individual testing. They were given a massive battery of tests, including medical histories; physiological tests of brain waves, heart function, allergies, and other reactions; psychological examinations tapping interests, values, phobias, and so on; and tests of intelligence and abilities. Many measures were repeated during the course of the eight days, in order to assess a given factor at different times.

The twins showed surprising similarities, from highly correlated IQ scores to odd "coincidences." Some of their life histories were full of similar names. One pair of men had sons named James Allan and James Alan. The same two had both married and divorced women named Linda and remarried women named Betty. A pair of women had sons named Richard Andrew and Andrew Richard and daughters named Catherine Louise and Karen Louise. Some of the similarities are quite perplexing. One pair of men, one raised in Germany and the other in the Caribbean and in Israel, led quite different lives but shared a host of idiosyncrasies, such as flushing toilets before using them, reading magazines from back to front, fidgeting with other people's rubber bands, and dipping buttered toast in their coffee. They had very similar profiles on the Minnesota Multiphasic Personality Inventory (MMPI). A pair of British housewives met each other at the Minneapolis airport, each wearing seven rings, two bracelets on one wrist, a watch and bracelet on the other. One pair suffered suspected heart attacks at the same time; another pair developed diabetes at the same time. Brain waves of the twins were similar in most cases, as were their abilities and interests. Vocational interest test results looked like those of one person tested at different times. Twins shared phobias and tended to have similar emotional styles. In fact, these twins raised apart seemed even more alike than identical twins reared together. We know that identical twins who are raised

Jim Springer and Jim Lewis, identical twins who were reared apart, have very similar interests. Their basement workshops are much alike. They both make miniature furniture.

together often strive for individuality by downplaying their similarities and emphasizing their differences. Separated pairs do not have to prove their individuality in this way, so similarities can come to the fore.

Twins' similarities, especially the strange "coincidences," cannot be fully explained. Take the twins with the seven rings—clearly, a gene could not be responsible for such a phenomenon. An idea suggested by David Lykken (Hanson, 1981) is that the twins could have inherited both their attractive hands and an attraction to sparkling objects, combining in a fondness for rings. An attraction to the sounds of certain names may be similarly based. Such notions suggest that genes may have a subtle, usually imperceptible, influence over many aspects of human individuality.

Because the research is new, and the coincidences between twins' histories are ripe for sensationalization, the similarities emerging from this study have received the most attention. But the differences are at least as fascinating because any difference between identical twins means that heredity is definitely not in control of the trait. Thus the fact that only one member of a pair of twins has a rare neurological disease thought to be hereditary means that it must have a partial environmental cause. As the data are analyzed, differences such as this one may offer the greatest insights to the question of nature and nurture. Bouchard cautions that the degree of similarity between twins will vary, and that no numbers will ever be put on the respective influences of heredity and environment (Hanson, 1981).

SUMMARY

Personality and other traits seem to be somewhat less heritable than intelligence, but genetic factors do influence them to some degree. Stuttering is an example of a trait that has generally been thought to derive from psychological causes but in fact seems to have a genetic component.

Both identical and fraternal twins are more alike on measures of intelligence than of personality, but identical twins are more alike than fraternal on both types of measures. Although the findings do not indicate a strong resemblance, the interests, attitudes, and certain personality traits of identical twins reared together are more alike than those of fraternal twins.

A major study of identical twins reared apart promises to increase our knowledge of the relative influences of nature and nurture on behavior. On the basis of preliminary analysis, these twins seem even more alike than identical twins reared together. Similarities show up in physiological and psychological tests and often in idiosyncrasies of behavior and remarkable coincidences of life histories. Surprising differences between twins are also emerging and are perhaps even more informative, since they rule out the possibility of complete genetic control of the trait in question.

HUMAN EVOLUTION

It is generally recognized that life began with a single cell, which somehow gave rise to the vast diversity of plant and animal life in existence today. Scientists have now begun to answer the profound question of how this came to be. Their new understanding comes from a rather strange way of looking at the nature of life. This point of view regards life as entirely the result of the properties of DNA molecules, which are the principal ingredient of genetic material. What differentiates these molecules from all other naturally occurring molecules is their ability to make perfect replicas of themselves. The trick is not difficult to imagine. Picture a template molecule floating in a watery soup of smaller molecules. The template molecule simply gathers and holds the smaller molecules together until another complete molecule, and another template, is constructed. Then the two molecules separate, and the process begins again in each one (Figure 2.13).

The environmental conditions under which genetic material reproduces itself are very stringent. The raw materials must be present in a medium of water, energy must be available, and the temperature and pressure must remain within narrow limits. When the proper conditions prevail, genetic material not only replicates itself but does so at a rate faster than it is destroyed. This is the crucial feature common to all forms of life.

The rather strange way of looking at the nature of life can now be stated. The structure and behavior of all living things are simply elaborate devices that reduce the destruction rate and enhance the reproduction rate of genetic material. This startling idea was stated metaphorically and long ago, in the late nineteenth century, by Samuel Butler: ". . . a hen is simply an egg's way of producing another egg" (quoted by Simpson, 1958).

The shift in emphasis from organisms to genetic material is extremely difficult for most people to accept, because the idea that human beings are being exploited by thoughtless molecules seems to demolish human dignity. But if this view is adopted, even temporarily and for the sake of the argument, it follows that humankind is just one of the many ways in which genetic material has maintained its reproduction rate over its destruction rate. Oak trees are another, bacteria still another.

The process by which genetic material has succeeded in covering the earth with bodies in the service of its own survival is called **organic evolution**. First, we shall examine how the various forms of life evolved from one another, with emphasis on how human beings acquired their humanism. Then we shall look at cultural and racial evolution, so that we may begin to understand human heritage and diversity in their overall biological context.

Phylogenetic History

Barely two centuries ago, the uncontested belief was that the world had been created six thousand years ago and that the earth's land, animals, and plants had from the beginning taken the same form and would remain the same forever. This idea was held so firmly that any suggestion to the contrary was heresy. But once the great exploratory voyages of the sixteenth and seventeenth centuries were underway, it became impossible to ignore the great diversity of

Figure 2.13
The way a hypothetical molecule may "reproduce." Small black and white squares are elemental particles. The larger rectangles consisting of two white and two black squares are genetic material. (*a*) A molecule is in the process of building a replica of itself by collecting elemental particles along its surface. (*b*) A completed daughter molecule is splitting away from its mother. (*c*) A molecule is disintegrating because of some lethal environmental event.

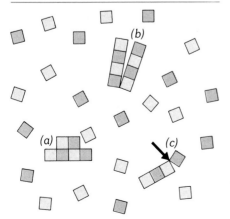

plant and animal life that existed in various parts of the world. Then in the seventeenth and eighteenth centuries the true nature of fossils and the depths of geologic time began to be understood. It became clear that the stratified rocks told stories of a world aeons old and of wonderful earlier creatures.

With these necessary preliminaries underway, the real explosion of evolutionary thought came when Charles Darwin published his *On the Origin of Species* in 1859. Darwin's theory of **natural selection** was based on observations of living and extinct animals, which he had made during a five-year scientific voyage around the world. According to Darwin, the variation that occurs in any population leaves some animals better adapted to their environment than others. These animals are the most likely to survive to maturity— **"survival of the fittest"**—and reproduce, passing their characteristics to the next generation.

In December of 1831, the H.M.S. *Beagle,* with Charles Robert Darwin (1809– 1882) aboard as ship naturalist, set forth on a five-year voyage through the waters and to the lands of the Southern Hemisphere. The voyage was the preparation for Darwin's lifework.

Early Phase of Evolution.   Biologists believe that the first primitive cells were **heterotrophs,** feeding and maintaining themselves on the same large molecules from which they themselves had been formed. Heterotrophs are organisms that obtain food from outside sources. These cells were the earliest animals. The supply of the large molecules in the waters in which they lived was limited, however. Fortunately, before the supply was exhausted, some of the early cells had acquired pigments by which to absorb sunlight. They began to synthesize organic molecules from their own carbon dioxide and from water. Able to feed themselves, these cells were the earliest plants. The heterotrophs, the animal cells, were then able to feed on these plant cells and, as they multiplied, on one another.

As animal forms evolved, competition between prey and predator, that is, between food and feeders, and between predator and predator, became major factors in natural selection. Certain physical characteristics were more advantageous than others. For example, greater size meant threat from fewer predators, so larger creatures survived. The animals had to move to find food, and the food, if it was also animal, had to move in order to avoid being destroyed. The selective pressure was for greater motility and speed.

The evolutionary process can be imagined as a chase for food, with those most adept in obtaining it the most likely to live on. To find more minerals and sunlight, some of the plant life moved from the sea onto the land. An arthropod was the first animal to follow this plant food. Amphibians evolved from lobefinned fish caught in dwindling pools, and insects evolved from a land arthropod. Later the reptilian line and then the mammalian evolved. Probably because of the intense threat imposed upon them as prey of the larger reptiles, our early mammalian ancestors led a nocturnal and subterranean existence. As soon as the large reptiles became extinct, mammals expanded their activities. They moved into the daylight, onto the land and into the sky, all previously dominated by the reptiles. The number and variety of mammals increased dramatically. One small shrewlike mammal followed the insects into the spreading forests. These creatures eventually gave rise to the smaller primates and then, later on, to the more advanced primates, the monkeys, apes, and hominids.

Hominid Ancestors.   Several major anatomical changes set the **hominids,** the branch of primates preceding and including human beings, apart from other primates: bipedalism, the ability to walk on two legs; a large and complex brain; and a decrease in the size of face and teeth. Bipedalism entailed a great many anatomical changes, one of which was a tilted, narrower pelvic region to permit smooth walking on two legs. Because of this development, female human beings have more difficulty giving birth than any other species. To add to the trouble, selection was also favoring comparatively larger-brained infants. The solution to this dilemma was for the young to be born at an earlier state of development. For ease at birth, they were smaller. But this shift left the hominid infants more dependent during their long period of growth and development after birth.

Most young animals can be relatively self-sufficient soon after birth—at least able to walk and attempt to escape predators. Hominid infants were at the mercy of the adults around them, and it is likely that the family was formed for the purpose of protecting and caring for infants. The long period of human infancy is ultimately highly adaptive because infancy and childhood are the time for socialization, for the passing on of culture and for learning the complex ways of living in social groups.

Cultural Evolution

The anatomical changes that marked hominid evolution interacted with our ancestors' development of culture. Biology both allowed for and was affected by emergence of human cultures. For example, the evolution of the most impressive human characteristic, the capacity for symbolic language, was made possible by changes in the physical structure of our ancestors' brains. Language, in turn, has surely promoted the rapid expansion of culture. Language made it possible for the products of learning to be passed from generation to generation, and for children to profit vicariously from the life experiences of their ancestors.

Another example of the harmonious development of biology and culture is bipedalism. This ability freed our ancestors' hands to make the items and carry out the behavior that their brains imagined. The ability to conceive of, construct, and use tools represented the beginnings of a uniquely human control over the environment. Since this stage, selective pressure for adaptation of the body has decreased because human beings have become ever more able to adapt to the environment by material means—to combat cold with clothing and fire and to make food palatable by cutting and cooking it. Consequently, once *Homo sapiens* began to act on the environment, evolution has proceeded in the realm of culture and social life rather than through changes in the anatomy of the body.

Cultural adaptations, however rudimentary, marked the transition in our ancestors' way of life from beastlike to human. The first step in this transition involved the means of finding food. Primates are foragers; they wander in search of food, usually plant matter, and each individual is primarily concerned with feeding itself. At some point in our distant past, however, our ancestors moved from forests into arid savannah land and began to hunt animals. Hunting requires cooperative efforts and usually provides food for more than one person. A major break from the primate pattern occurred, then, when human beings began to work together and share the results of their labor. The choice of hunting as a major means of subsistence probably encouraged the advancement of complex traits such as forethought and cooperation and increased the use of language and memory, for these would have been essential for the new way of life. Hunting also meant a sexual division of labor. Females were less mobile than men at times when they were pregnant or nursing infants, making it more feasible for women to stay behind when men went off on long hunts. Moreover, group cooperation in seeking life's necessities meant that each individual spent less time finding food to stay alive. Our ancestors were freed for leisure activities—visiting, playing, becoming creative with objects and thoughts. Perhaps the newfound leisure time paved the way for the development of abstract aspects of human culture such as art and religion. Fossils and artifacts provide

Copy of a prehistoric cave painting. Early in the course of cultural evolution, hominids worked and hunted together and recorded their hunts in paintings on the walls of caves.

evidence of this kind of culture by the time of the Neanderthals, from 125,000 to 40,000 years ago.

Approximately 10,000 years ago, our ancestors began to domesticate plants and animals and they shifted to a more settled, agricultural life-style. At this point the number of human beings increased enormously. In contrast to the demands of a hunter-gatherer's life, to keep group size down and to move in search of food, agriculture offered a stable food source, and permanent settling of large numbers of people was now possible. Thus societies grew, each adapting to their surroundings and developing appropriate material technologies and social institutions. For example, societies that lived near rivers developed technologies based on fishing.

Sociobiology

Sociobiology is a new and specialized discipline that is concerned with the biological basis of social behavior. Sociobiology looks to ethology and evolutionary theory to explain both nonhuman and human behavior. The basic premise of sociobiology is that biological evolution involves genetic competition between group members. That is, members of a species compete with one another in order to survive and to pass on their own genes. The individuals who do not survive and who do not conceive offspring are phylogenetic failures. The evolutionary process is permanently rid of their genetic material. According to sociobiological theory, all organisms are impelled by genetic forces to act in ways that maximize the probability of survival of their genetic material.

In this sense social evolution works counter to biological evolution. Complex urban societies require cooperation. If they are to evolve, they must overcome the biological selfishness of their members. They do so by formulating moral, religious, and social ethics which preach altruism, honesty, generosity, and selflessness. The most conspicuous social behavior that appears to run counter to biological evolution is **altruism,** the acts of individuals who sacrifice their own goals, even their lives, for the sake of another person or the group. Altruism seems totally inconsistent with a theory that sees every organism as struggling to pass its own genes on to future generations. The sociobiologists contend that the struggle to reproduce is not really among organisms themselves but among DNA molecules, and among organisms only because they are the carriers of DNA. Thus one individual's survival is less important than that of the group; altruism becomes a way of preserving the greatest amount of the group's genetic material.

Much of the supporting evidence for this theory is drawn from observations of other species. Darwin himself modified his theory of natural selection after observing certain social insects such as ants. He noticed a class of members who are essential to the survival of the colony but are incapable of reproduction. Darwin then argued that natural selection could operate at the level of the family or group rather than that of the individual. This can be seen clearly in the alarm calling of various species of rodents. An individual will call an alarm when a predator appears, endangering itself but warning the group. In one kind of squirrel, reproducing females give alarms more often than ones without offspring nearby, and individuals with relatives nearby call more often than those without (Barash, 1979). In each case making alarm sounds is most likely when large amounts of closely related genetic material are there to be protected.

Another behavior that sociobiology explains in terms of maintaining genes is reproduction. Since males can reproduce again and again, their genetic material is most certain to survive if they mate with as many females as possible. Females, on the other hand, are limited in the number of times that they can reproduce. For purposes of preserving genetic material, they should put more effort into bearing and rearing offspring. It is better for them for be "choosy" in selecting a mate and to be conscientious in caring for their offspring. It follows from this that competition among males will be far greater than among females, because males perpetually strive for as many females as possible. In support of this notion, sociobiological accounts provide numerous examples of fierce male competition or "harem" arrangements among animals, and of differences in the mating and reproductive behavior of men and women in primitive as well as modern societies.

Sociobiological reasoning attempts to cover virtually all social behavior, from human sexual mores to racism. Not surprisingly, reactions against the theory and its overriding emphasis on genetics abound. It is argued that the assumptions of the theory are untestable; that generalizations from animal behavior to human behavior are made too easily; that the theory attempts to rationalize social problems like sexism and racism. To some sociobiology may seem intuitively correct, to others abhorrently simplified, especially with respect to human behavior. As human beings we are unique in our capacity to think, predict, and plan the consequences of our behavior. We can thereby modify the dictates of our genes. Still, we do inherit a genetic makeup which defines our potentialities. Although we may not be at the mercy of our genes to the extent that some sociobiological reasoning suggests, this field of study highlights the potential scope of biological influences on our behavior.

SUMMARY

Evolutionary thought began as a mighty challenge to the religious concept of a permanently unchanging world. The major breakthrough was Darwin's theory of natural selection. Darwin reasoned that organisms with traits that help them adapt to the environment are more likely to survive and reproduce. Then eventually these traits come to characterize the population.

The evolution of life on earth can be traced through a number of major phases, beginning with the first animal and plant cells. In the search for food, and to avoid becoming food, animals evolved in a great number of forms. Because of our common ancestry, human beings share many of the characteristics of other primates.

Hominids, the primates preceding and including human beings, developed many of the traits that are now uniquely human, the most important a large and complex brain. Hominids also developed a culture in which the use of tools and language became important. Agriculture marked the beginning of settled existence 10,000 years ago. Ever since then human beings have adapted to their environments by cultural innovations; pressure for anatomical adaptations has decreased.

Sociobiology, a new field of behavior genetics, holds as its premise that genetic factors underlie all social behavior, which therefore serves the purposes of natural selection. Drawing evidence from studies of animal and primitive human cultures, sociobiology proposes that there are genetic reasons for acts of altruism, for sex roles, and for other social behavior. This strong emphasis on genetics has met severe opposition, chiefly on the grounds that sociobiological theory generalizes too freely from animal to human behavior. As with any extreme hereditarian position, the weakness of sociobiology is its tendency to downplay environmental forces. Its strength is that it forces us to consider the biological influences on aspects of behavior for which they may have been overlooked.

The long, slim bodies of the Bororo nomads of the Niger Republic give them a high surface-to-volume ratio, allowing their body heat to dissipate.

RACE AND THE INHERITANCE OF BEHAVIOR

Current social and political issues, such as desegregation in our public schools and our attitudes and national posture toward newly emerging nations, make the question of racial differences in behavior an important one. But the problem is complex. At least three difficult questions are posed. (1) Are there measurable racial differences in behavior? The answer to this question is "yes." (2) Are these differences inherent in the race, or can they be traced to dissimilarities in culture? This is the scientific issue to which our discussion will be directed. (3) Do any discovered differences in the races justify keeping the members of a particular race in a socially subservient position? Obvious as the answer is, this question cannot be ignored, for its presence in the background of what should be a straightforward scientific evaluation has often tainted the interpretation of data.

Evolution and Races

Different races are formed when groups of people are isolated from one another in differing environments. Over time a group may come to differ from other groups in the frequency of one or more genes. The biological definition of a **race** is in terms of gene frequencies. In this sense a race is a group of people distinguished from other groups by a gene frequency different from that found in other populations.

Natural selection is the most important process that brings about differences in the gene frequencies of races, in the same way that it brings about differences between species. Within every population there are people with different genetic makeups. Those with genes that help them adapt to their particular environment are the most likely to survive and to reproduce. Thus, over time, genes that provide a survival advantage become more numerous and eventually come to characterize the **gene pool,** the collection of genes available to the population. Since environments differ, we would not expect the genes that are advantageous in one environment to be advantageous in another. Over the course of evolution, populations in different geographic regions have come to vary from one another in their genetic makeups.

For example, the skin of early human beings was the filter that controlled the absorption of sunlight. Sunlight causes a layer of tissue just under the skin to produce vitamin D. If too little vitamin D is produced, the individual suffers from the softening of the bones associated with rickets. With too much vitamin D, bones become brittle and are easily broken. Thus in northern climates there was a selective pressure favoring fair skins that could pass the faint rays of the northern sun. Nearer the equator, however, natural selection favored a heavy pigmentation that reduced the amount of sun penetrating the skin. Since individuals suffering from either rickets or frequent bone fractures are less likely to produce offspring than are healthy individuals, the genes underlying the right degree of pigmentation for the particular climate came to multiply through progeny until they were representative of the population.

To cite another example, the long-limbed, slim bodies of African black populations yield a high surface-to-volume ratio that allows heat to dissipate into the environment. The short-limbed, fleshy body of the Eskimo is equally valuable in a cold climate, since it conserves heat. The survival value of many traits, such as the distinctive shapes of eyes, ears, and lips found in particular populations, is not as clear. Nor is it evident why males in some South American Indian tribes have blue penises (Goldsby, 1971). As we have already seen, intelligence and personality traits are influenced by genetic factors, just as physical structure is. It therefore seems probable that, in the process of natural selection, differing racial groups may have found certain psychological traits to be valuable in adapting to their particular environments. For example, aggression might very well be a more essential trait in hunting populations than in those whose diet is for the most part vegetarian.

As appealing as this notion may seem, the obvious environmental alternative is just as attractive. Consider how the social behavior of the Bantu tribesman differs from that of the Canadian Eskimo, and how both differ from that of the college student on an American campus. Does it not seem reasonable to explain these differences in terms of the tremendously diverse environments and cultural histories of their racial groups? Obviously we must be prepared once more for the conclusion that cultural and genetic factors both make their contributions. The exact nature and relative importance of these contributions remain to be determined.

Race and Intelligence

By far the largest number of investigations of behavioral differences in races have had to do with the intelligence of American whites and blacks. Since these two groups differ in respect to the frequencies of particular genes, they satisfy the definition for being different races. On the other hand, they are far from pure races, for there has been considerable intermating. As B. E. Ginsburg noted, ". . . American Negroes have received 20 to 30 percent of their genes from the white population [and] we are, therefore, closer to being brothers under the skin than phenotypic appearance would suggest" (1971, p. 232).

The empirical finding that American blacks and whites differ in average IQ has never been in dispute. But for many decades the interpretation of these findings has constituted one of the bitterest controversies in psychology. Considering the data from all studies, the indication is that the difference between the two groups is about 15 IQ points, with whites having a mean IQ of approximately 100 and blacks a mean of approximately 85. This 15-point difference quickly reduces to 11 points if the blacks and whites being compared are of the same socioeconomic status. What is responsible for this 11-point difference? This question raises the nature-nurture issue in a particularly controversial way.

The Jensen Controversy. In 1969 Arthur Jensen published a monograph in the *Harvard Educational Review* that captured the nation's attention and created a furor. The bulk of the monograph was a scholarly discussion of the evidence concerning the genetic component in intelligence and had nothing to do with racial differences in IQ. Jensen concluded that the genetic component was substantial and thought that the best estimate of the heritability ratio for intelligence was .80. This figure, you will recall, is on the high side, but within the range of values reported in Table 2.2.

Had Jensen written no more than this, his paper would have been counted as nothing more than another analysis indicating that heredity is indeed important in determining intelligence. In a relatively brief section of his paper, however, Jensen went beyond this and suggested that since the intelligence of individuals *within* races is so influenced by inheritance, it seemed possible that the mean IQ differences *between* races might also be caused by differences in genetic endowment. The mere mention of this possiblity created what came to be called the ''Jensen controversy.''

The bitterness aroused by Jensen's paper led John Loehlin, Gardner Lindzey, and James Spuhler (1975) to undertake an extensive review of the research on racial and ethnic group differences in intelligence. They examined studies of heritability of intelligence in black and white persons, studies of intelligence in mixed-race children, and studies of the patterns of abilities of different racial and ethnic groups. Their conclusion was that the observed average differences in the IQ test scores of American racial and ethnic groups could not be explained on the basis of genetic differences alone. Other factors, such as differences in the living conditions of the groups and inadequacies and biases in the tests, also affect performance. These factors will be discussed in turn.

Social Status.   We have seen that equating whites and blacks on socioeconomic status reduces their average IQ difference from 15 to 11 points. Such matching, however, does not truly equate the groups on their environmental experiences. Important differences remain.

- Even within the same social class, the two racial groups often have markedly different environments. In terms of health factors, for example, black children often receive poorer prenatal and early postnatal care than white children of the same class, as evidenced by the higher infant mortality rate among blacks.
- Of special importance for the type of achievement reflected in test scores is whether the child comes from a stable family headed by both parents. In all social classes more blacks have broken homes, defined by the absence of the father (Figure 2.14).

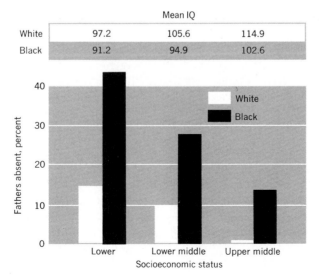

Figure 2.14
Nonverbal IQ scores of white and black children of different socioeconomic status, and the percentage of their fathers absent from home. (Adapted from Deutsch and Brown, 1964.)

Black children adopted and raised in well-to-do white homes show substantial increases in IQ.

• The effects of prejudice itself probably contribute to the difference. Until our society divests itself of the view that blacks are inferior to whites and abandons the prejudicial behavior that is associated with this view, we will never know exactly how much white racism has lowered the IQ scores of black children.

Some studies of racial differences in intelligence have done a great deal to reduce the differences in social status of the groups being compared. These are the studies of the IQ scores of black children raised in white homes. In one study (Scarr and Weinberg, 1978) black and interracial adolescents who had been adopted in their first year of life by white middle- or upper-class families were found to have a mean IQ of 110. There was no reason to believe that the biological parents of these adolescents were above average in intelligence. Thus being raised by white, well-to-do families apparently pushed their IQ scores 10 points above the mean IQ of the white population and approximately 25 points above the mean IQ of black children raised by their own families.

Tests. Differences in the IQs of blacks and whites are only differences in scores on tests of intelligence. These tests have been constructed primarily on the basis of the performance of whites and may have a cultural bias that favors whites (see page 418). For instance, many of the words in the vocabulary portions of the tests are much more likely to be encountered in the white culture than in the black.

Motivation and Test-Taking Behavior. Test scores are not perfect indicators of a child's ability. A number of factors have been found to depress the test scores of black children. In general, they may have less motivation to score highly on tests because their aspirations are lower (Katz, 1968); they often have greater anxiety about taking tests (Zigler, Abelson, and Seitz, 1973); and they are sometimes inhibited when tested by an adult member of a different race (Sattler, 1970). Given these drawbacks, the test scores of black children may very well be less adequate indicators of their intellectual abilities than are the test scores of white children.

Educational Opportunity. There is a geographical variation in the IQ scores of blacks and whites. This variation is probably related to the different amounts that states spend for education and to the amounts spent within each state to educate blacks and whites. Spuhler and Lindzey (1967) found higher intelligence scores for both blacks and whites who were residents of states that had a higher per capita expenditure for education. Although within states whites consistently scored higher than blacks, some groups of Northern blacks scored higher than some groups of Southern whites.

The effects of better schooling in the North were seen in a study of black children who had migrated to Philadelphia. As indicated in Table 2.5, the longer the children lived in Philadelphia, the higher their IQs became. The group who entered school in the first grade (1A) had a mean IQ of 86.5; this had increased to 92.8 by the ninth grade (9A). Furthermore, in virtually all grades the earlier children had begun their studies in the Philadelphia schools, the better they did in comparison with those who were latecomers to the school system.

Race Differences and Racism

The racial differences described in the preceding section represent differences between average values for groups. They reveal little about the traits of any one member of a particular race. Average differences between races are one

Table 2.5 Mean IQs of Black Children with Varying Periods of Residence in Philadelphia

Group	N	Mean IQ at Grade Listed				
		1A	2B	4B	6B	9A
Born in Philadelphia —no kindergarten	424	92.1	93.4	94.7	94.0	93.7
Southern-born— entered Philadelphia schools in grade: 1A	182	86.5	89.3	91.8	93.3	92.8
1B-2B	109		86.7	88.6	90.9	90.5
3A-4B	199			86.3	87.2	89.4
5A-6B	221				88.2	90.2
7A-9A	219					87.4

Adapted from Lee, 1951.

thing; differences between individual members of the same race are another matter entirely. The student will do well to learn and remember the following general principle because it is so basic. *The variation in the psychological traits of individual members of a race is always greater than the average difference between races.*

This principle is clearly demonstrated with IQ scores. For white children variations in IQ range from a rare low near zero to an equally rare high above 200. For black children the range is exactly the same. The 15-point difference in mean IQ scores of blacks and whites is therefore much less than the variability of scores of members of the same race (200 points). In addition, the fact that the range of IQ scores for blacks and whites is the same means that there is tremendous overlap in the scores of the two races.

Of late, the term racist has been used so gratuitously that it has been robbed of all meaning. In an attempt to restore a measure of sense to the discussion, we make the following distinction. An individual who investigates racial differences, while at the same time appreciating the variation within a race, is not a racist. A **racist** is an individual who ignores individual variation and concludes that because members of group A get a higher average score on some measure than members of group B, every member of group A is "superior" to every member of group B.

Whatever the outcome of investigations of racial differences, there is clearly no ethical basis for allowing either proven or unproven group differences to affect how people are treated.

SUMMARY

Biologically, races are groups that differ in a number of traits because they have different frequencies of particular genes. These varying genetic makeups emerged over the course of evolution as natural selection acted on groups living in different environments.

Studies of racial differences in behavior have been numerous, but their results have been difficult to interpret since so many factors are uncontrolled or uncontrollable when comparing races. For example, although racial differences in average IQ exist, there are also racial differences in environmental factors known to affect IQs. These include socioeconomic standing, quality of medical care, nutrition, and prejudice. In addition, cultural bias in tests, motivational factors influencing test-taking behavior, and quality of schooling favor the white group. An important principle to consider when comparing behavioral differences of races is that the variability found within any given race is large compared with the variation between any two races.

APPLICATION OF GENETIC PRINCIPLES

With rapid gains in knowledge in the fields of genetics and reproduction, we may soon attain incredible power over our genetic future. Before long we may be able to eliminate certain diseases, improve particular genes, and alter gene frequencies in the population. These possibilities evoke both enthusiasm and fear—enthusiasm that genetic manipulations may greatly improve the lot of humankind, and fear that this new power, if not used wisely, may become yet another tool that can ultimately destroy the human race.

Eugenics

Concern for the genetic potential of the human species has a long history. The ancient Greek philosopher Plato wrote in his *Republic* that if we do not wish to see the human race degenerate, we should apply some lessons learned from breeders of hunting dogs and birds of prey. That is, we should encourage unions between the better members of the population and limit matings of the worse. This concern for our genetic potential and methods for improving it have come to be known as **eugenics,** a term coined by Sir Francis Galton in 1883. Galton also made some practical recommendations for improving the human gene pool, such as urging men and women of superior family stock to have large families and giving fellowships to good students so that they could marry and produce children.

The eugenics movement was very influential in many parts of the world in the early part of the twentieth century. In America many states enacted compulsory sterilization laws to prevent the reproduction of "sexual perverts," "drug fiends," "diseased and degenerate persons," and "drunkards." In addition, restrictive immigration laws were written to limit the number of southern and eastern Europeans who could settle and thereby "mix" in the population. In England Karl Pearson, a disciple of Galton, continually employed genetic arguments in an effective effort to stem the immigration of Polish and Russian Jews. He wrote, "Taken on the average, and regarding both sexes, this alien Jewish population is somewhat inferior physically and mentally to the native population" (quoted in Hirsch, 1970, pp. 92–93). It is interesting to note that before fifty years had passed, another distinguished Englishman, C. P. Snow, argued that in light of the large number of Jewish Nobel laureates, Jews must be a superior people. We thus see how tenuous are assertions that a particular group is inferior or superior.

Medical Genetics

Today scientists have moved beyond the simplistic notions of genetic superiority and inferiority to the more humane problems of preventing and ameliorating genetic disease. About one in ten gametes in the general population carries bad genetic news (Gardner, 1975), in the form of a **mutation,** a fundamental change in genetic material. The majority of mutations are deleterious, and most embryos bearing abnormal genes are miscarried. About 2 percent of newborns, however, suffer recognizable genetic defects. Agents that can cause mutations

include toxic wastes, environmental radiation, certain drugs, some of the compounds in smog, certain pesticides and viral infections. The most effective single
way of preventing genetic disease is to prevent mutations by eliminating haz-
ardous materials from the environment and protecting people from those that
cannot be totally eliminated.

Genetic Screening and Counseling.   Another way to prevent, or at least
minimize, genetic disease is to screen potential parents for the existence of
defective genes. If individuals are discovered to be carriers of a genetic disease,
or have genetic disorders in their family backgrounds, they can receive advice
from genetic counselors on the risk of passing these on to their children. On
the basis of the odds, an individual can decide whether or not to have children.

Some of these genes are more frequently found in certain ethnic groups and
family lineages than in others. Jews of eastern European descent, for example,
are more likely than the rest of the population to carry the gene for Tay-Sachs
disease. This disorder causes blindness, brain deterioration, paralysis, and finally
death within the first two or three years of life. The disease is inherited as a
recessive trait and appears only in children who receive the Tay-Sachs gene
from both parents. A blood test now available can determine whether a man
and woman planning a family are carriers of the gene. If only one of them is a
carrier, none of their children will have the disease, although one in two will be
carriers. If both husband and wife are carriers, each child will have a 25 percent
chance of inheriting the disease. Blood tests are also available to detect carriers
of sickle-cell anemia, a blood cell disorder typically found in the black population, and thalassemia, a related anemia generally found in people of Mediter-
ranean origin.

Prenatal Diagnosis and Treatment.   Those at risk for passing on certain
genetic diseases can take the gamble with greater confidence now that there
are specific tests to determine whether an unborn child has a particular disorder.
A procedure that has enabled the prenatal detection of many genetic abnormalities is **amniocentesis.** In the uterus the baby is surrounded by the amnion,
a fluid-filled sac which contains, among other things, skin cells shed by the
fetus. In amniocentesis some amniotic fluid is withdrawn from the uterus of the
expectant mother through a special needle. Both the fluid and cells are then
tested for a variety of biochemical abnormalities that can signal the presence of
a genetic defect. Nearly eighty biochemical disorders can be detected prenatally,
including Tay-Sachs disease and thalassemia.

The cells of the fetus can also be tested for chromosomal abnormalities. The
cells are grown in the laboratory to a certain stage of cell division allowing
analysis of the chromosomes. For example, Down syndrome, a condition in
which the child has a broad face, slanted eyes, shortened limbs, and mental
retardation, can be detected in a karyotype by the presence of an extra number
21 chromosome. A woman's chances of having a baby with Down syndrome
increase dramatically each year after the age of thirty-five. For this reason it is
recommended that older pregnant women undergo amniocentesis so that the
fetal chromosomes can be analyzed.

An important goal of diagnosing a genetic defect prenatally is to treat the
child while still in the womb or soon after birth. Treatment can now be administered through the mother or directly to the fetus for a few disorders such as
Rh blood disease and methylmalonic aciduria, a biochemical defect which
causes poor muscle tone and mental retardation and prevents the infant from

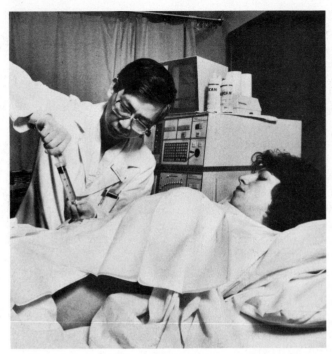

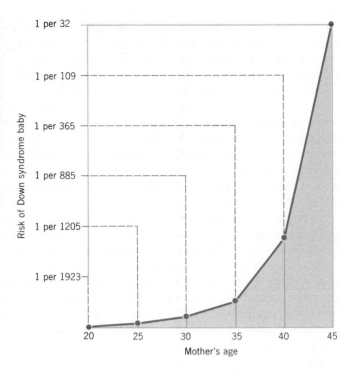

Although the great majority of pregnant women in their thirties and forties deliver normal babies, the risk of having a child with some form of abnormality increases sharply in these years. For one thing, aging eggs do not always halve the small chromosomes of pair 21. Amniocentesis, a procedure in which the physician draws a small amount of amniotic fluid from the uterus, makes it possible to detect the extra chromosome 21 causing Down syndrome.

thriving. No prenatal treatment is yet possible, however, for the majority of serious and fatal genetic diseases, although progress is being made. As more knowledge is gathered and as genetic counseling becomes more widely available, it is hoped that many of these tragic disorders can someday be eliminated.

Genetic Engineering

Many human disorders are associated with specific enzyme deficiencies that are known to be genetically determined. These disorders are sometimes called inborn errors of metabolism. One of them is phenylketonuria (PKU), in which a single defective gene causes an insufficiency in the enzyme phenylalanine hydroxylase. Because of the lack of this one enzyme, the brain becomes badly damaged and mental retardation results. Currently, newborns may be screened for PKU by a simple blood or urine test. Children who have the disorder are maintained on a very specialized diet. Although this treatment is effective in preventing the retardation, it is very expensive and must be strictly observed for a number of years.

A far simpler way of treating PKU and similar single gene disorders would be to repair the defective gene, if only we had the ability. Gene manipulation may not be as far off as we would imagine. For example, bacteria have now been given the ability to form the gene that carries instructions for producing the hormone insulin. Bacteria in nature do not have this gene. This feat has been accomplished by splicing into the genetic material of the bacteria the section of DNA from rat cells that specifies the hormone. In this way insulin and other substances necessary to human health can be artificially produced in laboratories and made more easily obtainable and affordable to people whose bodies are unable to manufacture them.

Despite the possible benefits of such programs of **genetic engineering,** many scientists and laymen are urging that research on transplanting and recombining genes of different animal species be discontinued. They fear that unnatural organisms harmful to human beings might be produced in the laboratory and escape into the environment. Since adequate safeguards are so essential, most recombinant DNA research is being conducted in conformity with stringent safety guidelines.

Another extreme form of genetic engineering is **cloning.** This is an asexual form of reproduction in which all progeny are genetically identical. A number of years ago an African clawed frog was produced by cloning. The experimenter, J. B. Gurdon (1968), obtained an unfertilized egg cell from a frog, destroyed the nucleus, and replaced it with the nucleus from an intestinal cell of a tadpole. The egg, now containing the full complement of chromosomes characteristic of its species, began to divide and grow as though it had been fertilized. The resulting frog was an identical replica of the tadpole that served as the nuclear donor. Not long after the first reports of cloning in other species appeared, a science writer caused a stir by claiming that the cloning of a man had already been achieved. This kind of publicity, and the fear that particular individuals and their many "carbon copies" will try to take over the world, have made people want to restrict further research on cloning. The consensus of scientific opinion is that, for now, cloning techniques have this degree of sophistication only in science fiction. With adequate safeguards cloning may prove useful in research on chromosomes, cancer, aging, and organ transplants.

Cloning and manipulating genes are the most spectacular but not the only means of altering genetic material. Even the relatively simpler procedures of genetic counseling, amniocentesis, abortion, artifical insemination, test tube conception, and contraception are powerful tools for tampering with the genetic inheritance of our species. These techniques can be used to increase our understanding and control of genetic disease, and they can greatly alleviate human suffering. Indiscriminate use of these tools to gratify selfish and temporary needs can be extremely dangerous, however.

The choice of a baby's sex is an example. An older pregnant woman reportedly underwent amniocentesis to discover whether her child had Down syndrome. Upon receiving the chromosomal analysis, the doctor gave her the good news that she was carrying a perfectly normal baby girl. The woman promptly elected to have an abortion, hoping that the next child she conceived would be a boy.

Most couples would probably be reluctant to undertake the expense and inherent physical danger of repeated amniocenteses and abortions for the mere pleasure of selecting their child's sex. If, however, a simple technique could increase the chances of their having either a boy or a girl, many couples might give it a try. Such a technique is now under study, but let us consider what might happen if a foolproof method were indeed available.

For whatever reasons, in most societies sons are preferred to daughters. If many couples practiced some technique to increase the probability of their having sons, drastic changes in society could conceivably occur. First there would be a decrease in the population, since fewer women would be available to have babies. This of course could alter the entire economic system. The institutions of marriage and the family might have to be revamped or even replaced by a system of polyandry, with women having more than one husband. Thus even a simple procedure for genetic control could have a tremendous impact on the whole structure of a society.

Of perhaps greater significance is the impact that procedures to control our reproduction and genes might have on the gene pool and ultimately on the survival of our species. If we were to decide that a particular combination of traits is desirable, we could use all the genetic engineering techniques at our disposal to promote these traits in the population. In time these efforts would decrease our genetic diversity. Since there is no way of knowing what the nature of the environment will be in the far future, we could breed out genes that might someday have survival value for our species.

As the techniques for choosing who shall or shall not be born, and what traits they shall have, become better developed and more widespread, we will need to examine the implications that these choices may have for our society and for humankind's genetic inheritance. It is clear that in applying even the simplest of these techniques, we are adding our hand to the force of natural selection. The question is whether we can ever be wise enough to direct the future evolution of the human race.

SUMMARY

People have long wanted to improve human genetic potential. The eugenics movement of the early part of the twentieth century focused on how to safeguard the quality of our gene pool. With gains in knowledge in the fields of genetics and reproduction, concern has shifted to the prevention of genetic disease. Today individuals can be screened to determine whether they are carriers of particular genetic disorders and counseled on the risk of passing on genetic defects to their offspring. Certain genetic diseases can be detected prenatally by examining a sample of the amniotic fluid surrounding the fetus, some of the fetal cells found in this fluid, or the maternal or fetal blood. A few diseases may even be treated while the child is still in the uterus.

Research of gene repair and cloning may someday help to alleviate the human suffering caused by genetic disease. The indiscriminate and widespread application of genetic engineering techniques, however, may have serious consequences for society. It is essential that human genetic diversity be maintained in order to preserve our ability to adapt in future environments.

TO BE SURE YOU UNDERSTAND THIS CHAPTER

This chapter introduces many important concepts. You should know the meaning of those in the following list.

Gene	Turner syndrome
F_1 or first filial generation	Klinefelter syndrome
Law of segregation	XYY male
Germ cell	Selective breeding
Allele	Nature-nurture interaction
Homozygous	Gene-environment interaction
Heterozygous	Heritability ratio (H)
Dominant gene	Variance
Recessive gene	Environmental variance
Law of independent assortment	$V_{environmental}$
Albinism	Genetic variance
Genotype	$V_{genetic}$
Phenotype	Phenotypic variance
Norm of reaction	$V_{phenotypic}$
Normal distribution	Monozygotic twins
Polygenic inheritance	Dizygotic twins
Chromosome	Organic evolution
DNA	Natural selection
Zygote	Survival of the fittest
Karyotype	Heterotroph

Hominid	**Racist**
Cultural evolution	**Eugenics**
Sociobiology	**Mutation**
Altruism	**Amniocentesis**
Race	**Genetic engineering**
Gene pool	**Cloning**

Several points that are not well covered by a listing of concepts should be reviewed.

Selective breeding studies of emotionality and maze learning

Twin studies and the inheritance of personality traits

The Jensen controversy

Variation in psychological traits among and within races

TO GO BEYOND THIS CHAPTER

In This Book. The nature-nurture issue comes up in connection with every psychological topic. There are briefer discussions of the heritability of psychological functions in Chapter 5, on perception, and in Chapter 8 in connection with alcoholism. Chapters 11 and 14 add to the discussion in the context of cognitive development. In Chapter 9 the issue becomes whether motives are inborn or learned. Chapter 12 examines the degree to which heredity and learning influence the development of emotions, temperament, attachment, and sex roles. Chapter 18 has substantial material on the inheritance of mental disorders.

Elsewhere. An excellent textbook of genetics is Eldon Gardner and D. Peter Snustad's *Principles of Genetics,* which contains detailed accounts of genetic mechanisms and genetic engineering. A clear and readable discussion of medical genetics can be found in Aubrey Milunsky's *Know Your Genes. Evolution, Genetics, and Man,* by Theodosius Dobzhansky, provides a thorough treatment of how natural selection and adaptation to the environment are important in the process of evolution. For a clear discussion of polygenic explanations of inheritance, G. E. McClearn's chapter in *Psychology in the Making,* edited by Leo Postman, is recommended. A book that brings together the best literature on the nature-nurture controversy over intelligence is N. J. Block and Gerald Dworkin's *The IQ Controversy.* A standard reference on behavior genetics, John Fuller and William Thompson's *Foundations of Behavior Genetics,* contains an excellent discussion of genetic principles and of animal and human behavior genetics studies.

CHAPTER 3   NERVOUS AND ENDOCRINE SYSTEMS

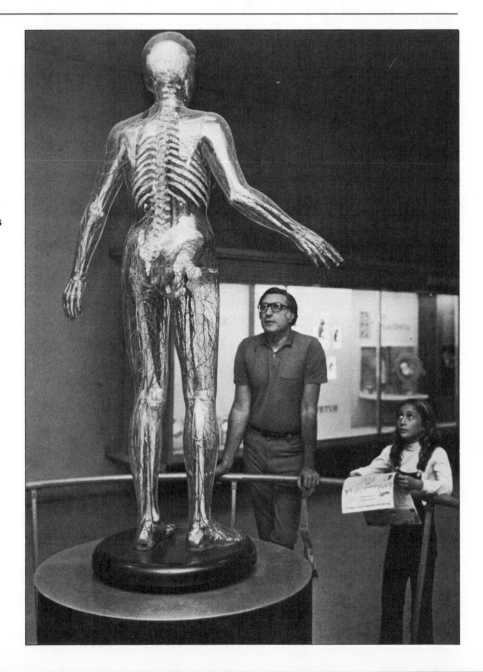

The study of the biological basis of behavior focuses on the two anatomical systems that are the most directly involved in regulating behavior, the nervous system and the endocrine system. These two systems, which are intimately interrelated both structurally and functionally, enable the organism to make the best possible adaptation to the demands of its environment. They permit individuals to detect events in their surroundings, to change their behavior and physiology in response to environmental requirements, and to maximize their own chances of personal survival as well the survival of their species.

Knowledge of how the nervous and endocrine systems influence behavior has been gained by a wide variety of methods, most of which may be divided into two groups: those that decrease the level of activity of one system or the other and those based on the opposite strategy of increasing such activity. Thus parts of the nervous system may be removed or destroyed to abolish their activity. Or brain regions may be electrically or chemically stimulated to increase activity. For obvious ethical reasons, these procedures are used almost exclusively with lower animals. In human beings affected by diseases, genetic abnormalities, and accidents, natural experiments are sometimes possible. For example, a stroke, which is caused by disruption of the blood supply to a region of the brain, may impair or destroy that region's ability to function. Genetic anomalies may cause too much or too little secretion of certain hormones, the chemical substances produced by endocrine glands. By studying the changes in behavior that occur with such disruptions of physiological functioning, we are able to gain considerable knowledge about how the nervous and endocrine systems work and govern behavior.

Overview of the Nervous System.   The human nervous system (Figures 3.1 and 3.2) consists of two principal parts, the **central nervous system** and the **peripheral nervous system.** There are, in turn, two parts of the central nervous system, the **brain** and **spinal cord,** which are contained within the skull and bony spinal column. Together they control bodily activity via the peripheral nerves. The peripheral nervous system consists of four types of nerve fibers: the **somatic sensory** fibers, which carry information from the receptors—the eyes, ears, nose, skin, and so on—to the central nervous system; the **somatic motor** fibers, which carry commands from the central system to the skeletal muscles, those attached to bones, instructing them to move the body; the **visceral sensory** fibers, which carry information about the internal state of the body and viscera to the central system; and the **visceral motor** fibers,

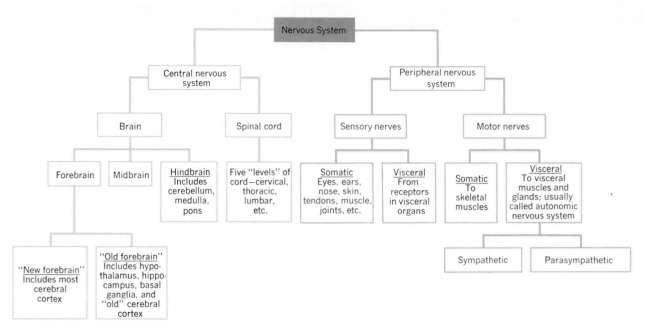

Figure 3.1
Major subdivisions of the nervous system. This chart provides an overview of the various sections of the nervous system to be covered in this chapter. Figure 3.2 presents some of the same information in an anatomical form.

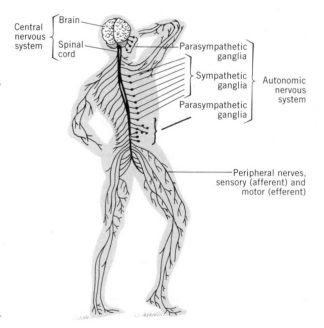

Figure 3.2
Plan of the human nervous system. The brain and spinal cord are the two parts of the central nervous system. Sympathetic and parasympathetic ganglia are two parts of the autonomic nervous system. Every organ of the body is connected with every other through the central nervous system.

which carry commands from the central system to the smooth muscles of the blood vessels and internal organs, to heart muscles, and to glands. The two types of sensory fibers are sometimes called **afferent** because they carry messages toward the central nervous system; the two types of motor fibers are sometimes called **efferent** because they carry messages away from the central nervous system. The visceral motor fibers are usually referred to as the *autonomic nervous system;* it plays an important role in a person's reactions to situations of psychological importance.

Examination of the most obvious physical features of the nervous system, such as the size of the brain, reveals little or nothing about psychological function. The brains of most adult males weigh about three pounds (1350

PHRENOLOGY

The pseudoscience of phrenology began at the turn of the nineteenth century and flourished through much of it; it has some adherents even today. Phrenology assumed correctly that different parts of the brain serve separate functions. From there, however, phrenology went on to make many false claims. The phrenologists proposed, for example, that some psychological characteristics such as religiosity, scientific aptitude, and patriotism have such localization. Certainly they do not. The phrenologists also assumed incorrectly that brain functions are bounded by neat, rectilinear boundaries. Finally, they assumed that the development of strong traits of personality would increase the amount of tissue in the appropriate part of the brain. This greater amount of tissue would in turn require that the area of the skull above it become larger in size. On these grounds the phrenologists claimed to be able to determine a person's characteristics of personality and talents by examining the bumps on his or her skull. These claims were very seldom tested and never verified.

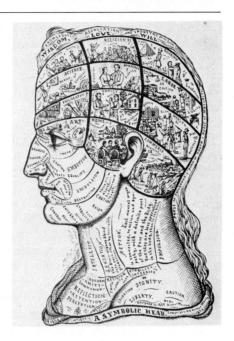

grams), but some weigh as little as two pounds (900 grams) or as much as four pounds (1800 grams). We wonder immediately, of course, whether these differences might not be related to psychological traits such as intelligence. A number of brains of brilliant men have been weighed and measured after death. When compared with the weights and sizes of the brains of average, or even subaverage, persons, these brains were neither heavier nor larger (Donaldson, 1900).[1] Moreover, for at least a hundred years investigators have studied the pattern of furrows and fissures in the brain, hoping to discover intimations of intelligence, personality, or moral fiber, but nothing of the sort was ever demonstrated. This means that the search for a relationship between brain and behavior must turn to a more detailed examination of the nervous system, of its cellular elements, the interconnections among these elements, and the functionings of particular parts of the system.

The almost infinite number of specific functions of the nervous system can be divided into two general categories, *communication* and *integration*. As a communicative network, the nervous system allows organs at one place in the body to respond to events occurring elsewhere. As an integrative system, it deals with the enormous amount of simultaneous stimulation that impinges upon the individual from inside as well as outside the body. It continuously evaluates the importance of all incoming stimulation and directs the activities of the organs into a unified and appropriate course of action.

[1] The brains of people with a few types of organic retardation have been found to be smaller and to weigh less.

THE NEURON

The entire nervous system is composed of only two kinds of cells, **glia cells** and nerve cells, or **neurons.** Glia cells provide a mechanical framework supporting the networks of neurons; they insulate one neuron from another; they police the nervous system for foreign materials and debris resulting from injury or infection; and they provide a chemical barrier, the **blood-brain barrier,** which prevents some substances in the blood from contacting the sensitive nerve cells.

The active elements of the nervous system are the neurons. The nervous system contains some ten billion of them and they take numerous specialized forms, one of which is shown in Figure 3.3. There are four main parts of a neuron: (1) the **cell body,** which contains the nucleus of the nerve cell and its nutritional mechanisms; (2) several **dendrites,** which are usually short and thick extensions of the cell body; (3) a single **axon,** which is a thin cylinder of cytoplasm extending for some distance from the cell body and eventually branching; and (4) numerous **terminal buttons,** each a small swelling at the end of one of the axon's many fine terminal branches. A neuron receives stimulation at its cell body and dendrites, conducts a signal along its axon, and emits its responses at the terminal buttons. The axon of a neuron is usually sheathed in a white, fatty, insulating substance called **myelin,** which is produced by the glia. In general, the conductive part of the neuron is myelinated and insulated; receptive parts and the fine terminal branches are not.

Communicative Action

The axons of most neurons are less than a millimeter long, but some peripheral neurons have axons or nerve fibers several feet in length. For example, the sensory neurons whose dendrites are in the skin of the feet have cell bodies near the spinal cord and terminal buttons near the base of the brain. Thus the site of a neuron's stimulation is usually at some distance, and may be a considerable distance, from the site at which it responds. Obviously, there must be a communicative mechanism by which stimulation of the dendrites and cell body of a neuron can trigger a reaction fairly far away. This communicative mechanism is the **nerve impulse.**

The Nerve Impulse.   When a neuron is adequately stimulated, an electro-chemical reaction occurs in the walls of the axon near the place where the axon leaves the cell body. This reaction is the nerve impulse; once established, it traverses the entire axon. The speed of the nerve impulse is fairly slow, 10 to

Figure 3.3
The neuron. The cell body and dendrites are receptive and integrative parts; axons are communicative parts; terminal buttons are transmitting parts. Insulating myelin sheaths the axon. Terminal buttons secrete a transmitter substance, the neurotransmitter, upon arrival of an impulse.

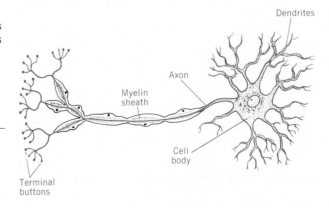

250 miles per hour, depending on whether the diameter of the axon is small or large and on the thickness of the myelin sheath.

The nerve impulse is accompanied by small electrical changes called an **action potential.** The existence of action potentials makes the nerve impulse relatively easy to observe and measure. Small wire electrodes placed near the surface of the axon detect the electrical activity generated by the neuron, which can then be amplified and recorded in visual form (Figure 3.4).

One fact revealed by these recordings is that the action potential of any given neuron is always the same size and shape and has the same speed as it travels the length of the axon. This means that the axon conducts whole impulses or none at all, sometimes called the **all-or-none law** of nerve conduction. The nerve impulse does not die out as it travels because it is a chemical reaction that takes its energy from within the axon itself.

This total absence of any variation in the action potential as it traverses the length of the axon raises a question. How can the nervous system react differently to stimuli of different strengths, as the fact that we perceive intensity differences suggests it must? One part of the answer to this question is that, as the intensity of stimulation increases, a sensory neuron increases the *rate* at which it generates impulses, up to the limit of its capacity—as many as 200 to 1000 impulses per second. A second part of the answer is that, as the intensity of stimulation increases, more and more neurons generate impulses. Different neurons have different thresholds of excitation; some require greater stimulation than others to make them fire. Therefore weak stimuli evoke low rates of response, few impulses in only a few neurons. Strong stimuli evoke high rates of response, many impulses in many neurons.

A final point about the action of the neuron is important. Even when there is no obvious stimulation whatsoever, for example, during sleep or even coma, almost every neuron in the nervous system emits occasional impulses. This spontaneous activity provides a refinement in the neuron's mechanism of communication. The neuron, like a gauge whose pointer rests at the center of its scale instead of at one end, can signal changes in stimulation either by increasing or by decreasing its rate of response. That is, the impulse rate of a neuron may be either *excited,* sped up, or *inhibited,* slowed down, by stimulation.

Synaptic Transmission. So far we have described only the mechanism by which a neuron communicates within itself, from its cell body to its many axon terminals. How do neurons communicate with one another and with the muscles or glands that they ultimately control?

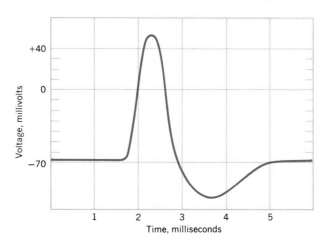

Figure 3.4
Tracing of an action potential. The action potential is a reliable pattern of electrical changes that accompany the nerve impulse.

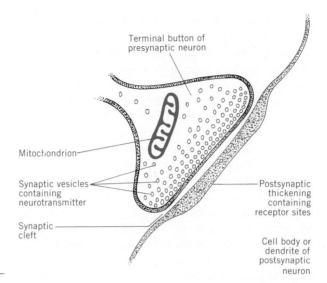

Figure 3.5
A synapse. The synaptic junction of the terminal button of one neuron with the dendrite of another neuron is the site of transmission.

The mechanism by which neurons stimulate other neurons is called **synaptic transmission.** Figure 3.5 illustrates a junction between two neurons in sufficient detail to reveal its typical structure and function. The entire junction is the **synapse,** the transmitting cell is the **presynaptic neuron,** the receiving neuron is called a **postsynaptic neuron,** and the space in between is the **synaptic cleft.** The terminal button of the presynaptic neuron contains many **synaptic vesicles** full of the neuron's chemical transmitter substance, called a **neurotransmitter.** The membrane of the postsynaptic neuron contains the synaptic **receptor sites.**

When an impulse in the axon of the presynaptic neuron reaches the terminal button, one or more of the synaptic vesicles release their contents, the neurotransmitter, into the synaptic cleft. After diffusing to the other side of the synaptic cleft, the neurotransmitter molecules attach to the receptor sites and stimulate the postsynaptic neuron.

After the neurotransmitter has stimulated the postsynaptic neuron by attaching to its receptor sites, the molecules are ejected or fragmented by another chemical, the **deactivating enzyme.** The presynaptic neuron may reabsorb unused whole molecules of transmitter. The duration of the process from arrival of the impulse at the terminal button to stimulation of the postsynaptic neuron is about 0.3 to 1.0 millisecond (thousands of a second, msec).

The chemical reactions that take place at synapses are of a very precise kind: one and only one kind of neurotransmitter can stimulate a given postsynaptic receptor site; and one and only one kind of receptor site can accept a given neurotransmitter. Some of the substances that have been identified as neurotransmitters are acetylcholine, norepinephrine, dopamine, serotonin, glycine, and gamma-aminobutyric acid (GABA). Another two dozen or more substances are thought to serve the same purpose. Each neuron manufactures and secretes only one of them. Depending solely on the effect of this substance on other neurons, the neurotransmitter and the neuron that secreted it can be characterized in general terms as either *excitatory* or *inhibitory*. For example, acetylcholine is generally an excitatory neurotransmitter whereas glycine and GABA appear to be mostly inhibitory. Since many terminal buttons from many different neurons converge on any one neuron, both excitatory and inhibitory neurons are themselves bombarded by both excitatory and inhibitory neurotransmitters from other neurons.

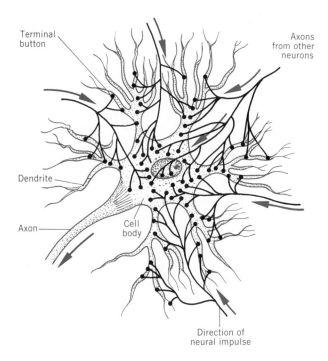

Terminal button

Axons from other neurons

Dendrite

Axon

Cell body

Direction of neural impulse

Figure 3.6
Synaptic terminals at the cell body of a neuron. In reality, the cell body and dendrites are almost completely covered by terminal buttons. The many synaptic connections allow for the integrative function of the neuron.

Integrative Action

The communicative function of a neuron is only one part of its contribution to the activities of the nervous system. As we have already stated, the nervous system has a second function, integration. The neuron integrates or weighs simultaneous and successive stimuli. Since the cell bodies and dendrites of most neurons are in synaptic contact with axon terminal buttons of a large number of other neurons, this means that most neurons receive stimulation from many other neurons and, in turn, stimulate many others. This complexity of interconnections in the nervous system provides for great flexibility of behavior. But for any single neuron it means that neurotransmitters at hundreds of synapses may be bombarding it at any one moment (Figure 3.6).

The cellular mechanism of integration, like the communicative mechanism, can be observed by means of electrical recording. When an electrode small enough not to kill the neuron is inserted through its membrane into its cell body and a second electrode is placed outside, it is possible to detect an electric charge called the membrane's **resting potential.**

The resting potential of a neuron is measured in volts, as is the charge in a battery, but the voltage is very small. A neuron has a resting potential of about -70 millivolts (thousandths of a volt, mv). The inside of the neuron is electrically negative in comparison to the area outside its membrane. As long as a neuron remains unstimulated and healthy, the resting potential stays at -70 mv, but any event that irritates the dendrites or cell body upsets the neuron's chemical balance and there is a change in the potential. Figure 3.7 shows the effect on the membrane's resting potential of irritations produced by electrical shocks of various intensities. Up to a point increasing intensities decrease the amount of the membrane voltage faster and to a greater extent, but the potential always returns to its resting level within a few milliseconds after the shock. Beyond this point, however, an entirely different set of events begins. A shock strong enough to decrease the membrane voltage to about -40 mv produces the reaction in the walls of the axon that is the nerve impulse.

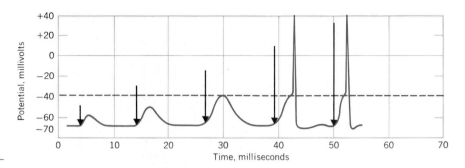

Figure 3.7

Effects of stimulation on the neuron's potential. Stimuli of increasing strengths have been applied at the arrows. The length of the arrow suggests the strength. When the potential reaches −40 mv, an impulse is generated and an action potential is recorded.

Temporal Summation. If two or more stimuli from excitatory transmitters are applied to a neuron in sufficiently quick succession, the series will decrease the membrane voltage more than one of them alone. Indeed, individual stimuli too weak to trigger a nerve impulse can in succession decrease the membrane voltage to −40 mv and generate a nerve impulse (Figure 3.8). This ability of the neuron to allow the effects of many single stimuli to add together over short periods of time is called **temporal summation.** Since the effects of any one stimulus are over after only about 5 msec or so, the stimuli in a train must be separated by less than this amount of time if temporal summation is to occur.

Spatial Summation. Figure 3.9 is a schematic drawing of a neuron with a *recording* electrode inside it near its axon and three stimulating electrodes that mimic terminal buttons located at three different places on its surface. With this arrangement it is possible to study the effect of stimulating the neuron at each point individually or at two or three points in combination. Even though the intensity of the stimulus is the same at each point, the effects are different,

Figure 3.8

Temporal summation. A single stimulus does not lower the membrane voltage enough to trigger an impulse, but trains of successive stimuli do. Repeated stimulation has a staircase effect on the neuron's potential.

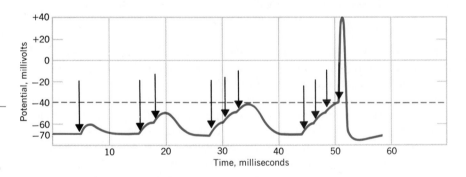

Figure 3.9

Spatial summation. The inset shows the location of three stimulating electrodes and one recording electrode. The effects of individual stimuli add together to produce a larger potential change, but only the simultaneous stimulation of points 1, 2, and 3 lowers the membrane voltage to −40 mv and triggers a nerve impulse.

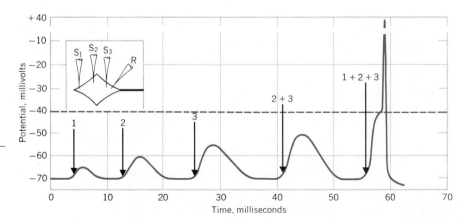

depending on the distance between the stimulating and recording electrodes. The greater the distance, the less the effect. Thus the terminal buttons contacting a neuron near the origin of the axon will have a greater effect on the axon's activities than those that make contact farther away. Terminal buttons with synapses far out on a dendrite have only slight effect on the axon's activities.

So far we have considered the effects of stimuli occurring at only one place at a time. For a neuron in its natural state, however, this would be a very unusual event. At any one moment a neuron may be bombarded with stimulation at many different places on its surface. We have already seen in Figure 3.9 that stimulation at point 1, 2, or 3 alone does not produce a nerve impulse. If points 2 and 3 are stimulated together, the effects add and the decrease in membrane voltage is greater; but again, the effect is not enough to fire the neuron and the potential soon returns to the resting level. If points 1, 2, and 3 are stimulated together, however, the membrane voltage decreases to -40 mv and an impulse is generated. The effects of simultaneous stimuli at different places on the neuron's surface add together, which is called **spatial summation.** For the integrative action of the nervous system, this is the neuron's most crucial ability.

Excitation and Inhibition.   Four factors work together to determine whether or not a neuron generates an impulse. These are (1) the rate of excitatory stimulation (temporal summation), (2) the distance of this stimulation from the origin of the axon, (3) the number of simultaneous stimuli (spatial summation), and (4) the fact that the stimulation received by a neuron may be **excitatory stimulation** or **inhibitory stimulation.** As a usual thing, the effects brought about by excitatory and inhibitory transmitters cancel one another, and the neuron's potential remains at or near its resting level. It is only when the total amount of excitation far outweighs the total amount of inhibition that the membrane voltage decreases enough for a nerve impulse to be triggered.

SUMMARY

Neurons or nerve cells are the active elements of the nervous system. A neuron receives stimulation at its dendrites and cell body in the form of small amounts of chemical neurotransmitter substances secreted onto its surface by the terminal buttons of many other neurons. If the excitatory component of this stimulation exceeds the inhibitory component, and the excitatory stimulation is persistent and widespread enough, the neuron will generate an impulse which travels down its axon and triggers the release of its own transmitter substance at each of its many terminal buttons. In this manner each neuron integrates the simultaneous and successive stimuli from a wide variety of sources and communicates its information to other neurons. The net effect of this process is an integrative and communicative network which is capable of weighing considerable, often contradictory, information, making decisions, and executing motor activities appropriate to each situation that arises.

THE FUNDAMENTAL PLAN OF THE NERVOUS SYSTEM

Much of what the nervous system does is to process information from sensory sources and initiate appropriate action in the form of motor responses. Thus a basic distinction of function in the nervous system is between *sensory* activity and *motor* activity. This functional distinction is imposed on the nervous system by other organs of the body—by **receptors,** such as the eyes, ears, and nose, and by **effectors,** the muscles and glands. In the peripheral system it is possible to distinguish between sensory and motor neurons. The sensory neurons carry impulses from receptors into the central nervous system. The motor neurons carry impulses originating in the central system outward to effectors. Once inside the central nervous system, however, the distinction begins to blur.

We shall examine in all five progressively higher levels of the central nervous system. Proceeding from the lowest of these levels to higher and higher levels, we find the peripheral or first-order sensory neurons making synaptic connections with more central second-order neurons, these with still more central third-order neurons, and so on. These higher-order neurons are not directly attached to a receptor and thus are less strictly sensory in function. Proceeding *backward* through the motor system, function becomes similarly diffused. Motor neurons which synapse directly upon effectors are usually stimulated by higher-order neurons whose entire lengths are in the central nervous system.

Spinal Cord

In a six-foot man the tissue making up the spinal cord is about the diameter of the little finger and two feet long. A cross section of the spinal cord at any level reveals the same basic internal arrangement (Figure 3.10). There is an area of **white matter** near the outside and a butterfly-shaped core of **gray matter.** White matter gains its color from the myelin sheath around axons. Thus the more exterior part of the cord consists of axons of nerve fibers and is communicative in function. The gray core consists of unmyelinated nerve cell bodies and dendrites and is integrative in function.

There are thirty-one pairs of peripheral **spinal nerves** connected to the spinal cord. Bundled together in each nerve are thousands of individual axons, some sensory and some motor in function. The sensory branches of the spinal nerves enter the cord at the back, or dorsal, portion (top of cross section in Figure 3.10). They bring into the spinal cord information originating in the sensory receptors in the skin, joints, muscles, and viscera. After making synaptic connections in the cord, the sensory activity flows toward the brain in nerve tracts. A **nerve tract** is a bundle of functionally associated axons which have a common point of origin and a common destination in the central nervous

Figure 3.10
Cross section of the spinal cord showing gray matter, white matter, roots, and a typical reflex arc consisting of sensory neuron, interneuron, and motor neuron.

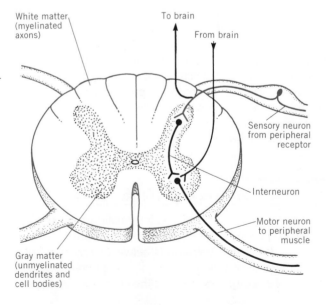

White matter (myelinated axons)

To brain

From brain

Sensory neuron from peripheral receptor

Interneuron

Motor neuron to peripheral muscle

Gray matter (unmyelinated dendrites and cell bodies)

Although paraplegics never regain voluntary control of the body below the place where their spinal cord is damaged, they do learn to make very effective use of the rest of the body.

system. The motor branches of the spinal nerves, receiving messages from descending nerve tracts, leave the front, or ventral, portion of the cord (bottom of cross section in Figure 3.10) and control the action of nearby muscles and glands.

Function. The communicative and integrative functions of the spinal cord can be deduced from observing the actions of a person who has survived a complete transection of the spinal cord. The resulting condition is called *quadriplegia* if the cut is above the level of exit of the spinal nerves to the arms and legs and *paraplegia* if the cut is below the arm level but above the leg level. Because neurons within the central nervous system do not regenerate their axons after they are cut, both conditions are permanent—there is no recovery. The most dramatic effects of quadriplegia or paraplegia are complete anesthesia and paralysis of the body below the level of the cut. Because axons of sensory neurons that run up the spinal cord to the brain have been severed, the patient feels nothing in the lower part of the body. The paralysis, an inability to make voluntary movements, is evidence that the axons of motor neurons running down the cord from the brain have also been cut.

Although transection of the cord destroys voluntary movement in the part of the patient's body below the cut, reflexive movements are not lost. In paraplegia the patient's limbs will respond reflexively to a variety of stimuli. If a toe is pinched or pricked with a pin, the leg withdraws. If the sole of the foot is tickled, the toes splay and the leg extends. If the tendon below the knee is tapped, the knee-jerk reflex occurs. Obviously the spinal cord is capable of responding integratively to simple stimuli. It is also capable of performing a crude kind of decision making. For if two stimuli, such as a pinprick and tickle, are applied simultaneously to one foot, the severed spinal cord withdraws the leg, the response to a pinprick, and inhibits the competing response of the foot to tickle.

A part of what is lost in paraplegia is the capacity to perform these actions upon command. Also lost is the moderating influence of the higher centers. Normally reflexes are under some sort of inhibition by the brain. In paraplegic or quadriplegic persons the reflexes are larger and more sudden than they are in intact individuals.

The ability of the brain to inhibit actions originating in the spinal cord is just one example of a more general principle that holds true at all levels of the nervous system. The successive levels form a chain of command. Each higher level is capable of achieving a more complete integration of sensory input than is possible at lower levels. If, on the basis of this more complete integration, a better or longer-range plan of action can be worked out, the higher levels can supersede the actions initiated by the lower levels. The higher levels of the nervous system evaluate the wide and subtle array of stimulation and direct the body to the most appropriate action.

Reflex Action. Figure 3.11 shows some of the spinal interconnections for the reflex withdrawal of the leg to avoid pain. When the foot is pricked with a pin, for example, sensory neurons carry impulses to **interneurons,** which in turn connect to motor neurons. Receiving stimulation from sensory neurons by way of the interneurons, the motor neurons cause the leg muscle to contract.

The three-neuron model of the **reflex arc** shown in Figure 3.11 is correct as far as it goes, but the sketch is simplified and incomplete. There are several additional points to make. (1) The action of just one neuron would have no effect at all. Simultaneous activity in many neurons is necessary to produce overt action. (2) Opposed or antagonistic muscles must also act. For the leg to withdraw reflexively, muscles that ordinarily extend the leg must relax as the muscles that make it bend contract. A reflex arc relaxing the extensor muscle must operate in parallel with the arc producing flexion. Otherwise the leg would not withdraw but become rigidly locked. (3) Pricking the foot with a pin would create impulses in sensory axons not shown in Figure 3.11. This neural activity goes to the brain and translates into the conscious experience of pain. (4) Impulses from the brain, traveling down the cord on motor neurons not shown in the figure, also affect the interneurons and the motor neurons in the reflex arc. They often inhibit the reflex.

Figure 3.11

The reflex arc. The effects of stimulation are transmitted to the spinal cord by sensory neurons. These synapse with interneurons, which in turn synapse with motor neurons, which in turn activate the muscle. A reflex act requires the stimulation of hundreds of neurons.

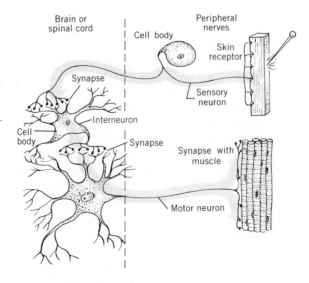

Hindbrain

The **hindbrain** consists of the **cerebellum, medulla,** and **pons** (Figure 3.12). The medulla and pons constitute the lower part of the **brainstem.** The upper part of the brainstem includes the **midbrain** and a portion of the **forebrain.** The cerebellum, a convoluted, two-hemisphere structure with a small wormlike central lobe between the two hemispheres, is behind the brainstem and is connected to the pons through three large pairs of nerve tracts. It is the second largest structure of the human brain. Like the cerebrum, which is the largest, it has a gray outer covering or cortex made up of layers of neurons.

The brainstem portion of the hindbrain occupies a key position in the nervous system. The narrow medulla serves as the main line of traffic for nerve tracts originating in the spinal cord and ascending to higher brain structures, and for nerve tracts originating in the brain and descending to the spinal cord. The pons, a conspicuous bulge on the anterior surface of the brainstem, consists mostly of nerve tracts passing up and down between medulla and midbrain and across from pons to cerebellum. The medulla and pons also receive sensory nerve fibers from the ears, skin, mouth, and muscles of the head and from the viscera. They send motor nerve fibers to the face, throat, neck, and some visceral muscles and glands. Outside the medulla and pons these fibers course together as eight pairs of peripheral nerves. They are called **cranial nerves** because they are confined mostly to the skull. In structure and function they are essentially similar to the spinal nerves. There are twelve pairs of cranial nerves in all.

The cerebellum receives sensory stimulation relayed to it from other parts of the nervous system. Some of the stimulation comes from the eyes, ears, and skin, but the largest portion originates in muscles and tendons and in the receptors of the inner ear that are responsible for the sense of balance. The cerebellum also receives from and returns to the pons motor commands from the higher brain.

Since the brainstem portion of the hindbrain provides the only route for communication between the receptor organs of the head and the effector organs

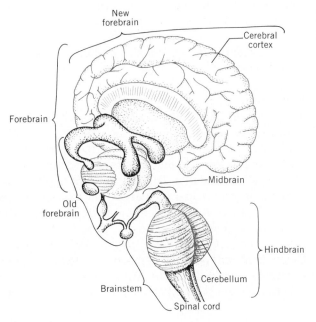

Figure 3.12
Levels of the human nervous system.

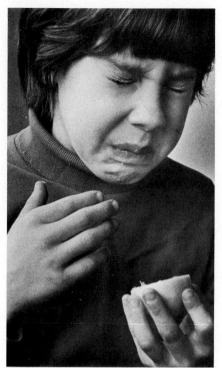

This easily identified reaction to a sour taste is the visible expression of a reflex act. Similar responses have been observed in babies.

of the trunk and limbs, communication is a large part of its total function. The hindbrain also has integrative duties which are performed by centers made up in part of the neuron cell bodies of the axons in its tracts. Other of the cell bodies in these islands of gray matter within the central nervous system have very short fibers making connections to neighboring neurons, thereby collecting and integrating the messages of the tracts. These centers are usually called **nuclei.** Most of the cranial nerves have nuclei within the brainstem. Some of the integrations of the medulla and pons are sensory-motor reflexes coordinated by these nuclei—withdrawal reactions to noxious stimuli to the head, eyeblinks to stimuli near the face, the tensing of muscles in the ears to loud sounds, gagging or coughing to a clog in the throat, increasing the depth of breathing when the level of carbon dioxide in the blood rises, and dilating the arteries when blood pressure increases. Each of these actions, like those controlled by the spinal cord, serves a protective or maintenance function; like the spinal reflexes, each is subject to some measure of inhibition from higher levels of the nervous system.

Second-order integrations of the brainstem mix stimulation from various sensory receptors and direct the product to higher levels of the system. The stimulation from the two ears is mixed to localize the source of a sound, and information from the two sets of vestibular organs is combined to reveal head movements.

The highest order of integrative activity of the hindbrain is much more complex that any integration accomplished by the spinal cord. The cerebellum, receiving information from skin receptors and from muscles and tendons, monitors the pressures on the skin in each limb and the current state of contraction of each muscle. In addition, the eyes and vestibular organs inform it of the body's position in space and its balance. By integrating all this information, the cerebellum helps to keep the body upright and balanced and the muscles in the slightly contracted condition necessary for their prompt and smooth coordinated action. In other words, the cerebellum helps to maintain equilibrium and muscle tone. Whenever the higher brain sends a command to a muscle, simultaneous instructions about the intent of the movement are relayed to the cerebellum. Because the cerebellum is also receiving messages from the muscle, it is able to fine-tune the command. The cerebellum smooths, refines, and coordinates the body's voluntary movements even as they are being made. It prevents them from overshooting and undershooting the mark and gives them good timing.

Midbrain

The midbrain (see Figure 3.12) lies just above the hindbrain. The optic tract from the eye sends axons here, providing the only direct sensory input to the midbrain. There are only two pairs of motor nerves leaving the midbrain. Their nuclei control some of the muscles for moving the eyes and also the muscles of the eye's iris and lens. The interior of the midbrain, as well as of the hindbrain below it, is gray matter interlaced with thin, crisscrossing tracts of myelinated axons. This structure is called the **reticular formation,** strictly a descriptive term. When viewed through a microscope, the core of the brainstem resembles white netting or lacing on a gray background; it is, therefore, "reticulated." Unless inhibited, neurons of this system tend to send forward a steady stream of impulses which keep the higher brain awake and alert and help the cerebellum maintain muscle tone. The system can filter out weak or familiar stimuli, allowing the brain to concentrate on a particular thought. When the midbrain reticular formation of an intact but sleeping animal is stimulated, the animal awakes with a bound and gives every indication that something has awakened it. But if the midbrain reticular formation is damaged, the animal falls into a prolonged coma. For this reason the ascending fibers have come to be called the **reticular activating system.**

The communicative function of the midbrain is much like that of the hindbrain. Tracts of the motor system originating in the forebrain stream down through the midbrain on their way to lower motor structures, and tracts of the sensory system from the spinal cord and hindbrain stream upward into the forebrain. The midbrain also has important integrative functions. One of these integrations can be illustrated by imagining the picture of the world that would be obtained with a movie camera hand-held in a moving car. The camera would jog with every bump in the road. If the film shot by this camera were then projected onto a screen, these bumps would make the world appear to jump and jerk. When you are riding in a car, your head and eyes are subjected to the same bumps as the camera, yet the world still appears steady. We achieve such stable perception because every slight movement of the head is sensed by the visual and vestibular systems and integrated by nuclei of the midbrain. Vision is momentarily suppressed, and the eyes instantly adjust to the new point of view. In spite of bumps, the world appears stable.

SUMMARY

The anesthesia and paralysis of paraplegic patients indicate how the communicative and integrative functions of the spinal cord are organized. Because sensory neurons that carry messages from the sense organs to the brain have been severed, such individuals lose all sensitivity to stimulation below the point at which the cord is cut. They also lose the ability to initiate voluntary movements of their legs, for nerve tracts that run from the brain to the spinal nerves serving the muscles in these limbs have been cut. On the other hand, not only do paraplegic and quadriplegic patients have reflexes but these reflexes are exaggerated. Reflexes are still possible because they are managed locally, entirely within the cord and the connecting spinal nerves. Similar responses cannot be initiated voluntarily, however, because there are no connections with the higher centers of the nervous system. Nor can higher centers exert their usual inhibitory control over reflexes.

The hindbrain consists of the medulla, pons, and cerebellum. The first two of these structures serve both communicative and integrative functions; the cerebellum is solely integrative. The communicative functions of the hindbrain make it possible for the individual to react to stimuli to the eyes, ears, and other head receptors. The simplest integrations of the brainstem portion of the hindbrain are reflexive in nature. Nuclei also mix stimuli, for example, in localizing sound. The cerebellum contributes more complex integrations, maintaining posture and muscle tone and refining all movements commanded by the higher brain. The simplest integrations of the midbrain are reflexes making the eyes move and adjusting pupil size and focus. The midbrain also provides the righting reflex and moves the head to improve vision and hearing. The reticular formation of the hindbrain and midbrain arouses the entire nervous system, keeping the individual in a state of alert wakefulness through ascending connections to the forebrain.

FOREBRAIN

The forebrain or *cerebrum,* the largest part of the human brain, can be divided into old and new portions. The **old forebrain** consists of structures similar to those that constituted the entire forebrain of our ancient vertebrate ancestors. From its evolutionary history the old forebrain can be expected to tend to bodily functions and regulations common to all vertebrates, such as appetite and thirst, water balance, sleeping and waking, temperature control, reproductive cycles, and activity cycles. It also has much to do with the patterns of the basic emotions rage, terror, and pleasure and with sexual arousal. The new forebrain evolved later. For this reason it may be expected to provide higher-order integrations which allow the behavior that is unique to mammals and particularly to human beings.

The largest part of the old forebrain is the **limbic system.** Although this system receives fibers indirectly from every sensory system, its most direct input is from the olfactory system and the viscera. It also sends out a pathway of fibers to the autonomic nervous system controlling the viscera. The limbic system consists of many parts, but only the hypothalamus will be discussed here. The **hypothalamus,** no larger than a peanut, is positioned in the base of the forebrain. Made up of a number of paired nuclei, it receives some fibers from the viscera and sends back others in return. It is also directly connected to the pituitary gland, which controls the activities of the other endocrine glands throughout the body. Thus the hypothalamus is the structure by which the old forebrain maintains control over the body's interior.

In turning from the contributions to behavior of the spinal cord, hindbrain, and midbrain to those of the forebrain, we need a new set of descriptive categories. Whereas structures below the level of the forebrain support behavior that we might call automatic or reflexive, the forebrain structures control behavior that is emotional or affective and thoughtful or cognitive. In general, the old forebrain serves more emotional or affective functions; the new forebrain serves more thoughtful or cognitive functions.

Autonomic Nervous System

The **autonomic nervous system** carries out many of the emotional and motivated activities initiated by the old forebrain and in particular by the hypothalamus. This system, which consists of peripheral motor fibers running to a variety of organs, is divided into two parts (Figure 3.13). Fibers leaving the brainstem and sacral regions of the spinal cord make up the **parasympathetic system.** Fibers leaving the central portion of the cord comprise the **sympathetic system.**

The contented grazing zebras are governed by the parasympathetic division of the autonomic nervous system. When startled and running away in fright, zebras are governed by the sympathetic division.

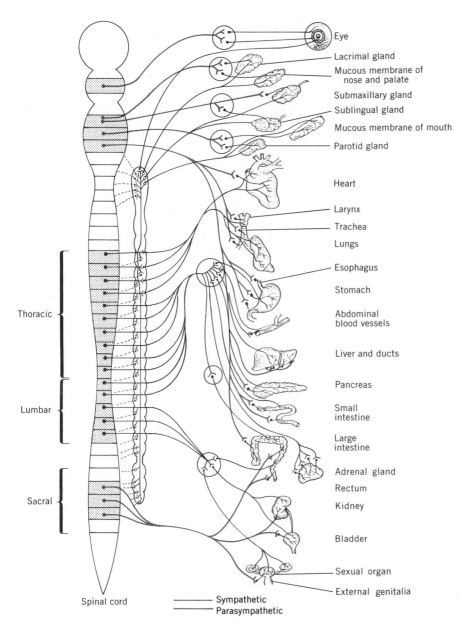

Eye
Lacrimal gland
Mucous membrane of nose and palate
Submaxillary gland
Sublingual gland
Mucous membrane of mouth
Parotid gland
Heart
Larynx
Trachea
Lungs
Esophagus
Stomach
Abdominal blood vessels
Liver and ducts
Pancreas
Small intestine
Large intestine
Adrenal gland
Rectum
Kidney
Bladder
Sexual organ
External genitalia

Thoracic
Lumbar
Sacral

Spinal cord

—— Sympathetic
—— Parasympathetic

Figure 3.13
The autonomic nervous system.
Sympathetic innervation is indicated by black lines, parasympathetic innervation by blue lines. When the fibers of the sympathetic system leave the spinal cord, they synapse almost immediately with other motor neurons located in the ganglia on either side of the vertebral column. These side banks of ganglia have connecting fibers to make them a coordinating chain. Fibers of the parasympathetic system synapse in ganglia close to the organs to be innervated and do not necessarily act in concert. Notice that most organs receive both sympathetic and parasympathetic nerves.

The sympathetic and parasympathetic systems tend to act in opposing ways. The sympathetic system prepares the body for action; the parasympathetic system usually functions when the body is at rest. When the sympathetic system is active, heartbeat increases to pump more blood. Blood is shunted away from the viscera to the muscles, providing extra oxygen and nutrients where they are most needed during activity. Breathing becomes deeper and more rapid, which ensures a plentiful supply of oxygen. The pupils of the eyes dilate to allow for better vision. The liver releases sugar for energy. All these actions mobilize the body's resources.

The parasympathetic system helps the body's organs to protect and conserve their resources. The heart slows down, blood is shunted from the muscles to the viscera, the pupils of the eyes contract, breathing is more relaxed and shallower. Because of the nature of the physiological processes that they initiate,

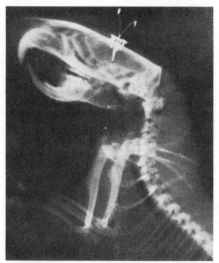

Figure 3.14
The technique of brain stimulation. This X-ray photograph shows the permanent placement of an electrode in the brain of a rat.

the two systems tend to be associated with emotional states. Sympathetic arousal is interpreted as nervous tension, anxiety, fear, and excitement, parasympathetic arousal as calmness.

Electrical Stimulation of the Brain

Peripheral nerve fibers of the sympathetic and parasympathetic systems terminate on many of the same organs. In the brain, however, the two systems are quite separate. The front and sides of the hypothalamus are parasympathetic, the back part sympathetic. The evidence for this division comes in part from observations of the behavior of animals when one of these regions is stimulated electrically. While the animal is anesthetized a hole is bored in the skull and a minute electrode is inserted into the hypothalamus (Figure 3.14). The electrode is anchored to the skull and equipped with a socket. This makes it possible for the experimenter to plug the animal into a source of weak electric current and stimulate the hypothalamus directly. At other times the animal leads a normal, healthy life.

Stimulation applied through an electrode in the back half of the hypothalamus brings sympathetic reactions. The animal becomes watchful, crouches, its hair erects, and by every other standard it acts frightened. Stimulation applied to the front part of the hypothalamus, on the other hand, induces parasympathetic activity. Stimulation of slightly different locations to the left or right makes the animal eat or drink, even if it has just eaten or drunk its fill. With stimulation in still other locations, there is sexual posturing.

A slightly different technique, called **self-stimulation,** also demonstrates that the old forebrain is intimately associated with emotion and motivation. James Olds and Peter Milner (1954), in testing the effects of electrical stimulation of the reticular system of rats, unknowingly but serendipitously missed and inserted the electrode into the septal region of one rat. Laboratory rats can be counted on to hug walls and avoid open spaces, but this particular animal repeatedly returned to the spot where he had last received brain stimulation. Olds and Milner realized that the rat must enjoy the shocks and discovered the misplacement of the electrode. They eventually decided to put the "pleasure center" at their rat's disposal and wired the source of electric current to a pedal which the animal could press. They also tested animals with electrodes implanted in other areas of the limbic system, hypothalamus, and midbrain.

Depending on the brain site of stimuation, these animals either stimulate themselves only once or stimulate themselves constantly. There seems to be little middle ground. Rats have shocked themselves at the rate of 500 to 5000 times per hour and often at the expense of their true needs. Hungry animals stimulate themselves rather than eat. Thirsty animals stimulate themselves rather than drink. One rat kept at it at the rate of 2000 stimulations per hour for twenty-six hours, until he fell exhausted. After sleeping for twenty hours, the rat resumed stimulating himself at the same rate.

The experiments just described provide clear evidence that the old forebrain participates in emotion and motivation. Other experiments have shown that it exerts both excitatory and inhibitory control over these reactions. Stimulating one area may make an animal eat. Stimulating a slightly different location may make even a very hungry animal stop eating. Still other locations excite or inhibit drinking, excite or inhibit sexual activity, arouse or inhibit fearful reactions.

Cerebral Hemispheres

The new forebrain consists of the thalamus and the cortex of the two **cerebral hemispheres.** The **thalamus,** a pair of egg-shaped collections of nuclei located above the hypothalamus, is the topmost part of the brainstem and a major relay center for sensory information. All sensory pathways, except the olfactory, reach the thalamus. Visual, auditory, taste, touch, temperature, and pain information arrives here. The thalamus processes this information and then transmits it to specific areas of the cerebral cortex. It also projects to the cortex feedback information for coordinating voluntary movements, collected from the cerebellum and several of the basal ganglia. The basal ganglia are groups of nuclei located deep within the cerebral hemispheres. The thalamus helps the reticular formation maintain alertness and focus attention. Crude pain and awareness of touch, the pleasantness or unpleasantness of sensations, the vibratory sense, and temperature discriminations are brought to consciousness in the thalamus.

The **cerebral cortex,** the gray-matter covering of the hemispheres, consists of six layers of densely packed and intricately connected neurons. In human beings the cortex is deeply fissured, folded upon itself and into itself, allowing for a very large surface. The cerebral cortex is thereby able to manage our complex human behavior—our sensitivities and motor dexterity, our language and extensive memory, our rapid learning and effective reasoning, our sense of time and interest in our own history, our imagination.

The cerebral cortex, which is only 2 to 5 millimeters thick, has many parts and many functions. Some areas are most closely connected to the receptors and serve a relatively sensory function. These areas are called **primary sensory cortex.** Other areas, called **primary motor cortex,** are most closely connected, via only two synapses, to the body's muscles. Immediately surrounding primary sensory and motor cortex are areas that are less directly sensory and motor in function but whose damage also results in perceptual or motor deficits. These areas are called **secondary sensory** and **secondary motor cortex** (Figure 3.15). Most of the cerebral cortex, however, is neither clearly sensory nor clearly motor in function. This vast area is usually referred to as **association cortex.**

Each cerebral hemisphere also has an anatomical division, into lobes. The central fissure, running sideways from the top of the head to the ears, separates the frontal lobe from the parietal. The division between the parietal and the occipital, at the rear of the hemisphere, is not as clear-cut. The deep fissure on the side of the brain is the upper boundary of the temporal lobe. Each lobe is named for the bone of the skull overlying it.

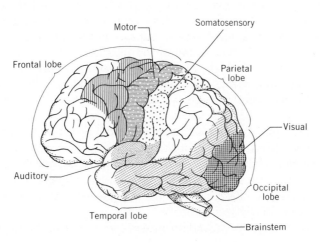

Figure 3.15
Lateral view of human cerebral cortex. Primary and secondary sensory and motor areas are shaded. Unshaded areas of cortex are "associative."

Organization of Sensory Cortex.   The sensory areas in each hemisphere are connected to the receptors in such a way that the right side of a person's perceptual world is predominantly represented in the left hemisphere, and the left side of the world is represented in the right hemisphere. For example, the visual system is arranged so that the right half of what each eye sees is represented in the left visual cortex. At the optic chiasma on the underside of the hypothalamus, the two optic nerves meet. There the fibers from the portions of the eyes nearest the nose cross over to the other side of the brain. Stare at a point on the wall. Everything to the left of a vertical line through that point is represented in the visual cortex of your right hemisphere, and everything to the right is represented in the left hemisphere. A patient in whom the right visual cortex has been destroyed cannot see anything to the left of the vertical line (Berkeley, 1978). Similarly, sounds coming from places to the left of the same line are represented for the most part in the auditory cortex of the right hemisphere, and skin sensitivity on the left side of the body is represented in the right somatosensory cortex. Consequently, damage to the right auditory or somatosensory cortex disrupts these perceptions of the left side (Thompson and Masterton, 1978; Vierck, 1978).

The secondary sensory areas surrounding primary sensory cortex receive a large part of their input from the primary areas and provide a higher level of perceptual organization. The symptoms of damage to secondary sensory cortex reveal something of the nature of this higher organization. The general name for these symptoms is **agnosia** (Greek *agnosia,* ignorance). We speak of visual agnosia when secondary visual areas are destroyed and auditory agnosia when secondary auditory cortex is destroyed.

In each of these syndromes the ability to understand or speak about what is being perceived is lost. People with visual agnosia, for example, may be able to see quite well but they are unable to understand or recognize what they see. Such individuals can see a book as well as they ever could, but they cannot call it a book or describe what it is used for. If, on the other hand, these patients hear the word *book* or are allowed to feel a book, they can say ''book'' and describe its use.

Organization of Motor Cortex.   Like the connections of sensory organs to sensory cortex, those of the motor cortex to muscles are crisscrossed. The right motor cortex controls muscles in the left half of the body and vice versa. When the left motor cortex is damaged, for example, the right side of the body is paralyzed, a **hemiplegia** (half-paralysis). Motor cortex has an orderly upside-down arrangement by body part, which is suggested somewhat metaphorically in Figure 3.16. Because this organization is not really as precise as depicted in the figure, a small area of damage in the motor cortex may appear to cause only a slight weakening of the muscles controlled by that area rather than a complete loss of their voluntary movements. This means that the adjacent area, which has some, but less efficient, control over the muscles, can compensate for the focal damage, at least to a degree. Such compensation is probably never perfect, but the deficit may be noticeable only in fine movements. For example, a pianist with damage in the area that controls the little finger of the right hand would probably lose the very precise control that is needed to perform, although somewhat more gross activities, such as writing, would appear to be unaffected. More extensive damage in primary motor cortex, of course, produces correspondingly greater loss of control, and recovery is correspondingly less complete.

Damage to secondary motor cortex, the area just in front of the primary

The precise coordination of movements managed by the motor cortex, cerebellum, and basal ganglia allows this young woman of northern India to carry with enormous grace both herself and water from the village well.

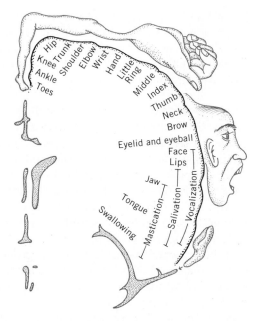

Figure 3.16
The motor homunculus. The size of the body part suggests the amount of cortex devoted to control of that part. The cortex controlling the toes is deep within the longitudinal fissure dividing the hemispheres. (Adapted from Penfield and Rasmussen, 1950.)

motor area, brings a subtler kind of motor deficit, affecting whole categories of actions rather than specific movements. With damage to secondary motor cortex, the pianist in our example might still be able to move each finger correctly and to perform all the basic movements needed in playing; these are controlled by primary motor cortex. But now he or she would be unable to execute a musical passage, or play a scale, or even drum the fingers rhythmically. In short, a higher order of motor organization, the timing and ordering of movements, is disrupted.

Cortical Areas Associated with Speech and Language.   The ability to speak appears to have two components. First, there is the utterance of sounds, which depends on the ability to move the vocal cords, throat, tongue, and lips in a coordinated fashion. Second, there is the utterance of words and sentences. Sounds are combined to convey ideas symbolically. The mere physical act of making sounds is managed by the brainstem. The cerebral cortex—in fact, a special area of cortex distinguished only in primates— directs coherent, meaningful speech.

   In almost everyone the speech area is located in the left hemisphere (Figure 3.17). Damage to this region brings about a disturbance of speech called **aphasia.** Aphasia is an inability to speak in coherent sentences, even though

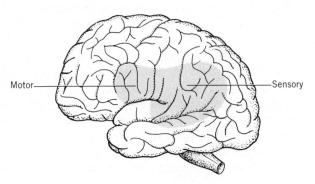

Figure 3.17
Speech areas of the brain. The sensory and motor aspects of speech are represented in different locations.

the ability to make speech sounds is unimpaired. There are two principal kinds of aphasia, depending on the location of damage to the brain. The entire speech area can be roughly divided into a front half and a back half. Although damage in either of these parts disturbs speech, the symptoms of the aphasias are quite different.

Sensory Aphasia.   The rear part of the speech area includes the primary and part of the secondary auditory sensory cortex. Damage in this general area causes **sensory aphasia** or *receptive aphasia.* The most glaring symptom is the person's inability to understand spoken words. The patient cannot repeat sentences or take dictation and may perceive spoken words in a jumbled way, much as we do when we hear someone speaking rapidly in a foreign language.

The inability to understand speech extends to the patient's own speech. Normally, we listen to the sounds we are uttering and correct our lip, tongue, and throat movements to make the sounds we want and to say the words we want with proper enunciation and in proper grammatical sentences. Persons with damage in the back part of the speech area, however, do not understand the words that they are saying and cannot be sure that what they wanted to say was in fact said. With their speech perception so muddled, these patients begin to speak and then slow down. They stutter and stumble until the coherence of the intended message is lost.

Motor Aphasia.   Damage in the forward part of the speech region interferes with the motor act of speaking, a syndrome called **motor aphasia** or *expressive aphasia.* Pure motor aphasia is easily distinguished from pure sensory aphasia. The critical question is whether the person can understand spoken words. Although neither a motor aphasic nor a sensory aphasic can speak in answer to a spoken question, a motor aphasic can give intelligent answers in writing or with gestures. A sensory aphasic cannot. The difficulty underlying pure motor aphasia seems to be an inability to put thoughts into speech. At best the motor aphasic, expending great effort, finds and stammers out words one at a time and leaves out a number of them. Since the motor aphasic is able to understand what others say, however, the disorder is not as disastrous as sensory aphasia (Peele, 1977).

Prefrontal Cortex.   The very large area of the frontal lobe that lies forward of the motor area (see Figure 3.15), the **prefrontal cortex,** has proved to be a very perplexing part of the cortex. We know little about its function. People with injuries to this area have no detectable motor or sensory disturbances.

It now appears, however, that damage to this area of the brain has subtle but important consequences. One such consequence is **perseveration deficit,** a loss of the ability to stop an activity when it is inappropriate. Perseveration deficit can be illustrated in this manner. Suppose you had a standard deck of playing cards with the usual four suits, clubs, diamonds, hearts, and spades, and the usual thirteen cards in each suit. If you were asked to separate the cards into piles, you might sort them either by suits or by the denominations of the cards. Not told which way to proceed, you would probably choose one of these and start building the appropriate piles. Then if, after you were halfway through the deck, the request came to stop sorting the cards by the method chosen and to sort the remainder of the deck by another method, you would have no trouble complying.

Individuals with damaged prefrontal areas have great difficulty making such a shift, although they can sort the cards on either basis as well as a normal person. Once started on a method of sorting, the person perseverates, in spite of seeming to know that the rule has changed. The patient may say, "I know this is wrong," but continue sorting card after card by the old rule.

The perseveration deficit suggests that normally the prefrontal cortex is able to forestall plans of action initiated at other places in the nervous system, assuring the deliberate thoughtfulness that is characteristic of much human behavior. The behavior of prefrontal patients, by contrast, is more automatized. They are unable to resume an activity at the point of interruption. If they are interrupted while counting, they start again at the beginning. Ordinarily, individuals can begin again at the point of interruption and have trouble only when a highly practiced series of movements or an extremely well-known pattern of words is interrupted.

People with prefrontal damage also have trouble with abstract thinking. Normal individuals, asked to copy simple arrangements of sticks such as those in Figure 3.18, have no difficulty reconstructing any of the patterns. Patients with prefrontal damage have great difficulty with some arrangements and no difficulty with others. Their comments about the problems are a clue to the nature of the deficit. Each construction that they can copy reminds them of a concrete object such as a "ladder" or a "house." The arrangements that they cannot reconstruct remind them of "nothing." Patients need to be able to give the sticks a name.

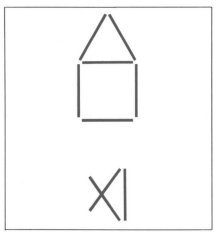

Figure 3.18
Stick arrangements for testing prefrontal patients. Meaningful arrangements such as one suggesting a house are easy for the patients to copy, but meaningless arrangements are not.

Connection Between the Hemispheres

The two hemispheres of the forebrain are interconnected by bundles of fibers called **commissures.** The largest of these is the **corpus callosum,** which connects the cortical parts of the two hemispheres. In a normal person information in the cortex of one hemisphere immediately reaches that of the other through this broad band of fibers. The commissures allow the sensations from both halves of the body to be integrated, and they guarantee that the movements of the two sides are coordinated.

As a treatment of last resort, these commissures are sometimes severed to alleviate the symptoms of severe epilepsy. **Epilepsy** is a chronic disorder in which the normal electrical activity of the brain is suddenly overwhelmed by a massive discharge of impulses, causing convulsions and loss of consciousness. Severing the commissures keeps the "electrical storm" of the neurons discharging in one hemisphere from passing over and exciting neurons in the other. For a time after these operations were first performed, the only symptoms noticed were an initial loss of fine muscle control on the left side of the body and some slurring of speech.

The symptoms of the so-called "split-brain" syndrome are revealed only by a very special set of tests. As we shall see, these symptoms raise profound questions about such basic matters as the concept of self. In fact, experiments with split-brain patients are about as astonishing as any you will meet in the study of psychology. Some thirty years ago Roger Sperry began his work on split brains. At first he studied cats, but later he worked with people who had been operated on for epilepsy. In 1981 he shared the Nobel prize in physiology for this work.

In order to comprehend the behavior of the split-brain patient, it is important to remember a number of things. The transection of the commissures does not disconnect the cortex from receptors or effectors. What happens on the right side of the visual field is projected to the left visual cortex; what happens on the left is projected to the right. Acts performed with the right hand continue to be controlled by the motor cortex of the left hemisphere, and control of the

Roger Sperry believes, on the basis of the evidence collected from split-brain persons, that our present-day educational system and modern society in general tend to discriminate against the whole right half of the brain, giving it a bare minimum of formal training.

left hand is by the right hemisphere. And as usual the left hemisphere contains the language areas. What is lost in split-brain patients because the hemispheres do not communicate is the normal ability to integrate the activities in the two halves of the brain. Experiments can be arranged so that the left and right parts of sensory fields and the movements of left and right parts of the body cannot be integrated.

If split-brain patients are presented with a list of six digits, three coming to the right ear and three coming to the left, they will be able to report only those delivered to the right ear. They are not deaf to those in the left ear, but the left ear projects predominantly to the right hemisphere, which is without the speech center required to name them. The fact that their difficulty is in responding verbally becomes clearer when they are confronted with visual stimuli.

In visual tests the split-brain subject stares at a spot in the center of a screen and words or pictures of objects are flashed to the right or left or to both positions for about 150 milliseconds (Figure 3.19). If the word or picture remains longer, the subject will have time to move his or her eyes and the information will be to both hemispheres. If the word "he/art" is flashed so that the "he" portion is positioned in the left visual field and "art" in the right visual field, split-brain patients say that they saw "art" when asked what the word was. That is, they report only the part of the word that the speaking left hemisphere saw. By contrast, when "heart" is flashed on again, and they are asked to identify the word they saw by *pointing with the left hand* to one of two cards, one containing "he," the other containing "art," they invariably point to "he." This is the part of the word seen by the right hemisphere, which controls the

Figure 3.19
Visual and touch tests for a split-brain subject. With a fixation as indicated, the retinal image of the spoon on the left goes to the right hemisphere. The subject cannot name the object as a spoon but can identify it by touch.

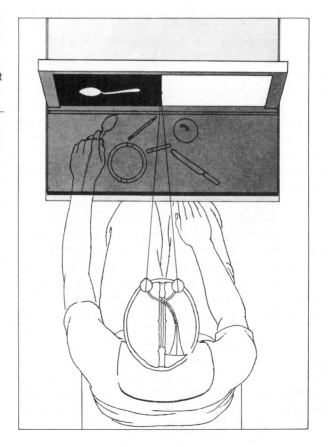

left hand. Neither hemisphere knows that the word was "heart" (Gazzaniga, 1967).

If the left hemisphere is required for giving spoken answers, is the right hemisphere best at any particular activity? The answer to this question is yes. The right hemisphere is superior for many tasks requiring spatial perception. Suppose that split-brain subjects are given the task of solving a block design puzzle (Figure 3.20). The right hemisphere, and therefore the left hand, is good at this kind of perceptual task, as long as words are not involved. The left hemisphere, and the right hand, is poor at such tasks. Because of this difference split-brain subjects are usually unable to do these puzzles when allowed the use of both hands, although they can solve them easily with the left hand alone. When they are free to use both hands, the right hand tries to help but often undoes the superior accomplishments of the left hand (Gazzaniga, Bogen, and Sperry, 1965).

When the two hemispheres are separated by damage to the commissures, the person becomes "two" individuals, a right-sided one, connected to the left hemisphere, who can talk, read, understand speech, and operate the right arm and leg; and a left-sided individual, connected to the right hemisphere, who is entirely without spoken language but can operate the left arm and leg and perform certain nonverbal perceptual and motor tasks in a manner superior to that of the right-sided individual.

Outside the laboratory, and to some extent within it, these two individuals tend to get along very well because each is attentive to the activities of the other and each makes use of the other's skills. For example, in the laboratory the left hemisphere of one man would make a guess about what the right hemisphere alone had seen. If the left hemisphere gave the wrong answer, his right would shake the head and the left would then say, "No, I mean. . . ." But as we might anticipate, peace and harmony do not always reign. The first man to have this operation some morning found his left hand casually unzipping the pants that his right hand had just zipped.

Although both hemispheres in these people can have emotions, there are differences. The left hemisphere can describe and explain the basis for the emotion; the right hemisphere cannot. Moreover, the emotions can be different in the two hemispheres. Half of one of these patients, the right-hemisphere half, once got angry with his wife, grabbed her with the left hand, and shook her violently while the left-hemisphere individual and right hand tried to intercede and bring this other half of himself under control. Suppose that the right hand had been unsuccessful and that the left hand had murdered the wife. Who would be guilty of homicide in such a case? Who should be punished, perhaps even put to death (Gazzaniga, 1970)?

SUMMARY

The forebrain integrates a greater range of stimulation than the spinal cord, hindbrain, and midbrain, for it initiates sequences of activity, such as eating; its actions are more complex and of longer duration than any controlled by lower levels of the nervous system. Via the hypothalamus the old forebrain controls food intake, regulates the water balance and temperature of the body, and adjusts the circulatory system to the needs of the body musculature. The hypothalamus exercises quick control over the viscera through the sympathetic and parasympathetic divisions of the autonomic nervous system. The divisions act separately either to mobilize or to protect and maintain bodily resources. Chemical and electrical stimulation of relevant sites in the old forebrain provide additional evidence of its contributions to motivation and emotions.

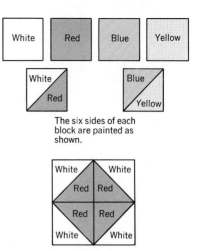

The six sides of each block are painted as shown.

The patient is asked to construct this pattern, using these four blocks.

Figure 3.20
A block design test showing superiority of the right hemisphere for spatial perception. A patient is given blocks with each of their six sides painted differently. The patient's task is to arrange these blocks so that they copy a pattern presented on a card.

The cerebral hemispheres are the largest part of the human brain. One area of the gray matter covering them, the primary sensory cortex, is most closely connected with sensory receptors. Destruction of this cortex causes perceptual deficits. Primary motor cortex is most closely connected to effectors. With its destruction voluntary movement is lost. Still other areas surrounding the primary sensory and motor areas, called secondary sensory and secondary motor cortex, are necessary for recognition of what is sensed and the execution of acts requiring sequences of movements. A large part of one hemisphere, usually the left, contains mechanisms necessary for speech and language. Damage to this area causes sensory or motor aphasia, depending on the exact site of the damage. Finally, the frontal lobe contains a large amount of cortex that is neither sensory nor motor. Subtle deficits in thoughtfulness and abstract thinking are noticeable after its destruction, but its function is still largely unknown.

In the normal individual the activities of the two hemispheres are integrated by the corpus callosum and other connecting fiber tracts. Studies of people with surgically bisected brains have revealed the special capabilities of the two hemispheres. These patients can speak only about information coming to the left hemisphere. The right hemisphere is found to be superior to the left in spatial perception. In the split-brain patient integration is lost. The two hemispheres lie side by side but cannot communicate directly.

NEUROENDOCRINE INTEGRATION

The nervous system brings about rapid changes in behavior and internal states. For states that are to be sustained, the nervous system activates the **endocrine system.** Anatomically, eight glands make up the endocrine system—pituitary, pineal, thyroid, parathyroid, adrenal, pancreas, kidney, and gonads. The secretions of these glands, called **hormones,** pass directly into the bloodstream and are carried to all the body's tissues, where they have a multitude of consequences, a few of which we shall consider here.

Of all the endocrine glands, the pituitary is foremost because it secretes many different hormones; in turn, many of them trigger the secretions of the other endocrine glands. The pituitary itself functions mostly under the control of the hypothalamus, to which it is attached. The hypothalamus regulates the pituitary in two ways. It stimulates a posterior neural part by way of neurons, and it influences the anterior part of the pituitary by releasing its own hormones into a specialized network of tiny blood vessels that interconnect the hypothalamus and anterior pituitary. One of the hypothalamic hormones is the gonadotropin-releasing hormone (GnRH). This hormone stimulates the anterior pituitary production of two hormones that affect the gonads or sex glands, the testes in the male and the ovaries in the female. These pituitary hormones, luteinizing hormone (LH) and follicle-stimulating hormone (FSH), stimulate production of sperm by the testes and maturing of ova by the ovaries; they also cause these gonads to secrete sex hormones, which can be divided into three groups. **Androgens,** the male sex hormones, are formed principally by the testes. An important androgen is testosterone. The other two groups, **estrogens** and **progestins,** are female sex hormones manufactured by the ovaries. At puberty testosterone stimulates maturing of the male reproductive organs and the development of secondary sexual characteristics—a heavy musculature, broad shoulders, pigmented face, pubic, and other body hair, a deeper voice. Thereafter it maintains them and contributes to sexual arousal. Estrogen stimulates maturing of the female reproductive organs, the onset of menstruation, and the development of female secondary sexual characteristcs—breasts, rounded body contours, and enlargement of the pelvis.

Although the hypothalamus controls hormonal secretions, the interaction of the nervous and endocrine systems is not one way (Figure 3.21). Endocrine hormones act reciprocally upon the hypothalamus and other parts of the nervous system and do much to regulate the secretion of hypothalamic hormones. Through a process of feedback, the endocrine hormones may either decrease—negative feedback—or increase—positive feedback—the release of their corresponding hypothalamic hormones. Knowledge of the feedback mechanisms of estrogen has been applied with practical benefits in the birth control pill. This pill acts as a contraceptive by preventing ovulation, the release of a mature egg from the woman's ovary. Ovulation occurs when increasing estrogen levels, through positive feedback, bring about a sharp rise in luteinizing hormone secretion. Most birth control pills contain relatively large amounts of estrogen. By taking these pills daily, the woman keeps her estrogen at a constant high level. This prevents the sharp rise in secretion of the luteinizing hormone and thus ovulation.

Hormones and Behavior

In addition to their feedback effects on neuroendocrine regulation, hormones act on the brain in two other major ways. They activate overt behavior or tendencies to behave, and they have an organizational influence, shaping the development of the brain and behavior early in life, even before birth. Since considerable research has been conducted on the activational and organizational effects of sex hormones, we shall examine these effects in some detail.

Activational Effects.   Hormones play an important role in sexual arousal. Males need androgens to maintain sexual interest and behavior. Castration causes a decline and the eventual disappearance of libido and copulating ability. Libido and potency return rapidly if testosterone is administered. Factors other than hormonal ones must contribute to sexual arousal, however. Some men lose potency immediately after castration; for others the decline is slow and gradual, over a number of years. Prior experience appears to be one factor accounting for these individual differences, at least in some mammals. In cats, for example, considerable sexual activity before castration prolongs potency afterward (Rosenblatt and Aronson, 1958).

The hormonal activation of femal sexual behavior is more complex. Females of the great majority of mammalian species are sexually receptive in cycles. Generally, the female is receptive to the male only when a ripe egg is ready for fertilization and the levels of estrogen and progesterone are high. At all other times these hormones are at low levels, and she is not receptive to the male. Removing the ovaries in females of these species abolishes the cyclic changes in receptivity—the females no longer come into heat. Administering estrogen and progesterone to these ovariectomized females restores their sexual receptivity.

Sex hormones affect behavior by activating various regions of the brain. Neurons in these regions of the brain have receptors that bind the hormones in a manner similar to that in which receptors bind neurotransmitters. Specific receptors exist for each hormone, as receptors exist for each transmitter. Each hormone attaches itself only to the receptor that matches its chemical structure. Once the hormone binds to the receptor site, it initiates a series of chemical reactions and alters the functioning of the neuron.

Neurons that have receptors to take up the hormones have been located by

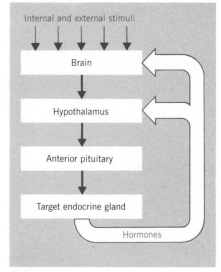

Figure 3.21
Neuroendocrine regulation. This simplified model indicates the basic elements, including feedback mechanisms. (Adapted from Frohman, 1980.)

injecting animals with radioactive hormones. A photographic emulsion discloses the whereabouts of the radioactivity in slices of the brain (Stumpf, 1970). These studies indicate that testosterone, estrogen, and progesterone bind to neurons in the anterior and lower hypothalamus and in the preoptic area, which is just in front of the hypothalamus. In neat correspondence, behavioral studies have shown that implanting minute quantities of hormones in these areas of the brain restores the sexual activity of castrated animals producing no sex hormones of their own. Estrogen implants in the preoptic area or basal hypothalamus will stimulate sexual receptivity in ovariectomized female rats (Davis, McEwen, and Pfaff, 1979). Testosterone implants in the anterior hypothalamus will restore male sexual behavior in rats castrated as adults (Johnston and Davidson, 1972).

Organizational Effects. Would men become women if their testosterone were removed and replaced with estrogen? Would women become men if their estrogen were exchanged for testosterone? The answer to both of these questions is no. Withdrawing testosterone and administering estrogen would alter a man's body—he would develop breasts and rounded contours and lose his beard—but he would not consider himself to be a woman or behave like one. In spite of his inability to have erections, he would not become interested in performing sexually like a female. Nor would be become homosexual, interested in sexual contact with other men. Similarly, a heterosexual woman treated with testosterone would neither lose her sexual interest in men nor wish to engage in sexual activity with other women.

Sex hormones do not alter the sexuality of adult men and women because the organizational effects of androgen have established it so decisively during fetal development. At seven or eight weeks after conception, the primitive gonads of the human embryo become testes and begin secreting androgen if the fetus is to develop into a male. Without androgen the female fetus develops the internal and external reproductive organs of a female.

The period of time in which androgen affects the organization of later behavior is limited. In rodents this "critical period" ends some time after birth. A normal adult female rat will not acquire male sexual behavior, even if her ovaries are removed and she is given injections of testosterone. If a female rat is given an injection of testosterone shortly after birth, however, and then again later in adulthood, her sexual behavior will become masculine. Male rats castrated immediately after birth—before androgen has had its organizational effects— will not mount females in adulthood, even when given testosterone. For most other mammals, including human beings, the critical period ends before birth.

Early **androgenization** affects behavior other than sexual activity. Parental behavior is more readily demonstrated by females and neonatally castrated male rats than by normal male rats. Normal male rats and females that have received androgen soon after birth are more timid in exploring new surroundings than normal females. Without prenatal androgenization a male dog will not lift his hind leg when urinating. Young male monkeys will not engage in rough and tumble play or make their normal threatening gestures without prenatal androgenization (Beach, 1970; Goy and Goldfoot, 1973).

Early exposure to androgen may bring later sex differences in behavior by determining how the brain develops. Differences in synaptic connections and branching patterns of dendrites have been observed in the preoptic region of male and female rats and hamsters (Field and Raisman, 1973; Greenough et al., 1977). In addition, the size of the preoptic area and of a group of motor neurons that bind androgen in the spinal cord differs in male and female rats (Gorski, 1980).

To what extent are the psychological and behavioral differences of men and women dependent on early androgenization? This question is difficult to answer because males and females are not raised in the same way. The effects of physiology are confounded with those of social learning. Some light may be shed on the question, however, by examining what happens when early hormonal exposure is not consonant with the socialization of the individual. The adrenal glands of girls normally secrete small amounts of androgen, but sometimes they secrete too much. At one time this exposure also happened as a side effect of a synthetic hormone given to mothers to prevent miscarriages. Some of their daughters were born with genitals indicating a degree of masculinization; they were corrected by surgery. Eleven of these girls were studied by John Money and Anke Ehrhardt (1972). Although the girls were raised as girls and perceived themselves to be female, they described themselves as "tomboys." They preferred toy trucks and guns to dolls, as well as male companions to females. They also had considerable athletic interests and skills. In adolescence they looked forward to a career first, marriage and maternity second; they became interested in young men at a later age than do most young women. The greater "masculine" interests of these females suggest that prenatal androgen may indeed affect later behavior in human beings.

Human upbringing may have the power to reverse some of the effects of prenatal androgenization. In another case studied by Money and Ehrhardt (1972), identical twin boys were born and raised normally until the age of seven months, when one of the boys had his penis removed in a carelessly performed circumcision. Given female genitals surgically, this boy was thereafter raised as a girl and acted in ways typical of girls. She was neat and tidy, in contrast to her rather messy twin brother. She helped with the housework and modeled her behavior on that of her mother. Through socialization, one of these genetically identical children became a girl in her behavior while her brother remained the boy he was born.

Pheromones

So far we have seen how the hormones of individuals can affect their physiology and behavior. Some chemical substances produced by individuals have the remarkable ability to change the physiology and behavior of *other* individuals of their own kind. These chemical substances, which are secreted by one individual, become airborne, and reach the olfactory systems of others, are called **pheromones.** One of the first pheromones to be identified was a substance manufactured by glands in the abdomen of the female gypsy moth. So powerful is its scent that, given proper wind conditions, males are attracted to a single female from several miles away. The effects of other pheromones are quite familiar from observations of domestic animals. Dogs are attracted, sometimes over considerable distances, by the scent of estrous bitches. An estrous cat will roll and rub and adopt the characteristic estrous posture when she smells the odor of a male cat's urine.

Pheromones released by a female rhesus monkey make her more attractive to a male. Studies were conducted by Richard Michael (1980) in which male rhesus monkeys were required to press a lever to gain access to females. They indicated little interest in doing so when the ovaries of the females had been removed. Treating these females with estrogen, however, made the males press the lever avidly. That the males were responding to a chemical signal in the air was demonstrated by blocking their sense of smell with nasal plugs. They no longer pressed the lever with the same amount of interest. A group of modified fatty acids in the female's vaginal secretions, whose production depends on estrogen, have been identified as the chemical signal. In one experiment these substances were collected from estrogen-treated females and applied to untreated females whose ovaries had been removed. Males earlier unresponsive to them immediately showed a great deal of sexual interest.

Michael has discovered similar chemical substances in human females. The quantity of these substances, which he calls "copulins," varies cyclically; amounts are greatest just prior to the time of ovulation. We do not know yet how these substances affect human sexual behavior.

Pheromones are also important in reproductive physiology. Some of the most dramatic effects have been described in laboratory mice. If within twenty-four hours of mating a female mouse is exposed to a male from a different strain, the fertilized egg is not implanted in the uterus and the pregnancy is blocked. The urine of a strange male is as effective as the presence of the male himself, but urine from males castrated before puberty is ineffective. The estrous cycle of female mice provides another example. Female mice separated from males and caged individually have a normal four- or five-day estrous cycle. If these females are then grouped together in a cage, their cycles become irregular and many of them develop a physiological state similar to pregnancy. If a male is introduced, however, nearly all of them will come into heat on the third day after the male's arrival. In addition to reproductive behavior and physiology, pheromones may help in body growth and maturation, maternal recognition of young, the mother-infant bond, and individual and species recognition.

Endorphins: Opiates in the Brain

One of the most startling revelations in recent years was the discovery of receptor sites for opiates. In the course of their studies on drug addiction, Candace Pert and Solomon Snyder found that morphine, heroin, and other substances derived from opium attached themselves to certain cells in the brain, spinal cord, intestines, and other places in the body (Pert, Kuhar, and Snyder, 1976). Binding was greatest to cells in the limbic system, the region of the brain concerned with the regulation of emotion. Once the opiate receptors had been discovered, the obvious question was why are they there. Could there be a naturally occurring opiate with pain-relieving properties that acts at these receptor sites? The existence of such a substance might explain the pain-free period commonly experienced by wounded soldiers and injured athletes. The search for the brain's own opiate led to the discovery of substances, peptides, with morphinelike properties. They were called **enkephalins** (Greek *en,* in; *kephalē,* head). Other peptides that bind to opiate receptors were later identified and named **endorphins,** for "endogenous morphine." When injected in minute quantities into the brains of animals, these natural substances suppress pain.

The possibility that endorphins and enkephalins are the brain's own analgesics suggests a provocative idea, that these substances may be responsible for the placebo effect (page 15) in pain relief. A placebo medicine is usually successful in treating at least 30 percent of the people taking it, relieving their pain, inducing sleep, reducing nausea, and so on.

Recent investigations have demonstrated that the placebo effect is more than just imagination. A placebo can actually act like a medication, altering body chemistry and helping to mobilize the body's defense in combating disorder or disease. In a study of people recuperating from wisdom tooth extractions, some patients received the usual postoperative treatment, morphine, others a placebo. The patients were then asked to report changes in their pain. As expected, about one-third of the people receiving the placebo reported a significant reduction in pain. When these individuals were subsequently given naloxone, a drug which prevents opiates from taking effect, they reported a significant increase in pain. Since naloxone cannot by itself cause pain, it was apparently blocking the action of endorphins in these placebo-responsive individuals. The researchers concluded that the placebo treatment probably activated the brain's endorphins in relieving the patients' pain (Levine, Gordon, and Fields, 1978).

Throughout this chapter we have examined the biological basis of behavior, demonstrating how the nervous and endocrine systems regulate behavioral and visceral responses. Evidence that a person's belief or expectation can actually release a brain chemical suggests that the interaction between physiology and mental activity is not unidirectional. Rather, the interaction may be reciprocal. Although the nervous system is absolutely essential for thinking and behavior, an individual's thoughts and behavior may also influence the activity of the nervous system. A new frontier of study in the brain sciences is the examination of how conscious or unconscious mental experience affects the nervous system. Although new, these studies of the reciprocal interaction of mental activity and the nervous system are addressing an important facet of the age-old question of how the mind and body are connected, a question whose study continues to fascinate us.

SUMMARY

The endocrine system, which consists of eight glands, is closely interrelated with the nervous system. Together, these two systems ensure the organism's best adaptation to the demands of its environment. By means of its own chemical substances or hormones, the hypothalamus regulates the secretion of hormones by the pituitary gland. The pituitary hormones, in turn, trigger the release of other endocrine gland hormones. In addition, the endocrine gland hormones are able to influence their own regulation by the hypothalamus through feedback mechanisms.

Hormones can have two types of effects on behavior, activational— actually stimulating behavior; and organizational—shaping the development of the brain and behavior early in life. They activate behavior in part by governing the activity of neurons regulating it. They organize the development of the brain by determining the size of specific areas, the branching patterns of dendrites, and so on.

Sex hormones are necessary for sexual interest and the expression of sexual behavior. The male sex hormone androgen must be present very early in life for male anatomy and behavior to develop. Without androgen the individual becomes a female. The early learning and socialization of human beings may reverse some of the effects of early androgenization.

Pheromones are odoriferous substances that are released by one individual and have specific effects on the physiology or behavior of another member of the same species. Pheromones can promote reproductive physiology and behavior, growth and maturation, the mother-infant bond, and individual and species recognition.

Endorphins and enkephalins, which may be neurotransmitters of the nervous system, have natural pain-suppressing properties. These substances may be responsible for the initial pain-free period of people who have just been injured and for the placebo effect in pain relief.

TO BE SURE YOU UNDERSTAND THIS CHAPTER

This chapter contains a very large number of concepts. The list that follows includes the most important. They are given in the approximate order in which they appeared in the chapter. If you can define them all in order, you will reproduce most of the content of the chapter.

Peripheral nervous system
Central nervous system
Brain
Spinal cord
Somatic sensory fiber
Somatic motor fiber
Visceral sensory fiber
Visceral motor fiber
Afferent neuron
Efferent neuron
Glia cell
Neuron
Blood-brain barrier
Cell body
Dendrite
Axon
Terminal button
Myelin
Nerve impulse
Action potential
All-or-none law
Synaptic transmission
Synapse
Presynaptic neuron
Postsynaptic neuron
Synaptic cleft
Synaptic vesicle
Neurotransmitter
Receptor site
Deactivating enzyme
Resting potential
Temporal summation
Spatial summation
Excitatory stimulation
Inhibitory stimulation
Receptor
Effector
White matter
Gray matter
Spinal nerve
Nerve tract
Interneuron
Reflex arc
Hindbrain

Cerebellum
Medulla
Pons
Brainstem
Midbrain
Forebrain
Cranial nerve
Nucleus
Reticular formation
Reticular activating system
Old forebrain
Limbic system
Hypothalamus
Autonomic nervous system
Parasympathetic system
Sympathetic system
Self-stimulation
Cerebral hemisphere
Thalamus
Cerebral cortex
Primary motor cortex
Secondary sensory cortex
Secondary motor cortex
Association cortex
Agnosia
Hemiplegia
Aphasia
Sensory aphasia
Motor aphasia
Prefrontal cortex
Perseveration deficit
Commissure
Corpus callosum
Epilepsy
Endocrine system
Hormone
Androgen
Estrogen
Progestin
Androgenization
Pheromone
Enkephalin
Endorphin

In This Book. Chapter 4 on the sensory processes is the chapter most closely related to this one. Additional related materials are to be found in Chapter 5 on perception, 8 on conditioning and learning, and 9 on motivation.

Elsewhere. The subject matter in this chapter is drawn from material of several disciplines, each of which is an entire science in itself and has its own name, such as physiological or biological psychology, psychobiology, neuropsychology, neurophysiology, neuroanatomy, neurochemistry, neuropharmacology, and so on. Texts with any of these words, or any other words with the prefix neuro-, in their titles will contain wider-ranging and more detailed discussions of the phenomena described here. Perhaps a hundred new books on these subjects are published each year. Examples of the more general ones are *Functional Neuroscience,* by Michael Gazzaniga, Diana Steen, and Bruce Volpe; *The Brain,* by C. U. M. Smith; *Handbook of Behavioral Neurobiology,* edited by F. A. King; and *Biological Psychology,* by Philip Groves and Kurt Schlesinger.

CHAPTER 4   SENSORY PROCESSES

One of the oldest ideas in the history of psychology is that mental life or consciousness has its origins in sensory experience. The best-known statement of this idea is that of the British philosopher John Locke. In *An Essay Concerning Human Understanding*, published in 1690, Locke maintained that the mind of a child is a blank tablet, a *tabula rasa*, and that what it becomes depends on what experience writes on it.

> Let us suppose the mind to be, as we say, white paper, void of all characters, without any ideas:—How comes it to be furnished? Whence comes it by that vast store which the busy and boundless fancy of man has painted on it with an almost endless variety? Whence has it all the *materials* of reason and knowledge? To this I answer, in one word, from experience.

John Locke is generally regarded as the founder of British empiricism, a school of thought gaining its name from the conviction that there are no innate ideas, that all knowledge comes from experience, by way of the senses. They give us our sensations, the raw material out of which knowledge is constructed.

When psychology turned to experimental work some two centuries later, such thinking still persisted and made the sensory processes logical early subjects for investigation. Our presentation breaks this study down into two parts. This chapter is devoted to the sensory mechanisms, which provide the raw materials out of which experience is created. The sensory processes relate closely to the physiology of the nervous system given in Chapter 3. Chapter 5 on perception describes some of the kinds of experience we create from the raw sensory materials. It ties the more physiological mechanisms to cognitive activities.

John Locke (1632–1704) believed that understanding the way in which the human mind works is a prerequisite to understanding everything else.

VISION

What we call light is a small, intermediate portion of the complete spectrum of electromagnetic energies, which range from cosmic rays to radio waves (Figure 4.1, color plate). The elemental unit of electromagnetic energy is called a **quantum** and can be thought of as a small, fast-moving packet or particle of energy. The quantum unit of visible light energy is called a **photon**; when lights are very weak, their strength can be expressed as some number of photons. Emitted by some source, photons travel through space at approximately 186,000 miles per second. When they strike an object, some of them are absorbed and some are reflected back. Certain objects of visual experience, such as the sun, a lighted lamp, a burning fire, are sources of light; but most of what we see comes to us by means of light that is reflected. In a very few instances reflected light is also a source of light; moonlight, which is reflected sunlight, is an example.

Basic Qualities of Visual Experience

As a quantum travels through space, the energy pulsates in a wave motion. The pulsations of quanta can be compared, somewhat imprecisely, to the ripples traveling away from the spot in a pond where a pebble has been dropped. Electromagnetic waves, like others, are distinguished by length and amplitude. The distance from crest to crest in the train of waves is the **wavelength** and represents the distance between pulsations of the quanta. The distance from trough to crest of a single wave is its **amplitude** and is greater the larger the number of quanta radiated in a given direction by a source during some period of time (Figure 4.2).

Wavelength and Hue. The wavelengths of quanta in the visible spectrum extend from about 380 to about 760 nanometers (nm, billionths of a meter). The length of these **light waves** is the major determiner of **hue,** what we refer to by the common color names red, yellow, blue, green, and so on. The shorter wavelengths are seen as violets and blues, the longer ones as yellows and reds (Figure 4.1, color plate).

The visual spectrum can also be depicted as bent into a **color circle** (Figure 4.3, color plate). If people are asked to arrange colors by similarity, they must necessarily put them in a circle—red, orange, yellow, yellow-green, green, green-blue, blue-green, blue, violet, red-violet, and red again. Some colors given in this circle, the purplish hues and the purest red, do not actually appear in the spectrum because they are mixtures. What we perceive as pure red needs a little blue from the other end of the spectrum to rid the most nearly pure spectral red of a slightly yellowish tinge. People throughout the world see four of the colors on the circle—red, yellow, green, and blue—as pure colors that resemble no other hue. They are called **psychological primaries.** All other colors, orange, chartreuse, and brown, for example, seem to be made up of two or more colors.

Wave Amplitude and Brightness. Colors that are identical in hue may differ in **brightness.** The differences between maroon and pink will give meaning to this concept. It would be possible to find a maroon and a pink that contain the same proportion of red. The maroon will appear blacker, however, the pink whiter, which suggests one way of describing brightness: it is the dimension from black to white.

The principal physical determiner of a color's brightness is the amount of energy, the number of photons of that particular wavelength, making up the reflected light. Graphically, it is the amplitude of the light wave. Light waves that are identical in length can differ in amplitude. Those of high amplitude, representing a large number of photons, are perceived as brighter than those

Figure 4.2
Wavelength and wave amplitude. In vision wavelength is the principal determiner of the psychological dimension of hue. Wave amplitude is the principal determiner of the psychological dimension of brightness.

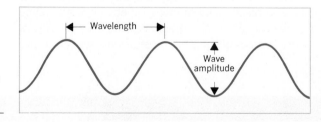

of low amplitude, representing a smaller number of photons. A secondary determiner of brightness is wavelength; certain colors appear intrinsically brighter than others, because our eyes are more sensitive to these wavelengths. In ordinary daylight the brightest color is a somewhat greenish yellow. That is, when this particular yellow and any reds and blues whose waves have the same amplitude are compared, the yellow appears brighter, the reds and blues noticeably duller.

Wave Complexity and Saturation. Our discussion of hue and brightness has assumed a monochromatic (*mono,* one; *chroma,* color) reflected light, made up of photons of a single wavelength. Such colors rarely, if ever, occur in nature. When light falls on objects in the world, some photons are absorbed and some are reflected back. The reflected light is made up of photons of different wavelengths, and the apparent color of an object depends on the pattern of wavelengths reflected. For example, an object that absorbs most of the waves of incident light, reflecting light waves predominantly 575 nm long with only small amounts of waves of other lengths, appears to be a very strong yellow. Light waves still predominantly 575 nm long but containing larger proportions of other wavelengths translate visually as a dull, grayed yellow. Light made up of all wavelengths appears to us as white. The dimension from white or gray to full color is the dimension of **saturation.** Saturation depends on the purity of the light, the number of different wavelengths that contribute to it. All the achromatic colors, the colorless colors from black through gray to white, are completely desaturated. The lights we see as white and gray are made up of photons of all wavelengths. They differ in brightness because of the number of photons producing them. White is produced by a great many photons of all wavelengths, gray of fewer photons of all wavelengths. Black objects reflect no appreciable fraction of incident light.

The double cone in Figure 4.4 summarizes these elementary aspects of visual experience. The circumference of the cone is hue; its radius is saturation; the vertical dimension is brightness. The figure is conical in order to make the point that a maximally bright, or dull, fully saturated hue is an impossibility. The highest and lowest degrees of brightness are white and black, which are colorless, that is, without saturation.

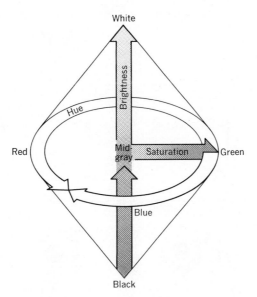

Figure 4.4
Dimensions of vision. This color solid is a three-dimensional representation of all possible visual experiences.

Structure of the Eye

The organ of vision, the eye, collects the energy called light and brings it to focus on a small region of the retina called the fovea. If the analogy is not pushed too far, the eye can be thought of as a simple camera (Figure 4.5).

The Iris.   The amount of light entering the eye is controlled by the **iris,** which corresponds to the diaphragm in a camera. The iris is a ring of smooth muscles whose outer pigmented layer gives the eye its color. It surrounds the **pupil,** the aperture or opening through which lights enters. In very bright light the iris closes to reduce the amount entering the eye. In dim light it enlarges to allow more light to enter.

Although the level of illumination is by far the most important factor, it is not the only one controlling pupil size. When we do close work, even under good light, the iris closes down still further because this increases the sharpness of the visual image. Foods, political personalities, sharks, beautiful landscapes, and nude human figures—emotional arousal or interest of any kind—will widen the pupils. For example, the pupils of males dilate when looking at pinup pictures of women, those of women when looking at pinup pictures of males. The third factor is mental activity. Eckhard Hess and J. M. Polt (1964) measured increases in the size of subjects' pupils as they solved a graded series of multiplication problems "in their heads." The pupils gradually dilated as the subjects performed the multiplications, reaching a maximum just before they gave their answers. The more difficult the multiplication, the greater the dilation.

Focusing Mechanisms.   For a person to receive a clear and unblurred perception of an object, its image must be sharply focused on the retina. A system

Figure 4.5
The structure of the eye and its similarity to the camera. The operation of the iris has been imitated in the diaphragm of the camera. The images formed on the retina and the film are both upside down.

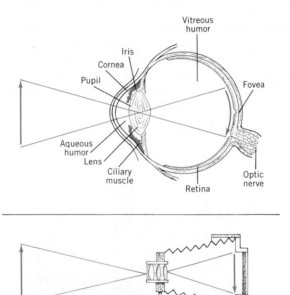

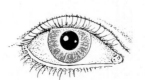

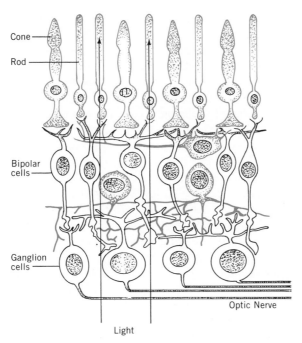

Cone
Rod
Bipolar cells
Ganglion cells
Optic Nerve
Light

Figure 4.6
The retina. Light travels through a complex network of cells before arriving at the rods and cones. Impulses generated in these receptors are transmitted to the bipolar cells and then to the ganglion cells. Lateral connections are made at the level of the bipolar and ganglion cells.

consisting of several elements accomplishes this focusing. The first element is the **cornea,** a deeply curved transparent membrane which is continuous with the tough, white opaque coat of the eyeball; the second is the **aqueous humor,** a pocket of clear fluid just behind the cornea which helps to maintain its rounded shape. Next in order is the **crystalline lens,** which with the help of the **ciliary muscles** flattens and bulges to obtain a sharp focus for objects distant and near. Finally, in the ball of the eye, between the lens and the retina, lies the **vitreous humor.** This is a jellylike substance which maintains the degree of focus produced by the earlier elements in the system and also maintains pressure to help keep the retina in place. The cornea provides about two-thirds of the focusing power in this system, sharply decreasing the size of the visual image. The lens takes over at that point and operates like a fine tuner, making precise adjustments as required.

The Retina. The photosensitive part of the eye corresponding to the film in the camera is the **retina.** The retina (Figure 4.6) is a thin sheet made up of several layers of interconnected nerve cells. The receptive cells of the retina, the **rods** and **cones**—named for their distinctive shapes—are at the back of the retina. Light must pass through the various layers of blood vessels and of the fibers and cell bodies of neurons before reaching the rods and cones, which are also neural structures. As we shall learn in more detail later, the cones respond in bright light, in terms of color, the rods in dim light, in terms of white, black, and shades of gray. The cones are the most heavily concentrated in the **fovea,** a small pit or indentation only about 0.5 millimeter across, where the image of an object viewed directly falls. The fovea contains only cones. The density of cones drops off drastically just beyond the fovea, however; few inhabit the periphery. The rods become greatest in density a short distance out from the fovea, and then they too become fewer in number in the periphery.

The rods and cones contain light-sensitive pigments, **rhodopsin,** sometimes called visual purple, in the rods, and **iodopsin** in the cones. Rhodopsin was

In this electron micrograph of a very minute section of the retina, the structures with blunt ends are rods, the tapered ones cones.

discovered in 1876 by Franz Boll, but little was known about the pigment of the cones until some eighty years later. When light waves reach the visual pigments, they are absorbed and initiate a chemical reaction which breaks down the pigments, in effect bleaching them. This reaction in turn initiates neural activity which moves on to the **bipolar** and **ganglion cells** in the retina (Figure 4.6) and eventually to the occipital lobes of the brain. At the level of the bipolar and ganglion cells there are also **lateral connections.** These connections make it possible for cells in different retinal areas to influence one another. The most important psychological contributions of these horizontal connections are to sharpen our perception of borders and edges. The ganglion cells translate information about color into the code by which such information is represented at higher levels of the nervous system (see page 115).

The retina contains some 6 to 8 million cones and at least 120 million rods, but only some 800,000 ganglion cells. Since there are so many rods and cones and relatively few ganglion cells, impulses from many rods and cones must converge on single ganglion cells. Such convergence is greater in the periphery of the retina than in the fovea, and for this reason greater for rods than cones. A great many rods converge on ganglion cells, but in the fovea the bipolar and ganglion cells are nearly one to one with cones. In the peripheral portions of the retina, several hundred rods may connect to one bipolar cell.

The pooling of impulses initiated in many rods allows the bipolar cells they converge on to be fired in low illumination. This spatial-summation aspect of retinal functioning plays a very important part in dark adaptation (see page 110). The heightened sensitivity of rod vision to dim light does not come cost free, however. The price we pay is lowered **visual acuity,** seeing fewer details. Vision is sharpest where individual receptors can respond separately and privately to details of whatever scene is before the eye. In peripheral rod vision signals from many receptors covering an aspect of the scene reach the bipolar cells and are blended, making precise perception of spatial arrangement impossible.

By contrast with the rods, the cones in the fovea are packed very closely together and are narrower in this area than elsewhere. Pursuing the comparison of the eye to a camera, we can say that in the fovea the retina is like a fine-grained film, one coated with more and smaller grains of the photosensitive silver halides. Cones also have nearly one-to-one connections to their bipolar cells. Moreover, the blood vessels and nerve fibers form a thinner layer in front of the fovea. Vision is at its sharpest and most detailed. Once more, however, there is a price to pay. Since the bipolar cell to which each cone connects is fired by its output alone, illumination must be good to supply the stimulation needed by each cone for temporal summation.

The axons of the ganglion cells run along the surface of the retina and collect together at the **blind spot,** where they leave the eye as the optic nerve. The blood vessels pass through the wall of the eye along with the nerve. Because the blind spot contains no rods or cones, it is, in fact, blind. With the aid of Figure 4.7, you can locate your own blind spot. The existence of the blind spot means that there is actually a gap in the visual field of each eye. We are usually

Figure 4.7
Locating the blind spot. Close the left eye and fixate the blue spot on the space ship. Move the book toward you. When the planet disappears, its image is falling on the blind spot. Now close the right eye and fixate the blue arrowhead. Move the book as before. When the bar of the arrow appears to be continuous, the white space is falling on the blind spot. The brain at this point takes over and fills in the visual field.

unaware of it, however, because when we are using both eyes, an object never falls within both blind spots at once.

Physiological Nystagmus.   Tiny tremors of the eye keep it in constant motion. This **physiological nystagmus,** as it is called, blurs vision to a slight degree, but it is also essential to the proper functioning of the rods and cones. Both of these facts can be demonstrated by removing the tremor of the eye optically. In one demonstration of this, experimenters attached a tiny slide projector to a contact lens worn by the observer. A slide was projected onto a screen (Figure 4.8). Since the contact lens and the projector moved with the individual's eye, the image from the screen always fell on the same area of the retina, which means that the pattern of rods and cones stimulated was always exactly the same. In short, the movements of physiological nystagmus could no longer have their usual effect of switching stimulation to neighboring rods and cones. At first, vision became somewhat sharper, confirming that this eye tremor does in fact blur the image. Soon, however, the image faded and disappeared. The fading of perception as the pigments of particular rods and cones are depleted gives physiological nystagmus an important function. If it did not exist and we looked at an object for more than a few seconds, the object would not be visible.

Two Mechanisms of Vision

The rods and cones, together with the bipolar and ganglion cells to which they send their messages, make up two different mechanisms of vision. The cones operate in daylight, requiring bright illumination to function; the rods function in dim illumination. There are two reasons for this. The rods contain deeper stacks of visual pigment than the cones and, as we have already seen, the output of many rods converge on single bipolar cells, thus increasing the probability that these cells will respond. The rods and cones are both sensitive to light waves in most of the visible spectrum, but there are differences. The rods and their connections produce the experience of achromatic colors, black, white, and shades of gray. The cones and theirs produce the experience of hue, although acting together in groups they can also yield the achromatic colors. The rods and cones differ in their sensitivity to various wavelengths. As indicated earlier, for this reason we see greenish yellow, a reflected light with a wavelength of about 550 nm, as the brightest hue. The right-hand curve of Figure 4.9 indicates the varying sensitivity of cones to the wavelengths of the visible

Lorrin A. Riggs, a professor at Brown University, was a pioneer in the study of the effects of physiological nystagmus on visual acuity. He and a student, Floyd Ratliff (Riggs et al., 1953), reported the initial sharpening and subsequent fadings of stopped images.

Figure 4.8
Stilling physiological nystagmus. With a tiny slide projector attached to a contact lens, the image projected to the retina falls on the same area however the eye moves. (After Cornsweet, 1970.)

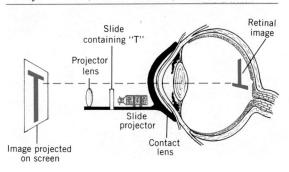

Figure 4.9
Visibility function for rods and cones.

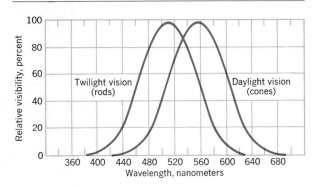

spectrum. And, as indicated by the left-hand curve, rods also vary in their sensitivity to different wavelengths, their peak sensitivity being to a wavelength of about 510 nm, a definite green. This is the wavelength that most effectively penetrates the atmosphere of our planet. The rod system records this wavelength as a light gray; other wavelengths appear as darker grays. Finally, Figure 4.9 shows that the cone system responds to certain long wavelengths—reddish colors—to which the rod system does not respond and, conversely, that the rod system responds—but with achromatic colors—to certain short wavelengths to which the cone system does not respond.

Dark Adaptation.   The bright illumination flooding the scene when a person spends time in daylight subjects the rods and cones to continual stimulation and reduces their sensitivity to illumination of any lesser degree. The sensitive rhodopsin has in fact been largely depleted. It has little time for reconstitution before it is broken down again. In darkness, however, cones gradually become somewhat more sensitive and rods very much more sensitive. Pigments build up, especially rhodopsin, helping the eye to become dark-adapted. Neural changes help too, but the precise mechanism is not known. **Dark adaptation** is measured by determining the dimmest light a person can see (absolute threshold, page 129) after successive amounts of time in the dark (Figure 4.10). After forty minutes in the dark, eyes are about 100,000 times more sensitive than before dark adaptation began. Since most of the process of dark adaptation takes place in the rods, which are concentrated in the periphery of the retina, night vision has an interesting aspect. We can see faint stars best by looking slightly to one side of them. A falling star is usually noticed out of the corner of an eye, where the rods prevail. It may disappear when we turn our eyes to look directly at it. The image is then cast on the fovea, where the much less sensitive cones are concentrated.

Dark adaptation has different time courses for the rods and cones. It begins to take place in the rods and cones at the same time. In five to seven minutes, the cones have become fully adapted. The additional, slower adaptation evident in the curve in Figure 4.10 is that of the rods alone. The discontinuity in the

Figure 4.10

Dark adaptation. The vertical axis is in fractions of the intensity of light that is visible to the light-adapted eye, set at 1.0. Until the rods and cones have been about seven to eight minutes in the dark, the curves for them are identical. Then they diverge. The cones adapt no further. The rods become very much more sensitive.

In dark-adapted vision color disappears, as does all the information that color conveys.

adaptation curve is called a **rod-cone break,** but it could more logically be called a cone-rod break, given the order of events. The more slowly adapting rods do not reach their maximum sensitivity until after thirty to forty minutes in the dark. The fact that the rods are responsible for dark-adapted vision following the rod-cone break can be demonstrated by tracing the course of adaptation in low-intensity red light. Rods are relatively insensitive to the wavelengths for red, but the cones are sensitive (Figure 4.9) to them. After the five to seven minutes required to adapt the cones, there is no further increase in sensitivity to the red light and no improvement in vision.

Important practical use has been made of the fact that the rods are insensitive to red. Rods can remain unstimulated and become dark-adapted in the light, if that light is red. The cones are used for seeing, since they respond to red. One way of making all light reaching the eyes red is to wear red goggles. Sentinels who must go on watch during the night often prepare themselves by putting on a pair forty minutes or so before their duty is to begin. During this period the world looks entirely red, but there is enough light to carry on activities that require vision. The last ten minutes of the forty sentinels spend in complete darkness, to adapt the cones. After this preparation they are able to see in the dark as well as they could had they spent the entire forty minutes in complete darkness.

The Purkinje Shift. The differential sensitivities of the rods and cones account for the changing brightness of different colors with dark adaptation. A red and green matched for brightness in daylight appear to differ under dim illumination, the green appearing much brighter than the red. This phenomenon may be observed easily as twilight falls in a rose garden. The green leaves remain bright for some time after the red blossoms appear black. The fact that the red roses are seen as black in dim illumination confirms again that the rods are totally unresponsive to red. This shifting of the relative brightness of the different colors in dim light is called the Purkinje phenomenon or **Purkinje shift,** after the physiologist who discovered it.

Color Vision

Most readers of this book already have fair amount of knowledge about the phenomena of color vision. After the blinding light of the photographer's flash gun, you have undoubtedly noticed the color afterimage that persists for at least several seconds. Since color blindness is not uncommon, you probably know someone with at least a degree of this condition. In art classes you have learned about one form of color mixture and, in this same context, many of you will have asked yourselves a very basic question. When I see the color green obtained by mixing blue and yellow paints, is my experience the same as what others have when they say that they see something green? How could I ever know whether we have the same experience? This question is a fundamental philosophical question, to which the most common philosophical answer is that we can never know whether the private experiences of different individuals are the same or not.

Color Mixture. There are two general kinds of color mixing to consider, mixtures of lights and mixtures of pigments. The results of mixing any two colored lights are easiest to explain with the aid of the color circle (Figure 4.3, color plate). In general, when any two lights are mixed, the resulting color is halfway between them on the circle, and there is a loss of saturation that depends on the distance between them. Consider the mixture of red and yellow wavelengths. Draw a line from red to yellow on the circle and notice where the center of this short line falls. As you could have predicted, it is in the range of hues called orange. The eye receives both wavelengths, which add together as orange. The result of mixing wavelengths for red and green, a yellow of very low saturation, is more surprising. The center of the line connecting red and green is in the range of hues called yellow, but the line passes very near the center of the color circle, which means that the color resulting from the mixture will be very low in saturation, almost a neutral gray. Colors that are exactly opposite to each other on the color circle are called **complementary colors.** When wavelengths of such hues are mixed, they have no detectable color and are seen as an achromatic gray or white. Yellow and blue wavelengths are complementary and mix together as gray.

As the part of Figure 4.11 (color plate) showing mixtures of lights suggests, most colors of the spectrum can be produced by combining, in proper proportions, three lights carefully chosen from different thirds of the spectrum. A blue-violet of wavelength 460 nm, a green of 530 nm, and a somewhat yellowish red of 650 nm are often selected. Such colors are called **physical primary colors,** as opposed to the psychological primary colors, red, yellow, green, and blue, mentioned earlier.

Mixtures of lights and mixtures of paints do not always produce the same result. The most dramatic case is that of blue and yellow. A mixture of blue and yellow lights produces gray; a mixture of these pigments is seen as green. The color seen can be understood in terms of the wavelengths absorbed and reflected by the two pigments. The blue pigment reflects blue wavelengths predominantly, but some for violet and green; it absorbs the other wavelengths in the spectrum. The yellow pigment reflects predominantly yellow wavelengths, but some for green and red, and absorbs the other wavelengths. When these two pigments are mixed, the blue pigment absorbs the red and yellow wavelengths reflected by the yellow pigment, and the yellow pigment absorbs the violet and blue wavelengths reflected by the blue pigment. The only wavelengths reflected back in any quantity are those for green. The mixture of lights or of reflected colors is sometimes called **additive mixture** because the eye receives all the wavelengths that are mixed. The mixture of pigments is sometimes called **subtractive mixture** because the pigments cross-absorb and the eye receives only leftover wavelengths (Figure 4.11, color plate).

Afterimages and Related Phenomena.   If you stare at the small black dot in the center of the upper left part of Figure 4.12 (color plate) for thirty or forty seconds and then at the dot in the gray circle to the right, you will soon see an ephemeral blue ring surrounded by a green one. The hue of the **negative afterimage** is always the complement of the fixated hue. A closely related effect is seeing **induced colors.** If a patch of gray paper appears against a colored background, the gray takes on a faint tinge of the color that is the complement of the background hue. If we replace the gray paper with a patch that is itself the complement of the background color, the hue of this patch intensifies. This is the phenomenon of **simultaneous contrast.**

Finally, there are the phenomena of color blindness, which comes in many gradations ranging from the complete absence of color vision to not being able to see red and green, to seeing all colors but red or green with some degree of weakness. The completely color-blind individual sees the world entirely in shades of gray. This condition is rare and usually occurs in albinos, whose bodies lack all pigments. Since their cones do not contain the usual photosensitive pigments, the cones in effect do not function. Another extremely rare form of color blindness, usually caused by disease, is the inability to distinguish yellows and blues. The most frequent types of color blindness are several hereditary varieties of red-green color blindness affecting 7 to 8 percent of males but less than one percent of the female population. Those with this defect cannot distinguish green from red, seeing them both as yellowish brown (Figure 4.13, color plate).

Theory of Color Vision

Research carried out in recent years has made it very clear that color vision is the result of processes that occur in two stages. First, the retina contains three types of cones, each of which responds to a range of wavelengths but is maximally responsive to a particular wavelength. Second, in ganglion cells and at higher levels of the nervous system, the neural activity initiated in these three types of cones is integrated and triggers an "opponent-process mechanism." Thus the facts of color vision coincide with elements of two classical theories of color vision proposed in the nineteenth century. Although the second one was originally offered as a competing theory, together they predicted the two stages of color vision.

Trichromatic and Opponent-Process Theories.

The two classical theories of color vision were developed on the assumption that the primaries, physical in one theory and psychological in the other, are fundamental to color vision. Early in the nineteenth century an English physicist, Thomas Young (1773–1829), proposed that the retina contains three kinds of "particles" which "vibrate" to the wavelengths of the three physical primaries, red, green, and blue, and that the eye mixes these stimulations to see the other hues. Initially, the theory received only limited acceptance. Fifty years later, however, the great German physiologist Hermann von Helmholtz (1821–1894) revived Young's theory and revised it. Helmholtz proposed that the three receptors, Young's particles, respond maximally to the wavelengths for the primary colors, but that each also responds less strongly to a range of wavelengths. Since it assumes three receptors, the Young-Helmholtz theory can be called a **trichromatic theory.**

Hermann Ludwig Ferdinand von Helmholtz, shown here in a classroom, was one of the great men of science. Theoretical physics, neurophysiology, optics and vision, physiological acoustics, and the psychology of the senses were all encompassed by his genius.

The second classical theory of color vision was put forward by Helmholtz's compatriot and fellow physiologist, Ewald Hering (1834–1918). Hering also proposed a three-component system, but with each component capable of a dual response. He theorized that three sets of receptor cells deal individually with the three linked visual experiences, blue-yellow, red-green, and black-white. Hering proposed that these receptors respond in one but not both of two mutually antagonistic ways. The blue-yellow cells, for example, can provide the experience for blue or yellow, but not both as the same time. When these receptors respond in one way, the other reaction tends to be canceled. For this reason Hering's theory can be called an **opponent-process theory** (Hurvich and Jameson, 1957).

Reconciliation of the Two Theories.

The Young-Helmholtz and Hering theories had both taken definite form by about 1870. From then, until the middle of this century, the two theories were in competition, each with its own adherents. For the greater part of this period, the Young-Helmholtz trichromatic theory was the dominant one, partly because of the enormous respect that science held for Helmholtz, but more importantly because the assumption of three receptors, each with just one function, seemed simpler than the assumption of three sets of receptors, each with opposing functions.

It is October 20, 1967, and George Wald, professor of biology at Harvard University, has just learned that he has won the year's Nobel prize in physiology, along with two other colleagues.

The three Young-Helmholtz receptors, maximally responsive to wavelengths for red, green, and blue, but also less strongly responsive to the other wavelengths in the spectrum, handled the facts of color perception and color mixture very nicely. Red, green, or blue will be seen when one of these receptors is stimulated more strongly than others, yellow when red- and green-sensitive receptors are stimulated simultaneously. Nonprimary colors will be seen when other combinations of receptors are excited, white and gray when all three are excited.

The theory also explained well the fact that negative afterimages have a color that is the complement of the fixation stimulus, assuming that receptors are subject to fatigue. Fixating the red stimulus in Figure 4.11 tires the red-sensitive receptors and renders them incapable of a maximal response. The gray background looked at after the fixation period would normally excite all three receptors equally. Since the red receptors are fatigued, however, they will respond with less vigor than the blue and green; hence the bluish-green hue of the negative afterimage for red.

Stronger evidence for the trichromatic theory of retinal function came in 1964 with George Wald's discovery that there are three kinds of cones, varying by their iodopsins. Three years later his work on vision won Wald a Nobel prize in physiology. A device called a microspectrophotometer makes it possible to study the absorption of light in a single cone. Each cone in the human retina contains one of three iodopsins which differentially absorb wavelengths of the visual spectrum (Figure 4.14). The absorption accomplished by one pigment peaks at approximately 445 nm, a blue; that of the second at 535 nm, a green. The third absorbs maximally at 570 nm, a yellow, but it also absorbs all the long wavelengths up to 650 nm, covering the reds (MacNichol, 1964).

The Young-Helmholtz theory had never explained color blindness very well, however. Since the experiences of red and green are produced by different Young-Helmholtz receptors, two kinds of red-green color blindness, one in which the red receptors do not function properly and another in which the green receptors are insensitive, might be expected. Indeed, in color-mixing experiments some people who are red-green color blind are relatively insensitive to red. In matching yellow with mixtures of red and green, they require an unusually large amount of red. A second kind of red-green color blindness is revealed as insensitivity to green. The red-green color-blind can see yellow, however. Since the experience of yellow would presumably depend on the simultaneous stimulation of the red and green receptors, weakness in either of these sets of receptors should distort perception of yellow. This does not seem to be the case. Red-green color-blind people, and the few individuals who are

Figure 4.14
The absorption spectra for three types of cones.

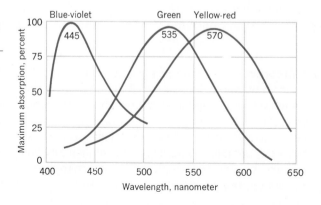

red-green blind in one eye only, report that red and green resemble the yellow-ish shades. There must be other processes whose deficiencies will explain color blindness.

Physiological studies have indeed shown that these additional processes resemble the opponent mechanisms proposed by Hering. In the lateral genic-ulate body of the thalamus, the nuclei which serve as a major relay station in the transmission of nerve impulses from the eye to sensory cortex, neurons that operate on what appears to be an opponent-process principle have been detected. As is true of neurons elsewhere in the nervous system, those in the lateral geniculate body respond continuously, at a relatively slow rate, even though they have not been stimulated. Russell DeValois and his associates discovered that this firing can be stepped up or slowed down, depending on the wavelength of the stimulus (DeValois, Abramov, and Jacobs, 1966). They inserted microelectrodes into single cells in the lateral geniculate of a monkey and then presented flashes of light of different colors (Figure 4.15). Presenting a blue or green light to a particular neuron might decrease its rate of firing; a yellow or red light would increase it. The firing of other cells follows the opposite pattern. The ganglion cells in the retina and neurons in several areas of the visual cortex were later found to alter their firing in the same fashion.

The physiological data strongly suggest the trichromatic theory describes visual mechanisms very well in the cones but that, at later stages of the visual system, three-color cone information is recoded into opponent neural processes.

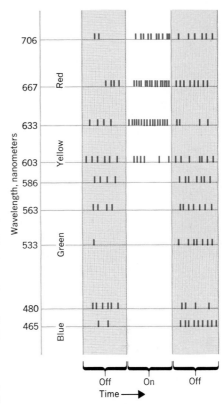

Figure 4.15
Opponent processes in the lateral geniculate body. The short vertical lines indicate the responses of a single microelectrode-implanted cell in the thalamus to stimulations of nine different wavelengths. The cells are of two kinds. Firing spontaneously at a fairly slow rate, the cell increases the rate of firing, decreases the rate, or ceases firing altogether when the stimulus is given. This particular cell increases its rate of firing at the presentation of yellow and red lights and ceases at the presentation of blue and green lights. (After DeValois, Abramov, and Jacobs, 1966.)

SUMMARY

Physics describes light in two different ways, as a flight of fast-moving particles or packets of energy, which are called photons; and as energy traveling in a wave motion. The waves have three properties, length, amplitude, and complexity. Each of these physical properties of light is the principal determinant of a particular psychological aspect of visual experience. The eye is sensitive to wavelengths of light that range from about 380 to about 760 nm. Different wavelengths produce the experience of different hues. Wave amplitude, but also to a degree wavelength, is responsible for brightness. Saturation depends on the purity of the light waves, on their all having the same wavelength.

The photoreceptive layer in the eye, the retina, contains two kinds of receptors, rods and cones. These receptors contain pigments rhodopsin and iodopsin that react to light and produce neural activity that is passed along to bipolar and ganglion cells in the retina. These cells, in turn, transmit their messages on to higher levels of the nervous system. Physiological nystagmus, a continual tremor of the eye, shifts the visual image as it falls on the receptors, preventing its loss of the image through a depletion of the pigments in the rods and cones.

The rods and cones are receptors for two different visual mechanisms. The cones function in bright illumination, the rods in dim illumination. Both become more sensitive in relative darkness. With dark adaptation the eye shifts from cone vision to rod vision, allowing us, after a time, to see more clearly in dim illumination. The rods and cones also differ in their sensitivity to different wavelengths, the rods being more sensitive to shorter wavelengths and totally insensitive to the longest. This difference is responsible for the Purkinje phenomenon, a shift in the relative brightnesses of colors at twilight.

In the cones color perception depends on three pigments which absorb selectively blue, green, and red wavelengths. The ganglion cells as well as neurons in the lateral geniculate body and in the visual cortex respond in terms of opponent colors —green versus red and blue versus yellow. They slow firing to short wavelengths and increase it to long wavelengths or vice versa.

AUDITION

The stimuli for hearing are sequences of compression and rarefaction of the air. Consider, for example, the vibrating tuning fork shown in Figure 4.16. As the fork vibrates to the right, it pushes the molecules of air, which are represented by the dots, to the right. When it moves to the left, a partial vacuum is created. Successive vibrations produce the pattern of compression and rarefaction indicated by the density of the dots. As in vision, sound stimuli can be represented as waves of energy. These pressure waves radiate outward in all directions from the source, however, and they are mechanical rather than electromagnetic. Another important difference between the description of auditory and visual stimuli is that the waves for sound are specified in terms of frequency, in cycles per second, or **hertz** (Hz), rather than by wavelength, although both could be described either way. One cycle is a single complete compression and rarefaction. Frequency is therefore the number of times per second that the complete cycle of the sound wave is repeated.

Physical Characteristics and Psychological Experience

Particular sound waves may differ in frequency, amplitude, and complexity, and these differences are responsible for certain aspects of auditory experience. The correspondences between vision and audition in terms of their dependence on the physical characteristics of stimuli are given in Table 4.1.

Pitch. The human ear is sensitive to frequencies ranging from about 20 to 20,000 hertz, the greater the frequency, the higher the **pitch.** One interesting phenomenon that is easy to understand in terms of this relationship is the **Doppler effect,** the change in pitch that a person who is stationary hears as a moving sound source approaches and then speeds past. The pitch of a train whistle or automobile horn, for example, rises as the vehicle nears and falls as it passes by. As an automobile approaches, the sound waves are, in effect, more frequent because the forward movement of the car crowds the compressions of the air together; as the car passes, the time between compressions increases back to what is normal for the pitch of the horn (Figure 4.17). Since frequency is the physical basis for pitch, it is to be expected that the pitch of the sound will increase and decrease, exactly as it does.

Loudness. **Loudness** in audition corresponds to brightness in vision, both of them reflecting wave amplitude. The amplitude of a sound wave depends on the degree of displacement of the vibrating body from its resting position. It is the strength or intensity of the wave, the extent of compression and rarefaction. The intensity of a sound is usually expressed in terms of **decibels** (dB), a unit

Table 4.1 A Comparison of Psychological Correlations for Vision and Audition

Vision		Audition	
Physical Feature	**Psychological Dimension**	**Physical Feature**	**Physical Dimension**
Wave length	Hue	Wave frequency	Pitch
Wave amplitude	Brightness	Wave amplitude	Loudness
Wave complexity	Saturation	Wave complexity	Timbre

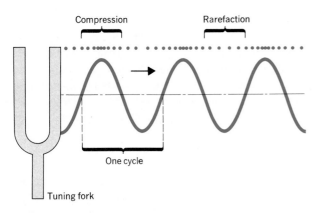

Figure 4.16
The nature of sound waves. As the tuning fork vibrates, it produces waves of successive compression and rarefaction of air molecules, represented by dots at the top of the figure. The horizontal line extending from the middle of the fork indicates the normal concentration of molecules. Denser concentrations are represented by the wave peaks above this line, less dense concentrations by the troughs below.

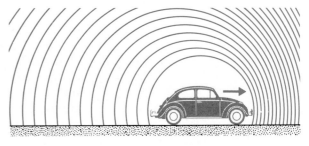

Figure 4.17
The Doppler effect. As the car moves forward, the sounds of its horn and engine are heard as high in pitch because the movement of the car, in effect, pushes the sound waves together. As the car speeds past, the waves stretch and the pitch lowers.

of measure related to that for physical pressure (see page 134). The loudness of sound, a psychological dimension, is usually measured in **sones**. Although the sone scale was originally developed from the judged loudness of tones by human subjects, sones are related to decibels in a simple way. A 1000-hertz tone at 40 decibels is arbitrarily defined as one sone. Then every 10 decibels in intensity doubles the number of sones, so that 50 decibels = 2 sones, 60 = 4, 70 = 8, 80 = 16, 90 = 32, and so on. The ear is the most sensitive in the frequency range around 500 to 4000 hertz: these tones can be heard at fewer than 10 decibels. Higher or lower tones require a great deal more intensity to make them audible. Human voices range from 100 to 3500 hertz, and conversation is usually conducted at about 60 decibels. The lowest piano note has a frequency of 27.5 hertz, the highest 4180 hertz. Prolonged exposure to sounds above 90 decibels can cause permanent deafness. Sounds above 120 decibels are painful to the ears.

Timbre. **Timbre** is the tonal quality of sounds that makes it possible to distinguish between different musical instruments that are all sounding the same note. When a violinist draws the bow across the open A-string, the string vibrates at a basic frequency of 440 hertz. This produces the dominant pitch or **fundamental tone** in what the listener hears. At the same time, however, the string also vibrates in segments that are exactly, a half, third, fourth, fifth, and so on of its entire length. The vibrations produce **overtones** of a higher pitch. With the fundamental tone taken as one, these overtones stand in the ratio 1:2:3:4:5. Thus the overtones produced with a fundamental tone of 440 hertz would have frequencies of 880, 1320, 1760 hertz, and so on. For different musical instruments the number and intensity of the overtones vary. The peaks and troughs of the fundamental tone are preserved, but the wave is not smooth. There is a mathematical way, called Fourier analysis, of breaking down any wave form, and thus any tone, into its components. These components are all pure tones of single but different frequencies.

The most complex waves are heard as what we call noise. They are composed of many frequencies that are not in harmonious relation with one another. A completely pitchless noise can be produced by generating a sound that contains all the frequencies in the audible spectrum. By analogy to white light, which contains all wavelengths of the visible spectrum, such a noise is called **white noise.** The nearest approximations to white noise encountered in everyday life are the hissing sounds of air or steam escaping from pressure, as in the sound of a tire slowly going flat.

The Structure of the Ear

Tracing the path of sound through the ear will serve to describe its principal functions (Figure 4.18). The pressure waves are first collected by the external ear and are carried to the **eardrum,** which they force to vibrate at the same frequency. In the air-filled cavity between the eardrum and another membrane, the **oval window,** are three small bones (ossicles) fastened together by ligaments: the **malleus,** or hammer; the **incus,** or anvil; and the **stapes,** or stirrup. These bones, the tiniest in the body, act as a series of levers when transmitting the vibrations of the eardrum, increasing the pressure as much as threefold. In addition, because the oval window is much smaller than the eardrum, the pressure per millimeter that it receives is much greater than that on the eardrum. The fairly small movements of the whole eardrum are transformed into much stronger movements of the minute oval window. The increase in pressure is necessary, for the oval window must move against the fluid of the inner ear or cochlea. Fluid is much more difficult to set in motion than air.

The bony and coiled **cochlea** is divided into three canals, each filled with fluid. The **perilymph** in the vestibular canal is set into motion by the vibrations of the oval window (Figure 4.19). These vibrations cause waves to travel up the vestibular canal and back down the lower tympanic canal, with which it is connected at the apex of the cochlea. The true auditory receptors are in the cochlear duct, which lies in between. They are tiny **hair cells** located on the **organ of Corti,** which rests on the **basilar membrane** dividing the duct from the lower canal. As the fluid waves travel through the upper and lower canals, they twist this tough but flexible membrane. These movements in turn bend the stiff, protruding cilia of the hair cells against an overhanging tectorial membrane, to which they are attached. These shearing movements of the hair cells translate into impulses. Nerve fibers connecting with the bottoms of the some 25,000 hair cells join together to form the auditory nerve and send their messages to the temporal lobes of the brain.

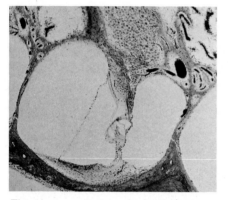

This electron micrograph shows the inner cochlear duct of the human cochlea.

Figure 4.18

Anatomy of the ear. The inner ear is sometimes called the bony labyrinth. In addition to structures for hearing, it contains the vestibule and semicircular canals, which are concerned with equilibrium.

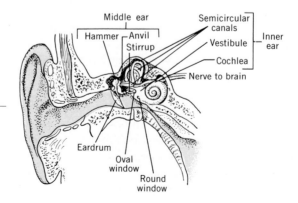

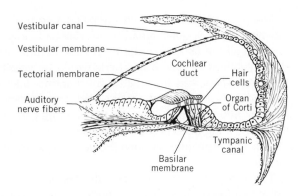

Figure 4.19
Structure of the cochlea. The vestibular and tympanic canals contain perilymph; the cochlear duct contains endolymph.

Theories of Hearing

The organ of Corti is smaller than a pea, and yet it can distinguish tens of thousands of tones ranging from hardly audible to damagingly and painfully loud. By what mechanism it manages these discriminations, in pitch and loudness or, physically speaking, in frequency and intensity, is not definitely known.

As with color vision, two competing theories have struggled for acceptance as the correct theory of hearing, but research now suggests that each of these two theories may tell one part of the story. And as with color vision, Helmholtz suggested one of these theories in 1873. George von Békésy (1899–1972) expanded on it and won a Nobel prize for his work. Helmholtz's theory is commonly called a **place theory.** The basic idea in the place theory of pitch is that particular regions of the basilar membrane respond, depending on the sound frequency. In fact, near the entrance to the cochlea the basilar membrane is narrow and stiff; it becomes progressively wider and is a hundred times more flexible at the tip. According to the place theory, the narrow portion of the basilar membrane would be expected to twist and the cilia of its short hair cells shear the most to high-frequency fluid waves in the cochlea. The wide tip should twist and the cilia of its taller hair cells shear the most to lower-frequency fluid waves. Therefore, according to this theory, nerve fibers connected to hair cells in different places on the basilar membrane are stimulated, depending on the frequency of sound vibrations. The neural code for pitch is the area of the basilar membrane that moves.

Von Békésy collected considerable evidence in support of the place theory of pitch. In one of his experiments he observed fresh cochlea taken from recently dead human cadavers. He cut windows into them at various locations and through a microscope watched the movement patterns of the basilar membrane as the oval window was vibrated with a small electrically powered pistion. He observed a traveling wave beginning in the stiffer, narrow region of the basilar membrane and moving to the broader portion. The maximum bulge of the traveling wave initiated by high-frequency vibrations occurred near the stapes, and thereafter the wave quickly dissipated. The traveling wave initiated by intermediate-frequency vibrations bulged the broader region near the tip of the cochlea. Unfortunately for the place theory, the wave set up by low-frequency vibrations also had its greatest bulge near the cochlear tip.

The place theory of loudness assumes that the more intense a vibration, the greater the proportion of the basilar membrane bulging in the traveling wave and the greater the number of hair cells and nerve fibers stimulated. Moreover, the organ of Corti contains two sets of hair cells, an inner one with one column of hair cells and an outer one with three columns. Evidence suggests that the inner column is responsible for registering pitch, the outer for registering loudness.

George von Békésy won his Nobel prize in physiology, awarded for his work on the ear, in 1961.

The principal difficulty with the place theory of pitch is that the lump in the traveling wave is quite broad for vibrations below several thousand hertz and engages all the far end of the basilar membrane. It is difficult to see how pitch discriminations of only a few hertz would be possible for lower frequencies. It has been suggested that neural mechanisms take over and produce a more focused pattern of neural activity. Auditory messages pass through at least four levels of neurons on their way to the auditory cortex. Experimental data indicate that the coding becomes more precise at each level (Brown and Deffenbacher, 1979). The problem is enough, however, to warrant consideration of alternative theories.

The most important of these alternatives is the **frequency theory,** which holds that the pitch we hear depends on the rate at which the basilar membrane as a whole vibrates. The entire basilar membrane and attached hair cells are assumed to vibrate, reproducing the vibrations of the sound. Thus we hear middle C, which has a frequency of 256 hertz, because their are 256 displacements of the membrane per second and 256 impulses travel up the neurons of the auditory nerve.

The chief problem with frequency theory is that a single nerve fiber cannot fire at rates faster than about 1000 impulses per second and therefore would not be able to transmit most of the frequencies of the audible range. Faced with this difficulty, frequency theorists advanced a **volley theory** of nerve conduction, proposing that every nerve fiber does not fire at the same moment, that groups of neurons in the auditory nerve respond together, in squads. While some neurons are refractory, others respond, only to become refractory themselves as other squads take over. In this turn-taking manner the nerve can communicate higher vibration frequencies—perhaps as many as 4000 hertz— but still not enough to represent the entire range of pitches.

The volley theory of loudness holds that more nerve fibers fire in each volley when the vibrations are strong, indeed that the groups of fibers may fire more frequently, so that two groups are firing for each volley. The greater number of impulses in each volley registers the greater amplitude of the sound wave.

It may well be that the two mechanisms proposed by the place and frequency theories both operate in our perception of pitch. The greater bulging of the near and narrow portion of the basilar membrane by the traveling wave probably codes all high-frequency sounds, perhaps all those above 3000 hertz. Lower frequencies, probably those below 400 hertz, are registered one for one in membrane vibrations and auditory nerve impulses. Sound frequencies in between may be handled by both mechanisms.

Impaired Hearing

Difficulty with hearing is a common physical affliction, affecting perhaps 5 percent of the population. Accumulations of wax in the outer ear, imperfect functioning of bones in the middle ear, damage to the receptive mechanism of the inner ear, and defects in the auditory nerve pathways are all possible causes. Some cases of impaired hearing are genetic in origin; some appear as a common symptom of aging. The hair cells on the organ of Corti close to the oval window gradually deteriorate. By age seventy most people cannot hear frequencies greater than 6000 hertz. Before the days of penicillin, deafness often followed middle-ear infection in children. Continued exposure to loud sounds, whether in the boiler room or at a rock concert, can also damage structures in the organ of Corti, causing **stimulation deafness.**

The first step in dealing with impaired hearing is to assess the extent and kind of hearing loss. The degree of loss is usually greater at certain frequencies

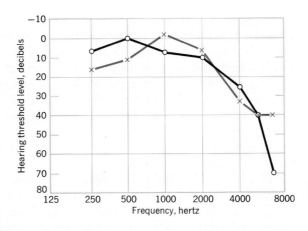

Figure 4.20
An audiogram. The vertical axis is a measure of hearing loss, showing in decibels the increase in intensity necessary to produce normal hearing at each frequency. O's are for the right ear, X's for the left.

than others. In order to obtain the necessary information, the examiner determines the lowest sound the person can hear (absolute threshold, page 129) for the range of pitches most essential in day-to-day living—from 125 or 250 to about 8000 hertz. With this information available, the individual's pattern of sensitivity can be plotted in an **audiogram,** which shows hearing loss throughout a range of pitches. The degree of loss consists of the additional decibels needed above those normally required to make a sound of a given pitch audible.

The audiogram for a typical patient, a fifty-four-year-old man, appears in Figure 4.20. The audiogram indicates normal hearing within speech frequencies, up to about 2000 hertz, but substantial loss of sensitivity at the higher frequencies. Does this pattern represent a serious problem and is there a remedy?

Rock bands performing at up to 150 decibels have impaired the hearing of a generation of young people.

The patient had come to the Hearing Evaluation Clinic because he had had some difficulty understanding speech in noisy surroundings for the last twenty-five years, and it seemed to be getting worse. His complaints are typical of **sensory-neural deafness,** resulting from some defect in the organ of Corti or in the higher neural pathways. Masking of speech by noise is common in such cases. At the present time little can be done to correct these disorders. Hearing aids are of limited usefulness, and no other corrective measures have been developed.

The other principal class of hearing disorder is **conduction deafness.** As the name implies, such deafness stems from problems in the mechanical transmission of sounds to the oval window. There are several causes of conduction deafness and several corresponding cures. If wax has accumulated in the auditory canal, a simple cleaning and flushing of the canal may restore normal hearing. In cases of middle-ear infection, the area may fill with liquid, hampering the function of the malleus, incus, and stapes. The physician will frequently pierce the eardrum of such patients. allowing the liquid to drain out.

Many cases of conduction deafness are caused by a hereditary disease called **otosclerosis.** A spongy growth in the middle ear turns to bone and fixates the stapes in the oval window or fuses the ossicles. Hearing aids that utilize the bones of the skull to transmit vibrations to the cochlea will help these people hear. Now it is also possible to remove the immobilized middle ear bones surgically and to install a plastic and wire replacement, all under local anesthesia. Recovery in these cases is sudden and spectacular. Even during surgery the patient may report the return of useful hearing.

SUMMARY

The ear responds to successive compressions and rarefactions of the air over a range of about 20 to 20,000 hertz (cycles per second). The frequency of the changes in air pressure determines pitch. The amplitude of the sound wave determines loudness, although perceived loudness also depends on pitch. With the intensity of sound waves at a generally comfortable level, tones in the range from 500 to 4000 hertz are the most easily heard. The complexity of the sound wave determines timbre.

The receptor for hearing works as follows. Sounds are collected by the outer ear and carried to the eardrum. Vibrations of the eardrum are amplified and transmitted to the oval window of the inner ear by three small bones. Waves established in the fluids within the inner ear travel up and down the canals of the inner ear. These waves stimulate the basilar membrane on which are located the true auditory receptors, the hair cells. The physiological mechanisms responsible for the experiences of pitch and loudness are not completely understood. The place theory of pitch maintains that particular regions of the basilar membrane are moved the most, depending on the frequency of the sound vibrations. The frequency theory of pitch maintains that the whole basilar membrane vibrates in one-to-one correspondence with the sound vibrations, and that this frequency is translated, by neurons firing in batches, into the same frequency of impulses in the auditory nerve. Common opinion holds that the mechanism proposed by place theory handles high tones and those proposed by frequency and volley theory handle low tones. The perceived loudness of a sound depends on the number of neurons activated by the sound wave and, according to the volley theory, their rate of firing. Perhaps the outer set of hair cells on the organ of Corti register loudness. Defects in the transmission of sound energy from the eardrum to the oval window cause conduction deafness.

In sensory-neural deafness functioning of the inner ear or neural mechanism is impaired.

THE OTHER SENSES

Taste

Substances must be in solution if we are to taste them, for they must seep into furrows and then into pores. The receptors for taste are spindle-shaped cells clustered together like orange segments to form a **taste bud.** Taste buds are especially dense in the small but visible bumps on the upper surface of the tongue (Figure 4.21). Each bump or papilla is a flat, disk-shaped elevation surrounded by a moatlike furrow, within which the taste buds lie. But taste buds are also found in microscopically small pits and grooves of the soft palate, the floor of the mouth, the mucosa of the cheeks, and the underside of the tongue. Human beings have between 9000 and 10,000 taste buds. Ten to forty taste cells group together to form a taste bud. These taste cells have a short life of several days. New cells continually move into taste buds to become taste cells, and the aging cells move from the edge to the center. Over any seven-day period a taste bud has a completely new set of taste cells. As we age, however, the taste cells are replaced at a slower rate and our sense of taste diminishes.

The tip, sides, and rear of the tongue are the areas most sensitive to tastes, the tip of the tongue being particulary sensitive to sweet, the sides to sour, and the rear to bitter. There is sensitivity to salt along the edges of the tongue. Partly because of such differential sensitivity of portions of the tongue to salt, sweet, sour and bitter, these tastes have often been proposed as primary taste sensations in the same way that red, yellow, green, and blue are psychologically primary colors. Recently, however, this proposal has been criticized (Schiffman and Erickson, 1980). When subjects try to analyze the tastes of a wide range of substances in terms of salt, sweet, sour, and bitter, they find that tastes cannot be rated in terms of these qualities. A substantial amount that is not one of them is always "left over." Anatomical and neurological information also raises questions. Although the suggested primary tastes tend to be sensed the most heavily in certain areas of the tongue, most individual taste cells and the nerve fibers connecting to them seem to respond to several taste qualities. In short, no set of receptors corresponding to the separate cones that register the blue, green, and red of vision exist. Single taste cells show mixed sensitivity, respond-

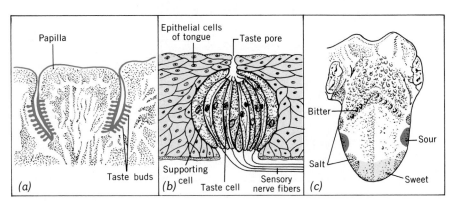

Figure 4.21
(a) Papilla with taste buds in its walls and in those of neighboring papillae. *(b) Structure* of an individual taste bud. Sensory nerve fibers enter the taste bud, then entwine and contact one or more taste cells. The taste cells project hairlike microvilli into the taste pore. *(c) Tongue areas* most sensitive to salt, sour, sweet, and bitter.

ing, for example, to sour and salty or to sour, salty, and sweet stimulation. In addition, evidence suggests that some substances may excite taste cells and other substances inhibit them and the firing of the nerve fibers contacting them. The neural code for taste apparently depends on a pattern of firing in a number of fibers.

Smell

About all that can be said with certainty concerning the stimulus for smell is that odorous substances must be volatile enough for their molecules to be carried by air currents to the receptors and water- and fat-soluble to penetrate the film covering them. Most substances whose molecules have odors are organic compounds, by psychophysical studies have failed to produce any dependable system of primary odors. The odor-sensitive **olfactory rods** are at the top of the nasal passage (Figure 4.22). There are perhaps ten million of these long, narrow, column-shaped neurosensory cells, each with six to twelve delicate hairs projecting down into the fluid covering of the mucous membrane. There they contact the dissolved odoriferous molecules. Extending from their other ends are nerve fibers which go to the olfactory bulbs of the brain directly above them. There these fibers converge on far fewer neurons whose axons form the olfactory tracts to other regions of the brain, including the temporal and frontal cortex. The olfactory epithelium is accessible both from the nostrils and from the mouth, which is what makes it possible for the sense of smell to contribute to taste.

As we have learned in the last chapter, odors play an important role in the lives of other creatures. The *pheromones,* secreted by the bodies of animals of many species, communicate information that is important to sexual arousal and reproduction and to the survival of the species. Pheromones serve other purposes too. The males of many mammalian species mark their territory by such secretions. When an intruder disturbs the hive, honeybees release an alarm pheromone which attracts other honeybees and makes them join in the attack against the intruder. Laboratory rats that were performing a task were given whiffs of the odor of their compatriots who had suffered electric shock. The odor served as an alarm pheromone and distracted the attention of these rats from their work (Valenta and Rigley, 1968).

There is quite substantial evidence that human beings can recognize gender

Figure 4.22
The olfactory system. (a) The human ofactory epithelium measures about half a square inch in each nasal cavity. *(b)* The olfactory cell is neurosensory, which means that it is a more primitive type of receptor having its own nerve filament. Neurosensory cells are able both to receive and to conduct stimulation.

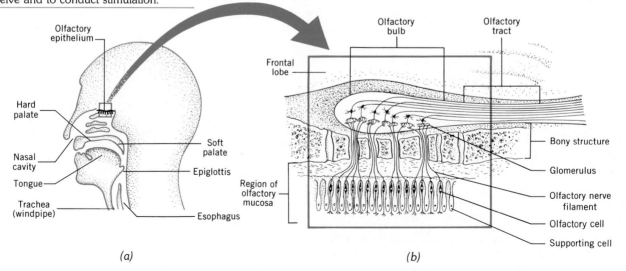

on the basis of the underarm odors left behind in clothing. In several studies (for example, Russell, 1976), subjects distinguished between the undershirts worn by men and women for a bathless twenty-four-hour period. Other evidence suggests that odors can affect our attitudes toward the unmet person who allegedly wore these clothes, and that women are more susceptible to such influences from their noses than men (Hopson, 1979).

In one of the most interesting studies, Martha McClintock (1971) reported that as the college year progressed, the menstrual cycles of women who were close friends and roommates in a dormitory at Wellesley College fell into synchrony, occurring nearly at the same time. These observations have been confirmed by a study of women living on a university campus (Graham and McGrew, 1980). This menstrual synchrony depends on the closeness of the women's relationships with one another and has nothing to do with the nature of their associations with males. Pheromones may very well be responsible for these phenomena.

The Skin Senses

Pressure. The classical instrument for studying the sensitivity of the skin to "touch" or pressure is a set of small sticks to which are attached at right angles a graded series of hairs which differ in stiffness. If the skin is explored with a hair of moderate stiffness, it will be found that, within a small area, some spots respond with a clear sensation of pressure; others do not. Other sensitivities of the skin, for warmth, coldness, pain, itch, tickle, and vibration, can be similarly mapped. When the maps for sensitivity to pressure, warmth, cold, and pain of a particular area are compared, the points that are maximally sensitive to these four types of stimulation do not match. For this reason these senses are considered separate. Maps for itch, tickle, and vibration, on the other hand, so overlap the others that they are usually considered derived senses. An itch is experienced when pain spots are gently and repeatedly pricked, or when they react to a chemical. Light, rapid strokes of pressure spots are felt as tickle, even faster and rhythmical stimulation of them as vibration. Thus itch, tickle, and vibration appear to be the experience of light and rapid excitations of the receptors for pain and pressure.

The tip of the tongue, the lips, the fingertips and the hands, the inner forearm are all extremely sensitive to pressure; the upper arm, outer thigh, and back are considerably less so. The more mobile the area, the greater precision in its detection of touch.

Temperature Senses. The normal temperature of the skin varies from one part of the body to another, ranging from perhaps 82°F in the ear, which is exposed and poorly supplied with blood, to 98°F in protected areas such as the armpit. On the hands and face, which have been the most used for experimental investigation, the normal temperature of the skin is about 90°F. The temperature of the skin area under investigation is taken as **physiological zero**. Temperatures that depart from physiological zero feel warm or cold, depending on the direction of the departure.

The experience of heat, as opposed to warmth, is ordinarily produced by stimuli much above physiological zero. Heat is also experienced in another way, which has implications concerning the mechanism of thermal reception. The alternate tubes of a heat grill (Figure 4.23) can simultaneously present neighboring areas of the skin with warmth (not heat) and coldness. If such a grill is applied to a large area of the skin, the heat felt is intense enough that the limb

Figure 4.23
A *heat grill*. Cold water circulates through one tube; warm, not hot, water circulates through the other. Together the warm and cold stimulations produce the sensation of intense heat.

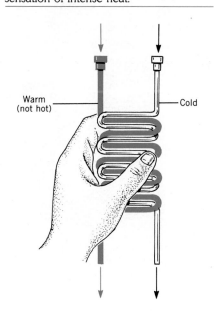

Warm (not hot) — Cold

or other body part is quickly withdrawn. In this experience of heat, nerve fibers for transmitting both warmth and coldness are apparently stimulated. This means that the experience of heat is not merely an intense sense of warmth; it is a synthetic experience made up of both warmth and cold.

Pain. Pain can be elicited by many different stimuli—mechanical, thermal, electrical, and chemical. It is also experienced in many different ways. A distinction is commonly made between "bright" pain, which is felt in the superficial layers of the skin, and "dull" pain, coming from the deeper layers of the body. Bright pains are usually well localized and are of the sort produced by brief electrical shock, a pinprick, or a superficial burn. Dull pains are poorly localized and have an aching, intensely unpleasant persistence.

The mechanisms responsible for the experience of pain have been very poorly understood. In the last twenty years, however, the gate-control theory of pain and the discovery of endorphins and enkephalins have advanced our understanding considerably. According to the **gate-control theory** of pain, developed by Ronald Melzack and Patrick Wall (1965), the experience of pain depends on the frequency of impulses sent to the brain by a set of "transmission cells" in the spinal cord. Two types of neurons running from the skin to these transmission cells carry the messages of pain. One type of neuron transmits the impulses for sharp pain, as well as those corresponding to other skin sensations, over large-diameter, myelinated axons which are rapidly conducting. The second type of neuron transmits the impulses for dull pain over small-diameter, unsheathed, slowly conducting axons.

In addition to making synaptic connections to the pain-transmitting cells, both types of neurons make other connections to a gating mechanism which modulates their effects on the transmission cells. Through these collateral connections the large fibers reduce their own capacity to fire the transmission cells and, in effect, close the gate to the experience of pain. The small fibers tend to open this gate, increasing their capacity to fire the transmission cells.

The experience of pain then depends on the balance of activity in the large and small fibers. Usually activity in the large fibers predominates, pain is sharp but short lasting before the gate is closed, and no additional pain is felt. High levels of activity in the small fibers open the gate and we feel dull, persistent pain.

In the gate-control theory fibers coming down from the brain also help to close or open the gate. Through these fibers' activities influences other than pain stimulation may affect the degree of pain perceived. For example, hypnosis appears capable of eliminating the experience of pain. Moreover, the relief delivered by the inserted and twirled needles of acupuncture probably depends on related phenomena. But even more important, there are many opiate receptors and enkephalin-containing neurons in the substantia gelatinosa, an area of small, densely packed cells extending the length of the spinal cord. The large- and small-diameter pain-carrying fibers have branches to the substantia gelatinosa. Enkephalin may inhibit the release of a neurotransmitter by the large-diameter fibers. The substantia gelatinosa may be the "gate" and enkephalin the mechanism for closing it and suppressing pain.

There is also considerable evidence (Sherman and Liebeskind, 1980) that the brain releases endorphins to help reduce long-lasting pain. When rats suffer thirty minutes of intermittent foot shock, from which they cannot escape, profound analgesia eventually relieves them, an analgesia which can be blocked by naloxone.

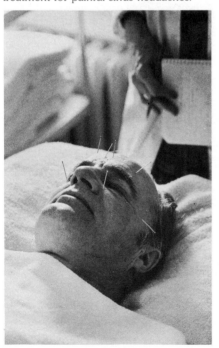

This patient is receiving acupuncture as a treatment for painful sinus headaches.

Two Senses of Movement

We experience two kinds of movement, that of parts of the body and that of the whole body through space. These experiences come from two quite different sensory mechanisms, kinesthesis and vestibular sensitivity.

Kinesthesis. The joints, muscles, and tendons contain receptors that give us a delicate awareness of where the parts of the body are and how they are moving. We know the position of our fingers, wrist, limbs, trunk, and other mobile parts of the jointed skeleton, as well as their precise and larger motions. Kinesthesis, as this sense is called, also tells us of muscle tensions and strains, of a poorly aimed hand movement, and of a trunk pitched too far forward, allowing us to relieve and right them. Through this sense we coordinate our movements automatically, putting one foot before the other as we walk, alternately lowering legs the correct distance as we negotiate stairs, stretching out a hand to an exact spot when picking up an object.

Receptors in the linings of the mobile joints are stimulated as the angles at which bones are held change. Free nerve endings among the muscle fibers signal when a muscle stretches. And in the tendons connecting muscles to bones there are nerve endings which signal when muscle contracts and puts pressure on them.

Vestibular Sensitivity. Detection of the position of the whole body and its motion in relation to gravity depends on structures of the inner ear which give us equilibrium, a sense of balance, and an awareness of changes in direction and in rate of motion. The nonauditory **vestibule** and **semicircular canals** of the inner ear are continuous with the auditory cochlea (Figure 4.28). The vestibule is in the central position of the inner ear at the "entrance" to the cochlea and consists of two sacs; beyond lie the three semicircular canals, at approximately right angles to one another so that they register the three planes of the head and body.

The cutaway portion of Figure 4.24 reveals something of the inner structure of the vestibule and semicircular canals. Within the outer bony structures, called the **bony labyrinth,** is a **membranous labyrinth;** the two are separated by a fluid, *perilymph.* The membranous labyrinth itself contains another fluid, **endolymph.** In one of the membraneous sacs of the vestibule, the utricule,

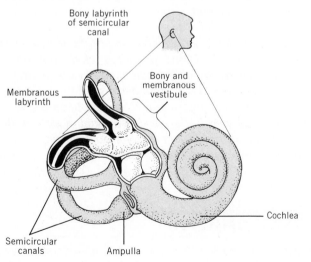

Bony labyrinth of semicircular canal

Bony and membranous vestibule

Membranous labyrinth

Cochlea

Semicircular canals

Ampulla

Figure 4.24
The bony and membranous labyrinths of the semicircular canals and vestibule.

are many tiny crystals of bonelike calcium carbonate loosely attached to a gelatinous mass embedding hair cells. Because of their inertia, the crystals bend the hairs against which they rest in the opposite direction whenever the head is tilted, or when the body is speeding up or slowing down in straight-line motion. The base end of each semicircular canal swells. Within this area is a patch of hair cells. Their hairs, embedded in a crest of gelatin, are deflected in the opposite direction by the lagging endolymph when the head is turned or rotated and when it comes to rest.

The nonauditory portion of the inner ear produces no sensations of its own but provokes sensations elsewhere. In everyday life dizziness is the most frequent experience associated with vigorous labyrinthine stimulation. Dizziness, upon analysis, turns out to be compounded of pressure in the chest, head, and viscera; a pulsating sensation from the blood vessels; and rapidly shifting visual experiences—the eyes move slowly in a direction opposite that of rotation and rapidly back to the normal position.

SUMMARY

The stimuli for taste are substances in solution. They are received by taste buds, most of which are distributed over the surface of the tongue. Because particular parts of the tongue tend to be strongly stimulated by salty, sweet, sour, and bitter tastes, these were once considered to be primary tastes. Neurological studies show that most of the nerve fibers contacting single taste cells can be fired by a variety of taste stimuli, although a few may respond more vigorously to a certain stimulus than to others. All this suggests that the neural code for taste consists of a pattern of neural firing.

We know even less about the sense of smell. There is no generally accepted system of primary odors and little understanding of how the odoriferous pheromones secreted by land animals help them communicate with their kind, marking off territory, signaling danger. Evidence that pheromones are, unbeknown to us, also important in human behavior is growing.

Maps of the skin, obtained with appropriate stimuli, suggest that pressure, pain, warmth, and coldness may be primary sensations. Others, such as heat, tickle, itch, and vibration, are derived sensations. According to the gate-control theory of pain, activity in large, myelinated pain-carrying fibers can activate a gating device, perhaps enkelaphin, to limit pain quickly. But a great deal of activity in unsheathed pain-carrying fibers will keep the gate open, and we feel dull, persistent pain. Endorphins released in the brain can eventually bring analgesia for long-lasting pain.

The kinesthetic sense, registered in the joints, muscles, and tendons, serves two important functions, providing information about the movements of the body and cues that aid in their coordination. Vestibular sensitivity, registered by minute hair cells in the nonauditory portions of the inner ear, gives us our sense of equilibrium. It informs us when the head is tilted, when linear movements of the head, and body, are accelerating or slowing down, and when the head and body are beginning to rotate or coming to rest. This stimulation affects other senses in a complex way, as we learn by analyzing the symptoms of dizziness.

PSYCHOPHYSICS

With our discussion of the individual senses complete, it will be useful to explore briefly the field of **psychophysics,** the study of how psychological events

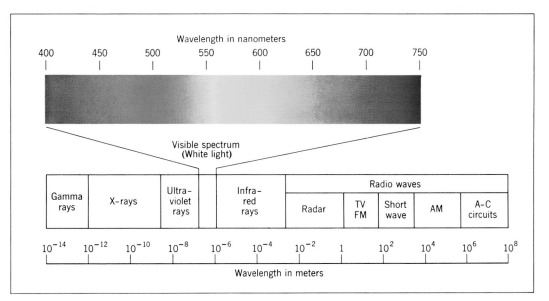

Wavelength in nanometers

400 450 500 550 600 650 700 750

Visible spectrum
(White light)

Gamma rays	X-rays	Ultra-violet rays		Infra-red rays	Radar	TV FM	Short wave	AM	A-C circuits
							Radio waves		

10^{-14} 10^{-12} 10^{-10} 10^{-8} 10^{-6} 10^{-4} 10^{-2} 1 10^{2} 10^{4} 10^{6} 10^{8}

Wavelength in meters

Figure 4.1
The electromagnetic spectrum. The visible portion of the spectrum is shown enlarged in the upper part of the figure.

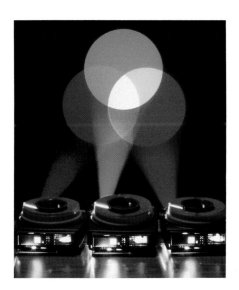

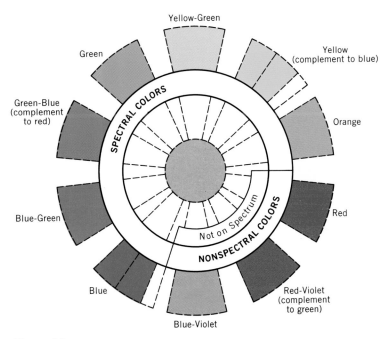

Spectral colors: Yellow-Green, Green, Green-Blue (complement to red), Blue-Green, Blue, Blue-Violet, Yellow (complement to blue), Orange, Red, Red-Violet (complement to green)

Not on Spectrum

Nonspectral colors

Figure 4.3
The principal complementary colors. Colors exactly opposite each other on this circle produce white or gray when mixed. They are called complementary colors. The mixture of any other two colors produces a hue halfway in between them on the circle, with a loss of saturation that is greater for colors far apart than for colors close together.

Figure 4.11
When lights of physical primary colors combine, the wavelengths of the three add together in the middle as white. When pigments are mixed and when color filters transmit light, the pigments and filters cross-absorb one another's reflected and transmitted wavelengths. Three primaries acting together absorb all wavelengths and are seen as black.

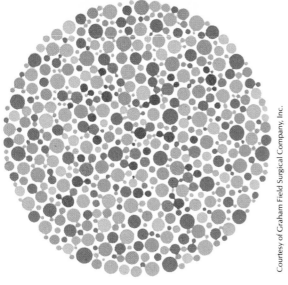

Figure 4.13
A plate from the Ishihara test for color blindness. A person with normal vision sees the number sixteen.

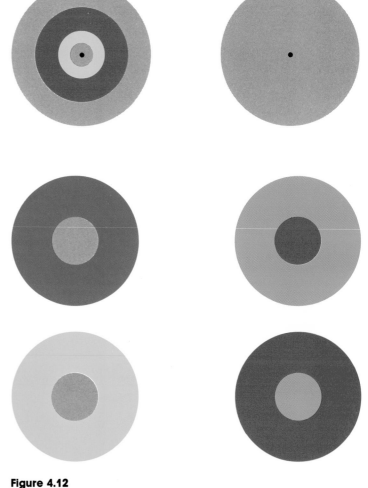

Figure 4.12
Stare at the black dot within the red and yellow rings (*top*) for thirty or forty seconds and then at the black dot on the gray circle. A gray circle within a colored one (*left*) takes on a faint hue complementary to that of the surrounding ring. When a colored circle is surrounded by a ring in its complementary color (*right*), both colors are enhanced through contrast.

YELLOW	RED
GREEN	GREEN
BLUE	YELLOW
RED	GREEN
YELLOW	BLUE
RED	YELLOW
GREEN	YELLOW
BLUE	RED
YELLOW	BLUE
BLUE	GREEN
GREEN	BLUE
GREEN	GREEN
BLUE	RED
YELLOW	YELLOW

Figure 6.17
Sample Stroop test. It is difficult to ignore the words and report only the colors. The words seem to take over and are responded to automatically.

depend on physical ones. One of the oldest areas of study in psychology, psychophysics asks two basic questions. How weak a stimulus can a person detect? How small a difference in stimulation can a person detect? These are questions respectively about the absolute threshold and the difference threshold. They can be asked about any sensory system.

Absolute Threshold

The **absolute threshold** in any sensory system is the weakest stimulus that it can detect. For any sense it is the smallest amount of physical energy that will produce a sensation. Studies of the absolute threshold for various senses have shown that they respond to levels of stimulation that are remarkably low, so low, in fact, that greater sensitivity would be maladaptive, given the nature of the physical world. If the dark-adapted eye were any more sensitive than it is, visual experience would be very peculiar. Steady light would appear to flash, and we would perceive, in visual terms, the chemical changes that take place within the eyeball. The absolute threshold for hearing is so low that, were the ears only slightly more sensitive, we would be able to hear the collisions of air molecules against the eardrums. The receptors in the inner ear detect movements smaller than one percent of the diameter of a hydrogen molecule. Threshold values for the different senses in terms that may be more meaningful are listed in Table 4.2.

Although the study of absolute thresholds has a long and honorable history in psychology, and although the exceeding lowness of actual thresholds is impressive, there is a problem with the concept. In order to make the essential points, we need to consider one of the techniques for determining an absolute threshold, the **method of limits,** as it applies in a practical way for the clinical diagnosis of deafness.

The important equipment for measuring the acuity of hearing, as explained in less detail earlier, is a tone generator that can present sounds of different pitches and intensities. The individual being tested listens to the sound being presented through earphones and indicates hearing it, usually by pressing a key. First a given tone is presented at an intensity so low that it cannot be heard. Then, trial by trial, the intensity is gradually raised, by small increments, until the individual always reports hearing the tone. On other trials testing starts with an intensity well above threshold, and the stimulus is decreased in stepwise fashion until the observer fails to hear it. The absolute threshold determined by the method of limits would be the intensity at which experience changes from not hearing the tone to hearing it, and vice versa.

The individual's responses can be plotted as a graph which indicates the probability that the subject will report hearing the sound against the intensity of the sound wave. If there were an absolute threshold, in the most obvious

Table 4.2 Approximate Absolute Thresholds

Sensory Modality	Threshold
Vision	A candle flame at 30 miles on a dark, clear night
Hearing	The tick of a watch at 20 feet in a quiet room
Taste	One ounce of quinine sulfate in 250 gallons of water
Smell	One drop of perfume diffused throughout a six-room house
Touch	Wing of a bee falling on the cheek from a distance of 1 centimeter

Figure 4.25

Two concepts of absolute threshold. (a) If the absolute threshold were absolute, there would be an abrupt shift from not sensing a stimulus to sensing it as the intensity of stimulation increases. *(b)* Actually, the increase in the probability of detecting a stimulus is gradual. The absolute threshold is determined by reading from the point on the vertical axis where the probability of detection is .50, over to the curve, and then down to the intensity.

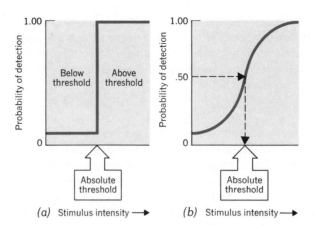

sense of this expression, the results would take the form illustrated in Figure 4.25*a*. There would be a range of intensities that the individual never detects and, above some single threshold intensity, an abrupt transition to a range of intensities that the individual always detects.

Such results are never obtained, however. Instead, as the intensity of the tone increases, there is a gradual increase in the probability that the listener will detect it (Figure 4.25*b*). It has become conventional to define the absolute threshold as the level of stimulation that is detected 50 percent of the time. Such results mean that the absolute threshold is not really absolute. Because of this basic ambiguity, procedures for studying the detectability of stimuli that avoid the concept of absolute threshold have been developed.

Theory of Signal Detectability

If you have ever had your hearing tested, you will remember that the experience is a strange one. You sit there, in an utterly silent room with the earphones on, and soon discover that your head is a noisier place than you would have thought. There is a constant background of noise, created partly by the testing equipment, partly by spontaneous neural activity in the auditory system, and partly by the sound of blood coursing through the arteries and veins. Sometimes this sound is indistinguishable from what you hear when the very weak signal that you are listening for is sounded. Moreover, when a signal is presented it sometimes gets lost in the noise of the background. The **theory of signal detectability** begins with a hypothesis presenting the principal features of such situations.

The theory of signal detectability assumes that judgments about stimuli are based on neural activity in the sensory system, which can vary in magnitude. The signal itself will produce neural activity, but the theory also recognizes the ever-present and interfering spontaneous activity of the nervous system and the disturbances stemming from other background factors, collectively termed background noise. The theory assumes that the magnitude of the effects stemming from background noise varies randomly from moment to moment. For example, in the hearing tests the amplitude of the background noise heard by the subject varies moment by moment in this way. If it were possible to measure the magnitude of the background noise at every instant and then plot a frequency distribution for these sometimes smaller, sometimes larger values, the result would be a normal distribution (page 35). Presenting a tone adds to the overall magnitude of effects, but the magnitudes heard by the subject when the signal is presented a number of times still have a normal distribution. If the signal is very weak and barely detectable, the two distributions will overlap; sometimes the magnitude of the background noise heard by the individual is as great as or exceeds the magnitude heard when both background noise and signal are present. Figure 4.26 summarizes the ideas presented so far. The figure deserves careful study before you read on.

Now suppose that you are a subject in an experiment in which the situation is that represented in Figure 4.26. You listen to a long series of trials in which a very weak signal is sometimes present, sometimes absent. On each trial you must indicate with a "yes" or a "no" whether you heard the signal. Although the intensity of your impression that a signal is present is greater on some trials than on others, you are never absolutely certain whether it is there or not. Discriminating with complete confidence between the effects sensed when only background noise is present and those sensed when both the noise and signal are present is impossible. So what do you do?

In general, you establish a **criterion** for saying "yes," you decide how certain you must be that you have heard the signal. If the magnitude of effects on a trial exceeded your criterion, you say yes; otherwise you say no. You can think of the criterion as a vertical line extending up from a point somewhere on the baseline of Figure 4.26. You respond "Yes, a signal is present" if the magnitude of effects is to the right of this line, no if it is to the left.

However you set your criterion, you are in a no-win situation. As Figure 4.26 shows, the intensity of the impression that a signal is present will be greater, on the average, on trials with a signal present than with it absent. But this is not always so, and no criterion you select will produce a perfect performance. You will sometimes miss a signal and at other times report one when none is there.

Figure 4.27 summarizes your situation in another way. There are two kinds of trials in such experiments: trials without the signal, called noise trials because the only stimulation present is the background noise; and signal-plus-noise trials, in which the effects of the signal are added to the noise in the background. On each trial you make one of two responses: "Yes, I hear the signal," or "No, I don't." Two kinds of trials on which you can make two different kinds of responses add up to four identifiable outcomes:

Hit—a "yes" response on a signal-plus-noise trial (a correct response).
False alarm—a "yes" response on a noise trial (an error)
Miss—a "no" response on a signal-plus-noise trial (an error)
Correct rejection—a "no" response on a noise trial (a correct response).

ROC Curves. The methods of signal detectability use two of these outcomes, hits and false alarms, to obtain a measure of the sensitivity of the observer. The method requires the construction of what is called a receiver-operating characteristic curve, abbreviated **ROC curve** (Figure 4.28). The expression comes from electronic engineering, where it refers to the signal-detecting capabilities of equipment. The most direct way to explain the construction of an ROC curve is to ask you to imagine an experiment with many observers, all of the same sensitivity, whose criteria range from strict to lenient. Each observer provides

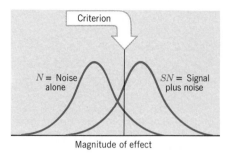

Figure 4.26
Theoretical distributions of internal effects assumed in signal detection theory. In considering this and later representations of this type, remember the following points. (1) The distributions are normal. (2) The distribution of internal effects of signal plus noise *(SN)* is obtained by adding a distribution of signal *(S)* effects to the distribution of noise *(N)* effects. (3) The two distributions are not present simultaneously; a sample drawn from one or the other is present on each trial.

Type of trial		Response	
		Yes	No
	Signal plus noise	Hit	Miss
	Noise	False alarm	Correct rejection

Figure 4.27
Possible outcomes on signal detection trials. Two kinds of trials with two possible responses add up to four kinds of outcome.

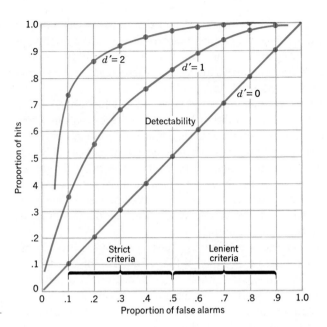

Figure 4.28
An ROC curve. Imagine a study with nine observers having very different criteria. On a trial with an undetectable stimulus ($d' = 0$), they have proportions of hits and false alarms of .1, .2, .3, and so on. With stronger signals these biases persist, but the proportion of hits now exceeds the proportion of false alarms. With a weak stimulus the curve bows ($d' = 1.0$), and with a strong stimulus it bows even more ($d' = 2.0$).

two measurements to be represented in the ROC curve, his or her proportion of hits and proportion of false alarms. The vertical and horizontal axes represent these proportions. The method for constructing an ROC curve is similar to that used to construct a scatter plot (page 19). A single point expresses the proportion of hits plotted against the proportion of false alarms. People with strict criteria have points to the left on the horizontal axis and toward the bottom of the vertical axis. Those with lenient criteria have points toward the upper right.

Response Bias and Criteria.   Imagine, in the experiment that we have been discussing, that the signal is so weak that the observers cannot detect it at all. Under these conditions they can only guess, and performance will depend entirely on the observer's criterion. Individuals with lenient criteria will say "yes" on most trials; individuals with conservative criteria will usually say "no." As we have just seen, the first group will have many hits but also many false alarms, the second group few false alarms but also few hits. The diagonal moving from lower left to upper right in Figure 4.28 represents this relationship, showing that hits and false alarms increase together when the signal cannot be detected.

Detectability, Sensitivity, and d'.   Now consider what can be expected as stronger and stronger signals are presented. The individual's bias will still influence the proportion of hits and false alarms, but with a signal that the observer can sometimes detect, the proportion of hits will exceed the proportion of false alarms. The stronger the signal, the greater will be the excess of hits over false alarms.

The two ROC curves in Figure 4.28 represent the detection of signals of two strengths, the upper curve being for the stronger signal. When the signal is stronger, the curve arches higher above the diagonal. The measure of the degree of arching above the diagonal is d'. The arching is also an indication of the signal's detectability and of the sensitivity of the observer to the signal. Both curves summarize the performances of individuals whose criteria varied from extremely strict to very lenient but whose sensitivities are the same. Every point on each curve represents exactly the same degree of sensitivity to the signal.

This is the great power and purpose of the methods of signal detectability. They provide a relatively pure measure of the observer's sensitivity that is independent of criteria.

Another way of representing the meaning of d' appears in Figure 4.29. The two normal curves are the same as those shown in Figure 4.26, but now three possible criteria have been drawn in. Criterion A is extremely reckless. The individual using this criterion always reports a signal when there is one, maximizing the number of hits. But notice that this individual also makes a very large number of false alarms. Criterion A_2 is extremely conservative. A person using this criterion never makes a false alarm, but he or she also misses a great many of the signals actually presented. Criterion A_3 is an obvious compromise. This subject detects most of the signals on the trials containing them, giving, however, a few false alarms. The point to understand from this figure is that d' remains the same wherever the observer sets the criterion for responding. This is another way of indicating that the signal detection method separates sensitivity from bias, providing separate indexes of each.

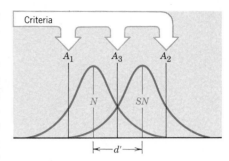

Figure 4.29
Criteria and d'. The N and SN curves are the same as in Figure 4.26. The added lines show three hypothetical criteria and the meaning of d'.

Differential Sensitivity

The second major question to which psychophysics addresses itself is that of differential sensitivity, the accuracy of our perception of differences among stimuli. Interest in this problem dates back about a hundred and fifty years. In the course of his study of what we now call kinesthesis, physiologist Ernst Heinrich Weber (1795–1878) performed experiments to determine the smallest difference between two weights that could be discriminated. On the basis of his investigation, he concluded in 1834 that the discrimination of stimuli is relative rather than absolute. To illustrate the meaning of this proposal, let us suppose that a person can just barely detect the difference between a 50-gram weight and a 51-gram weight. In absolute terms the difference is one gram; in relative terms it is one-fiftieth of the smaller weight. Now suppose that we want to predict the weight that a person can just barely discriminate as heavier than 500 grams. If such discriminations were on an absolute basis, requiring as before a one-gram difference in weights, the detectably heavier weight should be 501 grams. In actual fact, however, the discrimination is relative; the detectably heavier weight will be more like one-fiftieth greater than 500 grams or 510 grams.

A more formal statement of the concept that discriminations between stimulus intensities are relative is sometimes called **Weber's law,**

$$\frac{\Delta I}{I} = K$$

where I is an intensity of stimulation taken as a reference, ΔI is the difference in stimulation required to make the two intensities just noticably different, and K is a constant. The equation says that ΔI will be a constant fraction (K) of I, no matter what the absolute value of I. In the examples given, in which the differences between 50- and 51-gram weights ($\Delta I = 1$ gram) and 500- and 510-gram weights ($\Delta I = 10$ grams) turn out to be just barely discernible, the formula applies as follows:

$$\frac{\Delta I}{I} = \frac{1 \text{ gm}}{50 \text{ gm}} = \frac{1}{50}$$

$$\frac{\Delta I}{I} = \frac{10 \text{ gm}}{500 \text{ gm}} = \frac{1}{50}$$

It is conventional to refer to the absolute value (ΔI) necessary to produce a detectable difference as the **difference threshold** or as a **just noticeable difference,** often abbreviated **j.n.d.** The fraction $\Delta I/I$ is sometimes called the *Weber fraction.*

The value $1/50$ used in our example is approximately correct for sensing differences is lifted weights. Rough values of the Weber fraction for other senses are brightness vision, $1/60$; pain, $1/30$; skin pressure, $1/7$; odor, $1/4$; and taste, $1/3$. Research has established these constant fractions, but it has also revealed that they do not hold when stimulus intensity is very high or very low. In the middle ranges, however, the proposed relationships hold quite well.

Measurement of Sensation

Weber's work was enlarged upon by his brother-in-law, Gustav Theodor Fechner (1801–1887), who thought that he saw in Weber's law a universal statement of the relation between the mental and physical worlds. Fechner believed that it should be possible, by applying Weber's proposition, to measure the intensity of sensory experience produced by different magnitudes of physical stimulation. He assumed, as had Weber, that all j.n.d.s are equal, whether the two sensations being compared are registrations of small amounts or great amounts of physical energy. The j.n.d. becomes in effect a unit of measurement for sensation. It would follow that the intensity of any particular sensory experience is the sum of all the successive just noticeable differences between the absolute threshold and the stimulus responsible for the sensation whose value is to be stated. Fechner proposed that **sensation level** *(S)*, as the intensity of a sensory experience is sometimes called, is a logarithmic function of stimulus intensity,

$$S = K \log I + A$$

where S is sensation level, I is the intensity of the physical stimulus, A is the absolute threshold, and K is a constant that depends on the sensory system. In other words, as each arithmetic increase in sensation is registered, the amount of physical energy necessary to initiate the sensation has increased geometrically.

In less quantitative terms, what all this means is that the intensity of sensory experience increases less and less rapidly as stimulus intensity increases. Imagine hearing a sound that is barely at threshold. If you increase the physical intensity of that sound tenfold, its loudness will be an amount that we might arbitrarily call a sensation level of 10. Now increase the intensity of the sound tenfold again, to 100 times the threshold intensity. Sensation level (perceived loudness) increases but only to 20. Repeat the tenfold increase and sensation level is now 30.

The example just presented was chosen because it illustrates the meaning of the decibel (dB) scale for measuring the relative intensity or loudness of sounds. The decibel scale is logarithmically related to that for measuring physical pressure. The range of decibels is from zero to about 140 db, extending from the threshold of hearing to an intensity strong enough to produce pain. Each increase of 10 on the decibel scale represents a tenfold increase in the amount of physical pressure. The decibel scale, together with some psychological landmarks and a scale for which the unit is a just discernible sound, appears in Figure 4.30. The loudest sounds to which we are subjected are trillions of times louder than the faint sound we can just barely detect.[1]

---

[1] *To the instructor.* We have used the original definition of decibel in this account. The *Instructor's Resource Manual* has a brief discussion of other definitions.

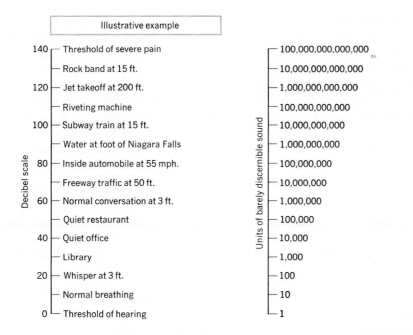

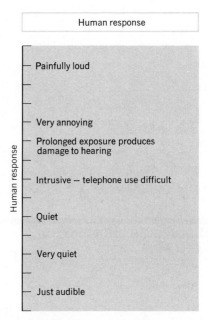

Figure 4.30
The loudness of some familiar sounds in decibels, units of discernible sound required to produce them, and a description of typical human experiences.

Difference thresholds have the same problem as absolute thresholds. If you glance back at Figure 4.25 and think of the horizontal axes as relabeled "stimulus difference," instead of "stimulus intensity," the point will be clear. The difference threshold is just as ambiguous as the absolute threshold. For this reason the difference threshold is usually arbitrary too, being the difference in stimulation that can be detected 50 percent of the time. And the methods of signal detectability provide the same solution for this problem as they do for that of the absolute threshold.

SUMMARY

Psychology operates on the empirical assumption that our knowledge of the world is based on experience. Since the senses provide our only contact with the world, an understanding of how the senses operate is basic to psychology. Two questions about the operation of the senses were among the earliest ones raised in the field. What for any sensory system is the weakest stimulus a person can detect? What is the smallest difference in stimulation that a person can detect? These questions concern the absolute and difference thresholds, respectively.

Experimental work has shown that absolute thresholds are all very low, which means that our receptor systems are extremely sensitive. The same work has also indicated, however, that there is no absolutely identifiable absolute threshold. Instead, the probability of detecting a stimulus increases steadily with increases in stimulus intensity. For this reason the absolute threshold of a sensory system is usually defined arbitrarily as the stimulus a person detects 50 percent of the time.

The absolute threshold poses another problem. In most methods of determining it, the results fail to separate sensitivity to the signal from the observer's criterion for giving a positive response. The methods of signal detectability have helped to solve this problem. Working with 'hits," when the observer has reported the presence of a signal correctly, and "false alarms," when the observer has reported a signal not there, makes it possible to obtain a measure, d', of sensitivity that is bias free. The receiver-operating characteristic curve (ROC) plots hits against false alarms to provide a graphic picture of sensitivity.

The concept central to the study of detecting differences in stimulation is the difference threshold, or the just noticeable difference (j.n.d.), a unit for measuring sensation first conceived by Weber. Within a wide middle range of stimulation of any sensory system, an increment that registers as a just noticeably different sensation is roughly a constant fraction of the intensity of the stimulus given first. Fechner enlarged upon Weber's work and proposed that the intensity of sensation has a logarithmic relation to the magnitude of the physical stimulus. The difference threshold, like the absolute, requires a statistical definition, the difference that can be detected 50 percent of the time.

TO BE SURE YOU UNDERSTAND THIS CHAPTER

The following concepts are listed in the approximate order in which they appear in this chapter. You should be able to define these new concepts and state the points made about each in text discussion.

Quantum	Complementary colors
Photon	Physical primary colors
Wavelength	Additive mixture
Wave amplitude	Subtractive mixture
Light wave	Negative afterimage
Hue	Induced color
Color circle	Simultaneous contrast
Psychological primary colors	Trichromatic theory
Brightness	Opponent-process theory
Wave complexity	Hertz (Hz)
Saturation	Pitch
Iris	Doppler effect
Pupil	Loudness
Cornea	Decibel (dB)
Aqueous humor	Sone
Crystalline lens	Timbre
Ciliary muscle	Fundamental tone
Vitreous humor	Overtone
Retina	White noise
Rod	Eardrum
Cone	Oval window
Fovea	Malleus
Rhodopsin	Incus
Iodopsin	Stapes
Bipolar cell	Cochlea
Ganglion cell	Perilymph
Lateral connections	Hair cells
Visual acuity	Organ of Corti
Blind spot	Basilar membrane
Physiological nystagmus	Place theory
Dark adaptation	Frequency theory
Rod-cone break	Volley theory
Purkinje shift	Stimulation deafness

Audiogram

Sensory-neural deafness

Conduction deafness

Otosclerosis

Taste bud

Olfactory rod

Physiological zero

Gate-control theory

Kinesthesis

Vestibular sensitivity

Vestibule

Semicircular canals

Bony labyrinth

Membranous labyrinth

Endolymph

Psychophysics

Absolute threshold

Method of limits

Theory of signal detectability

Criterion

Hit

Miss

False alarm

Correct rejection

ROC curve

d'

Weber's law

Difference threshold

Just noticeable difference

Sensation level

TO GO BEYOND THIS CHAPTER

In This Book.   A review of Chapter 3 at this point will reveal that the materials in this chapter contribute to your understanding of that one. Chapter 5 carries the discussion into the area of perception.

Elsewhere.   There are several excellent volumes on sensation and perception that treat sensory psychology materials in greater depth. Three are by Stanley Coren, Clare Porac, and Lawrence Ward (1978), E. Bruce Goldstein (1980), and Harvey Schiffman (1982). In the field of vision, the two books by Richard Gregory, *The Intelligent Eye* and *Eye and Brain* (third edition), are particularly useful.

PART THREE   COGNITION

Igler, Gustav. *Off to School.* Sotheby Parke-Bernet/Art Resource.

CHAPTER 5   PERCEPTION

"Relativity," 1953, by Maurits C. Escher

Perception can be thought of as the interpretation of sensory information, as a constructive, creative process which endows sensory experience with meaning. The most basic question to be asked about **perception** concerns the rules we use in making these interpretations. It is clear that painters and other graphic artists must have at least an intuitive grasp of these rules in order to create an acceptable representation of the world. Sometimes they use this understanding to give us wonderful, impossible phantasms. Holland-born Maurits C. Escher was the greatest of these artists. Using contradictory depth cues, reversible perspective, and figure-ground reversal, he created some of the most provocative graphic art imaginable. Escher's "Relativity" is a striking example. Look at it for a while and then read the artist's own interpretation.

> Here we have three forces of gravity working perpendicularly to one another. Three earth-planes cut across each other at right-angles, and human beings are living on each of them. It is impossible for the inhabitants of different worlds to walk or sit or stand on the same floor, because they have different conceptions of what is horizontal and what is vertical. Yet, they may well share the use of the same staircase. On the top staircase . . . two people are moving side by side and in the same direction, and yet one of them is going downstairs and the other upstairs. Contact between them is out of the question, because they live in different worlds and therefore can have no knowledge of each other's existence (1967, p. 15).

PERCEPTION OF OBJECTS

The most basic perception of all allows us to recognize that there is something out there. The first question to ask, then, concerns the circumstances under which the perception of objects occurs. One way of working toward an answer to this question is to start with a world without objects and see what happens when we introduce into it some of the features of objects.

Vision in the Ganzfeld

The German word **ganzfeld** (*ganz,* entirely; *feld,* field) is often applied to such an objectless world. For experimental purposes a ganzfeld has been produced in different ways. In some studies individuals have worn halves of Ping-Pong balls over their eyes or looked into a translucent globe. They see light but no sharp impressions of form. In other studies subjects have looked into a hemisphere so constructed that light is evenly distributed over the entire surface.

Physiologists Torsten Wiesel and David Hubel, of Harvard University Medical School, celebrating their winning of the 1981 Nobel prize in their field for their studies determining the specific responses of single cells in the cat's visual cortex.

The experience is something like looking into a large mixing bowl standing on edge, with even illumination across it.

Suppose now that the ganzfeld is illuminated with a gradient of light so that, from side to side, it changes from brighter to darker. If the gradient is very gradual, an observer does not notice it and the whole field seems to have a uniform brightness midway between the greater and lesser brightnesses on either side. Although differences in brightnesses of adjacent areas is one feature associated with the existence of objects, this condition alone is not enough for the perception of an object. Suppose, however, that a thread is stretched through the field just described, so that it bisects the imperceptible gradient. Now perception changes, and the two halves of the field appear to have distinctly different brightnesses separated by an apparent step at the line of the thread. This demonstration tells us that contours and edges provide essential information contributing to the perception of objects.

Specialized Feature Detectors

As it turns out, there are single neurons in the visual cortex that respond the most strongly to stimuli containing such basic perceptual information. These cells were discovered by David Hubel and Torsten Wiesel in studies of the visual system of the cat. In these experiments the cat is anesthetized and a microelectrode is implanted in an individual cell in the visual cortex. The eye of the partially paralyzed animal is held open and focused on a screen about five feet away. The investigators then project various patterns of light onto the screen in order to discover the pattern to which the cell responds.

Some cells, referred to by Hubel and Wiesel (1959) as **simple cells,** react to lines or edges that fall on a very specific region of the retina. They must also be of a particular orientation, such as vertical or horizontal. Figure 5.1 shows the firing of a cell that responds best to a vertical slit of white light. This cell also fires to slits that are slightly tilted but not to stimuli that depart very much from the vertical. Other cells, called **complex cells,** are excited by a sliver of light falling on a larger area of the retina. These complex cells respond most vigorously when the light has a particular orientation and is moving in a specific direction. Still other cells, **hypercomplex cells,** fire to a slit of light with a particular orientation, moving in a certain direction, and having a specific length.

Cells responding to entities with more detail than contours and edges have also been discovered. Activity in a particular cortical cell of the macaque monkey is triggered by the outline shape of a monkey's hand (Gross et al., 1972). Other information indicates that a large region of the human brain is given over to a very specific ability, identifying people by their faces, a skill which is important to a highly social creature. Individuals with prosopagnosia, the inability to recognize faces, have damage on the underside of both occipital lobes, extending forward to the inner surface of the temporal lobes. Within this region there must be a neural network for the rapid and reliable recognition of human faces. The disorder caused by damage to this network is remarkably specific. The identity of familiar people is not lost to individuals with prosopagnosia. Although they may not be able to recognize members of their own family, they know them immediately by their voices. The ability to describe the details of the faces seen also remains intact. Persons with the disorder are usually able to say that photographs of a full face and profile are of the same individual. The only difficulty a person with prosopagnosia has is linking together the faces and identities of the people they know (Geschwind, 1979).

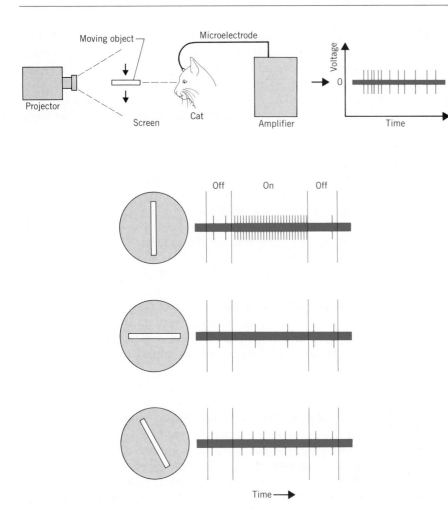

Figure 5.1
Neural effects of stimulation in the visual cortex. The upper figure shows the arrangement used in these experiments. The bottom figure shows the responses of single simple cells in the visual cortex of the cat to slits of light presented in different orientations. The stimuli are depicted on the left; the electrical responses of the cell (evoked potentials) are on the right. This particular cell responds maximally to a vertical slit. It also fires to slits that are slightly tilted but not to those that depart very much from the vertical. The responses to the horizontal are not responses at all but just the cell's normal, spontaneous firing. (After Hubel, 1963.)

Perceptual Organization

To describe the perception of an object in terms of joining together the responses of individual neurons to edges and angles is in the tradition of structural psychology. **Structuralism** was a school of psychology founded in the 1890s at Cornell University by Edward B. Titchener, one of Wundt's disciples. Wundt and his students had been trained in the physiology of the sense organs and the nervous system and in the philosophy of the British empiricists. Structuralism, which dominated the field through the turn of the century, held that the way to develop a scientific psychology was to discover the mental elements that combine to produce conscious experience. Structuralism was a part-to-whole psychology because of this hypothesis that consciousness is constructed of mental elements. The structuralists sought to develop a sort of "mental chemistry," in which the mental elements would be sensory—hues, loudnesses, and the like. Psychology's program of study would be to discover these elements and the laws by which they combine to create the contents of a mental experience. These psychologists emphasized the structure of the mind rather than its function; hence the name of their school, "structuralism."

A few years later, about 1910, a group known as the **Gestalt psychologists** began to argue for a very different position. *Gestalt* is a German word with no

Figure 5.2
Figure on ground.

Figure 5.3
An ambiguous figure. Notice that as the view shifts from vase to profiles and back again, the boundary always belongs to what you see as figure.

Figure 5.4
The wife and the mother-in-law. (From Boring, Langfeld, and Weld, 1948.)

exact translation in English, although form, organized whole, and configuration are close. The Gestaltists argued that objects are perceived as complete, unitary shapes, not as elementary constituents adding together. Gestalt psychologists took a whole-to-part position. When we percieve an apple, they maintained, it does not appear as a rounded contour with so much redness, so much greenness, and a stem on top. Rather it appears to be an apple, which has these characteristics.

Figure-Ground Relationships. Our experience of **figure-ground relationships** serves to emphasize the wholeness of perceived objects. In the visual field certain parts usually stand out in a distinctive manner from the rest. The distinguishable part is called a figure; what it extends against is called a ground or background (Figure 5.2). Figures tend to have a distinct shape, to be more solid and substantial, and to be in front of the ground. Boundaries seem to belong to the figure rather than to the ground, which is seen as formless. A reversible figure-ground makes this point. Figure 5.3 can be perceived either as a white vase against a colored ground or as two human profiles against a white background. As perception of it shifts from one version to the other, the boundary switches and the newly bounded figure acquires shape and a forward position. Figure 5.4 is a more complicated demonstration of a reversible figure. The drawing shifts back and forth, being seen as a picture of a young woman, then as that of an old woman.

Perceptual Grouping. The Gestaltists called attention to a number of organizing principles of perception. Items that have *proximity* are likely to be seen as belonging together and forming a group. So too are any constituents that have a point of *similarity*. Items of the same size, shape, and color group together as parts of a pattern. *Continuity* of line in an established direction will make the line seem unitary. And when enough of a pattern is present that a whole can be guessed at, *closure* takes over and fills in. We see incomplete figures as though they were complete (Figure 5.5).

Influence of Context. Although these simple demonstrations make a persuasive case that we perceive forms whole, the part-to-whole theorists have a very difficult question for the opposition. How is it physiologically possible to perceive objects except in terms of elementary features? As we saw in the last chapter and early in this one, there are reasonably well-understood physiological mechanisms for detecting hue, brightness, and contours. There is even a cell by which a monkey sees its hand and a neural network by which we recognize familiar faces. But there cannot be separate mechanisms for perceiving everything, for detecting apples and vases and profiles. The only answer the whole-to-part theorists have to this criticism is a stubborn, "Somehow we do!"

As so often happens in psychology, battles over an issue down through the years have led finally to the recognition that both sides of an argument have merit. The sense in which this could be true in the part-to-whole versus whole-to-part debate is demonstrated with the materials in Figure 5.6. In each of the three paired examples, the same pattern of lines takes on a different meaning and even a different appearance, depending on the context. At first blush such phenomena suggest that wholes are affecting the perception of parts. But once more we must face the hard-nosed observation that, as far as anyone knows, human beings have no detectors for words, series of symbols, or even individual symbols. Rather, they have detectors that respond to parts of symbols, to lines, angles, and the like.

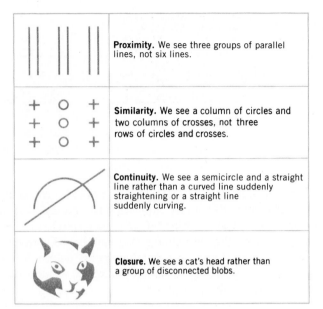

Figure 5.5
Gestalt principles of perceptual grouping.

Faced with this problem, current theorizing to explain such effects goes like this. The raw perceptual materials picked up by our visual system are information of the kind that the nervous system is sensitive to. These data initiate a part-to-whole mechanism—sometimes called "data-driven" or "bottom-up" processing—which makes numbers, letters, and words out of the information provided. Almost immediately, however, as the symbols take form, a whole-to-part—"conceptually driven" or "top-down"—mechanism enters the picture. Detecting the features that usually create numbers, the observer develops the hypothesis that the display is, in fact, a display of numbers, and this hypothesis controls perception from that moment on. The materials in Figure 5.6 are designed to illustrate this whole-to-part process of hypothesis formation. They bring past experience to bear on perception. Seeing one string of symbols made up of 12, ?, 14, 15, 16, and another made up of A, ?, C, D, E, the individual perceives the same item, which fills the second position of each string, as a different symbol. It becomes the number 13 in the first string, the letter B in the second. These different completions fulfill the expectations created by the concept of number in the first string, that of letter in the second. This is why the interpretation is "conceptually driven."

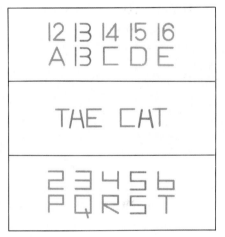

Figure 5.6
Part-to-whole versus whole-to-part processing.

Adaptation Level. The phenomena just described make it very clear that contexts can influence perception and that contexts are provided by earlier experience with similar objects. Put another way, past experience gives us a certain **adaptation level** with respect to the dimensions of objects; for example, we consider them great or small in terms of this level. Thus we judge a course as easy or difficult, a salary as high or low, a person as above or below average in attractiveness, the traffic in the city as light or heavy on the basis of such frames of reference. If the average grade on an examination were 35, your reaction to a grade of 50 would be quite different from what it would be were the average grade 85. On similar bases, Western visitors to Japan, even if they are short or of average height, report discovering that they feel like giants by comparison with the native Japanese people.

Experimental procedures make it possible to examine the influence of adaptation levels under conditions of better control. Harry Helson had observers

Figure 5.7
Adaptation level. Different subjective scales of weight were developed by observers, depending on whether the standard weight was very heavy or very light. The standard weights are sometimes said to anchor the scale of a subjective judgment. (After Helson, 1948.)

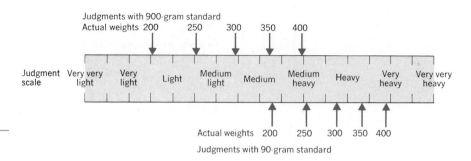

lift and judge the weight of a series of objects whose actual weights were 200, 250, 300, and 400 grams. Subjects were requested to make their judgment on a nine-point scale ranging from very, very light to very, very heavy. In one series subjects made their judgments after lifting a 900-gram weight, in another series after lifting a 90-gram weight. Judgments fell predominantly toward the light and heavy ends of the scale, depending on whether the weight originally lifted was heavy or light (Figure 5.7).

SUMMARY

Although the difference between sensory processes and perception is somewhat arbitrary, a roughly useful distinction holds that sensory processes provide the raw materials and that perception provides an interpretation of these materials. The most basic perceptual interpretation tells us that there are objects in the world. Psychologically, the basic condition for perceiving objects is the existence of contours. Physiologically, the detection of contours is accomplished by cells in the visual cortex that respond fairly specifically to lines, edges, and angles, as well as to their movements through their specific fields. The macaque monkey has a single cortical cell that fires at the sight of his hand; human beings have an extensive neural network to link the faces and identities of persons.

Structuralism, a classical position in psychology, assumed that the perception of objects is accomplished by combining simple elements, the aspects of sensations. An opposing position, Gestalt psychology, held that perception is not atomistic but provides an immediate interpretation in terms of whole units. The very obvious figure-ground relationships, perceptual groupings, and the effects of contexts on perception provide evidence for the Gestalt position. The differences in the two schools can be summarized by saying that for the structuralists perception is a part-to-whole process, for the Gestaltists a whole-to-part process. Current theorizing holds that perceptual experiences begin with the detection of elementary constituents. As these are combined to produce the impressions of objects, previous experience supplies an interpretation that controls to some extent what we actually perceive. Perception consists of both the structuralist's elements of sensations and the Gestalt psychologist's wholes interacting together. Previous experience provides a frame of reference or adaptation level which influences the quantities that people consider as small, large, or medium. People with different past experiences vary in their judgments of these matters.

PERCEPTION OF DEPTH, DISTANCE, AND MOTION

Having seen something of the processes by which we form perceptions of objects, we come to the next question. How do we know where these objects are—at what angle and at what distance? In order to discuss this question, we

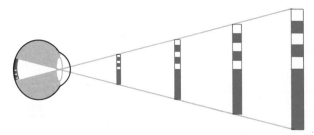

Figure 5.8
What retinal images fail to tell us. The same retinal image can be produced by an infinite number of objects of different sizes. This principle was pointed out by Bishop George Berkeley (1685–1753), a British empiricist. He also wrote about what are now called the primary and secondary cues to distance.

need to make a distinction between proximal and distal stimuli. We refer to energies in the physical world that excite the sense organs as **distal stimuli.** The light waves reflected by objects in space and the sound waves produced by vibrating bodies are examples. When these energies impinge on an individual's retina or eardrum, they bring about **proximal stimulation.** Thus the pattern of light energies reflected by the print that you are now reading is a distal stimulus; the image of the print cast on your retina is a proximal stimulus.

Any proximal stimulus is ambiguous because it can represent an infinite number of distal stimuli. Representation of the size of the objects is a good illustration, for a retinal image of a given size could be produced by any number of objects differing in physical size and distance (Figure 5.8). But obviously we have little tendency to become confused about such matters. Our perception of the sizes of objects is usually very accurate because our estimates of size always take distance into account. A number of cues aid us in our estimation of distance. Some of these cues, frequently called **primary cues** to distance, depend on the functioning of the visual system. Others, called **secondary cues,** depend not on the visual system but on certain physical characteristics of objects in the world.

Primary Distance Cues

The three primary cues to distance are accommodation, convergence, and retinal disparity. The third of these is by far the most useful.

Accommodation.   The shape of the lens of the eye changes in order to produce a sharp image on the retina. For near objects the lens bulges, for far objects it flattens. Called **accommodation,** these changes are initiated by the ciliary muscles surrounding the lens. Kinesthetic receptors in these muscles detect tension when the eye is viewing near objects but none when it is viewing from afar. Accommodation is a useful cue to distance only when the object at which we are looking is fairly near. Beyond three or four feet accommodation is relatively unimportant. Accommodation is a monocular cue; the lens of one eye will focus whether or not the other eye is being used.

Convergence.   The two eyes must turn toward each other, or **converge,** to fixate on a near object. Beyond a distance of thirty or fourty feet, the lines of sight of the two eyes looking at an object are essentially parallel, but to look at a near object, they must converge. Muscles attached to the eyeballs turn them and are in different states of tension for viewing near and distant objects. Kinesthetic receptors again send impulses, but this time they must come from both eyes. Convergence cues to distance are binocular, for both eyes contribute.

Several hundred years ago Berkeley hypothesized that convergence becomes a cue to distance through learning. His description of how sight and touch combine for the perception of distance, given in his *Essay Towards a New Theory of Vision,* published in 1709, was a landmark in the empiricist theory

Convergence is a binocular cue to distance and depth.

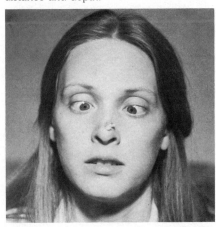

Figure 5.9
Double images of nonfixated objects. The figure on the left shows the procedure described in the text. The figure on the right explains the effect. Assume that fixation is on the near object. The image falls on the fovea (*F*) of both eyes. The images of the nonfixated object fall on the nasal retina of the two eyes, toward the nose, and not on the fovea. The two objects are interpreted as being to the two sides of the real object. The solid lines represent light reflected by the two objects, the dashed lines the paths of the projected images. Although such double images exist, they are usually suppressed and we pay attention only to objects whose images are foveal.

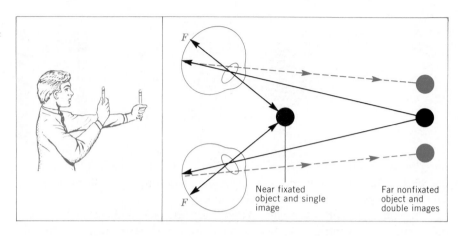

of perception. Empiricists believed that association is the means of binding one sensation to another. The baby links the sensation of convergence to the extent of its reach for an object in the crib. After these sensations have happened often enough together, convergence evokes a memory of reach and the baby knows from the sensation of convergence alone the distance of a toy.

Objects on which the two eyes do not converge create separate images on the two retinas, and if we paid attention to such images, these objects would be seen as double for reasons that are explained in Figure 5.9. A simple demonstration will make this point. Hold up two pencils, or two fingers will do. Fixate either the near pencil or finger, or the far one, but pay some attention to the other. You will discover that there are two images of the nonfixated object. The double images of extreme drunkenness come about in a related way. The two eyes fail to converge on the object that the intoxicated person wants to look at, and two images are seen. Closing one eye under those circumstances leaves the person with just one image and single vision.

Retinal Disparity.   The retinas of the two eyes are separated by about 2.5 inches. This means that in normal binocular vision they receive slightly different images of the same scene. Although we are almost never aware of this **retinal disparity,** the right eye sees more of the right side of a scene, the left eye more of the left side. When the brain combines these two scenes as a single view, it is in three dimensions and objects have solidity. Thus retinal disparity provides a binocular cue to depth and distance. Since good distance perception is important to the handling of an automobile, tests of an applicant's ability to use this most important cue to distance are a standard part of the eye test administered in driver's license examinations.

Secondary Distance Cues
The secondary cues to distance are all monocular cues, available separately to each eye. Because they depend on the physical aspects of the scene, artists can use them to create the illusion of distance on a two-dimensional surface. Several of these cues are used in Figure 5.10 in a somewhat exaggerated but appealing way.

Linear Perspective.   Parallel lines, such as the two sides of a road, appear to converge as they stretch into the distance. As objects become more distant, they decrease in size and appear closer together.

Figure 5.10
Illustration for Just So Stories, *by Rudyard Kipling, London, 1902.* Linear perspective, relative size, level of elevation, and interposition of objects all contribute distance information.

Figure 5.11
Distance and interposition. This figure makes several points. In the left-hand drawing relative size and linear perspective make one card seem farther away. The same is true in the middle drawing, presented here to show how this demonstration works. In the right-hand drawing the small card fills the cutout in the large card. Now it seems *closer*, illustrating the effect of interposition. It also seems smaller, although the size is unchanged. You will understand why after you read the discussion of the moon illusion later in the chapter.

Elevation in the Visual Field.   Objects that are farther away appear to be higher in the field of vision (Figure 5.10).

Aerial Perspective.   The dust and water vapor of the atmosphere diffract the reflected light waves coming from objects on the visible scene. We receive relatively more short wavelength in the light reflected by distant objects. For this reason they have a blue and hazy appearance, and we judge them to be farther away.

Relative Size of the Retinal Image.   When the retinal images of objects of the same or similar shapes differ in size, the object projecting the larger image is judged to be closer.

Aerial perspective. The dust and vapor of the atmosphere accumulate in this view to a very far horizon, until much is lost in haze.

Figure 5.12
Gradient of texture as a cue to distance.

Interposition.   If one object obstructs our view of another object in the same line of vision, the fully exposed one appears closer than the obscured one (Figure 5.11).

Gradients of Texture.   Most surfaces have a texture or grain. The texture gradually loses roughness or detail as the surface extends into the distance. The elements making up the texture become denser and finer the farther away they are (Figure 5.12).

Patterns of Light and Shade.   Since the sunlight and most sources of artificial light are above us, there is a certain dependability to the pattern of highlights and shadows on an object. They provide a cue to small differences in depth. The parts of an object that are lower and recede from the light are usually in shadows. Figure 5.13 illustrates the operation of this cue photographically. Turning the photograph upside down reverses the pattern of light and shade;

Figure 5.13
Light and shade as cues to depth. Turn the picture upside down and see the reversal of depth.

"Waterfall," 1961, by Maurits C. Escher.

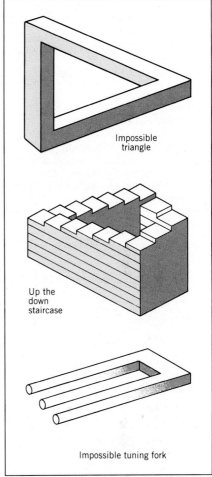

Impossible triangle

Up the down staircase

Impossible tuning fork

Figure 5.14
Impossible objects.

the indentations become bumps, and vice versa, because we continue to assume an overhead light source.

As we indicated at the beginning of this chapter, these secondary cues to distance are the stock-in-trade of artists, who sometimes manipulate them with great facility and draw "impossible" objects such as those in Figure 5.14. Small segments of these drawings are reasonable depictions of three-dimensional objects, but put together the segments conflict with one another. Escher has said that his drawing "Waterfall" incorporates the "impossible" triangle. This drawing and "Relativity" also use the pattern that we have called "up the down staircase."

Motion Perception

Our ability to detect movement is far more important to us than looking at stationary objects and scenes. In the simplest case we detect motion when a succession of neighboring rods and cones are stimulated. This is what happens when a breeze stirs the leaves of a plant in our line of sight or a bug unexpectedly flies by (Figure 5.15). We may almost immediately try to track the bug with our eyes, however, in which case the image of the bug falls rather consistently on the fovea, and objects in the background stimulate a succession of rods and cones. Yet we know that the bug and not the background moves. Similarly, our eyes can follow a dot of light moving in complete blackness, when there are no background images to pass across the retina, but we know that the dot moves. When we shift our head and eyes to survey a room and its contents, the objects passing before our eyes stimulate a succession of rods and cones, but we see the objects as still and stationary.

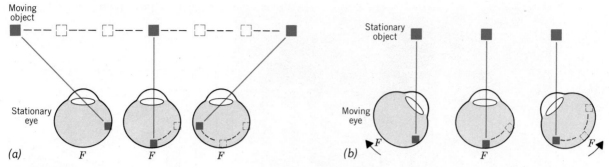

Figure 5.15
Motion perception. (a) Motion is perceived when rods and cones are stimulated in quick succession, which happens when an object moves across the field of vision. (b) When the eye moves, the image of a stationary object also stimulates a succession of rods and cones.

Richard Gregory (1973) has described the interplay of two neural systems, the image-retina movement system and the eye-head movement system. When the leaves stir and the bug flies through the field of vision of our stationary eye, the **image-retina system** registers the sequential firing of rods and cones and attributes movement to the leaves and bug. When we track the bug, however, the **eye-head system** registers the self-initiated neural signals to rotate the eyes in their sockets. In other words, the brain keeps track of its instructions to the eye and then relates them to the images on the retina. The eye-head system attributes movement to the tracked bug and cancels that implied by the flow of the images issuing from the background, registering objects there as stationary. When we survey the room before us, the eye-head system, knowing the eyes' purpose, stills the flow of images from the objects there. When we watch a dot of light moving in darkness, the eye-head system, again aware of the commands to the eye, attributes movement to the dot.

Helmholtz (1866) figured out the eye-head system long ago. He also pointed out that when the eyeball is moved by other than its own muscles, this system is not stimulated and the shifting images on the retina are interpreted as motion. The surroundings are erroneously seen as moving. You can observe the perceptions of the passively moved eye in a simple experiment. Close one eye and gently place a finger across the bottom lid of the open eye, just below the eyeball. Move the eyeball slightly upward. The visual field will be observed to move downward, since retinal events are the opposite of those in the outside world. The image of objects in the field now fall on a higher region of the retina, which is interpreted as a downward motion.

Apparent Motion. In certain other circumstances objects that are standing still are seen to move. Suppose that two lights, A and B, represented by the circles in Figure 5.16a, are flashed on one after the other and that the time interval separating the two flashes is about 0.06 second, which is nearly optimal. Under these conditions we see not first one light and then the other but one light moving across the field of vision from A to B. This is the **phi phenomenon.** Such apparent motion makes it possible to construct animated electric signs, in which "moving" arrows point to the entrance to a cafe or lights seem to travel around the periphery of the theater marquee.

The phi phenomenon, or stroboscopic motion as it is sometimes called, is basic to the motion seen in moving pictures. As almost everyone knows, the figures on the motion picture screen do not really move. The film consists of a series of still frames of people and objects in slightly different positions. When the frames are projected in rapid succession, usually at least twenty-four frames per second, continuous and smooth movement is perceived. Flicker would be evident, however, if the intense projecting light were not flashed three times for each frame. Projection is really at seventy-two flashes per second.

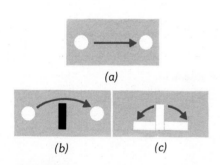

Figure 5.16
Apparent motion. (a) Flashing on first the left-hand light and then the right-hand light produces apparent motion from left to right. (b) If a barrier is interposed between the two lights, the light may seem to jump over the barrier. This is called bow movement. (c) If the center vertical bar of light comes on and then the two horizontal bars are flashed on simultaneously, the center light may appear to split and become two horizontal bars. This is sometimes called split movement.

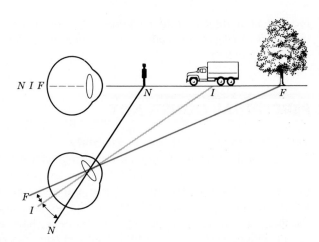

Figure 5.17
Motion parallax as a cue to distance. The diagram shows the shifts in retinal stimulation that make near objects appear to flash by in an opposite direction and far objects to "go along with us" as we ride in an automobile or on a train.

Motion Parallax. When the observer is moving, objects at various distances in the visual scene shift in relation to one another. This phenomenon is known as **motion parallax.** Let us say that we are riding in a rapidly moving train, looking out to the middle distance. Distant objects appear to move with us, those at the intermediate distance appear to remain in the same fixed position, and those nearest us whiz by in the opposite direction. The top part of Figure 5.17 shows a near (*N*) figure of a person, a truck at an intermediate (*I*) distance, and a far (*F*) tree all lined up along a single line of sight. At this moment the figure, truck, and tree all stimulate the same central area of the retina. A moment later our eye is in a new position. We are still fixating on the truck, so it still occupies the same position on the fovea. The image of the near figure has moved some distance in the same direction that the eye has traveled; that of the far tree has not moved as much in the opposite direction. But the movements of objects are interpreted as being in the direction opposite that in which the retinal images move. Far objects appear to move with us and near objects flee past us in the opposite direction. The blurred images of near objects and the stately immobility and clarity of the middle and distant countryside are important monocular cues to their distances.

SUMMARY

Proximal stimulation is basically ambiguous, because any such stimulus can be produced by a variety of distal stimuli. A retinal image of a given size, for example, may represent any of an infinite number of objects of different sizes at different distances. In spite of this ambiguity, we judge sizes and distances remarkably accurately. The cues to distance fall into two categories. Primary cues—accommodation, convergence, and retinal disparity—depend on the functioning of the visual system. Secondary cues depend on the physical arrangement of objects. Linear and aerial perspective, the relative size of the retinal image, interposition of objects, gradients of textures, and patterns of lights and shade all help us judge distances.

We detect motion when a succession of neighboring rods and cones are stimulated, as happens when an object moves across the visual field. In addition, the brain is aware of its instructions to the eyes to track and survey and relates them to images on the retina. It attributes movement to the object being tracked and perceives background objects as stationary. It knows that the surveying eye is moving, not the scene before it. In the phi phenomenon the stationary eye sees apparent motion when lights of a certain intensity and closeness are flashed at correct fractions of a second. In motion parallax the rapidly traveling eye focused at a middle distance perceives faraway objects as moving with it, intermediate objects as stationary, and nearby objects as speeding by in the opposite direction.

PERCEPTUAL CONSTANCY

What Constancy Achieves: Stability

The size of the retinal image varies inversely with the distance from which an object is viewed. Figure 5.18 indicates what happens to the retinal image of an object viewed at two different distances and also what happens to perception. When the square is near, the image on the retina is large. When it is far away, the image is smaller. Our perceptions, however, have a way of compensating for this difference in the size of the retinal image. Perceptual processes reinterpret the proximal stimulus to provide an object with **size constancy.** For familiar objects such as automobiles, people, animals, and the like, learning is important. As soon as we recognize an object for what it is, we judge it to have an appropriate size, whatever its distance. Our judgment of the size of unfamiliar objects apparently always takes into account the distance at which the object is viewed. We make an estimation based on the various distance cues described earlier. Experiments in which cues to distance have been eliminated demonstrate that size constancy then breaks down, and the perceived size of an object decreases rapidly with increasing distance.

Retinal images also vary when we look at an object from different points of view. Yet from many angles objects are perceived as maintaining about the same shape. **Shape constancy** is another of our valuable perceptual reinterpretations of the proximal stimulus. An opening door appears to have the same rectangular structure even when viewed edge on, although the retinal image changes considerably (Figure 5.19). The integrity of a coin's round outline is maintained, though when the coin is placed on the bureau, the retinal image of its surface becomes an ellipse. The order and stability of the visual world depend on this object constancy, this perception of objects as existing in the same size and shape, whatever the size and pattern of the retinal image.

Objects also tend to maintain their appropriate colors and brightness, in changing illumination. In the special case of **brightness constancy,** a white shirt looks white in bright light or in the shade, although much less light is reflected from the shirt when it is in shadows. A black suit looks black even in bright sunlight, when it reflects a great deal of light. The perception of blackness and whiteness depends not on the absolute intensity of stimulation reaching the eye but on relative intensities. If the amplitudes of the light waves reflected

Figure 5.18
Retinal images of near and far objects.
Although the two objects are the same size, they produce retinal images of different sizes. We tend to see objects in an appropriate constant size, however, as the lower part of the figure indicates.

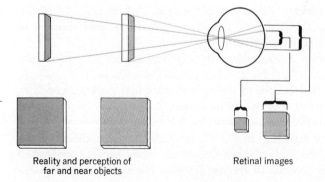

Reality and perception of
far and near objects

Retinal images

Size constancy. Bringing the background figure closer to the foreground shows how small the man really is when viewed from a distance. In both pictures the figure of the man is the same size.

by two adjacent objects differ by a ratio of about 16 to 1, the object reflecting the smaller amount appears black. The special signs used along some of our superhighways are an interesting application of this principle. They have white lettering, in ordinary paint, against a background of green paint which contains small particles of a light-reflecting material. At night, when the headlights of an automobile strike these signs, the lettering appears to be black on a white background, for the special green paint reflects much more light than the white lettering.

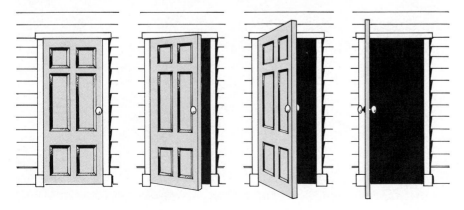

Figure 5.19
Shape constancy. The opening door is perceived as retaining its rectangular shape, even though the image projected on the retina may be a trapezoid or little more than a line.

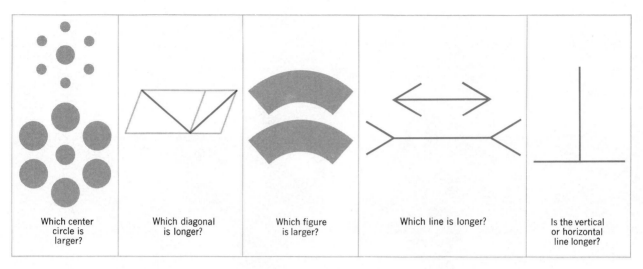

| Which center circle is larger? | Which diagonal is longer? | Which figure is larger? | Which line is longer? | Is the vertical or horizontal line longer? |

Figure 5.20

Illusions of extent. In every instance one of the two identical sizes appears to be larger. The figures with the angles at the ends make up the Müller-Lyer illusion.

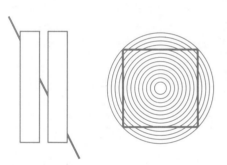

Figure 5.21

Illusions of direction. In these illusions straight lines appear distorted. Lay a ruler along the diagonal in the left figure to see where it actually goes. Do the same on the edge of the bent square to see that the line is actually straight.

When Constancy Fails: The Illusions

Although our perceptions are usually quite accurate, they are also subject to distortions called **illusions.** Illusions take a great many fascinating forms (Figures 5.20, 5.21).

The Moon Illusion. One illusion has been noticed and has generated speculation for millenniums. Near the horizon the moon looks larger than it does high in the sky, although the size of the retinal image is the same in both cases. A favorite explanation can be traced to Ptolemy, the second-century astronomer and mathematician. He maintained that an object seen through space that is filled with objects, as the terrain leading to the horizon is, seems farther away than an object at the same distance seen through empty space. The horizon moon therefore looks farther away and for this reason seems larger.

As we have indicated earlier, a large object far away or a small object that is closer can produce retinal images of the same size (Figure 5.22). There is a direct way to make this point. Obtain a good afterimage of the circles in Figure 4.7, top left, held at normal reading distance. Now cast the afterimage, first on a wall across the room, then on a sheet of paper held close to your face. Although the image on the retina remains unchanged, the circles you see on the wall are much larger than those you see on the sheet of paper. The sizes

The horizon moon can appear truly enormous.

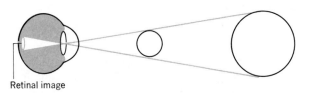

Retinal image

Figure 5.22
Basis for the moon illusion. Images of the same size can be projected to the retina by a small near object or a large distant object of the same kind. One theory holds that when retinal images are of the same size and we think that we know the distances of the objects, we automatically see the far objects as larger. Thus seeing the horizon moon as farther away than the zenith moon can only make the horizon moon seem larger.

of these circles illustrate what is known as **Emmert's law.** The perceived size of an afterimage is directly proportional to the distance of the surface on which the afterimage is viewed.

If, as Ptolemy suggested, the horizon moon does seem farther away than the zenith moon, people would interpret the retinal image of the horizon moon as coming from an object of *larger* size. As Ptolemy also pointed out, there is good reason for the horizon moon to seem farther away. Many more of the secondary cues to distance are present in a view of the horizon moon, interposition of objects, gradients of texture, linear and aerial perspective, to name the most important. If people do perceive the horizon moon as farther away, they may also conceive of the arching heavens as a flattened dome (Figure 5.23). They would interpret the retinal image produced by the zenith moon as being *smaller* because the vault of the heavens has been misjudged. Obviously, this estimate that the horizon moon is farther away is not a conscious judgement. It appears that the nervous system makes the **unconscious inference,** to use Helmholtz's expression, that the moon is farther away when it is on the horizon. Since the cues to distance are present, the nervous system takes them into account and arrives unconsciously at this interpretation.

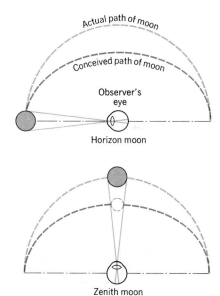

Actual path of moon

Conceived path of moon

Observer's eye

Horizon moon

Zenith moon

Other Illusions of Extent. The **Müller-Lyer illusion,** the two figures with standard and reversed arrowheads in Figure 5.20, has also been interpreted in terms of false adjustments for size constancy. In normal perspective the apparently longer line often means "far corner" of a room, and the apparently shorter one often means "near corner" of a building (Figure 5.24). The explanation

Figure 5.23
Imagined distant horizon and low-vaulted heavens. As the moon moves in its orbit, it may be considered farther away at the horizon, nearer at its zenith. Cues to distance are far fewer looking straight up than looking toward the horizon.

Figure 5.24
Interpreting the Müller-Lyer illusion. The photography indicates how the arrowheads in the Müller-Lyer illusion mean "near corner" of a building and "far corner" of a room.

Figure 5.25
Ponzo illusion. A powerful cue to distance, linear perspective, indicates that one of two identical lines and boats is farther away. Since the second line and boat project the same retinal images as the first, they are considered to be larger as well as more distant.

resembles that developed for the moon illusion. Although the retinal images of the two principal lines are the same, the size-constancy mechanism goes to work and adjusts the one farther away to a larger size. The retinal image supposedly coming from close by is similarly shrunk in size.

The Ponzo illusion, sometimes called the ''railroad track'' illusion, has converging lines which introduce a powerful cue to distance, linear perspective. On this basis the top horizontal line, or boat, in Figure 5.25 is considered to be farther away. Therefore, since the upper and lower objects make the same-sized projections to the retina, the upper one is perceived by ingrained processes as not only more distant but also larger.

SUMMARY

Perceptual constancy has been demonstrated for a host of attributes of objects. Size constancy is possible in part because of numerous cues to distance. Our

Les Promenades d'Euclide. The two cones in this painting have the same physical height, but cues to distance make us see the second as a lengthy but spectral avenue.

perceptions of the sizes of objects take this distance information into account. If the object is recognized, familiarity provides an additional cue. The shape, color, and brightness of an object are also perceived with some constancy, matching our vision to reality.

Although perception is usually accurate, sometimes it is subject to distortions, the so-called illusions. Most of these illusions are not well understood. There is, however, a particular class of illusions, of which the moon illusion is one, that have a currently accepted explanation. Two objects that are actually the same size and at the same distance seem to be different sizes because the situation leads the perceiver to infer unconsciously and incorrectly that one object is farther away. Because the retinal images for these objects are the same size, the perceiver necessarily sees the object considered more distant as larger.

PERCEPTUAL DEVELOPMENT

The important phenomena of perceptual organization, of form, distance, and motion perception, and of perceptual constancies are by now rather firmly established. But the questions how much of perception is accomplished through innate processes and how much is learned still remain to be answered. This is the **nativism-empiricism issue,** which dates back to the philosophers of the seventeenth and eighteenth centuries and to the nineteenth-century scientists. Nativism is the view that elements of knowledge and perception are native to the mind and are not derived from experience. Among the important nativists have been René Descartes, who held that ideas are innate; Immanuel Kant, who believed that the mind has a priori categories, such as causality, unity, and totality, and a priori intuitions of time and space; Johannes Müller, who put forth the doctrine of a specific nerve quality for each sensory system; and in this century Max Wertheimer, the founder of Gestalt psychology. Thomas Hobbes, John Locke, George Berkeley, David Hume, and Hermann von Helmholtz were all empiricists. Most contemporary psychologists believe that many perceptual capacities are available in some form very soon after birth and that experience and practice hone them. Their studies of perceptual activities tell us much about what we have of perception in the beginning and what we develop later.

New Sight in Adulthood

John Locke once received a letter from his friend William Molyneaux posing a now-celebrated question.

> Suppose a man born blind, and now adult, taught by his touch to distinguish between a cube and a sphere of the same metal, and nighly of the same bigness, so as to tell, when he felt one and the other, which is the cube, which the sphere. Suppose then the cube and sphere be placed on a table, and the blind man be made to see: query, whether by his sight, before he touched them could he distinguish and tell which is the globe, which the cube? (Locke, 1690).

Both Molyneaux and Locke believed the man could not, for ''he had not yet attained the experience, that what affects his touch so and so must affect his sight so and so.''

Evidence bearing directly on this issue has come from the study of persons who have had severe cataracts since childhood and have been given sight by surgical removal of the cataracts. Such evidence is less satisfactory than we might wish, however. For one thing, these patients have never been truly blind.

Rather, their vision has been obscured by cataracts, which usually allow them to see clouded patches of light but no patterns. Second, the sight restored is often in a physiological sense defective. Finally, there is an enormous problem in communicating with these patients. They do not have the vocabulary to describe their world, and we do not have the experiences to understand what they are trying to say. In spite of these difficulties, the information obtained has been important.

Richard Gregory and Jean Wallace (1963) have given a detailed case history of a Mr. S. B. The patient, an Englishman, had lost effective vision in both eyes at the age of ten months, through a disease which severely scarred his corneas, and had his vision restored surgically at the age of fifty-two. Gregory and Wallace saw him about one month after his operation. They discussed with him his visual experience following removal of the cataracts and conducted a number of visual tests. Describing his first visual experience, the patient said that he had heard a voice coming from in front of him and to one side. He turned to the source of the sound and saw a "blur." He realized that this must be a face. Upon careful questioning, S. B. seemed to think that he would not have known that this was a face had he not previously heard the voice and known that voices come from faces.

The strengths and weaknesses in the patient's vision were instructive. S. B. seemed not to have most of the illusions. The lines in the Hering illusion (Figure 5.26a) did not bend; the two "arrows" in the Müller-Lyer illusion seemed much more nearly the same length than for most people; the reversible staircase (Figure 5.26b) portrayed no depth for him and did not reverse. S. B. could make little or nothing of most photographs, and card 1 on the Rorschach test (see page 432) was merely a design. He misjudged depths badly, thinking that it would be easy to step from a second-story window to the ground, a distance of some thirty to forty feet.

The patient's performance on the Ishihara test for color blindness (Figure 4.13, color plate) was excellent. He read all the numbers accurately, including the most difficult ones. He could read a clock correctly and drew a recognizable picture of a bus, although he omitted the radiator and hood.

The less-than-obvious fact tying all the patient's perceptual strengths together was that every accurate perception was of objects with which he had become familiar by touch. He had learned to read a watch by feeling the position of the hands, and this transferred to sighted clock reading. The blind are taught to read numerals and capital letters by touch because these skills are useful in reading embossed signs; this skill transferred perfectly to the Ishihara test, although there the numbers are made up of dots. The patient was able to draw a picture of a bus and his drawings improved in quality, but they never included the hood, the one part of a bus with which he had never come in contact.

Figure 5.26
(a) *The Hering illusion.* Check it with a straight edge. (b) *Reversible perspective.* Fixate the near edge of the middle stair for a while and notice the change.

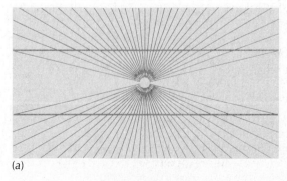

(a)

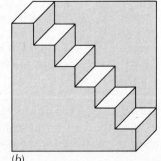

(b)

These observations seem to prove that Locke and Molyneaux were wrong; knowledge acquired by touch alone does transfer to the visual sphere.

S. B. was at first delighted with his newfound sight, rising at dawn each morning to gaze out his hospital window at the cars and trucks passing four stories below. He loved bright colors and was saddened each day when the light faded. Before his operation S. B. had been a very active man, making things with simple tools in a shed in his garden, riding a bicycle with his friend's hand on his shoulder to guide him. He had crossed the streets in the thick of London traffic, but after the operation he became terrified and could hardly be forced across by two people holding his arms. He found the world drab and was upset by flaking paint and the blemishes on things. Formerly a sociable man, he spent hours in the local tavern watching people in the mirror. Their reflections interested him more than their real-life images.

> Depression in people recovering sight after many years of blindness seems to be common. . . . Its cause is probably complex, but in part it seems to be a realization of what they have missed—not only visual experience, but opportunities to do things denied them during the years of blindness. . . . S. B. would often not trouble to turn on the lights in the evening, but would sit in darkness. . . . He gradually gave up active living, and three years later he died (Gregory, 1973, p. 198).

Perception in the Neonate
The experience of S. B. argues that learning is necessary for perception, but a great deal of other evidence indicates that some aspects of perception may depend only slightly on experience. For example, in infants every sensory system is functional at or soon after birth, and some more complex perceptual capacities are also known to be present.

Color Vision. In an early study of color vision (Peiper, 1926), the experimenter took advantage of the fact that infants reflexly throw back the head in response to light. Infants were presented with colored lights that were strong enough to produce this eye-neck reflex; then the intensity was gradually reduced until the reflex disappeared. In this manner it was possible to obtain an absolute threshold for lights of different colors. The threshold was lowest for a yellow light, to which adult observers are also the most sensitive.

More recent work has begun to describe the infant's visual sensitivity in more detail. There is now good reason to believe, for example, that four-month-old babies are able to distinguish the psychologically primary colors, blue, green, yellow and red. One demonstration of this fact (Bornstein, Kessen, and Weis-kopf, 1976) used the method of **habituation,** a way of detecting what the baby sees as new. When an infant is first presented with a stimulus, he or she looks at it and perhaps becomes active. With repeated exposures to the same stimulus, however, the baby becomes habituated to it and is inattentive. When a different stimulus is presented, the baby looks again. The two stimuli might be red and green lights. At first the baby responds to the red light, but not after fifteen fifteen-second presentations. Switching to the green light captures the baby's attention again, indicating that the baby sees the green light as new and different. In this experiment a switch from what adults perceive as one of the four primary colors to what they perceive as another made the baby attentive. For example, a switch from a blue of 480 nm to one of 450 nm did not interest the infant, but a switch from 480 nm to 510 nm, which is seen as green and is the same distance away in nanometers, did.

Audition. Michael Wertheimer's (1961) remarkable observations of his new-born daughter, at three to ten minutes of age, suggest that babies localize

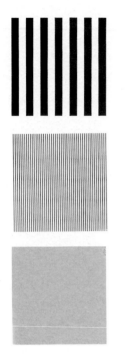

Figure 5.27
Squares used by Robert Fantz (1961) to study the visual acuity of infants.

Years ago, while Eleanor Gibson was enjoying a picnic meal at the rim of the Grand Canyon, she found herself worrying about the children near her. Would a very young child be able to perceive the enormous drop to the river far below?

sounds at birth. As the granddaughter of Max Wertheimer lay in a crib, a toy "cricket" was sounded next to her right or left ear fifty-two successive times. Two observers independently noted whether she looked to the right or left. On the twenty-two trials when she looked at all, eighteen were in the direction of the click, thus providing the evidence for sound localization. The fact that the baby failed to respond so often may mean either of two things. The amniotic fluid and connective tissue that babies retain in the middle ear for a few days after birth impeded her hearing. She may have been asleep; sleep and waking in babies are more difficult to distinguish than one might expect.

Visual Acuity.   The straightforward method employed by Wertheimer, of noting where a baby is looking, has become very important in the study of visual perceptual development. Robert Fantz (1961) has devised an apparatus for observing the visual preferences of infants. The infant is placed on its back in a small, drawerlike crib which slides inside a test chamber. There the baby looks up at two panels. The observer peers through a small hole in the ceiling of the chamber and is able to see a tiny reflection of the object the baby looks at on the pupil of the eye. The observer starts timing fixation as soon as the reflection appears on one or both eyes, stops when the baby turns away or closes its eyes. One study employing this procedure revealed that infants as young as one week old look longer at complex patterns such as a bull's-eye design or checkerboard than at simpler figures such as a cross, circle, or triangle. As a test of visual acuity, Fantz presented a solid gray square together with a striped square (Figure 5.27). The stripes of the first pairing were coarse and then trial by trial became finer. At two weeks of age the babies fixated on a square with one-eighth-inch-wide stripes, indicating that they could distinguish it from the gray square. At three months they looked at a square with very thin stripes in preference to the gray patch. Visual acuity in early infancy is very poor. Until they are about a month old, babies do not accommodate to focus on objects at different distances. Their eyes maintain a fixed focus at about 19 centimeters (White, 1971). This means that stimuli that are nearer or farther away would be blurred, making acute vision impossible. Improvement in visual acuity is rapid, and by the age of six months or so it is excellent.

Depth Perception.   Other evidence indicates that infants also have depth perception. The most interesting and important studies to make this point are those of Eleanor Gibson and her associates at Cornell University, using an apparatus called the **visual cliff** (Gibson and Walk, 1960). In these experiments the infant is placed on a slightly raised runway spanning the middle of a heavy plate glass table top about three feet above the floor. On one side of the runway, checkerboard-patterned material is affixed to the undersurface of the glass. This side of the table appears to be solid. On the other side the material extends down from the runway and onto a board near the floor. In an experiment with human babies aged six to fourteen months, only three of thirty-six infants could be coaxed to the "deep" side of the cliff by their mothers' calls and offerings of toys. Apparently, the perception of depth is present at least by the time the baby begins to crawl and needs this perceptual skill. The young of other species also have this skill as soon as they need it. We suspect that depth perception is present at birth or soon thereafter. Day-old chickens, goats, and lambs can stand, and they perceive and avoid the visual cliff. Other animals have been tested as early as they can stand or walk, and they too shy away from the cliff.

Person Perception.   Fascinating new research reveals that important aspects of the ability to perceive people as people are present very early in life. A number of studies have been done of babies' attention to faces. The infant may be placed on its back below a mirror in which a face is reflected. Infrared marker lights, which are invisible to the child, reflect off the baby's right eye, and a camera continuously records the image on the baby's pupil. Daphne Maurer and Philip Salapatek (1976) found that one-month-olds tend to concentrate their gaze on the edges of the face, on the hairline and the chin. At two months infants scan the features of the face, especially the eyes and mouth. Louise Hainline (1978) found that eyes are of great interest to two-month-olds. By this age the face may have become an entity, with the eyes occupying a central position, or the eyes may have acquired social meaning. At two months babies also distinguish between human faces and facelike configurations (Maurer and Barrera, 1981). Marshall Haith, Terry Bergman, and Michael Moore (1977) studied babies' attention to the reflections of faces during forty-five-second periods. Babies three to five weeks old fixated on the face only 22 percent of this period, seven-week-old infants 88 percent of the forty-five seconds, and babies nine to eleven months old 90 percent of this period.

Studies have shown that two other aspects of humanness are perceived very early. The first of these is **biological motion.** As adults we are very sensitive to the patterns of stimulation provided by human locomotion. We recognize the differences between male and female walks; we know what normal walking looks like and easily detect the limping caused by injury or even a pebble in another person's shoe; we can identify the characteristic walk of a friend. In the laboratory it has been shown that just seven to ten spots of light on the limbs and torso of a person are enough to convey this information (Cutting, 1981). In these experiments dots of luminous tape are attached to persons wearing very dark clothing (Figure 5.28). They are photographed or videotaped against a very dark background as they walk or run in place or move in other ways. The pictures and videotapes show only the dots in motion, but people are very good at identifying the particular activity. It has been proposed that the perception of human motion from such meager information may be innate.

Robert Fox and Cynthia McDaniel (1982) have done an important experiment that bears on this issue. Using a procedure similar to that of Fantz, they observed whether two-, four- and six-month-old babies tended to look at a pattern of randomly moving dots or a pattern of dots produced by a person running in place. Two-month-old babies showed no preference, but four- and six-month-old babies preferred the pattern of biological motion. In a further study Fox and McDaniel showed that six-month-old babies were interested in the pattern of motion made by "a pair of hands that appeared to come together to grasp an invisible glass and then withdraw."

Adult expressions of emotion are an aspect of humanness that babies apparently distinguish even earlier—and imitate. In the study making this startling discovery (Field et al., 1982),

> A series of three facial expressions (happy, sad, and surprised) were modeled by an adult for 74 neonates (mean age 36 hours). . . . The model held the neonate upright with the newborn's head supported in one hand and the torso in the other. . . . The neonate's facial movement patterns were recorded by an observer who stood behind the model in order to see the infant's face but remained unaware of the expression being modeled (p. 179).

The visual cliff. The child avoids the "deep" side, revealing depth perception.

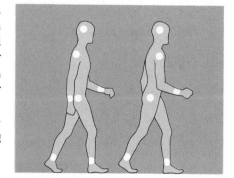

Figure 5.28
Detection of human locomotion. Pieces of luminous tape are placed on the head, right shoulder, hip, right and left wrists, and right and left ankles. (After Cutting, 1981.)

On the basis of the infant's facial expression, the observer tried to guess the emotion that the model was expressing (Figure 5.29). Since there were three emotional expressions, the observer could be correct by chance 33 percent of the time. The actual percentages of correct guesses were 76 percent for surprise, 58 percent for happy, and 59 percent for sad.

The Role of Experience

Although the research just presented makes the argument that important aspects of perception are present very early, we know that experience must play a part.

Visual Stimulation. Studying the effects of visual deprivation is one way of demonstrating the contribution of experience. Pigeons have been raised for a period of time with their eyelids sewn shut or with translucent hoods over their heads. When these restrictions are removed, the birds assume unusual postures as though they are disoriented in space. They find it impossible to avoid bumping into obstacles. Similar perceptual abnormalities have been observed in kittens, rabbits, and chimpanzees reared in darkness and in fish brought from dark pools into lighted aquariums.

In one of the earliest of these studies (Riesen, 1948), chimpanzees were raised in total darkness for sixteen months. When they were brought into the light, these animals behaved as though they were blind. And they were blind or almost blind because one effect of living in darkness from birth is a degeneration of the retina. The visual system requires some stimulation if it is to develop, and experience contributes in this very basic way. Later research, mostly with kittens (Hubel and Wiesel, 1963), has shown that visual deprivation disturbs the functioning of the cells in the visual cortex.

Since these cells respond to such stimuli as vertical and horizontal edges, we might expect that depriving the kitten of stimulation of these specific types would cause specific perceptual disabilities. This expectation has been confirmed (Blakemore and Cooper, 1970). Kittens raised in a cylinder with walls consisting entirely of vertical stripes developed both behavioral and neurological impairments. Although they showed normal kittenish interest in a stick held vertically before them, they ignored the same stick when it was held horizontally. Neurologically, there was a sharp decrease in the number of cortical cells responding to horizontal stimuli.

We now know that there is a **critical period** for the development of visual perception. If kittens are deprived of visual stimulation for only three days between the age of four and five weeks, they have extensive behavioral and neurological abnormalities. The damage is greater with greater deprivation. If adult cats are deprived of visual stimulation, however, their visual systems are unaffected.

Movement and Perceptual Development. A part of what is accomplished in the development of perception is to establish a delicate coordination between perceptual information and behavior. Early hints of the importance of such achievements came from a very famous experiment by George Stratton (1897). For a period of eight days Stratton wore over one eye a lens that reversed the visual world from right to left and from top to bottom. The other eye he kept blindfolded. At the beginning of the experimental period, the upside-down and backward nature of his world made it extremely difficult for Stratton to carry on his daily activities. He could perform tasks guided by sight only slowly and laboriously. To pour a glass of milk at the table was a major undertaking. Particularly interesting is his report that, initially, the world lost its stability. Head and eye movements seemed to make the world move and swing about.

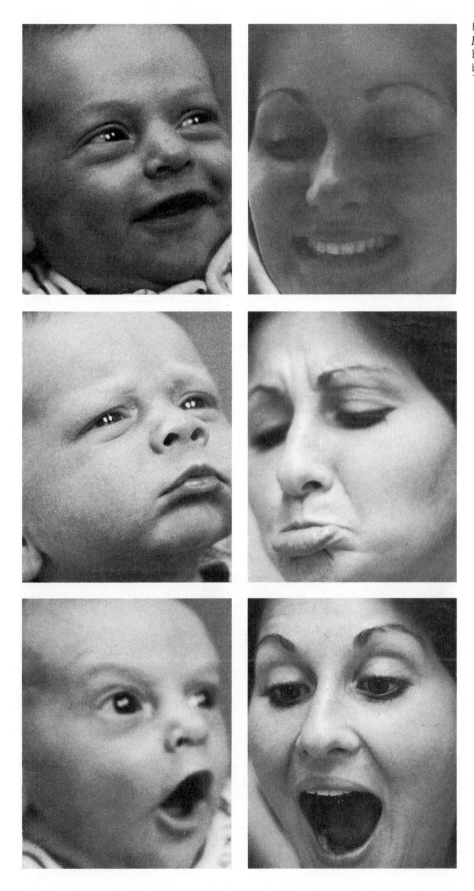

Figure 5.29
Imitation of facial expressions. A model's happy, sad, and surprised expressions are imitated by an infant.

Richard Held of the Massachusetts Institute of Technology tested the hypothesis that the young acquire their normal perceptual skills by being able to move about in and touch their surroundings.

With respect to uprightness and the inversion of things, Stratton perceived the world as being upside down, but the orientation of his body was the same as it had been before he donned his lens. Whereas we usually judge the orientation of our bodies by references to the outside world, Stratton now took his body as the standard and perceived the world as inverted and movement as reversed.

As the experiment wore on, Stratton became better able to function in his new environment. Movements were made with less deliberation. He ran into things less often and was able to wash his hands, sit down, and eat, which had been extremely difficult at the beginning of the experiment. Although Stratton never said that the world came to look right side up, he did learn to get around in it adequately and eventually came to regard the orientation of his body as consistent with that of his surroundings. Moving about in his visual surroundings seemed to be critically important.

There is a brilliantly simple demonstration of the importance of locomotion to the development of perception. Richard Held and Alan Hein (1963) reared twenty kittens in darkness until they were mature enough to pull a bit of weight, a matter of eight to twelve weeks. At this age the kittens, two at a time, spent three hours a day in an illuminated carousel apparatus (Figure 5.30). One kitten wore a body harness which allowed it to move of its own accord in a circular path within a cylindrical enclosure. The other was transported in a suspended carriage as the first kitten moved. The idea behind this procedure was to provide the two kittens with nearly the same view as they circled within the cylinder but allow only one of them an opportunity for visual-motor coordination.

After each pair had spent an average of about thirty hours in the apparatus, their perceptual capabilities were tested. The active kittens blinked at approaching objects, extended their forepaws in anticipation of contact as they were lowered onto a table, and evidenced depth perception by avoiding the "deep" side of the "visual cliff." The passive kittens did not blink or extend their forepaws in these circumstances, and they walked unconcernedly across the visual cliff. But all their deficiencies were righted after a few days of free movement in a lighted room. At a minimum, such results indicate that self-

Figure 5.30
The kitten carousel. The active and passive kittens had essentially equivalent visual experiences as they moved within the vertically striped cylinder, but for one kitten these experiences were initiated by its own locomotion.

produced movement in lighted surroundings is necessary for the development of fundamental perceptual abilities; visual experience alone is not enough.

Just what does self-produced movement contribute to the development of perception? Held and Joseph Bauer (1967) performed another rearing experiment, this time with infant monkeys. Within twelve hours of birth, the infant was transferred to a confining apparatus (Figure 5.31) which made vision of the hands impossible, although it did of course provide for feeding the infant and contained a bar covered with soft fur which the infant could fondle. We know that this kind of stimulation is necessary to prevent severe emotional disturbances in the monkey (see page 299).

After a monkey had been in this apparatus for thirty-five days, which is somewhat longer than the normally reared monkey needs to develop good eye-hand coordination, one hand and arm was exposed to view and the infant was handed a bottle. The baby monkey reached for the bottle, but the moment its hand came into view, it stopped reaching and for minutes at a time watched its own hand with apparent fascination. For the next twenty days the visually guided reaching of that limb for the nursing bottle was tested. The infant was also allowed to view the exposed arm for one hour each day.

With time the hand watching abated, and it was possible to determine the accuracy of the visually guided reach. It turned out to be much poorer than that of normally reared monkeys, but with practice it improved. A series of ten similar sessions with the other, previously unexposed hand followed training of the first limb. The sequence of events was similar. Reaching was inaccurate at first. With training, however, the ability to use the second limb improved rapidly. This study effectively demonstrates that for the visually guided movements of the very young to be accurate, both perceptual and motor practice are required.

Children's Perceptions

One of the most amusing scenes of childhood is that of a three-year-old "reading" with the book held upside down. Adults are likely to interpret such behavior as a reflection of intellectual immaturity, but in reality it tells us something important about a child's perception. It is much less rigidly tied to vertical-horizontal and left-right orientation than adult perception. Children apparently have much less trouble than we do in perceiving an upside-down figure correctly (Figure 5.32). Such perceptual flexibility also seems to be at the root of certain reading problems. Some children treat two letters that are the same except for their right and left orientations and letters that are in opposite sequences as identical. The fail to distinguish between *b* and *d, p* and *q, rat* and *tar* and *was* and *saw.* Appropriate teaching can help children to overcome this pliancy when it causes reading difficulties. Gregory Lockhead and William Crist (1980) have shown that special alphabets constructed to make letter discriminations easier to perceive are also beneficial (Figure 5.33).

A particularly striking phenomenon of children's perceptions is **synesthesia,** in which stimulation of one sensory system is also experienced as a stimulation of other senses. Probably the most common form of synesthesia is color hearing, which has been estimated to occur in 40 to 50 percent of children (Marks, 1975). Heinz Werner (1957) reported hearing children refer to "light- and dark-red whistling" and the "gold and silver striking of the hour." Color and smell may also be merged. For example, one child whose mother was wearing grape perfume said that her mother smelled purple. For children these are not poetic metaphors but descriptions of very real experiences. The child's sensory system is so undifferentiated that sensations are able to merge. It must be emphasized, however, that synesthesia does not refer merely to an association between two

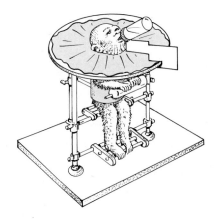

Figure 5.31
Perceptual restriction in the monkey. The apparatus kept the infant monkey from seeing its limbs and their movement for thirty-five days. (After Held and Bauer, 1967. Copyright © 1967, by the American Association for the Advancement of Science.)

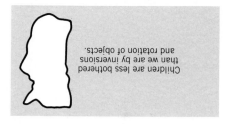

Figure 5.32
What do you make of the left-hand figure? Turn it 90 degrees counterclockwise and watch it become something else. (After Rock, 1973.)

d	b	p	q
d	b	p	q

b i d b i d
b i b b i b

Figure 5.33
Natural (upper) *and distinctive* (lower) *letters.* The words "bid" and "bib" are easier to distinguish when in the distinctive alphabet.

sensations. Rather, in synesthesia two or more sensory systems are registering connected sensations.

A child who has **eidetic imagery** can still see a picture "out in space" or "on a screen in my head" after looking at a picture in a book or on a screen. The child can examine this image and describe its components in great detail. For example, if the picture was of Alice and the Cheshire cat, the child can look at the image and count the stripes on the cat's tail (Haber, 1969). The child's eyes will move during the process of counting.

An eidetic image is not quite a "photographic memory," as it is sometimes called, nor is it quite a normal perception. As with perceptions, the eidetic image is actually "there" before a person; but more like memories, the image is subject to alteration and imaginative embellishment. For instance, an eidetiker— the individual who has eidetic images—can be shown a face, hold the face in an eidetic image, and then be told to put a beard on the face. The eidetiker then reports seeing the chin disappearing and being replaced with a beard. Studies suggest that up to 11 percent of children may have eidetic imagery, and that this ability is rarely found after adolescence (Gray and Gummerman, 1975). A variety of explanations of eidetic imagery have been advanced; an especially appealing one is that eidetic imagery, like synesthesia, is the product of an undifferentiated cognitive system. Early in the development of a child's cognitive functioning, sensory and imaginative phenomena have not yet become differentiated, and the two types of experiences are merged. This undifferentiated state gives way later in life to a system in which the individual has no difficulty distinguishing between perception of the outer world and a memory image formed by the inner world of cognitive processes.

Traces of the earlier processes remain even in adult perception. For example, many of the metaphorical expressions of poets are synesthetic. Synesthetic experiences are also quite common to persons under the influence of the drugs mescaline and hashish. Even when not intoxicated, all of us apparently retain some small degree of synesthesia. Most of us could readily answer the question, "What is the color of the sound that a trumpet makes?" Viewed objectively, the blare of a trumpet can produce no color sensation. Most individuals, however, describe the color as red, orange, or yellow. They never call it green, black, or white.

As is true of synesthesia, a few adults retain considerable eidetic imagery, and perhaps all adults retain some small remnants of it. It is not uncommon, for example, to call up an image of the page of a textbook when attempting to answer a test question. The image is seemingly before us, and we have a sense that the answer is on a particular portion of the page—there on the left side, halfway down. Unfortunately, our eidetic ability deserts us at this point, and we cannot quite make out the exact words occupying that position.

This common experience has the support of experimental data (Rothkopf, 1971). In one study students read passages of prose material. Later some were asked to describe the part of the page on which certain material had appeared. Others were asked to describe the information that appeared on specific areas of the page. Individuals found it easier to recall locations than words.

SUMMARY

The nativism-empiricism issue—whether our perceptual talents are inborn or learned—is several centuries old. Today psychologists believe that they are available very early and improved through learning. Studies conducted in laboratories allowing close control provide very direct evidence that perception can be affected by learning. Newly sighted people have the most accurate perceptions of objects that they have previously learned to know through touch. Other evidence supports the notion that some competencies are inborn. The sensory systems of the infant function at birth or soon after. Moreover, complex perceptual capacities such as form and depth perception are present very early. Movement and observation of it are essential to many aspects of perceptual development.

Children's perceptions are less rigidly bound by normal right-left and up-down orientations than adult perceptions are. Children may also have synethesias, fusions of sensations from different sensory systems, for which adults would have single sensations. A few children have eidetic images, which they can examine as if the original were still before them. These images may indicate that their sensory and memory systems have not yet been differentiated.

The following concepts are the important ones introduced in this chapter. You should be able to define them and state the points made about each in text discussion.

TO BE SURE YOU UNDERSTAND THIS CHAPTER

Perception	**Gradient of texture**
Ganzfeld	**Patterns of light and shade**
Simple cell	**Image-retina system**
Complex cell	**Eye-head system**
Hypercomplex cell	**Phi phenomenon**
Structuralism	**Motion parallax**
Gestalt psychology	**Size constancy**
Figure-ground relationship	**Shape constancy**
Adaptation level	**Brightness constancy**
Distal stimulus	**Illusion**
Proximal stimulus	**Moon illusion**
Primary cues to distance	**Unconscious inference**
Accommodation	**Müller-Lyer illusion**
Convergence	**Nativism-empiricism issue**
Retinal disparity	**Habituation method**
Secondary cues to distance	**Visual cliff**
Linear perspective	**Biological motion**
Elevation in the visual field	**Critical period**
Aerial perspective	**Synesthesia**
Relative size	**Eidetic imagery**
Interposition	

TO GO BEYOND THIS CHAPTER

In This Book. A review of Chapter 4 at this time would be appropriate. Perceptual development is an aspect of cognitive development, which is discussed in Chapter 11. The nature-nurture issue comes up again in various contexts. Chapter 2 covers behavior genetics and develops the topic very fully. Chapter 16 deals with the heritability of mental disorder.

Elsewhere. The references given for Chapter 4 are all appropriate for this chapter as well.

CHAPTER 6   MEMORY AND FORGETTING

From time to time psychologists discover people whose memories are truly astonishing. One such individual was studied by two psychologists at the University of Washington. This man, whom they called "VP," played up to seven chess matches blindfolded. He could simultaneously play bridge and chess and read a book. Without referring to notes, he could carry on sixty correspondence games of chess. In the laboratory VP's performance was equally outstanding. In one test he studied for several minutes normal and staggered matrices of numbers such as the following.

Standard matrix						Staggered matrix				
0	3	4	7	4	3	3	6	96	4	7
9	7	7	4	2	4	2	7	073	1	
3	1	6	7	6	6	42	1	0	5	0
1	2	5	6	8	5	2	6	2	78	6
5	5	5	9	5	6	1	24	1	9	4
1	6	2	2	7	7	9	30	21	8	
8	4	4	2	1	7	5	9	3	38	2
0	3	0	1	7	8	7	6	709	0	

He was then able to repeat either matrix without error and to give any row, column, or diagonal series of numbers upon request. Two weeks later he could still repeat the normal matrix without a mistake, except for the reversal of two numbers (Hunt and Love, 1972).

Such impressive performances raise questions, some of them about the specific individual being studied. Are people like VP a great deal more intelligent than ordinary mortals, or are their accomplishments ones that many of us could aspire to? Are there special circumstances in the histories of such individuals that appear to account for their mental feats? Are particular aspects of personal makeup important?

More general questions also come to mind. In what form do memories—for example, of the matrix—exist? As mental pictures, verbal sentences, or what? How does a person go about retrieving materials from memory? Why do we forget certain things and remember others? What skills might we develop to improve our memories? In this chapter we shall describe some of the basic knowledge about the phenomena of memory and forgetting. As we do so, we shall answer some of these specific questions and now and then describe other examples of phenomenal memories.

Information-Processing Theory.   At the present time the dominant approach to the study of memory and forgetting is the information-processing approach.

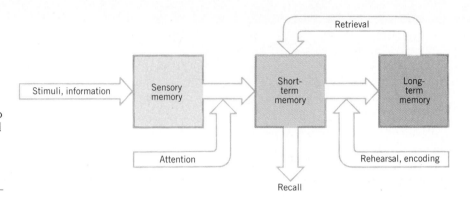

Figure 6.1
Information processing as stages of memory. Information remains briefly in sensory memory. Whatever is attended to enters short-term memory. Rehearsal and encoding transfer information to long-term memory. Recall retrieves information from long-term memory and brings it back to short-term memory.

According to the theory that also bears this name, an individual works on or processes materials as they are presented, putting them into a form that allows them to be stored in memory and retrieved again when needed. These first paragraphs present a brief summary of **information-processing theory.** The following sections give the substance and implications of the theory in more detail.

The simplest version of information-processing theory hypothesizes that there are distinct **stages of memory** through which information passes, and that certain **control processes** determine what information gets from stage to stage and what can be remembered later on (Figure 6.1). All the stimulation reaching the receptors resides in great richness yet only very briefly in *sensory memory.* The duration of this brief period varies from one sensory system to another but is probably no more than three to four seconds for any of them. During this period most of the information in sensory memory is lost but some moves on to *short-term memory.* The control process determining the information that survives is *attention.*

By contrast with sensory memory and its momentary holding of vast amounts of information, the storage capacity of short-term memory is small. A great deal of evidence suggests that something like seven items may be the limit. Short-term memory lasts for approximately fifteen to twenty seconds. During its brief existence in short-term memory, some of the information reaching there may be *rehearsed* and *encoded,* that is, put into a form that allows for storage in *long-term memory.* There is reason to believe that an important part of this code is auditory or acoustic.

Information that reaches long-term memory may stay there permanently, stored in terms of meanings and available for *retrieval* as needed. Such retrieval is accomplished by bringing materials back to short-term memory. The evidence for this surprising hypothesis is that acoustic information plays a key role in the retrieval of verbal materials.

The earliest versions of information-processing theory treated the three stages of memory as though they were quite separate. More recent accounts have tended to blur the distinction, particularly that between short-term and long-term memory, for reasons that will become clear as our discussion develops.

SENSORY MEMORY

If you have gone to a foreign movie or tried to follow a conversation in a language with which you are only vaguely familiar, you have probably found yourself wishing from time to time that the sound would stop for a moment so that you could translate what is being said. This suggests that the words must remain briefly in a stage of **sensory memory,** where they are available for us to attempt to give them meaning.

Duration of Sensory Memory

In an experiment that indicates the momentary lingering of visual images, George Sperling presented three short lines of letters and numbers for very brief periods of time (Figure 6.2*a*), asking observers to report as much as they could of the material in the complete display. Participants were able to report between four and five items correctly. If, however, very soon after the presentation of the materials, when they were no longer visible, participants were told by a high, medium, or low tone to report the letters and numbers in the first, second, or third lines, they were able to do so almost perfectly. This result suggests that all or almost all the twelve items in the display were available in sensory memory for a brief moment of time. A person participating in experiments of this type is very briefly able to inspect the fleeting image of the display after it has vanished from the visual field. To demonstrate just how fleeting this image is, the experimenter sounded the tone indicating which line was to be reported at various intervals before and after the presentation of the materials (Figure 6.2*b*). Given the instruction to report, for example, line three *before* the array was flashed, the observers were able to identify the items very precisely. When the signal *followed* the flashing of the array, performance deteriorated rapidly and after a second's lapse reached the same level as trying to remember the whole array.

Attention

The fact that so much of what is momentarily in sensory memory disappears in a second or two raises basic questions. The first is whether it is not unfortunate that we forget so much so quickly. The answer to this question seems to be that sometimes it is unfortunate but much more often it is not. Imagine how cluttered our minds would be with useless information if *every* stimulus to affect the receptors were retained forever. But such an answer leads to another question. Given that most materials in sensory memory are lost, what determines which survive for further processing? Which move forward into short-term memory? Part of the answer to this second question is that it is a matter of what we attend to. **Attention** is the mechanism that selects some materials for further processing and excludes the rest.

Theory of Attention. In one of the most important papers on attention published in the past many years, Donald Broadbent (1957) of Cambridge Uni-

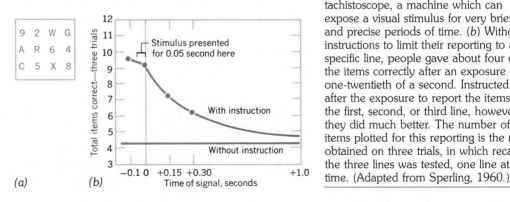

(a)   *(b)*

Figure 6.2

A study of sensory memory. (*a*) The displays were flashed by means of a tachistoscope, a machine which can expose a visual stimulus for very brief and precise periods of time. (*b*) Without instructions to limit their reporting to a specific line, people gave about four of the items correctly after an exposure of one-twentieth of a second. Instructed after the exposure to report the items in the first, second, or third line, however, they did much better. The number of items plotted for this reporting is the *total* obtained on three trials, in which recall of the three lines was tested, one line at a time. (Adapted from Sperling, 1960.)

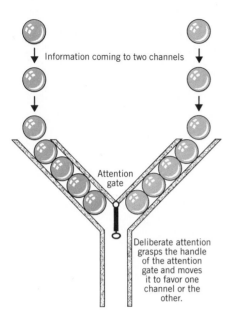

Figure 6.3
Broadbent's model of attention. The balls represent information coming into two channels. The little swinging gate is attention. It allows one batch of information to pass if characteristics of the input favor it or if the individual chooses to notice materials in one channel or the other.

versity in England proposed a simple, limited-capacity model to account for the selectivity of attention (Figure 6.3). Imagine that separate "channels," for example, the two ears, are receiving different information. Items of information are like small balls dropped into the two upper arms of the Y-shaped apparatus. They roll down their respective tubes, but at the stem of the Y they meet a little gate which normally hangs down and divides the intersection exactly in half, allowing only a single ball through. In effect, this little gate is attention. If it swings one way, items from one channel get through for processing; if it swings the other way, items in the other channel get through. But if the items in one channel get through, those in the other do not.

There are two general ways in which the gate may operate to favor one channel or the other. (1) Aspects of the stimuli may determine which way it swings. If the balls in one channel come with greater force, they will have the advantage, or if the items in one channel get there first, the gate will open for them and also will tend to allow others in this channel to get through. (2) A handle on the outside of the Y-tube can move the flap to favor one channel or the other. This second mechanism is the equivalent of deliberately paying attention to information in one channel or the other.

The "Cocktail Party Phenomenon." To apply Broadbent's gate theory of attention, think of a cocktail party or any other noisy gathering at which you were confronted with several conversations going on around you all at the same time—one about America's foreign policy, another about somebody's favorite sports event, a third about sex, and a fourth about the cinematography in a recent film. You found it impossible to listen to all these conversations at once. But you found it easy to exclude the other conversations and to attend to the one of greatest interest. This suggests the great functional value of attention. It selects certain stimuli for processing, excludes others, and allows us to monitor and remember materials that are interesting or important.

Does this mean then that unattended to stimuli are not processed at all, that they are totally ignored and not remembered? Broadbent's model certainly suggests that this would be the case, but information obtained from **dichotic** (two-ear) **listening** experiments which employ the method of **shadowing** suggests otherwise. In this method different messages are delivered to the two ears through earphones. The observer is asked to "shadow" the message being delivered to one ear or to the other, whichever the investigator chooses, by repeating each word immediately. Shadowing is a way of making sure that the observers are actually paying attention to the message that the experimenter wants them to listen to. Then the experimenter can manipulate the unshadowed message delivered to the other ear to determine what sorts of information may be picked up when attention is directed elsewhere.

The earliest shadowing experiments indicated that very little of the information in the unshadowed message got through. The observers knew that there was a message delivered to the unattended ear and that the message was speech. They remembered nonverbal signals, such as a whistle, but they sometimes did not notice when a voice was changed from a man's to a woman's. They were unable to recognize, as belonging to the message, a short list of words that had been repeated thirty-five times. Even if bilingual, they could not report the language of the rejected message or tell whether the language had changed during the course of the tape.

All of this might suggest that only physical features are processed by the unattended ear. There is, however, a commonsense problem with such a conclusion. If it were true, and the meaning of an unattended message were not

It is easy to select and pay attention to the conversation that interests us, even though we are in a sea of talk.

processed at all, we would never notice important bits of information in a cocktail party conversation other than the one attended to, and we would never be able to redirect attention to messages more important than the ones we are listening to. In other words, Broadbent's model of attention must be too simple.

We now know that the message to the unattended ear is, in fact, processed for meaning. Apparently the unattended message remains in memory for a few seconds and is briefly interpreted in terms of meaning. Then it fades away, just as visual memories do.

The evidence that the unshadowed message is briefly available is quite direct. If the experimenter stops the messages and immediately asks for a report of material in the unattended ear, observers can remember the last few words. The evidence for meaningful processing comes from several observations. If a message to the unattended ear is preceded by the listener's name, he or she is likely to recall at least part of it later on. If a coherent message changes ears, the observer may follow it briefly. Suppose that the messages to the right (R) and left (L) ears are familiar ones, and that the observer is supposed to shadow the message delivered to one ear or the other:

R   When in the course of MAINLY ON . . .

L   THE RAIN IN SPAIN STAYS human events . . .

When the message being shadowed switches to the unattended ear, there is a tendency for observers also to switch ears and follow the familiar sentence briefly.

Finally, Donald McKay (1973) had subjects shadow sentences like, "They threw stones toward the bank yesterday," and, at the same time, delivered either "river" or "money" to the unattended ear. Later on the subjects could not recall the word presented in the unshadowed message. But when they were asked to choose one of two sentences as being the one that they had shadowed,

"They threw stones toward the side of the river yesterday,"

versus

"They threw stones toward the Savings and Loan Association yesterday," the observers chose the sentence that was consonant with the word presented to the unattended ear.

The fact that unattended messages are processed for meaning as well as their physical characteristics is another bit of evidence that the stages of memory are not sharply distinguished. Although in the early stages of memory materials are chiefly represented by superficial physical characteristics, a deeper processing in terms of meaning also ocurs.

SUMMARY

The individual is constantly bombarded with more stimulation than can be processed, and only a small fraction of it "gets through." The great majority of this information resides in sensory memory for a second or two, during which it rapidly fades away. This disappearance of most material from memory is necessary because a person's processing capacity is severely limited. It is equally necessary, however, that people have some sort of mechanism to select the information to be retained. Attention serves this function. A well-known experience, the "cocktail party phenomenon," demonstrates how attention operates. In the midst of several conversations, all going on at the same time, we have no trouble at all in attending to just one of them and excluding the others. One of the most important theories of attention implies that we can attend to only one thing at a time. Further insights into the nature of attention, coming from dichotic-listening experiments employing the method of shadowing, find this theory too simple. Although we attend for the most part only to the shadowed message delivered to one ear, the unattended message is processed for meaning and may enter memory.

SHORT-TERM MEMORY

Attention provides the bridge that information crosses in moving from sensory memory to **short-term memory.** The fragility of this memory is a common source of inconvenience and embarrassment to all of us. We look up a telephone number, go to dial it, and for some reason it is gone and we have to look it up again. We are introduced to a man at a meeting but cannot recall his name when another person asks it moments later. Some materials are attended to, identified, and briefly memorized, but nevertheless disappear within a few seconds. Other materials are retained for very long periods of time. These very different spans of retention suggest the desirability of distinguishing between short-term and long-term memory.

Experimental evidence for the existence of two forms of memory comes from studies of **free recall.** The investigator has subjects first listen to a list of words, given one at a time, and then attempt to recall as many of the words as they can, usually by writing them down. One way of representing the pattern of recall is called a **serial position function** (Figure 6.4). The probability that a word will be recalled depends on its position in the list. If subjects attempt to recall the words immediately, they remember the first few words and the last few best. The better recall of the first items on the list is called a **primacy effect,** that of the final items a **recency effect.** If the test of retention is delayed for even a matter of seconds, the recency effect disappears. This indicates that the final items were in short-term memory and were lost, just as a telephone number sometimes is in the few seconds between looking it up and beginning to dial it.

Was it 5421 or 5621?

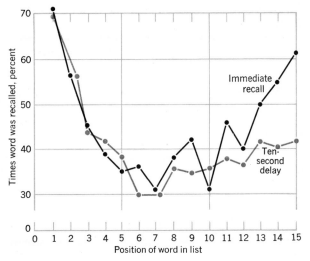

Figure 6.4
Serial position curve. Memory is best for the first few items in a list and the last few—primacy and recency effects—when retention is tested immediately after presentation. With a delay of only 10 seconds, the recency effect has almost disappeared. With a 30-second delay, it disappears completely. (After Glanzer and Cunitz, 1966.)

In an experiment that is now a classic, Lloyd and Margaret Peterson (1959) of Indiana University studied short-term memory in a different way, one best presented by quoting from their instructions.

> . . . In front of you is a little black box. The top or green light is now on. The green light means that we are ready to begin a trial. I will speak some letters and then a number. You are to repeat the number immediately after I say it, and begin counting backwards by 3s from that number in time with the ticking you hear. I might say ABC 309. Then you say 309, 306, 303, etc., until the bottom or red light comes on. When you see this red light come on, stop counting immediately and say the letters that were given at the beginning of the trial. . . .

Under these circumstances subjects' retention of the letters lessened with each passing second; after eighteen seconds they almost never recalled the letters. For later purposes it is important to mention that forgetting such as this happens only after three or four trials. Subjects remember the letters almost perfectly on the first trial (see Figure 6.5).

Acoustic Coding

Short-term memory holds information, at least verbal information, in predominantly acoustic form, a fact that has been demonstrated by errors in recalling letters. Even if letters are presented *visually,* the errors in recall are most often acoustic in nature. Consider the two sets of letters BCPTV and FMNSX. Those in the first set sound like one another but not like those in the second set and vice versa. Reuben Conrad presented these ten letters visually at a rate of 0.75 second per letter and then immediately asked subjects to write them down in the order that they had seen them, guessing wherever necessary. When he examined errors later on, Conrad found that most of them represented acoustic confusions (Table 6.1). Errors made in reporting "sound alike" letters were four times more frequent than confusion of letters that did not sound alike. Referring to the table, you will note, for example, that when the correct letter was B, C, P, T, or V and the subject made an error, 198 of these errors were B, C, P, T, or V and only 51 were F, M, N, S, or X. When the correct letter was F, M, N, S, or X, 190 of the errors were these letters and only 42 were B, C, P, T, or V.

Table 6.1 **Frequency of Acoustic and Nonacoustic Confusions in Recalling Letters in Order**

		Stimulus Letters	
		B C P T V	F M N S X
Erroneous Response	B C P T V	198	42
	F M N S X	51	190

The data in the four cells are numbers of errors averaged across letters. After Conrad, 1964.

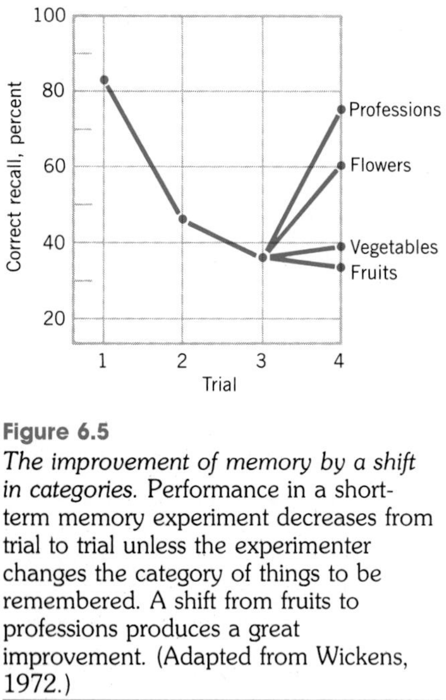

Figure 6.5
The improvement of memory by a shift in categories. Performance in a short-term memory experiment decreases from trial to trial unless the experimenter changes the category of things to be remembered. A shift from fruits to professions produces a great improvement. (Adapted from Wickens, 1972.)

Semantic Coding

Although a persuasive case can be made that verbal materials are represented acoustically in short-term memory, obviously some short-term memories must exist in other forms. If, after fifteen seconds, we recall a powerful painting, the smell of a rose, the taste of honey or a kiss, there is probably not much that is verbal, much less acoustic, about what we remember.

Experimental evidence proves that a part of the code for short-term memory is semantic. Delos Wickens and his associates at Ohio State University have done dozens of experiments in which on each of four trials the learner receives three related words to try to remember. On the first three trials the sets of three words all belong to the same category, such as fruits—*apple, orange, mango; pear, grapefruit, plum; apricot, cherry, peach.* On the fourth trial the words are fruits again—*tangerine, pineapple, banana*—for a control group. For an experimental group the words are from another category, perhaps professions—*doctor, teacher, dentist.* The results of the experiments are similar to those shown in Figure 6.5. On trials 1, 2, and 3 recall decreases. Because the words all belong to the same category, they become confused and memory suffers. On the fourth trial the retention of the experimental group, now freed of such confusion, shows a pronounced improvement. The retention of the control group decreases a bit more. Shifts from words to numbers, from feminine to masculine nouns, as well as shifts in categories, have improved the retention of experimental groups. These demonstrations all show that meaning as well as sound must play a role in short-term memory.

The Magical Number Seven

One important aspect of short-term memory is the limited amount of material it can deal with before it fades away. As early as 1859, Sir William Hamilton, the Irish mathematician and physicist, noticed that if a handful of six or seven marbles is thrown onto the floor, it is possible to perceive the correct number in a single glance, without counting. When more are thrown, the number cannot be instantly perceived. More recent work has shown that Hamilton's claim also applies to the number of things we can remember. With just one presentation we can remember an average of about seven numbers, letters, or simple words. The **memory span** is so dependable that George Miller, writing in 1956, referred to the "magical number seven." But people do vary in capacity, and materials do vary in memorability. In recognition of this fact, Miller modified the expression and referred to the "magical number seven plus or minus two."

The fact that the span of short-term memory is the same for letters and words suggests an important point of interpretation: words must be remembered as *words*, not as collections of letters. If they were remembered as letters, we would remember fewer of them. A similar thing happens with numbers. Most of us would find a string of ten numbers, say 2034178935, impossible to remember unless we thought of grouping the numbers and recalling them as telephone numbers broken down into three components, area code (203), exchange (417), and individual number (8935). This reduces the number of numbers to be remembered to three: two three-place and one four-place number, well within the span of immediate memory, 7 ± 2.

SUMMARY

The fraction of incoming information that we pay attention to enters short-term memory, where it remains for less than a minute. Only about seven items plus or minus about two can be held in short-term memory. In one demonstration of short-term memory, the last items of a list of words are remembered very well when recall is immediate, but they are partially lost after a matter of only ten seconds. In another demonstration subjects are asked to recall three-letter sequences after short periods of time, during which they are distracted by the task of counting backward from some number by threes. Under these circumstances retention of the letters declines essentially to zero in eighteen seconds. Although there is evidence that short-term memory holds verbal materials primarily in acoustic form, studies in which categories of items to be remembered are shifted and retention improves indicate that some coding is semantic.

LONG-TERM MEMORY

The fleeting forms of memory discussed so far prepare some materials for transfer to a more permanent memory. In these stages information is **encoded,** that is, put into the form in which it will be stored in **long-term memory.** Psychologists are just beginning to learn about the processes that allow materials to be stored in long-term memory.

Rehearsal

One of the processes promoting long-term storage is *rehearsal.* Operating in short-term memory, this process takes at least two different forms. One form of rehearsal, the mere repetition of new information, over and over again, without thinking about it, is sometimes called **maintenance rehearsal.** This form of rehearsal keeps information in short-term memory at least until it has served its purpose. This is the type of rehearsal by which we say a phone number again and again between the time of looking it up and making the call. After that the number is likely to be lost, as is any item in short-term memory. A more effective form of rehearsal is **elaborative rehearsal,** in which the individual deals with the new information in terms of its meaning.

Materials have many different attributes that might be emphasized by a person who wants to commit them to memory. A printed word, for example, is a set of marks on paper; it is a string of letters, perhaps capitals, perhaps lowercase; it creates an auditory impression when read that makes it rhyme with some words and not with others; it has meaning and calls forth other words and ideas by a process of association. As it turns out, people will follow instructions to

Table 6.2 Questions and Answers for Different Levels of Processing

Type	Question	Answer	
		Yes	No
Case	Is the word in capital letters?	TABLE	table
Rhyme	Does the word rhyme with SOUR?	flower	CARPET
Sentence	Would the word fit in the sentence: "He met a _____ in the street?"	FRIEND	cloud

After Craik and Tulving, 1975

pay attention to these different attributes and to attempt to remember materials in such terms. These instructions induce different **levels of processing:** paying attention to the visual appearance or the sound of a word is superficial processing; paying attention to meaning and associations is deeper processing.

In an experiment designed to show how these levels affect retention, Fergus Craik and Endel Tulving of the University of Toronto presented college students with lists of forty words, one by one. Sometimes they told the students that there would be a memory test, sometimes not. The results were similar in both cases. Just before each word was given, the students were asked a question about it. The questions for the words were designed to make the students process them at different levels. The case and rhyme questions, as indicated in Table 6.2, required attention to fairly superficial physical characteristics of the words. The sentence questions required thinking about the meanings of the words.

The results obtained on a test of free recall (Figure 6.6), given shortly after presenting the list, indicated that words processed at a deeper level were better retained than the others. The words processed at the two superficial levels were recalled with about the same frequency. In each kind of processing, more words for which the answer to its question was "yes" were recalled than were words for which the answer was "no."

In attempting to explain why questions answered by "yes" led to better memory for words than those answered by "no," Craik and Tulving proposed that *elaborateness* was probably a better concept than *depth* for effective processing, and that questions with positive answers brought about elaboration. Obviously, the ideas called up by meeting a friend in the street (Table 6.2) are richer, more personal, and more full of meaning than any connected with meeting a cloud in the street.

In an experiment that provides impressive support for this idea, Barry Stein and John Bransford (1979) compared recall for sentences such as those listed in Table 6.3. The sentence at the top of the table is a "base sentence," which expresses a certain idea. The second sentence in the table adds a congruent

Figure 6.6
Recall after different methods of processing. Words processed by putting them into sentences, or even finding that they did not fit, were recalled best. With all methods recall was better for words whose processing question was answered by "yes" rather than "no." (After Craik and Tulving, 1975.)

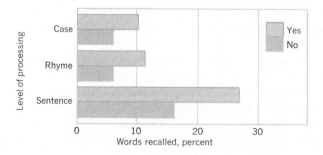

Table 6.3 Base Sentences, Type of Elaboration, and Recall

Type	Example	Recall, percent
Base sentence	The fat man read the sign	42
Base and congruent idea	The fat man read the sign that was two feet high	22
Base and elaboration	The fat man read the sign warning about thin ice	74
Base and self-generated phrase	The fat man read the sign [subject's completion of sentence]	58

After Stein and Bransford, 1979.

idea, but one that does not elaborate on the information carried by the base sentence in any important way. The third sentence does provide such elaboration. Four groups of college students participated in the experiment. Three groups heard a reading of ten sentences of one of the three types in Table 6.3. As a cover task they were asked to rate the sentences for comprehensibility. A fourth group heard the base sentences and were then asked to add their own brief phrase to each sentence. On a surprise test following these presentations, the students were asked to recall which man purchased the tie, read the sign, and so on.

There were no important differences in the comprehensibility ratings given the sentences, but there were large differences in recall, depending on which set of sentences the students had heard: 42 percent correct for the base sentences, 22 percent for the sentences with inconsequential additions, 74 percent for the sentences with meaningful elaborations, and 58 percent for the sentences which the students completed themselves. Apparently elaboration rather than mere additional content is the important aid to recall. In fact, the results show that an inconsequential addition interferes with recall, probably by increasing the amount of material to be remembered. A breakdown of the recall scores of the students who completed the sentences themselves strengthens the conclusion that elaboration is important. If independent judges rated the completion as a meaningful elaboration, recall was nearly perfect, 91 percent; if it added nothing of consequence the recall score was 49 percent.

Retrieval

Having completed our description of the processes that get information into memory, we turn to the question of how we get it out again. This is the process of *retrieval,* the incredible talent that each of us has of being able, upon command, to call up from a multitude of memories the exact one that meets the requirements of a particular situation. Of course, there are times when we "remember" things we never learned and others when we cannot quite remember something that we are certain we know. These instances in which retrieval fails may well be as instructive about the nature of memory as failures of function have been about the nervous system.

A familiar situation in which memory fails is the **tip-of-the-tongue phenomenon.** We try to recall a name we know, but it refuses to be remembered. Technically we say that the name is **available** in memory but that it is not **accessible.** Roger Brown and David McNeill (1966) studied this phenomenon by reading to a group of students the definitions of a series of obscure English words, such as *ambergris, apse, cloaca, nepotism,* and *sampan,* and asking them to supply the word. For example, one definition was, "A navigational instrument used in measuring angular distances, especially the altitude of the sun, moon, and stars at sea." The students were asked, upon hearing the definition, to indicate whether they knew the word, were sure that they did not know it, or had it "on the tip of the tongue" but could not produce it. In the event that they reported being in the last-mentioned state, the experimenters questioned them further. How many syllables do you think there are in the target word? What is the initial letter? What words that possibly sound like the target word are occurring to you? What words are you thinking of that may have a similar meaning?

Given the definition of the navigational instrument just stated, students with the word on the tip of the tongue were likely to guess correctly that it had two syllables rather than any other number; to guess, also correctly, that the first letter was "s"; to think of words like *sextet* and *secant,* which sound like the word; and to think of others, such as *compass,* which are related in meaning. Twice as many "sound like" words occurred to them as "mean the same" words.

These responses suggest something about the nature of storage and the process of retrieval. It would seem that an item in memory is stored in a form, or code, that includes certain of its physical features or attributes, such as number of syllables, initial letter, and general sound, as well as its meaning. Moreover, a word's location in memory is apparently within a network of related items. The word *sextant* is stored in a way that puts it in contact with words with similar physical features, such as *sextet* and *secant,* and with words related in meaning, such as *compass* and *protractor.* With such a system of cross-filing, retrieval must consist of a search through a region of memory with a particular range of meaning for an item with particular physical features. In this case the physical features are acoustic. This is the evidence mentioned earlier for believing that, in the process of retrieval, materials reenter short-term memory, where the code is also for the most part acoustic.

SUMMARY

New information is transferred from short-term memory to long-term memory by processing it for meaning. Although some have proposed that the effectiveness of this activity lies in its depth, the evidence suggests that elaborateness may be a better word for it. Once in long-term memory, information is usually both available and accessible; it is there and we can get to it. In the interesting tip-of-the-tongue state, however, information is available but temporarily inaccessible. Studies of the tip-of-the-tongue phenomenon suggest that retrieval is a search through a region in memory where words with related meanings reside for one that sounds a particular way.

REPRESENTATION OF INFORMATION IN MEMORY

Although the role of acoustic factors in memory is well established, it is clear that other sensory systems participate, and that the representation of information in long-term memory is for the most part verbal or semantic. The evocation of memory by tastes has been celebrated since Marcel Proust had his narrator piece together *Remembrance of Things Past* after eating a bit of tea-soaked madeleine cake. Odors, too, can trigger memories.

Consider the following description from a female undergraduate, age nineteen, who had just smelled an unlabeled bottle containing mothballs: "Musty corners of closets in our cottage in Michigan. I remember finding ancient toys, books from when my grandfather was little. . . . A treasure chest!" Her age at the time of the remembered event was reported as ten. A nineteen-year-old male who had just smelled an unlabeled bottle containing peppermint also reported a nine-year-old memory: "Candy Christmas canes at my aunt's house. They were on the tree, just a few left because it was after Christmas" (David Rubin, personal communication, July 28, 1980).

Dual-Coding Theory

The most studied of these other contributions to memory have been visual factors. According to Allan Paivio's **dual-coding theory,** information is represented in memory by two separate but interconnected systems or codes, a system of visual images and a verbal or semantic system. The theory goes on to say that the system of images handles concrete, spatial, imaginable objects and events. They are coded as though they were pictures in the head. The verbal system, using words and associations, handles abstract linguistic units and structures. To the extent that information can be handled by both systems, it will be represented in both.

One experimental result that dual-coding theory explains quite convincingly is the ease of learning and remembering certain types of materials. Consider the words *apple, daffodil, arrow,* and *mountain* on the one hand and *bravery, instance, happiness,* and *obedience* on the other. All are fairly familiar. The first group, however, consists of words that are concrete and capable of evoking a vivid image of the object to which they refer. The second group of words have less of this quality. A considerable amount of research indicates that words evoking images are easier to learn than words that do not. Dual-coding theory explains this ease by assuming that a concrete word enters into both the image and the verbal memory systems, whereas an abstract word is put only into the verbal system. Double representation also doubles the number of ways in which the concrete words can be retrieved. Hence we have a better memory for such words.

Allan Paivio believes that when we think we constantly form images in conjunction with words. Information is coded as though it were a picture in the head, whether or not we really "see" the image.

Shift from Images to Meaning

Other evidence suggests very strongly that in time the representation of materials in memory changes from images to a semantic code. Walter Kintsch and his colleagues at the University of Colorado have done experiments that make this point. In these experiments one group of college students presented with materials that expressed a proposition explicitly; a second group saw materials that expressed it only by implication. In one study (Keenan and Kintsch, 1974) sentences contained a proposition, for example, "The discarded cigarette started the fire," given in two ways.

Explicit: "A carelessly discarded burning cigarette started a fire. The fire destroyed many acres of virgin forest."

Implicit: "A burning cigarette was carelessly discarded. The fire destroyed many acres of virgin forest."

As you can see, the second version actually fails to state the proposition.

In a parallel experiment conducted by Pat Baggett (1975), the materials were series of pictures which told stories. One of them was about a long-haired youth entering a barber shop, getting his hair cut, and emerging with a crew cut. The

Walter Kintsch has found that people take longer to read a sentence expressing two propositions than to read a sentence expressing a single proposition, even though the sentences contain an identical number of words. Adding an adjective to a sentence adds a proposition. This proposition consists of the modified noun as the subject, the verb *is*, plus the adjective.

"Goin' Fishin'" is one of the picture stories used by Pat Baggett in her study of the representation of materials in memory. All subjects saw pictures 1, 2, and 4, but some saw the explicit version of picture 3, others the implicit version. For the crucial test given afterward, all subjects were shown either the explicit version or a picture showing the fisherman doing something that probably would not have occurred in connection with the story. They were asked to indicate as quickly as possible whether the test picture "fits in with your understanding of the event you saw earlier." (Adapted from sketches supplied by Dr. Baggett, 1975.)

EXPLICIT   IMPLICIT

explicit version of this story contained a picture of the youth getting his hair cut; the implicit version did not.

In both of these experiments, the subjects were presented later with the target proposition—"The discarded cigarette started the fire"; the picture of the hair-cutting episode—as well as with sentences and pictures concerning other subjects. They were asked to say as quickly as they could whether the item was "true" or "false" on the basis of what they had seen earlier. These tests came "immediately" (within thirty seconds) for half the students in each group and later on for the others. For the verbal propositions the delayed test was given after approximately twenty minutes. Because pictures are remembered much better than verbal materials, the delayed test for them came three days later.

The results are very similar for the two experiments (Figure 6.7). On the test given immediately verification was much more rapid by the subjects who had seen the explicit versions of the proposition. This seems to mean that the proposition as presented was still in memory and available to compare with the test sentence or picture, allowing a rapid check on its truth. Subjects given the pictorial proposition only by implication needed an additional second to interpret and verify the truth of the test picture. Subjects given the verbal proposition only by implication took an additional two seconds to interpret the meaning of the test sentence and recognize its truth. But after a delay the literal memory of the item had disappeared. Whether the proposition had first been presented explicitly or implicitly, the observer was forced to make an interpretation, which took time. These results suggest that, with time, memories are stored in a code that is chiefly semantic (but see page 194 for further discussion of this issue).

Episodic and Semantic Memory

Another way to describe the results of these experiments would be to say that they illustrate the difference between memory and knowledge. Immediately after reading a newspaper story, say of a specific forest fire started by a discarded cigarette, a person has a *memory* of reading the story, the information it contained, and a good bit of the precise phraseology: "The discarded cigarette

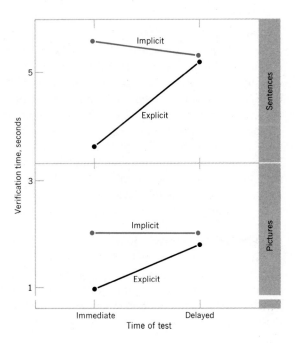

Figure 6.7
Verification times for propositions. The propositions to be verified had been presented earlier, either explicitly or only implicitly, in sentences or pictures. The very fast verification times in immediate tests with items that had been presented explicitly indicate the contribution of literal, explicit representation in short-term memory. (Adapted from Keenan and Kintsch, 1974; Baggett, 1975.)

started the fire." Later on the individual has the *knowledge* that a cigarette started the forest fire, but the precise phraseology is gone and even the fact that the information came from a newspaper story may have been forgotten. Perhaps it was heard on radio or seen on television.

Endel Tulving (1972) calls memories of personal experiences episodic memory and knowledge semantic memory. **Episodic memory** is memory for temporally dated, autobiographical events in the individual's own life. Episodic memories are tied to time and place. **Semantic memory** is organized knowledge about the world, including the verbal world of words and how they are used. Semantic memory consists of facts, principles, relations, and strategies. The information has been coded in ways that allow it to be retrieved in a form different from the one in which it was originally stored. After any fire caused by a cigarette left burning, whether we were there or heard about it, we have the general knowledge that cigarettes can cause fires, information that is above and beyond the specific occasion that gave us this knowledge. This general knowledge, semantic memory, plays a very important role in retention.

Semantic-Episodic Interactions.   To get an impression of one important way in which semantic memory controls retention, please read through the following paragraph quickly, asking yourself how much of it you think you could reproduce, if you had to, after this quick reading. You will find yourself saying, "Not much!"

> The procedure, actually, is quite simple. First you arrange things into different groups. Of course, one pile may be sufficient, depending on how much there is to do. If you have to go somewhere else due to lack of facilities, that's the next step. Otherwise, you're pretty well set. It is important not to overdo things. That is, it is better to do too few things at once than too many. In the short run, this may not seem important, but complications can easily arise. A mistake can be expensive as well. At first, the whole procedure will seem complicated. Soon, however, it will become just another fact of life. It is difficult to foresee an end to the necessity of this task in the immediate future, but then one never can tell. After the procedure is completed, one arranges the materials into different groups again, and then they can be put into their appropriate places. Eventually, they will be used once more, and the whole cycle will have to be repeated; however, that is a part of life.

John Bransford and Marcia Johnson (1972) presented this paragraph to two groups of students. One group knew when they read it that the passage is about "washing clothes." The other lacked this knowledge. The participants in the study were asked to rate the comprehensibility of the passage on a scale from one to seven and then to recall as much of it as they could. The informed group gave the passage a rating of 4.5 for comprehensibility and remembered 32 percent of the content of the passage. The uniformed group gave the paragraph a rating of 2.8 and remembered only 13 percent of the content. These results illustrate an important form of interaction between semantic and episodic memory. The experimental task was an episodic one, to remember the specific materials that had just been read. The knowledge that made these materials hang together for recall was in semantic memory, however.

Eyewitness Testimony.   Semantic memory obviously can have considerable control over how our episodic experiences are perceived, interpreted, and stored, but the manner of such control can be subtle. In an experiment on eyewitness testimony, Elizabeth Loftus and John Palmer (1974) had students watch a short film of a traffic accident and then asked them questions about what they remembered. The subjects were asked slightly different questions

Elizabeth Loftus, now at the University of Washington, is a specialist in learning and memory. She has won national recognition for her research on eyewitness testimony.

If a witness to this accident tells an inquiring passerby that the cars "smashed" into each other, both are likely later to remember the accident as causing considerable damage. If a witness describes the cars as "hitting" each other to a passerby, these two are likely later to remember less damage.

about the speed at which the cars were going: "About how fast were the cars going when they smashed into each other?" or "About how fast were the cars going when they hit each other?" The subjects who were asked the first question gave much higher estimates than those asked the second. Apparently "smashed" in semantic memory implies greater speed than "hit."

Would the verbs of these two questions affect the subjects' memory of the film, although the questions had been asked after the subjects saw the film? To find out, Loftus and Palmer called the subjects back a week later for a second interview. The critical question this time was whether in the film they had seen any broken glass after the accident. There had been none. Responses to this question differed, however, depending on the verb of the critical question asked a week earlier (Table 6.4). About twice as many subjects remembered seeing glass if they had been told that the cars "smashed into each other."

Apparently the episode of the accident has been stored according to the meaning of the words applied to it. Subjects asked about the cars that "smashed" into each other have it stored in terms of greater damage than subjects asked about the cars that "hit" each other. After this initial storage, memory will be constructive. Details will be included to fit the event as it is stored. The implications of this point for interrogation and for courtroom proceedings generally are of great importance and are just now beginning to be studied.

Organization of Memory. Semantic memory has an organizational effect that helps us to recall information. In an early demonstration of this point, students at the University of Connecticut were given a list of sixty nouns to memorize. Although the list was made up of fifteen words in each of four categories—animals, vegetables, first names, and professions—presented in random order, the students tended to recall them in categories, clusters, or "bursts," finishing one cluster before moving on to the next (Bousfield, 1953). The recall of words in categorized lists takes place in two stages. First the individual recalls the category, then the items in the category. Remembering one item in a category usually means that the majority of the other items in the category will come to mind. Lists that are made up of words falling into categories have a natural

Table 6.4 Responses to Question, "Did you see any broken glass?"

Response	Verb in Question Asked One Week Earlier	
	Smashed	Hit
Yes	16	7
No	34	43

After Loftus and Palmer, 1974.

organization for recall. If the materials lack such an organization, subjects in recall studies will invent one. They create a *subjective organization,* a consistent order in which they come to recall the items in the list.

Here is a little experiment that you might try on a group of friends to obtain evidence for a somewhat different aspect of this organizational tendency. Read the following list of words to them fairly rapidly—one per second or less—and ask your friends to remember as many of the words as they can: *bed, rest, awake, tired, dream, night, pillow, comfort, slumber, snore, drowsy, quiet, nightmare.* Then ask your subjects to write down the words that they remember. You will probably find that about half of them include *sleep* among the words they "remember," in spite of the fact that *sleep* was not one of the words in the list. In this case the related items in the category recreated the category itself.

Context Effects on Memory

Memories are tied to the situation in which learning originally occurred, but the tie may be weak or very strong. For example, recall is sometimes slightly better in the room where a person learned the set of materials, but not much better. At the other extreme, experiments suggest that sometimes an item can be retrieved only in the context in which it was encoded. Tulving and Donald Thompson (1973) interpret this fact in terms of an **encoding specificity principle:** "The effective cues for retrieval are the specific cues that were present at the time of encoding and participated in the process." This idea needs to be put more concretely. Suppose that you are a participant in an experiment that takes place in a series of steps.

Step 1. You are instructed to learn a long list of words printed in capital letters. Each word is paired with another word, a cue word, that "may help you remember it." One example is *train*—BLACK, in which the cue word is *train* and the word to be remembered is BLACK.

Step 2. You are presented with a list of new words and asked to write down as many associations as you can to each. One of the words is *white,* and you come up with *snow, wedding, black, paper,* and *china.*

Step 3. You are asked to encircle any of the words that you have just written down should you recognize it as a word you are supposed to be remembering. *You fail to encircle black.*

Step 4. On a final test the cues are presented again, but without the words to be remembered. When *train* appears, you immediately remember *black.*

In two experiments that followed the procedure just described, Tulving and Thompson found that subjects recognized only 15 to 24 percent of the target words when they were in a new context. By contrast, they remembered 59 to 63 percent of them when the original context word was repeated. This phenomenon of failing to recognize words that can be remembered in another context is surprising, for recognition is usually much superior to recall. Here memory for the word *black* depends on the specific context of its encoding, appearing with its partner word *train.* In a different context, in association with the word *white,* it is not even recognized.

Demonstrations of **state-dependent learning** also reveal the control of memory by context. These experiments employ a standard procedure with two groups of subjects and two stages. In the first stage one group of subjects learn a response or set of materials while they are in some special state, usually the physiological state produced by administering a drug. Marijuana, barbiturates, amphetamines, and alcohol have all been used. Other subjects learn in their

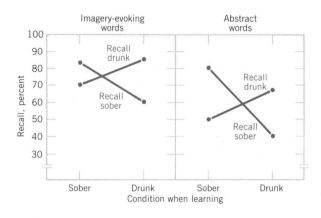

Figure 6.8
State-dependent learning.

normal undrugged state. In a second stage of the experiment, the subjects are tested for recall, either in the same state as existed at the time of learning or in the alternative state. The great majority of these experiments have been done with lower animals. The results can be summarized quickly: subjects do better on recall tests when in the same state as that in which they learned rather than in another state.

In an experiment with human participants (Weingartner et al., 1976), female subjects learned and attempted to recall lists of ten words. Half of the women learned when they were intoxicated, probably extremely intoxicated; they were served a screwdriver cocktail containing a triple shot of vodka and six ounces of orange juice. The other women learned while sober. For the recall test the subjects were either in the same state as at the time of learning or in the alternative state (Figure 6.8).

Half of the words learned in the experiment called up vivid images, half did not. Recall was better for the image-evoking words, but the pattern was the same for both kinds of words. The subjects remembered more words when they were in the same state in which they had learned them. Perhaps a parting word of warning is in order. Learning and memory in the drugged state are usually *much worse* than in the undrugged state. Getting high on something when you study and staying in that state for examinations will probably ruin your grade rather than raise it.

SUMMARY

Information is stored in memory in a complex code which includes both physical and semantic features. Paivio's dual-coding theory holds that information is represented in memory by two systems, a system of images and a verbal system. Both this theory and the topic of imagery have generated a great deal of experimental work. The theory maintains that information represented in both systems rather than in just one is more easily recalled. Evidence does indicate that concrete words, which can be served by both systems, are more easily learned and recalled than abstract words, which are served for the most part by the linguistic system.

Studies that test memory both immediately and after a delay reveal that, with time, the representation of materials in memory usually becomes less sensory and literal and more semantic and meaningful. This change is related to the distinction between episodic memory and semantic memory. Episodic memory stores the events of personal experience and of experiences recounted by others. Semantic memory stores knowledge. Research reveals that semantic memory has a strong influence on episodic memory. Sometimes, however, as has been revealed by studies of eyewitness testimony, semantic memory distorts information. Materials in semantic memory acquire a degree of organization and meaningfulness that is usually beneficial. Semantic memory also provides a context for episodic information. A particularly interesting example of the importance of context is the phenomenon of state-dependent learning: recall is best if the individual's physiological state is the same as at the time of learning.

FORGETTING

The first significant scientific experiments on verbal learning and memory were performed toward the end of the last century in Germany. The important pioneer was Hermann Ebbinghaus (1850–1909). Ebbinghaus was a loner. Having completed a degree in philosophy at Bonn in 1873, he spent the next seven years studying on his own. During this period his scientific work on memory took form. In 1880 he went to the University of Berlin as a docent, or lecturer, and in 1885 he published his major work, *On Memory,* reporting a long series of experiments done entirely on himself.

Ebbinghaus realized that the meaningfulness of materials would have an effect on how easily they could be learned and how well they could be remembered (see page 213). He set out to control for this problem by eliminating meaning. To that end he used nonsense syllables, typically three-letter, consonant-vowel-consonant sequences like LUN, ZIV, WEK, which are nearly devoid of meaning. He devised some 2300 of these syllables and kept them on separate slips of paper. Ebbinghaus drew seven to thirty-six of these slips at random to make up lists of various lengths. Then he learned the syllables in order, reciting them to the beat of a metronome, and tested himself for recall after different amounts of time.

Among Ebbinghaus's many contributions was the first careful tracing of the course of forgetting (Figure 6.9). The striking thing about forgetting is the speed with which it obviously occurs. The first point on Ebbinghaus's curve was obtained nineteen minutes after learning, but already 42 percent has been forgotten. Or, as the graph also expresses it, retention is 58 percent. Although the absolute amount forgotten in a given period of time depends on many variables, most forgetting takes a course similar to Ebbinghaus's curve.

Measures of Retention

The extent of forgetting usually depends on the method by which it is tested. In general, **recall tests,** which require a person to retrieve something from memory, are more difficult than **recognition tests,** in which materials are presented and subjects have to indicate only whether each item is one that they

Fechner's *Elements of Psychophysics* gave Hermann Ebbinghaus the idea of applying the scientific method to the study of processes "higher" than sensations.

Figure 6.9
Ebbinghaus's retention curve for nonsense syllables. The amount forgotten is the difference at any point between the level of the curve and 100 percent. The amount retained is the difference between this same point and zero.

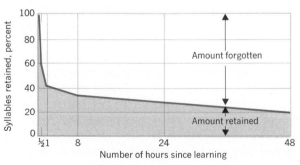

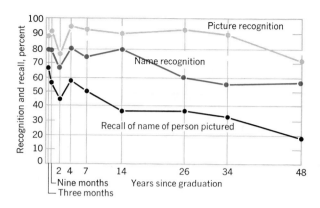

Figure 6.10
Memory for classmates after retention intervals ranging from three months to forty-eight years. As usual, recognition is better than recall. (Data from Bahrick, Bahrick, and Willinger, 1975.)

have learned or encountered earlier. An interesting experiment by Harry Bahrick and his colleagues (1975) at Ohio Wesleyan University makes the point very nicely. These investigators studied the memory of 392 high school graduates for the names and faces of their classmates at periods after graduation that ranged from three months to forty-eight years. Their subjects ranged in age from seventeen to seventy-four. In one measure of memory, the graduates were asked to *recall* the names of their classmates when shown a series of ten pictures drawn at random from their yearbooks. In two measures of *recognition,* they had to select first the picture of a classmate from sets of five pictures, and later the name of one from sets of five names, four in each set being those of individuals who had not gone to their school.

People who had graduated almost half a century earlier were still able to recognize 75 percent of the names and photographs of their classmates correctly (Figure 6.10). During the same period, however, recall of names declined to under 20 percent.

Interference

What causes forgetting? Although personal experience suggests that memories simply fade in time and eventually disappear, experimental studies tell us that this is not the case. What actually happens is that things we learn before and after a given event interfere with our recall of it.

Retroactive Inhibition.   One of the earliest hints that retention of something learned might be subject to some sort of interference from whatever followed learning came from the famous experiment of John Jenkins and Karl Dallenbach (1924), who compared retention after various periods of sleep and waking. The participants in this experiment were to male college students who worked with the experimenters over a period of almost two months in order to provide the necessary data. During this time they slept in a room next to the psychological laboratory so that they would be available for the experimental sessions that came at night. The materials were lists of ten nonsense syllables. The syllables were exposed briefly, one at a time, and the learner pronounced each syllable as he saw it. After each run-through of the list, he attempted to recall the syllables in order. The list was considered learned when the participant remembered all the syllables in the correct order. The students learned some of the lists in the morning, between 8:00 and 10:00 a.m., and the other lists at night, between 11:30 p.m. and 1:00 a.m. For the late-night sessions the participant got ready for bed and learned the list just before retiring. The daytime sessions were fitted into the normal course of daily activity. Tests for recall were

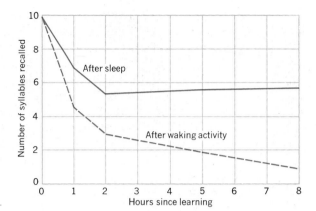

Figure 6.11
Retention after sleep and waking. These results were important in developing the concept of retroactive inhibition. (After Jenkins and Dallenbach, 1924.)

given at one of four intervals, at one, two, four, or eight hours after learning. Half the periods during which forgetting might take place were filled with sleep, the other half with waking activity.

Recall was shown to be much better after a period of sleep than after a comparable period of being awake (Figure 6.11). Forgetting then is not a passive function of the passage of time after learning. Intervening activity determines to a considerable degree how much the individual remembers.

More recent studies of **retroactive inhibition** have been carried out under conditions that allowed better control. The experimental design employed to demonstrate retroactive inhibition proceeds in three stages and requires at least two groups (Figure 6.12). In this design the two groups first learn the same materials, typically to a stated criterion, such as 80 percent correct. In the second stage of the experiment, the experimental group learns a second set of materials; the control group spends the same amount of time in some unrelated activity, such as solving a mechanical puzzle. In the third stage both groups are tested for recall. The control group usually remembers much more than the experimental group, showing that the interpolated learning interfered with the recall of the experimental group.

Proactive Inhibition.   In retroactive inhibition later learning hinders the recall of materials learned earlier; in **proactive inhibition** materials learned earlier hinder recall of those learned later. The experimental design for studying proactive inhibition appears in Figure 6.13. Somewhat surprisingly, proactive inhibition is responsible for a great deal of forgetting. In 1957 Benton Underwood summarized experiments by a dozen or more investigators. In all these experiments retention had been tested after twenty-four hours, but the individuals in some of the experiments had previously learned different numbers of other lists. Since the interval between learning the critical list and the test for recall of

Figure 6.12
Design of an experiment on retroactive inhibition. The two groups learn the same materials to the same degree of mastery in stage I and receive the same test in stage III. Thus any difference in recall is the result of the different activities in stage II.

Group		Stage of experiment		
		I	II	III
	Experimental	Learn materials to be remembered	Learn new materials	Test for recall
	Control	Learn materials to be remembered	Unrelated activity	Test for recall

		Stage of experiment		
		I	II	III
Group	Experimental	Learn first materials	Learn materials to be remembered	Test for recall
	Control	Unrelated activity	Learn materials to be remembered	Test for recall

Figure 6.13
Design of an experiment on proactive inhibition. The two groups learn the same materials to the same degree of mastery in stage II and receive the same test in stage III. Thus any difference in recall is the result of the different activities in stage I.

it had been the same in all these studies, any differences in retention could be attributed to previous experience in learning and recalling such materials. This effect was very great (Figure 6.14). Individuals without previous experience retained about 75 percent of the syllables; those who had learned as many as twenty earlier lists retained only about 15 percent. Ebbinghaus would be considered a highly practiced subject; he learned several thousands of these lists in three to four years, and he recalled a little less than 30 percent after twenty-four hours (Figure 6.9).

As we have seen, earlier learning also hinders short-term memory. In experiments on short-term memory, there are usually many trials with different items to be remembered and tests after various short intervals. This means, of course, that the materials learned on early trials could interfere with memory on later ones. In one study the memory of individuals tested after eighteen seconds on six successive lists gradually deteriorated. On the first test their recall was nearly perfect. On the last list it had reduced to 40 percent, and there was every indication that practice on more lists would have interfered even further (Keppel and Underwood, 1962).

The extraordinary memory of VP, reported by Earl Hunt and Tom Love, provides an interesting sidelight on this process of proactive inhibition. Among the tests given to VP was the classic one of short-term memory. First a syllable made up of consonants, such as TGV, was presented. Then VP did the successive subtractions by threes for the interval required and finally tried to recall the syllable. VP's performance in a series of such tests was superior. Whereas college students could report only 50 percent of the syllables during the course of the experiment, at the eighteen-second interval VP was able to report 85 percent of them. Further study showed that VP's performance was like that of the college students on their first test. The difference was that he showed no susceptibility to proactive inhibition. Asked to explain this, VP said that, knowing

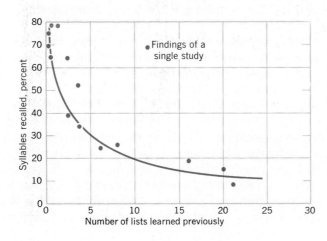

Figure 6.14
Cumulative interference by previous learning. The graph shows 24-hour retention of a list as a function of the number of lists learned previously. The greater the number of lists learned earlier, the less the retention. The data are from many different experiments. This is our most impressive demonstration of proactive inhibition. (After Underwood, 1957.)

several languages, almost every syllable suggested a word to him and he could therefore treat the three-consonant item as a single unit.

Autobiographical Memory

The phenomena of proactive and retroactive interference have important implications for everyday memory. For example, the bad memory that old people have for recent happenings can be blamed in part on proactive inhibition. Decades of accumulated memories prevent the recall of more recent events. But the determination of psychological phenomena is never simple. An opposite process also affects memory. Accumulating retroactive inhibition progressively destroys earlier memories so that people remember less and less of happenings farther and farther back in their lifetimes. Figure 6.15 provides a summary of the results of many studies (for example, Rubin, 1982) of this relationship. Autobiographical memory is poorer and poorer for events that are more and more remote in time. The decline is gradual for happenings back to the age of three or four or five. There the curve breaks sharply downward. We have very few memories of happenings in the first half decade of life.

Long-Lasting Memories. Some of the memories that do survive from earlier years are those that are protected from interference. Motor skills such as riding a bicycle, once learned, are notoriously impervious to the passage of time, probably because they have little or no contact with interfering and competing skills. The unreasonable learned fears called phobias (see page 527) are also retained for a long time, again because they are protected from interference. People with a phobic fear of heights stay away from high places, and their fear is never diminished by occasions when they might learn that nothing bad happens to them there.

A few memories seem to persist because they were particularly well learned. Some of these memories are **flashbulb memories,** vivid recollections of important events, often stressful ones. The very best example of a flashbulb memory is the recall that older people have of the assassination of President Kennedy. For college students, the most frequent memories of this type are of accidents (Rubin and Kozin, 1983).

Finally, some long-enduring memories are for passages that our teachers have drilled into us: the Gettysburg address, Hamlet's soliloquy, "The Star Spangled Banner," and the Twenty-Third Psalm. The interesting thing about these memories is that they are preserved as they were memorized, in very literal form, in exact wordings (Rubin, 1979). The memory code is not transferred from literal to semantic. In fact, the words are often remembered mechanically, with almost no attention to their meaning.

The Permanence of Memory. Long-lasting memories are the exception; most of what happens to us disappears from memory. But does this mean that the lost memories are truly lost, in the sense of being unavailable, or are they merely *inaccessible?* Until recently, most psychologists were at least inclined to accept the second interpretation, that once something is learned, it remains forever in the nervous system. There were several reasons for arriving at this startling conclusion. The neurosurgeons had reported that electrical stimulation of the human brain during surgical operations can elicit memories (Penfield and Roberts, 1959). Brain surgery is carried out with local anesthesia; the patient is awake and able to report experiences as they happen. In an effort to determine the areas that were associated with epileptic attacks, Wilder Penfield explored the surfaces of his patients' brains, applying a very weak electric current in

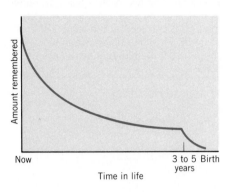

Figure 6.15
Retention of autobiographical memories.

many different locations. Sometimes these patients reported hearing voices or a long-forgotten song. A woman relived the experience of delivering a baby. Hypnotists, working both with clinical patients and with victims of crime, have claimed that under hypnosis individuals have recalled events that they were unable to remember earlier. Furthermore, psychoanalysts have described cases in which their procedures made it possible for people to remember things that had happened to them in the very early months of life. The analysts believe that these events had been repressed, creating an "infantile amnesia."

Over the years the case for a completely permanent memory has gradually crumbled. It turns out that memories are brought back by brain stimulation during surgery in only about five percent of the patients. Moreover, these patients may translate what happens in their stimulated brains into "memories" because this is one way to report an experience that is very difficult to communicate. As for hypnosis, studies have shown that some of the memories of hypnotized individuals are fictitious. Finally, it seems very likely that patients in analysis report memories of infancy because they feel that they are expected to. Patients tell the analysts what they believe the analysts want to hear (Loftus and Loftus, 1980).

All the early memories recalled raise the difficult question of validity. How can we ever be certain that whatever events are remembered from childhood actually happened? The following experience reported by Jean Piaget (1962), of whom we shall hear a great deal more in Chapter 11, makes this point very effectively.

> One of my first memories would date . . . from my second year. I can still see, most clearly, the following scene, in which I believed until I was about fifteen. I was sitting in my pram, which my nurse was pushing in the Champs Élysées, when a man tried to kidnap me. I was held in by the strap fastened round me while my nurse bravely tried to stand between me and the thief. She received various scratches, and I can still see vaguely those on her face. Then a crowd gathered, a policeman with a short cloak and a white baton came up, and the man took to his heels. I can still see the whole scene and can even place it near the tube station. When I was about fifteen, my parents received a letter from my former nurse saying she had been converted to the Salvation Army. She wanted to confess her past faults, and in particular to return the watch she had been given as a reward on this occasion. She had made up the whole story, faking the scratches. I therefore must have heard, as a child, the account of this story, which my parents believed, and projected it into the past in the form of a visual memory, which was a memory of a memory, but false (pp. 187–188).

All these considerations have led psychologists today to the conclusion that very few of the events of early childhood remain in memory. They believe that children lack the cognitive skills required to encode anything but the very simplest experiences. In this connection it seems relevant that the curve in Figure 6.15 drops abruptly at three to five years. Before that time language, which is so important to memory, is not well enough developed to encode a sequence of happenings. Probably your own earliest memory is of something very concrete, something which can be remembered in terms of visual images or possibly emotional reactions.

SUMMARY

Although our own subjective experience tells us that we forget because memories simply fade away in time, experiments reveal that other processes are responsible. A study of memory following periods of sleep and waking found that memory after sleep was better, suggesting that waking activity somehow interfered with retention of earlier learning. Technically, such an effect is called retroactive inhibition: new learning acts back upon earlier learning and inhibits memory of it. Retroactive inhibition has been demonstrated many times in controlled laboratory experiments with a standard three-stage design, consisting of original learning by two groups; interpolated learning by the experimental group and unrelated activity by the control group; and test of the recall of both groups.

By a comparable process, earlier learning interferes with the recall of more recently learned materials. This type of interference, proactive inhibition, is even more powerful than retroactive inhibition. It has been shown to hinder both short-term memory and recall after many hours. In everyday life proactive inhibition appears to be one of the factors responsible for the poor memory of older people. And as we grow older, retroactive inhibition makes us steadily lose our memories of early experiences. We retain very few childhood memories, probably because they were never encoded in a way that allowed them to be remembered.

TOWARD A BETTER MEMORY

In nearly the following words, Gordon Bower (1970), a psychologist at Stanford University, relates a story to begin a discussion of the practical uses of memory. Simonides, a Greek poet, was commissioned to compose a poem praising a Roman nobleman and to recite it at a banquet attended by a multitude of guests. After he had recited the poem, a message was brought to Simonides that two young men were waiting outside to see him. Simonides arose from the banquet and went out but could find no one, for the invisible visitors were the gods Castor and Pollux, whom he had also praised in his poem. While he was absent, the roof of the hall collapsed, killing all the guests. The corpses were so mangled that relatives were unable to identify them. But Simonides stepped forward and named each of the many corpses on the basis of his memory of where they had been sitting in the huge banquet hall.

Later on we shall describe the ''method of loci,'' which Simonides used to perform this feat of memory. But there is a good bit of other practical material to present first. If you are willing to work at it, the content of these next few pages may help to make you a slightly better student and a slightly better memorizer in general. But it will require work. The points made here are simple, but putting them to use takes practice.

The Feeling of Knowing

As a student you have the task of mastering a vast amount of material. Along the way to such mastery, you have probably already encountered the problem of judging when you have learned the materials well enough to handle the examinations that your professors inevitably inflict upon you. In the tip-of-the-tongue experiment described earlier, students were asked to decide whether they were certain that they did or did not know the word being defined, and they were able to do so readily. Other research has shown that our sense of what we know, perhaps even only marginally, is really quite remarkable. But this skill is not perfect. Particularly in the social sciences, the materials are of a kind that can seduce students into thinking that they know them when they do not. Many of the concepts of social science are quite familiar ones. Psychology, for example, is about such things as learning, memory, motives, emotion, intelligence, madness, and the like, which you knew something about even before you took a course in the subject. Under such circumstances it is not surprising that students can mistake familiarity with the topics for an understanding of what psychology has to say about them.

Have you ever gone to a friend, or if you are brave enough, to your instructor, and said, "I really studied for that last test and I really knew the materials, but somehow the test just didn't allow me to show what I knew"? Although there are times when you will be correct in this judgment, you should consider a possible alternative, that you did not know the subject matter as well as you thought. Your criteria for "knowing the materials" may have been too lenient; you may have known them well enough to meet your own standards of knowing but not well enough to meet those of the instructor.

What to do about it, if you decide that you have been lax in setting criteria? Clearly, you should try to find out what the instructor's criteria are like. If exams from previous years can be secured, try to take them. If a study guide is available to accompany your textbook, its most useful function may be to help you decide whether you know the materials as well as you should. Finally, having come to terms with the question of criteria, you should keep the following truism in mind: a good memory is really good initial learning. The only way to sharpen your memory is to develop techniques of effective learning. We turn to some of them now.

Overlearning

The process of mastering materials well enough to handle them on a test may very well mean **overlearning** them, that is, practicing beyond the point of bare mastery. An important question concerns the value of various degrees of such extra practice. Degrees of overlearning are usually expressed as percentages. If it takes ten trials to learn a list of words, and a person practices for five trials more, this is 50 percent overlearning; ten extra trials is 100 percent overlearning, and so on. In the best-known study of the effect of overlearning (Krueger, 1929), people learned lists of single-syllable nouns, just to the point of mastering them, with no overlearning, and to overlearning percentages of 50 and 100. There were recall tests after one, two, four, seven, fourteen, and twenty-eight days.

Three things are worth noting about the results (Figure 6.16). The first is that 50 and 100 percent overlearning clearly allows better recall than mere mastery of the materials. The second is that 50 percent overlearning produces a great improvement in recall, but 100 percent overlearning does not add many additional words to the number remembered. More than 100 percent overlearning would not be an economical procedure when learning lists of nouns, for the

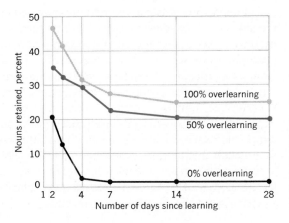

Figure 6.16
The effect of overlearning on retention. Overlearning aids retention, especially over long intervals. But these benefits probably follow a law of diminishing returns. Fifty percent overlearning adds a great deal to retention, but 100 percent overlearning does not improve recall that much more. (After Krueger, 1929.)

amount of extra time required to overlearn them would be out of proportion to the additional number recalled later on. Finally, the value of overlearning increases as the amount of time for forgetting increases; that is, the advantage of overlearning is greater after fourteen or twenty-eight days than after one or two. This last fact is of considerable practical importance. Overlearning is the most beneficial with materials that must be remembered for a long time.

Subjective Organization.   Why should overlearning aid retention? Probably there is more than one reason. Perhaps the most important is that learners impose their personal or **subjective organization** on materials as they memorize them, and this organization is strengthened through practice beyond the point of mastery. Practice on any set of materials to be memorized may soon bring learners to the point that, given a test, they could reproduce them all. But this does not mean that no further learning takes place with additional practice. On a number of successive practice runs learners may put materials into ever-better subjective order so that they feel surer of remembering them. Recall continues to become better ordered for some time after the list is nearly mastered. Given the importance of organization to memory, it seems to be one of the major contributions of overlearning.

Automatization.   Another important contribution of overlearning is that with more and more practice whatever you learn becomes more and more automatic. Everyone has experienced this effect. Without thinking about it or paying attention, you find your way about your home or from your home to class because the paths you take are so familiar. If you have considerable athletic or musical skill, you no doubt have practiced it well beyond the point at which practice brings noticeable improvement, in order to make your performance so automatic that you can do well under pressure.

For the most part such **automatization** of behavior appears to be advantageous. An activity that takes care of itself and proceeds without attention frees the mind to deal with more important problems. Sometimes, however, the process works against you. Having moved to a new house, you make a wrong turn on your way to the kitchen, a turn which would have been correct where you lived before. You call an attractive young woman whom you have just met to arrange a date, but your former girl friend answers the phone because you automatically dialed the old number. The poem that you practiced *ad nauseam* so that you could recite it in class keeps occurring to you instead of the one you want to remember now. On the Stroop test (Figure 6.17, color plate) your automatic reading habits are so powerful that you cannot quickly name the colors in which the words are printed.

Automatic processing in memory has just begun to receive from psychologists the attention it deserves. Some of the facts revealed in experiments on automatic processing are consistent with information obtained in studies of attention. For example, as dichotic-listening experiments have already indicated, the physical features of message tend to be remembered automatically. On this basis we know that the information that we are trying to recall came early in the professor's lecture, that he repeated the point, and that relevant information also appeared in the lower right-hand quarter of a page in the textbook. Thus the temporal, frequency, and spatial attributes of messages are among the types of information that are processed automatically (Hasher and Zachs, 1979).

As we also saw in our earlier discussion of attention, however, some semantic information appears to be processed automatically. In one of the most impressive demonstrations of this point (Hirst et al., 1980), subjects learned to take

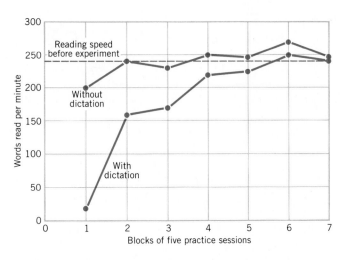

Figure 6.18
Learning to read at usual speed while taking dictation. With many hours of practice, taking dictation had less and less effect on reading speed. (Hirst et al., 1980.)

dictation while they were reading short stories or encyclopedia articles for content. The results were the same with both types of reading material. In one experiment the dictation consisted of short, related sentences, such as

Cookbooks contain recipes.

Susan owns several.

Mary hates cooking.

After thirty-five to forty hours of practice, the subjects were able to take these sentences down in longhand and read at their usual speed. Figure 6.18 shows that taking dictation had less and less effect on reading speed as practice progressed. The process of taking dictation was apparently becoming an automatic act which did not interfere with other mental activity (Kimble, 1981).

Even more impressive than being able to take dictation while reading, however, was the evidence that the subjects understood the sentences that they recorded automatically. They were tested with sentences that were dictated sentences, simple inferences that could be drawn from the dictated sentences, or unrelated statements that were usually wrong, for example

Cookbooks contain recipes.   (dictated)

Susan owns cookbooks.   (inference)

Susan hates cooking.   (unrelated)

The subjects were asked to rate the sentences for familiarity. The dictated sentences seemed the most familiar, the unrelated the least familiar, with the inference-containing sentences falling in between. The fact that the subjects could recognize the truth of the inferences means that, during dictation, they had extracted the meaning from the sentences and then stored them in memory in terms of their meaning.

Recoding or Chunking

In an earlier discussion we saw that one way to increase the memory span beyond its normal limit of seven plus or minus two is to group a set of items, that is to **recode** or **chunk** them. Another way to increase the memory span is to apply the organizing power of semantic memory. K. Anders Ericsson and William Chase, working with an undergraduate student, Steve Faloon, at Carnegie-Mellon University (1980), have shown that, with extended practice, mem-

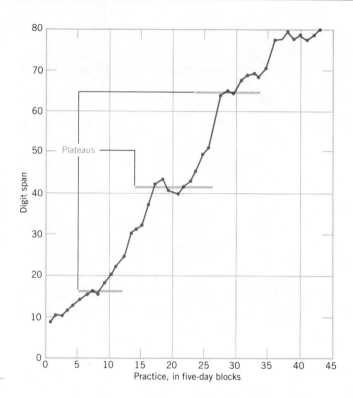

Figure 6.19
*Increase of Mr. Faloon's digit span with
many hours of practice.*

ory span may be increased from seven digits to more than eighty, the largest ever recorded in the literature (Figure 6.19). In this study random digits were presented at the rate of one per second, and Mr. Faloon attempted to reproduce the sequence. If he got the numbers right, the next list was one digit longer; if he made a mistake, the next list was one digit shorter. The experiment went on one hour a day, three to five days a week, for more than two years, providing Mr. Faloon with some 230 hours of practice.

Above and beyond the dramatic increase in his memory span, Mr. Faloon's feat was instructive in a number of ways.

1. One device Mr. Faloon used to expand his memory was to recode the items into chunks of three or four digits. He handled all but five or six digits in this way, retaining these five or six in a "rehearsal buffer." For example, he remembered eighteen digits by recoding twelve of them into three groups of four items each and holding the remaining six in his rehearsal buffer.

2. As the lists became longer and longer, Mr. Faloon began to form groups of chunks. One of these layer units might consist of two four-digit chunks followed by two three-digit chunks. Then he graduated to a more complex organization which might involve three four-digit chunks followed by three three-digit chunks, and so on. Eventually he devised a still higher organization, one made up of supergroups—groups of groups of chunks. Figure 6.20 shows the structure of Mr. Faloon's memory at the point when he could recall eighty digits.

3. The ability to recall eighty items organized as in Figure 6.20 does not represent a substantial increase in basic memory span. At most it is ten items: two supergroups, three groups of chunks, and five digits. If these five digits comprise even two roughly organized chunks, the subjects memory span is seven, what it was at the outset of the experiment.

4. Before Mr. Faloon was able to devise each next order of organization, his

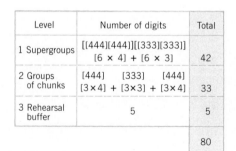

Level	Number of digits	Total
1 Supergroups	[[444][444]][[333][333]] [6 × 4] + [6 × 3]	42
2 Groups of chunks	[444]　[333]　[444] [3×4] + [3×3] + [3×4]	33
3 Rehearsal buffer	5	5
		80

Figure 6.20
*Structure of Mr. Faloon's memory for
eighty digits.*

memory span reached and stalled at several *plateaus* (Figure 6.19). It is a common and frustrating experience in the mastery of a high-level skill that there are periods of little or no improvement until new organizations develop and allow acquisition to proceed.

5. To aid in the development of this organization, Mr. Faloon made use of sets of numbers that he knew very well. Mr. Faloon was a good long-distance runner who competed in races throughout the eastern United States. Stored in his long-term memory were many running times for various races, from half-miles to marathons. He was able to put many consecutive digits into running times; he would think of 3492 as "3 minutes and 49 point 2 seconds, near world-record mile time." After about two months of practice, Mr. Faloon began supplementing the running times with ages and dates. The digits 893 became "89 point 3, very old man," 1944 "near the end of World War II."

Our friend with the wonderful memory, VP, used methods somewhat similar to Mr. Faloon's to increase his memory span. When originally tested, VP's immediate memory span was nine digits—high, but no higher than that of many college students. Given the task of trying to increase his memory span, he did so, reaching a span of seventeen numbers in just five trials. When asked how he accomplished this, he said that he (1) paid strict attention to the number of digits to be expected on each trial; (2) grouped the digits in sets of three and five, depending on their number; (3) decided his strategy of grouping before each trial; (4) made verbal associations to each group of numbers—weights, dates, anything he could think of; and (5) when he could, he made associations between groupings. Provided with these hints and given eleven trials of practice, a selected group of college students increased their span from nine to twelve digits.

Other Mnemonic Devices

Methods for improving memory, of which recoding or chunking is an example, are sometimes called **mnemonic devices** (Greek *mneme,* memory). As with recoding, most other mnemonic devices provide materials with some sort of organization. Usually they take advantage of some organizational structure already in memory and let it provide a way of grouping an unfamiliar set of items.

The Method of Loci. Some of these mnemonic devices have an ancient pedigree. One of them, the **method of loci** (*loci,* plural of Latin *locus,* place) was the means by which Simonides achieved perfect recall of all the guests at the banquet, in the tale of catastrophe with which this section began. Simonides was able to retrace in his mind's eye the seating of the guests at the long tables in the banquet hall. The seating arrangement provided a spatial structure wherein he could remember the guests. Any familiar spacial structure or setting can be used to help you remember a number of items. Take a mental tour of some area you know well and imagine the things you need to remember located at various places (loci) in this setting. For example, you might imagine that you are walking from home to campus. Now suppose that you have a set of things to remember, perhaps a shopping list consisting of hot dogs, cat food, tomatoes, bananas, and whiskey. The method of loci requires you to place each item to be remembered at some definite location on your mental tour, and to form a vivid image of the item in its spot.

Your route from home to campus might pass a picket fence, a huge tree, the

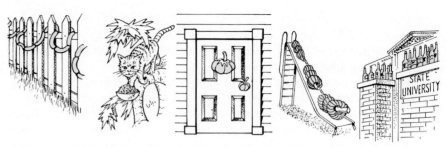

Figure 6.21
The method of loci. Putting images of items to be remembered at various places in a recalled scene would be an effective way to remember a grocery list.

entrance to an elegant house now used as a doctor's office, a children's park with a slide, and the main entrance to the college, marked by pillars on either side. Using the method of loci to memorize the shopping list, you might imagine long chains of hot dog links topping the fence, a cat eating cat food in the tree, tomatoes replacing the door knocker and doorknob on the elegant house, a parade of bananas sliding in bunches down the slide, and bottles of whiskey lined up on the pillars at the campus gate (Figure 6.21). Once you have committed your shopping list to memory in this way, you have only to take your mental walk again to remember the items in order. A common recommendation is to develop bizarre associations, but this is not necessary. The method of loci, by its very nature, however, will often have you imagining objects in places where it would be very unusual for them to appear.

Experiments have shown the method of loci to be quite effective. In one study students associated lists of forty unrelated concrete nouns with forty locations on campus, taking thirteen seconds to form each association. Tested immediately, the students remembered an average of thirty-eight of the forty items. A day later they still remembered thirty-four (Ross and Lawrence, 1968). Obviously these averages are so high that for many individuals recall must have been perfect. Such excellent recall depends on three important factors: using a previously mastered organization, taking a fairly long time to deal with each item, and making an effective use of imagery. Again, the images formed need not be weird or bizarre, as one sometimes hears, but it may be important to think of images in which the items to be remembered interact with the places where they are stored for retrieval. For example, the bananas should slide down the slide, not just lie there beside it.

Numerical Pegs.   You probably already know the following little series rhyming numbers and objects, or one something like it.

One is a bun,	six is sticks,
two is a shoe,	seven is heaven,
three is a tree,	eight is a gate,
four is a door,	nine is a line, and
five is a hive,	ten is a hen.

Such a series can become a mnemonic device. The procedure is not unlike that employed in the method of loci. As each to-be-remembered item is presented, the individual forms an image that relates it to the corresponding object in the series. If the list of objects consists of an ashtray, firewood, and a football, he or she might imagine an ashtray as the filling for a sandwich, made with a bun (one), a huge shoe (two) filled with firewood, a football lodged in a tree (three), and so on. The method works. Individuals after just one presentation can usually remember every item, sometimes to their surprise.

Narrative Stories. Another very effective mnemonic device is to put items that are to be remembered into a story form. In an experiment which makes this point very impressively (Bower and Clark, 1969), students learned twelve different lists of ten simple, unrelated words. Students in an experimental group put the lists into the story form. The second group was a **yoked control group.** Each member studied the words for the amount of time a partner in the experimental group needed to make up stories. Instructions to the members of the experimental group were as follows.

> A good way to learn a list of items is to make up a story relating the items to one another. Specifically, start with the first item and put it in a setting which will allow other items to be added to it. Then, add the other items to the story in the same order as the items appear. Make each [of the twelve stories] meaningful to yourself. Then, when you are asked to recall the items, you can simply go through your story and pull out the proper items in the correct order.

Three typical stories appear in Table 6.5

The results of the experiment can be stated quickly. On recall tests that were given immediately after each list was learned, there was no difference between the two groups; both remembered over 99 percent of the words. After all twelve lists had been memorized, however, the students who made up stories remembered 93 percent of the words in the correct order; the students in the control group remembered only 13 percent.

One explanation for this difference readily suggests itself. Learning twelve lists of words puts the individual into a situation in which retroactive inhibition and proactive inhibition would create powerful interference. The creation of a story made it possible to keep the lists separate and prevent the accumulation of retroactive and proactive inhibition. Moreover, stories tend to call up images which aid memory, as demonstrated by the clothes-washing example cited earlier.

Finally, making up stories applies elaborate processing to the words in the list. The stories created by the students accomplished the same thing as the elaborate sentences used by Craik and Tulving to improve recall for words. The relevance of this point to study, that you must engage yourself in it, is worth emphasizing. Whenever you find yourself "just reading words" as you study, your processing is superficial. The time has come to take a break, start over, and read for meaning.

Individual Differences

We come now to a point from which some of you will take comfort. For, as

Table 6.5 Narrative Stories

A LUMBERJACK DARTed out of the forest, SKATEd around a HEDGE past a COLONY of DUCKs. He tripped on some FURNITURE, tearing his STOCKING, while hastening toward the PILLOW where his MISTRESS lay.

A VEGETABLE can be a useful INSTRUMENT for a COLLEGE student. A carrot can be a NAIL for your FENCE or BASIN. But a MERCHANT of the QUEEN would SCALE that fence and feed the carrot to the GOAT.

One night at DINNER I had the NERVE to bring my TEACHER. There had been a FLOOD that day, and the rain BARREL was sure to RATTLE. There was, however, a VESSEL in the HARBOR carrying this ARTIST to my CASTLE.

From Bower and Clark, 1969.

with all psychological processes, there are great individual differences in what makes for effective memorization. There are those, for example, for whom visual images are a mystery. These people claim not to have them and therefore cannot use them as an aid to learning. One such individual was VP, who was not much of a visualizer and did not depend heavily on images. He was very sensitive to linguistic similarities and made extensive use of semantic groupings, even when tested for recall of pictures.

VP believed that the development of a memory as powerful as his begins early and depends on being placed in situations in which memorizing facts rather than manipulating them is the prized performance. For this reason he said that excellent memorizers are likely to be rather passive people, who are willing to abide by the "rules of the game." When these rules are to memorize, they do so without rebellion. Since current education places more emphasis on interpretation than memorization, VP believed that the number of people like himself may be decreasing. A willingness to work hard at memorizing is also essential. Whenever possible, VP would devote more time and effort to memorizing than most people. Another of VP's skills was a great ability to note details quickly. In VP's case this aptitude was particularly conspicuous with respect to semantic details.

SUMMARY

The study of human information processing has progressed to the point that we understand a fair amount and can make modest recommendations about how to develop an effective memory. Our recommendations have much more to do with learning or storage than with memory or retrieval. As a point of departure, we called attention to the fact that the feeling of knowing some set of materials is usually accurate, but that it is not always entirely so. This is the origin of some of the problems students have with study. Setting the criteria for knowing too low, they have a feeling of knowing when materials are less than completely mastered.

Among the procedures that may help correct this error is overlearning, which puts the materials to be learned more firmly into memory and, furthermore, improves the way that they are subjectively organized for recall. Overlearning also tends to make responses automatic.

The so-called mnemonic devices employ artificial but familiar forms of organization. The simplest procedure is to group or "chunk" materials. This reduces the number of elements so that they are within the span of immediate memory. More elaborate mnemonic aids include the method of loci, imagining items to be recalled in familiar places; the method of numerical pegs, imagining items in relation to the elements provided by the little rhyme that begins, "One is a bun"; and the method of narrative stories, creating a story to connect the items to be remembered. In all these methods imagery as well as organization contributes to superior recall. A narrative story also puts items through deep or elaborate processing, known from laboratory studies to improve recall.

We end with an escape clause: there are huge individual differences in what makes for effective memory. Students will need to shop around among these recommendations, selecting those that suit their individual talents best.

Here are the principal concepts presented in this chapter. You should be able to define them and state the points made about each in the text discussion.

Information-processing theory	**Accessibility of memory**
Stages of memory	**Dual-coding theory**
Control process	**Episodic memory**
Sensory memory	**Semantic memory**
Attention	**Encoding specificity principle**
Cocktail party phenomenon	**State-dependent learning**
Dichotic listening experiment	**Recall test**
Shadowing	**Recognition test**
Short-term memory	**Retroactive inhibition**
Free recall	**Proactive inhibition**
Serial position function	**Flashbulb memory**
Primacy effect	**Overlearning**
Recency effect	**Subjective organization**
Memory span	**Automatization**
Encode	**Mnemonic device**
Long-term memory	**Recoding**
Maintenance rehearsal	**Chunking**
Elaborative rehearsal	**Method of loci**
Level of processing	**Numerical pegs**
Retrieval	**Narrative story**
Tip-of-the-tongue phenomenon	**Yoked control group**
Availability of memory	

TO GO BEYOND THIS CHAPTER

In This Book. This chapter is a fairly self-contained unit. The most closely related materials are to be found in Chapter 5, on perception; Chapter 7, on language and problem solving; and Chapter 11, on cognitive development. The ties are not extremely close, however.

Elsewhere. Dozens of books covering information processing and memory have come out in the last ten years. Some that you may find particularly useful are the following: *Memory and Cognition,* by Walter Kintsch; *Human Memory: Structures and Processes,* by Roberta Klatzky; *Human Memory: The Processing of Information,* by Geoffrey and Elizabeth Loftus; and *Memory and Attention: An Introduction to Human Information Processing* (second edition), by Donald Norman.

CHAPTER 7   LANGUAGE, THOUGHT, AND PROBLEM SOLVING

We sometimes hear that language is the principal thing distinguishing the human organism from lower forms of life. However that may be, there is no doubt that our linguistic talents are truly impressive. Consider, for example, the following passage from *Alice in Wonderland,* by Lewis Caroll. The speakers in this conversation are Alice and the Knight.

"The name of the song is called 'Haddocks' Eyes.'"

"Oh, that's the name of the song, is it?" Alice said, trying to feel interested.

"No, you don't understand," the Knight said, looking a little vexed. "That's what the name is *called.* The name really is, 'The Aged Aged Man.'"

"Then I ought to have said 'That's what the *song* is called'?" Alice corrected herself.

"No, you oughtn't: that's quite another thing! The *song* is called 'Ways and Means': but that's only what it's called, you know!"

"Well, what is the song, then?" said Alice, who was by this time completely bewildered.

"I was coming to that," the Knight said. "The song really is 'A-sitting on A Gate': and the tune's my own invention."

To follow the subtleties of this conversation requires remarkable **linguistic competence,** that is, an understanding of how the language operates. Very few of us could put into words the nature of this understanding. We sense how language works without being consciously aware of all its devices. The existence of such knowledge is what makes the study of language appropriate to psychology. **Linguistics** is the study of language as language; the study of the psychological aspects of language is the relatively new field of **psycholinguistics.**

Language as a Set of Rules.   Although most of us could not describe them, sets of rules govern every aspect of our linguistic endeavors. These rules cover language at different levels of complexity.

Some of them are rules of **phonology,** which has to do with the units of sound that make up the stream of speech. For example, only particular sounds can be combined in making words. The rules differ somewhat for different languages. In English *trick* is a word. *Twick* is not but it could be, because *tw* is an acceptable phonological combination. In fact, some children who have not yet learned to pronounce *trick* find *twick* a simpler substitute. *Tbick* is not a word in English because the phonological rules do not allow the *tb* combination at the beginnings of words. (But compare *basketball.*) Although the phonological rules are fairly standard in a given language, they are not absolute.

For example, *sr* is a prohibited initial combination in English, but in some part of America the natives plant *srubs;* elsewhere they eat *srimp.*

Other rules are rules of **syntax.** They cover the ways in which words may be combined into phrases, clauses, and sentences that convey meaning. As an illustration, the improbable "Colorless green ideas sleep furiously" is a sentence in a way that "Furiously sleep ideas green colorless" is not (Chomsky, 1957). The first string of words obeys the rules that dictate the locations of adjectives, nouns, verbs, and adverbs in a sentence, but the order of the second string of words is completely haphazard. Words must be put into a sequence that indicates their mutual relations, and syntax is this ordering.

Another set of rules are supplied by **semantics.** These are the rules by which we put meaning into our own utterances and extract it from the utterances of someone else. An understanding of these rules allows us to recognize that a single syntactic form may carry a variety of meanings. Consider, for example, the following ambiguous headline in the *Durham Sun* for March 16, 1983.

SUSPICIOUS PERSON REPORTS SKYROCKET IN CHAPEL HILL

What does this announcement mean? Decide before you read on. Does the headline tell us that someone who suspected that a skyrocket had no business being in Chapel Hill reported seeing one? Or did that a person with a history of strange behavior report seeing a skyrocket? As it turns out, neither of these two obvious interpretations is correct. The headline actually means that, after a series of sexual assaults in the area, the number of reports of suspicious people seen in Chapel Hill has increased dramatically. Our knowledge of semantics lets us know that all these meanings are possible. The same understanding tells us that "They are eating apples" has one meaning as an answer to the question, "What are they doing?" and quite another in answer to "Are those apples better for cooking or for eating?"

Finally, some rules are rules of **pragmatics.** They describe the use of language in a social context, such as the fact that speakers take turns when carrying on a conversation. They also take the situation into account. The same language may mean quite different things in different circumstances. When your professor tells you that your grade in his course is a C and you say "Thanks a lot!" the inflection in your voice will indicate gratitude if you had expected a grade of F but something quite different if you had expected an A. When I say, "Can you open the window?" I probably mean it literally ("Are you able to?") if we are trying to get back into a house after locking ourselves out. But if we are inside and the room is hot, I may really mean, "Will you please open the window to cool the room off?" When you tell me that your head is spinning, you may mean, depending on the situation, that you are dizzy from a car trip on a winding mountain road, that you have consumed more of some intoxicant than you should have, or that you have had just about all the psychology of language that you can handle.

LANGUAGE COMPREHENSION

When you talk to someone on the telephone, you recognize that the speech you hear is distorted. In spite of this, it is possible to understand the person to whom you are talking. You can distinguish people by their voices and tell how they react to what you say. This is really quite remarkable because the auditory signal you interpret is very much different from the one that would be heard in face-to-face conversation. Studies have shown that as much as half the

/bɛ/

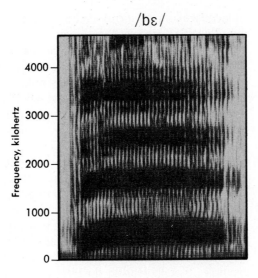

Figure 7.1
Sound spectrogram. The energies for
most speech sounds, more particularly for
their vowels, are concentrated in four
clear concentrations. The darkness of the
band reflects the intensity of that pitch in
the speech sound. The ɛ in "bet" has
four heavy concentrations of energy at
500, 1500, 2500, and 3500 kHz.

physical stimulus can be filtered out of a message without seriously degrading
its intelligibility. This means that nonacoustic, psychologically meaningful factors
must contribute to speech perception. We shall consider what these factors
might be after we have discussed the elementary speech sounds.

Physical Attributes of Speech Sounds

From our discussion of auditory stimuli, you already know that *every complex
sound is constructed of a set of tones and overtones that vary in numbers and
intensity.* The composition of any sound can be represented in several ways.
The sound spectrogram is a common way of representing the sounds that make
up speech. The horizontal axis of Figure 7.1 covers the brief time, about 0.3
second, required to say the syllable "bɛ," as in bet. The vertical axis covers the
range of frequencies, in kilohertz, making up the syllable. The darker the
smudged bar for a particular frequency, the greater the intensity of the tone at
that frequency.

The auditory signals for the syllable "bɛ" consists of a pattern of energies
changing in time. The sound spectrogram for a longer utterance consists of
patterns (Figure 7.2) similar to the single one in Figure 7.1. Detailed study of
sound spectrograms reveals that the same person saying the same syllable on
different occasions produces slightly different patterns of sound. When different
speakers utter the same syllable, the recorded patterns vary even more. In fact,
these patterns are unique to individual voices. Just as fingerprints are a means

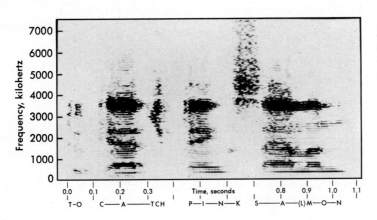

Figure 7.2
Sound spectrogram. The portions of the
spectrogram associated with the a's in
catch and salmon are quite similar. The
consonant sounds tch and s have higher
pitches than the other vowels and
consonants.

of identification, so too does the sound spectrogram serve as a sort of voice print by which to identify a speaker.

The fact that speech sounds can be analyzed so exactly means that the process can be reversed. With a sound spectrogram of an utterance available, a computer can be given this description and then programmed to operate sound equipment to reproduce speech. This is the basic nature of a speech synthesizer. The computer instructs the auditory equipment every few milliseconds to produce sounds made up of such and such frequencies in such and such relative intensities.

A speech synthesizer can reproduce speech fairly accurately but, perhaps more importantly, it can also modify sounds. It can speed speech up or slow it down. It can raise or lower the dominant pitch, thus speaking in a high voice or a low one. Being able to manipulate speech in such controlled ways allows us to determine the effects of these manipulations on how speech is perceived. Although data are sparse, those available indicate that rate and pitch of speech may affect our evaluation of a speaker's personality. One study found, for example, that increasing the rate of a man's speech made him seem less benevolent; decreasing the rate of speech made him seem less competent. When the pitch of the male's voice was raised, he was judged less benevolent and less competent (Brown, Strong, and Rencher, 1974). Newspaper reports have now begun to call attention to the fact that such manipulations might be used to influence voters' reactions to the recorded messages of candidates for political office or buyers' judgments of products being advertised on the radio.

From Sounds to Meanings

The simplest *functional* speech sounds in any language are called **phonemes.** They are the smallest units of sound that distinguish one utterance from another by signaling a difference in meaning. Phonemes have no meaning of their own, however; they must be combined with one another to make up meaningful words. Examples of phonemes are the "k" sound in *keep, cool, account, back,* and *liquor,* and the "t" sound in *atlas, gently, tulip,* and *fault.*

If you say the two words *keep* and *cool* and listen carefully as you do so, you will discover that the two "k" sounds are slightly different. You can also feel that the placement of your tongue is farther back in your mouth for the first than for the second. Considered just as physical events, the two "k" sounds are different *phones,* a phone being any individual and distinct speech sound, irrespective of how it fits into the structure of the language. The two "k"s are considered forms of the same phoneme, technically **allophones,** because the difference between them has no linguistic significance.

In Arabic things are different. The word for "dog," *kalb,* begins with the "k" as in *keep.* The word for "heart," *qalb,* begins with the "k" as in *cool.* Thus in Arabic the two "k"s are separate phonemes because they signal a difference in meaning. It is for exactly this same reason that /k/ and /r/ are different phonemes in English. In Arabic *kalb* and *qalb* are different in the same way that *keep* and *reap* and *cool* and *rule* are different in English (Glucksberg and Danks, 1975). The English language has approximately forty-five phonemes. Some languages use as few as twenty phonemes, others as many as sixty.

There is now strong evidence that phonemes have separate psychological reality. The nature of the evidence is as follows. With the aid of an electronic speech synthesizer, it is possible to control the physical composition of simple speechlike sounds very exactly. For example, the syllable "ba" can be altered in very gradual steps so that it becomes the syllable "pa." Through this set of small transforming steps, the phoneme /b/ becomes the phoneme /p/. The person listening, however, does not hear a gradual transformation. Instead, the syllable continues to sound like "ba" through a considerable range and then, more or less abruptly, shifts to "pa," which it continues to be through any additional small alterations (Eimas and Corbit, 1973). In short, the two phonemes /b/ and /p/ have a kind of integrity that permits them to be heard only in these terms and not as blends. Moreover, some evidence indicates that babies only one month old hear phonemes in the same categorical way (Eimas et al., 1971). The method employed in the experiment from which this conclusion was drawn was the habituation method, the one used in the experiment suggesting that babies perceive the same primary colors that adults do (page 161).

The simplest semantic units of language, that is, the smallest bits of sound carrying meaning, are called **morphemes.** Whereas phonemes are single speech sounds signaling meaning, morphemes are the smallest combinations of speech sounds possessing meaning. Morphemes are words and meaningful segments of words. Thus *pill* and *bill* are morphemes, as are *pillow* and *billow,* because none of them can be analyzed into simpler meaningful units. *Pills* and *pillows* both contain two morphemes, *pill* and *pillow,* and the final pluralizing "s." Other multimorpheme words are mark/s, mark/ed, mark/ing, mark/er, un/mark/ed, mark/er/s, and re/mark/able. Root words like *pill, mark,* and *dream* are referred to as **free morphemes,** because they can occur alone. Inflections that make a noun plural and indicate that the activity of the verb is ongoing or finished; prefixes such as un- and re- indicating the negative and "again," and suffixes such as -er and -able signifying agent and ability are called **bound morphemes.** They cannot stand alone and must be bound to free morphemes. Bound morphemes add to or change the meaning of the free morphemes to which they are attached.

Syntax

The rules of syntax govern the arrangement of elements to produce larger linguistic structures. For psychology the most important of these are the rules of grammar. As we learned them (and learned to hate them) in grade school, the rules of grammar tell us how sentences *must* be constructed. In the psychology of language, these rules tell us something slightly different, how sentences *are* constructed. Sentences are made up of phrases and subphrases which, in turn, are combinations of words. A phrase is a set of words that represents a single idea. The sentence "The dog buried the bone" consists of two major phrases, the noun phrase "The dog" and the verb phrase "buried the bone." The verb phrase further divides into "buried" and "the bone." The phrase "the bone" is a unit as "buried the" is not, for the single word "it" can be substituted for "the bone," but there is no similar substitute for "buried the." Groups of words that have a conceptual unity, that serve a single function in a sentence and can be replaced by one word, are called constituent structures or simply constituents.

The constituent structures of a sentence can be represented in a diagram which indicates its hierarchical organization. The diagram begins by dividing the sentence into its noun phrase and verb phrase.

The analysis of sentences into constituents is a linguistic analysis. An important question to ask is whether the constituents of a sentence also have psychological meaning. The answer from a number of studies is that they do. In a representative investigation Richard Graf and Jane Torrey (1966) broke the same materials up into lines in the two ways illustrated by the following sentence.

During World War II,	During World War
even fantastic schemes	II, even fantastic
received consideration	schemes received
if they gave promise	consideration if
of shortening the conflict	they gave
	promise of shorten-
	ing the conflict

The lines in the left-hand version correspond to constituents of the sentence. In the right-hand version they do not. In the experiment a machine exposed each line for a very short time. One group of participants read the passage broken into constituents, the other group the randomly broken passage, and immediately took a multiple-choice test of comprehension. The subjects who read the passage given in constituent form did better on the test.

Semantics

The primary function of language is a semantic function, to convey meanings. Studies of what words mean, the earliest semantic studies conducted in psychology, have indicated that it is useful to consider several types of meaning, denotative, associative, and connotative.

Denotative Meaning.   The **denotative meaning** of a word is the thing, event, or relationship that a word stands for or refers to. Hence it is also called referential meaning. Denotative meaning sometimes seems pretty arbitrary.

"When I use a word," Humpty Dumpty said, in a rather scornful tone, "it means what I choose it to mean—neither more nor less."

"The question is," said Alice, "whether you can make words mean so many different things."

"The question is," said Humpty Dumpty, "which is to be master—that's all." Alice was too puzzled to say anything. . . .

Humpty Dumpty was mostly correct in his observation. As a rule the meaning of a word is arbitrary. Occasionally, however, a connection between the sound of a word and its meaning makes the meaning less than completely arbitrary. In an important early book on psycholinguistics, Roger Brown (1959) dealt with this point as **phonetic symbolism,** the term he chose to express the idea that the sounds of words sometimes reflect attributes of the objects to which they refer. To illustrate, if speakers of English are told that one of the two objects in Figure 7.3 is a "takete" and that the other is a "maluma," they generally agree that the first is a "maluma" and the second a "takete." Other studies have tested the ability of subjects to choose the correct translation of words in languages with which they are unfamiliar. These studies indicate that subjects tend to agree on appropriate translations, and that the agreed-upon translation is correct much more often than not. For example, if English-speaking people are told that the two Chinese words *ch'ing* and *ch'ung* refer to our two concepts "heavy" and "light" and are asked to guess which is which, they will usually offer the correct translations, *ch'ing*—light; and *ch'ung*—heavy. At a more informal level, Brown points out that there could hardly be a better onomatopoeic rendition of the sound of water splashing back and forth in a flask than the German word *geschleudert,* that the very structure of the English word *God,*

Figure 7.3
Phonetic symbolism. Which is a "takete" and which a "maluma"? (After Köhler, 1925.)

or even better of *Jehovah* and *Gawd,* implies enormity, and that *tweeter* and *woofer* in hi-fi terminology suggest the functions of such speakers.

Associative Meaning. Words may call up associations with considerable speed and in considerable numbers, or they may not. If we are asked to respond to "house" as rapidly as we can with as many associations as possible, we will come up with "home" quickly and easily move on to "family," "school," "live," "window," and so on, giving a substantial number of associations to "house." For "zuren," which is not even a word, we may need a full five seconds to think of "zebra" or some other word, probably one beginning with *z*, then draw an utter blank. Both the number of associations and the speed with which they are given have been used as measures of the meaningfulness of words in this sense of having **associative meaning.**

For example, Clyde Noble (1952) chose as a measure of meaningfulness the average number of associations people could make in one minute. He used two-syllable words that varied all the way from the very familiar "kitchen" to nonwords like "gojey." A few of his words, together with the average number of associations made to them, were kitchen, 9.61; uncle, 6.57; sequence, 3.21; flotsam, 2.19; polef, 1.30; gojey, 0.99. The associative meaningfulness of words is an important factor determining the ease with which they are committed to memory. Lists and highly meaningful words are easy to learn. List of words with few associations are difficult (Figure 7.4).

Connotative Meaning. The simple listing of such terms as *poverty, freedom, nasty, elegant, slipshod,* and *success* will serve to make the point that words differ tremendously in the emotions and judgments they evoke. Charles Osgood and his associates have provided a method for measuring differences in connotations, the **semantic differential.** Subjects are asked to rate a series of verbal concepts that could be almost anything—for example, *polite, eager, burning, lady, Russian.* The scales on which they are rated, usually twenty to fifty of them, consist of two polar adjectives connected by a line divided into seven positions from left to right. The subject decides whether the concept is near one or the other of the pair of contrasting adjectives in its connotations and chooses one of the seven positions to indicate how close the word falls to one end of the scale or the other. The average placements of two concepts, *polite* and *burning,* on ten such scales are indicated in Figure 7.5. Both concepts were regarded as neutral on the angular-rounded scale, and both were rated relatively strong and active. On the other hand, the concept *polite* is midway on the cold-hot scale, *burning* near the hot end. *Polite* is rated as relatively good, whereas *burning* is rated as relatively bad. On the wet-dry scale, *polite*

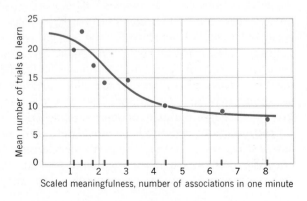

Figure 7.4
Learning and associative meaningfulness. Meaningfulness was measured by Noble's procedure. Learning was measured by the number of trials to master the list. The smooth curve is typical of the function obtained in several studies.

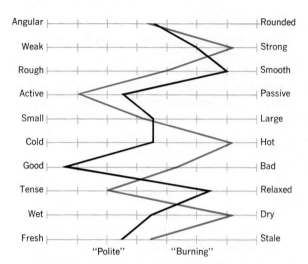

Figure 7.5

Semantic-differential profiles. The figure shows the placement of "polite" and "burning" on ten semantic-differential scales. (Adapted from Osgood and Suci, 1955.)

is neutral and *burning* relatively dry. Comparisons of the profiles for different words provide a picture of how concepts vary in their connotations. From an analysis of a large number of concepts rated by many subjects on many different scales of contrasting adjectives, Osgood and his associates concluded that the **connotative meaning** of a word can be specified by its position on three summary dimensions. They are *evaluation,* the good-bad dimension; *potency,* the strong-weak dimension, and *activity,* the active-passive dimension. A word like *terror* would be bad on the evaluation dimension, strong on the potency dimension, and active on the activity dimension. *Contentment* might be good, weak, and passive.

SUMMARY

Psycholinguistics, the psychology of language, is a study that goes on at several levels. At the most basic of these levels, it describes the nature of elementary speech sounds called phonemes and how they combine to form words. At the level of syntax it deals with the rules by which words combine to form phrases and sentences. Semantics is the study of meaning. Pragmatics concerns the use of language in real situations by real speakers and listeners.

Evidence suggests that we have an unconscious understanding of the linguistic rules that apply at each of these levels. Thus at the level of speech sounds we understand that shamble *and* scamble *could both be English words (both are) but that* sgamble *could not. At the level of syntax we know that "Mary hit John" is an acceptable sentence but "Hit Mary John" is not. At the level of semantics we can find out that the denotative meaning of* scamble *is "to struggle greedily for something," then guess that an associated word might be* scramble, *and that its connotations might place it at the bad end of the evaluative scale, the active end of the activity scale, and the strong end of the potency scale on the semantic differential. Still at the level of semantics we know that "Mary hit John" and "John was hit by Mary" mean the same thing, but that "John hit Mary" means something different. At the level of pragmatics we know, as William James once said, that it is one thing to step on a man's toe and apologize but quite another to apologize and then step on his toe.*

Psycholinguistic analyses have provided us with information that has psychological significance. The phonological characteristics of a person's speech affect our judgments of personality. Phonemes, the basic units of sound that signal differences in meaning, are perceived that way, categorically, as separate units of sound. Syntactic analyses of sentences divide them into constituents or units. Text arranged in short lines corresponding to these units is easier to understand than text that is not. The familiarity and meaningfulness of language, as revealed by semantics, affect its comprehension and the ease with which it is learned and recalled.

ANIMAL COMMUNICATION

It is clear that animals of many species communicate. They announce the location of food, state their claims on territory, proclaim a condition of sexual arousal, indicate their recognition of an acquaintance, and perhaps even reassure with sociability.

The "Language" of the Bees

One of the most carefully worked out descriptions of animal communication is that of the foraging bee. Karl von Frisch (1950), the great Austrian naturalist, had concluded that bees must be able to communicate, for when one bee found a supply of food and then departed, others from the same hive soon arrived in hordes. To find out how they communicated, von Frisch constructed a special hive that made it possible to observe the behavior of the bees directly.

Patient observation eventually revealed that a bee returning to the hive after discovering a new source of food can communicate its closeness at hand by a simple but vigorous circling dance, or the food's distance away and its direction from the hive with a more complicated sequence of straight runs, loops, and abdomen wagging. The platform on which the dance is performed is usually the vertical surface of a honeycomb within the hive. When the food is more than 150 yards away, the scout bee first runs in a straight line for a short distance, wagging its abdomen from side to side. Then it takes a semicircular loop in the clockwise direction, again makes the straight-line, abdomen-wagging run, now loops again, this time counterclockwise. And so on.

The angle of the straight-line run from the vertical communicates the direction of the food with respect to the sun. If the bees must fly with the sun 30 degrees to their left, the straight-line run of the bee scout points to about one o'clock. To indicate greater distance of the food from the hive, the bee dances ever more slowly. It makes a turn *every* second and a half when the food is a hundred meters away, every three seconds when the food source is a thousand meters distant.

Interestingly, the scout bee performs its remarkable feat in complete darkness and can dance its information about as well on a cloudy day as a clear one. Polarized light from the sky apparently indicates to the bee the correct location of the sun. And the bee's companions in the hive, receiving the information provided by touch—for they feel the dancing movements of the scout with their antennas—are able to find their way to a food source as many as three and a half miles away (Figure 7.6).

Communication of Primates

The number of vocalizations made by our fellow primates for purposes of communication is quite large. As many as thirty-two vocalizations of the chimpanzee can be distinguished. Apparently these sounds are uttered to express temporary emotional states, and other chimpanzees respond appropriately. The vocalizations evoked by social contact or made in an attempt to establish it are distinctive. So are vocalizations that express fright or assert superiority, that

Figure 7.6
The language of the bees. The direction of the dance indicates the direction, with respect to the sun, in which nectar can be found; the speed communicates distance.

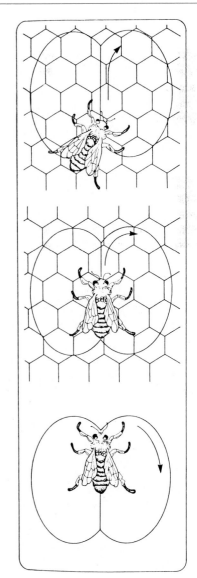

complain about isolation, strangeness, and suddenness, that herald aggression against hostile companions. There are also pained cries of frustration and the urgent calls for mating.

There is even evidence that monkeys use a low-level type of semantics in their communications. Although groups of vervet monkeys studied in Kenya fail to react with alarm to over a hundred species of mammals, birds, and reptiles that are common in their forests, they do make alarm calls when predators appear. Moreover, these calls are different for different threats. The alarm calls for leopards were short, tonal calls, usually made in a series on both exhalation and inhalation. The alarms for eagles were low-pitched, staccato grunts, and those for snakes were high-pitched "chutters." The animals being warned responded differently to the different calls. The leopard alarm caused them to run up into trees; eagle alarms caused them to look up, run into dense cover, or both; snake alarms made them look down at the ground around them. Even infant monkeys made these alarm calls but, as is generally the case with infantile responses, they were less differentiated. Baby monkeys gave the leopard alarm to many terrestrial mammals, the eagle alarm to birds in general, and the snake alarm to snakes or long, thin objects (Seyfarth, Cheney, and Marler, 1980).

Attempts To Teach Language to Chimpanzees.   Such information raises questions about the potential limits of communication in lower animals and specifically whether they might be able to acquire human language. In studies directly relevant to this question, a number of investigators have raised chimpanzees in their own homes, providing them with as close an approximation of a human environment as they could. Two well-known earlier studies were those of Winthrop and Luella Kellogg (1933) and Cathy and Keith Hayes (1951). Both couples made an effort to determine whether the chimpanzee could develop human speech. The baby chimpanzee Gua, raised along with the Kelloggs' infant son Donald, learned to understand some commands but never uttered any English words. The chimpanzee Viki, raised by the Hayeses, did learn to produce three recognizable words—"papa," "mama," and "cup"—but only with great difficulty and after very patient training, which included manipulating her lips directly. The failure of these studies led psychologists to conclude that chimpanzees must lack some part of the physiological equipment required to develop speech. Either the chimpanzee's vocal apparatus was inadequate or the deficiency was in the animal's brain.

More recent attempts to teach language to a chimpanzee have begun with the assumptions that the problem at least in part is the inability of the animals to control lips and tongue and that the chimpanzee does have the potential for true language. The psychologists have therefore sought ways to circumvent the need for vocalization.

David Premack, working first with a young chimpanzee named Sarah and later with three others, used as "words" variously shaped symbols cut out of colored plastics (Figure 7.7). The animals could "write" by placing the metal-backed symbols on a magnetized board. With practice they learned the meaning of a hundred symbols or more and were able to put them together in particular orders that resembled sentences. In the following examples the parentheses enclose the words denoted by each symbol.

"(Apple) (name of) [picture of apple]"
"(Mary) (insert) (banana) (bowl)"
"(Square) (not) (shape of) (banana)"
"(Red) (color of) (apple)"
"(Sarah) (drop) (glass) (if then) (glass) (break)"

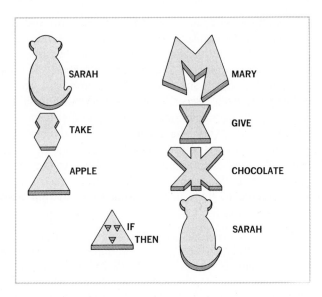

Figure 7.7
Sarah's vocabulary. This figure shows a few of Sarah's "words" as she arranged them to form a complex sentence. (Adapted from Premack, 1972.)

The identification of symbols with words and ideas and the construction of such sentences indicate that chimpanzees are capable of learning fairly sophisticated concepts—agency, color, shape, questioning, if then. Sarah also learned correct word order. It is questionable whether she actually learned syntactical rules, however, for she only constructed sentences that had already been shown her. Never on her own did she put new words in old orders, so to speak. Even so, her accomplishment was far more impressive than any chimpanzee's verbal behavior previously described (Premack, 1976).

In the meantime, Allen and Beatrice Gardner were taking a different approach to the problem. They began to teach American Sign Language, or Ameslan, used by many deaf people in North America, to a chimpanzee named Washoe (Figure 7.8). Washoe lived in a trailer in the Gardners' backyard and had the companionship of one, sometimes two, people during all her waking hours. They took care of her and played with her, signing to Washoe and to each other, but no one ever spoke in Washoe's presence. She was taught some signs by physically placing her hands in the desired position, some through imitation.

Figure 7.8
Washoe being shown a picture and then making the sign for "cat."

Sue Savage-Rumbaugh and Duane Rumbaugh believe that their chimpanzees Sherman and Austin were the first nonhuman primates to communicate with each other by symbols.

In a little over four years, Washoe had mastered 132 signs (Table 7.1) and had learned to combine some of them in sentences, such as "Please tickle more," and "You me go out there hurry." Washoe often seemed to chat with herself. When looking at pictures in magazines, she apparently enjoyed making the signs for objects she saw, and sometimes she signed "Hurry" as she rushed to her potty chair. Occasionally she also put two signs together as though she were attempting to describe a new object that way, for example, calling a swan a "water bird," when she saw one in a pond.

Finally, Duane Rumbaugh and his colleagues, working first with Lana and later with two other chimpanzees, Sherman and Austin, have taught these primates to do their communicating with the aid of a computer, which responds appropriately to their needs. Rumbaugh and his associates (1974) describe Lana's situation this way.

> For Lana, the world is a plastic cube, seven feet in each dimension. Her interactions with and adaptations to this unnatural plastic niche concentrate upon use of keyboard console that now holds 75 keys. On each key there is a geometric configuration or *lexigram* that represents a specific word. . . . As the locations of the keys are altered from time to time, Lana cannot rely upon the position of a key to define its functions or word meaning. She must attend to the lexigram on the keys to find her way to successful linguistic expressions. . . . Whenever the keys are randomly reassigned to the console, Lana's visual search for the locations of the word keys . . . becomes pronounced, but the search is basically accurate.

Pressing these keys in a correct order instructs the computer to deliver a requested substance or service. Lana might, for example, send the message: PLEASE MACHINE GIVE LANA BANANA (or M & M) PERIOD or PLEASE MACHINE MAKE MOVIE (or MUSIC or WINDOW OPEN) PERIOD. The PLEASE and PERIOD instructions are necessary to inform the computer that the message is beginning or ending. Lana developed a vocabulary of several dozen items and, like Premack's chimpanzees, she acquired more abstract linguistic concepts such as "name of." Lana lived in a situation in which she had to rely more on her linguistic skills than the chimps in most studies. Rumbaugh and his colleagues have described how well she applied them.

Table 7.1 A Few of the Signs Used by Washoe

Sign	Usage
Come-gimme (1)	For a person or an animal to approach, and also for objects out of reach. Often combined: come tickle, gimme sweet.
Please (16)	Asking for objects and for activites. Frequently combined: please open, please flower. Also, when ordered to ask politely.
Cat (34)	For cats and for meowing.
Enough (71)	Spontaneously, when rejecting food at end of meal. At the end of other routine activites such as a bath or a drill session on signing, when asking, you finished?
Time (97)	Equivalent to the English word "now," as in time food, time tickle, time out.
Hot (warm) (115)	For hot objects such as furnace or electric heater, and for hot substances such as soup or meat.
Mirror (117)	For mirrors.

Selected from Gardner and Gardner, 1975. The number following each sign indicates its order of appearance in Washoe's repertory.

And probably most important of all, she has learned to use the system on a [twenty-four-hours-a-day] basis to get the good life. . . . we know, for example, that not infrequently she gets up during the night for a drink of water and entertains herself with slides and music in the early hours of the morning. Perhaps she's just a swinger at heart. She also seems to ask for the window to be opened when the first light of morning is sensed. And when there is something novel to view out-doors—lawn mowers, trucks, people on the lawn, etc.—the requests for the window to be opened come hot and heavy.

But Is It Language?   Those who question whether chimpanzees are using language are usually asking whether their speech is somehow the same as *human* language. Behind this question often lies a concern that, with the work of the Gardners, Premack, and Rumbaugh, yet another mark of human unique-ness and dignity has been taken from us. First there was Darwin, who turned us into animals, perhaps the most highly evolved animals, but animals none-theless. Next came Sigmund Freud, who took away our special status as rational beings and exposed the primitive sexual motives that drive our simplest actions. Then there was Burrhus Frederick Skinner, who robbed us of free will and left us powerless puppets manipulated by a history of reward and punishment. In a very influential book entitled *Beyond Freedom and Dignity* (1971), Skinner had argued that free will is just an illusion, that who we are, what we are, how we feel, and everything we think is determined—determined by the rewards and punishments we have received in the past. And now Sarah, Washoe, Lana, and company seem ready to tell us that there is nothing unique about our greatest talent, language. Are we to be diminished to the point that our only uniqueness is being the one creature who worries about such matters?

Lana's computerized world.

Certainly the "language" acquired by the chimpanzees has many of the qualities of human speech. (1) It makes sense. When Sarah says that an apple is red but a banana is not, she is correct. (2) The sentences created by the chimps show acceptable grammatical structure. Washoe, whose syntax is some-times erratic, uses the order "You tickle me," as opposed to "I tickle you," appropriately. (3) Washoe's utterances have a self-determined beginning and an end. At the end of a sentence she drops her hands. (4) Washoe (W) responds appropriately to the so-called "wh-" (who, what, where) questions, as indicated by the following exchanges with an experimenter (E) (Gardner and Gardner, 1975).

Question	Answer
E: Who you?	*W:* Me Washoe.
E: Who pretty?	*W:* Washoe.
E: Whose that?	*W:* Shoes yours.
E: Now what?	*W:* Time drink.
E: What you want?	*W:* You me out.

(5) Two chimpanzees will communicate with each other in the language taught them. After a considerable amount of training in simpler exchanges, the two chimpanzees Sherman and Austin learned to tell each other about the food available from a container, using the computer keyboard.

[But] could they also simply ask one another for food on the keyboard? To answer this, we gave only one animal a variety of foods and allowed the other animal to watch through the window between the rooms [in which they were separately housed]. The observing animal spontaneously used the keyboard to request food. We encouraged the second animal to observe this request and comply with it. We then reversed the roles, giving food to the other animal. Again the observer spontaneously used the keyboard to request food and the animal with the food was encouraged to comply. From this point on, the animals began to exchange

Nim Chimpsky, trained in Ameslan by Herbert Terrace, here signs "Joyce" to his student-teacher Joyce Butler, who is asking, "What?"

roles and comply with each other's requests. . . . The initial encouragement was necessary to facilitate the social behavior of giving, but was not needed to facilitate the use of symbols or the nature of the communication. . . . Accuracy ranged across sessions from 70 to 100 percent, depending upon the willingness of the animals to comply with each other's requests. In general, the lower-ranking animal, Austin, always complied with Sherman's requests. Sherman also complied with Austin's requests but needed more frequent encouragement to do so (Savage-Rumbaugh, Rumbaugh, and Boysen, 1978, pp. 643–644).

Although all this sounds a great deal like human verbal behavior, the language of the chimpanzee actually falls considerably short of human language, so much so that many critics question whether it deserves to be called language at all. There are several reasons for taking this dim view. (1) Recent work has created doubts that the chimpanzee uses even a simple grammar. A careful analysis of one chimpanzee's multiword signs indicates that they usually reduce to two and occasionally three words, and that the order is an imitation of the order used by a trainer (Terrace et al., 1979). (2) There is also reason to doubt that the chimpanzees put signs together in new, creative ways. The much-quoted example of Washoe's seeming to call a swan a "water bird" could represent nothing more than the independent giving of the signs for birds and water, both of which would have been appropriate to the situation. (3) Although the "languages" taught to chimpanzees have provided them with at least some ability to handle abstractions, the skill imparted so far still falls short of the linguistic flexibility of human beings. As yet no chimps have developed the ability to use such concepts as *principle, justice,* or *abstraction.* (4) One distinctive feature of human language is what has been called its *self-reflexive* aspect: it can talk about itself. No chimpanzee, so far, has acquired the ability to use its language to speak about language. (5) Probably most important of all, the chimpanzee acquires language only with great difficulty. What the human child picks up naturally, quickly, and spontaneously takes years of patient tutoring of the chimp.

SUMMARY

All but the simplest animals communicate, which raises the question whether animals other than ourselves might develop something comparable to human language. Because of their evolutionary proximity, our fellow primates are the obvious animals of whom to ask this question. Attempts to teach chimpanzees human vocalization have always failed, but these same creatures communicate with considerable success by means of American Sign Language, plastic word forms, and symbols on a computer. The languages acquired so far by chimpanzees have many of the characteristics of human languages, but the chimpanzees' use of them falls short of human usage. Chimpanzee sentences have few if any self-generated, creative word combinations; syntax is very simple; there is little use of abstract conceptions, and the self-reflexive aspect of human language is lacking. Even the primitive languages that chimpanzees are able to acquire are very difficult for them to learn, which suggests that human beings must have a predisposition to learn language. There must be a biological basis for the development of linguistic competence.

ACQUIRING HUMAN LANGUAGE

The question of how children acquire language has intrigued scientists and laymen alike for centuries. Salimbene, a thirteenth-century monk and chronicler, wrote of his contemporary, Frederick II, king of Germany.

> He wanted to find out what kind of speech and what manner of speech children would have when they grew up if they spoke to no one beforehand. So he bade foster mothers and nurses to suckle the children, to bathe and wash them, but in no way to prattle to them, or to speak to them, for he wanted to learn whether they would speak the Hebrew language, which was the oldest, or Greek, or Latin, or Arabic, or perhaps the language of their parents, of whom they had been born. But he laboured in vain because the children all died. For they could not live without the petting and joyful faces and loving words of their foster mothers (quoted in Ross and McLaughlin, 1949, p. 366).

Only in recent years have there been many answers to the basic questions of what children acquire when they master a language and how they acquire it. The progress made has paralleled the new developments in psycholinguistics, developments which have called into question some commonsense "truths" in an earlier psychology of language.

The Traditional View

The traditional view of language acquisition is based on a number of assumptions which now appear either to be wrong or to be overstatements. These are that language is (1) learned (2) by direct experience, which includes the child's receiving (3) rewards and punishments as part of the learning process. Let us consider these points in order.

Learning. Since the language we acquire is that of our parents, the conclusion that learning is involved in language acquisition is inescapable. At the same time, however, there is a great deal of evidence that biological factors are important. As we mentioned earlier, phonemes may be innately recognizable, which suggests an inborn disposition to make certain of the perceptions that are basic to language acquisition. Moreover, children acquire language very rapidly between the ages of two and six, a period when brain development is rapid. This is a further indication that physiology is important.

Perhaps the strongest case for an innate disposition to learn language was presented by Eric Lenneberg (1967). He argued that the ability to produce and understand human language is an inherited, species-specific attribute based on a finely tuned vocal apparatus—the human larynx, mouth, and arrangement of teeth—specific brain centers for language, and an auditory system which processes speech sounds differently from other sounds. According to Lenneberg, language acquisition is tied to physiological maturation and requires only minimal exposure to examples of language. One line of evidence for this innate predisposition is that various aspects of language are acquired in a fixed order and at similar rates by children all around the world. When maturation is abnormally slow, as in the case of children with Down syndrome (see page 453), language is still acquired in the same stages but at a slower rate.

There also appears to be a critical period for the learning of a foreign language, which is another reason to believe that acquiring language is an innate, maturational ability. Learning a foreign language is easy before puberty. Children can become fluent in any language, or in several at once, with no special training. After puberty, however, learning a new language usually requires study, and individuals rarely achieve the fluency of a native speaker. Similarly, when brain damage disrupts speech in young children, they usually recover completely from their difficulties with language, but when brain damage occurs after puberty, the prognosis for recovery is not as good (Lenneberg, 1967).

By Direct Experience.   Learning theory once held that children acquire language by directly imitating the words, phrases, and sentences they hear, and then learning to combine and use them appropriately through reinforcement and generalization. There are several problems with this view. First of all, most of the speech we create or comprehend is new to us, and direct previous experience with new expressions is a contradiction in terms. Beyond that, it is easy to show that a lifetime would not be long enough to provide such experience. In a landmark paper that revolutionized the psychology of language, George A. Miller (1965) put the argument this way.

> By a rough, but conservative calculation there are 10^{20} sentences 20 words long, and if a child were to learn only these it would take him something on the order of 1,000 times the estimated age of the earth just to listen to them. . . . Any attempt to account for language acquisition that does not have a generative character will encounter this difficulty. . . .
>
> Since the variety of admissible word combinations is so great, no children could learn all of them. Instead of learning specific combinations of words, he learns rules for generating admissible combinations (pp. 176, 178).

Rewards and Punishment.   The principal point to be made against the view that children acquire language because their utterances are approved or disapproved is a factual one. Naturalistic studies have shown that parents use rewards and punishments not so much to establish correct language habits as to influence the content of their children's speech. They tend to reward statements that are factually accurate more than they do grammatical correctness. The following description of the verbalizations of two children, Adam and Eve, illustrates this point.

> Gross errors of words choice were sometimes corrected, as when Eve said, "What the guy idea." Once in a while an error of pronunciation was noticed and corrected. More commonly, however, the grounds on which an utterance was approved or

George Miller was one of several psychologists who in the early 1950s introduced linguistics into the psychological study of language. Thereafter the term psycholinguistics was applied to the research interests shared by linguists and psychologists.

disapproved . . . were not strictly linguistic at all. When Eve expressed the opinion that her mother was a girl by saying, "He a girl," mother answered, "That's right." The child's utterance was ungrammatical but the mother did not respond to that fact; instead she responded to the truth . . . of the proposition the child intended to express. . . . Adam's "Walt Disney comes on on Tuesday" was disapproved because Walt Disney came on on some other day. It seems then to be truth value rather than syntactic well-formedness that chiefly governs explicit verbal reinforcement by parents—which renders mildly paradoxical the fact that the usual product of such [training] is an adult whose speech is highly grammatical but not notably truthful (Brown, Cazden, and Bellugi, 1969, pp. 70–71).

Beyond this, there is evidence that the interventions of parents are not particularly effective if the child is not ready to move from one stage of linguistic development to a more advanced one.

Child: Nobody don't like me.
Mother: No, say "Nobody likes me."
Child: Nobody don't like me.
Eight repetitions of this dialogue.
Mother: No, now listen carefully; say "Nobody likes me."
Child: Oh! Nobody don't likes me (McNeill, 1966, p. 69)

The child has learned the rule that adding "don't" makes a statement negative but cannot yet absorb a new form, one in which "nobody" expresses negation and the rest of the sentence should remain declarative.

The New View
Most current theories recognize that both innate potential and experience contribute to language acquisition. Human beings are biologically prepared by nature to learn language, but exposure to expressed language is also necessary. In contrast to older views that children are passive learners of language, current theories recognize that children acquire language actively, formulating and testing hypotheses about the nature of the language they hear (Tagatz, 1976). Adults also have an important role in promoting children's language. But if, as we have seen, adults do not function chiefly as dispensers of rewards and punishments for children's verbal efforts, what do they do?

Adults of course provide children with a model of how language is spoken, but they do not talk to children in the same way that they talk to one another. Caretaker speech, often called "motherese," differs from adult speech in several ways.

Phonologically, it is higher in pitch than normal speech. Intonations are exaggerated. Caretakers speak slowly and distinctly and often repeat phrases. When children are very young, some words may be simplified to eliminate consonant sounds that are difficult for them—"mommy" for "mother" and "tummy" for "stomach."

Grammatically, motherese is also simplified. Sentences are short and have fewer tenses. Sometimes words and word endings are omitted, such as the articles "the," "a," and the plural and possessive "s" (Clark and Clark, 1977). The extreme form of motherese is "baby talk," a steady diet of which some believe may hinder rather than promote the child's facility with language.

Semantically, caretaker speech is concrete. It tends to be about the here and now and to avoid complex abstractions. The responsive caretaker chooses subjects at the child's level of comprehension and interest.

Pragmatically, motherese has the effect of helping the child learn to use language in socially proper ways. As we have already seen, caretakers reward

My, don't we look lively after our nap. Yes, dear. You've spent enough time in bed, haven't you? You want to see what the world is doing. What? It looks the same? You make your own fun, hon. You're showing me how strong you are, aren't you?

truthfulness in children's speech, and truthfulness is one of the pragmatic conventions. Another convention is that of taking turns in conversation. From the beginning caretakers emphasize this characteristic of conversation.

Mother: Hello. Give me a smile (gently pokes infant in the ribs).
Infant: (Yawns).
Mother: Sleepy are you? You woke up too early today.
Infant: (Opens fist).
Mother: (Touching infant's hand). What are you looking at? Can you see something?
Infant: (Grasps mother's finger).
Mother: Oh, that's what you wanted. In a friendly mood, then. Come on, give us a smile (Clark and Clark, 1977).

Although this "dialogue" is entirely one-sided as far as words spoken are concerned, the mother has treated anything that the child does as though it were a verbal "turn."

As children's language abilities increase, it is important that caretaker speech not remain so simplified that it hinders development. Adults usually vary their speech according to the age of the child, choosing a wider range of words and parts of speech as children get older (Phillips, 1973). A level of complexity just ahead of the child's seems to elicit attention the most effectively and to provide the greatest opportunity for learning (Shipley, Smith, and Gleitman, 1969).

The Chronology

Crying and Babbling.   At birth the infant has a limited repertoire of sounds. Vocalizations are little more than undifferentiated crying and perhaps a few grunts and gurgles. Within four to six weeks, noises that are not exactly cries are heard. They may well be of two general types—narrow, nasalized sounds of discomfort and relaxed, back-of-the-mouth sounds of comfort. This ability to express dissatisfaction and satisfaction appears to be an accident of the general muscular and physiological state of the tense and relaxed baby (Menyuk, 1971).

As sounds uttered by babies become more differentiated, those initially most prominent are vowels. Consonants gradually become more frequent as the baby begins to use consonant-vowel combinations and to repeat these syllables again and again. Some babblings resemble words—ma-ma-ma, choo-choo-choo, bye-bye-bye—but many do not—hey, hey, bup-bup-bup, erdah-erdah. The babblings of babies the world over are the same, whether or not these initial sounds will find their way into later speech. Eventually, at about nine months, babies whose language will be English start to lose their French nasals and German gutterals, largely because their parents do not make and cannot mimic them, and babies hear the sounds only from themselves.

As babbling continues, the baby begins to produce strings of sounds with patterns of stress and inflection that resemble the cadences of adult speech. At about the same time sounds that others interpret as words are heard with increasing frequency. If parental reinforcement is ever important in language development, it is at this stage. The attention and affection bestowed upon babies for producing wordlike vocalizations encourage the repetition of such sounds.

First Words.   The age at which babies speak their first words is difficult to determine because of this tie to babbling. Sixty weeks has been suggested as the average, but the range is considerable. Whatever the language of the child, the first words spoken are likely to contain the consonants p, t, b, m, and n, those for which the tongue is at the front of the mouth; and the vowels a and e, which come from the back of a relaxed mouth. Although the child has already made many of the other vowels and consonants when playing with sounds, the first-mastered words contain the sounds most easily formed.

The first words are likely to name animals, foods, and toys, to comment on things that have changed, moved, or disappeared, such as "Mamma" leaving the room, "Daddy" appearing at the door. The first action words are likely to be the prepositions that appear with verbs, such as "up" as in "Pick me up" or "down" as in "Put me down" (Nelson, 1973; Greenfield and Smith, 1976). During the six months following their first words, babies usually rather slowly add another fifty words to their vocabularies. After that the increase is rapid. Beginning sometime around the age of twenty-one months or so, the child's vocabulary increases at a rate of more than a word a day, probably because of a developing sense of the usefulness of language. At any age children's **passive vocabularies,** the number of words they understand, is much greater than their **active vocabularies,** the number of words they use (Figure 7.9).

Children's first words may function as complete sentences. Depending on how and when it is uttered and with what gestures, "Doggy" may be a simple declarative—"It is a doggy"; or a demand—"I want the doggy"; or a question— "Doggy, where are you?" Spectrographic analyses have shown that babies inflect these simple word sentences, called holophrases, in different ways and apparently with different linguistic intentions. Although these one-word sentences have meaning in themselves, they are often strung together in sequences to express ideas that are later handled with complex sentences, such as "Daddy," then "Eat," then "Apple."

Acquisition of Grammar. As children approach their second birthday, they begin to put two words together as sentences, revealing their earliest concepts of syntax. At this point their brief sequences may be their own and not an imitation of adult speech. Children first pair words haltingly and only occasionally, but soon new combinations are added daily. Within a few months children may be using two to three hundred word pairs.

Identical early sentences sometimes seem to have different meanings. Lois Bloom (1970) reported that twenty-one-month-old Kathryn used the sentence, "Mommy sock," twice in the same day, once when she picked up her mother's stocking and again when her mother put Kathryn's own sock on her. In the first sentence "Mommy" was used as a possessive: "This is Mommy's sock." In the second she was an agent: "Mommy put the sock on Kathryn." Two-year-olds may say "Doggy bark," "Milk fall," "More car," meaning "Drive around some more," "More cookie," "No carrot," "Allgone doggies," "Go store," "Kimmy swim," "Pretty dress," "Hand dirty," "Where ball?" "There Daddy," "Bye-bye please," to communicate other important aspects of their lives. All the world's children appear to go through this stage in which they string two words together to express a wide variety of relationships. Interestingly, the pattern applies to sign language as well as oral language. Deaf children begin to use two-sign strings just as their peers use two-word ones.

Apparently children's linguistic development is related to their cognitive development, no matter what their mode of communication. As children are beginning to speak, they are also learning about environmental relationships such as self-other distinctions, object permanence, and causality. Language expresses what they understand at a particular time. Thus all children understand and speak about possession, location, recurrence, agent-action, disap-

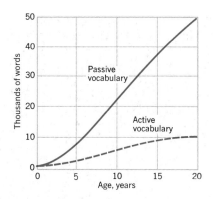

Figure 7.9
The development of active and passive vocabulary. As is common in language acquisition, understanding, as indicated by the size of the passive vocabulary, is always far ahead of usage, indicated in active vocabulary.

pearance, and reappearance in their two-word sentences, presumably because these are significant at their stage of cognitive development.

Children's early sentences are called telegraphic speech. They omit the connecting words, auxiliary verbs, articles, prepositions, and pronouns that serve a grammatical function. The reason for omitting these parallels that for leaving words out of telegrams. There they cost money. In children's speech they cost precious processing capacity. Children at this age hold two units of information in mind, three at the most. They therefore construct their sentences of the bare essentials, of words carrying the most meaning for them. The frills can come later.

And come they do. When children are two, going on three, and switching from two-word to longer sentences, the functional words omitted from telegraphic speech appear, and sentences increase in length, complexity, and precision. Children begin to use an occasional article, the definite pronouns "I," "me," "you," "we," and some demonstratives and modifiers—"I want candy," "That a flower." They are adding the bound morphemes to verbs and nouns— "Car backing up"; "Mommy changes sheets," "There is Daddy's shoe"; and a few prepositional phrases—"Doggy in box," "We goed to the store." Children can be heard constructing their sentences, so to speak. About a cat they may say, "Stand up. Cat stand up. Cat stand up on table."

Linguists have found that mastery is gained in a remarkably consistent sequence. For example, in one intensive study the three children Eve, Adam, and Sarah were found to add fourteen grammatical morphemes to their sentences in nearly the same order (Brown, 1973). A study of twenty-one American children, ranging in age from sixteen to forty months, confirmed this order (de Villiers and de Villiers, 1973). On the other hand, certain relationships are more difficult to express in some languages than in others. For example, noun plurals are relatively simple to form in English but very complex in Arabic. Although English-speaking and Arabic-speaking children probably understand the meaning of plurals at the same time, those who speak English acquire them early, and Arabic-speaking children acquire them last of all in mastering their language. Even more dramatically, bilingual children who speak Hungarian and Serbo-Croatian can express relations like "into," "out of," and "on top of" in Hungarian well before they can in the more complex Serbo-Croatian language. The children clearly understand the meaning of these relations, but their expression is limited by the complexity of the language.

By the age of three, many children use sentences in which verbs follow nouns that are used as subjects, verbs have auxiliaries, there are indefinite pronouns, and clauses are joined—"Then he played with toys," "I'm going to empty it," "You lookit that book and I lookit this book," "Make the car go." But they have not yet learned the transformational rules for questions. Children first form questions by means of inflection. They ask "Is Daddy coming?" by saying "Daddy coming?" For a relatively long period they may be unable to make the necessary change in word order to transform a declaration into a question. Beginning to use auxiliary verbs, they say "Daddy is coming?" rather than "Is Daddy coming?" Their wh-questions begin with the question word but do not immediately shift subject and auxiliary verb: "When Daddy is coming?" "Where you hide my dolly?"

One syntactic rule the child appears to learn early is that the order of words in sentences is *agent-action-object*. This is correct for sentences in the active voice—John hit Mary—but incorrect for those in the passive voice—Mary was hit by John. Once children become conscious of the word order rule, they may overgeneralize and believe that the passive sentence actually means that Mary hit John. Eventually, of course, they solve this problem.

Children have similar difficulties with the plurals that are formed in irregular ways—like foot, feet; child, children; deer, deer—and with irregular verb forms. Although many verbs change from present to past tense by adding "ed"— smile, smiled—some of the most basic verbs in the language are exceptions— go, went; come, came; fall, fell; bring, brought; take, took. Children have usually learned the correct irregular form at first. Later on, as vocabulary enlarges, children discover that the majority of words have a regular way of becoming plural or past. With the acquisition of this knowledge, they **overregularize** in applying these rules. The child who once said "Daddy came" and referred to "my feet" now says "Daddy comed" and speaks of "my foots" or "my feetses." The child is not a passive receptacle into which linguistic rules are poured by experience but rather an active creator, attempting to construct a theory of usage that will make him or her a competent speaker of the language.

Pronunciation. The ability to pronounce a sound correctly can lag behind knowing what it should be. This sometimes amusing effect has been called the *fis phenomenon,* after an incident reported by Jean Berko and Roger Brown (1960).

> One of us . . . spoke to a child who called his inflated plastic fish a *fis.* In imitation of the child's pronunciation, the observer said: "This is your fis?" "No," said the child, "My *fis.*" He continued to reject the adult's imitation until he was told, "That is your fish." "Yes," he said, "my fis."

In another exchange a little boy asked whether he could come along on a trip to "the mewwy-go-wound." An older child, teasing him, said, "David wants to go on the mewwy-go-wound." "No," said David firmly, "you don't say it wight!" (Maccoby and Bee, 1965).

Children eventually acquire correct pronunciation that is quite subtle in its distinctions. For example, given a problem such as the one shown in Figure 7.10, kindergarten and first-grade children commonly give the correct ending Wug/z/. Words ending with voiced consonants form their plurals with the voiced sibilant /z/, as in dogs, rows, bells, birds. Words ending with voiceless consonants add a voiceless /s/—cats, socks, pups. When English is learned by an older person, this distinction may never be mastered, even though the correct combinations are in fact easier to pronounce.

Semantic Development. Something very much like overregularization happens to the meanings of words. Very young children who are learning their first words often overextend the meaning of a word to a number of things that have a perceived similarity. For example, they may think that the word "doggy" applies not only to canines, but to cats, cows, horses, and any other four-legged creature that moves. Later, when the child learns other words and notices that dogs bark and are small, that cats meow, and that cows moo and are large, the process reverses and the meaning of the word narrows.

Three-year-old children have lost many of their overextensions, but they have trouble with antonyms. The meaning of one may be extended to cover both, as though the words really were synonyms. Margaret Donaldson and George Balfour (1968) showed three- to five-year-old children two toy apple trees, one with more apples on it than the other, and asked which tree had more apples and which tree had fewer. To answer *both of these questions,* the

This is a Wug

Now there is another one.
There are two of them.
There are two _____

Figure 7.10
Method for studying children's inflections. After children are shown a picture of a Wug and then a picture of two of them, the experimenter says, "Now, there are two _____." The fact that children normally respond Wug/z/ suggests that they know the rule for creating this plural. (From Berko, 1958.)

majority of the children pointed to the tree with more apples. Testing with other pairs of opposites, such as wide and narrow, tall and short, has revealed similar confusions.

One explanation for this phenomenon is that children first acquire general concepts for amount, more–less; breadth, wide–narrow; and height, tall–short. They know that the two adjectives apply to the same dimension, but they have not sorted out the quantitative meanings of the words themselves. Children apparently prefer whatever is more, and this preference together with their vaguely developed general concept of amount makes them select the greater when asked which is less.

SUMMARY

Most current theories recognize that human beings are predisposed by nature to acquire language, but that their specific language is learned. Rewards and punishments are relatively ineffective in helping children to learn language, especially since adults are more likely to reward correct meaning than correct grammar in children's speech. Children acquire language by interacting with other people who provide appropriate linguistic models When talking to children, adults may modify their speech in ways that facilitate language development.

Children the world over go through certain stages in acquiring language: babbling, followed by one-word sentences, followed by longer sentences; telegraphic speech followed by the use of complex grammatical rules. The linguistic development of children is a constructive struggle. At every stage and in every process the child appears to test hypotheses about appropriate usage, sometimes overgeneralizing rules of construction and overextending the meaning of words, but eventually mastering the language.

THINKING

By means of language, events and objects in the world can be expressed as verbal symbols. These symbols can then be manipulated in a way that physical reality cannot be. This manipulation of the world at a symbolic level is an important part of thinking. To observe these processes in your own thinking, try solving the arithmetic puzzle presented by Sir Frederick Bartlett of Cambridge University in England and keep a record of the steps in your solution. Bartlett's problem is this:

> DONALD
> + GERALD
> ROBERT

The problem is to be treated as an exercise in simple addition. All that is known is: (1) that D = 5; (2) that every number from 0 to 9 has its corresponding letter; (3) that each letter must be assigned a number different from that given for any other letter. . . (1958, p. 51).

The answer appears at the end of the chapter (page 243).

Concept Formation

A **concept** is a symbol that stands for the common properties of objects, events, or ideas that are otherwise distinguishable. Day by day we deal effectively with a vast array of concepts. Some of them are simple and objective, concepts like "dog," "automobile," "house," and "shoe." Other concepts are abstract and elaborate, like "avarice," "faith," "justice," and "mercy." Adding to the complexity of concepts is the fact that they exist in hierarchies. The concept "dog" includes the concept "poodle" but is included in the concept "animal." The concept "faith" includes "faith in God," "faith in the free-enterprise system," and "faith in the power of reason," but at least "faith in God" is included in the larger concept "cardinal virtue." Certainly the hierarchial ordering of concepts is anything but tidy.

Experimental Study of Concept Attainment.   The definition of a concept as a symbol that stands for the common properties of things indicates the process by which concepts are acquired. We form concepts by noting common properties and allowing the concept name to cover all objects that have these attributes. The experimental study of concept attainment takes the formation of concepts into the laboratory and makes the process somewhat simpler than what happens in everyday life.

To illustrate the general procedure, let us consider a famous old experiment by Kenneth Smoke (1932). He presented figures to help his research participants develop concepts such as DAX, which consists of a circle with one dot inside and another dot outside (Figure 7.11). The figures employed by Smoke have certain features: shape, size, number of dots, and location of dots. Some of these attributes are relevant—shape, number of dots, location of dots; others are irrelevant—size, aspects of dot location except for being inside or outside the figure. In order to attain this concept, it is necessary to figure out what attributes are relevant and reject those that are irrelevant.

In concept attainment, not only are there relevant attributes to detect, but the rule or principle governing them must be ascertained. DAX is a figure that is circular *and* has two dots, *and* the two dots are one inside, one outside the circle. Depending on the rules that apply to them, it is possible to identify different types of concepts. Three examples are the following. (1) Some very simple concepts, for example, the concept of "red," have only one attribute. Thus red is the feature shared in common by lipsticks, fire engines, sunsets, and blood. (2) Concepts like DAX are based on the conjunction of attributes. That is, an exemplar of the concept must have this attribute *and* this attribute—for as many attributes as define the concept. "Science fiction," "boring lecture," "cute dumb broad," and "male chauvinist pig" are all examples. (3) Other concepts are disjunctive: exemplars must have this feature *or* that feature. A "natural" in a game of craps is a 7 or an 11. In baseball a strike is a pitch that is swung on and missed, *or* a pitch that passes over home base at a height

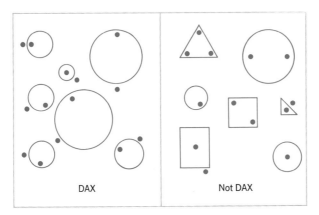

Figure 7.11
Samples of DAX *and non-*DAX *figures.*
(After Smoke, 1932.)

between the knees and shoulders of the batter. Investigators in the field of concept attainment have identified other rules that define more complicated types of concepts, but the varieties presented here will help to make certain additional points.

Hypothesis Testing and Concept Attainment.   An experiment on concept learning presents a series of examples and nonexamples of the concept, and the learner indicates whether or not each individual example represents the concept. The experimenter then provides appropriate feedback, telling the learner whether the response was right or wrong (Figure 7.12). Correct examples of the concept usually carry more information and aid concept learning more than do those that are incorrect. It would be extremely difficult to acquire the concept DAX without seeing an example of it.

The chief method employed by subjects in mastering the concepts they learn in these experiments is hypothesis testing (Levine, 1966). For example, after the first trial in Figure 7.12, the subject might hypothesize that the concept is a simple one, "a dot to the left of the figure whatever else is there." Testing this hypothesis on trial 2, the subject learns that it is wrong and develops the second hypothesis that the concept is "two dots, whatever else is there." Trial 3 eliminates this hypothesis. How about "two dots and a circle"? Trial 4 proves this to be a possibility, so the subject responds "DAX" on trial 5, only to be shot down again. Reviewing the sequence of trials, the subject concludes that the concept must involve two dots and a circle but that something else must be required. How about "one dot inside a circle and one outside"? A test of this hypothesis on trial 6 succeeds, and trials 7 and 8 confirm it.

Figure 7.12

Concept attainment. An experiment for identification of the concept DAX would consist of such a hypothetical series of trials. Successive rows show, trial by trial, the stimulus presented, the response given, and the feedback provided by the experimenter. By trial 6 the research participant has mastered the concept.

Trial	Figure presented	Response	Feedback
1	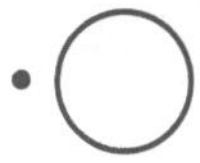	"DAX"	Wrong
2	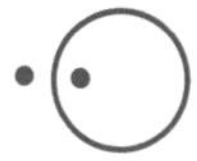	"Not DAX"	Wrong
3		"DAX"	Wrong
4		"DAX"	Right
5		"DAX"	Wrong
6		"DAX"	Right
7		"Not DAX"	Right
8		"Not DAX"	Right

Two aspects of the subject's hypothesizing in this sequence of trials are worth noting. First this particular subject's behavior is **analytic** in that the hypotheses tested attempt to isolate the attributes and rules that define the concept. Probably in such an experiment most participants would develop an analytic approach, but a few might not, relying instead on a **nonanalytic** one consisting of nothing more than remembering positive instances of the concept. In the formation of real-life concepts, the nonanalytic approach is more common. Because children are not analytical, their concepts of fish include whales and dolphins and their concepts of bird include bats.

Second, in the concept-learning strategy laid out in Figure 7.12, the subject used a **win-stay, lose-shift strategy**: stick with the hypothesis you have developed until it is proved wrong; then try another possibility. The number of potentially correct hypotheses gradually narrows until the concept is established. About 95 percent of the subjects in concept-learning experiments perform in this way.

Conceptual Fuzziness. As they are studied in the laboratory, concepts are usually quite definite; a given object is or is not an *exemplar* of the concept. In real life things are less clear-cut. Consider, for example, the conjunctive concept of *bird*. Birds fly, they are of a standard size, they have two longish legs, they have feathers, they build nests, they sing, they go to warmer climates when the weather turns cold. Now consider the following representatives of this concept: *robin, sparrow, eagle, crow, pheasant, goose, chicken, penguin.* You will recognize that the order in which they are given is a decreasing order of "birdness." *Robin* and *sparrow* are very good examples of the concept bird; *chicken* and *penguin* are less good. The first examples have more of the attributes of the concept *bird*; the last examples have fewer of them (Rosch, 1977).

Eleanor Rosch (1973) and others have demonstrated the importance of the

Some dogs fit the concept of dog better than others.

difference just described in studies in which people are asked to respond "true" or "false" as quickly as possible to sentences like

A robin is a bird.

A penguin is a bird.

Less time is required to say "true" when the objects are good examplars of the concept than when they are poor ones. The time required to decide that sentences like

A bat is a bird.

A stone is a bird.

are false makes the same point. It takes longer to reject the first sentence than the second, theoretically because bats have many of the attributes of birds whereas stones have none. In fact, some subjects in studies asking them to list examples of birds have included bats in their lists.

Prototypes and Transformations.   A robin, of course, is an example of what a bird is supposed to be like, a **prototype** with all the essential attributes of good members of this category. Research suggests that people tend to abstract such essential features in the course of their experience with exemplars of a concept. They may even develop prototypes without ever having encountered one. Jeffrey Franks and John Bransford (1971) did an experiment in which the prototypical member of a category was a card with a square above a triangle on the left and a heart above a diamond on the right (Figure 7.13). In the first part of the experiment, the subjects saw cards that were various *transformations* of the prototypical card, but never the prototypical card itself. In the second part they were shown a series of new and old cards, including the prototype, and were asked to rate their certainty of having seen each card before. As Figure 7.13 indicates, the subjects were the most confident that they had seen the prototype, although they had actually never seen it before! Their confidence in recognizing the other cards was less.

Linguistic Relativity

Another important fact about real-world concepts is that conceptual categories vary from culture to culture. The Eskimos have three words for snow, depending on whether it is falling, covering the ground, or made into igloos. We have only

Figure 7.13
False recognition of prototypes and variants of prototypes. Variant 1 reverses the halves of the prototypical card from right to left; variant 2 reverses the square and triangle; variant 3 reverses the heart and diamond; variant 4 omits the square.

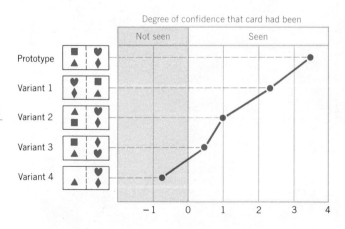

FLYING OBJECTS

English—three words

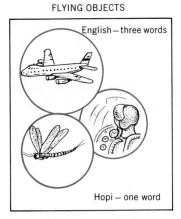

Hopi — one word

SNOW TERMS

Eskimo—three words

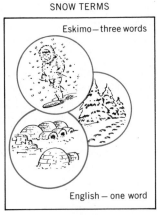

English — one word

WATER TERMS

Hopi — two words

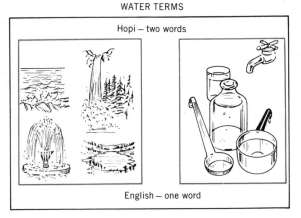

English — one word

Figure 7.14
Linguistic relativity. Certain concepts are handled differently in the English, Hopi, and Eskimo languages. We use three different words for a dragonfly, an airplane, and an aviator; the Hopi use one. We use one word for water; the Hopi have two. (Adapted from Whorf, 1940.)

one. The Aztecs go in the other direction and use the same word for cold, ice, and snow. The Hopis have a noun that refers to everything that flies except birds (Figure 7.14). We identify nouns and verbs as very separate parts of speech. Certain of the natives of Vancouver Island make no such distinction. They generally make verbs of nouns, as we might of "flame." Just as it is correct for us to say "it flames," for these people "it houses" is the correct way to refer to the building of a house.

Examples such as these led Benjamin Lee Whorf (1897–1941) to the hypothesis of **linguistic relativity**, which proposes that language determines the content of thought. In its strongest version the hypothesis holds that these peculiarities of language determine the content of thought, that what the indi-

We have the same word for falling snow, snow on the ground, snow packed hard like ice, slushy snow, wind-driven flying snow. . . . To an Eskimo, this all-inclusive word would be almost unthinkable; he would say that falling snow, slushy snow, and so on . . . are different things to contend with; he uses different words for them. . .(Whorf, 1956).

vidual can possibly think depends on the categories of language. A few experimental tests of this idea have now been carried out on the categories for colors.

Linguists have known that languages vary in the number of their terms for colors, and, arguing from the hypothesis of linguistic relativity, supposed that the different designations of the color spectrum affected the perception of colors. Anthropologists Brent Berlin and Paul Kay (1969) studied the basic and most often applied color terms in a number of languages, however, and found that they were restricted to a list of eleven, corresponding to our black, white, red, yellow, green, blue, brown, purple, pink, orange, and gray. Some languages do not refer to all these colors, but the order of this list of eleven is significant. Languages usually incorporate terms for colors in this fairly set order. Languages that name only two colors refer to black and white, which can be translated in terms of brightness, as light and dark. Those referring to three name black, white, and red. The languages naming six refer to these three plus yellow, green and blue.

The boundaries for the basic colors may not be the same in each language, depending on the number of basic colors designated, but people with terms for blue will all pick from several the same blue as the prototype for the category. They all regard the same blue as quintessential. Moreover, new color names are learned more easily and remembered better if they are grouped according to the eleven basic categories (Heider and Oliver, 1972). Members of the Dani tribe of New Guinea, whose language names colors on the basis of brightness, that is, light and dark, learned to give new color names to eight different groups of colors, each of which contained three different hues. In one case the three colors with the same name were grouped naturally, for example, an orangish red, a pure red, and a bluish red. The colors in the other groups crossed natural color boundaries, for example, a red, an orangish red, and a yellow. The Dani learned the natural group of colors much more rapidly, although linguistic relativity would predict no difference.

The Nature of Thought

The intimate relationship between language and thought led the early behaviorists, for example, John B. Watson, to propose that the two skills are identical—that language is just silent talking to oneself. This view consigned thought to the periphery. It held that the essential mechanism of thought is not neural activity in the brain but muscular activity in the vocal apparatus. There are many objections to this view, one of which is based on a dramatic experiment. In a classic display of heroism for the scientific good, an anesthesiologist, Scott Smith, allowed himself to be curarized to the point of complete paralysis and then introspected on his own thought processes.

Curare is a chemical that eliminates all muscular and skeletal activity by blocking the neural junction at which nerve impulses pass on directions to the muscle. Curare has been used as a poison by several South American Indian tribes, who put it on the tips of their arrows for battle and hunting. An enemy or quarry shot with a poisoned arrow dies almost immediately because breathing ceases. Smith took enough of the curare that he had to be kept alive with artificial respiration. In these bereft circumstances, Smith reported later, his mind was "clear as a bell" and he could solve problems (Smith et al., 1947). He recalled questions put to him while he was totally paralyzed. Thinking then can proceed when muscular activity is absent, belying the view that it is subvocal speech. It seems more likely that thoughts originate in the brain, and language expresses them.

SUMMARY

One of the great powers of language is that it provides a set of symbols by which to manipulate what we call thought. In large part the manipulations employed in thinking are the manipulations of concepts, that is, of the symbols which stand for the common properties of things that are otherwise distinguishable. Concepts develop as an individual notices these common properties and learns to treat objects that possess them in the same way. In laboratory research concepts are defined in terms of arbitrary attributes, and subjects are provided with positive and negative instances of the concept until they master it. The same processes probably account for concept attainment in everyday life. There are complexities, however. Examples vary in the degree to which they represent the concept. Moreover, different cultures develop different concepts. There is modestly convincing evidence that this process affects thinking, but nothing to suggest that these factors affect such basic processes as the categorization of colors.

The close relationship between language and thought suggested to the early behaviorists that thought might be nothing more than subvocal speech. Introspective observations made by an individual under curare, a paralyzing drug which would have eliminated any traces of the speech that this theory proposed as thought, confirmed that thinking must be a function of the brain.

PROBLEM SOLVING

Three missionaries and three cannibals come together on the bank of a river. They all want to get to the other side. The only method of transportation available is a boat that holds, at most, two people. The missionaries and cannibals decide to use the boat to cross the river, but there is a difficulty. If at any time the cannibals outnumber the missionaries on either side of the river, the outnumbered missionaries will be eaten. How is it possible to get all the missionaries and all the cannibals across the river without losing anyone? (See page 243 for the solution.)

This classic puzzle will serve to introduce the topic of problem solving. A problem consists of three components: (1) a current situation that must be changed to attain (2) a desired situation by the use of (3) certain legal moves. In the example, (1) the missionaries and cannibals are all on the same side of the river; (2) they want to be on the other side; but (3) they can go only two at a time, and cannibals must never outnumber the missionaries.

Steps in Problem Solving

The cannibal and missionary problem is complex, requiring some eleven steps in its solution. Table 7.2 follows the thinking of a young man solving a problem that is similar to the one given earlier—DONALD + GERALD = ROBERT— but is somewhat easier. This protocol illustrates the most important points about problem solving.

Note first that the subject used two different strategies in solving the problem. Most of his manipulations followed an **algorithm**, a precise set of rules for solving problems of a particular type. Here the rules are those of addition. An algorithm guarantees success if applied correctly and in the right circumstances. Steps 1 and 2 in the table provide good examples. In steps 3 and 4 the young man resorts to something different, a **heuristic**, a "best guess" or "rule of thumb" strategy. A heuristic is a conjecture which will often solve a problem

Table 7.2 How One Subject Solved an Arithmetic Problem

Problem at Each Stage of Solution	Steps in Solution
CROSS + ROADS —————— DANGER	*Given*: R = 6. Each of the other letters correspond to a number from 1 to 9.

1.   C60SS
    60ALS
——————
    1ANGE6
	1. D can only equal 1. Even 9 + 8 (the largest numbers allowed), even with 1 to carry, cannot produce anything larger.

2.   C6033
    60A13
——————
    1ANG46
	2. S must be 3 or 8 (3 + 3 = 6 and 8 + 8 = 16). It can't be 8 because S + 1 + 1 to carry would make E = zero; not used. Thus S = 3 and E = 4.

3.   96033
    60513
——————
    15NG46
	3. C cannot be 2; wouldn't produce 1 to carry. C cannot be 7 because 7 + 6 = 3 (already used) or 7 + 6 + 1 to carry = 4 (already used). C must be 5, 8, or 9 but I'm stuck; 8 seems least likely 8 + 6 = 4 (already used). Try 9 as a best guess. If correct A = 5. Remaining numbers 2, 7, and 8.

4.   96233
    62513
——————
   158746
	4. 0 cannot be 7 because 6 + 7 = 3 or 6 + 7 + 1 = 4 (already used). 0 cannot be 8 because 8 + 5 = 3 already used. Therefore 0 = 2 and N becomes 8; G becomes 7. C = 9 was a lucky guess!

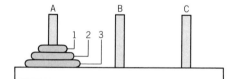

Figure 7.15
The Tower of Hanoi problem.

but not always. It does not entail the logical, if-then procedure of an algorithm, and its correctness cannot be proved.

At each step the problem solver uses a **means-end analysis**, comparing the current position with the desired end position and asking whether the particular act being considered will take him a step closer to the desired goal. He proceeds if it does, tries another alternative if it does not. You can observe yourselves using means-end analysis in solving the Tower of Hanoi puzzle shown in Figure 7.15. The problem is to move the three disks from peg A to peg C in as few moves as possible, shifting one disk at a time and never placing a larger disk on top of a smaller one. The problem is solved when the disks are on peg C in the same order as they are now arranged on peg A.

Suppose that you start by moving disk 1 to peg B. Thinking ahead, you will see that your next move must be to place disk 2 on peg C. But then the only possible placement of disk 3 would be to put it on top of a smaller disk. The initial move was not a means to the desired end, and you have to start over. Your only alternative is to place disk 1 on peg C and disk 2 on peg B. Then you can move disk 1 to peg B, on top of disk 2, disk 3 to peg C, disk 1 to peg A, and finally disks 2 and 1 to peg C in that order. The problem is thus solved.

Obstacles to Problem Solving

Problems are problems for many reasons. Sometimes initial states or final goals are not clearly defined. Many of our everyday human problems are caused by unclear definitions of present circumstances or ultimate objectives. For example, students sometimes have problems in selecting courses because they are not

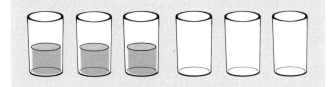

Figure 7.16
The water glass problem.

sure whether they have fulfilled certain college requirements; they are uncertain about their current academic situation. More often they have trouble choosing courses because they have not defined their goals. They have been unable to make a career decision or choose a major. Until they do so, they have no basis for selecting courses. Means-end analysis is impossible because, not knowing where they are headed, it is never clear whether taking any particular course is a step in the right direction. These open-ended problems of everyday life involve a great deal more than just techniques of problem solving. The establishment of goals brings in questions of motives and values, factors which make a complex process even more complicated. For these reasons psychologists have focused their research on problems with better definitions. The Tower of Hanoi problem is a good example.

Lapses of Memory. The most obvious obstacle to solving a problem is losing track of where you are. In the CROSS + ROADS = DANGER problem, step 3, it is easy to forget that C cannot be 6 or 7 unless you make a written note of this fact. Scientists very often keep a record of their thoughts about problems and possible solutions. Many keep diaries, which are sometimes published.

Unwarranted Assumptions. Another difficulty in problem solving is that people make mistaken assumptions about the moves that are and are not legal. To illustrate, consider the problem of rearranging the glasses in Figure 7.16. The glasses must be arranged to alternate: glass containing water, empty glass, water, empty, and so on, *but you are allowed to touch only one glass.* The solution is to pour the contents of the middle glass containing water into the middle empty glass. Many people assume that this straightforward solution is not allowed, although the instructions do not preclude it. Another problem which is more difficult but for similar reasons is the nine-dot problem (Figure 7.17). You are to connect the nine dots by drawing four continuous straight lines without lifting your pencil from the paper. Try it and discover the unwarranted assumption that most people make about this problem. The solution appears at the end of the chapter.

Figure 7.17
The nine-dot problem.

Seeing New Relationships. Many problems are solved with **insight**. Objectively, this means that the solution occurs to the individual suddenly, often after a long period of trial and error. Subjectively, the problem solver sees the problem in a new light. The higher apes sometimes solve problems suddenly and possibly, therefore, with something like the "Eureka" or "Aha" experience of human beings.

The most famous studies of insightful behavior in higher apes had chimpanzees as subjects. They were conducted during World War I by Wolfgang Köhler (1887–1968) on Tenerife, the largest of the Canary Islands. In most of Köhler's testing situations, the chimpanzees occupied a large enclosure, and a banana, or other lure, was placed at some point within or outside the cage, where it could only be obtained with the aid of a tool. In one problem, for example,

Figure 7.18
Chimpanzee Sultan at the moment of solving the two-stick problem. (Drawn from a photograph in Köhler, 1925.)

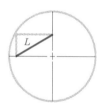

Figure 7.19
If the radius of the circle is 100, what is the length of line *L*?

the banana was suspended from the center of the ceiling. In the corner of the cage was a box, which could be moved and used as a platform to stand on to reach the lure. In another problem two boxes had to be stacked one on the other to get to the banana. In a third problem the banana had to be raked into the cage with a stick. And in a fourth problem two sticks had to be fitted together and used as a rake to reach the banana. At least some of Köhler's chimpanzees solved all these problems. Köhler saw in their behavior evidences of insight.

In one experiment a young chimpanzee, Sultan, had the problem of securing a banana placed out of reach outside the cage. Although Sultan was in the habit of using sticks to rake in desired objects, no stick long enough to reach the banana was in the enclosure. Instead, there were two short, hollow sticks, one thinner than the other. Sultan began by attempting to reach the banana in various ways, frequently poking one of the sticks through the bars toward the banana. Such fruitless efforts persisted for about half an hour. At this point the casual observer would have concluded from his behavior that Sultan had become discouraged. He sat indifferently in the cage; and then, as if by accident, he held the two sticks in either hand in such a way that they nearly touched (Figure 7.18). Sultan pushed the thinner one a little way into the opening of the thicker, jumped up, ran to the bars that separated him from the banana, and began to draw the banana toward him with the double stick. Thereafter Sultan would immediately put the two sticks together to reach the banana.

Figure 7.19 presents a problem for you to solve that requires a similar insight. It is surprisingly difficult. Again, the solution is provided at the end of the chapter.

Problems of Representation. Sometimes problems appear very difficult only because we have not figured out how to put them into a solvable form. One example is the old monk problem, which John Hayes (1978) presents this way.

> Once there was a monk who lived in a monastery at the foot of a mountain. Every year the monk made a pilgrimage to the top of the mountain to fast and to pray. He would start out on the mountain path at 6 a.m., climbing and resting as the spirit struck him, but making sure that he reached the shrine at exactly 6 p.m. that evening. He then prayed and fasted all night. At exactly 6 a.m. the next morning, he began to descend the mountain path, resting here and there along the way, but making sure that he reached his monastery again by 6 p.m. of that day.

ANTHROPOMORPHISM

We can never know, of course, whether the ape's experience in solving a problem insightfully is like our own. For this reason there is a widespread nervousness in psychology about interpreting the behavior of lower animals in terms of human experience, a practice called **anthropomorphism** (Greek *anthropos*, man; *morphe*, form). As an example, consider the following quotation from Aristotle's *Historia Animalium*:

> Some animals are good-tempered, sluggish, and little prone to ferocity, as the ox; others are quick-tempered, ferocious, and unteachable, as the wild boar; some are intelligent and timid, as the stag and the hare; others are mean and treacherous as the snake; . . . some are crafty and mischievous, as the fox; some are spirited and affectionate and fawning as the dog; others are easy-tempered and easily domesticated, as the elephant; others are cautious and watchful, as the goose; other are jealous and self-conceited as the peacock.

Although attributing human temperaments to lower animals is scientifically dangerous, because we have no way of knowing the actual experience of other animals, one purpose of studying animal behavior is to obtain information that is relevant to human activity. On this basis psychology makes occasional cautious attempts to bridge the species gap. The problem-solving behavior of chimpanzees at least suggests that they may solve problems in somewhat the same way as we do.

That evening as he was hastening to a much needed dinner, he was stopped by the monastery's visiting mathematician, who said to him, "Do you know, I suddenly realized a very curious thing. Every time you make your pilgrimage there is always some point on the mountain path, perhaps different on each trip, that you pass at the same time when you are climbing up as when you are climbing down." "What!" snorted the monk, annoyed. "Why, that's ridiculous! I walk at all manner of different paces up and down the path. It would be a great coincidence if I should pass any spot at the same time of day going up as coming down. The idea that such a coincidence might happen time after time surpasses belief!" The mathematician, who had a touch of fiendishness in his soul, smiled sweetly and said, "Bless you, Brother, not only should you believe it, but if you will just think about it in the right way, it's obvious." He then locked himself in his cell, confident that he had spoiled the monk's dinner and probably his night's sleep as well (p. 178).

This puzzle shows in a very elaborate way the importance of how a problem is represented. The mathematician's statement is, in fact, true, but this truth is difficult to grasp when we think in terms of the monk's going up the mountain one day and coming down the next. If we think instead of two monks, one ascending, the other descending by the same path, it is immediately clear that they will always meet some exact time and place. Or make the representation graphic, as in Figure 7.20, and the point, if anything, becomes clearer.

Effects of Set. As we have all learned to our sorrow, sometimes problems are difficult to solve because of our **mental set.** We tend to use again and again a procedure that has worked in the past. We become so stuck with a particular, but unsuccessful, way of solving a problem that the correct solution never occurs to us when it is different.

This fact is well illustrated by Abraham Luchins's (1942) experiments with problems which were versions of the following: "A mother sends her son to the well to get three quarts of water. She gives him a five-quart jar and an eight-quart jar. How can the boy get exactly three quarts of water, using only

Figure 7.20
However these lines are drawn, they cross. There must always be some exact time when the old monk is at the same place coming down the mountain that he was going up.

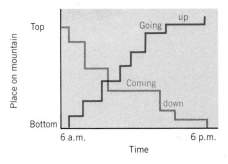

these containers and not guessing at the amount?'' The solution to the problem is to fill the eight-quart jar, empty out enough to fill the five-quart jar, and take the rest home. Luchins's problems were more complicated in that they involved three containers and numbers a little more difficult to handle. Eight of them are presented in Table 7.3. In order to get the point of the experiment, you should work through all eight of the problems. Begin with problem 1 and work down through the list. Do this before you read on.

Problems 1 and 7 follow a common pattern. Expressed algebraically, the solution is always of the form $b - a - 2c$; that is, to get 100 units of water as required in the first problem, you fill the 127-unit container, fill the 21-unit container from it once and the 3-unit container from it twice: $127 - 21 - 2(3) = 100$. Problems 1 through 5 can be solved only in this way, but problems 6 and 7 have much simpler solutions, algebraically $a - c$ and $a + c$. The eighth problem can only be solved in a simpler way, $a - c$.

The basic question asked by Luchins's experiments is whether solving problems 1 through 5 has any effect on the solving of subsequent problems? The answer is "yes." Luchins used two groups of problem solvers. About 80 percent of the people in the experimental group, who were presented with all eight problems, continued to rely on the same method that had solved the first five, in spite of the fact that the last three had an easier solution. Many actually failed to solve the last problem in the time allowed because the method would not work. A control group, presented with only the final three problems, had little trouble with the last one, and they almost always used the simpler method for solving problems 6 and 7. The set developed by solving problems 1 through 5 in a certain way interfered with the solutions to the later problems.

A set may also hamper logical reasoning. One experiment (Morton, 1942), for example, used abstract terms and emotionally loaded terms to state similarly faulty syllogisms. The following resemble those used in the study.

1. All x's are y's.
   All z's are y's.
   Therefore all z's are x's.

2. All communists are radicals.
   All labor leaders are radicals.
   Therefore all labor leaders are communists.

Table 7.3 **Luchins's Problem**

	Amount of Water Contained by Each Jar, quarts			Water To Be Obtained, quarts
Problem	a	b	c	
1	21	127	3	100
2	14	163	25	99
3	18	43	10	5
4	9	42	6	21
5	20	59	4	31
6	23	49	3	20
7	15	39	3	18
8	28	76	3	25

From Luchins, 1942

Which conclusion follows logically? Actually, neither, for the two problems are similarly faulty syllogisms. Should a logically false conclusion match a strong attitudinal bias, however, it is more readily accepted than an identical false conclusion expressed in terms of x's, y's, and z's. If you believe that all labor leaders are communists, you are likely to accept the statement as following from the premises, even though you would not accept the abstract equivalent that all z's are x's. An attitude provides a set that operates in the same way as the set established by prior experience in the Luchins experiment.

Functional Fixedness.   An obstacle to problem solving that is closely related to set, and possibly the same thing, is what has been called **functional fixedness.** A famous demonstration of this tendency to think that an object can be used only in its customary way was carried out by Karl Duncker (1945) using the problem presented in Figure 7.21. The subject's task in this experiment was to think of a way to mount a candle on the wall so that it would burn properly and give light. The solution to the problem is to empty the box, tack it to the wall, and let it function as a candle holder. For some of the participants the box was presented already empty, and there were a few tacks on the table. All these participants solved the problem, but only about half of the other group did. Apparently they were so fixated on the tack-holding function of the box that they were unable to perceive its possible use as a candle holder.

SUMMARY

A problem consists of an undesirable present situation that can be changed, using specified moves, to bring about a more satisfactory situation. Whenever possible, problem solvers make use of algorithms, moves that guarantee to correct solution to a problem. When algorithms are not available, they resort to heuristics or "rules of thumb." Problem solvers monitor their progress by a means-end analysis, asking at each step whether they are moving toward the desired goal.

Figure 7.21
Get the candle up on the wall so that it burns properly, using only the objects on the table.

Obstacles that keep us from finding a solution to a problem include unclear definition of the present state or of the desired goal, lapses of memory, unwarranted assumptions about what moves are legal, difficulty in seeing elements of a problem in new relationships, being unable to state the problem in a solvable way, having a mental set to solve all problems by the same means, and, finally, functional fixedness, thinking that objects can be put only to their customary uses.

TO BE SURE YOU UNDERSTAND THIS CHAPTER

The following concepts are the important ones presented in this chapter. They are listed in the approximate order in which they appeared. You should be able to use them to reconstruct the discussion of the chapter.

Linguistic competence	**Passive vocabulary**
Linguistics	**Active vocabulary**
Psycholinguistics	**Overregularization**
Phonology	**Concept**
Syntax	**Analytic concept formation**
Semantics	**Nonanalytic concept formation**
Pragmatics	
Phoneme	**Win-stay, lose-shift strategy**
Allophone	**Prototype**
Morpheme	**Linguistic relativity**
Free morpheme	**Algorithm**
Bound morpheme	**Heuristic**
Phonetic symbolism	**Means-end analysis**
Denotative meaning	**Insight**
Associative meaning	**Anthropomorphism**
Connotative meaning	**Mental set**
Semantic differential	**Functional fixedness**

A number of other important points made in Chapter 7 should be added.

Phrase structure of sentences
Hierarchical organization of phrases
Meaningfulness and learning
Communication and "language" in animals
Role of learning in language acquisition
Characteristics of caretaker speech
Methods of studying concept attainment
Components of a problem
Obstacles to problem solving

TO GO BEYOND THIS CHAPTER

In This Book. This chapter ties in very nicely with Chapter 11 on cognitive development. The two chapters supplement each other and should suggest a number of interesting connections.

Elsewhere. The psychology of language is a rapidly changing field, and many treatments are very technical. Recommended books are *Language and Speech,* by George A. Miller, and *Psychology and Language,* by Herbert and Eve Clark. An article on language acquisition by Bregne Arlene Moskowitz in *Scientific American* is first rate.

SOLUTIONS TO PROBLEMS

DONALD   =   526485
GERALD   =   197485
ROBERT   =   723970

Missionary and cannibal problem.   Let CCC be the three cannibals, MMM the three
missionaries, and < > the boat. The boxes show who is on which side of the river and
where the boat is before and after the eleven moves required to solve the problem.
These moves are indicated between boxes.

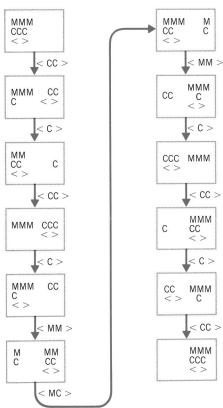

Figure 7.17.   This solution requires that lines be drawn beyond the boundaries of the
square defined by dots. Many people fail to consider the possibility of drawing these
lines, on the mistaken assumption that the instructions preclude it.

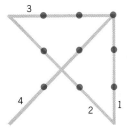

Figure 7.19.   Line *L* is 100. Consider the triangle half a rectangle. Then draw in the
other diagonal of the rectangle. It is a radius, and the radius of the circle is 100.

PART FOUR   LEARNING AND ADAPTIVE BEHAVIOR

Seurat. *The Circus*. Jeu de Paume. Scala/Art Resource.

CHAPTER 8

CONDITIONING AND LEARNING

As you begin the study of learning, it will be useful to look at events in the world in a special way, asking in effect about the extent to which your behavior controls them. There are a few events over which you have almost no control. Thunder follows lightning, however strongly you may wish away its awesome cracks and rumbles. Pain is a likely prospect once the dentist applies the drill. For many people an uncontrollable queasiness follows the sight of blood. There is no way to keep each of these second events from following the first.

More commonly what you do has consequences. You study hard for an examination and get a good grade. You leave your bicycle unlocked on campus and somebody steals it. You go to the auditorium early and find an eighth-row seat on the aisle. In such circumstances you are rewarded or punished, depending on how you have behaved.

Other situations seem to represent a combination of these two states of affairs. A displeased look on a mother's face means punishment is forthcoming, unless the child switches to behavior that forestalls it. The light and crackling of a fireplace means warmth and comfort in a chilly house on a cold evening, but only if a person moves near enough to feel it.

These examples suggest that, in any given situation, two rather different things may be learned: the sequences of events to be expected and what to do about them. Probably most, and possibly all, learning in practical situations involves both of these components. This makes the study of learning complicated. In order to simplify things, psychologists who study learning have developed two separate experimental procedures that seem to capture the essentials of these two processes. These procedures are called classical and operant conditioning. In **classical conditioning** events in the experiment follow a certain sequence no matter what the subject does. In **operant conditioning** specific behavior brings reward or punishment.

CLASSICAL CONDITIONING

The systematic study of classical conditioning began in Russia with the work of Ivan Petrovich Pavlov (1849–1936). A doctor of medicine and physiologist by training, Pavlov won a Nobel prize in 1904. The research that won him the prize was not on conditioned responses but on digestion. This work is worth describing briefly, because it seems to have provided the inspiration for the studies of conditioning for which Pavlov is now more famous. In some of these

Ivan Petrovich Pavlov, skeptical about psychology, avoided mentalistc and subjective terms and insisted that his work on conditioning was physiological.

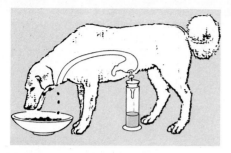

Figure 8.1
Dog with esophageal and gastric fistulas.
The esophagus was cut and the two openings were brought to the outside of the body. Thus the dog could be sham-fed, as shown: the animal could chew and swallow food that never reached the stomach. Food could also be introduced directly into the stomach, bypassing any chewing and swallowing. Connecting the two cut ends of the esophagus made it possible for the dog, with training, to eat normally. Gastric juices flowing from the stomach were collected and measured.

early studies, the esophagus of a dog was severed, and both cut ends were sutured to the outside of the animal's throat. Food could then be introduced directly into the stomach through the lower opening. Or, as is shown in Figure 8.1, the animal could eat, but the food, instead of reaching the stomach, fell back into the food dish through the upper opening. When the two openings were connected, the animal could eat normally. In addition, a fistula, a surgical opening into the animal's stomach, allowed the collection of gastric juice, Pavlov's principal object of interest in these studies.

Pavlov found that the complete act of eating, with the two ends of the dog's esophagus connected, produced a large amount of gastric secretion. Introducing food directly into the stomach reduced the secretion to about half this amount. Allowing the animal to eat when food did not reach the stomach, often called "sham feeding," also reduced the level of gastric secretion, again to about 50 percent of normal. It appears to have been this last fact that led Pavlov to a simple but very important thought. Even though the esophagus, the principal connection between the mouth and the stomach, had been severed in the sham-fed animal, and no food was reaching its stomach, the stomach was responding to events in the mouth by secreting gastric juice. This proved that some other connection must allow stimuli in the mouth to control reactions of the stomach. This other connection must be by way of the brain. Moreover, it seemed likely that this connection was not innate but acquired, a **temporary connection** in Pavlovian language. Putting all this together, Pavlov came to the idea of studying these acquired connections. The procedures he developed were those of his famous experiments on the conditioned reflex of salivation.

The Demonstration of Conditioning

In order to record the salivary response, the dogs first received a minor surgical operation which brought the duct of a salivary gland to the outside of the cheek. After the dogs had recovered from the operation, they were introduced to the laboratory, to the harness that would restrain them, and to the other apparatus that would make measurement during the experiment possible (Figure 8.2). When they had adjusted to these conditions, the experiment began.

In a typical procedure the animal was first presented with a neutral stimulus such as light, which produced no salivation. After the light had been on for several seconds, food was placed within the dog's reach. The chewing and swallowing of food typically produced copious salivation. After the light and food had been paired in this manner a number of times, the dog gradually came to salivate when the light was turned on. Such a response, called forth by a stimulus which earlier had no connection at all with salivation, is a **conditioned response** or *conditioned reflex.*

Pavlov's experiment provides us with a means of introducing the basic vocabulary of conditioning. The most important terms in this vocabulary are the following.

Figure 8.2
Dog in conditioning apparatus. The dog is restrained by a harness attached to a stand. The tube connected to the dog's cheek covers a salivary gland duct brought surgically to the body surface. Saliva can be collected in the test tube. Each drop of saliva, as it contacts the channel leading to the tube, activates a lever and stylus, which records the secretions on the revolving drum at the left.

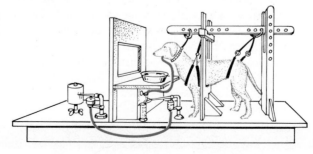

Unconditioned Stimulus (US). Any stimulus that produces a dependable response at the outset of an experiment. In the Pavlovian experiment just described, the US was food. Pavlov spoke of the US as a *reinforcer* to convey the idea that it strengthened and supported the conditioned response that was acquired in these experiments. With time the term came to refer to any reward or punishment employed to obtain learning in any situation.

Unconditioned Response (UR). The consistent reaction to the US just mentioned. Salivation was the UR in the Pavlovian experiment.

Conditioned Stimulus (CS). A stimulus which, for experimental purposes, is paired with the US and, at the outset of the experiment, does not produce the UR. In the experiment just described, the CS was the light.

Conditioned Response (CR). A response which is usually similar to the UR, now elicited by the CS. Figure 8.3, which is the kind of record Pavlov obtained, compares the salivary response at it might occur on a first conditioning trial and after a series of such trials. Note that the response comes to anticipate the US during the series of conditioning trials.

Illustrative Examples

To be sure that you understand the method of classical conditioning, let us analyze two additional examples. The first is a method for curing enuresis, or bed-wetting. The problem in enuresis is not so much to get the child to "control himself" as to get him to awaken to the stimuli provided by bladder tension. Unfortunately, these stimuli are relatively weak. In the cure for bed-wetting developed by O. Hobart Mowrer (1938), the child sleeps on a special pad consisting of two metallic foil sheets, the top one perforated, separated by a heavy cotton fabric. The pad acts as a moisture switch. When urine strikes the pad, it quickly penetrates the fabric and completes a circuit between the two foil sheets, which are wired to a battery and a buzzer alarm (US). The child awakens (UR) and goes to the bathroom. After such conditioning the child learns to awaken (CR) before the accident occurs and in response to smaller

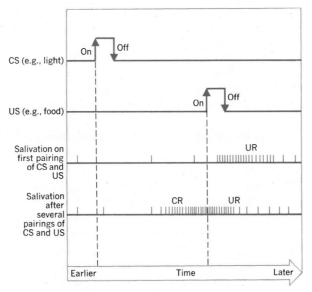

Figure 8.3
Hypothetical records obtained in salivary conditioning experiment. This diagram shows what goes on in time in a conditioning experiment. First the CS comes on and goes off after a brief period. Then the US is offered. Early in the experiment, before many pairings of CS and US, salivation occurs only as a UR to the US. In records of this kind each short vertical line indicates one drop of saliva. After several pairings salivation anticipates the US, as a CR, and blends with the UR made to the US.

Children have no natural fear of rats.

amounts of bladder tension (CS). In one study this method was found to be 90 percent effective (Geppert, 1964).

Our second example, one of the most famous experiments in the history of psychology, was conducted by John B. Watson and Rosalie Rayner (1920) more than sixty years ago. In this experiment the eleven-month-old Albert learned a conditioned fear of a white rat after its presence was paired with an unconditioned fear-producing stimulus. When Albert was first introduced to the tame white rat (CS) as he sat playing on a mattress, he showed no fear and indeed appeared happily curious. But just as he reached out to touch the rat, the experimenter struck a large steel bar immediately behind the child's head. At the sound of the very loud noise (US), Albert started, fell forward, and buried his head in the mattress (UR). When Albert had recovered enough to reach for the rat a second time, the bar was hammered again. This time Albert jumped, fell forward, and began to whimper. One week later Albert seemed afraid of the rat (CR). He reached for the rat when it was first put down near him but withdrew his hand before touching it, even though he had not seen the rat in the meantime. That day presentations of the rat were paired with the loud noise a few more times. Albert was soon crying and crawling away from the rat as fast as his knees would carry him, even when the bar was not struck. He also appeared to be afraid of objects resembling the rat, such as a fur coat, a ball of absorbent cotton, and a Santa Claus mask.

The early date of this experiment is significant. The ethical codes developed since then would almost certainly prevent carrying out such a study today. As a matter of fact, the experimenters had originally intended to remove Albert's fear, again through conditioning, but unfortunately Albert was taken from the hospital where he had been living before they could do so.

What Is Learned in Classical Conditioning?

The question of exactly what has been learned as a result of conditioning has been a matter of controversy for years. Early theorizing took a **stimulus-substitution** point of view and held that classical conditioning gave the CS the power to call out the response originally evoked by the US. From the beginning, however, it was clear that there was a problem with this interpretation, for conditioned and unconditioned responses are almost never identical. This meant that not only a new stimulus but a new response was involved in conditioning.

An alternative point of view holds that, in classical conditioning, the subject learns about the CS-US relationship. More specifically, the occurrence of the CS informs the individual that an important event, the US, is about to happen. This emphasis on the information-carrying feature of the CS receives support from two interesting phenomena of conditioning, overshadowing and blocking.

When the CS is a compound stimulus, say a light and a noise presented together, and one of the elements of the compound is more salient than the other, only the salient element becomes effective. If this compound stimulus is paired with a US, say a shock, only the salient element will call out the response when the stimuli are tested separately. This is called **overshadowing.** It is as though the other stimulus added no information to that carried by the salient stimulus. The second is redundant and although alone it would be an effective CS, in combination with the stronger stimulus this effectiveness is overshadowed.

The phenomenon of **blocking** is closely related. Suppose that light is paired with shock for a number of trials—until a CR is well-established—and then light and noise together are paired with the US. Later tests with the noise will show that it does not elicit the CR. Its effectiveness had been blocked by the previous trials with the light, again because the added stimulus is redundant. It adds no information not carried by the original CS.

OPERANT CONDITIONING

At about the time Pavlov was beginning his experiments on classical conditioning in Russia, work on operant conditioning began in America. Edward Lee Thorndike, at Columbia University, studied the learning of chicks, cats, dogs, and monkeys in a number of experimental situations. The best-known of Thorndike's work was that on hungry cats in a puzzle box. The puzzle box was a cage with a door so latched that a cat could open it from the inside by treading on a pedal (Figure 8.4), pulling a string, or turning a button. Outside the box, where the cat could see and smell it, was a bit of fish or liver.

When a cat was first put into the box, it became extremely agitated, clawing and scratching at the sides of the box and anything within, and trying to push it head and paws through the spaces between the slats. Sooner or later, in the course of its struggles, the cat, more or less by accident, released the door and escaped. In the typical Thorndikean experiment the cat was allowed to eat the bit of food but was immediately put back into the box and required to escape again. On this second trial the cat engaged in the same set of agitated movements but confined them for the most part to the region of the box that

Edward Lee Thorndike (1874–1948) put Harlem alley cats in his puzzle boxes, for he was still earning his degree. His study of them, a classic of the literature on learning, was his dissertation.

Figure 8.4
Puzzle box used by Thorndike. In this version the cat can escape from the box and get food outside by pressing the treadle inside the box. A cord and pulley system unlocks the door.

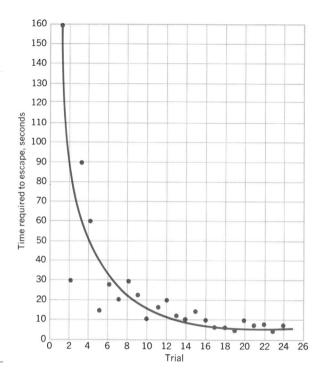

Figure 8.5
Learning curve for a single cat's escapes from the puzzle box. Although the cat's escape time decreased in a somewhat irregular fashion, Thorndike believed that learning is a regular, continuous process. The smooth curve represents this idea.

In his prophetic writings—*Walden Two* (1948) and *Beyond Freedom and Dignity* (1971)—Burrhus Frederick Skinner envisages a behaviorally engineered and controlled society. His basic claim is that we can arrange the conditions of a society so that its citizens will be more likely to do what is desirable.

contained the release mechanism. The animal usually escaped sooner than on the previous trial. On later trials the ineffective scrambling gradually ceased, and the act of opening the door of the cage became more and more precise. The measure of learning employed by Thorndike was the amount of time required by the cat to escape from the puzzle box. With practice, this measure steadily decreased (Figure 8.5).

For obvious reasons such learning was originally called **trial and error,** or sometimes trial and success, **learning.** Later on it came to be called **instrumental learning** because the responses that are learned, such as those that allowed Thorndike's cats to escape from the puzzle box, are instrumental to solving a problem and earning a reward. Burrhus Frederick Skinner of Harvard chose the term *operant conditioning* for such learning because it occurs while the learner is operating on the environment.

Varieties of Operant Conditioning
In his interpretation of the results of his early experiments, Thorndike put forth several principles of learning. The most important of these was the one he referred to as the **law of effect.** The law of effect held that organisms tend to learn responses that have rewarding consequences (effects) and not to learn those that have punishing consequences. This proposal takes us back to the point with which this chapter began, that the consequences of their actions are important in determining what individuals learn. It is time now to be more specific about such matters.

Rewards and punishers are often called, respectively, **positive reinforcers** and **negative reinforcers.** If there is any relationship at all between responses and these consequences, it must be one of two kinds. The response leads either to the presentation or to the withholding of a reinforcer. Since reinforcers can be either positive or negative, there are four possible relationships between behavior and its consequences and therefore four operant conditioning procedures: **reward training, omission training, active avoidance,** and **passive avoidance** (Figure 8.6). We shall deal briefly with each of them.

Reward Training.   In the 1930s B. F. Skinner began an extensive series of studies, first of rats learning to press a bar (Figure 8.7) and then of pigeons learning to peck at an illuminated window, usually called a "key" (Figure 8.8). The apparatuses, both of which have been called **Skinner boxes** by people other than Skinner, are similar. In the bar-pressing or lever-pressing experiment a hungry rat is put into a small compartment containing a short, movable lever on an inside wall. When the rat depresses the lever, an electrical device releases a pellet of food into a food tray. In this experiment food is the reinforcer. Sooner or later the rat learns to press the lever to obtain reinforcement. In the key-pecking experiment a hungry pigeon is placed in a cage which has the key in one wall, located at about eye level for the pigeon. The key is illuminated as a signal that food is available. If the bird pecks at the key, a door below opens, permitting the pigeon to peck from a dish of bird seed for two or three seconds. Again the most important outcome is that pigeons quickly learn to peck the illuminated key for reinforcement in the form of food.

Omission Training.   Although omission training represents a logical and physically possible procedure, it has not been studied much in the laboratory. Under this procedure the animal is rewarded if it *fails* to make a certain response. In one of the few studies of this type, the Polish physiologist Jerzy Konorski describes his method as follows. On the first few trials the ticking of a metronome serves as a signal that food is forthcoming. Then on omission training trials, the metronome is set in motion and at the same time the dog's leg is passively flexed with the aid of a string and pulley arrangement. On these trials the food is omitted. Konorski writes that under these conditions, ". . . the animal begins to resist the passive flexion of the leg by actively extending it. . . . Finally the movement of extension becomes so strong that we are almost able to raise the animal into the air by its extended limb" (1948, pp. 226–227). At least in this case the animal learned the opposite of the response connected with the omission of food.

Active Avoidance.   Active avoidance learning is an operant procedure in which a particular response allows the animal to avoid punishment. It is sometimes studied with a special apparatus which has electrifiable rods for a floor and, in one wall, a wheel that will turn off the electricity if it is rotated (Figure 8.9). In a typical experiment the procedure is as follows. A rat is placed in the apparatus and a warning signal, such as a light or sound, comes on five or ten seconds before an electric current passes through the rods of the floor. If the animal rotates the wheel during this interval, the current does not come on and the animal avoids the shocks. On the very first trials, of course, the rat has not learned this. There is no response to the light, and when the current comes on, the animal shows considerable agitation. It jumps, defecates, urinates, crouches, squeals, and finally clawing or bumping against the wheel, turns it. When the rat succeeds in turning the wheel, perhaps thirty or forty seconds after the beginning of the trials, the warning light and shock both go off immediately. On subsequent trials the rat makes the escape response more and more promptly, until it turns the wheel within a fraction of a second after the onset of shock. With further training the animal learns to turn the wheel when the light comes on and thus to avoid the shock completely. Such learning usually occurs quite rapidly.

Effect of response	Type of reinforcer	
	Reward	Punishment
Reinforcer presented	Reward training	Passive avoidance
Reinforcer withheld	Omission training	Active avoidance

Figure 8.6
Four basic operant conditioning procedures. In these four procedures reinforcers are either positive or negative and the response is rewarded or goes unrewarded.

Figure 8.7
A Skinner box for rats. The apparatus was developed by Skinner (1938) and called an operant chamber by Skinner himself, a Skinner box by others. Pressing the bar delivers a pellet of food from the hopper on the left.

Figure 8.8
Pigeon in a key-pecking apparatus.

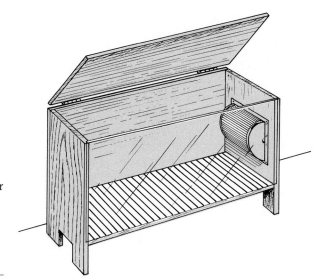

Figure 8.9
A wheel-turning apparatus for studying avoidance learning. In the usual procedure a conditioned stimulus (light or sound) comes on, and then 5 to 10 seconds later an electric current passes through the floor rods. Rotating the wheel after the shock comes on turns it off. Responding to the CS allows the animal to avoid the shock.

Passive Avoidance. In a passive-avoidance experiment the animal learns that a particular response leads to punishment. A common procedure is to place an animal on a platform in the middle of an electrified grid. If it steps down from the platform, it receives shock. Animals very quickly master the simple skill of remaining on the safe platform and thus passively avoiding the shock. This method is widely used to study the memory of lower animals.

Biofeedback and Self-Control

The responses made in operant conditioning are almost always of the kind that we would call "voluntary." The bar pressing, key pecking, and wheel turning just described are examples. In recent years there has been considerable interest in the question whether "involuntary" responses can also be conditioned through operant techniques.

For centuries reports have been reaching us from the East of the impressive accomplishments of the Yogis in gaining control of normally involuntary responses. It is claimed, for example, that the practice of Yoga permits voluntary control of heart rate, blood pressure, oxygen consumption, skin temperature, and a number of other bodily functions that are normally involuntary and managed by the autonomic nervous system. The same sources report impressive alterations in mental states. Within the last several decades the accomplishments claimed by the Yogis have been investigated in the laboratory. The general result came as a surprise to many psychologists; the reports of the Yogis are true. Achieving voluntary control over involuntary processes is actually quite easy for almost anyone. The method is a version of the operant conditioning procedure.

Developing Awareness. The secret of gaining such control is to provide people with some way of knowing what is happening to the bodily process that they are trying to influence. Normally, involuntary responses are also beyond awareness; we do not notice changes in blood pressure, heart rate, body temperature, and the like. But modern electronic technology makes it possible to monitor such functions and to let the individual know their state. The collection of techniques for giving a person knowledge of these physiological functions has come to be called **biofeedback.** With the development of these

This biofeedback equipment monitors muscle tension in the forehead and the temperature of the forefingers of this patient who has migraine headaches. The information obtained from this monitoring is presented on the video screen.

methods, a new specialty has appeared in psychology, the study of biofeedback and self-control.

A representative experiment is that of Jasper Brener and Roger Kleinman (1970), who quickly trained a group of college students to lower their blood pressure. The procedure was quite simple. Blood pressure was monitored by equipment of the type a physician uses to take blood pressure. An electronic monitor made the readings accessible to individuals in an experimental group. They were asked to attend to the signals from the monitor and to keep their blood pressure as low as they could. Individuals in a control group received the same feedback, but they did not know the significance of the signals; they were asked simply to lie still during the experiment. In less than half an hour the members of the experimental group succeeded in reducing their blood pressure by about 15 millimeters of mercury. The methods of biofeedback have been applied to many different clinical problems. In addition to cardiovascular symptoms, some success has been obtained in relieving tension and migraine headaches, bruxism (clenching and grinding the teeth), asthma, enuresis, and gastrointestinal disorders such as fecal incontinence (Miller, 1978).

Direct Control versus Mediation.   The most interesting scientific question raised by these studies concerns the mechanism of control. Is it direct or through some mechanism of mediation? What we mean by **mediation** can be illustrated with this example. Suppose that you are a participant in a biofeedback experiment in which you are supposed to elevate your heart rate on command. Striving to do your best for science, you jump up and down vigorously whenever the command is given. Your heart rate goes up and you receive feedback to that effect. In this way you learn to control your heart rate by jumping up and down, and you contribute to the positive outcome of a study on biofeedback and the self-control of heart rate. But this, you say, is cheating! The increase in heart rate was not direct; it was *mediated* by the response of jumping up and down. This is an important point to make, but it should be made a bit more subtly. Suppose you found that you could *elevate* your heart rate by *imagining* that you were jumping up and down. Would it be cheating to produce the desired response this way? It would also be a case of mediation. Jumping up and down in the imagination is merely less obvious than physically jumping

Neal Miller is a pioneer in establishing the medical legitimacy of biofeedback. He has pointed out the difficulty of patients' maintaining at home through biofeedback the same degree of control of a bodily function obtained in the laboratory or hospital. He also suggests that patients must be adept at discriminating and paying close attention to internal physical signals—their heartbeat, blood pressure, finger warmth, whatever they are trying to control.

up and down. Whatever position you wish to take on this issue, there are now these points to make. (1) Imagined exercise can as a matter of fact influence cardiac responses. (2) It is very difficult to eliminate such effects in studies of biofeedback. (3) The organs of the body function together; one affects others, adding to the possibilities for mediation. For all these reasons the question whether the control of involuntary responses in biofeedback experiments is direct control is still unanswered. Studies of several Yogis found that, to slow their heartbeats, they relied on mediating skeletal responses such as holding their breath and tensing their chest and abdominal muscles (Kimble and Permuter, 1970).

The most impressive attempts to condition visceral responses under circumstances in which possible mediating responses of the skeletal musculature are controlled were those of Neal Miller and his colleagues (see Miller, 1978). These investigators undertook the conditioning of visceral responses with curarized animals, in this case laboratory rats. The curare immobilized the skeletal musculature of the animals and eliminated the possibility that their skeletal responses could mediate the conditioned viscera reaction.

There are numerous technical problems with experiments of this type. Since curarization prevents the animals from breathing, they must be given artificial respiration. Food, water, and electric shock are ruled out as reinforcers because curare makes it impossible for the animals to use the muscles needed for ingestion and to avoid shock. Miller and his colleagues solved the problem by using electrical stimulation of a "pleasure center" in the brain (page 86) as a reinforcer. Before the experiment began, electrodes were placed in the rat's hypothalamus, and bar-pressing tests were carried out to ensure that electrical stimulation had a rewarding effect. In one experiment one group of rats received this rewarding brain stimulation for an increase in heart rate; another group received the same reward for a decrease in heart rate (Miller and DiCara, 1967). During the course of the experiment, the subjects in the first group learned to speed up their heart rate considerably; those in the second group learned to slow it down.

Clinical Applications.   For some still undiscovered reason later studies, even in Miller's own laboratory, were unable to reproduce the results obtained in the earlier investigations. Therefore the validity of the earlier data is now in doubt. In the meantime, however, accumulating clinical evidence had made a strong case that the conclusion drawn from these experiments was probably correct. Miller and Bernard Brucker (1979), for example, describe the case of a man paralyzed from the waist down by a gunshot wound which had severed the spinal cord. He had powerful arms and shoulders, but he found it impossible to walk with crutches and braces. Whenever he stood up, his blood pressure fell so low that he fainted. This patient was fitted with a blood pressure cuff that turned on an auditory signal whenever he raised his blood pressure to a criterion level. To everyone's surprise, because other therapy had been totally unsuccessful in helping this man, he learned to control his blood pressure and thus was able to walk with crutches and braces. Similar results were obtained with other paraplegic patients. In these cases mediating muscular control is impossible because of the nature of the spinal injury.

SUMMARY

Both in real life and in the laboratory, it is possible to identify some situations in which a person has almost no control over rewards and punishments and others in which there is considerable control. The first of these is the classical conditioning situation. The second is that for operant conditioning. In classical conditioning experiments a neutral conditioned stimulus (CS) is paired with a nonneutral stimulus (US) which produces a dependable response (UR). The result of such pairing is that the CS becomes capable of eliciting a response (CR) resembling the UR. During the process of classical conditioning what the individual learns is that the CS predicts the US is forthcoming. The phenomena of overshadowing and blocking show that noninformative stimuli, without predictive value, do not participate in the conditioning process.

The distinguishing feature of operant conditioning is that such learning takes place under conditions in which the learner's behavior has specific consequences. These consequences, referred to by Thorndike as "effects" in his law of effect, are either positive reinforcers (rewards) or negative reinforcers (punishments). The response may be rewarded or go unrewarded by either a positive or a negative reinforcer. Thus we can identify four operant conditioning procedures: reward training, omission training, active avoidance learning, and passive avoidance learning.

The responses that can be conditioned by operant methods are usually "voluntary" responses. This fact raises the interesting question whether "involuntary" responses can be conditioned in this way. For example, can we learn to control blood pressure and heart rate by the methods of operant conditioning? People learn such control quite readily when provided with feedback that indicates the state of the system over which they are attempting to establish control. An important question is whether biofeedback allows the person to exert direct control over involuntary responses or whether this control is mediated by voluntary processes. Although the issue has not been completely settled, a growing body of evidence suggests that direct control is possible.

BASIC PHENOMENA

Now that the procedures of classical and operant conditioning have been described, we are in a position to discuss the basic psychology of learning, to explain the phenomena and principles that have been discovered in experimental work on classical and operant conditioning.

Acquisition

Although learning is sometimes sudden and insightful, it is more commonly gradual. This fact makes it natural to present the course of learning in the form of a **learning curve.** The horizontal axis of such a graph is always some measure of practice, either the number of practice trials or the amount of time devoted to practice. The vertical axis is always some measure of performance. Some of the most common measures of learning are the percentage of conditioned or correct responses; the strength or magnitude of the response; the time required to complete a response; and response latency, the time between some signal, such as a CS, and the response. Depending on the measure, the learning curve may increase or decrease. Magnitude and percentage measures increase; time and latency decrease, as is shown in Figure 8.10.

Cumulative Response Curves.
The curves in Figure 8.10 show the progresss of learning in experiments in which there are separate trials. In the Skinner boxes, in which animals are free to respond as they choose, there are no trials. The animal remains in the experimental situation for a period of time and responds as it will. Performance in such experiments is often recorded auto-

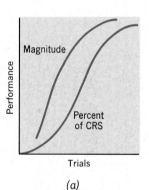

(a)

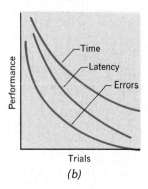

(b)

Figure 8.10
Characteristic forms of learning curves.
(a) Percentage of CRs and response magnitude increase with practice. (b) Latency measures and other time measures decrease, as do errors. Errors can decrease to zero.

Figure 8.11

The operation of a cumulative recorder.
The paper moves at a constant speed in
the direction indicated. A response, the
bar press or key peck, operates an
electromagnet, which moves the pen one
step upward. When the pen reaches the
top of the paper, it activates a switch,
which causes the pen to move back to
the bottom of the paper. In this way the
animal draws its own learning curve.
Responses are also counted by an electric
counter.

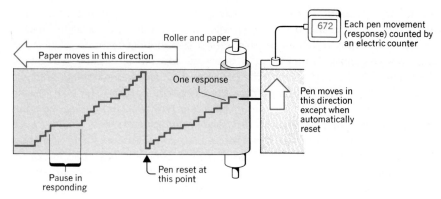

matically, as a **cumulative response curve.** A long sheet of recording paper
moves continuously and at a constant rate beneath a pen (Figure 8.11). Every
time the animal responds, the pen moves upward by a small fixed step. A
learning curve revealing the rate of responding is produced automatically. The
faster the rate of responding, the steeper the slope of the record.

Behavioral Shaping. Training a pigeon to peck at a key to obtain food in
the operant situation is often handled in a succession of steps. Such training
begins by teaching the bird to eat from the food dish. This is accomplished in
a series of trials in which the experimenter occasionally opens the food magazine
so that the bird can learn where the food is. Training the desired response
begins when this first stage is complete and the bird shows only positive
reactions to the sounds and sights produced by the food-delivery mechanism
as it offers the reward of bird seed. At first the experimenter opens the food
hopper whenever the pigeon is near the illuminated key. This keeps the pigeon
near it. In the next step the pigeon must be very near the key to receive
reinforcement. And, finally, it is required to peck at the key, which opens the
food hopper automatically. These three stages, near the key, very near the key,
and pecking at the key, represent a series of gradual approximations to the
response that the pigeon is to learn. For this reason the method is called the
method of successive approximations or, more often, **shaping.** The second term suggests a gradual molding of the response to the form desired by
the experimenter.

Schedules of Reinforcement. In the operant procedures described so far the
learner received a reward every time it made the required response. Such
continuous reinforcement, however, is not typical of learning as it goes on
in the everyday world. The gambler at the card table wins only part of the time.
A mother's efforts to teach her children the expected social graces are sometimes
successful, but sometimes not. A student's efforts to guess which questions will
be on the next exam are sometimes correct, winning a good grade, but sometimes the student makes bad guesses and the grade is poor. In all these situations
the reinforcement schedule is what would technically be called a partial or
intermittent schedule. **Partial reinforcement** or **intermittent reinforcement** is any arrangement in which the learner is rewarded only a fraction of
the time for making a certain response. The variety of schedules of partial
reinforcement developed for rats and pigeons performing in Skinner boxes is
enormous. Four schedules, however, are basic. These are the fixed-ratio, variable-ratio, fixed-interval, and variable-interval schedules. Rewards are given

after fixed or variable numbers of responses or after fixed or variable amounts of time.

In the **fixed-ratio (FR) schedule** the learner must make a fixed number of responses to receive reward. The fixed-ratio schedule is the piecework schedule of the sweatshop in which a worker is paid a particular amount for sewing a certain number of garments. In a bar-pressing experiment with a fixed-ratio schedule, a reward might be given for every second, tenth, or thirtieth response, in which case the ratios are 2 (responses): 1 (reward), 10:1, or 30:1. In the terms employed by those working in this field, these schedules would be referred to as FR (fixed ratio) 2, FR 10, FR 30.

In the **fixed-interval (FI) schedule** reward follows the first response to occur after a certain amount of time, such as thirty seconds (FI 30).

In the **variable-ratio (VR) schedule** rewards are irregular, but they come after a number of responses that average out to some particular number. On a VR 10 schedule reward would be given on the average after ten responses. For example, five rewards might occur after four, fourteen, ten, one, and twenty-one responses. Averaging, $4 + 14 + 10 + 1 + 21 = 50$; $50 \div 5 = 10$. Hence the designation VR 10.

In the **variable-interval (VI) schedule** rewards follow the first responses after varying amounts of time that average out to a certain value. If the average of these varying amounts of time were thirty seconds, the schedule would be called a VI 30 schedule.

Typical performances under these schedules are illustrated in Figure 8.12. Rats that are on a fixed-ratio schedule soon work very hard. They make a great many bar presses very rapidly, almost as though they know that a certain number of responses are required to earn the next pellet. They may pause immediately after receiving and eating a pellet, especially if they must press many times for the reward, but they soon start again with a great burst of fast bar presses. Rats on a fixed-interval schedule, once they have gained some experience, routinely pause after receiving a pellet and ignore the bar for a

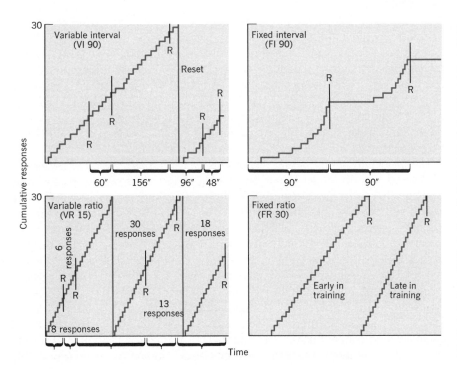

Figure 8.12

Hypothetical, but fairly typical, cumulative response curves under different schedules of reinforcement. Facts to note: (1) The vertical lines marked R mean reinforcement. (2) Performance under the variable-interval schedule is very steady. (3) Performance under the fixed-interval schedule shows a pronounced scallop. The animal has probably learned that it is never rewarded again immediately after receiving one reward. It responds slowly at this point, but it speeds its rate of responding as the moment of reward approaches. (4) On a variable-ratio schedule the animal responds very rapidly because it learns that rewards can be received soon after a previous reward, and that increasing the number of responses increases the number of rewards. (5) The difference between rates of responding early and late in training indicates that the animal learns that rapid responding brings reward quickly.

Habits acquired through partial reinforcement are extremely persistent.

while. Apparently they learn that immediately after receiving a pellet, whether they press or not, there is never another one. Then, as the time nears for the next pellet to be given for pressing the bar, they set to work again. Rats on a variable-interval schedule, however, work steadily for their pellets, for they may receive one at any moment. Those on a variable-ratio schedule press the bar very steadily and rapidly for this same reason and because a number of bar presses must be made to keep the pellets coming. The slot machines in a gambling casino are set to pay off on a variable-ratio schedule and are very effective in keeping the customers playing through long stretches for the occasional and unpredictable rain of coins.

Extinction

As we have seen, classical conditioning takes place when CS and US are paired, operant conditioning when reward or punishment follows a given response. Omitting the US in the classical procedure, or discontinuing reward or punishment in the operant procedure, can undo the process and extinguish the conditioned response. When Pavlov's conditioned dogs saw the light come on again and again but never received meat powder, the drops of saliva they secreted gradually decreased in number. The light was no longer a signal for food to them. The course of **extinction** of a salivary CR is shown in Figure 8.13a.

The extinction of an operant response is similar. If bar pressing or pecking at the lighted key no longer brings an offering of food, the rat and pigeon may continue these responses for a while, but eventually the rate falls off. The rat will press the bar, the pigeon peck the key only in the ordinary and haphazard explorations of their boxes.

The number of unreinforced trials or responses that are necessary to obtain extinction depends on many variables. In general, it is more difficult to extinguish well-learned responses than weak ones. A special condition that delays extinction is a prior schedule of partial reinforcement. That is, the individual who learned under a schedule of partial reinforcement persists longer in responding without any reinforcement at all than an individual who learned originally with continuous reinforcement. This heightened resistance to extinction is called the **partial-reinforcement effect.** Human gambling is probably

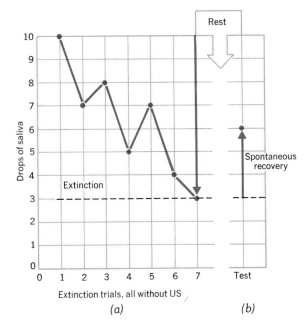

Figure 8.13
Extinction and spontaneous recovery.
The data are for a single dog described by Pavlov (1927). The arrow pointing downward indicates that unreinforced trials reduced the number of drops of saliva from 10 to 3. The arrow pointing upward indicates that, after rest, the number of drops increased from 3 back up to 6 through spontaneous recovery. Such incomplete recovery, 6 drops rather than 10, is usual.

the most important manifestation of the partial-reinforcement effect. Gambling persists even when the gambler has a long streak of bad luck, probably because the gambling habit was learned with partial reinforcement. If it had been established with continuous reinforcement in the first place, the gambler would probably give up after a few substantial losses.

The partial-reinforcement effect is explained by several factors that are not entirely different from one another. (1) During acquisition on a partial schedule, the individual learns to persist in the face of no reinforcement; this persistence continues when there are no rewards at all. (2) The shift from partial reinforcement to none is much less noticeable than the shift from continous reinforcement to none. (3) When individuals have learned to make responses which are only occasionally rewarded, their memories of earlier nonreinforcement are reminders that reward may be given only after a number of responses. In other words, nonreinforcement becomes one of the stimuli for responding. For a long time during the extinction process, nonreinforcement continues to be a cue that encourages a response.

Spontaneous Recovery

Extinction often only temporarily suppresses the conditioned response. When the animal is given an interval of rest following extinction, the CR may reappear spontaneously. During the rest period the previously extinguished CR regains strength and, on a new trial with a CS, the animal may again make the CR. After this **spontaneous recovery** the animal will continue to make the CR for a few more trials without reinforcement. The following example from Pavlov illustrates the point. A dog was conditioned to salivate to the sound of a metronome (CS). Then, on seven extinction trials, the metronome ticked on without the presentation of food (US). During this period the drops of saliva produced in response to the metronome decreased from ten to three; the salivary CR was extinguishing. At this point the dog was given a rest, and twenty-three minutes later the metronome was started again. On the first trial after the rest interval, six drops of saliva were secreted, indicating a stronger response than on the last extinction trial (Figure 8.13*b*).

In operant conditioning the rat's bar pressing and the pigeon's key pecking also show spontaneous recovery after these responses have been extinguished. Returned to the home cage overnight and then put back in the Skinner box, the rat or pigeon will often go immediately to the bar or key and begin responding.

In practical terms the phenomenon of spontaneous recovery is important because it shows that we cannot count on the permanent disappearance of a habit that we thought we had broken. With lapses of time it may reappear. As the data in Figure 8.13b indicate, however, the spontaneously recovered response tends to be weaker than responses before extinction began. This means that a second extinction will occur more rapidly. If the spontaneously recovered CR is not now reinforced by the US, it quickly reextinguishes. With a series of such extinctions, the response may disappear completely and be beyond spontaneous recovery. If the US is reintroduced, however, the reaction reconditions rapidly and reattains its original strength.

Figure 8.14 is a review of the phenomena of conditioning covered so far. The left-hand portion of the figure shows the acquisition of the learned response. The intermediate portion demonstrates the process of extinction. The extreme right-hand portion shows what happens to a response that has spontaneously recovered and then is reinforced (upper curve) or not reinforced (lower curve).

Figure 8.14

Review of some basic phenomena. The upper graphs are for classical conditioning. The lower graphs are the cumulative response curves for operant conditioning. You should notice the lengths of the horizontal lines for the various operant responses. The lengths of these lines represent times during which a response does occur. Shorter lines mean more rapid responding, that is, responding in a shorter time than that designated by longer lines. Both graphs will repay careful study.

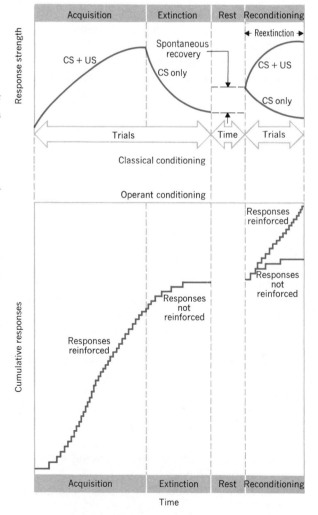

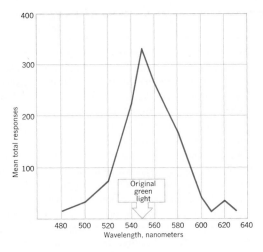

Figure 8.15
Stimulus generalization in key pecking of the pigeon. Originally the key was illuminated with a greenish light. When pigeons were tested with lights ranging from blue to red, their key pecking indicated a generalization gradient. (Data courtesy of Dr. Norman Guttman.)

Stimulus Generalization

The CS in a classical conditioning experiment is usually a very specific one, a light of a certain hue and brightness, or sound of a certain pitch and loudness. In the operant conditioning experiment the pigeon pecks at a key illuminated with a light of a certain color. It is natural to wonder whether other more or less similar stimuli can evoke the CR. A variety of experiments have shown that a CR can be elicited by such stimuli. This phenomenon is called **stimulus generalization.**

We have already met one example of stimulus generalization in classical conditioning, the transfer of Little Albert's fear of the rat to other fury objects. Pavlov also reported several instances of stimulus generalization. In an operant experiment pigeons were trained to peck at a key illuminated with a green light. Then the pigeons were tested with lights of different colors. The birds did tend to peck at any color (Figure 8.15), but the number of key pecks fell off as the difference between the color of the training stimulus and that of the test stimulus increased. This symmetrical falling off of the number of responses as the test stimulus becomes more and more different from the training stimulus is called a **generalization gradient.**

Discrimination

The concepts of acquisition, extinction, and generalization can be used in combination to account for the phenomenon of **discrimination.** An animal can learn to respond to a particular stimulus and not to a slightly different one. Pavlov described a discrimination experiment in which a dog was conditioned to salivate at the tone of a specific tuning fork. After such training the dog's conditioned salivation generalized to neighboring tones, although the response was not as strong as to the tone used as a conditioned stimulus. Then in a new procedure the dog heard the original tone and a different one on randomly alternated trials. Food continued to follow the original tone, but the second tone was never reinforced. As a result, the dog's generalized response to the second tone gradually extinguished, but the response to the original stimulus was maintained. This process of reinforcing one tone and withholding reinforcement for the other thus taught the animal a discrimination. The dog salivated when it heard the reinforced tone but not when it heard the other.

As this example shows, the development of a discrimination combines several of the processes described in previous sections. Through the pairing of a certain tone with the US, the dog (1) acquires a CR that (2) generalizes to a similar stimulus. Through the omission of the US following the presentation of this

EXPERIMENTAL NEUROSIS

Perhaps the most dramatic observations to come from Pavlov's famous conditioning studies were those of an animal required to make a very difficult discrimination. Pavlov first conditioned a dog to salivate when it saw a circular figure. Then he established a discrimination between the circle and an ellipse. Whenever the circle was presented, food followed; whenever the ellipse appeared, food failed to follow. Soon the dog came to salivate to the circle but not to the ellipse. When the discrimination was strongly established, the experimenter began, day by day, to widen the ellipse so that it became more and more

similar to the circle. Finally, the two stimuli were so much alike that the dog could not distinguish between them. At this point the dog's performance began to deteriorate. Salivation, the conditioned reflex, disappeared and, at the same time, the entire behavior of the animal underwent a marked change. Previously quiet and docile, the dog began to squeal in the restraining apparatus and tore at the equipment and at the tubes for measuring saliva. The dog also showed signs of great anxiety— whimpering, trembling, and refusing to eat—as well as drowsiness and yawning. And it barked frantically whenever it was

taken to the experimental room. Pavlov called his reaction an **experimental neurosis.**

Pavlov described experimental neurosis as a clash between excitation and inhibition. Translated into slightly more modern phrases, **excitation** is the animal's positive tendency to respond, acquired through reinforcement. **Inhibition** is its tendency to withhold a response because it has not been reinforced. This interpretation was very much in line with the view that human neuroses reflect conflict, a position held in Pavlov's time by Sigmund Freud.

similar stimulus, the dog's CR (3) is extinguished. A discrimination is established by reinforcing a response to a particular stimulus and extinguishing generalized responses to similar stimuli.

Animals can also be trained by operant methods to make discriminations. For example, a pigeon will learn to peck only when the key is illuminated with a light of a particular color if responses to that color are reinforced and responses to other colors are not reinforced. The processes involved seem to be the same as those responsible for the development of conditioned discriminations in the classical situation. Responses to a reinforced stimulus are maintained while generalized responses to nonreinforced stimuli are extinguished.

Higher-Order Conditioning

The final phenomenon to be described is **higher-order conditioning.** One of Pavlov's experimental demonstrations consisted of the following steps. A dog was conditioned to salivate at the ticking of a metronome. After this CR had been very well established, a card with a black square on it was brought into the dog's field of vision just before the ticking began. Food, the original US, was no longer given. In other words, the sound of the metronome, which was the original CS, now served as the US. The black square became a second-order CS. Through this pairing of the black square and the metronome, the dog came to salivate at the sight of the black square, even when there was no ticking. In this demonstration the amount of saliva secreted when the metronome was paired with food in the first-order conditioning procedure was about twelve drops. After ten pairings of the black square with the metronome in the second-order conditioning procedure, the black square evoked six drops of saliva, although the square had never been paired with food directly. Pavlov was successful in obtaining third-order conditioning as well. When a tuning fork was struck just before the black square was seen by the dog, salivation eventually followed its sounding. Pavlov had great trouble obtaining third-order conditioning and was never able to achieve higher than third-order conditioning in dogs. The difficulty with higher-order conditioning is that it is running a race against the extinction process. The procedure extinguishes the original CR because food is never provided. The dogs do not have a chance to learn to salivate to a higher than third-order CS because this response has already been extinguished.

Work on secondary reinforcement, to be described more fully in the next section, reveals that something like higher-order operant conditioning is also possible. In operant conditioning we say that the animal may learn to work for a *secondary reinforcer* because it has been associated with a *primary reinforcer*. For example, if the rat presses the bar and hears a click at the same time that the food pellet, the primary reinforcer, slides into the tray, the animal will continue to press the bar just to hear the click, even though food is no longer offered.

SUMMARY

The phenomena described in this section begin to show the rich variety of influences that learning brings to behavior. (1) Acquisition occurs as a result of reinforcement, when CS and US are paired in classical conditioning or when reward or punishment follows the response in operant conditioning. Schedules of reinforcement can be arranged to control the rapidity and strength of a response as well as whether the response is made. The progress of learning is often represented in graphic form, as a learning curve which shows how some measure of performance changes with the amount of practice. (2) Nonreinforcement leads to extinction of the conditioned response, but resistance to extinction varies with a number of conditions, the most important of which is the schedule of reinforcement. Partial or intermittent reinforcement, of which the four principal types are fixed-interval, fixed-ratio, variable-interval, and variable-ratio, increases persistence and slows up the extinction process. (3) An extinguished response often shows spontaneous recovery if the subject is allowed a brief rest following extinction. This recovery indicates that the extinguished response was suppressed rather than completely erased. (4) The responses conditioned to a particular CS in classical conditioning, or controlled by a particular discriminative stimulus in operant conditioning, are given to similar stimuli, a phenomenon called stimulus generalization. The greater the difference between training and test stimuli, however, the weaker the response to the test stimulus. A graph of this relationship is called a generalization gradient. (5) A discrimination is learned, in both classical and operant conditioning, when reinforcement maintains the responses to one stimulus and nonreinforcement extinguishes generalized responses to similar stimuli. (6) Higher-order conditioning is accomplished by making the CS from an earlier stage of a classical conditioning experiment the US in a later stage. In operant conditioning stimuli associated with primary reinforcers become secondary reinforcers and are sought for themselves

CLASSICAL-OPERANT INTERACTIONS

As we mentioned in the first pages of this chapter, classical and operant conditioning procedures are a means of simplifying the learning process as an aid to investigation, but in most actual learning situations both forms of learning occur together. Moreover, the two forms of learning affect each other.

Secondary Motives and Rewards

Some motives and their corresponding rewards are **primary motives** and **rewards.** They depend very little on experience. Hunger and food, thirst and water, and escape from pain are obvious examples. Other motives and satisfactions, including most of those that are important to human behavior, are acquired through experience. The needs for power, approval, and achievement and the means of their satisfaction are examples.

No doubt the mechanism for the establishment of these **secondary motives**

The "Chimp-O-Mat." If the chimpanzee puts a token into the slot, it receives a piece of food in exchange.

and **secondary reinforcers** is as complicated as learning itself. It appears, however, that classical conditioning is a part of the story. Stimuli that are associated with primary rewards become secondary rewards, and stimuli associated with primary motives become secondary motives. A description of some of the best-known studies on secondary motives and reinforcers will help to clarify these abstract statements.

Conditioned Positive Reinforcement. One of the investigations of secondary reinforcers is now a classic. In these studies (Wolfe, 1936) chimpanzees first learned to insert small disks, about the size of poker chips, into a vending machine to obtain a grape, banana, peanut, or other pieces of desirable food. Through this experience, which associated the tokens with food, tokens came to be secondary reinforcers. The chimpanzees then learned a number of other responses, for which the only reward was a token. One such response was lifting a weighted lever. Another was to pull toward them, by means of a cord, a sliding tray which was baited with a token. The animals would continue to work for and save these tokens, even though they could not be exchanged for food until later.

An important incidental point made by this study is that the motive-reward distinction is not a completely sharp one. Although the association of tokens with food made the tokens secondary rewards for the chimpanzees, the tokens were obviously also functioning as motivators. The animals were willing to work for them. In the terms that are generally used, the tokens became **incentives** at the same time that they acquired secondary reinforcing power.

The Token Economy. **Token economies** created for the management of hospitalized psychiatric patients are a direct application of these ideas to human problems. In the token economy of the mental hospital, patients receive plastic or metal chips, or sometimes paper money, for desired behavior such as dressing neatly, making beds, or talking to others. They may then exchange these tokens for specific goods from the commissary, for privileges such as a better room or choice of dining partners, for activities such as taking part in recreation programs and excursions, and for time away from the institution. The most dramatic successes of these methods have been with psychotic patients who had been kept out of sight in the back wards of state mental hospitals for a decade or more. Such people are out of social contact, slovenly, uncooperative; they spend their hours sleeping, in stuporous thought, or in aimless motor activity. If you have read *One Flew Over the Cuckoo's Nest* or seen the movie, you have the picture. With the installation of token economies, the attitudes, behavior, and appearance of patients have improved considerably (Krasner, 1976).

Conditioned Fear and Active Avoidance Learning

When the animal learns to turn the wheel to avoid shock in the avoidance learning situation described earlier, it learns two things. The first of these is a form of classical conditioning in which the light is the CS and the shock is the US. The pairing of light and shock produces a conditioned fear, a secondary motive; the CS becomes capable of arousing fear. This is important because now the animal has a motive for responding before the shock comes on. The motive is the fear evoked by the light.

The other thing that the animal learns is when to turn the wheel. At first this operant response is a means of escaping shock after it comes on. With practice, however, the animal, motivated by fear of the CS, turns the wheel *before* the shock comes on. When it does so, the light goes off and fear subsides; wheel turning is no longer rewarded by eliminating shock but by a sharp reduction in fear. This account is a **two-factor theory** of avoidant behavior. The avoidant reaction is *motivated* by conditioned fear and is *reinforced* by reduction of fear.

This simple learning process can explain important aspects of human behavior, such as the development of neurotic symptoms. The case of Mrs. A, described by John Dollard and Neal Miller (1950), will show the connection.

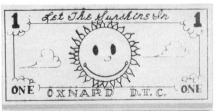

> Mrs. A., a strikingly beautiful twenty-three-year-old married woman who came for psychotherapy, complained of a number of fears, the strongest of which was a fear that her heart would stop beating. Because of this fear she had developed the annoying neurotic symptom of compulsively counting her heartbeats. Born an orphan, Mrs. A had been brought up by a harsh foster mother whose exceedingly repressive sex training had made her feel that sex was evil and dirty. In spite of this Mrs. A developed unusually strong sexual urges. Before her marriage she had slept with a dozen different men, on every occasion feeling painfully guilty.

These few details of Mrs. A's background are enough to show the basis of her fear and to explain why she counted her heartbeats. Mrs. A. was highly motivated sexually, but in the past the stimuli of sexual arousal had been conditioned to bring on an intense anxiety reaction. The conditioning sequence was CS, sexual stimuli, followed by US, punishment at the hands of her repressive foster mother. Mrs. A's predominant symptom, counting her heartbeats, was an avoidant response, motivated by anxiety, now interpreted as a fear that her heart would stop beating, and rewarded by reducing this anxiety. Whenever a sexual thought came to mind, Mrs. A became anxious about her heart and started counting. Since this took all her attention, the sexual fantasy and the resulting anxiety disappeared from consciousness.

In the token economy of the Oxnard Community Mental Health Center, the day-care patient receives paper money in the amounts listed on the bulletin board for accomplishing the work tasks listed.

Learned Helplessness

Another important phenomenon with relevance to human experience has been observed in experiments in which animals receive punishment that is in no way contingent on their behavior. Under these circumstances animals behave as though they have learned that they can do nothing to control the situation; they behave as though they were helpless.

Experiment with Dogs. Steven Maier and Martin Seligman (1976) have conducted several studies of **learned helplessness** with three groups of dogs. All dogs were eventually tested in a shuttle box like the one shown in Figure 8.16. By jumping the hurdle, the animal is able to avoid a painful electric shock. Before this test, however, the three groups received different treatments. One group received no shock at all. The dogs in another group were strapped into a harness and received shocks, which they soon learned were escapable. They were able to turn the shock off by moving their heads and pressing a panel. The third group of dogs was a **yoked control group**; these dogs were also

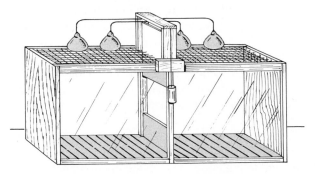

Figure 8.16
Avoidance apparatus for dogs. The animal is placed on one side or the other of the apparatus and must jump the partition to escape or avoid shock from the floor rods of that compartment. In some versions of the experiment the dog merely shuttles back and forth. In others the lights come on as a warning signal. (Adapted with permission of Richard L. Solomon.)

harnessed and were subjected to electric shock at the same time as the dogs in the second group. They could not control shock by pressing a panel, however. By means of electrical wiring, the animals receiving the escapable shock turned off the shock for their partners in the yoked control group. Maier and Seligman found that when the dogs in the three groups were put into the shuttle box, they behaved in the following ways.

> When placed in the shuttle box an experimentally naive dog (and also one that has experienced escapable shock), at the onset of the first electric shock, runs frantically about, until it accidentally scrambles over the barrier and escapes the shock. On the next trial, the dog, running frantically, crosses the barrier more quickly. . . . Within a few trials the animal becomes very efficient at escaping and soon learns to avoid shock altogether. . . . But the dogs first given inescapable shock . . . show a strikingly different pattern. Such a dog's first reactions to shock in the shuttle box are much the same as those of a naive dog. He runs around frantically for about 30 seconds, but then stops moving, lies down, and quietly whines. After 1 minute of this, shock terminates automatically. The dog fails to cross the barrier and escape from shock. On the next trial, the dog again fails to escape. At first he struggles a bit and then, after a few seconds, seems to give up and passively accept the shock. On all succeeding trials, the dog continues to fail to escape. . . .
>
> We believe that these phenomena are instances of "learned helplessness," instances in which an organism has learned that outcomes are uncontrollable by his responses and is seriously debilitated by this knowledge (p. 4).

Knowledge that its responses will not control outcomes is debilitating to the animal in three ways. It has the *cognitive* effect of interfering with the animal's ability to perceive contingent relationships between behavior and its consequences, the *motivational* effect of keeping the dog from initiating escape responses when they would be effective, and the *emotional* effect of calling out maladaptive responses, such as crouching and immobility.

Human Helplessness.   The earliest demonstrations of learned helplessness in dogs were published in the late 1960s (Overmier and Seligman, 1967; Seligman and Maier, 1967). By the early 1970s there had been successful demonstrations of similar phenomena with human subjects. The reference experiments with college students (Hiroto, 1974) used the same triadic design that had been employed with dogs. One group of students learned to turn off (escape from) a noxious loud noise by pushing a button. A yoked control group heard the same noise, but independently of their responses. A third group heard no noise. After these preliminary treatments the three groups were tested in a hand shuttle box where all they had to do to escape noise was to move the hand from one side of the apparatus to the other. The results were the same as in the animal experiments. The students who had heard no noise or were able to turn it off performed quite well, but most of those in the previously yoked group just sat there and accepted the unpleasant noise.

In the meantime it has been demonstrated that failure on cognitive tasks can teach helplessness, just as uncontrollable aversive physical stimuli had in the studies with dogs and college students (Dweck and Repucci, 1973). Learned helplessness is a common classroom experience of children. Some children find that failure in school is an uncontrollable aversive event, something that is independent of their behavior. No matter what they do, failure seems to follow. They therefore feel helpless and see no reason to keep trying to do their schoolwork.

Studies with children, most often third graders, have now revealed important aspects of learned helplessness, which contribute much to our understanding and add to the importance of the phenomenon. For the development of human helplessness, the experience of uncontrollable failure is not enough. An important additional factor is where the person puts the blame for failure. Children who feel helpless tend to attribute their failure to their own inadequate abilities or sometimes to impossible external cimcumstances. Children who attribute failure to a lack of personal effort are less likely to develop a sense of helplessness (Dweck, 1975). Moreover, the self-esteem of children who feel helpless through their failures and personal inadequacies is damaged. They think of themselves as ineffective, as losers, as unable to cope with the problems of the world.

Fortunately, there is evidence that the reaction of helplessness can be conquered with training. Children can be taught to attribute success or failure to the amount of effort they devote to a task rather than to personal adequacy (Fowler and Peterson, 1981; Johnson, 1981). In this connection it is very important to recognize that, contrary to common opinion, arranging events so that children are certain to succeed is not enough to erase their helplessness. Children who felt helpless and were given a series of successes were later as helpless in the face of failure as they had been before. Being successful whatever they do leaves children as much out of control as inevitable failure or punishment does. Children need to learn that there is a relationship between their behavior and such consequences and that what they do is the determining factor.

Biological Constraints on Learning

During the first half of the present century the dominant opinion in psychology was that almost every aspect of behavior was modifiable by experience. Research in the field of classical conditioning lent support to this interpretation, for it was demonstrated that a wide range of responses could be conditioned to many different forms of stimulation. As a result psychology came to accept a **premise of equipotentiality** (Seligman and Hager, 1972), according to which any reaction an organism can make can be conditioned to any stimulus it can detect.

Physiological Preparedness.   With time, however, it became clear that the elegantly simple view expressed in the premise of equipotentiality is too simple. Some responses are difficult and perhaps impossible to condition to certain stimuli, although they may be conditioned easily to other stimuli.

Sam Revusky and John Garcia (1970) have made this point by describing an imaginary experiment that goes as follows.

> [Suppose that while you are reading this account] . . . you find $100 on the floor. Presumably this functions as a reward for you. The $100 was left by an insane billionaire experimenter because, two hours ago at lunch [for the first time in your life] you ate gooseberry pie for dessert instead of your usual apple pie. The experimenter wanted to increase the future probability that you would eat gooseberry pie.
>
> It is very unlikely that this experiment will be successful unless you are actually told the connection between consumption of gooseberry pie and receipt of the $100. . . .
>
> Let us now change . . . our thought experiment: you are reading this paper and suddenly you become sick. Since the gooseberry pie was new to you, you would probably conclude that the pie caused the illness. . . .
>
> Thus associations over long delays must be explained in terms of natural restraints on the process of associative learning (pp. 21–22).

Revusky and Garcia are saying that a **principle of preparedness** appears to be at work to favor the establishment of certain associations rather than others. You are somehow biologically ready to form an association between a taste and the experience of sickness, but you are not prepared to associate a taste with the positive reactions brought on by a substantial amount of money. You may even be prepared not to make such associations.

Experiments with lower animals support this interpretation. In a typical experiment an animal—usually a rat, but cats, mice, birds, and monkeys have shown the same reactions—is allowed to taste and consume some substance with a novel taste. Water flavored with saccharine is a common example. Then, several hours later, the animal is made sick by subjecting it to X-rays or by administering a sublethal dose of poison. When the animal recovers from the effects of this treatment, it is given access once more to the substance with the novel taste. Now the animal avoids it, as though it thought the substance had made it sick (Seligman and Hager, 1972).

These results are very different from those obtained in other experiments. For one thing, associations between CS (taste) and US (sickness) are made after an interval of an hour or more. Usually conditioning does not occur if the time between stimuli is more than a few seconds. For a second thing, learning in this situation happens all at once, in a single trial. These results bring to mind a concept of "belongingness" that Thorndike proposed many years ago. Thorndike believed that certain pairs of events naturally belonged together and were easy to associate. The work on taste aversion seems to prove that taste and sickness are such a pair. Control studies have demonstrated that rats *do not* learn to avoid a *place* after being made sick there, although they do avoid the place where they have experienced electric shock. Just as Thorndike proposed, there apparently are certain sympathies between stimuli: sights and pain are easy for the rat to associate, as are tastes and sickness.

The phenomena of conditioned taste aversions are common in human experience. In the introduction to his book *Biological Boundaries of Learning* (1972), written with Joanne Hager, Seligman tells this personal story.

> Sauce Béarnaise is an egg-thickened, tarragon-flavored concoction, and it used to be my favorite sauce. It now tastes awful to me. This happened several years ago, when I felt the effects of the stomach flu . . . after eating filet mignon with Sauce Béarnaise. I became violently ill and spent most of the night vomiting. The next time I had Sauce Béarnaise, I couldn't bear the taste of it. At the time, I had no ready way to account for the change, although it seemed to fit a classical conditioning paradigm: CS (sauce) paired with US (illness) and UR (vomiting) yields CR (nauseating taste) . . . (p. 8).

There is now good reason to suppose that taste aversions can accompany vitamin deficiencies (Rozin, 1968) and diseases such as cancer in which nausea is a common symptom. Ilene Berstein and Ronald Sigmundi (1980), for example, found that rats implanted with a lethal tumor ate much less food than control animals, and that they did so because they developed aversions to the tastes of the foods eaten while the tumor was developing. The same authors point out that people also develop aversions to the foods that they consume while they are undergoing chemotherapy and radiation therapy, which have well-known nauseating side effects.

Preparedness and Conditioned Fears. The point so dramatically made by the taste aversion experiments is that a principle of preparedness applies to the establishment of these conditioned responses. Evidence that this principle might also apply to human fear conditioning became available shortly after Watson and Rayner (1920) reported the results of their experiment with little Albert. Attempts to repeat the experiment with other CSs were sometimes unsuccessful. For example, Charles Valentine failed to obtain fear conditioning in a child when he used objects such as a pair of opera glasses as the CS. He suggested that fears might be more easily conditioned to furry animals than to other objects.

Arne Öhman and his colleagues (1976) have now provided more formal evidence for the correctness of this point of view in an experiment on the galvanic skin response (GSR), which is commonly used for the experimental study of conditioning with human beings. If an electric current too weak to feel is passed between electrodes placed on two points on the body, there is a measurable resistance to the passage of this current. The level of this resistance depends on several factors, the most important one for psychological purposes being emotional arousal. When the individual is emotionally excited, resistance decreases. This change can be measured with sensitive electronic equipment and recorded in ink on moving graph paper. This change in resistance is the GSR. When the GSR is used in the conditioning laboratory, the procedure usually consists of pairing a neutral CS with electric shock, the US. After a very few such pairings, the CS usually comes to elicit the GSR.

The investigators conditioned the GSR to three different classes of stimuli—pictures of snakes and spiders, circles and triangles, and flowers and mushrooms—using electric shock as the US. The strengths of conditioning to these classes of stimuli were in the order listed: greatest to snakes and spiders, next greatest to circles and triangles, least to flowers and mushrooms. This suggests that the circles and triangles were truly neutral stimuli for the participants in this experiment, but that human subjects are prepared to acquire a fearful response to snakes and spiders, and prepared not to acquire such a response to flowers and mushrooms.

Prepared Responses.   Psychologists who have studied operant conditioning in the laboratory have made other observations that fit this general picture. It is very difficult, for example, to train pigeons to peck an illuminated key to turn off a shock but very easy to train them to make the same response to obtain food. It appears that some response-reinforcer relationships are more readily learned than others in a manner that parallels the biological preparedness to learn CS-US relationships. One of the most dramatic demonstrations of this point comes from studies of the interesting phenomenon called **autoshaping.** In these demonstrations the key in a Skinner box is illuminated for a few seconds and then food is delivered no matter what the bird does. The pigeon nevertheless begins spontaneously to peck at the key after it has been illuminated a few times. The birds train themselves to peck the key even though a key peck is not required to obtain food. The effects of autoshaping are very powerful. Key pecking persists even if, later on, conditions are arranged so that it *prevents* the delivery of food (Brown and Jenkins, 1968).

Instinctive Drift.   The power of these prepared responses is well known to animal trainers, who make use of them in teaching their animals clever tricks. The "dancing chicken" trained by Keller and Marian Breland (1961) is an example.

> The chicken walks over about 3 feet, pulls a rubber loop on a small box which starts a repeated auditory stimulus pattern (a four-note tune). The chicken then steps up onto an 18-inch, slightly raised disc, thereby closing a timer switch, and scratches vigorously, round and round, over the disc for 15 seconds, at the rate of about two scratches per second until the automatic feeder fires in the retaining compartment. The chicken goes into the compartment to eat, thereby automatically shutting the door. The popular interpretation of this behavior pattern is that the chicken has turned on the "juke box" and "dances."

The development of this behavioral exhibition was wholly unplanned. In an attempt to create quite another type of demonstration which required a chicken simply to stand on a platform for 12-15 seconds, we found that over 50 percent developed a very strong and pronounced scratch pattern. . . . we were able to change our plans to make use of the scratch pattern and the result was the "dancing chicken" [just] described. . . .

In this exhibit the real contingency for reinforcement is that the chicken must depress the platform for 15 seconds . . . (pp. 681–682).

The appearance of the food-related scratch pattern in this demonstration is an example of what has been called **instinctive drift.** Being trained to make a very different response, the animal gradually drifts into a form of behavior that is biologically more natural. The Brelands were able to incorporate the chicken's scratching into its performing sequence. But instinctive drift interfered with the stunts of some star performers. Racoons trained to put coins in a strong box became very miserly indeed, keeping them and rubbing them together again and again. They do this to shellfish to remove their shells. Pigs trained to put wooden coins in piggy banks threw them on the floor and rooted and tossed them about. A similar thing sometimes happens in avoidance-learning experiments. Occasionally a rat learning to turn a wheel to avoid shock will cease to make these responses and will "freeze" to the training signal. Freezing is a common fear reaction in animals of many species.

SUMMARY

The materials in this section have now spelled out the meaning of the assertion with which this chapter began, that in any learning situation there are two somewhat different things to learn: the sequence of events to be expected and what to do about them. As we have now seen, what is learned about sequences of events has motivational and emotional significance. For example, such learning provides neutral stimuli with secondary reinforcing power. Having been associated with primary reinforcement, such stimuli take on reinforcing properties themselves. They also acquire motivational or incentive value. In a similar way stimuli associated with pain become capable of evoking fear.

Such conditioning plays an important role in the establishment of operant responses. The mechanisms have been worked out best for avoidance learning. In such learning the animal acquires a fear of stimuli associated with an aversive stimulus, usually shock. Motivated by such fear, the animal then learns any response that removes the stimulus provoking fear or allows it to leave the situation provoking fear.

The roles played by secondary reinforcement and conditioned fear in the behavior of animals have surprisingly direct parallels in human behavior—in the workings of token economies in the first case and in the selection of neurotic symptoms in the second. The learned helplessness evident in animals when they have no control over aversive events is also found in human behavior. Uncontrollable failure in schoolwork makes children feel helpless, as does attributing failure to personal inadequacy rather than to lack of effort. Children's feelings of helplessness can be reduced by teaching them that success and failure depend on how hard they try in a situation.

At one time learning was believed to be a completely general process, that any response an organism can make can be associated with any stimulus it can detect. More recently, however, this premise of equipotentiality has been abandoned in favor of a principle of preparedness. There are biological constraints on learning. Some associations like tastes and sickness are made with remarkable ease; others like visual stimulation and sickness are impossible to make or nearly so. There are similar sympathies between responses and reinforcers. In pigeons pecking to obtain food is a response so natural that the birds teach it to themselves. Pecking to avoid shock is difficult, if not impossible, for these birds to learn. Sometimes these natural responses drift into training sessions and replace those that the experimenter is attempting to teach the animal.

TO BE SURE YOU UNDERSTAND THIS CHAPTER

These are the most important terms in this chapter.

Classical conditioning	**Fixed-ratio schedule**
Operant conditioning	**Fixed-interval schedule**
Temporary connection	**Variable-ratio schedule**
Unconditioned stimulus (US)	**Variable-interval schedule**
Unconditioned response (UR)	**Extinction**
Conditioned stimulus (CS)	**Partial-reinforcement effect**
Conditioned response (CR)	**Spontaneous recovery**
Stimulus substitution	**Stimulus generalization**
Overshadowing	**Generalization gradient**
Blocking	**Discrimination**
Trial and error learning	**Experimental neurosis**
Instrumental learning	**Excitation**
Law of effect	**Inhibition**
Positive reinforcer	**Higher-order conditioning**
Negative reinforcer	**Primary motive**
Reward training	**Primary reward**
Omission training	**Secondary motive**
Active avoidance	**Secondary reinforcer**
Passive avoidance	**Conditioned positive reinforcement**
Skinner box	**Incentive**
Biofeedback	**Token economy**
Mediation	**Two-factor theory**
Learning curve	**Yoked control group**
Cumulative response curve	**Learned helplessness**
Method of successive approximations	**Premise of equipotentiality**
Shaping	**Principle of preparedness**
Schedule of reinforcement	**Autoshaping**
Continuous reinforcement	**Instinctive drift**
Partial (intermittent) reinforcement	

TO GO BEYOND THIS CHAPTER

In This Book. You will find the ideas developed in this chapter reappearing at many points in this book. There is further discussion of learned motives in Chapter 9. Chapter 15 describes the relationship of the ideas of conditioning and learning to personality development. There is discussion in Chapter 16 of how the concepts of conditioning apply to the development of behavior disorders. In Chapter 17 you will find that most of the forms of behavior therapy are direct applications of the ideas you have learned from this chapter.

Elsewhere. Pavlov's 1927 book is well within the comprehension of the beginning student. For a contemporary treatment of conditioning and learning with more of an emphasis on operant conditioning, we recommend *Psychology of Learning and Behavior* (second edition), by Barry Schwartz. There are many other excellent books on this topic. You can locate them easily by a bit of browsing in the library.

CHAPTER 9   MOTIVATION

In his book *The Crime of Punishment* (1968), Karl Menninger tells the story of the beginnings of one man's day as reported by a California newspaper.

> With a defiant roar, he ripped back out of his driveway, across the street, and up onto a neighbor's lawn. Then . . . in forward gear not a block away he side-swiped a car. About a half-hour later police picked up his trail. When another car appeared in front of him he rammed the car in the rear, but instead of stopping, he just kept ramming. The driver in the front car jammed on his brakes but the angry man shoved him 125 feet out into the southbound traffic of the main highway, then backed off and proceeded south on the same highway. A policeman . . . sped after him. When the pursued car and the patrol officer whipped through a red light . . . , another traffic police officer joined in the chase. A car that appeared in front of the pursued driver was rammed, the nearly demolished station wagon bouncing off . . . onto the shoulder of the highway for 500 feet before it ran into a fence and finally stopped.

One of the first questions people ask when they read such an account is "Whyever did he do it?" They are usually satisfied with an answer that tells them about some personal characteristic of the individual. The driver was angry, frustrated, a hostile person, someone with an uncontrollable need to be destructive, a man with an overly strong aggressive trait. As we saw in Chapter 1, however, such "explanations" are circular; they may describe important aspects of behavior but as scientific explanation they are unacceptable. Acceptable attempts at explanation lead inevitably to the environmental and physiological conditions associated with the behavior we are trying to explain.

THE NATURE OF MOTIVES

Motivation may be defined as the process that gives behavior its energy and its goals. We experience motives as feelings of wanting, needing, and desiring. In order to explain the nature of motives more exactly, we must understand that motives are concepts, not things. We cannot see motives directly but must infer them from the behavior of people and other animals. When we see a student working longer and harder than anyone else on the material in a course, we infer that the student has a very strong need to succeed in the subject. When we see a ragged waif, wide-eyed before the pastry-filled window of a bakery, we infer that the child is hungry. When we see a wild animal in cowering

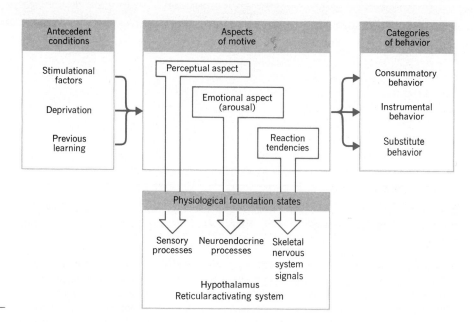

Figure 9.1
The nature of motives.

immobility, watching intently as a group of hikers go by, we infer from this behavior that it is afraid.

As we saw in Chapter 7, concepts serve the useful purpose of collecting together in one category items that share certain attributes in common, however diverse they may be in other ways. What then, as exemplars of the same concept, motivation, do states like fear, hunger, and the need to master a college course share in common. The answer to this question appears in Figure 9.1. The different motives all arise as consequences of certain *antecedent conditions* or causes; they manifest themselves in certain *behavioral expressions;* and certain *physiological foundation states* appear to be associated with motives.

The structure of Figure 9.1 explains why concepts like motivation are sometimes called **intervening variables.** These unobservable concepts stand between the observable antecedent conditions that give rise to the state and the observable behavior by which these states express themselves.

The materials presented in the previous paragraphs and Figure 9.1 are very important, because almost *every* significant topic in psychology has the status of an intervening variable. In discussions of these topics, it is very easy to lose track of the distinction between observable antecedent conditions, behavioral manifestation, and unobservable concepts. With some frequency a diagram like Figure 9.1 helps to clarify important issues. We shall meet such diagrams again.

Antecedent Conditions

The principal antecedent condition contributing to the strength of appetitive drives such as hunger and thirst is *deprivation,* the length of time the individual has been deprived of the object that is its goal. Other motives are largely determined by the *strength of stimulation.* The motive to avoid the pain of physical punishment is the clearest example. The stimulus properties of the object toward which motivated behavior is directed also affect the strength of the motive. Sexual arousal, for example, depends for the most part on the accessibility and desirability of appropriate sexual objects. To a lesser extent, but still importantly, the degree of an animal's hunger depends on the kinds of foods available.

A third set of antecedent conditions contributing to the creation of motives is the *history of the individual.* The degree to which experience shapes our motives provides a way of distinguishing different types of motivation. **Primary motives**—hunger, sex, pain avoidance, the need for rest, and so on—are unlearned motives, which depend principally on the functioning of the individual's physiology. **Secondary motives**—the need to outdo others in competition, achieve scholarly distinction, and so on—are acquired through experience. The distinction is only roughly useful, however, for both physiology and learning figure in all motives. Learning and experience have an influence even on motives that have a clear physiological basis. Within cultural groups tastes in food vary; some people love liver and brussels sprouts; others hate them. Between ethnic and national groups of people the differences are even greater. There are people who eat toasted grasshoppers, ants, soups made of birds' nests, and each other. There is no evidence that the bodily requirements of these people differ from ours. The differences seem certain to have been learned, just as particular tastes in food are learned. Much of human motivation derives almost entirely from experience.

Motivated Behavior

Motives are expressed in three forms of behavior. The most obvious expression of any motive is *consummatory behavior,* that is, behavior designed to fulfill the motive in question. Eating is the consummatory response for hunger, copulation that for sex, and so on.

A second general class of responses associated with any motive are those that are instrumental to its satisfaction. *Instrumental behavior* consists of the acts that secure what will satisfy the motive. It is the behavior studied in operant conditioning. The stronger the motivation, the greater the vigor with which we work for whatever satisfies the motive. One interesting incidental point about these instrumental acts is that they are sometimes the consummatory responses for another motive. A child eats, the consummatory response associated with hunger, in order to secure its mother's approval; the prostitute uses the consummatory behavior associated with the sexual motive to secure food, clothing, shelter, and sometimes power; a businessman may be aggressive, not because of a motive to hurt a competitor but to further his ambitions; students sometimes do scholarly work on some topic, not because of curiosity about the subject matter but because they hope to gain the professor's approval.

Finally, many expressions of human motivation are indirect and *substitutive* in nature. A study performed at the University of Minnesota during World War II serves to make this general point. This investigation was conducted with conscientious objectors, who voluntarily submitted to a six-month period of semistarvation. During this time the subjects in the experiment lived on a very restricted diet. Their weight dropped from an average of about 155 pounds to less than 120 pounds, and their daily existence became preoccupied with food. Favorite topics of conversation were food and eating, and cookbooks became fascinating reading material. Motives other than hunger became noticeably weaker. Sexual urges declined; romances collapsed; dancing was too much work. Many of the men were bothered with vivid dreams of breaking their diet. One man expressed his craving for food symbolically by stealing cups from a coffee shop. Thus extreme hunger initiated behavior that was only a substitute for the satisfaction of the hunger drive (Keys et al., 1950).

Physiological Bases and Aspects of Motivation

William McDougall (1926) had this to say in defining the concept of instinct, which he used in much the same way that we currently use the concept of motive:

> We may define an instinct as a psychophysical disposition which determines its possessor to perceive and pay attention to objects of a certain class, to experience an emotional excitement of a certain quality upon perceiving such an object, and to act in regard to it in a particular manner . . . (paraphrased slightly).

In this statement McDougall identifies three aspects of a motive or instinct: a perceptual aspect, an emotional aspect, and an action aspect. These aspects of motivation appear in Figure 9.1, which also shows that the physiology of motivation will certainly consist, not of a single physiological process but a set of them.

With all this complexity before you, it probably requires no special argument on our part to convince you that the complete psychology of motivation is far too large a topic to present in a single chapter. For this reason we have selected only a few motives for discussion.

SUMMARY

Although common sense often "explains" behavior in terms of motives, it is important to realize that such explanations are circular and nonexplanatory. More acceptable explanations relate behavior to environmental circumstances and physiological conditions. Motives, which we experience as desires, provide behavior with its energy and the goals toward which it is directed. The antecedent conditions that contribute to this energizing of behavior include deprivation, the strength and other characteristics of stimulation, and the history of the individual. Consummatory, instrumental, and substitute activities are the forms of behavior in which motives are expressed. The physiology of motivation is complex, for the individual is perceiving, feeling emotion, and acting.

HUNGER

As already indicated, the principal condition causing a person to be hungry is food deprivation. This deprivation initiates a complex set of chemical and neurological events that make the individual seek food. The longer the deprivation, the more urgent the search becomes. This relationship is a matter of first-hand personal experience for all of us.

Physiological Bases of Hunger

The most obvious physiological indicators of hunger are churnings of the stomach, what we experience as hunger pangs. The evidence for a relationship between the stimuli produced by these churnings and hunger is very straightforward. Many years ago Walter B. Cannon and his colleagues at the University of Chicago had subjects swallow a tube which ended in a balloon. The balloon was inflated to press against the walls of the stomach. Whenever the stomach contracted, it forced air up the tube. This air pressure was measured and recorded (Figure 9.2). The basic discovery made in these experiments was that the stomach contracted at the same moments that the individual reported having hunger pangs, indicating that the contractions must be the stimuli informing us that we are hungry.

Although the stimuli coming from an active stomach can inform us that we are hungry, they are not absolutely essential to the experience of hunger. People who have had their stomachs removed report a normal craving for food.

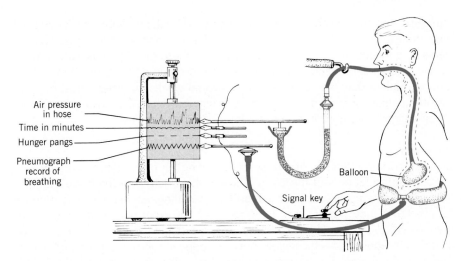

Air pressure
in hose

Time in minutes

Hunger pangs

Pneumograph
record of
breathing

Balloon

Signal key

Figure 9.2
*Recording stomach activity and the
experience of hunger pains.* Notice that
the record of stomach motility, indicated
by fluctuations in the top line, corresponds
with that of hunger pains, indicated by
the horizontal straight lines. The subject
produced these horizontal lines by
pressing a key whenever he felt pangs of
hunger. (After Cannon, 1934.)

Moreover, rats without stomachs learn a maze just as quickly for a food reward as do those with their stomachs in place; and rats whose nerve pathways to and from the stomach have been severed behave about as normal animals do. Clearly, physiological factors other than stomach contractions must be involved.

One of the effective physiological agents appears to be the amount of sugar in the blood, which increases soon after eating and then decreases as the hours without food pass. Sugar injected directly into the bloodstream inhibits stomach contractions; the injection of insulin, which lowers blood sugar, increases them. Other evidence argues against blood-sugar level as the final determiner of hunger, however. Attempts to establish correlations between low blood sugar and indices of hunger have not been very successful. Although some animal studies have shown a modest degree of relationship, other studies, particularly those with human subjects, have been unable to establish any relationship at all. The search for other physiological factors that might control hunger has uncovered important neuronal factors.

As usual, these discoveries reflect a history of scientific advance. In 1840 a pituitary tumor was discovered in a person who had been referred to a physician because of extreme obesity. Since the hypothalamus is located near the pituitary and has neural and circulatory connections to it, it was only a question of time before scientific interest was directed to this structure. It was eventually discovered that the hypothalamus contains nuclei that serve as centers for eating, drinking, and temperature regulation. Lesions in certain small regions of the hypothalamus, for example, will cause rats to eat to excess and become obese. Within two months lesioned animals may double their normal body weight. These findings indicate that this region is a *satiation center;* eliminating its function allows the animal to go on eating. Other lesions 1.5 to 2.0 millimeters away from the satiation center make the rats stop eating, suggesting that this is the locus of a *feeding center.* Hunger apparently is under dual contol. There is an excitatory center responsible for eating and an inhibitory center that registers satiation and halts eating.

Apparently these hypothalamic centers respond to some receptor system that monitors body weight and causes the individual to eat enough to keep that weight at a constant **set point** over fairly long periods of time. Our body weight remains remarkably stable, despite short-term variations in the amount we eat and the energy we expend. Indeed rats with damage to the satiation center in the hypothalamus do not gain weight indefinitely. Once they reach two or three times their normal weight, they reduce their food intake to slightly above normal and then maintain themselves at their established obese weight. The weight-regulating mechanism is set at a higher point in these rats. The rats with damage to the feeding center show an opposite pattern. They refuse all food for a time and die unless they are force-fed. After several weeks, however, most of them resume eating on their own, especially if highly preferred foods are available. Their weights then stabilize, but at a lower than normal level.

Obesity

Set-point interpretations of hunger and eating emphasize the stimulus role played by the fat cells of the body. These cells, which store the body's fat and are called adipocytes, can be enlarged by overeating, sometimes increasing up to five times their normal size. Laid down for the most part before the age of two (Knittle, 1975)—although there is some evidence that new ones may develop in adulthood—these cells never disappear. Obese adults may have as many as three times the normal number of fat cells (Hirsch and Knittle, 1970). The number of fat cells and their size are the basis of the individual's set point for weight. Once established, this set point is strongly resistant to change. From early childhood on, obese people have had a high set point. Whenever the obese person's weight falls below its set point, the hypothalamic centers receive

Obese people often experience guilt, shame, and rejection.

strong signals from the fat cells directing them to increase food intake and restore the obese person's usual weight.

Obesity is usually defined as body weight that exceeds the average for a given height and body build by 20 percent. About 35 percent of all Americans are obese. An overweight person is significantly more susceptible to heart disease, high blood pressure, and diabetes than a person of normal weight. And of course in American society the obese person suffers because fat is considered physically unattractive. Largely for this reason, the control of body weight has become an American obsession; "body fat" and "fat cells" are now a part of the everyday vocabularies of many people. Since the fat cells constitute adipose tissue, some have suggested calling this obsession to lose weight the "adipose complex." *Newsweek* (December 13, 1982) has supplied a richly descriptive account of the tyranny of the fat cells.

> If only we could learn to view them objectively, we might appreciate our fat cells for the truly remarkable structures they are. However one may feel about 70 billion of them jostling for space in a pantsuit, a single fat cell is one of nature's microscopic works of art, a shimmering droplet the color of Mazola. Far from being sluggish, they are among the most chemically active cells in the body, sniffing the blood for traces of dessert, ever ready to send a squall of protest brainward if they sense deprivation. But above all, we can admire them for their tenacity. Time and again they emerge phoenix-like from the ashes of last month's diet; even on the threshold of starvation, shriveled fat cells hang in limp clusters, clamoring for lipids. It is their most impressive and unlovable characteristic: Fat cells may shrink, but they never die.

Therapy for Obesity

The usual dietary regimes that have been offered as means of conquering obesity are based on the assumption that obesity is a learned disorder to be treated by therapies based on principles of learning. Unfortunately, the fact of the matter seems to be that unlearned physiological factors are more important than learning. The control of weight by physiological set-point mechanisms makes it easy to understand why these therapies are relatively unsuccessful. In the words of Albert Stunkard (1982), one of the leading investigators of the topic, "Obesity has a very strong biological basis, and treatment consists of persuading people to live in semi-starvation—because nothing else works."

In spite of this gloomy assessment, it will be useful to review the most important features of the behavior therapies (Stunkard, 1981) that have been used for obesity. They have already had at least modest success, and the methods appear to have promise.

- Patients carefully *monitor* their eating behavior, noting the foods they have eaten, how much they have consumed, at what times, where, and with whom. Using this procedure, fat people try to give up their casual and careless intake of food.
- In what is called *stimulus control* of eating, the dieter attempts to limit eating to certain times and places and to eat low-calorie foods rather than high-calorie foods.
- The patient practices *specific techniques* to control eating, such as counting each mouthful of food, each chew, each swallow; placing the knife, fork, or spoon down after every second or third mouthful; gradually lengthening the interval of time between mouthfuls.
- The dieter works out some scheme to *reinforce* maintenance of the diet: the opportunity to purchase a wished-for article, relief from a chore, an evening out, and so on. The reinforcer should be for short-term gains. Far-off goals

Table 9.1 Negative Self-Statements and Counterarguments in Cognitive Behavior Therapy for Obesity

Content	Negative Self-Statements	Counterargument
Weight Loss	"It's taking me so long to lose weight."	"But, I am losing it, and this time I'll keep it off."
Food thoughts	"I keep thinking how good chocolate tastes."	"Stop it! It's just frustrating you. Think of _____."
Excuses	"It's in my genes."	"That just makes it harder, but not impossible. If I stick with this program, I will succeed."

From Mahoney and Mahoney, 1976.

are not as effective, as witness this complaint from a middle-aged female patient Stunkard was seeing.

My husband was always offering to buy me a car if I lost 50 pounds. I used to work away at it and knock myself out and lost 30 pounds, which was a lot of weight, but what did it get me? I didn't get half a car. I got nothing. [Then, contrasting the past with her current behavioral weight reduction program, she added] I've only lost eight pounds in this program so far, and he's done all sorts of good things for me (Stunkard, 1982, p. 538).

- Obese persons attempt *cognitive restructuring.* They conduct carefully planned monologues in which they condemn and blame themselves but then respond with counterarguments to such negative self-appraisals (Table 9.1). The aim of these monologues is to help obese people revise the messages that they deliver to themselves.

Since 1967 many studies of the efficacy of these forms of behavior therapy for obesity have been conducted. Stunkard (1982) has summarized the results.

- The number of dropouts from treatment, a pervasive problem in other therapies, is low. More people stay with behavior therapy. Dropout rates in other programs were reported to be between 25 and 75 percent; they were 15 percent or less in the behavioral programs.
- Behavior therapy has fewer side effects than treatment with appetite-suppressing drugs, but the amount of weight lost—average amount 11.2 pounds—has not differed appreciably from the weight lost with drug treatments.
- Weight changes during and following treatment vary greatly, suggesting that unknown factors are influencing the results. It has proved difficult to determine the traits of individuals that predict who will and will not profit from treatment.
- Marked weight loss tends not to be maintained. The pounds stay off for a year following treatment, but then they begin to slip back on again. The goal of all the psychological therapies for obesity is the same, to get people to take pounds off and keep them off. The common outcome of these programs is depressing. The taking off is easy, or easier anyway; the keeping off is difficult, if not impossible.

Eating Disorders

The preoccupation with food and eating that leads to obesity has psychological consequences—shame, social discomfort, and separation from others. But these consequences are insignificant by comparison with those of two disorders whose symptoms are so severe that they are included in a group of psychiatric disturbances called eating disorders. These two conditions, **anorexia nervosa** and **bulimia,** frequently occur among college students.

Anorexia Nervosa. The parents of Mary, a fifteen-year-old high school student, brought her for medical attention because they had grown worried about her loss of weight.

> At the age of fourteen, Mary was five feet, three inches tall and weighed a hundred pounds. A year later, determined to become more attractive and convinced that she was too heavy, she began to diet with such intensity that she finally reduced her food intake to only a few vegetables each day. She also started a vigorous exercise program. Within six months her weight dropped to eighty pounds. Mary soon became preoccupied with food. She began to collect recipes from magazines and enjoyed preparing gourmet meals for her family. She also had trouble sleeping and grew depressed and irritable. She had begun to menstruate the year before, but she had had only a few normal periods. When interviewed, Mary insisted that she felt fat and expressed fears that she would become obese were she to lose control and overeat. The interviewer described her as an extremely conscientious person who made great demands on herself to perform perfectly at anything she undertook. She had never been socially active, had never dated, always obtained high grades in school, and spent much of her time studying (adapted from Spitzer et al., 1981, pp. 134–135).

This description is typical of anorexia. There is the intense fear of becoming fat; a distorted body image and a sense of being obese despite conspicuous thinness; and a loss of 25 percent of body weight without any known physical illness. Anorexics exercise vigorously to lose still more weight. They are often perfectionists and are easily depressed when they cannot meet the standards that they have set for themselves.

Many different psychobiological and sociocultural factors have been suggested as the causes of anorexia nervosa. It seems likely that both kinds contribute. On the biological side, there is strong evidence (Chapter 2) that our physiques are determined to a substantial degree by inheritance. On the sociocultural side, there has been a recent growing emphasis on slimness as a requisite of beauty in women. Middle-class educated women, in particular, seem to have accepted this concept (Hsu, 1983). Evidence for the existence of this emphasis are the models selected for advertisements and the highly publicized contestants in the so-called "beauty pageants." The women who appear in *Playboy* centerfolds and the Miss America pageant weigh 20 percent less than the average American woman their own age. The Miss America winners tend to weigh even less than the other contestants (Garner et al., 1980). One tragic consequence of this image of ideal American womanhood, which equates extreme thinness with sexual attractiveness, may be the increasing prevalence of anorexia nervosa.

Anorexia is a life-threatening disorder, because of the regimen of self-starvation that the individual imposes on herself. We say "herself" advisedly; the ratio of girls and women to boys and men with this disorder may be as high as twenty to one. Anorexia usually has its onset during adolescence, often shortly after the beginning of menstruation. The cessation of menstruation, or amenorrhea, may even precede noticeable weight loss. Like other starved people, anorexics are preoccupied with food, but for them it takes the form of collecting recipes and planning and preparing meals for others.

Anorexia nervosa is the most common among young women. American standards of feminine beauty and the young girl's rejection of adulthood, of the inevitability of becoming sexually mature, are believed to contribute to the development of the disorder.

Bulimia. Bulimia has been described as the "binge-purge" syndrome. It is a serious and spreading disorder marked by uncontrollable overeating, often followed by self-induced vomiting or overdoses of laxatives to eliminate the caloric intake. Persons of normal weight, as well as those who are anorectic or obese, may be bulimics (Loro and Orleans, 1981). *Newsweek* (November 2, 1981) began its report on the "binge-purge syndrome" with a brief case description.

> Sharon seemed to be a modern Wonder Woman: Successful, attractive and smart. At twenty-five, the enviably slim Harvard graduate was vice president of a big New York bank. But Sharon (not her real name) also had a dangerous, humiliating habit. Obsessed both by eating and staying thin, she would regularly gorge in secret, then purge away the guilt by forcing herself to throw up. After years of therapy, Sharon is only now beginning to conquer her compulsions, and she vividly recalls her shameful process. "If I deviated by one slice of bread from my diet, my day was shot" she says. "Then I'd have to eat a bag of cookies, two boxes of doughnuts, several candy bars, two bags of English muffins with jam, you name it. Afterward, I'd vomit" (p. 60).

The bulimic person attempts to counteract stress and depression by overeating—but does so in an uncontrollable manner. The typical bulimic is a female in her twenties, white, middle-class, with some college education, and has been a binge eater for a number of years. It is difficult to know exactly how many people are afflicted with the disorder, but some experts estimate that one in five college-educated women have been or will be affected at some time in their lives. The incidence may be greatest in able, young working women who are expected to have a career, to take care of a house, to raise children, and to retain the slim form that is highly admired in a male-dominated, sex-conscious, achievement-oriented society.

Reports indicate that some bulimics have consumed as many as 55,000 calories at a single sitting. This would approximate sixteen pounds of food. More commonly, they consume 2000 to 3000 calories of pastries, breads, cookies, and "junk food"; high-calorie foods are favored. The recurrent pattern of heavy binging and vomiting brings in its wake a number of devastating physical consequences: ulcers, gastric and dental problems, and acute disturbances in the chemical balance of the blood which can cause heart attacks. Other problems include sore throats, aching joints, feelings of weakness and dizziness, and apathy (Leon et al., 1982).

Bulimic college students sometimes report that immediately before one of their caloric binges they feel depressed, angry, and disgusted with themselves, and that vomiting may give them a pleasurable "high." Their problems with eating and weight affect their social lives, their work, and their family relationships. Binge-purge eaters may also have a history of overusing such substances as alcohol, marijuana, amphetamines, diet pills, and barbiturates.

Intervention. The most effective therapy for these eating disorders varies from patient to patient. The National Association of Anorexia Nervosa and Related Disorders recommends experimentation with several therapies and changing therapists or types of therapy if necessary. Patients in whom the disorder has produced the physical symptoms of starvation will need medical attention in order to bring the body back to normal functioning. In addition, some form of psychological therapy may be helpful. Possibly effective treatments include traditional psychotherapy, behavior modification, family therapy, and biofeedback for stress management. Drug therapy is sometimes necessary to deal with a patient's anxiety or depression. A general discussion of these therapies appears in Chapter 17.

SUMMARY

The experience of hunger depends for the most part on the bodily changes brought about through food deprivation, although external stimuli also play a role. Stomach contractions can serve as signals of hunger, but they are not essential to the experience. A low blood-sugar level contributes, and brain function, particularly hypothalamic activity, is also of demonstrated importance. The three disturbances of eating—obesity, anorexia nervosa, and bulimia—are common in twentieth-century life. The first of these is a chronic preoccupation of millions of American citizens. Weight control is difficult because obesity is more a physical problem than a psychological one. According to currently accepted set-point theory, people become obese because they have more fat cells than normal. These cells fill with fat, causing a gain in weight, the increase being one that set-point mechanisms strive to maintain. Behavior therapies have had some success in persuading people to lower their food intake. The same therapies have had some success with anorexia and bulimia, but other forms of intervention may be necessary in these cases.

SEXUALITY

As recently as twenty-five years ago, the sex drive was treated very nervously in most psychological writing, in spite of the strong case made by Sigmund Freud for its importance to human behavior and experience. Now, however, a liberalized moral climate has freed us from the Victorian shackles that prevented open discussion of the subject. In recent years a considerable body of research on sexuality has accumulated.

Sexual Behavior

Sexual behavior includes many more responses than copulatory ones. Most species precede sexual contact with some kind of preparatory activity to increase the excitability of both partners. Birds bill, coo, bow, and strut. Cats are excessively playful and make peculiar vocalizations. Primate partners and some tribes of human lovers spend hours grooming and delousing each other as a preliminary to coitus. In most mammals the sexual preliminaries include stimulation of the female genitalia. One interesting aspect of the preliminaries to human sexual behavior is that they often have an element of aggression. In our own society strong sexual arousal may lead to biting, scratching, and pinching, in other cultures to hair pulling and biting the eyebrows and neck.

Frequency.   On the average, young married couples in the United States have sexual intercourse about three times per week. By comparison with other cultures, this figure is low. The study of Clellan Ford and Frank Beach (1951), covering 190 societies, indicated that the most common frequency was about once a day. In many primitive cultures frequencies of five to six times a night are common, and eight to ten not unheard of.

In lower animals the frequency of copulation is more difficult to study because of the difficulties of observing these animals in their natural habitat. Such observations as have been reported seem to indicate a greater potency for many species than is found in any human society. In tests of only half-an-hour's duration, male rats and cats have been observed to copulate five to ten times. After a series of copulations, however, the male becomes less and less responsive and the time between matings becomes longer and longer.

Considering just the population of American men and women, nowhere is personal variation more apparent than in sexuality. Alfred Kinsey, Wardell Pomeroy, and Clyde Martin (1948) found that 3900 men below the age of thirty had an average of 3.27 orgasms per week, but the average was overshadowed by an extraordinary range. Some males had gone for years without ejaculating. One respondent had ejaculated only once in thirty years. Others had maintained average frequencies of ten to twenty orgasms per week for long periods of time. One scholarly, and ardent, lawyer averaged thirty per week for thirty years— 46,799 more than the man who had a single orgasm in that span of years.

Age Changes. These variations in sexual vigor persist over the life-span. Kinsey found that married couples at thirty had two coital acts per week; at forty they had one and at sixty one every two weeks. But, as an indication of the variability, the greatest frequency for any fifty-year-old man included in the study was fourteen per week. Men and women report a decline in sex drive as they get older, but sexual activity in old age is related to sexual activity earlier in life. Those who are sexually active in old age had also been active during their young and middle years (Masters and Johnson, 1966).

The sex drive, as indicated by sexual arousal, sexual fantasizing, and masturbation, usually appears in males at age thirteen, in females at fifteen, with a normal variation of plus or minus two years. Although young girls experience physiological puberty at an earlier age than young boys, their sex drive develops later and more slowly. Most individuals have their first sexual fantasies soon after the onset of sexual arousal. These fantasies are at first vague and only marginally sexual. As the sex drive increases during the first few years of adolescence, however, erotic fantasies become more vivid and detailed and contain explicit sexual activities and specific sexual partners. Then, as the sex drive becomes fully mature in later adolescence, most individuals develop very specific erotic fantasies (Storms, 1981). The ability of human beings to create and respond to fantasies seems to play a major role in sexual motivation (Byrne, 1976) and in impressionability and receptivity. Sexual fantasies are one of the complicated overlays of thought influencing this basic physiological drive.

Historical Trends. During the past forty years sexual activity has apparently stepped up. Morton Hunt's survey (1974) of the sexual attitudes and practices of 982 men and 1044 women found that, in their forties, married couples had intercourse twice a week, in their fifties once a week. These frequencies are approximately twice those reported by Kinsey. Techniques have also changed over the same period of time. There have been increases in oral sex in marriage, more variation in foreplay, and more experimentation with positions. Men and women also report more satisfaction in marriage. Judith Hyde (1982) has summarized several important ways in which attitudes currently influence heterosexuality.

- Liberal attitudes are correlated with premarital sexual experiences.
- Sexual behavior is shaped by the emotional quality of a couple's relationship. Particular forms of lovemaking are deemed appropriate or not on the basis of the depth of the emotional commitment to each other.
- Self-image, self-esteem, and gender-role definitions are unrelated to premarital sex.

• The double standard is disappearing, but most women are still seeking a greater emotional commitment in a relationship before accepting premarital intercourse as appropriate.

Homosexual Behavior.   So far, we have dealt only with **heterosexual** relationships, those between males and females. In all human societies, however, a minority of people are aroused by, and form **homosexual** alliances with, members of their own sex. Such behavior appears in lower species, too. Females of many species mount other animals, clasping them in the male fashion and making pelvic thrusts similar to those of the copulating male. Such behavior does not mean that these females are incapable of normal female sexual function. Actually, such reactions often occur at the peak of female receptivity. Similarly, males often mount other males, and they may behave sexually as females. And, again, this is no indication of a lack of masculine prowess. Such behavior in a male rat usually indicates that he will be a vigorous copulator when tested with a receptive female. Kinsey, Pomeroy, and Martin (1948) were told by 37 percent of the men they interviewed—a disproportionate number were prisoners—that they had experienced homosexual orgasm at some time since adolescence. Four percent of the male population reported being exclusively homosexual throughout their lives. Of the women interviewed (Kinsey et al., 1953), 13 percent had experienced homosexual orgasm and about 2 percent were exclusively homosexual.

The gay rights movement made homosexuality much more visible in our society in the 1970s, but there is no evidence that its incidence is increasing. Robert Sorensen (1973) found in his questioning of 393 adolescents that 11 percent of boys and 6 percent of girls had had at least one homosexual experience. They did not report encounters as continuing, however, nor did they regard themselves as homosexuals. Many more adolescents, 25 percent of them, had had homosexual advances made to them by other adolescents and adults. Alan Bell, Martin Weinberg, and Sue Hammersmith (1981), through interviews with about 1500 homosexual men and women living in the San Francisco Bay area, found that a strong inclination to be either heterosexual or homosexual seems to exist before sexual activity begins. Sexual preference appears to be "a pattern of feelings and reactions" present in individuals before they become sexually active. Adolescents are fairly tolerant of homosexuality; 41 percent of Sorensen's boys and 40 percent of the girls regarded such encounters as all right when both partners want them.

It is worth mentioning specifically that the individuals considered so far in this discussion are normal physiologically. Occasionally, however, children are born who possess the internal physiological makeup of one sex but external genitalia resembling the other. It sometimes happens that a child with ovaries is raised as a boy and one with testes is raised as a girl. When such people are later apprised of their true sex, they generally prefer to retain the social and sexual role to which they had been accustomed. This fact attests to the importance of learning in determining sexuality and gender orientation.

Antecedent Conditions

For the males of many species a short period of deprivation is sufficient to bring the sexual drive to its maximum. Longer periods of deprivation are therefore not a very important determiner of male sexual behavior. Most female mammals are receptive to the male only during **estrus,** when they are able to conceive.

Female rats come into estrus, or heat, every four or five days for fifteen hours; the sow every three weeks for three days; the female chimpanzee every thirty-six days; the bitch every six months, sometimes for up to two weeks. Primate females are not as closely bound by the estrous cycle as other female mammals. Female monkeys, apes, and chimpanzees will copulate during all phases of the cycle, although the most sexual activity is still at the time of ovulation. Some studies indicate that human females have a surge of sexual desire at the time of ovulation and are 20 percent more likely than usual to initiate sexual activity, but if they wish not to conceive, their caution may dampen the effects of their hormones.

The situational factors controlling sexual behavior in different species are highly variable. In some, illumination is important. Rats, for example, are nocturnal animals and mate at night. Toads mate in ponds and pools or slowly moving water. They may travel a mile to reach this water. The presence of a nest stimulates the sexual activity of some birds and fish. Many species are stimulated to sexual behavior by the presence of other animals, and some show no sexual behavior in the absence of other members of their own group. Caged female pigeons, for example, do not lay eggs if they are kept in isolation. The introduction of a mirror will occasionally help them lay eggs, however. Female mink come into heat more readily if they are caged near other mink. Herring gulls are sexually more active in large flocks than in small ones. Only human beings seem to prefer privacy—and not all cultures are so insistent on this matter as ours is.

Physiological Basis of Sexual Excitement

The physiological and anatomical considerations important to the understanding of sexual activity were presented in Chapter 3, and we make only a few additional points here. The most sensitive portion of the male sexual apparatus is the glans penis, which makes up about one-quarter of the total length of the erect penis. The extreme sensitivity of the glans is explained by its many rather hard structures, cornified genital papillae, which rest upon touch receptors. When it is engorged with blood, the diameter of the penis increases. This increases the pressure of the cornified papillae upon the touch corpuscles and provide some of the sensory basis for sexual excitement in the male. During coition the papillae rub on the underlying touch receptors, which supply the stimuli for orgasm and ejaculation.

The feminine counterpart of the male penis is a much less prominent structure called the clitoris. Located above the vaginal and urinary openings, it has a glans and is capable of erection. During intercourse the clitoris is between the pubic bones of the man and woman and is stimulated by the repeated pressures exerted against it. The stimuli for the female sexual climax may be provided by these pressures.

SUMMARY

The status of sex as a biological drive is unassailable, for the very survival of the species depends on it. Because sexual behavior is so variable within and between cultures, by age, and by gender, the conclusion that situational factors are at work is inescapable. Over the past forty years, sexual behavior and sexual attitudes have undergone a marked change. Sexual behavior has become even more variable; attitudes have become more permissive. In particular, many more young women desire premarital sex, provided only that it is the expression of an emotional commitment. This new acceptance of sexual expression has extended at least to some degree to homosexuality and masturbation.

PUNISHMENT AND THE AVERSIVE CONTROL OF BEHAVIOR

Hunger and sex are positive motives in that they lead the individual to eat and to mate. They are sometimes called **appetitive motives** because the direction of striving is toward rather than away from a goal. Thirst and aggression are other appetitive drives. Another group of motives associated with fear, shame, guilt, and anxiety are negative, causing the individual to avoid or flee from a situation. They are sometimes called **aversive motives.** As is true of other motives, the aversive ones are concepts or intervening variables (Figure 9.3). The antecedent conditions responsible for these motives are punishment in its various forms; the motivated behavior is avoidant behavior. The physiological bases for the motives include the autonomic nervous system and the mechanisms responsible for the experience of pain.

Historical Background

The study of punishment lagged behind work on appetitive motivation, for years and for a number of reasons. For one thing, Edward Thorndike had concluded very early in his career—on the basis of totally unimpressive evidence—that punishments were much less effective than positive rewards. William Estes (1944) supplied evidence supporting this position. He trained rats in a Skinner box and then extinguished their bar pressing either with or without the delivery of a slap to the rat's paws every time it pressed the lever. Estes found that the punishment only temporarily suppressed their bar pressing, and that punished rats eventually made just as many responses as unpunished rats did before bar pressing was extinguished. Punishment therefore seemed an ineffective procedure and was little investigated for this reason.

Paradoxically, psychologists were at the same time warning against the use of punishment in child rearing because it was *too* effective. After John Watson and Rosalie Rayner's famous experiment in which they conditioned an infant to fear a white rat (page 250), many further studies had indicated that fear was conditionable. This meant that parents who punish children can serve as conditioned stimuli and come to be feared. Some theorists began to relate neuroses to such patterns of child rearing.

Other investigators demonstrated that painful stimulation causes aggressive behavior (Ulrich, 1967). If two animals of any of several species are put together in an enclosure and subjected to electric shock, they begin to fight. This pain-elicited aggression, together with the fear that pain brings, makes for a very complicated situation. Punishment at the hands of parents appears to have the potential for producing conflicting attitudes of hostility and fear in children. Again, the clinical literature revealed that neurotic individuals have such conflicting reactions toward their parents. As the literature on punishment grew, its effects were found to depend on so many variables that the outcome of using it seemed very difficult to predict.

Variables That Influence the Reactions to Punishment

For obvious reasons, most research on punishment has been done with lower animals, primarily laboratory rats. The usual procedure is to train them to make a particular response in some situation, to punish them for making that response—usually with electric shock—and then to observe the effect of punishment on behavior. The question is whether the animal ceases to make the punished response.

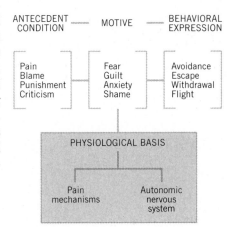

Figure 9.3
Motives based on pain and punishment. This figure is a more specific version of Figure 9.1, illustrating these negative motives.

Strength of Punishment. Very mild punishment does nothing more than attract attention and slightly arouse the animal. Such punishment may even strengthen the punished response rather than suppress it. Karl Muenzinger (1934), for example, found that punishing hungry rats with a mild electric shock when they made a correct turn in running a maze or food actually facilitated learning. Such punishment seemed to call attention to significant stimuli in the maze and to emphasize the correct response.

Shocks that are somewhat stronger than very mild have been found to suppress the punished response, but later the animal makes it as before, as dependably as though the response had never been punished. The punishment used by Estes, slapping the rat's paw, was at this level. Still stronger shocks bring suppression, from which there is only a partial recovery. Very strong shocks suppress responses completely and there is no recovery at all.

Delay of Punishment. As is true of positive reinforcers like food, the sooner punishment is delivered after a response is made, the greater its effect on behavior. A mild punishment administered immediately may have as much effect as a harsher punishment that is delayed.

Habituation. Animals subjected to a longer series of shocks may adapt to them, and the shocks may become less effective. In the extreme case a mild punishment repeated again and again can even come to serve as a sign of reward. An experimenter in Pavlov's laboratory succeeded in using electric shock as a CS in a salivary conditioning experiment.

Type of Response and Its History. Although strong, well-established responses are usually more resistant to punishment than others, one type of strong response is surprisingly susceptible. Consummatory activity, such as copulation and eating, are easily disrupted by mild punishment, probably because they are managed by the parasympathetic division of the autonomic nervous system. Punishment calls up antagonistic responses of the sympathetic division.

Responses that are learned through positive reinforcement are more easily disrupted by punishment than responses learned through punishment in the first place. For such responses punishment was one of the conditions of learning. Punishment is a stimulus for these responses. At least temporarily, punishment can strengthen responses learned by means of it.

Availability of Alternative Responses. Punishment is the most effective when it works collaboratively with reward. In a famous experiment making this point, John Whiting and O. Hobart Mowrer (1943) first trained rats to take a particular route to a goal. Then they punished them for taking this route but provided them with a new route, which they rewarded. The animals never took the original route again.

Dangers in the Practical Use of Punishment

Most of us would prefer not to use punishment as a way of controlling the behavior of children and other people for whom we are responsible, and with good reason. The use of punishment is a very dangerous procedure. For one thing, the same type of punishment will not be equally effective with everyone. For some people criticism is the most effective punishment. For others it is physical punishment; for still others it may be denial of privileges or restriction. What seems punishing to the punisher may not seem so to the one punished.

A second problem is that punishment seldom gets at the basic reasons for

For some children criticism is more effective than physical punishment.

misbehavior. There may be motives and rewards that continue to support misbehavior even though it is punished. In adolescence the approval by peers of drinking and taking drugs can nullify the effects of punishment given by adults.

Finally, punishment has side effects. As mentioned earlier, the person punished can come to fear the punisher, an undesirable consequence when the punisher is the parent and the person punished is his or her child. We know too that inescapable punishment can sometimes make a child feel helpless (Chapter 8). When children find that they have no control, they may become listless and depressed and lose self-esteem. Since active participation is necessary if we are to cope with the stresses of life, passivity can bring failure. Failure, in turn, is often punished further by a society that demands that we meet certain standards of effective performance.

Some Dos and Don'ts in the Use of Punishment

In spite of these dangers, there will be time when a parent, for example, must resort to punishment. One cannot stop to reason with a child who is about to run into a traffic-filled street, play with a wasp, or pull dinner off the table by climbing up a corner of the table cloth. When there are no alternatives, the literature on punishment makes some suggestions about effective ways to use it.

- Make the punishment intense enough to be effective. Do not use mild punishment out of thoughtless kindness. It may have no effect on the undesirable behavior. Or the punished person may become aggressive, behavior that is worse than the behavior being punished.

- Punish undesirable behavior immediately. Do not use warnings like "Just wait 'til your father gets home!" This is partly mild punishment, partly delayed punishment, both of which decrease the effectiveness of punishment.
- Do not begin with weak punishment and increase it until it reaches an effective intensity: "If that isn't punishment enough, how about this!" The administration of punishments in sequence leads to habituation, especially when the sequence is from weak to strong.
- Do not punish undesirable responses that are based on fear, responses that were learned to avoid or escape from punishment. Punishment only sets the occasion for making the same response.
- Suggest possible alternatives that may achieve what the punished behavior accomplished for the individual. When you must punish a person, do not take the position "That will teach you!" It won't; you must offer constructive suggestions.

SUMMARY

Motives may be classified as appetitive or aversive. Hunger is an example of an appetitive motive; those based on punishment are aversive motives. Until recently, psychology worked on the erroneous assumption that punishment is ineffective in controlling behavior. Research has now shown the error in this way of thinking. Punishment that is intense, immediate, and applied to responses learned through positive reinforcement is very effective, particularly if alternative responses are available to the individual being punished. Although punishment can be effective in controlling behavior, it may have negative side effects. One should use punishment in efforts to control the behavior of others only with great caution.

THE ORGANIZATION OF HUMAN MOTIVATION

Human beings share the basic physiological motives of lower species, although the expression of these motives tends to differ from individual to individual more than it does in other animals. Sometimes a physiological motive may even be denied. For example, most of us avoid pain, but this is not true of everyone. Patients with a curious psychiatric disorder called the **Munchausen syndrome**[1] (Enoch, Trethowan, and Barker, 1967) create a false medical history, hoping to secure admission to a hospital, not only for medical attention but also to have surgery performed to cure their imaginary illnesses. Multiple abdominal scars on the bodies of these patients often betray the syndrome.

Still other motives are almost exclusively human motives; they are minimally expressed at most by members of other species. Human beings strive for achievement, conformity, mastery, social approval, affiliation, and self-actualization as well as to dispel anxiety and to conquer fear of failure. One of the most appealing of these theories of human motivation is that of Abraham Maslow (1908–1970), who interpreted human motivation as a search for self-actualization.

---

[1] Baron Munchausen is famous in literary history for the highly colored mendacious stories known as the *Adventures of Baron Munchausen* (1785), written by Rudolf Erich Raspe and based on the exaggerated anecdotes of a certain Karl Friedrich Hieronymus von Münchhausen (1720–1797), a German huntsman and soldier.

Figure 9.4
A hierarchy of motives. Motives at the base of the pyramid must be at least partially satisfied before people have time, energy, and attention for higher needs. The hierarchy is an approximate developmental sequence. Most people probably never achieve self-actualization, as defined by Maslow.

For Maslow human needs are organized into a hierarchical structure (Figure 9.4) with basic physiological needs at its base and others at higher levels. Maslow believed that when the more basic needs are satisfied, other higher needs emerge.

Physiological Needs. In common with many psychologists, Maslow took the position that all other motives derive from the physiological drives. In human motivation, however, these needs are not very important because they are satisfied most of the time. This means that motives that are higher in the hierarchy can express themselves. In the behavior of the subjects in the study of human starvation, however, we saw how dominant the physiological needs can be when they are not satisfied.

Safety and Security Needs. The needs for safety and security, too, tend to be satisfied in most modern lives. The peaceful, smooth-running, good society ordinarily makes its adult members feel reasonably safe from wild animals, extremes of temperature, assault, and murder. Safety needs are of greater importance in childhood. Children want routines that they can count on and surroundings that have predictability and orderliness. The failure to satisfy the safety needs of children may make them fearful, insecure adults who are unable to cope with the ordinary demands of the environment.

Needs for Love and Belongingness. Maslow believed that human beings have needs for affection, affiliation, and acceptance, which come to the fore when the physiological and safety needs are satisfied. The secure individual will be able to reach out for friends, affiliate with a group, and ultimately take on the responsibilities in marriage of being both spouse and parent.

Self-Esteem Needs. Once people find themselves loved and loving members of an accepting circle, they then need to think highly of themselves and to have others think highly of them. They want self-respect and the respect, confidence, and admiration of others. They strive to achieve and be competent and to win recognition for their accomplishments.

The Need for Self-Actualization. According to Maslow, **self-actualization** is the highest human motive. It is the need for self-fulfillment, the sense that

Table 9.2 **Personal Characteristics of Self-Actualizing College Students**

1. They perceive reality as it is. They can make accurate judgments of themselves and others, undistorted by personal needs, fears, and anxieties.
2. They accept others and themselves, without pose or defensiveness.
3. They have great spontaneity, simplicity, and naturalness.
4. They have a sense of mission and purpose in life.
5. They have an air of detachment, a need for privacy, and great concentration.
6. They are autonomous and independent, assuming responsibility for themselves.
7. They have an always fresh appreciation for nature, art, and children.
8. Many have had a mystical experience, filled with ecstasy, wonder, and awe.
9. They identify with humankind.
10. They have deep emotional ties with a few especially loved persons.
11. They are democratic in their attitudes and behavior toward others.
12. They focus on ends rather than on means.
13. Their sense of humor is philosophical rather than hostile, and they are able to laugh at themselves.
14. They are creative and inventive.
15. They resist conformity, particularly in the face of injustice.

Adapted from Maslow, 1970.

Dr. Albert Schweitzer (1875–1965), shown here at his hospital with a tiny patient, was one of the rare self-actualizers.

one is becoming everything that he or she is capable of being. People do not inevitably become self-actualizing if all their more basic needs are satisfied. Once they have self-esteem, most people do not seek greater fulfillment. The personal characteristics of persons who strive for self-actualization, those distinguishing them from people who do not, are still not certain. Maslow's own major research effort went into a search for them. He set out to locate people who appeared to have achieved self-actualization and then to determine what attributes these people shared in common. He evaluated some of his friends and acquaintances and historical figures whom he considered self-actualizers. Among three thousand college students Maslow found only one or two dozen individuals who seemed likely to become self-actualizers at some future time (Table 9.2).

SUMMARY

One of the most interesting theories of human motivation is that of Abraham Maslow, who proposed that human needs form a hierarchy. From most basic to most highly derived, these needs are physiological needs, safety and security needs, love and belongingness needs, self-esteem needs, and the need for self-actualization. Only if the individual's lower needs are satisfied can the higher needs come into play. A very small fraction of the human population ever develops the need for self-actualization.

ETHOLOGICAL STUDIES

Ethology is an exciting new science which occupies a position at the boundary between zoology and psychology. The science originated in the 1930s in Europe when Konrad Lorenz of Vienna began to publish his careful observations of innate patterns of behavior in geese, ducks, goats, and other animals. At about the same time Niko Tinbergen was closely observing animals in a similar manner in Holland. In 1936 Lorenz invited Tinbergen to join him for a few months at an outdoor laboratory on an estate in Austria. There they collaborated on several studies. Whenever possible, ethologists study animals in their natural surroundings or in outdoor laboratories where they are able to observe the animals' natural patterns of behavior. Animal behavior is an interesting topic in its own right. Probably most students of animal behavior are little concerned about the relevance of their work to the understanding of human behavior. But such relevance clearly does exist. The pages to follow describe animal research that offers clues to the understanding of such behavior as courtship and mating, parent-child attachments, and territoriality, all of which are important at the human level.

Mating Behavior of the Stickleback

The three-spined stickleback is a small fish whose courting and mating behavior has been carefully studied by Tinbergen (1952). These fish, common in the fresh and coastal waters of the Northern Hemisphere, usually mate early in the spring and go through a complicated sequence of actions in doing so. First the male stickleback establishes a small area as his territory, chasing away all intruders, male and female. Territoriality is a component of mating behavior in many species. Next the male stickleback builds a nest by binding together weed stems on the water bottom. When the nest is completed, his dull gray underside turns pink and then bright scarlet; his back becomes a bluish white. Now a distinct pattern of courtship begins. Whenever a female happens by, showing him her egg-swollen abdomen by swimming with her head upward, the male approaches her with a seductive zigzagging motion and lures her to the nest. He sticks his head into the nest opening, as though to draw her attention to it, and then withdraws. She enters the nest, and he induces her to lay her eggs by prodding rhythmically at the base of her tail (Figure 9.5). After she has left the nest, the male stickleback enters, fertilizes her eggs, and then looks for another female. He follows the same pattern of courtship with three to five female fish. At some point, however, the strength of the male's mating urge subsides, his color pales, and from then on he occupies himself with fanning the water over the nest, which increases its oxygen supply. When the young are born, the male stickleback cares for them for a few days, until they are big enough to join a school of fish.

Instincts and Releasers

The description of stickleback mating illustrates some of the most important concepts of ethology. The first is the idea that behavior like that just described

Nikolaas Tinbergen won the Nobel prize for physiology in 1973, together with Karl von Frisch and Konrad Lorenz. This was the first time the prize had been awarded for studies of behavior.

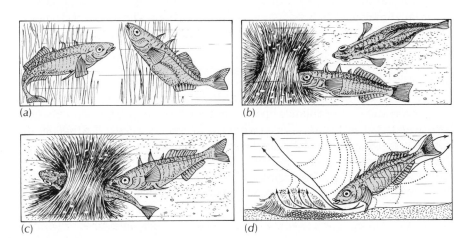

(a)

(b)

(c)

(d)

Figure 9.5
The courting behavior of the stickleback. (a) The male courts the female, (b) then he lures her into the nest, where (c) he induces her to lay her eggs. After the mating urge has subsided, (d) the male stickleback devotes himself to fanning the water over the nest to keep it in motion, as indicated by the arrows. (After Tinbergen, 1952.)

is instinctive. By **instinct** the ethologists mean a complex pattern of serially organized, unlearned behavior which is characteristic of a particular species. Ordinarily, the parts of an instinctive act tend to follow one another in a rigidly fixed sequence. The male stickleback does not build a nest until he has defended his territory for a while, he builds a nest before looking for females, and so on. Once the animal has completed a particular link in the chain of instinctive acts, the next one follows whether or not it is appropriate. Thus once a female stickleback is in the nest, she will lay her eggs in response to any nudging at the base of her tail, and she does so even if the male stickleback who led her to the nest is removed from the water.

According to ethological theory, the energy for instinctive behavior somehow exists in the nervous system in a form that makes it available only for specific instinctive actions, those related to mating in this example of stickleback behavior. This energy is released by specific stimuli called **releasers.** These stimuli have certain distinctive features. The reaction to an object is "blind" in the sense that it occurs to any object with these features whether or not the object is really appropriate. The male stickleback will attack any object that has the red color of a mating male and court any object with the approximate form of a gravid female. Occasionally the male stickleback takes a male gorged with food to be a female and courts it.

Releasing signals perform many functions. Some of them elicit feeding responses in parents. The herring gull's chicks peck at the red spot on the mother's bill to get her to regurgitate food for them. Other releasers protect members of the species. Some rodents and vervet monkeys give warning calls when they see predators; in response to these signals other rodents and monkeys take protective action. Releasers are very commonly used to attract a sexual partner. These signals may be odors or sights. As we have already seen (Chapter 3), the pheromones serve as powerful sexual attractants. Birds of paradise display their extraordinary feathers when courting. Some male birds hang from branches when they court females; others decorate trees with fruit, flowers, and colorful shells to create "love bowers."

Other signals indicate submission, greeting, or appeasement. The wolf of inferior status will prostrate itself before a superior male by lying on its side with its ears back and its tail between its legs. Rats squeal to indicate submission; the male sea lion intrudes himself between two fighting females and extends greetings to both as a means of calming them; chimps shake hands with each other, the more submissive holding the hand out in a begging gesture. Still other signals help animals to establish and maintain contact. Many animals can recognize the individual calls of their young. Some birds have duet calls by which they maintain their bonds to each other. Some signals are designed to maintain distance. Threat postures serve to ward off conspecifics or members of other species.

Imprinting

Lorenz has spent considerable time studying **imprinting,** which is the means by which many young animals become attached to their parents and are kept from wandering off alone. The newborn of many species tend to follow the first large, moving, noisy object they encounter and behave toward it as though it were their mother. Ordinarily, of course, the young animal's first experiences are with its mother, but sometimes a member of another species or even an inanimate object may happen to provide this first experience. The young animal will then become attached to it. Imprinting takes place in the young of a number of species—lambs, goats, deer, zebras, moose, buffalo, and seals—but most

Konrad Lorenz, the famous Austrian ethologist, swims with the goslings imprinted on him.

studies have been of ducks, geese, chickens, turkeys, quail, and other birds able to waddle or swim soon after they are hatched.

Early Observations.   The discovery of imprinting by European ethologists was actually a case of rediscovery. William James, writing in 1890, described such phenomena as though they were well known and cited Douglas H. Spalding (1873) as an important investigator. He quoted Spalding as saying that if baby chicks are born in an incubator, they

> . . . will follow any moving object. And, when guided by sight alone, they seem to have no more disposition to follow a hen than to follow a duck or a human being. Unreflecting lookers-on, when they saw chickens a day old running after me, and older ones following me for miles, and answering to my whistle, imagined that I must have some occult power over the creatures; whereas I had simply allowed them to follow me from the first.

Spalding also knew that imprinting occurs only during a critical period early in the life of the chick. If such experience was postponed until later, the initial reaction of the animals was not following but fear. As a demonstration of this, Spalding kept three chickens hooded until they were nearly four days old and had this to say about their behavior.

> Each of them, on being unhooded, evidenced the greatest terror to me, dashing off in the opposite direction whenever I sought to approach it. The table on which they were hooded stood before a window, and each in its turn beat against the window like a wild bird. One of them darted behind some books, and, squeezing itself into a corner, remained cowering for a length of time. We might guess at the meaning of this strange and exceptional wildness; but the odd fact is enough for my present purpose . . . had they been unhooded on the previous day they would have run to me instead of from me. . . .

Nearly a century later, laboratory experiments have fully confirmed both the fact of imprinting and Spalding's interpretation. Eckhard Hess (1958), for example, using mallard ducklings as subjects, showed that it was easy to imprint them on a circling wooden decoy of the male mallard (Figure 9.6). The decoy

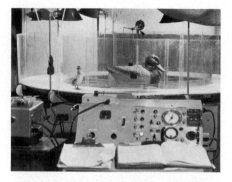

Figure 9.6
Imprinting in the duckling. This apparatus (*top*) is used to establish imprinting. A duckling (*bottom*) remains near a male decoy, on which it has been imprinted.

contained a heating element, emitting some warmth, and a loudspeaker equipped with a recording of a human voice saying, "Gock, gock, gock, gock." The duckling was placed on a circular runway near the decoy for ten minutes and allowed to follow it. Thereafter, when placed between a male decoy and a female mallard, the duckling tended to follow the decoy. In a pond the ducklings imprinted on a decoy congregated around it, in preference to a real adult duck. Moreover, ducklings that had been imprinted would climb over four-inch hurdles or up an inclined plane in order to remain near the decoy, suggesting that the process of imprinting creates an attachment with motivational properties.

One important element in imprinting is the call of the hen of the species as she leads the young from the nest. Young birds appear to be "tuned in" to the distinctive sound of the maternal call. If in the laboratory the maternal call is heard when replicas of different kinds of hens are seen, their visual qualities—size, color, and markings—can be varied markedly without reducing their attractiveness to the duckling. The use of a call different from that species' maternal call does reduce the visual effectiveness of different replicas (Gottlieb, 1973).

First Following, Then Fear. As we would expect from Spalding's observation that young animals tend first to follow and then to avoid novel objects, there is indeed a critical period during which imprinting is the most easily accomplished. Hess has investigated this relationship (Figure 9.7). The ducklings were placed in the enclosure with the circling decoy at various times after hatching, and a record was kept of whether they followed the decoy. Quite clearly, the tendency to imprint has some strength immediately after birth and increases for matter of fifteen or sixteen hours, as the ducklings are able to walk better. After that there is a decrease. Hess's interpretation, similar to Spalding's, is that the ducklings become more and more fearful of strange objects as they mature. In the normal life of the infant animal, this sequence of events is one of great adaptive significance. The infant develops an attachment to a protecting adult and, subsequently, a fear of all strange and potentially threatening creatures and a tendency to avoid them.

Later Consequences. The imprinting experience has a more permanent and more general effect on the animal's behavior than is at first evident. Much later,

Figure 9.7
Age and imprinting in ducklings. Imprinting occurs readily during a very limited age range and then falls off rapidly, beginning about 16 hours after birth. (From Hess, 1958.)

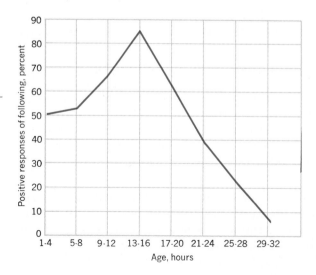

A crane imprinted on human beings performs a mating dance with Dr. George Archibald. Imprinting experiences determine later sexual preferences.

when the animal becomes mature, its sexual responses are directed toward the species or the object on which it has been imprinted. If the gosling has imprinted on a member of some other species, it will engage in other activities with its own kind, but it regards the creature on which it is imprinted as parent and sex partner. Hess, for example, cites one striking case in which a jungle fowl cock was imprinted on a person and kept away from contact with members of its own species for a month. Then it returned to the flock, but, even after five years with members of its own species, it courted human beings exclusively.

Attachments in Infant Monkeys

Harry Harlow and his colleagues at the University of Wisconsin Primate Laboratory have studied the attachments of young rhesus monkeys and found that they need what Harlow calls *contact comfort*. In Harlow's initial experiments infant monkeys were separated from their mothers at six to twelve hours after birth and were raised alone in a cage with substitute or "surrogate" mothers made either of a stiff and bare wire mesh cylinder or of a wooden cylinder covered with soft terry cloth (Figure 9.8). In one experiment both types of surrogates were available, but only one was equipped with a nipple from which the infant could nurse. Some infants received nourishment from the wire mother, and others were fed from the cloth mother. Even when the wire mother was the source of nourishment, the infant monkey spent a greater amount of time clinging to the cloth surrogate. Harlow's studies thus suggested that the contact comfort provided by the mother rather than her association with feeding fostered the infant's attachment, at least in rhesus monkeys.

Although the contact comfort provided by the terry cloth mothers seemed to allow normal behavior during infancy, the actions of monkeys raised by surrogates and without their peers became bizarre later in life. They had stereotyped patterns of behavior such as moving in circles or clutching themselves and rocking constantly back and forth while staring vacantly. They exhibited excessive and misdirected aggression, sometimes attacking infants or injuring themselves. They proved to be particularly deficient in their sexual and parenting behavior. Harlow colorfully described the sexual inadequacy of these monkeys.

Figure 9.8
Two surrogate mothers and the preference of the infant monkey. Although the wire mother provides food, the infant prefers the contact comfort of the cloth mother surrogate.

Figure 9.9
Normal mother's response to infant's need. Physical contact with the mother is constantly sought by the infant monkey. A normal mother responds positively.

Figure 9.10
Motherless mother's response to infant's need. The pathological quality of child rearing of the firstborn by a "motherless mother" is shown in this rebuff of the infant's need for physical contact. Despite the indifference of a motherless mother to her infant, the infant will continue to make futile but persistent efforts to cling to her.

Sex behavior was, for all practical purposes, destroyed; sexual posturing was commonly stereotyped and infantile. Frequently when an isolate (surrogate-raised) female was approached by a normal male, she would sit unmoved, squatting upon the floor—a posture in which only her heart was in the right place. Contrariwise, an isolate male might approach an in-estrus female, but he might clasp the head instead of the hind legs, and then engage in pelvic thrusts. Other isolate males grasped the female's body laterally, whereby all sexual efforts left them working at cross purposes with reality (1972, p. 47).

Some of the isolate females were finally impregnated, either through artificial insemination or after repeated and heroic efforts by the most persuasive of the normally raised males in the laboratory. The behavior of these monkeys as mothers—the "motherless mothers" as Harlow called them—proved to be very inadequate. The typical winsome appeal of an infant monkey seeking to be cuddled and the normal maternal response of supporting and protecting the infant may be seen in Figure 9.9. By contrast, Figure 9.10 reveals the motherless mother in full pathological bloom. These mothers tended to be either indifferent or abusive toward their babies. The indifferent mothers did not nurse, comfort, or protect their young, but they did not harm them. The abusive mothers bit or otherwise injured their infants, to the point that many of them died.

The rejection and brutality of these mothers raised the question whether their infants would become attached to them. Harlow found that the infants of motherless mothers were unceasing in their efforts to gain maternal contact. Over and over again, the infant would try to nuzzle and cuddle with the mother, despite repeated physical rebuffs. Interestingly, these persistent efforts had a rehabilitating effect on some of the motherless mothers. After several months these mothers became less rejecting and punishing; in fact, some of their infants established more contact with their mothers than did infants of normal mothers. The rehabilitated mothers proved to be adequate caretakers of their later-born infants. The motherless mothers that had never warmed up to their firstborn, however, continued to be inadequate or brutal mothers to their later offspring.

Human Ethology
A surprising amount of evidence suggests that the phenomena ethologists have observed in the behavior of other animals have parallels in human behavior.

Releasers. Babies themselves are to adults a conformation that elicits an affectionate, caretaking reaction. In common with the young of other species (Figure 9.11), they have a head that is large in proportion to the body, large eyes, a protruding forehead, upturned nose, and a soft, plump, rounded body with short, thick limbs. Possibly on an innate basis, mothers, fathers, and other people find babies of most species "cute" and want to pick them up and cuddle and care for them (Eibl-Eibesfeldt, 1970). They also respond to the smiles of babies, which begin in the first weeks of life (see page 372).

Territoriality. Like the stickleback and most animals, human beings show some form of territoriality. They lay claim to particular areas and make their claims of ownership known to others. Within the family father has his favorite chair in the living room, and each family member usually takes the same chair each night at the dining room table. Street gangs lay claim to a few urban blocks. When people spend time in libraries and cafeterias and must be temporarily absent, they try to preserve their territories by laying their personal possessions about on tables and chairs.

Human beings manifest territoriality in their need for privacy and for a certain

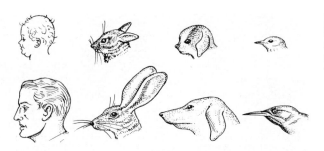

Figure 9.11
Biological bases of "cuteness." The differences between the young and adult members of many species are similar.

amount of control over their immediate surroundings. They tend to feel uncomfortable if other persons move within the invisible envelope of unoccupied space with which we all like to surround ourselves. Personal characteristics and social circumstances affect how large an envelope of space the individual prefers. For example, women choose closer physical proximities than do men (Mehrabian and Diamond, 1971), and southern Europeans stand closer than northern Europeans do (Little, 1968). People sit and stand closer to individuals whom they like or know than to strangers.

In general, people prefer to be a certain spatial separation from others. Five or six feet from nose to nose is a generally comfortable distance between two people conversing. If the people to whom we are talking are either nearer or farther away, we feel a certain amount of discomfort. Even though we are seldom able to attribute the discomfort explicitly to this distance factor, the person who comes too close is felt to be intrusive, overbearing, or ingratiating; the one who stays too far away is perceived as cold or hostile. More than physical distance defines this envelope of privacy, however. To some extent we trade off intrusion of one kind by maintaining distance in another (Argyle and Dean, 1965). Thus we can bring another person psychologically closer by enhancing eye contact or by smiling. If the other individual is intrusive in one of these ways, just as when he or she stands too close to us, we can reduce intimacy to an acceptable level by decreasing the amount of eye contact or the amount of smiling we engage in.

Children pictured on greeting cards are often drawn to have the features that bring affectionate responses.

In crowded public places people in pairs maintain as much distance from other pairs as they can manage, but they still sit closer than they would like. Birds also space themselves from one another.

Conclusion

Although the evidence presented in this section indicates that there probably is a connection between the instinctive activities of lower animals and our own motivated behavior, we should be prepared for differences. The "ascent of man" through evolution has produced an organism with a greater ratio of brain size to body size than any other. Human behavior is, therefore, more **encephalized,** more dependent on brain function, than that of any other animal. Whereas the behavior of lower organisms is dominated by reflex and instinct, ours is dominated by learning and reason. The simpler forms of behavior are still part of human behavior, but there is a heavy overlay of more highly evolved forms. Human behavior is for this reason much more variable than the behavior of other animals. With the understanding that human behavior will be more complex and varied, its ties to instincts, nevertheless, make us expect that human motives will follow certain patterns.

- The origins of human motivation are likely to be found early in life, much as Freud suggested.

- There may be critical periods when it is easier to acquire motives than at any other time. Such periods, if they do exist, will be important, for accidents of experiences may distort or prevent the development of significant motives.
- Situational factors will be important. Motives cannot be viewed as states that are entirely internal to the human being.
- The relationship between innately given and habitual components of motivation may be essentially that suggested by William James (1890). James argued that instincts exist only to form a basis for the establishment of habits, and that once the habit is formed, the instinct fades away.

SUMMARY

In the past few decades the concept of instinct has played an important role in psychology, as a result of work done by the ethologists. They study the instinctive behavior of animals, the complex sequences of stereotyped acts that are characteristic of species. The motivated behavior of higher mammals and human beings has parallels to the innate behavior studied by ethologists, but it has more flexibility and is affected to a greater extent by experience.

Here is a list of the important concepts in the chapter, in the approximate order in which they appeared.

TO BE SURE YOU UNDERSTAND THIS CHAPTER

Motivation	**Bulimia**	**Munchausen syndrome**
Intervening variable	**Heterosexual behavior**	**Self-actualization**
Primary motive	**Homosexual behavior**	**Ethology**
Secondary motive	**Estrus**	**Instinct**
Set point	**Appetitive motive**	**Releaser**
Obesity	**Aversive motive**	**Imprinting**
Anorexia nervosa		

In this chapter there are several more general themes that you should be able to apply.

The varieties of antecedent conditions determining hunger and sex as well as the varieties of behavioral expression

The variables controlling the effectiveness of punishment and the practical recommendations to which this information leads

Maslow's hierarchy of motives

The interaction of following and fearfulness in imprinting

Human ethology

In This Book. The following subjects are quite closely related to those covered in this chapter: sociobiology in Chapter 2, the physiology of sexuality in Chapter 3, classical-operant interactions in Chapter 8, all of Chapter 10, and Erikson's personality theory in Chapter 15.

TO GO BEYOND THIS CHAPTER

Elsewhere. Recently a number of new texts on motivation that provide good summaries of contemporary research have appeared. Among the best are Bernard Weiner's *Human Motivation,* Herbert Petri's *Motivation: Theory and Research,* Ross Buck's *Human Motivation and Emotion,* Robert Beck's *Motivation: Theories and Principles* (second edition). On the topic of punishment, see *Punishment,* by Gary C. Walters and Joan E. Grusec. Irenaus Eibl-Ebesfeldt's *Ethology: The Biology of Behavior* (second edition) is a useful volume on the subject.

CHAPTER 10   STRESS, EMOTION, AND COPING

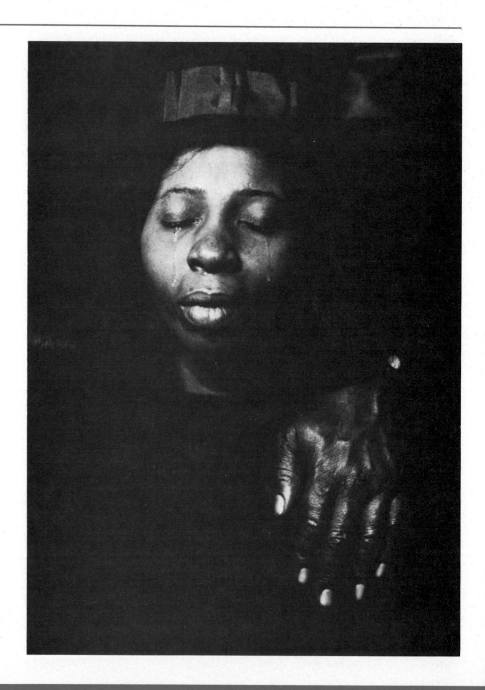

Although the concept of stress has had an important place in psychology for many decades, this subject and the related one of coping are particularly prominent in the field today. Hans Selye (1907–1983), an endocrinologist who was one of the pioneers of stress research, provided us with this perspective in 1980.

> Nowadays, everyone seems to be talking about stress. You hear it not only in daily conversation, but also through television, radio, the newspapers and the constantly increasing number of conferences, stress centers, and university courses that are devoted to the topic. . . . The businessman thinks of it as frustration or emotional tension, the air traffic controller as a problem in concentration, the biochemist and endocrinologist as a purely chemical event, the athlete as muscular tension. This list could be extended to almost every human experience or activity, and somewhat surprisingly, most people . . . think of their own occupation as being the most stressful. Similarly, most of us believe that ours is "the age of stress," forgetting that the caveman's fear of being attacked by wild animals while he slept, or dying from hunger, cold or exhaustion, must have been just as stressful as our fear of a world war, the crash of the stock exchange, overpopulation or the unpredictability of the future (p. vii).

THE NATURE OF STRESS

Whether the stresses of life today are less or greater than they were in prehistoric times cannot be determined. However that may be, there can be no doubt that modern life is stressful. Rape, assault, pollution, hurricanes, crowded surroundings, bombings, terrorism, overwork, death of a spouse, illness, poverty, unemployment, divorce, conflict, and undignified old age are some of the sources of **stress** in today's world. Such events are called **stressors.** When they are severe or last for a long time, they may produce many and varied symptoms. Those listed in Table 10.1 were identified by Selye (1976). Feelings of helplessness, reduced self-esteem, and the inability to complete assigned tasks have been named by others. Sometimes people have vivid flashbulb memories (page 194) of stressful events and experience intense guilt for having survived the traumatic event in which others have died (Gatchel and Baum, 1983).

The distinction between stressors and stress reactions is similar to the distinction between antecedent conditions and behavioral consequences of motives. The concept of stress intervenes between these two sets of factors and links them together. These similarities suggest that it should be possible to treat the

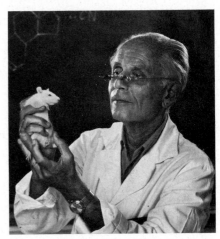

In medical school Hans Selye learned that each disease has its own symptoms and specific cause. But he noticed that people with many diseases had several symptoms in common—loss of appetite, muscular weakness, and loss of interest in what was happening in their lives. He theorized that there might be a common stress syndrome in addition to particular disease syndromes.

Table 10.1 Some Symptoms of Stress

1. Irritability, hyperexcitation, or depression.
2. Impulsive behavior, emotional instability.
3. Floating anxiety: fear without knowing what we are afraid of.
4. Tension and alertness: the feeling of being "keyed up."
5. Fatigue, loss of the joy of living.
6. The overpowering urge to run or cry.
7. Pounding heart.
8. Dryness of mouth and throat.
9. Frequent need to urinate.
10. Diarrhea, indigestion, upset stomach, vomiting.
11. Premenstrual tension, missed menstrual cycles.
12. Sweating.
13. Loss of or excessive appetite.
14. Increased smoking.
15. Increased use of legal drugs.
16. Alcohol and drug addiction.
17. Insomnia.
18. Trembling, nervous tics.
19. Easily startled, by small sounds.
20. Bruxism, grinding the teeth.
21. Hypermotility, restless moving about.
22. High-pitched, nervous laughter.
23. Inability to concentrate.
24. Feelings of unreality.
25. Stuttering and other speech difficulties.
26. Migraine headaches.
27. Nightmares.
28. Psychoses.
30. Accident proneness.

Adapted from Selye, 1976.

Figure 10.1

The nature of stress. A number of conditions called stressors are the causes of stress, which is expressed in many different physiological and behavioral reactions. The stressfulness for an individual of any stressor varies, depending on how he or she perceives the situation and on the resources available for coping.

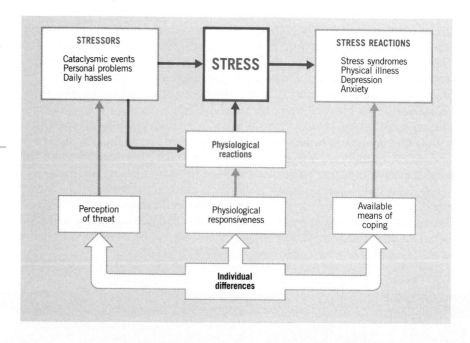

topic of stress according to the pattern laid out in Figure 10.1, which has the same general structure as Figure 9.1. In addition to the parallels to the concept of motivation, Figure 10.1 includes some ideas to which we shall return after developing necessary background materials.

The General Adaptation Syndrome

When Selye first discussed the concept of stress in the 1930s, it was in the context of medical experimentation. He exposed rats to a number of stressors—prolonged exposure to near-freezing temperatures, infections, injections of toxic drugs, confinement in small cages, fatigue, and X-irradiation. He observed a consistent sequence of reactions, which indicated that the body was mobilizing its resources to deal with these traumatic events. Selye called this sequence the **general adaptation syndrome** (GAS). The general adaptation syndrome (Figure 10.2) consisted of three successive physiological stages, which Selye called the *alarm reaction,* the *stage of resistance,* and the *stage of exhaustion.* The **alarm reaction** consisted of two phases: a *shock phase* in which there was an enlargement of the adrenal cortex, a withering away of the thymus gland, and the appearance of gastrointestinal ulcers; and a *countershock phase* in which the body temporarily recovered from these symptoms. Most of the effects on the body of the alarm reaction, particularly in the shock phase, are degenerative in nature; but Selye noted that " . . . the adrenal cortex actually seemed to flourish on stress."

If the stress was prolonged, a **stage of resistance** set in and most of the symptoms of the alarm reaction began to subside. The adrenals returned to normal size. The glucose and chloride levels of the blood, which were often depleted during the alarm reaction, were restored; and the thymus began to recover its normal appearance. In this stage the physiological adjustment of the rats seemed optimal. The state of the body was not as it appeared, however; there was a serious weakness in the animals' adjustment. Their resistance was strictly limited to the particular stress to which they had been exposed. The introduction of other stressors led to further degeneration and even death. It was as though the protective defenses of the animals were limited in amount. When they were given over entirely to handling one stressful situation, there were few or no reserves to use against other stressors.

Moreover, the stage of resistance did not persist indefinitely. If stress continued, the animals eventually weakened, and the **stage of exhaustion** began. In this final stage serious physical changes occurred, particularly in the brain. These included hemorrhages, cerebral arteriosclerosis, and epilepticlike seizures, which brought death.

Selye's research was carried out in a physiological laboratory. The stressors he employed were physical and physiological; the reactions he studied were bodily reactions. Behavioral consequences were not emphasized, although in the book Selye published (1976) he mentioned some of them in a discussion of what he called "the stressors of daily life." Very soon, however, the study of stress expanded its boundaries and it moved into the psychological arena. The concept of stressor was extended to include frustration, conflict, environmental deprivations, and threats to esteem and security. Reactions to these new stressors included of course emotional and cognitive processes, and *coping,* the efforts of the individual to adapt to stress, grew in importance.

Measuring the Stresses of Life

As we indicated at the beginning of this chapter, psychological stresses are clearly a simple fact of everyday living. Methods have been developed to measure the level of these stresses and to determine their consequences.

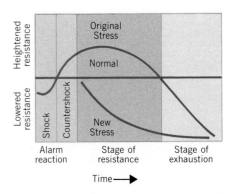

Figure 10.2
The general adaptation syndrome. Stress occurs in three stages. A new stressor has a destructive effect sooner than the original stressor. (Adapted from Selye, 1956.)

Life Events Scales.   Imagine that you have the task of putting the following events into a rank order that represents their degree of stressfulness. In terms of the intensity of the stress you would feel and the time that it would probably last, give a rank of 1 to the most severe stress and 10 for the least severe. You may want to make your rankings before reading further.

 1. Sexual difficulty   ( )
 2. Trouble with one's boss   ( )
 3. Son or daughter leaves home   ( )
 4. Pregnancy   ( )
 5. Minor violation of the law   ( )
 6. Major illness   ( )
 7. Death of a spouse   ( )
 8. Changing to a new shcool   ( )
 9. Retirement from work   ( )
10. Divorce   ( )

When a group of 400 men and women from several countries, who differed in age, race, religion, education, social class, and marital status, ranked these events, they put them in the following order: 1, death of a spouse; 2, divorce; 3, major illness; 4, retirement from work; 5, 6 (tie), sexual difficulty, pregnancy; 7, son or daughter leaves home; 8, trouble with one's boss; 9, changing to a new school; 10, minor violation of the law. A review of these rankings will reveal that the majority of these events, and all the most stressful ones, represent a loss or threatened loss of some type, loss of a mate through death or divorce, loss of health through illness, and loss of work through retirement.

The stressful events of this short list appear in a much longer one used in research on the stresses of everyday life, the Social Readjustment Rating Scale (Table 10.2). This, the most popular of the **life events scales,** was developed by Thomas Holmes and Richard Rahe (1967). Their 400 raters were told to compare the intensity of each of forty-three stressors with marriage, which was assigned an arbitrary score of 500. Ratings were averaged and divided by 10 to arrive at each life change value.

Correlates of Life Stress.   Hundreds of studies have now established the existence of modest correlations between the amount of stress a person lives with and various unhappy consequences. The general method employed in these studies is to ask people to check off the stressful events that they have experienced in the past six months or year. A score is then obtained by adding up the stress points corresponding to the events the person checks. Finally, a correlation coefficient is calculated to determine the degree of relationship between stress and its consequences. High numbers of stress points are found to correlate with such negative outcomes as illness, injuries, depression, and symptoms of emotional disturbance. To quote from one report, the consequences have included

> . . . sudden cardiac death, myocardial infarction, accidents, athletic injuries, tu-
> berculosis, leukemia, multiple sclerosis, diabetes, and the entire gamut of minor
> medical complaints. High scores on checklists of life events have also been repeat-
> edly associated with psychiatric symptoms and disorders . . . (Rabkin and Struening,
> 1976, p. 1015).

Other research suggests that stress increases vulnerability to infection and may even be related to the development of spontaneous cancers.

Table 10.2 The Social Readjustment Rating Scale

Rank	Life Event	Life Change Units
1	Death of a spouse	100
2	Divorce	73
3	Marital separation	65
4	Jail term	63
5	Death of a close family member	63
6	Personal injury or illness	53
7	Marriage	50
8	Fired at work	47
9	Marital reconciliation	45
10	Retirement	45
11	Change in health of a family member	44
12	Pregnancy	40
13	Sex difficulties	39
14	Gain of new family member	39
15	Business readjustment	39
16	Change in financial state	38
17	Death of close friend	37
18	Change to different line of work	36
19	Change in number of arguments with spouse	35
20	Mortgage over $10,000	31
21	Foreclosure of mortgage or loan	30
22	Change in responsibilities at work	29
23	Son or daughter leaving home	29
24	Trouble with in-laws	29
25	Outstanding personal achievement	28
26	Wife begins or stops work	26
27	Begin or end school	26
28	Change in living conditions	25
29	Revision of personal habits	24
30	Trouble with boss	23
31	Change in work hours or conditions	20
32	Change in residence	20
33	Change in schools	20
34	Change in recreation	19
35	Change in church activities	19
36	Change in social activities	18
37	Mortgage or loan less than $10,000	17
38	Change in sleeping habits	16
39	Change in number of family get-togethers	15
40	Change in eating habits	15
41	Vacation	13
42	Christmas	12
43	Minor violations of the law	11

Holmes and Rahe, 1967.

Evaluation of Life Stress Research. It is important to recognize that there are many shortcomings in such research.

1. Although the correlations between life stress and illness are statistically significant, they are low or moderate in magnitude. They are not precise predictors of disease or disorder.

2. As is always true with correlational information, the nature of causation is indeterminate. Stress probably *is* a causal factor in disease, but it could be that people who are vulnerable to illness for other reasons have a greater probability of becoming victims of stress.

3. The validity of the life stress measures is a problem. Respondents are usually asked to "check the events that have happened to you during the past year." They may forget some stressful events (Monroe, 1982). Because they are uncertain what some items in the list refer to, they may miss some they should have checked and report some that never happened.

4. The precise values assigned to the various stressors are suspect. Is it really correct to give "death of a spouse" twice the stress value of "marriage" and "change in living conditions" half the same value? Such precision seems unwarranted.

5. The calculation of scores implicitly assumes that the stress points assigned to each life event are equally appropriate for everyone who checks the schedule. A recurring theme in the rest of this chapter is that this assumption is unwarranted.

6. The events listed in the stress schedules are heterogeneous, covering many types of stress. This shotgun approach makes it impossible to sort out the effects of particular kinds of stress. Might it not be more informative to study stresses of special types, to discover their psychological meaning and consequences (Rutter, 1981b)?

SUMMARY

Stress is an ever-present fact of life; it takes many forms and reveals its malignant consequences in many ways. Selye's early studies of stress were carried out as medical research. They revealed a pattern of reactions to prolonged stress called the general adaptation syndrome, comprising an alarm reaction, with shock and countershock phases, then a stage of resistance, and, if stress continues, a stage of exhaustion. This research suggested that many different stressors cause the general adaptation syndrome, and that the effects of stress are cumulative.

Life stress inventories determine the stress under which an individual lives by means of a checklist of events that are known to be stressful. Scores on these tests are correlated with the development of physical and mental disorders, but the method has many flaws. Examining the effects of more specific stressors might be more revealing.

MAJOR STRESSORS AND THEIR CONSEQUENCES

Different stressors differ in a number of ways. Natural catastrophes and severe illness are more physical; overwork and separation from a parent are more psychological. Poverty is of long duration; a bombing is of short duration. Crowded living arrangements affect many people. The death of a loved one affects only a few. Unemployment is something we can hope to cope with by finding a job; a hurricane is beyond our control. Terrorism is a severe stressor; the irritating habits of a roommate are inconsequential. Obviously, these differences offer several bases for classifying stress. Designating them as cataclysmic events, personal stressors, and background stressors (Lazarus and Cohen, 1977) is one way (see Figure 10.1).

Combat, floods, earthquakes, nuclear accidents, and other disasters are **cataclysmic events.** They happen suddenly, have great intensity, and affect many people. **Personal stressors**—separation, divorce, death of a spouse, loss of one's job—may be as powerful as cataclysmic events, but they affect individual people. **Background stressors** are the hassles of everyday life. They are the persistent, nagging irritations at home, school, and work that affect us all. Interestingly, positive events such as election to office, promotion at work, even vacations and Christmas (see Table 10.2) can be stressful. In terms of stress, the best things in life are not free.

Background Stressors

A major finding of some fifty years of research has been that stress, even in relatively mild forms, has physiological and psychological consequences. Selye (1976) has cited many examples.

- Invoice clerks, shifted from fixed wages to a piecework pay schedule, became fatigued, developed backache and pain in their arms and shoulders, and excreted amounts of epinephrine in their urine.
- Workers on night shifts are particularly susceptible to peptic ulcers, probably because of fatigue and mental distress.
- At income tax time, when work is heavy, accountants have higher levels of serum cholesterol, a stress reaction which predisposes the individual to heart disease.
- In two studies of air traffic controllers, more than one-third of them were found to have peptic ulcers. The longer these people are on their jobs, the more they show such indications of stress as rapid pulse rate, sweating, and increased excretion of epinephrine. These symptoms are even present on the workers' days off.

Not everyone who is exposed to such stressors develops these physiological symptoms, which means that some people have resources that help them ward off the consequences of stress. But there is an important related point. The effects of stress accumulate. By comparison with the stressors yet to be considered, doing piecework and night work and working under pressure are not powerful stressors. A brief exposure to any of them would have little or no effect on anyone. Prolonged exposure to them, however, can leave the individual vulnerable to stress disorders in a process that is difficult to reverse.

Personal Stressors

Personal stressors are inevitable in the lives of all of us. Over the life-span we face separation from parents, the new responsibilities of a higher stage of development, taking a job, losing a job, divorce, bereavement, the infirmities of old age, and the prospect of death.

Separation. Very young children find it extremely distressful to be separated from their parents for any length of time.

> Ten children, ranging in age from thirteen to thirty-two months, have been brought to a residential nursery where they will remain for a while separated from their parents. The fathers work and the mothers are entering a hospital to deliver a baby or to undergo medical observation or treatment. When brought to the nursery, the children stay close to their fathers and mothers; they seem subdued and anxious.
>
> When the parents prepare to leave, the children begin to cry and scream and refuse to be comforted. When put to bed, they are inconsolable. One little girl screams until fatigue overwhelms her. She awakens intermittently crying, "Mommy . . . , mommy."
>
> The children refuse to eat. Eight of them, who had been toilet-trained, begin to

soil and wet themselves again. Weeks later, when their mothers reappear, all the children *seem* disinterested in them (Heinicke and Wertheimer, 1965).

Initially, when young children are separated from their mothers, they *protest* and attempt to recover the lost mother. When the mother fails to return, they are in *despair,* are continually preoccupied with her absence, and watch constantly for her return. Finally, there is *detachment,* a seeming loss of interest in the mother, which continues for a period following her return (Bowlby, 1973).

Although they are obviously not identical, this separation syndrome has some of the features of the general adaptation syndrome. There are three stages; the "protest" response resembles Selye's "alarm reaction"; the third stage, the "detachment" stage, is like Selye's low-energy "stage of exhaustion." We shall meet similar patterns again, in reactions to catastrophic disaster.

There are circumstances that can lessen the intensity of the separation syndrome. The presence of a sibling or another familiar person, the availability of familiar possessions, and good caretaking by a warmly responsive mother surrogate all help. Strange surroundings, unfamiliar people, painful medical procedures, and an earlier history of separation from home and mother, however, can intensify the syndrome.

The young of other species who are not with their mothers may suffer some aspects of the separation syndrome. Some, but not all species of monkeys, go through the protest-despair sequence whether they are separated from their mothers in the laboratory or in their natural surroundings (Mineka and Suomi, 1978). The infant monkeys who do not go through this sequence are those who easily transfer their attachments to other adult members of a troop (Rosenblum, 1971).

An important difference between monkeys and human beings is that infant monkeys indicate no detachment from their mothers when they are reunited with them. Infant monkeys rush to embrace their mothers; they cling to them and continue to remain close to them (Spencer-Booth and Hinde, 1971).

Transition Stress.   In the course of developing from infant to child to adolescent to adult, the individual experiences a series of new stressors connected with the transition from one stage of development to another. During these transitions individuals are likely to feel a discrepancy between the new demands placed on them and their assessment of their abilities to meet these demands. A **transition stress** can occur at an early age, as the results of a recent study by Jerome Kagan (1983) very clearly indicate.

Kagan's experiment was strikingly simple. One at a time, children came to the laboratory and played on the floor with toys as the mother sat near by. Soon a female examiner came in, knelt down by the child, and played with the toys herself in one of three very complex ways. Then, turning to the child, she said, "Now it's your turn to play," and sat down. This simple experiment has been carried out with several groups of children, with the following results. Children under seventeen months of age show no distress when the examiner tells them that now it is their turn to play. At sometime between seventeen and twenty-four months, however, children begin to be greatly distressed by this request. They cling to their mothers, cry, stop playing, protest vocally, and inform their mothers that they want to go home. Children of the Fiji Islands behave in similar ways, suggesting that this form of stressful experience may be very general (Figure 10.3).

Why should this behavior tend to peak at twenty-four months of age and then decline? The answer appears to lie in the great psychological changes taking place in toddlers of this age. They are acquiring new cognitive compe-

Jerome Kagan believes that basic intellectual skills are developed as physiological processes permit. Therefore we should concentrate more on motivation than on attempts to promote vocabulary, say, or reading. Helping children to have an expectancy of success, less obviously maturational, may be more crucial to their future lives.

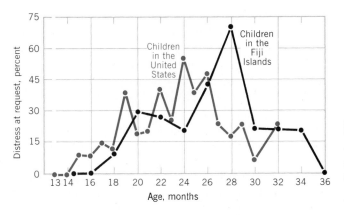

Figure 10.3
Transition stress. Young children in a transition stage of development are distressed when asked to play in a new and complex way. (Adapted from Kagan, 1983.)

tencies and rapidly mastering their language. With language their powers of thought improve. At the same time children are becoming sensitive to the evaluations of others. As they begin to acquire the standards of their parents, there is a surge toward autonomy and independence, and they have a need for achievement. Children now begin to have some skills and to take a pride in their accomplishments, but the enhanced sensitivity to others and a developing ability to anticipate the future combine to generate a painful fear of failure. As a result, these children do not feel that they are able to play with the toys as the examiner did, but they sense that they should be able to. Their crying, clinging, protesting, and attempts to escape the situation by going home are manifestations of the distress brought on by this discrepancy between their perceptions of the demands of the situation and their estimations of their abilities.

The experimental situation devised by Kagan reveals the existence of transition stress in very young children. Similar stress occurs at later ages when the

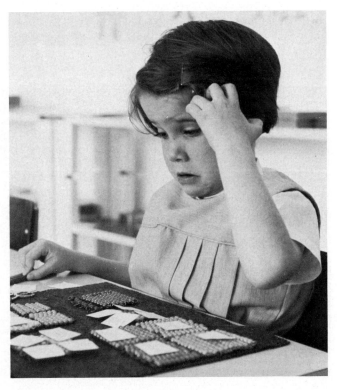

As children develop a need to achieve and face tasks demanding new skills, they may perceive their abilities as lagging behind.

life of an individual changes in important ways: going off to school, experiencing the pubertal changes of adolescence, leaving home for work or college, marrying and beginning a family, retiring. In the case of retirement, people often experience a reverse form of stressful discrepancy. The individual's abilities are greater than the demands of retirement. Competent people who are unemployed or underemployed face a similar stress-inducing discrepancy.

Unemployment.   Based on his analysis of thirty years of data, M. Harvey Brenner (1973, 1981–1982), the Johns Hopkins University expert on the long-term effects of stress on the nation's health, has projected the following unhealthy consequences of *every* one percentage point of increase in the unemployment rate: suicides, up 4.1 percent; homicides, up 5.7 percent; deaths from heart disease, stress-related disorders, and cirrhosis of the liver, up 1.9 percent; admission to state mental hospitals, men up 4.3 percent, women, up 2.3 percent.

Depressing as these statistics are, they cannot project the poignancy captured by one social worker's report of life in Flint, Michigan, where unemployment among auto workers hit 20 percent.

> I don't know how many cases I've had where the father admits that what his child did would normally not have been cause for a reprimand. Or it would be overlooked. But in the house of the unemployed there is so much tension it's like striking a match in a room full of gas fumes. The child misbehaves, the father loses his temper and smacks much harder than he intended. There is *no* evidence of sadism or serious emotional illness in most of the child-beating cases we have been seeing. . . . The hospital or the doctor shows me a child covered with bruises and when I ask the parents what happened, the father breaks down and tells me he did it. He says over and over again that he's sorry, that he simply lost control, that if he could only find a job he would make it up to the child (Woodcock, 1976).

This clinical account of the stressfulness of unemployment is reinforced by a study of the physiological consequences of joblessness (Kasl and Cobb, 1970). The participants in this study were married, stably employed men who lost their jobs when their plant was permanently shut down. Over a span of twenty-six months, their stress reactions were studied by means of their blood pressure.

Unemployment takes a heavy toll emotionally and physiologically and on all the members of the family.

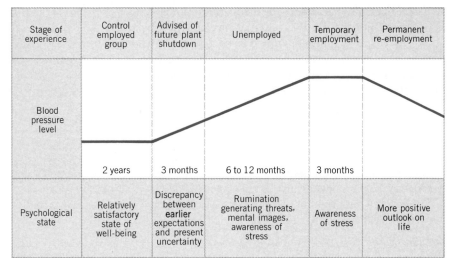

Stage of experience	Control employed group	Advised of future plant shutdown	Unemployed	Temporary employment	Permanent re-employment
Blood pressure level		2 years	3 months	6 to 12 months	3 months	
Psychological state	Relatively satisfactory state of well-being	Discrepancy between earlier expectations and present uncertainty	Rumination generating threats, mental images, awareness of stress	Awareness of stress	More positive outlook on life

Figure 10.4
Physiological and psychological reactions to the stress of unemployment. With the announcement that their plant would shut down, the blood pressure of workers began to rise and stayed high during subsequent unemployment and temporary employment. When the men had permanent jobs again, their blood pressure lowered. While anticipating the end of their jobs and while unemployed and temporarily employed, the men were psychologically distressed. (Based on Kasl and Cobb, 1970.)

During these months their jobs ended, some men were unemployed for a prolonged period, some took temporary work, and some found another job. The blood pressures of a group of men who kept their jobs during the same period were also studied. The major results (Figure 10.4) were these. (1) Individuals who continued to be employed showed no important changes in blood pressure. Psychologically they remained reasonably well satisfied with their situations. (2) When workers were advised that they would probably lose their jobs, their blood pressure began to rise as they were forced to deal with the discrepancy between their earlier expectations and their now uncertain situations. (3) With unemployment blood pressure rose further and remained high, even when men took temporary work. The men also reported a greater awareness that they were under stress. (4) When the men went back to work, their blood pressure began to decline, and their outlook on life become more positive. Extensive data obtained more recently support these findings (Kasl and Cobb, 1980, 1982).

Divorce. Divorce is now a major source of stress, especially in the lives of children. And the rate of divorce is on the increase.

- Nearly 40 percent of marriages in the United States end in the divorce courts.
- Each year from 1972 through 1979 one million new children below the age of eighteen experienced the trauma of family breakup through divorces.
- In the first eight months of 1979, the number of divorces and marriages in California were nearly equal.
- Primarily because of divorce, 20.1 percent of all children lived with a single parent in 1981, an increase of 53.9 percent since 1970 (Bureau of Census, 1982).
- By the 1990s only 56 percent of America's children are likely to spend their entire childhood with both natural parents. The comparable figure for 1960 was 73 percent.

Divorce places strains on children in three principal ways. The first is by removing one of the children's parents from the home. The second is by the decline in the economic status of their mothers, with whom they usually remain. California figures (Weitzman, 1981) show that the standard of living of men improved 42 percent after divorce, but that of divorced women declined 73 percent. The third source of pressure is from the heightened stress on the divorced mother herself. In a national survey (Campbell et al., 1976) divorced women gave more affirmative responses, even than widows, to questionnaire items such as the following: *feel life is hard, feel tied down, always feel rushed, worry about bills, feel frightened, worry about nervous breakdown.*

The effect of divorce on children is destructive. As E. Mavis Hetherington, a distinguished developmental psychologist, notes,

> Although divorce may be the best solution to a destructive family relationship and may offer the child an escape from one set of stresses and the opportunity for personal growth, almost all children experience the transition of divorce as painful. Even children who later are able to recognize that the divorce has constructive outcomes initially undergo considerable emotional distress with family dissolution. The children's most common early responses to divorce are anger, fear, depression, and guilt (1979, p. 851).

The following observations enlarge upon this theme.

> Most often, the children responded to the [divorce] announcement with apprehension or anger. Over three-quarters of the children opposed the divorce very strongly. Many burst into tears and pleaded with parents to reconsider. Some prayed for God's help. Sonia, age eight, first vomited, then hugged and kissed her mother, offering a new washing machine or a clothes dryer to placate her. Several children asked, "Will I ever see my daddy again?" A few children had delayed reactions. Five-year-old Fred watched television silently and a few days later began to sob. "We don't have a daddy anymore! I'll need a new daddy!" (Wallerstein and Kelly, 1980).

Divorced men and women, of course, also suffer. By comparison with non-divorced people, they are overrepresented in the statistics for motor vehicle accidents and fatalities; they are more frequently psychiatric patients; they visit physicians more often every year because of higher rates of illness, disability, and alcoholism. They are more frequent victims of homicide, and they more often take their own lives.

Bereavement. Death of a spouse is the very most powerful stressor on the life stress scales (see Table 10.2). This tragedy is particularly stressful since it must be endured alone. The death of a spouse brings in its wake the loss of companionship, sex, comfort, often a home, and the most important source of economic and social support. Friends are unable to understand or accept the grief and mourning of the widow or widower as it becomes prolonged, and they gradually drift away. Bereavement is a particularly common problem among the women in our older population. Because of the greater longevity of women, the ratio of widows to widowers is four to one.

The stress of bereavement is sometimes fatal. For men and women who become widows and widowers, the mortality rate increases abruptly, especially during the first six months after the death of a spouse. These mortality statistics prove that people do die of broken hearts, literally as well as figuratively (Lynch, 1977). Cardiac disorders take the lives of many widows and widowers, even of those who are under thirty-five years of age.

Other data indicate that widows younger than sixty-five consult physicians at thrice the expected rate for their ages (Greenblatt, 1978; Parkes, 1972). These widows also spend more time than other women of their ages sick in bed at home or in the hospital. They use sedatives at seven times the normal rate, they drink too much alcohol, and they use medication excessively. All these practices are ones that hasten dying. Suicides are an additional testimonial to

Bereavement.

the grief of bereavement. During the first year of widowhood, the suicide rate is 2.5 times that of other women their age. From the second through the fourth year, the rate is 1.5 times greater for widows than for other women of their age.

Conflict. Conflicting motives are a final important source of personal stress. States of **conflict** and the stress that accompanies them are familiar to all of us. We experience conflict in many ways. One of our common conflicts is deciding to forgo one goal to attain another, for example, giving up tonight's social evening to work on a term paper that is due tomorrow. In terms of emotions, conflict is a state in which opposing feelings tug at one another. We are irritated at the sight of another student's cheating and consider reporting the incident, but the feeling that we are not the sort of person who tells on another restrains us. The more important the opposed values in conflicts of this type, the greater the conflict. The wartime conflict between patriotic and religious values is one of the most difficult of these. Patriotism may require a soldier to slay an enemy; God's commandment insists that "Thou shalt not kill." General S. L. A. Marshall (1947), a distinguished military historian, believed that line commanders pay too little attention to the reality of this conflict, which makes some soldiers fear killing more than they fear being killed.

Some of the earliest theoretical analyses of conflict were by experimental psychologists who applied the basic principles of learning and motivation to the subject. They treated conflict in terms of positive tendencies to approach certain goals and negative tendencies to avoid others. They identified four major ways in which these tendencies could oppose one another and thus defined four major types of conflict: approach-approach, avoidance-avoidance, approach-avoidance, and double approach-avoidance.

In the **approach-approach conflict** a person is faced with two attractive alternatives, only one of which can be selected. There are two courses that you want to take, but they are scheduled for the same time. As this example suggests, approach-approach conflicts are usually easy to resolve; you choose one course and decide to take the other next semester. Presto, the conflict is

Approach-approach choices are not difficult to make.

resolved. Approach-approach conflicts become serious only if the choice of one alternative means the loss of an extremely attractive alternative. The course conflict will be more stressful if it occurs in your final semester, which means that you will never be able to take one of the courses, than if it happens in your sophomore year.

As an example of **avoidance-avoidance conflict,** think of yourself in the following dilemma. The term is over and your grades are disappointing. You promised to call your mother or your father today to tell them how you did. They will both be unhappy, expressing their feelings in different painful ways. Whom do you call? What you would like to do is to call neither, but you made a promise and besides that you need to find out when they are coming to take you home. So you have to do something. Obviously, avoidance-avoidance conflicts can be stressful. Usually they are resolved but only at an emotional cost.

In an **approach-avoidance conflict** the same object or state of affairs is simultaneously attractive and unattractive, generating tendencies both to approach and avoid it. An adolescent boy would like to have it out with his father, but feelings of guilt and fear of retaliation prevent him from getting into a direct confrontation. Instead, he goes to his room and, sitting there, has a daydream in which he challenges his father and wins.

Meanwhile, the boy's father has a conflict of his own. Strongly tempted by the possible sexual availability of his neighbor's wife, he nevertheless refrains from making any advances toward her. The thought of violating important moral values causes him intense anxiety and prevents him from approaching her. Instead, for a while, he devotes more attention to his own wife.

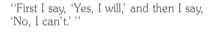

"First I say, 'Yes, I will,' and then I say, 'No, I can't.'"

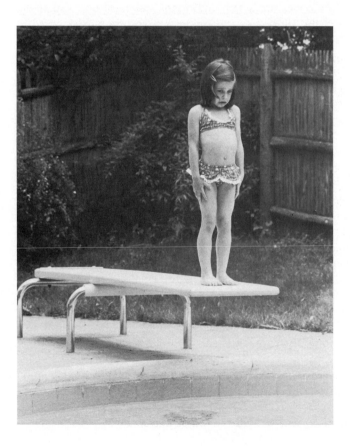

Aggression-anxiety conflicts and sex-anxiety conflicts such as these are common and important. In both cases a wish to approach—aggression or sex—clashes with guilt and anxiety. Resolution takes the form of some substitute activity—in our example daydreaming and greater attentiveness to the wife. Sometimes the symptoms of mental disorder seem ways of resolving approach-avoidance conflicts (see page 530).

Most of the important decisions people make in life force them to choose between two alternatives, each of which, by itself, is an approach-avoidance conflict. A **double approach-avoidance** conflict that almost everyone faces at least once is choosing between two job offers or between keeping a present job and taking a new one. Such decisions can be exceedingly difficult. One job might have certain advantages—desirable location, convenient distance from family, good salary; but also disadvantages—little chance of rapid advancement, poor "fringe benefits," long workweek. The alternative position has its own virtues—excellent housing available for employees, initial appointment at a higher level, a prestigious organization; but also its own drawbacks—company's reputation for letting employees go after a few years, probability of being required to move often, policies of management undergoing change.

It is very important to try to understand the behavior of people in a double approach-avoidance conflict because so often things go wrong. A man chooses one job over another, after what he believes is careful deliberation, but finds that he has made a mistake. Now, with the job market difficult, he is stuck with his wrong decision. A gifted woman artist chooses to marry rather than pursue a career but finds, in a few years, that running a household for husband and children seriously limits the time she can spend painting. Deeply frustrated, she thinks of divorce. President Kennedy, looking back and realizing how badly he had miscalculated in making the conflict-ridden decision approving the Bay of Pigs invasion, asked, "How could I have been so stupid?" (Janis and Mann, 1977).

Cataclysmic Events

The impact of catastrophe was vividly described by Dr. Hachaya (1955), a physician living in Hiroshima when that city was destroyed by an atom bomb on August 6, 1945.

> Those who were able walked silently toward the suburbs in the distant hills, their spirits broken, their initiative gone. When asked whence they had come, they pointed to the city and said, "that way"; and when asked where they were going, pointed away from the city and said, "this way." They were so broken and confused that they moved and behaved like automatons.
>
> Their reactions had astonished outsiders who reported with amazement the spectacle of long lines of people holding stolidly to a narrow, rough path when close by was a smooth, easy road going in the same direction. The outsiders could not grasp the fact that they were witnessing the exodus of a people who walked in the realm of dreams (p. 54).

A town in Appalachia was inundated when 132 million tons of debris-filled water crashed down on it after a makeshift mining company dam had broken. The flood destroyed what had for generations been a tightly knit community, leaving 125 persons buried in the muck. A survivor described his life after the flood waters had receded.

> My whole family is a family of fear. Fear of rain, storms, wind, or hail. If it will just cloud up, my family all wants to get to higher ground, but there's no place around that I can go to that'll beat where I am. And my wife, she's about to run

us all off. She is so nervous and she is so upset, she don't take no interest in what we've got. It's not there. In other words, our house is just a place to stay. It's not a home. And we don't have no neighbors, that's the whole lot of it (Erikson, 1976, p. 146).

Reaction to Disaster.   Tornadoes, hurricanes, floods, droughts, earthquakes, and volcanic eruptions—these disasters strike in an unpredictable pattern and often permit neither preparation nor escape. More detailed observations of persons living through such catastrophes indicate that they suffer from a disaster syndrome that is reminiscent of the general adaptation syndrome. It consists of three stages, the first of which is a **shock reaction.** In this stage some 10 to 20 percent of people remain calm, and another 20 percent go into a state of panic; but most individuals are confused, stunned, and paralyzed by the magnitude of disaster. This reaction may serve a useful purpose, for, like those in the silent exodus from Hiroshima, it isolates the victims from an overwhelming reality, at least for a time. In the second stage, a **recoil reaction,** people become aware of the disaster and begin to face reality. Depression and hostility are common parts of the reaction. In the third stage, the **stage of recall,** depression and hostility give way to tenseness and restlessness. People may relive the events of the disaster, or they may repress these traumatic experiences. Only later does the process of renewal and rehabilitation begin to take place. Usually, the victims do not require hospitalization. But high levels of anxiety and distress may continue to have debilitating effects on the individual. As we saw in Selye's work and shall see again in connection with the stress of combat, the individual who has suffered trauma often remains susceptible and breaks down when faced with other stress later on.

A woman weeps after being brought by heliocopter across a roaring stream, part of a wall of water that has destroyed her home. A dam had collapsed earlier during a furious wind and rain storm in Big Tujunga Canyon in California.

Relatives of one of seven miners killed in the Craynor mine explosion leave the church after his funeral service in Teaburry, Kentucky.

War and Combat.   Nature's catastrophes come in an unexpected fashion; there is relatively little anticipation of the threat. By contrast, war usually comes upon a people with some degree of warning, bringing with it the expectation of hunger, separation, bereavement, and terror. Actual combat adds an additional element of fearful expectancy and thus heightens the stress of men going into battle. Neuropsychiatric casualties are inevitable in wartime, but time has brought changes to the most common types of breakdown, the conditions that produce them, and the forms of therapy available. Three wars in America's history witnessed some of these changes.

Before World War I breakdown in combat was viewed as cowardice. A well-known regression to this view created a furor in the United States during World War II. General George S. Patton, while touring the wards of a military hospital, slapped a soldier who had been hospitalized as a neuropsychiatric casualty and called him a coward. On the orders of his commander, General Dwight Eisenhower, Patton later apologized for this behavior to assembled troops and hospital personnel.

During the First World War the perception of breakdown changed. At first dazed and confused soldiers were considered the victims of "shell shock," which was thought to be brain damage caused by the impact of nearby explosions. But as the war progressed "shell shock" came to be recognized as a psychological reaction to stress, and the causal factors were thought to be personal. The victims were seen as individuals in whom vulnerability to stress had been an aspect of their basic personality even before their wartime service.

In World War II stress reactions to combat were called **combat exhaustion,** a designation that put the blame once again on the stressful conditions of battle. The principal symptoms were extreme fatigue, sleeplessness, terror, tremors, strong startle reactions to the slightest sounds, mutism, and either stupor or agitated excitement. The treatment of these cases moved close to the front; casualties were given a respite from fighting, sedation to get them to sleep, warm food, a chance to clean up. Those who were the most severely affected had the opportunity to recount and discuss their battlefield experiences. Sodium Amytal, the so-called ''truth serum,'' was a frequent aid to therapy. A skilled interviewer induced the soldier to recall and relive the traumatic episodes of battle. Such therapy helped the victim develop ways to deal with his horrible memories.

In the Vietnam war a still different picture became evident. Except for those based on drug abuse, the psychiatric casualties were very few and were rarely diagnosed as combat exhaustion. They were considered instead to be disorders of prewar origin, unrelated to combat. Several aspects of the situation in Vietnam may have contributed to the decline in the incidence of combat exhaustion. The troops in Vietnam fought only intermittently in the field and were then flown back to more secure bases. After a few months of combat, they were allowed to leave the military zone for periods of rest and recuperation. Battalion physicians who were skilled in the use of different therapies were made available to the casualties. Three principles, *immediacy, proximity,* and *expectancy,* served as guidelines for the conduct of therapy. Treat the soldier as soon as possible and as near as possible to his unit and his comrades, with the expectation that recovery will make it possible for the soldier to return to active duty. Finally, the tour of duty in Vietnam was limited to one year. Every soldier had an exact DEROS, date expected to return from overseas, and thus a guaranteed day on which he would no longer face the possibility of combat (Bourne, 1970).

Posttraumatic Stress Disorder. Although these factors appear to have reduced the number of psychiatric casualties that occurred in Vietnam, the period following the war revealed that it had taken a greater toll than had originally been realized. Upon their return to the United States, many combat veterans appeared at the doors of the Veterans Administration hospitals and clinics complaining of what is now called **posttraumatic stress disorder.** The symptoms are similar to those of battle fatigue or combat exhaustion.

The existence of the posttraumatic stress syndrome might have been anticipated. Selye's research had revealed that, even when an animal resists the effects of one stress, it remains vulnerable to other stressors. In earlier conflicts the discharged soldiers had always been kept from undergoing further stress. The transition from combat to a peacetime existence was gradual. The soldiers came home by ship, as members of their own military units. They were with the men with whom they had fought the war. Counseling programs were set up, even on shipboard, to forewarn of the changes and stresses of shifting back to civilian life. Once the veterans were home, there were welcoming ceremonies to acknowledge their bravery, sacrifice, and service (Borus, 1976).

The returning Vietnam veterans enjoyed few if any of these benefits. Each of them flew back home alone, after he had finished his twelve-month tour of duty. Within a few days the soldiers went from the jungle battlefront back to home and family. They were given little or no warning of the nature or even the possibility of postmilitary stresses. There were no homecoming ceremonies, quite the contrary. Many soldiers were reviled, spat upon, and called ''baby killers'' by those who had fought against participation in the war. The hardest blow of all was the discovery that the nation had declared the war meaningless, leaving the veterans with the problem of finding a justification for the service they had given and the trauma they had experienced (Borus, 1976; Horowitz and Solomon, 1975).

Upon arrival home, the veterans at first felt a sense of relief. Coping by denial, they excluded the wartime experience from memory; but therein lay the trap. Once the men were relaxed, the memories of the war experience came rushing back, bringing with them the old traumatic conflicts and anxiety. The consequences for more than a third of those who had seen heavy combat were nightmares, emotional distress, fatigue, difficulties in relating to other people, breakdown in personal relationships, self-destructive or aggressive rages, and fear of losing control (Smith, 1981).

SUMMARY

Stress comes in so many different forms that some sort of classification is necessary. The one chosen here identifies three general kinds of stressors. Background stressors are the hassles of everyday life. Although these stresses are mild, their effects accumulate, causing mental and physical disorders in some people. The fact that some individuals are little affected by these stresses indicates that people vary in their vulnerability to stress.

Personal stressors are the problems that we all face in the normal course of life. Separation from parents, transition stress, unemployment, divorce, and death of a spouse are examples of such stress. They all strain the coping skills of the individual. Four forms of conflict—approach-approach, avoidance-avoidance, approach-avoidance, and double approach-avoidance—are other personal stressors.

People's reactions to cataclysmic events, to natural and man-made disasters, often occur in three stages that put one in mind of the general adaptation syndrome. They suffer first a shock reaction, then a recoil reaction, and finally a stage of recall.

Before World War I stress reactions to combat were considered cowardice, in World War I shell shock, in World War II combat exhaustion. Such reactions were the least frequent in the Vietnam war, but the later appearance of a posttraumatic stress reaction revealed that stress had taken its toll.

EMOTION

Until now in our discussion, whenever consequences of stress have been mentioned, they tended to be very objective consequences—physiological reactions, overt behavior, sickness, and death. There are also the less tangible psychological consequences that we call emotions. The misery experienced in bereavement, divorce, and unemployment has at least been alluded to. Emotions are also a part of happy occasions that we do not think of as stressful. Emotions light up our lives as well as darken our days. They give tone to our experiences and color to our passing moments. They are the richest aspect of our mental life. To match this richness, all languages have an enormous number of words to capture the great diversity of emotions and their many shadings.

We know in a general way that the emotions are acquired partly through experience and partly through maturation. We also know a fair amount about the physiological reactions that accompany our emotions. Activation of the sympathetic division of the autonomic nervous system readies the body for emergency action. Respiration, heart rate, blood pressure, and perspiration increase; the pupils of the eye dilate; blood sugar increases to supply the extra energy that will be needed. Digestive activity virtually stops as blood moves from stomach and intestines to the brain and muscles. The salivary glands may cease working, causing the mouth to become dry. Muscles just beneath the surface of the skin contract, causing body hairs to stand on end. Theories of emotion have attempted to explain the relationship of these physiological changes to our feelings as well as other aspects of emotions.

The James-Lange Theory

One of the most interesting early theories of emotion was proposed in 1884 by William James and independently in 1885 by the Danish physiologist Carl Lange. The **James-Lange theory** is intriguing because it is counterintuitive; it is not the theory of common sense. James described the position this way.

> Our natural way of thinking about [the] emotions is that the mental perception of some fact excites . . . the emotion, and that this latter state of mind gives rise to the bodily expression. My thesis on the contrary is that the *bodily changes follow directly the* PERCEPTION *of the exciting fact, and that the feeling of the same changes as they occur* IS *the emotion.* Common sense says we lose our fortune, are sorry, and weep; we meet a bear, are frightened, and run; we meet a rival, are angry, and strike. The hypothesis here to be defended says that this . . . sequence is incorrect . . . that the more rational statement is that we feel sorry because we cry, angry because we strike, afraid because we tremble, and not that we cry, strike or tremble because we are sorry, angry or fearful as the case may be (James and Lange, 1922, p. 13).

Lange expressed the same idea in the form of a question:

> And now we have the question: . . . If I start to tremble when I am threatened with a loaded pistol, does a purely mental process arise, fear, which is what causes my trembling, palpitation of the heart, and confusion; or are these bodily phenomena aroused immediately by the frightening cause, so that the emotion consists exclusively of these functional disturbances of the body?

And an answer:

> Take away the symptoms from a frightened individual; let his pulse beat calmly, his look be firm, his color normal, his movements quick and sure, his thoughts clear; and nothing remains of his fear (James and Lange, 1922, pp. 64–66).

Broadly stated, the James-Lange theory held that the consciousness of bodily disturbances constitutes the experience of emotion. In neural terms the theory proposed that an emotional event brings about visceral and motor reactions of the body—crying, striking, trembling—and these reactions then send afferent impulses back to the brain where they are interpreted in terms of emotional feelings. The James-Lange theory explains very well the sequence of events when a car we had not noticed is about to run us down. We jump first to avoid it, then notice our trembling, palpitations, and sweating. And finally we are conscious of our overwhelming sense of fear.

The Cannon-Bard Theory

The James-Lange theory never enjoyed total acceptance for several reasons. First, on the basis of timing, it is questionable whether physiological reactions can be responsible for emotions. Those of the viscera are slow, and we feel many emotions immediately. Second, these bodily changes are known to be very much the same for the range of intense emotions, even though a few differences have now been discovered. Moreover, clinical and experimental studies showed that emotional reactions occurred in human patients and lower animals deprived of a large part of the sensory feedback from the peripheral organs of the body. According to the James-Lange theory, it should be impossible for these subjects to perceive their bodily states and, therefore, impossible for them to have emotions. Finally, studies of damage to or stimulation of various subcortical areas of the brain demonstrated that these regions were involved in the expression of emotion. Such evidence seems to mean that what James called "our natural way of thinking" might be correct.

The two scientists who were primarily responsible for criticizing the James-Lange theory and formulating an alternative theory were Walter B. Cannon (1927) and Philip Bard (1934). Cannon first theorized in 1915 that perception of an emotional situation triggers a nerve impulse in the thalamus, which he then regarded as the control center for emotions. The impulse splits, with one signal traveling to the cerebral cortex and causing the conscious feeling of emotions, the other traveling simultaneously to the viscera and bringing about physiological changes. The subjective experience of emotion and the bodily changes are concurrent.

The most important neuroanatomical evidence for the **Cannon-Bard theory** came from studies of dogs and cats deprived of their cerebral cortexes. With only very minimal stimulation, such as a gentle pinch, these animals had reactions resembling rage; to gentle sounds they trembled as if in fear. Once or twice stimulation of the genitals elicited sexual behavior. At first Cannon had thought that these responses originated in the thalamus, but after Bard did a major summary of the evidence in 1934, it was clear that the hypothalamus was more important. We now know that parts of the limbic system play a role.

Cannon and Bard did *not* claim that the thalamus or hypothalamus was "the seat of the emotions." They knew that both the autonomic nervous system and the cerebral cortex contributed. The fact that decorticate animals have emotional responses to very weak stimuli made it apparent that the normal role of the cortex is inhibitory, restraining the expression of emotion. Another fact also suggested how the cortex contributes. The rage exhibited by the decorticate animals had more of an automatic, reflex quality than rage in intact animals—"sham rage" they called it. The cortex apparently adds meaning to the reaction, an interpretation which introduces a James-Lange element into the Cannon-Bard theory and which is also compatible with a more recent cognitive theory of emotion.

Cognitive Theory

Over half a century ago a Spanish physician, Gregorio Marañón (1924), injected 210 of his patients with epinephrine, or adrenaline, in an unemotional laboratory situation and asked them to introspect. The effect of epinephrine is to bring on the physiological state of arousal that is characteristic of emotion. In the experiment 71 percent of the patients reported only physical symptoms with no emotional interpretation. The remaining 29 percent responded emotionally. The emotions of this 29 percent were not, however, experienced as "real" emotions. They were reported instead as "cold" emotions or "as if" emotions: "I felt as if I had a great fright, yet I am calm"; or "I felt as if I were awaiting a great happiness." There was, in addition, some evidence that people who had been thinking about an emotional experience, such as sick children or dead parents, before the injection, and dealing with it calmly, became quite emotional about the subject after the injection. These individuals had already had an appropriate reason to feel emotional. Apparently providing them with physiological arousal had induced an emotional state. Does this mean that it would be possible to induce a variety of emotional states by manipulating the individual's thoughts and experiences as well as arousal?

A series of experiments by Stanley Schachter and Jerome Singer (1962) suggested a positive answer to this question. Research participants were told that they were in an experiment testing the effect of a new vitamin compound, "Suproxin," on vision. When Suproxin, actually epinephrine, was injected, some participants were given an accurate description of the effects of the drug: "What will probably happen is that your hand will start to shake, your heart will start to pound, and your face may get warm and flushed." Other participants received no such information. The physician who gave the injection told them that the substance was mild and harmless, and that there were no side effects.

After the injection the participants, both those informed of the probable physiological reactions and those not so informed, were treated in two different ways. Members of one group were individually put in a situation calculated, through the antics of the experimenters' confederate, to make them euphoric. The others were treated in a way that was calculated to make them angry. Then, on the pretext that moods might influence vision, the experimenters measured the participants' degree of irritation or happiness. The general results of the experiment, reflected in these measurements, indicated that the informed individuals, those who had received accurate information about the probable effects of Suproxin, showed little or no tendency to become euphoric in the first situation or angry in the second. The uninformed participants, in dramatic contrast, were happy following the euphoric experience and angry following the experience designed to irritate them. These results meant that when individuals were physically aroused, their emotions depended at least in part on how they perceived the situation. This is the **cognitive theory of emotion.** In Schachter's (1967) words,

> Given a state of physiological arousal for which an individual has no immediate explanation, he will "label" this state and describe his feelings in terms of the cognitions available to him . . . precisely the same state of physiological arousal could be called "joy" or "fury" or any of the great diversity of emotional labels, depending on the cognitive aspects of the situation.

Unfortunately, this assessment of the results of the studies by Schachter and Singer soon proved to be too optimistic. Attempts to repeat the experiments did not always produce the same results. In the original work the subjects who had been in the situation meant to provoke euphoria reported feeling elated more often than the subjects who had been in the irritating situation reported anger. In a later study by Christina Maslach (1979), all the subjects who experienced unexplained arousal—it had been induced by hypnosis—reported negative reactions, in spite of confederates' attempts to evoke elation in some and anger in others. This disorderly pattern of results indicates that a great deal remains to be learned about cognitive influences on emotion. But our lack of understanding appears to be about the details. The research leads to the conclusion that these effects are complex, *not* that they are nonexistent.

Opponent-Process Theory

Richard Solomon and John Corbit (1974), who developed the **opponent-process theory** of emotion, began their presentation this way.

> First, we describe the kind of phenomenon which has caught our attention . . . a woman at work discovers a lump in her breast and immediately is terrified. She sits still, intermittently weeping, or she paces the floor. After a few hours, she slowly regains her composure, stops crying, and begins to work. At this point, she is still tense and disturbed, but no longer terrified and distracted. She manifests the symptoms usually associated with intense anxiety. While in this state she calls her doctor for an appointment. A few hours later she is in his office, still tense, still frightened. She is obviously a very unhappy woman. The doctor makes his ex-

amination. He then informs her that there is no possibility of cancer, that there is nothing to worry about, and that her problem is just a clogged sebaceous gland requiring no medical attention.

A few minutes later, the woman leaves the doctor's office, smiling, greeting strangers, and walking with an unusually buoyant stride. Her euphoric mood permeates all her activities as she resumes her normal duties. She exudes joy, which is not in character for her. A few hours later, however, she is working in her normal, perfunctory way. Her emotional expression is back to normal. She once more has the personality immediately recognizable by all of her friends. Gone is the euphoria, and there is no hint of the earlier terrifying experience of that day (p. 119).

Over a period of time this woman's emotional reactions changed according to a pattern that Solomon and Corbit believe to be typical. An emotional stimulus produces an emotional reaction which first increases to a peak of intensity. Then there is adaptation, reducing the emotion to a steady level which may be maintained for some time. When the stimulus for the emotion is taken away, the emotion does not just disappear. Instead there is a transition to a very different state—from terror to euphoria in this example.

Solomon and Corbit believe that two opposed states or processes, opposed in the sense that the second has an effect that is exactly opposite to that of the first, underlie this pattern of emotional experience. They call the first of these hypothetical underlying states state A and the second state B. They assume that state B is a *slave process,* called forth whenever state A is in action (Figure 10.5). But state B is more slowly aroused than state A, and it also decays more slowly. When state B begins to be aroused, state A is diminished somewhat, for the opposing state B subtracts from it. In order to understand the details of emotionality, it is necessary to assume further that certain changes take place, that the first time an emotion is experienced these underlying processes are different from what they are after many such experiences.

The first time an emotion is experienced, state B is very weak and is overshadowed by state A, until the emotional stimulus is removed. When this happens, state A disappears quickly and the more slowly decaying state B persists and is able to express itself (Figure 10.5a). Later emotional experiences are different, and Solomon and Corbit explain this by assuming that state B is strengthened with use and weakened with disuse, whereas state A remains unchanged (Figure 10.5b). After many experiences of the same emotional situation, the A experience is hardly manifest and the B experience has great intensity (Figure 10.5b).

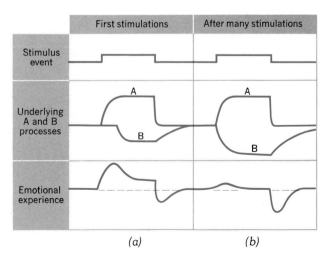

Figure 10.5

Opponent-process theory of emotional experience. (a) An emotional event turns on an emotional response A, to which an opposing reaction B is tied. (b) With many stimulations the B process becomes stronger, whereas the A process remains unchanged. Emotional experience is determined by the differences in strength between the A and B processes. The bottom boxes indicate when in time the A and B processes are operating. (Adapted from Solomon and Corbit, 1974.)

Solomon and Corbit believe that their theory applies to many emotional reactions that are otherwise difficult to explain. They describe the reactions of a dog receiving an intense electric shock in an experiment that went on for many sessions.

> The dog appeared to be terrified during the first few shocks. It screeched and thrashed about, its pupils dilated, its eyes bulged, its hair stood on end, its ears lay back, its tail curled between its legs. Expulsive defecation and urination, along with many other symptoms of intense autonomic nervous sytem activity, were seen. At this point, the dog was freed from the harness, it moved slowly about the room, appeared to be stealthy, hesitant, and unfriendly. Its "state" had suddenly changed from terror to stealthiness.
>
> . . . When the same dog was brought back for the same treatment day after day, its behavior gradually changed. During shocks, the signs of terror disappeared. Instead, the dog appeared pained, annoyed, or anxious, but not terrified. For example, it whined rather than shrieked, and showed no further urination, defecation, or struggling. Then, when released suddenly at the end of the session, the dog rushed about, jumped up on people, wagged its tail, in what we called at the time "a fit of joy." Finally, several minutes later, the dog was its normal self: friendly, but not racing about (p. 121).

Solomon and Corbit have applied their opponent-process theory of emotion to many interesting situations. They draw from the work of Seymour Epstein (1967) on the reactions of sport parachutists for one illustration. On their first few jumps novice parachutists are terrified (state A) in the period just before and during the jump; after the jump they are stunned and stonily silent (state B). After many jumps their state A experience is one of tense and eager excitement, much less intense than the fear they felt earlier. Their state B reaction is jubilant exhilaration, which sometimes lasts for hours and is very different from their earlier numbness.

Or take the case of a man who has a wife or a lover whom he loses. His early state A emotional responses to the woman are full of ecstasy, excitement, and happiness. If he loses her at this point, the state B response to her loss is a relatively brief period of loneliness. After many years the first reaction (state A) has weakened to one of contentment and comfort. But now the experience of losing her (state B) is intense agony and grief of long duration. The fact that the opponent-process theory of emotions attempts to deal with these changes is one of its important strengths.

Conclusion

Now that you have some knowledge of the four principal theories of emotion, you naturally wonder which theory is correct. As is always the case in psychological theorizing, the answer is none of them and all of them. A complete theory remains to be developed. When one is available, it will probably include these components: (1) autonomic nervous system arousal, as recognized in all the theories; (2) hypothalamic and limbic systems responses and inhibiting cerebral activity, as proposed by the Cannon-Bard theory; (3) the cognitive contributions of perception and labeling, stressed in the James-Lange theory and the cognitive theory; and (4) the way emotional reactions change with time and after repeated experiences, which is emphasized by the opponent-process theory.

SUMMARY

The individual experiencing an emotion is in a stirred-up, agitated mental and physiological state. Although we know many of the details of emotionality, no single theory has yet succeeded in bringing all the facts of emotional behavior together. The oldest theory, the James-Lange theory, considers emotions to consist of consciousness of physiological changes; we feel emotions by interpreting our bodily sensations. The Cannon-Bard theory proposes that impulses causing the brain to feel emotions and the body to be aroused travel to their destinations simultaneously. Cognitive theory maintains that physiological arousal is much the same for all emotions, and that the individual's interpretation of this pattern of arousal is responsible for the emotional experience. Finally, the opponent-process theory sees emotional experience as the result of an interaction between a state A brought on by an emotional stimulus and an opposing state B elicited by state A. According to this theory, state A is unaffected by experience but state B is strengthened with use and weakened with disuse. Thus, after we have gone through some emotional experience a number of times, state A is hardly noticeable and state B prevails. This theory is the only one that accounts for changes in emotionality with time.

At the present time none of these theories is universally accepted as "true." No doubt such a theory will contain elements of all of them.

VULNERABILITY AND COPING

Some people adapt with ease to the stressful events that prove crushing to others. This means that the stressfulness of events is not the sole cause of breakdown. The different reactions of people must also be important. By the same token, individual differences cannot be the whole explanation. People who crumble under one stressful pressure may later survive another; the events must also have something to do with their reactions. Such reasoning indicates that the destructiveness of stress depends on the interaction between the stressfulness of precipitating events and the predispositions of individuals to react inadequately to stress. The threshold model of vulnerability and stress given in Figure 10.6 diagrams this interaction. The baseline of the graph represents the range of vulnerability of people to stress, the vertical axis the amount of stress they encounter. The concept of threshold, as you know, is applied in sensory psychology. There it refers to the lowest level of stimulation that a person can detect; here it refers to the lowest level of stress that will cause the person to break down. People who have little vulnerability can withstand a great deal of stress; those of great vulnerability withstand little. The threshold model for stress reactions is a specific interpretation of what is called the diathesis-stress view of psychopathology. According to this view, whether or not people develop a mental disorder depends on the interaction of their predisposition to illness, the diathesis, and of the distressful conditions and happenings of their lives (Davison and Neale, 1982).

Type A Behavior

At the turn of the century heart disease was a comparatively rare phenomenon. Now it is the leading cause of death in this country and costs the economy some fifty-four billion dollars a year (Kaplan and Kimball, 1982). A search for the factors responsible for coronary disease has uncovered a number of culprits, including hypertension, cigarette smoking, obesity, and lack of exercise. Genetic factors seem to play a role, and we know that an inability to tolerate frustration makes one group of people especially vulnerable. In 1896 William Osler, a physician at the Johns Hopkins University Medical School, suggested that angina attacks were common in vigorous, ambitious persons "whose engine is

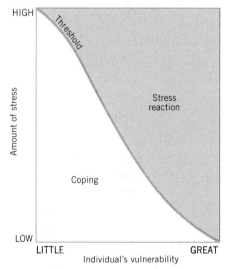

Figure 10.6
Threshold model of the interaction between the individual's vulnerability and stress. People vary in vulnerability. Those who are very vulnerable have stress reactions to low levels of stress. Those with little vulnerability have stress reactions only when they face a great deal of stress.

Table 10.3 **Type A and Type B Behavior**

Behavior	Type A	Type B
Speech	Loud, rapid, single-word answers; immediate answers; sentences short and to the point; interrupts others; uses obscenities	Soft, slow, measured answers with frequent pauses; pauses before answers; sentences long and rambling; rarely interrupts others; rarely uses obscenities
Motor Behavior	Tense; alert; harsh laughter; on edge of chair; smiles with side of mouth	Relaxed; calm; gentle chuckle; quiet attentiveness; broad smiles
Attitudes and emotion	Competitive, wants to move up in job; hates delay; humorless, ambitious, hostile	Cooperative, satisfied with job; does not mind delay; humorous, unambitious, friendly

From Chesney, Engleston, and Rosenman, 1981.

always set at full speed ahead." More than half a century later, in 1958, Meyer Friedman and Ray Rosenman described a "coronary prone behavior pattern," which they called **Type A behavior.** People with Type A behavior are intensely ambitious and competitive; they are preoccupied with occupational deadlines and have a sense of urgency about time. An eight-and-a-half-year study of 3524 men, aged thirty-nine to fifty-five, some of whom initially showed the Type A pattern, was revealing. In comparison to a **Type B** group of men who did not have the Type A symptoms (Table 10.3), the Type A men had twice the rate of coronary disease, twice the rate of fatal heart attacks, and five times the rate of recurring coronary difficulties (Rosenman and Friedman, 1983).

Type A persons are often identified by means of a structured interview which covers the respondent's health history and the family history of coronary disease. On the behavioral side, it inquires about their habits, attitudes, and typical ways of behaving. Portions of such an interview appear in Table 10.4. Type A people are hard-driving, ambitious, and achievement-oriented. They work at maximum effort and try to ignore fatigue, particularly when it will interfere with accomplishment. They are impatient with delay and do more poorly than Type B people when they cannot deal with a task immediately. They grow irritated with slower colleagues. They are assertive and aggressive and seek to maintain a sense of control. They desire and receive relatively little social support from others.

Compared to Type Bs, Type A people are more prone to avoidance and denial in dealing with frustration and conflict. They show a greater tendency to express negative feelings. They try to endure stress for longer periods of time despite higher and higher levels of discomfort. This last fact is probably especially important in making Type A persons vulnerable to cardiac disorder.

It is important to understand that people do not fall neatly into the Type A and Type B categories. As is usually the case, reactions are normally distributed. Most people have both Type A and Type B characteristics. The Type A and Type B personalities are persons who show certain types of behavior to an extreme degree.

Can Type A behavior be changed? Obviously the Type A person's health

Table 10.4 Excerpts from Type A Interview

Would you describe yourself as a hard-driving, ambitious type of person in accomplishing the things you want, or would you describe yourself as a relatively relaxed and easygoing person?

    a. Are you married?

    b. (If married) How would your wife describe you in those terms—as hard-driving and ambitious or as relaxed and easygoing?

Do you think you drive harder to accomplish things than most of your associates?

When you play games with people your own age, do you play for the fun of it, or are you really in there to win?

When you are in your automobile, and there is a car in your lane going far too slowly for you, what do you do about it?

    a. Would you mutter and complain to yourself? Honk your horn? Flash your lights?

    b. Would anyone riding with you know that you were annoyed?

Most people who work have to get up fairly early in the morning. In your particular case, what time do you ordinarily get up?

If you see someone doing a job rather slowly and you know that you could do it faster and better yourself, does it make you restless to watch him?

    a. Would you be tempted to step in and do it yourself?

    b. Have you ever done that?

    c. What would you do if someone did that to you?

Do you eat rapidly? Do you walk rapidly? After you've finished eating, do you like to sit around the table and chat, or do you like to get up and get going?

Do you always feel anxious to get going and finish whatever you have to do?

Do you have the feeling that time is passing too rapidly for you to accomplish all the things that you think you should get done in one day?

    a. Do you often feel a sense of time urgency or time pressure?

Adapted from Chesney, Eagleston, and Rosenman, 1981.

would benefit if prevention or modification of the pattern were possible. The therapeutic programs that have been initiated rely heavily on the use of relaxation to dampen anxiety (Suinn and Bloom, 1978) and on the methods of behavior modification (Thoreson, Telch, and Eagleston, 1981). The behavior therapy methods have been shown to decrease the probability that a Type A person who has had one heart attack will have another by about 40 percent. In the course of these studies, an interesting complication has been discovered, however. It is hostility more than Type A behavior, per se, that is responsible for placing the Type A person at risk for cardiac disorder.

The effectiveness of these therapies also raises an intriguing question. Do we really want to eliminate Type A behavior? Many Type A characteristics are prized strengths in the worlds of commerce, science, and industry. The personal payoffs of Type A behavior include better jobs, upward social mobility, and the fulfillment of important motives. Suppose that it were possible to eliminate the driving ambition of Type A persons. Would they be any happier? More importantly, would society be better off? There is reason to think that advances in science, technology, and business are often the contributions of people who have the Type A pattern of behavior. There are those who believe that the existence of a healthy economy and even Western culture as we know it depend on Type A values. Perhaps the people who hold those opinions are wrong, but such a judgment is not ours to make.

Appraisals of Situations

Studies of stress have suggested that individuals perceive different degrees of threat (see Figure 10.1) in potentially dangerous situations. A black man and a white woman entering medical school might assess the effect of their being a member of a minority group in different ways. They might see their status as *irrelevant.* "Color and gender have nothing to do with success in med school." They might see it as *benign,* "My status ought to give me a bit of an edge that the others don't have." Or they might see their situation as *dangerous,* "I know that they'll go out of their way to give me a hard time here." Only the last appraisal of the situation is likely to be threatening and stressful (Lazarus and Launier, 1978). When the individual perceives a situation as threatening, its stressfulness is greater if the threat appears to be one that cannot be controlled.

Effective Coping

Coping is facing and finding effective means of overcoming problems and difficulties. People vary in the means they have of coping with stress (see Figure 10.1). Frances Cohen and Richard Lazarus (1979) have suggested that the behavior of people who cope effectively with stress has five primary characteristics.

1. Information seeking.   What is the problem? What do I need to know to deal with it? What are my alternatives?
2. Direct action.   What can I do that will help solve the problem?
3. Inhibition of action.   How can I avoid impulsive, ill-timed actions that make the problem worse instead of helping?
4. Intrapsychic processes.   These processes, which may be out of awareness, include the various defense mechanisms (see page 492) that people use when they feel endangered, anxious, insecure, and threatened. For example, they may deny that the situation exists. Or they may try for an intellectualized detachment. They may block the emotions aroused by their distress from conscious awareness, becoming calm and detached in the stressful situation.

   There is no hierarchy of adaptativeness in these processes. Even denial, which has long been considered the hallmark of immaturity, may be a healthy choice in overwhelming situations. Denial may buy us the time that is needed before we move against an intolerable situation.
5. Flexibility.   Overriding all these more specific modes of coping is a general one, flexibility. Functional fixedness (page 241) is an obstacle to solving the problems of stress, just as it is an obstacle to the solution of other problems. Flexibility is the hallmark of adaptive behavior.

Social Supports

People's coping with stress does not happen in a vacuum. For everyone effective modes of coping will be more successful in some situations than others. Coping is more successful if certain types of social support are available. One source of such support is the family. A family marked by discord can have a powerful negative effect on a child's development of effective coping strategies. Families that are integrated and responsive to the needs of all their members can increase the likelihood that a child will grow up to become a competent adult. And members of the family can of course be the best, most dependable, and closest source of comfort and aid for the person in trouble.

Other sources of social support are the various agencies of the community and government. These can be informal, such as the friends and neighbors who come to the aid of people in distress, or they may be formal. For example, community resources are available to attenuate the distress of handicapped children. Support groups, such as Al-Anon, can be a source of strength to families facing the problem of alcoholism in one of their members. The processes whereby such support systems facilitate adaptation to stress is not entirely clear, but their effectiveness is evident.

SUMMARY

Whether a person copes with a stressful experience or succumbs to it depends on the interaction between the individual's vulnerability to stress and the stressfulness of the situation. A threshold model, which is a specific interpretation of the diathesis-stress view of psychopathology, describes this interaction. Vulnerability to stress seems to reflect the enduring personal characteristics of the individual. For example, the impatient, hard-driving, achievement-oriented Type A individuals, who may be responsible for much of the world's progress, are more likely than calmer persons to develop heart disease.

People vary in their vulnerability to stress partly because some see more threat in situations than others and partly because some have better coping skills. People who cope successfully with stress are flexible; they seek information, look for appropriate lines of action, try to find ways to curb impulsive, maladaptive acts, and sometimes make unconscious use of the defense mechanisms that protect us all from anxiety. Their coping is likely to be even more successful if they receive support from family, friends, and social institutions.

TO BE SURE YOU UNDERSTAND THIS CHAPTER

The major concepts contained in this chapter are listed in the order in which they appeared in the chapter.

Stress	**Approach-avoidance conflict**
Stressor	**Double approach-avoidance conflict**
General adaptation syndrome	**Shock reaction**
Alarm reaction	**Recoil reaction**
Stage of resistance	**Stage of recall**
Stage of exhaustion	**Combat exhaustion**
Life events scale	**Posttraumatic stress disorder**
Background stressor	**James-Lange theory**
Personal stressor	**Cannon-Bard theory**
Cataclysmic event	**Cognitive theory of emotion**
Transition stress	**Opponent-process theory**
Conflict	**Type A behavior**
Approach-approach conflict	**Type B behavior**
Avoidance-avoidance conflict	**Coping**

TO GO BEYOND THIS CHAPTER

In This Book. Stress is present and evident in the lives of all of us. Such broad experiences must tap into many areas of psychology. It is not surprising then to learn that materials found in chapters on personality (15), psychopathology (16), therapy (17), and social psychology (18, 19) are particularly relevant to the study of stress and emotion. We also recommend a rereading of the chapters on nervous and endocrine systems (3) and motivation (9), for these areas too are central to an understanding of stress.
Elsewhere. Figuratively speaking, there has been an explosion in the publication of

books focused on stress. Here are several that you would enjoy reading. The outstanding overview of the field of stress is provided by a recently published *Handbook of Stress: Theoretical and Clinical Aspects,* edited by Leo Goldberger and Shlomo Breznitz. A paperback written by Tom Cox, *Stress,* provides an appropriate, somewhat abbreviated overview of this complex field. For a review of stress and combat we urge a reading of Charles Figley's edited volume, *Stress Disorders Among Vietnam Veterans.* Two volumes of interest are *Women Under Stress,* authored by Donald Morse and M. Lawrence Furst, and *Stress at Work,* edited by Cary Cooper and Roy Payne.

A recommended volume on *Stress Responses Syndromes* has been written by Mardi Morowitz, a national leader in the analysis and treatment of stress reactions.

PART FIVE PSYCHOLOGICAL DEVELOPMENT

Cassatt, Mary. *The Family.* (1887). The Chrysler Museum. Gift of Walter P. Chrysler, Jr.

CHAPTER 11

COGNITIVE DEVELOPMENT

Historically, psychologists have studied cognitive development in two ways. The **psychometric approach,** which will be discussed in Chapter 13, emphasizes the measurement of intelligence and individual differences in intelligence, often focusing on the extremes of mental retardation and giftedness. In contrast, the **developmental approach** emphasizes the development of thinking and related processes, particularly in the average individual. Psychologists who favor the developmental approach believe that although test scores can be informative, they do not tell the whole story about cognitive development. For example, a "wrong" answer to a test question may sometimes reflect more sophisticated thinking than a "right" answer. For such reasons the cognitive developmentalists are more interested in how children arrive at their answers than in the number of items they answer correctly.

Both approaches have contributed much to the psychologist's understanding of intelligence, and both have been concerned with similar questions. How is early intelligence related to later intelligence? What is the pattern of cognitive abilities at different ages? Before turning to a discussion of such issues, we will present a few useful background ideas.

MATURATION

The nature-nurture question, which we introduced in Chapter 2, reappears in the study of **maturation,** the behavioral changes that result from physiological growth. In this context, we want to know the extent to which age-changes in behavior are the result of maturation and the extent to which they are the result of learning. For example, we want to know how much of a child's mastery of language is learned and how much is the result of maturation.

Animal Studies of Maturation

Studies of maturation in animals have provided useful principles for understanding the role of maturation in human development. Although these studies traced the development of motor behavior, the patterns discovered apply to cognitive development. A classic study of maturation was reported by George Coghill over fifty years ago (1929). In a series of experiments spanning a period of almost forty years, Coghill studied development in the salamander and the frog. He discovered that, as their neural system developed, these animals progressed through a series of clearly defined behavioral changes.

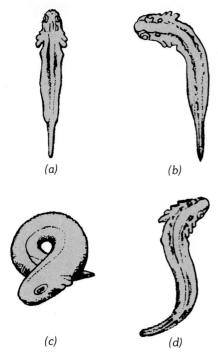

Figure 11.1
Responses of the salamander tadpole at various stages of development: (a) at rest, (b) turning away from the source of stimulation, (c) the coil reaction, and (d) the S or swimming motion. (From Coghill, 1929.)

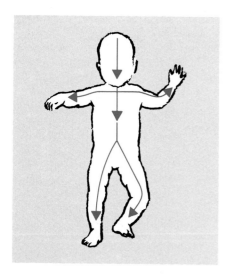

Figure 11.2
Cephalocaudal and proximodistal control of movements. The baby is able to control its head before its feet, its shoulders before its arms, its arms before its hands, its hands before its fingers. (From Vincent and Martin, 1961.)

The development of the salamander as an aquatic animal proceeds through five stages (Figure 11.1). Initially, the salamander is immobile; in this stage it moves in response to stimulation such as a needle jab, but the motion is produced by muscular tissue and does not involve neural control. The first true movement appears in the second stage of development, as a contraction of the muscles located immediately behind the head. This reaction gradually moves down the trunk and, in about thirty-six hours, the entire trunk of the salamander is involved in the response. These contractions bring about a coil reaction, which is characteristic of the third stage of development. In the fourth stage a second opposite flexion is superimposed upon the coil reaction. The salamander is now making its S reaction. In the fifth stage the speed and duration of the S reactions increase until sufficient pressure is exerted against the water to force the animal forward. It can swim.

The development of the salamander demonstrates two important principles of maturation. The first principle is that larger movements of an organism tend to be made earlier than smaller, more precise movements. Thus the coil reaction, which involves the whole organism, precedes the S reaction, in which the head and tail react in a semi-independent manner. This first principle, the principle of **mass action–differentiation,** is evident in the developing behavior of many organisms. The second principle is that bodily control tends to proceed from the head (cephalic) to the tail (caudal) regions of the organism. This is the **cephalocaudal sequence** of development. The muscles near the head respond first, and control then moves down the trunk. These two sequences of development operate simultaneously. A third sequence can be seen the most clearly in the development of the land-going locomotion of the salamander. The salamander acquires control over its shoulder joints before it controls its elbow joints, and control of the hand is acquired last of all. In this pattern of development, control moves from regions of the body near the trunk (proximal) to regions more distant (distal). This is called the **proximodistal sequence.**

Human Motor Development

The patterns of development discovered by Coghill also appear in human motor development. Much of the behavior of the fetus and newborn infant is generalized mass action. By the time of birth, however, the infant is capable of a remarkable amount of specific behavior. The newborn can open and close its eyes, secrete tears, open and close its mouth, suck, yawn, frown, "coo," sneeze, swallow, vomit, turn its head, close its hand, arch its back, and make stepping movements, to cite only a fraction of its accomplishments. As the baby develops, new behavior is constantly added to its repertory. The sequence of its development continues to reflect the principles identified by Coghill in the salamander.

Grasping. A good example of the proximodistal principle (Figure 11.2) appears in the development of prehension, or grasping. When a very young infant is offered an object such as a cube, it is likely to react with a sweeping motion involving the whole arm and shoulder, and the hand is unlikely to make contact with the object. This reaction, which is characteristic of children approximately twenty weeks old, gives way by approximately twenty-eight weeks to a response in which the arm moves outward beyond the cube, but eventually brings the hand into contact with it. Only in subsequent stages does the baby's approach to an object include the hands and fingers.

Grasping also exemplifies the trend from mass to more differentiated specific activities. During the first year the infant's increasing use of small muscles makes

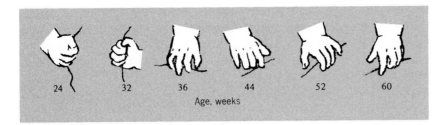

Figure 11.3
The use of the hand in grasping string, as it changes with age. The number below each sketch is the age in weeks when these grasping movements are typical. (After Halverson, 1931.)

grasping become increasingly precise. Figure 11.3 shows how the gross, sweeping motions characteristic of the twenty-four-week-old child are replaced in the one-year-old by precise, coordinated use of hands and fingers.

Walking. The development of walking presents a good example of cephalocaudal development. At birth the baby's behavior gives little indication that it will ever walk. It cannot roll over or support the weight of its own head. Yet by one month of age the maturational sequence leading to walking has definitely begun. Now the baby can lift its head from a flat surface. By two months it can raise its chest. By seven months it can sit alone. By nine months it can stand with help. Soon will come the baby's first steps, control of the body now reaching from its head to its feet. These stages and several intervening ones are illustrated in Figure 11.4.

Although this sequence of motor development is relatively constant in all babies, the age at which any particular behavior occurs varies from child to child. The average child walks unassisted at fifteen months, some children walk as early as ten months, and others do not walk until they are almost two years old. The age at which babies began walking was studied in five European cities: Paris, London, Brussels, Stockholm, and Zurich (Hindley et al., 1966). Within no city were differences in age of walking found to be associated with the sex

Figure 11.4
The developmental sequence by which the infant progresses from lying, to sitting, to standing, and finally to walking. The approximate ages in months are indicated, but normal children accomplish these steps at widely different ages. (From Shirley, 1931.)

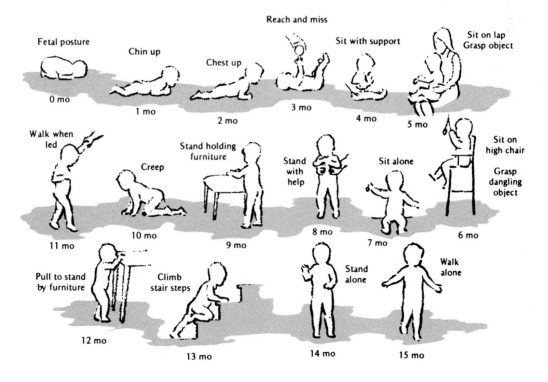

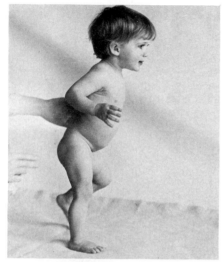

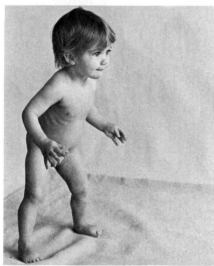

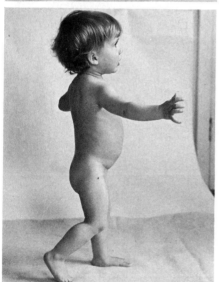

Walking with support. First, tentative steps. Walking alone with confidence.

or social class of the child. There were variations from city to city, however. The average baby in Stockholm walked the earliest, and the average Parisian baby walked the latest. There is no clear explanation for these national differences. Genetics, nutrition, encouragement of locomotion, or some combination of such factors may account for them.

Surprising as it may seem, practice apparently does not influence the age at which babies start walking. Decades ago Wayne Dennis (1940) studied two groups of Hopi Indian babies; the infants of the first group were on cradleboards, and the others were not. The cradleboard is a plank on which a baby, wrapped in a blanket, is firmly bound. Mothers who use the cradleboard place their babies on it the day they are born and leave them there, except for brief periods required to change them, for an average of nine months. Hopi mothers who have abandoned the traditional cradleboard allow their babies more freedom of movement and therefore more opportunity to make the movements used in walking. If this early experience has an effect, the two groups of children would be expected to walk at different ages. Dennis found almost no difference in the average age at which these Hopi mothers reported that their babies first walked. Confinement to the cradleboard had no retarding effect. Many other studies of the effects of maturation and practice on a variety of motor behaviors—climbing a ladder, cutting with scissors, roller skating—have provided little support for the notion that early practice results in superior performance.

SUMMARY

Studies of psychological development sometimes employ a psychometric approach, sometimes a developmental approach. This chapter will emphasize the developmental, in which the concept of maturation is central. Maturation refers to changes brought about by physical and physiological growth. Grasping and walking are examples. Whether maturation or learning is responsible for behavior is the version of the nature-nurture issue that applies to development. Research with lower animals has revealed the existence of patterns of maturation that are relatively impervious to the effects of learning. These patterns— the sequence from mass to specific action, the cephalocaudal sequence, and the proximodistal—are as evident in the development of human beings as they are in that of lower animals.

COGNITIVE STAGES

Everyone agrees that through cognitive development the child becomes a more adequate individual, capable of a greater number of intellectual accomplishments. People disagree, however, whether cognitive power is gained through a steady, gradual increase in intellectual strength or in a sequence of stages, each qualitatively different from the others. Although psychologists continue to argue whether cognitive stages have any reality, the theories that assume the existence of stages have contributed much to our understanding of cognitive development.

One useful means of identifying cognitive stages is to ask children of different ages carefully selected questions, the answers to which reveal their reasoning processes. For example, when we ask a child how a peach and an orange are alike, the child must engage in a series of mental operations. The child must recall what a peach and an orange are, determine their similarities and differences, and then produce an answer. If a child tells us that a peach and an orange are alike because they are both round, the child's answer is based on the inherent physical attributes of the pieces of fruit, a mode of thinking called *concrete*. If the child says that a peach and orange are alike because you could eat them both, this child has used a *functional* principle to classify the objects, based on what can be done with them. If the child says that a peach and an orange are both fruit, he or she has applied a high-level *abstraction*. Children's reasoning typically proceeds from concrete to functional to abstract in the course of cognitive development.

Models of Cognitive Stages

The simple model given in Figure 11.5 may help to clarify several important aspects of cognitive development. First, there is a definite sequence of cognitive growth. Stage 2 is always preceded by stage 1 and always followed by stage 3. To use our earlier example, the child always moves from the concrete to the abstract but never in the reverse order. Second, the stages are qualitatively different, as though the individual uses quite different processing systems at different stages of cognitive development. Finally, this model helps to make the point that, although cognitive development is a continuous process that takes place over time, the individual does not go through the sequence of stages merely as a function of getting older. Time is simply a backdrop against which the rate of cognitive growth is assessed. To understand cognitive development, we must ask what causes the individual to move from one stage of development to the next.

Maturation versus Learning. The model presented in Figure 11.5 would be perfectly acceptable to psychologists who take an extreme maturationist view of human development. This position considers development to be the inevitable expression of an internal plan by which the human being is propelled through a sequence of stages, each stage being reached at a particular point in the life cycle. In such a view intellectual growth depends entirely on physiological development. An equally extreme, contrasting point of view attributes all cognitive development to experience. According to this position, behavior at any stage of development depends on what the child has learned up to that time. The cognitive stages seem to occur in an invariant sequence because our methods of educating children force the sequence upon them. The environmentalists would explain progression from concrete to functional to abstract thought, for example, as the result of teaching the child to discriminate first

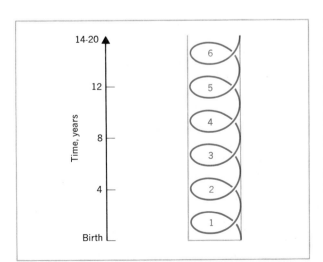

Figure 11.5
Simple model of stages of cognitive development. The vertical arrow represents the passage of time. The individual's cognitive development appears as an internal ascending spiral, in which the numbered loops represent successive stages of cognitive growth. This model shows only the growth of intelligence, not its decline. The time arrow stops in the fourteen-to-twenty-year range, when a number of cognitive abilities have been found to peak.

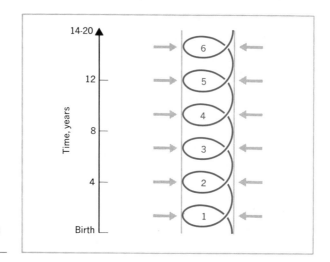

Figure 11.6
Interactionist model of cognitive development. The horizontal arrows represent the environmental experiences affecting the developing individual.

simple dimensions such as shape and later more abstract dimensions such as function and category. Environmentalists would argue that children could move from one stage to any other if they received the appropriate training.

Most workers in cognitive development reject both of these extreme positions. Instead, they take a middle ground and consider the stages to emerge in an invariant order through a process of individual-environment interaction (Figure 11.6). They view the infant's mind as coming equipped with a primitive structural organization, which allows the child to process information in a certain way. As the child matures and has more and more contact with the environment, this structure is reorganized and with these reorganizations new stages emerge.

Although the cognitive-developmental approach has much to recommend it, one of its weaknesses is that it pays too little attention to individual variations. Children go through the stages of development at different rates, and they attain different upper limits. One of the most fascinating truths for students of human development is the unique combination of developmental sequences any one child will demonstrate at any age. Thus one baby of eighteen months may walk awkwardly but talk well and manipulate small objects gracefully with its fingers. Another eighteen-month-old may walk well, say few words, and

Figure 11.7
Developmental model showing individual variation in rate of intellectual growth and in final level attained. The number of stages at each intellectual level has been selected arbitrarily. The actual number of stages that can be identified varies with the particular cognitive process being examined.

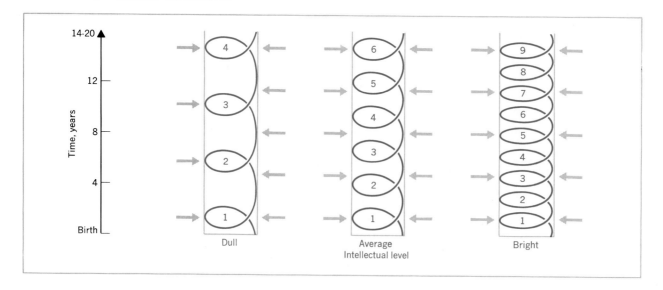

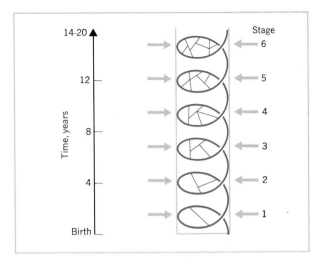

Figure 11.8
Developmental model showing greater cognitive differentiation at each successive stage. The increasing number of "regions," as Lewin called them, indicated by the subdivisions at each stage represent the increasing number of cognitive activities of which the person is capable.

have a sophisticated grasp of spatial relations. Another model, depicting courses of development for below average, average, and bright individuals, takes this variation into account (Figure 11.7).

Differentiation and Cognitive Stages.   Early in life there is a gross, all-or-none quality to thinking. Later it becomes more fine-grained, discriminating, and complex. One of the most striking examples of the early lack of differentiation is the very young child's failure to discriminate between "me" and "not me." Even body boundaries are fuzzy to very young children, and they have great difficulty differentiating what is inside themselves, and therefore private, from what is outside and therefore public. It is not uncommon to find young children who believe that their thoughts are accessible to others. Even after they have successfully differentiated "me" from "not me," they are still unable to step outside themselves to take the perspective of someone else, and to view themselves as objects distinct from other objects. One adult's conversation with six-year-old Pippa illustrates this phenomenon. " 'Pippa, what is your sister's name?' 'Heather.' 'And who is Heather's sister?' 'Heather hasn't got a sister.' 'But who are you then? Aren't you Heather's sister?' 'No, I'm Pippa' " (Nash, 1970, p. 359). Pippa has still not totally escaped her *egocentricity,* her tendency to see herself as the center of all experience. As her thinking develops, Pippa will be able to differentiate herself from others and her perspective from theirs. If we add to our model certain aspects of a model suggested by Kurt Lewin (1936), we can express the view that each cognitive stage is more differentiated than the one preceding it (Figure 11.8).

Illustrations of Stagelike Thinking

Explaining Dreams.   The development of children's stages of thought, and the greater differentiation at each stage, can be seen in children's explanations of their dreams. If adults are asked where their dreams come from, they have no difficulty in saying that they come from within themselves. But this comprehension is a demanding cognitive task. Young children do not have the cognitive equipment to understand dreams in adult terms. At every stage children can use only the abilities that they have developed so far to deal with the phenomena they experience. A bright five-year-old boy explained dreams in this way.

Dreams come from God. God makes the dreams and puts them in balloons. The balloons float down from heaven, and enter a dream bag under your stomach. In the dream bag there are some little men and a sergeant. They have a cannon that shoots the dream-balloons up into your head where they burst into pictures outside your head (reported by Kohlberg, 1971, p. 112).

We can be fairly certain that no adult taught the child this intricate and appealing explanation of dreams. Rather, the boy actively attempted to come to grips with the problem of dreams by using the cognitive abilities available to him.

Children only gradually sort out their dreams from other happenings (Laurendeau and Pinard, 1962). At the age of four, children believe that dreams are real events existing apart from themselves and taking place in their room. In the next stage of comprehension, when they are about six, children recognize that the dream is not taking place in the room; they often believe that dreams are in their eyes or in their head. If another person could look inside their head, that person would see the dream, like a little show, being played there. By the age of eight, children realize that dreams take place inside of themselves, cannot be seen by others, and are produced by their own thoughts or imagination.

Studies have shown that children's conceptions of dreams develop in an invariant order. Children who have passed a particular step in their thinking about dreams will also have passed through all the earlier steps in the sequence. Lawrence Kohlberg (1969) pointed out that these steps in the understanding of dreams represent progressive differentiations, which logically cannot have any other order. First, the real and the unreal are differentiated. Then, internal events are differentiated from external events; the dream is like a movie taking place inside the person rather than outside. Finally, the dream is differentiated as psychic and immaterial rather than as physical and material; it is no longer a picture projected in the head but a psychic projection of the imagination.

Problem Solving.   Children's learning ability also shows stages of increasing differentiation, a point that has frequently been made in experiments using a two-choice size discrimination problem (Figure 11.9). In this problem children see two wooden squares of different sizes. On each trial they see the same two squares, but the positions vary; the larger square is sometimes on the right, sometimes on the left. A reward such as a marble or small piece of candy is always placed under a square of a particular size, either the larger or the smaller one. Children are told to find the hidden object as often as possible.

Children need several cognitive abilities to solve this kind of problem. They must have advanced from the egocentricity of the very early years and realize that the blocks and rewards exist in the external world, that they cannot make rewards appear simply by wishing them to be there. They must have developed the verbal skills to understand the instructions and the ability to perceive the size difference between the two blocks. Finally, they must sense that there is a problem to be solved and be able to develop hypotheses about its solution.

Suppose that the experimenter decides to reward a young girl for picking up

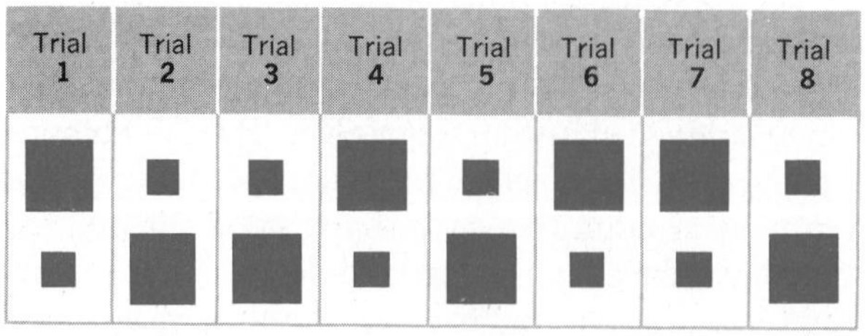

Figure 11.9
The first eight trials on a size discrimination problem. The child must learn always to pick up the same-sized block, either the larger one or the smaller, whichever the experimenter has determined will be correct.

the larger block and that on trial 1 the child by chance picks up the larger block, which happens to be on the left. At this point she might generate any of three hypotheses that would affect her behavior on trial 2. One hypothesis is that the experimenter is a nice person who likes to give her candy, and that she will get candy for picking up any block. A second hypothesis is that the candy is always on the left. A third hypothesis is that the candy is under the larger block. To avoid getting bogged down with erroneous hypotheses, the child must be flexible enough to reject hypotheses that bring only occasional reward. The older the child, the greater the likelihood that she can generate the correct hypothesis as well as reject erroneous ones. As the cognitive system becomes more differentiated, the child is able to generate a much greater variety of hypotheses. An older child might develop the hypothesis that the correct block is first on the left and then on the right. A still older child might even entertain more elaborate hypotheses, for example, that the block is first on the left, twice on the right, three times on the left, and so on. The number of hypotheses that can be generated is limited only by the cognitive ability of the individual.

For this reason greater cognitive capacity is not always helpful in solving problems. If the individual entertains only complex hypotheses and rejects all simpler ones, he or she may be slow to reach the solution. This effect was actually observed in a study comparing the performance of different age groups on a simple, two-choice task. Children in grades five to eight needed only about one-third as many trials to learn the correct hypothesis as did preschool or second-grade children (Figure 11.10). But tenth graders and college students required almost as many trials as the youngest children. Questioning the older students revealed that they were hypothesizing complex sequences of alternating positions or sizes or both. Some of them even hypothesized that there was no logical solution and that success depended on chance alone, in itself a highly differentiated hypothesis.

Morton Weir (1964) obtained similar results in another study, in which children were shown three knobs and told that if they pressed the correct one a marble would be delivered. The task was complicated by the fact that although there was only one correct knob, a marble was not delivered every time it was pressed; there was no way to win on every trial. Weir found that younger children learned to press the correct knob quickly and continued to press it, but older children either came to choose the reinforced knob more slowly or continued to make different choices on different trials. Weir's explanation was that the younger children responded to reinforcement—only one knob ever

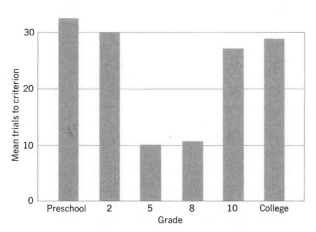

Figure 11.10
Mean number of trials required by individuals in different grades to solve a two-choice size discrimination problem. Mean trials to criterion were nearly as great for college students as for preschoolers. (After Stevenson, Iscoe, and McConnell, 1955.)

paid off, even though it did not pay off all the time. The older students, however, believed that there was a solution that would be right all the time. The ability to interpret the problem in this manner and to generate many complex solutions indicates a higher level of cognition than that of the younger children, who outperformed them.

SUMMARY

It is useful to describe cognitive development as a progression through a series of stages. A simple cognitive-stage model presents this development as a continuous process that follows a definite sequence. More complex models indicate that at every stage the individual actively interacts with the environment and grows further, and that individuals proceed through the stages at different rates. The principle of mass action–differentiation can also be included in these more complex models. Individuals at higher stages of development show more differentiation than those at lower stages.

Children's reasoning in explaining dreams and their use of increasingly complex hypotheses in problem-solving tasks demonstrate this progression through cognitive stages. Children first believe that dreams are real events which take place outside themselves. Then they realize that dreams are inside their heads, but they believe that others could see their dreams if they could look inside their heads. By about age eight children realize that dreams are products of their imagination and cannot be seen by others. The increasing differentiation of the cognitive system can also be seen in problem-solving behavior. The ability to understand and solve problems generally increases with age. With simple problems, however, older children may hypothesize so many complex solutions that they are outperformed by younger children.

LANGUAGE AND COGNITIVE DEVELOPMENT

At birth the infant can cry; a few months later it can coo; then come babbled strings of sounds; one day the baby says something that sounds like "Ma!" or "Da!" and is on the threshold of the world of human speech. Children's growing ability to use language provides them with labels to identify objects in the world and supplies the materials that can be used to reduce the events in the world to reason. With the help of language, the child can remember that "Our car is the green car; Mary's car is the yellow one." And parents can also take advantage of the existence of this new and powerful tool: "Tell me in <u>words</u>!" the parent begs the frustrated, whining little boy to stop him from hitting and kicking.

As an illustration of the importance of this connection between language and cognition, many studies have shown that a failure to apply words hinders problem solving. When asked to memorize the order in which some common objects are presented, kindergarten children who know the names of the objects do not necessarily use them. Second graders spontaneously say the names of the objects more often than kindergarteners, and fifth graders name them even more frequently. A transitional stage occurs at about age seven, when some children do and some do not produce the names of objects. At this age children who do not spontaneously use names will do so if asked, and their performance improves markedly. When told that they may either use words or not use them during the task, however, children in this transitional stage typically do not verbalize (Keeney, Cannizzo, and Flavell, 1967). For these children more cognitive development must take place before they spontaneously produce the **verbal mediators** that can make their behavior more effective.

Luria's Stages of Language-Action Relationship

Language is available to children long before they use it effectively to direct their behavior. This fact was convincingly demonstrated by Alexander Luria (1961), a distinguished Russian psychologist, who studied how language comes to control behavior. Luria believed that children begin with a relatively undifferentiated system in which motor responses can be made in the absence of language. With the advent of language, he believed that children are more differentiated, for then they have two systems at their disposal. But the verbal and motor systems are separate systems at this stage. What remains to be accomplished is the integration of the two systems.

Luria demonstrated this developmental progression by studying how children of different ages follow verbal instructions. When he put various toys before children and said, "Give me the fish," six-month-old babies were not at all influenced by this command; at most they simply looked at the speaker. By eighteen months of age, the children almost always looked at the fish and would sometimes give it to the experimenter. They did not follow the instruction consistently, however, until the age of two. And even at two language does not truly regulate behavior; it merely impels it. Language may stimulate a two-year-old to act, but the action is not necessarily appropriate. For example, Luria found that after the children had been asked for the fish several times and he changed the instruction to, "Give me the horse," the children often continued to hand Luria the fish.

In a more complicated experimental procedure, a child sat before a panel containing a light bulb. There was a rubber bulb for the child to squeeze, and the child's squeezes were recorded (Figure 11.11). Children were given commands such as, "When the light comes on, squeeze the bulb," or "When the light comes on, don't squeeze the bulb." Most two-year-olds would look at the light whenever they heard "light" and squeeze the bulb whenever they heard "squeeze." They could not appreciate the full meaning of the instructions. Their behavior was guided by the meaning of individual words. Moreover, when

Figure 11.11
Luria's bulb-squeezing task. This apparatus is used to investigate the relationship between language and action. In its simplest use the child is instructed to squeeze the bulb when the light on the display panel comes on. An event recorder keeps a sequential record of the child's responses, including when he squeezes the bulb, the number and duration of his squeezes, and his verbalizations.

children were following instructions to squeeze the bulb and were then told, "That's enough," they did not stop squeezing but rather intensified it! In short, although language can direct simple activities in the two-year-old child, the motor system is clearly dominant. Adult speech may impel children to initiate an activity, but it cannot inhibit actions they have already started or make them switch from one action to another.

Luria found that, by the time children are three, most of them are able to follow instructions to squeeze the bulb, to stop squeezing, and to wait until the light comes on before squeezing. But they cannot follow more complicated instructions. For instance, when told to "Squeeze when the red light comes on but not when the green light comes on," they usually squeeze to both lights (Figure 11.12). If the command was, "When the light comes on, squeeze twice," they were likely to squeeze more than twice. They perseverated, not because they did not understand the meaning of "twice" but because, like younger children, they could not stop an activity once they had begun it. The children often performed better on these tasks if they were asked to verbalize as they acted. For example, if trained to say "Go" when the red light came on, but not when the green appeared, they were more likely to squeeze the bulb at the correct times. Similarly, the children squeezed only twice if they were trained to say "Go, go."

Only when the child reaches five or six years of age does language gain a genuine regulatory function over behavior. When children of this age are given the bulb-squeezing instructions, they respond appropriately. They can follow the instruction to "Squeeze when the red light is on but not when the green is on." By this stage language not only activates children but can direct patterns of action and terminate them. The meanings of words are now more dominant than the motor system.

This shift in the function of language from impelling children's activity to directing its course is paralleled by a shift from an external to internal mode of verbal control. At first children's behavior is directed by the spoken instructions of others. Later, children will give themselves spoken instructions, saying aloud, "Don't touch the lamp." Finally, they internalize their speech. This internalized speech, which according to Luria (1957) is "indissolubly linked" to thinking, continues to fulfill the function of regulating behavior.

Figure 11.12

Two records from Luria's bulb-pressing experiment, illustrating how language gradually comes to control behavior. Children are asked to squeeze the bulb when the red light comes on but not when the green light comes on. Three-year-old Sasha squeezes when either light is on. Language has an impelling function for him, regardless of its meaning. Five-and-a-half-year-old Vasili, on the other hand, squeezes when the red light is on but is able to refrain from squeezing when the green light comes on. (Adapted from Luria, 1961.)

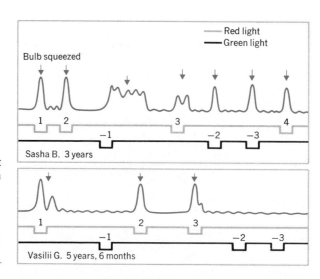

Bruner's Stages of Cognitive Growth

It is clear from the discussion so far that language gives children greater flexibility and power in solving problems and regulating their own behavior. But how does language do this? Jerome Bruner views language as a tool provided by culture that actually expands the use of the mind. Language provides the child with a means of processing information and dealing with experiences in symbolic form. According to Bruner, children grow cognitively as they acquire techniques that enable them to represent the regularities and consistencies of their surroundings with ever greater efficiency. In the ultimate stage of cognitive growth, children use language, and symbols in general, to code and store the products of experience in memory.

Before reaching this stage, which Bruner considers the third and last stage of cognitive growth, children use two other means of representation. The first of these is **enactive representation:** infants understand the world only by the actions they perform in it. To a baby girl in this stage, a rattle exists only when she is playing with it. If she accidentally drops the rattle over the edge of the crib, she will look puzzled and will seem to attempt to regain it by repeating the shaking movements she had just made. It is as though the rattle will be in her hand because she is enacting the movements that the rattle represents to her. A few months later she may look in the direction where the rattle went when it disappeared, but her hand and arm will remain still. To Bruner, this change in behavior indicates that she now has an image of the rattle that persists independently of her movements in connection with it. She can form a picture of the rattle in her mind, now that she has advanced to Bruner's second stage of cognitive development, that of **ikonic representation.** During this stage, which usually begins toward the end of the first year of life, imagery is the most effective means of processing information.

Bruner's third stage, **symbolic representation,** begins around age three, when children first start speaking grammatically. Language is much more flexible than images; it not only allows children to represent their experiences more efficiently than images, but it also permits them to organize and reorganize these experiences.

Children's performances on a simple matrix task illustrate how they proceed in the ikonic and symbolic stages (Bruner and Kenney, 1966). Three- to seven-year-old children were shown a matrix of nine plastic glasses, which varied in three degrees of diameter and three degrees of height (Figure 11.13). The investigator removed one, two, and then three glasses at a time from the matrix

Jerome Bruner, an American psychologist now teaching at Oxford University, considers the child's first two-word utterance a special landmark. "At this particular point, as far as I'm concerned, [the child] enters the human race as a speaker."

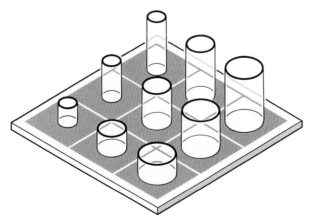

Figure 11.13
The matrix of glasses used in an ordering task. (After Bruner and Kenney, 1966.)

and asked the children to replace them. Then the glasses were scrambled and the children asked to make "something like what was there before," that is, to reproduce the matrix. Finally, the glasses were scrambled again, with the glass from the southwest corner now placed in the southeast corner. The children were asked once more to make something like what was there before, but to leave this particular glass in the southeast position.

The three- and four-year-olds were very poor at such tasks. They did not really grasp the meaning of the instructions, but they eagerly went about moving glasses around, putting them here and there more or less at random. The five-, six-, and seven-year-olds were all adept at replacing the missing glasses, and they could reproduce the matrix once it had been scrambled. The only difference within this group was that the older children were quicker. When one of the glasses was put in a different corner, however, none of the five-year-olds and only a small percentage of the six-year-olds could reconstruct the matrix. Most seven-year-olds succeeded.

The five-year-olds failed on this task because they seemed to rely on an image of the original matrix. Many of them would put the transposed glass "back where it belongs," or rotate the cardboard base on which the glasses were placed so that it would "be like before." Some five- and six-year-olds simply built the original matrix around the transposed glass. In contrast, the seven-year-olds were more likely to view the transposition as a problem that required thought rather than reliance on their mental images of the earlier matrix.

The language that the children used to describe the dimensions of the matrix had no bearing on how they replaced the glasses or how they reconstructed the matrix, but it did seem to correlate with how well they carried out the transposition task. When the children were asked how the glasses were alike and how they differed, they answered in three ways. The most precise answers were *dimensional;* they employed words that described two ends of a continuum, such as "fat" and "skinny," "tall" and "short." Some less precise answers were *global;* the children used undifferentiated terms such as "big" and "little" to describe differences in both diameter and height. Other answers used *confounded* terms; the children described one end of a continuum globally and the other end dimensionally: "That one is tall, and that one is little." Among the five- to seven-year-olds, those who used confounded descriptions were the most likely to fail on the transposed-matrix problem.

Bruner concluded from these findings that the five- and six-year-olds can develop an image of the two-dimensional array and can reproduce it quite efficiently. If asked to alter the image, however, they cannot do so because they are not yet capable of translating the matrix into a verbal or symbolic formula. The seven-year-olds, who use the correct dimensional language, have a principle for ordering the matrix that helps them deal with the transformation.

SUMMARY

Children acquire language long before they use it effectively to regulate their behavior. Alexander Luria traced a developmental sequence in the relationship between language and action and found a progression in which a process of differentiation is followed by integration. Initially, children's responses to language are undifferentiated; an adult's words serve merely to stimulate activity. As children develop, they respond in an increasingly appropriate and differentiated manner to the meaning of words. Children also learn to direct their behavior by their own internalized speech.

For the first six months of their lives, babies understand the world in terms of their activities. The movements they perform with objects represent the objects themselves. Bruner calls this representation of the world "enactive." Soon, however, infants develop an "ikonic" representation; they form mental images of objects. At the age of three, when children begin speaking grammatically, they come to have more flexible, symbolic representation. Bruner views language as a tool that actually expands the use of the mind because it permits individuals not only to represent their past experiences but to transform them as well.

THE WORK OF JEAN PIAGET

Jean Piaget (1896–1980) was the world's most renowned investigator of cognitive development and one of the seminal thinkers of our age. Using concepts from biology, psychology, philosophy, and mathematics to examine how children come to know the world, Piaget gave us an extremely well-elaborated and integrated theory of cognitive development. Despite criticisms of the limitations and the lack of objectivity in Piaget's methods, our understanding of children's intellectual development could never have progressed as far as it has without his work. His formulations and theory have stimulated a vast amount of research. As psychologists continue to confirm, question, and refine the Piagetian view of cognitive development, our understanding of children's mental processes continues to grow.

Piaget's Theory

For Piaget the function of intelligence was adaptation to the world. He saw the cognitive apparatus as an adaptive structure which individuals use to regulate their interactions with the environment. Piaget believed that since the use of intelligence is crucial to the adaptive process, intellectual activity should be considered a basic biological urge.

Perhaps Piaget's most significant contribution was to show how the intellect of children is fundamentally different from that of adults. At birth infants are not conscious either of themselves or of objects as independent structures. From this primitive level children's cognitive systems change and grow to become more adaptive and to provide a more realistic understanding of the world. Central to Piaget's theory is the view that knowledge of the world is not simply a "copy" of what is "out there." Rather, this knowledge is a creative structure, which depends on and is limited by the cognitive processes that the child has developed. For example, a two-month-old baby has only a few ways of knowing, by sucking, by touching, and by focusing on round, facelike objects. The infant's understanding of the world cannot go beyond what is provided by these first cognitive resources.

To consider sucking and touching cognitive activities seems strange, but Piaget believed that actual physical actions at first, and later in life mental actions, are the basis of all knowledge and cognitive growth. Piaget believed that actions are so important that he used a special terminology in describing them. He spoke of **schemes** to refer to organized patterns of physical action, such as sucking or grasping. A scheme does not refer to specific motor actions but is a generalization based on different instances of specific physical actions and summarizing what they have in common. For example, a child's scheme of grasping is made up of the features that are common to all the child's many acts of grasping. When schemes are carried out mentally, they are called **operations.** Both schemes and operations are ways of knowing.

ORIGINS OF PIAGET'S WORK

Piaget gave early signs of genius. As a boy, he was interested in biology, and his first article describing a rare albino sparrow was published in a natural history journal when he was only eleven. Throughout his adolescence Piaget mixed his interest in biology and his interest in epistemology (the development of a theory of knowledge). He never abandoned his biological orientation, and his investigation of the foundations and nature of human knowledge was cast solidly within the framework of biology.

As a young investigator, Piaget accepted a position as assistant to Théophile Simon in Alfred Binet's laboratory in Paris. His initial assignment was to standardize Cyril Burt's reasoning tests by giving them to Parisian grade school children. This work allowed him to observe firsthand the psychometric approach (see Chapter 13) to the understanding of cognitive development. That he found this approach limited can be seen in the following account.

. . . From the very first questioning I noticed that though Burt's tests certainly had their diagnostic merits,

Jean Piaget.

based on the number of successes and failures, it was much more interesting to try to find the reasons for the

failures. Thus I engaged my subjects in conversations patterned after psychiatric questioning, with the aim of discovering something about the reasoning process underlying their right, but especially their wrong answers. I noticed with amazement that the simplest reasoning task . . . presented for normal children up to the age of eleven or twelve difficulties unsuspected by the adult (1952, p. 244).

Thus Piaget realized that complete information about the nature of the evolving mind could not be gleaned from test responses alone. His technique of verbal probing has come to be known as Piaget's *méthode clinique*.

Piaget had been launched on his life's work. From 1921 until his death, he was engaged in studying child psychology; the development of logic, causal reasoning, language, and thought; the growth of moral judgment; the child's conception of the world; and the emergence of intelligence during infancy and early childhood. This work led to the evolution of his theory of intelligence and its development.

Cognitive growth takes place as schemes and operations change and become more complex. The process by which this is accomplished consists of two complementary components, assimilation and accommodation. When a child encounters an object or event for the first time, that object or event is assimilated, or taken in, to the child's existing cognitive framework. The child may then reorganize the cognitive structure to accommodate the new experience. In short, **assimilation** is the process of taking in new information and interpreting it—sometimes even distorting it—to make it agree with the available mental organization. **Accommodation** is a changing of the cognitive system so that it provides a better match to outside information.

For example, newborn infants reflexively suck the breast. They literally assimilate the breast into one of their existing schemes for behavior. If a finger or the corner of a blanket is placed on their lips, they also suck the finger or blanket. They continue to assimilate objects into one of the few organized responses that they possess. To continue treating a finger or a blanket as though it were a breast is ineffective, however. Therefore, in the process of sucking the blanket, they must reorganize their responses and their cognitive representation—their scheme—of the blanket. They must shape their lips differently and, in so doing, change their schemes of sucking. This reorganization in response to the demands presented by an alien object is an example of accommodation.

The child's explanation of dreams is another example of cognitive growth

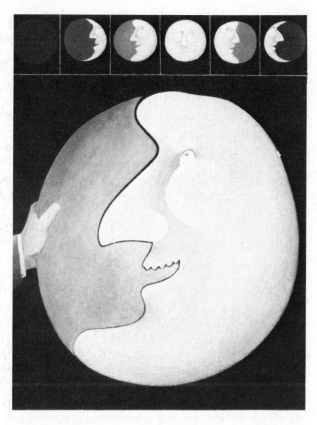

. . . Several children in the four to six age-groups told me that the sun and moon were "made" by a gentleman who lighted them up (Piaget, 1971).

through assimilation and accommodation. The boy who said that dreams come in balloons sent from God has assimilated the experience of dreaming into his existing cognitive framework. Since dreams have certain visual qualities, which make them similar to external events, he has associated them with balloons, external objects with which he is familiar. But in saying that the balloons "burst into pictures outside your head," the child has begun to show some degree of accommodation; he has made a distinction between inside and outside. Later he will be forced to come to grips with certain unacceptable aspects of his explanation, and he will have to make further accommodations. For instance, having had a number of dreams, he will realize eventually that dreams are unreal and without substance, that they differ in these ways from objects like balloons and from events taking place outside the head. The differences that he notices between dreams and not-dreams, as well as the greater differentiation of the cognitive system, will lead the boy to the next cognitive level of understanding dreams.

Each instance of assimilation and accommodation stretches the mind a bit, and this stretching will enable the individual to make new and somewhat different assimilations and accommodations in the future. These, in turn, will bring additional small increments in mental growth. Thus by repeated assimilations and accommodations the cognitive system gradually evolves and provides the child with an increasingly accurate view of the nature of things. When the child makes a startling leap in understanding phenomena, he or she moves onto the next stage of cognitive development. Piaget therefore viewed the development of intelligence as an active and constructive process. Children play an active role in learning about the world and in altering their cognitive processes.

Stages of Cognitive Development

Piaget charted four major stages of cognitive development: the sensorimotor stage, the preoperational stage, the stage of concrete operations, and the stage of formal operations. During each stage certain critical cognitive abilities are achieved, abilities that make it possible for the child to process information in ways that were previously impossible. The age ranges cited for each stage are only rough approximations, for they vary considerably from child to child and task to task.

Sensorimotor Stage—Birth to Two Years.   During the **sensorimotor stage** the most fundamental and rapid changes in cognitive structure take place. Piaget called this the "sensorimotor stage" to reflect his belief that knowledge is built up initially from sensory perceptions and motor actions.

At birth the infant has no self-awareness, no sense of an "I" that can act on the world, and no sense of the world as a separate entity. The infant is the center of the universe, a universe that consists of ever-changing perceptions but no permanent objects. Piaget (1973) described development during this stage as a Copernican revolution. Cognitively, the child is dethroned as the center of the universe and reduced to the status of one object among other objects. In this stage children also learn that they and other objects exist in space and that objects can cause things to happen to other objects. Children gain all this knowledge before they acquire language.

At birth infants make only isolated movements and have only isolated schemes. As they repeat and coordinate their movements, the schemes are elaborated by new assimilations and accommodations. The sensorimotor intelligence typical of this stage allows the child to pull a blanket that has a toy resting on its far end, in order to obtain the toy. This task may appear simple, but Piaget has shown what a cognitive feat it really is. Before children can perform this task, they must have constructed and mastered several relationships, in particular "resting upon" and "moving an object from one place to another," and then coordinated them for their purposes.

Perhaps the most significant achievement during this period is the development of the *object concept* or a sense of **object permanence.** As noted earlier, infants do not at first realize that objects, including people, exist independently of their perceptions of them. They may gaze at a toy held within their view, but when the toy is removed, they do not reach for it. The object simply ceases to exist for them once it leaves their visual field. This lack of the concept of object explains the delight infants derive from playing peekaboo. If a mother removes her face from her infant son's view and then reappears, he is surprised and pleased by her re-creation. Later in the sensorimotor stage children will gaze at the point where an object disappeared, and by the end of the sensorimotor period they will actively seek to find an object after it has vanished. By this time children have a sense that objects exist even when they cannot see or find them, a sense of object permanence.

Their inadequate concept of objects explains why infants less than a year old cannot successfully play the "guess which hand" game. When they watch you hide a coin in your hand, place your hands behind your back, and return an empty hand, they will begin to search where they believe the coin disappeared. Early in the sensorimotor stage children will think it disappeared when you first hid it in your hand, and they will begin the search among your fingers. By the end of the sensorimotor period, they look behind your back, for that is where they lost track of its whereabouts.

Preoperational Stage—Two to Seven Years of Age. During the **preoperational stage** children can engage in symbolic activities that draw upon mental imagery and language. For example, they can now mentally represent an object to themselves when it is not visually present. Their intellectual functions are no longer restricted to physical actions. By the end of this period, children are able to talk about objects, draw them, tell stories, and assemble three-dimensional constructions. They also learn to use language to direct their behavior. The stage is called preoperational, however, because children are unable to engage in certain basic mental operations. They cannot focus on two dimensions, such as height and width, at the same time; they cannot reverse or change actions mentally. They can repeat old actions in their minds, but they cannot think of actions that they have not yet engaged in or seen themselves. Their thinking is **egocentric:** they cannot see another person's point of view or put themselves in another's place. (As our discussion of social cognition will show, however, recent research suggests that young children may not be as wholly egocentric as Piaget thought.)

The use of language by preoperational children is very different from that of adults. When children first learn that objects have names, they believe that the names are an essential part of the objects. For instance, the word "ball" is considered just as much an inalienable property of a ball as its physical shape and color. This mode of thinking about the names of things is called **nominal realism.** In the earliest stage of nominal realism, the child finds it nonsensical to question why certain objects have the names they do. Since the name is part of the object, the child reasons, the object could have no other name. Furthermore, children feel that an object could not have existed before it had its name. In later stages children will abandon this view and realize that names are assigned to objects. It is not until the age of eleven or twelve, however, that children fully comprehend how arbitrary the naming process is. Until then, they

Toward the end of the preoperational period, children can draw objects and create sculptures.

Figure 11.14
In a study of identity constancy, a cat was
masked as a dog.

will insist that the names of objects are assigned by God or by the people who made them, and that the objects could not possibly have a different name.

Another characteristic of preoperational thinking is **animism,** a belief that inanimate objects have mental processes. Preoperational children ascribe thoughts, feelings, and motives to clouds, streams, trees, and bicycles. Plants may hurt when they are picked; clouds may chase each other; bicycles may like to run quickly. In accordance with the child's egocentric thought, the motives of external objects are based on the child's activities; the sun and moon "follow" as the child walks.

One of the important intellectual achievements of the preoperational period is the development of **identity constancy.** The child comes to realize that an object remains qualitatively the same despite alterations in form, size, or general appearance. Rheta DeVries (1969) devised an interesting way to study the development of identity constancy in three- to six-year-old children. The children were individually shown a very docile cat. After they had identified it as a cat and petted it, the experimenter told them that soon the animal would look different. She asked the children to look only at the tail end of the cat. Then, while screening the cat's head from their view, she placed a mask of a ferocious-looking dog over the cat's head (Figure 11.14). The cat was turned around, and the children were asked what animal it was now. DeVries found that the older children understood that the cat had retained its identity. Many of the younger children, however, thought that the cat had become a dog, even though its tail end had been visible to them while the mask was put on. They often seemed fearful of the animal and refused to pet it. When questioned, they asserted that it was indeed a real dog and could bark. The older children were more likely to think that a trick had been played, that a cat could not possibly become a dog, not even "by magic."

Concrete Operations Stage—Seven to Eleven Years of Age. In the stage of **concrete operations,** children organize into structural wholes many of the scattered schemes and conceptualizatons developed during the earlier stages. They form mental representations that adequately reflect possible actions and transactions in the physical world. As indicated earlier, operations are mental actions, schemes carried out in the head. During the stage of concrete operations, the child is able to act on objects and transform situations mentally. The operations are "concrete," however, because the child can only reason about physical things like blocks and lumps of clay. Reasoning about abstractions such as words and mathematical symbols is not possible until the next stage of development.

Flexibility. During the stage of concrete operations, children develop the concept of **hierarchical structures,** the ranking of classes within classes, and they develop the ability to order objects or people on more than one dimension. For instance, when ten red and five green wooden beads are shown to pre-operational children, they can tell us that there are more red beads than green. When asked whether there are more red beads or wooden beads, however, preoperational children often reply that there are more red beads than wooden ones. This simplistic approach to classification is overcome in the stage of concrete operations, when the child develops a more abstract notion of classes of objects as well as the concept of multiple classification. For example, during this stage children learn that people can be classified into more than one category, that a father can also be somebody's brother, an accountant, and a golfer. An example of the earlier inability to do so was given by David Elkind, a major interpreter of Piaget to American psychologists. Professor Elkind (1973) asked a preoperational child whether he (Elkind) could be a Protestant and an American at the same time. The child replied "No" but then after a second's thought added, "Only if you move."

Since a child's cognitive structure is an adaptive mechanism for dealing with all aspects of the world, it is not surprising that social interactions take on a different quality as the child develops cognitively. During the concrete operations stage children become less egocentric; they are able to consider the views of others as well as their own. They can share their thoughts with others, adopt others' perspectives, are less contradictory and inconsistent, and engage in meaningful and prolonged communication with others.

We see this change in the child's use of and attitude toward rules. Early in the stage of concrete operations the child regards rules as absolute and unchangeable, often considering them to have been handed down by God. Rules are thought to exist in the very fabric of the universe, to have existed always, and to permit no deviation. Piaget (1932) investigated children's conceptions of rules by playing marbles with youngsters of various ages and seeing whether he could induce them to change the rules. It was clear from the young children's responses that they viewed Piaget as a troublemaker who simply did not comprehend the inviolability of these rules. Despite their verbal commitment to rules, however, these children often break them. Toward the end of the concrete operations stage, a more abstract and useful approach to rules develops. Children come to realize that rules are established because they are in the best interests of those who construct them, and that since rules are made by people, they can be changed by people, including themselves. Once this transition has been accomplished, Piaget noted, children adhere to rules much more consistently.

Conservation. The perceptual world in which we live is remarkably invariant. Although an object projects radically different images to the retina, depending on its distance and our angle of regard, it remains the same size and shape (Chapter 5). We also know, however, that an object remains the same thing

Although early in the concrete operational period children regard rules as inviolable, they violate them. Toward the end of the period, they understand that rules are established for the good of the people who use them and obey them more dependably.

when it changes in its appearance. The ability to understand what changes and what does not change under various perceptual circumstances is an indispensable cognitive activity for an adapting individual (Flavell, 1977). Children must discern the consistencies, regularities, and order in the world in order to deal with it effectively.

The invariants that the child understands by the end of the preoperational period—object permanence, size and shape constancy, identity constancy—are fundamentally qualitative rather than quantitative in nature. During the concrete operations stage a notion of quantitative invariants develops. Piaget has called this ability **conservation.** During the concrete operations stage children acquire the ability to conserve such concepts as number, substance, and quantity. Let us use the concept of number as an example. By the concept of number, Piaget is not referring to the child's ability to count from 1 to 10 or to tell us that 2 + 2 = 4. These can be learned by rote and do not in themselves indicate that the child really possesses an understanding of the concept of number. Such understanding includes the awareness that 1 is less than 5 and that the number 7 means the same thing, whether there are seven mice or seven battleships. Shown pictures of seven mice and seven battleships, the young child may well feel that there are more battleships because they are so much bigger.

In mastering the concept of number, the child first must comprehend one-to-one correspondence. Suppose that we place five wooden balls in a row before a preoperational girl, give her a box containing a large number of square wooden blocks, and ask her to put out on the floor the same number of squares as there are balls. For an individual who has mastered the concept of number, this is an extremely simple task; the adult would immediately grasp that there are five balls and simply count out five squares. The young child, however, engages in quite a different process in order to solve the problem. Typically, she takes a block and places it directly under the first ball in the row, then places a second block directly beneath the second ball in the row. When she has put a block beneath every ball, she tells us that there are the same number of blocks as there are balls. She has used a strategy of one-to-one correspondence in order to produce two collections of objects, each collection having the same number.

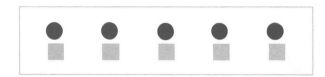

But understanding one-to-one correspondence is not the same as understanding the concept of number. It is just a necessary part of the process. Suppose we rearrange the objects this way.

Now when the child is asked whether there are as many squares as balls, she will answer that there are more balls. Since this simple difference in physical arrangement alters the child's answer, we know that she has not mastered conservation of number. The child's perception of length is overriding her conception of number; she reasons that there must be more balls than squares because the row of balls is longer. This single-minded riveting of attention on one particularly salient or interesting perceptual attribute Piaget calls **centering.** Only when children can **decenter** and attend simultaneously to several perceptual aspects of a thing or a collection of things can they conserve concepts.

The principle of conservation of substance is mastered when the child becomes aware than an amount of material stays the same even when the shape is changed. If a child is given two equal balls of clay and asked whether they contain the same amount of clay, the child will usually examine them closely and reply that they do. Then, while the child watches, one clay ball is rolled into a sausage shape. Asked which has more clay, the child who has mastered conservation is often amused at the stupidity of the question and replies that of course the two objects still contain the same amount of clay. A few years earlier, however, while in the preoperational stage, this same child would have replied that the round ball had more clay because it was fatter, or that the sausage had more clay because it was longer. Children in the earlier stage center so much more on the one dimension of length or breadth that they cannot conserve the concept of substance.

Closely related to the conservation of substance is the child's ability to conserve a quantity of liquid. If two glass beakers of the same size are filled with the same amount of water, the child will agree that they contain the same amount. As the child watches, the water from one of these containers is poured into a shorter and wider beaker. Children who cannot conserve believe that the shallow glass does not contain as much water. When the same liquid is poured into a tall, thin, beaker, they believe that this glass contains more water. They may even believe that when the water is poured back into the original container, the liquid will reach a higher level on the glass.

Pouring the liquid into the other beakers transforms the perceptual aspects of the liquid, making it appear shorter in the shallow container, taller in the other. Preoperational children, dominated by their perceptions, will say that the liquid has changed in amount, even though they observed the actual pouring. The child who has reached the stage of concrete operations, however, understands that the act of pouring has not changed the amount of liquid and conserves the quantity of liquid despite perceptual alterations.

The ability to conserve is connected with two aspects of thought, in addition to centering, that change during the concrete operations phase. The first way in which children's thought changes is that their attention shifts from states to transformations, from how things appear to how they come to appear that way. Piaget observed that when younger children are solving problems, they are more likely to focus their conceptual energies on states. They are less likely to recall how objects appeared in the past or to anticipate possible future changes in appearance. Children who are able to conserve, on the other hand, are more disposed to keep in mind the process of transition from one state to another. In justifying a conservation judgment, they can point out that pouring the liquid merely transformed its appearance, not its state.

The second way in which thought changes is that children become able to *reverse* it. They can interrupt a sequence of thought at any point and return to the beginning of the sequence. Young children cannot conceive that the two pieces of reshaped clay or the amounts of water in different-sized beakers are identical because they cannot think them back to their original states. Conservers recognize that, in their original states, the amounts of water were identical and that the act of pouring cannot change the volume of the liquid. The principle of reversibility is important to a number of mental operations. A child's numerical ability is greatly enhanced once he or she can reverse $4 \times 2 = 8$ by

Failure to conserve quantity. (a) Two equal volumes of fluid (b) poured into different containers may not be recognized as still equal until (c) they are returned to identical containers.

(a)

(b)

(c)

performing the operation $8 \div 2 = 4$. The process of reversibility is also a prerequisite for engaging in transitive reasoning, which takes this form: If A is smaller than B, and B is smaller than C, then A must be smaller than C. If Kirk is heavier than Loren, and Loren is heavier than Mark, who is heavier, Kirk or Mark? Conservers have the ability to reason transitively.

Formal Operations Stage—Eleven Years On. During the final stage of development, children become able to consider a problem in the abstract without needing a concrete representation of it. They will search for alternatives in trying to solve problems, rejecting those that seem inappropriate without physically testing their inadequacy. Children now are free to manipulate all sorts of conceptual hypotheses about the world, thinking not only about what is but about what could be. When younger children are confronted with the supposition, ''If coal is white, snow is _____," they will respond by insisting that coal is black. The adolescent will answer that snow is black. This problem makes cognitive demands because the reality of the situation is that coal is not white and snow is not black. Through **formal operations** children free themselves from such physical "givens" and are able to consider a totally hypothetical realm of possibilities, which nevertheless retains some orderliness. This new ability of the person to deal in hypothetical terms is described by John Flavell.

> No longer exclusively preoccupied with the sober business of trying to stablize and organize just what comes directly to the senses, the adolescent has, through this new orientation, the potentiality of imagining all that might be there—both the very obvious and the very subtle—and thereby of much better insuring the findings of all that is there (1963, p. 205).

The questions that older children ask when playing the game Twenty Questions indicates the higher level of abstraction in their formal operational thought. In guessing what object the experimenter has in mind, eleven-year-olds, like adults, will begin with general questions to narrow the range of their alternatives: "Is it alive?" "Is it a tool?" Six-year-olds, however, immediately guess at specific objects: "Is it the dog?" Eight-year-olds often combine these strategies. They begin with a general question but move straight to specific guesses. Thus they might follow, "Is it a tool?" with "Is it a hammer?" whereas the eleven-year-old's next question might be, "Can you cut with it?" This use of questions that progressively restrict the alternatives demonstrates a broad conception of the range of potential answers, which is not evident in the questions of younger children (Mosher and Hornsby, 1966).

Formal operations are the basis of adult thought. In addition to abstract, logical reasoning, they make possible the creative reasoning that brings about some of humanity's most impressive achievements; a grasp of truth and beauty and other ideals; being able to think about thinking; the ability to delve into probabilities and improbabilities; imagining other worlds. Not all adolescents or even adults attain the stage of formal operations. The ability to deal logically with abstractions becomes *possible* in this stage, but whether or not it is exercised depends in part on cultural and educational factors. Further, individuals who are somewhat below average in intelligence may never attain formal operational thought (Inhelder, 1966; Jackson, 1965); and very bright children may perform as well or better than some adults (Neimark, 1975; Neimark and Lewis, 1967). In any case, both psychometricians and cognitive developmentalists agree that by late adolescence individuals have developed all the cognitive processes that they are ever to possess. They can of course learn new things, and they may even become more intelligent with added years (Chapter 13), but the processes that underlie cognitive interchange with the world are pretty much established by the age of twenty.

Cross-Cultural Piagetian Studies

Cross-cultural studies of Piagetian theory have addressed the basic question of whether human cognition follows the same course of development in children the world over. Piaget's notions have sometimes been criticized as being a theory of cognitive development for Western scientists (Greenfield, 1976), a theory that may be no more than an ethnocentric description of mental development in the urban, technological cultures of Europe and North America. People of other societies may develop other cognitive processes more adaptive to their own surroundings and of greater cultural value to them.

Cross-cultural studies, conducted in countries as far afield as Thailand,

Rwanda (Africa), Papua (New Guinea), Iraq, Iran, Jordan, Ghana, Australia, and Mexico yielded two important findings (Dasen, 1977). The first is that the developmental stages observed by Piaget in Switzerland also appear in these very different civilizations. The sequence of cognitive development—sensorimotor, to preoperational, to concrete operations, and finally to formal operations—seems to be universal. The second finding is that the *rate* of cognitive development may vary from one society to another. Children may pass from one stage to another at different ages.

Since intelligence fosters adaptation to the environment, it would not be surprising to discover that children gain concepts that are important in their culture relatively early. This prediction has proved true of children in a number of different cultures (Dasen, 1975, 1977; Price-Williams, Gordon, and Ramirez, 1969). For example, Mexican children who grow up in pottery-making families are accelerated in their development of conservation of substance. Infants and toddlers living in rural Baoule on the Ivory Coast were found to have greater sensorimotor skills than their contemporaries in France, even though the African children were unfamiliar with the plastic toy cars and dolls that were used in the evaluation. Apparently the particular experiences of children as well as their general ways of life and the values of their culture can affect the rate of cognitive development.

Within a given cultural group cognitive development may also be affected by education and whether a child's residence is urban or rural. In Rwanda, a country in central Africa where mandatory education was only recently instituted, schooling was found to help children master tasks requiring concrete operations (Laurendeau-Bendavid, 1977). Another investigator found that rural Thai children lagged behind urban children in mastering several concepts requiring concrete operations (Opper, 1977). Urban children acquired the concepts over a period of five years, beginning at the age of six. The rural children did not begin to acquire the concepts until the age of nine, but then mastered all of them in a period of only three years.

Accelerated Progression Through the Stages
Whether special training can accelerate children's progression through Piaget's cognitive stages is a subject of continuing interest to those who study cognitive

This East African child is learning to count with the help of a handmade device schoolchildren bring from home. Just as with American and European children, the children in this school learn counting well before the conservation of numbers.

development. Many investigators have attempted to help children develop certain aspects of cognition by providing specific training, and a number of them have apparently succeeded. One of these demonstrations was carried out by Rochel Gelman (1969), who trained five-year-old children in conservation of number and length. First, she pretested the children on four standard Piagetian tasks to show that they could not conserve. She then gave them one of three types of special training. Children in one group were presented with sets of three toy objects, two identical and one different, and were asked to point either to two objects that were the same or to two that were different. They were given a prize whenever they chose correctly. Children in a second group were shown other sets of three items, two of them identical in number or length and the third one different. For example, there might be two rows of five chips and one row of three chips, or two six-inch sticks and one ten-inch stick. The children were asked to point either to two rows that had the same or different numbers of chips, or to two sticks that were the same or different in length. Since preoperational children often define number in terms of length, Gelman deliberately varied the distance between the chips in the number problems, so as to confound quantity with the length cue (Figure 11.15). Again, the children were rewarded for correct responses. Children in the third group were shown the same set of items and asked the same questions as children in the second group, but they received no rewards. Thus they had no way of learning when they had succeeded or failed in making the necessary discriminations.

The children in the first group performed almost perfectly. Apparently these five-year-olds came to the training session with an understanding of "same" and "different." Those in the second group quicky began to learn the required discrimination between length and number. The children in the third group, however, learned very little.

All children were given tests of conservation the day after training and again two to three weeks later. The results were quite remarkable. Neither the children in the first group, who were not trained to discriminate the appropriate dimensions, nor the children in the third group, who received no feedback to guide their attention, demonstrated much capacity for conservation. In contrast, the children in the second group performed almost flawlessly on both tests. More-

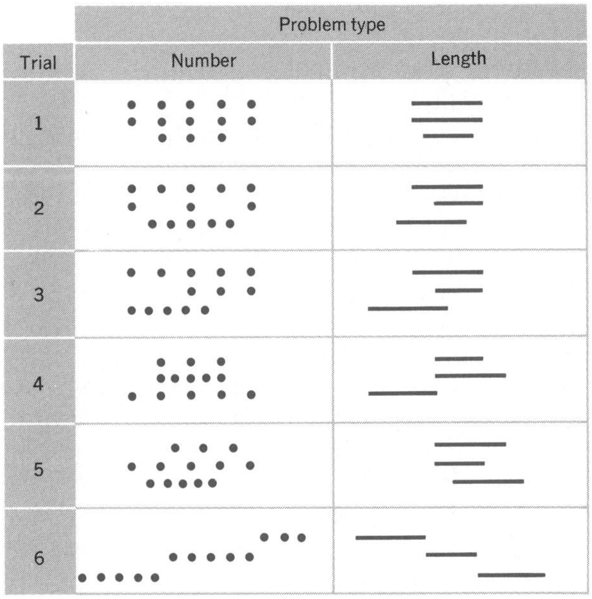

Figure 11.15
Examples of the sets of three items given children in number and length discrimination training. (Adapted from Gelman, 1969.)

over, although they had been trained specifically to conserve number and length, they were now able to conserve liquid and mass as well.

Gelman's study appears to be a powerful demonstration that training and experience may help children acquire the principle of conservation. Howard Gardner (1978) pointed out, however, that Gelman studied only five-year-old children. It is possible that they were already on the verge of learning conservation on their own, and Gelman's procedures may simply have nudged them a bit prematurely into operational thinking. Gardner did not think it likely that the training would have had any significant effect on four-year-olds. We must await additional research to learn the extent to which mental growth can be accelerated and the conditions that may encourage it. At this time the best conclusion appears to be that children will attain the cognitive abilities described by Piaget, provided they have had broad enough experiences and have reached the maturational level of the stage in question.

It is conceivable that hurrying a child from one stage to the next might interfere with normal cognitive development and that such acceleration might lessen the child's cognitive achievements. Joachim Wohlwill (1970) has noted that the reasoning of very young children, although generally outgrown, may be useful to them later in life, especially in their imaginative and creative acts. If children are hurried through early stages, the early processes may not be properly incorporated in the overall cognitive apparatus, and certain useful ways of thinking will be lost to them as adults.

SUMMARY

Piaget emphasized the biological, adaptive significance of intelligence and charted its growth through an apparently invariant series of four stages. Each of these stages is distinct in important respects from those preceding and following it.

Piaget stressed that human beings have an existing cognitive structure, which they use in their interactions with the outside world. They are never mere passive receptacles for environmental input. Even infants have behavioral sequences and generalizations, which they attempt to use in coping with the demands of their surroundings. To some extent infants can deal successfully with the environment by using their existing abilities and "schemes," for they will incorporate or "assimilate" new experiences into existing patterns of thought and action. But when an outside stimulus fails to conform to their expectations, they must modify some of their schemes. Such a changing of the cognitive apparatus is called "accommodation." Through assimilation and accommodation cognitive growth will occur. With certain major reorganizations of the cognitive processes, the child is said to enter a new stage.

The first cognitive stage is the sensorimotor stage, when infants acquire the concept of an object as a permanent structure whose existence is independent of their perception of it. Intelligence at this time is restricted primarily to the level of physical actions. Next comes the preoperational stage, when children begin to use symbols, imagery, and language and come to understand identity constancy. In the concrete operations period children acquire the ability to conserve number, length, quantity, weight, volume, space, and time. In the final stage, formal operations, the child becomes capable of considering a problem in the abstract without needing a concrete representation of it.

Cross-cultural studies have indicated that the stages Piaget observed in Western children also occur in children of very different societies. The rate of development, however, appears to differ, depending on schooling, cultural values, and experiences.

Research on acceleration of cognitive stages suggests that special training may possibly hasten mastery of abilities such as conservation, but firm conclusions are not yet possible. An unanswered question is the wisdom of hurrying children through the stages, since their early thought processes may remain useful or become the foundation for later modes of thinking.

SOCIAL COGNITION

So far our discussion has focused on the cognitive processes that give people an understanding of the physical world. But what about people's understanding of the social world, of other people, and of interpersonal relationships? Traditionally, it has been assumed that people use the same cognitive processes in social domains that they use in physical domains. The contexts in which we learn about social and physical events are different, however, and may have different influences on cognition. For this reason psychologists have begun to consider **social cognition** as a distinct process whose development can be studied independently as well as in relation to physical cognition.

Social and Physical Cognition

The social world is more complex and unpredictable than the physical world. Inanimate objects are subject to dependable physical laws and their behavior is predictable. People behave in ways that are less predictable. Their responses are determined more complexly, by subjective motives and needs and by the mutual intentions, shared perspectives, and coordinated actions that are part of relationships with other people. Given this complexity, it is, perhaps, surprising to discover that social cognition actually seems to develop more rapidly than physical cognition (Hoffman, 1981). In fact, some of the findings of research in social cognition challenge Piaget's statements about the cognitive capacities of young children.

For example, children apparently develop the concept of person permanence well before that of object permanence. They may respond anxiously to separation from a familiar adult before they seem to know that an object still exists when it is out of sight. There are several possible explanations for this devel-

Babies develop the concept of person permanence long before that of object permanence. This little girl pulls away the towel to find her mother's face.

opmental difference. The people a child interacts with are likely to be more familiar than objects. The child may have a greater emotional investment in people than in objects. Martin Hoffman (1981) has suggested that social cognition is entwined with emotion much more than physical cognition is. When we interact with people with whom we are emotionally involved, our motivation for learning and cognitive development is intensified. Furthermore, such interactions provide children with a constant source of feedback—other people's reactions—and this feedback may promote cognitive development by showing children when their hypotheses about the appropriate social interactions are right or wrong.

There is some evidence that social interaction can promote cognitive development as well as social development. William Doise and his colleagues demonstrated that children working together could master a spatial task—copying a model village when the model was rotated to change the child's perspective— that children of the same age working alone could not complete (Mugny and Doise, 1976). In related studies children who were initially unable to conserve acquired this operation after working on conservation tasks with peers (Doise, Mugny, and Perret-Clermont, 1975) or with an experimenter who challenged their assessments by offering either correct or incorrect alternatives (Doise, Mugny, and Perret-Clermont, 1976). In all these studies children's progress did not depend on offers of a correct strategy but on questioning and coordinating different approaches to the task.

Discussing these results, William Damon (1981) has suggested that social-coordination tasks require children to restructure their cognitive processes, and that this may influence their modes of thinking in lasting ways. The existence of such a relationship between social interaction and physical cognition makes good sense when we consider that children often explore the physical world, as well as the social one, in the context of interacting with other people.

Role Taking and Empathy

If children never outgrew the egocentricity of their earliest years, human social interaction would be very different from what it actually is in adult life. There could be no cooperation, sharing, or selflessness. The capacity to put oneself in another person's place, to take another's role, is vital in social interactions. But children are certainly not born with this capacity. **Empathy,** the recognition and vicarious sharing of the emotions of others, depends on being able to see things from the perspective of others. According to Piaget, the capacity for role taking develops gradually as a result of social interactions. A good example of egocentric thought comes from a study in which children were told a story while their mothers were out of the room and were then asked whether their mothers knew what had happened in the story. Two-year-olds demonstrated their egocentrism by assuming that their mothers knew what had happened. But most four-year-olds recognized that their mothers could not possibly know (Mossler, Marvin, and Greenberg, 1976).

Other research suggests that young children are not as egocentric as Piaget considered them, and that egocentricity declines gradually during the preoperational period, rather than suddenly at the transition from preoperational to concrete operational stages. For example, adults use simpler terms, speak more slowly, and repeat themselves more often when talking to young children than when talking to other adults (page 223). In one study four-year-olds were also found to modify their speech patterns when they talked to two-year-olds (Shatz and Gelman, 1973). The four-year-olds seemed to recognize and respond to the needs of the younger children. In short, by the age of four children in our

Earlier than Piaget proposed, children give up their egocentric notions of the world and are able to share the emotions of other children.

culture can engage in role taking. They have developed levels of social cognition that seem more advanced than their cognition of physical properties.

Scripts

One hypothesis of how children learn about their own and other people's social roles holds that they develop **scripts** for what happens in familiar situations. They develop scripts for what one does at lunch time, when meeting a stranger, when eating in a restaurant (Abelson, 1981; Nelson and Gruendel, 1981). These scripts reflect cultural regularities in a child's experience and can act as cognitive mediators of the child's behavior.

Children acquire some scripts, such as that for eating dinner, by participating directly in the activity. Since children eat dinner, but do not plan or prepare the meal, the dinnertime script that they learn through direct participation is only their part in dinnertime (Nelson, 1981). Scripts are also learned through observation. Children reveal some knowledge of other people's roles in their fantasy and role playing. For example, Katherine Nelson (1981) cites a dialogue in which two four-year-olds indicated some understanding of a dinner-planning script. They carried on a make-believe telephone conversation in which they played mother and father planning dinner.

Scripts are important guides for activities because, once learned, they allow people to attend to new features of the environment. For example, on the first day of school, when every aspect of experience is new, children must attend to everything, to the teacher, peers, desk, snack, and lesson. If the routine aspects of the school day did not become familiar, there would simply be too much to attend to for a child to learn much beyond these routines. By the second week of school, however, the child's classroom script has made the routines almost second nature, and the child can focus on each day's special activities, undistracted by the need to pay attention to these now-familiar details.

Scripts foster cognitive development because children are capable of more advanced cognitive functioning in familiar situations than they are in novel situations. For example, although four-year-olds are egocentric in their discussions with peers, recent evidence shows that they can in fact communicate cooperatively, sticking to a given topic while they take appropriate turns in speaking. Nelson (1981) has suggested that two young children can communicate competently when both of them know the script for the event they are discussing. Speech may be egocentric when there is no shared script, as when a situation is new to either or both children. Thus scripts have a meaningful place in development, although blind adherence to the scripts learned in childhood may prevent adults from adopting more suitable behavior later on.

Perceptions of Others

Perceptions of other people are another important aspect of social cognition. Research has revealed that the capacity to perceive other people, like role taking, develops gradually. For example, in studies in which children and adolescents were asked to describe people they know (Peevers and Secord, 1973; Livesley and Bromley, 1973), young children tended to refer to very concrete aspects of behavior—"She give me candy"—and to use undifferentiated adjectives such as "nice" or "kind." Older children and adolescents tended to use more informative, differentiated, and other-oriented descriptions—"She is always ready to help people who are in trouble"—and to draw abstract and general inferences from concrete events. These inferences about psychological states become more common with increasing age.

Similar trends are evident in children's descriptions of people they do not know. When describing brief vignettes, six-year-olds tended to focus on the events—"He hit the girl"—whereas nine- and twelve-year-olds were more likely to explain the events—"He hit the girl because she made him angry by teasing him" (Flapan, 1968). In one study children and adolescents of different social classes were asked to describe rich and poor people and how they are similar to and different from each other (Leahy 1981). Younger children emphasized "peripheral" characteristics—possessions, appearances, behavior—in their descriptions, but adolescents emphasized traits, thoughts, and "sociocentric" factors such as life chances and class consciousness.

According to Piaget (1932), young children evaluate others' behavior by its consequences, and older children consider the actors' motives and intentions. For example, children might be told one story about a boy who accidentally trips and breaks several cups while helping to clear the table, and another story about a boy who breaks a single cup while trying to steal from the cookie jar. Most children under age six or seven consider the first child naughtier because of the greater damage done. Older children and adults usually consider the second child naughtier because the accident occurred during a forbidden activity. It appears, however, that even younger children can recognize clearly specified intentions, and that this capacity develops before the ability to infer others' motives (Irwin and Ambron, 1973).

SUMMARY

Children seem to acquire social cognition, an understanding of other people and relationships with them, more rapidly than they do physical cognition. The process, one in which children must take into account the perspectives and intentions of others, is very complicated. Social interactions, which provide the context for learning about others, also provide the motivation for this learning and the feedback that aids it. Moreover, when children act together to solve problems, they further their general cognitive development.

Piaget believed that the egocentricity of preoperational children makes them incapable of role taking, but recent evidence suggests that children as young as four years old can and do take into account others' perspectives. They develop empathy for others gradually through cognitive growth and social interaction. Young children may shed their egocentricity in simple, familiar situations but still retain it in more complex ones.

One way in which children learn social roles is by developing scripts for familiar situations. They learn their own parts by participating directly in activities, others' parts through observation. Scripts allow children to adjust quickly to routines and to spend their attention on new aspects of their surroundings.

Children's descriptions of other people show developmental changes, being at first concrete and undifferentiated and later abstract and differentiated. Their inferences about the psychological states of others increase with age. Young children tend to make their value judgments of others' behavior by its consequences, and older children make their judgments according to the actors' intentions.

TO BE SURE YOU UNDERSTAND THIS CHAPTER

These are the important concepts introduced in this chapter.

Psychometric approach

Developmental approach

Maturation

Mass action–differentiation

Cephalocaudal sequence

Proximodistal sequence

Verbal mediation

Enactive representation

Ikonic representation

Symbolic representation

Scheme

Operation

Assimilation

Accommodation

Sensorimotor stage

Object permanence

Preoperational stage

Egocentrism

Nominal realism

Animism

Identity constancy

Concrete operations

Hierarchical structures

Conservation

Centering

Decentering

Formal operations

Social cognition

Empathy

Script

This chapter has also introduced some important concepts and issues that are not easily identified by single terms. You should recall and understand the discussions of each of them.

Cognitive capacity and problem solving

Universality of Piagetian stages

Accelerated progression through Piagetian stages

Development of role-taking abilities

TO GO BEYOND THIS CHAPTER

In This Book. The tie between the materials in this chapter and those in Chapter 7 is very close. It will be useful to review the earlier discussions of language, thought, and problem solving, putting the context of the two chapters together. Stagelike development is hypothesized too for personality, which is also studied both psychometrically (Chapter 13) and developmentally (Chapter 16). Chapter 18 carries on the discussion of social cognition.

Elsewhere. The following books give detailed accounts of theories and empirical data on development: *Cognitive Development,* by John Flavell; *The Growth of Competence,* edited by K. J. Connolly and Jerome Bruner; *Piaget's Theory of Intelligence,* by Charles Brainerd; and *Jean Piaget: The Man and His Ideas,* by Richard Evans.

CHAPTER 12   SOCIAL AND EMOTIONAL DEVELOPMENT

The newborn infant is a social being, but indiscriminately so. With development its social responses become increasingly specific. The occasions that provoke emotional reactions also change. Social tasks that delight or distress a young child are very different from those that cause the same reactions in an adolescent or an adult. In this chapter we focus first on emotional behavior in infancy. Then we consider how parents, other individuals, and the culture as a whole affect social and emotional development. Finally, we turn to a few of the basic "tasks" of social and emotional growth, the development of a self-concept, a sex role, and a set of moral values.

EMOTIONAL BEHAVIOR IN INFANCY

Because some of the basic aspects of personality, such as trust or mistrust of others, appear to be established in the first year or so of life, infants' social and emotional responses are of special interest and importance to psychologists. Charles Darwin was one of the first scientists to investigate emotional behavior in infants. In his book *The Expression of the Emotions in Man and Animals* (1872), he suggested that the emotions of the human newborn are innate. Some years later John Watson and J. J. B. Morgan (1917) modified Darwin's view, arguing that there are only three innate emotions—fear, rage, and love—and that all other emotional reactions are derived from these primary ones through learning. According to this theory, fear could be elicited by pain, an unexpected loud noise, or sudden loss of support; the infant felt rage when immobilized or restrained; and love was a response to stroking and gentle touching. You will recall from Chapter 8 that Watson and Raynor used a sudden loud noise as an unconditioned stimulus in their experiment to condition Little Albert to fear a white rat. Watson and Morgan made a persuasive argument that the responses of rage and love could be conditioned in the same way.

Watson and Morgan's theory was very popular in the 1920s and 1930s, but it is now only of historical interest because investigators were unable to confirm the existence of the basic emotions. An important reason for this failure was that observers rarely agreed on the type of emotional reaction an infant was making unless they knew the stimulus or incident that provoked it. Although an infant who is hungry usually cries, observers who do not know why a hungry baby is crying may call it grief, fear, anger, sleepiness, or some other emotion. When the stimulus *is* known, it usually becomes the entire basis for labeling the emotion. An observer who sees an infant crying when a threat appears to

Figure 12.1

Approximate ages of differentiation of various emotions. Early in development excitement is first differentiated into general positive (delight) and general negative (distress) affects; these emotions are then differentiated into more specific emotional states. (Adapted from Bridges, 1932.)

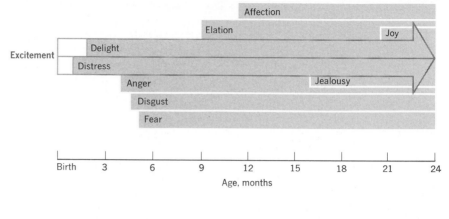

Katharine Banham Bridges determined what emotions children have by observing them day after day for the first two years of life. She theorized that at first some large-scale physiological stimulation induces a large-scale physiological response. By the time the children entered their third year, however, she found them expressing such subtle emotions as anger, envy, jealousy, and disappointment.

be present will almost certainly say that the baby is afraid, although the real reason for crying might be loneliness or hunger.

A theory that competed with Watson and Morgan's and still enjoys some popularity is that of Katharine Bridges (1932). She maintained that infants are born with just one basic emotional reaction, a generalized excitement. As they mature, this excitement is differentiated into delight and distress. These reactions give way in turn to more specific emotional expressions. This process of differentiation continues, and still more specific emotions emerge (Figure 12.1). The general pattern parallels the one we described for cognitive and motor development in Chapter 11.

Smiling

Some time in a baby's first month or two of life it smiles its first smile. Laughter appears later, at about four months of age. It is reasonable to conclude that smiling and laughing have a physiological basis because even children born deaf, dumb, and blind smile and laugh. Experience is also important, however; research has shown that the development of smiling in blind infants is slower than that in sighted children (Freedman, 1964).

The Development of Smiling.   In their development of smiling, babies appear to go through three stages. Soon after birth there is **spontaneous** or **reflex smiling,** which occurs in the absence of appropriate external stimuli. The infant will smile in response to stomach disturbances or to high-pitched voices. In the second stage, which begins between two and eight weeks of age, the infant smiles at visual and social stimuli. In this stage of **nonselective social smiling,** the infant smiles the most readily at human faces. At about five or six months of age, **selective social smiling** begins. Now the infant smiles mostly at familiar faces; unfamiliar faces sometimes make the baby cry.

Theories of Smiling.   How much children smile depends in part on how they are reared. Infants smile more when an adult coos and cuddles and smiles back at them, and their smiles cease if the adult is unresponsive (Brackbill, 1958). These observations suggest that babies smile because they are rewarded for smiling, the principle concept in the **reinforcement theory of smiling.** Jacob Gewirtz (1965) examined the smiling of two- to eighteen-month-old infants raised in three different settings in Israel. One group were with their families. Another group lived in an institution where the babies rarely saw their parents. A third group were kibbutz infants, who stayed in large children's houses with

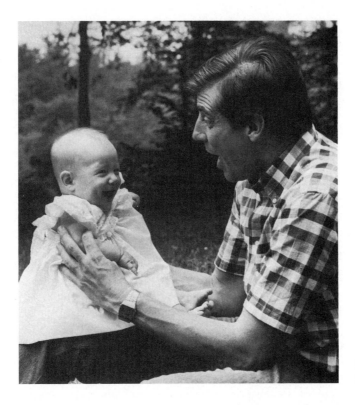

Smiling is universal in human infants and appears to be unlearned.

professional caretakers, but their mothers visited them at feeding times. Gewirtz found that the groups of children varied in how much they smiled at the face of an unfamiliar, unsmiling adult during a two-minute period (Figure 12.2). As they get older, all children showed an increase in smiling, followed by a decline. The children raised in the institution were about a month slower than the others in reaching the peak number of smiles observed, and the later decline was more rapid. The kibbutz children resembled the family-raised children in the early months, but later the number of their smiles was intermediate between those of the institutionalized and family-raised groups. Gewirtz attributed these findings to the children's histories of reinforcement. He suggested that children who live in a family are much more likely to be picked up, fondled, and spoken to when they smile than children in an institution or kibbutz. Because they are

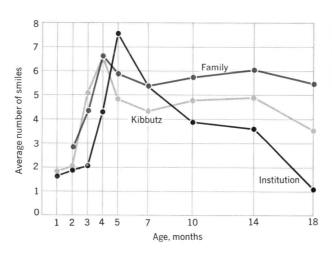

Figure 12.2
The amount of smiling at strangers during a two-minute period by infants reared in three different manners. (Adapted from Gewirtz, 1965.)

rewarded oftener for smiling, these children are likely to smile more than the other children.

The reactions of other people to a child's smile also form the basis of the **evolutionary theory of smiling.** This theory emphasizes the adaptive and survival value of infant smiling (Freedman, Loring, and Martin, 1967). At birth a baby can both cry and smile. Crying has obvious survival value, for it usually gets a parent to feed, cover, burp, or otherwise tend to the baby's bodily needs. But smiling may also have survival value, for parents feel pleasantly rewarded by their baby's smile and are likely to increase the attention they give the smiling infant. Thus the smile, like the cry, assures that the infant's needs will be met, and both responses help to solidify the attachment between parent and child.

The **cognitive theory of smiling** explains smiling as a reflection of an innate joy that children experience when they master cognitive tasks (Shultz and Zigler, 1970). According to this view, the infant finds a new experience puzzling if it does not fit easily into its cognitive framework—if, in Piaget's terms, the baby cannot assimilate the experience. This inability to assimilate the experience means that the infant must accommodate or reconstruct its internal representation of it. Once this is done and the child can assimilate the object, the child is gratified and smiles.

The cognitive theory predicts that a child will take longer to smile at a more complex visual stimulus than at a simpler one. To test this prediction, investigators (Shultz and Zigler, 1970) showed three-month-old infants a clown doll that was either stationary or swinging. The swinging doll was the more complex stimulus, because the contours of a moving object are more difficult to define than those of a stationary object. The prediction of the cognitive theory of smiling was born out. Although the infants smiled at both presentations of the doll, they smiled more quickly when the clown was stationary. That their smiles were preceded by hard cognitive work was reflected in the very quiet and serious way the infants studied the doll before smiling. A similar phenomenon probably explains the amusement we experience when hearing a joke. Certainly a portion of our pleasure derives from our success in using our cognitive abilities to get the point of the joke. For the same reason a joke that we have heard and figured out before never seems as funny in the retelling, and jokes that must be explained to us are never as funny as those we master on our own.

Fear

Watson's view that fear is an innate response to loud noises or to the sudden loss of support is no longer accepted, but many psychologists do continue to feel that there is an innate component to many fears. For example, Donald Hebb (1949) suggested that fear of snakes is a product of maturation rather than of learning. He called attention to the fact that five-year-old children show little fear of a harmless snake, but adolescents recoil in horror. Interestingly, the same pattern is found in chimpanzees; the young do not fear snakes, but adults do.

Learning Fear. Whether or not some fears may be innate, psychologists agree that many fears are learned and that such learning is a form of classical conditioning. For example, pain is a natural stimulus for fear, and people learn to fear things, persons, and events associated with pain. Thus pain from the physician's needle and the dentist's drill can lead to fear of the doctors them-

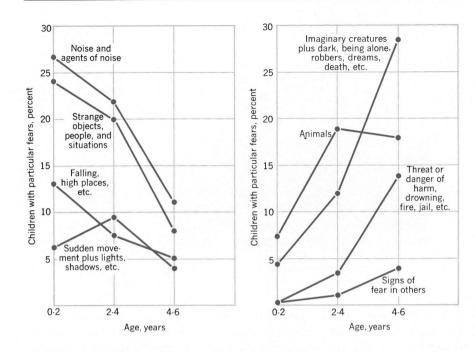

Figure 12.3
Frequency of fears at different ages.
(Adapted from Jersild, 1960.)

selves. Children also acquire fears of things that are not associated with pain. There is evidence, for example, that they learn, presumably by imitation, the fears that their mothers have.

Newborn infants appear to have very few fears, but with age a steadily increasing number of real and imaginary stimuli can frighten a child. The succession of such stimuli reveal increasing levels of cognitive development. At first children tend to fear physical events directly associated with pain. Later on they still fear concrete objects, such as lions and tigers, but the connection of these fears with pain must be indirect, for children have little or no first-hand contact with these animals. Still later children begin to fear intangibles such as failure in school. The increasing and decreasing frequencies of specific fears between birth and six years of age are summarized in Figure 12.3. The finding that brighter children express more fears than their less intelligent age-mates is another indication that children's fears are related to their level of cognitive development.

Fear of Strangers and Separation Anxiety. Two complementary fears that appear toward the end of the baby's first year of life are stranger anxiety and separation anxiety. **Stranger anxiety** is the baby's pronounced negative reaction to a stranger. **Separation anxiety** is the baby's unhappiness, crying, and fretting when a parent or other adult to whom the baby is attached is absent. The developmental course of stranger and separation anxieties has been traced in a study of infants from four to twelve months old (Morgan and Ricciuti, 1969). Each infant was sitting either on its mother's lap or four feet away from her, when a stranger approached. Before eight months of age, the infants cooed, smiled, and were generally positive toward the stranger whether or not they were close to their mothers (Figure 12.4). By twelve months, however, those who were separated from their mothers reacted much more negatively to the stranger than the infants sitting on their mothers' laps.

Figure 12.4

Reaction to strangers. Infants become more afraid of strangers as they grow older, especially when they are not in mother's lap. (From Morgan and Ricciuti, 1969.)

Harriet Rheingold is a leading experimental researcher on attachment. A decade ago she and Carol Eckerman demonstrated that "fear of strangers" was not the common developmental milestone that psychologists had considered it to be.

Many psychologists have considered stranger anxiety a universal phenomenon appearing at a certain age in all children, to be taken as a sign of normal development. This widely accepted view was challenged by Harriet Rheingold and Carol Eckerman (1973). These researchers found that infants between eight and twelve months of age are not always afraid of strangers. The infants in their study repeatedly looked and smiled at the stranger, played peekaboo, and permitted the stranger to hold them, whether or not the mother was present. Rheingold and Eckerman (1970) also found that babies were willing to leave their mothers, even in strange surroundings, to explore a distant empty room. The distinction between voluntary and involuntary separation was important,

When babies are about a year old, they often seem to be afraid of strangers.

however, for children whose mothers were unavailable if they needed them became very distressed and did not explore. This research indicates that stranger and separation anxieties are complex phenomena which appear only under certain conditions. When the reactions do occur, the child may indicate symptoms of considerable stress (page 311).

SUMMARY

During infancy emotional development shows a pattern of increasing differentiation, from a generalized excitement into progressively more precise emotional reactions. Particular emotions, such as smiling and laughing, also have their own developmental courses. Smiling is an important social response, which appears to be universal among human infants. Young babies smile at many different stimuli, but their smiling becomes a specific response to particular people as they mature. The frequency of smiling in infants can be increased by rewarding their smiles. Smiling has a significant cognitive component, for infants and older children smile to express their joy at having mastered a challenging task. Smiling, like crying, may also have survival value for the child.

Some fears may be innate, but many are learned. Children's fears are related to their level of cognitive development. Younger children fear concrete objects and events, especially those associated with pain, whereas older children fear more abstract things such as ghosts and failure in school. The most widely studied fears of infants are separation anxiety and fear of strangers. These appear to be related; infants are more likely to have negative reactions to strangers when separated from their mothers.

INDIVIDUALITY IN DEVELOPMENT

From the time they are born, children differ from one another in many traits, and some of these differences appear to be innate. Because of such inborn differences, even children who are exposed to similar circumstances and child-rearing practices do not turn out to be the same. Moreover, as we shall see, individual children seem to invite social experiences that affect their development in particular ways. As Piaget said of children's cognitive growth, youngsters appear to play an active role in bringing about their own social and emotional development.

Temperamental Styles

Although newborn babies may look alike to the unpracticed eye, they differ greatly in general activity level, sensitivity to external stimuli, social responsiveness, and sleeping and feeding patterns. Many of these individual characteristics seem to persist as the infant grows older. Alexander Thomas, Stella Chess, and Herbert Birch (Thomas and Chess, 1977; Thomas, Chess, and Birch, 1968) have identified some of these persistent traits which constitute an individual's **temperament** or **temperamental style.**

In a major longitudinal study these investigators observed children from infancy through adolescence, in an effort to determine the relation between temperament and mental health. They identified three types of temperament in infants, although many babies were not of a pure type. The majority had the temperament of the **easy child,** a pleasant mood, regular patterns of hunger, sleeping, and excretion, and little fear of new objects or persons. The intensity of their responses was generally low or moderate. A second group of children were **slow to warm up.** These children had a slightly negative mood and were wary of new situations and of strangers. They were somewhat variable in biological functions, and the intensity of their responses was generally low. About one in ten babies was a **difficult child,** who often became the tyrant of the household. These children had irregular feeding and sleeping patterns and were slow in accepting new foods or in adjusting to new routines and activities. They tended to cry often and quite loudly; they seemed generally unhappy, unfriendly, and unpleasant; frustration usually sent them into a tantrum.

These three temperamental styles appeared to be unrelated to sex or intelligence, but they were associated with the development of behavioral problems in childhood or adolescence. Only 18 percent of the easy children developed behavioral problems judged serious enough to warrant psychiatric attention, whereas 40 percent of the slow-to-warm-up children and 70 percent of the difficult children needed such help in later years.

Origins of Temperament

What accounts for the differences in temperament of children? Why is one baby a gurgling smiler who sleeps soundly and eats with gusto and another— equally loved and cared for—a cautious, easily frightened crank who sleeps fitfully and rejects virtually every new food, toy, face, and game? Evidence that inheritance may help determine temperamental style was obtained by a Norwegian investigator, A. M. Torgersen (cited in Segal and Yahraes, 1978), who found that identical twins were more likely to have similar temperaments than fraternal twins. Research by Arnold Sameroff and Melvin Zax (Sameroff, 1977; Sameroff and Zax, 1973) has suggested that temperament may be fashioned by physiological and chemical influences on the brain as it develops before birth. These investigators interviewed women in their later months of pregnancy and then studied their children soon after birth and at four, twelve, and thirty months of age, using a variety of neurological and psychological tests. Many of the children who were labeled difficult at four months of age had mothers who had suffered high levels of anxiety in late pregnancy. Difficult children were also more likely to have many siblings, to be black, and to be of low socioeconomic status. The quality of a mother's health and nutrition is affected by all these sociological factors. Poor, black women with many previous pregnancies are more likely to be less healthy and less well nourished than white, middle-class women. The mother's health and nutrition are known to affect—quite strongly—the developing fetus and the baby during the first few months of life.

Implications of Temperamental Differences

These temperamental differences observed in early infancy imply that behavior patterns once thought to be the outcome of poor child-rearing practices may actually be constitutional traits of the child.

A child who stands at the periphery of the group in nursery school may be anxious and insecure, but he may also be expressing his normal temperamental tendency to warm up slowly. An infant with irregular sleep cycles who cries loudly at night may possibly be responding to a hostile, rejecting mother, but he may also be expressing his temperamental irregularity. A six-year-old who explodes with anger at his teacher's commands may be aggressive and oppositional, but he may also be showing the frustration reactions of a very persistent child when he is asked to terminate an activity in which he is deeply absorbed. A mother's guilt and anxiety may be the result of a deep-seated neurosis, but they may also be the result of her problems and confusion in handling an infant with a temperamental pattern [of] a very difficult child (Thomas, Chess, and Birch, 1968, p. 191).

Such reasoning suggests that by knowing and understanding a child's temperament, parents may be better able to guide the development of their child. For example, parents who have slow-to-warm-up children can learn not to pressure them to accept new situations immediately, for this pressure may only strengthen the fears and tendencies to withdraw of these already wary children. Parents are more likely to succeed if they sensitively and slowly encourage such children to try new things and experiences. Mishandled, a slow-to-warm-up child may turn out like a boy named Bobby. Whenever Bobby rejected new food, his parents never again gave it to him; because he shied away from the kids at the playground, they kept him at home. At the age of ten, Bobby had no friends and ate only hamburgers, applesauce, and medium-boiled eggs (Segal and Yahraes, 1978).

Difficult children need very special handling. They appear to do best under a kind, consistent, and firm regime. Permissiveness seems to be the wrong strategy, often allowing the child to become a "holy terror." Parents of difficult children must learn to grit their teeth and sometimes to ignore the crying, for continually placating difficult children only teaches them that they can get anything they want by howling. With proper handling difficult children improve as they grow older; they can develop into positive and charming individuals.

How parents and others react to a child's temperament has many important consequences for the child's development. As we have already noted, Thomas, Chess, and Birch found that difficult babies are more likely than others to develop behavior problems later on. The reason for this may not reside in the children's temperaments per se, but rather in the type of interactions difficult children typically have with their parents and other people. A child who is difficult to manage, whose every waking hour is a battle, who tries the patience of everyone is very likely to drain the resources of an entire family. The parents' responses to a difficult child may become as negative as the child's behavior. Thus a vicious circle begins. As the parents scold, frustrate, ignore, or spank their child, the child grows ever more difficult. And the difficult baby turns into a child with serious behavior problems in school, on the playground, and elsewhere.

An example of this kind of vicious circle has been described by Arnold Sameroff. In his longitudinal study Sameroff found that children having difficult temperaments at four months of age were the most likely to obtain low scores on an infant "intelligence" test at thirty months. Although this finding might indicate that temperament and intelligence have a common genetic basis, it is more likely that the two are linked behaviorally. Sameroff observed children and their mothers at home when the children were twelve months old. He found that the mothers of difficult children tended to avoid them more and to look at, stimulate, and play with them less than did mothers of other children. Children whose mothers spent a great deal of time in social interactions with them had higher intelligence test scores at thirty months of age. Apparently the child with a difficult temperament may "turn off" the mother, so that she, in turn, may not engage the child in playful and stimulating interactions. A mother's lack of attention may then depress the child's intellectual functioning.

SUMMARY

Temperamental differences in infants affect both how they are likely to be treated by caretakers and how they are likely to respond. One classification of infants' temperaments includes the three categories of "easy," "slow to warm up," and "difficult." These differences may stem from genetic factors, from prenatal physiological and chemical influences, or from environmental conditions during the infant's first few months of life. Probably all these influences contribute. Studies of these three types of temperament suggest that parents would benefit from recognizing their children's temperamental styles and tailoring their child-rearing practices to them. Not only can parents' behavior affect the child, but the opposite is also true. Children, to some degree, control the behavior of their parents. In this way children play an active role in their own personality development.

THE NATURE OF SOCIAL ATTACHMENTS

One striking characteristic of human infants is their desire to be close to other human beings. Babies enjoy physical contact with and attention from other people and become unhappy when they cannot be near them. This cluster of behaviors is what psychologists call **attachment.** Probably no process is more important to later development than infants' attachments to their primary caretakers, typically in our society their mothers.

The Formation of Attachments

Psychologists' views of how infants form attachments have been changing in recent years. An earlier view, based on learning theory, held that an infant becomes emotionally attached to the mother because she is a source of relief from discomfort or pain. The mother is originally a neutral stimulus for her child, but after repeated pairings with pleasurable events such as feedings, she becomes a *secondary reinforcer* (Chapter 8); that is, she takes on rewarding properties and becomes a desired object.

A later view, advanced by the British psychoanalyst John Bowlby (1969), is that attachment is an innate response which serves to protect the young from predators. Consistent with ethological thought (Chapter 9), Bowlby believes that infants seek contact with their mothers, especially when they are frightened, in order to elicit protective responses from their mothers. Bowlby believes that punishing attachment behavior does not extinguish it but actually intensifies it. Punishment is itself a threat, and it inclines the infant to attach itself to the mother.

H. Rudolph Schaffer and Peggy Emerson (1964) have also suggested that infants have an innate need to be near other people. They studied the development of attachment in a group of human infants from the early weeks of life to the age of eighteen months, measuring attachment by the infants' reactions to common types of separation, such as being left alone in a room. They found striking individual differences in the age at which attachments developed and in their intensity. Some babies focused their attachment on one person; others were attached to several people. The mother's responsiveness to the child's crying and the amount of interaction she initiated with the child were found to be related to the child's attachment, but the mother's general availability, defined by the amount of time she spent with the child, was not.

Schaffer and Emerson's work refutes the idea, drawn from learning theory, that infants form attachments to the person who relieves their hunger and pain. In 39 percent of the cases, the principal object of attachment was not the person primarily responsible for the infant's feeding and care; in 22 percent of the cases, the person did not participate even to a minor degree in the child's physical care. What seemed to determine the infant's choice was the amount of stimulation and attention the adult provided, not the adult's association with satisfaction of physical needs.

Infants' striving for nearness to other people has no single preferred form. It appears in many patterns which differ from child to child and from one developmental level to the next. Mary Ainsworth and Silvia Bell (1973) described three different kinds of attachment that children can have with their mothers. When babies were reunited with their mothers after a brief separation, the majority of them wanted to be close to their mothers. Ainsworth and Bell interpreted this response to mean that the child had a *secure* attachment to its mother. Another group were *ambivalent* in their attachment; they sought contact but at the same time resisted it. A third group, called *avoidant,* sometimes did not seek contact with the mother upon her return or, if they did, they then turned and looked away from her. It may be that this last reaction is the common one after long periods of separation (page 312), and that, depending on the duration of separation, children will show any of these responses when they are reunited with their mothers.

This brings up the issue of the mother's attachment to her child. Marshall Klaus and his colleagues (1972) studied the impact of mother-child contact soon after birth. Some mothers were allowed an extra sixteen hours of contact with their babies during their maternity stay in the hospital. A control group of women with similar backgrounds were permitted contact only for the brief periods then customary in many hospitals. The findings were remarkable. One month later the mothers who had been allowed the extra contact stayed closer to their infants, soothed them more often during a physical examination, fondled them more, and engaged in more eye contact. Similar results were found at one, two, and five years. The results of this study suggest that even the relatively short periods of separation that take place after normal births may be detrimental to the attachment between mother and child. On the basis of these findings, the investigators offered an intriguing hypothesis concerning the high percentage of premature infants who fail to thrive or are later battered by their parents. Because premature babies typically require prolonged medical treatment from the moment of birth, they are often kept in incubators and their mothers have no contact with them for long periods of time. Through this long early separation the mother may fail to develop an attachment to her premature infant.

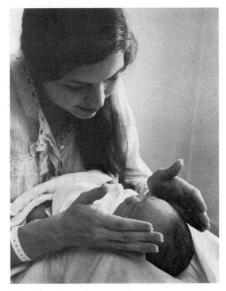

The attention that mother gives her baby and the stimulation she provides are the basis of the attachment between them.

Importance of Attachment for Later Development

Attachment between parent and child may be as vital to the child's survival as food or protection from bodily harm. One study of institutionalized infants has shown that, even when their physical needs are met, infants become markedly disturbed unless there is someone available with whom they can develop a warm and secure relationship. René Spitz (1972) examined infants in institutions and found that those who received good physical care but no sustained personal contact or perceptual stimulation suffered definite ill effects, including depression and withdrawal, susceptibility to illness, and retarded development. Longer-term effects of the lack of attachment in infancy may be to impair the formation of social bonds later in life.

The process of attachment also has important implications for *detachment,* the child's becoming an autonomous human being who can get along without the parents. Unless an infant forms a secure attachment, he or she cannot develop the trust and confidence necessary to go on to the next stage of development.[1] Overt indications of attachment usually become fewer when infants start to engage in another basic human activity, the exploration of their surroundings. In these explorations a child frequently encounters objects and situations that are simultaneously interesting and frightening. Exploration therefore requires that the child have a sense of safety, a self-confidence that only a secure attachment to a caretaker can foster.

The role that attachment plays in encouraging successful exploration was demonstrated in the Rheingold and Eckerman study (1970) mentioned earlier. When infants were placed alone in a room with strange objects, they appeared insecure and frightened. Often they remained immobile and did little exploring. When their mothers were present, however, they felt confident enough to wander rather far afield and examine strange objects, returning afterward to their mothers as a base of security. Infants who felt a secure attachment would then venture forth again to explore at ever greater distances before returning to their mothers for reassurance. In contrast, children without a secure attachment often protested loudly when their mothers put them down and did not readily go off into independent activity. Thus children's independence, revealed by their willingness to explore, appears definitely to be related to the quality of the mother-child attachment and to the degree of trust children have developed.

SUMMARY

Many theorists believe that an infant's attachment behavior is an innate response. Babies typically develop attachment relationships with their most significant caretaker, but studies show clearly that strong attachments can be formed even to someone who does not satisfy the infant's basic physical needs. Infants whose mothers are not responsive may not develop secure attachments. They may become ambivalent or avoidant in their relations with their mothers. There is some evidence that early contact between mother and child soon after birth may promote a mother's attachment to her infant.

Infants who are unable to develop such relationships may suffer severe developmental disturbances, even when their physical care is adequate. A trusting relationship with a caretaker can provide the emotional security a child needs to be able to explore strange surroundings and eventually to become an autonomous individual, a process called detachment. Infants with insecure attachments remain dependent and fearful in novel situations.

CHILD-REARING PRACTICES

Parents have long sought the advice of experts to aid them with the job of child rearing, and the experts have been more than ready to respond, always claiming their advice to be based on the most advanced scientific information of the day. Each historical shift in expert advice has been accompanied by assurances that, if only parents follow the prescription, their child will grow up to become the wholesome person they so avidly hope for. It is difficult to believe that parents in the 1920s and 1930s took seriously the advice of John Watson:

[1] See the discussion of Erik Erikson's theory of personality development in Chapter 15.

There is a sensible way of treating children. Treat them as though they were young adults. Dress them, bathe them with care and circumspection. Let your behavior always be objective and kindly firm. Never hug and kiss them, never let them sit in your lap. If you must, kiss them once on the forehead when they say good night. Shake hands with them in the morning. Give them a pat on the head if they have made an extraordinarily good job of a difficult task. Try it out. In a week's time you will find how easy it is to be perfectly objective with your child and at the same time kindly. You will be utterly ashamed of the mawkish, sentimental way you have been handling it (1928, pp. 81–82).

Only twenty years later mothers were being urged to fondle and play with their children and to allow the infants themselves to initiate feeding, weaning, and toilet training, lest parental mismanagement leave indelible scars on a child's developing personality. Ideas on child rearing can change this radically within a generation because our theories about social development often far outrun their empirical foundations.

Styles of Parenting

Whatever the advice put forth by the experts of the day, parents translate their love and concern for their children into very different styles of parenting, especially when it comes to guiding and controlling their children's behavior. In 1964 Wesley Becker evaluated the effects of different parental styles on children's development. He divided parents' disciplinary techniques into two broad categories, **love-oriented** and **power-assertive.** The first category included praising and reasoning with the child as well as temporarily withdrawing love and separating the child from the parent. The second category contained all the methods involving physical punishment. Becker reported that children whose parents used love-oriented techniques were more likely to be cooperative, to feel responsible for their actions, and to have appropriate feelings of guilt. Children whose parents asserted power tended to be uncooperative and aggressive.

More recently, Diana Baumrind (1975) has reported her findings from an eight-year longitudinal study of 150 nursery school children and their families. Instead of styles of discipline, Baumrind identified three types of parent: the **authoritarian parent,** who "values obedience as a virtue and . . . believes in restricting the child's autonomy"; the **permissive parent,** who seeks "to give the child as much freedom as is consistent with the child's physical survival"; and the **authoritative parent,** who "attempts to direct the child's activities in a rational, issue-oriented manner." Baumrind found the authoritative parents to be the most effective of the three types of parents. Their children seemed the most socially responsible, independent, oriented toward success, and vigorous. Baumrind also found that corporal punishment—the kind of nonbrutal physical punishment that a parent metes out in response to behavior the child knows is not acceptable—does not inevitably lead to psychological damage. In fact, the authoritative parents who were the most effective preferred physical punishment over other negative sanctions. On the basis of her own and other research in this area, Baumrind recommended most of the same rules for making punishment an effective tool of discipline that we outlined in Chapter 9. (1) Punishment should be given as soon as possible after the undesirable behavior; (2) it should be consistent and unavoidable; and (3) it should be accompanied by an explanation of why the behavior is unacceptable and what behavior would be more desirable.

Is Mother Essential?

Today, when over half the American mothers with school-age children, and about one-third of those with children under age six work outside the home, the question of whether a mother's continuous care is indispensable for her child's normal development is one of great urgency. According to Helen Bee (1974), who reviewed the research related to this question, children of working mothers suffer only if there is instability in the family or in the child care arrangements. For example, boys from unstable families are more likely to be delinquent if their mothers work, but the sons of working mothers in stable families are no more likely than other boys to be delinquent. Unstable substitute care may also make children more dependent and anxious about being separated from their mothers, whereas stable substitute care does not have these effects.

The consequences of having a mother who works seem to differ according to the sex of the child. According to a review by Urie Bronfenbrenner and Anne Crouter (1981), working mothers appear to have a beneficial effect on their daughters, who come to admire their mothers more, to have a more positive conception of the female role, and to be more independent than the daughters of women who do not hold outside jobs. The effects on sons are less clear, but the evidence suggests that they are more negative than they are for daughters.

Bronfenbrenner and Crouter pointed to several factors that may influence how a mother's employment can affect her children. One is the mother's attitude toward working. Children fare best when their mothers are satisfied with their life situation and feel that they are doing what is best for themselves and their children, whether that be working or remaining at home. Only a few studies have compared part-time and full-time working mothers, and most of these have concerned consequences for adolescent children. These studies indicated that the part-time work of mothers had a positive effect on their adolescent children, probably because the pattern of their availability met their children's needs for both dependence and independence.

According to Bronfenbrenner and Crouter, the most important factor determining how a mother's work affects her children is the nature of the mother-child relationship. For example, some working mothers may compensate for their absence by setting aside time to be with their children. Mothers who do so may develop a better relationship with their children than they would if they were not working. In these families the mother's working benefits her children.

Exclusive Mothering versus Substitute Care.   The effects of a mother's employment depend in part on the quality of the substitute care the child receives in her absence. One of the most extensive studies of the long-term consequences of exclusive mothering versus substitute care was conducted by Terence Moore in England (1975). To determine the effects of one type of care or the other on later personality development, Moore studied the records of children whose behavior and personality had been assessed at ages up to fifteen years. Children in an exclusive-mothering group had received full-time care from their mothers up to the age of five. Those in a diffuse-mothering (substitute care) group had spent at least twenty-five hours per week apart from their mothers for at least one year before the age of five. On the average, the substitute care began at 2.6 years and lasted approximately two years. All the children came from intact homes, and the two groups were matched on several dimensions including IQ at three years of age. Moore found few differences between girls who had experienced the two types of mothering. For boys, those who had diffuse mothering were somewhat more active, aggressive, independent, and relatively free from fear. They were also less likely to study for school examinations and more likely to drop out of school than the boys who had exclusive mothering. In contrast, boys who had exclusive mothering were anxious for adult approval and not very assertive. They were more conforming to adult standards than the boys in the diffuse-mothering group. Moore's study suggests that children, particularly boys, who have mothers providing full-time care tend to internalize adult standards of behavior, especially in regard to self-control and scholastic achievement. Children in substitute care, on the other hand, tend to be less concerned with adult approval and more interested in approval from peers.

The Effects of Day Care.   The effects on children of the substitute care received in day-care centers are difficult to assess. One problem is that day-care conditions are so varied. A day-care center may be an institution with large groups of children and large numbers of caregivers, or a single child or a few children may stay at the home of a neighbor or relative. In terms of quality, there are some superb centers with well-trained staffs and ample facilities; others are understaffed and ill-equipped places where children have been left mesmerized before television sets or even tied to chairs. Family day care also ranges in quality, from the most desirable and homelike to the most horrifying. In some arrangements ill-trained "caregivers" neglect and even abuse the children in their charge. A further problem in assessing day care is that even under the best conditions the various types of day care have different effects on different children, depending on such factors as the child's age, temperament, relationship with parents, and prior experiences with substitute care.

A particularly important concern about day care today is that it may interfere with children's attachments to their parents. Research suggests that there is little reason to worry about such consequences. In a recent review of the findings of many studies, Michael Rutter (1981a) reported that children develop primary bonds with their parents and form them in similar ways and at similar times, whether they are at home or in day care. For example, babies raised by nurses in kibbutzim in Israel develop attachments to their mothers even though they spend relatively little time with them. Rutter concluded that day care need not have adverse effects if it offers sufficient contact with adults, cognitive stimulation, and opportunity for play. In fact, spending more time with peers and becoming attached to supplementary caregivers as well as to parents are potential benefits of day care. Psychologists cannot yet be definite about the long-term effects of day care. Their present knowledge indicates that it is important for children to receive day care from well-trained caregivers in centers that have a high proportion of adults to children and that offer supportive social and physical activities.

Role of the Father

Studies of parental influences on social development have given little attention to the role of the father. Most of these studies have emphasized early infancy, a time when fathers have until recently played a relatively minor role. It has also been difficult to secure fathers as research participants. Despite these problems, the accumulated evidence indicates that the father's personality and behavior are no less important than the mother's to the social and emotional development of their child.

The baby opens his mouth wide for spoonfuls of food given him by Dad. His father's patience, attentiveness, and other personality traits will affect his development as much as the personality traits of Mom.

The research of Michael Lamb (1977a, b) and his colleagues has shown that children develop attachment relationships with their fathers as well as with their mothers. These workers also found that a father's interactions with his children are qualitatively different from a mother's. For example, fathers hold their babies to play with them, whereas mothers hold them for caretaking. Fathers play more physically stimulating games than mothers. These father-child interactions, which differ from mother-child interactions, broaden the scope of children's social experiences in unique ways.

The importance of the father was clearly established in a study that compared the attitudes of parents whose children were well adjusted with those whose children had problems of adjustment (Peterson et al., 1959). The investigators were surprised to discover that both the mothers and the fathers of children with adjustment problems were themselves less well adjusted, less friendly, and less democratic than parents of the well-adjusted children. The maladjusted children whose problem was unacceptable aggressiveness tended to have weak and ineffectual fathers. Children who were shy and felt inferior tended to have fathers who were dictatorial and unconcerned about their children. These findings indicate that how a father treats his child is quite important in determining not only whether the child will become maladjusted but what form the maladjustment will take.

The largest body of research involving fathers has examined how their presence or absence affects children's personality development. Boys from fatherless homes have been found to be less well adjusted and less skillful in peer relations than boys whose fathers are regularly at home. The usual explanation given is that the boy without a father lacks a masculine model with whom to identify. Normally children develop their **sexual identification**—the interests, attitudes, and behavior appropriate to their sex—by imitating or modeling the behavior of the same-sex parent. If the father is not present, a boy has difficulty in forming a strong and appropriate sexual identification. Boys without fathers tend to be less masculine, although at times some of them behave in an overly masculine manner and at other times in a highly feminine manner (Biller, 1970). Some boys from fatherless homes do not learn how to be appropriately aggressive, thinking that masculinity consists of constant aggression toward others.

This may explain the relation discovered between father absence and juvenile delinquency. Sheldon and Eleanor Glueck (1950), for example, found that more than 40 percent of the adolescent delinquent boys they studied came from fatherless homes, as compared with fewer than 25 percent of the boys in a group of nondelinquents.

In many of the fatherless homes studied, family discord was the reason why the father had left home and abandoned his family. An analysis by Rutter (1971) suggests that parental conflict and disharmony play an essential role in causing antisocial behavior in boys from families without fathers. Rutter noted that, in comparison with boys from unbroken homes, delinquency is twice as frequent in those whose fathers are absent because of divorce. Boys whose fathers have died, however, are no more frequently delinquent than their peers with fathers.

The effect of a father's absence on girls has also been studied. E. Mavis Hetherington (1972) found that adolescent girls growing up without fathers had difficulties in heterosexual behavior. Those whose fathers had died tended to be shy around males and were anxious about sex. Girls whose fathers had divorced or deserted their mothers, on the other hand, tended to be promiscuous or inappropriately assertive in their relations with men.

However negative the consequences of a father's absence may be on a child, the father's presence alone does not guarantee the child's optimal development. The quality of the father-child relationship is also very important. Mark Reuter and Henry Biller (1973) gave college men a questionnaire concerning their relationships with their fathers and then looked at these students' personality adjustments. They found that those who were well adjusted remembered their fathers as either highly nurturant and at least moderately available or only moderately nurturant and very much available. Men who were insecure tended to remember their fathers either as at home a great deal and not paying much attention to them or seldom at home but highly nurturant.

At a time when rising divorce rates and the demands of work are making fathers less available to their children, this body of research has some practical social implications. The father is not merely an economic necessity to his children but a psychological one as well. Divorced fathers should be encouraged to spend more time with their children. It is also important to help young boys to value their future role as fathers. They should be taught that fatherhood is no less important than motherhood and that their warm and supportive presence can do much to promote the psychological well-being of their children.

In her research on the young girl's need for her father, E. Mavis Hetherington studied three groups of thirteen- to seventeen-year-olds from working-class families. The girls in one group had grown up in intact families; those in the other two had no brothers and had lost their fathers before the age of five through death or divorce. At school dances the daughters of divorceé gathered near the stag line. Some painfully shy daughters of widows remained in the ladies' room about 90 percent of the time.

SUMMARY

Advice on how to rear children has changed drastically over the years, but it appears that parents' attitudes rather than their practices shape the child's development. Parental disciplinary techniques have been identified as love-oriented or power-assertive; parents themselves have been described as authoritarian, permissive, or authoritative in guiding their children. Love-oriented authoritative parents are probably the most effective. Punishment has been found to be a useful method of discipline, but only when it is used in accordance with rules that eliminate its destructive quality. Punishment should be immediate and given along with advice about more appropriate behavior.

Evidence is accumulating that children can thrive despite temporary absences from their mothers, provided they have a stable relationship with warm and attentive adults. How the mother's employment affects children depends on the stability of the home, the type of substitute care that children receive, the mother's attitude toward her work, the nature of the mother-child relationship, and the amount of time the mother spends working. The age and gender of the children are often factors to consider; maternal employment may be less detrimental to daughters than to sons. The quality of the day care children experience largely determines whether substitute care will have ill or beneficial effects.

Investigators have paid more attention to the attitudes and behavior of mothers than of fathers. Fathers can broaden their children's range of social experiences by playing with them more often and in a more physical way than their mothers do. A father's availability and way of interacting with his child are related to whether the child becomes maladjusted and in what way. A father's absence from the home can affect both sons and daughters. Boys from fatherless homes are more likely than other boys to be juvenile delinquents, but familial discord rather than the father's absence may be the root cause. Daughters without fathers may develop problems related to their sexuality.

OTHER INFLUENCES IN SOCIALIZATION

Although parents' influences on their children's development may be particularly significant, many other forces contribute to the socialization process. **Socialization** is inculcating in children the values of the culture to which they belong. As children grow older, the people they encounter—teachers, other adults, friends—become increasingly influential as agents of socialization. Children also learn social behavior through their own experiences in play and by what they observe on television.

The Influence of Peers and Play

As children grow up and spend greater amounts of time with their friends, the importance of acceptance in the peer group grows, and interactions with peers become a major source of social learning. Studies show that children's aggressive, altruistic, competitive, and moral behaviors, to name a few, are all influenced by peers. At a minimum, the influence of peers supplements that of parents and other adults. It has been suggested, however, that peers may be even more effective agents of socialization because their ideas about acceptable behavior are less flexible than those of adults (Kohlberg, 1966, 1969). For example, children in the process of developing sex roles may be less tolerant of nontraditional sex-role behavior in play than their parents would be.

When children play with friends their own age, they engage in interactions with their social equals, something that is impossible in their relationships with bigger and more powerful adults (Hartup, 1978; Mueller and Vandell, 1979). This equality of status may have a special significance for children's development of social competence. Children also play together in ways that are different from how they play with adults. For example, children slip easily into fantasy play, but most adults have lost the ability to abandon reality. Children are willing to play the same game repeatedly, strengthening each player's competence, whereas adults often get bored after the first few rounds. In ways such as these, relationships with friends expand the child's horizons and encourage the development of new social behavior. Children who are isolated from their peers may be unable to make friends or to initiate and maintain social interactions.

Whether they play alone, with peers, or with adults, play is one way in which children participate in their own socialization. Through play children learn about the environment, how to get along with others, and how to use their imagina-

The play of young children slips easily into fantasy and sessions of pretend.

tions. Dorothy and Jerome Singer (1977) have suggested that children's play fosters the development of self-awareness, a sense of control over the environment, verbal skill, emotional awareness, a sensitivity to the social roles they are expected to play, and the ability to explore new situations.

Children's play follows a characteristic pattern of development from reality-based and self-centered to symbolic and socially oriented. Greta Fein (1978) has described this progression. She notes that children's earliest play is exploratory and manipulative. Infants learn about their surroundings by such activities as touching, banging, and throwing the objects that are around them. At about fifteen to eighteen months of age, play begins to be more symbolic, and children use objects for pretend purposes, such as eating from an empty spoon. By thirty months of age, the pretend activities have become more elaborate; dolls may be fed, dressed, and spanked. With development the need for play activities to resemble real life gradually decreases. **Sociodramatic play,** that is, play about social situations, begins about age three; by five it has become a complex system of improvisation and plot. Of course, children as young as two or three create pretend social exchanges over which they have control, and it is not uncommon for a four-year-old to create an imaginary companion with whom to talk, play, and give orders. True play with others, in which children interact with one another, cannot begin until development takes the child out of the self-centered stage described by Piaget. For example, toddlers may play *next* to each other but not *with* each other, a far cry from school-age buddies who must do *everything* together.

Television

Many children spend so much time watching television that its influence has become a subject of national concern. The focus of the concern is the violence seen on television. Violence is a dominant theme in programs generally, but children's programs often contain more violence than adult programs do. Most children's cartoon programs, for example, contain violent episodes. Although we know that television violence influences children's behavior, the extent of this influence is not altogether clear. Research has demonstrated that children who watch violent shows are more likely than nonviewers to play and act aggressively. Similarly, children who had watched more violence on television in the elementary school years engaged in more aggressive behavior as adolescents than those who had watched less (Murray and Lonnborg, 1980).

Other concerns about children and television are, first, that children may neglect important tasks of childhood. Children who sit in front of the television for hours and hours each day are not exercising, not playing, and not developing the cognitive, physical, and social skills that they normally should in childhood. The second concern is that television may have a bad effect on attitudes and values. Children have no direct experience with the subjects that they see on television, and there is reason to fear that they may come to expect real life to be as it is on the screen. Moreover, television's stereotyped portrayal of sex roles and of ethnic and socioeconomic groups may lay foundations for sexist and racist prejudices.

But television can also have very positive effects. It can be used to spark interest and to teach children about people and their surroundings; it can aid language development; and it can foster a wide range of interests and knowledge. When parents limit the time their children spend watching television, monitor the shows their children see, and watch along with them, the much maligned television set can become a powerful educational tool.

SUMMARY

Many sources besides parents are important in socialization; children's contact with peers is one of the most crucial. Peers supplement adult influences by reinforcing appropriate behavior; they also provide opportunities for children to interact with their equals. Children who do not have contact with peers may have difficulty later with social interactions.

Play, whether alone, with peers, or with adults, is an important way for children to explore physical and social environments, to try out social roles, and to use their imaginations. Play shows a developmental progression from the concrete and physical to the symbolic and socially oriented. Even in their solitary play children gradually introduce social interactions and often create imaginary playmates.

Television can have a profound influence on children's behavior and development. Watching violence can lead some children to aggressive behavior. Since children do not have the backlog of experiences that adults do, they are especially vulnerable to television's stereotyped portrayal of groups of people. Too much time with television also takes time from other important activities of childhood. But television can be a powerful educational tool, particularly when parents watch with their children and discuss what is likely to alarm or confuse them.

CULTURAL INFLUENCES IN SOCIALIZATION

Sometimes parents transmit cultural values to their children quite consciously. Chinese parents begin training children in the sayings of respected figures very early in life. More often, however, parents have no awareness of the extent to which culture determines their child-rearing behavior. They teach certain values and engage in certain practices simply because "that is the way that one raises children."

Economic Influences

Child-rearing practices often grow out of the economic needs of a culture and are unconsciously directed at producing adults who can fulfill that culture's requirements. How the economy affects child rearing can be seen in the results of a worldwide study of more than a hundred societies, categorized according to how much their economies depended on accumulations of food (Barry, Child, and Bacon, 1959). Societies that accumulate large amounts of food, such as those practicing agriculture and animal husbandry, were found to put strong pressure on their children to be responsible, obedient, and compliant. In contrast, societies that accumulate little food, such as those relying on hunting and fishing, emphasized achievement, self-reliance, independence, and assertiveness. These findings indicate that economies encourage the child-rearing practices that provide training in the motives and behavior necessary to carry out expected adult roles. If members of a herding society, for example, raised their children to be assertive rather than compliant, as adults they might not have the patience and cooperative attitude required for tending crops and livestock. On the other hand, societies that engage primarily in hunting and fishing need adult members who are resourceful in obtaining food, so they teach their children to be individualistic, assertive, and venturesome. The chosen child-rearing practices are deeply ingrained in social norms, having evolved gradually through many generations. People use them automatically and without awareness of the fact that the way they treat their children serves the purposes of their culture.

American parents seem to foster personality characteristics in their children appropriate to the niche they will probably fill in the economy. Daniel Miller and Guy Swanson (1958) divided all occupations in the United States into two major categories, **entrepreneurial** and **bureaucratic.** Entrepreneurial occupations are those in which rewards are based solely on the individual's own performance. Small-business owners and salespeople whose salaries consist entirely of their commissions are examples. Success in these occupations depends on risk taking and competition. It should be noted that entrepreneurial occupations cut across conventional socioeconomic and class lines. An entrepreneur could be a wealthy lawyer or a small-scale gardener who sells door-to-door and earns only a subsistence income.

In large organizations employing many kinds of workers, the positions are bureaucratic. Incomes are in the form of salaries or wages, and rewards are based on specialized abilities. These bureaucratic positions offer employees a degree of security that is not available to the entrepreneurs, and working with and getting along with others are extremely important. Bureaucratic occupations can also cut across class and economic boundaries. A bureaucrat might be the vice-president of a large bank, a teller in the same bank, or the janitor.

Miller and Swanson suggested that parents socialize their children to have the traits that they will need if they go into the parents' occupations. Thus entrepreneurial families tend to adopt child-rearing practices that promote the development of self-control and independence. They are likely to be more severe than other families in toilet training, and they deal with transgressions through appeals to the child's conscience, attempting by both means to develop internal restraints. The economically more secure atmosphere of the bureaucratic family favors child-rearing practices that are less severe and stress the child's ability to get along with others and to be considerate. Because bureaucratic families depend on rewards and punishments that flow from sources outside of themselves, they tend to employ more external controls, such as spanking, in punishing misbehavior.

Additional evidence on how economic outlook and child rearing are related comes from a study of over 300 adolescent boys (Berkowitz and Friedman, 1967). On a task requiring cooperation, boys from entrepreneurial homes were found to give help only to the degree that they themselves had received help from their work partners. Boys from bureaucratic families helped their partners no matter how little assistance they had received. The entrepreneurial boys employed a philosophy of "Scratch my back, and I'll scratch yours," whereas the bureaucratic boys were organizationally oriented and more willing to help others in order to get the job completed.

Effects of Poverty

Many myths surround the poor. In particular, the poor tend to be viewed as homogeneous, and the diversity among them is usually ignored. Eleanor Pavenstedt (1965), a child psychiatrist, demonstrated the importance of distinguishing different subtypes of poverty in discussions of child-rearing practices. She conducted intensive clinical studies of two subgroups in a poor urban population. In one impoverished group the family structure tended to be disorganized. Marital separation, divorce, desertion, and neglect of the children were common. The households of many of these families were chaotic. The youngest child was often found in a crib in a back room, untended and unchanged, crying and unheeded by the mother. There were no set patterns for eating, dressing, bathing, or other daily activities. The mother might be away from home for hours, leaving a four- or five-year-old in charge of an infant. Many of the children owned nothing that they could call their own, and a gift made to one child could be appropriated immediately by a sibling. If one child did something wrong, another child might be punished for the misdeed.

When the children from these disorganized families entered nursery school, they tended to conceal their emotions, turning away when frustrated or angry. They often failed to discriminate one adult from another and could not sustain relationships with them. Few learned their teachers' names. They did not try to solve problems; they rarely asked questions; they could not carry over what they had learned from one day to the next.

> The saddest, and to us the outstanding characteristic of this group . . . was the self-devaluation. One little boy, when encouraged by the teacher to have her put his name on his drawing, wanted her to write "shitty Billy." Their lack of confidence in their ability to master was painfully reenacted with each new encounter (1965, p. 96).

In striking contrast, Pavenstedt found other poor families who lived in the same skid-row neighborhood as the disorganized multiproblem families, but their homes were stable. Children were shown much affection and were seldom separated from their mothers. These parents emphasized neatness, conformity, and respectability. When the children entered school, parents helped them with their homework and expressed concern about poor achievement. Children from these homes posed few behavior problems in school and learned to read sufficiently well in the first grade to warrant promotion.

Comparison of Child Rearing across Social Classes

A few reasonably consistent findings have emerged from the many studies comparing the child-rearing practices of higher and lower socioeconomic groups. For example, parents of all social classes have been found to share certain values—wanting their children to be honest, happy, considerate, obedient, and dependable—but the emphasis given these values varies somewhat with socioeconomic class (Kohn, 1959). Middle-class parents are more likely to stress internalized standards or goals such as honesty, self-control, consideration, and curiosity, whereas working-class parents stress qualities that assure respectability, such as obedience, neatness, and cleanliness.

One factor that influences how lower- and middle-class parents behave toward children is their experience with authority on their jobs (Kohn, 1979). Lower-class adults often hold subservient positions in which they are expected to obey without question the unexplained instructions of their supervisors. As parents, Kohn suggests, they expect the same obedience from their children. Lower-class mothers tend to guide or teach their children with directives and instructions. By contrast, middle-class adults often hold jobs in which they participate in decision making and are given explanations for the instructions they receive. These parents adopt a more democratic mode of supervising their children. Middle-class mothers ask questions and give hints that encourage children to discover answers for themselves (Hess and Shipman, 1965).

General conceptions of the parents' role have also been found to vary with social class (Table 12.1). Lower-class mothers tend to feel responsible for making their children obey commands immediately; they expect their husbands to be directive and to set strict limits on their children's activities. Middle-class mothers tend to feel a long-term responsibility for their children's growth, development, affection, and satisfaction. Middle-class parents have more egalitarian relationships with their children and are more accessible to them than lower-class parents.

Some words of caution are in order concerning the relation between child rearing and social class. The differences in the child-rearing practices of lower-

Table 12.1 Behavior and Philosophy of Parents of Two Socioeconomic Classes

Philosophy	Lower Class	Middle Class
Concept of good parent	Elicits specific behavior	Promotes development, affection, satisfaction
Behavioral requirements	Obedience, neatness, cleanliness	Internalized standards
	Qualities assuring respectability	Honesty, self-control
		Boys, curiosity; girls, consideration
Role differentiation	More rigid, more paternalistic	More flexible, more egalitarian
Response to misdeed	Focuses on immediate consequences of child's actions	Takes into account child's intentions and feelings
Discipline techniques	More physical punishment	More reasoning, isolation, appeals to guilt
Permissiveness	Less to infant and young child	More to infant and young child
	More to older child	Less to older child
Achievement demands	Less	More
Father as companion to child	Less	More

Adapted from Smart and Smart, 1967; data from Clausen and Williams, 1963

and middle-class families exist within a context of tremendous similarity. Often a statistically significant difference in such practices consists of nothing more than the finding that 60 percent of the parents of one social class and 45 percent of the parents of another social class follow a particular child-rearing practice. In every social class parents adopt a variety of child-rearing practices. It would be a serious mistake to conclude that just because parents have a particular socioeconomic status, they raise their children in a particular fashion.

SUMMARY

Parents' attitudes and child-rearing practices reflect the culture in which they live. The culture's economic base may foster child-rearing practices that help future adults to meet the economic needs of their society. In a similar way, parents who are entrepreneurs may adopt child-rearing practices that encourage their children to develop self-control and individuality, whereas bureaucratic parents may stress cooperation. A family's socioeconomic status may influence the values stressed by parents, the strategies they use in supervising and teaching their children, and their feelings of responsibility for their children's socialization. Although there are social-class differences in typical child-rearing practices, these practices vary greatly within any class, and the overlap between classes is substantial.

SELF-CONCEPT

Developmental Changes in Self-Concept

Your **self-concept** consists of everything that you know, believe, and feel about yourself, what you see as your strengths and weaknesses, what you pride yourself on, and what you hate about yourself. As children mature, their self-concepts change in content, basis of evaluation, and even in how highly they regard themselves. Young children tend to have self-concepts that emphasize specific and concrete features, activities, and interests: "I am a girl," "I can run fast," "I like books." As children become more comfortable with inner thoughts and feelings, they tend to conceive of themselves as having more abstract traits, such as "I am friendly" or "I am a good person." Because young children see parents and teachers as all-knowing authorities, they base their opinions about themselves largely on adults' evaluations. Older children rely more on their own judgments or on those of peers, friends, and people they most admire (Rosenberg, 1979).

Because of the limits of their cognitive abilities, young children are oriented outward toward activities that they enjoy and things that interest them in their surroundings. They are not very self-reflective. Their self-concepts are relatively stable and satisfactory. As children get older, however, they focus their attention inward and become more critical of themselves. As they learn about society's judgments of appropriate and valued behavior, they create more demanding images of themselves, and they set new standards that are more difficult to live up to. As a result, the gap between their self-concepts and their ideas of the people they would like to be often increases as children develop (Phillips, 1978). This gap is partly responsible for the identity crisis of adolescence.

Encouraging Positive Self-Concepts

Considering oneself a capable person is basic to a positive self-concept. A positive self-concept allows a person to approach life eagerly, to explore new interests, to challenge oneself, and to lead the life of a happy individual. Children with positive self-concepts are enthusiastic and able to take initiative, to work independently, to feel proud of their accomplishments, and to recover from experiences of failure. Children with negative self-concepts, in contrast, may feel inadequate, refuse to try a new task or problem, and give up before they begin because they always assume that they are sure to fail.

One way that children form impressions of themselves is by comparing themselves with other children. Although they make these comparisons in many contexts, a particularly important one is school, where children are faced with classroom evaluations and grades that make the differences in their abilities evident. Children also receive subtler messages from the way that parents and teachers treat them. These adults encourage some children to keep trying at a difficult task but quickly give the solution to others, thereby expressing a judgment that these children have little competence and simultaneously denying them the possibility of feeling pride in finding the answer by themselves (Brophy and Good, 1974). Stifling children's opinions can make them feel that their views, and they themselves, are worthless. By the same token, allowing children to express themselves and make decisions helps them develop confidence (Phillips and Zigler, 1980).

Since all children need support from people who are important to them, the most effective way of promoting a positive self-concept may be the same for all children: relating to them in a way that lets them know they are valued and accepted. This acceptance may be especially important for children from minority and poor families, because their day-to-day experiences tend to be so damaging (Phillips and Zigler, 1980). When disadvantaged children compare themselves with their white, middle-class peers, the differences in their experiences and backgrounds may make them feel strange and, therefore, inferior. Black children who attend predominantly white schools, for example, have less self-esteem, but higher grades, than those who attend black schools and can compare themselves with other children more like themselves.

SUMMARY

The self-concepts of children develop from their perceptions of themselves in social and physical environments and from the reactions of others to their behavior. Young children see themselves as having concrete features and base their self-evaluations on adults' views of them. Older children see themselves as having abstract traits and rely more on self-perceptions and the evaluations of peers. Black and disadvantaged children may have poorer self-concepts than their more advantaged peers if they must judge themselves against majority group children in an integrated setting. For these and all children positive self-concepts can be promoted by supportive interactions with adults and experiences that allow them to express initiative and to experiment with their environments.

GENDER AND SEX-ROLE DEVELOPMENT

Consciously or unconsciously, and willingly or unwillingly, all of us make assumptions and hold expectations about ourselves and others on the basis of gender. There are behavioral as well as physical differences between the sexes, and a question of great concern today is the extent to which the behavioral differences come from child-rearing practices and learning and the extent to which they come from biological factors.

Sex Differences

One place to look for traits with a biological basis is among newborn babies, but studies of the behavior of newborns have not shown very reliable sex differences. Moreover, it is difficult to tease apart biological and environmental factors even early in life. For example, male infants appear to be more irritable and physically active than females (Richards et al., 1977), but we know from other studies that mothers give baby boys more attention than they give girls. Which factor, the mother's attention or the infant's activity, is the cause and which is the effect? Similarly, mothers talk to their daughters more than to their sons (Endsley et al., 1975; Lewis, 1972, 1975; Moss, 1967). Do mothers foster the greater verbal ability found in girls later on, or are they reacting to a greater verbal responsiveness that already exists?

One sex difference in behavior that does seem to have a biological basis is the greater aggressiveness of males. Evidence on this point comes from cross-cultural, animal, and hormonal research. For example, young boys play more rough-and-tumble games than girls, not only in America but in the vastly different cultures of Ethiopia, Mexico, and Okinawa (Maccoby and Jacklin, 1974). Young male monkeys play more roughly than young females (Harlow, 1962). In human beings and a wide range of species, high levels of testosterone, a male hormone, accompany greater aggressiveness, and lower levels of the hormone are associated with little aggressiveness (Davis, 1964).

A second sex difference that appears to have some biological basis is our pattern of cognitive abilities. On the average, females do better on tests of verbal ability, and males do better on tests of spatial and mathematical ability. This does not mean that all boys will be better than all girls at spatial tasks, merely that, on the average, boys have more potential for acquiring spatial skills. It is important to remember that, for any trait, characteristic sex differences refer to *averages,* not individual cases. Although, on the average, males are more aggressive than females, an individual girl may be relatively aggressive and an individual boy relatively passive.

In discussing the relative influence of nature and nurture on sex differences, we must distinguish between two concepts, gender identity and gender role. Although they are often confused, these concepts are quite different. **Gender identity** refers to individuals' knowledge of their gender as one of their personal traits. **Gender role** refers to society's expectations of how females and males should behave. Anthropological evidence indicates that these expectations vary considerably from culture to culture. In her classic studies of three South Pacific societies, Margaret Mead (1935) described some of this variability. In one group, the Arapesh, both males and females had what we in this society would consider typical feminine traits; both sexes were nurturant and unaggressive. Among the Mundugumor people, by contrast, she found that both males and females were hostile and aggressive, traits we tend to think of as masculine. Among the Tchambuli there was a reversal of the Western gender roles; women were aggressive whereas men were nurturant. The plasticity of gender roles, however, does seem to have some limitations. In the vast majority of societies, males have *instrumental* roles and females have *expressive* roles (Munroe and Munroe, 1975). That is, men carry out the tasks to ensure that the society runs smoothly; women are concerned with interpersonal relationships and are responsible for binding the family together.

Sex Typing

In most cultures little boys and little girls are subjected to very different child-rearing practices because social expectations differ for the two sexes. In keeping with their different treatments of boys and girls, many parents actually perceive major differences between their sons and daughters. For example, when middle-class American parents were asked to describe their seventh-grade children, they spontaneously described their sons as tough-minded activists who were ambitious, energetic, competitive, confident, stable, and capable of being leaders. Daughters were described as expressive and sociable, and their parents perceived them as having such qualities as warmth, charm, popularity, and eagerness to please (Hill, 1964).

Sex-role typing begins at birth. Distinctions are made in the clothing, toys, and even the colors, pink and blue, selected for boys and girls. As children

Little girls, by imitating their mothers, prepare themselves for the roles of wife and mother.

grow older, pressures for role differentiation escalate. Boys are encouraged to be active and aggressive and to take responsibility. Girls, being considered more "fragile," despite the physiological evidence contradicting this stereotype, are taught to be dependent and helpful to others; tomboyishness gains them few rewards. In general, child-rearing practices are directed at preparing boys for the role of protector and provider and girls for that of wife, mother, and homemaker.

Many sources of influence besides parents contribute to sex typing. Peers are especially influential. Children as young as three years of age have been found to reinforce one another's gender-appropriate behavior and to punish inappropriate behavior (Lamb, Easterbrooks, and Holden, 1980). From the time that they are introduced to a peer group, children prefer to play with same-sex peers. This preference appears to arise partly because parents and teachers encourage it and partly because children like to play with other children who have similar interests. This playing with same-sex peers increases the likelihood that children will engage in gender-appropriate activities in the company of gender-appropriate models. Around the time that they enter school, children's understanding of the importance of socially approved behavior increases (Kohlberg, 1966). At this age children begin to socialize themselves and to pay special attention to people of their own gender as models to imitate (Slaby and Frey, 1975).

SUMMARY

It is difficult to assess the relative roles of nature and nurture in determining sex differences in behavior, even for infants. Two differences that appear to have some biological basis are the male's greater aggressiveness and better spatial ability and the female's superior verbal ability. As with any sex difference in behavior, however, it is important to remember that these are average differences between males and females generally, not differences between every male and every female.

Gender identity refers to an individual's knowledge of his or her gender as a personal trait. Gender role denotes expectations of how females and males in a given society should behave. These expectations vary in different cultures, but in many cultures boys are encouraged to become independent and assertive breadwinners, and girls are encouraged to develop social abilities and to become homemakers and mothers.

MORAL DEVELOPMENT

A very important part of socialization is learning right from wrong and behaving accordingly. Before we turn to discussion of what is known about moral development, however, we should make a distinction between **moral knowledge** and **moral behavior.** This distinction is important because the two do not necessarily go together. For example, most people would agree that cheating is morally wrong, yet studies show that a great many individuals will cheat if they think there is little chance of being caught (Feldman and Feldman, 1967). In this case, moral behavior, or the lack of it, appears to depend on practical consequences rather than on moral knowledge.

The Development of Moral Knowledge

Within psychology today the major approach to moral development is that of the cognitive-developmental theorists, who suggest that moral reasoning pro-

Table 12.2 Kohlberg's Stages of Moral Reasoning

Level I. Preconventional: Behavior is dominated by hedonistic considerations and conformity with those who are the most powerful.

Stage 1. *Heteronomous morality.* Physical consequences of the action define its "badness"; punishment and reward control behavior.

Stage 2. *Instrumental behavior.* The individual pursues his or her own needs and lets others pursue their own within the limits of equitable exchange.

Level II. Conventional: Obedience and loyalty are viewed as desirable ends in themselves.

Step 3. *Mutual interpersonal expectations.* The individual tries to please those around him or her, seeking to be viewed as good.

Stage 4. *Social system and conscience.* Rules are defined by institutions of the society; obedience is viewed as a civic duty.

Level III. Principled (Postconventional): The individual attempts to define moral values and principles that are valued in themselves.

Stage 5. *Social contract.* Rules are formed through a process of consensual definition; they are essentially arbitrary, but it is only fair that all obey the laws defined by the majority in order to ensure the smooth functioning of society.

Stage 6. *Universal ethical principles.* Some moral principles are not arbitrary; they have universal significance and supercede societal rules when the two sets conflict.

From Kohlberg, 1976.

ceeds through a series of stages. At present, the most prominent theory of the development of moral reasoning is that of Lawrence Kohlberg. Kohlberg first concluded that there are six developmental stages of moral judgment (Table 12.2), but so few peope reach the sixth and highest stage that he later combined this stage with stage five. In the first two stages, termed the **preconventional** level, children do not understand morality; they simply obey rules in order to avoid punishment and obtain approval. In the next two stages children are concerned about **conventional** conformity; they recognize that rules exist so that a society can function smoothly, and they perceive the rules as dictates from a higher authority. Unlike children in the earlier stages, those with conventional morality obey rules because it is in the interest of society, not just of themselves, to do so. The last two stages are called the **postconventional** level. In the fifth stage rules are seen as the products of social consensus, and their arbitrariness is recognized. Finally, in stage six—the stage attained by very few people—the individual recognizes certain universal principles, such as justice and equality, and feels morally obligated to disobey rules that violate these ethics.

Kohlberg assesses the individual's level of moral development by means of interviews in which he or she answers questions about stories that pose a moral dilemma. For example, one story is about a man who stole money to buy drugs for his cancer-stricken wife. Was the stealing a moral or an immoral act? An individual's stage of moral reasoning is determined by the kind of justification he or she provides for a moral decision in such situations. Kohlberg's work has been criticized by other psychologists. Some have objected to his methods; others have disagreed with his ideas about the development of moral reasoning. William Kurtines and Ester Greif (1974) argued that empirical evidence has failed to confirm Kohlberg's postulation of a sequence of developmental stages, and they have shown that people do not operate consistently at a particular level of moral development.

Moral Behavior

Research on moral behavior has proceeded somewhat independently of that on moral knowledge. Two of the most important approaches are those of Justin Aronfreed (1968) and Martin Hoffman (1970a, 1970b).

Aronfreed's approach is based on social-learning theory. He believes that children learn what forms of behavior are approved and disapproved much as they learn other principles of behavior. At first, children behave "morally" only because they expect to be rewarded for doing so and to be punished for behaving otherwise. Children then internalize the rules that they have learned. In this way their behavior comes to be monitored by an internal conscience. They start to "reward" and "punish" themselves for conforming to or deviating from social rules.

Hoffman's study of the development of moral behavior focuses on the type of disciplinary strategy parents adopt. Hoffman (1960, 1970b) has distinguished two such strategies, punitive and inductive. **Punitive techniques** emphasize the personal consequences of breaking rules: "If you hit your little brother, you will not be allowed to watch TV." **Inductive discipline** stresses the effects of misbehavior on the victims of moral transgressions: "If you hit your little brother, he will be hurt." Inductive discipline has proved to be a more effective strategy than the punitive techniques for teaching children to behave morally (Hoffman, 1970b). The reason for this may be that encouraging children to empathize with those who have been wronged makes them feel guiltier when they do wrong themselves than they feel if their parents have not encouraged such empathy (Hoffman and Saltzstein, 1967). Inductive discipline also appears to be a better disciplinary strategy than withdrawal of love, a strategy which makes children feel that their parents' respect and love are contingent on the children's behavior (Hoffman, 1970b).

Teachers, parents, media personalities, and peers all communicate moral standards and provide models for children to emulate. There is substantial evidence that children behave in a more altruistic or prosocial fashion after observing models who behave in these ways (Rushton, 1980). It also appears that, when there is a discrepancy between what models say and do, children are more likely to pay attention to what models do (Bryan, 1975).

SUMMARY

In the earliest stages of moral development, children's "moral" behavior is little more than an attempt to obtain rewards and avoid punishment. In the next stages moral behavior takes the form of observing rules that are perceived to emanate from a higher authority. At still later stages people realize the consensual nature of rules and may develop a morality based on such abstactions as justice and equality.

Behavior becomes moral through learning and the internalization of rules of conduct. Discipline for unacceptable behavior that encourages empathy with a victim has been shown empirically to lead more effectively to moral behavior than discipline that emphasizes punitive consequences for the individual. Children will imitate moral behavior; when there is a difference between what models say and do, children are more likely to follow what they do. Psychologists do not yet know how close the relationship between moral reasoning and moral behavior is.

The following concepts are the major ones introduced in this chapter. You should be able to define them and state the points made about each in the text discussion.

Spontaneous (reflex) smiling

Nonselective social smiling

Selective social smiling

Reinforcement theory of smiling

Evolutionary theory of smiling

Cognitive theory of smiling

Stranger anxiety

Separation anxiety

Temperament (temperamental style)

Easy child

Slow-to-warm-up child

Difficult child

Attachment

Love-oriented discipline

Power-assertive discipline

Authoritarian parent

Permissive parent

Authoritative parent

Sexual identification

Socialization

Sociodramatic play

Entrepreneurial occupations

Bureaucratic occupations

Self-concept

Gender identity

Gender role

Sex-role typing

Moral knowledge

Moral behavior

Preconventional morality

Conventional morality

Postconventional morality

Punitive discipline

Inductive discipline

The topics that you might miss in reviewing just this list are these:

Watson's and Bridges's theories of emotional development

Management of children with different temperaments

Attachment and later life

Child rearing and social development

Comparison of exclusive mothering and substitute care

Cultural influences on development

Social class and child rearing

Influences on, and implications of, sex roles

In This Book.   Some of the themes of this chapter were touched on in Chapter 9 (Motivation) and Chapter 10 (Stress, Emotion, and Coping). The discussions of personality in Chapter 15 are also related.

Elsewhere.   Many recent works discuss topics covered in this chapter. Some recommended books are *A Child's Journey,* by Julius Segal and Herbert Yahraes; *The Role of the Father in Child Development* (second edition), edited by Michael Lamb; *The Psychology of Sex Differences,* by Eleanor Maccoby and Carol Jacklin; and *Contemporary Issues in Developmental Psychology* (second edition), by Norman Endler, L. Boulter, and H, Osser.

PART SIX   INDIVIDUALITY

Metzinger. *Profile of a Woman.* (1917). Musee National d'Art Moderne, Paris. Scala/Art Resource.

CHAPTER 13   PSYCHOLOGICAL ASSESSMENT

The existence of differences among people is one of the things that make life worth living. Imagine the dreary lives we would all lead if every person were an exact replica of everyone else. On the other hand, these differences are also a source of much unhappiness. Hostility in personal relationships, competition for status, marital discord, failure in college, painful shyness, and sibling rivalry are just a few of the consequences of the uniqueness of individuals. Resigning themselves to the pervasiveness of such differences, some people have remarked that, "It takes all kinds of people to make a world," to which the cynics have responded, "It doesn't take all kinds, but they're all here."

In psychology the word **trait** refers to any relatively enduring and consistent way of behaving in which people differ from one another. Introversion, intelligence, anxiety, aggressiveness, prejudice, musical aptitude, honesty, sensitivity, seriousness, and friendliness are all examples. The traits that people possess and the degree to which they possess them are part of their psychological makeup. The idea of permanence is essential to the concept of trait. We think of traits as remaining with a person over long periods of time.

It is important to recognize that traits are not items of concrete reality. They are concepts, shorthand expressions which summarize the patterns of behavior that set one person apart from another. Thus the concept of aggressiveness refers to all sorts of ways in which one person relates offensively to another. Aggressiveness may take the form of hostile remarks, physical assault, social assertiveness, or economic competitiveness. A person who behaves in these ways on numerous occasions has a strong trait of aggressiveness.

The fact that traits are concepts does not diminish their importance. Traits are of enormous practical significance because they relate to success in college or in employment, to suitability for holding positions of leadership, and so on. If we could do so, the best way to predict these important performances would be to observe how people act in the actual situations in which the traits are thought to be significant. Usually this is impractical. We want to know whether a person will succeed in school, be a good leader, profit from psychotherapy, or be a trustworthy employee in government *before* he or she encounters the practical situation. In the exercise of some responsibilities, such as that of military command, too much is at stake to permit us to decide, after observing the performance of several candidates and watching some of them fail, who should be given the position. The decision has to be made ahead of time. For this reason psychological tests have been developed to measure the traits thought to be relevant to performance in particular practical situations.

In psychology we tend to think of traits in terms of two somewhat arbitrary clusters: traits of personality such as extroversion, gregariousness, aggressiveness, and prejudice; and aptitudes, such as clerical, mechanical, and artistic aptitudes. This last cluster includes intelligence which, for many purposes, is scholastic aptitude.

INTELLIGENCE TESTING

In popular usage **intelligence** is the ability to learn, to reason, to deal with abstract concepts, to adapt to novel situations, and to get along in society. Everyone recognizes that we differ greatly in these talents. Differences in intelligence are so important that attempts to assess them began early in the history of psychology.

History of Intelligence Testing

The earliest tests of intelligence, developed toward the end of the nineteenth century, were based on the assumption that intelligence has a physiological basis. Many scientists were convinced of the heritability of intelligence; moreover, physiologists had discovered that neural impulses took time to traverse the nervous system, and some thought that speed of neural functioning might determine intelligence. It made sense, then, to attempt to assess intelligence by measuring physiological processes.

Early intelligence tests measured such abilities as sensory acuity, eye-hand coordination, and reaction time. Even muscular strength and breathing capacity were sometimes tested, perhaps because Sir Francis Galton (1822–1915) believed that the fine-tuning of the nervous systems of intelligent people benefited their bodies and made them physically vigorous. By the end of the nineteenth century, however, psychologists were aware that such tests did not assess mental functioning in any useful sense. Children's performances on these tests were not related to how well they did in school or how intelligent their teachers thought them to be. It became clear that adequate indicators of intelligence would have to test higher mental abilities rather than physiological processes. This view was central to the work of Alfred Binet (1857–1911), the French psychologist who developed the first widely used tests of intelligence.

Alfred Binet. Binet devoted his career to the study and measurement of intelligence, and he was particularly interested in the intellectual differences of individuals. Although he never totally abandoned tests of sensorimotor behavior, Binet rejected them as measures of intelligence. Instead, he recommended tests of ten "mental functions": memory, imagery, imagination, attention, comprehension, suggestibility, aesthetic appreciation, moral sentiments, muscular force (will power), and motor skill. Binet did not view these functions as independent and unrelated elements of the mind, but rather as specific abilities that reflected some more basic underlying general ability.

By 1900 Binet had developed a number of intelligence tests. He administered many of these to his two adolescent daughters over a three-year period, and in 1903 he published *The Experimental Study of Intelligence,* an exhaustive report of the test results.

During the course of this investigation, Binet noticed that the girls performed better on the tests as they grew older. Herein lay the seed of a major breakthrough in our understanding of intelligence. As obvious as it now seems, it

In 1889 Alfred Binet cofounded the first French psychological laboratory at the Sorbonne. His early interests were "imageless thought," suggestibility, hypnotism, mental fatigue, and semipathological "alterations of personality."

was extremely important to recognize explicitly that whatever intelligence might be, older children have more of it than younger ones. Once intelligence was recognized to be age-related, test constructors began to define the difficulty of a test item in terms of the average age at which children could first respond to it correctly.

The Binet-Simon Tests. In Binet's day the French schools were struggling with the problem of determining which children could benefit from normal schooling and which could not. Compulsory education had been established, and since classes were age-graded, less intelligent children often fell behind their age-mates in school. The Ministry of Education wished to set up classes for "dull" children so that they too could profit from the "benefits of instruction." Binet was given the task of developing an instrument that could objectively identify children in need of special education.

In 1905, in collaboration with Théophile Simon, Binet constructed a test consisting of thirty items which were presented in an ascending order of difficulty. Item 1 required the child to follow a lighted candle with the head and eyes; item 4 tested the child's ability to distinguish between a square of chocolate and a square of wood; item 20 called for a discrimination between two lines of slightly unequal length; item 30 asked for the definitions of several abstract words. Binet and Simon again found that older children could pass more of the items than younger children.

In 1908 and 1911 Binet and Simon published revisions of the 1905 scale. The 1908 revision included almost twice as many items as the original test and was organized in a way that was to be embodied in all future versions of the test. The items were classified by age levels extending from three to thirteen years. An item was placed at the age level at which 50 to 90 percent of the children could pass it. The 1911 version had five different items at each age level except for one.

American Revisions of Binet's Scales. The major force in bringing the Binet test into the mainstream of academic psychology in America was the work of Lewis Terman (1877–1956) of Stanford University. In 1916 Terman issued the first American revision of the Binet, which was called the Stanford-Binet Intelligence Scale. This version was quite similar to Binet's 1911 scale, but Terman revised, dropped, added, and modified the age placement of many test items on the basis of the performance of children in the United States. The Stanford-Binet scale contained ninety items placed at ages three through ten, plus items at twelve and fourteen and at "average" and "superior" adult levels.

In 1937 the 1916 Stanford-Binet was replaced by a more refined revision, which appeared in two different forms, L and M. This revision was actually two intelligence tests with items that differed in content. In 1960 the Stanford-Binet again became a single test composed of the most satisfactory subtests from the two 1937 tests. The last change came in 1972, when the scoring methods were revised to make the test a better indicator of the intelligence of American children regardless of ethnic or socioeconomic background. Table 13.1 presents a comparison of sample items from the 1908 and 1960 Binet scales.

Wechsler Scales. An important point implicit even in Binet's work is that intelligence is a complex trait made up of many contributing talents. An effective measurement of intelligence must sample performance on a wide array of intellectual tasks. David Wechsler has constructed several intelligence tests that

David Wechsler first published his intelligence scale for children in 1949, his scale for adults a decade earlier in 1939. He also constructed the Wechsler Pre-school and Primary Scale of Intelligence (WPPSI), for children from four to six and a half.

Table 13.1 Comparison of Test Items for Years Five, Eight, and Twelve in the 1908 and 1960 Revisions of the Binet Scale.

1908 Binet Test (Binet and Simon)	Form L-M, 1960 Stanford-Binet (Terman and Merrill, 1960)
Year 5*	**Year 5**
1. Compares two boxes of different weights.	1. Completes a drawing of a man with leg missing.
2. Copies a square.	2. Folds a paper square twice to make a triangle after demonstration by examiner.
3. Repeats a sentence of ten syllables.	3. Defines two of the following three words: *ball, hat, stove*
4. Counts four sous.	4. Copies a square.
5. Puts together two pieces in a "game of patience."	5. Recognizes similarities and differences between pictures.
	6. Assembles two triangles to form a rectangle.
Year 8	**Year 8**
1. Reads selection and retains two memories.	1. Defines eight words from a standard vocabulary list. Some of the easier examples are: *orange, straw, top.*
2. Counts nine sous (three single and three double).	2. Remembers most of the content of a simple story.
3. Names four colors.	3. Sees the absurdities in such statements as, "A man had flu (influenza) twice. The first time it killed him, but the second time he got well quickly."
4. Counts backward from 20 to 0.	4. Distinguishes such words as *airplane* and *kite, ocean* and *river.*
5. Compares two objects from memory.	5. Knows what makes a sailboat move, what to do if you find a lost three-year-old, etc.
6. Writes from dictation.	6. Names the days of the week.
Year 12	**Year 12**
1. Repeats seven figures.	1. Defines fourteen words such as: *haste, lecture, skill.*
2. Finds three rhymes.	2. Sees absurdity in such items as, "Bill Jones's feet are so big that he has to pull his trousers on over his head."
3. Repeats a sentence of twenty-six syllables.	3. Understands the situation depicted in a fairly complicated picture.
4. Interprets pictures.	4. Repeats five digits reversed.
5. Solves problems of facts.	5. Defines such abstract words as: *pity, curiosity.*
	6. Supplies the missing word in such incomplete sentences as, "One cannot be a hero . . . one can always be a man."

*The average child of the ages for which items are given, five, eight, and twelve, can do the problems correctly.

Reproduced with permission of Houghton Mifflin Co.

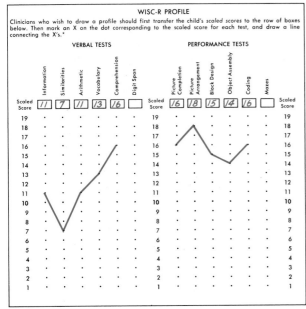

WISC-R PROFILE

Clinicians who wish to draw a profile should first transfer the child's *scaled* scores to the row of boxes below. Then mark an X on the dot corresponding to the scaled score for each test, and draw a line connecting the X's.*

	Year	Month	Day
Date Tested	___	___	___
Date of Birth	___	___	___
Age	9	2	3

	Raw Score	Scaled Score
VERBAL TESTS		
Information	13	11
Similarities	8	7
Arithmetic	11	11
Vocabulary	31	13
Comprehension	23	16
(Digit Span)	( )	( )
Verbal Score		58
PERFORMANCE TESTS		
Picture Completion	23	16
Picture Arrangement	40	18
Block Design	38	15
Object Assembly	25	14
Coding	51	16
(Mazes)	( )	( )
Performance Score		79

	Scaled Score	IQ
Verbal Score	58	109
Performance Score	79	141
Full Scale Score	137	127
*Prorated from 4 tests, if necessary.		

Figure 13.1
The Wechsler Intelligence Scale for Children. Test scores of a nine-year-old have been entered on the WISC record form. Mazes may be substituted for the coding test; the digit span test is optional. Scaling raw scores makes them comparable to one another so that they can be added.

The block design test for the WAIS. A student at Teachers College, Columbia University, is being timed as she arranges varicolored blocks to match designs in the spiral-backed copybook.

A cartoon simulation of the picture-ordering subtest of the WAIS. The correct ordering of the panels is given on page 439. (Drawing by CEM; © 1974 by The New Yorker Magazine, Inc.)

assess a broader range of abilities and are appropriate for different age groups. The best known of these are the Wechsler Adult Intelligence Scale (WAIS) and the Wechsler Intelligence Scale for Children (WISC).

Wechsler's original problem was to devise a test to evaluate the intelligence of patients at Bellevue Hospital in New York. Most of the patients were adults; many were from the working class and had been poorly educated. Because they were at a disadvantage on the usual verbal tests, Wechsler included nonverbal items in his tests along with the verbal ones.

Wechsler's tests now contain separate verbal and performance sections (Figure 13.1). The verbal section poses questions on general information, finding similarities, mathematical reasoning, vocabulary, comprehension, and recall. In the performance section the individual is asked to name the missing parts of incomplete pictures, to order a series of pictures so that they make a story, to copy printed designs by arranging multicolored cubes, to assemble jigsaw pieces to form an object, and to substitute unfamiliar symbols for letters according to a special code.

Wechsler's tests provide three intelligence scores, a verbal IQ, a performance IQ, and a composite IQ based on all subtests combined. Verbal and performance IQs are rather highly correlated, but the magnitudes of the correlations (+.77 to +.81) are far enough from perfect to suggest that the two scales, to some extent, measure different abilities.

Measures of Intelligence

When Binet and Simon decided to place the items on their tests at appropriate age levels, the way was paved for the development of a measure of intelligence that is still in use, namely **mental age (MA).** The examiner first finds the age level at which the child passes all the test items—now known as the **basal age** or basal level. The examiner then tests the child with the more and more difficult items for later age levels, until a level, called the terminal or **ceiling level,** at which the child passes none of the items is reached. Since there were five items at each age level on the Binet test, the child's MA was the basal age plus one-fifth of a year for each of the items passed above the basal. Table 13.2 illustrates the computation of mental age on the Stanford-Binet Intelligence Scale. Since the Stanford-Binet has six items at most age levels instead of five, one-sixth of a year, or two months, of MA credit is given for each item passed beyond the basal level.

The MA is interpreted quite literally. A nine-year-old child who receives an MA of six is functioning at the intellectual level expected of the average six-year-old and would be considered below average in intelligence. A six-year-old child who attains an MA of nine is functioning at a level expected of the average nine-year-old and would be considered quite bright.

The MA is thus a measure of the absolute level of intelligence. For many purposes it is useful to assess relative intelligence by considering the relation between the individual's mental age and **chronological age (CA).** A relative measure indicates how a child's absolute level of intelligence compares to that of other children of the same age. Such a measure was first computed in 1912 when the German psychologist Louis Stern (1871–1938) recommended the division of MA by CA. This brightness ratio was later developed into the **intelligence quotient,** or **IQ,** which is obtained by multiplying the MA/CA ratio by 100 in order to eliminate decimals. The formula $IQ = MA/CA \times 100$ was used for many years to compute intelligence scores.

For reasons that we come to in a moment, the average person's IQ is 100. People above average in intelligence receive IQs above 100; those below average receive IQs below 100. Besides being a measure of relative brightness, the IQ is also a measure of the individual's rate of intellectual development. An IQ of 100 indicates the rate of intellectual development of the average person in the population. For example, the eight-year-old child who attains eight years of MA credit on the test (IQ = 100) is average in rate of development. The child of twelve who attains eight years of MA credit (IQ = 66) is slow in rate

Table 13.2 Computation of MA from a Hypothetical Distribution of Test Items Passed on the Stanford-Binet Intelligence Scale

Year Level of Test		Number of Items Passed	Credit	
			Years	**Months**
Basal level	–Year 8	All items	8	0
	–Year 9	4	0	8
	–Year 10	3	0	6
	–Year 11	2	0	4
Terminal level	—Year 12	0	0	0
		Total MA =	8	18
			or 9 years, 6 months	

of development, since this child took twelve years to acquire the intellectual ability found in the average eight-year-old.

The Frequency Distribution of IQs.   Intelligence quotients are normally distributed. The majority of people have IQs in the neighborhood of the average, but the scores are scattered symmetrically along the IQ dimension with higher and higher or lower and lower IQs occurring with decreasing frequency. Figure 13.2 presents this **normal curve** for IQs. The **mean** of the IQ distribution is 100. The mean IQ is 100 for arithmetic reasons. Tests like the Binet test were constructed so that average children always have mental ages that are the same as their chronological ages. The average nine-year-old child has an MA of 9.0, and

$$IQ = 100\left(\frac{9}{9}\right) = 100$$

Intelligence quotients range from a low near zero to a high of over 200. The variability of some other normally distributed values—the lengths of daisy petals, for example—is less; the variability of others—SAT scores, for example—is greater. By methods that need not concern us here (see page 643), we may calculate a measure of variability called the **standard deviation.** By such calculations the standard deviation of the IQ distribution is about 15 IQ points. Some tests and some populations have yielded slightly different values. Since a standard deviation of 15 is commonly obtained on the most widely used tests, however, we will adopt this value for the purposes of our discussion.

The most important property of the standard deviation is that it permits us to specify exactly what percentage of values will lie between any two points in a normal distribution. With the help of special tables, such calculations are easily made. For example, in an ideal normal curve 68.26 percent, or more than two-thirds of the values, are found between one standard deviation below the mean and one standard deviation above the mean. This figure confirms our observation that the majority of cases cluster about the mean. In addition, 99.72 percent of the values in an ideal normal curve are found between three standard deviations below and three standard deviations above the mean. In our example, since the standard deviation is 15 and the mean is 100, a full 99.72 percent of the IQ scores would be predicted to lie between 55 and 145. Since the percentage 99.72 includes nearly all cases, a practical range of values in a normal distribution is only six standard deviations wide, three above and three below the mean. This fact helps in predicting which values are actually likely

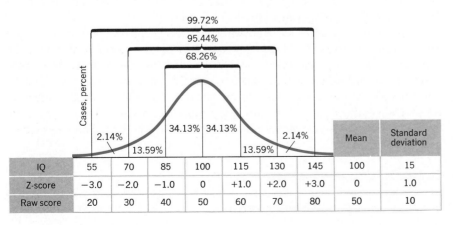

								Mean	Standard deviation
IQ	55	70	85	100	115	130	145	100	15
Z-score	−3.0	−2.0	−1.0	0	+1.0	+2.0	+3.0	0	1.0
Raw score	20	30	40	50	60	70	80	50	10

Figure 13.2
Idealized normal curve of intelligence. This figure is important at several points in the text. Notice first the IQ scale. The figure shows the percentage of cases within three ranges of IQ. This distribution is approximately correct for all the most widely used tests of IQ. The raw score and Z-score scales indicate the procedures involved in calculating deviation IQs. Imagine a test whose raw scores have a mean of 50 and a standard deviation of 10. The transformation first to Z-scores (middle scale) and then to IQs (top scale) gives these scores values that correspond to the standard IQ scale.

to occur. Although IQs below 55 and above 145 have been recorded, their relative frequency is low.

Deviation IQs.   An important innovation originated by Wechsler and incorporated into the 1960 Stanford-Binet test was the **deviation IQ** based on normal-curve statistics. To calculate a deviation IQ, we first convert the individual's raw test score to a **Z-score** by the formula

$$Z = \frac{\text{Individual's score} - \text{Mean score for person the same age}}{\text{Standard deviation of distribution of scores for persons the same age}}$$

The Z-score for each individual indicates how far the test score is above or below the mean in terms of standard deviations. Because a normal distribution is about six standard deviations wide, Z-scores tend to range from approximately -3.0 to $+3.0$. It is a simple matter to transform Z-scores into a distribution with a mean of 100 and a standard deviation of 15 to obtain the deviation IQ. The equation is: deviation $IQ = 100 + 15Z$. The IQ thus obtained is roughly comparable to that calculated by the traditional formula (Figure 13.2). Appendix A gives further information on Z-scores.

Two problems led to the replacement of the MA/CA ratio by the deviation IQ. The first was the discovery that intelligence as measured by IQ tests does not increase steadily with chronological age but increases more slowly in late adolescence and eventually levels off. With the MA/CA formula the only way an intellectually average middle-aged person could attain an IQ of 100 was by the rather artificial trick of assigning that person an arbitrarily adjusted CA. The age of sixteen was chosen for the 1937 Stanford-Binet test because it was believed that intelligence did not grow after that age. Thus beyond age sixteen the IQ formula became $MA/16 \times 100$. Since intelligence may develop for a longer period of time, and different intellectual abilities may develop at different rates, any arbitrarily selected age poses a problem. The deviation IQ, which assesses the individual's test performance in terms of the distribution of test scores of others of the same age, avoids this problem.

The second problem with the MA/CA formula was that, because of certain statistical factors, children received different IQ scores at different ages, even though they maintained the same position compared to other children their age. With the deviation IQ the individual who maintains his or her relative position within each succeeding age group will always have the same IQ. For example, an intellectually superior person who maintains a Z-score of $+3.0$ on the Stanford-Binet will always be assigned an IQ of 145, regardless of whether the person is five or fifty years old.

Although the deviation IQ dealt with most of the problems inherent in the MA/CA ratio, it created others. The deviation IQ is a good indicator of the individual's level of intelligence compared to that of others of the same age, but it can be misleading with respect to a person's absolute level of intelligence. For example, at the age of seventy an average individual may still obtain an IQ of 100, even though this score may represent a lower level of absolute intelligence, as measured by the number of test items passed, than was evident at the age of thirty.

Standardizing Intelligence Tests

A score on an intelligence test or any other test has meaning only if the test has been standardized. **Standardization** is an arduous procedure, which we shall describe for an age-scale test. The test constructor begins with many more test items than will eventually be used and gives these to a sample of persons known as the **standardization sample.** Items for the final version of the test are selected on the basis of the performance of these people. If the same percentage of people of differing ages pass an item, it is considered a poor item and is not included in the final test. On the other hand, if an item is passed by 10 percent of four-year-olds, 60 percent of five-year-olds, and 90 percent of six-year-olds, the item is an ideal one for inclusion at the fifth-year age level. A sufficient number of children answer the item correctly and a sufficient number fail it for the test constructor to conclude that a correct answer reflects the intellectual ability of the average five-year-old.

The characteristics of people in the standardization sample should be as similar as possible to the characteristics of the total population for which the test will be used. There should be the correct proportion of males to females, of urban to rural dwellers, of people residing in various parts of the country, and of persons of various socioeconomic classes and ethnic backgrounds.

The adequacy of the standardizing procedure increases as the numerical size and representativeness of the standardizing sample increase. By this criterion Binet and Simon's 1908 scale was poorly standardized, since their sample included only 300 children. Over 3000 children were tested to standardize the 1937 Stanford-Binet. Although some care was taken to make this sample representative of the total population, only American-born whites were included. For this reason the test proved to be of doubtful value for evaluating the intelligence of foreign-born and racial minority children, and for comparing their intelligence with that of native-born white children. Some 4500 individuals participated in standardizing the 1960 Stanford-Binet, but once again the sample was limited to whites. This problem was addressed in 1972, when the test was standardized with samples of English-speaking Americans of varying ancestries (Terman and Merrill, 1973).

For IQ scores to remain accurate indicators of intellectual level, intelligence tests must be restandardized at periodic intervals. Changing social conditions may alter the amount or type of knowledge expected at different ages. For example, television has significantly increased the information available to preschoolers, and compulsory education has made today's young people more knowledgeable than their age-mates tested a few decades ago. Restandardization is also necessary because particular items may become easier or more difficult with time. Take, for instance, the question, "What is Mars?" At one time this was a relatively difficult item, but with the advent of the space age, even very young children have heard so much about Mars that they can give the correct answer. On the other hand, the word "coal" was once familiar to the smallest of children, since coal was used for heat in many homes and for the features of snowmen. Today's children may not encounter the word until later in life.

Reliability and Validity

An important aspect of the process of standardization is determining the extent to which tests meet two statistical criteria, reliability and validity.

Reliability. A test is reliable if it measures anything consistently, that is, if people receive the same score on the test whenever it is given. Since an individual's traits are assumed to remain fairly constant from day to day, psychologists strive for a reflection of this consistency in their tests. A test of intelligence would not be reliable, and would certainly not be useful, if individuals commonly received an IQ of 150 on one testing and an IQ of 75 on a second testing administered soon afterward.

The most direct way of determining the **reliability** of a test—the **test-retest method**—is to administer it to the same group of individuals twice to see whether their scores are similar on the two testings. If the scores correlate highly, the test is reliable. A reliability coefficient of about +.80 is commonly accepted as the minimum level for a psychological test, although the reliability of many tests is higher than this. That of the Stanford-Binet is about +.90.

Two other methods are also used to assess reliability. In the **split-half method** scores on one-half of a test are correlated with scores on the other half. For example, scores on the odd-numbered items may be correlated with scores on the even-numbered items. The third, the **alternate-forms method,** can be used only when there are two versions of the same test. If scores on the two tests correlate highly, it is evident that they measure the same thing. The correlation between scores on Forms L and M of the 1937 Stanford-Binet was +.91.

Validity.   The degree of a test's **validity** is the accuracy with which it measures what it is supposed to measure. A so-called intelligence test would not be a good one if performance on the test failed to agree with other independently observed facts about this trait. Psychologists recognize four different types of validity: predictive validity, concurrent validity, content validity, and construct validity.

Predictive validity is a measure of how well a test can predict an individual's performance in some important situation. As we have seen, intelligence tests were originally developed to predict school performance. Today the criterion of school success is still used to determine the predictive validity of intelligence tests. A number of studies have shown that the correlation between IQ scores achieved on the Stanford-Binet and school grades is about +.60. In other words, this test of intelligence is a valid predictor of school performance, although not as accurate a predictor as we might wish.

There seem to be three reasons why the correlation between tested intelligence and school grades is not higher than it is. School performance depends on many factors in addition to intelligence, including motivation, interest, and the quality of instruction. Measures of school performance are not completely reliable because teachers make errors and also have their own standards in assigning grades. Finally, the reliability of intelligence tests, although high, is not perfect.

We say that a test has **concurrent validity** when individuals obtain scores on it similar to the scores they obtain on another test of established validity. If the scores on a new intelligence test correlate highly with Stanford-Binet or Wechsler IQs, for example, the new test has concurrent validity.

A test has **content validity** if its coverage of a given subject is adequate and appropriate. An achievement test for a foreign language or mathematics is a good example of a test that strives for content validity. The items allow individuals to demonstrate their knowledge of these subjects. Achieving this type of validity is not a goal in the construction of intelligence tests which try *not* to rely on specific knowledge.

Finally, a test has **construct validity** if scores on it bear out theories about the trait or *construct* being tested. For example, since intelligence is expected to increase with age, an intelligence test will have at least an element of construct validity if older children obtain higher scores than younger children.

Whatever the special method employed, establishing the validity of a test comes down in the final analysis to the computation of a correlation coefficient (or some comparable statistic) that provides an estimate of the accuracy with which test scores predict behavior in some criterion situation, either in real life or on another test.

SUMMARY

Binet, who devised the first successful instrument for measuring intelligence, was able to do so through a series of brilliant insights. First, he aligned intelligence, not with sensorimotor functioning but with the complex higher mental processes. Second, he measured the effectiveness of his tests against an important criterion, the ability to achieve in school. Third, he viewed intelligence as age-related, as a configuration of different mental abilities that matured as the child grew older. Intelligence test constructors generally recognized that intelligence consists of many abilities, but Wechsler was the first to develop effective tests to measure a broader range of talents. His scales included a number of separate verbal and performance subtests.

Test scores expressed in terms of mental age provide a measure of absolute intelligence, but they do not indicate an individual's relative intelligence compared to that of others of the same age. This drawback was originally corrected by defining IQ as MA/CA $\times$ 100, but the resulting measure had certain inherent limitations. For this reason the deviation IQ was adopted. The deviation IQ expresses a person's relative intellectual status within his or her age group by a measure derived from Z-scores.

Standardization is a process of evaluating test items in order to choose those actually to be used on the test and of establishing standards with which to compare an individual's performance. Many possible test items are administered to a large sample of individuals who should be representative of the population for which the test will be used. On the basis of their answers, final test items are selected and placed at the appropriate age or difficulty levels. The value of a test, whether of intelligence or anything else, depends on the degree to which it meets the criteria of reliability and validity. Reliability is the consistency of the scores obtained on a test. Validity is the extent to which scores are related to some other criterion or measurement. "Test-retest," "split-half," and "alternate forms" are procedures for assessing reliability. "Predictive," "concurrent," "content," and "construct" are different types of validity.

PROBLEMS OF INTELLIGENCE TESTING

Although most existing intelligence tests have been standardized and are reliable and valid, unsolved problems remain in using them to measure intelligence. The composition of intelligence changes with age; what tests of infant intelligence tap is quite different from what tests used for older children and adults measure. Moreover, we have so far been unable to obtain pure measures of intelligence. Scores on intelligence tests are always contaminated to some degree by the test taker's previous experience, past opportunities, and motivation or lack of it to do well on the test.

Tests of Infant Intelligence

How early can differences in intelligence be detected? In efforts to answer this question, a number of intelligence tests have been constructed for use with infants. Most of the items on infant tests, like those on the original adult tests,

Arnold Lucius Gesell established schedules of ages at which most children reached sequential milestones of maturation.

are of sensorimotor skills. What the infant tests measure is probably not the same thing as is measured by adult tests of intelligence.

One of the earliest tests of infant intelligence was a set of developmental schedules devised by Arnold Gesell (1880–1961). As with the Binet tests, Gesell's schedules contain items which show a clear age progression. In this case the age levels are from one month to two years. The items at each level are divided into four categories: motor, adaptive, language, and personal–social. Items in the motor category assess such behavior as head balance, standing, walking, jumping, and the child's ability to reach for, grasp, and manipulate objects. Adaptive tests determine babies' reactions to objects, such as a toy cube and a dangling ring, and their ability to fit variously shaped blocks into forms on a board. Language items cover the prelinguistic vocalizations of babies, their comprehension of the speech of others, and their ability to point to objects and pictures named by the examiner. Personal-social items are administered for the most part by interviewing the mother. They cover smiling, self-feeding, toileting, play, and how the infant asks for things.

Gesell viewed his tests as measuring not intelligence but the child's level of development. The score an infant obtains is therefore called a **developmental quotient (DQ)** and is calculated with the same formula used for IQ. That is, performance is scored in months and is expressed as a developmental age (DA), which is divided by CA and multiplied by 100. For example, if a twelve-month-old girl passes all the items passed by the average sixteen-month-old, her DQ equals 100(16/12) or 133.

An important question is whether the infant whose DQ indicates accelerated development will be brighter later in life than the infant who is not so advanced. Study after study has failed to find evidence for such a relationship. Although children do vary widely in their rates of development, the DQs obtained early in life do not correlate with IQs achieved at maturity. Representative of these studies is the Berkeley Growth Study (Bayley and Schaefer, 1964), in which children were tested every month for the first fifteen months, then every three months up to three years of age, and finally semiannually from three to eighteen years. Figure 13.3 charts the correlations of IQs obtained at ages sixteen, seventeen, and eighteen with the DQs and IQs of the same individuals obtained at several earlier ages. There is no relationship between the earliest scores and those obtained later. From age four on, the relationship becomes increasingly greater, and by age seven the correlation is useful for predicting adult intelligence.

Figure 13.3
Correlations of earlier mental scores with sixteen- to eighteen-year scores. Before age two the correlations are low. Not until age seven does the correlation of early scores with late scores become sufficiently high to have predictive value for both boys and girls. (Data from the Berkeley Growth Study, Bayley and Schaefer, 1964.)

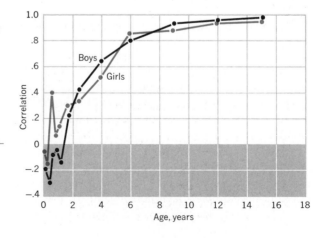

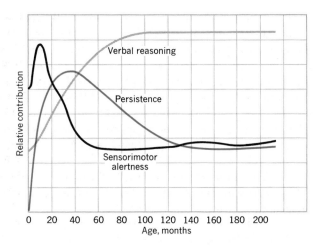

Figure 13.4
Three factors differently related to intelligence scores at different ages. The height of each curve at each age indicates the relative importance of the factor in determining the total score at that age. (Adapted from Hofstaetter, 1954.)

The failure to find a strong relation between infant DQs and later IQs indicates that the two scores reflect different abilities, suggesting again that intelligence is not a single capacity but rather a collection of abilities, some being found in the young child and others only in the older child. Several studies that have attempted to isolate the specific abilities assessed by early and later tests agree unanimously that scores on the two types of tests do indeed reflect different talents. Moreover, the relative contributions of the abilities sampled change with age. In one study (Hofstaetter, 1954), for example, early test scores were found to depend primarily on sensorimotor alertness, whereas test scores from age two to four depended on persistence (Figure 13.4). Through the preschool period verbal reasoning rapidly became more influential and was the most important determinant of test scores as the child became older. These findings indicate that as intelligence grows, mental functioning changes qualitatively as well as quantitatively.

Predictive Validity

Testing is a very practical enterprise. Tests are constructed to predict some particular behavior, technically called a *criterion*. Tests are valid to the extent that they predict criterion behavior. For historical reasons school performance came to be the ultimate criterion of intelligent behavior. The tests were constructed to predict scholastic behavior. Although the cognitive processes assessed by intelligence tests are useful both in and out of school, test scores are, because of this history, much better predictors of school performance than they are of other types of functioning. For one thing, a number of cognitive processes important in other activities are not important to school success and are therefore not sampled by intelligence tests. For this reason the common question, "Do the IQ tests measure true intelligence?" cannot be answered yes or no. Instead, the answer to this question will be, "If you can identify the criterion of true intelligence, it will be possible to determine the extent to which the tests measure it."

Intelligence versus Achievement

From Binet onward psychologists have agreed that it is important that intelligence tests keep intelligence separate from achievement or knowledge. Have they been able to do so? To make this question clear, suppose that an intelligence test includes the question, "What is a cable car?" More children in San

Francisco than in New York would answer this item correctly, but this certainly would not mean that San Francisco children are more intelligent. Rather, the West coast children would be showing greater achievement because they live in a city where cable cars are an everyday fact of life.

Theoretically, if two people have had the same opportunity to acquire the information or skills assessed on a test, and if one of them has learned them but the other has not, the test is a measure of their intellectual aptitude. But if they have not had the same opportunity to acquire the information, the test may yield only a measure of their achievement. It would be rare, of course, to find two people who have had exactly the same opportunities to acquire information. In practice, therefore, intelligence tests are measures of both intellectual ability and achievement, although the concept of intelligence emphasizes the former.

Culture Fairness

A test does not assess intelligence fairly if passing the items depends on belonging to one particular culture rather than another. Many theorists believe that our standard intelligence tests contain items that give an advantage to middle-class white children and place minority groups at a disadvantage.

Jerome Kagan (1971) has called our attention to a number of culturally biased items in our current tests. Vocabulary items often ask for the definition of words that are most likely to be heard in middle-class white homes. Children are asked how a piano and violin are alike, not how a tortilla and a frijole are alike. On a reasoning problem they are asked such questions as, "What should you do if you were sent to the store to buy a loaf of bread and the grocer said he didn't have any more?" Kagan points out that the correct answer—"Go to another store"—assumes a middle-class, urban neighborhood with more than one grocery store within safe walking distance. Rural or ghetto children who respond "Go home" receive no credit, even though this is a perfectly reasonable answer where they live.

One of the most serious consequences of using culturally unfair tests is that they can sometime lead to an incorrect diagnosis of mental retardation. Jane Mercer (1975) has argued that this is more likely to happen to children from minority groups and lower socioeconomic levels. She notes that a disproportionate number of these children are labeled mentally retarded and placed in special-education classes. She claims that these are incorrect diagnoses and blames them on the improper use of IQ tests. She believes that it is unfair to use an IQ test to assess the intelligence of children whose sociocultural backgrounds are significantly different from those of the majority of children on whom the test was standardized.

To prove her point, Mercer divided Mexican-American and black children into five groups according to how closely their family backgrounds corresponded to the dominant Anglo-American culture. She found that children whose homes were more similar to the Anglo-American homes scored higher on IQ tests than children whose homes were less Anglicized. For example, Mexican-American children from the most-Anglicized homes had a mean WISC IQ of 104.4, compared to a mean of 84.5 for those children from the least-Anglicized homes. The corresponding scores for black children were 99.5 and 82.7. In some school districts the least-Anglicized children in both groups would be candidates for special class placement.

In an effort to reduce the influence of culture on test results, a number of so-called **culture-fair tests** have been constructed. These tests cut down on verbal materials and include in their place tests of spatial reasoning, often about

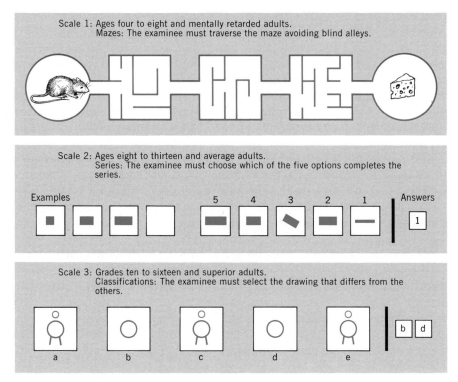

Scale 1: Ages four to eight and mentally retarded adults.
Mazes: The examinee must traverse the maze avoiding blind alleys.

Scale 2: Ages eight to thirteen and average adults.
Series: The examinee must choose which of the five options completes the
series.

Examples

5   4   3   2   1   Answers

1

Scale 3: Grades ten to sixteen and superior adults.
Classifications: The examinee must select the drawing that differs from the
others.

a   b   c   d   e

b d

Figure 13.5
Culture-fair measures of intelligence.
These sample items are from the IPAT
Culture-Fair Intelligence Test. (Reprinted
with permission of Professor Raymond B.
Cattell and the Institute for Personality
and Ability Testing. Copyright © 1949,
1953.)

the relations between geometric forms. They also ask children to complete
drawings, fit irregularly shaped blocks into holes, and copy designs with multicolored cubes. One such instrument is the IPAT Culture-Fair Intelligence Test,
devised by Raymond Cattell at the Institute for Personality and Ability Testing
(hence, IPAT). Samples of items from the test's three scales appear in Figure
13.5. Research suggests that the test has been only partially successful in
providing a measure of innate ability uncomplicated by cultural influences.
Although the scores of people in Taiwan and France appear to be comparable
to those gathered in the United States, scores of other nationality groups show
marked differences.

Taking culture-dependent items out of tests has proved to be a difficult if not
impossible task, and to date no test has been devised that can be considered
totally free of cultural influences. In interpreting intelligence test performance,
we must therefore consider the disparity between the groups on which the test
was standardized and the specific group to which the test taker belongs. Even
if a perfectly culture-fair test were devised, it would probably be a poorer
predictor of school performance than our present tests, inasmuch as successful
school performance is also culturally biased. Schools encourage the achievements and ways of performing considered valuable in the white middle-class
culture.

Motivational-Emotional Factors

Intelligence tests have also been criticized for being sensitive to personality and
motivational factors. For example, some test items require persistence or close
attention, but these are not necessarily intellectual abilities. To demonstrate that
emotional factors can have a dramatic effect on intelligence test performance,
one group of researchers (Zigler, Abelson, and Seitz, 1973) gave economically
disadvantaged children an intelligence test and then retested them a week later.

Their average scores increased a full ten points. That the earlier lower scores were related to emotionality was suggested by the test scores of a second group of children. The IQ scores of children who had an opportunity, before the initial testing, to play games with the examiner in a warm and friendly session were not much lower than their retest scores. These results suggest that in an unfamiliar testing situation the children's anxieties may have impaired their performance. When the children could become familiar with the testing situation through a retest or an amicable exchange with the examiner, their scores were substantially higher.

Going a step further, the researchers (Zigler et al., 1982) investigated whether scores might be influenced by two distinct types of emotional factors, those that are specific to the test situation, such as test anxiety, and more general ones that affect behavior other than test taking. They administered tests to a group of children in a Head Start program and a group of otherwise similar children who did not participate in Head Start. The children were tested once before the Head Start group began the program, once shortly after they began, and once several months later. Although the scores of all the children increased from the first to the second tests, only those of the Head Start children increased between the second and third tests. Apparently test-specific motivational difficulties were alleviated for all the children by their first experience in the testing situation. Participating in the Head Start program, however, affected the children's motives and emotions in a broader way, and they were able to increase their test scores further.

The results of these studies indicate that general life experiences do affect children's performances on tests. With special care an examiner may be able to alleviate some motivational-emotional factors detrimental to test performance, but testing cannot be kept totally free of them. The individual's willingness to perform on a test and his or her general emotional state will always be important determinants of the test score actually achieved.

SUMMARY

The development of standardized intelligence tests has been one of psychology's major contributions, but many problems of intelligence tests still remain to be solved. One is the measurement of intelligence in infancy. Infant tests, which emphasize sensorimotor abilities much more than tests of later intelligence do, yield a developmental quotient, an index of the relative rate at which the tasks of infancy are mastered. Little relation has been found between DQs and later IQs, indicating that with the growth of intelligence mental functioning undergoes qualitative changes.

Although intelligence test scores are useful in predicting school achievement, they are less successful in predicting everyday adult functioning. Clearly intelligence cannot be defined on the basis of abilities related to school performance alone, since other cognitive abilities are important in other situations. Intelligence tests fail to measure all the cognitive abilities that contribute to intelligence, broadly defined.

A third problem is that these tests inevitably measure both intellectual ability and achievement. Unless two people have had similar opportunities to learn the information and practice the skills measured by an intelligence test, their differing IQ scores are not valid indicators of their intellectual abilities but merely reflections of their differing experiences.

Performance on standard intelligence tests is partially dependent on the culture in which an individual has been raised. Despite careful standardization, our tests may give an advantage to middle-class whites and penalize those from minority and lower socioeconomic groups. The culture-free tests that have been constructed have not been completely satisfactory. Items requiring specific knowledge have been eliminated to some extent, but testing is still affected by culturally derived motives, attitudes, and values.

Emotions can also affect performance on intelligence tests. Children who are unfamiliar and uncomfortable with testing do better after they become acquainted with the procedures. Since persistence and paying attention contribute to school performance and since anxiety interferes with it, the motives and anxieties of children taking tests may actually contribute to predictive validity, because these factors influence test performance and school performance in the same way.

APTITUDE TESTING

From one point of view, intelligence is scholastic aptitude, the capacity to profit from training in school. Defined in this way, intelligence is closely related to other aptitudes. The general meaning of **aptitude** is the capacity to benefit from training in some particular line. Thus musical aptitude is the capacity to profit from training in music, legal aptitude the capacity to profit from law school. It is conventional to distinguish between aptitude and ability. Whereas aptitude is a capacity or potential to benefit from training, **ability** refers to an individual's present level of performance. A person with a high level of mechanical aptitude may, for lack of training, have little mechanical ability.

Constructing Aptitude Tests

The problems of constructing tests for the various aptitudes are similar to those encountered in constructing intelligence tests. First there is the problem of definition. Take the aptitude for learning to drive a car. In one sense it is the potential to profit from driver training. Or it could be defined in terms of contributing traits, such as fast reaction time, good distance perception, and an emotional stability that keeps the potential driver from taking too many chances. Tests based on these two definitions would be somewhat different.

With driving aptitude defined as the potential to profit from driver training, a test might resemble the practical situation very closely. Such tests are **work sample tests,** which are sometimes indistinguishable from the work or training itself. In the case of automobile driving, such a test might involve letting potential trainees try to drive an automobile. If they do well in a brief test, one might predict that they would do well with further training. Such methods are sometimes used in industry. Very often, however, the work sample test is not feasible. A work sample driving test would expose the trainee to the hazards of traffic and traffic to the hazards of the trainee. It is sometimes possible, however, to use an artifical situation that resembles the real one. Testing could be conducted on one of the simulators used in driver-training classes.

Most aptitude tests try to tap relevant abilities, which are often identified by a formal process of **job analysis.** In industry, for example, observing and interviewing workers and supervisors may reveal the talents that are important for particular jobs. Once these capacities have been identified, the next task is to make up tests to measure them. The final task is to demonstrate that the tests possess the statistical properties required of all tests.

Reliability and Validity

The reliability of an aptitude test is established by the same methods as those used for intelligence tests and requires no special comment. The validity of

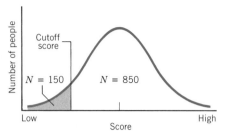

Figure 13.6
Theoretical distribution of scores on an aptitude test for computer programming.

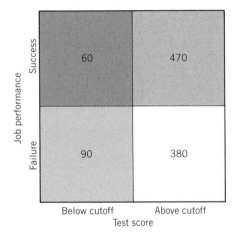

Figure 13.7
Numbers of people who succeeded and failed in the computer programming training program, separated into groups by whether their scores were below or above the cutoff score on the aptitude test. The validity of a test can be determined by these figures.

Figure 13.8
Effects of placement of a cutoff score. (a) With a low cutoff score most applicants are accepted, but the majority of them are destined to fail. (b) With a high cutoff score fewer applicants are accepted, but now the majority of them succeed.

aptitude tests, however, requires further explanation. Suppose that someone develops a test that is intended to assess the aptitude for computer programming and gives the test to 1000 applicants for admission to a training program for this skill. The distribution of scores might be roughly normal, looking something like that in Figure 13.6. The horizontal axis represents the range of scores on the test from low to high, and the vertical axis represents the number of persons obtaining each score. In the graph something called a **cutoff score** is indicated by a vertical line. The placement of this line depends on factors to be discussed in a moment. For the present, just notice that the cutoff score identifies two groups of people, the relatively large group with scores above the cutoff score and the relatively smaller group with scores below it.

Now suppose that all the individuals represented in the figure—those below the cutoff score as well as those above it—are admitted to the computer programming training program. If the people who fail and succeed in the course are those who scored below and above the cutoff score, respectively, the test can be considered valid. The results might turn out to be something like those in Figure 13.7. Obviously, people scoring above the cutoff score do better than those scoring below it, but the relationship is very far from perfect. These results indicate that the test can be used to select people so that more potential successes than failures enter training, but mistakes of two kinds are inevitable. Some of the people admitted to training turn out to be failures, and some potential successful candidates are excluded from training. You should note that this unhappy outcome cannot be avoided.

Against this background, we can now explain the location of the cutoff score. It is set, at the completion of a study such as the one just described, at a place where it admits as few potential failures and excludes as few potential successes as possible. The "as possible" provision depends on the size of the pool of candidates available for training or a job. The greater the number of candidates, the higher the cutoff score may be set. In general, the higher the cutoff score is set, the greater the proportion of potential successes accepted if the test has any validity at all. This last point can be made clear with the aid of scatter plots that depict the correlation between test scores and success in training or on the job. Figure 13.8 shows what happens when high and low cutoff scores are used for selection. The low cutoff actually admits more future failures than successes; the high cutoff does the opposite.

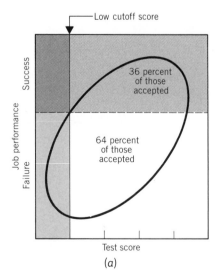

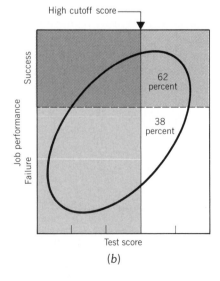

Specific Aptitudes

The validity of aptitude tests may be very specific. They sample very limited skills and are often standardized for particular job situations. For example, some tests measure aspects of manipulative skill, such as finger dexterity and steadiness. The tweezer dexterity test illustrated in Figure 13.9 is one example. It has some validity as a predictor of success in dental school. Correlations (validity coefficients) of +.15 to +.30 are typical.

Other tests tap perceptual skills. One of the most widely used is the Minnesota Paper Formboard (Figure 13.10). Scores on it correlate about +.50 with the production speed of merchandise packers but essentially zero with the production speed of lampshade sewers. Tests of clerical aptitude, such as the Minnesota Clerical Test, require people to go through two long lists, consisting of items like the following, as rapidly as possible, noting where items in the two lists differ.

84192	84182
296305	296035
John Wiley & Sons, Inc.	John Wilie & Sons, Inc.
1567 Pine Crest	1567 Pinecrest

Scores on this test correlate about +.40 with performance in various clerical jobs.

Valid tests for aptitude in more complex occupations are more difficult to construct, art aptitude being a case in point (Figure 13.11). Validities of these tests tend to be low, probably because they often fail to test for significant aspects of the aptitude, some of which may be as yet unknown.

Another aptitude that has proved difficult to assess is the aptitude for scientific research. In one of the few studies of this aptitude, Anne Roe (1951) interviewed and tested twenty-two of the most eminent experimental and theoretical physicists in the United States. Perhaps her most striking finding was that intelligence is not the decisive factor in determining a high-level aptitude for physical science. Although all the physicists were obviously intelligent, they were not more so than their less eminent colleagues. In fact, no single characteristic was sufficient to predict the degree of eminence attained by the group of physicists. Clearly the problems of assessing aptitude for theoretical physics are not the same as those of determining aptitudes for operating a machine on a production line. Personality and social factors play a much greater part.

Academic Aptitude Tests

Aptitude tests are used sometimes in educational settings to determine which individuals are likely to do well in particular fields or institutions. These tests

Figure 13.9
The O'Connor Tweezer Dexterity Test. The test taker must pick up metal pegs and insert them in small holes in the correct order.

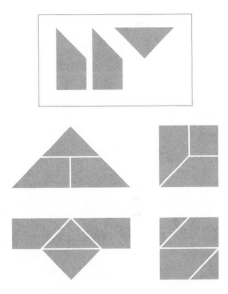

Figure 13.10
An item of the sort used in the Minnesota Paper Formboard. Which of the figures at the bottom are constructed from the pieces at the top?

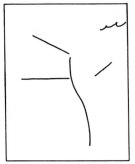

Figure 13.11
An item from the Horn Art Aptitude Inventory and pictures that two individuals made using the lines on this card. (From Horn and Smith, 1945.)

are necessarily achievement tests of a sort. People who have never taken mathematics in high school are likely to do poorly on the mathematics section of a college admissions exam. Their scores on the test do not indicate a lack of aptitude for mathematics, but they do suggest that these students would have a difficult time in the type of math courses taught in college. Some academic tests are purposefully designed to show achievement rather than aptitude. Placement or waiver exams, for example, are meant to assess achievement and to indicate the level at which a student should be placed, for example, in a beginning or advanced French course, or whether the student needs to take the course at all.

Of the tests that strive to tap aptitude more than achievement, the most familiar is the Scholastic Aptitude Test (SAT). Scores on this test are required for admission to most colleges, although some states have their own testing systems, and some colleges rely on SAT scores more than others. The validity of the SAT is determined by comparing individuals' scores on the test with their grades in college. Validity coefficients for both the verbal and quantitative sections of the test are approximately $+.30$ to $+.40$. The most probable reason for this relatively low validity is that people with low scores are excluded from many colleges, and this lowers the possible correlation (see page 648).

The national average scores on the SAT began to decline in 1963 and, although the downward trend appears to have ended, current average SAT scores are nearly ninety points lower on the two scales combined. Some have blamed the content of the tests for the decline in scores. Others have pointed the finger of shame at television for undermining basic academic skills, or for causing students to learn in a different manner, from images rather than from the written word. Schools have been taken to task for emphasizing electives instead of basic subjects. Lyle Jones (1981) pointed out that before 1972 changes in the population of test takers were the most important factors behind the change in scores. Since more students from disadvantaged backgrounds were taking the SAT, this shift in the test-taking population could have lowered the national average. More recently, however, the population of test takers has been more stable, and only about one-quarter of the decline since then can be attributed to this factor. Whatever the actual cause—and it is almost certainly a combination of many factors—the decline of SAT scores has highlighted controversies surrounding this particular test and psychological tests in general.

One subject of debate concerns culture fairness, which we discussed in connection with intelligence tests. Originally adopted in 1926 as a tool which admissions officers might use to screen applicants, the SAT was meant to give a fair chance to all students without the potential discrimination of subjective evaluations. More recently, however, the SAT has been criticized as biased against poor and minority students.

A second issue is whether the SAT truly tests aptitude rather than achievement. If it is an aptitude test, scores should not be affected by coaching. If coaching does help, this would suggest that the test is partly a test of achievement. The Educational Testing Service (ETS), which publishes the test, reports that coaching can raise scores by twenty to thirty points, depending on the amount of coaching. According to ETS, however, any individual, coached or uncoached, who repeats the test has a two-thirds chance of earning a second score that is thirty points above or below the first. Consequently, it is unclear how significant raising scores thirty points through coaching may be in practical terms.

SUMMARY

Aptitude tests are constructed to predict success in training or on a job. These tests must fulfill the standard criteria of reliability and validity. Reliability is assessed by the methods used for intelligence tests. In the assessment of validity, a cutoff score is often established; the validity of the test becomes the degree to which this score divides the people tested into groups who succeed and fail in the training or employment situation for which the test is constructed.

Tests used for personnel selection and placement range from tests of general intelligence to special tests of manipulation, perceptual skill, and clerical aptitude. Aptitude tests for more complex occupations such as that of the artist do not attain the validity of many aptitude tests, perhaps because success in such callings depends to a greater degree on unique personality factors.

Scholastic aptitude tests such as the SAT are routinely used in the admission procedures of educational institutions. Achievement tests are also used, both for admissions to particular programs of study and for certification in professional fields. Controversies surround the use of the SAT. A seventeen-year decline in national average scores raised questions whether the test is culturally biased and whether it is truly a measure of aptitude.

THE ASSESSMENT OF PERSONALITY

The development of tests to assess the general dispositions and psychological adjustment of people has been an active field for decades. There are currently in existence more than 500 different **personality tests.** They differ from one another both in content and in the specific traits of personality that are measured.

Constructing Personality Tests

Psychologists who develop personality tests make use of three different methods: the rational-construct method, the empirical-criterion method, and the factor-analytic method. The developers of many tests have used all three.

The **rational-construct** method relies on the psychologist's understanding of the trait to be measured. Someone developing a test for introversion by this method might begin with the intuitive belief that introverts are hesitant, reflective, withdrawn, reserved, and intellectual and then proceed to write items designed to tap these characteristics. In and of itself, the rational-construct method makes no claims of validity. Some other method must be used to determine whether the test is valid.

The **empirical-criterion** method, in contrast, begins by establishing a criterion of validity. Someone developing a test for introversion by this method might start out by selecting two groups of individuals who seem to differ in this trait. The 100 students at some university who have the most dates and the 100 students who have the fewest dates might serve this purpose. Then these students would respond to a large number of potential test items, perhaps items developed by the rational-construct method. For the final test of introversion, only the items to which the two groups responded differently would be retained. This method is an *empirical*-criterion method because very little theory is involved. The chosen items are those that, as a matter of fact, distinguish between different groups of people. It is an empirical-*criterion* method because the two samples of subjects who provide the data differ in a way that is related to the trait being measured.

The **factor-analytic** method of personality test construction begins by selecting a very large number of items and administering them to many different people. The statistical procedures of factor analysis make it possible to identify groups of items that cluster together, in the sense that answering one item in a given way is correlated with the tendency to answer the others in the cluster in a given way. The items so identified then become a scale, which is named on the basis of the content of the items. A test of introversion developed by this method would contain clustered items that seem to reflect this trait. The criterion for selecting items is that answers to them relate rather than that they differentiate groups of people.

Self-Rating Tests of Personality

The traditional paper-and-pencil personality tests are self-rating inventories. They ask the individuals taking the test to respond "yes" or "no," or "true" or "false," or in some cases "can't say" to indicate whether certain statements describe them. Examples are "I am easily embarrassed" and "I often become impatient with people." One of the difficulties with such questionnaires is that too often the "correct" answer to each question, in the sense of indicating good adjustment, is obvious. Answers can be "faked" to make a person look good. But a growing sophistication in test construction has done much to remedy this situation, as can be seen by reviewing the structure of the personality inventory used most extensively throughout the world.

Minnesota Multiphasic Personality Inventory. The **Minnesota Multiphasic Personality Inventory** or **MMPI** consists of 550 statements that respondents evaluate in terms of their own behavior, answering "true," "false," or "cannot say" to each of them. The test was created by the empirical-criterion method in which the responses of persons with particular psychiatric diagnoses and those of normally adjusted people were compared. The content of the items covers a wide range of topics, including physical conditions, psychosomatic symptoms, social attitudes, family and marital factors, and psychiatric symptoms. More than 200 empirically derived scales have now been constructed from the items on this test. They measure anxiety, ego defensiveness, self-control, and so on. Fourteen basic scales, however, are commonly used for the analysis of personality. Four so-called validity scales measure the test-taking attitude of the individual and provide evidence of attempts at deliberate faking. The remaining ten scales are called clinical scales, eight of which bear the names of clinical diagnoses; one is a scale of masculinity–femininity and one measures social introversion. These fourteen scales, with illustrative items and the behavior reflected by each, are listed in Table 13.3

The MMPI has been found useful in a number of clinical and nonclinical settings. It has been used for screening job applicants, for college counseling, for making diagnostic decisions, and for assessing whether people can be helped by therapy. The MMPI enjoys worldwide favor as a clinician's technique for assessment. There are more than fifty translations of the MMPI into approximately twenty-six languages. For some translations items must be changed. In the Hebrew version for use in Israel (Butcher and Gur, 1974), the American item, "Christ performed miracles such as changing water into wine," became "God performed miracles such as dividing the Red Sea."

After a person has taken the MMPI, the test is scored for each of the scales, and these scores are plotted in the form shown in Figure 13.12. The ordinate is in terms of standard scores, or T-scores, which have a mean of 50 and a standard deviation of 10. High scores, especially those of 70 or more—two standard deviations above the mean—are taken as particularly significant.

Table 13.3 Basic Scales of the Minnesota Multiphasic Personality Inventory

Name of Scale	Psychological Significance	Illustrative Item with Keyed Response
Validity Scales		
? Cannot say scale	Not a scale in the ordinary sense. Failure to answer more than ten items taken as significant.	
L Lie scale	Fifteen items which reflect minor faults that most people have, such as minor aggressions, temptations, and lack of control. High L means faking in the "good" direction.	Once in a while I put off until tomorrow what I ought to do today. (False)
F Validity scale	Sixty-four items which measure how often subject chooses a response only rarely chosen by most subjects. High F means all subject's responses are invalid because of carelessness in answering or deliberate malingering.	It would be better if almost all laws were thrown away. (True)
K Correction scale	Measures test-taking attitude. High K indicates personal defensiveness, low K a desire to "look bad" by revealing personal defects to an excessive degree.	At periods my mind seems to work more slowly than usual. (False)
Clinical Scales		
(Hs) Hypochondriasis	Indicates how often subject worries about bodily functions, although not physically ill.	I am bothered by acid stomach several times a week. (True)
(D) Depression	Reflects feelings of hopelessness, unworthiness, slowness in thought and action, and a pessimistic view of life.	I usually feel that life is worthwhile. (False)
(Hy) Hysteria	Indicates the use of somatic complaints to solve difficult problems or avoid responsibilities, the denial of any kind of difficulties when facing stress.	I can be friendly with people who do things which I consider wrong. (True)
(Pd) Psychopathic deviate	Measures emotional shallowness in interpersonal relations, a disregard for rules of social conduct, and inability to profit by past experience.	My way of doing things is apt to be misunderstood by others. (True)
(Mf) Masculinity–femininity	Measures the feminine interests of men and the masculine interests of women. High scores for men reflect cultural and aesthetic interests, passivity, and emotionality; for women high Mf identifies vigorous, active, and masculine orientation.	If I were an artist, I would like to draw flowers. (True)
(Pa) Paranoia	Indicates delusions of being influential and the center of attention, or of being victimized. High scores reveal an extreme suspiciousness and excessive sensitivity in interpersonal relations.	I have no enemies who really wish to harm me. (False).
(Pt) Psychasthenia	Indicates obsessive thoughts and compulsive actions. High scores suggest vacillation, rumination, ritualistic concerns, an emphasis on morality, and a lack of esteem.	I usually have to stop and think before I act even in trifling matters. (False)
(Sc) Schizophrenia	Reveals bizarre and unusual thinking, disorientation and withdrawal, and sometimes delusions and hallucinations.	I often feel as if things were not real. (True)
(Ma) Hypomania	Reflects hyperactivity, an elated mood, rapid flights of disconnected ideas, and emotional excitability.	When I get bored, I like to stir up some excitement. (True)
(Si) Social introversion	Indicates little interest in people, withdrawal from social contacts and responsibilities. Low scorers are extroverted.	At parties I am more likely to sit by myself or with just one other person than to join in with the crowd. (True)

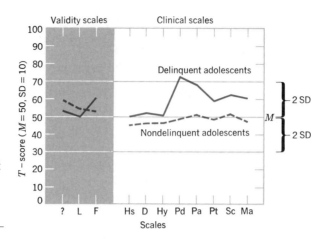

Figure 13.12
Plotting a profile of scores from the MMPI. The scores of delinquent adolescents and nondelinquent adolescents are compared. Notice the extreme score on the psychopathic deviate scale. This "Pd spike" is characteristic of delinquents. Scales Mf and Si are omitted. The scale to the right shows the range of scores, 30 to 70, falling two standard deviations on either side of the mean value of 50. (Adapted from Hathaway and Monachesi, 1953.)

When the test is used for diagnostic purposes, the diagnosis is based on the individual's pattern of scores (see Figure 13.12). This profile can be compared with the configurations of persons with known disorders, and a diagnosis can be arrived at on the basis of matching patterns. This approach makes automated machine scoring of the MMPI possible. Computer printouts provide interpretations based on the similarity of the individual's profile to those of other individuals whose data are stored in the memory banks of the computer.

The California Psychological Inventory.   The MMPI has served as the prototype for many other personality inventories, but none of these offspring is closer to the parent than the **California Psychological Inventory (CPI).** Although it draws 178 of its 480 items from the MMPI, the CPI has a different purpose and fills a great need. The MMPI, as we have seen, was created to diagnose psychopathology. One objection to the test has been that too many items describe people in pathological terms. Normal individuals who take the MMPI are likely to be affronted by the relatively large number of items inquiring whether they are followed everywhere by suspicious people, hear things other people cannot hear, are afraid of using knives or other sharp and pointed objects, whether someone is trying to poison them, whether parts of their body have feelings of burning, tingling, or crawling, and whether someone is trying to control their mind. The CPI was constructed for use with general populations from age thirteen and up, and particularly for high school and college students.

Retaining the true-false format, the CPI consists of eighteen scales, three of which are again so-called "validity scales" that measure the test-taking attitudes of the respondent. The fifteen other scales were designed to measure what its creator, Harrison Gough (1960), called "folk concepts, descriptive and classificatory notions concerning behavior and disposition that people everywhere use easily in their daily interaction with one another." The CPI has little symptom-related content; both its language and interpretive scales are appropriate for ordinary people. The CPI was standardized on the responses of 6000 men and 7000 women of varying ages, occupations, levels of education, and socioeconomic status and from different geographical areas. Scores are reported in the form of a profile. Gough divided the scales into four classes (Table 13.4) to facilitate interpretation.

There has been a great deal of research on the CPI, much of which has been brought together in a CPI handbook (Megargee, 1972). The handbook de-

Table 13.4 The Psychological Significance and Illustrative Items of the CPI Scales

Name of Scale	Psychological Significance	Illustrative Item with Keyed Response
Class I Scales: Measures of Poise, Ascendancy, Self-Assurance, and Interpersonal Adequacy		
Dominance	Indicates strong, dominant, influential person, able to exercise initiative and leadership.	I have a natural talent for influencing people. (True)
Capacity for Status	Measures ambition, self-assurance.	I get very nervous if I think someone is watching over me. (False)
Sociability	Measures outgoing sociability, participation.	I am a good mixer. (True)
Social Presence	Reveals poise, self-confidence, verve, and spontaneity in social situations.	I like to go to parties and other affairs where there is lots of loud fun. (True)
Self-Acceptance	Measures sense of personal worth, self-acceptance, and capacity for independent thinking and action.	I am certainly lacking in self-confidence. (False)
Sense of Well-Being (Validity scale)	Indicates health and verve, or the inability to meet demands and a lack of vitality.	I usually feel that life is worthwhile. (True)
Class II Scales: Measures of Responsibility, Socialization, Maturity, and Intrapersonal Structuring of Values		
Responsibility	Indicates conscientious, responsible behavior and belief that reason should govern actions, emphasis on values and controls.	When I work on a committee, I like to take charge of things. (True)
Socialization	Measures social maturity, integrity, the internalization of values.	As a youngster in school I used to give the teacher lots of trouble. (False)
Self-Control	Indicates degree of self-control and freedom from impulsiveness and self-centeredness.	I would do almost anything on a dare. (False)
Tolerance	Indicates permissive, accepting, nonjudgmental social beliefs and attitudes.	I feel sure there is only one true religion. (False)
Good Impression (Validity scale)	Infrequent items indicating random responding.	I usually try to do what is expected of me to avoid criticism. (True)
Class III Scales: Measures of Intellectual Efficiency and Achievement Potential		
Achievement via Conformance	Reveals strong need for achievement, combined with an appreciation of structure and organization.	I always try to do a little better than what is expected of me. (True)
Achievement via Independence	Reveals need for achievement through independence of thought, creativity, and self-actualization.	For most questions there is one right answer, once a person is able to get all the facts. (False)
Intellectual Efficiency	Reveals personality traits highly correlated with measures of intelligence.	I seem to be as capable and smart as most others around me. (True)
Class IV Variables: Measures of Intellectual and Interest Modes		
Psychological Mindedness	Measures insight into how others think and feel.	I have frequently found myself alone, pondering such abstract problems as free will, evil, etc. (False)
Flexibility	Indicates flexible, accepting, changeable person.	I like to have a place for everything and everything in its place. (False)
Femininity	Indicates feminine patterns.	I get very tense and anxious when I think other people are disapproving of me. (True)

Adapted from Megargee, 1972.

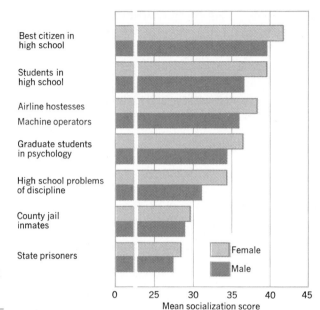

Figure 13.13
Validity of the California Psychological Inventory. The score on the socialization scale of the CPI distinguishes in expected directions male and female members of different groups. (After Gough, 1960.)

scribes the usefulness of the test as a "wide-band" instrument in this summarizing paragraph.

> The studies . . . have found significant associations between the CPI and various measures of achievement in elementary school, high school and college, as well as in military and police training programs, medicine, dentistry, nursing and teaching; moreover, the CPI can identify those who are likely to partake in extra-curricular activities or cheat on exams. The inventory has been found to relate to leadership, managerial ability, employability, and adjustment. It can forecast juvenile delinquency, parole success and can reliably discriminate alcoholics from marijuana and cigarette smokers. It has been found to relate to conformity, creativity, . . . physiological responsiveness to stress, . . . political participation, marital adjustment, and to one's choice of family planning methods. The [parent's] CPI can also be used to predict whether an infant is likely to suffer from colic, and it can chart the short and long term effects on such infants if the marriage should end in divorce (p. 247).

The power of the socialization scale in distinguishing various groups appropriately (Figure 13.13) is one example of how the test functions in actual use.

Projective Techniques
Some of the potentially most powerful ways of measuring personality come from the evaluation of materials created in the test taker's imagination. Collectively, the methods that tap these imaginings are called **projective techniques.** The procedures may ask the individual to make up a story about a picture, interpret an ambiguous figure such as an inkblot, create a drawing, or complete an incomplete sentence. One helpful feature of the projective tests is that their purposes are not obvious to those taking them. Psychologists who use these methods assume that people project important aspects of their personalities—their feelings, desires, and wishes—in their responses on the test.

Thematic Apperception Test. The **Thematic Apperception Test (TAT)** consists of a set of pictures (Figure 13.14); the person being tested makes up a story about each. The instructions indicate that the story should describe the events that led up to the scene pictured, what the participants in the story are thinking and feeling, what is currently happening, and how the story will end. The following case study shows how a clinical psychologist used the TAT to achieve a greater understanding of a patient's problem.

> Mrs. T., a twenty-two-year-old white woman, was admitted to a hospital because of promiscuity, alcoholism, obesity, and depression. Five months before hospitalization she had taken an overdose of drugs. Then followed an episode in which she was violent and suffered from hallucinations and a sense of unreality regarding herself and her environment. The question of a psychotic disorder was raised.
>
> Six years before hospitalization the patient's parents had separated and her mother subsequently committed suicide. Two years later the patient entered college but subsequently transferred to several other institutions. Two years before her admission she married a student who remained uncertain about his career plans, switched courses of study repeatedly, and was contemplating leaving school at the time of her hospitalization.

Mrs. T. gave this interpretation of the picture in Figure 13.14 as part of her TAT:

> This is a picture of a woman who all of her life has been a very suspicious, conniving person. She's looking in the mirror. And she sees reflected behind her an image of what she will be as an old woman—still a suspicious, conniving sort of person. And she can't stand the thought that that's what her life will eventually lead her to. And she smashes in the mirror and runs out of the house screaming and goes out of her mind and lives in uh-a- institution for the rest of her life. That's it.

To give you a taste of how a TAT story is interpreted, we reproduce some of the clinical psychologist's commentary on this story. Remember this is only one story. The full test was given, and all stories were used in a more complete interpretation.

> From a perceptual point of view, looking in a mirror and seeing an image . . . behind oneself is peculiar . . . a disruption in the perceptual process. . . . Some of the other content in the protocol—suspiciousness and conniving—cannot be fully appreciated in this instance unless we also consider that frank perceptual distortion is evident and, therefore, that projective trends may reach psychotic proportions.
>
> Since the older woman is commonly described as a maternal figure, we can assume that the patient is communicating something about her relationship vis-à-vis this maternal figure. There is the attempt to destroy the ties to a dreaded negative maternal figure by violent means, a process which is seen as resulting in the inevitable destruction of the patient as well. . . . In that her thinking becomes peculiar on this card, the depth of identification with the mother seems extreme and may reach psychotic proportions.
>
> The feeling of being doomed to become like the maternal figure is of special significance for Mrs. T. since we know that her mother committed suicide. Her need to break the bond with the mother, therefore, becomes even more urgent, in order to free herself from being fated to repeat the mother's suicide (Allison, Blatt, and Zimet, 1968, pp. 121–122).

In this interpretation the clinician does several things. First, he conveys his opinions about the patient's mental state: there is a disturbance of her perceptual functioning; she is also attempting to break—by violence if necessary—a destructive tie to her mother. Second, he begins the development of a diagnosis: both the perceptual distortions and the quality of Mrs. T.'s identification with her mother suggest psychosis. Finally, the imaginative story is related to the patient's life history—her mother committed suicide and she is terrified that her fate will be the same.

The themes in the TAT stories play only one part in the clinician's effort to understand the patient; other aspects are equally important. These include the

Figure 13.14
A sample picture from the Thematic Apperception Test. The pictures are usually ambiguous but potentially emotional scenes which the subject can interpret in the light of personal experience and fantasy.

Hermann Rorschach (1884–1922), a Swiss psychiatrist, tested the reactions of patients to thousands of inkblots beginning in 1911. The ten he finally published in 1921 were selected because they provoked the most vivid and emotional responses. Rorschach died only eight months later.

Figure 13.15
Card 1 of the Rorschach inkblot test.

length of the story, its organization, originality, and continuity. Attention is also given to the emotional tone of the stories, the attributes of the hero or central figure, as well as those of the other characters in the story, the locations mentioned in the stories, and the interpersonal situations described.

The Rorschach Test. The most widely used of all projective tests is the **Rorschach inkblot test.** It consists of ten inkblot pictures like the one shown in Figure 13.15. All the blots are symmetrical, half of them are in black, white, and shades of gray, two contain splotches of red, and three of them are in full pastel color. The blots are presented to the individual one at a time, in a specific order, with the instruction to tell what the inkblot looks like or what it might be. After these responses have been recorded, the examiner and the subject go through the cards again. This time the subject indicates what parts of the inkblot suggested each response and why.

The average person will give thirty to forty responses to the blots, each of which is scored on four bases: location, determinant, content, and quality of the response. Location is the part of the inkblot selected by the subject for interpretation. This can be the whole blot, a large section of the blot that is commonly reacted to, a small detail that is less frequently reacted to, or a white space in the blot. The scoring for determinant describes the characteristic of the blot or part of it that is responsible for each interpretation. The possibilities include shape, color, shading, impressions of depth, and impressions of movement. The content of the response is the type of association given by the respondent, such as animal, human being, fire, clouds, and so on. Finally, as an indication of quality, each response is scored plus or minus, depending on whether the particular response is appropriate to the section of the blot to which it is given. Scoring and interpretation of the Rorschach responses are complex, and we would do a disservice to summarize rules the clinician uses in the analysis. It should be mentioned specifically, however, that the content of a response—animal, fire, and the like—has less significance than the other scoring categories.

Behavioral Assessment

In recent years research psychologists have grown increasingly dissatisfied with the projective techniques for several reasons. For one thing, the ambiguity of the stimuli, which are chosen deliberately to provide free play for the individual's responses, is a marked disadvantage. The more ambiguous and nonrepresentational these test materials are, the greater the problems of interpretation. Rorschach inkblots are at the far extreme in this regard, TAT pictures less so. But even with the TAT a great deal is inferred in making statements about the personality of a respondent. Reread the psychologist's commentary on the patient's TAT story and note the importance of such inferences. The young woman is assumed to be the patient, the old lady her mother. The assignment of these roles is based on clinical probabilities: "Since the older woman is *commonly* described as a maternal figure, we can assume that the patient is communicating something about her relationship vis-à-vis this maternal figure." Many psychologists criticize such inferences as being of dubious validity and useless for personality assessment. In a search for more substantial methods, they have developed techniques of **behavioral assessment** which have brought a new look to personality testing.

Traditional personality tests start with the assumption that responses to test items are signs of the underlying traits that account for the consistencies in an individual's behavior. Behavioral assessment, taking a somewhat different view

(Ciminero, 1977), concentrates on what a person does in specific situations, on the assumption that the observed behavior is a sample of how the person would behave in other, similar, situations (Goldfried and Kent, 1972). In this section we describe two methods of behavioral assessment, self-reports and direct behavioral observations.

Among the most popular **self-report** procedures are the *self-monitoring* techniques. These require individuals to record various aspects of their own behavior. For example, individuals in weight-reduction programs monitor their weight. In some programs to reduce smoking, a cigarette case that automatically records the number of times it has been opened is used. In this way the self-report, which might otherwise be untruthful, is supplanted by a mechanical device which records behavior honestly and has no need to make its owner look better.

In a second method, **direct observation,** an independent observer records the individual's behavior. Called "the hall mark of behavioral assessment" (Ciminero, 1977), this method has a long history in psychology. For example, during World War II situational tests were devised by staff psychologists of the Office of Strategic Services to select candidates for espionage and other dangerous military assignments. The candidate was placed in a very realistic, complex, and lifelike stressful situation. Those who behaved as though they were likely to think effectively and provide leadership under conditions of extreme stress were selected. In one test, called the Stress Interview, the candidate had to imagine that he had been caught in a government office, rifling through the contents of "secret" files. He was given twelve minutes to construct an alibi to explain his presence, then had to defend this explanation under a rapid, harrowing interrogation. At the end of each interview, the candidate was told that he had failed, and his reaction to this disturbing news was carefully observed. Later an interview was conducted by a friendly, informal interviewer to see whether the candidate would violate security in a situation where, unexpectedly, he could relax.

Tasks such as these are called **laboratory analogues** because they simulate possible real-life events. Some assessors who use these methods invite the person "to respond as you usually would to the following situation" (Nay, 1977). Others create wholly novel situations with which the individual has had no earlier experience. In one study (Arkowitz et al., 1975) the analogue method was used to study the social competence of male undergraduates who were frequent and infrequent daters. Descriptions and conversations for ten social situations were recorded on tape and then played back to the subjects. In one situation a male voice said, "At a party, you go over to a young woman and ask her to dance." Next a female voice was heard: "I'm not really much of a dancer." A signal on the tape then indicated that the subject was to respond. Ratings of the effectiveness of the responses revealed significant differences between the young men in the two groups.

Observations are also carried out in naturalistic settings. For example, observers have visited in homes to observe family interactions. Gerald Patterson (1980) has studied the interactions between mothers and delinquent offspring in their homes in an effort to evaluate the contribution of the family to adolescent aggression. Marital interactions have been observed in the course of treating couples who had come for counseling. Other studies have been made of anxiety states, addictive behavior, depression, sexual behavior, social skills, behavior problems in children, problem-solving skills (Ciminero, Calhoun, and Adams, 1977; Merluzzi, Glass, and Genest, 1981), and even human curiosity (Maw and Maw, 1977).

The expansion of the behavioral methods of personality assessment is one of the major developments of recent years, but the procedures are not without their critics. It has been pointed out that experimental rigor often requires that complex behavior be simplified (Pervin, 1980). But simplification brings a possible disadvantage. The complexities of human thinking and information processing may not be adequately reflected in observations that do little more than count frequencies. Social and interpersonal interactions may not lend themselves to simple categories. Acts of self-monitoring or direct observation may attenuate or modify the behavior we want to assess. These shortcomings can be remedied, however, and behavioral assessment bodes well for the future of personality measurement.

Responses to Personality Tests

Research on personality tests has led to an important distinction between the content of the response and the individual's characteristic style of responding. An anxious person may be extremely cautious and hesitate to guess when uncertain. The uninvolved person may be a cavalier test taker, guessing recklessly whenever an answer is not obvious. Some people have a tendency to acquiesce; they are "yea-sayers" who endorse or agree with most items. Others have a tendency to dissent; they are "nay-sayers" who respond "no" or "false" to most items. These **response sets** or response biases may reveal as much about an individual's personality as the test score. For example, the nay-saying tendency may be diagnostic, for maladjusted people often disagree with items describing them in a positive way (Rundquist, 1966).

Another response set has to do with the **social desirability** of alternative test answers. When one choice on a test item appears more socially acceptable than the others, whether or not it is an accurate description, a person may purposely try to make a good impression by choosing such answers. For example, job applicants often try to answer in a way that they think will please a prospective employer. In some instances, of which malingering may be the most important example, people attempt to make a bad impression by choosing answers with negative implications. Malingering is acting in a way that will secure the person a diagnosis of psychopathology. The individual may hope to receive treatment for perceived problems. Someone being tried for a criminal offense may hope to be acquitted for reasons of insanity. Or the malingerer may wish to avoid the consequences of a healthy performance on the test, such as induction into the army.

Research has demonstrated that such attitudes really can affect test responses. For example, examinees respond differently when told to answer as though they were a well-adjusted person or a maladjusted person, or as though they were applying for different types of jobs. Thus test results may not reflect the person's own thoughts and feelings but those they want to convey. The social-desirability response set may operate unconsciously. Motivated by a desire for conformity, approval, attention, or sympathy, the individual may adopt a social-desirability response set without being aware of it.

Interpreting Personality Data

There are two ways of interpreting the data obtained from personality tests. One is **clinical prediction.** The clinician arrives at an interpretation based on intuition, knowledge, impressions, and judgment. In the alternative, statistical or **actuarial prediction,** the test scores and other information about people, such as life history and interview data, are referred to some actuarial table, or "diagnostic cookbook," which gives the "recipe" for interpreting the personality data. Actuarial interpretations are arrived at by comparing the information collected on an individual with the large array of information collected on many people with different personal characteristics.

Some psychologists are more comfortable with the actuarial method because of its straightforward application of objective rules, mathematical procedures, and tables of data (Meehl, 1954). Others scoff at such mechanization. For example, Robert Holt (1977) calls the clinician's role in this type of analysis that of a "second-rate calculating machine." Sophisticated clinical predictions, asserts Holt, require consideration of an individual's needs, conflicts, defenses, and fantasies, and these pose problems far too difficult for an equation or a statistical table to handle. Furthermore, Holt argues, clinical assessment must often be made of unusual people, who are unlikely to be represented anywhere in mathematical equations or tables of data.

The real question, of course, is whether more accurate interpretations are made by the actuarial or the clinical methods. In 1959 Paul Meehl compared thirty-five studies that had appeared in the research literature. He found that the actuarial method was superior in twenty-three studies, and that there was no difference in twelve. More than two decades and many additional studies later, the actuarial method still retains its lead. It is premature, however, to decide on this basis that clinical methods are not useful. The problem seems to be to discover the bases of clinical insights and to subject clinical information to the same analysis employed in evaluating other forms of psychological assessment. Only then will it be possible to judge the relative effectiveness of the actuarial and clinical methods.

Computerized Personality Assessment.   A revolutionary development in actuarial assessment has been the computerization of personality diagnosis and interpretation. Usually such a system operates on MMPI test scores together with other data such as age, sex, and specific case history information. These data for an individual are fed into a computer, which compares them with information filed in its memory bank. On the basis of this comparison, the computer provides a test profile, a data sheet summarizing the scale scores, and a note about unusual answers to specific items. The main body of such a report is a computer-generated narrative which describes the individual's test-taking attitudes and behavioral symptoms, provides a general diagnosis, and makes a prognostic statement of the person's likely future adaptation. The following case history and the computer analysis, both supplied by Dr. James N. Butcher of the University of Minnesota, illustrate the method.

Case History.   Charles B., a twenty-one-year-old college senior, was referred for psychological treatment following his hospitalization for an ulcerated stomach. Charles is the oldest of three children. His two younger brothers, sixteen and eighteen, are in high school and living with their parents. His parents are both professionals, his father a physician in general practice and his mother an attorney with a large law firm. Both parents have high aspirations for Charles, for he has demonstrated a great deal of ability since he was a child. He maintained a high academic average during the first few years of school; however, he has slipped somewhat in the present quarter and may not make the Dean's List for the first time. He is presently majoring in premed but lately he has been unhappy with the prospects of facing "another five years of pressure."

Charles is a slender young man (5 feet, 11 inches; 145 pounds) who appears, in an interview, to be quite shy and introverted. He reports that he has had a number of health problems in the past—stomach upset, nausea, fatigue, and inability to sleep—and has missed a great deal of school. His inability to sleep and his nausea have been bothering him more lately, as school pressures have increased and the need to make decisions about future professional training has become imminent. Charles has a great deal of insight into his present conflict situation. He thinks that the pressure on him to go on to medical school has been weighing heavily on him. He has not been able to tell his parents that he doesn't feel that he can pursue a career in medicine, although he has no other plans at this time.

In the initial interview Charles appeared to be somewhat depressed and anxious over his inability to deal with his present situation. He revealed that he has a strong sense of failure and that he feels he has let his parents down. He reported that he couldn't face his parents about his school problems and that he really did not have any close friends with whom to talk over his problems. He lamented the fact that he is so much alone, that no one seems really to care about how he is feeling. He described himself as "a true introvert"—having few friends and preferring to spend time alone reading and listening to music. He appears to be somewhat effeminate in manner. He has always had some problems initiating conversations with women and has not dated since he has been in college. He reported that he is not "gay."

Charles appears quite motivated to secure psychological treatment. He expressed an interest in trying to learn why he is feeling so "down" lately, and why he has not been able to deal directly with his problems. He realizes that he has to initiate some changes in his life, but he does not know where to start. He was referred to a clinical psychologist for further evaluation and therapy.

Analysis. The following statements were computer-generated on the basis of the similarities between Charles B.'s MMPI and others stored in the memory of the computer.

> *Profile validity.* This client's approach to the MMPI was open and cooperative. The resulting MMPI profile [Figure 13.16] is valid and probably a good indication of his present level of personality functioning. This suggests that he is able to follow instructions and to respond appropriately to the task, and may be viewed as a positive indication of his involvement with the evaluation.
>
> *Symptomatic pattern.* The client's MMPI profile reflects much psychological distress at this time. He is experiencing intense feelings of self-doubt and low morale in the context of a mixed pattern of psychological problems. He has major problems with anxiety and depression. He tends to be high-strung and insecure, and may also be having somatic problems. He is probably experiencing loss of sleep and appetite, and a slowness in personal tempo.
>
> Individuals with this profile often have high standards and a strong need to achieve, but they feel that they fall short of their expectations and then blame themselves harshly. This client feels quite insecure and pessimistic about the future. He also feels quite inferior, has little self-confidence, and does not feel capable of solving his problems.
>
> He has diverse interests that include aesthetic and cultural activities. He is usually somewhat passive and compliant in interpersonal relationships, is generally self-controlled, and dislikes confrontation. He may have difficulty in expressing anger directly and may resort to indirect means.
>
> *Interpersonal relations.* He appears to be quite passive and dependent in interpersonal relationships and does not speak up for himself even when others take advantage. He avoids confrontation and seeks nurturance from others often at the price of his own independence. He forms deep emotional attachments and tends to be quite vulnerable to being hurt. He also tends to blame himself for interpersonal problems.

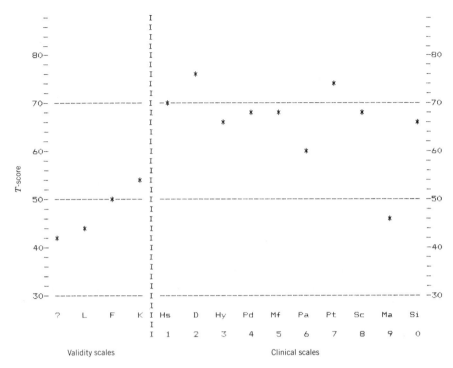

Figure 13.16
Computer-generated MMPI profile.
Check how Charles's performances on the validity scales and three clinical scales (D, Pt, and Ma) are represented in the computerized report. Do these tendencies appear in the case history?

He appears to be rather shy and inhibited in social situations, and may avoid others for fear of being hurt. He has very few friends, and is considered by others as "hard to get to know." He is quiet, passive, submissive, and conventional, and lacks self-confidence in dealing with others. Individuals with this passive and withdrawing life-style are often unable to assert themselves appropriately.

Behavioral stability. Individuals with this profile are often experiencing psychological distress in response to stressful events. The intense affect [emotion] may diminish over time or with treatment.

Treatment considerations. Individuals with this profile tend to seek help for their psychological problems. Psychotherapy, particularly cognitive-behavioral treatment, may be beneficial. They may also respond to brief, directive psychotherapy. Their symptoms are often relieved by antidepressant medication.

The passive, nonassertive personality style that seems to underlie this disorder might be a focus of behavior change. Individuals with these problems often learn to deal with others more effectively through assertiveness training.

Evaluation. How good are these computerized evaluations? A comparison of Charles B.'s case history with the analysis provided by the computer reveals a fair amount of correspondence between the two. On the other hand, experts in MMPI diagnosis such as Dr. Butcher (1978) accept the promise of the procedures but caution that the "computer systems are still pretty rudimentary and most MMPI interpretations made out of context produce either superficial (general) information or highly fallible descriptions." Since actuarial prediction, of which computerized assessment is an example, is usually superior to alternative methods of interpretation, our conclusion must be that no method is very accurate. The reliability and validity of personality tests are not as great as users might desire. Why, then, do psychologists bother to use tests at all?

A study by Terry Wade and Timothy Baker (1977) sheds some light on this question. In a survey of 500 clinical psychologists, they found that the great majority of them used test results in assessment, therapy, or both. Most of the respondents regarded reliability and validity as relatively unimportant factors in the decision to use tests. In spite of the inadequate psychometric credentials of projective tests, for example, clinicians use them more often than objective tests. The probable reason is that most clinicians regard testing as an insightful process rather than as an objective skill. Most said that they used personalized rather than standardized evaluation procedures for projective tests, and many did so even for objective tests. Further, most said that they would accept their own hypotheses over test results in cases of conflict. Of course, the apparently substantial component of personal judgment used in evaluating tests may increase the possibility of human error. Nevertheless, this study indicates strongly that those who use psychological tests find them useful tools, and that a great many clinicians prefer to interpret tests on their own.

SUMMARY

Personality assessment techniques vary in their degree of objectivity. The most objective tests are the personality inventories, which ask people to respond to statements by indicating whether they describe themselves. The most widely used inventory is the MMPI, which rates people on ten clinical scales, including one on masculinity–femininity and one on social introversion. Four other scales assess test-taking attitudes. The CPI is a similar inventory developed for nonclinical use with high school and college-aged people. Its fourteen scales assess personal adequacy, social maturity, cognitive efficiency, and interests. The MMPI and CPI both provide rich descriptions of personality.

Projective techniques evaluate people's imaginary creations produced in response to ambiguous stimulus materials. The hypothesis is that people project their deep-seated needs and personality problems in their stories about TAT pictures and interpretations of Rorschach cards, in their drawings and sentence completions. Themes that run throughout people's responses to these and other projective tests are interpreted in terms of their case histories.

Individual response styles or sets can affect test results. People vary in conformity, resistiveness, and acquiescence, which may be reflected in a tendency to yea-say or nay-say. Others may try to make themselves look good or bad by answering according to the social desirability of test choices. Many personality inventories contain validity or lie scales to expose such attempts. A comparatively new approach to personality testing is behavioral assessment, through self-reports and behavioral observations.

One way to interpret data from personality tests is clinical prediction, based on the psychologist's knowledge, intuition, and judgment about individual cases. Another is actuarial prediction, which makes interpretations of people's personalities objectively by comparing their test performance, life history, and so on with similar data of other people whose behavior has already been interpreted. Computerized personality assessment is one version of this approach. Whether an actuarial table can beat the sophisticated clinician is a matter of controversy.

TO BE SURE YOU UNDERSTAND THIS CHAPTER

The following are the major concepts in the chapter.

Trait	**Ceiling level**
Intelligence	**Chronological age (CA)**
Mental age (MA)	**Intelligence quotient (IQ)**
Basal age	**Normal curve**

Mean

Standard deviation

Deviation IQ

Z-score

Standardization

Standardization sample

Reliability

Test-retest method

Split-half method

Alternate-forms method

Validity

Predictive validity

Concurrent validity

Content validity

Construct validity

Culture-fair test

Aptitude

Ability

Work sample test

Job analysis

Cutoff score

Personality test

Rational-construct method

Empirical-criterion method

Factor-analytic method

Minnesota Multiphasic Personality Inventory (MMPI)

California Psychological Inventory (CPI)

Projective technique

Thematic Apperception Test (TAT)

Rorschach inkblot test

Behavioral assessment

Self-report

Direct observation

Laboratory analogue

Response set

Social desirability

Clinical prediction

Actuarial prediction

TO GO BEYOND THIS CHAPTER

In This Book. The two chapters to follow relate directly to this one. Chapter 14 discusses variation in intelligence, and Chapter 15 provides a further treatment of traits of personality. The discussions of the heritability of intelligence and personality in Chapter 2 are also relevant.

Elsewhere. We recommend the following treatments of individual differences and assessment: Leona Tyler, *Individuality;* Philip Vernon, *Intelligence: Heredity and Environment;* Lee Willerman, *The Psychology of Individual and Group Differences.*

(Drawing by CEM; © 1974 by The New Yorker Magazine, Inc.)

CHAPTER 14   THE RANGE OF INTELLECT

Variations in intelligence were probably recognized by the prehistoric cave dwellers, who knew that their animal hunt would be more successful if dumb Throg was left at home and smarter Zeeg went in his place. But what abilities did Throg lack and Zeeg have that led to this evaluation by their peers? A better sense of smell? Tracking ability? Courage? Fleetness of foot? Whatever the specific answer, intelligence to the cave dwellers was intimately related to an individual's effectiveness in carrying out real-life tasks—such as catching dinner.

In the centuries since the Stone Age, not much has changed in what we consider to be intelligence. To most of us, the intelligent person still is one who effectively meets life's challenges, and the unintelligent person is one who does not. What have changed are the specific abilities that are useful for coping with life's problems. In this age of high-speed communication and computers, intelligence has much more to do with verbal and mathematical abilities than with the skill to track large animals. Modern definitions of intelligence thus emphasize cognition, the capacity to think, reason, remember, and understand. This change highlights an important feature of our everyday definition of intelligence, namely that it is arbitrary and culture-bound. Intelligence consists of the abilities that a society values because they are useful in meeting that society's current needs.

However intelligence is defined, individual differences in intellectual abilities are impressively large. The two extremes of this range of intellect are mental retardation and giftedness. As these terms are used conventionally, people who obtain low scores on IQ tests are considered retarded, and those who get very high scores are considered gifted. Within both groups, however, there is significant individual variation. Two people with the same IQ, whether low, high, or average, may be very different in their everyday behavior and accomplishments. To understand the meaning of individual differences in intellect, therefore, we must consider both the nature of human intellect and the factors that determine how effectively people use their intellectual abilities.

THE STRUCTURE OF INTELLECT

There is controversy in psychology over the question of which specific traits constitute intelligence, but there is surprising agreement on one general point of interpretation. Almost everyone will agree that intelligence has two different aspects. One is the individual's intellectual *potential,* which mysteriously resides within the chemistry of the brain and cannot as yet be measured directly. The other is intellectual *behavior*, which can be observed and assessed reasonably well. These two aspects of intelligence identify two different ways in which the term "intelligence" is used.

To illustrate this distinction, consider Donald Hebb's (1972) notion of intelligence A and intelligence B. **Intelligence A** refers to a person's innate potential for the development of intellectual capacities. **Intelligence B** refers to the level of that person's intellectual functioning. A similar theory was advanced by Raymond Cattell and his associates (Cattell, 1963; Horn and Cattell, 1967) in their definitions of "fluid" and "crystallized" intelligence. **Fluid intelligence** is the type of cognitive analytic ability that is relatively uninfluenced by prior learning, that shows up the most clearly on tasks requiring adaptation to new situations. **Crystallized intelligence** involves skills and talents that depend more on learning and experience.

Types of Intelligence

Although the deep-down nature of intelligence remains to be discovered, people's commonsense ideas of what intelligence must consist of commonly identify several different types of intelligence. Robert Sternberg and his colleagues (1981) compared laypeople's conceptions of intelligence with those of experts and discovered that the two groups described similar basic components of intelligence. These components include (1) "verbal intelligence"—general learning and comprehension abilities, such as good vocabulary, verbal fluency, and good reading comprehension; (2) "problem-solving ability"—abstract thinking and reasoning, such as applying knowledge to problems at hand, posing problems in an optimal way, and identifying the connections between ideas; (3) "practical intelligence"—sizing up situations well, determining how to achieve goals, taking an interest in the world at large, and being socially competent.

This interesting breakdown of intellectual categories leads to the question whether the several types are related. If the truly intelligent person is good in all three, we might conclude that the three types of intelligence spring from a general intellectual source. If not, we might conclude that different types of intelligence are separate from one another.

General Trait versus Specific Abilities. Psychologists have long argued whether intelligence is a single ability, which permeates all cognitive processes, or whether it is composed of many independent abilities. Early workers attempted to answer this question by determining whether individuals who score high on one type of intellectual task also perform well on others. They found that the scores were significantly related, but not perfectly so.

To explain these findings, Charles Spearman (1863–1945) in 1904 advanced a two-factor theory of intelligence. He thought that there was a general ability that people use to cope with a variety of intellectual tasks. Spearman called this general ability g, for **general factor,** and thought of it as basic mental energy. But, since an individual does not perform equally well on different types of cognitive tasks—mathematical, verbal, and so on—Spearman thought that each type of task requires a specific intellectual ability as well. Spearman called these specific abilities s, for **specific factors.** Thus Spearman thought of intelligence as composed of the g factor and a number of s factors.

Other psychologists have challenged the view that there is a general ability that contributes to all intellectual functions. Edward Thorndike, for example, argued (1926) that intelligence consists, instead, of a large number of independent abilities. Louis L. Thurstone's (1887–1955) view was somewhere between the theories of Spearman and Thorndike. Thurstone (1938) suggested that the intellect is comprised of specific abilities, but so few of them that each has broad generality. He called these components **primary mental abilities** and subdivided Spearman's general factor, g, into seven of them: spatial perception, perceptual speed, verbal comprehension numerical ability, memory, word fluency, and reasoning. Thurstone found that an individual's scores on tests of these primary abilities were often interrelated, a discovery which again pointed to some factor in intelligence reminiscent of Spearman's g.

Adaptation and Profiles of Abilities.   Throughout the history of mental testing, most test constructors have emphasized personal effectiveness in their definitions of intelligence. Binet, for example, saw intelligence as the abilities to become oriented toward a goal, to make adjustments in the process of achieving the goal, and to know when the goal has been reached. This problem-solving orientation also appears in Henry Goddard's (1866–1957) definition of intelligence as "the degree of availability of one's experiences for the solution of immediate problems and the anticipation of future ones" (1946, p. 68). David Wechsler saw intelligence as "the capacity of an individual to understand the world about him and his resourcefulness to cope with its challenges" (1975, p. 139).

Expanded versions of these views came from both William Charlesworth and Robert Sternberg. Charlesworth (1976) saw intelligence as specific cognitive abilities that enable an individual to adapt to the environment. Sternberg included the abilities "to adapt oneself to the vagaries of a changing and uncertain real world environment" and "to motivate oneself to accomplish expeditiously the tasks one needs to accomplish" (1981, p. 16). One difference between these and the earlier views concerns the difference between being effective and adapting. To be effective is to have a set of unchanging capacities that allows one to cope with a changeable environment. To adapt is to change oneself in response to unchanging reality. A second difference is a somewhat expanded concept of environment.

Although the early proponents of the effectiveness view recognized that intelligence operates in a broader environment, their research for the most part was limited to the school. Even in preparing tests for adults, they assumed that the cognitive abilities important for children's success in school would also determine adults' success outside of school. The proponents of the adaptation view of intelligence, in contrast, argue that school and the real world make different demands of people, and furthermore, that the real world varies tremendously for different groups of people. The daily experiences of the ghetto resident, Appalachian poor, and Peruvian peasant certainly differ from one another as well as from those of the middle-class North American white person. The cognitive abilities that make a person effective in one of these environments may not be equally useful in the others. Thus for these different groups of people intelligence may actually consist of different patterns of abilities.

Evidence that different patterns of cognitive abilities may exist in different cultures was provided by a study of four ethnic and racial groups of children living in the United States (Lesser, Fifer, and Clark, 1965). Six- and seven-year-old black, Chinese, Jewish, and Puerto Rican children were tested on verbal ability, reasoning, number facility, and space conceptualization. No group performed well or poorly on all the tests. Rather, the groups of children ranked differently on each of the cognitive abilities (Figure 14.1). Within each ethnic or racial group children from the lower economic class scored below those in the middle class, but their overall *pattern* of scores was still the same.

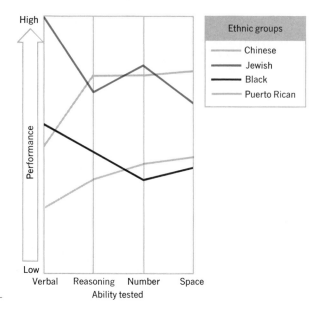

Figure 14.1
Patterns of ethnic and racial intelligence.
These profiles show that different groups
have different patterns of intelligence.
Jewish and black children score highest
on measures of verbal ability. Chinese
and Puerto Rican children are strongest
in spatial intelligence. (Adapted from
Lesser, Fifer, and Clark, 1965.)

Intelligence over the Life-Span

When Binet's intelligence tests were first given to people of different ages, the testers were surprised to find that average scores reached an upper limit at about age sixteen. On the Wechsler scales, developed many years later, they peaked at about age twenty. After that performance remained at a plateau until age forty-five or so and then began to decline. Before jumping to the conclusion that people are as intelligent as they will ever be in their late teens, however, we must realize that these data came from **cross-sectional studies.** That is, different people—a cross-section of the population—of various ages were tested at about the same time. This means that the younger participants undoubtedly had had greater educational opportunities than the older people. A way of eliminating this problem and obtaining a more accurate picture of the growth of intelligence would be to do a **longitudinal study,** in which the same individuals would be tested at various points in their lives.

By now several longitudinal studies have shown that general intelligence increases all the way up to age fifty or so, but that various abilities show different courses of development over the life-span. Figure 14.2 charts the results from tests of three intellectual abilities (Schaie and Strother, 1968). The ability to understand verbal meaning, ideas expressed in words, did not peak until age fifty-five, and at age seventy verbal understanding was still better than it had been at age twenty-five. On the reasoning test, which assessed the ability to solve logical problems, scores peaked at forty and showed no substantial decrement until age sixty. In contrast to these results, scores on a test of word fluency, which required individuals to write as many words beginning with a certain letter as they could in a brief period of time, declined markedly and consistently with age.

In general, longitudinal studies have shown that capacities that depend on accumulated experience, such as one's vocabulary and store of general information (Cattell's "crystallized intelligence"), increase with age for decades and decline only with the approach of very old age. Capacities that depend on speed, flexibility, and adaptation to the novel and unfamiliar (Cattell's "fluid intelligence") peak much earlier. We should note, however, that longitudinal studies are not completely free of difficulties of their own. These studies cover

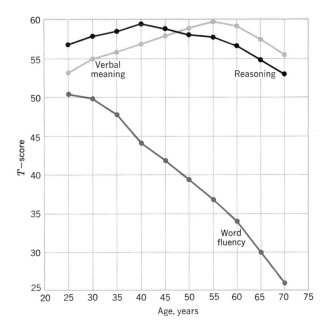

Figure 14.2
Estimated change over time for three intellectual abilities. The data are based on longitudinal findings. A *T*-score is a standard score (resembling a deviation IQ) which has a mean of 50 and a standard deviation of 10. (Adapted from Schaie and Strother, 1968.)

so much time that they often must continue on beyond the lifetimes of the original investigators. For one reason or another, subjects drop out of longitudinal studies, and a great many of them may be unavailable by the time the final results are tallied. Results lose reliability if those who drop out differ in any systematic way from those who remain—if they are predominately of one sex, more or less intelligent, sickly or better educated, for example. Finally, longitudinal studies do not eliminate completely the problems of cross-sectional studies. Over a lifetime the richness of a person's environment may change with shifts in that person's situation. The test scores of the older person who maintains an active interest in ideas and continues to engage in intellectual pursuits will probably decline less than those of the older person who does not.

SUMMARY

Definitions of intelligence depend on the abilities that are valued in particular societies. Nevertheless, psychologists and laypeople have similar conceptions of intelligence. Both groups consider general intelligence to include verbal intelligence, the type of intelligence required for problem solving and abstract reasoning, and practical intelligence or social competence.

Several psychologists have recognized a difference between pure intelligence and measured intelligence. The first is an innate potential, relatively uninfluenced by the environment. The second is the actual functioning level of intelligence and is the product of learning and experience. IQ tests measure only the second type of intelligence. Although these tests reflect innate intelligence, there are no direct measures of this capacity.

Whether intelligence is a general trait, which permeates all realms of functioning, or a number of specific abilities is a matter of controversy. Individuals who do well on one type of cognitive task tend to do well on others, a tendency which suggests but does not prove the existence of a general underlying ability. Spearman interpreted such data to mean that there is both a general factor and several specific factors. Thurstone identified seven primary mental abilities.

Definitions of intelligence have commonly emphasized individual effectiveness, but a relatively recent focus has been on adaptation. Defining intelligence as effectiveness implies that people have a set of unchanging capacities with which to cope with a changeable environment. Defining it as adaptation implies that they change themselves according to their surroundings. Because different groups of people must adapt to greatly different environments, the measured intelligence of each group—but not their pure intelligence—might consist of a particular pattern of abilities.

Although intelligence develops the most rapidly during childhood, longitudinal evidence indicates that it continues to increase until the later years of life. Abilities such as verbal reasoning, which require the accumulation of information, are the most likely to continue growing. Abilities that depend on flexibility of mental functioning peak earlier in adulthood and then decline.

FACTORS RELATED TO IQ CHANGES

Psychologists usually picture the growth of intelligence as a steady process, rapid in the early years and slower as the person grows older. Individual patterns of growth, however, are much more idiosyncratic. As can be seen in the growth curves in Figure 14.3, there may be spurts, plateaus, and even drops in an individual's test scores as a function of age. Although a person's IQ generally remains within the same range, it may be a bit higher or lower from time to time. Some of the fluctuations in IQ scores can be traced to intelligence tests themselves. Since the intelligence tests cover different topics at different ages, an individual may just happen to know the answers to many questions when he or she takes the test at one age and not know the answers to other questions later on. Such chance knowledge or lack of it at various testings can make a person's scores vary somewhat.

Other circumstances of life can also affect test performance. In one study of over 200 children, such factors as physical illness and environmental stress were found to correspond to shifts in IQ scores (Honzik, Macfarlane, and Allen, 1948). For example, one child's IQ improved markedly after the child's father had regained employment. In another case a boy who compensated for his physical problems through intellectual achievements raised his IQ from the below-average range to the superior range. In many children, however, the link between changes in life events and in IQ is not so clear.

Figure 14.3
Individual mental growth curve. (After Bayley, 1955.)

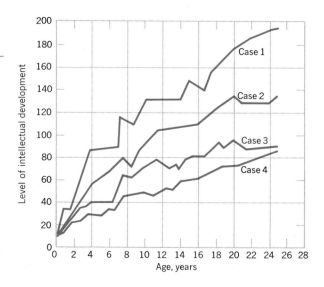

Personality and Sex Differences

Some evidence indicates that changes in IQ are related to the child's pattern of adjustment or personality. In a longitudinal study conducted at the Fels Institute, in Yellow Springs, Ohio, 140 children were tested at intervals between two and twelve years of age (Sontag, Baker, and Nelson, 1958). The 35 children whose IQs rose the most sharply over the years and the 35 children whose IQs showed the greatest decrease were rated on several personality measures. Children whose IQs had increased were found to be aggressive, independent, self-initiating, and competitive. Those with decreasing IQs lacked these traits. Other studies have suggested that the aggressiveness associated with an increasing IQ must be socially acceptable rather than destructive and uncontrolled. For example, children who have temper tantrums also have drops in their IQs (Peskin, 1964). To function well intellectually, a person must be able to harness emotions and utilize them in a constructive manner.

Personality factors may also contribute to gender differences in intellectual ability. The overall scores of boys and girls on standard intelligence tests are similar, because the tests were standardized to ensure that both sexes receive the same IQs. Any item on which one sex did better than the other was rejected. Nevertheless, there is some evidence that girls generally do better on verbal tasks and boys excel on numerical and spatial tasks. Some psychologists argue that the way boys and girls are reared and what they are taught to regard as important explain these intellectual differences. That such attitudes can affect intellectual performance was confirmed in a study by Gloria Carey (1958). She found that college women considered problem solving less acceptable behavior than did men. Carey attempted to change these attitudes by conducting group discussions with both men and women, during which she emphasized that it is socially acceptable to excel at problem solving. After these discussions the problem solving of women improved but not that of men. Thus the women's attitudes had been an impediment that was overcome once they felt that problem solving was appropriate behavior.

Not everyone would agree that male-female differences in such traits as intelligence and aggressiveness can be explained solely by learning. Others argue that basic constitutional differences in males and females also have a role. It has been discovered (Waber 1977) that teenagers of *both* sexes who reached puberty late performed better on spatial tasks than those who reached puberty early. Perhaps the better spatial ability of males is related to the physiological fact of their later maturation. More generally, differences in the maturation rates of the sexes may be associated with certain neurological and psychological changes that affect intellectual functioning.

Social Deprivation

Some theorists believe that social experiences are of utmost importance to intellectual development and that social deprivation can cause IQ changes. One of the most frequently cited investigations of social deprivation was conducted by Harold Skeels (1966). He studied twenty-five children who as infants had been placed in an overcrowded orphanage where they received little stimulation or personal attention. They saw only their busy nurses, who barely had time to feed and change them. At the age of eighteen months, thirteen of these children, all below average in intellectual development, were transferred to an institution for retarded women. Here they were considered "house guests," and each was "adopted" by a retarded woman, who lavished considerable attention and affection on "her" child. The children also received additional stimulation in the new setting, for they had toys to play with and were taken on excursions.

After two years these children showed an average IQ increase of 28 points. The IQs of the children who had remained in the orphanage dropped an average of 26 points in the same period—a total difference of 54 points!

The two groups also had quite different patterns of adjustment as adults. Of those who had been removed from the orphanage, most had completed high school and some had attended college. All were employed or married to wage earners. As adults, the other group remained at a retarded or borderline level of intellectual functioning. Only one had finished high school, only one was married, and just half of them had jobs. Four were still wards of the state. An unresolved issue is whether the effects of early deprivation are reversible. Studies such as this have indicated that the effects of severe deprivation in childhood are permanent and even cumulative. Other examples are the decline with age in the IQs of English children raised on canal boats and of American children raised in extremely isolated and impoverished regions of Appalachia.

Such evidence is on the side of the irreversibility of the intellectual damage done by early deprivation, but other data promote the opposite conclusion, that the effects are reversible. Jerome Kagan's (1972) study of child rearing in Guatemalan villages is especially persuasive. In these villages infants are confined to dark huts, for their parents believe that if allowed outside, they will catch diseases. Adults seldom play with or even talk to the infants; the children cannot see well enough to reach and crawl. At the age of two they are listless, apathetic, and retarded in development. Eventually, however, they learn to walk; then they leave the huts and participate in community life. By the age of eleven, the children are active and intellectually competent.

A study by Wayne Dennis (1973) may help to clarify the inconsistency in these studies. Dennis found that children raised in a foundling home in Beirut, Lebanon, under conditions of extreme social deprivation—the ratio of adults to children was one to twenty—were retarded in development. Those who continued to live in these deprived conditions through adolescence never achieved IQs much beyond 55. But the development of children who were adopted before the age of two became completely normal. In between were those adopted after the age of two but before adolescence. These children had degrees of intellectual impairment as adults that were related to how long they had lived at the foundling home; the older the child at the time of adoption, the lower the adult IQ. Thus the effects of social deprivation may depend on its duration.

Socioeconomic Status

Studies find repeatedly that socioeconomic status and intelligence are related: the higher a family's socioeconomic status, typically defined by occupation, income, and type of dwelling, the higher the IQs of both parents and children. By the same token, people who fill professional positions usually have higher IQs than those who fill unskilled positions (Table 14.1). These data raise an important question. Do people have high IQs because of greater economic means or greater economic means because they have high IQs?

At least four hypotheses, by now familiar to us, have been offered to explain the social-class–IQ relationship. The first is that intelligence tests are culturally unfair; they underestimate the IQs of people in lower socioeconomic classes. This possibility was assessed in a large-scale study (Eells et al., 1951) in which the performance of lower- and high-status children was compared test item by test item. Some culturally unfair items were found, but many others passed more frequently by high-status children were not unfair. These items tended to assess the ability to think abstractly rather than to require information.

A second explanation is that the personalities and motives of persons in different social classes influence their approaches to intelligence testing and therefore their performances. In one study (Yando, Seitz, and Zigler, 1979) economically advantaged children were found to be more curious and self-confident in their approach to academic tasks and more concerned about the quality of their responses than economically disadvantaged children. Disadvantaged children were spontaneous and flexible in their approach to problems, but they were less self-confident on academic tasks, even when they had the same level of ability as the advantaged children. Thus children of lower and higher socioeconomic status may bring different attitudes and styles to problem solving that could indeed affect their performance on intelligence tests.

A third explanation of social-class differences in IQ is that children of higher status are exposed to more enriching environments and, as a result, develop more intelligence. Unfortunately, there are few clues to just which particular "enriching" experiences might enhance intelligence. Could it be a greater availability of books and educational materials; or higher aspirations conferred upon children by parents, who themselves have high aspirations? Probably not. Many homes and parents can be so described, whatever their socioeconomic level.

The fourth explanation is that social-class differences in intelligence reflect genetic differences. Table 14.2 shows the IQs of children of differing socioeconomic groups as they grow up. The stability of these average IQs at all ages has been used to argue for a hereditary basis of intelligence. If the quality of the environment were responsible, its effects would be cumulative; the IQs of higher-class children would increase with age and those of lower-class children would decline. This prediction was tested in a unique study (Schiff et al., 1978) in which French school children of unskilled, working-class parents were compared with their half-siblings who had been adopted early in life into upper-middle-class families. The mean IQ of the adopted children was 111, that of their unadopted half-brothers and sisters 95. In spite of the genetic similarity of these two groups, the differences in their IQs were about the same as IQ differences between classes in the population at large. These findings therefore suggest that the social classes do not differ significantly in intellectual endowment. An alternative interpretation, however, is that the genetic disadvantage of the children born to working-class parents was allayed by the environmental advantages given them when they were adopted into upper-class homes. For example, there is the very real possibility, in this and other studies, that adopted

Table 14.1 Average Scores Obtained on the Army General Classification Test by Men in Various Occupations

Occupation	Mean Score
Accountant	128.1
Engineer	126.6
Chemist	124.8
Teacher	122.8
Pharmacist	120.5
Purchasing agent	118.7
Salesman	115.1
Receiving and shipping clerk	111.3
Sales clerk	109.2
Mechanic	106.3
Machine operator	104.8
Bartender	102.3
Auto mechanic	101.3
Chauffeur	100.8
Truck driver	96.2
Lumberjack	94.7
Miner	90.6
Teamster	87.7

Adapted from Harrell and Harrell, 1945.

Table 14.2 Mean IQs of Children Grouped by Fathers' Occupations

Father's Occupational Level	Chronological Age			
	2–5½	6–9	10–14	15–18
Professional	114.8	114.9	117.5	116.4
Semiprofessional and managerial	112.4	107.3	112.2	116.7
Skilled trades, clerical, and retail business	108.0	104.9	107.4	109.6
Semiskilled, minor clerical, and business	104.3	104.6	103.4	106.7
Slightly skilled	97.2	100.0	100.6	96.2
Day laborers	93.8	96.0	97.2	97.6

Adapted from McNemar, 1942.

children receive extra amounts of care and attention from parents who are truly committed to them.

Whatever causes psychologists eventually find to account for socioeconomic differences in IQ, it must be emphasized that these IQ differences are average differences and have nothing to do with the intelligence of any one individual in any socioeconomic class. In Table 14.1 we see that, as a group, teamsters have the lowest average IQ, but one teamster had an IQ of 145, far above the average for individuals in professional occupations. It should also be recognized that although the proportion of high-IQ individuals will be greater in very high-status groups, the absolute number of high-IQ individuals will be greater in lower-status groups for the simple reason that these groups contain so many more people.

SUMMARY

Group curves depict intellectual development as a smooth and continuous process. Individual curves, however, show sudden increases, periods of stability, and even declines in intellectual growth. Some of these fluctuations are caused by the way that the tests were constructed, others by changes in life circumstances, although these have not been found to affect children in a predictable manner.

Changes in IQ are also related to personality traits. Children whose IQs rise are more aggressive, independent, and competitive than those whose IQs decline. Aggressiveness, independence, and competitiveness may be more evident in males than females, but there are no sex differences in overall IQ. Sex differences have, however, been found in patterns of ability. Females tend to do better on verbal tasks; males do better on mathematical and spatial tasks. Both cultural and physiological factors have been advanced to explain these differences.

Extreme and prolonged social deprivation may produce permanent intellectual impairment. Shorter periods of deprivation usually have less severe effects. Socioeconomic-class differences in IQ have been explained in terms of social deprivation, cultural biases of the tests, personality and motivational differences among members of different economic groups, and possible genetic differences. Whatever the explanation, the relation between socioeconomic status and IQ is only moderate, and individuals with high and low IQs can be found in all socioeconomic groups.

MENTAL RETARDATION

Mental retardation is usually defined by arbitrarily drawing a line through the distribution of IQ scores so that individuals with scores above the line are considered intellectually normal, and those with scores below it are considered retarded. Through the years the exact position of this line has changed considerably. For a time the lowest 3 percent of the population was considered retarded; then the definition changed so that people whose IQ scores were more than one standard deviation below the mean, or less than 85, were considered retarded. In 1973 the American Association on Mental Deficiency (AAMD) shifted the IQ criterion of mental retardation again, this time to two standard deviations below the mean, or below about 70 on the most widely used tests of intelligence. On the basis of this most recent criterion, about 2.3 percent of the population is considered mentally retarded. Table 14.3 lists some of the ways in which mentally retarded persons have been classified. Retarded

subjective and unreliable. Behavior that is adaptive in one situation may be maladaptive in another. Moreover, adaptive behavior is highly susceptible to environmental influence. Consider a child with an IQ of 70 who fails in school and thus can be judged mentally retarded. Given just a little attention, perhaps by an understanding teacher, this child might succeed and no longer fit the classification. Thus the social adaptation criterion makes it possible for a person to shift categories with no change in mental abilities. Problems such as these have led some workers to the conclusion that, despite the importance of adaptive behavior, IQ should be the sole defining feature of mental retardation (Zigler and Balla, 1983).

Perhaps the most basic issue here is whether it is good or bad to apply the label "mentally retarded" to people who are mildly retarded. As Edward Zigler and David Balla (1983) have argued, the label may be stigmatizing, something to be avoided. On the other hand, if the label makes available services that improve an individual's life, it can be beneficial. Zigler and Balla have described a practice in Sweden to illustrate this second point. When Swedish children are labeled mentally retarded, they are eligible to receive vocational training that enables them to obtain employment upon graduation from school. Mildly retarded children who were not so labeled, however, receive no special assistance. Often they find themselves unemployable and request the status "mentally retarded" in order to obtain vocational training. If services are available, then, labeling may be constructive; at present IQ scores may be the best means of determining when to use the label.

Organic Disorders

Knowing that an individual has a low IQ and inadequate adaptive behavior tells us nothing about the origin of these deficiencies. There are at least 200 different **etiologies,** or causes, of mental retardation. These many etiologies can be classified into two basic groups: retardation associated with a recognized organic disorder and retardation for which no organic cause can be detected. **Organic retardation** makes up about 25 percent of the retarded population. This type of retardation is caused by an abnormal physiological process, brought on by chromosomal anomalies, genetic disorders, brain damage, and a variety of environmental insults.

Down Syndrome.   Approximately one infant of every 700 live births suffers from **Down syndrome.** The infant's physical appearance alone is usually enough to permit a rapid diagnosis. The infant typically has a broad but short skull, round face, and low-bridged nose. Eyes are almost almond-shaped and slant upward and outward, the corners of the mouth droop, and the rather thick and furrowed tongue may protrude a good deal of the time. As the child grows older, stubby hands and legs and small stature for age become evident. Many children with Down syndrome have congenital heart defects, and some die young from these and other ailments. Individuals with Down syndrome have a rather wide range of intelligence, but many are in the severe and moderately retarded ranges. Postmortem examinations usually reveal that their brains weigh less than normal and that the frontal lobes, brainstem, and cerebellum are particularly small (Crome and Stern, 1972).

Down syndrome was first described by Landon Down, an English physician with some misguided views about the intelligence of various racial groups. The slanting eyes of the retarded children reminded him of the Mongolian eye fold. He concluded that these children had undergone some sort of evolutionary regression from the Caucasian race to what he considered the inferior "Mongol"

This little girl's round face, almond-shaped eyes, and stubby fingers are physical indications that she has Down syndrome. Plastic surgeons have recently tried removing some of the signs of the disorder from the faces of young people, who have been enormously pleased to become indistinguishable from others.

race. These children were said to suffer from "mongolism" and to this day they are often incorrectly referred to as "mongoloids."

The major cause of Down syndrome was not discovered until 1959, when it was found that afflicted individuals have forty-seven chromosomes rather than the normal complement of forty-six (Figure 14.5). Instead of two, they have three chromosomes in group 21, so Down syndrome is often called **trisomy 21.** The genetic material in the extra chromosome is thought to be responsible for the physical and mental abnormalities of Down syndrome.

The risk of giving birth to a child with Down syndrome rises as a woman becomes older and increases dramatically after she reaches the age of forty

Figure 14.5

A karyotype of chromosome pairings from a boy with Down syndrome. Notice that there are forty-seven rather than forty-six chromosomes. The extra chromosome (trisomy) appears in group 21. Karyotypes of fetal cells obtained through amniocentesis (page 63) can now reveal the syndrome in the fourth month of pregnancy. (Adapted from a photograph by Dr. Jorge J. Yunis, Medical Genetics Laboratory, University of Minnesota Medical School. Reproduced with permission of *New England Journal of Medicine.*)

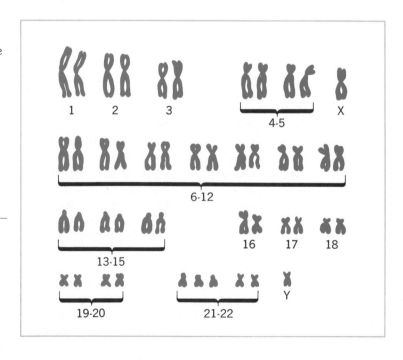

(page 64). A woman's egg cells are as old as she is, and with age they may deteriorate or suffer damage because of exposure to environmental influences, such as irradiation, viruses, and certain chemicals known to cause chromosomal damage.

Cretinism.   All retarded people who suffer from **cretinism** resemble one another. They have round and yellowish faces with wide, flat noses, thick lips, and enlarged, often protruding tongues. Their bodies are dwarflike, with a grossly swollen abdomen and short, stubby extremities. Cretinism also brings a sluggish disposition and severe retardation. This disorder occurs when thyroid glands are unable to synthesize the hormone thyroxine. The condition is often caused by a pair of recessive genes, but it may also develop when the body is deprived of thyroxine. This can happen when the thyroid glands are damaged or are congenitally absent, or when the pregnant mother's diet or her child's after birth is deficient in iodine. Iodine is essential in the synthesis of the hormone. At one time cretinism was much more prevalent in the United States than it is now, especially in regions where soil, air, and water have low concentrations of iodine. Today iodine is added to table salt. An infant born with a deficient thyroid can be given thyroid hormone, but early diagnosis and treatment are imperative, for even a few months of hypothyroidism (low thyroid function) will diminish intelligence.

Other Causes.   Other causes of organic mental retardation were mentioned in Chapter 2. One set of causes are inborn errors in the body's ability to metabolize certain substances. *Phenylketonuria* (PKU) and *Tay-Sachs disease* are two examples. Many of these disorders are transmitted through a pair of recessive genes and are rare. Other organic disorders may have either a genetic or an environmental cause. For example, *microcephaly,* in which neither the brain nor skull expands to normal size, can be hereditary, it can be induced by the mother's exposure to radiation or rubella during the first three months of pregnancy, or it can be caused by injury to the baby during birth. Maternal malnutrition; exposure of the mother to certain drugs and toxins; diseases such as syphilis; prematurity; anoxia, lack of oxygen at the time of birth; lead poisoning; and certain illnesses in infancy and childhood are other environmental causes of retardation.

In rare cases a developing retardation can be treated and severe retardation can be avoided. For example, special diets are effective in treating infants with PKU and cretinism if they are begun early enough. Another condition, *hydrocephaly,* literally "water head," is usually caused by tumors or disease. If left unchecked, the skull grossly enlarges as excess cerebrospinal fluid accumulates within the cranium. An operation that permits the excessive amounts of this fluid to drain off may prevent mental retardation. Special diets that diminish the accumulation of fluid also help. These treatments are best begun early, so most infants born in the United States are checked for the disorder before they leave the hospital.

Familial Retardation

Unlike those with organic disorders, people with **familial retardation,** sometimes called *cultural-familial retardation,* are invariably mildly retarded, having IQs above 50. Although they comprise the vast majority of the retarded population, about 75 percent, the causes of this condition remain a mystery. A combination of environmental and hereditary factors is probably responsible, but the relative contributions of the two are difficult to assess.

Environmental Evidence.   Familial retardation is the most prevalent in the lower socioeconomic classes. This evidence lends support to the notion that this form of retardation is environmentally caused. The widespread acceptance of this view is reflected in the current designation of familial retardation as "retardation due to psychosocial disadvantage," a terminology which implies that only environmental factors are important. But what those who use this label seem not to recognize is that very few of the children so classified have experienced truly serious "psychosocial disadvantage." Many of them live in homes which, although not affluent, should fulfill their developmental needs quite adequately. The only shortcomings of the parents who care for such children appear to be that they themselves do not score very high on intelligence tests. The term "familial retardation" is used in this text in preference to "cultural-familial retardation" because it more accurately describes one of the few things that are known with certainty about this condition: it tends to run in immediate families.

Some workers in the field of mental retardation are not convinced that people with familial retardation are free from organic difficulties. They point out that mothers in impoverished circumstances are often in poor physical condition; they are frequently malnourished and they receive poor obstetrical care (Kugel and Parsons, 1967). As a consequence, their children, who are diagnosed as familial retarded, may actually have organic damage. Some theorists assert that advances in our understanding of what is now called familial retardation will reveal the organic bases of this form of retardation, just as happened in the case of PKU, Down syndrome, and the other organic types of retardation.

Genetic Evidence.   Investigations of the inheritance of nonorganic retardation have a long history. In 1877 Richard Dugdale published his book describing a

Children raised in extremely impoverished homes may suffer from mild, familial retardation.

genealogical study of a family he called the Jukes. Dugdale reported that, for many generations, this family had produced a very large number of criminals, paupers, and people with mental retardation. Some forty years after Dugdale's report, Arthur Estabrook followed up the more than 1200 living members of the Jukes family and found half of them to be retarded. Both Dugdale and Estabrook noted the poor environmental conditions in which the Jukes children were raised. They suggested that both environment and heredity were to blame for the incompetents in the Jukes family.

Another famous genealogical study, conducted by Henry Goddard (1912), traced two lines of descent from Martin Kallikak, a Revolutionary War soldier. "Kallikak" is a name made up from the Greek words *kalos,* good, and *kakos,* bad. One line of Kallikak progeny began when Martin sired an illegitimate child by a retarded tavern maid. The second line stemmed from his later marriage to a woman of normal intelligence and some social standing. Goddard found that the descendants in the first line included a large number of drunkards, harlots, paupers, convicts, and horse thieves. Many were mentally retarded. The descendants of Kallikak's legitimate marriage showed no intellectual deficits, and some were of outstanding reputation. Goddard ignored the differences in rearing and environmental advantage in the two lines and claimed that heredity was the overriding determinant of intelligence and social competence.

Polygenic Evidence.   Today we know that Goddard's genetic interpretation of mental retardation was far too simple. Current thinking recognizes that intelligence is a polygenic trait influenced by a number of genes. This newer view allows us to anticipate an important fact about the intelligence of the offspring of retarded people. The simplistic genetic position predicts that all offspring of two retarded parents will be retarded. The present-day **polygenic model** predicts that the children of low-IQ parents will range in intelligence, with many but not all testing low in IQ. Findings such as those shown in Table 14.5 bear out these predictions.

Although the mathematical details need not concern us here, calculations reveal that the polygenic model of the inheritance of intelligence predicts a distribution of IQs for the entire population ranging from approximately 50 to approximately 150 (Gottesman, 1963). The predicted distribution is the distribution theoretically produced by genetic factors alone. It does not deny the importance of environment in the determination of an individual's IQ score, but it implicitly assumes a constant environment for all people. Actual environmental variation would determine where a person's IQ falls within a genetically provided range or *norm of reaction* (Chapter 2).

Since the effective lower limit of the polygenetically determined IQ distribution is 50, it is reasonable to conclude that the group with familial retardation, whose

Table 14.5 Percentage of Children in Various IQ Ranges Who Were Born to Retarded Parents

	Children's IQs						
Parents	0– 49	50– 69	70– 89	90– 110	111– 130	131+	Average IQ
Both parents retarded	7%	33%	40%	19%	1%	0	74
One parent retarded	2%	10%	28%	45%	13%	1%	92

Data from Reed and Reed, 1965.

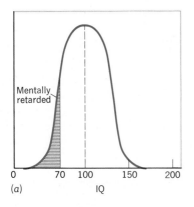

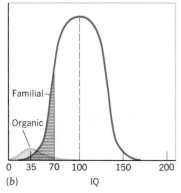

Figure 14.6
Two conceptions of the IQ distribution in mental retardation. (a) The conventional representation of the distribution of intelligence. (b) The distribution of intelligence represented by the two-group approach. The familial retarded group is seen as part of the normal distribution, the organically retarded group as having a separate distribution. (After Penrose, 1963.)

IQs range from 50 to 70, represent the lower portion of this normal distribution. That is, individuals with familial retardation may be quite "normal" in the sense that they are an integral part of the distribution of intelligence produced by variation in our population's gene pool.

The polygenic model is not readily applicable to those with organic retardation, many of whom have IQs below 50. Large-scale surveys have indicated that more individuals have very low intelligence than a simple normal curve allows for. This fact suggests that the distribution of IQs and the definition of retardation presented in Figure 14.6a should be modified. A more appropriate representation might consist of two curves (Figure 14.6b). Within this two-group approach the intelligence of the bulk of the population, including those with familial retardation, would be depicted as forming a normal distribution having a mean of 100 and a range of approximately 50 to 150. Superimposed on this curve would be a second distribution having a mean of approximately 35 and a range from zero to 70. The first curve would represent the polygenic distribution of intelligence; the second would represent the distribution of those with some type of physiological damage. Perhaps we should mention once more that Figure 14.6 does not include the contributions of environment, which would expand the range of the distribution.

Personality Factors in Retardation

Another common myth about mentally retarded individuals is that their behavior is an inexorable product of their low intelligence—that they behave as they do simply because they are retarded. Actually their behavior is no more or less determined by their IQs than is the behavior of people with average or superior intelligence. Indeed, many studies have revealed that the social adjustment of retarded persons depends as much on their personalities as on their levels of intelligence. Some of the personality traits found to be associated with poor social adjustment include anxiety, overdependency, hostility, hyperactivity, resistance, and a failure to follow orders, even when the orders are well within the individual's intellectual ability. A growing body of research has begun to explain how such personality traits might develop in retarded people and how they affect behavior.

Consider the fact that retarded individuals frequently do less well on cognitive tasks than might be predicted from the absolute level of their intelligence. For example, a twelve-year-old retarded child with a mental age (MA) of eight may do worse on academic tasks than average eight-year-old children with the same MA. The maladaptive motives, attitudes, and ways of solving problems that retarded children develop is one probable explanation. From their earliest years retarded children are almost certain to fail more often than nonretarded children. These many failures may give retarded children an expectancy of failure. They may therefore try harder to avoid failure than to achieve success and not even attempt tasks that are well within their intellectual capabilities. These consequences of their repeated failures are reminiscent of those of learned helplessness (page 268).

A high rate of failure can also make retarded children *outerdirected* when they are presented with a problem. They come to distrust their own solutions and seek guidance from their surroundings. Compared to nonretarded children of the same mental age, they are more sensitive to smiles, frowns, praise, and other cues from an adult and imitate the behavior of adults and peers to a greater extent. This **outerdirectedness** may explain the great suggestibility so frequently observed in retarded children. Research indicates that when retarded children are guaranteed success and are rewarded for independent thought, they can give up their overreliance on external cues, develop more trust in their own abilities, and improve their problem solving (Achenbach and Zigler, 1968).

All young children need reassurance and love, but as they develop they become more competent and autonomous and less dependent on adults. Socially deprived children are often slow to make this transition from dependence to independence. Relatively late in their development they still hunger for attention and nurturance from others. This is a common problem for mildly retarded children, who frequently come from socially deprived environments. When presented with a task, they may be more interested in socializing with the person who presented it than they are in solving the problem.

Although the social deprivation experienced by retarded children apparently gives them a strong desire to interact with a supportive adult, it can have the opposite effect as well. Many retarded children are suspicious, mistrustful, fearful, and avoid strangers, attitudes that can hinder anyone's everyday effectiveness. People can do their best only when they feel secure and safe from harm. These reactions of retarded children make it clear that they do not all have one personality pattern and all nonretarded children another. Although retarded and nonretarded children may differ in general patterns of personality, individuals within each group are unique.

Care and Training of Retarded Persons

Throughout history the care and training of retarded people have been determined as much by superstition, religion, fear, and various social aims as by any understanding of retardation. Treatments have ranged from infanticide and concealment to tender loving care. The work of Jean Itard in the early nineteenth century was the first systematic attempt to educate and train a retarded person (Lane, 1976). Itard was a French physician who undertook the task of teaching "the wild boy of Aveyron." When captured in the woods, Victor, as the boy was later named, was twelve or thirteen years old and could not speak. He grunted and shrieked, crouched and trotted like a beast. Dirty and naked, indifferent and inattentive, he had subsisted on roots and raw potatoes. Medical authorities diagnosed him as an "idiot" and felt that he had probably been abandoned for this reason. Itard, however, believed that the boy might have become retarded as a result of his social isolation. By providing Victor with the necessary educational and social experiences, Itard hoped to bring about his mental and moral development. Itard worked on the boy's senses, intellect, and emotions. Victor eventually learned to discriminate objects by sight, touch, taste, color, and to communicate by writing the few words he understood. Although Itard was unable to educate Victor to the point of normalcy, the success he did have created much enthusiasm for educating retarded people. It soon became apparent, however, that education could not *cure* mental retardation. Enthusiasm for training declined, and interest focused on protecting retarded persons from society. With time the opposite concern of protecting society from retarded persons became the dominant one. Residential institutions were built far from population centers, and laws were passed that required retarded people to be sterilized so that they could not pass their deficit on to future generations. This view continued into the twentieth century. During World War II, however, it was discovered that retarded citizens inducted into the army or working in defense industries did better than expected. This discovery had an important impact on the care and training of retarded individuals.

Normalization. Today much of the care and training of retarded people are guided by the principle of **normalization.** This concept, which originated in

Retarded children may remain overly dependent on others and mistrust their own judgment. This little girl has sought comfort from her teacher.

Normalization, making the conditions of everyday life available to the mentally retarded, may help them lead more satisfying lives. This nine-year-old is looking at books in the children's corner of a bookstore.

Sweden, is described by Bengt Nirje (1969) as "making available to the mentally retarded patterns and conditions of everyday life which are as close as possible to the norms and patterns of the mainstream of society." **Mainstreaming,** a related idea, is integrating handicapped with nonhandicapped people in schools and in the community whenever possible. The United States Congress wrote these concepts into the Education for All Handicapped Children Act of 1975, mandating that public schools provide appropriate educational services to all children and educate handicapped children with nonhandicapped children to the greatest extent possible. Separate classes or schools for handicapped children are permitted only if the regular educational environment plus supplementary services are not sufficient to serve their needs.

This law, especially its mainstreaming position, has become a source of great controversy among educators and psychologists. Those who champion mainstreaming view it as necessary for providing equal rights and opportunities to handicapped children and for reducing the stigma attached to special education. Opponents argue that handicapped children's needs are best met by the more individualized instruction of specially trained teachers in separate classrooms. To date, research on the consequences of mainstreaming has done little to abate this controversy, for the results have been mixed. It remains unclear whether mainstreamed children do as well academically as children in special classes. There is, however, evidence that mainstreaming does not reduce the stigma associated with special education. Most research indicates that mainstreamed retarded children are accepted less well by their peers than are children in self-contained special classes (Gottlieb and Budoff, 1973). Other studies found that retarded children in mainstreamed classes had higher expectancies of failure than those in special classes (Gruen, Ottinger, and Ollendick, 1974). Perhaps retarded students endure greater stigma and fail more often in a regular classroom, where their limitations are more evident in comparison with the abilities of their classmates.

Residential Care.   Normalization has had a profound effect on social policy concerning residences for retarded individuals. Until the 1960s large, central institutions were their most common housing. These were intended to provide total care, serving the educational, health, recreational, and social needs of the residents. Recently, however, dissatisfaction with large institutions has grown. The whole pattern of life in large institutions—the extreme regimentation, the limited choices, and the almost complete lack of privacy—is in conflict with the normalization principle. The current trend has been to shift retarded individuals, whenever possible, into smaller, community-based group homes, halfway houses, and foster homes.

There are those who argue that large institutions should be phased out completely and that all retarded individuals should be cared for at home or in small residential settings (Wolfensberger, 1971). In rebuttal, others have noted that different kinds of settings probably work best for different kinds of individuals, and at different times in their lives. Less severely retarded individuals may fare best in smaller, community-based homes where the more normal environment may help them become more self-sufficient. Others may do well at home if the family situation permits and collateral services are available to help retarded individuals and their families. But large institutions will continue to be necessary for some retarded persons, and efforts should be directed at making these facilities habitable and humane rather than at eliminating them entirely.

Providing appropriate care and training for retarded persons is not only humane but also sound social policy. Follow-up studies of adults who had been classified as retarded in childhood have found that the large majority were self-supporting and making good social adjustments. Retardation may not be reversible, but retarded people can contribute to society more than is commonly acknowledged.

SUMMARY

The American Association on Mental Deficiency defines a mentally retarded person as someone who has an IQ below about 70 and a deficit in adaptive behavior. The concept of social adaptation, however, remains vague, and its assessment is highly subjective. Whether it is helpful or harmful to label a child retarded depends on whether the label will make services available to the labeled individual.

The causes of retardation are numerous. Conventionally, a division is made between organic and familial retardation. About one-quarter of retarded persons have recognized organic causes for their lower level of functioning. The majority suffer from familial retardation, for which no organic defect can be identified. The cause of familial retardation remains unclear, but it seems safe to reject explanations based solely on heredity or on environment.

On the average, organically retarded individuals have lower IQs than those with familial retardation. The familial retarded group may represent the lower portion of the normal curve of polygenically determined intelligence, whereas organically retarded people may constitute a separate group whose intellectual potential may originally have been normal but failed to be realized because of unfortunate physiological damage.

Certain distinctive personality traits are found in many retarded persons— expectancy of failure, outerdirectedness, a strong need for attention and support, and often a fear of adults. These traits can interfere with learning, problem solving, and everyday effectiveness. Such personality factors probably do not stem from the poor mental functioning of retarded persons but rather from a lifetime of social deprivation and efforts marked by failure.

The concepts of normalization and mainstreaming have guided recent efforts to educate, care for, and generally ensure retarded persons the same opportunities and patterns of living that the rest of the population enjoys. Residential institutions and special-education classes are giving way to smaller, community residences and education in regular classrooms. Evidence on the effectiveness of these practices is not convincing, however. It seems likely that different arrangements will turn out to be best for different individuals.

LEARNING DISABILITIES

Mental retardation is sometimes considered to be a **developmental disability,** a term used to identify a wide variety of mental and physical disabilities that are manifested before an individual reaches the age of twenty-two. **Learning disabilities** also fall within this category. Like mentally retarded children, those with learning disabilities require special educational attention. Unlike retarded children, however, they are of average or even above-average intelligence. Their problems are in specific areas of learning such as reading or mathematics.

Because so many different kinds of problems are considered learning disabilities, the term is quite ambiguous. In general, it refers to children who show a major discrepancy between achievement and ability that is not caused by other known handicapping conditions or circumstances (Federal Register, 1976). To a certain extent learning disabilities are defined by exclusion. Learning-disabled children are those whose difficulties are not caused primarily by mental retardation, social deprivation, or visual, auditory, or motor handicaps. According to most estimates, between 2 and 5 percent of the school population are learning-disabled, although some claim the figure to be as high as 20 percent. Boys are more commonly diagnosed as learning-disabled than girls.

Dyslexia and Dyscalculia

Perhaps the best known of the learning disabilities is **dyslexia,** a disturbance in the ability to read. Dyslexic children have unusual difficulties in learning to break down words and sentences into their components and then in integrating these elements back into wholes. They also have problems with writing and spelling. In dealing with letters and numbers, dyslexic children may confuse direction—substituting *b* for *d,* or *p* for *q;* and sequence—reading *was* for *saw,* or *14* for *41.* They may also confuse words relating to time and direction—*up* for *down,* or *go* for *stop* (Bryan and Bryan, 1978).

Children with another learning disability, **dyscalculia,** have difficulty with mathematical concepts and computations and with spatial and size relationships. Although children sometimes have both types of disability, children with dyscalculia do not necessarily have dyslexia, and vice versa.

Many researchers believe that, whatever their specific symptoms, children with learning disabilities have problems with information-processing strategies, with attention, and with language. More specifically, these children may find it difficult to focus their attention on the critical aspects of a task and to maintain their attention to the task. They have trouble understanding others and express themselves poorly. Their companions may become irritated by their difficulties with language and react to the children in a negative manner, compounding their problems (Bryan and Bryan, 1978).

Hyperactivity

Children with and without learning disabilities may be afflicted by **hyperactivity.** Hyperactive children are extremely active, restless, inattentive, and unable to stop moving or talking in situations that call for sitting still. Approximately 3 to 20 percent of school-age children are described as hyperactive (Whalen and Henker, 1976), and an estimated 50 percent of all children referred to professionals for behavior disorders are hyperactive (Langhorne and Loney, 1976). Contrary to popular assumptions, hyperactive children are not hyperactive in every situation. In unstructured situations that do not require attention to a given task, hyperactive children do not have higher activity levels than their peers. In structured situations, however, hyperactive children show a great deal of motor restlessness; they are unduly impulsive and unable to keep their attention on the task at hand (Whalen and Henker, 1976).

Learning-disabled children in general, and hyperactive children in particular, seem not to be liked by the people around them (Bryan and Bryan, 1978). Teachers rate them as less cooperative, less attentive, less able to cope with new situations, and less tactful than other children—in general, less desirable in a classroom (Bryan and McGrady, 1972). Learning-disabled children are more often rejected by their peers and are less popular than other children (Bryan, 1974). Parents tend to describe their learning-disabled children as obstinate, disobedient, and difficult to manage (Bryan and Bryan, 1978).

A child who attracts such reactions may respond by becoming even more difficult to manage. On this basis it should come as no surprise that hyperactive children have problems in school and that they seem to have other problems as well. For example, in one study of hyperactive children that covered a period of five years, they were found to show no improvement in school grades, to have few friends, and 15 percent of them had been referred to courts for antisocial activities (Weiss et al., 1971). In interpreting such findings, we should remember that labeling itself can affect people's judgments of others. Behavior that might be tolerated in a more easygoing child may be judged unacceptable in one who is labeled "learning-disabled."

Causes and Remediation

Theories and Explanations. Interpretations of the learning disabilities were once dominated by the theory that these problems were the result of brain damage, for no better reason than that the behavior of learning-disabled children showed similarities to the behavior of brain-damaged adults. For example, since dyscalculia is observed in adults with brain damage, it was assumed that the disorder must have a neurophysiological basis when it occurs in children as well. Today this assumption is considered highly questionable, for a given symptom—think of coughing or mental retardation, for example—can be produced by many different causes. Although brain-damaged children may sometimes have learning disabilities, learning-disabled children do not necessarily have brain damage (Bryan and Bryan, 1978).

Many current explanations of learning disabilities still assume a physiological basis. Some workers continue to attribute them to structural brain damage, perhaps so minimal that it is difficult or impossible to detect (Cruikshank, 1967). Others believe that learning disabilities are caused by impairments in the functioning of the brain, perhaps through confusion in the brain systems controlling visual, auditory, and tactile perception (Johnson and Myklebust, 1967). Such confusion would explain why learning-disabled children have problems with the processing of auditory and visual sensory information and with integrating the information from different modalities, for example, from auditory and visual processes in reading. Other interpretations attribute learning disabilities to disturbances in children's perceptual-motor development or to organically based linguistic difficulties.

Some theorists advance quite a different type of explanation and argue that many children called learning-disabled are not essentially different from other children but suffer a **developmental lag** (Lerner, 1971). That is, learning-disabled children are simply slow in developing important brain functions. A more psychological approach suggests that the symptoms of learning disabilities are manifestations of anxiety, that children with mild learning problems may become unable to persist at schoolwork because of anxiety resulting from their initial failures. These reactions lead to additional failure, which leads in turn to more anxiety. Alternatively, worries and anxiety, whether related to schoolwork or some other activity, may exacerbate mild learning problems which, under better circumstances, children would be able to overcome (Hart-Johns and Johns, 1982).

Assessment and Treatment. When learning disabilities are evident in infants or preschoolers, parents tend to seek medical advice. When these problems occur after children enter school, assessment and treatment often take place within the school system, where the services of several different professionals may be available. Psychological evaluations are conducted to assess a child's emotional and intellectual status. These evaluations are based on observations of the child's behavior, the results of standardized tests, and the child's case history (Bryan and Bryan, 1978). Neurological examinations may be carried out to determine whether disorders of the nervous system or visual or auditory problems are responsible for the learning difficulties. As with children who are mentally retarded, the question is whether learning-disabled children should be educated in separate classrooms or mainstreamed. Many schools use a combination of special education and mainstreaming. For example, some schools have resource rooms where children are given special instruction for a certain portion of the day. In other schools special-education teachers serve as consultants to regular classroom teachers.

There are many different treatments for the learning disabilities. Some methods aim to alleviate the underlying causes of the problem and vary with the theory of learning disabilities to which the educator subscribes. For example, if an educator believes that the confusion of letters and words in dyslexia results from a child's failure to learn spatial orientation, treatment might include training in this sensorimotor skill. Other programs employ language exercises intended to correct children's linguistic weaknesses. Behavior modification techniques that focus directly on the manifestations of learning disabilities, regardless of their causes (see page 565), have had some success in improving academic skills and eliminating undesirable behavior in learning-disabled children. Token economy programs have been somewhat effective, but the effects of token economies seem to disappear when the programs are discontinued, and they do not generalize to other situations. Methods of behavior modification that reward positive behavior and ignore negative behavior seem to be the best strategy with learning-disabled children, possibly because attention to negative behavior, even if the attention takes the form of punishment, may encourage children to continue it.

One controversial treatment is the use of drugs to control hyperactivity. Drugs, usually amphetamines or Ritalin, are sometimes given to help children control their behavior and maintain attention (Bryan and Bryan, 1978). Although amphetamines usually work as stimulants, they have a paradoxical calming effect on some hyperactive children. Over time, however, the effectiveness of drugs lessens and gradual increases in dosage are necessary. The positive effects of drugs on hyperactivity seem not to last after medication is stopped, and while they are taken, drugs may have negative side effects for some children. Psychologically, the use of drugs may harm children's self-esteem, by leading them to believe that their problems are beyond their personal control and that any improvements come from the drugs rather than their own efforts (Whalen and Henker, 1976).

SUMMARY

Learning-disabled children may be average or above average in intelligence, but they have problems in specific areas of learning, such as reading—dyslexia; or in mathematical concepts—dyscalculia. The basis for the problems of learning-disabled children may be that they have difficulties with information processing, language skills, and paying attention to a task. Whether learning-disabled or not, some children are hyperactive. These children seem not to be liked by people around them, and so treated they become even more difficult to manage.

The causes of learning disabilities are not well understood. Various explanations include structural damage to the brain, impaired brain functioning, and physiological problems related to language or perceptual-motor development. Still other theories attribute learning disabilities to a developmental lag or to psychological problems such as anxiety. Physical and psychological examinations will help to ascertain whether a child is learning-disabled or suffers other physiological or emotional problems.

Treatments for learning disabilities that focus on the manifestations of the problem have fared better than those that try to remedy its underlying cause. Behavior modification techniques, such as token economies, have been somewhat successful, but the long-lasting effects and the generalizability of the benefits of these treatments are questionable. As with mental retardation, there is controversy whether learning-disabled children should be mainstreamed or placed in special-education classes. Controversy also surrounds the use of drugs to control hyperactivity.

GENIUS AND GIFTEDNESS

Just as one end of the distribution of intelligence is made up of a small percentage of individuals whose IQs are considerably below average, the other is made up of a small percentage of individuals who have very high IQs. This group is referred to as *gifted*. In terms of IQ scores, giftedness has been variously defined as scores over 125, over 140, over 180, or as the top 2 to 4 percent of the population. Although intelligence has never been disputed as a fundamental determinant of giftedness, there has been controversy about whether gifted individuals' intelligence differs from that of the general population in degree or in kind, whether gifted individuals merely have more of something like g or whether their cognitive functioning is qualitatively different. In addition, factors other than intelligence may be considered dimensions of giftedness. Creativity is one, and productivity and demonstrated achievement might be others.

Genius

A small number of individuals in the gifted group are considered to be geniuses. Although at one time the convention was to consider a genius someone with an IQ above 150, it is clear that genius must be something more than that. The academic woods are filled with faculty and students whose IQs are high enough

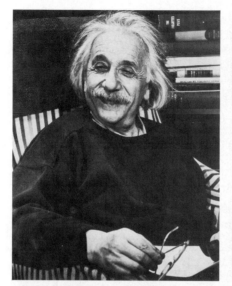

The mark of true genius is a lasting contribution such as those made by Albert Einstein, Marie Curie, Georgia O'Keefe, and Louis Armstrong.

to qualify on this criterion, but these same woods are notably devoid of geniuses. For an individual to become a **genius,** an exceptional pattern of basic talent must bring transcendent accomplishment. Furthermore, the individual's accomplishments must stand the test of time, for what is judged original and creative in one period may be considered derivative and unimportant by succeeding generations. People who receive widespread recognition for their accomplishments in their own lifetimes are more appropriately called "eminent" rather than geniuses.

The term genius is often applied to individuals whose accomplishments in a specialized area such as music or art have been impressive. For example, *Life* magazine wrote of Louis Armstrong:

> It is a simple fact of jazz music, the only art form America ever wholly originated, that virtually all that is played today comes in some way from Louis Armstrong. More than any other individual, it was Armstrong who took the raw spontaneous folk music of the honky tonks and street parades and, quite unconsciously, built it into a music beyond anything musicians had previously imagined. It was a spectacular outpouring of born, unschooled genius (quoted in Ashby and Walker, 1968).

A Superior Environment Is Not Enough.   There does seem to be something extraordinary about geniuses, and their special qualities are often observed early in their lives. Some hold to the myth that children with exceptional talents will never fulfill them unless their abilities are recognized early and they have the further good fortune to spend their childhoods in relatively advantaged homes, where parents diligently cultivate their child's gift. Yet many geniuses have not been blessed this way. Armstrong was a neglected child whose father deserted the family and whose mother was usually "out on the town" (Goertzel and Goertzel, 1962). As a child he was caught firing blank cartridges from his stepfather's revolver and placed in the New Orleans Colored Waifs Home for Boys, where he was taught to play an instrument. The father of Isaac Newton, the great physicist, was a humble farmer who died before his son was born; Karl Gauss, perhaps the greatest mathematician of all time, was the son of a bricklayer; James Watt and Abraham Lincoln were sons of carpenters; Martin Luther and John Knox were sons of peasants; and Johannes Kepler's father was a drunken innkeeper (Burt, 1955).

The circumstances of these lives lend credence to the "great person" view of the genius as a dedicated individual who overcomes all obstacles to fulfill an inspired, burning destiny. Others have argued that a genius is simply a highly intelligent person whose unique accomplishments are only the final, inevitable step in work brought to near fruition by many individuals who lived and labored earlier. Being considered a genius is largely a matter of luck for these individuals, it is argued, because they just happened to be at the right place at the right time. Both views appear to pierce through to a truth: geniuses are probably both born and shaped by circumstance.

Francis Galton: A Case History of Genius.

My dear Adele,

   I am 4 years old and can read any English book. I can say all the Latin Substantives and Adjectives and active verbs besides 52 lines of Latin poetry. I can cast up any sum in addition and can multiply by 2, 3, 4, 5, 6, 7, 8 [9], 10, [11].

   I can say the pence table. I read French a little and I know the clock (reported by Terman, 1917, p. 210).

So wrote Francis Galton to his sister on "Febuary" (his only spelling error) 15, 1827, the day preceding his fifth birthday. There are brackets around the numbers 9 and 11 because little Francis scratched out one with a knife and pasted some paper over the other, apparently in an effort to appear less boastful.

Galton's extreme precocity in a number of intellectual spheres has been colorfully described by Lewis Terman (1917). That Galton read at an incredibly early age, not mechanically but with real comprehension, is attested to by his ability to offer quotations appropriate to given situations. For instance, Terman reports a delightful story about Francis at age six, when he had already attained a scholarly understanding of the *Iliad* and *Odyssey*.

   At this age, a visitor at the Galton home made Francis weary by cross-questioning him about points in Homer. Finally, the boy replied, "Pray Mr. Horner, look at the last line in the twelfth book of the *Odyssey*" and then ran off. The line in question reads, "But why rehearse all this tale, for even yesterday I told it to thee and to thy noble wife in thy house; and it liketh me not twice to tell a plaintold tale." (pp. 211–212).

Young Galton grew up in advantaged circumstances. His early intellectual interests and his family's support of them are evident in the following letter written at the age of ten.

December 30, 1832

My Dearest Papa:

It is now my pleasure to disclose the most ardent wishes of my heart, which are to extract out of my boundless wealth in compound, money suffcient to make this addition to my unequaled library.

The Hebrew Commonwealth by John	9
A Pastor Advice................................	2
Hornne's commentaries on the Psalms	4
Paley's Evidence on Christianity	2
Jones Biblical Cyclopedia	<u>10</u>
	27

The ability to compose such letters would of course be unremarkable in an adult. Yet to be able to read and write at age five, as Galton did, suggests that he had then a mental age of ten and thus an IQ of 200! Just to indicate the rarity of his intelligence, when Terman examined thousands of children, the highest IQ he discovered was 170. In spite of all these clear indications of extremely high intelligence, Galton was not generally considered a child prodigy. Indeed, as Terman points out, since the intellectual feats that earned Galton his reputation were accomplished late in life, he was often referred to as a late-maturing genius. (Galton made breakthroughs in meteorology, anthropology, and genetics; he established the field of eugenics; he devised the correlation coefficient in statistics, invented a heliograph or mirror for signaling with the sun's rays, and originated a technique for identifying individuals through their fingerprints.) Like Galton, most geniuses are extremely bright as children, but the exceptional intellectual abilities that characterize their genius often do mature relatively late (Figure 14.7). As children they do nothing truly amazing in terms of creative accomplishment.

The Price of Genius.   Throughout history there has been a popular belief that geniuses pay a price for their creative intellect in madness and emotional instability. The view that the line between genius and insanity is very thin is based on striking instances of emotional instability among the ranks of the gifted. Galton, for example, suffered nervous symptoms throughout life and had two breakdowns. Gregor Mendel had several breakdowns or depressions, and Charles Darwin was plagued by a chronic and mysterious illness which depleted his energies and made him nervous and unable to sleep. Isaac Newton and Michael Faraday, two of the greatest physicists in the history of science, both became psychotic around the age of fifty, although after a period each recovered his sanity. The lives of such greats as Van Gogh, Blake, da Vinci, Nietzsche, Socrates, Swift, Kant, Coleridge, Raphael, and Rousseau all had their dark aspects. Some gifted individuals have even felt that their accomplishments stemmed from their instability. Thus Edgar Allen Poe wrote,

> I am come of a race noted for vigor of fancy and ardor of passion. Men have called me mad; but the question is not yet settled, whether much that is glorious, whether all that is profound, does not spring from disease of thought, from moods of mind enacted at the expense of general intellect (quoted in Marks, 1925, p. 22).

It has been suggested that creative giftedness may be genetically linked to schizophrenia. In a review of the empirical findings in support of this claim, Jon Karlsson (1974) found that the degree of association between the incidences of schizophrenia and giftedness in families is high; that individuals having schizophrenic family members are more creative thinkers than the rest of the population; and that persons suffering from schizophrenia are more likely than

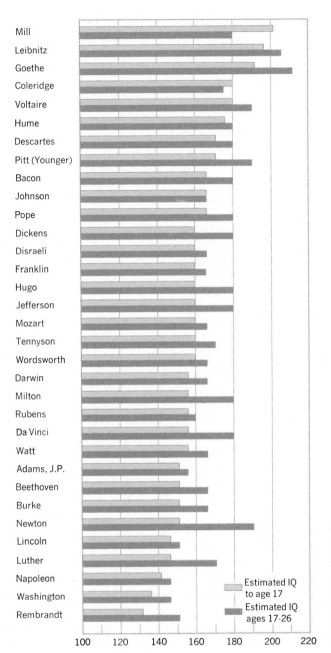

Figure 14.7
Estimated IQs of great men of the ages. The judgments were made by Cox, Terman, and Merrill on the basis of achievements of each person at ages 17 and 26. Many were "late bloomers," although all showed great potential at a very early age. (Adapted from Cox, 1926.)

others to have been the top graduates in their high schools and to have earned doctorate degrees.

An interesting theoretical speculation is that people with exceptionally high intelligence may differ in ways that affect adjustment. Although the gifted, unlike retarded persons, cannot be divided into separate groups on the basis of the etiology of their giftedness, it may be possible that they differ in other ways, for example, in neurophysiological functioning, creativity, or cognitive style. It has been argued (Hollingworth, 1942) that there is an "optimum intelligence" between IQ 125 and 155 and that too much intelligence may present a serious obstacle to normal psychological development. Edward Zigler and Rosa Cascione (in press) suggest that if further evidence confirms this point, we may be able to distinguish at least two groups of gifted individuals. Individuals in one group, with comparatively lower IQs, would fit in with the rest of the population and have no qualitatively different cognitive or neurological functioning. Individuals in the second group, with higher IQ scores, might be characterized by unusual neuropsychological functioning; the factor or factors responsible for the much higher IQs might also make these individuals more susceptible to psychological maladjustment. Individuals who become true geniuses would be found in this second group.

Another theory is that seeming madness "may be not so much the price of genius as the result of mismanaged lives" (Ashby and Walker, 1968, p. 219). The single-mindedness with which geniuses focus their talents may make them ignore or mismanage the details of everyday living, which seem insignificant in comparison to their work. Moreover, the prodigious labors necessary to bring forth monumental achievement leave little time for society and friendships. Michelangelo illustrates the extreme of the solitary genius in his statement, "I have no friends of any kind, nor do I wish any, and I have not so much time that I can afford to waste it" (quoted in Clements, 1963, p. 114).

Studies of Giftedness

Although there may be some connection between genius and madness, no such relation exists for giftedness in general. Longitudinal studies of individuals who had exceptionally high IQs as children have shown no evidence of an inordinately high incidence of maladjustment. The most notable study was that of Terman (1925; Terman and Oden, 1947, 1959), which should set to rest many of the popular stereotypes about gifted individuals. In 1922 Terman reported the results of an initial study of 1470 schoolchildren with IQs of 135 or over. They were for the most part in grades three to eight and averaged eleven years old when they were selected. In comparison with a control group of children of average intelligence, members of the gifted group were found to be taller, heavier, more socially poised, more outstanding in educational accomplishments, more avid readers, more active in play, and less prone to headaches, nervousness, tics, and stuttering. All in all, members of the gifted group were remarkably well adjusted. Terman's data shattered the erroneous belief that some mythical law of compensation would hold and put the brilliant mind into a fragile, weakened body.

Follow-up studies of these children were made every five to ten years; the last one was done in 1972, when these individuals were entering their sixties. These subsequent studies were equally telling. Educationally, the gifted children grew up to excel on all counts. About two-thirds of them went to college. By comparison with the average college graduate, six times as many who graduated continued their studies and received doctorate degrees. Occupationally, over 70 percent held positions in professional and semiprofessional fields. Many had international reputations. Social, marital, and sexual adjustments were as satisfactory as in the general population.

Gifted Women.   Terman's original sample included 671 girls. Although many became eminent women, they did not over the years report as many easily identifiable accomplishments as did the men. Nonetheless, at the time of the last survey more of these gifted women were employed than were homemakers, and compared to other American women their age, they had higher incomes, better educations, and more of their numbers in the professions. According to Pauline Sears (1976), who analyzed the women's responses in the 1972 survey, the women achieved less because many of them were less ambitious than the

Martha Graham, the dancer and choreographer; Margaret Bourke-White, the photographer; Katharine Graham, the owner of *The Washington Post*; and Dr. Sally Ride, the astronaut, are gifted women whose accomplishments have won them considerable recognition.

men. They were more likely to settle for work that they enjoyed than to strive for success. Compared to the men, this generation of women had not been offered the same opportunities or the social encouragement to develop their full potentials. Undoubtedly, as women are given equal opportunities and the encouragement to cultivate and apply their abilities, more of them will join the ranks of famous achievers.

Personality in the Gifted. Not all gifted individuals whom Terman studied could be counted as successes. Some failed in college, some drifted aimlessly from job to job, and some committed crimes. What factors distinguished the successful from the unsuccessful groups? Certainly IQ was not the critical element, because those considered most successful had an average adult IQ of 139, whereas those considered least successful had an equally potent average of 133. What did seem to distinguish the unsuccessful group were poorer motivation and poorer emotional adjustment. Thus, as with retarded persons, the gifted individual's everyday social effectiveness is determined not only by IQ but by other personality factors.

Several studies of personality traits in gifted individuals have confirmed that, in general, the gifted do not have an abnormally high incidence of maladjustment. When maladjustment was discovered, the complaints were of "too much time spent in reading, or being self-centered and bossy, and in a few instances of mixing poorly, being teased easily, [and being] solitary, resistant, or bumptious" (Miles, 1954, pp. 1025–1026). In addition, the gifted who were maladjusted often failed to develop good work habits and appeared stifled when forced to cope with circumstances that provided too little stimulation (Witty, 1940).

Nevertheless, gifted children, like retarded children, generally do have social and cognitive experiences different from those of their peers, and these may make them more vulnerable to personality difficulties. One psychoanalyst found in the gifted a hypersensitivity to stimuli in the external world, a disparity between intellectual and emotional development, and a deep unhappiness with their own exceptionality (Keiser, 1969). Part of this unhappiness may be explained by the greater demands gifted children make upon themselves and, surprisingly, by the fact that they consider themselves less adequate than children with lower IQs consider themselves (Katz and Zigler, 1967). This disparity between the high aspirations of very intelligent children and their low self-assessment may make them feel considerable guilt and personal dissatisfaction.

Others too can place high expectations on gifted children, who may react by feeling that they are failures for "not living up to potential" and may lose their motivation to try. In one study of over 100 high-achieving fifth-grade students, 20 percent had low self-concepts, and these children also set lower achievement standards for themselves and had lower expectations for success in school (Phillips, 1981).

Whether gifted children's dissatisfaction with themselves makes them maladjusted depends on whether their reaction is adaptive—for example, working harder; or maladaptive—perhaps withdrawing from social situations. Brilliant individuals by dint of their brilliance can make problems for themselves, but they bring to the solution of such problems tremendous intellectual resources. In light of these resources, we might expect them to attain better personal adjustments rather than worse.

Training the Gifted. Of the brilliant Isaac Barrow, who preceded Newton as professor of mathematics at Cambridge, it was said, "Endowed with a restless body and a vivid mind, he so plagued his teachers and was so troublesome at home that his father . . . prayed that if it pleased God to take away any of his children, he could best spare Isaac'' (Moore, 1924, p. 3). There is little question that the budding genius can sometimes be difficult and a trial to parents and teachers. Yet it is clearly to society's advantage to ensure that gifted children develop their full potentials.

There is little agreement about what form of education is best for the gifted child. Some feel that gifted children should be given special attention but remain in regular classrooms. Others champion the concept of teaching exceptionally talented children together in their own groups. Still others favor "acceleration," that is, promoting children until they reach a grade offering activities commensurate with their intellectual abilities.

Whatever methods are chosen, the fact remains that our nation does rather poorly in nurturing the abilities of the gifted. A report from the United States Office of Education (1971) concluded that a very small percentage of the nation's gifted children receive any kind of special services. Gifted children among minority groups and in economically disadvantaged populations appear to be particularly neglected.

Gifted individuals themselves are often unhappy with their school experiences. In one survey of the 400 most eminent men and women of our century, the majority of whom had had exceptional talent as children, three-fifths remembered being dissatisfied with school and teachers (Goertzel and Goertzel, 1962). Assigned work that did not challenge them, they became bored, frustrated, and disinterested.

Creativity

Creativity has been described in various ways, but most definitions view its essence as placing things in new perspectives and seeing connections that were previously unsuspected. Creativity thus entails originality, but originality is not always creativity. The thinking of mentally ill persons, particularly those with schizophrenia, is marked by originality and uniqueness, but it is hardly creative. The same holds for most of the new and unusual thoughts we all have. To be creative, an idea or product must be original and appropriate; it must fit the context or make sense in light of the demands of the situation. Although the process by which creative insights are achieved is little understood, research has provided some understanding of the attributes of very creative people and the environmental factors that may enhance creativity.

Frank Barron (1958) conducted intensive studies of people considered "highly original scientists and artists." Among those tested were painters, writers, biologists, economists, anthropologists, physicists, and physicians. They were assigned many tasks, such as interpreting inkblots, creating mosaics from colored squares, creating a stage design on a miniature stage, completing unfinished drawings, and expressing an artistic preference for various figures and designs. They were also asked to suggest new uses for commonplace objects and to wrestle with the consequences of untoward events, such as, "A nation finds a way to increase the average IQ of its citizens by 50 points—what would the consequences be?" Another task was to create a story using as many words as possible from a list of randomly drawn nouns, adjectives, and adverbs.

Among the findings of these studies were the following. The creative person, whether artist or scientist, prefers drawings and paintings that are asymmetrical, complex, and vital rather than those of balanced simplicity (Figure 14.8a). Their own mosaics and drawings (Figure 14.8b) have the same asymmetrical and complex qualities. What Baron considered the "most difficult and far-reaching

Figure 14.8
*Test responses of creative persons and
individuals chosen "at random."* (a) In
the Welsh Figure Preference Test people
state whether they do or do not prefer
abstract line drawings shown them on
cards. Persons chosen at random liked
those at the top, creative persons those
on the bottom. (b, page 475) In the
Drawing Completion Test individuals
elaborate on sample figures. Creative
persons did those on the far right.
(Created by Kate Frank.) (c) For the
Inkblot Test people describe what they
perceive in the configuration. (Created by
Frank Barron.) (d) In the Symbolic
Equivalent Test they say what a
"stimulus image" brings to mind.
(Adapted from the Welsh Figure
Preference Test, by George Welsh,
copyright 1949, in Barron, 1958.
Reproduced with permission of the
author, *Scientific American,* and
Consulting Psychologists Press, Inc.)

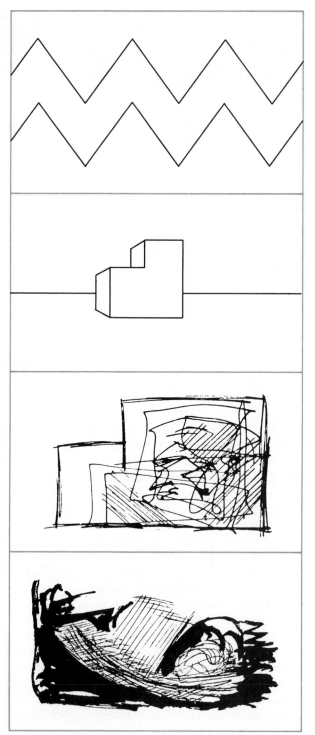

(a)

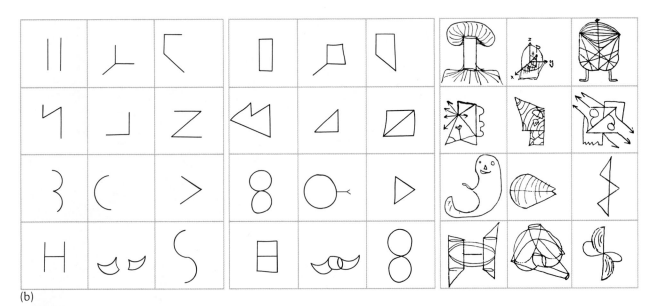

(b)

Common responses
1. Smudges
2. Dark clouds

Uncommon responses
1. Magnetized iron filings
2. A small boy and his mother hurrying along on a dark, windy day, trying to get home before it rains.

(c)

Common responses
1. An African voodoo dancer
2. A cactus plant

Uncommon responses
1. Mexican in sombrero running up a long hill to escape from rain clouds
2. A word written in Chinese

Stimulus Image:

Empty bookcases

Common resources
1. An empty mind
2. A deserted room

Uncommon responses
1. The vacant eyes of an idiot
2. An abandoned beehive

Sound of a foghorn

Common responses
1. A belch
2. A frog's croak

Uncommon responses
1. The cry of despair of a great unseen animal
2. A public address system announcing disaster

(d)

ordering'' were the efforts to interpret inkblots in a single comprehensive and synthesizing percept. ''It . . . illustrates the creative response to disorder, which is to find an elegant new order more satisfying than any that could be evoked by a simpler configuration'' (Figure 14.8c). A symbolic meaning test (Figure 14.8d) revealed the same quality of originality. We can also gain some insight into the creative person from responses to Barron's true-false questionnaire.

- I like to fool around with new ideas, even if they turn out later to be a total waste of time. (True)
- The unfinished and imperfect often have greater appeal for me than the completed and polished. (True)

Jackson Pollock fitted well the image of the creative person who explores new methods and imposes order where it does not exist.

- A person should not probe too deeply into his own and other people's feelings, but take things as they are. (False)
- Young people sometimes get rebellious ideas, but as they grow up they get over them and settle down. (False)

The image of the creative person that emerges is of someone who challenges the unknown, willingly attempts tasks that are too difficult and that test the limits of his or her abilities, seeks to impose order where it does not exist, and is independent in judgment, nonconforming in views, and often open and honest in expression.

Creativity and Intelligence.   Although it is generally assumed that creativity is one aspect of giftedness, the creative person is not necessarily highly intelligent. In several studies of individuals with high intelligence scores, surprisingly few were judged highly creative (Getzels and Jackson, 1962; Hollingworth, 1942; Terman and Oden, 1947, 1959; Torrance, 1962). Of course intelligence tests were designed to assess academic ability, and creativity may play only a small part in academic performance. In fact, Michael Wallach and Nathan Kogan (1965b) constructed several tests of creativity that correlate positively with one another but not at all with traditional tests of intelligence. Their data suggest that essential to the creative process in children are the ability to make multiple and unique associations and a playful and permissive attitude toward intellectual tasks. Wallach and Kogan found children who are both creative and highly intelligent to be confident, able, and sociable. Children with considerable creativity but less considerable intelligence were not so well adjusted (Table 14.6).

Promoting Creativity.   Is it possible to increase our creativity? Countless popular books contain advice on how to become more creative, and Sunday newspaper supplements regularly feature articles or quote experts on this topic. But whether people can actually learn to be creative by practicing prescribed lessons remains unclear. As is true for intelligence, we can probably do little to

Table 14.6 Personality Correlates of Intelligence and Creativity in Children

	Intelligence	
	Low	**High**
Creativity — High	". . . .in angry conflict with themselves and with their school . . . feelings of unworthiness and inadequacy. In a stress-free context . . . can blossom forth cognitively."	"These children can exercise . . . both control and freedom, both adultlike and childlike kinds of behavior."
Creativity — Low	"Basically bewildered . . . engaged in various defensive maneuvers ranging from useful adaptations such as intensive social activity to regressions such as passivity or psychosomatic symptoms."	" . . . addicted to school achievement. Academic failure . . . perceived . . . as catastrophic. So they must continually strive for academic excellence."

Adapted from Wallach and Kogan, 1965a.

increase our basic creative potential; we can only hope to exercise that potential to its fullest.

Whether or not creativity can be learned, its expression may be fostered by activities as simple as children's play. Dorothy and Jerome Singer (1977) have shown that people who demonstrated creative achievements early in their lives engaged in a good deal of fantasy as children, such as developing imaginary playmates and playing pantomime games. Creativity is certainly evident in children's symbolic play, such as when they come up with imaginative possibilities for functions of objects (Fein and Clarke-Stewart, 1973). Since creativity is so striking in children and so rare in adults, it can be argued that the trait is subdued during the process of education or socialization.

The psychoanalyst Silvano Arieti (1976) conjectured that a society can promote or inhibit the creativity of its citizens by its values and resources. He specified several factors that foster a "creativogenic" society: the availability of cultural means to all citizens, without discrimination; an openness, tolerance, and interest in diverging views; and a stress on becoming, not just on being. By emphasizing becoming as well as being, society would make individual growth and development as important as immediate gratification, pleasure, and comfort.

SUMMARY

Gifted individuals are those whose IQs are at the upper end of the distribution of intelligence. A few gifted people are considered geniuses, but their special qualities are difficult to stipulate. The requisites for genius are very high intelligence and accomplishments of such great significance that they continue to be recognized long after the individual's death.

Gifted individuals are often precocious as children. There is no evidence that they must be raised in a superior environment if they are to fulfill their potential, for many geniuses have bloomed in impoverished circumstances. Nor is there strong support for the popular notion that giftedness or genius is akin to madness. Although many creative geniuses have been severely maladjusted, the group of gifted individuals studied by Terman were, in general, better adjusted than the average. It has been suggested that gifted individuals with comparatively higher IQs may have qualitatively different cognitive or neuro-psychological functioning, and that whatever factors cause the exceptionally high IQs would also cause a greater susceptibility to psychological maladjust-ment.

Although the gifted are generally not maladjusted, they often have social and cognitive experiences different from those of their peers, and these experiences may make them more vulnerable to personality difficulties. Gifted children actually consider themselves less adequate than other children consider them-selves, perhaps because they erect such high standards for themselves or because of expectations others place upon them. On the other hand, the intellectual resources of the gifted may enable them to make better-than-average personal adjustments.

Creativity is an important aspect of giftedness and has been investigated extensively in its own right. Highly creative individuals have originality, can see things in new perspectives, dare to undertake tasks at which they may fail, and examine ideas in new ways. Although the extremely bright individual is often creative, creativity does not necessarily go hand in hand with intelligence. It is not clear whether creativity can be learned, but creative potential can be promoted by activities literally as simple as child's play, which stimulates the imagination.

TO BE SURE YOU UNDERSTAND THIS CHAPTER

The following are the major concepts employed in this chapter. You should be able to use them to reconstruct most of the discussion in the chapter.

Intelligence A	**Familial retardation**
Intelligence B	**Polygenic model**
Fluid intelligence	**Outerdirectedness**
Crystallized intelligence	**Normalization**
General factor *(g)*	**Mainstreaming**
Specific factors *(s)*	**Developmental disability**
Primary mental abilities	**Learning disability**
Cross-sectional study	**Dyslexia**
Longitudinal study	**Dyscalculia**
Mental retardation	**Hyperactivity**
Deficit in adaptive behavior	**Developmental lag**
Etiology	**Giftedness**
Organic retardation	**Genius**
Down syndrome (trisomy 21)	**Creativity**
Cretinism	

Much of the content of Chapter 14 concerns relationships and contrasts that you should also understand. These are some of the important ones.

IQ changes and personality, sex differences, social deprivation, and socio-economic status

Test scores (IQ and MA) versus adaptive behavior

Genetic and environmental interpretations of familial retardation

Two-group approach to mental retardation

Personality traits that may either contribute to or be the result of retardation

Attitudes of general population toward retarded persons
Mental retardation versus learning disabilities
Giftedness versus genius
Genius and maladjustment
Personality traits of the gifted

In This Book. The materials in Chapter 2, 13, and 14 are complementary. You might want to review the first two of these chapters at this point. The organic versus familial distinction reappears in the discussion of psychopathology (Chapter 16). It might be of interest to look at some of those materials now.

Elsewhere. A comprehensive treatment of intelligence is contained in H. J. Butcher's *Human Intelligence,* and statements of current views of intelligence are contained in Lauren Resnick's *The Nature of Intelligence. Intellectual Functioning in Adults,* edited by Lissy Jarvik, Carl Eisdofer, and June Blum, contains the results of various long-term studies of intellectual changes with aging.

For a comprehensive treatment of the field of mental retardation, see Peter Mittler's three-volume work, *Research to Practice in Mental Retardation.* Volume 1 is devoted to issues of care and intervention, volume 2 to education and training, and volume 3 to biomedical aspects of mental retardation. Robert Edgerton's *The Cloak of Competence* and Edgerton and S. Bercovici's follow-up report in the *American Journal of Mental Deficiency* (1976) provide insightful accounts of how retarded adults attempt to adjust to community living after being discharged from an institution.

TO GO BEYOND THIS CHAPTER

CHAPTER 15   THEORIES OF PERSONALITY

It has been said that every person is in certain respects like all other people, like some other people, and like no other person. All human beings share with everyone the physiology that is universal to the species. They also share with some people, who are members of their society, the general characteristics of people in that society. But they do not share their entire makeup with anyone. You can say about yourself that in the long history of the human race and in the future that lies ahead, there has never been and will never be anyone quite like you. The way you think, feel, perceive, and behave has a pattern which, in its finest details, has never been and never will be matched in another human being. You simply cannot be duplicated!

Theorists who have searched for a framework within which to understand the complexity of human personality usually adopt one of two orientations. The first is a descriptive view, which emphasizes the structure of personality. The descriptive theories resemble the psychometric approach to the study of psychological development (page 337), in that they too rely heavily on tests. The second approach, which also has a parallel in the study of psychological development, is a developmental orientation, in which the task is to describe how personality develops and how individuals adapt to their diverse environments.

DESCRIPTIVE PERSONALITY THEORIES

The descriptive theories of personality take one of two forms, **trait theory** or **type theory.** The difference between the two is that trait theories describe people in terms that are more specific, type theories describe people by their membership in broad categories.

Trait Theories

As we have seen elsewhere, a *trait* is a stable and enduring attribute of a person that is revealed consistently in a variety of situations. Were a trait theorist to study all the different characteristics that have been ascribed to people, the number of possibilities would be overwhelming. The most-cited number in the psychology of personality may be 17,953. This is the number of distinguishing adjectives that Gordon Allport and Henry Odbert (1936) were able to extract from the English language when they set out to create a dictionary of trait names that was intended to be exhaustive and to be used to distinguish all aspects of one person's behavior from another's. Nearly thirty years later Warren

GORDON ALLPORT'S THEORY OF TRAITS

Gordon Allport (1897–1967), one of the first and most influential of modern personality theorists, believed that people have common traits and individual traits. A common trait is one that appears to some degree, or in an opposing form, in every person. Common traits—generosity, friendliness, dominance, aggression, responsibility, kindliness—are related to social adjustment. The extent to which people indicate them can be measured by personality tests. An individual trait, one possessed by few people, gives uniqueness to the personality. Individual traits can be studied only through observation and the analysis of personal records, such as letters and diaries. The individual may have a quirky wit or a certain infectious ebullience, a cutting sarcasm or a streak of malevolence.

Allport also rated common and individual traits by how pervasive of the personality they are. A *cardinal trait* is a disposition around which the individual organizes his or her whole life—power, ambition, greed, self-sacrifice, humanitarianism. Not all people have cardinal traits, but a few from mythology, literature, and history have given their names to these determining motives of life—narcissistic, quixotic, puckish, sadistic, Byronic, Napoleonic, Rabelaisian, Machiavellian. Allport believed that instead of cardinal traits most people have five to ten *central traits*. These important values and interest patterns color their lives and pretty well describe their personalities—such as a love of gardening or dancing or cooking, an urge to simplify, quarrelsomeness, a preoccupation with sex, sentimentality, being artistic, independence. In addition, people have secondary traits that are evident only in particular situations. Taking note of these traits, which have for the most part been learned, allows a more complete picture of the individual. Being grouchy in the morning, or having

Gordon Allport studied normal, productive adults rather than animals, children, and mental patients. He wrote with a brilliant style and expressed "certain doubts concerning the ultimate power of psychological methods to represent adequately and to understand completely the enigma of human behavior" (Hall and Lindzey, 1978, p. 437).

a preference for French food, or harboring a strong dislike of crowds, of rock music, of vegetables, or of going to bed are examples.

Allport was interested in the unusual traits that are possessed by few people and that give uniqueness to the personality. He believed that the individual's whole personality could be discerned only through an intensive, long-term analysis, for each trait is unique in the way that it functions within a person's total makeup. To study personality for Allport was to study single individuals. Most psychologists feel, however, that psychology must make generalizations about people and about personality.

Norman (1963) developed a new pool of some 40,000 trait-descriptive terms. Using experimental and statistical methods, however, Norman was able to reduce this number dramatically. He began his search for simplicity by creating a set of paired polar-opposite adjectives drawn from the Allport-Odbert list

Table 15.1 Consistent Trait Dimensions and Polar Adjectives Used When Peers Rate Acquaintances and Strangers

Trait Dimension	Polar Adjectives	
	A	**B**
1. Extroversion	Talkative	Silent
	Frank	Secretive
	Sociable	Reclusive
2. Agreeableness	Mild, gentle	Headstrong
	Good-natured	Irritable
	Not jealous	Jealous
3. Conscientiousness	Fussy, tidy	Careless
	Responsible	Undependable
	Scrupulous	Unscrupulous
4. Emotional Stability	Poised	Nervous, tense
	Composed	Excitable
	Calm	Anxious
5. Culture	Polished	Crude
	Imaginative	Simple
	Artistically sensitive	Artistically insensitive

Adapted from Norman, 1963.

(Table 15.1). Participants in his study were then asked to rate peers whom they knew well on these word pairs. Factor analysis revealed that five personality traits seemed to account for the way in which the ratings grouped together. Table 15.1 lists these "basic" traits and some of the adjective pairs that define them.

Before the five were accepted as the basic traits of personality, a follow-up study was conducted by Frank Passini and Norman (1966). The data of the first study had been based on persons rating others they knew. In this study, by contrast, college students were brought together, one to rate the other after an acquaintance of only fifteen minutes. Each did know that the other was a student. Curiously, the dimensions of personality that these strangers used to describe each other produced the identical quintet of "basic" traits. Because these traits were being used by some individuals to evaluate others whom they did not even know, Passini and Norman concluded that the similarities in traits obtained in the two studies must depend not on solid information but on the stereotypic ways in which people label other people. We all use an "implicit personality theory" in our commerce with others. We believe that certain personality traits go together and are shared in common by people who belong to certain groups. Knowing only that the individuals to be rated were classmates was enough to evoke this set and produce the clusters of adjectives.

Surface Traits and Source Traits.   In another important attempt to classify traits of personality, Raymond Cattell (1965) analyzed the judgments that people made of close acquaintances and came up with a list of thirty-five trait clusters. He called these clusters **surface traits** because they were overt expressions of personality. These attributes are, figuratively speaking, close to the surface and are expressions of more basic traits of personality (Table 15.2). Using factor analysis, Cattell isolated sixteen of these more basic factors. He called these **source traits** and developed a self-administered personality questionnaire, the Sixteen Personality Factor Questionnaire (16PF), to measure them.

Raymond Bernard Cattell was born in England in 1905. From 1944 until his retirement in 1973, he directed the Laboratory of Personality and Group Behavior Research at the University of Illinois. His research over three decades was a massive attempt to penetrate personality through traits and factor analysis.

Table 15.2 A Surface Trait and a Source Trait, with Examples of Their Relevant Dimensions

Surface trait		
Sociability, sentimentalism	vs.	Independence, hostility, aloofness
Responsive	vs.	Aloof
Affectionate	vs.	Cold
Sentimental	vs.	Unsentimental
Social interests	vs.	Lacking social interests
Home and family interests	vs.	Lacking home and family interests
Dependent	vs.	Independent
Friendly	vs.	Hostile
Frank	vs.	Secretive
Genial	vs.	Cold-hearted
Even-tempered	vs.	Sensitive
Source trait		
Dominance		Submission
Self-assertive, confident	vs.	Submissive, unsure
Boastful, conceited	vs.	Modest, retiring
Aggressive, pugnacious	vs.	Complaisant
Extrapunitive	vs.	Impunitive, intropunitive
Vigorous, forceful	vs.	Meek, quiet
Willful, egotistic	vs.	Obedient

Questionnaire items	*Dominance indicators*
Do you tend to keep in the background on social occasions?	*No*
If you saw the following headlines of equal size in your newspaper, which would you read?	*a*
(a) Threat to constitutional government in foreign country by dictator.	
(b) Physicists make important discovery concerning the electron.	

From Cattel, 1950, 1965.

Over the years Cattell has given this test to many varied groups of people and reports some interesting findings. For example, in comparing successful and troubled marriages, Cattell has observed that, for marriage at least, unlike charges do not attract. Couples with stable marriages have greater similarities of personality than couples with unstable marriages, which are marked by striking differences between husband and wife. The similarities of personality in stable marriages and the differences in unstable ones seem to bring forth three important differences in the marital relationship: warmth as opposed to aloofness; trust as opposed to suspiciousness; and self-sufficiency rather than overdependence.

The test profiles for three different groups of individuals—airline pilots, neurotics, and creative artists and writers—on the sixteen factors of Cattell's scale are given in Figure 15.1. The two profiles of the artist groups are very similar to each other and both are quite different from that of the neurotic sample. Contrary to popular opinion, creativity and neurosis need not go hand in hand. The fact that personality profiles of creative writers are similar to those of creative artists suggests that the personality components of creativity are similar, wherever the creative spark exists. As for the pilots, they appear to have the traits

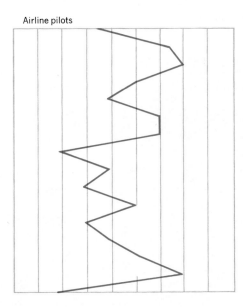

Airline pilots

Reserved	Outgoing
Less intelligent	More intelligent
Affected by feelings	Emotionally stable
Submissive	Dominant
Serious	Happy-go-lucky
Expedient	Conscientious
Timid	Venturesome
Tough-minded	Sensitive
Trusting	Suspicious
Practical	Imaginative
Forthright	Shrewd
Self-assured	Apprehensive
Conservative	Experimenting
Group-dependent	Self-sufficient
Uncontrolled	Controlled
Relaxed	Tense

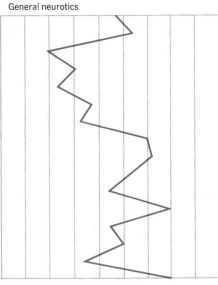

General neurotics

Reserved	Outgoing
Less intelligent	More intelligent
Affected by feelings	Emotionally stable
Submissive	Dominant
Serious	Happy-go-lucky
Expedient	Conscientious
Timid	Venturesome
Tough-minded	Sensitive
Trusting	Suspicious
Practical	Imaginative
Forthright	Shrewd
Self-assured	Apprehensive
Conservative	Experimenting
Group-dependent	Self-sufficient
Uncontrolled	Controlled
Relaxed	Tense

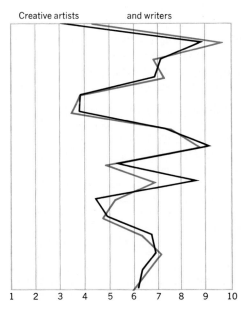

Creative artists   and writers

Reserved	Outgoing
Less intelligent	More intelligent
Affected by feelings	Emotionally stable
Submissive	Dominant
Serious	Happy-go-lucky
Expedient	Conscientious
Timid	Venturesome
Tough-minded	Sensitive
Trusting	Suspicious
Practical	Imaginative
Forthright	Shrewd
Self-assured	Apprehensive
Conservative	Experimenting
Group-dependent	Self-sufficient
Uncontrolled	Controlled
Relaxed	Tense

1 2 3 4 5 6 7 8 9 10

Figure 15.1
16PF personality profiles. The fact that groups differ in appropriate ways is evidence of the validity of the test. (After Cattell, 1973.)

In a stable marriage husband and wife tend to have similar interests and traits of personality.

most plane passengers would find reassuring. They are relaxed, controlled, tough-minded, emotionally stable, self-assured, and practical.

Inflexible Personality Traits. Traits are enduring patterns of behavior that are manifested in many different contexts. The degree of permanence and resistance to change varies a great deal from person to person, however. In the next chapter we will describe different forms of psychopathology, including certain personality disorders that demonstrate vividly how highly inflexible and maladaptive personality traits can significantly impair social and occupational functioning.

By way of a preview, we have chosen a case example that illustrates *compulsive personality disorder*. Individuals with this disorder tend to be perfectionists, insisting that their way is the best way and that others should follow their example; they are unable to express warmth and tenderness; they work meticulously, keeping their surroundings extremely neat and orderly; they are preoccupied with rules, efficiency, and trivia; they work at attaining pleasure but cannot manage to enjoy themselves.

> J., a twenty-five-year-old corporation executive, came for psychiatric treatment after physically assaulting his girlfriend. He reported that this was the first time he had ever struck a woman and was afraid that he might completely lose control of himself. All his adult life J. had led an extremely orderly existence, controlling to an incredible degree both his own behavior and that of people who came into contact with him. He refused to entertain in his apartment for fear that the precisely arranged furnishings might be moved out of place. When driving his car with his girlfriends, he wouldn't let them touch the glove compartment because its contents were meticulously arranged. Handsome and charming, he was attractive to many women, but he sooner or later found fault with them (Weintraub, 1974, p. 89)

When J. began to have an affair with a psychiatric nurse, his modes of adaptation grew more difficult. She reacted to his controlling efforts by interpreting his behavior, pointing out how he had no control over the way of life he had created. J. tried to demonstrate to her that he could be more flexible if he chose to be, but he was unsuccessful in changing his behavior. His trait of meticulousness took a somewhat different direction. Preoccupied by the thought that his anus was unclean, he began to wash it repeatedly after defecation. He was unable to make decisions, and new thoughts began to encroach upon him. He found himself unable to use his hi-fi system because he was certain the pressure of the tone arm was destroying his records. As his companion continued to "analyze" his behavior, he grew more distressed and finally lost control and hit her. Alarmed at his act he sought treatment.

Type Theories

Types of personality are broad, inclusive categories by which some psychologists and others have attempted to pigeonhole people. The very first theory of personality was a type theory, a theory of temperaments put forth by Galen, a Greek physician who practiced in Rome in the second century. It was based on the four "humors" or bodily fluids of Hippocrates' physiology, blood, black bile, yellow bile, and phlegm. A preponderance of blood caused a person to be sanguine—cheerful and optimistic; of black bile to be melancholic—depressed and pessimistic; of yellow bile to be choleric—quick-tempered and irritable; of phlegm to be phlegmatic—calm, slow, and uninvolved with the world.

Perhaps the most famous of all present-day typologies is that of introversion–extroversion, first described by Carl Jung. According to Jung, the extrovert is outgoing, exuberant, lively, and inclined toward direct action. The introvert presents the opposite side of the behavioral coin and is more prone to thoughtful reflection. This typology unfortunately shares the two major shortcomings of all simple typologies. First, they put people into extreme categories that apply only to a few individuals. As with most dimensions of human variation, the gradation from introversion to extroversion is a continuous one on which people are normally distributed. Most people fall in the middle of the dimension and show both introversion and extroversion to a degree. Second, in their simplicity, typologies ignore one of the most important facts about personality, that it is multidimensional and consists of many attributes.

These shortcomings have been partially overcome in the work of a famous British psychologist, Hans J. Eysenck. Eysenck is a typologist whose focus has been on a small number of personality types, defined by three major dimensions: *introversion–extroversion, neuroticism–stability,* and *psychoticism.* During World War II Eysenck used many different procedures to classify more than 10,000 individuals, including neurotic soldiers. The symptoms of this neurotic group helped him to identify the end points of the introversion-extroversion dimension. The introverts showed anxiety, depression, apathy, ruminative thinking, and psychologically created physical symptoms. The extroverts had poor occupational histories, imaginary physical complaints, and sexual difficulties and performed poorly on intelligence tests. Neuroticism–stability, Eysenck's second dimension, has at the neuroticism or "unstable" pole people whose emotions are labile, easily aroused, and strong. These individuals are moody, touchy, anxious, restless. At the other "stable" end of the dimension are individuals with emotional control. They are reliable, even-tempered, calm, and carefree (Eysenck and Rachman, 1965). Figure 15.2 is Eysenck's diagrammatic illustration of the relationship of various traits to the first two of the three major dimensions.

Hans Eysenck, a German-born psychologist who lives in England, believes that extroverted people have a reticular formation little activated by sensory inputs and therefore a naturally low level of arousal in the cortex of the brain. They are moved to seek excitement and companions in order to raise cortical arousal to an optimal level. Introverts, whose reticular formation is well activated by sensory inputs according to Eysenck, already have a naturally high level of arousal and therefore seek quiet and solitude.

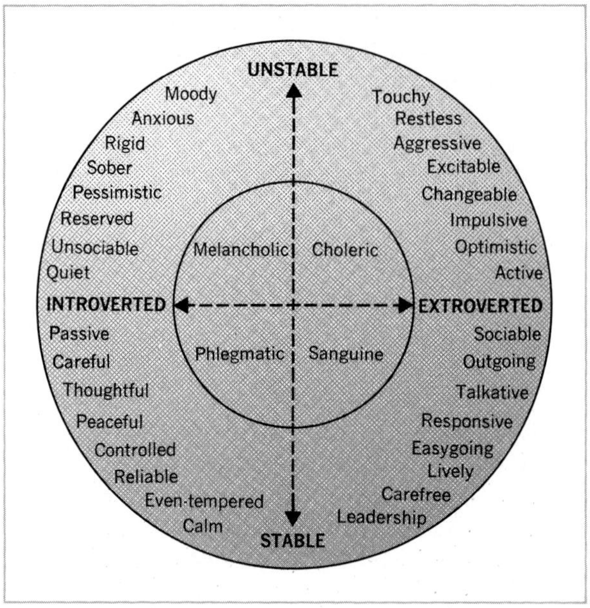

Figure 15.2
The result of modern factor-analytic studies of the intercorrelations of traits. To illustrate the long-term nature of such views, Eysenck provided an inner circle showing the four classical temperaments proposed by Galen in the second century, on the basis of the four body fluids of Hippocrates' physiology. (After Eysenck, 1964.)

Traits versus Situations

As a part of the nature-nurture controversy, personality theorists have long debated whether traits or situations are the determiners of our behavior. In 1968 Walter Mischel, in his influential book *Personality and Assessment,* challenged traits as determiners of behavior, maintaining that they have little power to predict it. Mischel's analysis of the evidence indicated that the behavior of people is often not very consistent from situation to situation. Trait advocates joined the battle. Jack Block (1971, 1977) of the University of California at Berkeley, examining evidence from longitudinal research, concluded that behavior had both consistency and continuity over time, but that the degree of consistency and continuity varied with different types of data. The consistency of personality ratings and self-observations, made by people about their own behavior, temperament, and feelings, is "undeniable and impressive." In sharp contrast, the behavior that occurs in artificial and contrived test and laboratory studies is erratic and unreliable. In other words, Block's criticism was that personality investigations had been inadequate and had failed to show that traits do make behavior consistent and predictable.

The debate over this issue has gradually been resolved in an intelligent compromise. Seymour Epstein (1977) of the University of Massachusetts has observed that a complete psychology of personality must make use of the concept of traits, defined as "enduring response dispositions . . . that allow us to predict long-term behavior [of the individual] averaged over many situations without having to specify the nature of particular situations." At the same time, however, this psychology of personality will have to recognize the effects of certain situations, which allow us to predict the behavior of a great many individuals in these situations without specifying the traits of the individual. After situations have been classified by their effects, Epstein proposes studying interactions between traits and situations—the behavior of people with certain traits in certain types of situations.

In tackling the trait-versus-situation question, we can take a page from the heredity-environment literature and anticipate that neither traits nor situations will be identified as the single determiner of behavior. Rather we may expect these two sets of factors to interact, with the strength of a trait determining the range of situations in which it is likely to be expressed. Very powerful traits will be revealed in many and varied situations. Weak traits will be revealed in very few. As mentioned earlier, the best examples of powerful traits finding wide-ranging expression are those of the psychopathological disorders discussed in Chapter 16. These traits are evident in almost everything the person does and over long periods of time.

SUMMARY

Trait and type theories are ways of describing and systematizing the variability in human personality. Traits are considered to be stable and consistent descriptive attributes of individuals. Type theories have used broad categories to characterize human beings. The basic assumption of the trait theories is that individual personalities can be described in terms of a limited number of dimensions. This view has been criticized as an oversimplification. Typologies, which employ an even smaller number of characteristics, have been criticized for the same reason. Since persons differ in quantitative as well as qualitative ways, efforts to categorize individuals on an "either-or" basis—either introverted or extroverted—do an injustice to the variety of behavior. Proponents of type theories, such as Eysenck, have increased the numbers of dimensions employed in their typologies in an effort to make such descriptions applicable to a larger number of people. In the field of personality, a controversy similar to the nature-nurture issue questions whether traits or situations determine our behavior. As with the nature-nurture issue, the answer is both; behavior results from an interaction of these two sets of factors.

DEVELOPMENTAL PERSONALITY THEORIES

Freud and Psychoanalytic Theory

If we accept as a criterion of greatness the influence of a person upon society, the roster of great names in the history of ideas must surely include that of Sigmund Freud. Freud contributed to psychology and psychiatry, to our language, and to the arts and literature. He put forward theories of personality structure and personality development. He developed a method of psychotherapy. As a result of Freud's work, "ego," "unconscious," "repression," and "neurosis" became everyday expressions. In a more general way, the lenient social and sexual mores of the twentieth century are attributable in part to Freud's influence.

Here is how Edwin Boring (1950), psychology's leading historian, wrote about Freud more than three decades ago. The intervening years have given us no reason to change the evaluation.

> In Sigmund Freud (1856–1939) we met a man with the attributes of greatness. He was a pioneer in a field of thought, in a new technique for the understanding of human nature. He was also an originator even though he picked his conceptions out of a stream of culture . . . [he] remained true to his fundamental intent for fifty years of hard work, while he altered and brought to maturity the system of ideas that was his contribution to knowledge. He was a leader who gathered about him an effective group of competent supporters, some of whom remained loyal to him throughout their lives and others of whom rejected the father image, criticized Freud's doctrine and started competitive schools of their own. His work passed first from obscurity into the notoriety of contumely, and then gradually, bit by bit . . .

his ideas spread until they pervaded all thinking about human motivation both among the psychologists and among the lay public for whom the adjective *Freudian* is almost as familiar as *Darwinian*. He gave the concept of the unconscious mind to common sense. . . . It was Freud who put the dynamic conception of psychology where psychologists could see it and take it. They took it, slowly and with hesitation, accepting some basic principles while rejecting many of the trimmings. It is not likely that the history of psychology can be written in the next three centuries without mention of Freud's name and still claim to be a general history of psychology. And there you have the best criterion of greatness: posthumous fame. The great man is he whom the historian cannot ignore (pp. 706–707).

Freud spent almost his entire life in Vienna. There over a span of more than fifty years, sitting in his study, surrounded by his books and Egyptian art objects, Freud listened to his patients, observed their distress, and watched their struggles to conquer it. On this basis he formulated, revised, and revised again his theory of psychoanalysis. When the Nazis moved into Austria, Franklin D. Roosevelt and many others urged Freud to leave Vienna. Reluctantly, he finally did so. He traveled to London a dying man, ravaged by the terminal stages of cancer of the mouth and jaw, the result of decades of relentless cigar smoking. When he died in September 1939 within days following the outbreak of World War II, his work had been finally acknowledged, his place in history assured.

The Emergence of Psychoanalysis.   If one had to point to the first great milestone in the historical development of **psychoanalysis,** it would be Freud's meeting with Josef Breuer, a noted Viennese physician. Breuer was treating a young woman, now celebrated in the psychoanalytic literature as "Fraulein Anna O." Anna suffered from a number of what were then called hysterical symptoms, including paralysis, an inability to swallow, blurred vision, and visual hallucinations. To refer to these symptoms as *hysterical* is to say that they were physical symptoms with no detectable physiological basis. Breuer, using hypnosis to treat her, would place Anna in a semitrance. During these states Anna would cry out, as though she were in the throes of an anguishing experience. Breuer found that when he asked Anna what was tormenting her, her answers led back to the events of a period during which she nursed her dying father. If Breuer allowed her to "talk out" these experiences, Anna would awaken relaxed and comfortable, her hysterical symptoms obviously relieved.

These sessions also offered hints about the source of some of Anna's symptoms. For example, in her waking state one of Anna's complaints was double vision. Under hypnosis she recounted an event in which her dying father asked her for the time. Through her tears the hands of the watch appeared blurred. Her symptom of blurred vision dated from this experience. Several days after recounting this episode, she reported to Breuer that her vision had cleared. In this systematic way Breuer removed Anna's symptoms one by one.

Breuer and Freud tried this new method on other cases of hysteria and, in 1895, described their work in *Studies in Hysteria*. Although the two men agreed in their descriptions of hysterical symptomatology, each wrote his own interpretive section for the book because they were unable to agree on the origins of the disorder. Freud emphasized repressed sexual factors; Breuer tended to blame the "hypnoidal state" of the neurotic. Later these differences became very acute and led to a breakup of the relationship between the two men. Breuer was evidently disturbed by the sexual implications of their analyses, Freud was not.

Breuer's concerns deepened when Anna declared her love for him, an event which made him believe that the method of treatment was dangerous. He

Sigmund Freud published only the cases in *Studies in Hysteria* and six others. Professional ethics restrained him from revealing to the world the histories of his other patients. The vast amount of raw case material from which his theory of personality was fashioned can never be examined.

ANNA O—THE STORY OF BERTHA PAPPENHEIM, FEMINIST

The story of Anna O did not end with her hysterical vision that she was giving birth to Breuer's child. The new physician who stepped in when Breuer stepped out of the case prescribed morphine to calm Anna. In time Anna became an addict and had to be institutionalized. In *The Story of Anna O,* Lucy Freeman (1972) has traced the events of Anna's subsequent life.

In 1888 Anna, recovered from her addiction, left Vienna to return to Germany. The daughter of a wealthy Jewish family, with a distinguished lineage on both sides, she could have immersed herself in art, music, and handiwork until an eligible man appeared to marry her. She rejected that role and began a career as one of Europe's first social workers. From volunteer worker in an orphanage for destitute and illegitimate children who were unacceptable to the Jewish community, she rose to the post of director of the institution. She soon set about creating other institutions to train and educate unwed mothers, and she pro-

Bertha Pappenheim—"Anna O."

vided residences for them, as well as adoption and foster homes for their children.

Orthodox Judaism relegated women to a secondary role, but Bertha Pappenheim, Anna's true name, would not accept such inferior status. She converted her orphan-

age from a custodial to an educational institution, helped to establish educational seminaries for young women, wrote and translated tracts in favor of women's liberation, fought anti-Semitism in the governments of Europe, founded the Federation of Jewish Women, and became its first president. It was Bertha Pappenheim who broke the power of wealthy Turkish Jews, who were surreptitiously running a white-slave traffic that forced illiterate, impoverished Jewish girls from the ghettos into prostitution and transported them to brothels in South America.

Bertha Pappenheim died in May 1936 and thus escaped witnessing the final desecration of her work by the Nazis. Nazi soldiers invaded one of the educational seminaries for young women that she had helped to establish in Poland. Informed that their school would be converted to a brothel, the ninety-three women students in a final act of dignity and courage all took poison and died by their own hands.

decided to abandon it. The specific event that led to Breuer's retreat occurred after eighteen months of treatment. Breuer had paid his last visit to Anna, before leaving on a vacation trip. He and Anna had said their good-byes. That night Breuer was called from his dinner table, summoned by Anna's mother. A new and extremely disturbing symptom had appeared. When Breuer came to Anna, she was lying on her bed, writhing about in an agonizing replica of birth pains and muttering, "Now Dr. Breuer's baby is coming! It is coming!" Breuer hypnotized her to get her to sleep and provided the posthypnotic suggestion that when she awakened in the morning she would realize that what she had experienced was entirely in her imagination. But the experience was so frightening to him that he asked a colleague to take over Anna's treatment.

Freud, who had been confronted with similar experiences, brought his intellectual powers to the task of analyzing such fragments of behavior and gradually formulated the concept of **transference**—a view which holds that the analyst acts as a parent substitute, attracting the patient's love for this reason. This point illustrates the most basic difference between the two men. One was caught in, and under the control of, the morality of his time; the other was freed from such control by a driving desire to know and to understand human behavior. Thus was Freud able to make his many contributions, among them his theory of personality structure.

The Structure of Personality. Freudian theory divides personality into three major components, *id, ego,* and *superego.* The **id,** the original and largest component of mental organization, is the reservoir of instinctual energy, made up of all the basic biological needs for food, water, warmth, elimination, sex, and aggression. It represents the inner world of subjective experience, knowing nothing of objective reality. Because the id cannot tolerate painful increases of tension either from external stimulation or from internal excitation, it acts immediately to discharge tension and return to a lower energy level. This impulsive method of reducing tension by which the id operates is called the **pleasure principle.** Thus the id is governed by a search for pleasure and immediate gratification, whatever the circumstances. The id remains an unchanging, powerful force throughout life.

The **ego** develops out of the id in the second six months of life, when the infant begins to distinguish between itself and the outer world. Knowing the difference between things in the mind and things outside, the ego is the rational, largely conscious component of personality. Unlike the id, the ego is governed by the **reality principle** and acts to prevent the discharge of tension until an object appropriate for the satisfaction of need has been discovered. It tries to satisfy the id, but it considers what is practical and possible as well as what is urged. It decides what id impulses will be satisfied and in what manner, thus protecting the person from the dangers of indiscriminately satisfying the urges of the id. The ego perceives, learns, remembers, and reasons.

The **superego,** which emerges in childhood sometime between ages three and six, is the equivalent of *conscience,* for it contains the values and moral standards of society as conveyed to the child by its parents. Like the id, the superego does not know reality. It would stifle all sexual and aggressive impulses. In addition to conscience, the superego has a second part, the *ego-ideal,* which is an image of what the individual ideally can be. The ego-ideal pushes the ego in the direction of moral action and self-sacrifice and urges it to strive for perfection. Thus the ego serves three masters, the pleasure-seeking id, the moralistic superego, and reality. It knows anxiety when it cannot reconcile the divergent demands of these three masters.

Anxiety and the Mechanisms of Defense.   When under pressure from extreme anxiety, the ego is sometimes forced to resort to mental strategies, called **mechanisms of defense,** to relieve this pressure. Since the purposes of these mechanisms are not obvious to those who use them, psychoanalysts speak of them as "unconscious." It should be noted, however, that people are not unaware of their behavior, but only of the motivation for it. It is also important to understand that the mechanisms are adaptive, because they reduce anxiety. Defense mechanisms are neither uncommon nor deviant, but they do represent self-deception. To this extent they prevent an individual from learning more effective and rational ways of coping with frustrations. The most important mechanisms of defense are the following.

Repression, the most basic of the defense mechanisms, is the pushing of unacceptable impulses back into the unconscious. It is the banning from memory of traumatic, dangerous, or embarrassing thoughts, events, and desires, thus preventing the arousal of anxiety. For example, Anna O had repressed the painful memory of the events surrounding the death of her father. Repression differs from *inhibition,* holding back a response for fear of punishment, and also from *suppression,* a conscious pushing aside of an unpleasant thought.

Denial, one of the most primitive of the defense mechanisms, is frequently used by children and severely disturbed adults. After being told by her mother that Daddy has died, a little girl may act as though she has not heard her mother's words and may ask where her father is. In denial, the individual rejects an intolerble reality by denying its existence. Persistent denial as an avoidance of reality can, in time, produce more serious signs of disorder.

Repression and denial serve to block the expression of a wish or thought.

Another group of mechanisms express a wish or thought in a modified form designed to disguise its true nature.

In **displacement** unacceptable feelings about a person or a situation are transferred from their true target to another against which they can more safely be vented. Angry at your professor, you may find yourself yelling at your best friend or a server in the cafeteria. Freud saw dreams as a form of displacement in which the contents of the dream serve as symbols of actions or persons that evoke severe anxiety and thus require repression.

One way to block objectionable thoughts or feelings is to attribute them to another person. This defense mechanism, which is called **projection,** locates the responsibility for unacceptable personal characteristics outside the self. The miser who believes that everyone else is stingy and the unscrupulous executive who considers all businessmen connivers are projecting. So is the man who has lustful desires for his sister-in-law but perceives instead that she is making advances toward him.

The mechanism of **reaction formation** consists of replacing unacceptable feelings with their exact opposites. The jealous boy who hates his older brother may show him exaggerated respect and affection, running errands for him and ''covering'' for him when he might be caught disobeying his parents.

Rationalization is the most common and most harmless of the mechanisms, probably because it comes closest to being a conscious way of dealing with unacceptable material. Through rationalization we can fool ourselves by substituting ''good'' reasons for ''bad'' ones in order to make our behavior appear more ethical and more moral than it really is. The father who punishes his children too severely says that he does so because he loves them and because ''it is for their own good.''

Two final mechanisms appear as new and socially acceptable forms of behavior, replacing unacceptable behavior or dissatisfaction with the self.

Sublimation is a mechanism whereby the expression of an impulse in its original form is repressed, but the impulse emerges in a socialized manner, diverted toward a socially acceptable goal. Sublimation has the quality of maturity since it enables a person to meet reality instead of fleeing from it. Freud suggested that Leonardo da Vinci's urge to paint Madonnas was a sublimation of his desire for intimacy with his mother, from whom he had been separated at a very young age.

Compensation is a mechanism by which we handle our deficiencies, ''making up'' for them in some other way. The defect that is being compensated for may be real or imaginary. Sometimes compensation is achieved through the development of a high level of personal skill, sometimes through the achievements of others. Parents who push their children toward specific occupations may be compensating for their own unfulfilled ambitions.

Psychosexual Theory of Personality Development. The individual, according to Freud, has a certain amount of psychic energy or **libido** that can be devoted to any of a number of different interests and enterprises. **Psychosexual development** is the history of the various activities and objects to which the libido attaches itself. In the normal course of development, the individual goes through a number of stages in which the libido is invested first in one kind of activity and then in another.

Freud associated the id's striving for sensual pleasure in infancy and childhood with the manipulation of the body parts for pleasure. Tensions that build up in these areas are reduced by manipulation, and such relief is pleasurable. The major areas for such satisfaction, termed *erogenous zones,* are the mouth, anus, and genitals. Each is associated with a primary drive—hunger, elimination, and sex—and each, in turn, becomes the central focus of the child's activity in the successive stages of development. Freud called all the strivings of the id for sensual pleasure "sexual," to emphasize the fact that they derive from the same reservoir of libido or psychic energy as does the striving for genital sex.

It is important to understand that when Freud wrote about "sex" he meant far more than sexual union. Perhaps it would be more appropriate to talk of "love," including love of parents, affectionate behavior, comradeship, and even a love of humankind. But it is equally important to understand that the concept of libido included sexuality in the narrower sense. Libido, for Freud, represented the life instinct or Eros. Freud also postulated a death instinct, but this construct is far less developed, and less accepted, in psychoanalytic theory.

The **oral stage,** the first stage of psychosexual development, occurs during the first year of life. In this stage the baby gains its most intense pleasures from nursing, sucking, and mouthing. Because oral activities are so pleasurable, aside from satisfying hunger, babies in this stage suck, lick, bite, and chew whatever they can get into their mouths. The oral drive expressed by these activities is usually satisfied through the efforts of the mother. If this drive is frustrated, as when infants are deprived of adequate mothering, the baby's behavior reveals its distress: breathing is shallow, crying is exaggerated, and there is tension and muscular rigidity. Other babies may become lethargic, their body muscles may grow lax, and tube feeding may even become necessary. When mothering becomes adequate again, these acute symptoms often disappear.

The second stage of psychosexual development is the **anal stage,** during which the baby derives pleasure from the process of elimination. In Freudian theory libidinal energy settles in the organs of excretion. For the first few months of life, the eliminative processes are automatic; apparently the baby is unaware of them. As the child matures, there is increasing pleasure in excretion. Parents in our society are likely to frustrate this satisfaction by initiating toilet training too early, often before the child has either the necessary muscular control or the use of language. Later on, parental discomfort with defecation can provide the growing child with a new means of exercising control over the parents. If the child is incontinent, the parents are distressed; if feces are retained and offered at the proper time like presents, the child gains praise and reward. In the Freudian view the experiences of the child during toilet training can exert a profound influence on later adjustment.

The third stage in psychosexual development is the **phallic stage,** spanning the ages from two or three to five or six. In this period the child's libidinal energy is directed toward genital activities. Children have now discovered the genital differences between the sexes. Definite signs of sexuality appear, sometimes as masturbation, sometimes as a desire for contact with the parent of the opposite sex. At least in our culture, many factors lead to the suppression of this childhood sexuality. Parents may be disturbed by the child's behavior, and they may avoid answering questions that they find embarrassing or even punish this early form of sexual interest. During this period the male child develops and resolves the **Oedipus complex,** a desire to have sexual relations with his mother. The name of the Oedipus complex comes from Greek mythology. Oedipus, the king of Thebes, unwittingly slew his father and married his mother. Freud reasoned that the early sexual desires of the little boy are directed at his mother, but that he rejects the desire out of fear of retaliation from his father, whom he now hates as a love competitor. The boy fears that his father will harm his genital organs, the source of his lustful feelings. Because of this

castration anxiety and his guilt for unseemly thoughts toward his father, the little boy strives to become just like him. He adopts his manner, his attitudes and interests, so that his father will not hurt him. By becoming like his father, he hopes also to win his mother's sexual love vicariously. At the same time he converts his erotic feelings for her into tender affection.

The little girl has a comparable **Electra complex** to resolve. In Greek mythology Electra helped her brother slay their mother and her lover in retaliation for the earlier murder of Agamemnon, their father. The little girl enters this stage retaining her early closeness to mother, but she becomes devoted to her father when she discovers that he has a penis. She wants one too and blames her mother for her penisless state. But her rebellious thoughts bring intense feelings of fear and guilt. She decides to settle for a baby from her father instead of a penis. Like the boy, however, she realizes that she can accomplish union only vicariously and identifies with her mother. Through identification with the same-sexed parent, both boys and girls acquire a conscience and, of course, their masculine and feminine ways.

The child now moves into a **latency period,** which extends from age six until adolescence; during this period little direct sexuality is observed. The pressures of the Oedipus and Electra complexes have given children reason to repress their sexuality. Boys play only with boys, girls only with girls; they want nothing to do with the opposite sex. Less concerned with their bodies, they are putting their energies into acquiring cognitive and social skills. They turn their attention to school and play.

At the onset of puberty, when the child matures physically and sexually, heterosexual interests reemerge and the individual enters the adult or **genital stage** of psychosexual development. In this stage young people, seeking more than self-satisfaction, turn their sexual interests toward others and become able to love them in a mature way.

In the Freudian view, failure to find ways of satisfying the needs that dominate the earlier stages of psychosexual development leaves the individual partially fixated at these levels. Some of the person's libidinal energies remain invested in the activities appropriate to an early stage of development. Such *fixations* are evident in adulthood in the form of immature behavior. The individual may have an "oral" or an "anal" personality. Oral personalities are said to smoke, chew gum, and overeat, to talk and gossip excessively, and to use "biting" sarcasm. Anal-explosive personalities, fixated at the stage when the infant took pleasure in defecation, are sloppy, disorganized, and overly generous; anal-retentive personalities, fixated at the stage when the infant retained the feces, are obstinate, stingy, and overly concerned with cleanliness, orderliness, and possessions.

Evaluation of Freudian Theory. Most critics who have read widely in Freud's writings—whether they agree or disagree with psychoanalytic theory—regard Freud's work as one of the revolutionary milestones in the history of human thought. As observations of the dynamics of human behavior, Freud's insights have never been equaled. Some of the concepts for which we are indebted to him are those of the unconscious, the ego, repression, anxiety, symbolization, regression, and projection. It was not that Freud was the first to use these concepts, and many others, but rather that he showed their potentialities for understanding human personality. In addition, Freud is responsible for the idea that childhood experience can influence adult life, and for the recognition that sexual difficulties are often involved in personality maladjustment and disorders.

Whether the connection with Freudian psychology is admitted or not, human development is now commonly recognized as proceeding in stages of some sort.

Despite these contributions, any appraisal of Freud's psychoanalytic theory of personality must include criticisms. As a theory it is inexact and literary in tone. At a factual level Freudian ideas distort the picture of personality. Freud drew his data from the limited and biased sample of late-nineteenth and early-twentieth-century Viennese upper-middle-class neurotic women who were his patients. There is little in the way of experimental evidence to support his dynamic analysis of behavior. For example, although there is evidence that the so-called oral and anal personalities may have particular identifying traits, little proof links these traits to child-rearing practices or to frustrations during an early period. The theory of infantile sexuality also evokes criticism. Does the little boy who expresses a wish to marry his mother or the little girl who speaks of growing up to marry Daddy—we have all heard young children make such statements—do so out of sexual motivation or out of a desire to imitate and model the parents? Contemporary thinking would place the emphasis on the child's strivings to be like the adult parent and to imitate his or her behavior.

Opponents also criticize the rigidity and a narrowness in the stage sequences set out by Freud. They point out that too little attention is paid to the personality changes that come with adulthood. We sense in psychoanalytic theory an entrapment in problems rooted in childhood, without adequate attention to the ever-changing nature of people's adaptations as they grow older. In a similar way the broader social environment is neglected in Freud's theory. Consideration of the social context of behavior was an important addition proposed by analytic thinkers who followed Freud.

Other Psychoanalytic Theorists

Of Freud's many followers, Carl Jung, Alfred Adler, and Karen Horney were among the important contributors to an extension of psychoanalytic thinking. The brief mention we give to them here is not commensurate with either their productivity or their originality.

Carl Jung.   Carl Jung (1875–1961) was Freud's greatest disappointment, for Freud had intended him to inherit the mantle of leadership of the psychoanalytic movement. But this was a secondary role that ill-befitted the independent Jung. Jung had been impressed with his reading of Freud's *Interpretation of Dreams* when that important volume first appeared at the turn of the century. He soon became one of Freud's most outspoken supporters, so outspoken that, at one point, Jung's academic career was jeopardized by his public and printed espousal of Freud. Jung's reply to two German professors who warned him of that danger attests to his scientific ethic and character. "If what Freud says is the truth, I am with him. I don't give a damn for a career if it has to be based on the premises of restricting research and concealing truth" (Brome, 1978, p. 95). In fact, Jung voluntarily relinquished his academic career and retained his independence of action throughout his life—an independence which finally culminated in his break with Freud.

Jung challenged not only Freud's preoccupation with the sexual basis of neurosis but his very concept of the unconscious. Jung argued that sexual thoughts were not alone in being subject to repression. He believed that repression could lead to the forgetting of any frightening event or threatening thought. Jung also believed that these forgotten experiences and repressed thoughts form "complexes" in what Jung termed the **personal unconscious**. Always

The Swiss psychologist Carl Gustav Jung accepted Freud's premise that the unconscious is the ultimate source of human behavior, but he saw it for the most part as fruitful and life giving, as supplying, for example, the desire and energy to formulate goals. The collective unconscious, the pool of ancient images possessed by all human beings, he considered the source of life's richness and mystery. Because of his respect for the racial past, Jung probed into human history and became the most erudite of psychologists.

interested in myth and mysticism, Jung believed that there is also an impersonal collective unconscious. This **collective unconscious** contains the images of humanity—the inherited archetypes that reflect the great mythical ideas of the past and the repeated experiences of humankind. Part of those experiences are represented in the concept of **persona**, the social mask people wear as they assume the roles that societal conventions and traditions impose on them.

A final point should be made about another major theoretical shift that Jung introduced. He saw human development as growth-oriented. As such it was aimed not so much at the resolution of conflict as at achievement, maturity, and "self-actualization." The last-named is Jung's term. Abraham Maslow, the humanistic psychologist, elaborated upon it in his own theory of personality growth, which had a pronounced impact in the 1960s and 1970s (page 292).

Alfred Adler. Alfred Adler (1870–1937) also departed from Freud in his rejection of sexuality as the primary force controlling human behavior. For Adler it was the sense of *inferiority*, not repressed sexuality, that underlay maladjustment. Adler believed that all children are born with a deep sense of inferiority because of their small size, physical weakness, and dependence on adults. Adler coined the term **inferiority complex** to identify this feeling. The goal of children, therefore, is to develop superiority, to accomplish self-perfection. The patterns of behavior that children use to reach these goals become, in time, their life-styles or most characteristic traits. One person tries to become superior by developing the intellect, another by athletic proficiency, and in any case all daily routines, relationships, and social activities are arranged to this end. Adler believed eventually that people have a creative self which strives with full self-awareness to develop potential and overcome obstacles. For this reason there is a sense in which people create their own personalities. Adler also believed that people have social interests and a feeling of responsibility toward others. They will not be happy unless they are actively engaged in improving life for everyone and in helping to construct the best possible society.

Adler seems a more contemporary figure than many who were part of the early psychoanalytic movement. His emphasis on the social context of behavior, his belief that people can cope with stress, his sense that individuals can exert control over their lives, his view of human motivation as directed toward growth, competence, and superiority—all these convey his view that people have the strength to meet life's difficulties. Adler's views on the structure and development of personality proved helpful not only to parents but to some of the major humanistic psychologists who came later, such as Carl Rogers and Abraham Maslow.

Karen Horney. With the growth of the feminist movement, Sigmund Freud has come to be viewed as the mortal enemy of women. This reaction is understandable because Freud (for example, 1925) cast women in a role inferior to that of men and used the ugly metaphor "penis envy" to summarize what he saw as women's dissatisfaction with their status. In Freud's opinion women envied men both their social roles and their sex roles.

Since Freud wrote his 1925 paper, things have changed radically. Women have challenged the Freudian assumption of their inferiority. In our time power in the family has shifted. Outside the family women have taken on many roles, including those of breadwinner and taxpayer. Identification with mother today brings the young daughter an increment, not a decrement, in her sense of power.

Within the psychoanalytic circle it fell to Karen Horney (1885–1952), one of

Born in Vienna in 1870, Alfred Adler settled in the United States in 1935. He observed that the personalities of the oldest, middle, and youngest child are likely to be quite different because of their distinctive experiences as members of the family. Pampering of children was his anathema, for it prevents them from developing social feelings and leaves them, according to Adler, the potentially most dangerous members of society.

Karen Horney saw the personality as being largely shaped in childhood through social relations, especially with parents. By being indifferent, erratic, or disparaging, parents can instill feelings of helplessness and isolation in children, what Horney called *basic anxiety*, and a deep resentment of the parents, *basic hostility*. Through the conflict between the two, the misused child adopts one of three rigid strategies: moving toward people, becoming compliant in order to win love; moving against them, finding security in power; and moving away from them, finding security in aloofness and independence.

the first women to be admitted to a medical school in Germany, to challenge Freud's views on female sexuality. Horney came to see that the source of women's feelings of inferiority resided in their powerless position in the society of the 1920s. Outlets for satisfactory personal expression for women were few, and the few there were were often limited by restrictive male power. Horney believed that masculine influences have a distorting effect on feminine development, not only within the family—favoritism shown a brother, punishment of the young girl's sexual curiosity, her dependence; but also in external events—the greater social value placed on maleness and women's sense of inferiority and their lack of self-esteem, which grow from unrewarded expressions of femininity and unrewarded achievements.

The artificial separation of "sexual" and "romantic" love forces women to repress one aspect of their emotional responsiveness. Women are also subjugated and debased by the male's need to reaffirm his dominance and need for conquest. They know greater disappointments and less fulfillment, not because of their physiology but because they have few opportunities and are allowed few aspirations and goals. Why, Freud had asked, did men often choose hysterical and uneducated women to be their wives or turn to prostitutes to satisfy their sexual drives? Freud's answer: sexuality can only be expressed to one who is inferior to the "pure" mother idealization. Horney's answer: a superior woman would pose too great a threat to masculine pride, and therefore debasement becomes the male solution to the problem.

Later in her life, in 1932, Horney came to America and wrote papers based on her observations of the social-cultural scene as she saw it here. She made this comment.

> Woman's efforts to achieve independence and enlargement of her fields of activity are continually met with a skepticism which insists that such efforts should be made only in the face of economic necessity, and that they run counter to inherent character and natural tendencies. Accordingly, all efforts of this sort are said to be without any vital significance for women, whose every thought should center upon the male or motherhood . . . (1934, p. 605).

For thirteen years, from 1923 to 1936, Horney wrote in this vein, creating a psychology of women that was strongly positive. Her pioneering efforts have served as an impetus to those who have since followed in her courageous path.

Ego Psychology

The most important development in psychoanalytic theory since Freud's death has been the emergence of a new theory sometimes called **ego psychology,** which emphasizes the relationship of individuals to the society in which they live. The theorists who founded ego psychology grew increasingly dissatisfied with the emphasis on conflict and defense that was implicit in Freud's formulation about ego functioning. They also argued that Freudian theory was outdated, that interpretations conceived at the beginning of the twentieth century no longer seemed to provide a sound basis for understanding personality. These theorists updated psychoanalysis by expanding the conception of ego and giving it functions that go beyond merely defending against anxiety and resolving unconscious conflicts. They did not believe that the ego emerges from the id but rather has its own origins and course of development. They allowed the ego a conflict-free sphere in which it uses its cognitive processes of perception, learning, memory, and attention for other than purely instinctual objectives. Its satisfactions are exploration, manipulation, and being competent in accomplishing tasks. This conception of the ego as autonomous represents a far-reaching change in psychoanalytic theory. Freud had given primacy not to the ego but to the id, which he believed exercised the most important influence throughout an individual's life.

Erik Erikson.   The psychoanalytic point of view has permeated all his intellectual endeavors, but Erik Erikson is certainly not an orthodox analytic thinker. Although continuing to appreciate the importance that Freud ascribed to the instinctual forces and to the erogenous zones, which underlie Freud's psychosexual stages, Erikson also emphasized the great importance to personality development of the child's interactions with the social environment. For Erikson any complete understanding of the process of personality development required a sensitivity to external social forces, as well as to intrapsychic biological factors. Thus, with other neo-Freudians, Erikson has made Freudian thought more social in nature.

Stages of Personality Development.   Erikson's anthropological interests had led him to fieldwork among a number of American Indian tribes. His observations of the sense of uprootedness among Indians and the disparities between their cultural history and current life-styles set him to thinking about how people develop their identities. This thinking led, in turn, to the promulgation of the eight-stage theory of psychosocial development (1963, 1964) for which he is best known. In each successive stage the individual passes through a major crisis, which must be successfully resolved if healthy development is to take place. At each of these points of conflict, society presents the developing individual with a particular task, and a particular component of personality comes to its ascendance, meets its crisis, and finds a solution. Erikson is aware that even though a conflict at an early stage is successfully resolved, it may recur at later stages of development and again have to be conquered. Conversely, a conflict unresolved at an earlier stage can be successfully resolved at any of the later stages of development.

  Stage 1: *Basic trust versus basic mistrust (first year of life).*   The infant's relationship with its mother during the first year is critical. Children develop trust if their caretaking has predictability and warmth and provides nourishment and tranquility. They develop a sense of being loved and of there being rhyme, reason, continuity, and consistency in what the parent is doing. The child relies on and trusts the parent and learns that hopes are within the realm of possibility. If the infant's world is chaotic and unpredictable and the parent's affection cannot be counted on, the infant develops a sense of mistrust.

  These basic attitudes are not set down in all-or-none fashion in the first year of life. Events in later years can modify the child's basic orientation. Figures other than family members may generate trust in a distrustful child, or the development of trauma in the family later on may rupture a previously developed sense of security and safety.

  Stage 2: *Autonomy versus shame and doubt (ages two through three).*   In the second stage children acquire skills, such as walking, climbing, exploring, speaking, and countless others. If parents welcome these important steps toward independence, children can continue to explore and master their surroundings and, in the course of doing so, they will begin to exert control over their impulses and to become autonomous. This stage also sees the development of self-expression and lovingness. If children are not allowed freedom, if they are overprotected, have things done for them, are criticized for what they do,

Erik Erikson was born in Germany of Danish parents, in 1902; he became an American citizen in 1939. He has studied the personalities of Harvard students; the Sioux children of South Dakota, to find the source of their apathy; the preoccupation of the Yuroks of northern California with their possessions; adolescents in the Berkeley Growth Study; soldiers discharged from World War II; and civil rights workers. He has also pondered the circumstances of life that bring forth leaders.

Basic trust versus basic mistrust—the first year of life.

Autonomy versus shame and doubt—
ages two through three.

Industry versus inferiority—ages six
through eleven.

Intimacy versus isolation—young adulthood.

shame, doubt, and uncertainty about themselves and their capabilities will be the consequence. Such a self-image will be particularly limiting when society demands autonomous behavior in later years. The problem for parents is to establish a delicate balance between the two extremes of an overly protective home atmosphere and one that provides little or no supervision of the child's activities.

Stage 3: *Initiative versus guilt (ages four through five).* In the third stage the child is ready to engage in self-initiated motor and intellectual activities. To cope effectively with the environment rather than being the passive recipient of whatever the environment provides, the child must develop initiative in play, in thought, and in activity generally. The child explores, plans, works for goals, and acquires a sense of purpose. At this stage the parents must still protect the child from undercontrolled activities and fantasies and yet encourage the child's initiative. If the parents downgrade the child's activities or if curiosity is discouraged, the child may be prevented from setting future goals by a doubt about the value of these goals and a sense of shame for holding these ambitions.

Stage 4: *Industry versus inferiority (ages six through eleven).* The fourth stage consists of the school years, during which children widen their array of skills. These skills become the vehicles through which life's work is accomplished. Children become responsible for homework and assignments. They develop the awareness that either tasks can be accomplished through industry or they will be failed. If parents reinforce their efforts with praise and reward, children will develop a sense of esteem based on achievements. They learn the rewards of diligence, perseverence, and being industrious. If children's work is derogated, a sense of inadequacy or inferiority may take over. To avoid this, children need success and a satisfactory resolution of earlier crises. Such growth results in further development of the sense of trust, autonomy, and initiative that began to form in earlier stages. The expansion of the child's world beyond the family means that other experiences can now begin to modify the child's sense of industry or inferiority.

Stage 5: *Identity versus role confusion (ages twelve through eighteen: adolescence).* Childhood proper comes to an end in the fifth stage, and youth begins. As the number of roles the adolescent is expected to play increases, there is a growing concern with the impression made on others. Puberty brings on what Erikson has called a "physiological revolution," which adolescents must cope with at the same time that they try to come to grips with an identity crisis—questioning who they are, what they value, and how they define themselves as people. In this process of trying to find themselves, adolescents experiment with many different identities. But the danger in these efforts is potential role confusion. The individual may not be able to piece together from the many roles attempted a coherent sense of self. In their striving for a sense of identity, adolescents often develop a very strong sense of loyalty to the cliques or gangs to which they belong, a loyalty that is more than matched by an outgroup hostility. If, at this age, the adolescent is permitted some freedom in the exploration of roles with appropriate structuring and advice from adults, a firm sense of ego identity is assured.

Stage 6: *Intimacy versus isolation (young adulthood).* Only after people have developed a sense of identity and are comfortable with it can they reach out for intimate relationships with other human beings. Forming close relationships, of love and commitment, both sexual and nonsexual, offers great potential gratifications, but close relationships also pose potential dangers. One can be rejected, or the relationship may fail through disagreement, disappointment, or hostility. If this fear is excessive, the individual may be tempted not to take a chance on intimate relationships but to opt instead for withdrawal and isolation. Persons who fail to resolve this conflict successfully may engage in a great deal of social activity, but their relations with others are of a superficial sort.

Stage 7: *Generativity versus stagnation (middle age).* For Erikson generativity includes marriage, parenthood, and the sense of working productively and creatively. It also means possessing a degree of selflessness and wanting to take care of those who need it. Generativity is expressed in a concern not only with one's own children but with future generations; it implies a willingness to extend oneself on behalf of all younger people. The generative individual enjoys work and family and is continually ready to come to the aid of others. The opposite of this person is the individual who cares little for other people, whose life is in a state of stagnation, and whose only pleasures derive from personal gratification.

Stage 8: *Integrity versus despair (old age).* Toward the end of life, all human beings must take stock of what they have accomplished and of the type of people they have been. This is the stage in which the individual looks back on life either with a sense of integrity and satisfaction or with a sense of despair. There is a period in the lives of all men and women when they realize that major changes in life-styles are no longer likely. What they are now and what they do now are what they will always be and do. This is a time of totaling up life's balance sheet and reflecting on what has been achieved. If earlier crises have been met successfully, the ledger reflects integrity. The individual sees that his or her life has meaning within a larger order. Such an individual has developed wisdom, "a detached concern with life itself, in the face of death itself" (1964, p. 133). If earlier crises have not been met, the balance sheet reflects despair, "the feeling that time is now short, too short for the attempt to start another life and to try out alternate roads to integrity." For individuals who experience such despair, death is indeed a bitter pill. A parallel between the first and final states of life is seen in Erikson's interesting observation: "Healthy children will not fear life if their elders have integrity enough not to fear death."

Integrity versus despair—old age. "Healthy children will not fear life if their elders have integrity enough not to fear death."

Evaluation.   Erikson's theory provides a welcome balance to traditional psychoanalytic theory. His emphasis on adult development does not deny the powerful effects of childhood experience, but it reduces the exclusive preoccupation with the early years that was the outgrowth of Freud's thinking. It assigns to experiences outside the family a role that also contributes to healthy or unhealthy personality formation. Erikson's life cycle theory places responsibility on the individual for his or her own maturity, but it also sets forth a climate of optimism in its view that at each stage people can modify their behavior and find new hope for a healthy psychological future. Erikson's belief that there are no fixed and immutable patterns that cannot be changed by time and appropriate experiences is a more positive and less depressive view of personality than orthodox Freudian theory.

Learning Theory

Three decades ago a classic volume was written by two distinguished learning theorists, John Dollard and Neal Miller of Yale University. Their book, *Personality and Psychotherapy* (1950), was one of the most significant efforts to link psychoanalysis and learning theory. Despite the differences between the two orientations, learning theory and psychoanalysis share the assumption that the causes of behavior are to be found in the previous history of an individual.

Personality and Psychotherapy was by far the most successful of a number of efforts that had been made to translate the concepts of psychoanalysis into the terms of learning theory. Since then the learning point of view has gained increased acceptance in personality theory. In the process the trappings of psychoanalysis have largely been discarded.

We consider now two contemporary views of personality that have gained wide acceptance. One is based on the work of B. F. Skinner of Harvard University. The other is social-learning theory, identified with the work of Albert Bandura of Stanford University.

The Skinnerian Approach. One important contribution of Dollard and Miller was to treat the learning of neurotic symptoms in the same way that they treated the acquisition of any other behavior. Although this conception was novel in 1950, it now has such general acceptance that it is no longer an issue for debate. If any further support were needed to make this point, it has been provided very forcefully by psychologists who take the Skinnerian approach to the study of personality development.

The emphasis of the Skinnerian school is on overt behavior—what the organism does in a specified situation. It avoids theory and all inferences of drives, motives, traits, and the like. The Skinnerian treatment of personality development emphasizes the gradual shaping of behavior that takes place as a result of planned or unplanned schedules of reinforcement.

In contrast to Dollard and Miller, Skinner's rejection of theory in general led him also to reject psychoanalysis. We take as an example Skinner's criticisms of Freud's views about a significant factor in his own early life.

Freud had suggested that sibling rivalry, which played a significant role in his psychoanalytic theorizing, had also been important in determining the nature of his own personal relationships with others. He traced his problems in relationships to the death of an infant brother and to his later experiences with a playmate and rival, a nephew who was older and stronger than he. Skinner suggests that, instead of looking to rivalry, Freud should have examined his earlier behavior and asked what he had been punished and rewarded for.

> An emphasis upon behavior would lead us to inquire into the specific acts plausibly assumed to be engendered by these childhood episodes. In very specific terms how was the behavior of the young Freud shaped by the special reinforcing contingencies arising from the presence of a younger child in the family, by the death of that child, and by later association with an older playmate who nevertheless occupied a subordinate family position? What did the young Freud learn to do to achieve parental attention under these difficult circumstances? How did he avoid aversive consequences? Did he exaggerate any illness? Did he feign illness? Did he make a conspicuous display of behavior which brought commendation? Was such behavior to be found in the field of physical prowess or intellectual endeavor? Did he learn to engage in behavior which would, in turn, increase the repertoires available to him to achieve commendation? Did he strike or otherwise injure young children? Did he learn to injure them verbally by teasing? Was he punished for this, and if so, did he discover other forms of behavior which had the same damaging effect but which were immune to punishment?
>
> We cannot, of course, adequately answer questions of this sort at so late a date, but they suggest the kind of inquiry which would be prompted by a concern for the explicit shaping of behavior repertoires under childhood circumstances. What has survived through the years is not aggression and guilt, later to be manifested in behavior, but rather patterns of behavior themselves (1972, pp. 244–245).

It is this type of systematic analysis of situations, behavior, and reinforcement contingencies that is necessary, the Skinnerians assert, if we are to understand personality processes. To push the translation of psychoanalytic theory into learning theory any further is a futile task and one that would do little to enhance personality theory or personality research. Personality psychologists should instead direct their attention to using learning principles to achieve an understanding of normal and abnormal personality development. The most significant current efforts along these lines have come from social-learning theory, which does not, however, accept the antitheoretical Skinnerian outlook (Skinner, 1974, 1978).

Social-Learning Theory.   Social-learning theory receives its name from the emphasis that Albert Bandura (for example, 1977), from the very beginning, has given to the social context of behavior and to the concept that behavior is formed and modified by patterns of social interaction. It is this emphasis that links social-learning theory so intimately to personality development.

Observational Learning versus Reinforcement.   A major difference between Skinnerian interpretations and social-learning theory are their assumptions about the conditions that are essential to learning. For Skinner the essential condition is the direct reinforcement of behavior. The social-learning theorist concedes the importance of reinforcement but insists that many forms of learning occur simply as a result of observing others. In such **observational learning** as espoused by Bandura, direct reinforcement is not essential for learning. People can experience rewards and punishments vicariously by seeing the consequences for others who behave in a particular way. These observations lead to the imitation or the **modeling** of the behavior of another. In social-learning theory the basis for changes in behavior is cognitive. Imitation is not automatic; people choose to imitate a model on the basis of their perceptions of the consequences of an act or their anticipation of what the consequences for behaving in a specific way are likely to be (Schultz, 1976).

In comparing modeling with direct reinforcement, Bandura argues that direct reinforcement is too inefficient a way to be the primary basis for learning how to behave in a complex world. We could not possibly learn our way to school, how to drive a car, or the corner on which to wait for a bus by trial, error, and direct reinforcement. The great majority of what we learn is learned by example. We observe what others do and what happens to them, and then we proceed to do the same thing or to avoid that particular behavior. As Duane Schultz (1976) has written,

> Some behaviors can be learned only through the influence of models; language is perhaps the best example of this. How could a child learn to speak if he or she never had the opportunity to hear words, phrases, and sentences. If learning to speak could be accomplished by operant conditioning alone, it would mean that the infant would not be reinforced for saying words (or approximations of them) until after he or she had said them spontaneously, having never heard them before (p. 303).

Evidence from studies of language acquisition (page 223) attests to the wisdom of this observation.

To broaden our understanding of the power of observational learning, let us look at some of the facts that seem to reflect modeling in our society. There is a relationship between the antisocial behavior of children and the antisocial

Early on Albert Bandura concluded that the learning views of the behaviorists were too narrow to account for socialization and the development of behavior. He proposed that from infancy individuals learn a great deal simply by observing what other people do and noticing what their actions gain or lose them. Because individuals ruminate about what has happened to them in the past and what may happen to them in the future, their behavior cannot always be manipulated by reinforcement. Their appraisals of their own weaknesses and strengths and their expectations do much to determine their behavior. Bandura sees individuals as freer to choose and to make changes in their lives than do the behaviorists.

behavior of their parents. Mobs of people act in concert in ways in which individuals are unlikely to act when alone. Adolescents model peers in ways that often seem aberrant to their families. College students may even model professors, although this type of observational learning seems in short supply these days. There is probably a causal relation between watching violence on television and hostility. Given the power of modeling, it is obvious that parents will inevitably transmit their fears, attitudes, and values to their children.

Schultz, commenting on the difference between the views of Skinner and Bandura, makes a telling point: the control of behavior in Skinner's system resides with whoever controls the reinforcers; in Bandura's system it resides with who controls the models. The explosive impact of television has advanced enormously the availability of models to be emulated, so much so that some psychologists fear that television can attenuate the power of parents as models. Others suggest that the typical middle-class portrayals of life seen on television have encouraged in viewers a rising tide of expectations which, if left unfulfilled, will cause a spiraling cycle of frustration and despair in poor people.

Component Processes in Observational Learning. What is required for modeling to be effective? Bandura has described four mechanisms that govern observational learning.

Attention. People cannot learn by observation without attending to the behavior being modeled. Such attentional behavior depends on many factors including the observer's characteristics, the activity being observed, the characteristics of the person who is engaging in the activity, and the rewards that accompany the activity. For example, children who are very dependent are more likely to be influenced by a model than independent children (Jakubezak and Walters, 1959). Moreover, children are likely to imitate another child whom they respect and who is similar to themselves in sex and age and status. They will imitate an older person who is warm, affectionate, competent, powerful, and in control of resources that children want. Children are also responsive to a model's enthusiasm (Waxler and Radke-Yarrow, 1975).

Retention. Behavior can be modeled only if it is remembered. The two memory systems discussed in our earlier treatment of dual-coding theory (page 183) are both necessary. The imaginal system allows us to call up an image of modeled behavior. The verbal system serves as a substitute for images. Thus ''hot'' can warn a child away from a radiator as effectively as can the pain of a burnt finger.

Retention is enhanced by rehearsal. The more a person mentally rehearses a behavioral pattern, the more proficient will be his or her behavior and the better it will be retained. In one experiment Bandura and his colleagues (1966) had children view a film of a model engaged in a series of novel actions and, according to assigned group, behave in one of three ways while watching: (1) the subject described aloud the sequence of acts as they were performed by the model; (2) the observer merely watched the model carefully as the acts were performed; (3) the subject had to count rapidly while observing the model, thus interfering with learning and retention of the observed acts. Later the subjects were asked to imitate the behavior they had witnessed. The quality of their performances, from best to worst, followed the order of the assigned ways of watching.

Motor responses. For modeling to occur, the symbolic representations of an action in memory, in images and words, must be converted into action. This requires the organization in sequence, time, and space of the modeled actions.

These actions must be practiced. Corrective feedback from self-observation helps the individual learn them. Complex behavior patterns may have to be segmented into basic components, which are practiced separately before they are all put back together again in the appropriate sequence.

Incentive. There is an important difference between learning and performance. Even well-learned motor responses become overt activity only when the individual has an appropriate incentive. In the case of modeling, social-learning theorists believe that rewards are more effective than punishment in providing such incentives. It is certain that acts that bring satisfaction are more likely to be modeled than are those that earn disapproval. Moreover, from our earlier discussion of punishment (Chapter 9) it is clear that one of the disadvantages of punishment is that it is effective only if accompanied by suggestions of alternative behavior that will be rewarded.

With this background we can now link together the Skinnerian and social-learning points of view in the following manner. If we wished to have an individual learn a social skill and use it optimally, the first step would be to have the person observe a competent model demonstrate it; then, with the aid of appropriate reinforcement, the person would practice the skill until he or she attained a high level of proficiency. The amount of time to give to modeling and the amount to give to reinforced practice would depend on the specific skills to be acquired.

The Phenomenological-Humanistic Tradition

The phenomenological-humanistic tradition, which emphasizes the human being's potential for health, goodness, creativity, and freedom, has been called the "third force" in American psychology to identify it as an alternative to psychoanalysis and learning theory. The most prominent figures associated with this movement are Carl Rogers and Abraham Maslow. Maslow's self-actualization theory was discussed in Chapter 9. Here we present the position of Rogers (1961).

Phenomenology, the central tenet of the Rogerian theory of human behavior, places primary emphasis on the conscious experience of individuals and their subjective awareness of themselves and the world in which they exist. We react, asserts Rogers, to the world as we perceive it. Our perceptions of the world, our perceptual environment or phenomenal field as it is sometimes called, depends on everything potentially available to our awareness at any moment. It is made up of the totality of earlier perceptions and is known only to us. The subjective reality of our experience, rather than external, objective, physically described reality, determines our behavior, our responses to events and to others. If we can keep ourselves open to the world of our internal experiencing and to information from experiencing the external world, we have established the basic condition necessary for growth, maturity, and the realization of our potential. Such statements reflect a position that is radically different both from the psychoanalytic view, with its stress on unconscious causality, and from learning theory, with its emphasis on external stimuli and overt measurable responses. For Rogers this striving for self-enhancement or "actualization" is a process that begins at birth and moves forward to fulfillment only if conditions are favorable for doing so.

The concept of "self," or "self-concept," is so important in Rogers's theory of personality that his has been termed a self-theory and a person-centered theory. How does the self emerge? Its basic roots are to be found in the earliest interactions with parents, for these form the background out of which emerge

Carl Ransom Rogers, originally a student of agriculture, realized his need to help others and switched first to religion. Then, discouraged by the attention to dogma and hierarchy in his seminary studies, he turned to psychology. Emphasizing the personal experiences of individuals, he sees each as the center of a self-created, unique reality. Rogers was the first to tape-record therapy sessions for later analysis. He has conducted and stimulated considerable research into the nature of the processes of clinical treatment.

the perceptions, values, attitudes, and cognitions that mark a person's relationships with others. But the sense of self is not fixed and immutable. The effects of poor relationships with parents can be modified by subsequent experience if the individual is able to be open rather than defensive, flexible rather than rigid, and strives successfully to gain freedom from external controls. How the individual interprets experiences depends on his or her interpretation of the self. A constricted sense of self can bring further restrictiveness as the individual shuts out events, experiences, and emotions that are considered to be incompatible with the self-image.

The **humanistic** principle in Rogers's thinking is his belief that all human beings are innately good and seek to grow and to expand their horizons. Such growth is dependent on love and acceptance from others—what Rogers calls "unconditional positive regard." Its presence or its absence in the individual's life determines whether that person's self-concept is one of worthiness or unworthiness.

Another basic concept in Rogerian theory is the principle of **congruence–incongruence**. Congruence is a state of internal harmony, incongruence one of disharmony. The achievement of a congruent state implies that the individual's self-concept is consistent with what he or she experiences. Successfully achieved consistency makes the "integrated" or whole person. Incongruence reflects basic estrangement, which develops when "unconditional positive regard" is lacking, when love and acceptance are made conditional by others. If conditions are demanded by others before love and acceptance are offered, a phenomenon comparable to repression takes place. The individual denies awareness of experiences that are unacceptable to the self, further narrowing the personal world.

SUMMARY

We have looked briefly at several dominant psychological models of personality development. The first was psychoanalytic theory, which brought many changes to psychology's views of the origins of behavior. It emphasized stages in development, a conflict between pleasure seeking and reality demands, and sexuality as both the source of this conflict and the source of human growth. The inflexibility of psychoanalytic doctrine threatened its viability and led other psychoanalytic thinkers to introduce new concepts that reduced the power of instinct and stressed the importance of social factors and the role of conflict-free cognition in influencing behavior.

Interpretations of personality in terms of learning theory began as an attempt to translate psychoanalytic concepts into some more acceptable to psychology, an effort that seemed promising because learning theory and psychoanalysis both assume that the causes of behavior are to be found in previous experience. Early learning theory and the Skinnerian approach today put greatest emphasis on the process of direct reinforcement in personality development. This approach is clearly too narrow, however. On this basis social-learning theory has stressed the importance of observational learning and modeling.

Although the extension of learning theory to much of human behavior has been nothing short of phenomenal, certain aspects of it do not easily reduce to learning principles: values and beliefs, powerful emotional states such as love and grief, patterns of self-actualization, the sacrificial behavior of people under stress, the quality of humanity in some, its absence in others, and so on. The deficiencies of learning theory define the emphases of the humanistic theories of personality. Although these theories have provided a renewed appreciation of the human striving to grow and find fulfillment, their formulations remain imprecise and their statements of the origins of personality weak and inade-quate.

Despite the shortcomings of each of the major perspectives on personality theory, each point of view has enlarged our understanding of human behavior. Psychoanalysis broadened our awareness of the continuity between infant and adult. Learning theory provided insights into how behavior is acquired, maintained, and extinguished. Humanistic psychology enlarged our horizons by emphasizing human strivings toward self-fulfillment and growth.

TO BE SURE YOU UNDERSTAND THIS CHAPTER

Here are the major concepts for you to know.

Trait theory	**Libido**
Type theory	**Psychosexual development**
Surface trait	**Oral stage**
Source trait	**Anal stage**
Psychoanalytic theory	**Phallic stage**
Psychoanalysis	**Oedipus complex**
Transference	**Castration anxiety**
Id	**Electra complex**
Pleasure principle	**Latency period**
Ego	**Genital stage**
Reality principle	**Personal unconscious**
Superego	**Collective unconscious**
Mechanism of defense	**Persona**
Repression	**Inferiority complex**
Denial	**Ego psychology**
Displacement	**Observational learning**
Projection	**Modeling**
Reaction formation	**Phenomenology**
Rationalization	**Humanism**
Sublimation	**Congruence–incongruence**
Compensation	

TO GO BEYOND THIS CHAPTER

In This Book. The topic of personality is so broad that every chapter in this book has some relation to this one. Among the most pertinent discussions are those of personality tests in Chapter 13, of the concept of stages in cognitive development in Chapter 11, and of social and emotional development in Chapter 12. Chapters 10, 16, and 17 are particularly relevant. Chapter 10, covering individual responses to stress, Chapter 16, treating psychopathology, and Chapter 17, on therapy, all contain further discussion of topics in this chapter.

Elsewhere. A number of excellent texts provide in-depth coverage of the personality theorists cited in this chapter and others as well. Foremost among the texts are Calvin Hall and Gardner Lindzey's *Theories of Personality* and Salvatore Maddi's *Personality Theories: A Comparative Analysis.* Briefer volumes are provided by Duane Schultz, *Theories of Personality,* and by Larry Hjelle and Daniel Ziegler, *Personality Theories: Basic Assumptions, Research, and Application.* The personological point of view can be found in *Personality Theory: The Personological Tradition,* by Robert Hogan.

PART SEVEN BEHAVIOR DISORDERS

Edvard Munch. "Young Woman on the Beach." Munch Museum, Oslo. Scala/Art Resource.

CHAPTER 16   PSYCHOPATHOLOGY

BREAKDOWN

About three years ago, in my mid-forties, I had a sudden and severe mental breakdown. There was nothing ususual about the breakdown itself, nor about the events in my own life that led up to it. The only exceptional feature was that I am a psychologist and should therefore be able to view the events of my illness from two standpoints—subjectively as the patient and more objectively as the detached professional observer.

Until I broke down I had always regarded myself as reasonably well-balanced: although I had sometimes worried about physical illness, the thought that I might be subjected to the torture and humiliation of a severe mental illness had never entered my head. For many years I had been outgoing, efficient, continually active and reasonably cheerful: I thought of myself as well-meaning, though possibly somewhat insensitive both to my own and others' feelings. It never occurred to me that one day my existence would disintegrate within the space of a few hours. For half a year I lived in mental anguish, a prey to obsessive and agonizing thoughts. I had neither interest in nor ability to cope with the outside world which formerly I had found so fascinating. I hated myself and I hated others, and so unremitting and painful were my thoughts that I was virtually unable to read: I could not even concentrate sufficiently to peruse the daily paper. In five months all I read were a dozen case histories of breakdowns which were sufficiently similar to my own to seize my interest. For someone accustomed to spending most of the day reading and writing, the complete inability to do either was a singularly refined torture.

There were two aspects of the breakdown that were particularly painful, and took me by surprise since I had never experienced anything similar. The onset . . . was marked by levels of physical anxiety that I would not have believed possible. If one is almost involved in a road accident, there is a delay of a second or two and then the pit of the stomach seems to fall out and one's legs go like jelly. It was this feeling multiplied a hundredfold that seized me at all hours of the day or night. My dreams were often pleasant, but as soon as I woke panic set in and it would take a few moments to work out what it was about. The realization brought anguish: an irrevocable and cataclysmic event had occurred from which I could imagine no recovery. Sleep was difficult to come by even with the help of sleeping pills, to which I soon resorted. I would awake in terror twenty or thirty times a night. I would sometimes doze off in the daytime, and dream pleasant dreams for what seemed an eternity only to wake panic-stricken to discover that I had been asleep for no more than a few minutes.

The second unexpected consequence of the breakdown was the most extreme boredom. I could concentrate on nothing except my own pain. At first I would try to go to the theater, or the cinema, but invariably I had to leave after a few minutes.

Since recovering from his breakdown, Professor N. S. Sutherland has become the editor of a series of books, called *Tutorial Essays in Psychology: A Guide to Recent Advances,* which attempt to describe what is going on in a particular speciality so that it can be easily understood by workers in other branches of psychology.

In my previous existence, there had always been something to look forward to: now there was nothing, except the fitful mercy of sleep. I spent the day longing for the night to come (Sutherland, 1976, pp. 1–2).

With these words Professor N. S. Sutherland of the University of Sussex in Great Britain begins one of the most candid accounts of a mental breakdown available in our literature. It is the story of a talented psychologist's journey through an affective disorder, a depressive episode that began with a *panic state.* This passage raises questions of fundamental importance. How did Dr. Sutherland's personality prior to his breakdown differ from his personality after the onset of the depressive disorder? Was it a matter of degree or did some basic qualitative change take place? Could a similar breakdown happen to anyone? Are we all vulnerable to the development of abnormal reactions? Such questions are similar to those raised in Chapter 10 on stress; the answers are also somewhat the same.

Normal versus Abnormal: The Thin Line That Divides. Psychopathology is the study of deviant behavior, sometimes referred to as *behavior pathology, behavior disorder, mental disorder,* or *abnormal behavior.* All these terms carry implications of a departure from normality. In fact, in many cases deviant behavior appears to be an extreme version of normality. We have often seen in others neatness that borders on compulsiveness, suspiciousness that seems tinged with irrationality, extreme sensitivity and fear that damage relationships with others or limit freedom and choice. At one time or another everyone experiences headaches brought on by nervousness, a vague sense of foreboding, an overwhelming anxiety in the midst of crisis, or uncertainty about his or her own identity and goals in life. On the behavioral side the line between normal and abnormal is a thin one, indeed. As we show now, the same is true of environmental conditions and experience.

Several years ago one of us taught a course in abnormal psychology in which 185 bright and healthy undergraduates were enrolled. At the very first class session, the instructor presented the students with this hypothetical situation.

Imagine that I am capable of dropping a drug into your drink that will, shortly thereafter, induce what appears to be a marked psychosis. You, however, have no awareness of what I have done. Your roommate, several hours later, finding you in a disturbed condition, takes you to the Student Health Service and the Dean's Office is notified of your illness. Your parents are asked to come to the campus and take you home for treatment. Within a day your worried folks take you to a mental health clinic in your community where you are interviewed and asked to fill in the details of your life. Consider this situation tonight. Spend some time reviewing your life and the things that have happened to you in some detail. At the next class session, I will ask you whether or not, on the basis of your previous life experiences, you can justify this "psychosis."

At the next meeting, when asked for a show of hands by those who believed that their lives could justify a psychotic outcome, a sea of hands went up, making a count difficult. The opposite question, "Whose lives can't justify it?" brought two hands into view! Only 2 of 185 competent students considered a severe breakdown incomprehensible in terms of their past history.

This example illustrates an important point about attempts to find the causes of psychopathology in reconstructions of a person's past. If you know the outcome of a life history, you will always, in looking backward into the life history, find events and factors that seem to explain the outcome. A successful outcome, normality, presses you to stress the more positive events in that person's life; an unsuccessful one, mental disorder, encourages emphasis on a person's negative experiences and relationships. For the moment it does not matter whether these experiences actually produce the disorder. The point is that they are available in the lives of most of us and, when needed, can be used as possible explanations for our behavior.

What then does distinguish abnormal behavior from normal behavior? Three criteria contribute to the distinction. The first criterion is *statistical;* abnormal behavior is unusual, uncommon, an extreme departure from ordinary behavior. The intensity of Professor Sutherland's anxiety illustrates this point. The second criterion is *cultural;* abnormal behavior is different from the expected behavior of the society. Some of the case histories to follow illustrate this criterion better than anything in Professor Sutherland's experience. The third criterion, however, is very well illustrated in the Sutherland passage; abnormal behavior impairs the individual's *personal adjustment.* Professor Sutherland's intense anxiety made it impossible for him to carry on the simplest daily activities.

APPROACHES TO PSYCHOPATHOLOGY

The apparent continuity of normal and abnormal behavior poses the principal problem addressed in one approach to psychopathology. What is the best way to describe and categorize disordered behavior? This is the question posed by **descriptive psychopathology.** The existence in the lives of all of us of conditions that might lead to breakdown poses the problem addressed in a second approach. What are the causes and origins of such behavior? This is the question for **developmental psychopathology.** Two giants in the history of psychiatry sought to answer these questions, and both made enduring contributions to the study of disordered behavior.

One of the giants was Emil Kraepelin (1856–1926), a brilliant descriptive psychiatrist who contributed more to the development of a classification system for mental disorders than any other figure in medical history. Kraepelin believed that personal investigation and continuous observation of the greatest possible number of different cases would provide a scientific foundation for psychiatry. Such investigations would have to include a study of the language, perceptions, thoughts, and emotions of disturbed people. With such information on hand, first steps could be taken to identify patterns of behavior or syndromes characteristic of different types of patients. These syndromes would evolve into a taxonomy of the mental disorders. But description alone would leave unanswered the question of how different types of mental disorder develop. A very different figure, but one of equal brilliance, Sigmund Freud, struggled to answer this question. It is essential that we contrast these two historical figures and their orientations: Kraepelin, the descriptive psychopathologist; Freud, the developmental psychopathologist.

Emil Kraepelin originated the classification system for mental disorders on which all subsequent ones have been based, distinguishing each, like physical illnesses, by symptoms, origin, course, and outcome. He proposed two major psychoses, dementia praecox, an early term for schizophrenia, and manac-depressive psychosis. Throughout his career Kraepelin observed large numbers of manic-depressive patients over long periods of time. His case histories are still among the best that we have.

Kraepelin and Descriptive Psychopathology

In the year 1904 Emil Kraepelin stood at the summit of his profession, occupying the chair in psychiatry at the Medical School in Munich, Germany. His influence was worldwide, his *Compendium on Psychiatry* was the definitive work of its time. Kraepelin believed that the future of psychiatry rested on observation and careful description, the methods of the natural sciences. His actions had followed his faith. After graduation from medical school, Kraepelin had elected to study with Wilhelm Wundt, the world leader of experimental psychology, in order to learn the procedures of laboratory investigation.

Kraepelin as a master of descriptive psychopathology wrote a case book titled *Lectures on Clinical Psychiatry* (1904), choosing a style he would have used were he addressing a medical school class. In the lecture that follows he describes a thirty-year-old woman, suffering from *hysteria*. We have chosen this disorder because it will allow you to compare Kraepelin's orientation with that of Freud, whose views follow.

> Gentlemen, the young lady, aged thirty, carefully dressed in black, who comes into the hall with short, shuffling steps, leaning on the nurse, and sinks into a chair as if exhausted, gives you the impression that she is ill. She is of slender build, her features are pale and rather painfully drawn, and her eyes are cast down. Her small, manicured fingers play nervously with a handkerchief. The patient answers the questions addressed to her in a low tired voice, without looking up, and we find that she is quite clear about time, place, and her surroundings.
>
> After a few minutes, her eyes suddenly become convulsively shut, her head sinks forward, and she seems to have fallen into a deep sleep. Her arms have grown quite limp, and fall down as if palsied when you try to lift them. She has ceased to answer, and if you try to raise her eyelids, her eyes suddenly rotate upwards. Needle pricks only produce a slight shudder. But sprinkling with cold water is followed by a deep sigh; the patient starts up, opens her eyes, looks around her with surprise, and gradually comes to herself. She says that she has just had one of her sleeping attacks, from which she has suffered for seven years. They come on quite irregularly, often many in one day, and last from a few minutes to half an hour.
>
> Concerning the history of her life, the patient tells us that her parents died sixteen years ago, one soon after another. Her father's stepbrother attempted suicide, and her brother is most fantastically eccentric. I must add that two other members of her family give the impression of being very nervous. She did her work easily at school. She was educated in convent school, and passed the examination for teachers. As a young girl she inhaled a great deal of chloroform which she was able to get secretly, for toothache. . . .
>
> During her present residence here, so called "great attacks" have appeared in addition to her previous troubles. We will try to produce such an attack by pressure on the very sensitive left ovarian region. After one or two minutes of moderately strong pressure, during which the patient shows sharp pain, her expression alters. She throws herself to and fro with her eyes shut, and screams to us loudly, generally in French, not to touch her. "You must not do anything to me. . . ." She cries for help, pushes with her hands, and twists herself as if she were trying to escape from a sexual assault. Whenever she is touched, the excitement increases. Her whole body is strongly bent backwards. Suddenly the picture changes, and the patient begs piteously not to be cursed, and laments and sobs aloud. This condition, too, is very soon put an end to by sprinkling with cold water. The patient shudders, wakes with a deep sigh, and looks fixedly round, only making a tired, senseless impression. She cannot explain what has happened (pp. 252–254).

There are many things to be said about this description. First, it is meticulously accurate in all details. Second, it illustrates Kraepelin's preference for experimentation and demonstration. Notice how Kraepelin produces an experiment-in-miniature to show how pressure near the ovarian region generates an attack, a sexualized sensitivity for which the patient will have no memory afterward. Finally, as a descriptive psychopathologist, Kraepelin is relatively uncommunicative about the origins of this woman's strange behavior because such speculations were alien to him. He introduces the patient's family background, but only for the purpose of indicating the hereditary "tainting" he perceives there. Kraepelin believed that the roots of disorder were to be found in biology and in genetics. This hereditarian emphasis led Kraepelin to a fatalism about mental disorders and virtually guaranteed his loss of influence later in the twentieth century, even as he pressed forward with his formulation and sharpening of the classification system. Looking back, a historian of psychiatry was to write of Kraepelin that "he seems to have been almost unaware that in his careful study he lost the individual" (Zilboorg, 1941).

Freud and Developmental Psychopathology

No one will ever be able to say of Freud that he lost sight of the individual. From the beginning of his career until the closing months of his life, when he began to succumb to cancer of the jaw and cheek, Freud was a practicing clinician who saw patients. His psychoanalytic writings, which were to fill twenty-four volumes, began with five case histories entitled *Studies in Hysteria,* written in collaboration with Josef Breuer.

Although these cases represented the birth of psychoanalysis, to say that their impact was negligible when first published in 1895 is to be charitable. The book was greeted with a stony silence in some medical quarters and with poisonous criticism from others. Why? Certainly not because of the symptoms that were described. Breuer and Freud's description did not differ markedly from that of Kraepelin. Instead, it was because Freud set forth a developmental view that stressed the sexual origins of the symptom. Kraepelin could not have been unmindful of the sexual implications of his demonstration that the pressure of his hands on the patient's ovarian region generated a response as if "she were trying to escape from a sexual assault." But he ignored their implications. Freud did not turn away from the possibility of sexual trauma as an etiological factor, as the account of one of the cases in *Studies in Hysteria* (1895, pp. 125–133) clearly reveals.

The setting for Freud's observations was a mountainside in the Alps where he had gone to "forget medicine and more particularly the neuroses." But even at 6000 feet Freud could not escape his destiny. As he sat and rested after an arduous hike up the mountain, he was approached by a young woman whom he recognized to be Katharina, the waitress who served him his meals at the inn where he was staying. Katharina, aware that Freud was a physician, solicited his help in alleviating her symptoms, for the medication she was taking provided no relief for her.

Beginning two years previously, she had, on occasion, felt giddy and become breathless without reason. She would then become afraid that she would suffocate and felt a great hammering sensation in her head. Her chest ached as though it were being crushed, and she imagined a figure behind her who threatened to catch her.

After hearing this brief case history, Freud inquired, "When you have an attack, do you think of something?" "Yes. I always see an awful face that looks at me in a dreadful way so that I'm frightened." "Do you recognize the face?" "No." "Do you know what your attacks come from?" "No." Freud then wrote

> Was I to make an attempt at an analysis? I could not venture to transplant hypnosis to these altitudes, but perhaps I might succeed with a simple talk. I should have to try a lucky guess. I had found often enough that in girls anxiety was a consequence of the horror by which a virginal mind is overcome when it is faced for the first time with the world of sexuality.

Freud's inner debate is of interest for two reasons. The first is his uncertainty whether to attempt to find the origins of Katharina's physical symptoms; the second is the mention of hypnosis. Breuer had used this method successfully with several similar cases of hysteria. Early in his career Freud too relied on hypnosis, but he would later discard it as he developed the psychoanalytic techniques of free association and dream interpretation. Having decided to go forward, Freud offers his hypothesis of probable early trauma with a rapidity entirely uncharacteristic of later psychoanalytic procedures.

> So I said: "If you don't know, I'll tell you how I think you got your attacks. At that time, two years ago, you must have seen or heard something that very much embarrassed you that you'd much rather not have seen."

Freud's speculation produced an immediate response. Katharina recalled that two years previously she had observed through a window her uncle, the owner of the inn, and a cousin engaged in sexual intercourse.

> "I came away from the window at once" [she told Freud] "and leaned up against the wall and couldn't get my breath—just what happens to me since. Everything went blank, my eyelids were forced together and there was a hammering and buzzing in my head."

But the face retained its mystery; it remained unclear and unrecognizable to Katharina. And so Freud encouraged her to continue her narrative. Gradually Katharina revealed that this same uncle had on at least two occasions crept into her own bed while she slept and had made sexual advances to her, which she had successfully repulsed. She was finally compelled to tell her aunt of her uncle's behavior; the uncle was turned out and a divorce was arranged. Now Katharina could provide the key to unlock the puzzle of the recurring image of the face. Reliving her traumatic experiences, she told Freud the face had now become recognizable. It was that of her uncle who, whenever he saw her, became enraged and made threatening gestures. Someday she feared he would catch her unawares and injure her.

Freud did not believe that he had effected a cure. His conclusion was appropriately modest; he hoped only that Katharina had "derived some benefit from our conversation."

By contrast with Kraepelin's case history, Freud's was developmental, emphasizing quite different elements. The stress was not on symptoms but on events that seemed to precede the onset of symptoms and might possibly be of etiological significance. The linkage of these events to disorder is twofold: (1) they were initially traumatic and therefore (2) gave the person who experienced them a reason to repress or forget them. Freud's basic goal was not descriptive but therapeutic—to undo the repression through recall. By the act of recalling the event in a supportive context, Katharina with Freud's help lifted the repression, and the symptom that presumably served as a substitutive response for it was relieved.

Just as Kraepelin searched for regularities in the physical symptoms, Freud looked for psychological regularities in the traumas preceding the hysterical attack and sought to develop a theory that would include these regularities as elements of causation. Reviewing the five cases of hysteria described in the volume on hysteria, plus twelve others, Freud finally concluded that a repulsion against sexuality was always involved. All seventeen of these seventeen patients recalled with great difficulty traumatic events marked with sexual overtones. Freud could only reason that the events and the patients' moral values were incompatible and that the memory of the events had to be driven from consciousness. The forgetting was only partial, however, and thus the conflict between event and values had induced the formation of hysterical symptoms. Freud did not come to these conclusions easily. "I regarded the linking of hysteria with the topic of sexuality as an insult—just as the women patients themselves do.'' But the conclusion seemed inevitable, and Freud courageously set it forth and earned, as he had anticipated, the vilification of society.

SUMMARY

Psychopathology is the scientific study of the problem of abnormal behavior, defined as behavior which is statistically rare, culturally unacceptable, and personally disruptive to the individual's psychological adjustment. Abnormal behavior is difficult to define exactly, however, because the symptoms of psychopathology are often extreme forms of normal behavior. Life histories only increase the difficulty because events that lead to breakdown in some people occur in the lives of all of us.

In the past and extending up to the present, there have been two major approaches to the study of psychopathology. One is to investigate the different forms that mental disorders take. This is the study of the structure of mental disorder, and it is a task carried on by descriptive psychopathologists. The second traces the origins of disorder, and this task falls to developmental psychopathologists. We have briefly reviewed the contributions of two of psychiatry's greatest figures—Kraepelin, who led the effort to create a descriptive classification system covering all forms of disordered behavior, and Freud, whose towering achievements were directed toward tracing the development of disordered behavior.

In Kraepelin's work we saw a greater concern for careful description than for the origins of disorder, a preference for experimental demonstrations, and a leaning toward biological and genetic interpretations of psychopathology. In Freud's work, by contrast, we saw an emphasis on origins, a search for the causes of disorder in experience, and a greater concern for psychological therapy than for classification.

PROBLEMS OF DESCRIPTIVE PSYCHOPATHOLOGY

The principal task of descriptive psychopathology is **diagnosis,** the description of symptoms of mental disorder, and the classification of forms of deviant behavior on the basis of these descriptions. There are those who object to this whole enterprise on humanistic grounds. Why should we diagnose at all? What damage do we do to people when we label them as having some specific form of mental disorder? What justification can there possibly be for classifying together individuals simply because they share certain behavior or experiences in common?

The descriptive psychopathologists counter by asserting that it is absolutely essential for any field, including psychopathology, that aspires to scientific status, to develop some system for describing the phenomena with which that field is concerned. It is difficult to see how there could be any understanding, much less a scientific one, of phenomena that are not described and classified. A science, after all, must be about something! This strongly suggests that achieving a sound descriptive psychopathology is an essential precondition for working out an equally sound developmental account of different types of mental disorder.

Reliability of Diagnosis

Diagnoses are useful only if they are reliable in the same sense that psychological tests must be reliable. In this case *reliability* usually means consistency of diagnosis, agreement among two or more clinicians on the diagnostic category to which a patient is to be assigned. Unfortunately, the **reliability of diagnosis** can be unsatisfactorily low, even when it is done with utmost care. One study (Beck et al., 1962) obtained agreement on only 54 percent of the cases.

Reliability can be low for a number of reasons. Perhaps the most important is that many symptoms are not unique to a given type of psychopathology. They can be present in groups of patients who show very different types of disorder (Zigler and Phillips, 1961). For example, bizarre ideas are present not only in some schizophrenics but in psychotically depressed patients as well; assaultive behavior is the most typical of antisocial disorders, but it occurs in other disordered states too. From the point of view of diagnostic reliability, this means that no single symptom can uniquely identify a diagnostic category. Obviously, this means, in turn, that the clinician must rely on patterns of symptoms or **syndromes.** This will not be entirely satisfactory either, however, for even the dependable components of such patterns may be absent in many cases of like diagnoses.

Other important factors that influence the reliability of diagnosis include the following. (1) Symptoms change spontaneously over time and therapy may also change them. Diagnosticians seeing a patient at different times may see different symptoms, and reliability may fade or even vanish completely. (2) Severe disorders are diagnosed more reliably than mild ones. (3) Diagnoses made early in the development of a disorder are likely to be less reliable than those made later on. (4) Diagnoses confined to broad categories are more reliable than highly specific diagnoses. (5) When reliability is based on separate examinations by different clinicians, reliability may be low because patients may provide different information to the different examiners. (6) Moreover, different clinicians may put different interpretations on, or assign different importance to, the same information. (7) And most important, diagnostic manuals often lack the precision needed to make distinctions among categories.

Reliability can be improved if the clinical judges receive common diagnostic training, if the diagnoses are based on the same information, and if there is agreement on the criteria that are to be used in making a specific diagnosis. This is a tall order but one that must be filled if satisfactory levels of diagnostic reliability are to be achieved.

Types of Psychopathology: DSM-III

The most widely accepted criteria for the diagnosis of mental disorders appear in the third edition of the *Diagnostic and Statistical Manual of Mental Disorder*, popularly known as DSM-III, published by the American Psychiatric Association in 1980. This manual was designed to spell out in great detail specific behavioral definitions for many of the more severe mental disorders. This attention to detail has paid off in terms of increased reliability of diagnosis (Eysenck, Wakefield, and Friedman, 1983; Strober, 1981).

Like so many things in contemporary society, DSM-III is inflationary. When DSM-I appeared in 1952, it contained a listing with brief descriptions of 60 disorders; DSM-II, published in 1968, covered 145 disorders; DSM-III lists and describes approximately 220 disorders and 13 other conditions "not attributable to a mental disorder," such as *academic problem, phase of life problem, parent-child problem, marital problem,* and *occupational problem.* Unfortunately, this expanded version includes some clearly nonpathological conditions mislabeled as "mental disorders," such as *avoidant disorder of childhood* (initially called "shyness disorder"), *identity disorder* (Who am I?), *developmental reading disorder,* and *developmental arithmetic disorder.* These types of behavior are so far removed from mental disorder that their inclusion has been sharply attacked by researchers and clinicians (Garmezy, 1978). Such mislabeling of nonmedical developmental problems could burden millions of American's children with the pejorative term "mental disorder." In the words of Hans Eysenck and his colleagues (1983),

> DSM-III includes many behaviors which have little or no medical relevance and belong properly in the province of the psychologist, for example, gambling, malingering, antisocial behavior, academic and occupational problems, parent-child problems, marital problems, and the curious "substance use disorders," which apparently would bring about any kind of behavior within the compass of psychiatry. . . . Psychiatry has always been ill-defined as a specialty, but this is going well beyond the pale (p. 189).

These are powerful negative features of DSM-III. On the positive side is the fact the DSM-III has taken a giant step forward in describing the well-established severe psychiatric disorders. The single paragraph associated with a global description of schizophrenia in the 1968 version of the manual has now been expanded to thirteen pages of excellent descriptive content. In a similar fashion, the affective disorders, which took up two pages of description in DSM-II, now occupy twenty pages. Size itself, of course, is not a criterion of excellence, but a reading of the description of these two historically significant categories of traditional psychiatric disorders suggests that careful, scholarly attention has been paid to the recent findings of research in psychopathology.

Another significant addition to DSM-III is the use of what has been termed a *multiaxial classification system* (Table 16.1), which provides for five different categories of diagnostic information. Each of these five categories is termed an **axis.** Axes I and II list the specific disorders. Axis III notes the existence of any current physical disorder that may be relevant to the patient's mental disorder, such as a neurological disorder in a child diagnosed as showing an anxiety disorder. Axis IV provides a seven-point rating scale of the severity of psychosocial stressors that may have contributed to the person's disorder. Axis V provides for an evaluation of the individual's highest level of adaptive functioning during the past year. This rating is a composite of social relations, quality of occupational functioning, and the use of leisure time. Why this emphasis on *stress* and *premorbid*—that is, before the onset of the disorder—*adaptive functioning?* There are many studies that indicate that both are important in understanding the patient's present state and in predicting the course of the disorder. Did something happen to the patient that might have precipitated the disorder? Stressful events of great intensity that precede breakdown are generally indicators of a more favorable prognosis than breakdown in the absence of stress. High levels of premorbid functioning predict recovery; low levels of functioning predict a poorer outcome. Thus information of these sorts helps us to understand more about a mental disorder and its context than the diagnosis alone.

If it is demanded of a classification system that it spell out not only symptom description but also etiology, course, and treatment of disorders, DSM-III falls far short of the mark. But here there is a reality to consider. In some instances, such as the organic mental disorders, how the disturbances arose is known. For most other disorders etiology is not yet known, forcing designers of DSM-III to focus on a description of psychopathological symptoms.

Over the next few years there will be many critical studies forthcoming, and gradually the strengths and the weaknesses of DSM-III will unfold. You should recognize that DSM-III is not the final word on diagnostic classification. There

Table 16.1 DSM-III Multiaxial Classification System: A Selective Listing

Axis I	Axis V
Disorders Usually First Evident in Infancy, Childhood, or Adolescence	Highest Level of Adaptive Functioning Past Year
Organic Mental Disorders	1. Superior: usually effective in social relations, occupation, and use of leisure time (e.g., single parent in reduced circumstances takes excellent care of children, has warm friendships and a hobby)
Substance Use Disorders	
Schizophrenic Disorders	
Paranoid Disorders	
Affective Disorders	2. Very good: better than average in job, leisure time, and social functioning (e.g., retired person does volunteer work, sees old friends)
Anxiety Disorders	
Somatoform Disorders	
Dissociative Disorders	
Psychosexual Disorders	3. Good: no more than slight impairment in either occupational or social functioning (e.g., individual with many friends does a difficult job extremely well but finds it a strain)
Psychological Factors Affecting Physical Condition	

Axis I

Disorders Usually First Evident in Infancy, Childhood, or Adolescence

Organic Mental Disorders

Substance Use Disorders

Schizophrenic Disorders

Paranoid Disorders

Affective Disorders

Anxiety Disorders

Somatoform Disorders

Dissociative Disorders

Psychosexual Disorders

Psychological Factors Affecting Physical Condition

Axis II

Personality Disorders:
    paranoid, schizoid, schizotypal, histrionic, narcissistic, antisocial, borderline, avoidant, dependent, compulsive, passive-aggressive

Specific Developmental Disorders:
    reading, arithmetic, language, articulation

Axis III

Physical Disorders and Conditions

Axis IV

Severity of Psychosocial Stressors
1. None
2. Minimal (e.g., small loan)
3. Mild (e.g., argument with neighbor)
4. Moderate (e.g., pregnancy)
5. Severe (e.g., serious illness)
6. Extreme (e.g., death of close relative)
7. Catastrophic (e.g., natural disaster)

Axis V

Highest Level of Adaptive Functioning Past Year
1. Superior: usually effective in social relations, occupation, and use of leisure time (e.g., single parent in reduced circumstances takes excellent care of children, has warm friendships and a hobby)
2. Very good: better than average in job, leisure time, and social functioning (e.g., retired person does volunteer work, sees old friends)
3. Good: no more than slight impairment in either occupational or social functioning (e.g., individual with many friends does a difficult job extremely well but finds it a strain)
4. Fair: moderate impairment in either social or occupational functioning or some impairment in both (e.g., lawyer has trouble carrying through assignments, has almost no close friends)
5. Poor: marked impairment in either social or occupational functioning or moderate impairment in both (e.g., man with one or two friends has trouble holding a job for more than a few weeks)
6. Very poor: marked impairment in social and occupational functioning (e.g., woman is unable to do any housework and has violent outbursts)
7. Grossly impaired: gross impairment in virtually all areas of functioning (e.g., elderly man needs supervision in maintaining personal hygiene, is usually incoherent)

From Davison and Neale, 1982.

will be a DSM-IV, a DSM-V, and as many as are needed to solve the problem of creating a sound and reliable system of classifying various types of behavior pathology.

SUMMARY

A sound descriptive psychopathology will be necessary for a scientific understanding of mental disorders. This raises the question of the accuracy of current description and the issue of the reliability of psychiatric diagnosis. The evidence is that this reliability is often uncomfortably low, the most important reason being the imprecise way in which diagnostic manuals describe mental disorders.

New developments are beginning to correct the diagnostic situation. A revised classification manual, DSM-III, is the major current effort to overcome the unreliability of psychiatric diagnosis. DSM-III provides improved descriptions of the more severe and traditional psychiatric disorders, such as schizophrenia and the affective disorders. It also uses a multiaxial classification, which can indicate how physical disorders, stress, and level of premorbid functioning impinge on the person's behavior disorder. A marked weakness in DSM-III is the inclusion as mental disorders behaviors of children that would more aptly be classified as developmental disabilities, lags, or behavior deficits.

SUBSTANCE ABUSE

It will not be possible in a single chapter to present examples of all the categories of mental disorder covered in DSM-III. Instead we will describe a sampling of disorders in order to illustrate their almost bewildering variety. Let us begin with the group of disorders that everyone has some acquaintance with, substance dependence, abuse, and addiction. The use of drugs is widespread, and there is no indication that the extent of use is soon to decrease (Richards, 1981). The disorders based on the abuse of various substances afflict every segment of society—the well-educated, the competent, and the economically advantaged as well as those who have known only disadvantage and deprivation.

Alcohol

Eighty percent of the young adult population of the United States have had some experience with alcohol before they are seventeen years old; by the age of twenty-five the figure is over 96 percent. In 1977 alcohol abuse cost the nation an estimated 49.4 billion dollars, over 200 dollars for every man, woman, and child in the country (Research Triangle Institute, 1983).

The reasons why young people drink are readily evident. Drinking is a part of the process of socialization; young people are mimicking the behavior of adults and their peers. Drinking also provides a temporary means of coping with the discomforts of adolescence, with the threats to self-esteem, the fear of failure, and the sense of alienation from family and adults faced by young people in the transition from childhood to maturity. Unfortunately, many of these who begin to drink in adolescence increase their drinking later on and become addicted alcoholics.

Problem drinkers are a heterogeneous lot. No special personality type, family background, social class, or stressful experience predicts the development of alcoholism. When people who have an alcohol problem are sober, their thinking, judgment, memory, insight, and appearance are no different from those of people without one.

Symptoms and Causes. Persons with a chronic history of severe **alcoholism,** or any person who has been drinking heavily for two weeks, may suffer delirium tremens (DTs) three to four days after they have stopped drinking. With the sudden drop of alcohol in the blood, the brain does not receive the supply to which it has grown physiologically accustomed. Individuals become disoriented and extremely agitated; they sweat profusely and are severely tremulous. They have a high fever, a racing heart, and they see and feel small animals and insects crawling over walls and up their bodies, advancing to destroy them. The condition requires immediate hospitalization and may cause death.

It was Aristotle who declared that drunken women "bring forth children like themselves." More recent information supports the view that alcoholism runs in families. One expert in the genetics of alcoholism indicates that with only a single exception, "Every family study of alcoholism, irrespective of country of origin, has shown much higher rates of alcoholism among the relatives of alcoholics than in the general population" (Goodwin, 1979). Such evidence does not prove that a genetic factor is at work, for drinking by parents, the attitudes they express, and the level of stress they put their children under are not always controlled in family studies of alcoholism. Studies that have incorporated such controls suggest a modest genetic predisposition to alcoholism, although the precise nature of the inheritance is not clear. A lack of tolerance for alcohol has been suggested.

Outlook. It was once believed that the prognosis for the problem drinker was inevitably a grim one, but recent evidence questions this view. Surveys of drinking practices indicate that within years of initial reports of problem drinking, 20 percent of individuals state that they have solved the problem and have an improved level of social and physical functioning (Mendelson and Mello, 1979). Scientific debate concerning the long-held belief that alcoholics cannot return to social drinking after treatment continues. Here too individual variability is probably a strong factor.

The Sedatives

Sedatives such as alcohol and the synthetic barbiturates act to depress the central nervous system. The barbiturates—representative trade names are Luminal, Amytal, Nembutal, Seconal—account for 25 percent of mood-changing prescriptions and are powerful sleep inducers. Unfortunately, the barbiturate hangover affects activity into the next waking day. Barbiturates are physiologically addictive. With prolonged use tolerance develops, and larger doses must be taken for the drug to have the same effect. At this point, if use of a barbiturate is abruptly terminated, the withdrawal reactions are severe. The person may go into convulsions and die or suffer a prolonged toxic psychosis.

In testimony before a United States Senate investigating committee, a noted expert in the field of drug abuse, Sidney Cohen, spoke of the overuse of barbiturates by the young.

> For the youngsters barbiturates are a more reliable high and less detectable than "pot." They are less strenuous than LSD, less "freaky" than amphetamines, and less expensive than heroin. A school boy can "drop a red' and spend the day in a dreamy, floating state of awayness untroubled by reality. It is drunkenness without the odor of alcohol. It is escape for the price of one's lunch money (quoted by Ray, 1978, p. 292).

Small doses of the barbiturates induce a euphoric "high" and sometimes aggressive behavior; larger doses can bring confusion, cognitive impairment, exaggerated emotionality, and a loss of motor coordination. Barbiturates are used by people who wish to commit suicide. They are responsible for 5000 deaths annually and five times that many trips to hospital emergency rooms. As drugs of abuse, the barbiturates are bad medicine indeed.

The Stimulants: Amphetamines and Cocaine

The amphetamines are synthetic drugs that act as **stimulants** to the central nervous system, bringing a sense of euphoria and heightening activity. Used to prevent sleepiness, to suppress appetite, and to counteract depression generally, the amphetamines are the "ups" in a world of ups and downs, but they are dangerous "ups." In large doses the amphetamines can cause convulsions and also heart attacks by affecting the heart muscles.

"Speed." The most threatening of all the amphetamines is "speed" or Methedrine, which is injected intravenously by "speed freaks." Hyperactivity, eventual exhaustion, paranoid thinking, and destructive, violent behavior may all be aftermaths of this "mainlining." In the 1960s the danger of methamphetamine was tellingly conveyed by the watchword "Speed kills." The attraction of speed lies in its ecstatic "high," but to maintain it requires heavier and heavier doses of the drug. The "speed freak" injects the drug every few hours for several days and goes without sleep and food. Irritability, confusion, and fears mount, culminating in collapse or sometimes a paranoid psychosis. Of all the drug-induced mental aberrations, amphetamine psychosis, although uncommon, is the one that most clearly resembles paranoid schizophrenia. Unfortunately, the prognosis for recovery from the psychologically addictive power of speed is a poor one.

Cocaine. Cocaine was one of the earliest stimulants to be used medicinally, and one of its prime advocates was Sigmund Freud. He had read an account of the isolation of cocaine, an active ingredient of coca leaves, at a time when he was suffering a bout of depression and fatigue. He decided to try the drug and found that it not only relieved the depression but gave him newfound energy with which to continue his work. Freud became a proselytizer for the drug. In his *Cocaine Papers* (1885) Freud wrote of its numerous therapeutic benefits. Not only was it exhilarating and an aphrodisiac, but it was effective, he stated, as a local anesthetic and for treating asthma, digestive disorders of the stomach, and alcohol and morphine addiction. Freud's enthusiasm vanished after he had spent a night nursing through an acute cocaine psychosis a physician friend who had taken the drug on his recommendation. Thereafter he was bitterly opposed to the drug.

Cocaine is now the extremely expensive "in" drug for inducing a sense of euphoria and intense stimulation. Inhaled or "snorted" into each nostril, the drug is absorbed from the mucous lining into the bloodstream and reaches the brain almost immediately. The short high peaks within minutes and may be over within thirty. A more dangerous method for ingesting cocaine is by intravenous injection, either alone or in combination with heroin. Cocaine increases heart rate and blood pressure; it may make the abuser feel strong and become talkative. Prolonged use can induce a psychosis and terrifying tactile hallucinations not unlike those of delirium tremens.

The Narcotics or Opiates

In the latter part of the nineteenth century, the dispensing of opiates was so open in this country that, in the words of one distinguished journalist, America was a "dope fiend's paradise." Opium was sold legally, costs were low, usage high; in fact, morphine, a derivative of opium, had been administered so extensively in treating the wounded of the Civil War that by the end of the conflict 45,000 soldiers were addicts. Not only drugstores but grocery and general stores sold opiates across the counter; if no store was nearby, mail-order houses were ready to fill the need. Patent medicines containing opium and morphine were abundantly available, ranging from Mrs. Winslow's Soothing Syrup to McMunn's Elixir of Opium. Teething syrups for children and medicines for "women's troubles" contained opiates (Brecher, 1972). Heroin, much stronger than the morphine from which it is derived, may induce a sense of euphoria and contentment which lasts for some four to six hours. Sometimes the reaction includes a "rush," "kick," or "bang," which is often sensed as a sexual equivalent, an "abdominal orgasm."

Many narcotic addicts go untreated and those who receive treatment often fail to profit from it. A treatment that looked promising for a time was the potent synthetic drug **methadone,** used medically as a substitute for morphine. The effects of methadone are similar to those of heroin but side effects are less severe and withdrawal symptoms are milder.

The first major test of the effectiveness of methadone in counteracting the addict's craving for heroin was conducted by Vincent Dole and Marie Nyswander (1966) at the Rockefeller Hospital in New York. In this study a large group of hard-core addicts were kept on a high level of methadone for a period of four years. During this time the addicts became more constructive in their activities, attending school or achieving some employment stability. Very few were arrested. Since methadone is both legal and inexpensive, it permitted the addicts to pursue a life free from the crime, despair, and terror so often a part of maintaining a heroin habit.

Unfortunately, methadone also has serious disadvantages as a treatment. Methadone is itself addictive; when discontinued, a craving for heroin, not methadone, becomes intense. Pregnant women who are methadone users frequently give birth to infants whose withdrawal symptoms are not unlike those of infants born to mothers on heroin. Moreover, although they tend to be mild, methadone does have physical side effects; overdosages can be fatal. Most important, 50 percent of street addicts on methadone maintenance reject the programs and prefer heroin.

The British program, called heroin maintenance, has long been advocated by some as the ultimate solution. In Great Britain heroin addicts are treated as sick individuals; clinics dispense the drug to them free. The number of addicts in England in extremely small, 3000, the rate of addiction has been slowed, and drug-connected crime is minimal by American standards.

The Hallucinogens

The **hallucinogens** are a class of drugs known for their power to affect perception, thinking, self-awareness, and emotion as well as for expanding consciousness. Slowing of time and extension of space, vividness of thoughts and sensations, empathy and enlightenments, delusions and hallucinations may be mild or overwhelming, depending on the dose and quality of the drug, the people around the user, the place and time the drug is taken, the user's previous experience, and his or her expectations.

The Psychedelics. In 1943 a chemist in Basel, Switzerland, Dr. Albert Hofmann, was experimenting with d-lysergic acid diethylamide and somehow, without his knowing it, some of this substance got into his system. Hofmann's report of the experience is as follows.

> Last Friday, April 16, in the midst of my afternoon work . . . I had to go home because I experienced a very peculiar restlessness which was associated with a slight attack of dizziness. At home I went to bed and got into a not unpleasant state of drunkenness which was characterized by extremely stimulating fantasy. When I closed my eyes (the daylight was most unpleasant to me) I experienced fantastic images of an extraordinary plasticity. They were associated with an intense kaleidoscopic play of colors. After about two hours this condition disappeared (Ropp, 1957).

These effects of LSD, obviously hallucinogenic, were at first sometimes called psychotomimetic because they appeared to mimic some of the symptoms of psychosis. Then the term **psychedelic** (Greek *psychē,* soul; *dēloun,* to reveal) was applied to LSD to emphasize the expansion of consciousness reported by its users. Within the class of psychedelic drugs, LSD was one of the most abused in the 1960s. Other psychedelics popular in those years were mescaline from the peyote cactus and psilocybin from a Mexican mushroom. Today they have been replaced by a drug of infinitely greater power of human destruction. Its chemical name is phencyclidine (PCP), but on the street it has many bynames: angel dust, dust, crystal, cyclone, embalming fluid, elephant or horse tranquilizer, killer weed, super weed, mint weed, mist, monkey dust, Peace Pill, rocket fuel, goon, surfer, KW, and scuffle.

A very powerful case against PCP appeared in a monograph published by the National Institute of Drug Abuse. Here is an excerpt.

> A young man smokes some PCP and proceeds to rob a gas station at gunpoint. A juvenile smokes PCP and rapes his baby sister. . . . A police officer encounters a young man who may have ingested an analog of PCP. The man, naked and unarmed, reportedly becomes combative and assaultive and is shot to death by the officer. Two lovers are smoking PCP alone in their bedroom; within a few minutes one is bleeding to death from a knife wound which may or may not have been self-inflicted. A middle-aged woman takes some cocaine which has been adulterated with PCP and tries to rob a bank armed only with a broom which she manipulates as if it were a gun (Siegel, 1978, p. 272).

Small doses of PCP can generate striking psychotic symptoms. The drug users, disassociated from their surroundings, may be both analgesic, insensible to pain, and amnesic; they may believe that their bodies have been altered in some way and feel completely estranged and isolated. Attention span is minimal, coherence of thought lost, and learning grossly impaired. Severe language disturbances may be evident (Lerner and Burns, 1978).

Marijuana and Hashish.   Marijuana is a mild hallucinogen that has been used as an intoxicant in Eastern cultures for thousands of years. It found its way to North Africa, Europe, South and Central America but was little used in the United States until after 1920. Marijuana is derived from the leafy portion of *Cannabis sativa,* the hemp plant, which is now widely distributed across the world's temperate and tropical areas. The major psychoactive element of the plant, tetrahydrocannabinol, is concentrated in its resin, which is found in the plant's flower tops. The leaf contains less of the resin and the fibrous portion of the plant the least of all. Marijuana is prepared from the leaf, hashish or hash from the flowering portion. The greater concentration of resin in the hashish explains why it is likely to be anywhere from three to ten times more potent than marijuana. In large doses marijuana itself can cause reactions that resemble those of the stronger hallucinogens.

Recent data relating to marijuana's effect on health indicate impairment of lung function to an even greater extent than by ordinary cigarette smoking. Extensive use may also impair reproductive functioning through diminished sperm count and motility in males, and interference with ovulation in females (Petersen, 1980). Smoking the amounts of marijuana commonly used is detrimental to driving, whether performance is measured in laboratory studies or on city streets (Klonoff, 1974). This impairment in driving skill by marijuana has now been firmly established as contributing to fatal accidents (Sterling-Smith, 1976). Marijuana has also been shown to interfere with immediate memory and with a wide range of intellectual tasks. There is also the possibility that classroom performance may be impaired by marijuana.

SUMMARY

Alcohol is the most common drug of abuse in most segments of society. There is no standard pattern in the development of alcoholism and no standard alcoholic personality. Some evidence suggests a genetic predisposition to alcoholism. Research has revealed that within three years of the onset of a drinking problem, one-fifth of the people have solved it and are functioning well again socially and physically.

The barbiturates, which are sedatives and physiologically addictive, and the amphetamines, which are stimulants and psychologically addictive, are both dangerous to the body and mind. The narcotics too are powerfully addictive, making it difficult to treat abuses. Heroin addicts do not remain long in therapeutic communities, and methadone itself is addictive. The British system that allows clinics to dispense free heroin to addicts may be the best means of caring for them.

Of the psychedelic drugs, a newer one on the street, phencyclidine or angle dust, is a menace. It has been directly implicated in violence and murder. Research on marijuana, the most widely used hallucinogen, has shown that its effects on behavior are as dangerous as those of alcohol.

ANXIETY, SOMATOFORM, AND DISSOCIATIVE DISORDERS

The anxiety, somatoform and dissociative disorders were formerly grouped together in the diagnostic category **neurosis.** As our description of cases in this grouping will show, however, their symptoms are so heterogeneous that it is doubtful that anything useful is accomplished by treating them as though they were a single disorder. In the sections to follow, we have attempted to provide a description of the essentials of these disorders with very brief case histories. The reader should understand, however, that the cases were very carefully selected in order to make the intended points. Single cases seldom illustrate the disorders this clearly and dramatically.

Anxiety Disorders

Panic Disorder. The symptoms of **panic disorder** are recurrent panic (anxiety) attacks—a sudden, intense, and pervasive apprehension and uncontrollable dread; labored breathing, heart palpitations, and chest pains; dizziness, faintness, and sweating; and feelings of unreality and impending doom. An attack may last for minutes, more rarely for hours. Panic disorder may be limited to a single brief period lasting several weeks or months, recur during several periods, or become chronic. When anxiety is a more generalized and persistent tenseness and apprehensiveness and lasts continuously for at least a month, it is called *generalized anxiety disorder.*

A forty-six-year-old businessman who was having serious difficulties in his work and marriage described his anxiety attack.

I was almost down to work, close to the White House on Pennsylvania Avenue. I got caught in some traffic. Suddenly I began to shake all over. I felt something awful was going to happen. I couldn't go on. . . . I wanted to hide my face in my arms. My chest hurt. I was afraid to drive. . . . I got a policeman to call up a friend to come down. He drove me home. I thought I was dying. . . . I've gotten afraid to drive downtown by myself now and I feel I want to have someone with me (Laughlin, 1967, pp. 91–92).

Obsessive-Compulsive Disorder. The principal symptoms of **obsessive-compulsive disorder** are constantly recurring, often absurd ideas, called **obsessions,** and impulses to perform some specific act, called **compulsions.** These actions may be quite simple mechanical movements or complex rituals such as repetitive hand washing. Efforts to resist performing the compulsion heighten anxiety.

A large jewelry firm regularly found one or two of their more perfect diamonds missing at periodic inventories. For a considerable period of time these irregular and seemingly inconsistent losses remained unaccountable. Finally, however, the recurring losses were traced to one of their most devoted and trusted diamond experts. He had not stolen them for himself. His rationale for their appropriation was most interesting and unique. The expert had developed such a tremendous obsessive need for perfection that he simply could not stand an imperfect stone. A diamond *must* be "just-so." As a result, when a customer occasionally brought in a chipped gem for resetting, or an imperfect one, he simply replaced it with a perfect stone from the firm's extensive stock, and threw away the poor or damaged diamond brought in by the customer (Laughlin, 1967, p. 335–336).

Phobic Disorders. A **phobic disorder** is a fairly common reaction in which the individual has a pathological but persistent and irrational fear of an object, activity, or situation that is not inherently dangerous. The person may show intense panic even in anticipation of confronting the feared object. The most common phobias are simple, specific phobias, of dogs, snakes, insects, mice, of closed spaces and of heights. Agoraphobia, fear of being alone and in public places, and social phobia, fear of situations in which the individual faces scrutiny by others, can be incapacitating and restrict daily living.

An eighteen-year-old woman had been given strict "moral training" concerning the evils of sex, and she associated sex relations with vivid ideas of sin, guilt, and hell. This basic orientation was reinforced when she was beaten and sexually attacked by a young man on her fifteenth birthday. Nevertheless, when the young man she was dating kissed her and "held her close," it aroused intense sexual desires—which were extremely guilt arousing and which led to a chain of avoidance behaviors. First she stopped seeing him in an effort to get rid of her "immoral" thoughts; then she stopped all dating; then she began to feel uncomfortable with any young man she knew; and finally she became fearful of any social situation where men might be present. At this point her life was largely dominated by her phobias, and she was so "completely miserable" that she requested professional help (Coleman, Butcher, and Carson, 1980, p. 221).

Somatoform Disorders

In **somatoform disorders** there are complaints of bodily symptoms that suggest a physical disorder. **Conversion disorder,** formerly called *hysterical neurosis, conversion type,* is an example. The serious physical ailments of conversion disorder—blindness, deafness, mutism, seizures, tics, anesthesias, motor paralysis—suggest neurological diseases but have no demonstrable organic or physiological base and are assumed to be an expression of psychological conflict or need. The incidence of these disorders appears to be declining.

A doctor was called to examine a rancher's adolescent daughter who had lost the use of both legs. The neighbors attributed [her disability] to an epidemic condition

A person's phobic fear of enclosed places may cause him or her to panic when entering a closet or small room.

which was raging through the ranch animals, but her parents knew this explanation to be untrue. While their daughter was in the house alone one afternoon, a male relative had come in, embraced her, and then attempted rape. The young girl screamed for help, her legs gave way, and she fell to the floor. The man fled. The mother, returning from an errand moments later, found her daughter on the floor. Efforts to help her stand were fruitless, and she was carried to her bedroom. Medical examinations revealed no organic basis for the paralysis which lasted several weeks (Cameron, 1963).

Dissociative Disorders

The **dissociative disorders,** which are relatively uncommon, involve some temporary change in consciousness, such as loss of memory for the past. In **psychogenic amnesia,** for example, there is the sudden inability to recall significant personal information accompanied by severe memory failure. Such memory loss is not caused by organic factors or simple forgetting. When the reaction does occur, it is often an object of attention in the media because of its intense, dramatic quality. Jules Masserman (1961) reported the case of Bernice L., who disappeared from her home and four years later was found in the college town of her youth, living under a different name and identity. She had lost all her memory of her previous life. Under treatment this patient gradually regained her memory and was able to provide the background for her **psychogenic fugue,** her sudden travel away from her home.

> Her parents were "fantastically religious." They fought constantly and accused each other of infidelities so often that the patient questioned her own legitimacy. Faced with this worry and subjected to general mistreatment, the patient, in her misery, sought comfort from an older sister. Tragically, this sister died when Bernice was seventeen years old, and she was left unconsolable.

> The patient entered college to prepare herself for a lifetime as a missionary. Her roommate, Rose P., a warm-hearted and gifted young woman, introduced her to people, guided her to new interests, and encouraged her to develop her skill as a pianist. Bernice fell in love with Rose's fiancé, but he ignored her, married Rose, and the couple moved to Canada. Following this loss, Bernice suffered a severe depression and she left the University for a brief period.

> Upon graduation, Bernice entered into a loveless marriage with a minister. They spent six unhappy years in missionary outposts in the Far East and then returned, with their two children, to begin an unbearable life in a small community where the parishoners imposed impossibly rigid moral standards on the pastor and his family. Gradually, Bernice began to daydream of her college days, finding her sole satisfaction in her memories of her friend Rose.

> When the patient was thirty-seven years old, her younger and favorite child fell ill and died. On the following day the patient disappeared; her family searched frantically for her but to no avail.

> Four years later Bernice was recognized by someone who had known her in college, and she was reunited with her family. In the course of her treatment, Bernice recollected that when in the college town, she had thought that her name was Rose P. She had begun to earn her living playing and teaching the piano. Within two years she had become the assistant director of a conservatory of music.

> Bernice's husband proved unexpectedly understanding and cooperative, and she eventually readjusted to a fuller and more acceptable life under happily changed circumstances (adapted, pp. 35–37).

Multiple personality, in which a person takes on two or more distinct and separate personalities, is a relatively rare dissociative disorder. Each personality is independent of the other, yet each is a reasonably stable one with its own thoughts and feeling. One of the personalities is usually dominant over the others. The other self is usually quite aware of the behavior of the dominant

Chris Sizemore and her painting "Three Faces in One." The most famous case of multiple personality is that of Chris Sizemore, three of whose personalities were portrayed by Joanne Woodward in the film *The Three Faces of Eve.* The first Eve, Eve White, was a retiring and gently conventional figure. Eve Black, the second Eve, was a devil-may-care, irresponsibly erotic individual. The third "Eve," Jane, was a mature, resourceful, and capable person. With Jane's emergence in about 1953, Chris seemed to have found a good personal adjustment, but such was not the case. Chris's dissociative disorder was based on a deep-seated fear of death; it took the form that it did because several childhood experiences had suggested to her that a single individual can be more than one person. Nine personalities had taken over her body before Eve Black did. As time passed, others appeared, until there had been twenty-two in all. It was some twenty years after her "Eves" before continued therapy and family support gave Chris a single, stable personality. *I'm Eve,* by Chris Sizemore and Elen Pittillo, tells Chris's story.

self, but the dominant personality may remain unaware of the activities of its lesser partner or partners.

One case of multiple personality became evident when a twenty-seven-year-old black man, Jonah, was admitted to a university psychiatric hospital after prolonged complaints of severe headaches. These headaches lasted for varying periods of time, and during them Jonah was unable to "remember things." Three weeks before his hospital admission, the patient had attacked his wife with a butcher knife, chasing her and his three-year-old daughter out of the home. Although the patient could not recall these events, his wife reported that during such episodes of violence, the patient referred to himself as Usoffa Abdulla, son of Omega. The patient's history contained many such acts of violence. While a soldier in Vietnam, he had suffered a lapse and fired his gun wildly in all directions until he was subdued. These and other episodes had led to his honorable discharge for medical reasons.

The ward physician in the university hospital noticed that each of the patient's lapses of memory was accompanied by a marked personality change. To the psychiatrist's surprise, one of four separate and distinct personalities would appear, each bearing a different name.

Jonah, the "square," was the primary personality, a shy, sensitive, conventional, fearful individual who appeared confused and whose emotional responses were shallow.

Sammy, the "lawyer," claimed to be aware of the other personalities but knew Jonah best. He was the rationalist, intellectual, legalistic, and capable always of talking his way out of trouble. This personality had emerged when Jonah was six years old, after Jonah's mother and stepfather had fought violently and she had stabbed her husband. When the family was finally reunited, Sammy emerged, announcing to both parents that their irresponsible behavior was bad for their children and urging that they never fight in front of them again. Jonah reported that from that day onward he had never again witnessed a fight between his parents.

King Young, the "lover," claimed that he appeared whenever Jonah was unable to "make out" with women. Pleasure-oriented, King proved to be a ladies' man who was incapable of taking "no" for an answer to his demands. King had also appeared when Jonah was six or seven years old. Jonah's mother had in those years taken pleasure in dressing him in girl's clothes, which had confused him about his sexual identity. When in first grade Jonah had expressed confusion over the identities of Jerry and Alice in the stories in his school reader, King had emerged to "set Jonah straight." Ever since then, King indicated, he had looked after Jonah's sexual interests.

Usoffa Abdulla, the "warrior," was a "god" who appeared briefly whenever

Figure 16.1
Self-portraits of each of Jonah's multiple personalities.

Jonah was unable to defend himself physically. Usoffa, cold, belligerent, and protective, first came on the scene when Jonah, then nine years old, was attacked by a gang of white children who beat him for the "sport" of it. Terrified, Jonah thought it was his end and lost consciousness. Usoffa emerged and fought so viciously that he almost killed two of his attackers. From that moment on, Usoffa exercised a protective watch over Jonah.

Through therapy the personalities of Jonah were encouraged to fuse together as a single individual, *Jusky,* a name made up of the first letters of all four Jonah's names. Unfortunately, Jusky turned out to be, if anything, more disturbed than any of the earlier personalities (Ludwig et al., 1972).

Self-portraits were drawn by each of the four personalities (Figure 16.1). The psychiatric investigator (Ludwig et al., 1972) concluded that their separate functionings may have been a more effective way of handling the patient's problems. Four heads, he suggested, may be better than one.

The Roots of Anxiety

Most psychologists agree that much of the behavior just described is learned during the early years of childhood. The roots appear to lie in the conflict between powerful drives and the anxiety aroused by their expression. Sexual expression versus sexual inhibition, aggression versus fear of retribution, and a striving for autonomy and independence as opposed to being compliant and dependent (page 312) are important anxiety-inducing conflicts faced by children. Their parents are also making multiple and particularly heavy demands of them: cleanliness training, toilet training, self-feeding, delay of immediate gratifications, achievement pressures, control of sexual and aggressive behavior. Yet such socializing experiences are the typical pattern of our society. Most children are subjected to these demands. Why then do some acquire the burdens of disordered behavior, whereas others remain free of such symptoms?

Two factors appear to be particularly critical, parental child-rearing attitudes and individual vulnerability. Two forms of early parental attitudes seem to be the most important. Either childhood tendencies are excessively indulged, with minimal emphasis on growing up, or they are excessively suppressed, with the expectation that the child can grow up all at once. The slow learnings that result in channeling or renunciation are minimized or ignored.

The second factor, individual vulnerability, has its locus in the child. Children differ in their susceptibility to threat and frustration. Such predispositions are basic factors in anxiety arousal, although it is not entirely clear to what extent this is determined by temperament and to what extent it is determined by the long-term stresses provided by living with inadequate parents. At any rate, it appears that faulty child-rearing practices focused on a vulnerable child and poor parental models form the basis for maladaptive personality formation.

Symptom Selection

A more specific question remains. How do the specific forms of disordered behavior develop? Why a phobia rather than an obsession? Why amnesia rather than an effort to control anxiety or undo guilt by compulsive hand washing? The answers to such questions can be only speculative, but again we are probably safe in suggesting that a nature-nurture interaction is involved (Klein, 1981). The typical makeup of the obsessional individual may help to clarify this point.

The symptoms of the obsessional person are intellectual. The obsessional person is essentially a thinker, meticulous and rigid, but a thinker nonetheless. One young widow summed up her experiences with a dating service by describing an obsessional "neurotic" she had met.

> He had to count everything, all the time. His small change, the number of cars parked in a street, how many people there were in a room—just everything. Most of the time he couldn't talk, he was that busy counting (Godwin, 1973).

Counting is an intellectual activity. To make effective use of a defense of obsessive overintellectualization requires intelligence in a way that many other symptoms do not. Because intelligence is, in part, a genetically determined trait, it can be viewed as an inherited component that can contribute to an obsessive-compulsive disorder.

It seems likely that nurture plays a greater role in the development of such disorders. In fact, it is common to treat the "neuroses" as learned disorders. In cases of maladaptive behavior like this man's counting, it is common to find that the response serves to reduce anxiety. If we could look back into the man's history, we would probably be able to find the situations in which counting was first used successfully to counteract anxiety. Now, whenever anxiety threatens to overwhelm him, perhaps when dating, he begins to count.

There is reason to believe that child-rearing practices have something to do with symptom selection. Obsessive-compulsive people tend to have had meticulous, perfectionistic parents of middle-class professional backgrounds. These parents have been described as overambitious for their children, demanding achievements that are appropriate to a later stage of development. Given this background, we can conjecture about the familial factors that predispose an individual toward an obsessional disorder. The first would be the role played by the parental model. Through modeling the child copies the responses of the parents, but usually without the appropriate discriminative ability that is necessary to keep the behavior from becoming a parody of the original model. Imitation is an easy and effortless way for children to acquire a variety of responses, including the disturbed behavior of the parental model.

There is the factor of selective reinforcement to be considered. Middle- and upper-class professional parents tend to reward their children for intellectual achievement, for problem solving by reflection as opposed to action, for verbal skills rather than for motoric ones, and for the inhibition of behavior rather than the expression of impulsive acts. Thus for the child from such a family background, the aggressive and sexual impulses of childhood are more likely to be displaced into efforts at orderliness, meticulousness, ritualistic behavior, and overintellectualized rumination. Extended to disorder in the obsessional person, hostility and sexuality may take the form of plaguing and distressing thoughts—not acts—of anger or promiscuity.

SUMMARY

The concept of neurosis in psychiatric classification has now been supplanted by several new categories, anxiety, somatoform, and dissociative disorders. The behavior covered by these categories consists of exaggerated symptoms that presumably serve to modulate and prevent the arousal of anxiety. This means that the disordered behavior is learned in situations that arouse distress and is maintained and strengthened by the extent to which it successfully reduces anxiety. Many types of behavior can be reinforced in this manner, including the avoidance of feared objects or situations—phobic disorder; ruminative thoughts or repetitive actions—obsessive-compulsive disorder; physical complaints that lack an organic basis—conversion disorder; loss of memory and flight from familiar surroundings—psychogenic amnesia and psychogenic fugue; and the like.

An interaction of environmental and genetic factors probably causes these disorders. Although psychologists have tended to emphasize social learning and operant conditioning in the acquisition of behavior, a more basic predisposition of the individual could explain why he or she is more likely to develop a certain disorder.

ANTISOCIAL PERSONALITY DISORDER

The personality disorders make up a heterogeneous category covering inflexible and maladaptive personality traits. DSM-III lists a number of personality disorders (see Table 16.1); they are generally recognizable by adolescence or earlier and continue throughout most of adult life, although they are often tempered by time and become less obvious in middle and old age. A major personality disorder, **antisocial personality disorder,** is described here in detail.

The antisocial personality has a long-term history of disruptive behavior that brings injury to others. In childhood, lying, fighting, stealing, promiscuity, and running away can be early signs of the disorder. In adulthood, the same pattern of behavior is retained. The individual is unable to keep a job, to plan ahead, to be a good parent. Personal relations are generally poor; the individual cannot sustain close and meaningful contacts with others. *Sociopathy* and *psychopathy* are other psychiatric terms for this pattern.

A Typical Case History

Several years ago *The New York Times* published a story that can stand as an illuminating case study of the antisocial personality.

A thirty-four-year-old man who had tried to extort more than $300,000 from TWA after hijacking one of its jetliners failed to be convicted because of a hung jury. The skyjacker had had a long history of crime. He had robbed seven banks, had forged thousands of dollars in checks, pulled off a $100,000 jewel heist in the Bahamas, had been arrested at least twenty times for major criminal acts, but had spent less than two years in jail.

A singular achievement! How did he manage to do it? By repeatedly assuming the mantle of a multiple personality, the skyjacker had recurrently fooled psychiatrists and psychologists who were required to testify at his trials. Basically, he asserted, he was a sane, honest man whose mind was repeatedly taken over by a sinister and criminal alter ego. The crimes were committed by this criminal personality and were not of his own doing.

The skyjacker's past was an interesting one. Both his father, who was a naval officer, and his mother, who came from an old New England family, drank heavily. The father was later dismissed from the Navy for running a brothel in the Caribbean area. The parents were subsequently divorced and the young man, then eleven years old, went to live with his father and stepmother, who threw him out of the house when the father died. The boy, then fifteen, moved into a brothel euphemistically called the "House of Love" and began his long criminal career. But in most cases he avoided criminal prosecution by being sent to a mental hospital from which he equally promptly escaped. At his trial four of six psychiatrists testified that he was mentally ill, the other two indicating that he was sane and "malingering."

Under the intriguing title *The Mask of Sanity* (1976), Hervey Cleckley produced a classic volume on the behavior of antisocial personalities. In it he listed the following characteristics of this disorder. (1) The behavior of these individuals is impulsive, destructive, and inadequately motivated; (2) they lack conscience, disregard truth, and have no sense of responsibility; (3) there is a lack of depth in their feelings, which makes them unable to form meaningful relationships with others; (4) they are unable to learn from experience, even when punishment has followed their actions; (5) and yet many psychopaths are able to maintain a pleasant and even impressive exterior (Bootzin and Acocella, 1980).

Etiology

The origins of antisocial personality or sociopathy are not at all clear. The term sociopathy places emphasis on its possible social basis. What are these social-developmental roots? Clearly implicated are faulty parental models. Case histories of sociopathic individuals often reveal parental behavior that is antisocial— a mother's alcoholism, a father's physical abuse of the child, a family history of thievery and crime. Often cruel abuse and physical neglect are noted, providing the child with occasions to observe and later to imitate coldness, unconcern, brutality, a lack of involvement, and a rejection of others. Some of this neglect and brutality is apparent in the case history of Derek, an example of sociopathy in the making.

Derek, a seven-year-old boy of averge intelligence, was referred for "uncontrollable and aggressive behavior, enuresis and encopresis [lack of bladder and bowel control], speech and sleep disturbances, sexual offenses, jealousy, truanting, stealing, lying, wandering at night, exaggerated masturbation, destructiveness and retardation at school."

Derek's behavior rightfully earns him the dubious distinction as one of the worst delinquents seen at the tender age of seven in a large-scale British study. Here are some of the behaviors that were recorded by the investigators.

Derek is the oldest of two children; his sister aged four is the object of his cruelty and aggressiveness; he expresses his hatred of her and she, in turn, is terrified of him. The mother reports that he constantly interfered with the sister and at age five achieved sexual intercourse with her which has been repeated several times. Mother has frequently found the children in bed together despite her reproofs. Derek openly masturbates day and night. He remains incontinent even at age seven. He has been unresponsive to toilet training. He is still unable to dress himself. He began to talk with a stutter at age three and it has persisted. Because he was difficult, he was placed in a foster home by a child guidance clinic, but was so troublesome he could not be kept there. At the age of four he ran away from home, he has set fires in hotels on several occasions, has stolen, and although professing a liking for animals, he has stomped two cats to death and has been cruel to other pets. He is a sleepwalker who is beset with night terrors. Sent to school at age four and a half, he refused to learn, truanted, and was the victim of attacks by other children. His teachers report that he seems far away. He performs poorly in all subjects despite his average IQ, although he seems better adjusted at school than in the home. He has peculiar mannerisms, used only his left hand, interrupts conversations to describe "incomprehensible fantasies and to play weird games." Mother reports that Derek never shows his feelings; he has never wanted affection, kicking her away from him even when very young.

The family picture provides a bleak spectacle. The mother, who is thirty years old, is described as "apathetic and tearful." She married Derek's father at twenty-one and he deserted her when Derek was six years old. Only poverty forced her to return to him when her children were younger. Mother is fatalistic about Derek. Her controls are feeble and inconsistent. Derek has beaten her and remains defiant. At present mother lives with a truck driver, a friendly man whom she would like to marry, but cannot do so without divorcing her husband. The mother wants Derek sent away because she fears that he will be perverted sexually like his father. Derek's father, thirty-one, is a gardner who was dismissed from the army for beating other soldiers. Mother describes him as "sex-mad." He has been brutal, jealous, sexually demanding and likely perverted. While mother was in the hospital having Derek, father impregnated a young girl in the neighborhood. Derek "idolized" his father who treated him severely (he was frequently beaten for masturbation) and preferred the younger sister. The father's family history shows a background of epilepsy, mental retardation, and psychosis.

Treatment of Derek was attempted at a clinic for children but his attendance was irregular because of the chaotic home conditions and the rejection of a treatment plan by the parents. Foster home placement has been achieved with only moderate success. He was brought to juvenile court for stealing and destructive behavior and remanded to the care of education authorities until he is eighteen (Bennett, 1960, adapted, pp. 247–250).

The outlook for Derek seems bleak. But can we be certain that Derek is on the path to adult psychopathy? That he appears headed in this direction is suggested by a classic follow-up study of deviant children by Lee Robins (1966). The children of this study—524 of them—had been seen in a psychiatric clinic as youngsters, some thirty years earlier. Many had been seen because of antisocial behavior, others for different forms of behavior disorders. When traced in their adult life, many showed signs of very poor adaptation, including sociopathic behavior. From her study Robins developed a set of childhood predictors of antisocial behavior in adulthood. We have introduced numbers into the Robins quotation as a count of the criteria against which to apply Derek's history by the age of seven.

Robins's Criteria

If one wishes to choose the most likely candidate for a later diagnosis of sociopathic personality from among children appearing in a child guidance clinic, the best choice appears to be: [1] the boy referred for theft or aggression who has shown [2] a diversity of antisocial behavior in many episodes, [3] at least one of which could be grounds for a Juvenile Court appearance and whose antisocial behavior involves him with [4] strangers and organizations as well as with [5] teachers and parents. With these characteristics more than half of the boys appearing at the clinic were later diagnosed sociopathic personality. Such boys had a history of [6] truancy, [7] theft, [8] staying out late and [9] refusing to obey parents. They [10] lied gratuitously, and [11] showed little guilt over their behavior. They [12] generally were irresponsible about being where they were supposed to be or [13] taking care of money. They were [14] interested in sexual activities and had experimented with [15] homosexual relationships (p. 157).

Measured against these fifteen criteria, Derek's score would be 14, a bleak portent of things to come.

Genetic and Environmental Factors in the Antisocial Personality. The history of Derek illustrates certain familial factors known to be associated with antisocial personality: parental violence, incapacity, inconsistency and indecision with regard to discipline, marital discord, maternal rejection, early separation from home, and a family history of psychopathology. This last factor of deviant history or defect in relatives raises anew the question of environmental and hereditary influences in psychopathology. Research suggests that hereditary factors may be quite important.

A study conducted in Denmark (Schulsinger, 1972) of the biological and adoptive relatives of children who were adopted early in life, and were diagnosed psychopathic when adults, provides some highly relevant data on the importance of genetic and environmental factors. A control group of nondisturbed adoptees was used for comparison purposes. The basic question asked in the study was this. For the two adoptee groups was there a greater proportion of deviance in the biological or the adoptive relatives? If the data indicated a higher incidence in the biological relatives as opposed to the adoptive relatives, it would suggest a genetic linkage, for the children were not raised by their biological parents. Were the reverse true, it would suggest the operation of environmental factors, for the adoptive parents were the primary caretakers of the adoptees. The results showed that the rate of psychopathy of biological parents was higher than that of adoptive parents for the index group. It was also higher than the rate of psychopathy of both biological and adoptive parents of the normal control adoptees (Table 16.2).

SUMMARY

A heterogeneous collection of inflexible and maladaptive personalities make up the personality disorders. Antisocial personality disorder, sometimes known as sociopathy or psychopathy, is one form of personality disorder that has received a great deal of attention. The symptoms of antisocial personality disorder include disruptive behavior that brings injury to others, lying, cheating, fighting, stealing, and sexual promiscuity. Recent findings seem to implicate hereditary factors, but depriving environments and disorganized families play a very important role as well.

Table 16.2 Psychopathic-Type Disorders in Biological and Adoptive Relatives of Adoptees with and without a Diagnosis of Psychopathy

Status of Adoptees	Relatives Showing Deviances, percent	
	Biological	**Adoptive**
Psychopathic	14.4	7.6
Nondisturbed	6.7	5.3

From Schulsinger, 1972.

AFFECTIVE DISORDERS

The term **affect** refers to the conscious, subjective aspect of an emotion or mood. Thus the **affective disorders** are disorders of emotion or mood. Mood refers to a pervasive and sustained emotion that colors the whole psychic life. A severe disturbance of mood may be felt as depression, elation, or alternation between the two. If the disturbance is extreme, there is a loss of contact with the surroundings. How debilitating such a disorder can be, even in a person of superb intellectual achievement, is seen in the following case of a depressive disorder.

A distinguished fifty-five-year-old college professor who had been a very productive and meticulous scholar began to ruminate about his past transgressions which were really quite minor in nature, such as taking a towel from a hotel room when a youth. Unable to concentrate and overwhelmed by guilt, he despaired that he would ever work again. He found himself unable to sleep as his anxiety and agitation mounted. He grew more depressed, talked of suicide and cried intermittently.

Increasingly worried about his threats to take his own life, his wife had him admitted to a private psychiatric hospital. To his therapist he repeated his assertion that his career was ended and nothing could be done for him. After a case consultation it was decided to institute a brief course of electric convulsive shock treatments [see page 560]. These were followed by a rapid recovery and return to his home and campus where he was able to resume his research, writing and teaching activities (confidential case history).

The young woman has tried to commit suicide a number of times.

Depression is so commonplace in our country that estimates of the size of the group of people prone to mild or moderate manifestations of these states range up to 20 to 25 percent of the adult population. A figure this large suggests that moods of depression are simply part of the normal human condition that includes "the blues" or being "down-in-the-dumps." At a more severe level there is a growing concern about our suicide statistics (cited in Davison and Neale, 1982).

- Every thirty minutes someone in the United States commits suicide.
- Three times as many men kill themselves as women.
- Three times as many women as men attempt suicide but do not die.
- Suicide ranks tenth as a leading cause of death among adults, second (accidents are first) among college students.
- Suicide rates are increasing for children and adolescents.
- Suicide rates among black and American Indian youth are more than twice those for whites.

Classification of the Affective Disorders

The affective disorders occur in episodic and chronic forms, as well as in an *atypical* one, which will not be discussed here. In an **episodic disorder** periods, or episodes, of disturbance last from a few days to several months. They may be separated by years of normal functioning, or they may recur more frequently. A **chronic disorder** is a sustained and long-lasting disturbance. In either form symptoms may consist of **mania**—a pattern of excessive activity, talkativeness, flight of ideas, inflated self-perceptions, grandiosity, and a rapidly changing mood; or **depression**—pervasive feeling of sadness, tearfulness, discouragement, hopelessness, loss of pleasure, motoric agitation or excessive slowness and retardation, a sense of personal worthlessness, and negative views of the self. In some cases, called **bipolar disorder,** both manic and depressive episodes occur. In this disorder the initial episode is usually a manic one, with subsequent manic and depressive episodes tending to be more frequent and of briefer duration than in the episodic form. The following case illustrates the cyclical mood swings of a patient diagnosed with a bipolar disorder.

Depression: sadness, hopelessness, and despair.

A thirty-eight-year-old woman was admitted to a state hospital for the first time, although since childhood she had had marked mood swings, some of which were of a psychotic nature. Her first depression at age seventeen prevented her from working. At thirty-three, pregnant with her first child, [she suffered a second] depressed episode. One month after the birth of the baby excitement seized her and she was hospitalized for a brief period. Sent to the seashore to recuperate, she took a hotel room for a night. The next day she signed a lease on an apartment and bought furniture for it, going heavily into debt.

She recovered and for two years functioned reasonably well until she again became overactive, spoke of countless business activities, pawned jewelry and wrote checks indiscriminately although she had no funds with which to cover them. She recovered after several months of hospitalization and resumed her life, but felt mildly depressed. One year later she again had a manic episode and in a single day purchased fifty-seven hats!

She has since been in and out of hospitals with sequences of severely manic and less severe depressive episodes. During one manic episode she became enamored of a physician and sent him the following telegram:

"To: You; Street and No. Everywhere; Place: the remains at peace! We did our best, but God's will be done! I am so very sorry for all of us. To brave it through that far. Yes, Darling—from Hello Handsome. Handsome is as Hand-

some does, thinks, lives and breathes. It takes clear air, Brother of Mine, in a girl's hour of need. All my love to the Best Inspiration one ever had."

At age fifty-nine this woman is now making an excellent adjustment in home and community. Her ill husband has needed her assistance and she has met these responsibilities admirably. Recurrent episodes of excitement and depression, however, remain a likely outcome (Kolb, 1977, pp. 455–456).

Origins of the Affective Disorders

When the affective disorders are more fully understood, it seems likely that a complex interactive explanation will emerge to take into account genetic vulnerability; significant early disheartening circumstances, such as loss of a parent in childhood (Brown, Harris, and Copeland 1977); stressful circumstances in adult life that overwhelm the individual's ability to cope, such as childbirth; physiological stressors, such as levels of particular biochemical substances; and specific detrimental aspects of personality, such as a pessimistic view of life or becoming quickly anxious under stress.

Twin studies show the importance of genetic factors. If one of a pair of identical twins develops a depression, the likelihood that the other twin will also be depressed has been estimated, in different studies, to range between 50 and 93 percent. The range for fraternal twins is 3 to 38 percent.

Several lines of evidence point to the importance of disrupted attachment and separation from a loved relative or friend. A study by Colin Parkes (1964) of more than 3000 psychiatric inpatients of various diagnoses revealed that patients whose psychiatric disorder followed within six months of a family member's death were more likely to develop an affective disorder. Research done by George Brown and Tirril Harris (1978) in London indicates that a major loss for women occurring nine months before the onset of psychiatric symptoms tended to precipitate a depressive disorder. Four specific factors were found to heighten vulnerability to depression: (1) loss of mother before the age of eleven, (2) presence at home of three or more children aged less than fourteen, (3) lack of a confiding relationship with a husband, and (4) lack of full- or part-time employment.

With regard to cognitive factors, evidence points to differences between depressive and nondepressive individuals, depressives having negatively distorted views of events. They are pessimistic and have a negative self-concept. Depressives tend to attribute negative outcomes to personal incompetence (Abramson et al., 1978). When performing a task requiring skill, depressed subjects fail to expect more of themselves on the basis of earlier success, whereas their expectations for other individuals are similar to those of controls (Garber and Hollon, 1980). Depressed subjects are also more likely than nondepressives to recall negative events (Lloyd and Lishman, 1975).

SUMMARY

The affective disorders are disorders of mood or emotion, the disturbance being so severe that it interferes with normal patterns of living. Affective disorders take several different forms. In episodic disorders the periods of disturbance are brief; chronic disorders endure for longer periods of time. Another dimension of classification concerns the type of mood change. Mania is characterized by extreme elation, depression by extreme sadness. In bipolar disorder manic and depressive phases alternate.

Twin studies have provided strong evidence for a genetic basis for the affective disorders. Other data implicate experiential factors such as loss of a mother, poor relationships with a spouse, and difficult situations of employment.

SCHIZOPHRENIA

Every year between 25,000 and 30,000 people enter public or private hospitals with a diagnosis of schizophrenia. In the course of a lifetime as many as one person in a hundred may develop the disorder. Schizophrenia is a malignant disorder with a presence that extends outward to the most distant parts of the world and ranges backward in time to antiquity. Historical records indicate that the disorder was recognized in ancient India as early as 1400 B.C. as well as in Greece, Rome, and other civilizations of antiquity.

As far back as the seventeenth century, a British anatomist, Thomas Willis, recorded observations of a large number of persons who, initially talented and even brilliant in childhood, deteriorated while still young. Such observations explain why the disorder was first called **dementia praecox.** "Dementia" indicated the deterioration of intellectual abilities; "praecox" referred to the early or precocious appearance of this disorder in the young. The term seemed firmly established when Emil Kraepelin used it in the fifth edition of his major text on psychiatry, published in 1899, but this acceptance was to be short-lived.

In 1911 a famous Swiss psychiatrist, Eugen Bleuler (1857–1939), published a classic volume, *Dementia Praecox or the Group of Schizophrenias,* in which he introduced the term **schizophrenia** because he did not see the disorder as terminating in dementia, but rather as one characterized by a "splitting off" of various types of mental or cognitive functions. The word *schizophrenia* combines two Greek words, *schizein,* to split, and *phren,* the mind. Unfortunately, this derivation makes it easy for lay persons to confuse schizophrenia with multiple personalities and to think in terms of Dr. Jekyll–Mr. Hyde cases of double identities. This interpretation is completely false. The split is not in terms of personal identities but rather in terms of inappropriateness of a function, such as emotion when linked to a thought. An example of this split is seen in a schizophrenic patient who describes a personal tragedy but without the signs of sorrow that one anticipates; or a patient may recount the manner in which he murdered his mother without any emotional expressiveness at all.

Clinical Criteria of Schizophrenia

DSM-III summarizes a number of general and specific characteristics of the schizophrenic disorders.

- First, there is a general deterioration from a previous level of functioning; individuals slip in self-care and in meeting their obligations in work and social relations. This is one of the cardinal characteristics of schizophrenia.
- Second, there are a number of typical, more specific, symptoms involving a variety of psychological processes.

Thinking. One of the fundamental symptoms of schizophrenia is disordered thinking, both in form and in content. Associations are disturbed; speech is rambling, incoherent, and disconnected; weird and unusual associations spill forth; new words, *neologisms,* are constructed to describe peculiar thoughts. The patient may be given to rhyme without reason. In some instances the rhyme dictates the association, producing a "clang association" readily observable even to the untutored, such as this greeting of a patient to a physician who walked through the ward: "Hi guy, my sty is in your eye."

Some patients report their awareness that *every* thought seems to generate an association, some of them related only by sound; other associations are markedly idiosyncratic and based solely on personal experience.

> I couldn't read [newspapers] because everything that I read had a large number of associations with it. I mean, I'd just read a headline, and the headline of this item of news would have . . . very much wider associations in my mind. It seemed to start off everything that I read, and everything that sort of caught my attention seemed to start off, bang-bang-bang, like that, with an enormous number of associations, moving off into things so that it became difficult for me to deal with, that I couldn't read (Laing, 1967, cited in Freedman, 1974, p. 335).

Patients sometimes believe that they have extraordinary cognitive powers—flashes of brilliant insight; a great gift for generating original, creative thoughts; a unifying system to provide greater coherence in thinking; "racing thoughts" that come so swiftly they cannot be sorted out. Other patients experience "slowed thoughts" which creep at a snail's pace. In still others there is an enveloping awareness that they can no longer control their thinking and that some external force must be responsible for such as extraordinary event.

An excellent example of the bizarre nature of schizophrenic thought is provided by a patient who had the delusion that he was God. Before hospitalization he had been going with a woman for many years but had never had sexual relations with her. Eventually, she turned to another man and became pregnant by him. When she informed the patient of this, the patient maintained that, because he was God, she must be the Virgin Mary and the pregnancy the Immaculate Conception (Rosen, Fox, and Gregory, 1972).

Affect. As you will recall, *affect* refers to emotion. Some schizophrenics have "flattened affect," others "inappropriate affect"; some show both types of emotionality simulaneously. *Flattened affect* refers to a shallowness or blunting of emotion so that situations that would normally be expected to produce an emotional response elicit only apathy from the patient. *Inappropriate affect* refers to an emotional response that is inconsistent with a situation. Although the patient may speak of some great tragedy, it is without the expected display of sorrow. A patient, the mother of three children, threw them from a bridge into the river below. Her explanation was that she wished to save them from having to live in a world of evil. In the hospital her manner was bland, her emotional reaction shallow; having saved her children, there was no need for grief. Because her tone was consistent neither with her situation nor her actions, we speak of her affect as inappropriate. The blandness of her response also indicates the blunting of her affect.

Perception. Perceptual disturbances take the form of **hallucinations,** perceptions of things that other people do not preceive. The most common hallucinations are auditory. Patients may hear their thoughts spoken aloud; they may hear voices arguing about them, referring to them in the third person; they may hear voices describing the patient's ongoing activities as they take place (Mellor, 1970).

Distorted perceptions may lead by stages to the development of a **delusion** or false belief. A normal perception is given a private meaning by the patient; the perception is then almost immediately elaborated into a delusion. For example, a young man in a boarding house, while having breakfast with his fellow lodgers, had a growing sense of unease that something frightening was about to happen. One of his companions pushed a salt cellar to him; as it moved forward, the young man suddenly developed the conviction that he had to return home to greet the Pope, who was going to visit his family to reward them (Mellor, 1970).

Other delusions take the form of a belief that some external agent is at work putting thoughts into the patient's mind, physically extracting them, or broadcasting them to others by means of television or mental telepathy. Other examples of delusions appear in the following paragraphs and in the section on subtypes of schizophrenia.

Self-Control. The schizophrenic patient may experience feelings or impulses to act or engage in actions that are seemingly imposed by an external power. Usually a delusion is used to explain the mechanism behind these events. When the patient carries on normal activity, he or she may perceive the self as a passive automaton commanded by another.

> A twenty-nine-year-old shorthand typist described her actions as follows: "When I reach my hand for the comb it is my hand and arm which move, and my fingers pick up the pen, but I don't control them. . . . I sit here watching them move, and they are quite independent, what they do is nothing to do with me. . . . I am just a puppet who is manipulated by cosmic strings. When the strings are pulled my body moves and I cannot prevent it" (Mellor, 1970, pp. 17–18).

Contact with Reality. Schizophrenic patients are often out of contact with the world. They are likely to be disoriented in time and place and without a sense of personal self. They are unable to tell what month or day it is, where they are or who they are, living instead in their own inner worlds. A young schizophrenic girl who had mislaid her violin case insisted that she must have swallowed it, in spite of assurances that it would not have been possible for her to do so.

Motor Activity. In severely chronic or acutely disturbed patients various forms of disturbed motor behavior may be evident. There may be a significant reduction in spontaneous activity. The patient may become stuporous, rigid, posturing, and stereotyped in the movements he or she makes. Mannerisms, grimacing, and readiness to hold to any position to which the patient is moved may be evident; pacing, rocking and immobility may be other characteristics of the patient's motor stance.

Subtypes of Schizophrenia

Certain of the symptoms just described were the basis of a classification of subtypes of schizophrenia that was once widely accepted. It is less so today, but the terms remain in common use.

This schizophrenic man indicates explicitly that he has withdrawn from contact with humankind and that he is out of touch with reality.

Simple Schizophrenia. The primary symptom of simple schizophrenics is their lack of emotions, interests, and activity. These people are often apathetic, withdrawn, and without conversation and interests. They daydream and spend their time alone in their rooms. **Simple schizophrenia** usually begins in adolescence and is so gradual in onset that families are not aware of the seriousness of the disorder. Some simple schizophrenics are never hospitalized; if they leave their families, they live out their lives as vagrants, drifters, tramps, and prostitutes. Others may be recognized as the town eccentrics, but because they do not disturb anyone, they are allowed to go their own ways unmolested.

Disorganized (Hebephrenic) Subtype. **Disorganized schizophrenia** has an early but gradual onset. It is characterized by inappropriate emotional re-actions—hebephrenic "silliness"—which consists of giggling, inappropriate laughter, and unexplained weeping; and flat, incongruous, or silly emotional expression. These patients have lively hallucinations and often have delusions of grandeur, but these are usually bizarre and fragmented. The patient often shows marked regression, soiling, and wetting. Withdrawal tends to accelerate and, when seen years later in the ward, the patient may have suffered profound disintegration of personality. With the advent of phenothiazine medication, however, the depth of such deterioration has been lessened.

Catatonic Subtype. **Catatonic** patients have periods in which they are stuporous and immobile and others in which they are highly excitable and seem under great "pressure of activity," or one or the other state may predominate. During the stuporous periods there may be posturings; the patient assumes a rigid, often uncomfortable position and resists attempts to be moved from it. When in this state, the catatonic reacts only to the most painful of stimuli. This is not to suggest that the patient lacks awareness of what is going on. In some cases catatonic patients have shown a remarkable memory for events that took place when they were in this state. The excited motor disturbances may take the form of pacing, ritualistic motions, repetitive and stereotyped actions. At other times such expressions of the psychosis may be verbal, with simple phrases and words being repeated over and over. Under the impact of the drug therapies, catatonia too has begun to disappear from the psychiatric scene.

Paranoid Subtype. The most impressive symptom of **paranoid schizo-phrenia** is the delusional system. In many instances these delusions are delu-sions of persecution. Patients believe that some person or group is out to get them. Voices may torment the patients or force them to unusual actions. By comparison with other schizophrenics, the thought processes of the paranoid schizophrenics are far more adequate. The basis for their thinking may be a little difficult to accept, but, if this is done, the rest of the argument can appear sensible. Paranoid thinking contrasts so sharply with the illogicality and rambling incoherence of other schizophrenic subtypes that some psychiatrists question whether the paranoid subtype should be included among the schizophrenias.

The prepsychotic personality of the paranoid patient is often that of a person who resents and distrusts others and is excessively suspicious and hostile. Such persons have been called "litigious characters." They often feel that they are being wronged; they may seek court action against others on the slightest provocation, or they may demand justice and retribution in situations in which others would not perceive injury at all. Onset is later in life than for the other subtypes.

Process Schizophrenia versus Schizophreniform (Reactive) Disorder. As we have seen, schizophrenia does not necessarily imply deterioration, for some patients recover from the disorder. Psychopathologists therefore began a search for the correlates of different outcomes. The results of these studies are so consistent that they have led to a typology aimed at distinguishing process from reactive schizophrenia.

In **process schizophrenia** development of the disorder is a long process. The slow, insidious onset usually begins in the late teens or the early twenties. When the life histories of such patients are reviewed, they show early signs of inadequacy in work, school, and in their sexual and social lives. The process of withdrawal follows, and the person grows apathetic and indifferent and finally must be hospitalized. Before the advent of drug therapy, prognosis for these patients was poor. Their average stay in the hospital was thirteen years. The use of drugs has changed all that, and many of these individuals can now be maintained in the community, often residing with their families or in halfway houses.

By contrast, the patient with **reactive schizophrenia,** called **schizophreniform** in DSM-III, reveals a good premorbid history. It is not unusual to find that the person has been a good student and even a class leader in high school. Such patients are usually married and have been able to raise and support a family. Their breakdown, when it takes place, comes later in life, often when they are in their thirties; occurs suddenly; and frequently is not preceded by evident stress. Most important of all, the response to treatment is good, the patient recovers and returns to family and community, and he or she may never be seen in the hospital or clinic again.

When these two types of patients are studied in the laboratory, the responses of the reactive patients are more similar to those of normal individuals than to those of their process counterparts. Furthermore, genetic studies suggest that hereditary influences are present in process cases, but less so, if at all, in the reactive ones. This has led recently to speculation whether they are forms of the same disorder or quite different disorders, an issue that remains unresolved at the present time. The data seem to tilt in the direction of viewing reactive schizophrenia as different from process schizophrenia, but having sufficient similarities to it to be thought of as a "schizophrenic spectrum disorder" (Kety et al., 1975).

Origins of Schizophrenia

As the most serious of the psychopathological disorders, schizophrenia has also been the most studied. Various lines of investigation converge on the conclusion that many different factors contribute to the condition. In order to understand schizophrenia, we will have to understand what these variables are and how they interact.

Genetic (Hereditary) Factors in Schizophrenia. Suppose that a family has one schizophrenic child. What are the chances that a second child in the same family will also be schizophrenic? If neither parent is schizophrenic, the probability is 9 to 10 percent. If one parent is schizophrenic, it is approximately 17 percent. If both parents are schizophrenic, the probability ranges between 36 and 46 percent. But, you may argue, with two parents so severely disturbed, family life would be so chaotic that an equally strong case for etiology could be made in favor of detrimental environmental influences. This is a good point and more powerful data are needed to deal with it. Some of these data have come from studies of twins.

Twin Studies. In one twin study fifty-seven schizophrenic index cases were drawn from a special twin register of people admitted consecutively over a sixteen-year span to one of the largest and most famous of England's psychiatric hospitals. Of this group twenty-four pairs were identical twins and thirty-three pairs were fraternal sets. Psychiatric diagnosis was checked by a distinguished assemblage of psychiatrists and psychologists. On this basis the investigators have reported an identical-twins **concordance rate** of 40 percent, compared to 10 percent for the fraternal pairs. The fact that concordance in the identical pairs fell far short of 100 percent is one of the best indicators we have that, although genes may be necessary, they are not apparently sufficient for the later development of schizophrenia. Environmental factors are also important in the etiology of the disorder (Gottesman and Shields, 1972).

Adoption Studies. The fact that genetic factors may at least partly determine who becomes schizophrenic is revealed by studies that find the disorder present in relatives of schizophrenics, but these studies are unable to separate out the possible influences of environmental factors. Because of this uncertainty a group of American and Danish investigators have studied the prevalence of schizophrenia in the biological and adoptive relatives of adopted children who later became schizophrenic (Kety et al., 1968, 1978). The reasoning behind the research design is straightforward. Adopted children secure their genetic endowment from the biological parents, their environmental influences from the adoptive parents. The younger the child at the time of adoption, the more striking will be the differentiation. By examining the siblings and half-siblings of thirty-three index cases, adoptees who later became schizophrenic; and the siblings and half-siblings of a closely matched age group of thirty-four control cases, adoptees who were never admitted to a psychiatric facility, the investigators were able to evaluate the relative weightings of hereditary versus environmental influence (Kety et al., 1975).

This study revealed that 21 percent of the biological relatives of the schizophrenic adoptees fell into a "schizophrenia spectrum," having such disorders as "acute schizophrenia," "uncertain schizophrenia," "inadequate personality," and "schizoid personality." Only 11 percent of the biological relatives of the controls fell into the schizophrenia spectrum. For the adoptive relatives the comparable figures were 5 and 8 percent, respectively.

Children Separated from a Schizophrenic Mother at an Early Age. Another method for studying the relative contributions of genetics and environment to schizophrenia is revealed by this question: Do children born to a schizophrenic parent but separated from their biological parents at an early age tend nevertheless to develop the disorder? This is the question asked in an extraordinary study by Leonard Heston (1966), who learned that a particular foundling home in Oregon had been used as a repository between the years 1915 to 1945 for infants who had been born to schizophrenic mothers confined in a neighboring state hospital. It had been hospital policy at that time to remove the baby from the hospitalized mother within three days and to place it either with members of the father's family or in the foundling home. Later the infants were placed for adoption or settled in foster homes. Heston decided to compare these children with a matched control group made up of children who had also been placed in the same foundling home, but whose mothers had not had an earlier history of institutionalization for a mental disorder. The search for these grown offspring took Heston into fourteen states and Canada. Whenever he located one of the individuals in either group, Heston sought permission to

Table 16.3 **Adult Statuses of Children Born to Schizophrenic and Nonschizophrenic Mothers and Removed from Their Care at Birth**

	Offspring of	
Adult Outcomes	Normal Mothers	Schizophrenic Mothers
Number (N)*	50	47
Males	33	30
Mean age	36.3	35.8
Schizophrenia	0	5
Mental deficiency (IQ < 70)	0	4
Sociopathic personality	2	9
Neurotic personality disorder	7	13
More than one year in a penal or psychiatric institution	2	11
Felons	2	7
Services in armed forces	17	21
Discharged on psychiatric or behavioral grounds	1	8
Mean IQ	103.7	94
Years in school	12.4	11.6
Total number of children	84	71
Total number of divorces	7	6
Never married; > 30 years of age	4	9

* Totals greater than N are possible because more than one outcome may have applied to the individuals studied.

Adapted from Heston, 1966; Heston and Denney, 1968.

interview the person and to administer both an intelligence and a personality test (MMPI).

The results of the study (Table 16.3) indicate how much more disturbed were the adjustments made in adulthood by the children whose biological mothers had been schizophrenic. Five of the children had already become schizophrenic, many had been arrested for committing thefts and assaults, and for others life had been a marginal existence—they held low-level jobs or had only seasonal employment, lived alone, and remained unmarried. Examining all these studies of genetic influence, we conclude two things: the case for the role of heredity in schizophrenia has been effectively demonstrated; and the role of environmental influences has also been demonstrated, particularly given the failure to find 100 percent concordance rates in identical twins.

Neurochemical Factors. If there is a genetic basis for schizophrenia, this means that there must be a biochemical correlate of schizophrenia, for genes exert their influences through biochemical processes. A noted neurophysiologist, Ralph Gerard, once expressed this view with a dramatic sentence: "No twisted thought without a twisted molecule." But the search for the "twisted molecule" for a long time seemed fruitless.

A revolution and new discoveries in the neurosciences portend the end of this frustrating search. The synapse, once thought to be simply an electrical junction for the transmission of nerve impulses, is now recognized as a biochemical "switch" (Chapter 3).

It is these chemical switches that can be affected by hormones, drugs, and metabolic processes and, in turn, affect behavior. Recent research indicates that the neurotransmitter dopamine may play an important role in schizophrenia. An excess of dopamine may be present in special tracts in the brain. Chlorpromazine, a powerful phenothiazine, may block the dopamine receptors, thus containing the would-be transmission of impulses by this excess dopamine—which accounts for the therapeutic action of this antipsychotic drug.

A similar story is unfolding in the study of depression, in which levels of a group of neurotransmitters, serotonin, norepinephrine, and dopamine, may be abnormally low. These neurotransmitters, which are monoamines, can be destroyed by an enzyme, monoamine oxidase (MAO). Drug treatments are directed to the inhibition of MAO or to increasing the life of the monoamines presented in the synapse. The antidepressant drugs that keep norepinephrine from being taken up again by the nerve cell after firing are called tricyclics.

Sociocultural Factors.   That schizophrenia and lower social-class status are highly correlated is unequivocal. In their classic study of social class and mental illness, August Hollingshead and Frederick Redlich (1958) located all residents of New Haven, Connecticut, who were in psychiatric treatment during a six-month period from May 31 to December 1, 1950. This group was compared with a control sample drawn from the same community. Subsequently, all patients were sorted into five social classes on the basis of available demographic data. They ranged from unskilled laborers and semiskilled workers (class V) to business and professional leaders who held highly prestigious positions in the community (class I). The data show that the frequency of schizophrenia in class V was almost nine times the rate in social class I and II. Some years later Barbara and Bruce Dohrenwend (1974) reviewed all the studies done throughout the world that had looked at the relationships between mental disorder and social class. In twenty-eight of thirty-three studies that reported social-class data, the lowest class had the highest rate of mental disorder. This relationship was strongest for schizophrenia, fifteen of seventeen studies; and personality disorder, eleven of fourteen studies. Another study of first hospitalization providing data on the relationship between mental disorder and education found that the most highly educated group, college graduates, were at only one-tenth the risk for schizophrenia that the group with the lowest level of education were (Eaton, 1980).

What can account for the higher incidence of schizophrenia found in the class V population? Some suggest that the answer lies in the stresses that accompany poverty; others reflect on the powerlessness of the poor. Still other theorists believe that lower-class living creates resistance to change, particularly disadvantageous in a rapidly changing technological society; distrust of others; lessened self-esteem; self-deprecation; and heightened anxiety and a belief, which is not unrealistic, that one's efforts bring very little reward (Kohn, 1972). Others have advocated an explanation based on "social drift"—schizophrenics drift to the slums through their own inadequacy. The problem with both positions is that there is not a universal pattern in all individuals who live in poverty. Individual variation is present in class V just as it is in the other social-class groups. Only through comparative studies of those in class V who resist schizophrenia and those who capitulate will there be a clearer answer to the question why a heavy loading of schizophrenia is to be found among the poor.

Models of Psychopathology: Two Contrasting Views
Schizophrenia provides a striking example of the range of views that surround issues of etiology in psychopathology. A marked contrast is provided by two orientations. One is the medical model with its emphasis on disease; the other

denies the disease concept and stresses the negative effects of labeling a person as mentally disordered.

The disease concept of mental disorder has roots that extend back to the previous century. Perhaps the most significant event in the history of mental illness was the identification of the cause of syphilis, a disease that had spread like wildfire over Europe in the fifteenth century, leaving in its wake thousands upon thousands of infected people. The symptoms of the later neurological and paralyzing part of the disease, which affects about 30 percent of those infected, were partly psychological: disturbed thinking, loss of memory, impaired judgment, inability to concentrate, disorientation in time and place, and apathy or violent rages. This disease, **paresis,** occurred the most commonly in thirty-five- to fifty-year-old men, when the syphilitic microorganism destroyed tissues of the brain. Imagine the difficulty of associating these symptoms with an act of sexual intercourse that took place decades earlier. The tie was finally established, however, in 1897, when Richard von Krafft-Ebing inoculated paretic patients with matter from syphilitic sores. They did not develop syphilis, indicating that they had been infected earlier. In 1905 the particular microorganism causing syphilis was identified. The discovery of the organic basis of paresis provided an analogy whereby diseases of the mind could be viewed as diseases of the brain, an interpretation that came to be called a medical model of psychopathology.

The **medical model** of psychopathology begins with the assumption that mental disorders are *diseases.* On this basis it is appropriate to refer to afflicted people as *sick* and to treat them as *patients.* The manifestations of their *illnesses* are *symptoms* which can be used to arrive at a *diagnosis.* Therapy requires the discovery and removal of the *cause* of the disease in order to *cure* it. The treatments of choice are the various somatic therapies. Supported by recent demonstrations that some forms of mental disorder have a neurochemical basis and are partly inherited, the medical model is currently very much in evidence. Not only paresis but also schizophrenia, the affective disorders, alcoholism, phobias, and learning disabilities are all considered by some clinicians to be physiological problems to be treated with drugs and, in some severe cases, electroconvulsive shock therapy.

Opponents of the medical model hold that mental illnesses are not medical diseases, but rather disturbances of behavior that develop in the same way that normal behavior develops. One point that the opponents of the medical model have in their favor is the one made earlier, that no sharp dividing line separates normal and abnormal behavior. The particular view of psychopathology that stands in direct opposition to the medical model, **labeling theory,** holds that disordered behavior is caused by the labels that are assigned to people. Call a person a schizophrenic and that individual will behave as a schizophrenic is expected to behave. Labeling theory clearly goes too far. Although labels may push people toward behavior that is consistent with them, there is too much evidence for physiological contributions to psychopathology for us to take labeling theory with complete seriousness.

Paul Meehl, a wise scholar and experienced clinician in the field of schizophrenia, tells an amusing story about his confrontation with an adherent of labeling theory when he was presenting a seminar in which he described his theory of the genetics of schizophrenia. He was interrupted in his talk by a faculty member who informed him that it was now well known that people behaved in a schizophrenic manner primarily because others had so labeled them. Ignoring some of Meehl's richer language, we quote part of his later comment to us.

Paul Meehl (1962) has identified three primary signs of schizophrenia: *cognitive slippage,* losing the semantic or syntactic rules of communication, such as in the statement "I'm growing my father's hair"; *anhedonia,* a lessening or loss of the zeal for life, of the ability to find pleasure; and profound *ambivalence,* in motives, thoughts, and feelings. Meehl believes that these conditions may stem from a basic and inherited neurological dysfunction, which makes the brain unable to integrate thoughts and emotions and which he calls *schizotaxia.*

I just stood there and didn't quite know what to say. I was thinking of a patient I had seen on a ward who kept his finger up his ass to "keep his thoughts from running out," while with the other hand he tried to tear out his hair because it really "belonged to his father." And here was this man telling me that he was doing these things because someone had called him a schizophrenic. What could I say to him?

Perhaps what one could say is that the labeling theorists have spoiled an important argument by carrying it to extremes. Their promotion of an oversimplified behavioral explanation of disordered behavior encourages rejection of the idea that behavioral factors are even important. It is essential to recognize that physiological and psychological influences both contribute to mental illness.

SUMMARY

The most malignant form of psychopathology, schizophrenia, is a deterioration of considerable psychological functioning, thought, emotion, perception, sense of self-control, contact with reality, and motor activity.

Depending on the symptoms that predominate, it is possible to identify several subtypes of schizophrenia: disorganized or hebephrenic subtype, marked by silliness, hallucinations, and bizarre delusions; catatonic subtype, stuporous, immobile postures and excited, ritualistic motion; paranoid subtype, delusional beliefs and systems. A different classification distinguishes schizophrenias on the basis of their onset, course, and outcome. Process schizophrenia is identified by a gradual onset, a poor premorbid history, a poor prognosis, and a probable hereditary component; reactive schizophrenia, or schizophreniform disorder, is identified by a sudden onset, a good premorbid history, a good prognosis, and probably little if any hereditary component. Reactive schizophrenia may be one of a spectrum of related schizophrenic disorders.

Studies of the concordance rates for identical and fraternal twins, adoption studies, and pedigree analyses of families with heavy concentration of schizophrenia strengthen the case for genetic transmission of the disorder. It is equally evident that environmental factors also pay a key role, but these have not as yet been unequivocally identified.

Still a different model looks to the larger social scene for explanations. The poor bear many burdens, including schizophrenia, which tends to be heavily concentrated in the lowest economic strata. The problem, as with other etiological theories, is how to explain the correlation between poverty and mental disorders. Does it lie in the drift downward of incompetent people, circumstances not uncommon in the life histories of schizophrenic patients? Or does poverty add unbearable stresses, disorganization, and a rootlessness that heighten the likelihood of disorder?

The discovery of a physical basis for the neurological disorder paresis fostered the development of a medical model of psychopathology that treats mental disorders as sickness and discounts the importance of experience. Labeling theory takes the opposite position. It rejects the medical model and maintains that mentally disordered people are merely acting out the behavior demanded by a diagnosis that has been assigned to them. Both of these positions are two simple and too extreme.

TO BE SURE YOU UNDERSTAND THIS CHAPTER

Here are the major concepts of the chapter in their approximate order of appearance.

Psychopathology	Diagnosis
Descriptive psychopathology	Reliability of diagnosis
Developmental psychopathology	Syndrome

Axis (in DSM-III)

Alcoholism

Sedative

Stimulant

Narcotic (opiate)

Methadone

Hallucinogen

Psychedelic

Neurosis

Panic disorder

Obsessive-compulsive disorder

Obsession

Compulsion

Phobic disorder

Somatoform disorder

Conversion disorder

Dissociative disorder

Psychogenic amnesia

Psychogenic fugue

Multiple personality

Antisocial personality disorder

Affect

Affective disorder

Episodic disorder

Chronic disorder

Mania

Depression

Bipolar disorder

Dementia praecox

Schizophrenia

Hallucination

Delusion

Simple schizophrenia

Disorganized (hebephrenic) schizophrenia

Catatonic schizophrenia

Paranoid schizophrenia

Process schizophrenia

Schizophreniform (reactive) disorder

Concordance rate

Paresis

Medical model

Labeling theory

TO GO BEYOND THIS CHAPTER

In This Book. For a complete understanding of the materials in Chapter 16, you will find it useful to review the discussions of behavior genetics (Chapter 2), neurotransmitters (Chapter 3), avoidance learning (Chapter 8), stress (Chapter 10), and personality testing (Chapter 13). The therapies discussed in Chapter 17 are also important related materials. **Elsewhere.** There are many excellent textbooks on psychopathology. All of them amplify considerably on the treatments presented in this chapter. Three that are widely used as textbooks in courses on abnormal psychology are James Coleman, James Butcher, and Robert Carson, *Abnormal Psychology and Modern Life* (sixth edition); Gerald Davison and John Neal, *Abnormal Psychology* (third edition); and Robert White and Norman Watt, *The Abnormal Personality* (fifth edition).

CHAPTER 17   THERAPY FOR BEHAVIOR DISORDERS

Every year in America a million or more students withdraw from college because of emotional problems, another one million people are actively schizophrenic, six million children are considered emotionally disturbed, ten million of us have alcohol-related problems, twenty million individuals suffer from some form of neurotic disturbance, and many millions more live at various times with mild to moderate feelings of depression. No wonder mental health "has been designated the country's number-one health concern" (Coleman, Butcher, and Carson, 1980). The question we face now is what to do about it.

History of the Mental Health Movement. We begin our presentation of the history of therapy by putting to rest a popular misconception. Anthropologists have discovered skulls, with holes in them, of Stone Age cave dwellers who lived some half a million years ago. Some of these holes show evidence of healing. On these bases others have proposed that the cave dwellers recognized psychopathology, that they had developed the theory that mental illness is caused by evil spirits who enter the skull. The holes are considered *trephine* holes, drilled into the heads of the victims of spirit possession to cure them of their madness by driving out the evil spirits. Popular as this speculation has become, the evidence is now recognized as too flimsy to warrant the conclusion. It is more probable, but also just speculation, that the holes were spear wounds acquired in battle or through ritualistic torture, or that the trephining was carried out to serve some other purpose (Maher and Maher, 1984).

Although we cannot accept the imaginative trephining theory, the history of the search for a cure for mental illness is quite an old one. Written records going back 3000 years or more reveal that psychopathology was recognized at least that long ago. By the fifth century before the Christian era, treatments consisting of potions brewed from various forms of plant life and procedures resembling psychoanalysis had been proposed.

For the last 750 years and more the treatment of the mentally disordered has oscillated between neglect and cruelty on the one hand and kindness and concern on the other. In the fifteenth and sixteenth centuries madness was considered evidence of witchcraft and devil possession. An alliance, even including "carnal relations," supposedly existed between the afflicted and the devil. Such interpretations were supported by the clergy and by political, academic, and scientific figures of the time. In 1487 two theologians wrote a notorious tract, *Malleus Maleficarum* ("The Witches' Hammer"), which became "the most authoritative and the most horrible document of the age" (Zilboorg, 1941). It gave license to inquisitors to denounce disturbed behavior as the

The thin and ragged inner rims of the skull holes are new bone, indicating that the individuals survived at least for a time their spear wounds or operations.

manifestation of witchery and sorcery. Any uncommon behavior, such as having hallucinations and delusions, was seen as a sign of witchcraft. This conclusion then justified the medieval mode of "treatment": burn the body and save the captive soul.

The recipients of these inhumane forms of "therapy" included, in addition to the mentally ill, people who belonged to certain religious groups, the herbalists who sometimes administered mind-altering potions, and those with various physical disorders. In America, the witchcraft trials that took place in Salem, Massachusetts, in 1692 claimed among their victims some individuals suffering from chorea, often called Saint Vitus's dance. This disorder, caused by alterations in the cerebral cortex that sometimes follow rheumatic fever, is marked by symptoms that might have suggested that a person was possessed by the devil—irritability, emotional instability, jerky and purposeless involuntary movements of the face and extremities, and explosive speech.

By the late eighteenth century a more humane view—madness as sickness—had emerged, and the treatment of the mentally ill turned to sanctuary and care. In the mid-nineteenth century a period of "moral," that is, humane, treatment began. Great emphasis was placed on the need for a warm relationship between physician and patient and for a cheerful and pleasant hospital milieu (Bockhoven, 1963). Wards were made homelike, and patients were treated as though they were members of a family. They were encouraged to rest and to participate in recreational activities in keeping with a view that mental disorder was brought on by being too preoccupied with work. Hospital discharge rates were high, and hospitals competed to see which had the best recovery rate.

With the tidal wave of immigration in the late nineteenth century, racial and ethnic prejudice arose and moral treatment went into decline. The term "foreigner" began to appear in state hospital reports and, on bases that were totally inadequate, psychiatry began to "explain" mental disorder as caused by genetic factors. With this formulation a mood of pessimism about recovery settled over the hospitals. "If madness is genetic, it cannot be cured." Slowly the mental hospitals expanded into monolithic institutions to house the "genetically disabled" who would be hospitalized for a lifetime. Far removed from population centers, the mentally disturbed suffered neglect by families and society. For the patient lost in the back wards of hospitals, the phrase "out of sight, out of mind" became tragically apt.

THE MENTAL PATIENT IN SOCIETY

The patient rolls of state mental hospitals continued to increase until the mid-1950s, when the introduction of the phenothiazines initiated a decline in their populations. In 1955 the resident population of these institutions was 559,000; in 1975 it was 191,000. Length of stay grew shorter and the mental hospitals began to empty, but not always to the advantage of the patients or their families.

Consequences of Early Discharge

By the 1970s the closing of mental hospitals was in full swing in this country. California was in the vanguard of the movement. As the state hospitals began to discharge, often prematurely, even the chronically disordered, a heavy burden was placed on the families of these patients. In the Los Angeles area Eliot Rodnick and Michael Goldstein (1974) of the University of California decided to look at what happened to children when their disturbed mothers were returned home after brief periods of hospitalization, still suffering the effects of an acute schizophrenic disorder.

The investigators selected a sample of twenty-seven schizophrenic women, all of whom were mothers, from the roster of a community mental health center. Each patient and a close relative were interviewed to secure data on the quality of the patient's adjustment before breakdown, on such indicators of competence as outside activities, participation in community organizations, friendship and leadership patterns with same-sex peers, dating, and a stable sexual attachment. The mothers were then divided into a *good premorbid* group, those having higher competence before the disorder, and a *poor premorbid* group, those having lower competence prior to the disorder.

The average period of hospitalization of the patients was ten days, after which they returned to their homes. At six months and one year following discharge,

Eliot Rodnick has studied the relation between family factors and schizophrenia, in its etiology and treatment.

This photograph of a ward in the North Carolina Mental Hospital is from an earlier decade. Treatment with phenothiazines has emptied many of these wards of their severely disturbed patients and even closed some of the hospitals.

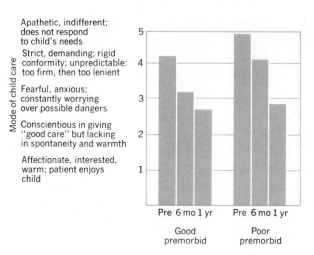

Figure 17.1
Ratings of maternal care of good and poor premorbid schizophrenic mothers after early release. The ratings, made on the basis of interview information, are for three periods: before hospitalization (pre) and for six months and one year after release. (Adapted from Rodnick and Goldstein, 1974.)

the investigators again held interviews with the patient and the relative. Clinicians made blind evaluations of maternal behavior, using a five-point scale that ranged from warm responsiveness to indifference to the child. The results (Figure 17.1) clearly indicated that, by comparison with the good premorbid mothers, those in the poor premorbid group were inferior caretakers, both before their hospitalization and six months after discharge. At the end of a year there were no significant differences between the groups of patients, all of whom appeared to be "conscientious and giving good care but lacking spontaneity and warmth."

The inferior early mothering of the poor premorbid group seems likely to have had negative consequences for their children. The poor premorbid mothers on the average were seven years younger than the more competent good premorbid mothers. This is to be expected because poor premorbid competence correlates with breakdown at an earlier age. The children of these younger mothers were also younger, of course. They were at an age when mothering is of particular importance. Unfortunately, these mothers could not meet their infant's needs because of their "apathy . . . indifference, neglect, or even anxious fearfulness during the baby's first year of life."

As we saw in the last chapter, there is a growing belief among researchers that a genetic factor figures in schizophrenia. Thus the babies whom these poor premorbid schizophrenic mothers tended may have already had a genetic vulnerability, to which was added the stress of inadequate caretaking. Both factors might contribute to the children's heightened risk of developing mental disorder in later life.

The Revolving Door

As mental hospitals began to close and patients went back into the community, only the most chronic cases remained behind. But investigators who checked new admissions data soon began to question the inference that the recovery rate had become remarkable. They detected a **revolving door** pattern of admissions and readmissions. Soon after the discharge trend began, a survey (Miller, 1966) of 1045 patients from the San Francisco-Oakland area revealed that 71 percent of them had returned to the hospital at least once during a five-year period following their release, and that 24 percent had been rehospitalized an average of 4.4 times.

A decade later other statistics proved equally discouraging. Rehospitalization rates for schizophrenic patients released to the community were 50 to 60 percent within just two years following discharge (Mosher, 1971; Talbot, 1974). In another follow-up study 34 percent of patients discharged from mental hospitals had to be readmitted within a year. Elsewhere there has been a 30 percent rise in the readmission rates to state and county hospitals (cited in Liberman, 1979).

Who Comes Back? Who Stays Out?

Studies conducted during the past two decades, most often with schizophrenics, have uncovered a number of factors related to the success these patients have in staying out of the mental hospital, once they have been released. The best indicator that a former patient will remain in the community seems to be a good work and social adjustment before the disorder. In general, schizophrenics with more adequate premorbid social and heterosexual adjustment tend to have shorter hospital stays, to recover more rapidly, to show greater initiative on discharge, to make decisions more readily, and to conform to the social rules of society. Such behavior increases the likelihood that they will be able to remain in the community (Evans et al., 1972; Evans, Goldstein, and Rodnick, 1973).

One of the most difficult problems for the patients who have been released from a mental hospital is obtaining the social support they need to help them function more adequately in the outside world. Here the role of the family is critical, and it has been studied and clarified by a team of British investigators (Brown, Birley, and Wing, 1972; Leff, 1976; Vaughn and Leff, 1976).

In one investigation of male schizophrenic patients who had been released from mental hospitals, a surprising finding was an unexpected relationship between adjustment outside the hospital and the patient's type of living arrangements. Severely disturbed behavior was reported for 30 percent of the patients who were living with their families, but for only 11 percent of the patients who were living alone. Half of the first group, but only 30 percent of the second, were readmitted to the hospital within five years after discharge. Through an intensive interview one factor responsible for this striking difference was finally determined to be the intensity of the emotional atmosphere in the family to which the patient had returned. Hostility, censure, and critical comments about the patient reflected the family's emotional intensity and were the key indicators that a patient might return to the hospital.

Families were rated on a dimension of **expressed emotionality** (EE) covering these aspects of family atmosphere. When these ratings were related to relapse rate, it was found that 59 percent of the patients from high-EE homes returned to the hospital compared to 16 percent of those from low-EE homes. Additional interviews indicated that a great deal of emotionality had prevailed in the homes of relapsed patients even before their hospitalization. How, the investigators asked, could the situation be improved?

Patients from high-EE homes seemed to benefit to some extent if they were on tranquilizing drugs; those from low-EE homes had the same low rate of relapse whether they were medicated or not. Another important variable was the amount of social contact that patients had with family members. Patients in high-EE homes had a lower relapse rate if they had fewer than thirty-five hours of face-to-face contact with family members during the week and higher rates if they had more than thirty-five hours. The amount of such contact had no significant effect on readmission rates of patients from low-EE families. Figure 17.2 shows the nine-month relapse rates for a group of 128 schizophrenic patients separated by their low- and high-EE families. The category ''on drugs'' denotes patients receiving tranquilizing medication. A careful scan of this figure

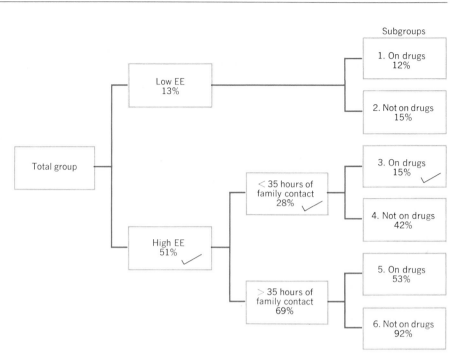

Subgroups

Figure 17.2
Nine-month relapse rates for schizophrenic male patients with low- and high-EE families. The percentages in the boxes are those of patients who had been released and then returned to the hospital. The check marks call attention to the important points. Relapse rates for patients in high-EE homes were high (51 percent), but they were less (28 percent) if these patients had fewer than thirty-five hours of contact with family and were even less (15 percent) if these patients were also using drugs. But hours of family contact and drugs were not important to the relapse rates of patients from low-EE families. (After Vaughn and Leff, 1976.)

provides two important suggestions about measures that might be taken to reduce the relapse rate. Patients should be urged to follow a carefully regulated drug regimen, and efforts should be made to increase the social distance between patient and relatives. Day centers or day hospitals, aftercare clinics, and transitional living arrangements provide a supportive environment in which a patient can spend time away from the family. A job or a sheltered workshop is another possible inoculant against further breakdown (Mosher and Keith, 1980). Finally, changing the pattern of patient-family interaction and developing new social skills may serve as good mental hygiene measures (Liberman, 1982).

Social-Skills Training

At present a number of methods for fostering social skills in patients and members of their families are being tested. The therapist may model ways of making communication more effective. Videotapes of actual family interactions show viewers how emotional situations in the family might be handled with less conflict. Patients are taught how to develop better problem-solving techniques, ways of expressing negative feelings, how to make requests of others. They are also given practice in listening more effectively and responding more rationally to others. Reinforcement of desired behavior sometimes helps to achieve these goals. There may be trips into the community under the guidance of a therapist or a well-trained aide, followed by discussions of the patient's performance while away from the hospital.

The most extraordinary program of research in **social-skills training** is the ten-year project that Gordon Paul and his associates conducted at the University of Illinois (Paul and Lentz, 1977). When Paul began his project in 1968, his intention was to compare two forms of psychosocial treatment of typical mental patients in two different wards of a state hospital. One program of therapy was to be milieu therapy, the other a program of therapy based on the principles of social-learning theory (page 503). A control group in a similar state hospital was to receive the traditional treatment services available to such patients, including an extensive drug regimen.

Milieu therapy is a type of ward management that encourages social interaction and relevant communication among patients, group activities, and group pressure directing patients toward more normal behavior. Patients are free to move about and are regarded as responsible people, not as burned-out custodial cases. **Social-learning therapy** emphasizes principles of operant conditioning. The physical and social environment of the patient is controlled to ensure that appropriate behavior of the patient receives positive reinforcement and that inappropriate behavior does not.

It is difficult enough to try to maintain a research program for six consecutive months in a state hospital. To do it for a decade is nothing short of incredible! In the course of those ten years, the hospital where Paul's study took place emptied in the same way as others did throughout the country. Paul and his colleagues saw their most improved patients discharged, until finally they were left with a group of patients for whom the probability of recovery and return to the community was negligible. These patients had been in the hospital for an average of seventeen years, about two-thirds of their adult lives. Their disorder was the process type of schizophrenia. They had very low levels of social functioning in the hospital. All the patients had a history of unsuccessful treatments of many types, including drug therapy.

Prospects for improvement in such chronic patients are so gloomy that the positive results of the study are extraordinary. Social-learning therapy proved to be the most effective treatment. Milieu therapy was second best and significantly more effective than traditional hospital procedures. This finding held for improvement in hospital behavior (Figure 17.3), for maximizing release from the institution—all but one social-learning participant achieved release—and for obtaining release in the shortest period of time. The patients improved with relatively little use of antipsychotic drugs and without regard to their individual characteristics or their earlier treatment history. The social-learning ward also cost less per patient than did the other two modes of treatment.

Finally, rehospitalization rates for the social-learning group were less than 3 percent for all patients over a follow-up period that extended from eighteen months after release from the hospital to five years after release, when the study

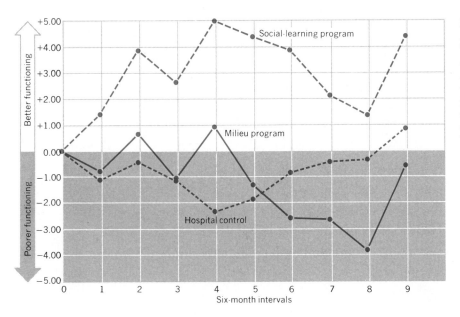

Figure 17.3
Improving social behavior in the hospital. The general level of hospital functioning of three groups of twenty-eight patients, each undergoing one of three kinds of treatment, was assessed at six-month intervals for signs of improvement. These were the most evident in the patients in the social-learning program.

Table 17.1 Status of Three Treatment Groups at Termination of the Hospital Programs and at Final Follow-up

Treatment Program	Patients Released by Termination of Hospital Program, percent	Patients Still in Community at Time of Final Follow-up, percent	Condition of Patients in Hospital at Final Follow-up, percent		
			Worse	No Change	Improved
Social learning	96.4	92.5	2.5	2.5	2.5
Milieu therapy	67.9	71.0	16.1	9.7	3.2
Hospital control	46.4	48.4	29.0	9.7	12.9

Adapted from Paul and Lentz, 1977

ended (Table 17.1). Paul believes that a social-learning program such as he conducted would result in community placement of most chronic mental patients within twenty-six to thirty weeks. Given an additional two to three years of continued training in the community, he asserts, these patients would function well enough to live independently and be self-supporting.

Ghettoization of the Released Mental Patient
The plight of the released mental patient who roams the streets of every major city in the United States should provoke national concern. Here is what Gerald Klerman (1977), formerly the director of the federal government's Alcohol, Drug Abuse and Mental Health Administration (ADAMHA) and now a research professor in psychiatry at Harvard University, had to say about the problem.

New forms of "community chronicity" have been developed in many large urban areas such as New York City, Chicago, Los Angeles, and San Francisco. In the absence of any adequate network of aftercare facilities, community residences and halfway houses, sheltered workshops, or day treatment centers, large numbers of patients are relegated to "lives of quiet desperation" in welfare hotels in segregated

The streets of our large cities have become the habitats of former mental patients. Whatever aftercare programs they are assigned to are often inadequate or quickly fail them. They cannot find affordable housing and the few able to work jobs. Without a permanent address they cannot manage the red tape necessary to keep their monthly Supplemental Security Income checks, to which they are entitled, coming to them.

neighborhoods. They are subsisting on minimal incomes from social welfare or disability payments, and receiving poorly monitored, often poorly prescribed, psychotropic medication. . . .

. . . Patients often live under conditions of minimum supervision and poor drug management, so that they often may be overdrugged, heavily sedated, stuporous, or dulled. Their limited ability for social interaction often means they wander the streets or sit aimlessly looking at television. . . .

In cities, particularly inner city neighborhoods, they are often at the mercy of various predatory groups, such as youth gangs and criminals, and are subject to beatings, robberies, and various forms of abuse (pp. 628–629).

There is evidence to support these assertions. When the state mental hospital in Santa Clara County (California) was closed in 1970, 3000 patients were sent back to the community. The majority grouped together into one square mile in the heart of downtown San Jose where they lived in decrepit board-and-care homes. In 1977 this area had a rate of public mental health treatment services sixty times the average for the county. At the same time, across the country in New York City, 25,000 chronic mental patients were living alone in cubical hotel rooms or in seedy boarding houses. Community living for the mental patient has become reinstitutionalization outside the mental hospitals instead of inside them.

SUMMARY

Although the theory that prehistoric cave dwellers drilled holes in the skulls of the mentally ill to drive out evil spirits has little merit, psychopathology has been recognized for some 5000 years. There were ancient proposals directed at its cure. During the fifteenth and sixteenth centuries psychopathology was tied to witchcraft and demon possession; "cures" involved numerous forms of punishment. During the eighteenth century it became more common to view psychopathology as a form of sickness, and therapy was more humane. The asylums, which had for the most part merely confined the mentally ill, became or were replaced by small, retreatlike, caring hospitals. In this century, with the advent of antipsychotic drugs, the now-traditional large mental hospitals have been emptied. Some former patients have gone back to homes in which there may be considerable conflict and censure if the family members are too emotionally intense about them. How to dampen these high levels of "expressed emotionality" (EE) has begun to occupy investigators. Early evidence suggests the importance of a carefully monitored drug regimen and social-skills training of patients and family members.

Other former patients have returned to communities that are poorly prepared to house and to provide for them. The ghettoization of these citizens is a growing national problem. They are in effect reinstitutionalized in boarding houses or deteriorated hotels in run-down sections of cities. Here they receive almost no care and are socially isolated. New methods of rehabilitation and social-learning programs are needed to help former patients become more self-sufficient.

FORMS OF THERAPY

The mental health practitioner uses two major forms of therapy in the effort to treat disorder. The first are the **somatic** or physical therapies, such as drug and shock therapy. These therapies are based on physiological and biochemical hypotheses of mental disorder. The second group consists of the methods of **psychotherapy,** which are based on psychological theories of mental disorder.

During the past twenty-five years two distinctly different treatment revolutions have brought drastic changes in the practice of both somatic therapy and psychotherapy. The first revolution occurred in somatic therapy when advances in the understanding of brain chemistry led to the introduction of a number of promising drug treatments. The second revolution was the development of behavior therapy, which applies the principles of learning to mental disorder. As a result of these advances, drug therapies and behavior therapies have largely replaced more traditional forms of therapy. In addition, they reach more people. In 1955 the National Institute of Mental Health estimated that only one percent of the population had some contact with a mental health practitioner, mostly as inpatients. By 1980 the utilization rate was 10 percent, most of it conducted as psychotherapy outside of mental hospitals. Ten percent of the population also took some form of psychotropic medication, for the most part minor tranquilizers (Klerman, 1983). In the pages to follow, we present a brief discussion of the older therapies and then move on to these newer ones.

Somatic Therapies

Electroconvulsive Shock Therapy. In 1938 two Italian neuropsychiatrists, Ugo Cerletti and Lucio Bini, introduced the form of **electroconvulsive shock therapy** (ECT) now in use. By means of electrodes fastened to the temples, 70 to 150 volts of electric current pass through the patient's head for 0.1 to 1.0 second. The effect is a convulsion resembling a grand mal epileptic seizure. The use of special muscle relaxants, a general anesthetic, and short-acting intravenous barbiturates has now reduced the likelihood of bone fractures during treatment, but such injuries sometimes still occur. After the electroconvulsive stimulation, the patient is often confused and usually suffers a loss of memory for events just prior to the convulsion. The memory loss is not permanent, however, and within a few weeks following treatment the patient's ability to learn and to retain what he or she has learned appears unaffected. There is somewhat equivocal evidence that ECT produces permanent brain damage, however (Salzman, 1978), and this is a major reason that therapists are reluctant to use the procedure.

Electroshock appears to have its greatest success with certain groups of severely depressed patients. Current evidence suggests that ECT is not effective with mild long-term depressions, in which the patient complains about many imaginary body ailments; with young people; or with chronic depression associated with the personality disorders. More systematic studies of treatment are necessary to determine when ECT should be used rather than some other form of therapy.

Psychosurgery. The original procedure used in **psychosurgery** was **lobotomy,** a severing of the connections between the thalamus and the frontal lobes. Such procedures have fallen into disrepute for three reasons. (1) The long-term results have been questionable; (2) drugs, which came into use in the mid-1950s, have proved to be far more effective as tranquilizers for acutely disturbed patients; and (3) moral objections have been raised against such a radical and irreversible procedure. Today the application of psychosurgery for the control even of violent behavior is a hotly debated topic and has led to court action. As a result, there has been a dramatic decline in the use of the procedure, despite improvements in the precision with which psychosurgery is now done.

Drug Therapy.   The most widely used and abused drugs prescribed for the treatment of mental problems are so-called "minor tranquilizers," which go by such trade names as Miltown, Equanil, Librium, and Valium. General practitioners with little training in psychiatry are increasingly prescribing these drugs for tense and anxious people, whatever the basis for the problem. One study found that 17 percent of all prescriptions filled in a small American city were for these mood-altering substances. Although they are called minor tranquilizers, these drugs are dangerous because, if taken frequently and over a period of time, they can become physically addictive.

Phenothiazines and Schizophrenia.   Although a number of different antipsychotic drugs appear to be equally effective for the treatment of schizophrenia, the most widely used drugs are the **phenothiazines,** of which the best known is **chlorpromazine.** A plausible hypothesis to account for the success of these drugs is that the symptoms of schizophrenia are caused by an excess in the brain of the neurotransmitter dopamine (page 545). According to this hypothesis, the phenothiazines alleviate the schizophrenic symptoms by reducing the excessive dopamine levels or possibly by modifying the activity of postsynaptic dopamine receptors.

Studies of the effectiveness of the phenothiazines and similar substances have demonstrated that they produce improvement in more schizophrenic patients than treatment with a placebo, but some patients are unaffected and a few even get worse. Patients treated with these drugs or the drugs combined with psychotherapy do significantly better than those receiving psychotherapy alone, but still the success rate is far from 100 percent (May, 1968, 1974).

Some 15 percent of previously inaccessible patients improve to the extent that they can be returned to their communities. Others have become less of a custodial problem despite their failure to recover. Still others can leave the hospital provided they can receive a maintenance dosage of the drug on an outpatient basis. The phenothiazines, however, are not miracle drugs. Unless some form of environmental support can also be provided for these patients, there is always the possibility of a subsequent relapse and return to the hospital. A special problem with the phenothiazines is that prolonged usage can cause **tardive** (late) **dyskinesia,** ticlike involuntary movements of the face, mouth, and shoulder effects, which are sometimes irreversible (Baldessarini, 1977).

Drug Therapies for Emotional Disorders.   The two drugs most commonly used in the treatment of depressions are the several different **tricyclics** and **monoamine oxidase (MAO) inhibitors,** both of which elevate mood. The MAO inhibitors are highly toxic. They can cause damage to the liver and the cardiovascular system and are used less than the tricyclics as therapy for depression.

One particular tricyclic, **imipramine,** has promise as therapy for panic disorder (page 526), of which the following description (Klein, 1981) is typical.

> Such people, often feeling quite well, are doing something innocuous, such as walking down the street or having a meal, when suddenly they are struck by the worst experience of their life: they become suffused by terror, with a pounding heart and inability to catch their breath; the very ground underfoot seems unstable, and they are convinced that death from a stroke or heart attack is imminent. They may blindly appeal for help to passersby and eventually make their way to a doctor (p. 236).

Physicians tend to be reassuring and, although this is momentarily helpful, there is little long-term benefit. A second and then a third panic attack may follow. Donald Klein (1981) has reported that imipramine gradually reduces the patient's anticipatory anxiety and then eliminates the spontaneously occurring panic attacks. Behavior therapy has also been used effectively in treating severe anxiety states.

Finally, **lithium carbonate** has become the standard drug for treating mania (Shopsin, 1979). This substance dampens a manic episode and, even more important, helps to prevent subsequent manic and depressive episodes. Lithium carbonate, like the MAO inhibitors, is a potent drug and can be dangerous when used with patients suffering from kidney problems or heart disease.

Psychoanalysis

The forerunner of all psychotherapies is Freudian **psychoanalysis.** In the classical psychoanalytic session the patient reclines on a couch in a softly lighted room and is instructed to talk about everything that comes to mind, no matter how trivial, irrelevant, senseless, embarrassing, or vulgar. This is the technique of **free association.** It is one of the keystones of psychoanalytic treatment. The task of free association is more difficult than it may seem. It is something the patient must learn in the early stages of treatment. During this procedure the analyst is passive; the patient is the active contributor to therapy.

The patient at first talks about what appears to be an aimless, directionless stream of topics, but gradually it drifts toward the repressed events that are presumably responsible for the neurosis. When this trend begins, the first of the many problems for the analyst, **resistance,** appears. Psychoanalysis assumes that conflicts and unpleasant events responsible for neuroses are repressed, and that **repression** is a protective device, keeping these events out of the individual's awareness. Repression is not easily abandoned and, as free associations begin to touch on the repressed material, various things may happen to keep the repressed ideas from being brought to consciousness. A dream with latent content that reveals the resistance may appear, or the patient may say that there are no thoughts, that the mind is a blank, or that the content of thought is too foolish or too meaningless to record. Or a flood of associations may appear, all quite irrelevant but not quite "free" because they are designed to avoid the distressing areas.

Freud's consulting room was splendid with Persian rugs; small statuary, paintings, reliefs, and fragments from ancient frescoes; and a fine tile stove with special tubes for humidifying the room. The couch was piled high with pillows, to put the patient in a near-sitting position, and supplied with shawl and throw, should he or she need protection from drafts.

FREUD AS PSYCHOTHERAPIST

Freud's emphasis on the transference relationship as a means of changing the patient's behavior has sometimes obscured his view that there is need for a "working alliance" between therapist and patient. Such an alliance allows the patient to develop warm and positive feelings toward the therapist, which is a necessary component not only in psychoanalysis but also in all therapeutic methods. In the interests of creating such an alliance, Freud was flexible in a way that is not always manifest in contemporary psychoanalytic practitioners. Sometimes his methods departed drastically from standard psychoanalytic procedures.

Richard Sterba (1951) has reported Freud's efforts to assist one of the great orchestral conductors of our time, Bruno Walter. In his autobiography Walter (1946) recounted that shortly after the birth of his first child, he was seized with an arm ailment that bordered on paralysis and made it impossible for him to conduct an orchestra or to play the piano. Visits to a number of physicians proved fruitless, and finally the great conductor decided to call on Freud, "resigned to submit to months of soul searching." To his surprise, Freud did not plumb the depths of his unconscious in a search for sexual trauma. Instead he recommended that Walter leave immediately for a vacation in Sicily. Unfortunately, the rest did little good, and Walter returned to Vienna and again presented himself in Freud's office. Walter's description of the exchange is illuminating.

[Freud's] advice was to conduct!
"But I can't move my arm."
"Try it at any rate."
"And what if I should have to stop?"
"You won't have to stop."
"Can I take upon myself the responsibility of possibly upsetting a performance?"
"I'll take the responsibility," Freud responded.

Walter took Freud's advice, again took up his conducting, and gradually succeeded in returning to his musical career.

Forty years later Sterba interviewed Walter about these events. Walter recalled the indelible impression that Freud had made upon him, an impression unchanged despite the passage of four decades. Walter felt immediate confidence and trust in Freud's decisiveness and sincerity. Although discouraged with the failure of his arm to heal during his trip, he retained the strong belief that Freud could help him. When Freud indicated that *he* would take the responsibility for the satisfactory performance of the concert, Walter believed that he could now try to conduct again. Freud, in turn, reinforced Walter's efforts to overcome his handicap.

All this was accomplished in six interviews. First, Freud sought to dampen Walter's anxiety by urging him to escape the site of his affliction. Second, Freud used the power of the therapist's authority and the patient's faith in him to suggest that the concert would go off satisfactorily. The treatment of Walter illustrates the flexibility of Freud's therapeutic views.

I believe it quite justifiable to resort to more convenient methods of healing as long as there is any prospect of attaining anything by their means.

Assured that the analyst is interested in everything that comes to mind, the patient may forget appointments—and be charged for the missed session in recognition of the dynamics of such behavior—or begin to feel that the therapy is getting nowhere and should be discontinued. Actually, the opposite is true. The patient is getting too close to repressed material for comfort, and these defenses are designed to prevent the exposure of ego-threatening material.

In psychoanalytic theory it is essential to the therapeutic process that the individual recall and relive the events behind the personality disorder in all their emotional intensity. Thus it is critical that the resistance to such revelation be overcome. The most powerful ally of the therapist in this and other phases of analysis is **transference.** This term is used in various therapies and has come to have several meanings, all referring to the therapeutic relationship. In a general sense it refers to the warmth or rapport that exists between patient and therapist. In psychoanalysis it has the more specific meaning of a repetition of past relationships that the patient introduces into the therapeutic relationship, called the *transference neurosis.* By the mechanism of transference, the analyst comes to represent an important figure in the person's early life. The emotions originally directed at that figure are now turned toward the analyst. Early in treatment at least, these emotions are usually love responses that were originally directed toward a parent. In **positive transference** the patient unconsciously seeks to recapture the past and to relive it, but with a more satisfactory resolution than had been encountered in childhood.

Because the therapist will not go along with such neurotic behavior, the person is once again doomed to disappointment. The patient's attitude toward the therapist may therefore shift from affection and admiration to one of anger and derogation, called **negative transference.** This marks a critical point in therapy, for here the interpretation of such behavior can reveal to the patient that the repetitive neurotic pattern he or she brings to all relationships originated in unresolved emotional conflicts of childhood. The therapist seeks to analyze these reactions, trying to make clear to the patient that the emotions experienced are related to infantile reactions and repressions. The growing awareness and acceptance of these interpretations and a conscious redirecting of attitudes and views toward the self and others are the important elements in the restructuring of personality.

With the interpretation and resolution of the transference neurosis, the analysis begins to move toward its final stages. It is important to understand that neither this interpretation nor others are offered until the analyst is confident that the patient is ready to receive them. Initially, the analyst may concentrate on showing connections between certain areas of the patient's verbalizations. Later the interpretations may become more specific, with the analyst indicating how certain dynamic conflicts are being reflected in behavior. At certain points it may be necessary for the therapist to interpret the patient's resistance to facing the contents of his or her thoughts. The process is a gradual one in which the person "works through" the materials and the interpretations. There is no sudden blossoming of insight and no spontaneous, miraculous "cure," as is so often suggested in television or Hollywood movies. The same thought content may reappear, resistances may show a type of spontaneous recovery, and interpretations, although previously accepted, may have to be offered again and again. But in a successful analysis the individual moves toward awareness and understanding. Often symptoms are reduced, but sometimes, curiously enough, they remain unmodified during treatment.

The benefit derived from psychoanalysis seems to come about through an emotional catharsis or **abreaction** produced by reliving the traumatic experiences responsible for the patient's maladjustment. This catharsis takes place in a setting in which the therapist is neither disapproving nor distressed by the patient's innermost thoughts. There is a readjustive or reeducative process, which gives the patient new responses to replace the neurotic ones.

SUMMARY

Somatic therapies for the mental disorders are electroconvulsive shock therapy, brain surgery, and drugs. Psychosurgery is rarely used today. It, along with ECT, has been subjected to strong criticism on moral grounds. Objections to ECT must be evaluated against its beneficial effects in relieving certain forms of severe depression. Drugs are the most widely used of these therapies. Powerful beneficial effects of drugs have been demonstrated, particularly of chlorpromazine, the antidepressants, and lithium carbonate.

Psychoanalysis is the respected elder in the family of the psychotherapies. Its fundamental aim is to make unconscious conflicts conscious and thus bring irrational neurotic behavior under rational and constructive control. To this end, the psychoanalyst, over an extended period of time, demonstrates to the patient his or her tendency to foist onto people in the present the qualities of important figures of the past who were involved in the development of the neurosis. During treatment the patient may come to view the therapist as one of these past figures, in the hope this time of achieving satisfactions denied in the past. The therapist counters by utilizing such transference to help the patient under-

stand these early conflicts and the disturbance wrought when he or she tries to carry them into adulthood. Before this goal can be achieved, however, powerful resistances to allowing such thoughts into awareness must be overcome through the analysis of free associations, dreams, fantasies, slips of the tongue, and other symbolic acts that betray the presence of the unconscious.

BEHAVIOR THERAPIES

Beginning in the 1960s, clinical and experimental psychologists, joined by a small band of behaviorally minded psychiatrists, set out to modify various forms of behavior disorder by applying the principles of classical and operant conditioning. This revolution in therapy was exclusively psychological in its origins, for its basis lay in a history of laboratory research and theory in the field of learning that extended back to the beginning of the century (Kazdin, 1978). The results have been impressive.

> In behavioral research, theoretical advances by some of the world's greatest experimental psychologists have led to new therapeutic techniques. The techniques of behavior therapy and behavior modification have exercised a profound influence on our capacity to treat a wide-range set of disordered behaviors: obesity and anorexia; the addictive disorders involving drugs, alcohol, and tobacco; sexual aberrations; obsessive-compulsive neuroses; psychosomatic disturbances; severe phobias and anxiety states; delinquent behavior in the classroom; social incompetence of schizophrenics; severe depression; self-injurious behavior in institutional settings; biopsychological feedback treatments of various somatic disorders; . . . learning disability and hyperactivity due to attentional dyscontrol in children (Report of the Research Task Panel of the President's Commission on Mental Health, 1978, p. 1536).

The basic belief of the first wave of behavior therapists was that neurotic behavior stemmed from learning experiences in which responses that were initially acquired as a means of avoiding anxiety subsequently developed into persistent and inflexible habits. Because the aim of both psychotherapy and learning is to produce behavioral change, this commonality suggested that the techniques of classical and instrumental conditioning could be used to help maladjusted people acquire more adaptive behavior and extinguish their older, maladaptive habits.

The behavior therapists rejected the psychoanalytic doctrine that the primary task of therapy was to unmask the causes of symptoms, to identify and resolve the unconscious conflicts underlying them. Hans Eysenck provided a declaration of independence of brevity and force: "There is no neurosis that underlies a symptom, but merely the symptom itself. Get rid of the symptom and you have eliminated the neurosis!" (1960, p. 9).

We can sense in this declaration the view that there was no need to search for the roots of disorder in childhood trauma, no necessity to interpret dreams and to free-associate in order to escape the bonds of repression, no two to five years of tenure on the psychoanalytic couch. The task to be accomplished was to effect change, through learning principles, in the disturbing habits that others called symptoms. Reflecting these values, the behavior therapies differ from psychoanalytic therapy in a number of ways. They emphasize the specific problems that the client faces in the here and now. There is little or no attention to early childhood experiences, unconscious processes, and the early sexualtiy of the child.

Systematic Desensitization

In 1958 Joseph Wolpe, a psychiatrist, reported experiments in which he had induced experimental neurosis in cats by shocking them when they approached food in a cage. He then tried to overcome the neurosis by therapy. His technique involved counterconditioning, the principal element being to get the cats to feed in the presence of stimuli that only minimally evoked distress and then gradually to expose the animals to stimuli that formerly had aroused greater and greater intensities of anxiety.

This was Wolpe's principle of *reciprocal inhibition,* and it consisted of the following components. (1) In the presence of anxiety-evoking stimuli, therapy must provide a means whereby (2) a response antagonistic to anxiety can be made, so that (3) the anxiety reaction is suppressed, resulting in (4) a weakening of the bond between these stimuli and the anxiety that they have produced in the past.

The Technique. Because the therapeutic method consisted of systematically desensitizing the individual to situations that aroused anxiety, it was called **systematic desensitization.** The theory was performed according to a certain set technique. First, the therapist had to know the specific stimuli that triggered the person's anxiety, what situations the client feared, and how intense these fears were. There could be no guessing about this; the person who came for treatment had to describe exactly the stimuli that created fear. The first step in the treatment process was to have the client make a list of anxiety-evoking stimuli, ranked in order from the one that made the patient most anxious down to stimuli that produced little or no anxiety.

The second step was to train the person to make a response incompatible with anxiety whenever these stimuli were present. Wolpe decided that the response would be deep relaxation, and he set about to train patients in how to achieve it. Subsequently sexual responses and assertive responses have also been used successfully as incompatible responses.

The third step was to join the feared stimuli in the patient's ordered list with the incompatible response of relaxation. This step is the heart of the procedure of desensitization. The patient in the treatment room must first relax deeply and

Arnold Lazarus conducts a group desensitization therapy session at his home. Here his clients are learning deep relaxation.

Table 17.2 Partial Desensitization Hierarchy for Test Anxiety in a College Student

First Fear Rating	Second Fear Rating	Anxiety Hierarchy Items
0	0	Beginning a new course
15	10	Hearing an instructor announce a small quiz two weeks hence
20	25	Having a professor urge you personally to do well on an exam
40	45	Reviewing the material that you know should be studied, listing studying to be done
60	50	Hearing an instructor remind the class of a quiz one week hence
75	75	Hearing an instructor announce a major exam in one week
80	85	Talking to several students about an exam right before taking it
90	90	While studying in a group, hearing some "pearls" from another student that you doubt you'll remember
95	95	Talking with several students about an exam immediately after taking it
100	100	Thinking about not being adequately prepared for a particular exam

Ratings: 0 = "totally relaxed"; 100 = "as tense as you ever are."
Adapted from Kanfer and Phillips, 1970.

then imagine the situations that are feared. Wolpe has the patient begin with an image of the least-threatening situation. Being already relaxed, the patient responds to the image with relaxation rather than tension. In this way anxiety is extinguished to the stimulus the patient fears least. The procedure of imagining anxiety-producing stimuli is then repeated for stimuli higher and higher in the hierarchy. Step by step the patient visualizes and relaxes to the stronger and more feared stimuli.

Table 17.2 lists a part of one college student's **anxiety hierarchy** over being tested. The fear ratings given by the student on two separate occasions appear in the left-hand columns. Two things are notable, the reliability of the ratings and the preciseness of item descriptions. The latter requires the therapist to be a sophisticated interviewer with good clinical skills. Expressed another way, systematic desensitization is not a simple-minded technique that can be performed by just any believer in behavior therapy. Carelessness in creating a hierarchy can result not only in a treatment failure but also in heightened anxiety for the client.

If the client begins to feel anxiety as a scene is visualized, his or her imagery must cease. The person is asked to relax, and a pleasant scene is then substituted. If no fear is felt, the client continues visualizing for ten to fifteen seconds followed by fifteen to thirty seconds of relaxation. The client may repeat the scene for two or three trials and then imagine the next item in the hierarchy. If the client feels afraid, he or she repeats a less disturbing item, then when fear has decreased, returns to the distressing item until its anxiety-arousing properties have been extinguished.

The Effectiveness of Desensitization. The following case illustrates Wolpe's procedures.

> A twenty-three-year-old bus driver was brought to the physician in a state of great anxiety, eight hours after hitting a pedestrian. The victim had been knocked down and, although she was not serously injured, her head bled profusely following the accident. It was the sight of human blood that brought on the anxiety attack. This fear dated back to age thirteen when the patient's father had been killed in an accident. Since then, the sight of even a few drops of blood would precipitate an anxiety attack.
>
> To overcome the patient's phobia, the first five interviews were initially devoted to learning more about the patient's background and to inducing hypnotic relaxation. The patient was told to drive his bus again for a short distance.
>
> During the sixth interview, a series of stimulus situations was arranged in ascending order in terms of the amount of anxiety these evoked. During later interviews (under hypnosis) the patient was told to visualize "blood situations." For example, one that evoked very little anxiety was a blood-tinged bandage. Later the patient was presented with tiny drops of blood on his face while shaving. By presenting several images at these sessions, the patient was finally able to visualize and accept with equanimity a whole ward full of injured patients.

Wolpe concludes his case presentation with dramatic evidence of the potency of this form of therapy: "Two days before the last interview the patient saw a man knocked over by a motorcycle. The victim was seriously injured and was bleeding profusely. The patient was absolutely unaffected by the blood and when the ambulance arrived, helped to load the victim on it" (1960, p. 109).

One of the best comparative studies of the effectiveness of desensitization procedures was performed as a doctoral study by Gordon Paul, who was soon to conduct the decade-long mental hospital study of social-learning–milieu therapy described earlier. Paul (1966) chose five carefully matched groups of college students who shared a strong fear of public speaking. These "clients" were assigned to one of five treatment programs: insight-oriented psychotherapy, traditional interviewing aimed at the development of insight into the basis of the problem; systematic desensitization, in which the aspects of anxiety aroused by public speaking were graded into a hierarchy and imagined during relaxation; attention–placebo, a "pseudotherapy" consisting of attention from a therapist plus prescription of a placebo described as a "fast-acting tranquilizer."

Figure 17.4
The effectiveness of three psychotherapies in reducing stage fright. The mean scores for signs of anxiety are based on checklist items observed, and tallied, when speeches were made before and at the end of psychotherapy. (Data from Paul, 1966; graph adapted from Strupp, 1971.)

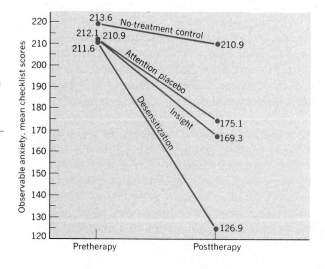

Table 17.3 Percentages of Cases in Various Improvement Categories Following Treatment for Stage Fright

Treatment	N	Unimproved	Slightly Improved	Improved	Much Improved
Desensitization	15	0%	0%	14%	86%
Insight	15	7	47	27	0
Attention–placebo	15	20	33	47	0
No-treatment control	29	55	28	17	0

From Paul, 1966.

Two no-treatment control groups were also used. To control for therapist differences, all therapists administered all forms of therapy.

Each person who received therapy delivered a pretreatment test speech and then entered into a series of five hours of individual therapy extending over a period of six weeks. At the end of that time, they gave a posttreatment test speech. One set of results—observable manifestations of anxiety during test speeches—is presented in Figure 17.4. All measures tended to favor the desensitization group; "attention–placebo" and "insight" students also benefited from their therapy, but the no-treatment controls did not benefit at all (Table 17.3).

Implosion Therapy

Instead of beginning with the first scene in a hierarchy, the one that arouses the least anxiety, the **implosion therapy** procedure begins with the most fear-arousing, hair-raising stimulus imaginable in an effort to provide intensive and dramatic extinction. In this technique there is no counterconditioning or relaxation and no hierarchy of stimuli. The model is Pavlovian, and the emphasis is on extinction by presenting the feared stimulus in the absence of anything punishing or painful. In the view of its founders, Thomas Stampfl and Donald Levis (1967), the most rapid extinction takes place if the stimulus used most closely resembles the stimulus to which anxiety was originally conditioned. The technique therefore consists of "forced reality testing" and therein lies its danger. If the anxiety that is generated is so excessive that the client cannot cope with it, the anxiety itself may be exacerbated.

In his book *Living with Fear,* Isaac Marks (1978), a well-known British behavioral psychiatrist, describes an actual implosion procedure used with a young male student who had failed a previous exam because of an attack of panic. The therapist with the student's collaboration decided to have the client experience his examination anxiety fully without providing an escape from it.

The student was made to sit up in bed and try to feel his fear. He was asked to imagine all the consequences that would follow his failure—derision from his colleagues, disappointment from his family, and financial loss. At first as he followed the instructions, his sobbings increased. But soon his tremblings ceased. As the effort needed to maintain a vivid imagination increased, the emotion he could summon began to ebb. Within half an hour he was calm. He was instructed to repeatedly experience his fears. Every time he felt a little wave of spontaneous alarm he was not to push it aside but was to enhance and try to experience it more vividly. The patient was intelligent and assiduously practiced his exercises methodically until he became almost unable to feel frightened. He passed his examinations without difficulty (p. 212).

Flooding

If the therapeutic procedure exposes the individual to a real situation rather than an imagined one, the method is called **flooding** rather than implosion. There are suggestions of the method in the writings of Freud (1955). In his discussions of the use of psychoanalysis with **agoraphobic** patients, people with a morbid fear of open spaces, Freud said that it was essential for these people to attempt actively to conquer their phobias before analysis could proceed. They must, he wrote, "go into the street . . . to struggle with their anxiety while they make the attempt [to overcome their phobia]. Only when that has been achieved [do the conditions exist] which enable the phobia to be resolved."

Marks (1972) compared desensitization with flooding in treating chronic phobic hospital patients. Both treatments produced improvement, but flooding was more successful. Despite the high level of anxiety it generated, it proved to be a "surprisingly acceptable treatment" to the patients. Anxiety levels that were high in the first session dissipated quickly over subsequent sessions. It is Marks's view, based on years of experience, that rapid prolonged exposure to the feared real-life public situation is the treatment of choice with phobic individuals. It is simply quicker and more effective than fantasizing exposure through the medium of imagery.

Paradoxical Intention

The **paradoxical intention** procedure is a variation of flooding. Clients are asked to stop fighting their fears and instead to express them openly and even to exaggerate them (Marks, 1972). For example, a patient who lived in fear of having a heart attack was told by the therapist, "Go ahead. Right now. Try to make your heart go so fast that you will die of a heart attack right on this spot." The patient laughingly said, "Doc I'm trying but I can't do it." With repeated instructions to try to die three times a day, the patient began to supplant fear with laughter. Marks writes,

> In the moment he started laughing at his symptoms and when he became willing to produce them (paradoxically) intentionally, he changed his attitude toward his symptoms . . . [and] interrupted the vicious cycle and strangled the feedback mechanism (p. 179).

The Power of Operant Conditioning

Systematic desensitization, implosion therapy, flooding, and paradoxical intention are all based on the methods of classical conditioning. In one way or another they aim at the extinction of an undesirable conditioned response. Other therapies employ an operant conditioning model. The operant methods employ rewards and punishment to remove a client's symptoms and to encourage more desirable behavior. The methods derived from procedures developed in the laboratory include (1) *positive reinforcement,* in which the patient receives rewards for desired behavior; (2) *extinction,* in which the therapist withholds reward for undesirable behavior; (3) *avoidance training,* in which the patient may avoid punishment by producing healthy responses; and (4) *punishment,* in which the patient is punished for undesirable behavior. Positive reinforcement and extinction are often used in combination, as are avoidance training and punishment. These last two methods are often classed together and called *aversion therapy.*

Positive Reinforcement.   The treatment of an adolescent girl with *anorexia nervosa* (page 283) provides an illustration of the use of **positive reinforcement** for therapy. This example also illustrates an application of the methods of small-*N* research described in Chapter 1. The patient, a five-foot-tall, thirteen-year-old girl, was admitted to the hospital after her weight had dropped from 117 pounds to 77 pounds. The severe weight loss had occurred because the patient was on a very strict diet which her mother had insisted she adhere to. The girl's menses had ceased, she now ate very little, and she had grown depressed. Treatment followed a series of four stages that allowed the therapists (Agras et al., 1974) to demonstrate the effectiveness of the therapy they used.

Stage A: *Baseline observation.* At the beginning of treatment, the patient was told that the staff was concerned about her, that she was expected to eat as much as possible, and that four meals of 1500 calories each would be served at set times during the day. She was asked to count and plot on a graph the mouthfuls of food she swallowed. After she had entered the number on the graph, she was given a card that informed her of the number of calories she had consumed. In addition, each morning she was told her weight. During this baseline phase, for reasons that will become obvious as the next phase of treatment is described, the patient was given a minimum amount of nursing attention and was confined to her room, except for three scheduled periods each day when she could go to the dayroom. Her room was without reading or writing materials, television or radio.

Stage B: *Introduction of the independent variable, privileges for weight gain.* During this second phase, for each 3.5-ounce gain in weight over her previous high weight, the patient received privileges for the day. These privileges were the positive reinforcement that was made available for desired behavior. The patient could leave her room or have a radio or television brought to it, play games with the nurse, or converse with other patients in the dayroom. As stage B progressed, in order for the patient to have a day of privileges, the necessary additional weight that she had to gain slowly rose to 8.8 ounces.

Stage C: *Privileges given whether or not weight was gained.* Stage C was an interesting modification of stage B. The treatment team wanted to know whether weight was gained in stage B because the privileges depended on it. One way of answering this question was to give the patient the same privileges in stage C as in stage B, whatever her daily caloric intake and weight gain.

Stage B: *Reintroduction of the independent variable, privileges again made contingent on weight gain.* Making privileges again contingent on weight gain would confirm their power to encourage eating. The final stage B was simply a repeat of the earlier stage B.

Weight, expressed in kilograms, is measured along the ordinate on the left side of Figure 17.5, caloric intake on the right ordinate. In stage B the increase in food intake and weight gain were steady. In stage C, however, when receiving privileges was no longer dependent on eating, caloric intake dropped markedly and weight gain slowed considerably. When receiving privileges depended again on weight gain in the second stage B, both food intake and weight increased once more.

Positive reinforcement has been used on a broader scale in the **token economies,** in which individuals earn tokens for desirable behavior and are able to exchange them for goods and services, privileges, and being able to participate in favored activities (page 266). Token economies have now been successfully set up in schools, mental hospitals, clinics, reformatories, homes for the mentally retarded, and other institutions.

Extinction. The method of **extinction** removes an undesirable response by withholding the positively reinforcing stimulus that maintains it. Teodoro Ayllon

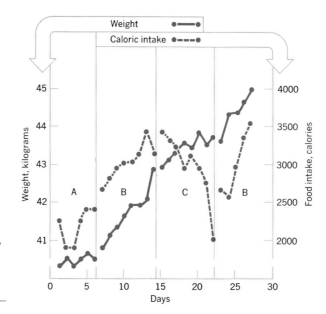

Figure 17.5

Control of anorexia nervosa through reward for eating. The four panels are A, baseline observation; B, privileges depend on eating; C, privileges continue but are not contingent on eating; B, privileges are again contingent on eating.

(1963) reports the case of a forty-seven-year-old chronic schizophrenic patient who was the bane of the ward's nursing personnel because of three undesirable activities: she stole food, hoarded towels in her room, and insisted on wearing an excessive amount of clothing. To control her food stealing, the nurses and attendants had in the past coaxed, wheedled, cajoled, and finally forcibly induced the patient to return the food. Ayllon arranged that they discontinue these attentions and had the nursing staff carefully record all such food-stealing episodes over a period of one month. The patient was then assigned to sit alone at a table in the dining hall; whenever she approached another table to steal food or attempted to take food from the counter, she was removed from the cafeteria and deprived of her meal. Thus a positive reinforcer, food, was withheld whenever the undesirable behavior occurred. Results of this regimen were dramatic (Figure 17.6). Within two weeks food stealing had extinguished; at the end of fourteen months the patient's weight had declined from 250 to 180 pounds. Over a subsequent one-year period there were only three occa-

Figure 17.6

Successful extinction of food stealing. Food stealing *(lower curve)* disappeared almost as soon as food was withdrawn by sending the woman from the cafeteria whenever she attempted to steal. The dots not on the curve indicate that food stealing recurred on only three occasions. The upper curve indicates the decline in the patient's weight. (Adapted from Ayllon, 1963.)

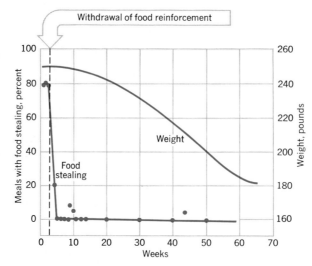

sions when the patient attempted to steal food. The alert staff reinstated the extinction procedure on these occasions and the behavior reextinguished rapidly.

Aversion Therapy. The methods of **avoidance training** have been commonly used for the treatment of alcoholism and certain sexual disturbances. More than fifty years ago a Soviet physician paired a painful electric shock with the sight, taste, and smell of alcohol as a therapy for alcoholism. He reported that 70 percent of a small group of patients who received this treatment abstained from drinking for periods ranging from three weeks to twenty months. Medication and hypnotic suggestion used with a control group of patients were less effective.

Other therapists who tested this **aversion** method were unsuccessful, and they turned from the use of electric shock to chemical aversion therapy. Subjects took a nausea-producing drug such as Antabuse, and then the therapist watched for the first signs of sickness. When they appeared, the patient drank his or her favorite alcohol beverage. The hypothesis behind this treatment came from the studies of conditioned taste aversions described earlier (page 270). Patients were expected to associate alcohol and sickness, perhaps even becoming nauseous when they drank, and would for this reason give up drinking. The method has been somewhat successful, but not with the most severely alcoholic patients (Mendelson and Mello, 1979). Partly for that reason, but at least as importantly because the aversion therapies raise grave ethical questions, they are currently used only as a treatment of last resort.

One of the most dramatic uses of the aversion method of **punishment** was in treating a nine-month-old infant whose life was seriously endangered by persistent vomiting and chronic ruminative rechewing of the vomitus. The case was unusual because of the extreme youth of the patient and because the conditioning procedure was attempted only after all other physical and psychological treatments had been ruled out or had proved unsuccessful (Lang and Melamed, 1969).

> The infant had been hospitalized three times for persistent vomiting, which began in the fifth month of life, and failure to gain weight. The mother related the onset to a broken ankle she had suffered which forced the family to live with her parents for several weeks. There followed a period of conflict between mother and grandmother over the care of the baby; the parents were also having marital difficulties at this time.
>
> During the infant's hospitalization all medical tests had proved negative; exploratory surgery had been performed; dietary changes had produced no changes nor had the use of antinauseants. Intensive nursing care to provide security and warmth for the infant was eliminated when it seemed to heighten the baby's anxiety and restlessness. The psychologists were called in as a last resort when the infant's weight had declined to twelve pounds and feeding had to be continued through a nasogastric pump.
>
> After two days of observation, treatment began. It took the form of administering a brief repeated sequence of shocks—one second in duration, one second apart—to the infant's calf whenever he started vomiting after feeding. A tone signal was sounded before shock, as soon as vomiting began, and stopped when vomiting ceased. The pairing of vomiting, signal, and shock was managed by a nurse who observed the infant and signaled when he was beginning to vomit. After two sessions shock was needed only rarely; the infant would cry when he heard the noxious tone, but vomiting would cease. Shock was then administered not just after feeding but whenever the baby vomited during the rest of the day, while he was lying down, playing, or being held. Weight started to increase steadily as soon as treatment

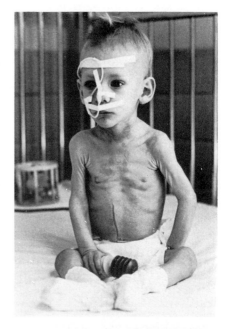

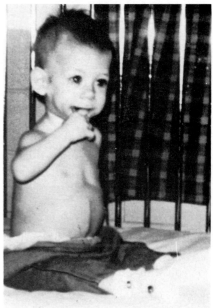

Before aversion therapy the infant was debilitated, his body fat gone and his skin hanging in loose folds. The tape on his face holds the tubing for nasogastric feeding. Thirteen days later, after behavior modification and immediately before discharge, the child's body weight had already increased 26 percent. His face had filled out, and his arms and trunk were rounded and substantial.

Figure 17.7
Changes in body weight of an infant hospitalized and treated for chronic vomiting. Conditioning began on day 13. Dots indicate days on which shock was administered. Notice the weight gain from days 13 to 18. On day 19 the infant started to vomit again. Additional conditioning on days 20 and 21 reinstituted weight gain. (From Lang and Melamed, 1969.)

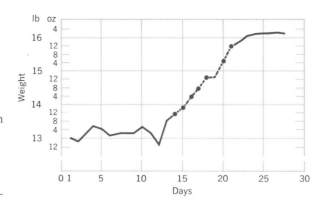

began [Figure 17.7]. After the last conditioning trial had ended, the mother was reintroduced into the picture and gradually took over the responsibility of feeding and caring for her young son. The infant was discharged from the hospital five days later. On follow-up the infant was eating well and gaining weight, sought attention from others, and was declared to be fully recovered by the family physician. A year later the baby was continuing to thrive, and there was no evidence that another symptom had been substituted for the vomiting.

Cognitive Behavior Therapy

One of the most important developments in recent years has been to include among the behavior therapies the procedures now collectively referred to as **cognitive behavior therapy.** These methods are designed to help clients understand how the thoughts and beliefs that they harbor about themselves and others contribute to their distress. The goal of the cognitive behavior therapists is to help individuals develop more realistic evaluations as a way of coping with their problems.

Rational-Emotive Therapy. Albert Ellis, the creator of **rational-emotive therapy** (RET), is one of the pioneering figures in the field of cognitive behavior therapy. For Ellis cognition and emotion are closely linked. To control one's thoughts is to provide control over one's emotions. Neurotics are so because they think irrationally, engage in "self-sabotaging" behavior, and either cannot or will not behave more appropriately. RET is clearly a cognitive therapy, as can be seen by looking at what Ellis (1977) has called the ABCs of the method.

The symbol A represents an activating experience or event—you are fired from a job; C represents the emotional and behavioral consequences that follow—you can go home, become depressed, and sit around the house, your self-esteem nearing the zero point. Does A cause C? No, says Ellis, because interpolated between A and C is B, your belief about A. It is B that causes C— if you loved the job, you are depressed; if you disliked it, you are noncommittal or even relieved. So beliefs are the essential elements that give rise to the irrational views that people have about themselves and the situations they encounter.

Here is Ellis (1962) describing his behavior as he confronts a patient who has failed to carry out a work assignment that he was given as part of his therapy. The harsh language is designed for its shock value in jolting the patient out of his lethargy.

If a patient says to me, "You know, I just don't feel like doing the homework assignment you gave me, and I didn't like you for giving it to me, so I just forgot

Albert Ellis believes that people are governed by unreasonable, hidden expectations, such as "I must make everyone like me." He helps patients to search out, admit to, and question these unexamined yet guiding silent sentences.

about it," I rarely nondirectively reflect back to him: "So you didn't like the assignment and hated me for giving it to you?" And I often fail to say, in an approved psychoanalytic manner: "What is there about the assignment and about me that you didn't like?"

Rather, I am likely to say: "So you didn't feel like doing the assignment. Tough! Well you're goddamn well going to have to do it if you want to overcome the nonsense you keep telling yourself. And you didn't like me for giving you the assignment. Well, I don't give a shit whether you like me or not. We're here not to have a lovey-dovey relationship—and thereby to gratify you for the moment so that you don't have to work to get better—but to convince you that unless you get off your ass and do that assignment I gave you and many equivalent assignments, you're probably going to keep stewing in your neurotic juices forever. Now when are you going to cut out the crap and do something to help yourself?" (p. 198)

In his attempts to change a destructive pattern, Ellis will cajole, attack, lecture, upbraid, direct, suggest, support, criticize, evaluate, and argue with patients. He has no hesitancy in contradicting the patient, in denying the validity of his self-defeating behavior, or in combating his illogicalities and demanding that he follow an alternate form of action—all with the professed aim of educating the patient in the direction of developing a new, more positive, better-reasoned, and less self-destructive set of beliefs. Several of the irrational ideas that create neurotic disturbances and the rational transformations that Ellis seeks to induce by means of therapy are listed in Table 17.4.

Ellis's mode for coping directly with the patient's illogicalities in therapy is revealed in the following passage.

Table 17.4 The Rational-Emotive Therapist's View of Some Irrational Beliefs That Create "Neurosis"

Irrational Beliefs	Rational Transformations
1. Individuals must be loved or approved by virtually everyone for the things they do. People should consider what others think of them and depend on others.	1. There is nothing horrible or catastrophic in not being loved by everyone. True self-respect comes not from the approval of others but from liking yourself and following your interest. "What do I want to do in life?" is more important then choosing an action on the basis of what others wish you to do.
2. To be worthwhile, people must be thoroughly competent, adequate, and achieving in all respects.	2. This confuses extrinsic and intrinsic values. The principal goal in life consists of discovering what are your own most enjoyable and rewarding interests in life.
3. Human unhappiness has its roots in external events, and people cannot control their sorrows.	3. Unhappiness comes from within and is created by the individual; you therefore must forthrightly face the fact that since you create, you too can eradicate your own unhappiness.

Adapted from Ellis, 1962.

> Convincing oneself, if one is a therapist, that the usual concepts of self-worth are illogical and illegitimate and convincing one's patients of this fact are, unfortunately, two different things. I must say that I have had the devil of a time, in recent years, showing many of my clients that they are not as worthless as they think they are . . . I . . . put the onus on them of proving that they are valueless. . . .
>
> I, therefore, often say to my patients: "Look, you insist that you are worthless, valueless, and no damn good. Now give me some evidence to prove your hypothesis." Of course they can't. They almost immediately come up with some statement such as: "Well, I am worthless because I'm no good at anything" . . . but as I soon show them, these are tautological sentences which say nothing but: "I am worthless because I consider myself to be worthless" . . . .
>
> I then go through a whole battery of reasons with these clients which indicate why it is untenable for them to consider themselves worthless. [By the same token, I usually attempt to show them that they (that is, their totality or essence) cannot be legitimately rated at all, but only their many traits, deeds, and performances can be accurately given some kind of rating or worth.] (1962, p. 154).

This description captures Ellis's view of how he uses the therapeutic exchange to extinguish an old belief system while reinforcing another. He has called this method **insightful countersuggestion** to describe how he teaches the client to understand the forces that have shaped his or her behavior, thereby providing some degree of control over actions. Such procedures are consistent with the methods used by a new breed of cognitive behavior therapists.

Cognitive Therapy with Depressed Patients. In the wake of Ellis's pioneering work, many versions of cognitive behavior therapy have been developed. One of the most significant is the method devised by Aaron Beck (1976, 1979), a psychiatrist distinguished for his contributions to therapy with depressive patients. Beck was trained in psychoanalysis, but his clinical experience with patients convinced him that the central task in treatment was changing the faulty ways in which they think about themselves. Patients, particularly depressives, have arbitrary, broad, and inclusive negative views of the self, and these in turn are reflected in painful rather than pleasurable emotional states. Events are invariably given a negative interpretation. Self-appraisals are marked by self-blame and self-dislike. The future is inevitably perceived as bleak and punishing.

Here is an example of an exchange between Beck and a twenty-six-year-old graduate student who had a four-month recurrent depression. Note how Beck focuses on the *meaning* of an event and the powerful, exaggerated interpretation that the student gives it.

P: I agree with the descriptions of me but I guess I don't agree that the way I think makes me depressed.

T: How do you understand it?

P: I get depressed when things go wrong. Like when I fail a test.

T: How can failing a test make you depressed?

P: Well, if I fail I'll never get into law school.

T: So failing the test means a lot to you. But if failing a test could drive people into clinical depression, wouldn't you expect everyone who failed the test to have a depression? . . . Did everyone who failed get depressed enough to require treatment?

P: No, but it depends on how important the test was to the person.

T: Right, and who decides the importance?

P: I do.

T: And so, what we have to examine is your way of viewing the test (or the way that you think about the test) and how it affects your chances of getting into law school. Do you agree?

P: Right.

T: Do you agree that the way you interpret the results of the test will affect you? You might feel depressed, you might have trouble sleeping, not feel like eating, and you might even wonder if you should drop out of the course.

P: I have been thinking that I wasn't going to make it. Yes, I agree.

T: Now what did failing mean?

P: (tearful) That I couldn't get into law school.

T: And what does that mean to you?

P: That I'm just not smart enough.

T: Anything else?

P: That I can never be happy.

T: And how do these thoughts make you feel?

P: Very unhappy.

T: So it is the meaning of failing a test that makes you very unhappy. In fact, believing that you can never be happy is a powerful factor in producing unhappiness. So, you get yourself into a trap—by definition, failure to get into law school equals "I can never be happy" (Beck et al., 1979, pp. 145–146).

Stress-Inoculation Therapy.   As we saw in Chapter 10, the task of coping with stressful life events is a very significant one. Cognitive behavior therapy has made important contributions by training people to modify their ways of dealing with situations that provoke anxiety (Meichenbaum, 1977; Meichenbaum and Cameron, 1983). There are three phases to such training. In the first phase clients are helped to examine their modes of responding to stressful situations. In the second phase they are provided with new behavioral and cognitive coping techniques and given the opportunity to practice them. In the third, the test phase, clients test their coping responses in a variety of stressful experiences. Read Table 17.5 carefully. It provides examples of how clients are assisted in rehearsing coping self-statements.

How effective is such **self-inoculation** training? Philip Kendall and his colleagues (1979) compared the method with three others in an attempt to answer this question. The participants in the study were patients who were undergoing the painful medical procedure of cardiac catheterization. The self-inoculation procedure helped the patients label the stress and identify the cues associated with it. The patients received information about the event to come and engaged in positive self-talk about means of coping with it. They were provided with the opportunity to rehearse these coping skills. Other groups of patients received standard hospital care, were taught about heart disease, or were allowed to discuss their concerns and fears. Self-ratings of anxiety and more objective ratings provided by physicians and nurses revealed that the most effective procedure was self-inoculation training.

THERAPY IN GROUPS

Individual psychotherapy, the one-to-one confrontation of a client and therapist, has always been the dominant form in therapeutic practice. Then this traditional method of treatment was challenged by a group of brash newcomers—the group therapies. **Group therapy** came to the fore during World War II when the shortage of therapists available to soldiers who had broken in combat made it necessary to introduce more efficient treatments. That shortage is still in evidence today and, together with the growing expense of individual treatment, has fostered the development of short-term group therapy.

Whatever the forces that led to the growth of group therapy, there is an important justification for the movement. People are social beings. They can

Table 17.5 Examples of Coping Self-Statements Rehearsed in Stress-Inoculation Training

Preparing for a stressor
What is it you have to do?
You can develop a plan to deal with it.
Just think about what you can do about it. That's better than getting anxious.
No negative self-statements: just think rationally.
Don't worry: worry won't help anything.
Maybe what you think is anxiety is eagerness to confront the stressor.

Confronting and handling a stressor
Just "psych" yourself up—you can meet this challenge.
You can convince yourself to do it. You can reason your fear away.
One step at a time: you can handle the situation.
Don't think about fear; just think about what you have to do. Stay relevant.
This anxiety is what the doctor said you would feel. It's a reminder to use your
    coping exercises.
This tenseness can be an ally; a cue to cope.
Relax; you're in control. Take a slow deep breath.
Ah, good.

Coping with the feeling of being overwhelmed
When fear comes, just pause.
Keep the focus on the present; what is it you have to do?
Label your fear from 0 to 10 and watch it change.
You should *expect* your fear to rise.
Don't try to eliminate fear totally; just keep it manageable.

Reinforcing self-statements
It worked; you did it.
Wait until you tell your therapist (or group) about this.
It wasn't as bad as you expected.
You made more out of your fear than it was worth.
Your damn ideas—that's the problem. When you control them, you control your
    fear.
It's getting better each time you use the procedures.
You can be pleased with the progress you're making.
You did it!

From Meichenbaum, 1974, 1977.

exist only marginally when alone. When they experience distress, it is often a product of their relationships with others. If people are to learn new methods of relating to others, what better way is there for them to do so than by using a group as a place to practice and develop the necessary skills? Furthermore, retraining in a group should promote the generalization of adaptive behavior to the social world beyond the treatment setting.

Irvin Yalom (1975), one of the nation's leaders in group therapy, sees a more intimate function for group therapy. He observes that "without exception, patients enter group therapy with the history of a highly unsatisfactory experience in their first and most important group—their primary family" (p. 14). An aim of group therapy must be to remove the effects of such negative experiences. To foster the identification with the family, it is common for a male-female cotherapist team to lead the group. Group members often assign them the symbolic roles of parents. They interact with these leaders and members as they once interacted with parents and siblings. For this reason group therapy invites an enormous number of possibilities for emulating past relationships. Yalom continues:

> There are an infinite variety of patterns: [The group members] may be helplessly dependent upon the leaders, whom they imbue with unrealistic knowledge and power; they may defy the leaders at every step because they regard them as individuals who block their autonomous growth or strip them of their individuality; they may attempt to split the cotherapists and to incite disagreements or rivalry between the two; they may compete bitterly with other members in their efforts to accumulate units of attention and caring from the therapists; they may search for allies among the others in an effort to topple the therapists; they may forgo their own interests in a seemingly selfless effort to appease or provide for other members (pp. 14–15).

Groups detect such manipulations and group correctives are applied. Behavior is challenged, new relationships develop, the group encourages different and more adaptive behavior; a new pattern of social learning is achieved and new social skills are acquired, sometimes through imitation and modeling, sometimes by rapid and personal feedback. Yalom observes that the senior members of a therapy group acquire marked social skills, by helping others, withholding judgments, assisting in the resolution of conflicts, and becoming capable of empathy and compassion. Skills such as these go beyond the therapy room and transfer to the social world beyond.

EFFECTIVENESS OF PSYCHOTHERAPY

Research in psychotherapy often begins with a very basic question. Does psychotherapy work? Some psychologists, considering the results of many studies, have taken a pessimistic view, suggesting that, except possibly for behavior therapy, there is little evidence that psychotherapy is effective at all. One of the strongest critics, Hans Eysenck (1961), reviewed 19 studies that covered more than 7000 cases seen in psychoanalysis and other types of treatments. Patients were divided into several groups, including *cured, much improved, improved, slightly improved,* and *unimproved.* On the basis of his survey, Eysenck reported that only 44 percent of those treated by psychoanalysis showed improvement, whereas 64 percent of those treated by other psychotherapeutic methods and 72 percent of those who received primarily custodial care improved. Eysenck took a dismal view of the field and concluded that recovery and psychotherapy seem to be inversely related: the more psychotherapy, the lower the recovery rate.

Eysenck's conclusions did not go unchallenged. A reappraisal of his analysis by Allen Bergin and Michael Lambert (1978) suggested that Eysenck's original judgments of improvement were far too harsh, and that there were too many differences in the studies cited to permit ready comparison. Types of cases, measures of improvement, and extent of follow-up varied considerably. In contrast with Eysenck, Bergin and Lambert found the results encouraging and concluded that the best results of psychotherapy occur with longer and more intense treatment. Psychotherapy, they asserted, has "modestly positive results," with a larger proportion of the studies cited by Eysenck reporting favorable outcomes than chance alone would suggest.

A recent survey (Smith, Glass, and Miller, 1980) has provided one of the most thorough appraisals of the psychotherapy and drug therapy literature. The evaluation included 475 studies, involving tens of thousands of persons, in which a group receiving psychological treatment had been compared with a roughly equivalent untreated group. The investigators found that, in terms of psychological well-being, a person who obtained therapy was better off than 80 percent of those who needed therapy but went untreated. They concluded that "psychotherapy is beneficial, consistently so and in many different ways. Its benefits are on a par with other expensive and ambitious interventions such as schooling and medicine." But there was a final caution: "The benefits of psychotherapy are not permanent, but then little is" (p. 183).

Health Psychology

While controversy continues over the effectiveness of therapy for emotionally disturbed people, a new and broader approach to intervention has begun to take form. Sometimes called *medical psychology, health care psychology,* and *behavioral medicine* (Millon, 1982), **health psychology** represents an important transition from clinical psychology's former preoccupation with the behavior disorders to a concern with the interface between physical health and behavior (Matarazzo, 1983).

> Health psychology is the aggregate of the specific educational, scientific, and professional contributions of the discipline of psychology to the promotion and maintenance of health, the prevention and treatment of illness, and the identification of etiologic and diagnostic correlates of health, illness, and related dysfunction (Matarazzo, 1980).

As this statement by one of the pioneers in health psychology indicates, the new discipline has turned its attention to a wide range of physical disorders. The areas to which health psychologists are now contributing are so extensive that the new field is beginning to redirect the energies of the entire science and profession of psychology. For health psychology has begun to attract the interests of physiological, experimental, developmental, and social psychologists; some of them are now doing clinical work along with their laboratory studies. Common problems have now brought together in a common calling psychologists who a decade or two ago were going very different ways.

The list of areas of research and treatment with which health psychologists have concerned themselves reads like a catalogue of human infirmities. Elsewhere in this book we have covered many subjects that come together under the umbrella of health psychology.

- Genetic counseling, which helps people understand the contributions of inheritance to disease.
- Biofeedback to alleviate migraine headache and other pain and to lower blood pressure or sometimes to raise it to help patients with spinal damage stand upright and move around.
- The diagnosis of sensory impairments as an aid to therapy.
- Memory training for old people and those with brain damage that causes losses of memory.
- Therapy for the various learning disabilities.
- Stress control and therapy for people with the Type A pattern of behavior.
- Application of the methods of classical conditioning to enuresis.
- Behavioral methods of treating obesity, alcoholism, drug abuse, and smoking.
- Programs designed to apply psychology's knowledge of compliance to one of the most important present-day medical problems: getting people to fill prescriptions, take their medication, and stick to recommended diets and programs of physical exercise.
- The various methods of therapy for disordered states covered in this chapter.

Joseph D. Matarazzo is head of the Department of Medical Psychology at the University of Oregon Medical School. A graduate of Northwestern University's doctoral program in clinical psychology, he has been a pioneer in the field of health psychology.

The payoff for society of these and a host of other applications of health psychology can be substantial, in terms of the nation's physical, psychological, and economic well-being. It has been shown, for example, that the simultaneous referral of various types of medical patients to both a psychologist and a physician leads to a reduction in the total number of days patients stay in the hospital, fewer required visits to a medical outpatient clinic, and a decrease in the number of unnecessary laboratory and diagnostic services.

SUMMARY

The current psychotherapeutic scene has been invigorated by one of the genuine revolutions of our time—behavior therapies. The roots of these new forms of therapy are to be found in the principles of classical and operant conditioning. Their impact is evident in the diversity of the conditions to which behavior therapists have turned their attention, with results that are impressive. Some of the methods based on classical conditioning include systematic desensitization, implosion and flooding, and paradoxical intention. Others based on operant conditioning principles include positive reinforcement, extinction, and aversion therapy. More recent additions to the group of behavior therapies place great emphasis on the client's cognitions, expectations, and problem-solving strategies and are identified as cognitive behavior therapies.

Group therapy meets a need not served by individual psychotherapy. Exchanges within the group provide a means for portraying the role of the family. Sometimes the pattern of these exchanges resemble those of earlier exchanges in group members' families. Members of successful therapy groups may detect manipulative behavior and encourage the adoption of new social skills.

Evaluations of the effectiveness of psychotherapy have sometimes been very negative, seeming to show that these procedures have an impact that is either nil or negative. Reevaluations of these criticisms reveal that they were too pessimistic. When the results of hundreds of studies are considered, the data indicate that psychotherapy is beneficial.

A new field of application, health psychology, standing at the boundary between medicine and psychology, brings the skills of both fields to bear on health and illness. The field is growing rapidly, has found application to many health problems, and shows promise of making great contributions to the health problems of the world.

A PERSONAL NOTE

You and Psychotherapy

Two lengthy chapters on behavior pathology and its treatment may cause some concern in students regarding their own mental health. Such concerns can easily be brought on by similarities between normal and disordered behavior. This is not to deny that minor and severe maladjustments exist on the college campus, but in the individual case the probabilities always favor health and effectiveness, and the ability to adapt to college life does serve as one criterion of good mental health.

Suppose you are concerned with your psychological state. Does this reflect a morbid attitude on your part? Not necessarily. It may be one of the realistic self-appraisals you make as you move toward maturity. And it may be that you will conclude, after such an appraisal, that you can profit from psychological help. This is not a sign of weakness and it may well be a sign of strength to seek such counsel. If you feel a sense of pervasive unhappiness, a lack of accomplishment, and marked self-dissatisfaction, a counseling center on your campus—or a casework agency or a clinic in your community—may help you to achieve greater comfort, self-understanding, and self-acceptance.

For others, help may be found in friendship. Freedom to talk about your feelings and concerns—not indiscriminately but with a trusted friend, relative, or adviser in whom you have confidence—may help you to clarify your situation and see solutions that you might otherwise have missed or evaluated incorrectly. This, of course, is the way most people in our society gain help. Psychotherapy at present exists only for the few. The availability of a mature person who will honor your confidences is one alternative that can be helpful.

The advice to rely on friends is one of several suggestions that mental health experts have provided as ways of managing personal problems. These may be self-evident, but they may also be helpful.

- Do not hesitate to share your concerns with a trusted and respected person. You can choose a professional, a teacher, a faculty adviser, a friend. It is not a sign of weakness to choose judiciously someone with whom to discuss what is troubling you, what your options are, how you might solve the problem you face.
- Be aware that there may not be a *present* solution to your problem. If it is beyond your control at the moment, live with the problem until you can resolve it.
- Stay away from drugs, alcohol, and those other addictive substances designed to make you forget. You will not forget and you will feel worse in the morning.
- Take care of your physical self. Physical debility and mental disablement go hand in hand.
- Try getting outside yourself. Do things with others or, better yet, try doing some things for others. It will serve to boost your self-esteem at a time when such a boost is needed.
- Try to order your priorities. If a number of troubles have hit you simultaneously, tackle the ones that need handling first—after you have thought through what your hierarchy should be.
- Try getting exercise as an outlet for relieving some of the anxiety you feel. A few studies suggest that jogging is psychotherapeutic.

The patient ear and understanding of a friend can help a troubled person talk through an emotional problem.

- If you are going to read self-help books, stay away from those whose covers promise to solve all your problems. Self-help books are flooding the market and most of them are worthless. But there are some that have been written by wise people. Browse in the library; compare the credentials of the authors. Avoid the ones that make promises, promises, promises. If there is anything you do not need when you are under stress, it is soft-mindedness and fakery.

Questions Frequently Asked about Psychotherapy

Q: *What sort of qualities should I look for in a therapist?*
A: There is no universal set of desirable attributes. What is important is the relationship you develop with the therapist. It helps to know, however, that certain characteristics of the therapist seem to increase the likelihood that therapy will be successful: a solid level of experience, evident skills, a quality of empathy, similarities in values, attitudes, and interests with your own.

Q: *Who is most likely to benefit from psychotherapy?*
A: The person who is highly motivated to change, who has had a previous history of achievement, who is competent in terms of work, social, and sexual history, and who has the good fortune to secure an able, experienced, empathic therapist.

Q: *Can people be injured by therapy?*
A: There are reports of what have been called "deterioration effects" or "negative effects" (Strupp, Hadley, and Gomez-Schwartz, 1977). Some clients worsen with therapy. Those who do are fragile and disturbed to begin with and are made more vulnerable by the ministrations of inept, careless, or poorly trained clinicians. There are some forms of therapy that foster "leave-taking" by clients. These include flooding, implosive therapy, and aversive conditioning. There have been unfortunate reports of the development of depression in some phobics treated by desensitization. More traditional approaches in the hands of a competent, experienced therapist generally show positive effects (Bergin and Lambert, 1978).

Q: *Is one type of therapy superior to another?*
A: There is virtually no evidence of the superiority of any one traditional school of psychotherapy over another traditional school. Behavior therapy appears to have the best track record.

Q: *Are there any things I should watch out for?*
A: Yes, never pay much attention to therapists who advertise in the media. The shoddier the newspaper or magazine in which the advertisement appears, the more cautious you should be. Never join an encounter group impulsively. Beware of a group that is given to excessive bullying of its members, seeks to exploit specific individuals, uses jargon, or spends too much time interpreting the behavior of its participants.

These are the major concepts of the chapter, in the approximate order in which they are presented.

TO BE SURE YOU UNDERSTAND THIS CHAPTER

Revolving door	**Social-learning therapy**
Expressed emotionality (EE)	**Somatic (physical) therapy**
Social-skills training	**Psychotherapy**
Milieu therapy	**Electroconvulsive shock therapy (ECT)**

Psychosurgery	Reciprocal inhibition
Lobotomy	Implosion therapy
Phenothiazine	Flooding
Chlorpromazine	Agoraphobia
Tardive dyskinesia	Paradoxical intention
Tricyclic	Positive reinforcement
Monoamine oxidase inhibitor	Token economy
Imipramine	Extinction
Lithium carbonate	Avoidance training
Psychoanalysis	Punishment
Free association	Aversion therapy
Resistance	Cognitive behavior therapy
Repression	Rational-emotive therapy
Transference (positive and negative)	Insightful countersuggestion
Abreaction	Stress-inoculation therapy
Systematic desensitization	Group therapy
Anxiety hierarchy	Health psychology

TO GO BEYOND THIS CHAPTER

In This Book. For links to understanding the materials in Chapter 17, we suggest a review particularly of Chapter 16, Psychopathology. It would also be of interest at this point to review the various applications mentioned in the discussion of health psychology. **Elsewhere.** For extended discussions of therapy, somatic and psychological, we again refer you to the various abnormal psychology texts that appear at the end of Chapter 16.

There are a variety of overview books on psychotherapy. Here are some suggestions: Raymond Corsini, *Current Psychotherapies* (second edition); Isaac Marks, *Living with Fear,* available in paperback; Robert Martin and Elizabeth Poland, *Learning To Change: A Self-Management Approach to Adjustment,* one of the responsible self-help books; and Harry Kalish, *From Behavioral Science to Behavior Modification.*

PART EIGHT   SOCIAL PSYCHOLOGY

Oskar Schlemmer. "Bauhaus Stairway" (1932). Collection The Museum of Modern Art, New York. Gift of Philip Johnson.

CHAPTER 18   SOCIAL COGNITION AND SOCIAL BEHAVIOR

This chapter was written by Edward E. Jones
and Charles G. Lord.

You hardly need to be reminded that your daily, moment-to-moment behavior is greatly affected by social considerations. The choice of clothing you made this morning was probably influenced by your expectations of the particular people you might meet during the day to come. Your decisions about what to do this evening depended on who was going where and doing what. In the supermarket your familiarity with brand names touted by the commercials on television, which is inordinately concerned with social effects, is likely to guide your choices. Or consider what happens when you are irritated by the thoughtless behavior of a friend. Do you express your anger? How? You find yourself on a committee charged with a set of complex decisions. How should the committee be organized? Who should assume leadership? Your college classmates elect you to the judicial board, and a friend is accused of plagiarism under cloudy circumstances. How do you sort out all the moral and social pressures weighing on you in order to reach a decision that you can live with? These everyday incidents make the simple but important point that the presence and actions of other people make a difference in how we behave in many situations. The special field of **social psychology,** to be presented in this chapter and the next, is concerned with such influences.

UNDERSTANDING OUR SOCIAL ENVIRONMENT

Our perception of the social environment, like our perception of the physical, depends partly on our interpretation of events in it. The behavior of a particular person affects each of us in different ways, depending on the meaning we assign to that behavior. This meaning in turn grows out of our perceptions of a person's behavior, the setting in which the behavior occurs, and the inferences we make about the other person's motives and intentions. If a friend fails to greet us on campus, we react in one way if we conclude that the friend did not see us, but in quite a different way if we think that we have been ignored. Our perceptions of other people and their perceptions of us are obviously basic to the interactions that we have with others.

Person Perception
People emit sounds, they reflect different wavelengths of light, and they are more or less solid to the touch. On these bases we perceive people as physical objects, just as we perceive rocks, trees, and skyscrapers as physical objects. In addition, however, we perceive the psychological characteristics of people and

interpret the significance of their words and actions. These inferences are the hypotheses we form about the dispositions of other people—their motives, purposes, and intentions toward us. We see the behavior of others as caused by these dispositions. Fritz Heider (1958), a distinguished student of interpersonal behavior, suggested that our perception of the causes of people's behavior is just as much a part of perception as our perception of their physical characteristics.

In many situations other people can make decisions and carry out actions that strongly affect our well-being. Am I involved with him in a test of strength? Will she laugh at me if I tell her I need her help? If she finds out about my financial situation, will she bring an end to our relationship? Will he be embarrassed if I tell him he is attractive? How we answer these private questions depends on our perception of the other people. We process the witting and unwitting communications of these others and draw from them our inferences about their dispositions.

Heider emphasized the importance of our need to be able to understand the various states of our environment in order to maintain control over it. In our efforts to locate dependable bases for such understandings, we search for stable categories for important events in the environment, including the behavior of others. We impose stability on behavior by assigning causal status to the dispositions that we perceive to be behind it. If a man opposes us and helps our opponent, we are likely to perceive him as "hostile" rather than "sometimes hostile" and "sometimes friendly." Although the man's behavior is certainly friendly from our opponent's point of view, we frequently ignore such complexities and infer a single, stable, disposition "to explain" varying behavior: "He is against me because he is a hostile person."

Attribution Theory

When Heider proposed that the perception of cause and effect in people's behavior is primitive and basic, he set the stage for what came to be known as **attribution theory,** so called because it concerns the ways in which we attribute behavior to causes. In its treatment of the perception of causality in human behavior, attribution theory distinguishes between the instances when we perceive these causes to be in a person's dispositions and those when we attribute the causes to environmental factors. "Sorry I'm late," says your guest, "but my car broke down." How you react to this excuse indicates the kind of cause to which you attribute your guest's behavior. If you say, "Yes, old cars are a nuisance," you have attributed causality to something in the environment. If you say—or more likely just think—"If you took care of it, the car wouldn't break down," you have attributed causality to one of your guest's personal dispositions. The philosophical question of what *really* causes behavior is a nest of unsolved riddles. Attribution theory, however, concerns *perceived* causes. It attends to the assumptions people make and is moot regarding the validity of these assumptions.

Most psychologists agree that behavior can tell us either a little or a lot about the dispositions of the actor. If the situation seems to cause a person's action— "anyone would have behaved the same way"—the implication is that the behavior reveals little about this particular person. If it appears that the individual chooses one course of action over another, however, we conclude that the person's behavior reveals something about his or her personal characteristics. If you write a forty-page term paper because the professor assigned a paper that long, people will perceive the causes of your behavior to be environmental, the professor's assignment. If you write a forty-page paper when the professor assigned a paper "at least ten pages long," people will attribute your behavior to a personal disposition—you are really interested in the topic, you are a terribly compulsive person, or you are trying hard to improve your grade.

Edward E. Jones and Keith Davis (1965) have put forth this reasoning in the version of attribution theory known as **correspondent-inference theory.** This theory assumes that behavior tells us something distinctive about the person when there are few external reasons for engaging in the behavior and these reasons would not impel everyone to behave in the same way. By choosing a particular line of action when several alternatives are available, people reveal more about themselves than when their choices are coerced, obviously popular, or the "natural thing to do." When people make such choices among many alternatives, we say that they "wear their hearts on their sleeves," and we infer a corresponding disposition—hence "correspondent-inference theory"—to be part of the person's psychological makeup.

An example might be helpful here. John Thibaut and Henry Riecken (1955) conducted an early experiment in which each male subject was induced by the experimenter to try to persuade two other "subjects," who were actually accomplices of the experimenter, to a course of action. One of these accomplices had presented himself as a high-status person, a graduate student or law student, whereas the other student had presented himself as a lowly freshman. In one version of the experiment, subjects attempted to persuade the two accomplices to give blood to the blood bank. They both complied, and the subjects were then asked to evaluate each student for a number of pertinent characteristics signifying perceived intent and personal attractiveness. The subjects tended to see the compliant behavior of the high-status accomplice as internally caused—he complied because he spontaneously wanted to. They saw the low-status accomplice as complying because the situation forced him to—he had no alterantive. The subjects also reported greater liking for the high-status accomplice. The correspondent-inference theorist would say that the low-status accomplice had more reasons for complying and therefore less choice than did the high-status accomplice. The behavior of the high-status complier was consequently more informative about his intrinsic generosity, spontaneous good will, and related personal traits. Harold Kelley later christened these tendencies to diminish the importance of one cause or the other the **discounting effect:** "The role of a given cause in producing a given effect is discounted if other plausible causes are also present" (1971, p. 8).

In many respects, the average person attributes causality to personal or situational variables in the same way that a careful scientist might, by noticing whether behavior covaries with the person or with the situation (Kelley, 1967). When Jane tells us that she enjoyed the new movie, for example, we are more likely to attribute the cause of Jane's enjoyment to the movie than to her disposition if we discover that she does not enjoy other movies, if her reaction to this particular movie is **distinctive.** We are also more likely to regard the movie as causing Jane's reaction if other people also liked it, if there is **consensus,** and if Jane saw the movie twice and liked it both times, that is, if she showed **consistency.** When distinctiveness and consensus and consistency are low, we are likely to believe that Jane's reaction tells us more about her as a person than it does about the movie. If Jane likes all movies and no one else liked *The Creature That Ate Indianapolis,* we behave like rational scientists by attributing the cause of her endorsement to her peculiar preferences—and probably decide to save the price of admission.

Harold Kelley's work on attribution theory, a principal concern of social psychologists, has probably advanced it the most in recent years. He has now applied the theory to close and long-enduring personal relationships, those that exist between husbands and wives, lovers, close friends, roommates, and close co-workers.

Attributional Biases

The judgments that we make about the dispositions of others are not always so rational and scientific. Sometimes we act less like scientists than like "cognitive misers," taking mental shortcuts that save us time and effort (Fiske, 1981). Rather than taking the time to think through all the implications of an attributional problem, we rely on our expectations and intuitions—a reliance that usually serves us quite well but sometimes leads us astray.

The Fundamental Attribution Error. One mistake in attribution that people often make is to underestimate situational factors and to overestimate personal dispositions as causes of behavior. If people are shown essays that are clearly described as prepared under conditions that allowed the writer no choice—for example, as an assignment of the debating coach—they will still usually assume that the essayists believe in the position taken. This assumption turns out to be a serious mistake in light of the self-rated attitudes of the people who actually wrote the essays (Snyder and Jones, 1974).

A more dramatic example of this **fundamental attribution error,** as it is called by Lee Ross (1977), has been demonstrated by Ross, Teresa Amabile, and Julia Steinmetz (1977). These experimenters asked pairs of subjects to participate in a quiz game. One member of the pair was randomly assigned to the role of "questioner" and the other to the role of "contestant." *In the presence of the contestant,* the questioner was instructed to make a list of the hardest questions he or she could think of and knew the answers to. These questions were then given to the contestant as a quiz. During the quiz the contestant, naturally, did not fare very well. After the questioning both subjects were asked to evaluate their own general knowledge and that of their partner. Observers who had watched the proceedings also evaluated the general knowledge of both participants. The questioner considered the contestant's knowledge and his or her own to be that of the average student. The contestants as well as the neutral observers, however, saw the questioner as much more knowledgeable than the contestant, even though the observed discrepancy in knowledge was to an important degree preordained by the arbitrary role assignments. Ross and his fellow experimenters have speculated that for just this reason doctoral students invariably finish their oral exams feeling like dunces, whereas the examiners are impressed with the wisdom of their colleagues (Table 18.1).

Table 18.1 Questions for a Quiz Game*

1. Who was originally supposed to play Dorothy in *The Wizard of Oz* movie?
2. Who was the author of *As I Lay Dying?*
3. Who was president of France during World War II?
4. Who makes Crayola crayons?
5. "I buried Paul" can be heard at the end of what Beatles song?
6. Which weighs more, a proton or a neutron?
7. What was Richard Adam's next book after *Watership Down?*
8. Who was the only United States president to be elected, having lost the popular vote?
9. Which trilogy won the Hugo award as the best science fiction series of all time?
10. Who was the last player to bat against Tom Seaver while Seaver was still a Met?

* Is the person who thought up these questions, after being asked by the experimenter to devise ten "challenging but not impossible" questions, more knowledgeable than you are? Try to think of ten such questions yourself and see whether a friend finds them any easier to answer.

Actor-Observer Differences.   Jones and Richard Nisbett (1971) have proposed that the fundamental attribution error contributes to a socially important divergence of the opinions of people who observe a bit of behavior from those of people doing the behaving. They theorize that actors tend to attribute their behavior to the situation, whereas observers see the same behavior as reflecting personal dispositions.

Although this theory that actors are more aware of the situation and observers more aware of personal dispositions remains somewhat controversial, considerable evidence compatible with it has been collected. Whereas the angry man feels that he has been clearly provoked, and assumes that anyone would have reacted the same way he did, the bystander sees him as hostile and "trigger tempered" by disposition. Whereas failing students blame their failures on a broken love affair, their advisers are convinced of their fundamental academic inertia. Whereas the cabinet officer attributes his or her ineffective behavior to political pressure, the observer explains it as a lack of courage, persistence, and resourcefulness. Fortunately for the mutual understanding of actors and observers, these differences in the perception of causality may be partly overcome by inducing observers to put themselves in the shoes of actors. For example, the better the observer knows the actor and the better each is at taking the role of the other, the more comparable their perceptions of causality will be.

False Consensus.   We make another common error of social judgment when we assume that a majority of others would agree with us and would respond as we do. Suppose, for example, that you volunteer for a psychology experiment and that the experimenter hands you a large "sandwich board" sign of the kind depicted in cartoons. The experimenter asks you whether you would be willing to walk around campus for half an hour wearing this sandwich board, which proclaims in garish lettering "REPENT!" Would you agree to do this? How many other students do you think would agree, and how many would refuse? How confidently could you describe the traits of those who would agree and those who would disagree? Lee Ross, David Greene, and Pamela House (1977) conducted this experiment and found that about half the students agreed to wear the sign and half refused. More interestingly, the half who agreed claimed that about 62 percent of their peers would agree, whereas the half who refused claimed that only 33 percent of their peers would agree. In addition, in line with correspondent-inference theory, each half claimed that they could be much more confident in attributing traits, usually negative ones, to the "minority" of students who did not behave as they did.

Heuristics.   Social psychologists study attributional errors for the same reasons that perception psychologists study illusions or that physiological psychologists study split-brain patients. One of the best ways to find out how something works is to observe what happens when it malfunctions. Using this technique, psychologists have discovered that many attributional errors are made because we rely too heavily on certain **heuristics** (page 235), or "rules of thumb," that we apply to a variety of social judgments. One such heuristic is **representativeness.** To use an example drawn from a recent volume on social judgment (Nisbett and Ross, 1980), suppose that your psychology professor tells you that he or she has a faculty friend who is short, rather shy, and likes to write poetry. The professor asks you to guess whether his friend is a professor of Chinese studies or of psychology. What would your answer be? If you even considered responding "Chinese studies," you were probably using the representativeness heuristic as a guide. The odds are overwhelming that "psychology" is the

Table 18.2 Read This List of Names

Queen Elizabeth	Nadia Comeneci
Alben Barclay	Darrell Waltrip
Raymond Chandler	Edward Brooke
Cheryl Tiegs	Richard Helms
Edward Teller	Mother Theresa
Katharine Hepburn	Brooke Shields
Grace Kelly	Fletcher Knebel
Earl Weaver	Jake LaMotta
Tom Weiskopf	Jacqueline Onassis
Golda Meir	Jackson Pollock
Nancy Reagan	Elizabeth Taylor

After you have finished reading the list, return to the text.

correct answer. Given the fact that professors of psychology vastly outnumber professors of Chinese studies at most colleges and universities, there are probably many more short, shy poets who teach psychology than short, shy poets who teach Chinese studies. In addition, your professor is much more likely to have acquaintances in his or her own discipline. The fact that the description—"short, rather shy, writes poetry"—is representative of your image of a Chinese professor is what suggests the highly improbable answer. We make similar attributional errors based on representativeness if we identify people with narrow eyes as "suspicious" or those with bushy eyebrows as "criminal types."

Another commonly used heruistic is **availability**. Read the list of names in Table 18.2 before continuing. Without looking back at the table, can you remember whether there were more male or female names? Make your best guess, and then determine the answer by counting. Most readers report that the list contained more female names. This is an example of the availability heuristic. When judging the likelihood or frequency of an event, we rely on the subjective ease with which the event "pops into our heads," or comes to mind. Presumably, when you try to recall the names, the famous women like Elizabeth Taylor and Queen Elizabeth are more easily brought to mind than the less famous men like Alben Barclay, a vice-president of the United States, and Richard Helms, a former CIA director. Because the ease of bringing a person's name or event to mind is usually an excellent indicator of the actual frequency with which it occurs in our daily lives, we may follow this rule of thumb even when it leads to an erroneous conclusion.

Construct Accessibility. Availability, in turn, is closely related to **construct accessibility**. Say the following words out loud until you can repeat them three times in a row without looking back at the list:

RECKLESS CONCEITED ALOOF STUBBORN.

When you have memorized the list, read the next paragraph.

Donald spent a great amount of his time in search of what he liked to call excitement. He had already climbed Mt. McKinley, shot the Colorado rapids in a kayak, driven in a demolition derby, and piloted a jet-powered boat—without knowing very much about boats. He had risked injury, even death, a number of times. Now he was in search of new excitement. He was thinking that perhaps he would do some skydiving or maybe cross the Atlantic in a sailboat. By the way that he acted, one could readily guess that Donald was well aware of his ability to do many things well. Other than business engagements, Donald's contacts with people were rather limited. He felt that he did not really need to rely on anyone. Once Donald had made up his mind to do something, it was as good as done, no matter how long it might take or how difficult the going might be. Only rarely did he change his mind, even when it might well have been better if he had.

What did you think of Donald? Did you like him or not? Subjects in a study by Tory Higgins, William Rholes, and Carl Jones (1977) first memorized a list of traits or constructs like those given earlier and then participated in an "unrelated experiment," in which they read an evaluated the story about Donald. They evaluated Donald's behavior rather negatively. Other subjects memorized the following list: ADVENTUROUS, SELF-CONFIDENT, INDEPENDENT, PERSISTENT. After reading the same story, they liked Donald. These findings suggests that our attributions about other persons may be influenced by the constructs that have been made salient by recent exposure to them. You should hope that your date has been watching *Love Story* rather than *The Thing* just before you go out for what you hope will be a romantic evening.

Visual Salience. People tend to see other people as more influential than they are, and it may be that "see" is quite literally the word for it. By virtue of where our eyes are placed in our heads, the other person always "takes center stage" in our visual field, and we stand perpetually "waiting in the wings." To demonstrate that visual salience promotes attributions of influence, Leslie McArthur and David Post (1977) had subjects watch a panel discussion and judge the effectiveness of the participants. The subjects attributed greater influence to whichever panelist happened to be sitting under the brightest light and remembered more of what that person had to say. A brilliantly simple study by Shelley Taylor and Susan Fiske (1975), in which two subjects sat behind one of two conversationalists, so that they were facing the other one, had a similar outcome. When asked who led the conversation, who decided what would be talked about, and who set the overall tone, both subjects thought that the person whom they faced was more influential. They interpreted the same conversation quite differently, depending on mere **visual salience.**

Egocentric Biases. It has been said that all of us rewrite our personal histories to cast ourselves in the leading role and to make ourselves look good, in much the same way that totalitarian governments rewrite history to glorify their achievements (Greenwald, 1980). Michael Ross and Fiore Sicoly (1979) demonstrated the pervasiveness of these **egocentric biases.** They asked spouses to estimate their personal responsibility for various household activities, such as washing dishes, caring for the children, shopping for groceries, and taking out the garbage. Husbands and wives both claimed more responsibility for these activities than their spouses attributed to them. For example, both might claim that they took out the garbage 70 percent of the time. In a second experiment players on college basketball teams were asked to describe the "one important turning point in the last game." Almost invariably, the turning point was attributed to an action of a teammate rather than to something the other team had done. For example, members of the winning team might mention their defensive steal in the closing minutes, whereas members of the losing team might point to their own premature shift in offensive strategy just after halftime.

In their original discussion of correspondent-inference theory, Jones and Davis (1965) recognized that attributions may be affected by **personalism.** It is one thing to make causal attributions about events that involve others, but quite another to make attributions about events that involve ourselves. In an experiment by Michael Enzle, Michael Harvey, and Edward Wright (1980), for example, subjects observed an interview and learned that the interviewer had given the interviewee a negative rating. Then they were told that the interviewer had rated four previous interviewees rather positively. As would be predicted by Kelley's (1967) model, these subjects took the distinctiveness of the event into account and decided that the negative rating revealed something about the particular interviewee rather than the interviewer's personal disposition. Other subjects saw and heard exactly the same information, except that *they* were the interviewees. These subjects disregarded the distinctiveness information and decided that the negative rating said quite a bit about the interviewer's rather nasty disposition.

Knowledge Structures. The preceding account shows that the perception of others is an active process, in which the perceiver goes beyond immediate information to construct an impression of unseen personal traits and the environmental forces that control behavior. Psychologists have long understood that these impressions are a combination of the given and of the expected. Perceivers do not confront the social environment empty-handed—or empty-minded. They have richly developed expectancies about people in general, about classes or types of people, and about people who engage in certain behavior in certain situations. The network of expectancies that guide social perceivers are called **knowledge structures.**

Two types of knowledge structures are schemas and scripts. **Schemas** are the knowledge that resides in sematic memory; **scripts** are more closely related to personal episodic memory (page 185). We have schemas about groups of people. For example, we "know" what politicians are like and how they behave. We "know" that they are extroverted and that they kiss every baby in sight. Scripts help us to interpret and fill in gaps in familiar events (Abelson, 1976). Even though our view of a wedding ceremony may be blocked, we "know" that the groom is taking so long because he is having difficulty putting the ring on the bride's finger, and not because he is cutting her nails. The availability of certain scripts may even dictate foreign policy, as when presidents, cabinet officers, and congressional leaders refrain from involving the United States in foreign disputes for fear of "replaying the Vietnam script" (Gilovich, 1981).

SUMMARY

Social psychologists use the phrase "person perception" to refer to inferences that others make about the dispositions, motives, and intentions of a person. These inferences are derived by complex attributional processes that integrate information about behavior with information about the situation. It has been well established that people tend to attribute causality too readily to the disposition of a person and to underestimate the influence of the situation. People also often incorrectly assume behavioral consensus, that is, that others, in any situation, will behave as they would. These errors may occur because people rely too heavily on certain heuristics. Actors, through visual salience, egocentric biases, and personalism, may make errors different from those of observers. Social perceivers go well beyond the information that is immediately available, using schemas, scripts, and other general knowledge about the world to help them interpret the words and deeds of other people.

STEREOTYPES AND SELF-FULFILLING PROPHECIES

Because of the damage they do, stereotypes are perhaps the most important social-knowledge structures that people have. A **stereotype** is a schema about a group or category of persons. Some of us have better-elaborated or more-articulated stereotypes than others, but from time to time, when we meet people to whom they apply, we all think in facile stereotypes of redheads, feminists, Chicanos, artists, and politicians.

Stereotypes are social-knowledge structures that are based on inadequate information. They are overly concrete and specific and are relatively unaffected by evidence that the stereotype does not really apply to all, or even to many, members of the stereotyped group. Stereotypes often accompany and "justify" ethnic prejudices and, as such, they bring disadvantage to whole classes of people. The mistreatment of the groups against which prejudice is directed is typically buttressed by distorted cognitions that provide a rationale for discrimination (Hamilton, 1979). For example, the rationale for prejudice usually includes a tendency to see greater personal variety within one's own group than within other groups (Quattrone and Jones, 1980). A Yale student is likely to feel that Iowa State students are more similar to one another than Yale students are; the Iowa State student no doubt feels the same way about "Yalies." This tendency to perceive **outgroups** as more homogeneous than the **ingroup,** the group to which the perceiver belongs, can be explained in part by the greater likelihood of limited contact with outgroup members. But merely increasing contact may be insufficient to break down stereotypes. Extended and favorable contacts and the opportunity and leisure to observe personality differences in members of the outgroup are probably necessary if the stereotype is to be eroded away.

How Stereotypes Affect the Target of Prejudice

It has become increasingly clear that negative stereotypes have great impact on the actions and self-concepts of members of the targeted groups. As Gordon Allport (1954) has noted, prejudice often creates traits of victimization: "One's reputation whether false or true, cannot be hammered, hammered, hammered into one's head without doing something to one's character" (p. 142). More specifically, many social expectancies or stereotypes are self-fulfilling in nature. Not only can prejudice affect and determine certain traits in the targets of prejudice, but the target group's subsequent manifestation of these traits can convince prejudiced people that they were right all along.

It was Robert Merton who in 1948 first argued that prophecies about social events may increase the possibility that the prophesied events will happen. According to Merton's notion of **self-fulfilling prophecy,** a false definition of a situation may invoke new behavior that makes the false conception come true. The prophet then may mistakenly cite the actual course of events as proof that the prophecy was correct. For example, imagine that an authoritative public figure predicts a stock market decline. This prediction leads to a frantic wave of selling, causing in this way the prophesied decline. Another example comes from research in the classroom (Rosenthal and Jacobson, 1968). Teachers were told that a test had identified certain of their pupils as "late bloomers" and that these students, who were identified by name, would soon be displaying their latent academic ability. As predicted, several months later the late bloomers had spurted ahead of their peers both in schoolwork and in IQ scores. In reality, the children so identified had been chosen at random. Yet the teachers had somehow caused the false prophecy to come true. How did it happen?

Biased Hypothesis Testing. As shown in Figure 18.1, a prophecy may begin to be fulfilled when a perceiver entertains a tentative hypothesis or expectancy about another person. This tentative hypothesis may be based on a stereotype or second-hand information. In an experiment designed to determine whether tentative hypotheses can confirm themselves through biased interpretation of ambiguous behavior, John Darley and Paget Gross (1983) relied on the high probability that people will have heard, or developed in some other way, the stereotype of ghetto children as academic underachievers. They showed subjects a videotape of a little girl on a playground. In one version of the tape, the playground was located in an obviously well-to-do neighborhood; in a second version the playground was located in a ghetto. When asked to estimate the child's academic achievement level, subjects who had watched the two different tapes made almost identical estimates. Next, both groups watched another videotape in which the same child took an achievement test. The child missed some easy problems but was correct on some difficult ones—an ambiguous performance. After watching this second tape, which was identical for both groups, the subjects again rated the child's academic achievement. The subjects who believed the child's background to be upper-middle class now saw her as

Figure 18.1
Hypothetical sequences by which social expectancies are fulfilled.

Perceiver (A)	Partner or Target (B)

1. Tentative expectancy, hypothesis
   a. Ghetto kids are often slow learners.
   b. Is he an extrovert?
   c. Beautiful women are often socially adept.
   d. He is said to be competitive.

2. Ambiguous behavior
   a. Sometimes fails problems.
   b. Sometimes outgoing.
   c. Sometimes sociable.
   d. Sometimes competitive.

3. Expectancy or hypothesis
   a. Ghetto kids are slow learners.
   b. He is an extrovert.
   c. Beauty means being socially adept.
   d. He is competitive.

4. Behavior in line with expectancy
   a. More attention given to middle class.
   b. Asks leading questions.
   c. Warm, affiliative comments.
   d. Competitive actions.

5. Reciprocation
   a. More failures, few successes.
   b. Describes outgoing behavior.
   c. Warm sociability.
   d. Arousal to competition.

6. Strengthened expectancy ("I was certainly right.")

7. More behavior in line with now-strengthened expectancy

8. More reciprocation.
   a. Even more failures.
   b. Describes extroversion.
   c. Warmer, more sociable.
   d. More competitive behavior.

   Eventually???

9. New self-definition
   a. I am a failure.
   b. I am an extrovert.
   c. I am sociable, attractive.
   d. I am competitive, aggressive.

having a higher achievement level; subjects who believed the child's background to be lower class now saw her as having a lower achievement level.

Darley and Gross attributed these results to **biased hypothesis testing.** The playground scene set up a tentative hypothesis about the child's achievement level, namely that it would be low. This hypothesis did not influence the initial estimates because nothing in the first tape provided a basis for testing these tentative hypotheses. The achievement exam tape did provide a test of the hypothesis, but the child's ambiguous behavior allowed the subjects' biases to distort their ratings. Those who started with one hypothesis were more likely to notice the child's successes; subjects who started with the other hypothesis were more likely to notice the child's failures. Thus tentative hypotheses were transformed into firm conclusions.

Mark Snyder and William Swann (1978a) provided a direct test of the tendency of hypotheses to confirm themselves through the perceiver's actions. They told subjects that they would soon interact with another student and that they were to choose a set of "interview questions" that would give them the best chance of discovering whether the other student was an extrovert. These subjects chose to ask questions like, "What would you do if you wanted to liven things up at a party?" Other subjects were asked to choose a set of interview questions that would give them the best chance of discovering whether the other student was an introvert. They chose questions like, "What factors make it hard for you to really open up to people?"

Such leading questions could make almost anyone look extroverted or introverted, although the subjects were not intentionally trying to bias the results of their interviews. Like most people, the subjects in this experiment tended to put more stock in confirming evidence than in disconfirming. This tendency is one of which people are unaware. As proof of this, Snyder and Swann offered a reward of $25 for the best, or most diagnostic, set of questions and got much the same results as in their first experiment. The perceiver can act in ways that help to make prophecies self-fulfilling without appreciating the extent of his or her own contribution to the process.

Behavioral Confirmation. A hypothesis or expectancy may fulfill itself through a process of **behavioral confirmation.** As was shown in Figure 18.1, when perceiver A meets and interacts with partner B, there is a possibility that A will act on his or her hypothesis about B and elicit a response from B that confirms and therefore strengthens the initially false hypothesis. For example, we might assume from Darley and Gross's findings that teachers are likely to be very receptive to information confirming their hypothesis that ghetto children have little academic aptitude. It is then easy to imagine that teachers, acting on this hypothesis, might give preferential attention to middle-class children, and that the academic performance of these children might benefit. This interaction could produce further evidence of greater aptitude in middle-class children and reinforce the initial belief. This kind of preferential treatment based on expectations is probably a part of the explanation for the improved classroom performance of the "late bloomers" reported by Rosenthal and Jacobson. Figure 18.1 gives other examples to show how behavioral confirmation works toward the fulfillment of a prophecy. It would be a good idea to work through the whole series of steps for one or two examples to be sure you understand the argument.

Experimental demonstrations of the reciprocating behavior outlined in Figure 18.1 require that there be independent evidence in B's behavior that A's hypothesis has affected it. It is not enough that A *thinks* that B has behaved competitively, aggressively, or warmly. It must be shown that B has actually been induced to behave as A predicted. In one experiment (Snyder, Tanke, and Berscheid, 1977) that meets this criterion, pairs of undergraduate students, one male, one female, carried out spontaneous conversations by microphone

The children who were identified as and indeed became "late bloomers" may have received special attention from their teachers.

and headphones, believing that they were getting acquainted with each other. Male subjects were shown a snapshot, allegedly of their female partner, and each believed that a Polaroid snapshot of himself had been shown to her. In fact, the females knew nothing about any photographs. The experimenters showed the men one of several specially selected snapshots; the women in one group of photographs were very attractive, in the other rather unattractive, as judged by other undergraduates. The spontaneous conversations were tape-recorded, with each voice on a separate channel. The male subjects shown a photograph of an attractive woman were expected to find their partner warmer, more sociable, poised, and humorous than were the men with a supposedly unattractive partner. The results confirmed this expectation.

Twelve introductory psychology students subsequently evaluated the conversation of the female subjects for intimacy, enthusiasm, and other similar qualities. Although these judges knew nothing about the hypothesis, and neither heard the male side of the conversations nor saw the pictures, they considered the "attractive" females warmer and more sociable, poised, and humorous, just as the male subjects had. In ways that can only be guessed at, the males were able to elicit from the females the kinds of verbal responses that confirmed their own stereotypes about attractive and unattractive women, stereotypes which had been triggered in the first place by the randomly assigned photographs.

Expectancies and Self-Concepts

The same processes that bring about fulfillment of our prophecies about other people may fulfill our prophecies about ourselves (see Figure 18.1). Just as we interpret the ambiguous behavior of others as confirming our tentative hypotheses, we may, as perceivers of our own reactions, pick and choose and tend to be influenced by those that confirm our self-concepts. We may also deliberately solicit confirming feedback from others, as when we want to be lifted out of a temporary depression and indirectly solicit comfort from a loved one by remarking, "I can't imagine what you see in me." In a study of this process (Swann and Read, 1981), subjects first rated themselves as either assertive or unassertive. Then they were allowed to choose which of several evaluations of them, prepared by partners, they wanted to read. Those who had previously rated themselves as assertive chose to read their partner's responses to questions like, "What makes you think that this is the type of person who will complain in a restaurant if the service is bad?" Those who had previously rated themselves as unassertive preferred to read their partner's answers to such questions as, "Why would this person not be likely to complain if someone cuts in line in front of him or her at a movie?" This study shows that we can control our self-concepts, to some extent, through **self-verification,** by seeking feedback that fits what we believe about ourselves. One way to accomplish this is by choosing to associate only with others who react in ways that match our concepts of ourselves. We must point out, however, that not everyone is able to exercise such control over the ways in which people react to them. Children in school usually cannot escape the consequences of their teachers' expectations; the members of minority groups cannot easily avoid the stereotypes associated with their groups.

Self-fulfilling prophecies sometimes may form a "chain," in which the target changes his or her behavior to accord with a perceiver's label and then carries that changed behavior over into a subsequent interaction with an unsuspecting third party. In a complicated experiment (Snyder and Swann, 1978b) male subjects participated in a reaction-time contest with male partners whose performances they could try to disrupt with a "noise weapon" at their disposal. Before the contest began, the perceiver was arbitrarily informed that his partner was either a hostile, competitive person or a mild, gentle person. The partner was told that the first man's use of the noise weapon would depend on the kind of person he, the partner, was, as well as on what he considered to be the best way to win in competitive tasks. The men each had a number of turns at pressing a button as soon after hearing a bell as possible. As the contest proceeded, the perceiver who thought that he confronted a hostile partner delivered louder, more disruptive noises than the perceiver with a supposedly nonhostile partner. The partner understandably responded in kind when it was his turn, thus confirming the perceiver's belief that his partner was hostile or gentle. The supposedly hostile or gentle target was then asked to engage in a similar contest with a third person, who had no advance expectations about him. Now the man who had been initially, and quite arbitrarily, labeled as hostile was much more aggressive in his use of the noise weapon on a third party than was the man who had been initially labeled as gentle.

This study indicates that in certain well-defined circumstances, in which the actions of another are to be attributed to the self rather than to the situation, the perceiver can induce a response in a partner in line with an arbitrarily assigned disposition. Then the responder will continue to make that response when confronting another partner, showing that he or she has internalized the newly established disposition.

SUMMARY

The self-fulfilling prophecy represents a set of important social phenomena. Our expectations about others affect our interpretations of ambiguous social behavior and cause us to act in ways that may create the very reality we expect. And yet we often remain unaware that we affect the behavior of others in this way; we imagine that we are only observers. Not only does an expectancy produce confirming behavior, but the person expected to act in a certain way may actually internalize dispositions to account for this behavior, failing to appreciate the controlling influence of perceivers, their expectations, and the actions they tend to instigate.

ATTITUDES AND BEHAVIOR

In 1935 Gordon Allport wrote that "attitude" was the central concept of social psychology. This observation probably no longer holds true, but for many years it was believed that if we could understand how attitudes were formed and how they could be changed, we would have the key to social progress and to the elimination of prejudice. At first social psychologists were concerned with identifying and measuring attitudes. During World War II, however, the emphasis shifted to questions of how attitudes can be changed. How could American soldiers be made to understand the evils of the Axis powers and feel justified in combating them? How could they be made to realize that the war would be a long one? What are the attitudes of blacks and whites when white and black platoons fight side by side? When they fight together in fully integrated platoons? Work growing out of these war experiences and several years of subsequent research on attitude change culminated in an important book by Carl Hovland, Irving Janis, and Harold Kelley, entitled *Communication and Persuasion* (1953).

These important studies defined new areas for further investigation. Many of the results were quite consistent with common sense: credible, expert, sincere communicators are more effective than those with the opposite characteristics. Messages that give both sides of an argument are more effective than one-sided communications, but only with better-educated, more skeptical subjects. Groups can help their members resist outside persuasion. These were important "bench mark" findings, but they left ample room for exploring many intriguing subtleties. William McGuire (1964), for example, conducted a brilliant sequence of studies on the vulnerability to attack of truistic beliefs such as, "It is good to brush your teeth twice a day." He found that it was surprisingly easy to get people to give up these beliefs, probably because they are almost never challenged. McGuire then set out to show how people's resistance to persuasive attacks on these truisms can be increased by "inoculating" them before the attack. An effective kind of **inoculation** is to give the individual a brief, one-sentence argument attacking the truism, such as "Too frequent brushings tend to damage gums and expose the vulnerable parts of the teeth to decay." McGuire showed that this procedure stimulates the individual to find rebuttals to the argument. As a result the truism is no longer a truism, and it becomes more resistant to a subsequent full-scale attack. McGuire also found that attempts to defend the truism by offering arguments in its support are less effective than the inoculation procedure in protecting the truism against subsequent attack (Figure 18.2).

Cognitive Dissonance and Attitude Change

The 1960s were the decade of dissonance theory in social psychology. In 1957 Leon Festinger had proposed that when two thoughts or cognitions contradict each other—when one implies the opposite of the other—individuals experience an unpleasant tension, a state of **cognitive dissonance,** which leaves them uncomfortable. Dissonance motivates people to try to restore consonance to their clashing thoughts. Sometimes they do so by changing one of their beliefs. Let us assume that a young woman has eagerly agreed to go on a blind date, but her first glance at her companion tells her that he is about as unattractive a man as she has ever met. There is clearly potential dissonance between her recognition that she chose, with considerable enthusiasm, to go on the date and the undeniable perception that her date is unattractive. Assuming that there is no way in which she can distort her perceptions enough to convince herself

Leon Festinger originated and coined the name for cognitive-dissonance theory, which holds that, because people are always trying to make things fit together logically in their minds, they will sometimes change their attitudes to fit their behavior. The "hearts and minds" of people are not necessarily shifted first.

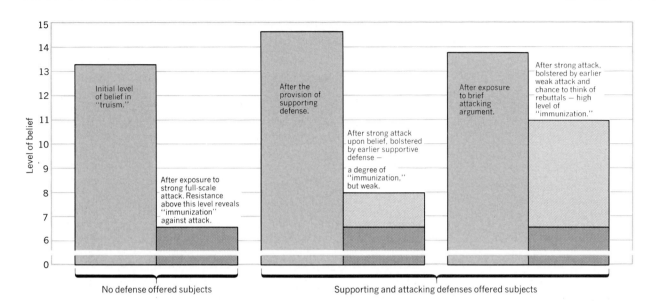

Level of belief

15
14
13
12
11
10
9
8
7
6
0

Initial level of belief in "truism."

After exposure to strong full-scale attack. Resistance above this level reveals "immunization" against attack.

After the provision of supporting defense.

After strong attack upon belief, bolstered by earlier supportive defense — a degree of "immunization," but weak.

After exposure to brief attacking argument.

After strong attack, bolstered by earlier weak attack and chance to think of rebuttals — high level of "immunization."

No defense offered subjects

Supporting and attacking defenses offered subjects

Figure 18.2
Immunization against persuasion. This experiment demonstrated that hearing earlier weak arguments against a truism allowed subjects to build up a defense against stronger arguments. (Data from McGuire, 1964.)

that the man is handsome, she might reduce her discomfort by noting that he has a lively personality, a wealth of knowledge on interesting topics, or contacts with other people whom she wants to meet.

When Behavior Can Affect Attitudes. One of Festinger's insights was that cognitions associated with overt behavior are highly resistant to change. It would be difficult for the young woman to convince herself, for example, that she is not really on a date with this man. Because thoughts about behavior are so resistant, this raises the crucial possibility that our behavior may influence our attitudes—the complement of the traditional assumption that our attitudes predict our behavior. Having made this assumption, dissonance theory goes on to point out that behavior affects attitudes only when people feel fully responsible for their behavior. They must feel that they had freedom of choice, that they were not coerced, and that they could have anticipated the consequences of their actions, or there will be no dissonance. Thus if the young woman had accepted the blind date at the urging of her roommate, who promised that she would return the favor, or if the roommate had insisted persuasively beforehand that the man was very handsome, the young woman would not subsequently have been so prone to emphasize the man's sparkling personality, for there would have been little or no dissonance to reduce. In the first instance she would be purchasing a favor in return, one she might need rather desperately at some time in the future. In the second she could hardly have foreseen that her date would be so unattractive, in view of her roommate's insistence on his appeal. In these situations the date's unattractive appearance might be a minor disappointment, but no real dissonance would develop.

A lengthy series of experiments have clearly shown the validity of this reasoning. If subjects are induced, for a barely sufficient reward, to write an essay that goes against their initial belief, for example, that the marijuana laws should be liberalized when they believe otherwise, they will subsequently show a change in attitude in the direction of that taken in their essay. Such a change does *not* occur if the essay is written for a large reward—an offer they could hardly be expected to refuse—or under conditions allowing them no choice.

ILLUSION OF CHOICE

Attitude change follows compliance only, it would seem, when the complying individual is given the **illusion of choice.** In a typical compliance-dissonance experiment subjects who are to experience the crucial dissonance are often assured that they can choose to write an essay consonant with their own attitude rather than the counterattitudinal essay the experimenter prefers that they write. Although all subjects end up writing the counterattitudinal essay, for their attitude to change it is crucial that they believe they could have done otherwise.

The illusion of choice may also operate in establishing statewide social policy. After the Supreme Court's desegregation decision of 1954, many Southern states vowed eternal resistance. When schools began to be integrated a few years later, there was often interracial violence and massive public resistance. In 1956 the legislature of the state of North Carolina debated various ways of complying with federal law while avoiding violent confrontations between the races. A controversial law was finally passed that ordered desegregation but offered state tuition aid to any student who wished to attend a private school instead. Although prointegrationists, a minority in the state at the time, were appalled at the potential use of state funds to support prejudice, the massive opposition to desegregation was more or less defused. Over the next several years schools were integrated with surprisingly few incidents of racial confrontation, in spite of the fact that no one took advantage of the tuition support option. In fact, the legal status of the support plan was never clearly established, and funds for its implementation were never appropriated. The people of North Carolina indeed shared an illusion of choice.

A question that can never be answered is whether more North Carolinians privately became less militant segregationists than citizens of other states because of the cognitive dissonance created by their illusion of choice. The theory would hold that there was greater dissonance in North Carolina over this issue because the citizens' cognition that desegregation would harm their children was dissonant with the cognition that they were freely—they had the illusion that another course of action was available—sending their children to a desegregated school. One way to reduce this dissonance would be to change their initial belief and to adopt the opinion that desegregated schools would not really harm white children. Changes of this sort may have helped to avoid militancy during the desegregation process. It is doubtful, however, that any legislator voting for the plan was aware that it might change private attitudes.

Actually, the important condition is only that the subjects *think* they have a choice, even though this choice is really illusory.

Effort Justification. An important implication of Festinger's theory was that people attempt to make their behavior *seem* reasonable and justified. If a man undergoes an especially severe initiation into a fraternity, he is likely to become a very committed member of the group (Aronson and Mills, 1959; Gerard and Mathewson, 1966). If a suitor has to argue long and persuasively to convince a woman to marry him, he is more likely to be faithful later. Joel Cooper (1980) suggested that this principle of **effort justification** plays a large part in the recoveries from mental illness that are attributed to psychotherapy. The patient might reason that "If I've chosen to pay thousands of dollars and to bare my soul to a complete stranger, then I *must* be getting better." To test this idea, Cooper enlisted as subjects a group of people with snake phobias. After determining how closely each subject was willing to approach a live snake, the experimenter administered either a frequently used form of psychotherapy or an essentially meaningless procedure called "physical exercise therapy," in which the subject exerted great physical effort by running in place and winding a Yo-Yo attached to a heavy weight. The two "therapies" were successful in enabling the phobics to approach the live snake more closely, but only when the subjects had been told that they had a choice of whether to engage in the therapeutic procedure. Phobics who were merely *told* to engage in either form of therapy showed no improvement. Without the illusion of choice, these phobics did not have to justify the effort that they were exerting and so remained afraid of snakes.

Insufficient Deterence. Just as dissonance may develop when we are lulled into doing something for reasons that are not clearly sufficient, so will we experience dissonance when we do *not* do something we would otherwise like to do, for reasons that are only marginally sufficient. In the classic study of this principle, by Elliot Aronson and Merrill Carlsmith (1963), three- and four-year-old children were individually brought into a playroom containing a table on which were five rather attractive toys. After the children had played briefly with each of the toys, the experimenter asked them to rank the toys by preference, from most-liked to least-liked. The toy that turned out to be the second-most-preferred was left on the table, and the remainder were spread around the room on the floor. The experimenter then told the child that he, the experimenter, had to leave for a few minutes but would be back soon.

What else he said at this point varied, depending on the situation in which children were put. In a no-threat situation the experimenter told the children that they could play with any of the toys in the room until the experimenter returned. He took the second-ranked toy with him as he left. In the severe-threat situation the experimenter told the children that they could play with any of the toys except the one on the table. Furthermore, they were warned,

> I don't want you to play with the _____. If you play with it, I would be very angry. I would have to take all of my toys and go home and never come back again. You can play with all the others while I am gone, but if you played with the _____, I would think you were just a baby. I will be right back.

In the mild-threat situation the child was also forbidden to play with the second-ranked toy, which was again left on the table, but the admonition was gentler.

> I don't want you to play with _____. If you played with it, I would be annoyed but you can play with all of the others while I am gone and I will be right back.

The experimenter then observed the subject for ten minutes through a one-way mirror. None of the children actually played with the forbidden toy, although some appeared tempted. When the experimenter returned, each child was asked to rank the toys again by preference. If the hypothesis of **insufficient deterrence** is correct, we would expect the second-ranked toy to be down-graded in the eye of the child who had been mildly admonished not to play with it. This child should be motivated to develop extra reasons for not engaging in forbidden behavior, including the "sour grapes" reason that the toy is not so much fun anyway. The results (Table 18.3) offer strong support for the hypothesis. Children who were severely threatened or not threatened at all increased their preference for the forbidden toy, whereas children who were mildly threatened either did not change the toy's preference rank or lowered it.

Table 18.3 Change in Preference for Forbidden Toy

Situation	Preference		
	Increased	Unchanged	Decreased
No threat	7	4	0
Severe threat	14	8	0
Mild threat	4	10	8

Adapted from Aronson and Carlsmith, 1963.

The theoretical reasoning leading to this experiment has been buttressed by many subsequent experiments. Jonathan Freedman (1965) showed that children would not play with a very attractive mechanical robot forty days after a mild prohibition against playing with the toy had been imposed in a totally different setting. Children who had earlier been more severely prohibited from playing with the robot, however, did so later. The children who had been gently admonished had apparently internalized the prohibition.

Mark Lepper (1973) later made an even more striking finding. Children who were mildly prohibited from playing with an attractive toy, and children who were severely prohibited from doing so, were asked three weeks later to play a game for prizes. The children soon realized that the game could be won only by cheating. Children who had earlier been mildly admonished were better able to resist the temptation to cheat. Apparently they viewed themselves as honest, moral people, who had been strengthened by their ability to resist the initial temptation to play with the forbidden toy. The children who had been mildly admonished were personally more responsible for avoiding the attractive toy than children who had been severely admonished. The abstinence had bolstered their self-image.

The Self-Perception Alternative

The experiments done within the framework of dissonance theory, and there were a great many from 1958 to 1973, were often provocative in suggesting that people would change their attitudes, perhaps permanently, after they had been subtly induced to act contrary to their beliefs. A common consequence of provocative research is that other investigators are provoked into looking for other explanations of the findings. This happened to dissonance theory. One of the most interesting counterproposals was Daryl Bem's (1972) **self-perception** explanation of findings supposedly explained by dissonance. Bem argued that people continue to learn about themselves from their own behavior, just as outside observers do. An observer who notes that a friend always stands by the dill pickles at a party and eats more than his share would probably conclude that the friend likes dill pickles. Bem's twist was in his suggestion that should the observer ask the friend whether he likes dill pickles, the friend might say, "I must like them; I eat them whenever I get the chance."

In several experiments inspired by dissonance theory, subjects' attitudes were changed more by paying them a trivial sum than a substantial one to write an essay taking a position that was contrary to their attitudes before writing the essay. Dissonance theory held that subjects who wrote a counterattitudinal essay for little money changed their attitudes to make them more consistent with those of the essay in order to reduce the dissonance for their otherwise inexplicable behavior.

To apply self-perception theory to these findings, Bem proposed that subjects who, for a pittance, write an essay contrary to their beliefs must conclude that they do not really feel very strongly against the position taken in the essay; otherwise they would not have written it for so little. Bem argued that subjects in a dissonance experiment do not *change* their attitudes; when asked, after the experiment, what their attitudes are, subjects who are paid very little simply remember them differently than do those who were amply reimbursed for taking a counterattitudinal position. In other words, the position taken in the essay, the subject's most recent act, is more salient than any attitude he or she may originally have held.

The crucial difference between Bem's theory and dissonance theory is that the first depends on a state of tension. According to dissonance theory, people are uncomfortable when they act contrary to their beliefs, and this motivates them to change their attitudes. Bem's theory, by contrast, is purely cognitive. People observe their own behavior and attempt to explain it, taking the situation into account. Tension created by inconsistent cognition plays no part in the explanation.

Mark Zanna and Joel Cooper thought that they saw a way to pit the two theories against each other to determine which was correct. In their reasoning they went back to Stanley Schachter's theorizing and research on the labeling of emotion (page 326). Schachter and Jerome Singer (1962) had shown that subjects who were given an injection of epinephrine, and a correct description of what to expect as a result of it, were unlikely to interpret the autonomic arousal brought on in this way as an emotion. Those who were given the injection and misinformed about its effects, or not told there would be any, attributed the arousal to the situation. They caught the mood of an experimenter's stooge, whether he was playful and full of hilarity or irritated and disgruntled. Zanna and Cooper (1974) thought that these findings could be exploited to distinguish between the dissonance and the self-perception explanations of why people change their beliefs after compromising them for very little purpose.

These experimenters convinced college students that they were to participate in two separate, unrelated experiments. In the first experiment, supposedly dealing with the effects of drugs on memory, subjects were given a powdered-milk placebo. Different groups of participants were told that the pill might make them tense, relax them, or have no side effects. Before the expected memory test, while giving the "drug time to take effect," subjects were asked to engage in another and ostensibly separate experiment on opinions. They were asked to write a forceful essay in favor of a ban on inflammatory campus speakers, a position that is counterattitudinal for most college students. The experimenter in charge of the opinion experiment then gave some subjects the illusion of choice, saying that they were completely free not to write the essay. The others heard nothing about such an option. All subjects did, in fact, write the essays.

The subjects who had been given a choice should have felt some dissonance, for they had willingly "decided" to write an essay countering a firmly held attitude. This dissonance, according to Festinger's theory, should have created a state of tension or arousal. But, following the logic of Schachter's emotion-labeling theory, subjects who also thought that they had just ingested a tension-producing pill might quite reasonably attribute any arousal symptoms to the pill itself. If they did so, presumably they would be less motivated to change their attitude on the speaker ban issue than subjects who were given no opportunity to attribute their discomfort to a pill. This is exactly what happened (Table 18.4), suggesting that people do experience dissonance as an uncomfortable

Table 18.4 Average Shift of Subjects' Later Opinions about Banning Inflammatory Speakers from Campus

Freedom of Decison	Expected Side Effect of Drug		
	Arousal	None	Relaxation
High	3.40	9.10	13.40
Low	3.50	4.50	4.70

Notice that the larger this average shift in opinion, the greater the later agreement with the position taken in the essay. The average for the control group—subjects who wrote no essay and took no pill—was 2.30.

tension and that they do change their attitudes in an effort to reduce this tension. These results then favor dissonance theory over the self-perception alternative.

When Self-Perception Applies. The two theories, cognitive dissonance and self-perception, have recently been integrated by Russell Fazio, Zanna, and Cooper (1977). They have suggested that both theories are valid descriptions of attitude change, but that they apply to different kinds of discrepancy between attitudes and behavior. They believe that the tension associated with dissonance comes about only when we are somehow induced to perform actions "of our own free will" that so violate our true attitudes that they fall outside what has been called our "latitude of acceptance" and within our "latitude of rejection." When our behavior and attitudes are only slightly discrepant, we sit back like uninvolved observers and calculate our attitudes from observations of our own behavior. If you feel, without much passion, that the legal drinking age should be lowered from twenty-one to sixteen and someone persuades you to write an essay arguing for retention of the present law, you may subsequently change your attitude, perhaps to the belief that the drinking age should be lowered to only eighteen rather than sixteen. You might do so quite coolly and without tension, because what you did fell within your latitude of acceptance. Although you initially preferred sixteen, eighteen was an acceptable alternative. By way of contrast, if you initially preferred sixteen but were induced to write an essay arguing that the drinking age should be raised to twenty-five, you would probably feel a great deal of tension and be motivated to reduce the discrepancy. Again, you might end up feeling that eighteen is the proper legal drinking age, but this time the process of attitude change would be different from that in the earlier case. You would presumably have reduced your dissonance rather than merely changing your perception of yourself and your beliefs.

Overjustification. One of the strong points of self-perception theory is that it addresses attitude change within the latitude of acceptance. Mark Lepper, David Greene, and Richard Nisbett (1973) were quick to realize that many of the attitudes that people try to change fall within this latitude, including the appreciation for learning that parents and teachers attempt to instill in their children and pupils. Children, after all, are naturally inquisitive and usually eager to learn to read, write, and work with numbers. If adults want to increase this thirst for knowledge, how should they proceed? A frequent answer to this question has been through rewards. Parents pay children for every "A" they bring home on their report cards, and teachers hand out candy and gold stars for completing school assignments. These seem like good ideas until we consider a self-perception analysis. Bem's theory predicts that people who see themselves performing an activity in order to gain some extrinsic reward will conclude that their intrinsic liking for the activity must be small, just as we would conclude that an actor who donates time for a television commercial must like the product being advertised more than an actor who wants $1000 to make the same commercial. According to this analysis, children paid to engage in activities that they already enjoy will be less interested in engaging in these activities on their own, and will perform them more poorly, than children who are not paid. Lepper, Greene, and Nisbett (1973) tested this self-perception prediction by offering nursery school children a "Good Player Certificate," complete with gold stars, if they would draw pictures with magic markers, an activity that most children of this age enjoy for its own sake. As compared to children who either received no reward or got the same reward as a surprise rather than as "pay," the contingent-reward children later avoided playing with magic markers in a free-play situation in which they did not know that they were being observed. In addition, they drew pictures that were inferior artistically (Amabile, 1979). In other words, to avoid turning play into work, we should offer only the minimum reward necessary to induce compliance, even when that reward is no reward at all.

Attitude-Behavior Consistency

Social psychologists were initially interested in studying attitudes because they believed that attitudes could predict behavior—that a racist would be likely to vote against civil rights legislation, or that a feminist would support women who are candidates for office. Years of research, however, have shown that we cannot count on such **attitude-behavior consistency.** In fact, the classic study on the consistency between attitudes and behavior found behavior to be not just inconsistent with, but diametrically opposed to, attitudes. Richard LaPiere (1934) toured the southwest United States with a Chinese couple. Despite the fact that anti-Chinese sentiments were running high at that point in the country's history, the trio were served courteously at all but one of 250 hotels and restaurants. In a later questionnaire, more than 90 percent of the proprietors of these same 250 establishments expressed an attitude totally opposed to serving Chinese. This study was just the start of a long line of experiments that have found little or no attitude-behavior consistency, and that have led some investigators to question the usefulness of the attitude concept itself.

But such a reaction is clearly too extreme, for attitudes often do predict behavior remarkably well—in voting behavior, for example. A more constructive approach to the issue is to ask when behavior is likely to be consistent with attitudes and when it is likely not to be. Several interesting hypotheses have been advanced. Allport (1943) noted that attitude-behavior consistency increases dramatically when people are deeply involved in an issue and committed to a position. For example, a member of the National Association for the Advancement of Colored People would be expected to have greater attitude-behavior consistency on civil rights legislation than a nonmember, but not necessarily on legislation about abortion. A related hypothesis is that being reminded of your position, or being self-conscious about it, can increase attitude-behavior consistency (Carver, 1975). Others have noted that the attitudinal questions asked in research are usually specific actions (Fishbein and Ajzen, 1974). If we want to predict whether Sally will be on time for her 8 a.m. class tomorrow, we should not expect to learn much by asking her, "How do you feel about education?" We are likely to obtain much greater attitude-behavior consistency if we ask a much more specific question, such as, "How do you feel about showing up for 8 a.m. classes?" The problem with this approach is that, although our research may now reveal attitude-behavior consistency, we may along the way lose the concept of a general attitude.

The issue of attitude-behavior consistency continues to be an important one in social psychology because it forces us to examine both cognitive processes and observable behavior at the same time. It is one thing to develop a psychology of how people perceive and draw inferences about others. It is quite another to specify how these mental events are "translated" into social behavior —how cognitions become actions. This second task appears to be much more challenging.

SUMMARY

Not only do attitudes sometimes affect behavior—we behave in ways that could have been predicted from our attitudes—but behavior induced by other means can affect subsequent attitudes. The great insight of cognitive-dissonance theorists is that people who are induced to behave in a manner inconsistent with their beliefs, when they have the option of not doing so, will change their attitudes to bring them more in line with the implications of their behavior. Furthermore, such changes in attitude appear to be quite long lasting. People may feel that they have to justify their actions by adopting favorable attitudes toward their jobs or toward psychotherapists just because they cost so much in training, money, or effort. Children may develop a sense of morality by justifying their own barely sufficient resistance to temptation, and they may have their intrinsic interest in learning stifled by the heavy-handed application of unnecessary rewards. Research continues on the conditions under which attitude-behavior consistency can be expected.

TO BE SURE YOU UNDERSTAND THIS CHAPTER

The following concepts are the major ones for this chapter. You should be able to define them and state the points made about each in the text.

Social psychology	**Personalism**
Person perception	**Knowledge structure**
Attribution theory	**Schema**
Correspondent-inference theory	**Stereotype**
Discounting effect	**Outgroup**
Distinctiveness	**Ingroup**
Consensus	**Self-fulfilling prophecy**
Consistency	**Biased hypothesis testing**
Fundamental attribution error	**Behavioral confirmation**
Actor-observer differences	**Self-verification**
False consensus	**Inoculation**
Heuristic	**Cognitive dissonance (theory)**
Representativeness	**Illusion of choice**
Availability	**Effort justification**
Construct accessibility	**Insufficient deterrence**
Visual salience	**Self-perception (theory)**
Egocentric bias	**Overjustification**
	Attitude-behavior consistency

In This Book.   The treatment of social and emotional development in Chapter 12 discusses the development of scripts. The treatment there of moral development is also related to topics covered in this chapter. Our coverage of social psychology continues in Chapter 19.

Elsewhere.   We recommend two textbooks, *Understanding Social Psychology* (third edition), by Stephen Worchel and Joel Cooper; and *Human Inference: Strategies and Shortcomings of Social Judgment,* by Richard Nisbett and Lee Ross.

TO GO BEYOND THIS CHAPTER

CHAPTER 19   SOCIAL INFLUENCE AND GROUP PROCESSES

This chapter was written by Edward E. Jones
and Charles G. Lord.

Social psychologists, sociologists, and anthropologists have long understood that the **cultural norms** shared by the members of every society—norms about acceptable values, beliefs, forms of speech, dress, and economic organization—are established and maintained by social pressures that others bring to bear on individual members of the society. Similar pressures are also applied for more limited purposes when a single individual tries to persuade another to buy a certain product, to join a particular political party, to abandon a prejudice against members of a minority group, or to give up a life-threatening habit, such as smoking. These examples all draw attention to the importance of the processes called **social influence**.

SOCIAL INFLUENCE

The process of social influence consists of one or more *sources* of influence who attempt to direct the behavior of one or more people who are the *targets* of such influence. Bibb Latané has proposed that the amount of pressure a person being subjected to social influence experiences depends on the *number* of sources communicating the influence and the *strength* and the *immediacy*, that is, the proximity in time and space, of the source of influence. For example, an adolescent boy is much more likely to volunteer to join a group to visit a local museum when the pressure to do so comes from many important people, his peers, who are right there urging him to come along with them, than when he reads an announcement on the school bulletin board that the principal has invited students to join such a group.

These ideas are depicted diagrammatically in Figure 19.1, which represents a *number* of sources of influence by a corresponding number of circles. The different sizes of the circles indicate different *strengths* of influence, and the nearness of the circle to the target represents *immediacy*. The size of the arrows represents the magnitude of social influence. One thing that the figure does not show is Latané's hypothesis that increases in the number of sources of influence become less and less significant as the total number increases. For example, more additional influence is exerted when the number of people trying to get you to do something increases from two to three than when the number increases from 397 to 398.

Latané and his associates have found evidence for his principal hypothesis in many different types of situations. People who imagine that they are reciting a poem in front of an audience report more embarrassment as the imagined

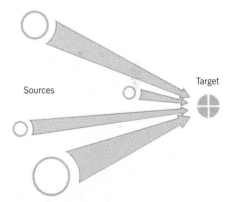

Sources

Target

Figure 19.1
Determiners of social influence on a target. The four circles to the left represent four people who, as sources of influence, affect another person, the target. The sizes of the circles represent the strength of the source. The distance of the source from the target represents the dimension of immediacy. The width of the arrows represents the amount of influence. (Adapted from Latané, 1981.)

Social influence is the greatest when many important people, such as our peers, exert it.

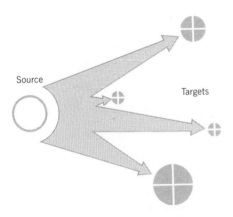

Figure 19.2
Influence of a single source on four targets. The division of what begins as a single, very wide arrow into four smaller ones represents the fact that each one of many targets receives less influence. (Adapted from Latané, 1981.)

number of people in the audience increases. The number of column inches that newspaper editors assign to a disaster story increases with the number of the victims, their status, and the proximity of the disaster (Latané and Harkins, 1976).

Figure 19.2 presents a situation of social influence that is the reciprocal of the one in Figure 19.1. In this case a single source attempts to influence the behavior of several targets. In general, the amount of social influence a source exerts decreases as the number of targets increases, although, as Figure 19.2 suggests by the different sizes of the target circles, some people are easier to influence than others.

Examples of the decreasing influence of single sources of influence on increasing numbers of targets are not difficult to find. The proportion of an audience, the targets, that an evangelist, the source, convinces to "inquire for Christ" decreases as the size of the audience increases. Restaurant tips received by servers in a restaurant, the source of influence, increase as the number of people in a dinner party, the targets, increases, but the tip per customer decreases. In many group endeavors there is a phenomenon called "social loafing." As the number of members of a group increases, the amount of effort exerted by each participant decreases (Latané, Williams, and Harkins, 1979). In this last example the group members are the targets; the influence brought to bear might be the implicit requirement to "do a good job."

Helping Others

The second, reciprocal version of Latané's model of social influence is useful in analyzing when people will help one another. If we imagine the person in need of help as a source of social influence, sending out verbal or visual distress signals, the model tells us that the impact of these signals on any one target will decrease as the number of targets increases (see Figure 19.2). In more practical terms, the probability that a witness to a crime will come to the aid of a victim decreases as the number of witnesses increases. As the notorious case of a young woman who was murdered in full view of her neighbors made sadly clear, the presence of many witnesses is, in fact, no guarantee that anyone will come to the aid of a victim of crime (Figure 19.3).

> On a March night in 1964, Kitty Genovese was set upon by a maniac as she came home from work at 3 a.m. Thirty-eight of her Kew Gardens neighbors came to their windows when she cried out in terror—none came to her assistance. Even though her assailant took over half an hour to murder her, no one even so much as called the police (Latané and Darley, 1969).

Single events, no matter how sensational and tragic they may be, say nothing about the effects of different numbers of witnesses. Would Kitty Genovese have received help had her emergency been witnessed by one or five or fifteen of her neighbors, rather than thirty-eight? We can never know. We can, however, study the phenomenon of **bystander intervention** in the laboratory. In one experiment (Darley and Latané, 1968) university students were placed in an isolation booth which the experimenters falsely told them was connected to several other booths by an intercom system. The experimenter explained that the students in the booths would take turns telling the others about their problems in adjusting to college life. In reality, no other subjects were present. The "other participants" were tape recordings, and the actual subjects talked into an unconnected microphone. This elaborate deception was necessary so that the experimenters could vary the number of other students believed to be present, and so that the subjects would have no way of knowing whether any other witness to a contrived emergency was summoning aid.

Figure 19.3
The Genovese murder scene. Kitty Genovese was fatally stabbed at a doorway (1) just a few yards from her home (2). Her assailant had attacked her twice in the parking lot adjacent to the Kew Gardens railroad station, shown at the left. She was unable to free herself a third time.

The "emergency" occurred when one of the tape-recorded "others," who had previously mentioned that he was prone to seizures during times of stress, became very agitated and ended his turn with "I-er-um-I think I-I-need-er-if-if could-er somebody er-er-er-er-er-er- give me a little-er give me a little help here because I-er-I'm . . ." The voice choked and then went quiet (p. 379). The experimenters measured how long the subjects waited before leaving the isolation booth to seek aid for the seizure victim, if indeed they left the booth at all. Just as Latané's model of social influence would predict, the students who thought that they were the only potential helpers came quickly to the aid of the victim. Eighty-five percent of them responded by the end of the seizure, and the average wait was fifty-two seconds. By contrast, only 13 percent of the students who believed that four others had also heard the emergency responded by the end of the seizure, and the average wait was 166 seconds. These and other experimental results support the notion that when more witnesses are present at an emergency, less social pressure falls on each of them, and the less likely is the victim to get help from any one of them.

Latané's model also explains why a greater number of victims are more likely to get help when the number of witnesses is held constant (Wegner and Schaefer, 1978). Increasing the number of sources of social influences increases the total amount of pressure on the targets (see Figure 19.1).

Dependence on Others

When people fail to come to the aid of someone who needs help, they violate expectancies that grow out of the trust we have in others. Erik Erikson (Chapter 15) considered such trust to be the most basic of all the human needs. People acquire this trust in very early childhood as they learn to depend on their parents for the satisfaction of their needs for food, physical comfort, affection, and approval. Later on children learn to depend on teachers, siblings, and peers, as well as parents, for information about their surroundings, information that is useful in attaining important goals. These two forms of dependence, for food, physical comfort, affection, and approval and for information, are intertwined and difficult to separate when the individual becomes an adult, but it is nevertheless useful to maintain their theoretical distinctness in analyzing how social pressures are exerted.

Social Comparison Defines Reality.   Leon Festinger, who emphasized (1954) that social pressures have diverse origins, gave psychology a detailed description of how, even as adults, people depend on others for information. Festinger pointed out that people have a powerful need to know the nature of their world and that much of this knowledge must come from others. If we want to know how heavy an object is or whether it will burn, we can perform obvious physical tests and get the answers without the help of other people. But if we want to know whether we should be fearful of nuclear disasters, or whether job opportunities in psychology are good or bad, we must seek such information through communications with others.

One of Festinger's key assumptions was that we are confident in the accuracy of our socially derived knowledge to the extent that others agree with us. The process of reaching such agreement is a major source of social pressure and has important attitudinal consequences. If there is a discrepancy between what others believe or see and what we believe or see, it is natural for us to conclude that one of us must be wrong. Festinger's **social-comparison theory** holds that usually we try to reduce this disconcerting discrepancy by trying to win others over to our point of view or by changing our own position to conform to theirs. Sometimes, however, we may decide that those who hold views different from our own are not really relevant judges, and we may stop comparing our opinions with theirs.

Conforming to a Unanimous Majority. The impact of social pressure is strikingly clear in the classic conformity studies of Solomon Asch (1956). A typical Asch experiment consisted of a number of trials in which each subject in a group expressed his judgment concerning which of three lines was the same length as a standard line. Through seating arrangements and instructions Asch maneuvered a particular subject into a position where he would hear the reports of several others before giving his own. Unbeknownst to the subject, these other "subjects" were accomplices of the experimenter, previously instructed to make unanimous incorrect judgments on a number of critical trials. These reactions of the accomplices, of course, placed the subject in a dilemma, for his eyes clearly told him one thing, but his companions told him something different. Asch actually launched his experiments to show the various ways in which people can maintain their independence of judgment in the face of disagreement. To his surprise, however, he found considerable yielding to social pressure. Although subjects in isolation rarely made errors on these tasks, when

Well, the middle line on the comparison card certainly seems the same length as the line on the first card.

I don't believe it, but they say with such certainty that the left line matches that on the first card.

"I suppose that the rest of you must be right, but I have to call them as I see them. I see the middle line as the matching one."

they were confronted by the conflicting opinions of others, three out of four subjects made at least one error. The average subject made between four and five errors out of a possible twelve. This proportion of yielding was confirmed in a number of later studies. Consistent with Latané's (1981) model, conformity increases as more confederates, and therefore more social influence, are added to the situation. And as Latané's model also predicts and Harold Gerard and Edward Connolley (1972) have shown, the impact of each new confederate decreases as the size of the mistaken majority increases.

When he asked his subjects about their private experiences after the experiment, Asch found ample evidence that some depended on the opinion of others. Many subjects discounted the evidence of their own eyes and concluded that the unanimous majority must be right because they could find no other explanation for the consensus. In their view it seemed more likely that they, themselves, would be wrong than that two, three, or more others would all be

HOW TO CREATE CONSENSUS IN ATLANTIC CITY

The immense success of Resorts International, the first legal gambling casino in Atlantic City, New Jersey, naturally attracted other developers anxious to purchase land near the famed Boardwalk. In one such block of valuable land, the buildings consisted almost entirely of two- and three-story row houses owned largely by Italian-American working people who had purchased them in the forties and fifties for but a few thousand dollars. Richard Bloom, a young real estate man, offered the owners on the block $100,000 each if they would sell him their property. But Bloom included an intriguing stipulation: everyone had to sell at that price or no one would get anything! When some owners complained that their houses were bigger or better maintained, Bloom noted that he was only interested in the land under the houses and the condition of the property was immaterial. Initial reactions to the proposal ranged from extreme eagerness to sign to firm reluctance. Within a month, however, all but fifteen owners had signed, and most of them too had indicated that they would sign. People eager to sell had exerted heavy pressure on the reluctant holdouts.

Owners of businesses in Atlantic City were under considerable pressure to sell their properties to developers.

> At one meeting, the son of a homeowner angrily demanded the names of those who had not signed. Bloom declined to provide the names, but the sentiment reflected by the request was an indication that his plan was working. "I'd hate to be the last guy,"

he said to a reporter. "It'd be hard to live here." As the signers became a majority, "Have you signed yet?" became a common question for people on the block.

Eventually, the signers mounted a bitter petition addressed to the holdouts, accusing them of extreme selfishness. When Bloom's original forty-five-day deadline arrived, only three property owners had failed to sign. The problem, according to Bloom,

is that the two whose "wishes and needs" are most difficult to satisfy— they simply want more money—live in South Philadelphia, out of range of pressure from the neighbors with whom they could have a common bond.

Quotations and general story line from Calvin Trillin, U.S. Journal: Atlantic City, N.J.: Assemblage, *The New Yorker*, January 8, 1979.

wrong at the same time. Other subjects revealed that their need for social approval accounted for their behavior. They went along with the majority *in spite of believing that the majority was wrong.* These subjects wanted to avoid appearing odd or being laughed at.

Subsequent research has verified that we accept the opinions of others sometimes because we think that they are right—we depend on them for information; sometimes because we wish to avoid censure or embarrassment—we depend on them for approval. Of course, there is nothing to prevent both dependencies from operating in a given situation, and we suspect that together they are responsible for considerable agreement within a group.

The Asch experiments were deliberately designed to minimize the likelihood of discussion among the group members. As Donald Campbell (1961) has noted, the rational thing for the subject to do in this situation would be to announce what his eyes have told him while conceding that the group is probably correct. This response would give the group the advantage of his input without his questioning their probable wisdom. This adaptive response was apparently very rare in the Asch experiments.

Obedience and Reactance

In a conformity experiment the subjects' perceptual judgments or opinions are only one of the things that are at stake. Their concepts of themselves as competent, yet responsive and agreeable human beings are also under attack. For this second reason the conflict produced can be quite severe, in spite of the fact that subjects know that they are in a psychology experiment. Some subjects in an Asch-type setting have experienced severe anxiety and autonomic disturbances.

The personal anguish of subjects was undoubtedly more extreme and pervasive in the obedience experiment designed by Stanley Milgram (1965). Milgram investigated whether people would conform even when their yielding might have extremely negative consequences for other people. In his experiments participants delivered what they believed to be unendurable and possibly lethal electric shock to other people for their failure to learn.

Male participants were solicited by a newspaper advertisement, which said that the experiment would be "a study of memory and learning." As each volunteer arrived at the laboratory, he met the experimenter and a mild-mannered, likable man in his late forties. In reality this man was an accomplice, but he was introduced by the experimenter as another subject. The experimenter, middle-aged, stern, impassive, and dressed in a gray lab coat, gave both men a description of the experiment. One was to be the "teacher" and inflict shock as punishment to the "learner" whenever he failed to remember the correct pairing of words to be taught him by the teacher. A rigged drawing made the naive subject the teacher. The teacher went with the experimenter and learner into an adjacent room, where the learner was strapped into an "electric chair," "to prevent excessive movement" during shocks. Electrode paste was applied to his wrist, "to avoid blisters and burns"; then the electrode, which led back to a "shock generator" in the first room, was attached. The learner became somewhat apprehensive and confided that he had a history of heart trouble, but the experimenter reassured him.

The shock generator had an impressive keyboard of thirty switches, which were marked as delivering from 15 to 450 volts. The 195-volt switch was labeled "very strong shock," the 255-volt switch "intense shock," the 375-volt switch "danger: severe shock"; the last two switches were labeled an ominous "XXX." The naive subject was required to raise the level of shock by 15 volts each time the learner made a mistake, and he made them regularly. The experimenter was at the naive subject's side, prodding him on through any demonstration of reluctance as the learner began to express discomfort. In Milgram's words,

> The responses of the victim are standardized on tape and each protest is coordinated to a particular voltage level. . . . Starting with 75 volts, the learner begins to grunt and moan. At 150 volts, he demands to be let out of the experiment. At 180 volts, he cries out that he can no longer stand the pain. At 300 volts he refuses to provide any more answers to the memory test, insisting that he is no longer a participant in the experiment. . . . In response to this last tactic, the experimenter instructs the naive subject to treat the absence of an answer as equivalent to a wrong answer and to follow the usual shock procedure. If the naive subject protested at any point the experimenter told him, "You have no other choice, you must go on!"

It is difficult to read about these experiments without intensely disliking the subjects, disapproving of the ethics of the experimenter, or both. The concern that led Milgram to conduct these studies was the cold-blooded extermination of millions of victims in the Nazi concentration camps during World War II, a gigantic enterprise carried out, not just by a few madmen but, in the final analysis, through the obedience of many individuals performing the jobs assigned them. Milgram was especially interested in pinning down the aspects of a social situation that make destructive obedience to authority such a routine happening.

Milgram's results (Figure 19.4) indicate that the unyielding persistence of an authoritative experimenter can induce almost anyone to harm others. Over half of the participants inflicted the most severe shock on the learner. That a person

Figure 19.4
Obedience to commands to punish. The graph itself shows the percentage of participants remaining in the experiment as the "punishment" they were required to deliver increased, from mild—a shock of 75 volts—to one of lethal strength. The textual material behind the graph is a verbatim transcript of a portion of one subject's verbal comments, together with Milgram's (1965) observations.

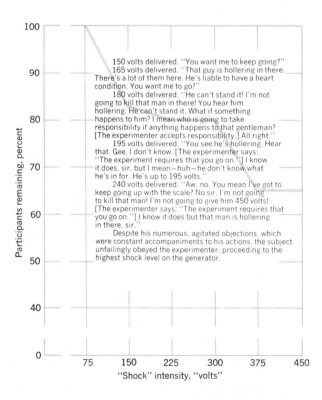

150 volts delivered. "You want me to keep going?"
165 volts delivered. "That guy is hollering in there. There's a lot of them here. He's liable to have a heart condition. You want me to go?"
180 volts delivered. "He can't stand it! I'm not going to kill that man in there! You hear him hollering. He can't stand it. What if something happens to him? I mean who is going to take responsibility if anything happens to that gentleman? [The experimenter accepts responsibility.] All right."
195 volts delivered. "You see he's hollering. Hear that. Gee, I don't know. [The experimenter says: "The experiment requires that you go on."] I know it does, sir, but I mean—huh—he don't know what he's in for. He's up to 195 volts."
240 volts delivered. "Aw, no. You mean I've got to keep going up with the scale? No sir, I'm not going to kill that man! I'm not going to give him 450 volts! [The experimenter says: "The experiment requires that you go on."] I know it does but that man is hollering in there, sir."
Despite his numerous, agitated objections, which were constant accompaniments to his actions, the subject unfailingly obeyed the experimenter, proceeding to the highest shock level on the generator.

(y-axis: Participants remaining, percent; x-axis: "Shock" intensity, "volts")

might damage others in a fit of rage, or that a few people with very serious psychological problems might inflict senseless violence on others may not surprise us. It is more disconcerting to learn that ordinary citizens, of various ages, are willing to damage an unoffending stranger simply because an experimenter insists that it is "required." This insight into human nature is not a pleasant one, but it is better to recognize it than to pretend that ordinary human beings have too much character knowingly to inflict such pain on others.

Social psychologists are as much interested in the phenomena of resistance to group pressure as they are in obedience. Any theory of social influence must come to terms with instances of personal autonomy and defiance of authority as well as with instances of imitation and conformity. Jack Brehm (1966) has proposed that certain circumstances arouse **psychological reactance:** we strive to assert our freedom when someone threatens to exert control over our options. Children told not to play in a rubble-strewn lot fuss about not being allowed to go there, although they might otherwise have preferred the playground. We may become more determined to see a play when an acquaintance tries to persuade us that it is not worth our time. We are likely to show resistance when anyone attempts to persuade us in ways that threaten our freedom to hold any opinion we want to.

Presence of Others

Social influence is exerted by the people whose help we seek, by those on whom we depend for the validation of our beliefs, and by authority figures. The oldest problem in experimental social psychology, though, is whether people can exert a social influence *just by being there.* In 1898 Norman Triplett, who had noticed that bicycle racers pedal faster when racing together than when racing against the clock, reported an experiment in which children were asked to wind fishing reels as fast as possible. He discovered that the children wound their reels faster when other children were present. This finding sparked a long line of experiments on the "energizing" effects that the mere presence of others has on task performance.

One of the most intriguing outcomes of these studies was that several of them obtained results exactly opposite to those expected. Quite often, the presence of others seemed to impair rather than facilitate performance. Robert Zajonc (1965) integrated these seemingly contradictory findings by suggesting that the **mere presence** of others facilitates the performance of simple, well-learned, repetitive tasks but impairs the learning of new skills or the performance of complex tasks. For example, riding a bicycle is an overlearned, almost automatic performance for most people. It should be facilitated or "energized" when others are watching; but imagine trying to learn to ride a unicycle in front of a large audience of strangers!

Alternative explanations have been offered for the effects of the presence of an audience on people's performance. The most persistent of these is that the effects are yet another example of social influence through dependence on others. Since we depend on others for our self-esteem, what appears to be social facilitation or impairment may actually be brought on by the thought of being evaluated rather than by the mere presence of others (Cottrell, 1972). This alternative explanation is supported by the finding that subjects' performances show no impairment when they perform in front of a blindfolded audience (Cottrell et al., 1968); but it is made less plausible by the fact that cockroaches also perform simple tasks better and complex tasks worse when other cockroaches are present (Zajonc, Heingartner, and Herman, 1969).

SUMMARY

Social norms, that is, universally accepted beliefs, attitudes, and behavior, are a fact of social life in every culture. So are the efforts of one individual to influence the behavior of another. Bibb Latané's theory describes the nature of such social influence and predicts many phenomena associated with the process. In Latané's model the number of sources of social influence, their individual strengths, and their nearness determine the pressure brought to bear on the person who is the target of such influence. If social influence from a certain source is directed at many targets, the impact is scattered and divided. This weakening of social influence accounts, in part, for the fact that there is an inverse relationship between the number of witnesses present when someone needs help and the probability that any individual witness will offer it.

Seeking help in times of distress is but one example of general dependency that human beings have on one another, a dependency which is learned from early childhood onward. One of the most studied forms of such dependency is the way in which we depend on others for information. Experiments have shown that we depend so much on such information that, through the process of social comparison, we sometimes conform to the incorrect judgments of a unanimous majority.

Studies of obedience show that, although people have a need to maintain autonomy, in most this need is easily overridden by a tendency to obey the orders of those in authority. In situations in which obedience or resistance to authority are not an issue, the performance of people may be hindered or enhanced by the mere presence of others. The explanation of such effects remains controversial.

TWO-PERSON INTERACTIONS

The interactions between two people take many forms and serve many purposes. For example, a conversation between two persons may be an occasion for expressions of anger, joy, or affection. It is a context in which the participants generally influence each other and in the process learn about their own social impact.

One way to classify two-person interactions is in terms of how much each person's behavior depends on the preceding responses of the other. At one extreme are ritualistic occasions, during which such mutual dependencies are nearly nonexistent. The behavior of people in a formal receiving line is an example. At the other extreme are the occasions when the two parties to the interaction share a rich involvement full of subtle influences, which unfold gradually and change over time. If we were to observe a relatively unstructured conversation between two friends, between a brother and sister, or between a husband and wife, we would quickly develop an intuitive feel for the nature of this interdependency. We would see that when one person talks, the other listens, perhaps nods and smiles, or lifts an eyebrow and looks thoughtful; and that a suitable break in the conversation leads the listener to contribute his or her own remarks to the developing conversation. As this intricate pattern unfolds, we might be able to separate out two forms of social influence, cue control and outcome control. **Cue control** refers to the kind of influence that exploits personal or social habits. If John asks Sally for the time, Sally will automatically look at her watch and tell him. Cue control elicits responses that have been triggered so frequently in the past that they now play an automatic role in social life. **Outcome control** refers to the kind of influence that is provided by the rewarding and punishing responses each partner makes to the behavior of the other. Thus parents manipulate a child's self-esteem by expressions of approval and disapproval. Employers influence employees by special recognition as well as by monetary benefits. An important approach in social psychology looks at two-person interactions as the exchange of outcomes.

Social Exchange

The **social-exchange approach** can be fruitfully applied in terms of each person's power to benefit or harm the other. Many people do not like to think of interpersonal relationships in terms of distributions of social power, but once we recognize that people routinely make other people feel better or worse by what they say and do, some such notion is inevitable. John Thibaut and Harold Kelley (1959) have defined Sally's power over John as the range of outcomes that Sally can provide for John. To the extent that Sally can benefit John greatly, and also harm John deeply, she has power over him. In most cases, of course, John has some *counter power* over Sally, so that their relationship is likely to avoid the extremes of mutual sacrifice and mutual injury.

The next step in our analysis is to attempt to describe how power is likely to affect the allocation of outcomes in a relationship. A convenient device for doing this is an interaction matrix such as that shown in Table 19.1; the matrix allows us to show how the outcomes for person A depend on person B's behavior, or vice versa. Let us choose a plausible but fictitious example, substituting Sally for the letter A and John for the letter B, as in Table 19.2, and fill in the outcomes for John when he adopts one of his two behavioral alternatives, and Sally responds with one of hers. John's imaginary alternatives are to express affection for Sally or to tell her the latest ethnic joke he has heard. Sally's alternatives are to smile or to frown. As you can see from the arbitrary numbers in Table 19.2, John is always happier when Sally reacts with a smile rather than a frown, and this difference is much greater if the smile is in response to a declaration of affection rather than to the latest joke about how many whoev-

Table 19.1 An Interaction Matrix

| | | Person A's Behavioral Alternatives | |
		Behavior 1	**Behavior 2**
Person B's Behavioral Alternatives	**Behavior 1**		
	Behavior 2		

Table 19.2 Outcomes for John

| | | Sally's Alternatives | |
		Smile	**Frown**
John's Alternatives	**Declare Affection**	John is elated ($+3$)	John is miserable (-3)
	Tell Latest Ethnic Joke	John is happy ($+1$)	John is disappointed (-1)

ers it takes to change a light bulb. The plot will thicken later when we consider how Sally's actions depend on John's choice of behavioral alternatives. For the time being, however, we can note that Sally has **behavior control** (Thibaut and Kelley, 1959) over John because the particular way in which their actions combine determines John's outcomes.

In recent years a considerable body of evidence suggesting that much of our behavior is influenced by factors of which we are quite unaware has accumulated (Nisbett and Wilson, 1977). In our example John may not realize that his own elation is really triggered by Sally's smile when he discloses affection. In view of these findings, it seems reasonable to assume that people may be unaware of the precise causes of their social outcomes in an ongoing relationship.

Awareness in the "Minimal Social Situation." A novel way to approach the question of awareness in two-person interactions was introduced by investigators who wanted to determine what would happen in a **minimal social situation,** a situation in which a person's outcomes depended on the actions of another person but were otherwise stripped of the rich embellishments that accompany most social situations (Sidowski, Wycoff, and Tabory, 1956). Each subject was directed to a cubicle, unaware that another subject was also serving in the experiment. Each subject, who was hooked to electrodes that could deliver shock to his left hand, was shown two buttons and told that he could push these buttons in any order and as frequently as he wished. "The object of the experiment," the experimenter explained, "is to make as many points as you can. Your point score will appear on this counter. The red light will blink and the counter will turn each time you score a point" (p. 116).

Whether one subject received a score or a shock was determined entirely by the button presses of the other subject. If subject A pressed the left button, for example, subject B received a point regardless of his own response. If A pressed the right button, B received a strong shock. B's button presses had similar consequences for A. The average subject learned quickly to press the button that gave the other subject points rather than shocks and continued to press only this button throughout the experiment. No subject expressed any awareness of the social nature of the experiment—the fact that another person was involved. Most of them apparently assumed that they were on some complicated learning schedule that was controlled by an automatic device. A later experiment revealed that subjects who were explicitly informed of the other subject's presence and of their mutual dependency performed no differently from subjects who were not informed (Sidowski, 1957).

It is easy to see why the subjects in these experiments behaved as they did, if you consider what your own reactions might be. Suppose that you first push the left button, giving the other subject a point, and, unbeknownst to you, the other person pushes the right button, giving you a shock. From your point of view, because you are unaware of any other subject, you pushed the left button and received a strong shock. You will probably switch to the right button next time, and the other person will stay with the right button, but this time you will both receive shocks. Now, you might well switch back to the left button, and so will the other subject. Now when you both receive a point, you will both push the left button again and, satisfied with that result, keep pushing the left button throughout the experiment. In fact, a close analysis in a subsequent experiment (Kelley et al., 1962) revealed that sooner or later most subjects will arrive at what might be termed a "win-stay, lose-shift" rule (page 231) that is guaranteed to bring them to a state of positive mutual interdependence. These investigators also challenged the previous conclusion that awareness was irrelevant in such a setting. Though subjects *may* apparently learn without being aware of the social contingency involved, they do learn faster when the contingency is clearly explained to them.

In seeking real-life parallels of minimal social behavior, Kelley and his colleagues (1962) suggested that partners in casual conversation often drift toward topics of mutual interest, and that eventually they may come to talk almost entirely about certain topics and to avoid others. This tendency may be especially prominent in long-married couples who tacitly agree to avoid certain touchy topics of conversation. This tendency is also evident in the way that conversationalists adjust their accents, their vocabulary level, their seriousness of tone, and their level of self-disclosure to match the other person's. The important point is that "underneath the more explicitly attained social arrangements the mechanism illustrated by [the] experiments provides a primitive and pervasive set of interpersonal adjustments of which the participants are hardly aware" (Kelley et al., 1962).

Non-Zero-Sum Interactions.   Some dyadic interactions are characterized by what has been called a "zero-sum mutual contingency." The distinctive feature of the **zero-sum interaction** is that one participant always gains precisely what the other loses, and vice versa. Good examples are games like chess, checkers, and tennis. At the other extreme are interactions in which the pattern of outcomes favors pure cooperation, as might be the case among members of a college crew. Much more interesting to social psychologists than either of these extreme patterns are **non-zero-sum,** or **mixed-motive interactions.** They are called non-zero-sum because, in contrast to a zero-sum game, both players may be able to gain positive outcomes from these patterns of behavior. The sum can be better than zero. They are often called "mixed motive" games because neither unremitting competition nor cooperation is an effective strategy for obtaining the largest individual outcomes from the game. Proper play requires a mixture of these two strategies based on a recognition of mutual self-interest. Consider the matrix in Table 19.3, which is another variation of the matrixes given in Tables 19.1 and 19.2. Here we present a set of behavioral alternatives commonly found in the getting-acquainted process, and we include Sally's outcomes along with John's. Sally and John like each other and want to get to know each other better. They realize that this calls for mutual self-disclosure, but they also recognize the penalties of self-disclosure that is not reciprocated. Such exchanges require that the two trust each other. If Sally and John do trust each other, they will each disclose intimate facts about themselves and experience mildly positive (+ 1) outcomes. But what happens if Sally bares her soul to John, only to find that he refuses to self-disclose in return? She may

Table 19.3 An Example of Mixed-Motive Mutual Contingency

		Sally's Alternatives	
		Self-Disclose	**Not Self-Disclose**
John's Alternatives	**Self-Disclose**	John is happy (+ 1) Sally is happy (+ 1)	John is miserable (− 3) Sally is elated (+ 2)
	Not Self-Disclose	John is elated (+ 2) Sally is miserable (− 3)	John is sad (− 1) Sally is sad (− 1)

feel miserable (-3) as she imagines the elation ($+2$) John will feel when he regales his fraternity house brothers with her most intimate disclosures. John, of course, faces exactly the same dilemma. And yet if they are both overly cautious and lacking in trust, they both will be sad (-1). In other words, neither can guarantee a specific outcome by his or her own choices. Each has to consider the most likely responses of the other, because the *combination* of responses is crucial.

It is easy to see how this type of two-person interaction could be turned into a game that is played for points or money, and how experiments using such mixed-motive games could reveal much about human nature. One of the most interesting findings has been that subjects in such experiments spontaneously adopt and stay with one of three strategies (Messick and McClintock, 1968). These three strategies are best illustrated by the "decomposed" matrix in Table 19.4. The matrix is called decomposed because it breaks down Sally's options in a mixed-motive game into three choices that produce different outcomes. Sally can choose to maximize her and John's joint satisfaction—total points for choice A $= +2$; she can choose to maximize her own satisfaction—Sally's points for choice B $= +2$; or she can choose to maximize her satisfaction relative to John's—Sally's advantage in choice C $= +4$.

Ecological Validity. Non-zero-sum games and their decomposed counterparts have been thought to model many natural situations, from lovers' quarrels to labor-management negotiations to nuclear disarmament talks. That is, it has been proposed that these games have **ecological validity,** applications in the real world. In fact, some investigators (Lave, 1965) have confronted naive subjects with "other players" who follow the "Stalin" strategy of unrelenting exploitation, which usually evokes matching noncooperativeness; the "Khrushchev" strategy of competition randomly interspersed with cooperation, which generally lulls subjects into foolish cooperation; or the "Gandhi" strategy of unconditional cooperation, which typically elicits exploitation. In spite of these results, the mixed-motive games have been criticized by some as artificial laboratory situations that have no relevance to the real world.

The question of the games' ecological validity comes down to this. Do subjects in these laboratory experiments behave as they do when confronted with interpersonal situations outside the laboratory, or do they leave their natural inclinations at the door and adopt a special "subject in an experiment" demeanor? In order to answer this question, Daryl Bem and Charles Lord (1979) asked university students to make a series of decomposed game choices of the type depicted in Table 19.4. The subjects in the experiment played the games for money, not just for points, and they always thought that the "other person"

Table 19.4 An Example of "Decomposed" Choices

	Sally's Alternatives		
	Choice A, Maximize Joint Satisfaction	Choice B, Maximize Own Satisfaction	Choice C, Maximize Relative Satisfaction
Sally's Outcome **John's Outcome**	Sally is happy ($+1$) John is happy ($+1$)	Sally is elated ($+2$) John is sad (-1)	Sally is happy ($+1$) John is miserable (-3)

was their own sex. Bem and Lord also obtained descriptions of the students both from them and from their roommates. The results supported the ecological validity of mixed-motive games. Although the students' own self-descriptions were largely unrelated to their choices of game strategies, their roommates' descriptions of them matched their strategies quite well. Subjects whose choices consistently maximized the joint gain accruing to themselves and the other person were described as "cooperative" by their roommates; those who maximized their own gain were described as "predictable."

The most interesting group were women who consistently chose to sacrifice their own gain just so that they could beat the other person by as much as possible. These women pursued a strategy quite at variance with the sex-role stereotype of the female, and yet they described themselves as the essence of femininity: physically attractive, socially poised, liked and accepted by others, never condescending or distrustful. Their roommates did not agree, finding them instead to be aloof, power-oriented, negativistic, tending to undermine or sabotage relationships, and not at all sympathetic, considerate, or giving. Not surprisingly, these women saw themselves as having much greater insight into their own motives and behavior than did their roommates. It appears, then, that mixed-motive laboratory games do tap some aspects of a subject's behavior outside the laboratory and are useful tools for unraveling the secrets of dyadic interaction.

Strategies for Enhancing One's Power

If the distribution of power in a two-person relationship is fairly equal, outcomes tend to be balanced. The two people engage in something like a fair exchange of economic commodities: within limits each will comply with the wishes of the other. In many dyads, however, one person is more powerful than the other. In these cases the outcomes of the person with less power are more affected by the action of the person with more power than the other way around. Such differences in power place less powerful people in an uncomfortable position of uncertainty about their situation, and we might expect them to attempt to reduce the uncertainty by reducing the power differential.

Compliance. The first and most obvious strategy available to the less powerful person who is willing to settle for just reducing uncertainty is to comply with the more powerful person's wishes. By complying the less powerful person may at least avoid the most negative outcomes that can be imposed by the more powerful person. As long as the more powerful person is aware of this **compliance,** the less powerful one can be fairly confident of maintaining good outcomes. But this position is precarious because the less powerful person has no way to retaliate should the more powerful person erroneously or capriciously administer punishment rather than rewards. In addition, compliance in and of itself tends to reinforce and perpetuate the power differential. The more reliable the worker becomes in meeting the supervisor's demands, the more confident the supervisor is that these demands are reasonable and that the worker is happy with the bargain symbolized by their differential power. Therefore, except in situations such as the military, where differences in power are based on status and are accepted by everyone, we would expect to find less powerful people often engaging in strategies designed to increase their power.

Outcome Masking. One common strategy for increasing relative power in a dyad is to mask or conceal the extent to which the other person's responses are rewarding or punishing. Thus John may not let Sally see that her smiles and frowns are important to him; he might accept her smiles as a matter of course, implying that he deserves even more. Both the buyers and the sellers of used cars commonly employ this tactic, seeming unimpressed with the other's offer until the last possible moment.

When outcomes are punishing, matters are more complicated. Two conflicting tactics are available, minimizing the hurt and exaggerating it. Minimizing the hurt or pain may induce the other to desist or shift to responses that induce less pain. This seems to be the strategy employed by the fictional prisoner—hero who is exposed to torture by the enemy. If the hero feigns stoic indifference to his captor's torture, the captor may give up or shift to punishing tactics that the prisoner secretly prefers. Brer Rabbit openly pleaded not to be thrown into the briar patch. The risks of stoic indifference are great, however. The more powerful person may be driven to even more extreme punishments in order to achieve control. The alternative tactic of exaggerating the pain apparently experienced may be successful, particularly if the person with less power has attractive alternative relationships available. The person with greater power is then prevented from applying any more pain for fear of forcing the person with less power out of the relationship.

Self-Presentation. The most common interaction strategies used by the less powerful person are all efforts to move the power relationship toward greater parity. We shall discuss five such tactics very briefly. They are all essentially ways of presenting oneself as a particular kind of person and attempting to "manage" a particular impression (Jones and Pittman, 1982).

Ingratiation is a strategy for gaining power by getting a more powerful person to like you. People ingratiate themselves by showing visible signs of appreciation of the other person's talents, agreeing with his or her opinions, or doing favors. The more dependent a person is on another, the greater the temptation to ingratiate. Yet dependency is the very condition that makes ingratiation least likely to succeed. The **ingratiator's dilemma** is that the more obvious his or her dependence, the less successful the flattery, favors, and kowtowing are likely to prove, because the more powerful person is more likely to interpret such behavior as insincere. When the ingratiator seems to slip across that fine line between likability and obsequiousness, a "boomerang" effect usually makes the ingratiator seem far less likable than if there had been no attempt at ingratiation at all. This effect often prevents subordinates from voicing *genuine* admiration for their superiors, lest their behavior be misinterpreted as ingratiation.

Intimidation is an attempt to convince another person that one is dangerous. In order for intimidation to succeed, the intimidator must appear to be *capable* of and *willing* to inflict harm on the other. Although it is more common for more powerful people to intimidate those with less power, intimidation can sometimes serve as a powerful weapon for those who are otherwise defenseless. We have all seen the four-year-old who, denied candy at the supermarket, throws a tantrum calculated to intimidate the hapless parent. Student sit-ins and prison riots often have the similar goal of "making a scene" that will be picked up by the media and force the administrators into making concessions. On an individual level, consider the advantages that accrue to the person who lets it be known that he has a "short fuse." The intimidator, whether of great or little power, is usually willing to be considered less likable in return for the power that goes with being thought dangerous, and therefore worth mollifying.

Self-promotion is a strategy to make others feel that one is competent.

Name-dropping, references to first-hand experience with exotic foods, wines, or vacation spots, and exaggerated tales of one's athletic prowess are all forms of self-promotion. Many such claims are difficult either to verify or to disprove, but just as the ingratiator must beware of the "ingratiator's dilemma," so must the self-promoter beware of the **self-promoter's paradox.** The paradox consists of the fact that people are more likely to claim competence when their competence is shaky than when it is secure. The Olympic decathlon gold medalist can afford to be modest about his or her athletic prowess, and the multimillionaire does not need to wear expensive suits. Research by George Quattrone and Edward Jones (1978) reveals that when success is likely to be forthcoming on a task, subjects will work to assure that this success is attributed to them rather than to helpful circumstances. Thus a female job applicant may mention her Harvard M.B.A. frequently while seeking the job but play down its significance, or even conceal this "facilitating circumstance," once the job is hers.

Exemplification is a bid for sainthood. The exemplifier wants to be regarded as a morally worthy person—as an individual of high principle and integrity—whom others will accept as a model. Exemplifiers, whether they are sincere or insincere in projecting self-sacrifice and moral worth, risk being regarded as hypocritical. They can arouse only so much guilt in others before they are perceived as having a "holier than thou" attitude, which hampers their ability to influence other people. One danger in exemplification as a way of influencing others is that its effectiveness can be canceled so abruptly; one slip and the game is lost. Woe betide the exemplifier who mars a lifetime of rectitude with a single moral lapse.

Supplication is the only strategy available to those who lack the ability or resources to employ any of the other methods of self-presentation. This method exploits one's own weakness and dependence. The supplicant relies on the cultural norm that prohibits "kicking someone who is already down." The strategy works best when it is possible to convince the other person that the supplicant's weakness and dependence are accidental and undeserved. In the relationship between the sexes, women may play helpless at sawing a board or changing a tire, and men may play helpless at changing diapers and preparing a meal. Using one's own weaknesses is a weapon of last resort, not only because its costs in self-esteem are high, but also because the other person may decide to treat the weaknesses as sufficient reason for breaking off the relationship.

SUMMARY

When two people interact, they sometimes do so only minimally. They may observe the proprieties of turn taking, but neither person's behavior either depends on or affects the behavior of the other. More frequently people genuinely interact and have relatively different degrees of power and control. Most dyadic interactions drift toward a condition of mutual dependency. Simple contingencies exist in games like chess, in which one person's loss is the other's gain, and in those in which all team members either win or lose. More complex contingencies, in which each person's outcomes are determined by the conjunction of his or her own behavioral choices with those of the other person, elicit mixed motives or strategies. Such situations have been studied in laboratory games that bear some resemblance to natural interactions such as labor-management negotiations and international arms limitation talks. In both the laboratory games and their more natural counterparts, outcomes depend on such psychological variables as trust and interpersonal attributions. At least five self-presentational strategies—ingratiation, intimidation, self-promotion, exemplification, and supplication—are available to less powerful people who want to maintain or increase their power and control within an uneven relationship.

PEOPLE IN GROUPS

The importance of group membership to the average individual can hardly be exaggerated. We are educated in groups; we play games in groups; we join "societies," clubs, sororities and fraternities; we make plans as a family; we come together to protest or to bargain for higher wages. Psychologists have long been fascinated by the complex processes of interaction in groups and have frequently been puzzled by them. One particularly challenging fact is that members of a group sometimes accomplish more than an equal number of individuals acting alone could. The clearest examples are ventures that require highly coordinated, complementary activities such as building a space shuttle or playing a Mozart quartet. As much as anything, it is these unpredictable phenomena in group activities that make psychologists want to identify the processes of effective interaction.

What Makes a Group?

Cohesiveness. Thibaut and Kelley (1959) have suggested that an individual's satisfaction with and continuing membership in a group depend on how the actual rewards of group membership compare with those expected and with those available from alternative groups. When the members of a group are highly committed to continuing membership, when morale is high and the group holds together well under stress, we say that there is great **cohesiveness.** This is usually reflected in feelings of belonging, comfort, and attraction to other members. Similarity in the attitudes of members of a group increases cohesiveness; dissimilarity of attitudes decreases it. Groups whose members have similar values and philosophies, such as the major religions of the world, are likely to last longer than groups formed to promote a single issue, whose members may disagree radically on other important issues. Two other factors that promote cohesiveness are success in group projects (Lott and Lott, 1974) and the existence of an external threat. For example, when small grocery store owners were told that a large supermarket chain was thinking of locating a store in their neighborhood, they decided to get together as a group much more frequently (Mulder and Stemerding, 1963). Perhaps the bickering nations of our planet might show greater cohesiveness if they were faced with an invasion from outer space.

Given that cohesiveness promotes group harmony and productivity, it is not surprising that creative management techniques include incentives for continued membership. Many Japanese business firms, for example, advance cohesiveness by hiring people who have been friends through school, by providing economical company housing, and by guaranteeing jobs for life. They are careful to avoid the development of group norms that limit productivity through co-worker censure of the "rate-busters" who work too hard (Roethlisberger and Dickson, 1939). And they discourage the tendency of very cohesive groups to avoid taking chances and to reject innovative solutions to problems (Blake and Mouton, 1979). Group cohesiveness can have negative implications for certain individual members of the group, as well as for the products of the group as a whole. Members of a highly cohesive group will sometimes gang up on a hapless member whom they perceive to be at all deviant. They will at first direct most of their communications at the member who holds a deviant opinion and then ignore the person totally or figure out ways to drive him or her from the group (Schachter, 1951). It is as though the group has been psychologically redefined to exclude the deviant member, whose opinions are no longer considered relevant for social comparison.

The fact that group membership is *psychologically* defined has led some social psychologists to wonder whether an uninformative label indicating group membership might not be enough to produce the phenomena of group membership. If someone were to remind you that you were born on Tuesday, would you feel a special kinship and sense of attachment to others born on Tuesday? According to the traditional view of how and why groups develop, and of what holds groups together, this reaction would seem unlikely.

In a classic experiment which favors the traditional view of group cohesiveness and intergroup rivalry, Muzafer and Carolyn Sherif (1953) found that boys at a summer camp developed intergroup rivalry when group interests and goals were in conflict; they came to like and associate freely with members of other groups when the groups were induced to adopt common goals. This *functional* theory of group formation and maintenance assumes that the best way to reduce intergroup animosity is to get the rival groups, be they street gangs or people of different races or nations, to cooperate in achieving some superordinate goal.

Social Categorization.   In 1971 Henri Tajfel and his colleagues challenged this traditional view of cohesiveness and intergroup rivalry, claiming that group membership per se is sufficient to produce ingroup favoritism and outgroup competition. These researchers asked subjects to estimate the number of dots in each of a set of pictures and then told them that everyone in the world could be divided into overestimators and underestimators, and that "You are one of the overestimators (or underestimators)." That is, the experimenters established *minimal groups* on the basis of a trivial distinction that should have had little to do with conflicts of interest. Then, with no group interaction of any sort, the subjects were asked to assign monetary rewards to anonymous others who were identified only by their group label. Subjects consistently gave more money to members of their own group than to members of the other, even though there had been no history of intergroup hostility, no utilitarian link with self-interest, and no face-to-face interaction (Tajfel el al., 1971). Critics objected to this study. They felt that, even though the subjects had been labeled overestimators or underestimators in a rather capricious fashion, they themselves might have assumed that, sharing one characteristic with members of their group, they probably shared others. More recent research has found ingroup-outgroup discrimination even when assignment to groups is explicitly random (Billig and Tajfel, 1973), a result that appears to meet this criticism.

The explanation offered by Tajfel and his associates is that the mere act of categorization accentuates similarities within a category and differences between categories (see Bruner and Rodrigues, 1953). This purely cognitive phenomenon is supplemented by a social-comparison process in which social categorizations are internalized to define the self. One's own self-esteem seems to depend on how the group fares (Tajfel and Turner, 1979). That is, not only do Mormons, or blacks, or Southerners assume certain similarities to other Mormons, or blacks, or Southerners, but these similarities will be exaggerated and contrasted with their differences from Roman Catholics, Asians, or Midwesterners. This "edge sharpening" occurs as a natural concomitant of categorization and of drawing distinctions between categories. In addition, people come to feel that when other members of their group do well—for example, by achieving leading positions in society—their own status is increased accordingly.

If this interpretation is correct, these tendencies of people in groups suggest a rather different way to reduce intergroup hostility: remove or make less salient any characteristics that differentiate the two groups, and create shared self-identifications. This strategy may help to explain why the United States was relatively successful in bringing together people of diverse ethnic backgrouds. By encouraging them to adopt similar life-styles and a common language, the country systematically deemphasized characteristics that set the groups apart and emphasized shared characteristics that promoted a new self-identification. Instead of regarding the other ethnic groups as the outgroup, new citizens were encouraged to regard non-Americans as the outgroup. Tajfel's hypothesis also suggests, unfortunately, that the "melting pot" strategy may not succeed with blacks, because feelings of ingroup-outgroup enmity may not be eliminated with the provision of superordinate goals. Distinctive and undeniable physical differences will still remain to "trigger" the categorization process. Under these conditions any temporary cooperation between groups could well be attributed to external constraints and thus have no lasting effects.

Group Problem Solving

Do groups solve problems better than individuals do? A great deal of research indicates that groups may enjoy advantages in acquiring correct information, in coordinating people's complementary skills, and in refining thought and making it more objective. But groups also run the risks of premature closure and stultifying conformity, the hallmarks of "group think," to be considered later.

Acquiring Correct Information.   Most problems or tasks confronting a group require the generation and application of information for their solution. Since the needed information is usually unevenly distributed within the group, and some of it is incorrect, a way must be found to ensure that the correct information is available and prevails over the incorrect. Fortunately, there is considerable evidence that groups tend to converge upon the answers held by the most proficient group members. They do so in part because the most proficient members have been found to be right in the past and are therefore taken seriously. In addition, the most proficient members tend to speak up more quickly and with greater confidence. These two factors probably help explain a successful college quiz team. In a winning team the knowledge of the members is complementary, and there is little dispute over who is likely to know what.

In addition to these social factors, which help push them to the fore, correct information and answers are likely to dominate for two additional reasons. Members can often determine whether answers are correct by checking whether they actually solve the problem. Moreover, correct answers are likely to be more common than incorrect answers. That is, if each of seven group members offers answers, and three of these are the same, this answer is more likely to be correct than any of four other, different answers. This reasoning is consistent with the results of Marjorie Shaw's classic study (1932). She found that problem-solving groups rejected many more incorrect solutions than correct ones for a problem, even though more correct solutions were actually offered. It seems reasonable to conclude that when the ideas of each group member are made known to each other member, a number of mechanisms operate to promote the adoption of the correct solution. This explains why groups can function much of the time at the level of their most proficient members.

Coordination of Complementary Skills. Often, however, even more is expected from groups than functioning at the level of the most proficient member. After all, if this were all groups could do for us, why not simply identify the most competent group member and dismiss the remainder? One reason is that the member who is most proficient on one problem or phase of a problem may not be the most proficient member on the next. On this basis, it is certainly possible to understand how, in fact, a problem-solving group could perform *beyond* the level of its most proficient member. For example, if Mary knows only that $X + Y = 8$, and Helen knows only that $X - Y = 4$, they must join forces to discover that $X = 6$ and $Y = 2$. Similarly, if memory is crucial to the task, it is quite likely that all members together can remember more than the single member who recalls the most. Thus all members of a jury, working together, are usually better able to reconstruct the testimony of a trial than any single jury member can, and they will feel confident of its accuracy. Even though some members cannot spontaneously recall some information, they can readily recognize its accuracy when someone else recalls it.

But are there also circumstances in which the members of a group are able to generate new and creative solutions that were not available to them as individuals beforehand? It seems very likely that there are times when an incorrect suggestion by one group member triggers off an associated response in another member, one which is correct and would otherwise not have come to mind. The possibility of such group-induced creativity underlies the procedure of **brainstorming.** This procedure advocates the suspension of criticism, so that participants will offer all their ideas, no matter how preposterous. It also encourages "free wheeling" or "taking off" from others' ideas, at least during the early phases of discussing a problem. Unfortunately, there are very few well-controlled studies of the effectiveness of brainstorming or, more generally, of the role that groups can play in bringing forth creative solutions not otherwise available. Brainstorming instructions, when given to groups, do yield a greater number of creative ideas than instructions emphasizing the quality of suggestions produced, but they also do so when given to individuals working alone (Meadow, Parves, and Reese, 1959). On occasion members of brainstorming groups actually produce inferior solutions as compared with those thought up by the same number of individuals working in isolation, possibly because groups tend to pursue a single line of thought for a longer time than individuals do (Taylor, Berry, and Block, 1958; Dunnette, Campbell, and Jaastad, 1963).

Refinement and Objectivity of Thought. M. C. Bos (1937) suggested that the very act of formulating an opinion or an idea for communication to the group may help the individual member sharpen and refine the idea. The results of an experiment conducted by Dean Barnlund (1959) supported this suggestion. In Barnlund's experiment the group had to choose the appropriate conclusion to a series of logical syllogisms. Each syllogism was so constructed that the content of either the premises or the alternative conclusions was attitudinally charged. For example, one correct syllogistic conclusion was ". . . then some communists are conservative Republicans." Barnlund concluded from his comparisons of how groups and individuals handled these syllogisms that the prospect of group discussion made members more cautious and deliberate in their thinking. As members of the group, they were less likely than individual problem solvers to act on their prejudices in proposing solutions. They were, for example, *more* likely to accept the conclusion that some communists are Republicans because they were less distracted by the loaded and irrelevant attitudinal content of the conclusion.

In discussions of why great errors are sometimes made in planning national policy, Irving Janis (1973) has singled out excessive need for consensus as a major culprit. Great cohesiveness and a desire to preserve unanimity at almost any cost lead to what Janis calls **group think.** He considers it a syndrome of group decision making. Group members are no longer rational and open to information but are directed by a blinders-on spirit of rallying around the flag, the leader, or the previously adopted plan. Speculating why there was a lack of critical debate about Vietnam war policies in the high policy-making circles of the government, Bill Moyers suggests that

> One of the significant problems in the Kennedy and Johnson Administrations was that the men who handled national security affairs became too close, too personally fond of each other . . . great decisions were often made in that warm camaraderie of a small board of directors deciding what the club's dues are going to be for the members next year. . . . So you often dance around the final hard decision which would set you against . . . men who are very close to you, and you tend to reach a consensus (quoted in Janis, 1973, p. 106).

The Risky Shift

In a landmark study reported in 1961, James Stoner asked male students in an industrial management program to make private decisions about the level of risk that they would accept in each of twelve "life dilemmas." For example, each subject was asked to consider what he would do if he had a satisfying, well-paying job with long-range security but was given an opportunity to go into business for himself. There would be some risk of failure but also a chance for great financial gain. The subjects had to decide how sure they must be that the new business venture would be successful before they would resign a secure job and devote their energies to it. Working alone, the subjects answered a set of questions about twelve such dilemmas. Then these subjects responded to a comparable set of questions, after engaging in a group discussion. The final decision was made either by members of the group acting together or by each individual acting separately after the group discussion. The question was whether the subject is more willing to make a risky choice—quitting the secure job and going into business for himself—when deciding by himself or after the

Sometimes group decisions are riskier, sometimes more conservative, than decisions made alone.

group discussion. Over a series of hundreds of experiments, far more individuals advocated a riskier solution to the problem after group discussion than when deciding on their own. The phenomenon was dubbed the **risky shift,** and the tendency was hailed as one of the most robust empirical phenomena in social psychology.

After researchers had accepted the validity of the risky shift, they tried to discover the factors responsible for the shift. Paradoxically, however, they soon learned that the phenomenon itself was not so general, universal, and robust as had been thought. Investigators such as Allan Teger and Dean Pruitt (1967) started to pay attention to the fact that the risky shift referred to a score obtained by combining results from many items. They noted that, for some dilemmas, the group opinion actually shifted in the cautious or conservative direction. For example, groups deciding on bets at the racetrack are more cautious than are individual bettors (Knox and Safford, 1976). The investigators also discovered an intriguing relationship between the mean initial response to an item and the mean shift on that item. If the mean initial response had been on the risky side, group discussions tended to shift opinion in the direction of further risk. If the mean initial response had been cautious, however, the groups tended to shift in the direction of even further caution.

Group Polarization

Serge Moscovici and his colleagues (for example, Moscovici and Zavalloni, 1969) came to the rescue and restored order to the situation with the new concept, **group polarization.** This concept holds that the average response of group members increases in extremity after discussion. Thus if we imagine an opinion scale ranging from -3 to $+3$, and a group whose initial, prediscussion ratings average $+1.5$, discussion might polarize the opinions of the members and the group average might move to $+2.3$. What support is there for such an effect? Actually, the support is quite remarkable and is not restricted to the domain of choice dilemmas, where the risky shift once ruled the roost.

In the realm of attitudes, Moscovici and Marisa Zavalloni (1969) were the first to report the strengthening through discussion of French students' initially positive attitudes toward De Gaulle and negative attitudes toward Americans (Figure 19.5). A variety of experiments assessing other attitudes before and after group discussions obtained the same pattern of results (Myers and Lamm, 1976). Similar experimental findings of polarization have been obtained in studies of ethical dilemmas, decisions of simulated juries about guilt and innocence, and evaluations of people. Recent experiments on risk taking have

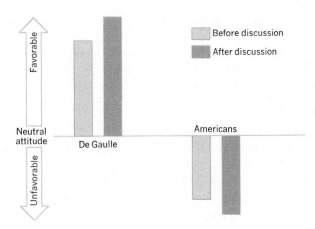

Figure 19.5

Effects of discussion on attitudes. Before their discussion the French students in this study had been favorable toward De Gaulle and unfavorable toward Americans. Discussion made them even more so. When group members are polarized on some issue, discussion may drive them even farther apart. (Adapted from Moscovici and Zavalloni, 1969.)

Figure 19.6
Effects of dramatic events on polarized attitudes. Before President Eisenhower ordered troops sent to Little Rock to enforce desegregation rulings, Texans were polarized in their attitudes toward compliance (*a*) by socioeconomic class as well as (*b*) geographically. Eisenhower's dramatic order increased the polarization. (Adapted from Riley and Pettigrew, 1976.)

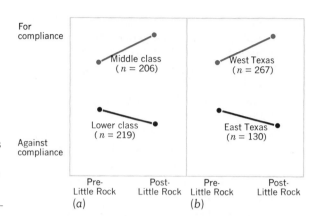

shown strong support for Teger and Pruitt's initial hunch; in general, when the betting odds favor risk, groups will take more risks than will individuals. When the odds are against risky bets, groups will take fewer risks than individuals.

In further support of the concept of group polarization, Helmut Lamm and David Myers (1978) have reported that, compared with independents, college students who join fraternities become increasingly conservative and prejudiced as they move from their sophomore to their senior year. In a different context, Robert Riley and Thomas Pettigrew (1976) report data to support the notion that dramatic events tend to polarize groups with different initial biases. A sampling of opinion in Texas shortly before President Eisenhower ordered federal troops to Little Rock, Arkansas, in 1957, indicated that respondents from the lower socioeconomic class were against compliance with desegregation rulings and respondents from the middle class were slightly for it. After the intervention of troops, opinions shifted to more extreme versions of the earlier inclination. Lower-class respondents were even more against compliance; those of the middle class were more in favor. The same tendencies were revealed when samples were reconstituted along regional lines (Figure 19.6). East Texans, originally against compliance, were more against it after the episode at Little Rock. West Texans, originally for compliance, favored it even more.

A number of explanations have been offered for the polarization effect, some of them borrowed from those accounting for the risky shift. One explanation is that the extreme members of a group argue more persuasively for their point of view during the discussion. A second explanation suggests that social comparison prompts divergent members to converge on the group mean and then to go a little farther than the group in the direction apparently preferred by the members. A third explanation is based on the diffusion of responsibility: the pressure of being held responsible for the decision is less when there are other people available to share the blame. Therefore each member may be willing to endorse an extreme position if everyone else does. This last explanation has also been used to explain the excessive violence of such groups as lynching parties and looting mobs, and the failures of witnesses to come to the aid of victims of crime, discussed earlier in the chapter.

SUMMARY

High morale, commitment, holding together under stress, feelings of belonging, attraction to other members, similar values and philosophies, success in group endeavors, and external threat all promote group cohesiveness. Research on minimal groups has challenged the functionalist view that intergroup rivalry and ingroup favoritism depend on conflicts in interest, however. Mere group labels seem sufficient to elicit preferential treatment of one's ingroup, perhaps because the very act of categorization accentuates intragroup similarities and intergroup differences, and because we identify with and base some of our self-esteem on the outcomes of the ingroup. Theories of ingroup-outgroup competition and cooperation suggest possible ways of achieving international understanding.

Much of what researchers have learned about the advantages of individuals working in groups rather than separately seems to support the conclusions of common sense. Groups are usually formed and maintained when individuals feel more rewarded by belonging than by not belonging to them. Members of a group can often summon the information required to solve a problem, even when none of the members working alone could do so. The knowledge of the group exceeds the capacity of any individual member. But studies of brainstorming by group members, sessions in which they offer all their ideas in the hope that perhaps even an incorrect one will bring to mind a brilliant solution, show that this is not necessarily an effective procedure. Groups can sometimes develop an illusion of invulnerability and can punish or expel those who propose innovative but deviant ideas.

A once widely held assumption, that group members would converge toward the average opinion, was rudely violated by the consistent finding that they did not do so in situations in which risk was a major consideration. They generally favored taking greater risk after group discussion. In attempting to explain this "risky shift" phenomenon, researchers found a more symmetrical tendency toward polarization. Thus there is a shift to the risky position or to the conservative one, depending on whether the group members' initial positions favored risk or caution. Moreover, social attitudes also seem to become polarized through group activities, by dramatic events, or even over time. One likely explanation for polarization is that diffusion of responsibility allows individuals to espouse more extreme positions. People also want to differentiate themselves from the average, in the direction of the majority leaning.

The following concepts are the major ones for this chapter. You should be able to define them and state the points made about each in the text.

TO BE SURE YOU UNDERSTAND THIS CHAPTER

Cultural norm

Social influence

Bystander intervention

Social-comparison theory

Psychological reactance

Mere presence

Cue control

Outcome control

Social-exchange approach

Behavior control

Minimal social situation

Zero-sum game

Non-zero-sum game

Mixed-motive game

Ecological validity

Compliance

Outcome masking

Self-presentation

Ingratiation

Ingratiator's dilemma

Intimidation

Self-promotion

Self-promoter's paradox

Exemplification

Supplication

Group cohesiveness

Brainstorming

Group think

Risky shift

Group polarization

TO GO BEYOND THIS CHAPTER

In This Book.   A review of Chapter 18 at this point would leave you with a complete overview of the field of social psychology. Some of the examples used to illustrate psychological methods in Chapter 1 relate to this chapter. The discussions of human motivation in Chapter 9 and social and emotional development in Chapter 12 are also pertinent.

Elsewhere.   Recommended textbooks on social psychology are *Principles of Social Psychology,* by Kelly Shaver; *Understanding Social Psychology* (third edition), by Stephen Worchel and Joel Cooper; and *Social Psychology,* by David Myers. Leonard Berkowitz edits the highly respected series, *Advances in Experimental Social Psychology. The Handbook of Social Psychology,* by Gardner Lindzey and Elliot Aronson, is another useful reference.

APPENDIX A
STATISTICS

H. G. Wells once described the importance of statistics this way: "Statistical thinking will one day be as necessary for efficient citizenship as the ability to read and write." For all of us, Wells's "one day" appears to be near at hand; for psychology it arrived a long time ago. Most of psychology is an inexact science at best. In such a discipline, which must muster and make sense of ill-assorted materials, the methods of statistics are the most important tools available, because they provide the means of dealing with imprecision and uncertainty.

In psychology statistical methods serve two basic purposes. (1) They offer efficient ways of describing sets of data. (2) They make it possible to evaluate the confidence that can be placed on data and to draw general conclusions from limited information. **Descriptive** and **inferential** statistics, named for these uses, are the subjects of this appendix. We hope that the presentation will demonstrate three things. (1) Statistics has some very useful things to say and clarifies important issues. (2) Statistics is more a way of reasoning than a branch of mathematics. (3) There is nothing very difficult about the subject. The presentation of whatever we need to know, in an elementary introduction to the topic, requires only grade school arithmetic.

DESCRIPTIVE STATISTICS

Benjamin Disraeli's and Fiorello LaGuardia's views of statistics were different from that of Wells. LaGuardia claimed that "Statistics are like psychiatrists—they will testify for either side." Disraeli was more unkind; he insisted that "There are three kinds of lies: lies, damned lies, and statistics." LaGuardia and Disraeli were talking about problems raised by descriptive statistics. In its most common meaning, to lie is to misrepresent the facts in some situation, or to describe them incorrectly, with intent to deceive. Descriptive statistics are especially subject to misrepresentation, but the distortion of truth may come either through innocent misunderstanding or through deliberate trickery. The materials in this section will include examples of both these mishaps in usage.

Incidence and Frequency
In everyday life the statistics we encounter most often are rates of the occurrences of things. Crime rates, rates of automobile accidents, and rates of unemployment are all vital pieces of information. Psychology provides comparable statistics. Thirty-five percent of the American public are obese. Ten percent

of the population have some form of mental disturbance. Two percent of the children in school stutter. Every thirty minutes someone in America commits suicide. The rate of mental illness throughout the world has been relatively stable for fifty years. The frequency of alcohol abuse increases with age; one out of every twenty adults is an alcoholic.

All statistical statements of this type share a particular problem. The rate referred to will go up or down, depending on how other terms that contribute to the determination of the rate are defined. Take the last case as an example. The frequency of alcohol abuse increases with age. To make the rate of alcoholism higher or lower, we need only raise or lower the age that defines adulthood. The definition of alcoholism adds to the problem. If having been drunk once is considered alcoholism, the rate will be very high indeed—even if we ignore the subsidiary problem of how being drunk is defined. If only people whose problems with alcohol have required medical or psychological help are considered alcoholics, the rate of alcoholism is considerably lower. Obviously it will often be important to give close attention to the meaning of the terms employed when making statements about the rate at which phenomena occur.

Trends in Data

Measures of the type we have been discussing often change with time or with other conditions. Frequently such materials are presented graphically. You have already discovered that psychology uses this mode of presentation frequently. With the aid of an example, we shall use this section to make some points about the use and misuse of graphs.

The example, which will be important to readers of this book, concerns apparent trends in the intellectual caliber of students coming to college. Measured by such instruments as the Scholastic Aptitude Test (SAT), which most students take before admission to college, it has until the last several years been declining. Figure A.1 depicts this widely discussed trend. The horizontal axis, the **abscissa** of the graph, represents the years 1969 through 1977. The vertical axis, the **ordinate,** is the average SAT score. This graphic presentation makes its sad point eloquently.

One question to ask about the decline in SAT scores shown in Figure A.1 is whether it is big enough to worry about. The answer to this question is "Yes," for reasons that you will understand better after you have read the rest of this appendix. The decline is about a third of a standard deviation of these scores, and that is a large decline.

In the meantime it is worth noting that the decline can be made to seem

Figure A.1
Nine-year trend in SAT scores.

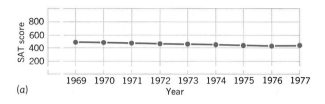

(a)

large or small by some simple graphic trickery. Figure A.2 will show you how to perform such statistical magic, or how to expose it for what it is, depending on your purposes. The top half of the figure makes the decline all but disappear by compressing the ordinate. The bottom half of the figure is what Darell Huff (1954) calls a "gee-whiz graph" in his book *How To Lie with Statistics*. Expanding the ordinate exaggerates the decline unrealistically.

Frequency Distributions

A graphical representation of data that is basic to a number of statistical concepts is the **frequency distribution**. We begin with an example. The scores below were obtained by a hundred college students on a twenty-one-item true-false test of psychological information.

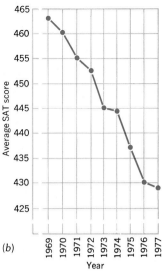

(b)

Figure A.2
Figures don't lie but liars sometimes figure. The significant decline in SAT scores over the years (a) can be made to disappear, or (b) it can be exaggerated by manipulation of axes.

```
19  16  18  19  12  18  15  15  15  14
16  13  15  15  13  15  14  19  20  18
14  15  17  16  18  19  18  16  10  19
15  11  20  14  13  12  19  13  18  15
13  16  13  16  21  16  16  16  14  13
18  12  19  18  15  11  13  17  15  15
17  19  17  13  14  17  20  18  19  18
21  17  14  16  16  16  17  17  16  17
16  18  17  16  19  16  11  14  17  16
19  14  16  17  12  17  15  15  17  18
```

Because of the large number of scores in this array, it is difficult to get an accurate grasp of them. A cursory glance tells us that the scores vary somewhat and that the typical student probably made a score of 15, 16, or 17. For many purposes, however, these statements are not precise enough. One way of bringing greater clarity to such collections of numbers is to put them into a frequency distribution, which presents the data graphically. In Figure A.3a, one version of a frequency distribution, the range of test scores has been marked off on the horizontal axis from low to high. Then single x's for each of the

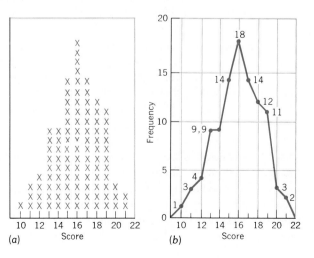

(a)   (b)

Figure A.3
Two forms of frequency distribution. (a) An x indicates the performance of each individual. Such figures are never actually used because they are tedious to construct. (b) A *frequency polygon* employs points and lines to present the same data. Notice that a scale has been added on the ordinate.

hundred scores have been put above the proper numbers. The graph thus shows us in a detailed way how the students distribute themselves by their scores. A more common frequency distribution is presented in Figure A.3*b*. This figure is a **frequency polygon**. The horizontal axis is the same as in Figure A.3*a*, but here a vertical axis has been added. And, instead of counting x's, we simply refer to this vertical axis to read the number of individuals who made a particular score.

Measures of Central Tendency

The shape of the graphs in Figure A.3 indicates that these scores tend to pile up in the middle of the distribution. This is typical of most psychological and biological data. Several different measures can be used as an index of this clustering or central tendency, but three of them are very common. Two of these measures can be determined by inspecting the set of data in Figure A.3. The third you already know about. The first and easiest number to determine is the **mode**. In Figure A.3 you will find that the most frequent score is 17. The mode of this distribution is 17. The mode is the most frequent score in a given distribution.

The second single number representative of the distribution and its clustering is the **median,** or the middle score. The scores of the distribution must be ordered by rank to determine the median. The middle score in Figure A.3 would fall between the fiftieth and fifty-first, since there are a hundred of them. If you count the x's in Figure A.3*a* from either end of the distribution, you will find that the median falls at the score of 16.

The third representative number, the **mean**, is the familiar arithmetical average. It is obtained by adding up all the scores and dividing by the number of scores. The mean of the test scores is 15.97, a value very close to those previously obtained for the mode and median.

Symmetry and Skewness

To be useful, any measure of central tendency should indicate the typical. Depending on the situation, and the shape of the frequency distribution, different measures of central tendency are differentially useful. The distributions of scores in Figure A.3 were symmetrical; that is, there were just about as many below the mean as there were above it. In such distributions the mode, mean, and median will have nearly the same value; they all describe the central tendency of the distribution quite well. For distributions that are not completely symmetrical but not remarkably asymmetrical either, the mean is the most useful measure of central tendency because it is familiar to everyone and it also allows other statistical manipulations.

In other situations one of the other measures of central tendency may be more appropriate. Let us start with an extreme case, the behavior of the American motorist at stop signs. The motorist will come to a full stop, decelerate to a very slow speed, slow down only slightly, or keep going at the same speed. These four categories of behavior, ranging from "full stop" to "no change in speed," can be arranged along the abscissa, the number of motorists falling into each category along the ordinate (Figure A.4). The resulting curve is sometimes called a **J-curve**. Although some motorists behave in other ways, the great majority of them conform to the law and stop completely at traffic signals. The mode of the distribution describes the typical behavior most exactly.

An asymmetrical distribution like the J-curve in Figure A.4 is said to be **skewed**. Distribution of yearly taxable income in the United States is always skewed in another way, because individual incomes can range from nothing to

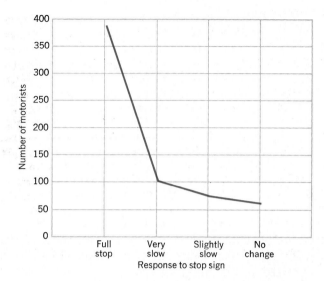

Figure A.4
A J-curve. This frequency distribution shows the number of motorists behaving in different ways at a stop sign. The experimenters sat in a parked car at an intersection and observed the motorists' reactions. Most of them came to a full stop.

enormous. Although in the late 1970s some families had yearly incomes between $5000 and 10,000 and even more earned between $10,000 and $20,000, some incomes were considerably higher (Figure A.5). The highest single yearly income in the United States was something like $6,000,000, skewing the distribution far, far to the right. The mean income in the United States during this period was approximately $12,500, whereas the median income was only $10,500. In the computation of the mean, the extreme values of the distribution, those of its very long tail, have pulled the mean toward them. But the median is obtained by counting, which means that extreme values are no more important than any other. Earnings of many times $6,000,000 would have no greater effect on the median than any other income above the median. Because it is unaffected by the extremely high incomes of the few, as is the mean, the median is a much more accurate measure of typical income.

A distribution like that in Figure A.5, which has a tail to the right toward the high numbers, is said to be **positively skewed**. Distributions in which the tail is to the left, toward the low numbers, are said to be **negatively skewed**. The median is again the better measure of central tendency. Scores on course examinations often have a negatively skewed distribution (Figure A.6). A number of students make a nearly perfect score on the test, which creates a ceiling effect, a bunching at the top scores. The usual test does not give the very best students a chance to show how good they are. They are not separated out but instead are part of the substantial group whose scores pile up toward the high

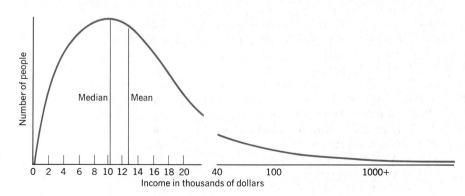

Figure A.5
Taxable income in the United States. Points on the abscissa are placed arbitrarily after $20,000. Median and mean have been indicated to show their relationship in a positively skewed distribution.

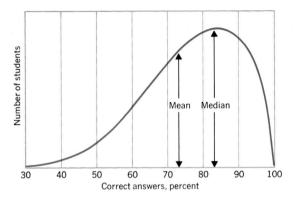

Figure A.6
Distribution of grades on a typical course examination. This distribution is negatively skewed. Notice that, as in Figure A.5, skewness affects the relationship between median and mean.

end of the distribution. The only straightforward solution to this problem is to make tests much longer than they usually are, but the limitations of time generally rule out this possibility.

Variability

The frequency distributions already presented have provided you with a glimpse at one of the most obvious facts of human nature. People vary enormously on almost every dimension you can think of. This simple observation is so basic that it identifies one way of expressing the whole purpose of psychology. Our aim is to account for the variance in human and animal behavior.

Variance and Standard Deviation. Two closely related measures of variability are important in statistical thinking. The reason for the existence of two measures is that each has a useful feature that the other does not. The two measures are *variance* and *standard deviation.* We shall describe these measures now and explain their useful features in later sections. Both measures serve the same descriptive purpose. They indicate the degree to which measurements cluster about the mean. The mean centers the distribution and the curve that expresses it. The variance and standard deviation indicate how measures spread out from the mean. The less the measures in a distribution cluster, the wider is the dispersion, and the larger are the variance and standard deviation (Figure A.7).

Both variance and standard deviation are numbers obtained by simple calculations. To find the **variance** of a set of scores, first obtain the mean—by adding the scores and then dividing the sum by the number of scores. Then determine the deviation of each of the scores from the mean—by subtracting the mean from each of these numbers. For scores below the mean, these deviations will be negative; for those above the mean, the deviations will be positive. Having obtained the deviation of each score from the mean, next square them all. Then add the squared deviations, whose signs will all have

Figure A.7
Features of frequency distributions. A frequency distribution is a plot of the number of individuals (ordinate) receiving each score on some scale of measurement (abscissa). Cases cluster around the mean but also scatter around it. The two distributions to the left have the same mean but differ in variability. The same is true of the two distributions to the right. The upper and two lower distributions each have the same variability but differ in their means.

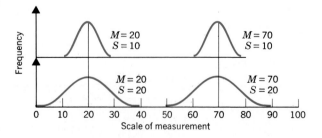

become positive in the process of squaring them. Finally obtain the mean squared deviation by dividing by the number of them. The statistic obtained is the variance of the distribution. The **standard deviation** is just one short step beyond variance. It is the square root of the variance.

The numbers in which variances and standard deviations are stated are in the same point system as the measurements on which they were based. The principal thing you need to know about variance and standard deviation is that these measures express something factual about a distribution. They do not come from on high but must be calculated. Such calculations have yielded the following values for some distributions with which you are familiar.

1. As measured by most IQ tests, the average IQ is 100 points. Scores range from near zero to over 200, with a mean of 100. The variance of the distribution of IQ scores is about 225 points and the standard deviation is about 15 points.
2. The range of SAT scores is some 600 points, from a little less than 200 to a little more than 800. On the original sample of students who took this test, the mean was 500. Reflecting the large range of scores, their variance was 10,000 and the standard deviation ($\sqrt{10,000}$) was 100.
3. For data in Figure A.3, with a mean of 15.97 and range from 10 to 21, the variance is 5.66, the standard deviation 2.38.

Symbols. Although it is possible, as we have been doing, to present statistical ideas in words, it is much more efficient to put them in symbolic form. This step is essential to the presentation of calculations.

The Mean. The formula for the mean, M, is

$$M = \frac{\Sigma X}{N}$$

where Σ stands for the process of addition, X refers to each and every individual score, and N is the number of scores for which the mean is computed.

As you can see, this formula describes simply and quickly the methods used to calculate the mean: add up (Σ) all the scores (X) and divide by the number of scores (N).

Variance and Standard Deviation. The formula for variance, S^2, sometimes symbolized V, is

$$S^2 = V = \frac{\Sigma d^2}{N}$$

where Σ stands for the process of addition and d refers to the difference between each and every individual score (X) and the mean (M). Thus $d = X - M$ and $d^2 = (x - M)^2$. The process of squaring makes all terms in the equation positive. As before, N is the number of measurements for which variance is computed.

The formula for the standard deviation is

$$S = \sqrt{\frac{\Sigma d^2}{N}}$$

where all terms have the meanings previously presented.

Computations. Since the formulae for the standard deviation and variance include terms that depend on knowing the mean, the calculation of either of these will illustrate the calculation of the mean as well. The following sets of

Table A.1 Computation of Variance and Standard Deviation

X	d	d²	
46	$46 - 49 = -3$	9	$M = \dfrac{\Sigma X}{N} = \dfrac{343}{7} = 49$
47	-2	4	
48	-1	1	
49	0	0	$S^2 = \dfrac{\Sigma d^2}{N} = \dfrac{28}{7} = 4$, the variance (V)
50	$+1$	1	
51	$+2$	4	
52	$+3$	9	$S = \sqrt{\dfrac{\Sigma d^2}{N}} = \sqrt{4} = 2$, the standard
343	0	28	deviation

X	d	d²	
1	$1 - 4 = -3$	9	$M = \dfrac{\Sigma X}{N} = \dfrac{28}{7} = 4.0$
2	-2	4	
3	-1	1	
4	0	0	$S^2 = \dfrac{\Sigma d^2}{N} = \dfrac{28}{7} = 4$, the variance
5	$+1$	1	
6	$+2$	4	
7	$+3$	9	$S = \sqrt{\dfrac{\Sigma d^2}{N}} = \sqrt{4} = 2$, the standard
28	0	28	deviation

numbers will provide two simple examples: (a) 1, 2, 3, 4, 5, 6, 7; and (b) 46, 47, 48, 49, 50, 51, 52. Please note that the two sets are very different in the sizes of the individual numbers. You should expect the means to be different. The ranges of the two sets of scores are the same, however, and you should not be surprised to find that S and S^2 are the same for the two sets. The calculations appear in Table A.1.

Having dealt with two sets of numbers for which the means differ and variability is the same, we present for comparison examples for which the reverse is true, for which the means are the same and variability differs. The two sets of numbers in the left-hand column of Table A.2 have these properties.

SUMMARY

The data of psychology commonly take the form of descriptive statistics that tell us what we need to know about behavioral phenomena—their frequency, the relation of one phenomenon to another, their distribution, their "average" values, and their variability. Most of the time descriptive statistics are useful and informative. Through innocent misunderstanding or otherwise, however, they can sometimes distort and mislead. Rate measurements may vary, depending on definitions of the terms that enter into the computation of the rate. The meaning of a given rate is unclear unless these definitions are given. Graphic representations of rates can be misleading if the vertical axis is made too long or too short.

A frequency distribution arranges the set of numerical data from lowest to highest and shows the number of measures at each value. Most distributions of data tend to pile up at the middle. There are three measures of this central tendency: the mean, the well-known arithmetic average; the mode, the most common value in the distribution; and the median, the middle score. Depending on the shape of the distribution curve, one or the other measure of central tendency will be the most appropriate. For symmetrical distributions the mean, mode, and median will all have the same value. In such situations the mean is

Table A.2 Computation of Variance and Standard Deviation

X	d	d^2	
4	$4 - 16 = -12$	144	$M = \dfrac{\Sigma X}{N} = \dfrac{112}{7} = 16$
8	-8	64	
12	-4	16	$S^2 = \dfrac{\Sigma d^2}{N} = \dfrac{448}{7} = 64$, the variance (V)
16	0	0	
20	$+4$	16	$S = \sqrt{\dfrac{\Sigma d^2}{N}} = \sqrt{\dfrac{448}{7}} = \sqrt{64} = 8$, the
24	$+8$	64	standard deviation
28	$+12$	144	
112	0	448	

X	d	d^2	
10	$10 - 16 = -6$	36	$M = \dfrac{\Sigma X}{N} = \dfrac{112}{7} = 16$
12	-4	16	
14	-2	4	$S^2 = \dfrac{\Sigma d^2}{N} = \dfrac{112}{7} = 16$, the variance
16	0	0	
18	$+2$	4	
20	$+4$	16	$S = \sqrt{\dfrac{\Sigma d^2}{N}} = \sqrt{\dfrac{112}{7}} = \sqrt{16} = 4$, the
22	$+6$	36	standard deviation
112	0	112	

the most useful measure. For skewed distributions that have a long tail, with data piled up at one end, the mean will be pulled too high by the extreme values in the tail and will not represent typical performance. Then the median or sometimes the mode becomes the better measure of central tendency.

Variance and the standard deviation are the most important indices of the degree to which measurements cluster about or spread out from their mean.

MORE DESCRIPTIVE STATISTICS

Variance and standard deviation have different special properties that make them useful in different ways. The variance for any set of scores can be broken down into additive components in order to estimate the degree to which several different variables contribute to the variation in a trait or aspect of behavior. We deal with this idea in the next section. The usefulness of the standard deviation derives from its precise relationship to the normal curve.

The Normal Curve

The normal distribution is actually a complex mathematical function, but almost everyone has seen the graphic version of it. The familiar bell shape and mirror-image symmetry of the **normal curve** describe the frequency distribution of many biological and psychological traits. Among the real-life happenings described by the normal curve are most body measurements, such as chest sizes, and reaction times in stopping a car. The normal curve in Figure A.8 is a somewhat idealized distribution of the IQs for the white population of the United States. The mean of the distribution of IQs is 100, the standard deviation of the distribution about 15. Once we have these facts and are aware that IQs are normally distributed, we know a great deal about the distribution of intelligence. It should be understood that knowledge about this distribution applies generally to any normal distribution.

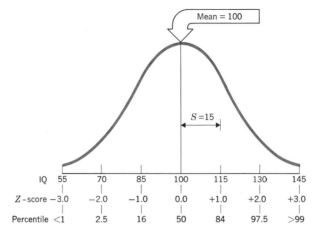

Figure A.8
IQs, Z-scores, and percentiles. This idealized distribution of IQs indicates their relation to Z-scores and percentiles.

Z-Scores. In Figure A.8 the abscissa is marked off into units corresponding to 15 IQ points. In other words, it is marked off in units of the standard deviation (*S*). We can now understand the second row of numbers beneath the abscissa, the one labeled ***Z-score***. The numbers on this scale represent deviations of scores from the mean in *S*-units. Since the mean does not deviate from itself, it has a *Z*-score of zero. An IQ of 85 is 15 IQ points, or one standard deviation, below the mean and therefore has a *Z*-value of −1.0. For an exactly analogous reason, an IQ of 115 corresponds to a *Z*-score of +1.0; an IQ of 70 is the equivalent of a *Z*-score of −2.0; and so on. A *Z*-score is computed by dividing the deviation of a raw score by the standard deviation. That is, from any raw score (*X*) subtract the mean (*M*) and divide by the standard deviation (*S*). The mathematical formula is very simple, $Z = (X - M)/S$. To illustrate the conversion of raw IQ scores to standard deviation units, let us take an IQ that does not appear in Figure A.8, for example, an IQ of 110: 110 − 100 = 10 ÷ 15 = +.667. Our computation tells us that in IQ of 110 falls two-thirds of a standard deviation above the mean, making the *Z*-score +.667. A more exact understanding of *Z*-scores requires an appreciation of the areas under the normal curve as they are marked off by various *Z*-score ranges. We shall present the important points in two slightly different ways.

Percentile Ranks. The **percentile rank** of a score is the percentage of other scores in a distribution that the particular score equals or exceeds. Thus if a score is at the fiftieth percentile (the median), it equals or exceeds 50 percent of the scores; if it is at the thirty-seventh percentile, it equals or exceeds 37 percent of the scores. Now look at the very bottom scale in Figure A.8, which ranges from < 1 (percent) to > 99 (percent), and compare it with the middle scale, which is in terms of *Z*-scores. As you can see, percentiles and *Z*-scores are very definitely related. Each *Z*-score has a particular percentile rank; for example, a *Z*-score of −1.0, which corresponds to a raw IQ of 85, has a percentile rank of 16. Another way to put it is to say that 16 percent of the area in a normal curve falls below a *Z*-score of −1.0.

Standard Deviations and Areas. The relationship of areas within the normal curve to *Z*-scores can be expressed in another way, one which is in terms of the standard deviation on which the *Z*-score is based. Figure A.9 shows the percentages of total area falling within a normal distribution curve as they are marked off by different *S*-distances on either side of the mean. The range from

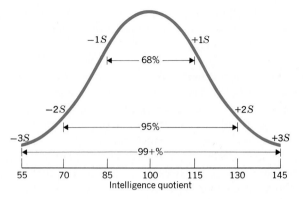

Figure A.9
Areas under the normal curve. This idealized distribution of IQs indicates what percentages of them fall within various *S*-ranges. If you understand this figure, you can derive Figure A.8 from it. A small fraction of one percent of the population have IQs over 145 and below 55.

$-1S$ to $+1S$ covers 68 percent of the area under the curve and of the distribution of scores. The range from $-2S$ to $+2S$ covers about 95 percent of the area and the scores, and the range from $-3S$ to $+3S$ covers over 99 percent of them. For any curve to be a normal curve, the areas bounded by the various standard deviation markings must be exactly these particular percentages of the total area beneath the curve. We know a normal curve only by these percentages; inspection alone will not tell us that a bell-shaped curve describes a normal distribution. For later purposes it will also be important to note that the percentages of area and of scores *not* included in each of the three standard deviation ranges shown in Figure A.9 are 32, 5, and 1.

Correlation

The methods of **correlation** tell us whether and how closely two different sets of measures are related. They also tell us whether the relationship is positive or negative. When high scores on one measure are associated with high scores on the second, the scores are said to be **positively correlated**. Figure A.10 is a **scatter plot** presenting such a correlation for scores obtained by thirteen students on two different examinations. When high scores on one measure are associated with low scores on the other, the scores are said to be **negatively correlated**. Figure A.11 presents an example of a negative correlation, that between the time required to decide that one of two lights was brighter and to press a button and the difference in brightness of the two lights, ranging from

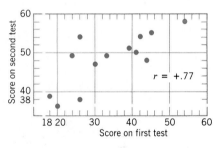

Figure A.10
Scatter plot of scores obtained by thirteen students on two tests. The correlation coefficient, $+.77$, is calculated in Table A.3.

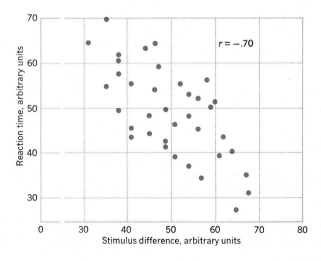

Figure A.11
A negative correlation. The *x*-measures on the abscissa are differences in the brightness of two lights. The *y*-measures on the ordinate are the times required by subjects to press a button to indicate that they detected a difference in brightness. The greater the stimulus difference, the less time required to detect it. (Data from Blommers and Lindquist, 1960.)

a small difference to a large one. The smaller the difference in brightness, the greater the amount of time required to decide that there was a difference and to press the button.

Correlation Coefficients. The relationships presented verbally and graphically so far in this section are more commonly expressed numerically. Called **correlation coefficients,** these numbers range in value from $+1.00$, indicating a perfect positive correlation, through zero or no correlation, to -1.00, indicating a perfect negative correlation.

The correlation coefficient can be computed with the help of Z-scores, which allow us to put measures as different as reaction times and differences in the brightness of two lights on the same scale and compare them. Whatever the scales of measurement in which scores are expressed, they can be converted to Z-scores and meaningfully compared with each other, for Z-scores state positions within distributions. The Z-score is sometimes called a standard score for just this reason.

In the computation of a correlation coefficient, we call the two sets of measures to be correlated x and y. The calculations proceed in these steps. First compute each person's two Z-scores for raw scores on x and y. The mean and standard deviation will of course have to be computed first. The Z-scores above the mean will have positive values and those below will have negative values. Then multiply each person's two Z-scores together. The processes of multiplying positive by positive and negative by negative Z-scores will both yield positive products, but multiplying negative by positive and positive by negative Z-scores will yield negative products. Finally, add together the Z-score products for all individuals and divide by the number of individuals. In other words, average these Z-score products. Their average is the correlation coefficient, denoted by r. The formula for the computation just described is

$$r = \frac{\Sigma(Zx \cdot Zy)}{N}$$

If you think through these calculations, keeping in mind the meanings of positive and negative correlations, you will see that correlations will be positive when high scores on x go with high scores on y and low scores on x go with low scores on y, for positive will be multiplied by positive and negative by negative. Correlations will be negative when high scores on either measure are associated with low scores on the other, for positive will be multiplied by negative. The final two steps, adding Z-score products that are positive or negative, or that are for the most part one or the other, and dividing them by their number, will obviously not change their signs.

Another measure of correlation, a rank-order coefficient called rho (R), may add to your understanding. The formula for rho is

$$R = 1 - \frac{6\Sigma D^2}{N(N^2 - 1)}$$

In this formula, instead of converting to Z-scores, the x and y measures are converted to rankings. The subjects are ranked 1, 2, 3, . . . , N on x and 1, 2, 3, . . . , N on y, from high to low, or vice versa. Then the individual's rank on x is subtracted from his or her rank on y or vice versa. The term D in the formula refers to the difference in each individual's rank on the x and y measures. With D defined, the meaning of the formula for r should be clear.

An Example. A professor gave his first examination to a small undergraduate class, graded it, and, addressing the class later, described the problem that the grades had created in this way. "Either I gave a rotten examination that was way too hard, or else you students didn't study. Since it is important for my examinations to be reasonable from your point of view, and it is just as important for you to understand my expectations, I will give another examination on the same materials a week from today. For my part, I will try to adjust the level of the exam. For yours, you should do a bit more studying if your conscience tells you that you did less for this exam than you should have."

One week later the second test was given. Table A.3 lists the scores of the thirteen students who took the two examinations, each sixty items long. As you can see, performance on the second exam was uniformly better than on the first, but there is also a positive correlation between the scores. The rest of the materials in the table make this point by computing r and R. For the computation

Table A.3 Computation of r and R

Computation of r

Student	First Exam Score (x)	Second Exam Score (y)	Z_x	Z_y	$Z_x \cdot Z_y$
1	24	49	$-.94$	$+.10$	$-.09$
2	45	55	$+1.04$	$+1.03$	$+1.07$
3	26	38	$-.76$	-1.61	$+1.22$
4	30	47	$-.38$	$-.21$	$+.08$
5	33	49	$-.09$	$+.10$	$-.01$
6	20	37	-1.32	-1.77	$+2.34$
7	18	39	-1.51	-1.46	$+2.20$
8	54	58	$+1.89$	$+1.50$	$+2.84$
9	39	51	$+.47$	$+.41$	$+.19$
10	26	54	$-.76$	$+.87$	$-.66$
11	44	48	$+.94$	$-.06$	$-.06$
12	42	54	$+.76$	$+.87$	$+.66$
13	41	50	$+.66$	$+.25$	$+.17$
					total $+9.95$

$$r = \frac{\Sigma\, (Z_z \cdot Z_y)}{N} = \frac{9.95}{13} = +\,.77$$

Computation of R

Student	First Exam Score (x)	Second Exam Score (y)	Rank on x	Rank on y	D	D^2
1	24	49	3	6.5	3.5	12.25
2	45	55	12	12	0	0.00
3	26	38	4.5	2	2.5	6.25
4	30	47	6	4	2	4.00
5	33	49	7	6.5	0.5	0.25
6	20	37	2	1	1	1.00
7	18	39	1	3	2	4.00
8	54	58	13	13	0	0.00
9	39	51	8	9	1	1.00
10	26	54	4.5	10.5	6	36.00
11	44	48	11	5	6	36.00
12	42	54	10	10.5	0.5	0.25
13	41	50	9	8	1	1.00
					total	102.00

$$R = 1 - \frac{6\Sigma D^2}{N(N^2 - 1)} = 1 - \frac{6(102)}{13(169 - 1)} = 1 - \frac{612}{2184} = 1 - .28 = +\,.72$$

of r, it is necessary, first, to compute the means and standard deviations for the two tests. Without going through the mechanics, the values obtained were these: for test 1, $M = 34.00$ and $S = 10.59$; for test 2, $M = 48.38$ and $S = 6.43$. Next it is necessary to compute Z-scores for each student's x and y scores. The scores for student 1 are taken as an example. Recalling that $Z = (x - M)/S$, we have

$$Z_x = \frac{24 - 34}{10.59} = \frac{-10}{10.59} = -.94$$

$$Z_y = \frac{49 - 48.38}{6.43} = \frac{+.62}{6.43} = +.10$$

With these values computed, the next steps are to multiply Z_y by Z_x for each student and to average these products, as required by the formula for r. The result is $r = +.77$ (Table A.3).

The calculation of R begins by converting the scores to ranks. Then differences between ranks are obtained. These differences are squared and added, and the sum is entered into the formula for R. The result of the computation is $+.72$, which approximates the value of r. The scatter plot in Figure A.10 is a graph of these data.

Accounting for Variance. A correlation coefficient is used principally for purposes of prediction. Correlation coefficients can be used to predict college grades from SAT scores (page 424), to predict the IQ of one identical twin from that of the other (page 47), and to predict cardiac disorder from scores on a stress inventory (page 308). A more exact way to describe the predictive power of a correlation coefficient is in terms of the proportion of variance in one measure that is accounted for by its correlation with another measure.

Take the case of SAT scores and college grades, for example. The distribution of grades for the entire freshman class of some university might be like the large distribution in Figure A.12 labeled "All SAT groups combined." This large distribution of course includes the scores for students with very different SATs. Suppose now that we look at the distribution of grades for five groups of students who have the similar SAT scores, identified in Figure A.12 by the labels 800 to 999, 1000 to 1199, and so on. There would of course be fewer

Figure A.12

Accounting for variance. Students with differing SAT scores receive different freshman grades on the average. The SAT scores account for these average differences. Each subgroup shows considerable variance around its individual mean, however. This variance is unaccounted for. The small distributions added together would reproduce the total distribution. The variance in the means of the groups plus the variance within individual groups equals total variance.

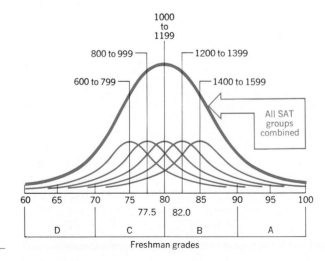

of them in each group and their distributions would be smaller. Notice that the means of grades for these groups differ; they are 75, 77.5, and so on. But the range of grades within each small group is very wide. One way to describe what we see in Figure A.12 is to say that SAT scores predict grades to a degree, reflected by the different means of the five subgroups, but the prediction of grades for individual students is seldom accurate, reflected by the wide range of grades within individual SAT subgroups.

Another way to describe the situation is in terms of the useful property of variance, to which we have finally come. Variance can be separated into additive components that are assignable to different causal factors. Figure A.12 shows that the total distribution of grades has been broken down into two components. The first component is the variation in mean grades for the five subgroups. The second component is the variation in grades within each subgroup. It would be reasonable to say that the first of these components is *accounted for* by SAT scores; the second component is *unaccounted for.* If the small distributions were all added back together, they would recreate the large distribution. This should begin to give you a feel for what it means to say that variance can be broken down into additive components. Accounted-for variance plus unaccounted-for variance, in this case, equals total variance.

What does all this have to do with correlation? The connection is surprisingly direct. If the correlation between x and y is r, the proportion of variance in y accounted for by x is r^2. In our example x is SAT scores, y is freshman grades. The proportion of variance of grades accounted for by SAT scores is whatever fraction the variance in the means of the grades of the five subgroups (variance accounted for, as we have already seen) is of total variance. These calculations, performed on actual data, yield values that range from about .09 to about .16. Since the proportion of variance accounted for is r^2, r will be the square root of the proportion of variance accounted for. This means that the correlation between SAT scores and freshman grades is in the neighborhood of $\sqrt{.09} = .30$ to $\sqrt{.16} = .40$. Clearly the correlation between SAT scores and grades accounts for only a small proportion of the variability of grades. This explains why college administrators do not put much faith in any except extremely high and low SAT scores—or at least why they should not.

SUMMARY

The normal curve is a symmetrical, bell-shaped frequency distribution. It describes the distribution of most biological and psychological traits. The most important aspect of the normal curve is the relation of proportions of area beneath it to Z-scores.

A Z-score is a number that tells us, in units of standard deviation, where a raw score of the distribution falls with respect to the mean. That is, it tells us that a score is so many standard deviations above or below the mean. For any normal curve there is a precise and known correspondence between proportions of the distribution and Z-scores: 68 percent of the distribution falls between Z-scores −1.0 and +1.0; 95 percent of it between Z-scores −2.0 and +2.0; 99.7 percent of it between Z-scores −3.0 and +3.0.

A correlation coefficient is a number between − 1.0 and + 1.0 that indicates the direction and degree of relation of two distributions of measurements obtained on the same individuals. The most direct interpretation of the meaning of a correlation coefficient is that it allows the prediction of one measure from another. A less direct interpretation is that the existence of a correlation, r, between x and y means that a proportion of the variance equal to r^2 in one variable is accounted for by variation in the other.

INFERENTIAL STATISTICS

It will be understandable if, by now, you have forgotten a major point with which this chapter began, that statistics is a tool for dealing with imprecision and uncertainty. Having seen a parade of means, standard deviations, and correlations presented with two-decimal precision, you may have come to the conclusion that statistics must be pretty accurate measures after all. It is time now to explain why this is an erroneous conclusion and how the other part of the statistical enterprise, inferential statistics, is able to manage imprecision.

Samples and Populations

The procedures of inferential statistics provide a means whereby information obtained on a sample is used to draw conclusions about a larger population. That is why the procedures are called **inferential statistics:** data on samples are used to draw inferences about populations. The terms population and sample mean about what you would expect them to. A **population** is the entire universe of individuals, objects, or events potentially available for study; a **sample** is a smaller set of individuals, objects, or events drawn from the population.

The general rule for drawing inferences about populations from sample data is straightforward. The statistic obtained on a sample provides an estimate of the same measure for a population. If the mean IQ of a sample of college students is 110, an estimate of the mean IQ of the entire population of college students would also be 110. If the correlation between the IQs of parents in a sample and of their children is +.60, we would infer that the same correlation applies to the IQ of parents and of children in the population. If 52 percent of a sample of voters say that they will vote Democratic in the next election, Dr. Gallup uses this percentage as his best estimate of the outcome of the election, even if it is an estimate in which he has little confidence.

The Accuracy of Estimates. As this *last* example suggests, the estimates based on samples must carry two cautious provisos. *First,* it is important to understand that, since samples *are* samples, the measure obtained on a given one will almost certainly differ from that obtained on another. In other words, measures obtained on samples are subject to error. If the values obtained on two samples differ, at least one of them and probably both must differ from the value for the population. It is the recognition of such errors that may lead Dr. Gallup to decide that the outcome of an election is "too close to call," in spite of the 52 percent majority who say they plan to vote one way or the other. *Second,* these estmates assume that the sample upon which they are based is representative of the population for which conclusions are being drawn. If the sample is not representative, the estimate may be very much in error.

No doubt the most famous error of this sort is that committed by the 1936 Literary Digest Poll. In that year the magazine *Literary Digest* mailed out ten million ballots on the presidential election and received over two million of them in return. On the basis of these straw votes, *Literary Digest* predicted the election of Alfred M. Landon to the presidency of the United States. But November 2, 1936 came and went and President Franklin D. Roosevelt received 60 percent of the popular vote in a landslide victory.

In the Literary Digest Poll ballots had been mailed to subscribers of the magazine, to individuals selected from telephone directories, and to persons on lists of automobile registrations. This meant that the sample contained far too many well-to-do people. The year 1936 was a depression year, a year in which many people could not afford an automobile or a telephone, much less the *Literary Digest*. In all years there is some tendency for individuals with high incomes to vote Republican. It was this basic failure to obtain a **representative sample** that led to the downfall of the Literary Digest Poll and the magazine itself.

Randomization. We have just seen that one of the great dangers in making inferences about a population from samples is that the sample selected may not be representative of the population. Furthermore, we have seen that large numbers of cases do not protect against this danger. The ideal procedure, in research, would be to select members of samples at random. A **random sample** is one in which each individual in the population and every combination of individuals have an equal chance of being selected. Selecting a truly random sample is rarely possible, because this would require the identification of every individual in a population and devising a scheme to give every person an equal chance of being selected. Because of the obvious difficulties in such procedures, investigators usually take liberties with randomness by selecting haphazardly from a phone book, advertising for volunteers in the newspaper, contacting people living at different addresses, or approaching people as they pass by some location. The representativeness of samples suffers as a result. Any lack of representativeness limits the confidence we can place in the outcomes of research, for reasons which will become clear as the discussion proceeds.

The Significance of a Difference

In recent years a feud has been raging between the bottlers of Coca Cola and Pepsi Cola over the question of which drink tastes better. Although it is difficult to imagine anyone other than the two corporations taking sides on this issue, suppose that someone actually does become interested enough to do an experiment, to try to answer the question with data.

There are eighteen participants in all, nine who will rate the taste of Pepsi, the other nine the taste of Coke. The experimental design is a double-blind one (page 15). The drinks are poured into identical glasses, so that the participants do not know which they receive. Someone else does the pouring so that the experimenter is also in the dark. The instructions direct the subjects in the experiment to rate the unidentified drink on a scale from zero to 100, with 100 the value that they would give to their most favorite taste in any food or drink. When the results are in, it turns out that the mean rating for Coca Cola is 53.5, that for Pepsi Cola 48.5. Apparently Coke tastes better than Pepsi—or does it?

Any experimental result of this type is subject to two interpretations. (1) The result obtained is a true one. It represents a difference that exists in the population. (2) The difference obtained is a misleading result. No difference exists in the population, and one was found only because the samples selected just happened to be unrepresentative.

The second of these two interpretations is called the **null hypothesis,** the hypothesis of no difference. The commonest procedure for determining whether an experimental difference is significant, that is, whether it has been caused by something other than mere chance, is to test the null hypothesis, almost always with the hope that the hypothesis can be rejected. If the null hypothesis can be rejected, whatever two situations were used in the experiment must have had, by implication, two distinguishable outcomes. Since we cannot say that there is *no* difference, the one found must truly exist and must be attributable to the difference between the two situations explored in the course of the experiment.

A test of the null hypothesis really asks this question. If the null hypothesis is true, what is the probability that a difference as large as the one obtained in the experiment would occur by a chance error in sampling? Statistical procedures provide an estimate of the probability. Through appropriate analyses it is possible to say that this probability is one in two (.50 or 50 percent), in ten (.10 or 10 percent), in twenty (.05 or 5 percent), in a hundred (.01 or 1 percent), or one in some other number. These probabilities define the **level of confidence** with which the null hypothesis can be rejected. To reject the null hypothesis at the .03 (or 3 percent) level of confidence is to say that if no difference actually exists in the population as a whole, the one obtained would occur by accident only three times in a hundred. It is more reasonable to conclude that the null hypothesis is false and that the experimental result is true. In practice, experimenters tend to reject the null hypothesis if they can do so at the .05 level of confidence or less.

The *t*-Test

Table A.4 Data for Determining Significance of Difference

Statistic	Coke Tasters	Pepsi Tasters
Mean rating	53.5	48.5
Σd^2	648	1152
N	9	9

In order to introduce the *t*-test, one of the most common statistical tests employed to evaluate the significance of a difference, let us stipulate the results of the Coke–Pepsi-tasting experiment in a little more detail. The numbers in Table A.4 are contrived to simplify as many calculations as possible.

The first and third rows in the table require no comment. The reason for including Σd^2 is related to a point that will be made after we compute the standard deviations for the two sample groups, using the formula $S = \sqrt{\Sigma d^2/N}$. For the Coke tasters

$$S_{\text{Coke}} = \sqrt{\frac{648}{9}} = \sqrt{72} = 8.49$$

And for the Pepsi tasters

$$S_{\text{Pepsi}} = \sqrt{\frac{1152}{9}} = \sqrt{128} = 11.31$$

As inferential statistics, that is, as estimates of the standard deviations for whole populations, there is a problem with these numbers. Standard deviations for sample groups slightly underestimate the standard deviations for populations, for reasons that are beyond the purposes of this presentation. A new statistic, $\hat{S}$ (sometimes called "S-hat"), must be calculated to correct for this small error and to obtain a better estimate of the population standard deviation. The formula for $\hat{S}$ is almost the same as that for S:

$$\hat{S} = \sqrt{\frac{\Sigma d^2}{N-1}}$$

For the Coke tasters this value is

$$\hat{S}_{\text{Coke}} = \sqrt{\frac{648}{8}} = \sqrt{81} = 9$$

And for the Pepsi tasters

$$\hat{S}_{\text{Pepsi}} = \sqrt{\frac{1152}{8}} = \sqrt{144} = 12$$

These numbers are slightly larger than the values for S and are better estimates of the population standard deviations, usually symbolized by sigma, σ, the lowercase Greek letter equivalent to *s*.

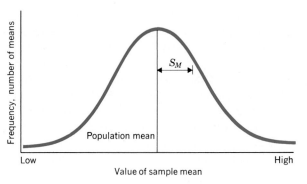

Figure A.13
Sampling distribution of the mean. If a large number of samples were drawn, their means determined, and these means plotted in the form of a frequency distribution, the distribution would be normal. The standard deviation of this distribution of means is the standard error of the mean.

Accuracy of the Estimate of the Mean. The mean calculated after the testing of a sample group is a fair estimate of the population mean, provided the people in the sample were randomly chosen. It is, however, only an estimate. If a very large number of sample groups were drawn and tested, the means of these many group testings would form a normal distribution. And the *mean* of this distribution of sample group means would be a very good estimate of the population mean. From this normal distribution of sample means, the **sampling distribution of the mean** as it is called, a standard deviation could be figured. It is referred to as the **standard error of the mean** and is symbolized by S_M. Figure A.13 gives these statements pictorial meaning.

In actual practice, of course, it is almost never possible to test sample after sample to obtain the sampling distribution of a mean and calculate its standard error. Fortunately this value can be estimated. The standard error of the mean, which would really be the standard deviation of a large number of sample means from *their* mean, is estimated by dividing the population standard deviation by the square root of the number of individuals in the sample:

$$S_M = \frac{\sigma}{\sqrt{N}}$$

Since the value of σ is rarely known, the working formula substitutes $\hat{S}$, our best estimate of σ, and thus becomes

$$S_M = \frac{\hat{S}}{\sqrt{N}}$$

For the Coke drinkers in our tasting experiment,

$$S_{M,\,Coke} = \frac{9}{\sqrt{9}} = \frac{9}{3} = 3$$

For the Pepsi tasters

$$S_{M,\,Pepsi} = \frac{12}{\sqrt{9}} = \frac{12}{3} = 4$$

These numbers are needed in the next step of our test of the null hypothesis.

Accuracy of the Estimate of Difference. To repeat a point, the difference between the average ratings of Coke and Pepsi was 5 points (53.5 − 48.5) in favor of Coke. This is only an estimate of a population difference, however. Since the means of samples will vary with the testing of one sample group and another, so too will the difference between these means. If a very large number of pairs of sample groups were drawn and tested, and if the differences between means were calculated for each and every sample pair, then put into a frequency distribution, the result would be a normal **sampling distribution of differences.** Its mean would be a very good estimate of the population difference. The standard deviation figured from this distribution would be the **standard error of the difference,** symbolized by S_{diff}. Again, it is possible to estimate this value without having data on large numbers of pairs of samples.

The standard error of the difference would really be the standard deviation of a large number of sample pair differences from *their* mean. It is calculated by squaring the standard error of the mean (S_M) for each of the two samples actually drawn and tested and compared, then adding these two squared terms, and finally taking the square root of their sum:

$$S_{\text{diff}} = \sqrt{S_{M1}^2 + S_{M2}^2}$$

With statistics for the tasters in the Coke-Pepsi experiment inserted, this becomes

$$S_{\text{diff}} = \sqrt{3^2 + 4^2} = \sqrt{9 + 16} = \sqrt{25} = 5$$

The meaning of this number is presented pictorially in Figure A.14.

Testing the Null Hypothesis. With S_{diff} available, we are finally in a position to use normal curve statistics to ask the following question. If the true difference between means that would be obtained by testing large numbers of pairs of sample groups were zero, what is the probability of obtaining by chance a difference as large as that revealed by our experiment? More concretely for our example, if people in the general population would give the same tastiness ratings to Coke and Pepsi, what is the probability of obtaining a difference in rating as large as the 5.0 points we obtained?

The answer to this question involves the **t-test,** a statistic which under certain circumstances is exactly the same as a Z-score. The formula for t is

$$t = \frac{\text{mean difference}}{S_{\text{diff}}}$$

Figure A.14
Sampling distribution of differences. The distribution of differences between a large number of pairs of sample means would be normal. The distribution in this figure is for the test experiment, in which the standard error of the difference was 5.0 by calculation. If the null hypothesis is true, differences of 5.0 or larger would be obtained by chance in 32 of 100 pairs of samples. Such an outcome is therefore too likely to allow rejection of the null hypothesis.

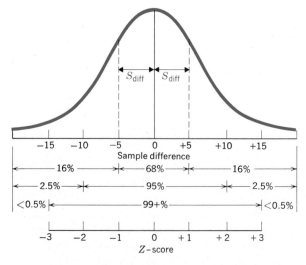

For our example

$$t = \frac{53.5 - 48.5}{5} = \frac{5}{5} = 1.0$$

As Figure A.14 may help you see more clearly, this value of t tells you that a difference rating of 5.0 points or more, in *favor of one drink or the other*, would occur by chance in 32 of 100 comparisons, almost a third of the time. In terms developed earlier, we can reject the null hypothesis at only the 32 percent (or .32) level of confidence. In practice no one rejects the null hypothesis when the probability of a difference being found through unfortunate chance sampling is this high. More commonly the .01 (1 percent) or .05 (5 percent) levels are required.

SUMMARY

The term "inferential statistics" refers to a set of procedures for drawing con- clusions about populations from measures obtained on samples. In most cases— the standard deviation is the most important exception—statistics obtained on a sample can be taken as estimates of the corresponding values for the popu- lation. An important point to understand, however, is that these estimates are merely estimates. The statistics obtained on different samples would vary from sample to sample. A second important point to understand is that these samples must be representative if statistics collected from them are to be fair estimates. The most straightforward procedure for assuring representativeness is through the selection of random samples.

Our discussion has concentrated on applying inferential statistics in the eval- uation of experimental data. A difference obtained in an experiment may be either a true one brought about by the different conditions of the experiment or an accident of unfortunate sampling. The second possibility, that there is actually no difference—the "null hypothesis"—is evaluated in the most common statistical tests. These procedures allow us to calculate the probability of finding a difference of the order obtained in the experiment should the null hypothesis be true. If that probability is low, the null hypothesis is rejected at a level of confidence corresponding to the probability. Rejecting the null hypothesis then lends support to the alternative, that the different situations explored by the experiment have different outcomes.

Here are the most important concepts in the materials just presented. You should be able to define and apply them.

TO BE SURE YOU UNDERSTAND THIS APPENDIX

Descriptive statistics	**Positive skew**
Inferential statistics	**Negative skew**
Abscissa	**Variance**
Ordinate	**Standard deviation**
Frequency distribution	**Normal curve**
Frequency polygon	**Z-score**
Mode	**Percentile rank**
Median	**Correlation**
Mean	**Scatter plot**
J-curve	**Positive correlation**
Skewed distribution	**Negative correlation**

Correlation coefficient	Level of confidence
Population	Sampling distribution of the mean
Sample	Standard error of the mean
Representative sample	Sampling distribution of differences
Random sample	Standard error of the difference
Null hypothesis	t-test

The list just given omits symbols and formulae, which have been collected for presentation.

$$M = \frac{\Sigma X}{N}$$

$$\hat{S} = \sqrt{\frac{\Sigma d^2}{N - 1}}$$

$$S^2 = \frac{\Sigma d^2}{N}$$

$$S_M = \frac{\hat{S}}{\sqrt{N}}$$

$$\hat{S} = \sqrt{\frac{\Sigma d^2}{N}}$$

$$S_{\text{diff}} = \sqrt{S_{M1}^2 + S_{M2}^2}$$

$$t = \frac{\text{mean difference}}{S_{\text{diff}}}$$

In addition to these terms and equations, you should be able to handle these materials.

Constructing and interpreting graphs, including frequency distributions and scatter diagrams.

Relationships between mean and median under conditions of symmetry and skew.

These relationships between Z-scores and areas under a normal curve: $-Z = 1.0$ to $+Z = 1.0$, 68 percent; $-Z = 2.0$ to $+Z = 2.0$, 95 percent; $-Z = 3.0$ to $+Z = 3.0$, 99 percent.

Relationships between correlation and variance accounted for.

The argument used in rejecting the null hypothesis and interpreting experimental data: since there is no difference, the obtained difference must be real.

TO GO BEYOND THIS APPENDIX

In This Book. Statistical considerations come up in almost every chapter, most importantly in Chapters 1, 2, 13, and 14. It seems likely, however, that you will review materials in this appendix in connection with those chapters, rather than the other way around.

Elsewhere. Any of a number of introductory statistics books will provide further discussion of most of the topics in this chapter. The most useful recommendation we can make, if you want to go further into the study of statistics, is to select a book that applies statistics to your major field of interest. A general book that will be well within your grasp is *How To Use (and Misuse) Statistics*, by Gregory A. Kimble.

APPENDIX B
ETHICAL PRINCIPLES
OF PSYCHOLOGISTS

CODE OF ETHICS

Psychology's code of ethics (American Psychological Association, 1981) covers the ethical obligations of psychologists as teachers, researchers, and providers of psychological services in ten areas.

1. **Responsibility.** Psychologists are responsible for their own acts and must make every effort to ensure that their services are appropriate to the situation.
2. **Competence.** Psychologists limit their professional activities to those for which they are prepared by training and experience.
3. **Moral and legal standards.** Psychologists' moral standards are a personal matter, but psychologists must not allow their personal standards to compromise the fulfilling of their obligations or to reduce the public trust in psychology and psychologists.
4. **Public statements.** Public statements, announcements of services, and promotional activities of psychologists must help the public make sound judgments and choices.
5. **Confidentiality.** Psychologists respect the confidentiality of information obtained about others in the course of their work as psychologists. They reveal such information only in the very rare circumstances when not to do so would clearly endanger the persons who have consulted them or others.
6. **Welfare of the consumer.** Psychologists respect the integrity and protect the welfare of their clients, students, and research participants.
7. **Professional relationships.** Psychologists respect the prerogatives and obligations of other colleagues and the institutions or organizations for whom these colleagues work.
8. **Tests and other techniques of assessment.** In the development, publication, and dissemination of assessment techniques, psychologists make every effort to promote the welfare and best interests of the individuals who are assessed.
9. **Care and the use of animals.** Psychologists who work with animals protect the welfare of the animals, treat them humanely, and make the protection of their well-being a matter of personal conscience.
10. **Research with human participants.** Psychologists conduct their research with respect and concern for the dignity and welfare of the people who participate and with cognizance of the official standards that govern such research.

CODE OF ETHICS

CARE AND USE OF ANIMALS

ETHICS OF RESEARCH WITH HUMAN PARTICIPANTS

The last two items in this code are closely related to the subject matter of this book. Both have been developed in detail. The following two sections present material from the codes for conducting research with animal and human subjects.

CARE AND USE OF ANIMALS

An investigator of animal behavior strives to advance understanding of basic behavioral principles, to contribute to the improvement of human health and welfare, or both. In seeking these ends, the investigator ensures the welfare of animals and treats them humanely. Laws and regulations notwithstanding, an animal's immediate protection depends on the scientist's own conscience.

- The acquisition, care, use, and disposal of all animals must be in compliance with current federal, state or provincial, and local laws and regulations.
- A psychologist trained in research methods and experienced in the care of laboratory animals closely supervises all procedures involving animals and is responsible for ensuring appropriate consideration of their comfort, health, and humane treatment.
- Psychologists ensure that all individuals using animals under their supervision have received explicit instruction in experimental methods and in the care, maintenance, and handling of the species being used. Responsibilities and activities of individuals participating in a research project are consistent with their respective competencies.
- Psychologists make every effort to minimize discomfort, illness, and pain of animals. A procedure subjecting animals to pain, stress, or privation is used only when an alternative procedure is unavailable and the goal is justified by its prospective scientific, educational, or applied value. Surgical procedures are performed under appropriate anesthesia; techniques to avoid infection and minimize pain are followed during and after surgery.
- When it is appropriate that the animal's life be terminated, it is done rapidly and painlessly.

ETHICS OF RESEARCH WITH HUMAN PARTICIPANTS

For several years, beginning in 1968, a committee of the American Psychological Association, under the chairmanship of Professor Stuart Cook, devoted itself to the development of guidelines to be applied in the treatment of human subjects. They were developed empirically. Almost 20,000 members of the association were asked to contribute actual incidents that they believed raised ethical problems. The committee received thousands of examples, which they sorted into such groupings as stress, invasion of privacy, and deception. With these categories established, instructions were developed for psychologists to use in handling the ethical issues that had been identified. The American Psychological Association published the guidelines in 1973. They were revised in 1982 and now include the following recommendations.

- In planning a study, the investigator must make a careful evaluation of its ethical acceptability. To the extent that the weighing of scientific and human values suggests a compromise of any principle, the investigator incurs a correspondingly serious obligation to seek ethical advice and to observe stringent safeguards to protect the rights of human participants.

- The investigator always retains the responsibility for ensuring ethical practice in research. The investigator is also responsible for the ethical treatment of research participants by collaborators, assistants, students, and employees, all of whom, however, incur similar obligations.
- The investigator must establish a clear and fair agreement with the research participant that clarifies the obligations and responsibilities of each. The investigator must honor all promises and commitments made to the participant.
- The investigator respects the individual's freedom to decline to paticipate in, or to withdraw from, the research at any time.
- The investigator protects the participants from any physical or mental discomfort, harm, or danger that might result from research procedures.
- After the data are collected, the investigator provides the participant with information about the nature of the study and attempts to remove any misconceptions that may have arisen.
- When research procedures result in undesirable consequences for the participant, the investigator has the responsibility to remove or correct these consequences.
- Information obtained about the research participant during the course of an investigation is confidential unless otherwise agreed upon in advance.

Further protection for participants in research is provided by institutional review boards of organizations that do research. These groups, which often include representatives of the subject populations to be studied, review proposals for research and evaluate them against ethical guidelines. Review boards may require revisions of procedures and, in cases in which the risks to participants are too great, deny approval.

DICTIONARY OF PSYCHOLOGICAL TERMS

This Dictionary includes the key concepts from the text and, in addition, psychological terms that the student is likely to come across in lectures and outside readings. We have culled a range of sources and used our collective judgment in choosing terms and concepts for their significance and frequency of use.

IMPORTANT NOTE TO THE STUDENT

Sometimes just knowing the definitions in this dictionary will be enough to handle the questions that you will encounter on exams, but often it will not. You will also need to understand what the textbook and your teacher had to say about these terms. Once you have checked the term in the dictionary, you should reread the text and your class notes.

A

ABAB design. An experimental design of the small-*N* type. ABAB refers to a sequence of treatments in which A stands for a baseline condition, without the experimental treatment, and B stands for a condition in which the experimental treatment has been introduced.

Ability. Present level of performance on some task. Contrast with *aptitude*.

Abreaction. In psychoanalysis, removal of emotional tension by reliving the original traumatic experience.

Abscissa. The horizontal or *x*-axis of a graph. Usually represents the values of the independent variable. Contrast with *ordinate*.

Absolute refractory phase. Period immediately after firing, during which a neuron is completely unresponsive to stimulation.

Absolute threshold. Minimal level of stimulation that the organism can detect.

Abstract reasoning. The ability to comprehend relationships among things; to respond to symbols and concepts as opposed to thinking in terms of specific objects and events.

Acceptance–acquiescence. A response set marked by a ready acceptance of all statements as self-descriptive.

Accessible memory. Information in memory which comes immediately to mind without prodding. Contrast with *available memory*.

Accessory symptoms. The secondary symptom effects of schizophrenia suggested by Bleuler—delusions and hallucinations. Contrast with *fundamental symptoms*.

Accommodation. (1) In vision, the flattening and bulging of the lens of the eye that serve to produce a sharp image of objects on the retina. A primary cue to depth and distance. (2) As used by Piaget, the process by which the individual, in adapting to new experiences, modifies internal cognitive structures.

Acetylcholine. A neurotransmitter.

Achievement motive. A need to achieve for its own sake rather than for the benefits derived from such achievement.

Acquiescence set. See *acceptance–acquiescence*.

Acquired drive. A learned motive.

Acquisition. Learning; the establishment of a habit.

Action potential. The electrical changes accompanying a nerve impulse, muscle contraction, or gland secretion.

Action-specific energy. In ethology, the energy available for specific sequences of instinctive behavior when certain stimuli called "releasers" are present.

Active avoidance. A form of operant conditioning in which a specified response allows the organism to avoid some noxious stimulus. Contrast with *passive avoidance*.

Active vocabulary. The words a person actually uses in speech. Contrast with *passive vocabulary*.

Actor-observer differences. The attributions of ineffectiveness to the situation by the person acting, to the disposition of the actor by the person observing.

Actuarial prediction. Statistical interpretation of the personality based on the known probabilities that certain patterns of test results are signs of particular traits. Contrast with *clinical prediction*.

Adaptation The adjustment of the senses to environmental conditions. In dark adaptation the *eye* adjusts to low levels of illumination.

Adaptation level. The concept that the judgment of the value of a stimulus depends on the context in which it occurs. See *frame of reference.*

Adaptive behavior deficit. Inability to meet the standards of personal independence and social responsibility expected of an individual's age and cultural group. Sometimes part of the definition of *mental retardation.*

Additive mixture. In vision, the mixture of lights, each contributing its wavelengths to the color seen. Contrast with *subtractive mixture.*

Adoptee study. A method for the study of gentic factors in behavior, in which adopted children are compared with their foster parents and their true parents, To the extent that genetic factors are important, there is greater resemblance to the true parents.

Adrenal glands. A pair of endocrine glands at the top of the kidneys.

Adrenaline. A hormone secreted by the adrenal glands under conditions of strong emotion. Its action is like that of the sympathetic nervous system. Also called *epinephrine.*

Aerial perspective. The blurring by the atmosphere of the images of distant objects; a secondary cue to distance.

Affect. In psychiatric terminology, emotion.

Affect, flattened. Lack of emotional responsiveness. Typical of schizophrenic patients.

Affect, inappropriate. Emotion which is incongruent with the objective situation.

Affective disorder. Mental disorder marked by great emotionality, by depression or elation so extreme that the individual cannot function and may even lose contact with the environment. See *depression* and *mania.*

Affective disorder, bipolar. Severe disorder of mood in which the same individual has both manic and and depressive episodes.

Affective disorder, chronic. Sustained and long-lasting mood disturbances marked by extreme elation or depression.

Affective disorder, episodic. Short-lasting mood disturbances marked by elation or depression. Episodes may be separated by months or even years.

Afferent neuron. A neuron which conducts impulses toward the central nervous system. Contrast with *efferent neuron.*

Afterimage. In vision, the image which the perceiver has after looking at a stimulus for several seconds and then removing it; the image is like the original stimulus in shape but is of the complementary color.

Age norms. The representative performance of children of a given age with regard to some specific characteristic, e.g., IQ.

Age scale. A type of intelligence test in which items are arranged in order of difficulty, and credit for passing is assigned in age units.

Agnosia. Inability to recognize objects. Usually results from brain damage. See *aphasia* and *apraxia.*

Agoraphobia. Fear of being alone or of being in public places from which escape might be difficult or where help might be unavailable were the individual to become suddenly incapacitated. For these reasons agoraphobics are usually unable to leave home.

Alarm reaction. The first stage of the *general adaptation syndrome.* Consists of two stages: a shock phase characterized by severe physiological symptoms and a countershock phase in which there is temporary recovery from these symptoms.

Albinism. An inherited condition in which the individual lacks pigmentation. The albino person has white hair, pale skin, and a colorless iris.

Alcoholism. A substance use disorder in which consumption of alcohol is excessive, either continuously or episodically, impairs some significant part of the drinker's life, and eventually causes progressive damage to the body.

Algorithim. A particular set procedure for solving a certain type of problem. Contrast with *heuristic.*

All-or-none law. The property of a neuron, muscle cell, or gland cell, either to respond to its fullest extent or not to respond at all.

Allele. One of the alternate forms of a gene situated at a given locus on a chromosome and affecting a particular characteristic.

Allophone. One of two or more forms of a speech sound which are used in a particular language as equivalent. They are different forms of the same *phoneme.*

Alpha rhythm. An approximately 10-cycle-per-second rhythm of the electroencephalogram, or EEG, typically obtained from the occipital region of the cortex during relaxed wakefulness.

Alternate-forms method. A method of establishing the reliability of the test by correlating the scores obtained on two versions of the test.

Altruism. Unselfish concern for and devotion to the welfare of others.

Amacrine cell. Cell making lateral connections in the retina.

Ambivalence. In conflict theory and elsewhere, a reaction toward an object that is simultaneously positive and negative.

Ambivert. In type theory, a person who is both introverted and extroverted.

Amnesia. Loss of memory, as a result of physical or psychological trauma.

Amniocentesis. The procedure of withdrawing amniotic fluid from the uterus in order to detect biochemical and chromosomal characteristics of the fetus.

Amphetamine. A dangerously addictive central nervous system stimulant which induces euphoria.

Ampulla. A swelling at the base of each semicircular canal. It contains hair cells embedded in a gelatinous mass.

Anagram. A word or phrase made by rearranging the letters of another word or phrase.

Anal stage. In Freudian theory, a stage of psychosexual development in which the one- and two-year-old child's most intense pleasures are derived from activities associated with elimination. See *oral stage, phallic stage, latency period,* and *genital stage.*

Anal triad. The syndrome of parsimony (stinginess), pedantry (meticulousness), and petulance (ill humor) assumed in psychoanalytic theory to result from fixation at the anal stage of development.

Analytic concept formation. Arriving at a concept by analyzing the characteristics of different exemplars to determine the defining attributes of the concept.

Androgen. Any of several male sex hormones, secreted especially by the testes and adrenal cortex; they stimulate development of sex characteristics in the male. Testosterone, secreted in the testes, is the best known.

Androgenization. In prenatal development, the secretion of androgen by the genetic male; necessary for the development of masculine characteristics.

Androgynous. Having the characteristics of both male and female.

Animism. Attributing conscious life, intentions, and feelings and an indwelling spirit to objects and to natural phenomena, such as lightning and sunshine, especially by children.

Anorexia nervosa. A life-threatening disorder in which the individual, usually a female adolescent, has an intense fear of becoming obese, either eats very little or binges and then induces vomiting, loses at least a quarter of her body weight, and feels fat even though emaciated.

Antagonistic muscles. Pairs of muscles so arranged that contraction in one member of the pair requires extension of the other.

Anthropomorphism. Interpreting animal behavior in terms of human psychological processes.

Anticipation method. In serial rote learning, the method in which the subject must respond to each item in a list with the one that follows.

Antidromic impulse. An impulse from axon to dendrite in a single neuron. The opposite of the normal direction of conduction.

Antisocial personality. The personality disorder of the guilt- and anxiety-free individual whose impulsive and often destructive behavior repeatedly brings this offender into conflict with society. Often truants, runaways, and vandals before the age of fifteen, these individuals are not able to form enduring attachments, take responsibility for children, hold jobs, honor financial obligations, plan ahead. Also called sociopathic or psychopathic personality.

Anxiety. A vague but persistent apprehension, uneasiness, and dread without appropriate cause. Can be defined by intensity, as in normal or pathological anxiety; by focus of response, as in somatic or psychological anxiety; or by locus of arousal, as in objective or neurotic anxiety.

Anxiety, state. A transitory experience of fear and apprehensiveness, specific to the situation.

Anxiety, trait. A stable, long-term predisposition to the easy arousal and maintenance of a state of apprehensiveness.

Anxiety disorder, generalized. Disorder in which the anxiety is persistent and pervasive, lasting at least a month. The individual is jittery and tense, feels "on edge" and apprehensive that something

bad is about to happen, and has physical symptoms such as sweating, a pounding heart and rapid respiration, clammy hands, dizziness, an upset stomach, and aching muscles.

Anxiety disorders. Disorders in which incapacitating and irrational fear and tension are the primary symptoms: phobic disorders; anxiety states, which are panic disorder, generalized anxiety disorder, and obsessive-compulsive disorder; and posttraumatic stress disorder.

Anxiety hierarchy. A list of events ordered by their power to evoke anxiety in an individual. Systematic desensitization extinguishes these anxieties, beginning with the least powerful stimulus.

Aphasia, expressive. A speech disturbance in which patients know what they wish to say but cannot utter the word. Also called motor aphasia or Broca's aphasia. Occurs with damage to Broca's area.

Aphasia, receptive. A speech disturbance in which patients are unable to understand the meaning of speech, including their own speech. Also called sensory aphasia or Wernicke's aphasia. Occurs with damage to Wernicke's area.

Apparent motion. Perception of motion under conditions in which no physical movement occurs. See *phi phenomenon*.

Appetitive motive. Drive derived from an internal organ condition and for which striving is toward a goal.

Approach-approach conflict. Conflict produced by the necessity of choosing between two desirable objects.

Approach-avoidance conflict. Conflict produced when a single object or activity is simultaneously attractive and unattractive.

Approach gradient. In conflict theory, the concept (often depicted graphically) that the tendency to approach a positive goal increases with nearness to the goal. Contrast with *avoidance gradient*.

Apraxia. Inability to execute skilled movement, usually as a result of brain damage. See *aphasia and agnosia*.

Aptitude. The capacity to profit from training in some particular skill. Contrast with *ability*.

Aqueous humor. A fluid transparent to light filling the space between the lens and the cornea of the eye.

Assimilation. In Piaget's theory, the process whereby a child, in taking in new information, modifies it or even distorts it to

agree with the internal cognitive system. The child gives meaning to an act by assimilating it to something already known.

Association area or neuron. An area in the nervous system or a neuron that allows communication from relatively sensory structures to relatively motor structures.

Association cortex. See *prefrontal association cortex*.

Association disturbance. One of Bleuler's fundamental symptoms of schizophrenia in which the individual is unable to retain a train of thought. Cognitions appear to be confused, illogical, and bizarre.

Associative meaning. The associations called up by a word.

Astigmatism. A structural defect, usually of the cornea, which prevents rays of light from being brought into common focus on the retina and hence blurs vision.

Asymptote. A straight line which a given curve approaches but never reaches as one of the variables of the curve's equation nears infinity.

Attachment. The emotional tie of an infant to mother or other caretaker.

Attention. Active selection of some aspects of complex experience by the perceptual process, heightening awareness of them and blocking out others.

Attention defect. Disturbance in the ability to maintain a set or a goal-directed idea.

Attitude. A tendency to respond positively or negatively to other individuals, to institutions, and to courses of activity and events.

Attitude scale. A test for measuring attitudes.

Attitudes-behavior consistency. Correspondence between a person's attitudes and behavior. Often there are discrepancies.

Attribution error. Tending to discount the importance of situational factors and to overestimate personal characteristics in judging the causes of another person's behavior.

Attribution theory. The conception that we find meaning by attributing motives to people's actions and purpose to events.

Audiogenic seizure. Usually in lower animals (e.g., mice), an epileptiform attack brought on by prolonged exposure to high-frequency auditory stimulation. Depends in important ways on hereditary factors.

Audiogram. A graphic representation of a person's absolute threshold of hearing at different frequencies. In cases of deafness shows where the individual's loss of hearing occurs.

Audiometry. Procedure for determining a person's hearing or the degree of hearing loss.

Authoritarian parent. A parent who places great value on a child's obedience.

Authoritarian personality. A type of personality identified by rigid adherence to middle-class values, extreme awareness of authority relationships, denial of personal sexuality, a tendency to exploit others but also to feel exploited, categorical thinking, and a tendency toward projection.

Authoritative parent. A parent who seeks to guide a child's behavior in a logical and issue-oriented manner.

Autism. Absorption in fantasy to the extent that thought is devoid of reality. One of Bleuer's fundamental symptoms of schizophrenia.

Autokinetic effect. The apparent movement (-kinetic) by itself (auto-) of a small, stationary spot of light in complete darkness.

Automatiztion. A descriptive term for the fact that greatly overlearned responses are carried out without conscious attention.

Autonomic nervous system. The part of the nervous system that consists of the sympathetic and parasympathetic divisions and is involved in control of the body's internal environment.

Autoshaping. A procedure, most commonly used with pigeons, in which the key in a Skinner-type apparatus is illuminated, and food is made available a few seconds later. Under this procedure the pigeon comes to peck the key without special training.

Availability. In attribution theory, the subjective ease with which something comes to mind, relied on but sometimes causing the individual to make an error of judgment.

Available memory.. Information in memory which does not immediately come to mind and requires prodding. Contrast with *accessible memory.*

Aversion therapy. A form of behavior therapy based on punishment. The unwanted behavior or its stimulus is paired with a discomforting outcome.

Aversive control. The use of negative reinforcement to induce *escape* or *avoid-ance conditioning.*

Aversive motive. Drive which causes the individual to avoid or flee from a situation.

Aversive stimulus. A negative, unpleasant, or punishing stimulus; a *negative reinforcer.*

Avoidance-avoidance conflict. Conflict produced by the necessity of choosing between two undesirable alternatives.

Avoidance gradient. In conflict theory, the tendency to move away from an undesirable object or state of affairs decreases with distance from this object. Often depicted graphically. Contrast with *approach gradient.*

Avoidance learning. Operant learning in which an individual learns to prevent the occurrence of a noxious stimulus by responding appropriately to a warning signal.

Avoidance training. A behavior therapy in which the sight, taste, or smell of what the patient desires but should not have is paired with electric shock.

Avoidant personality. The self-denegrating individuals with an avoidant personality disorder are hypersensitive to potential rejection and ridicule and therefore keep their distance from others, even though they hunger for affection and acceptance.

Axis. In DSM-III, a category of diagnostic information.

Axon. A thin extension of a neuron's protoplasm, which acts as the communicative part of a neuron.

B

Background stressor. One of the persistent hassles of everyday life. See *stressor.*

Bar graph. A form of frequency distribution in which bars are used to indicate numbers of cases.

Barbiturate. One of a class of synthetic drugs which depress the central nervous system. These sedatives are addictive.

Basal age (basal level). In the Binet-type test, the highest age level at which all test items are passed.

Basal ganglion. One of four deeply placed masses of gray matter within each cerebral hemisphere: the caudate nucleus, the lenticular nucleus, the amygaloid nucleus, the claustrum.

Baseline. Rate of occurrence of some phenomenon under normal conditions. See *ABAB design.*

Basilar membrane. A membrane in the cochlea of the inner ear that supports the organ of Corti.

Behavior control. The control which one person has over another because of the way in which their behaviors combine to determine outcomes for each.

Behavior modification. See *behavior therapy.*

Behavior therapy. A variety of psychotherapeutic techniques based on learning principles—classical and operant conditioning and modeling procedures used to shape and adjust the behavior of emotionally troubled people.

Behavioral assessment. Evaluations of personality made by observing behavior in representative natural situations.

Behavioral confirmation. Eliciting from others behavior that confirms our often false hypotheses about them. See *biased hypothesis testing.*

Behaviorism. A school which originated with John Watson and his proposal that psychology be limited to the observation of overt behavior.

Belongingness, principle of. The theory that certin stimuli and responses are naturally and easily associated in conditioning experiments.

Beta rhythm. The dominant pattern, a 14- to 25-cycle-per-second rhythm, of the electroencephalogram, or EEG, found in the alert adult paying concentrated attention.

Biased hypothesis testing. Interpreting the causes of ambiguous behavior according to an earlier tentative hypothesis based on stereotype or second-hand information.

Bilateral transfer. The effect of practice with one hand (usually) on learning the same skill with the other.

Bimodal distribution. A frequency distribution with two modes, i.e., two points at which there is piling up of frequencies.

Biofeedback. Providing an individual with information on the state of some physiological function, usually in the effort to help the individual gain voluntary control over that function.

Biological constraint. Limit on what an organism learns readily, imposed by its inborn characteristics. See *belongingness, principle of; preparedness, principle of.*

Biological motion. Recognizable pattern of human locomotion.

Bipolar cell. In the retina, a cell connecting the rods and cones with ganglion cells.

Bipolar disorder. An affective disorder in which the individual suffers episodes of mania and depression or, more rarely, only episodes of mania.

Blind spot. A region of the retina where a person is effectively blind. Fibers leave the retina at this point to become the optic nerve.

Blocking. (1) A sudden cessation in a train of thought or verbal expression. The person may be unable to explain the reasons behind sudden cognitive stoppages. (2) In conditioning, the difficulty in conditioning a response to one component of a complex stimulus after it has been conditioned to other components. (3) The prevention of a response by frustrating circumstances or conflict.

Blood-brain barrier. A barrier which prevents most foreign substances in the bloodstream from entering the brain. The extra layering in capillary walls, the presence of cerebrospinal fluid, and the selective action of glia cells constitute the barrier.

Boilermaker's deafness. See *stimulation deafness.*

Bonding drive. In ethology, a drive which facilitates attachment behavior and social cohesion in group members.

Bony labyrinth. The cavity in the temporal bone which contains the membranous labyrinth; consists of the vestibule, bony semicircular canals, and cochlea.

Borderline personality. The individual with a borderline personality disorder has intense but unstable and manipulative relations with others, is subject to shifting moods and fits of anger, may indulge in self-damaging sprees of spending, sex, gambling, shoplifting, and the like, has problems with identity and goals, and finds it very difficult to be alone.

Bound morpheme. A morpheme which has meaning only in combination with another, the pluralizing "s," for example. Contrast with *free morpheme.*

Brain. All the central nervous system except the spinal cord.

Brain waves. Rhythmic fluctuations of voltage between paired locations of the always electrically active brain, resulting in the flow of an electric current. Recorded from the skull by the *electroencephalograph.*

Brainstem. The forward extension of the spinal cord to which the cerebrum and cerebellum are attached.

Brainstorming. An undisciplined, freewheeling situation in which groups attempt to solve a problem.

Brainwashing. Techniques of influence used to modify the thinking of those who stand in a subjugated status to some control agent (e.g., prisoners of war, concentration camp victims). The goal of such methods is to induce people to do things or accept values that they ordinarily would not.

Brightness. A dimension of visual experience that depends for the most part on the energy of the stimulus. An experience of intensity, the dimension from black to white.

Brightness constancy. The tendency for objects to be seen with the same relative brightness under various levels of illumination.

British empiricism. A school of philosophy holding that knowledge is come by through the experience of the senses, that there are no innate ideas.

Broca's area. An area in the frontal cortex hypothesized by Broca to be responsible for speech. The function of Broca's area is primarily motor. See *Wernicke's area.*

Bulimia. Binge eating. A mental disorder in which the individual overeats and then induces vomiting.

Bureaucratic occupation. Type of occupation in which income is in the form of wages or salary, and specialized abilities rather than success in risk taking are needed. See *entrepreneurial occupation.*

Bystander intervention. Tendency of people who witness a crime to come to the aid of a victim. Often they do not.

C

California Psychological Inventory (CPI). A personality inventory for the general population of young people, assessing personal adequacy, social maturity, interests, and thought efficiency.

Cannon-Bard theory. The theory of emotion according to which an emotional stimulus activates the cerebral cortex and bodily processes at the same time. Bodily changes and the experience of emotion occur together.

Case history method. The investigation of psychological problems through the assembling and examination of people's biographies.

Castration anxiety. In Freudian theory, a fear on the part of a little boy that his father will castrate him because of his sexual attraction toward his mother. See *Oedipus complex.*

Cataclysmic event. A momentous, violent, sudden happening affecting many people, such as natural disasters and combat; a powerful stressor.

Catalepsy. Disturbed condition in which the body and limbs are retained in a muscularly rigid position for a considerable period of time; consciousness appears trancelike.

Cataract. A clouding of the cornea that impairs vision to the point of effective blindness. In severe cases only differences in brightness in different areas of the visual field are perceived.

Catatonic schizophrenia. See *schizophrenia, catatonic type.*

Categorial perception of phonemes. The abrupt shift in perception of phonemes as a sound is gradually altered from that of one to that of another. The sound is perceived first as one phoneme and then as the other. The gradual transformation is not perceived.

Catharsis. In psychoanalysis, elimination of a complex by bringing it to consciousness and allowing it expression. More generally, any relief from emotional disturbance that follows expression of the emotion. See *abreaction.*

Cathexis. Psychic energy invested in an idea, object, person, or action.

Ceiling level. The age level in Binet-type intelligence tests at which an individual fails all the test items of a given age.

Cell body (of a neuron). The part of the neuron that contains the nucleus and nutritional mechanisms.

Centering. Riveting of a person's attention on a particular attribute of a problem or stimulus array. See *decentering.*

Central nervous system. The brain and the spinal cord.

Central tendency. The clustering of values toward the center of a distribution. Measured by such statistics as the mean (arithmetic average), median (middle value), and mode (most frequent value).

Cephalocaudal sequence. A pattern of maturation in which development is from the head downward.

CER. See *conditioned emotional response.*

Cerebellum. A two-hemisphered structure of the central nervous system just below and behind the cerebrum and above the medulla. Covered with transversely fissured gray matter, the cerebellum is involved in the maintenance of muscle tonus and in the coordination of movements.

Cerebral arteriosclerosis. Hardening of the arteries of the brain, which produces marked neurological and behavioral changes in the individual.

Cerebral cortex. The surface layer of gray matter of the mammalian cerebral hemispheres, deeply infolded in human beings.

Cerebral dominance. The concept that one hemisphere of the cerebral cortex controls the person's behavior and thus dominates the other hemisphere.

Cerebral hemisphere. One of the two nearly symmetrical halves of the cerebrum, the left hemisphere controlling the right side of the body, the right hemisphere the left. The hemispheres are deeply separated by the longitudinal fissure, well joined by the corpus callosum.

Cerebral peduncle. Either of two large bulges in the bottom of the midbrain consisting of axons of neurons whose bodies are in the cerebral cortex.

Cerebrotonia. In Sheldon's theory, a personality type characterized by thought rather than action, restraint in social relations, introversion, and need of privacy. Associated in theory with *ectomorphy.*

Cerebrum. The main division of the brain in vertebrates, consisting of a left and right hemisphere.

Character disorder. A defect of personality structure characterized by immaturity, antisocial reactions, and lack of social responsibility.

Chloretone. A drug which inhibits movement without disturbing growth.

Chlorpromazine. Generic term for one of the most widely used tranquilizing drugs. Sold under the name Thorazine.

Cholinergic. The physiological functions and bodily processes that are stimulated by acetylcholine; also refers to a group of nerve fibers which act upon effectors (muscles, glands) by the release of *acetylcholine.*

Chromatic. Possessing *hue.*

Chromosomes. Long, threadlike strands which are located in the nucleus of the cell and play a central role in heredity. The genes—the genetic determiners—are to be found in the chromosomes. The human cell contains twenty-three pairs of chromosomes. One of each pair has been derived from the sperm cell (father), the other from the egg cell (mother).

Chromosomes X and Y. Sex chromosomes. An XX pair produces a female offspring, an XY combination a male.

Chronic disorder. A long-lasting, persistent disorder.

Chronological age. Age in years and months. Used in computing IQ.

Chunking. Grouping items as an aid to memory. Also called *recoding.*

Ciliary muscle. Muscle which controls and focuses the lens of the eye.

Classical conditioning. A learning procedure in which an organism is presented with a neutral stimulus (CS) and a biologically significant stimulus (US) in fixed order, without respect to the organism's behavior. Contrast with *operant conditioning.*

Client-centered therapy. Nondirective therapy devised by Carl Rogers in which the emphasis is on increasing the client's awareness of feelings and potentialities. The therapist offers the client unquestioning acceptance and encourages the client's self-growth.

Clinical prediction. Prediction of behavior based on clinical impressions. Contrast with *actuarial prediction.*

Cloning. A sexual form of reproduction in which all progeny are genetically identical.

Clustering in free recall. The tendency to recall a list of items, typically words, in groups or categories.

Cocaine. An addictive central nervous system stimulant.

Cochlea. A bony, fluid-filled canal, coiled like a snail, containing within it a smaller, membranous, fluid-filled spiral passage, wherein lie the receptors for hearing.

Cocktail party phenomenon. The ability of the individual to sort out two or more messages coming in simultaneously and to attend to only one of them.

Coding. Putting materials into a form (code) that permits their storage in memory.

Cognition. Knowledge. In psychology, the processes by which individuals acquire and make use of knowledge.

Cognitive behavior therapy. Therapy designed to help an individual understand and deal with the irrational beliefs and values that cause or exacerbate distress.

Cognitive dissonance, theory of. The general proposition that the tension felt when an individual holds one opinion and acts on another strongly motivates the person to reduce the inconsistency by action or thought.

Cognitive stage. A qualitatively different level of cognitive development.

Cognitive theory of emotion. The theory that the experience of emotion results from the interpretation the individual places on physiological arousal.

Cognitive theory of smiling. The theory that baby smiles because of the satisfaction associated with solving problems.

Cold spot. Area on the skin particularly sensitive to cold stimuli below 32°C.

Collective unconscious. According to Carl Jung, a portion of the unconscious—a pool of ancient images which come forth in ghost stories, dreams, literature, art, religious beliefs—inherited and common to all humankind. Contrast with *personal unconscious.*

Color circle. An arrangement of colors in which the spectrum is bent back on itself and to which are added the nonspectral reds and purples. The complementary colors are opposite each other.

Combat exhaustion. Extreme fatigue, sleeplessness, terror, tremors, startle reactions to the slightest sounds, mutism, and either stupor or agitated excitement in the aftermath of battle. A World War II term. See *shell shock.*

Commissure. Tracts connecting corresponding areas in the two cerebral hemispheres or other structures in the central nervous system.

Communicative action of nervous system. The activity of the nervous system that allows stimuli impinging on organs in one part of the body to evoke responses from organs in another part of the body.

Community psychology. Clinical psychology freed from its traditional concerns with individual assessment and treatment and focusing usually on the individual's adaptation within the community structure of which he or she is a part. It is sometimes preventive and attempts to resolve community problems fostering emotional disorders.

Compensation. A defense mechanism wherein an individual frustrated by failure or defect makes a strenuous effort to excel at a substitute activity.

Complementary colors. Colors which, when mixed, produce an achromatic color.

Complex cell. A single cell in the visual cortex that responds to stimuli registering in a small area of the retina and responds vigorously to stimuli of a particular orientation and moving in a particular direction. See *simple cell* and *hypercomplex cell.*

Compliance. (1) Yielding to the perceived judgments of the majority. (2) In two-person social interactions, attempts of a less powerful person to gain power by going along with the wishes of the more powerful person.

Compulsion. An irresistible impulse to perform some act again and again, even though it is inappropriate and sometimes harmful (e.g., handwashing). Together with obsessions, a symptom of obsessive-compulsive disorder.

Compulsive personality. This perfectionist, preoccupied with trivial details, rules, and schedules, is unable to grasp the "large picture." People with compulsive personality disorder, so devoted to work that they eschew pleasure, insist that others do things their way and have great difficulty expressing warm and tender emotions and making decisions.

Concept. A representation of the common properties of objects, events, or ideas that are otherwise distinguishable.

Concept formation. Acquiring a concept by grouping the objects, events, or ideas, all of which share common attributes or properties.

Concordance. A term in behavior genetics to describe the sharing of traits by pairs of individuals, usually relatives. If both show or fail to show the trait in question, the pair is described as concordant; if only one shows the trait, the pair is discordant for that trait. Usually expressed as a concordance rate, the percentage of a sample showing concordance.

Concordance rate. See *concordance*.

Concrete operation. In Piaget's theory, the mental ability to think logically about physical objects and their relations.

Concrete operational stage. In Piaget's developmental theory of intelligence, a phase extending from age seven to eleven years, characterized by conservation, ability to reverse thought, coherent play, flexible thinking, and evaluativeness but an inability to engage in abstract thought.

Concurrent validity. Validity established by comparing scores on a test with those obtained on another test of established validity.

Conditioned emotional response (CER). A form of conditioned fear produced in rats by pairing a neutral stimulus with electric shock. Its effect is demonstrated by a reduction in the rate of bar pressing for food.

Conditioned positive reinforcement. The reinforcing power of a conditioned reinforcer.

Conditioned reinforcer. A reward which is satisfying as a result of its pairing with reinforcement.

Conditioned response (CR). A response resembling the UR that is evoked by the CS as a result of repeated pairings of CS and US.

Conditioned stimulus (CS). A neutral stimulus which, for experimental purposes, is presented to an organism together with a nonneutral stimulus (US) for the purpose of studying the development of conditioned responses.

Conduction deafness. Deafness produced by imperfections in the mechanisms that conduct sound stimulation from the outer ear to the inner ear.

Cone. Retinal receptor cell which responds in terms of color and gives vision acuity.

Conflict. Simultaneous instigation toward two or more incompatible responses. See specific types (e.g., *approach-approach conflict*).

Congruence–incongruence. A Rogerian principle which emphasizes the internal harmony or disharmony between the concept of the self and the nature of the individual's experience.

Conjunctive concept. A concept for which all examples have in common two or more attributes.

Connotative meaning. The emotional tone of a word; its implications.

Consensus. Group agreement.

Conservation. The ability of a child to maintain such concepts as number, substance, and quantity, despite perceptual cues that seem to deny them.

Consistency. In attribution theory, term for behavior which is typical of a person and is attributed to personal characteristics rather than situational factors. See *distinctiveness*.

Consolidation. A process theoretically occurring for several minutes after learning, in which memories become more firmly established. During the period of consolidation, a blow to the head may obliterate the unconsolidated memory.

Construct accessibility. The influence on the evaluation of others in which people judge them as possessing characteristics that have been made salient in the thinking of the person making the judgment.

Construct validity. Validity established when scores on a test conform to what is generally understood about the trait being tested.

Consummatory behavior. Behavior which fulfills (consummates) some motive. Involves consumption (e.g., of food) only part of the time.

Content validity. Validity established when a test has adequate and appropriate coverage of a given area.

Contingency. In connection with operant conditioning procedures, the dependence of reward or punishment on the occurrence or nonoccurrence of a specified response.

Contingent reward. A reward which follows specific behavior and only follows that behavior.

Continuity. In personality study, the consistency of behavior through stages of development.

Continuous reinforcement. A schedule of reinforcement in which a subject is rewarded for *every* correct response. Contrast with *partial reinforcement*.

Control group. A reference group in an experiment. Typically subjected to the measurements performed on the experimental group, but not given the experimental treatment.

Control process. In information-processing theory, a process which determines whether information moves from one stage of memory to the next.

Controlled variable. A variable whose value is held constant for all groups in an experiment.

Conventional morality. The conception of morality that recognizes that rules exist for the good of society. See *preconventional morality* and *postconventional morality*.

Convergence. Kinesthetic stimuli, produced when the eyes turn slightly inward to obtain clear images on both retinas, providing a primary cue to depth and distance.

Convergent thinking. Thinking which moves toward the selection of a single solution to a problem. Contrast with *divergent thinking*.

Conversion disorder. A somatoform disorder marked by a variety of bodily symptoms such as paralysis and loss of sensation, sensory disturbances, and insensitivity to pain. The symptoms, which usually suggest neurological disease but cannot be explained by any physiological disorder, are apparently an expression of psychological conflict or need. They are not under voluntary control.

Coping. Facing and finding necessary expedients to overcome problems and difficulties.

Cornea. The outermost, transparent coating at the front of the eye.

Corpus callosum. The massive commissure at the base of the longitudinal fissure linking the two cerebral hemispheres.

Correct rejection. In signal detection procedures, indicating that no signal is present on trials when the signal is, in fact, absent.

Correlation. Co-relation. The way in which pairs of measures obtained on the same individuals are related. See *correlation coefficient.*

Correlation coefficient. A number from +1.00 to −1.00 which indicates the degree of relationship or correspondence of two measures obtained on the same unit, usually an individual.

Correlational method. A method of psychological investigation estimating the extent to which two variable phenomena are related.

Correlational study. See *correlational method.*

Correspondent-inference theory. A theory proposing that we assume a person's behavior tells us something more important about him or her when there are few reasons for engaging in the behavior than when there are many strong reasons. See *attribution theory.*

Cortex. The rind or bark; a layering of cells near the surface of any organ. Thus cerebral cortex is the surface layer of cells in the cerebrum.

Co-twin control. A method of experimentation, used in research on the nature-nurture problem, that employs a pair of twins as participants; one twin is assigned to the experimental condition, the other to the control condition.

Counterconditioning. The replacement of one conditioned response by the establishment of an incompatible response to the same conditioned stimulus.

Countertransference. In psychoanalytic practice, a form of transference in which the analyst develops strong emotional attachments for the patient.

CR. Conditioned response.

Cranial nerves. The twelve pairs of peripheral nerves containing fibers running to and from the brainstem.

Craniosacral system. An anatomical term for the parasympathetic nervous system.

Creativity. The ability to generate many new and useful ideas.

Cretinism. A form of mental retardation and stunted physical development usually caused by an inborn failure of the individual to synthesize thyroxin.

Criterion. (1) In signal detection theory, the standard an individual sets for giving a positive response. (2) In connection with tests, the performance (usually in a practical situation) which a test attempts to predict.

Criterion situation. A situation external to a test in which performance is observed to obtain an indication of the validity of the test.

Critical period. A stage in development during which the organism is optimally ready to acquire certain new responses.

Cross-sectional study. Research study which compares the performance of groups of people of various ages but at the same point in time, in order to determine how a particular characteristic changes with age. Contrast with *longitudinal method.*

Crystalline lens. The doubly convex, transparent, lenslike body in the eye, situated behind the aqueous humor and focusing rays of light on the retina.

Crystallized intelligence. Term used by Raymond Cattell to denote cognitive capacities that depend on learning. Contrast with *fluid intelligence.*

CS. Conditioned stimulus.

Cubical model of intelligence. J. P. Guilford's view of intelligence as consisting of three dimensions—the contents, the operations, and the products of thought.

Cue control. The kind of influence that one person has over another by presenting the stimuli for strong personal or social habits. Contrast with *outcome control.*

Cued recall. An experimental procedure in which the individual receives some cue as an aid to recall. The term is used the most frequently in connection with free recall, in which a category name may be provided as a cue.

Cultural evolution. The development of cultures through prehistorical and historical time.

Cultural-familial retardation. See *familiar retardation.*

Cultural norm. Accepted way of behaving in a given culture.

Culture-fair test. A test (usually an intelligence test) which is free of cultural bias.

Cumulative response curve. A record of performance in operant conditioning in which every response of the participant moves a pen a step of a certain size on a constantly moving paper.

Curare. A drug which immobilizes the skeletal musculature by blocking the junction between nerve and muscles.

Cutoff score. A score below which applicants for some job or training are rejected. The cutoff score is selected to maximize the number of successes and to minimize the number of failures.

D

d′ In signal detection theory, detectability. The distance between the means of noise and signal-plus-noise distributions.

Dark adaptation. Adaptation of the eye to low levels of illumination.

Db. The abbreviation for *decibel.*

Deactivating enzyme. A chemical which breaks up a neurotransmitter following synaptic transmission.

Decenter. To focus attention simultaneously on several perceptual attributes of a stimulus. See *centering.*

Decibel. A measure of the intensity of an auditory stimulus. The intensity of any stimulus in decibels (db) is ten times the common logarithm of the ratio of the sound in question to a standard reference intensity which is typically in the region of the absolute threshold.

Dedifferentiation. Regression in thought in which a mature individual engages in undifferentiated thought processes characteristic of an earlier age.

Deep structure. Noam Chomsky's term for basic meaning underlying a surface structure utterance that takes many forms—active or passive voice, or question form, for example.

Defense mechanism. Some type of behavior which allows a person to remain unaware of uncomfortable anxiety and scorned personal traits and motives.

Deficit in adaptive behavior. See *adaptive behavior deficit.*

Degeneration. Deterioration of a neuron following damage. Degeneration is a method for studying connections in the nervous system. Damage created in one area leads, by degeneration, to damage in the cell bodies of neurons connected to the damaged area.

Delirium tremens. An acute agitation and mental confusion occurring after years of alcoholism and usually precipitated by abrupt cessation of drinking. Symptoms are disorientation, sweating, severe tremors, and hallucinations of crawling creatures.

Delusion. A false belief; a common symptom of paranoid schizophrenia. **Grandiosity,** a false belief in one's power and greatness; a false sense of omnipotence. **Persecutory,** a false belief that others seek to destroy or take advantage of the perceiver, or in some manner render him or her incompetent.

Delusion, somatic. Perception by schizophrenic patients that their bodies are disturbed or distorted in some extremely aberrant manner (e.g., a snake in one's intestine).

Demand characteristic. A participant's perception of what is demanded by an experimental procedure. This perception may be very different from the experimenter's intention.

Dementia praecox. An earlier term for schizophrenia.

Demographic data. Vital and social statistics including such factors as dates of birth and marriage, place of residence, race, socioeconomic status, and history of disease and disorder.

Dendrite. Relatively thick extension of a neuron's protoplasm which receives impulses from other neurons.

Denial. See denial mechanism.

Denial mechanism. A mechanism of defense in which an unpleasant external reality is rejected and replaced by a wish-fulfilling fantasy.

Denotative meaning. The thing, event, or relationship which a word stands for.

Dependent personality. Lacking self-confidence, individuals with a dependent personality disorder allow others to make major decisions for them. They subordinate their needs to those of persons on whom they depend for fear of jeopardizing the relationship and being forced to rely on themselves.

Dependent variable. In psychology, any aspect of behavior that the psychologist attempts to predict or control through manipulation of the independent variable. More generally, the events that any science attempts to predict or control. See *independent variable.*

Depression. An emotional state consisting of marked sadness, fearfulness and apprehension, extreme sense of guilt, self-

condemnation, withdrawal from others, and loss of sleep, sexual interest, and appetite. The person may be highly agitated or extremely withdrawn and lethargic.

Depressive behavior. Behavioral expression of depression.

Depressive disorder. Any of several mental disorders of which depression is the principal symptom.

Descriptive psychopathology. The diagnostic aspects of behavior disorders; the study and classification of these disorders by their symptoms, etiology, course, and outcome.

Descriptive statistics. Measures (e.g., mean, standard deviation, correlation coefficient) which describe the characteristics of some set of data. Contrast with *inferential statistics.*

Determinism. In its most general sense, the philosophical point of view which denies the existence of free will and asserts that all phenomena can be explained in terms of their antecedents. Determinism asserts that if we knew all antecedent conditions, we could predict behavior.

Development quotient (DQ). Similar to intelligence quotient, but typically based on an infant test that provides a developmental age (DA) as a measure. $DQ = DA/CA \times 100$.

Developmental disability. A physical or mental disability which occurs before the individual reaches the age of twenty-two.

Developmental lag. Delay in development; development occurs more slowly than in other children but is otherwise normal.

Developmental psychopathology. The study of the origins and longitudinal development of various forms of behavior disorders.

Developmentalist, cognitive. One who studies the development of thinking processes and related ones in the maturing child.

Deviation IQ. A measure of intelligence based on Z-scores. In order to make the deviation IQ comparable to the MA/CA IQ, the formula is: deviation $IQ = 100 + 15Z$ (or sometimes $100 + 16Z$), where Z is an individual's Z-score on the untransformed measure of the test.

Diagnosis. The classification to which a mental disorder is assigned. The process of making such a classification.

Diathesis-stress theory. A theory of

psychiatric disorder that emphasizes the interaction of fundamental biological predispositions with life stresses, which potentiate them into disorder.

Dichotic-listening experiment. A technique for studying attention and information processing in which simultaneous but differing messages are presented to the two ears via earphones.

Difference threshold. The smallest difference between two stimuli that can be detected dependably. Compare with *absolute threshold.*

Differentiation, cognitive. Applied to cognitive development, the shift with age from gross, all-or-none types of thinking to complex, highly discriminative thought.

Difficult child. A child whose temperament is marked by an unpleasant mood, difficulty in accepting and adjusting to new situations, and irregularity in biological functions. See *easy child* and *slow-to-warm-up child.*

Direct observation. A method of behavioral assessment in which a person's behavior is observed in a practical situation. Contrast with *self-report.*

Disaster syndrome. A specific sequence of reactions to a natural or man-made disaster. Includes initial shock reaction, recoil reaction, and a stage or recall of the traumatic experience.

Discounting effect. In our interpretations of the whys of another person's behavior, playing down a given cause if other causes are plausible.

Discrimination. In conditioning and learning experiments, responding to a reinforced stimulus and not responding to a nonreinforced stimulus.

Disjunctive concept. A concept for which examples have one or another of several characteristics.

Disorganized (hebephrenic) schizophrenia. See *schizophrenia, disorganized type.*

Displacement. A defense mechanism in which unacceptable feelings about a person are redirected from their true target to someone against whom they can more safely be vented.

Displacement behavior. In ethology, the elicitation of common instinctive behavior in inappropriate circumstances, usually thwarting ones.

Dissociation. A process whereby a group of mental processes—certain feelings, motives, and ideas—is split off from the rest and from consciousness. So compartmentalized, aspects of personality and memory function quite independently.

Dissociative disorders. Disorders in which the normal integration of consciousness, memory, identity, and sometimes stationary behavior is suddenly, but temporarily, altered. Memory of personal information and previous life history or identity may be lost (psychogenic amnesia); a completely amnesic person may suddenly flee to new surroundings and establish a new identity (psychogenic fugue). See *amnesia, fugue,* and *multiple personality.*

Distal stimulus. The energy in the physical world that excites a sense organ. Contrast with *proximal stimulus.*

Distinctiveness. In attribution theory, the unusual quality of a given person's behavior that encourages the observer to attribute it to the situation rather than disposition. See *consistency.*

Distributed practice. In learning, practice which includes substantial rest pauses between trials. Contrast with *massed practice.*

Divergent thinking. Thinking which goes off in many directions in a search for solutions to a problem. Contrast with *convergent thinking.*

Dizygotic twins. Twins who develop from two fertilized ova. "Fraternal" twins. Contrast with *monozygotic twins.*

DNA (deoxyribonucleic acid). Molecules found in the cell nucleus that are the fundamental determiners of the heredity of the organism; made up of a sugar, deoxyribose; a phosphate group; and four nitrogenous bases—adenine, guanine, cytosine, and thymine.

Dominant gene. A gene which expresses itself in trait or appearance, even when paired with a *recessive gene.*

Dopamine. A neurotransmitter in the central nervous system believed to play a prominent role in schizophrenia, when produced in excess.

Doppler effect. The rise in pitch of a sound as it approaches us and its lowering as it moves away.

Double approach-avoidance conflict. Complex conflict in which the individual must choose between two alternatives, both having positive and negative aspects and consequences.

Double-blind procedure. An investigational procedure best exemplified by studies of the effects of drugs on psychopathological states in which neither the investigator nor the patient knows whether he or she is in the drugged or undrugged group. Applied more generally to all studies of therapy.

Down syndrome. A form of mental retardation with noticeable physical signs—slanted eyes with extra lid fold, thick tongue, stubby limbs and fingers, sparse, fine, straight hair—induced by a genetic anomaly, usually trisomy in the twenty-first chromosome.

Drive. A motive.

DSM-III. The present revision of the *Diagnostic and Statistical Manual of Mental Disorders,* published by the American Psychiatric Association in 1980. DSM-III was preceded by DSM-I and DSM-II.

Dual-coding theory. The theory that materials in memory are represented in two systems, a system of images and a verbal system.

Duplicity theory of vision. The theory, which has essentially the status of fact, that vision consists of two separate mechanisms. See *rod* and *cone.*

Dyadic interaction. Interaction between two people.

Dyscalculia. A learning disability, of which the major symptom is difficulty with calculations.

Dyslexia. A learning disability, of which the major symptom is difficulty in reading.

E

Eardrum. The membrane at the entrance to the middle ear that is set into vibration by sound waves striking it.

Easy child. A child whose temperament it is to have a pleasant mood, to approach new stimuli, and to be regular in biological functions. Contrast with *difficult child* and *slow-to-warm-up child.*

Echoic memory. A very brief sensory memory for auditory stimuli corresponding to iconic memory in vision. Auditory impressions persist in awareness for a second or so.

Ecological validity. Applicability of theoretical ideas or research findings to the real world.

Ectomorphy. One of the body types identified by Sheldon. The long, thin, angular, lightly muscled person has this one. Contrast with *endomorphy* and *mesomorphy.* See *cerebrotonia.*

EEG. See *electroencephalogram.*

Effector. An organ capable of producing a response; a muscle or gland.

Efferent neuron. A neuron which conducts impulses away from the central nervous system toward an effector. Contrast with *afferent neuron.*

Effort justification. The assumption that an accomplishment must be good or bad, or important or unimportant, because of the amount of effort, much or little, required to attain it.

Ego. In psychoanalytic theory, the portion of the personality that behaves realistically, postponing pleasures of the id and directing the energies of the id into socially acceptable channels.

Ego psychology. Revised versions of psychoanalytic theory emphasizing the functions of the ego as opposed to those of the id. Ego theory allows the ego its own origin and course of development and its use of perception, learning, memory, and attention for its own satisfactions of exploring, manipulating, and achieving competence.

Egocentric bias. The tendency to attribute outcomes more to the actions of ourselves or the group of which we are members than to the actions of others.

Egocentricism. Behavior characteristic of children in which there is little differentiation of self from others in the external world.

Eidetic imagery. A clear, vivid, and identical image of an object or event evoked after it has been experienced. Eidetic imagery is often, but inaccurately, referred to as photographic memory.

Elaborative rehearsal. Rehearsal in which the individual relates an item to be remembered to other times with which it can be associated. Contrast with *maintenance rehearsal.*

Electra complex. In psychoanalytic theory, the little girl's erotic attachment to her father and antagonism toward her mother at about age four during the phallic stage. These id impulses are usually repressed in some way through fear of punishment.

Electroconvulsive shock therapy. A therapeutic procedure often used with severely depressed patients; convulsions are produced by passing an electric current through the brain.

Electroencephalogram. A record, typically ink-written, of the spontaneous electrical activity of the brain, obtained by attaching electrodes to the scalp and greatly amplifying the voltage changes. Commonly referred to as a record of "brain waves."

Elevation in the visual field. Positioning of faraway objects above nearby objects; a secondary cue to distance, used in graphic representations.

Embryo. In the human species, the conceptus from the second to the eighth week following conception.

Emotion. A "stirred up" state of the organism. An excited state of mind based on a physiological departure from homeostasis.

Empathy. The capacity to recognize and share vicariously the emotions of others.

Empirical-criterion method. A method for developing personality tests that selects items that people who differ in the trait to be tested answer differently.

Enactive representation. First stage in Jerome Bruner's theory of cognitive growth, during the first half year, when infants know the world only by their actions, thus representing objects and past events through motor responses.

Encephalization. The concept that, in the higher levels of phylogenetic development, the cerebral cortex becomes increasingly important in the control of behavior.

Encoding. Putting materials into a form (code) that the memory system can handle.

Encoding specificity. The tendency for memories to be stored or encoded in terms of a specific context and to be accessible only in that context.

Encounter group. Small therapeutic group which emphasizes personal growth through emotional expressiveness, candor, and interpersonal honesty.

Endocrine system. The glands which excrete their products directly into the bloodstream.

Endolymph. A fluid within the membranous labyrinth of the vestibular system. Within the sacs of the vestibule, it contains small crystals of calcium carbonate which rest against and stimulate hair cells, giving us a sense of motion whenever the head tilts or changes in acceleration.

Endomorphy. One of the body types identified by Sheldon. The round, corpulent person has this one. Contrast with *ectomorphy* and *mesomorphy*. See *viscerotonia.*

Endorphin. One of several morphinelike substances occurring naturally in the brain; endorphins are apparently released from neurons during stress and act to lessen pain.

Engram. A hypothesized memory trace; supposedly a permanently altered state of living brain tissue underlying retention.

Enkephalin. One of several neuropeptides which counteract pain. Discovered before the endorphins, they were given a name made up of the Greek words *en* (in) and *kephalē* (head).

Entrepreneurial occupation. Type of occupation in which rewards are based on the person's performance, such as business ownership or selling, the salary for which consists of commissions. See *bureaucratic occupation.*

Environmental variance. The range of expression of a particular trait in a population that is attributed to different environmental conditions and experiences.

Epilepsy. Name for a variety of disorders brought on by widespread discharge of neurons in the brain. See *grand mal epilepsy, petit mal epilepsy,* and *psychomotor epilepsy.*

Epinephrine. A hormone secreted by the adrenal medulla, active in emotional arousal. Adrenaline is a synonym.

Episodic disorder. A disorder which occurs in brief periods separated by periods of normality.

Episodic memory. Memory for temporally dated personal events. Contrast with *semantic memory.*

Erogenous zone. Area of the body able to become sexually excited or to be libidinally gratified when stimulated.

Estrogen. One of several female sex hormones, secreted by the ovaries; they stimulate the maturing of the female's sex organs and the development of her secondary sex characteristics.

Estrus. A period in the sexual cycle of most female mammals when she is attractive to males, receptive to their advances, and able to conceive; also called heat.

Ethology. A branch of zoology concerned with the behavior of animals, particularly in their natural habitat, and in this sense allied to psychology.

Etiology. All the factors contributing to the occurrence of a disease or abnormal condition.

Eugenics. The study and application of principles to improve the genetic qualities of a population.

Evoked potential. An electric discharge in a neural center produced by stimulation elsewhere.

Evolution. The development of organic species through natural selection.

Evolutionary theory of smiling. The theory that smiling has evolved because the response has adaptive value.

Excitation. A general term for positive influences favoring the occurrence of a response. Contrast with *inhibition.*

Exemplification. Method of a person with little power to try to gain more by presenting the self as morally worthy.

Existential psychology. A psychology which emphasizes immediate, subjective human experience as the basic reality rather than psychical events and overt behavior.

Experimental design. The plan of an experiment. The simplest design involves two groups of subjects, an experimental group and a control group. It proceeds in three stages devoted to equating groups, introducing the experimental treatment, and evaluating the effect of this treatment.

Experimental group. In an experiment, the group to which some special manipulation is applied. Contrast with *control group.*

Experimental method. Method of investigation which relies on laboratory experimentation. Contrast with *correlational method.*

Experimental neurosis. Emotional disturbance produced in Pavlov's demonstration, by requiring the dog to make a very fine discrimination.

Experimenter bias. Distortions of experimental results produced by the investigator's tendency to see wished-for effects in the data. A source of experimental error.

Expressed emotionality (EE). A construct used to characterize the families of schizophrenic patients whose behavior to the patient is marked by intense criticism, hostility, and anger.

Extinction. The (1) procedure and (2) result of eliciting a learned response without reinforcement.

Extirpation. The removal of brain tissue for experimental purposes.

Extrasensory perception (ESP). Awareness of thoughts and objects without direct participation of the senses.

Extrovert. In type theory, the personality who is oriented outward, requiring continual stimulation from the environment. Contrast with *introvert.*

Eyedness. The tendency for one eye to dominate the other in vision. The two eyes receive different views of an object. When these are very different, we "see" the view obtained by the dominant eye. Otherwise things would be seen double.

Eye-head system. In perceiving motion, system in the brain that keeps track of its instructions to the eye to move and cancels flow of images from the background so that it is not seen as moving.

F

F₁. First filial generation. The first generation of descent from a given mating.

Face validity. The appearance of validity produced by the fact that a test requires a performance very similar to the job for which it is designed to make predictions.

Factor analysis. A statistical technique, employing the methods of correlation, designed to detect the components (factors) that contribute to a complex trait.

False alarm. In signal detection experiments, the report of a signal on trials when none is there. Contrast with *hit*.

False consensus. The erroneous belief that the majority of people would behave as the individual making that judgment would.

Familiar retardation. Mild retardation which is nonorganic. Sometimes called cultural-familial retardation.

Fantasy. Daydreaming, imagining another private and pleasant world.

Fechner's law. $S = K \log I + A$. The perceived intensity of a stimulus *(S)* varies with the logarithm of physical intensity *(I)*. *A* is an intercept constant.

Fetus. In the human species, the conceptus from the eighth week following conception to birth.

Figure-ground relationship. In the visual world, the tendency of a pattern to stand out sharply and definitely against an extended background.

Final common path. In reflex physiology, the motor pathway upon which many neural pathways converge.

First-rank symptoms (FRS). Hallucinatory experiences and delusional beliefs considered by Kurt Schneider, psychiatrist, to be the prototypic indicators of schizophrenia. Hence called Schneiderian signs, of which there are eleven.

Fis phenomenon. The refusal of a child who mispronounces a word (e.g., "fis" for "fish") to accept that pronunciation when it is used by someone else.

Fixation. (1) Stereotyped response developed as a consequence of conflict. (2) In psychoanalytic theory arrested development of the libido in some particular stage of psychosexual development through excessive gratification or deprivation.

Fixed-action pattern. In ethology, a stereotyped instinctive act.

Fixed-interval schedule. In operant conditioning, a schedule of partial reinforcement in which the subject is rewarded for the first response made after a certain fixed amount of time.

Fixed-ratio schedule. In operant conditioning, a schedule of partial reinforcement in which reward is given after a certain fixed number of responses.

Flashbulb memory. An immediate and vivid recollection of a notable event, often a stressful one.

Flight of ideas. A nearly continuous flow of rapid speech, with abrupt shifts of topics, usually according to superficial associations or a play on words, but sometimes incoherent.

Flooding. A form of implosion therapy in which individuals confront real rather than imagined stimuli in order to desensitize themselves to feared objects or situations. See *implosion therapy.*

Fluid intelligence. Term used by Raymond Cattell to denote cognitive ability that is not influenced by prior learning. Contrast with *crystallized intelligence.*

Forebrain. The uppermost portion of the brain which shows its most advanced development in the higher vertebrates; comprises the cerebrum, thalamus, hypothalamus, and related structures.

Formal operation. In Piaget's theory, the mental ability to think logically about abstractions, to speculate, and to consider the future, what might and what ought to be.

Formal operational stage. In Piaget's developmental theory of intelligence, a phase, extending from eleven years to maturity, in which reasoning and judgment come to full development.

Fovea. Region in the retina that is closely packed with cones; the region stimulated by the image of an object at which the eye looks directly.

Frame of reference. The background of experience against which a person's judgments are made. See *adaptation level.*

Fraternal twins. See *dizygotic twins.*

Free association. In psychoanalysis, the technique of having the patient report all thoughts as they come to mind.

Free morpheme. A morpheme which has meaning when it stands alone, a word for example. Contrast with *bound morpheme.*

Free recall. A method of studying memory in which the participant, after the presentation of materials, is allowed to reproduce them in any order.

Free responding. In operant conditioning, an experimental arrangement in which the participant is allowed to respond spontaneously rather than to promptings.

Frequency distribution. An array of measurements from lowest to highest, indicating too the number of times each occurs.

Frequency polygon. A frequency distribution in which points are plotted, along the *x*-axis for the measurement or score and along the *y*-axis for the number of times each measurement occurs. Points are connected by straight lines. Contast with *bar graph.*

Frequency theory. Theory of audition in which the perception of pitch depends on the rate at which the basilar membrane vibrates.

Frontal lobe. The upper or forward half of a cerebral hemisphere, lying in front of the central sulcus.

Frustration. Any state of affairs which prevents a person from obtaining a desired goal; the condition of being thwarted in some purpose.

Frustration tolerance. The amount of frustration that a person can undergo without a disintegration of behavior.

Fugue. A dissociative disorder in which a person, with almost complete amnesia for the past, relinquishes his or her identity and activities, flees accustomed surroundings, and establishes a new identity.

Functional fixedness. The inability to recognize that an object might serve a purpose other than its usual one. An obstacle to problem solving.

Functional mental disorder. A form of psychopathological reaction without a known physiological basis. Contrast with *organic mental disorder.*

Fundamental attribution error. A tendency to underestimate situational factors and to overestimate personal dispositions as the causes of behavior.

Fundamental symptoms. Bleuler's basic symptoms of schizophrenia: association and affect disturbances, ambivalence, and autism. Contrast with *accessory symptoms.*

Fundamental tone. The lowest tone in a complex tone; the one whose pitch identifies the note. Contrast with *overtone.*

G

Galvanic skin response (GSR). A lowering of the resistance of the skin to the passage of electric current. Occurs in emotional states.

Gamete. A cell of either sex, egg or sperm, that combines with a cell of the opposite sex to form a new organism.

Ganglion. A group of nerve cell bodies lying outside the brain and spinal cord, forming a sort of nerve center.

Ganglion cell. In the retina, one of the nerve cells whose fibers form the optic nerve.

Ganzfeld. A field of vision without objects and with homogeneous illumination.

Gate-control theory of pain. A theory of pain perception that attributes pain to the joint function of two sets of neurons. Activity in large-diameter fibers closes a gate determining whether stimulation to be experienced as painful will be transmitted; activity in small-diameter fibers opens it.

Gender identity. A person's inner, deeply felt sense of being a man or a woman.

Gender role. The patterns of behavior that a society expects of a male or a female person.

Gene. The basic unit for the transmission of hereditary attributes—an amount of DNA located on a chromosome.

Gene-environment interaction. The principle that the same surroundings may have different effects on different genotypes.

Gene pool. The total collection of genes in a particular population.

General adaptation syndrome. A sequence of physiological reactions produced by protracted periods of stress. Consists, in order, of the *alarm reaction,* the *stage of resistance,* and the *stage of exhaustion.*

General factor. Spearman's *g* factor, which statistical analysis suggests is applied in taking all tests of intelligence.

Generalization. The automatic transfer of a response conditioned to a particular stimulus to similar stimuli.

Generalization gradient. A graphic representation of the strength of response evoked by stimuli that vary in similarity to

a stimulus to which the organism has been previously trained to respond.

Generalized anxiety disorder. See *anxiety disorder, generalized.*

Genetic engineering. Processes and techniques for changing the structure of individual genes or sections of DNA or for changing the genetic makeup of individuals or populations.

Genetic variance. The range of expression of a particular trait in a population that is attributed to different genotypes.

Genital stage. In psychoanalytic theory, a stage of psychosexual development characterized by heterosexual interests. See *oral stage, anal stage, phallic stage,* and *latency period.*

Genius. Person of unparalleled achievements; formerly, a person with an IQ exceeding 150 to 180, but more recent discussions impose the additional criterion of supreme accomplishment. Contrast with *giftedness.*

Genotype. The inherited characteristics of an organism; also the totality of genes possessed by it. Contrast with *phenotype.*

Germ cell. Reproductive cell, a sperm or an egg, which unites with the other to form a new individual of species.

Germinal period. The first two weeks of prenatal development in the human species.

Gestalt psychology. A school of psychology which emphasized the wholeness of behavior, especially perception. The whole, according to this school, dominates and gives meaning to the parts.

Giftedness. Having very high intelligence. Contrast with *genius.*

Glial cells or glia. Literally "glue"; neurally inactive cells of the brain and spinal cord that perform supportive, nutritive, and phagocytic (i.e., ingests microorganisms) functions.

Gradient of texture. The lessening in amount of surface detail seen as distance increases; a secondary cue in judgment distance.

Grand mal epilepsy. A form of epilepsy characterized by loss of consciousness and violent convulsions.

Gray matter. Areas of the central nervous system made up of nerve cell bodies and dendrites and unmyelinated short axons. It is integrative in function. Contrast with *white matter.*

Group cohesiveness. The tendency for a group to remain a group. High morale, feelings of belonging, expectations of sat-

isfaction, similar values and philosophies, commitment to continuing membership, holding together under stress and against external threat, success in group endeavors all contribute.

Group polarization. Increase in the extremity of the position taken by a group on a controversial issue. Discussion can so polarize opinions. Segments of groups holding different opinions before discussion draw farther apart.

Group therapy. Therapeutic intervention in which group interaction is the central focus for understanding and bettering the behavior of individuals.

Group think. A symptom of group decision making in which the group rallies around the leader, an earlier plan, or a slogan, instead of finding an adequate solution to a problem.

Growth curve. A graphic representation of growth in which age units are represented on the abscissa and progressive or incremental units on the ordinate.

Guinea pig effect. The change in behavior, from what it would be under more natural conditions, of people who know that they are being observed.

H

Habituation. The weakening and disappearance of a response through repeated elicitation.

Habituation method. Method of investigating sensory abilities in infants. One stimulus is presented until habituation occurs. Then there is a test with another. If the new stimulus again evokes a response, the investigator knows that the baby senses it as different.

Hair cell. A hearing receptor in the organ of Corti; so called because the cell contains hairlike projections.

Halfway house. A self-governing residence within the community for persons who are or have been mentally disordered.

Hallucination. A sensory experience without known physical basis.

Hallucinogen. A drug which produces hallucinatory experiences.

Halo effect. In making judgments of people, the tendency to rate an individual high or low on all traits because he or she is known to be high or low on one or a few.

Health psychology. The application of psychology to the promotion and maintenance of health, the prevention and treatment of illness, and the identification of what makes people healthy and what causes illness.

Hemiplegia. "Half paralysis"; paralysis of one side of the body or part of it through brain damage.

Heritability ratio. An estimate of the relative contribution of heredity to the total variance of a given trait in a specific population.

Heroin. A white crystalline powder derived from morphine; a habit-forming drug.

Hertz (Hz). Unit of frequency of a periodic process equal to one cycle per second.

Heterosexual behavior. Male-female sexual behavior; interest in and attachment to a member of the opposite sex. Contrast with *homosexual behavior.*

Heterotroph. An organism obtaining nourishment from an outside source; one requiring complex organic compounds of nitrogen and carbon for metabolic synthesis. Most animals and plants that do not carry on photosynthesis are heterotrophs.

Heterozygous. With respect to a trait, having a gene pair consisting of a dominant and a recessive allele. Either may be transmitted to the offspring. Contrast with *homozygous.*

Heuristic. A best guess or rule of thumb employed in problem solving. Contrast with *algorithm.*

Hierarchial structuring. In Piaget's theory, a concrete operation by which the child is able to classify people and objects on the basis of more than one attribute or dimension and to rank classes within classes.

Hierarchy of needs. Maslow's concept of the sequential emergence of motives: physiological, safety and security, love and belongingness, self-esteem, and self-actualization.

Higher-order conditioning. Classical conditioning in which the US is the CS from a previous experiment.

Hindbrain. The lowest portion of the brainstem just above and continuous with the spinal cord and just below and continuous with the midbrain. Consists of medulla oblongata, pons, and cerebellum.

Histrionic personality. Individuals with a histrionic personality disorder are overly dramatic, always drawing attention to themselves. They crave excitement, cannot tolerate minor annoyances, are dependent, inconsiderate, and manipulative, though they may be superficially charming.

Hit. In signal detection experiments, the report of a signal on trials when one is present.

Homeostasis. The tendency of the body to maintain a stable internal condition through interacting physiological processes.

Hominid. The family of animals to which human beings and their ancestors belong.

Homosexual behavior. Gay male or lesbian sexual behavior; interest in and attachment to a member of the same sex. Contrast with *heterosexual behavior.*

Homozygous. With respect to a trait, having a gene pair made up either of two dominant or of two recessive alleles.

Horizontal cell. Cell making lateral connections in the retina.

Hormone. A substance excreted by any of the endocrine glands, secreted into the bloodstream and effective at some distance from its source.

Hue. The aspect of color determined by the length of the light wave and giving it its name.

Humanism. Devotion to and concern for human welfare; any mode of thought or action or way of life in which human interests, values, and dignity predominate.

Humanistic psychology. A view of human functioning that emphasizes the uniqueness of individuals, their subjective experiences of the world, and their strivings and potential for growth. Often identified as a third force in psychology, in contrast to psychoanalytic theory and behaviorism.

Hurler syndrome. A disorder of metabolism transmitted as a recessive trait. The head becomes abnormally large, with protruding forehead, bushy eyebrows, coarse lips and tongue. Limbs become deformed, and there is mental retardation.

Hydrocephaly. Literally "water head," a condition produced by an accumulation of cerebrospinal fluid in the cranial cavity. When this happens early in life, the head enlarges. The condition is associated with mental retardation.

Hyperactivity. The disorder of children who cannot remain quiet and attentive and cannot apply themselves in situations requiring their concentration.

Hypercomplex cell. A single cell in the visual cortex of the cat that fires to stimuli with a particular orientation, moving in a certain direction, and having a specific length. See *simple cell* and *complex cell.*

Hyperphagia. Literally "overeating,"

produced by injury to certain regions of the hypothalamus.

Hypochondriasis. A somatoform disorder in which the individual misinterprets physical signs and sensations as abnormal and is preoccupied with fears of having a serious disease.

Hypothalamus. A group of nuclei in the forebrain that controls many emotional and motivational processes.

Hysteria. A disorder, known to the ancient Greeks, in which there are physical ailments—paralyses, sensory disturbances, lack of sensation, analgesia—that make no anatomical sense and that have no demonstrable organic base.

Hysterical neurosis, conversion type. DSM-II category for *conversion disorder.*

Hz. See *hertz.*

I

Iconic memory. Sensory memory for visual stimuli corresponding to echoic memory in audition. Images of removed objects persist for a second or so.

Id. In psychoanalytic theory, the portion of the personality that is concerned with the immediate gratification of basic bodily needs and urges.

Idea of reference. An individual's falsely held notion that unrelated events and activities of others in the immediate surroundings concern him or her personally and significantly.

Identical twins. See *monozygotic twins.*

Identification. The process by which children assimilate the values of the parents and see themselves in some sense as "the same" as the parents. See *introjection.* Also, a mechanism of defense in which the individual imitates or attributes to the self the acts and qualities of another.

Identity constancy. Cognitive awareness that an object remains qualitatively the same despite alterations in form, size, and general appearance.

Idiographic law. A law applying to the behavior of a single individual. Contrast with *nomothetic law.*

Ikonic representation. The second stage of Jerome Bruner's theory of cognitive growth, beginning at about nine months of age, when children can process information in the form of imagery, that is, picture things to themselves.

Illusion. A misperception of a real external stimulus. Contrast with *hallucination.*

Illusion of choice. In situations in which individuals change their attitudes because they have behaved in a contradictory manner, the essential perception, sometimes false, that they could have chosen to act in another way.

Image-retina system. In the perception of motion, the system which registers the sequential firing of rods and cones and attributes motion to the images so produced.

Imagery. The products of the imagining process; mental pictures.

Imipramine. An antidepressant drug, one of the tricyclics, which appears to reduce anxiety and forestall panic attacks.

Implicit personality theory. The rich collection of expectations that each of us has about people in general and about people of a certain type in a particular situation. See *stereotype*.

Implosion therapy. A form of behavior therapy in which patients imagine themselves in the circumstances they fear the most in order to extinguish anxiety and fear. See *flooding*.

Impression formation. In social psychology, the process of forming opinions of people. See *person perception*.

Imprinting. The development in the young of many species of a filial attachment to the first large moving object they see.

Incentive. Any goal or external condition which impels an organism to action.

Incidence. In epidemiology, a statistic which states the frequency of new cases of a given disorder occurring within a given period of time. This term contrasts with *prevalence*, which is the percent of a population that has a given disorder at some particular time.

Incus. Commonly termed the anvil; the middle bone of three in the middle ear that transmit sound stimulation from the eardrum to the cochlea. See *malleus* and *stapes*.

Independent variable. (1) Any variable which serves as a basis for making a prediction. (2) In an experiment, a factor which can be manipulated for the purpose of determining the effect of such manipulation. Contrast with *dependent variable*.

Induced color. The complementary color induced in a small achromatic patch by the colored surface it is placed on.

Inductive discipline. In the moral training of children, reasoning with them and stressing the effects of any misbehavior on the victims of their moral transgressions. See *punitive technique*.

Inferential statistics. Statistics which are used to generalize findings from a representative sample to a broader population. Contrast with *descriptive statistics*.

Inferior colliculus. The hindmost pair of bulges in the tectum of the midbrain; a lower coordinating center for hearing.

Inferiority complex. Alfred Adler's term for a pervasive feeling of personal inadequacy.

Information-processing theory. A theory of memory modeled on the flow of information through a communication system.

Ingratiation. Method of a person with little power to gain more by expressing appreciation for the virtues of a more powerful person.

Ingratiator's dilemma. The less powerful person's quandary about how much to praise or give the more powerful person, for the more dependent he or she is, the more likely are the words and favors to be interpreted as insincere.

Ingroup. The group of which one is a member.

Inhibition. In general, any temporary interference with a response. Used more specifically in many contexts: (1) in motor learning, the suppressive effect of massed practice; (2) in reflex physiology, the diminished strength of the reflex under various circumstances; (3) in personality (especially psychoanalytic) theory, an interference with the expression of some tendency or with the recall of some event; (4) in Pavlovian theory, suppression of the CR during extinction; in discrimination learning, acquiring the ability not to respond to the nonreinforced stimulus.

Innate releasing mechanism. In ethology, the mechanism which releases instinctive behavior in the presence of appropriate stimuli. See *action-specific energy*.

Inner ear. The internal portion of the ear, made up of the bony and membranous labyrinths; contains the cochlea, semicircular canals, and vestibular sacs.

Inoculation (against persuasion). A technique for developing resistance to persuasion by exposing persons to brief counterarguments against their beliefs. They are stimulated to find refutations.

Insight. (1) The process assumed to be responsible for the sudden solution of a problem. (2) Seeing into the self and into the origins of motives and conflicts.

Insight-oriented therapy. Therapy aimed at helping an individual discover the

nature of his or her symptoms and their origins.

Insightful countersuggestion. A method in Albert Ellis's rational-emotive therapy whereby the client's self-denigrations are counteracted by the therapist's penetrating reasoning. Old and inappropriate value systems are replaced by new, less self-punitive ones.

Instinct. An unlearned, biologically based form of behavior. (1) For psychologists such as McDougall, a rough equivalent of biological or primary drive. (2) In ethology, a rigidly stereotyped, complex pattern of behavior that is specific to a species. (3) Popularly and incorrectly, an automatic, almost reflexive reaction.

Instinctive drift. The tendency for what the organism learns in a situation gradually to take on the characteristics of the normal responses to the reinforcer.

Instrumental behavior. Behavior which leads (is "instrumental") to the attainment of a goal.

Instrumental conditioning. Learning in which the new response is "instrumental" in achieving an end. Now usually called *operant conditioning*.

Insufficient deterrence. Giving a child only mild admonition not to behave in some way that he or she wants to. If the child then resists behaving in this way, the activity and its goal are downgraded in his or her mind. Children become more personally responsible for their actions.

Integrative action of nervous system. The activity of the nervous system that weighs simultaneous or persistent stimuli originating in organs throughout the body.

Intelligence. (1) The complex of traits measured by intelligence tests and revealed the most directly in school performance. (2) The ability to grasp novel relationships, to remember important information, to reason well, and to cope effectively with daily living.

Intelligence A and B. Terms used by psychologist Donald Hebb to denote the innate potential for the development of intellectual capacities (A) as opposed to the actual level of intellectual functioning (B).

Intelligence quotient (IQ). Traditionally MA/CA × 100. See *deviation IQ*.

Intermittent reinforcement. Reinforcement given irregularly rather than on every conditioning trial. Also called *partial reinforcement*.

Internalization. Adopting the ideals,

values, and goals of another person (usually admired) as one's own.

Interneuron. A neuron which connects a sensory and a motor neuron within the central nervous system.

Interoceptive conditioning. Classical conditioning in which some important component (CS, US, or response) is inside the body.

Interposition. The obstruction of the outline of one object by that of another, which is seen as closer; a secondary cue in judging distance.

Interstimulus interval. In classical conditioning, the time interval separating CS and US.

Intervening variable. A concept or logical construct theoretically standing between independent and dependent variables.

Intimidation. Attempt of an individual to gain power by trying to convince another person that he or she is capable and willing to inflict harm.

Introjection. The unconscious assimilation of the values of another, usually a parent, into the self.

Introspection. The process of examining and reporting the content of one's own consciousness.

Introversion-extroversion typology. The theory that persons may be divided into two types of personalities, introverts and extroverts, depending on direction of attention inward or outward, difficulty or ease of social adjustment, secretive or open behavior.

Introvert. A person who shows a strong tendency to find satisfaction in an inner life of thought and fantasy. Contrast with *extrovert.*

Involutional melancholia. A DSM-II affective disorder of women who are going through menopause and of men somewhat older whose sexual adequacy is diminishing. Their symptoms are depressive and sometimes regressive and paranoid.

Iodopsin. Light-sensitive substance—a pigment—found in the cones of the eye.

IQ. See *intelligence quotient.*

Iris. The set of autonomically innervated, flat and circular muscles that controls the amount of light entering the eye. The anterior surface of this diaphragm is variously pigmented in different individuals.

J

J-curve. A frequency distribution in which the modal value is the most extreme measure, typically zero.

James-Lange theory. The theory of emotion that awareness of it follows upon bodily changes—visceral arousal and actions of the skeletal muscles—in response to a stimulus: We see the bear, are aroused and run, and then experience fright. As opposed to: We see the bear, are frightened, and then are aroused and run.

Job analysis. An determination of the skills required for success on a job.

Just-noticeable difference (j.n.d.). The smallest difference between two stimuli that can be detected reliably.

K

Karyotype. A systematic array of the chromosomes of a single cell in a drawing or photograph.

Kibbutz. Communal, typically agricultural, setting in Israel in which children live in quarters separate from those of the parents. They are watched over by professional caretakers and see their parents in the evenings and on Saturday.

Kinesthesis. Sensory impressions which come from the joints, muscles, and tendons and provide information about the positions and movements of parts of the body.

Klinefelter syndrome. A disorder of males in which an extra X chromosome keeps the testicles small at puberty, disrupts hormonal balance, and is likely to cause sterility.

Knowledge structures. In attribution theory, the network of social expectancies about people and events in general and about particular types of people and events that guide social perceivers.

L

Labeling theory. The view that mental disorder is caused by attaching a label (e.g., schizophrenia) to the individual.

Laboratory analogue. In behavioral assessment, an artificial situation which simulates a complicated real-life situation.

Latency period. In psychoanalytic theory, a period of psychosexual development, from about age six to puberty, in which the child shows little or no interest in sexual matters. See *oral stage, anal stage, phallic stage,* and *genital stage.*

Latent dream content. According to Freud, the underlying, repressed information of the dream, which is camouflaged by the *manifest content.*

Lateral connections. Connections across the retina, allowing the sharp definition of borders and edges.

Law of effect. Thorndike's statement that we learn rewarded responses and unlearn responses that are not rewarded.

Law of independent assortment. A Mendelian law that a pair of genes governing a single trait segregate independently of other gene pairs in the formation of germ cells.

Law of segregation. A Mendelian law that the paired paternal and maternal alleles governing a trait separate in the formation of germ cells.

Learned helplessness. A condition of apathy following experience with unavoidable punishment. The organism then accepts punishment even when it could avoid the aversive situation.

Learning. A fairly permanent change in behavior which occurs as a result of experience.

Learning curve. Graph relating proficiency in a learning situation to practice. What is actually plotted is performance, learning being the assumed underlying state.

Learning disability. A failure to develop a normal capacity to learn, usually of some specific skill. See *dyslexia, dyscalculia.*

Lens. A transparent structure of the eye that focuses light rays directly on the retina by changes in convexity.

Lesion. A localized abnormal change in body tissue through injury or disease; sometimes for experimental purposes.

Level of aspiration. A level of accomplishment which a person sets as a goal. Attaining the goal is perceived as success, the inability to do so as failure.

Level of confidence. In testing the null hypothesis, the confidence with which the hypothesis can be rejected. Low probabilities mean a high level of confidence that a statistic was not obtained by chance.

Level of processing. The physical form (visual shape or sound) of an item to be remembered, its rhymes, or its meaningful associations. These levels of processing are from superficial to deep. The deeper the processing, the better the item is remembered.

Libido. In Freudian theory, general sexuality which provides the energy for all behavior.

Lie detector. An apparatus which measures blood pressure, pulse, respiration, and skin resistance changes during the course of questioning an individual. The assumption is that lying is accompanied by changes in these emotional indices.

Life events scale. A list of emotion-arousing life events by which to measure the stressfulness of a person's life; the person checks the events experienced recently.

Life instinct. In psychoanalytic theory, the basic instinct or drive under the control of the pleasure principle; called Eros.

Life space. A term used by Kurt Lewin to denote all the phenomena making up the world of actuality for a person, thus determining behavior.

Light wave. Electromagnetic radiation whose wavelength is measured in angstrom units.

Limbic system. A set of structures in and around the core of the old forebrain that supposedly integrates motivational-emotional patterns such as arousal, sleep, feeding.

Limen. See *threshold.*

Linear perspective. The convergence of parallel lines as they become more distant; a secondary cue to distance.

Linguistic competence. Possession of the rules of language. The ability to create and understand an indefinitely large number of expressions.

Linguistic determinism. The general conception that language determines what thoughts are possible. Part of the Whorfian hypothesis.

Linguistic relativity. The conception that the content of thought depends on how language categorizes objects and events in the world. Part of the Whorfian hypothesis.

Linguistics. The study of human speech in its various aspects, including phonetics, phonology, morphology, syntax, and sematics.

Lithium carbonate. A naturally occurring chemical compound which has proved effective in the treatment of manic states.

Lobotomy. A psychosurgical procedure, now used sparingly, in which the nerve tracts connecting the frontal lobes with the thalamus are cut.

Local-stimulus theory of drive. The hypothesis that motives are intense stimuli. For example, hunger is the stimulation provided by hunger pangs.

Lock-and-key specificity. A way of describing the fact that a neurotransmitter can affect only one type of receptor site and the receptor site can be affected by only one type of neurotransmitter.

Long-term memory (LTM). A memory system of long duration, following after short-term memory.

Longitudinal study. Research study which follows individuals over long periods of time to investigate development. Contrast with *cross-sectional study.*

Loudness. A dimension of auditory perception related to the intensity or amplitude of the sound wave; measured in *sones.*

Love-oriented discipline. Discipline based on praise, reasoning, witholding love, and separating the child from the parents. Contrast with *power-assertive discipline.*

LSD (lysergic acid diethylamide). A hallucinogenic drug which can induce vivid perceptual experiences, seeming expansiveness of the mind, hallucinations, and disorganized thinking.

M

MA. See *mental age.*

Mach bands. Light and dark edges of a visual pattern; an intensification brought about by lateral inhibition, in which stimulation of retinal cells inhibits activity of adjacent cells.

Macrocephaly. An abnormally large head; a condition which causes mental retardation.

Mainstreaming. The practice of educating handicapped children with the main group in regular classrooms, although special classes are provided as needed.

Maintenance rehearsal. Repeating an item over and over, thus keeping it in short-term memory until needed. Contrast with *elaborative rehearsal.*

Malleus. Outermost of the three bones of the middle ear; hammer-shaped and attached to the tympanic membrane or eardrum. See *incus* and *stapes.*

Mania. Intense emotional state in which the individual is elated, talkative, and distractible, has flights of ideas and grandiose delusions, and engages in purposeless, frenetic activity.

Manic-depressive disorder. An affective disorder in which the individual has extreme swings of mood, from elation to depression and back again, or more rarely only episodes of mania. Called *bipolar disorder* in DSM-III.

Manifest dream content. Freud's term for the picture or story of a dream, without reference to its symbolic or wish-fulfillment quality. Contrast with *latent content.*

Maple Syrup Urine disease. A disorder in the ability to metabolize certain amino acids, causing mental retardation.

Marasmus. Profound physiological decline in infants, sometimes associated with deprivation of activities (rocking, soothing) typical of good mothering.

Marijuana. The dried leaves of the hemp plant; a mild hallucinogen which enhances mood and the senses of touch, taste, and sound; makes space seem larger, time drawn out; interferes with reaction time, coodination, visual perception.

Marked expression. In pairs of words (e.g., short–tall), the one which implies an end of the continuum when used in the question, "How—is he?" Contrast with *unmarked expression.*

Masking. In hearing, the obliteration of one sound by another.

Mass action— differentiation sequence. In psychological development, a progression from activity that involves the entire body to a more precise control over parts of the body.

Massed practice. Practice in which the trials are crowded closely together. Contrast with *spaced practice.*

Maternal deprivation. Lack of adequate mothering of the infant, often with severe psychological and physiological consequences for the child.

Maturation. The developmental acquisition of skills by normal children through physiological (probably chiefly neural) growth, provided the environment is suitable.

Maturational readiness. A stage of development at which the organism is optimally prepared to acquire some particular kind of habit. See *critical period.*

Mean. The average: the sum of the measures divided by the number of them. A measure of central tendency.

Means-end analysis. In problem solving, an individual's determining whether the act under consideration will be an advance toward his or her goal.

Median. The middle score, or fiftieth percentile. A measure of central tendency.

Mediation. Internal processes which are

assumed to occur between an observed stimulus and an observed response.

Medical model. In psychopathology, a model of mental disorders which assumes that they are diseases similar to the traditional physical diseases treated by medical practitioners.

Medulla. The hindmost part of the brainstem. The lower part of the hindbrain containing major ascending and descending tracts between the spinal cord and higher centers; its nuclei maintain breathing, heartbeat, and blood pressure.

Meiosis. The particular type of cell division by which the gametes are formed. The chromosomes do not double, so that each germ cell receives only half the number of chromosomes characteristic of all other cells of the organism. Thus, when a sperm and egg cell are united during fertilization, the newly fertilized ovum then has the full complement of chromosomes, half contributed by the mother (via the egg cell) and the other half by the father (via the sperm cell).

Membranous labyrinth. Sensory structures of the inner ear, contained within the bony labyrinth; consists of the vestibular sacs, membranous semicircular canals, and cochlear duct.

Memory span. See *span of short-term memory.*

Mental age. For a tested person, the mean age of individuals who obtain the same score on the test as he or she does. More generally, the score on an individual test of intelligence, expressed in terms of years and months.

Mental retardation. A condition of significantly subaverage intellectual functioning and of deficits in adaptive behavior which are first manifested during childhood.

Mental set. A readiness to respond in a certain way. Sometimes called "mind set" or just "set."

Mentally retarded, educable. Retarded persons whose intellectual level indicates that they are capable of acquiring self-help skills, of becoming socially adaptive, and of handling unskilled or semiskilled jobs.

Mentally retarded, trainable. Retarded persons who are expected to learn self-care skills and to maintain a social adjustment within a relatively restricted social environment.

Mere presence. An aspect of being with other people that can affect the individual's performance, enhancing that of well-learned, repetitive tasks, interfering with the learning of new skills.

Mescaline. A psychotomimetic drug derived originally from the peyote cactus.

Mesomorphy. In Sheldon's typology, the vigorous, powerfully boned and muscled type of body build. Contrast with *ectomorphy* and *endomorphy.* See *somatotonia.*

Methadone. A synthetic dependence-inducing narcotic. Used chiefly in rehabilitating heroin addicts, since the drug blocks the craving for heroin and its euphoric effects.

Methamphetamine ("speed"). A synthetic drug which acts as a stimulant.

Method of limits. A psychophysical method for determining thresholds in which stimuli are presented in increasing and decreasing orders of intensity, trial by trial. The trials begin with stimuli below threshold or above.

Method of loci. A memory device to recall people or objects by imaging them in specific locales known to the individual.

Method of successive approximations. See *shaping.*

Microcephaly. An abnormally small head and brain area caused by disease, trauma, or a pair of defective recessive genes; a condition which brings mental retardation.

Midbrain. The middle section of the brainstem continuous with and just above the hindbrain and just below the forebrain. Contains the tectum, tegmentum, and cerebral peduncles.

Middle ear. The air-filled space between the eardrum and the inner ear. Contains the three auditory bones, *malleus, incus,* and *stapes.*

Milieu therapy. A form of therapy in which the climate and management of the wards of a mental hospital stress group activities, freedom of the patients to move about, and communication among patients and staff. Responsibility for the ward is housed to some extent in the patients.

Minimal social situation. A two-person social situation in which modes of possible interaction are extremely limited. One person's outcomes depend only on whether or not the other makes some single, simple response.

Minnesota Multiphase Personality Inventory (MMPI). An inventory consisting of 550 statements evaluating personality by psychiatric categories, masculinity–feminity, and social introversion.

Miss. In signal detection procedures, failure to detect a signal when one is presented.

Mitosis. The process of cell division in which the chromosomes duplicate, then line up in pairs within the cell nucleus. The pairs split, with one member of each duplicated pair going to one of the two daughter cells, which have been formed through division of the original parent cell.

Mixed-motive game. A social exchange of two people that comes out the best when the two are both cooperative *and* competitive. See *non-zero-sum game.*

MMPI. The Minnesota Multiphasic Personality Inventory.

Mnemonic devices. Artificial techniques for helping an individual to remember items to be learned.

Mode. The most frequent score. A measure of central tendency.

Modeling. Learning through the observation and imitation of others. Stressed in social-learning theory.

Monoamine oxidase inhibitor. One of several antidepressant drugs which keep the enzyme monoamine oxidase from deactivating norepinephrine and serotonin in limbic and hypothalamic synapses, increasing their concentrations and elevating mood.

Mongolism. See *Down syndrome.*

Monotonic relationship. Any relationship in which either steady increases or steady decreases of the dependent variable are associated with increases of the independent variable.

Monozygotic (identical) twins. Twins who develop from a single egg, hence genetically identical. Contrast with *dizygotic twins.*

Moon illusion. A visual illusion in which the moon appears larger the closer it is to the horizon.

Moral behavior. Behavior taken to be ethical in any culture.

Moral knowledge. Understanding of expected moral behavior.

Moral treatment. A method of treatment of the first half of the nineteenth century whereby patients in mental hospitals were treated with compassion and dignity. They were encouraged to discuss their problems and to pursue daily purposeful activity.

Morpheme. A unit of meaning of language. Basic words as well as prefixes and suffixes which change the meaning of the basic word are examples.

Motion parallax. Apparent motion, seen when the eye is fixed on a particular stimulus and the body is in motion. For example, in riding in an automobile, the individual has the illusion that objects nearer than the point of fixation are moving in a direction opposite that in which the person is traveling. Distant objects appear to move in the same direction.

Motivation. An intervening variable which gives behavior its energy and goals and is felt as wanting, needing, or desiring. **Primary,** the energizing of behavior by physiological drives such as thirst, hunger, need for warmth and rest, etc. **Secondary,** the energizing of behavior by acquired or learned drives such as achievement, affiliation, etc.

Motor aphasia. See *aphasia, expressive.*

Motor neuron. A neuron which transmits neural impulses from the central nervous system to muscles and glands. Also called *efferent neuron.*

Motor theory of consciousness. The theory that mental experience depends on stimulation from muscular activity.

Müller-Lyer illusion. A visual illusion in which two lines of equal length are perceived to be unequal if one ends with arrowheads (perceived as smaller) and the other with reversed arrowheads or "feather" marks (perceived as larger).

Multiple personality. A dissociative disorder in which a person may assume alternative personalities; the acts and memories associated with each are not within the awareness of the others or at least that of the original personality.

Munchausen syndrome. The disorder of people who come to physicians or hospitals for treatment of invented symptoms of disease. Named for the character "Baron Munchausen," a confirmed liar.

Muscle action potential. An electric discharge associated with the activity of muscles.

Mutation. An unusual and abrupt change in gene structure and hence in the bodily characteristic it governs. A change in DNA.

Myelin sheath. A fatty covering which encases the axons of larger motor and sensory neurons; allows impulses to travel faster.

Myopia. Nearsightedness as a result of a crystalline lens which focuses images in front of the retina rather than on it. In this condition near objects can be properly focused through accommodation; far objects cannot be.

N

N-of-1 design. An experimental design for use with one subject, for example the *ABAB design.*

Narcissism. In psychoanalysis, erotic feelings associated with the individual's own body or self. More generally, self-love, egocentrism.

Narcissistic personality. Individuals with a narcissistic personality disorder have a grandiose sense of self-importance and fantasies of achieving perfections. They crave attention and admiration from others, exploit them, and lack empathy for them.

Narcotic. A drug which in moderate doses blunts the senses, relieves pain, and brings profound sleep but in heavy doses causes stupor, coma, or convulsions; addictive when used constantly.

Narrative story. As a mnemonic device, the story sequence by which the individual links together a large number of items.

Nativism-empiricism issue. The question whether elements of knowledge and perception are native to the mind or learned through experience.

Natural selection. The Darwinian proposition that the inheritance of structures is determined by their usefulness to the species in the struggle for survival. Individuals of the species who can best meet environmental demands survive and reproduce.

Naturalistic experiment. A type of naturalistic observation in which the investigator pays systematic attention to behavior occurring in unmanipulated normal circumstances.

Naturalistic observation. The observation of behavior in the ongoing normal circumstances of life.

Nature-nurture interaction. The interplay between heredity or what is inborn and environment on the development of individual traits and behavior.

Nature-nurture issue. The pervasive question of the extent to which heredity (nature) and environment (nurture) determine behavior.

Negative afterimage. An image which is complementary in color to that of the original stimulus, seen after looking long at the original stimulus and then at an achromatic surface.

Negative correlation. A relationship between two measures in which high values of x are associated with low values of y, and vice versa. Contrast with *positive correlation.*

Negative reinforcer. A punisher; an event which an organism will learn to escape or avoid.

Negative relationship. A relationship in which increases in the independent variable are associated with decreases in the dependent variable. Contrast with *positive relationship.*

Negative skew. Describes a skewed distribution with the long tail toward the left, toward low numbers. Contrast with *positive skew.*

Negative transfer. Process in which learning one task interferes with the learning of another task. Contrast with *positive transfer.*

Neocortex. Literally new cortex. The part of the cerebral cortex that is unique to mammals.

Neologisms. New words; sometimes made up by schizophrenic patients.

Neonate. A newborn infant.

Nerve. A bundle of axons in the peripheral system, generally with a protective and supportive sheath.

Nerve impulse. An electrochemical excitation in the walls of a nerve cell that allows the cell body and dendrites to communicate with the terminal buttons by way of the axon.

Nerve tract. A collection of axons in the central system having a common origin, termination, and function.

Neuromuscular junction. The point of contact of a motor neuron with a muscle.

Neuron. Nerve cell; the active element of the nervous system.

Neurosis. Originally, a disorder of the nerves. In DSM-II, one of a large group of nonpsychotic disorders in which anxiety was believed to be paramount—phobias, obsessions, compulsions, anxiety attacks, hysteria, hypochondria.

Neuroticism—stability. A factor in the personality model espoused by Eysenck. At one pole is a "genotypical proneness" to neurosis, at the other stability or normality.

Neurotransmitter. A chemical substance released by a presynaptic neuron. It crosses a synapse and excites or inhibits a postsynaptic neuron.

Nominal realism. A mode of thinking in

the preoperational stage in which the child assumes that the name of an object is a concrete and essential attribute of the object.

Nomothetic law. A general law that applies to groups of persons. Contrast with *idiographic law.*

Nonanalytic concept formation. Remembering examples of the concept, the common way of forming them, especially by children.

Nondirective therapy. See *client-centered therapy.*

Nonmonotonic relationship. A relationship in which increases in the independent variable are associated first with increases (or decreases) in the dependent variable and then with decreases (or increases). Contrast with *monotonic relationship.*

Nonselective social smiling. See entry under *smiling.*

Nonsense syllable. Relatively meaningless three-letter sequence; such syllables are often used in studies of rote learning.

Non-zero-sum game. A social exchange of two people in which one person does not win what the other loses; both have the possibility of coming out ahead if they compete *and* cooperate with each other. Contrast with *zero-sum game.*

Noradrenaline. See *norepinephrine.*

Norepinephrine. A catecholamine which acts as a neurotransmitter and has some of the properties of epinephrine. Also called noradrenaline.

Norm of reaction. The range of phenotypes which are possible for a given genotype under different environmental circumstances.

Normal curve. The bell-shaped function characteristic of frequency distributions of many psychological measures.

Normal distribution. In statistics, a theoretical distribution of probability—of the frequencies with which the different values of a variate will occur; bell-shaped and symmetrical when graphed.

Normalization. The principle of providing mentally retarded and other handicapped persons with environmental conditions that are as close as possible to those of the rest of society.

Nucleus. (1) The area within a cell that contains the genetic material. (2) A relatively compact collection of the cell bodies of neurons.

Null hypothesis. The hypothesis that there is no true difference between experimental and control groups after they have been treated differently in an experiment.

Numerical peg system. A mnemonic device in which the memorizer uses some numerical system like "One is a bun, etc." as pegs on which to hang items to be remembered.

O

Obesity. Excessive fatness; 20 percent overweight, by arbitrary definition.

Object constancy. The perception of objects as relatively unchanged, despite variations in placement, illumination, distance from the observer, and so on.

Object permanence. The realization that objects continue to exist even though they are out of sight or hidden from view. Develops gradually in children between six and eighteen months of age. A term used by Piaget.

Objective test of personality. A personality inventory, questionnaire, or rating scale. Contrast with *projective test of personality.*

Observational learning. A form of learning that takes place through watching others, without direct reinforcement, although the individual may be rewarded or punished vicariously by seeing the consequences to others of the observed behavior.

Obsessions. Recurring, intrusive, and uncontrollable thoughts.

Obsessive-compulsive disorder. An anxiety disorder in which the mind is flooded with constantly recurring and often absurd ideas—obsessions; or the individual has impulses to perform a specific act repetitively—compulsions.

Occipital lobe. The hindmost part of either cerebral hemisphere, concerned with the processing of visual information.

Oedipus complex. In Freudian theory, the erotic attachment of the four-year-old boy in the phallic stage for his mother and his desire to eliminate his father as a rival. These id impulses are usually repressed in some way through fear of punishment.

Old forebrain. The more primitive parts of the forebrain. Consists of olfactory apparatus, basal ganglia, limbic system, etc.

Olfactory bulbs. Protrusions of the old forebrain that receive the olfactory nerve.

Olfactory rod. Long, narrow, column-shaped cell with projecting hairs; the receptor for smell.

Omission training. In operant conditioning, a procedure in which reward fails to follow a designated response but is given if that response is not made.

Operant conditioning. A form of training in which responses, which do something to or "operate" on the environment, are strengthened through positive or negative reinforcement. Also known as *instrumental conditioning.*

Operation. In Piaget's theory, basic and logical mental manipulation and transformation of information.

Operationism. A position in the philosophy of science that maintains that abstract concepts and internal events acquire their meaning from observations performed to observe and measure them.

Opponent-process theory. (1) The theory of color vision originally proposed by Hering, that three pairs of opposing processes account for color vision: black–white, blue–yellow, and red–green. (2) A theory of emotion proposing that specific emotional experiences are followed by their opposite emotional states—terror by euphoria. If the emotional experience is repeated a number of times, the second emotion becomes stronger.

Optic nerve. One of a pair of cranial nerves made up of axons of ganglion cells of the retina and connecting, through relay centers of the thalamus, with the visual centers of the brain.

Oral stage. First stage in psychosexual development, in which the infant acquires its most important pleasures from activities of the mouth—chewing, sucking, biting, etc. See *anal stage, phallic stage, latency period,* and *genital stage.*

Ordinate. The vertical or y-axis on a graph.

Organ of Corti. A structure located on the basilar membrane of the spiraling cochlea of the inner ear; it contains the hair cells, the receptor cells for hearing.

Organic evolution. The process by which genetic material has succeeded in covering the earth with bodies that ensure its own survival.

Organic mental disorder. Mental disorder in which intellectual and emotional functioning are impaired through brain pathology. The dysfunction can be caused by aging, excessive drug usage, or specific physical or physiological factors.

Organic retardation. Mental retardation caused by physiological disorder; examples are Down syndrome, phenylketonuria, microcephaly.

Orienting reaction. In Pavlovian terminology, paying close attention to novel stimuli—looking, listening, touching, sniffing—to discover what they are about.

Orthogenetic principle. Werner's principle that development proceeds from a relatively global undifferentiated response toward one of increasing differentiation and hierarchical organization of the elements constituting it.

Ossicles. The three small bones in the middle ear that transmit movements of the eardrum to the fluids of the inner ear.

Otosclerosis. A condition in which a growth of spongy bone immobilizes the stapes at the point where it transmits sound to the oval window, causing deafness.

Outcome control. The kind of control that one person has over another through the power to deliver or withhold rewards as punishments.

Outcome masking. A strategy of a person with little power to gain more by concealing the importance he or she places on the rewards and punishments that are under another's control.

Outerdirectedness. An orientation to the world in which an individual's tendencies to act are determined from without (i.e., by environmental events) rather than from within the self.

Outgroup. A group of which one is not a member.

Oval window. Membranous "window" at the entrance of the cochlea; its movement is passed on as pressure changes in the fluid in the vestibular and tympanic canals.

Overextension. In learning language, a child's tendency to overgeneralize the meaning of words; for example, his or her mistaken notion that all large, four-legged creatures are cows.

Overjustification. Giving a greater incentive than is necessary to induce another to behave in a certain way. Such overjustification reduces the value of the activity for the person.

Overlearning. Practice beyond the point of mastery in learning a set of materials.

Overregularization. The tendency of the child, during the course of acquiring language, to use regular verb and plural inflections for irregular words: "I comed" rather than "I came," "foots" rather than "feet."

Overshadowing. In conditioning to a compound stimulus made up of two or more components, the service of one element as the effective CS while the other gains no control over the CR.

Overtone. In a complex tone, any of the tones of higher pitch. The frequencies of the overtones are multiples of those of the *fundamental tone.*

P

Paired-associate learning. Learning pairs of words (e.g., "wagon"—"cold") after the manner of a foreign language vocabulary. The learner's task is to give the second member of the pair ("cold") when presented with the first ("wagon").

Panic attack. Sudden and inexplicable fear and intense apprehension, along with physiological symptoms—dyspnea, palpitations, chest pains, choking and smothering sensations, dizziness, faintness, sweating, shaking. A sense of impending doom, fears of dying, going crazy, or doing something uncontrolled are often part of a panic attack.

Panic disorder. An anxiety disorder in which, within a three-week period, the individual has at last three sudden panic attacks, with incapacitating and overwhelming physiological and emotional symptoms, that cannot be explained by physical exertion or a life-threatening situation.

Paradoxical intention. A variation of flooding in which the client is urged not merely to express fears but to confront them in exaggerated form. See *flooding, implosion therapy.*

Paranoia. General term for delusions of persecution, grandiosity, or both, found in paranoid disorder, paranoid schizophrenia, and paranoid personality disorder. These delusions can be isolated from the rest of the personality and intellect. Paranoia can be brought on as well by large quantities of cocaine and alcohol.

Paranoid disorder. A disorder in which the individual's symptoms are persistent delusions of persecution or delusional jealousy, an unfounded conviction that his or her mate is unfaithful. The individual is often seclusive, eccentric, contentious, and given to litigation but has no thought disorder.

Paranoid personality. Persons with a paranoid personality disorder are, without justification, unduly suspicious and mis-

trustful of others, hypersensitive—quickly taking offense and "making mountains out of molehills"—and cold, unemotional, and humorless.

Paranoid schizophrenia. A form of schizophrenia in which the patient has many systematized delusions and ideas of reference as well as hallucinations.

Parasympathetic ganglion (plural: ganglia). Cluster of nerve cell bodies in the head and alongside the sacral cord serving parasympathetic functions of the autonomic system.

Parasympathetic nervous system. A division of the autonomic system concerned with protecting and conserving the body resources, preserving normal functions, and maintaining a calm emotional state. Contrast with *sympathetic nervous system.*

Paresis. A consequence of syphilis in which organic damage to the brain by invading microorganisms produces profound mental and neurological symptoms.

Parietal lobe. A major division of either cerebral hemisphere lying between the frontal and occipital lobes and above the temporal lobe.

Partial reinforcement. Reinforcement which occurs at a rate less often than for every correct response or on every trial.

Partial-reinforcement effect. The greater resistance of responses developed through partial reinforcement to extinction than of those developed through continuous reinforcement.

Passive-aggressive personality. Persons with a passive-aggressive personality disorder express hostility in passive ways, by being resistant at work and socially through procrastination, dawdling, intentional inefficiency, stubbornness, and "forgetfulness." These people are often dependent and seldom win promotions.

Passive avoidance. A form of operant conditioning in which making a specified response brings punishment. The participant learns not to make the response and in this passive way avoids punishment. Contrast with *active avoidance.*

Passive vocabulary. All the words a person understands. Contrast with *active vocabulary.*

Patterns of light and shade. The ways in which the world is lighted from above by the sun and other dependable patterns of illumination, providing a cue to differences in depth.

Pavlovian conditioning. See *classical conditioning*.

Payoff matrix. (1) In social psychology, a diagrammatic representation of the gains and losses incurred by various combinations of acts on the part of persons who are competing. (2) In signal detection experimentation, the gains for reporting correctly that a signal is present when there is one and absent when there is none, as well as the losses for reporting that a signal is present when there is none or absent when one is present.

Peak experience. Abraham Maslow's term for a powerful emotional experience, bordering on ecstasy, that serves to transform the individual's perception of self and environment. At such moments people experience fully, vividly, selflessly, with full concentration and total absorption. They feel spontaneous and masterful and are almost unaware of space and time.

Percentile rank. The percentage of scores in a total distribution that a given score equals or exceeds.

Perception. The interpretation of sensory information.

Perceptual constancy. The tendency to perceive objects in their correct sizes, shapes, and colors in spite of great variations in the pattern of proximal stimulation.

Perceptual defense. A hypothetical, but not fully validated, tendency for a person to fail to perceive psychologically threatening stimuli.

Performance IQ. An IQ score based primarily on nonverbal tests of intelligence. Such tests investigate perceptual skills, spatial abilities, speed, etc.

Performance test. In intelligence testing, a test requiring minimal language; one measuring perceptual skills, spatial abilities, speed, etc. Contrast with *verbal test*.

Perilymph. The fluid between the bony and membranous labyrinths of the ear.

Peripheral nervous system. The portion of the nervous system that connects receptors with the central nervous system or the central nervous system to glands and muscles.

Permissive parent. A parent who gives a child as much freedom as is consistent with his or her physical safety.

Perseveration deficit. An effect of damage to perfrontal association cortex. Once started on an activity, the patient perseverates—is unable to stop and shift to something else more appropriate.

Person perception. Inferences made about the disposition, motives, and intentions of a person. Also called *impression formation*.

Persona. Carl Jung's term for the socially conforming mask maintained by each person.

Personal stressor. Disturbing situation affecting the lives of single individuals; e.g., death of a spouse, divorce, unemployment.

Personal unconscious. According to Carl Jung, the portion of the unconscious that contains specific experiences of the individual. Contrast with *collective unconscious*.

Personalism. In attribution theory, the tendency for the individual to disregard information indicating that his or her disposition is the cause of a bad outcome.

Personality. The unique organization of fairly permanent characteristics that sets the individual apart from other individuals and, at the same time, determines how others respond to him or her.

Personality disorders. A heterogeneous category of disorders of individuals with inflexible and maladaptive personality traits. The disorders are recognized by adolescence or earlier and impair social and occupational functioning. They may lessen in middle or old age.

Personality inventory. Self-appraisal test consisting of statements about personal characteristics; the individual decides whether or not they apply.

Personality test. A test to determine the general disposition and adjustment of the individual.

Petit mal epilepsy. Form of epilepsy in which there are momentary losses of consciousness.

Phallic stage. In psychoanalytic theory, a stage in psychosexual development from the third to the fifth or sixth year, during which children become interested in their sexual organs and develop and resolve their Oedipus and Electra complexes.

Phenomenology. In psychology, a theoretical point of view advocating the study of subjective awareness and experience. May also refer to the naive reports of experience made by untrained individuals. See *humanistic psychology*.

Phenothiazines. A group of antipsychotic drugs which reduce anxiety and distress; particularly effective with schizophrenic patients.

Phenotype. In genetics, the characteristics which actually appear in a living organism, depending on dominance of genes and the interaction between genotype and environment. Contrast with *genotype*.

Phenotypic variance. Total variance of some trait in a population.

Phenylketonuria (PKU). A disorder in the ability to metabolize the amino acid phenylalanine; it is inherited as a recessive trait and causes mental retardation. The mental retardation can be largely prevented by a special diet.

Pheromone. One of a class of hormonal substances that are secreted by an individual, become airborne, reach the olfactory system of another member of the species, and affect its physiology and behavior.

Phi phenomenon. Apparent motion of what is regarded as a single light, seen when two lights a short distance apart are flashed alternately in rapid succession.

Phobia. An unreasonable and excessive fear of a specific object, activity, or situation which is often not dangerous.

Phobic disorder. An anxiety disorder in which the individual has a persistent and irrational fear of a specific object, activity, or situation and is compelled to avoid it. The fear is pervasive enough to disturb daily living.

Phoneme. The smallest unit of sound that signals a difference in meaning in a particular language.

Phonetic symbolism. Meanings conveyed by the sound of an utterance.

Phonetics. The branch of linguistics which analyzes and classifies spoken sounds as they are produced by the organs of speech and register on the ear.

Phonology. The study of language in terms of speech sounds.

Photon. A very small, fast-moving particle—the unit—of light energy.

Photopic vision. Vision as it occurs under illumination sufficient to permit a full discrimination of colors; dependent on the cones.

Phrenology. The study of the bumps and configurations of the skull as indicating mental faculties and traits of character, according to the hypothesis of German physicians Franz Joseph Gall (1758–1828) and Johann Kasper Spurzheim (1776–1832).

Physical primary color. In vision, a color which, when mixed with two others from the two other thirds of the spectrum, contributes to the production of all visible hues. Contrast with *psychological primary colors.*

Physiological nystagmus. A continuous small tremor of the eyes.

Physiological zero. The temperature which is experienced as neither warm nor cold.

Pitch. The psychological attribute of hearing which depends for the most part on the frequency of the sound wave.

Pituitary gland. A gland of the endocrine system located at the base of the brain. It is the "master gland" or "key gland" because its hormones control the secretions of many other glands of the system.

Place theory. Helmholtz's theory that a particular place on the basilar membrane and the resonating fibers there are stimulated by a particular frequency of sound waves.

Placebo. Originally, a medicine without medicinal value given merely to satisfy a patient. More recently, a treatment (usually a pill, but could be any form of treatment) identical in all respects with the one under experimental test, except that it lacks the active ingredient. See *placebo effect.*

Placebo effect. In various therapies, including psychotherapy, the improvement of patients as a result of the attention they receive rather than through the treatment itself.

Placenta. The vascular structure within the uterus of mammals to which the fetus is attached by the umbilical cord, and through which the fetus receives nourishment and oxygen from the mother's bloodstream.

Pleasure principle. In Freudian theory, the principle that the individual impulsively seeks to satisfy id urges, either directly or in fantasy. Contrast with *reality principle.*

Polygenic inheritance. Inheritance which is determined by many sets of genes all affecting the same characteristic.

Pons. The upper part of the hindbrain; contains tracts which connect the lobes of the cerebellum to the cortex.

Population. A concept in statistics that refers to all the individuals of a stated kind at a particular time and location in some real or imagined universe.

Positive correlation. A correlation in which high measures on one trait are associated with high measures on the second trait, or low values on one are associated with low values on another. Contrast with *negative correlation.*

Positive reinforcer. A reward; an event which increases the probability that the response it follows will be made again in similar circumstances.

Positive relationship. A relationship in which increases in the independent variable produce increases in the dependent variable. Contrast with *negative relationship.*

Positive skew. Describes a skewed distribution with the long tail toward the right, toward high numbers. Contrast with *negative skew.*

Positive transfer. Process in which learning of one skill aids in the learning of a second. Contrast with *negative transfer.*

Postconventional morality. A conception of morality which sees rules first as being decided upon, and sometimes changed, through the consensus of members of a particular society; and then as instruments of certain universal principles, such as justice. See *conventional morality* and *preconventional morality.*

Posthypnotic suggestion. A suggestion given to a hypnotized person by the hypnotist that he or she perform a prescribed act later when in the waking state.

Postsynaptic neuron. In synaptic transmission, the receiving neuron. Contrast with *presynaptic neuron.*

Posttraumatic stress disorder. An anxiety disorder following in the aftermath of a traumatic event outside the range of usual human experience. The individual has intrusive recollections and recurrent dreams of the event, feels estranged from others and has lost interest in ongoing activities, is easily startled, and has trouble concentrating and sleeping.

Power-assertive discipline. Discipline based on physical punishment. Contrast with *love-oriented discipline.*

Pragmatics. The rules which govern the use of language by real people in real situations.

Preconventional morality. The first stage of moral development. Children obey rules in order to obtain approval and avoid punishment. See *conventional morality* and *postconventional morality.*

Predictive validity. The extent to which scores on a test can predict performance on some later task.

Prefrontal association cortex. Large area of frontal cerebral cortex that is neither sensory nor motor in function and is often assumed to serve an associative purpose.

Premise of equipotentiality. The false assumption that associations are formed with equal ease between any and all stimuli or between any and all stimuli and responses. Contrast with *principle of preparedness.*

Preoperational stage. In Piaget's theory of cognitive development, the stage extending from age two to seven years during which children acquire representational skills—mental imagery, language, drawing—and come to understand identity constancy. They focus on the striking states and conditions of objects and events, ignoring others, and cannot manipulate information logically.

Preparedness, principle of. The theory that the biological makeup of the organism predisposes it to form readily associations between certain events or between certain responses and their consequences. Contrast with *premise of equipotentiality.*

Presynaptic neuron. In synaptic transmission, the transmitting neuron. Contrast with *postsynaptic neuron.*

Prevalence. In epidemiology, the percent of a population that has a given disorder at some particular time.

Prevention, primary. A public health term denoting procedures designed to *prevent* the development of disorder in vulnerable populations. **Secondary,** a public health term for the early diagnosis of disorder in an effort to shorten its duration and impact. **Tertiary,** a public health term denoting efforts to reduce the difficulties and long-term consequences of having a disorder.

Primacy effect. In memory, a tendency to remember first-learned things best. Contrast with *recency effect.*

Primary circular reactions. In Piaget's theory, the movements repeated for pleasure by one- to four-month-olds. The repetition prolongs, refines, and extends their simple reflexes and motor acts. Called primary because movements involve only the infant's body.

Primary color. See *physical primary color, psychological primary colors.*

Primary cues. Cues to depth or distance derived from the functioning of the visual system. See *accommodation, convergence,* and *retinal disparity.*

Primary drive. An unlearned biological motive. Contrast with *acquired drive.*

Primary mental abilities. Thurstone's subdivision of Spearman's general factor into the primary abilities of spatial perceptions, perceptual speed, verbal comprehension, numerical ability, memory, word fluency, and reasoning.

Primary motive. See *primary drive.*

Primary motor cortex. Areas of the cerebral cortex most closely connected to the muscles, in number of intervening synapses. Contrast with *secondary motor cortex, primary sensory cortex,* and *secondary sensory cortex.*

Primary process. In Freudian theory, means of the id to secure immediate and direct satisfaction of an instinctual wish, making no sharp distinction between imagination and reality. A wish-fulfilling dream is a primary process. Contrast with *secondary process.*

Primary projection area. An area in the brain to which the neural effects of stimulation are conducted (projected) directly.

Primary reinforcement. Reinforcement which depends little or not at all on previous learning. Contrast with *secondary reinforcement.*

Primary reinforcer. Any stimulus or event which is innately reinforcing because of its biological significance to the organism, such as food, water, sex, and termination of pain.

Primary reward. See *primary reinforcement.*

Primary sensory cortex. Areas of the cerebral cortex most directly connected to the receptors, in number of intervening synapses. Contrast with *secondary sensory cortex, primary motor cortex,* and *secondary motor cortex.*

Primary taste qualities. Salty, sweet, sour, and bitter.

Prisoner's dilemma. A game involving two people that permits the study of cooperation and competition.

Proactive inhibition. Process whereby earlier learning interferes with the learning and later recall of new material.

Proband. In genetic studies, the family member who originally bears the trait or diagnosis in which the investigator is interested.

Process schizophrenia. See *schizophrenia, process.*

Production deficiency. In studies of verbal mediation, the failure of children to use labels of objects to facilitate performance.

Progestin. One of several female sex hormones, secreted by the ovaries; they prepare the uterine lining for pregnancy and the breasts for lactation.

Programmed instruction. The presentation of materials to be learned in carefully planned sequences, often with the aid of a computer.

Project Head Start. A national preschool educational, social, and health intervention program for economically disadvantaged children.

Projection. Defense mechanism in which individuals unwittingly attribute their own usually undesirable traits to others.

Projective test of personality. Test allowing relatively free responding to suggestive material, on the assumption that interpretations will reveal important aspects of personality. Contrast with *objective test of personality.*

Prototype. The standard or ideal exemplar of a concept.

Proximal stimulation. The effect of a potential stimulus or distal stimulus on the receptors.

Proximodistal sequence. A pattern of development that proceeds from near the trunk outward to the extremities.

Psilocybin. A psychedelic drug extracted from the mushroom *Psilocybe mexicana.*

Psychedelic drug. A hallucinogen perceived as providing a "mind-expanding" experience.

Psychoanalysis. The therapeutic methods developed by Freud and his followers.

Psychogenic amnesia. A dissociative disorder in which the individual is suddenly unable to recall personal information so extensive that the loss cannot be explained by ordinary forgetfulness.

Psychogenic fugue. A dissociative disorder in which the person, with all personal memory gone, suddenly moves from home to a new location and establishes a new identity, often more gregarious than before.

Psycholinguistics. The study of the psychological aspects of language and its acquisition.

Psychological primary colors. Red, green, blue, and yellow, hues that seem pure and untinged by neighbors in the spectrum. Contrast with *physical primary color.*

Psychological reactance. The tendency of individuals to assert their freedom of choice when someone threatens to control their options.

Psychometrics. The techniques and theories of mental measurement.

Psychomotor epilepsy. Form of epilepsy in which the individual loses contact with the surroundings but appears conscious and engages in confused, repetitive acts.

Psychoneurosis. Behavior pathology (DSM-II) in which anxiety always plays a part. Symptoms in addition to anxiety are the more specific ones of hysteria, phobias, and other neuroses.

Psychopathology. (1) The systematic study of mental disorders. (2) Disordered behavior and psychological functioning as in a mental disorder.

Psychopathy. Antisocial activity without evident feelings of anxiety and guilt. Psychopathic personalities are constantly in conflict with the law, have no loyalty or allegiance to others, and are markedly selfish and motivated by personal gain. See *antisocial personality.*

Psychophysics. The procedures used in the study of the relationships between physical stimulation and psychological judgment. Also the science resulting from such study.

Psychophysiological disorder. See *psychosomatic disorder.*

Psychosexual development. See *psychosexual stages.*

Psychosexual disorders. A DSM-III category of disorders grouping together all those having to do with psychosexual functioning: gender identity disorders; paraphilias—fetishism, transvestism, exhibitionism, voyeurism, sexual masochism, sadism; psychosexual dysfunctions—inhibited female orgasm, inhibited male orgasm, premature ejaculation, dyspareunia, vaginismus; and ego-dystonic homosexuality.

Psychosexual stages. In psychoanalytic theory, stages of development—oral, anal, phallic, latency period, and genital. Each stage has a focal bodily point for stimulation (e.g., in the oral stage the mouth plays a central role) and specific external objects for sexual attachment.

Psychosis. A general term for severe mental disorders adversely affecting mental functioning and social competence. In most psychoses there is (*a*) loss of contact with reality, (*b*) extended withdrawal from social relationships, (c) marked deviance in emotional expression, (d) severely disordered thought, and (e) pervasive regressive behavior.

Psychosocial retardation. Mental retardation for which no organic cause has been identified, usually of mild degree and prevailing in lower socioeconomic classes.

Psychosomatic disorder. Physical disorder which is precipitated or aggravated by emotional stress and other psychological factors. Also called psychophysiological disorder.

Psychosomatic medicine. The branch of medicine concerned with the study of psychosomatic disorders.

Psychosurgery. Brain surgery performed as treatment of mental disorder.

Psychotherapy. The treatment of mental and emotional disorders by psychological methods such as direction, suggestion, reconstruction, persuasion, and counseling.

Psychotomimetic drug. Drug which induces psychoticlike symptoms and behavior. The most important is LSD.

PTC. Phenylthiocarbamide, a substance to which some individuals are "taste blind."

Puberty. The time of transition from sexual immaturity to maturity.

Puberty praecox. Early onset of puberty as a result of a glandular disturbance.

Punishment. The application of painful or discomforting stimulus in order to decrease the probability that the undesirable behavior it follows will persist.

Punitive technique. In the moral training of children, discipline which emphasizes the personal consequences of breaking rules.

Pupil. The opening surrounded by the iris through which light enters the eye.

Purkinje phenomenon. The shift in the relative brightness of colors that occurs at twilight with the shift from rod to cone vision.

Purkinje shift. The *Purkinje phenomenon.*

Q

Quantum. A very small, fast-moving particle—the unit—of electromagnetic energy.

R

r. The symbol for the Pearson product-moment *correlation coefficient.*

R. The symbol for the rank-difference *correlation coefficient.*

Race. A large division of humankind distinguished by common ancestry and by the greater frequency of a collection of inherited bodily traits than is found in other groups.

Racist. A person having a constellation of derogatory beliefs about race: (a) that race is the primary determiner of negative psychological traits; (b) that members of a particular race do not vary from one another; and (c) that some races are biologically superior to others and thus dominant.

Random sample. A sample chosen so that every individual and every combination of individuals in the population stand an equal chance of being selected.

Range. The measure of variability indicated by the distance between the highest and lowest scores in a distribution.

Rapid eye movements. See *REM.*

Rational-construct method. A method for developing personality inventories or tests in which the test developer initially defines the construct represented by his or her test and then creates items reflecting behavior fitting that definition.

Rational-emotive therapy. A form of therapy originated by Albert Ellis, in which the therapeutic goal is the modification of the patient's inappropriate thoughts about the self and his or her relations with others.

Rationalization. Providing oneself with "good" reasons for one's undesirable behavior or position in life.

Reactance. The tendency of people to assert their freedom when others threaten to control them.

Reaction formation. Engaging in behavior that is the opposite of strong and unacceptable unconscious wishes in order to protect against them.

Reaction time. The interval between the onset of a stimulus and the beginning of the individual's response.

Reactive disorder. Disorder marked by acute distress in reaction to specific, traumatizing life events, such as bereavement, separation, natural disasters, and catastrophes.

Reactive effects of measurement. The unwanted side effects of psychological investigations, for example, the "guinea pig" effect produced in many participants in experiments.

Reality principle. In Freudian theory, the principle that the ego becomes aware of and adapts to the realities of life situations, thereby inhibiting or delaying the expression of the id's impulses or drives. Contrast with *pleasure principle.*

Reality testing. In Freudian theory, the exploratory probing by which the young person learns about the environment.

Recall test. A test in which the individual, provided with a cue or sometimes nothing more than request to do so, must remember something learned earlier.

Recency effect. In memory, the tendency to remember best the things learned last in a list. Contrast with *primacy effect.*

Receptor. A cell or group of cells which receives stimulation.

Receptor site. Location on a postsynaptic neuron that receives a neurotransmitter molecule in synaptic transmission.

Recessive gene. A gene which will not express itself in a trait or appearance unless paired with another recessive gene.

Reciprocal inhibition. In Wolpe's theory, weakening anxiety to certain stimuli by providing a means of responding that inhibits anxiety. See *systemaic desentization.*

Reciprocal innervation. The neural arrangement whereby one of a pair of antagonistic muscles relaxes as the other contracts.

Recoding. The reorganization of perceptual or other materials that makes it possible to deal with a collection of units as a single item.

Recognition test. An experimental procedure in which participants first see a collection of materials and then attempt to pick them from a list containing some new items.

Recoil reaction. The second stage of the disaster syndrome in which there is a growing awareness of the traumatic event, with an attendant sense of depression, helplessness, and anger.

Reference group. In social psychology, a group which provides an individual with attitudinal and behavioral standards.

Reflex. A relatively simple, rapid, and automatic unlearned response to a stimulus.

Reflex arc. A pathway which extends from a receptor to an effector and is followed by a neural impulse to produce a reflex.

Reflex schemas. In Piaget's theory, the reflex patterns of action, such as sucking and grasping, which are practiced by the infant from birth to one month.

Reflex smiling. See entry under *smiling.*

Refractory period. The three- or four-millisecond interval immediately following a nerve impulse in which the neuron is first absolutely and then relatively incapable of generating another impulse.

Regression. A return to an earlier, simpler, and less mature form of behavior as a consequence of stress, frustration, and failure.

Regression to the mean. A statistical concept referring to the fact that the measurement predicted from another on the basis of a correlation is closer to the mean and less extreme than the predictor measurement.

Reinforcement. Any process which increases the probability of occurrence of a response that is being learned.

Reinforcement theory of smiling. The theory that babies learn to smile because they are rewarded for it.

Relative refractory period. A brief period following stimulation of a nerve or muscle during which it is unresponsive to all but a very strong stimulus.

Relative size. A seconday cue to distance in which an object producing a smaller retinal image is seen as farther away than an object that is known to be of the same size but produces a larger retinal image.

Releaser. An ethological term to designate a stimulus which initiates ("releases") an instinctive behavioral cycle.

Reliability. The extent to which a measuring instrument yields consistent results at each time the same individual is tested. Contrast with *validity.*

Reliability of diagnosis. The dependability of psychiatric diagnosis; the extent to which separate diagnoses of the same individual made by two or more clinicians agree with one another.

REM (rapid eye movement). Eye movements which occur during sleep and usually denote dreaming. The movements of the eyeball generate electrical activity, which can be recorded by attaching electrodes near the eye.

Replication. The repetition of an experiment under the identical conditions

Representative sample. A sample whose characteristics match those of the population.

Representativeness. In attribution theory, an error in which an individual assigns another person to a particular group because that person has the characteristics

thought, often mistakenly, to be typical of the group. See *stereotype.*

Repression. The exclusion from consciousness of anxiety-provoking impulses and traumatic experiences, by a process of which the individual is not directly aware.

Resistance. In psychoanalytic therapy, the common tendency of a patient to use many ruses in order to avoid unpleasant topics.

Response bias. A redisposition to respond in a particular way, for example, (a) to answer "false" to items on a personality test, or (b) to turn left at a choice point in a maze.

Response set. A tendency (set) on the part of an individual to respond to test questions in characteristic ways without regard to content of the question.

Resting potential. The electric charge between the inside and outside of a neuron when in its resting state. Usually about −70 millivolts.

Retention. The ability to recall material learned earlier.

Retention curve. A graph depicting the retention over time of previously learned material.

Reticular activating system. The fibers and nuclei making up the reticular formation of the brainstem, originating near the spinal cord and extending to the thalamus; when stimulated, activates the entire nervous system, providing attention, wakefulness, and alertness and making perceptual associations.

Reticular formation. The innermost portion of the brainstem, which appears reticulated or netted under the microscope, for it consists of a network of delicate myelinated fibers and clumps of cell bodies and unmyelinated fibers.

Retina. The light-sensitive inner layer of the eye; it contains the receptors (rods and cones) for vision.

Retinal disparity. The slight difference in images of the same object received by the two eyes. Provides a very sensitive primary cue to depth.

Retrieval. The process of calling an item up from memory.

Retroactive inhibition. The interference with retenton by learning interpolated between the original learning and attempted recall of it.

Retrograde amnesia. Forgetting of events immediately preceding some injury or other traumatic experience.

Retrospective report. Recollection by an individual of a past event.

Return to baseline. See *ABAB design.*

Reversibility. In Piaget's theory, the ability to think of a manipulation that will reverse a sequence of events and restore the original condition; mentally returning a quantity to its original state to verify sameness. A concrete operation.

Revolving door. Pattern of release of mental patients, only for them soon to be readmitted again.

Reward training. A form of operant conditioning employing a positive reinforcer.

Rhodopsin. A light-sensitive substance found in the rods of the retina.

Risk population. In psychopathology, a group which has a higher probability of developing a mental disorder than the general population.

Risky shift. The tendency for people in groups to take bigger risks in collective decision making than they would as individuals.

RNA (ribonucleic acid). Complex molecules which are believed to be the "enforcers" of the genetic code by directing the formation of enzymes out of amino acids found in the cell.

ROC (receiver-operating characteristic) curve. In signal detection research, a function in which the probability of a "hit" is plotted against the probability of a "false alarm."

Rod. Visual receptor of the retina extremely sensitive to low intensities of light and thus employed in twilight and night vision; but rods are insensitive to hue. Contrast with *cone.*

Rod-cone break. In the curve of dark adaptation, the sudden increase in sensitivity (drop in the curve) that occurs after a few minutes, reflecting the transition from primarily cone vision to primarily rod vision.

Role. The behavior expected of an individual by reason of his or her social situation or membership in a particular group.

Role playing. Acting out the behavior an individual believes is expected of a certain role, in a hypothetical and staged situation.

Rorschach test. A projective test of personality in which the individual is asked to interpret freely the symmetrical inkblots on ten cards, shown one at a time.

Rote learning. Learning of verbal sequences, with little attention to meaning.

Round window. The membrane-covered

aperture located just below the oval window and separating the tympanic canal of the cochlea from the middle ear. It absorbs the pressure waves coming from the stapes via the fluid in the vestibular and tympanic canals.

S

Saccule. A fluid-filled sac of the vestibule of the inner ear.

Sample. A group from some population selected for special study; should be representative of that population.

Sampling distribution of differences. A distribution of the differences between means of each pair of sample groups that would be obtained were a very large number of pairs of sample groups drawn and tested.

Sampling distribution of the mean. A distribution of means that would be obtained were a very large number of samples of the same size selected, their means determined, and these means cast into a frequency distribution.

Saturation. The "richness" or purity of a color; the dimension from gray or absence of color to full color.

Savings method (relearning method). An experimental procedure for studying retention in which the learner relearns materials previouly learned, and the measure is the decrease in errors and in time or number of trials needed for relearning as compared with original learning.

Scapegoating. The displacement of hostility by directing it against the innocent, sometimes as anger toward a particular person, but more often as prejudice toward all members of a minority group. See *displacement*.

Scatter diagram. A graphic representation of a correlation.

Scatter plot. See *scatter diagram*.

Schedule of reinforcement. The specific pattern of partial reinforcement.

Schema. A theoretical structure in memory that organizes information about some experience, event, or concept.

Scheme. In Piaget's theory, the aspect of a capacity for knowing the world that is always constant, such as the infant's pattern of physical action in relation to an object; later, forming images of objects; still later, formulating complex ideas. Schemes are organized thought processes.

Schizoaffective disorder. A diagnosis to be applied when the clinician cannot determine whether the patient has an affective disorder or either schizophreniform disorder or schizophrenia.

Schizoid personality. Individuals with a schizoid personality disorder are cold, aloof, and indifferent to praise, criticism, and the feelings of others. Self-absorbed, daydreaming "loners," with solitary interests and hobbies, they have one or two close friends at the most.

Schizophrenia. A group of disorders marked by major dysfunctions of thinking, emotion, and behavior. Disturbances in thinking take the form of illogicality, numerous faulty associative interferences, and delusional beliefs. Perception is also disturbed, with hallucinations—auditory, visual, and tactile—common. Affects is flattened or extremely labile and often inappropriate. Motor behavior can be faulty and bizarre. Social relationships are minimal; withdrawal from others is the more characteristic pattern.

Schizophrenia, catatonic type. A form of schizophrenia in which the individual holds unusual and rigid postures for long periods or in great agitation makes many purposeless as well as stereotyped, repetitive movements.

Schizophrenia, childhood. A DSM-II form of psychosis in childhood occurring between five and eleven years of age, in which the chief disturbances are autistic withdrawal, an inability to establish affective contact with other people, and gross immaturity.

Schizophrenia, disorganized (hebephrenic) type. A form of schizophrenia in which the symptoms are bizarre ideas, silliness, and regression.

Schizophrenia, paranoid type. A form of schizophrenia in which the major symptom is a set of delusions, usually of persecution.

Schizophrenia, process. Schizophrenia which begins its long, insidious onset early, in the teens or early twenties of a poorly integrated individual. The prognosis is usually unfavorable.

Schizophrenia, reactive. Schizophrenia which is later and sudden in onset in a fairly well-adapted individual. The prognosis is usually favorable.

Schizophrenia, simple. A DSM-II form of schizophrenia in which the principal symptoms are apathy, withdrawal, and indifference to the world.

Schizophrenic, good premorbid. A term used to denote a schizophrenic patient whose life course before the disorder was socially, sexually, and economically adequate. In these patients breakdown usually follows an evident stress. Recovery prospects are good. Such conditions are also called *reactive*.

Schizophrenic, poor premorbid. A term used to denote a schizophrenic patient whose life course before the disorder was socially, sexually, and economically inadequate. In these patients the disorder often takes a chronic course. Such conditions are also called *process*.

Schizophreniform disorder. Disorder in which the symptoms are those of schizophrenia—emotional turmoil, fear, confusion, and particularly vivid hallucinations are evident—but which lasts less than six months and more than two weeks. It does not appear to be brought on by stress.

Schizotypal personality. The individuals with a schizotypal personality disorder are likely to believe in magical thinking, clairvoyance, and telepathy and have recurrent illusions. They may be digressive and overelaborate in their conversation and are usually socially isolated.

Scotopic vision. Vision in dim light with dark-adapted eyes; dependent on the rods.

Script. Knowledge of the structure of events that allows the individual to interpret happenings and to fill in unobservable gaps.

Secondary circular reaction. In Piaget's theory, the infant's repetition of an action, beginning at about four months of age, because something or someone has responded to the action in a way that pleases the child. The infant is preoccupied with the effects of its movements on the environment.

Secondary cues to distance. Cues which derive from features of the environment. See *linear perspective, aerial perspective, interposition, gradient of texture*, and *patterns of light and shade*.

Secondary motive. A motive learned through experience; a stimulus which becomes a motive through association with a *primary drive*.

Secondary motor cortex. Areas of the cerebral cortex indirectly connected to the muscles, through a number of intervening synapses. Contrast with *primary motor cortex, primary sensory cortex*, and *secondary sensory cortex*.

Secondary process. In Freudian theory, behavior which is reality-oriented and under the control of the ego. Contrast with *primary process.*

Secondary reinforcer. A stimulus which becomes a reinforcer through association with a reinforcing stimulus.

Secondary sensory cortex. Areas of the cerebral cortex indirectly connected to the receptors, through a number of intervening synapses. Contrast with *primary sensory cortex, primary motor cortex,* and *secondary motor cortex.*

Secular trend. Changes in patterns of bodily development or populations over an extended period of time.

Sedative. A drug which slows bodily activities, relaxing muscles and inhibiting thinking processes; used to allay irritability, nervousness, and distress, to induce relaxation and sleep.

Selective breeding. The method of investigating genetic factors in which subjects with specified characteristics are mated so that the transmission of these characteristics to the offspring can be studied.

Selective social smiling. See entry under *smiling.*

Self-actualization. The highest order of need in Maslow's hierarchy; the desire for self-fulfillment and realization of one's potential.

Self-concept. The individual's awareness of his or her identity as a person, starting with the infant's discovery of bodily parts and becoming eventually an encompassing, organized perception of the person's thoughts, feelings, attitudes, values, and goals.

Self-fulfilling prophecy. The principle that an expectation, belief, or prediction by a participant that an event will happen works toward fulfillment of the expected.

Self-perception (theory). The hypothesis that we continue to learn about ourselves by observing our own behavior and attempting to explain it.

Self-presentation. A general term to cover the many ways in which people attempt to gain influence, by giving the impression that they are particular kinds of individuals.

Self-promotion. Attempts of the person with little power to gain power and influence by making himself or herself appear competent.

Self-promotor's paradox. The fact that claims of competence are usually put forth by the incompetent. Hence expressions intended to convey an impression of competence are likely to be discounted.

Self-reflexive character of language. The power which true language has to be about itself.

Self-report. A method of behavioral assessment in which the individual monitors and reports on his or her own behavior.

Self-stimulation. Electrical stimulation of a "pleasure center" of the brain by means of an implanted electrode, administered by the animal's pressing a pedal.

Self-verification. Seeking feedback from others that confirms what we believe about ourselves.

Semantic differential. A rating scale by which a concept is located in one of seven positions between polar adjectives—good–bad, strong–weak, and active–passive, for example. These ratings yield measures of connotative meaning.

Semantic memory. Organized knowledge of the world, including knowledge of language and how it is used. Contrast with *episodic memory.*

Semantics. The study of the meaning of words.

Semicircular canals. Three curved and tubular fluid-filled canals of the inner ear, perpendicular to one another and registering three planes; they sense the turning of the head and its coming to rest.

Sensation level. The intensity of sensory experience.

Sensorimotor stage. In Piaget's developmental theory of intelligence, the period extending from birth to two years, during which time the child knows the world through sensory perceptions and motor actions but finally comes to realize that objects exist independently of his or her perceptions.

Sensory aphasia. See *aphasia, receptive.*

Sensory memory. Retention of sights and sounds as sense impressions, lasting a bare second or so. See *echoic memory* and *iconic memory.*

Sensory-neural deafness. Deafness caused by damage to the structures of the inner ear or auditory nerve. Contrast with *conduction deafness.*

Sensory neuron. Neuron which is in contact with receptors and carries messages to the central nervous system. An *afferent neuron.*

Separation anxiety. Crying, fretting, and discomfort reflective of a child's unhappiness when separated from an adult (typically a parent) to whom he or she is attached.

Serial position function. A graph showing that the ease with which each item in a serial list is learned depends on its position.

Serial rote learning. Learning lists of usually unrelated materials that must be committed to memory mechanically.

Set. An inclination to respond in a particular way. Also *mental set.*

Set point. The fairly constant level at which hypothalamic centers maintain an individual's weight over a long period of time.

Sex-linked trait. A trait which is determined by a gene transmitted on the sex chromosome.

Sex-role typing. The reinforcement and emphasizing of stereotypic behavior and attitudes assumed to be characteristic of males and females.

Sexual identification. Adopting interests, attitudes, and behavior which are perceived as appropriate for one's own sex.

Shadowing. A procedure in which a subject repeats one of two messages as it is heard. This assures that the individual attends to the shadowed message, although interest is in the extent to which the unshadowed message is processed.

Shape constancy. The tendency for an object viewed from different angles, which distort the retinal images, to be perceived as having a constant shape.

Shaping. An operant conditioning technique in which initially all responses approximating the desired one are rewarded but then only ever-closer approximations of the desired response.

Shell shock. The dazed loss of self-command, memory, speech, sight, or other powers, formerly believed brought on by the shock of shells exploding in battle. So named by a British pathologist in World War I. Now explained as the cumulative emotional and psychological strain of warfare. See *combat exhaustion.*

Shock reaction. Initial phase of the disaster syndrome in which the individual is confused and unable to act, under the impact of the stunning event.

Short-term memory (STM). Memory which lasts for about fifteen to thirty seconds. Contrast with *sensory memory* and *long-term memory.*

Signal detection theory. A theory of the sensory and judgmental processes involved in psychophysical determinations. According to this theory, when people must report whether a signal is present or absent, they decide whether what they experience is background stimulation or an actual signal.

Significant difference. In statistics, a difference which is unlikely to have occurred by chance.

Significate. Piaget's term for an external object or some aspect of reality.

Signifier. Piaget's term for the internal or symbolic representation of an external object.

Simple cell. A single cell in the visual cortex that respond to simple stimuli like lines or edges registering in a very specific region of the retina and having a particular orientation. See *complex cell* and *hypercomplex cell.*

Simple schizophrenia. See *schizophrenia, simple.*

Simultaneous contrast. The tendency for adjacent complementary colors to take on added saturation at the border between them.

Size constancy. The tendency for objects to be seen as their correct size from different distances.

Skewed curve. An asymmetrical frequency distribution in which the range of scores on one side of the mode is greater than on the other.

Skin map. A diagram showing the spots on the skin that are sensitive to cold, warmth, touch, etc.

Skinner box. A device for the study of operant conditioning: (*a*) a bar-pressing apparatus used with rats or (*b*) a key-pecking apparatus used with pigeons.

Slow-to-warm-up child. A child whose temperament it is to be wary of new situations, to be somewhat variable in biological functions, and to have a slightly negative mood.

Small-*N* design. An experimental design devised for use with a small number (*N*) of participants. Whereas traditional experimental designs subject some individuals to the experimental treatment and withhold it from others, all subjects receive the experimental treatment in small-*N* designs.

Smiling, nonselective social. Smiling of the two- to eight-week-old infant in response to a variety of visual social stimuli, particularly the human face.

Smiling, selective social. The third phase of smiling in the human infant at about five or six months of age, in response to familiar faces.

Smiling, spontaneous or reflex. The first stage of smiling, in the earliest weeks of life in the human infant, in which smiles are elicited without appropriate stimuli, perhaps even to stomach disturbances.

Social class. A grouping of people according to social status, determined by income, nature of occupation, area of residence, family and moral standing, and so on. Often conceived as ranging from upper-upper to lower-lower.

Social cognition. The individual's understanding of the social world, of other people, and of personal relations with them.

Social-comparison theory. A social psychological theory asserting that an individual verifies socially derived knowledge by comparing his or her opinions with those of others.

Social competence. A general term for the social, vocational, and sexual adaptation patterns of individuals. Everyday effectiveness in dealing with the environment.

Social-desirability set. A response style in which subjects respond to items in personality tests according to the social approval their answers might elicit.

Social-drift hypothesis. A sociological hypothesis which assumes the relation of lower-class social status to the incidence of psychopathology to be correlational but not causative. People, such as schizophrenics, migrate to the slums because of their inability to cope in a complex society.

Social environment. A general concept in social psychology referring to the many important social factors in the environment.

Social-exchange theory. The concept that we react to another person in terms of the rewards and costs of the encounter.

Social influence. The effect of societies, other people, or both on individuals.

Social-learning theory. The view that much of personality is formed through observation and imitation of others. This theory, identified with Bandura, emphasizes modeling and observational learning.

Social-learning therapy. The utilization of learning principles and a controlled physical and social environment to enhance the social adaptation of persons.

Social psychology. The study of the effects of social organizations and groups on individual behavior.

Social-skills training. A form of therapy designed to train patients in more adequate ways of responding to other people and to environmental demands.

Socialization. The child's acquisition through experience of the values and habits of the culture.

Sociobiology. A controversial branch of biology which attributes social behavior to genetic predispositions.

Sociodramatic play. Play in which children, beginning at about age three, assume roles and act out scenarios about social situations—mother and baby, house, doctor and patient, teacher, fire, death. By age five plots are elaborate.

Sociopathic personality. See *antisocial personality.*

Somatic motor fibers. Axons which carry commands from the central nervous system to the muscles attached to bones; efferent neurons.

Somatic nervous system. All the peripheral nerve structures not in the autonomic system; the sensory fibers serving the sensory receptors and the motor fibers serving skeletal muscles.

Somatic sensory fibers. Axons which carry information from the receptors to the central nervous system; afferent neurons.

Somatic therapy. The treatment of mental and emotional disorders by physical methods acting on bodily processes, e.g., *electroconvulsive shock therapy, psychosurgery,* and drugs.

Somatization disorder. Disorder in which the person complains of many recurrent physical symptoms and continually seeks medical care. Physicians, however, cannot find sufficient physiological explanation for the symptoms.

Somatoform disorders. Disorders with physical symptoms for which there is no evident accompanying condition, strengthening the assumption that psychological conflict underlies them. Includes somatization disorder and conversion disorder.

Somatotonia. In Sheldon's system, the personality associated with mesomorphy. The person tends to engage in vigorous muscular action rather than thought and is extroverted.

Somatotype. A scheme for classifying individuals by physique, with the assumption that psychological characteristics are associated with body type.

Sone. A subjective unit of loudness equal to that, in the judgment of a group of listeners, of a 1000-Hz reference sound having an intensity of 40 decibels. Contrast with *decibel.*

Sound spectrograph. An electronic device which records changes in intensity-frequency patterns of sounds as a function of time.

Source trait. In Raymond Cattell's theory of personality, an underlying basic trait which is expressed in a number of less fundamental *surface traits.*

Spaced (distributed) practice. Practice with relatively long pauses between trials. Contrast with *massed practice.*

Span of short-term memory. The number of items which can be remembered following a single, brief presentation. The span tends to be about seven with a range from five to nine.

Spatial summation. The adding together of two or more subthreshold stimuli, applied to different parts on a neuron, to produce a neurve impulse when none of the stimuli alone is strong enough.

Species-specific behavior. Patterns of response which are characteristic of members of a given species under the same or makedly similar conditions.

Specific energies of nerves. Johannes Mueller's law that afferent nerve fibers, being connected to specific receptors, can respond only to certain types of stimulation and can yield only certain types of experience.

Specific factor. In the factor analysis of intelligence, a skill which is applied when taking a particular kind of test. Contrast with *general factor.*

Spectrum. The range of physical stimuli to which a receptor responds. Most often used in connection with the full range of lengths of light waves.

Spinal cord. The nervous tissue within the vertebral column.

Spinal nerves. Thirty-one pairs of peripheral nerves extending from spaces between the vertebrae of the spinal column to various parts of the body.

Spinal reflex. A complete reflex circuit which passes through the spinal cord but not directly through a higher center.

Split brain. A brain in which the two hemispheres are no longer joined together because the corpus callosum has been cut, thus separating their functionings.

Split-half method. A method of establishing reliability of a test by comparing a person's performance on two halves of it, such as on all odd- and all even-numbered items.

Spontaneous or reflex smiling. See entry under *smiling.*

Spontaneous recovery. Reappearance of an extinguished conditioned response after a lapse of time.

Stabilized image. An image on the retina presented in a way that prevents the small movements of *physiological nystagmus* from affecting it.

Stage of exhaustion. In the general adaptation syndrome, the third stage, marked by physical deterioration and death.

Stage of recall. The third stage of the disaster syndrome in which the traumatic event is recalled and reviewed with tenseness and restlessness. Or the event is repressed. High levels of anxiety and distress may continue even after the need for renewal and rehabilitation begins to dominate the individual's thinking.

Stage of resistance. In the general adaptation syndrome, the second stage, in which the organism's physiological resources are restored after the effects of stress.

Stages of memory. The stages assumed by the information-processing approach: *sensory memory, short-term memory,* and *long-term memory.*

Standard deviation. The most commonly used measure of the dispersion or variability of a distribution.

Standard error of the difference. The standard deviation of a sampling distribution of differences between the means of a large number of pairs of samples all selected in the same way.

Standard error of the mean. The standard deviation of a sampling distribution of means that would be obtained in theory from a large number of samples all selected (or treated) in the same way.

Standardization. In test construction, the process of trying the test out on a group representative of the people for whom the test is meant, in order to establish appropriateness of items and standard methods of scoring and interpretation.

Standardization sample. A sample of persons used to pretest the adequacy of a test or tests and to establish norms for test performance.

Stanford-Binet tests. The test originally created by Alfred Binet and revised for use in the United States at Stanford University, by Lewis Terman and Maude Merrill. One of the most frequently used tests for children.

Stapes. Third of the three bones of the middle ear that transmit sound vibrations from the eardrum to the inner ear; stirrup-shaped and attached to the oval window. See *incus* and *malleus.*

State-dependent learning. The phenomenon that an individual's memory for learning that took place in a special condition (drunk) is greater when the individual is again in that state than when in the ordinary condition (sober).

Statistical inference. Drawing conclusions about populations from data obtained from samples.

Statistical significance. The extent to which the data obtained from studies permit rejection of (most commonly) the null hypothesis that the differences between groups were obtained by chance. Expressed in terms of the probability that the obtained results would occur were the null hypothesis true. See *level of confidence.*

Stereotype. Expectations and opinions about large groups of people, allowing the persons holding them to disregard individuality. A stereotype is overly concrete, specific, and resistant to disconfirming evidence.

Stimulant. A drug which steps up thought processes and motor activity, or some other vital process; it reduces fatigue, allowing the individual to stay awake for an extended period of time.

Stimulation deafness. Deafness produced by long-term exposure to high-intensity auditory stimulation. Also called boilermaker's deafness.

Stimulus. In general, any antecedent condition or "cause" of behavior. More specifically, physical energy causing physiological activity in a sense organ.

Stimulus generalization. See *generalization.*

Stimulus substitution. A theory of classical conditioning according to which the CS comes to serve as a substitute for the US.

Storage. Putting materials into memory. Some accounts refer to short-term and long-term storage, depending on the stage of memory involved.

Strabismus. Inability of one eye to focus on a spot with the other, usually because of imbalance in the eye muscles.

Stranger anxiety. A fear of strangers which may appear from about eight to twelve months of age in the human infant.

Stress. A general term which includes situations that threaten the adaptation of an organism; and the physiological and psychological responses of an individual to a threat to his or her integrity.

Stress-inoculation therapy. Donald Meichenbaum's cognitive therapy consisting of three phases: educational phase, patients learn about their emotional and stress reactions; rehearsal phase, patients are usually given relaxation training and practice four stages of positive coping statements to counteract their maladaptive thoughts, feelings, and behavior; application phase, patients apply their coping statements to handle graduated stressful conditions in the therapist's office.

Stressor. A difficult situation which strains the individual's physiological or psychological capacities. See *background stressor, cataclysmic event,* and *personal stressor.*

Structuralism. A school of psychology which saw the task of psychology as attempting to understand the structure of the mind. The major method of structuralism was introspection. Mind was reduced by this school to a set of sensory elements.

Subjective organization. The organization of materials to be remembered that a person creates for himself or herself as opposed to an organization imposed by the nature of materials.

Sublimation. Conversions of one's unacceptable impulses into socially acceptable outlets. A *defense mechanism.*

Substitute behavior. Any behavior which provides indirect or symbolic satisfaction of a need.

Subtractive mixture. Mixture of pigments, each of which absorbs some of the wavelengths reflected by the other pigments. Contrast with *additive mixture.*

Successive approximations. See *shaping.*

Summation. See *spatial summation* and *temporal summation.*

Superego. In Freudian theory, the portion of personality containing the parental and social standards internalized by the ego; the individual's conscience and ego-ideal or aspiration.

Superior colliculus. The foremost pair of bulges in the tectum of the midbrain; lower coordination center of the visual system.

Superstition. In operant conditioning, complex behavioral sequences brought on by presenting reinforcement at fixed intervals, whatever the bird happens to be doing.

Supplication. Attempts of the person with little power to gain more by claiming weakness and dependence.

Surface structure. In Noam Chomsky's theory, language as spoken or written. Surface structure is a transformation of materials in deep structure, the intended meaning, by a set of transformational rules which put it into a sentence in active voice or passive voice, into question or implied question form, or into some other sentence structure.

Surface trait. In Raymond Cattell's theory of personality, one of a cluster of manifest traits that seem to belong together in expressing an underlying *source trait.*

Surrogate mother. Substitute mother figure; also pseudomother, such as Harlow's cloth and wire mother-substitute forms.

Survival of the fittest. In evolutionary theory, the heightened probability that the best-adapted (fittest) variants of a species will survive and reproduce.

Symbiosis. The living together of two species on terms that are usually advantageous to both. Sometimes applied to pairs of individual members of the same species, including the human species.

Symbolic representation. Third stage in Jerome Bruner's theory of cognitive growth, beginning at age three, when children use language, and symbols in general, to process their experiences.

Sympathetic ganglia. Chains of clustered nerve cell bodies alongside the thoracic and lumbar spinal cord; they serve the sympathetic functions of the autonomic system.

Sympathetic nervous system. A division of the autonomic system concerned with emotional excitement. Prepares the organism for emergency and, in general, acts in opposition to the *parasympathetic system.*

Synapse. The very close but not touching connection between the axon terminals of one neuron and a dendrite or cell body of another.

Synaptic cleft. The extremely small space between presynaptic and postsynaptic neurons.

Synaptic transmission. The process whereby the neurotransmitter of one neuron crosses the synaptic gap and excites or inhibits an adjacent neuron.

Synaptic vesicle. Container for the neurotransmitter, located in the terminal button of an axon.

Syndrome. A pattern of symptoms characteristic of a disease or a disorder.

Synesthesia. Registration of a stimulus by both its own and by another sensory system.

Syntax. The rules by which words may be combined into phrases and sentences. Grammar is the most familiar example.

Systematic desensitization. A form of behavior therapy devised by Wolpe and based on the principle of counterconditioning. A person in a state of deep relaxation imagines threatening objects or situations in a hierarchy from least to most feared.

T

***t*-test.** A statistical test to determine whether a difference is significant.

Tardive dyskinesia. A muscular disturbance, often irreversible, of older patients who have taken phenothiazines for a long time. They grimace and smack their lips and have ticlike movements in their shoulders.

Taste bud. Flask-shaped mass, usually lying in the wall of a tongue papilla, made up of supporting cells and of taste cells which project short, hairlike processes into the pore of the structure.

TAT (Thematic Apperception Test). A projective test of personality, devised by Henry Murray, consisting of ambiguous pictures about which an individual is required to create stories.

Tay-Sachs disease. A disorder of metabolism transmitted as a recessive trait and causing mental retardation. It is confined for the most part to children of northeastern European Jewish ancestry.

Tectum. The roof of the midbrain consisting of superior and inferior colliculi.

Tegmentum. The medial portion of the midbrain, consisting for the most part of a dense feltwork of neurons, which are a section of the reticular formation.

Temperament. A very general aspect of personality typically associated with characteristic mood, level of activity, adaptability. Increasingly, a constitutional factor is thought to underlie it.

Temporal lobe. The part of the cerebral hemisphere lying in front of the occipital lobe; the most lateral of the four lobes.

Temporal summation. A form of summation in which two subthreshold stimuli occurring in rapid succession succeed in firing a neuron.

Temporary connection. Pavlov's expression for the conditioned connections between conditioned and unconditioned stimuli.

Terminal button. The responsive part of a neuron at the end of its axon. The terminal buttons store a neurotransmitter and discharge it upon arrival of a nerve impulse.

Tertiary circular reactions. In Piaget's theory, repeating actions, but modifying them slightly each time, to test the effect of the change, from the twelfth to eighteenth month. The "little scientist" begins "active experimentation" with his or her surroundings and finds out the consequences of actions.

Test-retest method. A method of establishing reliability in which the test is given twice to the same sample of persons.

Thalamus. A fairly large bilobed structure at midline within the cerebral hemispheres, each lobe consisting of collections of nuclei. The anterior and medial groups make up the center for the crude perception of pain and for the pleasantness and unpleasantness of sensations. The groups on the sides serve as the great relay station for optic and other somatic sensory paths to the cerebral cortex. Other nuclei help the reticular formation maintain wakefulness and concentration.

Therapeutic community. A form of therapy encompassing all ongoing activities and personnel of the hospital so that the patient's environment may contribute to the cure of mental illness.

Thought disorder. A symptom of schizophrenia: incoherence, loose associations, and concrete reasoning; neologisms and clang associations in speech.

Thoracicolumbar system. An anatomical term for the sympathetic nervous system.

Threshold. The point, statistically determined, at which a stimulus is just barely adequate to elicit a sensation (absolute threshold) or at which a stimulus is just enough greater in magnitude than another that a difference in intensity of sensation is just noticeable (difference theshold).

Timbre. The quality of sounds which enables us to tell one kind of sound from another when they are all of the same fundamental frequency.

Tip-of-the-tongue phenomenon. The temporary inability to call forth a word or name that the speaker is quite certain he or she knows.

Token economy. A therapy technique used in institutions or by the family in which rewards (tokens) are given for socially constructive behavior and can later be exchanged for material goods, services, and privileges.

Trait. An enduring attribute of a person that is manifested in a variety of situations.

Trait theory. A theory of personality that emphasizes traits as enduring and persistent aspects of the personality.

Tranquilizer. Drug designed to reduce anxiety and manifestations of psychosis.

Transactional model of development. A theoretical model which holds that the development of personal traits and behavior occurs through reciprocal actions between the individual and the environment over time.

Transfer of training. The process whereby learning one skill has an effect, beneficial or interfering, on learning another somewhat similar skill.

Transference. The close emotional attachment of the patient in psychoanalysis to the analyst.

Transference, positive. The patient's unconscious seeking to relive the past with a more satisfactory resolution than in childhood. **Negative,** hostility toward the analyst who will not allow the patient a positive transference.

Transference neurosis. A phenomenon encountered in psychoanalytic therapy in which the affect originally directed at another person (often a parent) is directed at the analyst.

Transformational rules. In Noam Chomsky's theory, the rules by which the intended meaning in deep structure is processed into a sentence of particular surface structure having one of several possible syntactical arrangements.

Transition stress. Stress created by conflict that occurs as children move from one stage of development to another. The conflict is between their perceptions of the demands of new situations and of their abilities to fulfill these demands.

Transmitter substance. See *neurotransmitter.*

Transvestite. A person who derives erotic satisfaction from cross-dressing, i.e., dressing as a member of the opposite sex.

Treatment milieu. The total physical and psychological qualities of an environment in which therapy occurs; usually applied to clinics and mental hospitals.

Trial and error learning. Complex operant or instrumental learning in which the organism selects the correct response in a particular situation by eliminating erroneous responses.

Trichromatic theory. The Young-Helmholtz theory of color vision which assumes that the elementary processes of three receptors account for it.

Trick vocabulary. The use of language, as by children (and probably birds), without respect to meaning.

Tricyclic. One of several antidepressant drugs—named for their molecular structure of three fused rings—which prevent the reuptake of norepinephrine and serotonin by limbic and hypothalamic presynaptic neurons, thereby prolonging their activity and elevating mood.

Trisomy 21. A condition of having three rather than two of the number 21 chromosome, the cause of Down syndrome.

Truncated distribution. A distribution which covers less than the complete range of scores through failure to obtain classes of observations that would fall at one extreme or the other.

Turner syndrome. A disorder of females in which the absence of an X chromosome keeps stature short and the breasts incompletely developed and brings sterility.

Two-factor theory. A theory of learning which assumes that feelings and attitudes are acquired through classical conditioning, and that learning what to do about them is acquired through operant conditioning. Avoidance is motivated by conditioned fear and reinforced by reduction of fear.

Type theory. In personality theory, any position that views persons as fitting into categories rather than as having many dimensions.

Type A behavior. The behavior of the impatient, hard-driving, aggressive individual who is susceptible to heart disease.

Type B behavior. The patient, relaxed, unaggressive reactions of someone who does not have Type A behavior and who is not as susceptible to heart disease.

U

Unconditioned response. A response elicited by the US without special training.

Unconditioned stimulus. A stimulus which produces a consistent response (UR) at the onset of training.

Unconscious. A general term for classes of activities that are not open to conscious awareness. In psychoanalytic theory, the region of the mind wherein reside all the experiences of life that have been repressed or never become conscious.

Unconscious inference. Interpretations of which we are unaware, made automatically by the brain; for example, the inference that the horizon moon is far away, which contributes to the moon illusion.

Unmarked expression. In pairs of words (i.e., short–tall), the one which merely asks for information when used in the question, "How _____ is he?" Contrast with *marked expression*.

Unobtrusive measures. Measures of behavior which the participants in research do not know are being made, designed to minimize reactive efforts of measurement.

UR. See *unconditioned response*.

US. See *unconditioned stimulus*.

Utricle. A fluid-filled sac of the vestibule of the inner ear, containing hair cells which are bent by crystals when the head is tilted or the body is in straight-line motion.

V

V$_{environmental}$. The variance of a population trait attributed to different environments.

V$_{genetic}$. The variance of a population trait attributed to different genotypes.

V$_{phenotypic}$. The total variance for a given population trait.

Valence, positive or negative. A term proposed by Kurt Lewin for the attractive (positive) or unattractive (negative) properties of an object that imply movement of an organism toward or away from it.

Validity. The extent to which test scores measure what they are intended to measure. Contrast with *reliability*.

Variable-interval schedule. A schedule of partial reinforcement in which the participant is rewarded for a response after a period of time that varies from one reinforcement to the next.

Variable-ratio schedule. A schedule of partial reinforcement in which the participant is rewarded after a number of unrewarded responses that varies from one reinforcement to the next.

Variance. A measure of dispersion; the square of the standard deviation.

Verbal IQ. Intelligence test scores derived from tests measuring the use of language, reasoning, vocabulary, general knowledge, comprehension, etc.

Verbal mediation. The use of language to intervene between the perception of outside events and acting upon them.

Verbal test. See *verbal IQ*. Contrast with *performance test*.

Vertical-horizontal illusion. A tendency for vertical lines to seem longer than horizontal lines of the same length.

Vestibular sensitivity. The "sense of balance" and detection of motion in relation to gravity conveyed by the two sacs of the vestibule and the semicircular canals.

Vestibule. Cavity of the membranous labyrinth containing two fluid-filled sacs; within the sacs otoliths or crystals lag against hair cells when the head is tilted or the body is in straight-line motion.

Vicarious functioning. The assuming of function by another area of the brain after the portion usually responsible has been destroyed.

Visceral motor fibers. Axons which carry commands from the central nervous system to the internal organs of the body. See *autonomic nervous system*.

Visceral sensory fibers. Axons which carry information from the viscera to the central nervous system. See *autonomic nervous system*.

Viscerotonia. In Sheldon's classification, the personality type associated with *endomorphy*: gluttonous, comfort-loving, sociable, and easygoing.

Visual acuity. The ability of the eye to distinguish fine details.

Visual cliff. A device with an apparent but not actual drop-off, designed to study infants' depth perception.

Visual purple. Rhodopsin.

Visual salience. In attribution theory, the prominence of people in our visual field, making us believe that they have influence.

Vitreous humor. The transparent jelly-like substance filling the eyeball between the retina and the lens.

Volley theory. A theory of neural action in audition that holds that squadrons of neurons fire out of phase with other squadrons, in order to increase the frequencies with which neurons can respond.

W

WAIS (Wechsler Adult Intelligence Scale). An individual intelligence test developed by David Wechsler for adults. Provides for verbal, peformance, and composite IQ scores. See *WISC*.

Warm spot. A small area on the skin that is sensitive to warm stimuli.

Wave amplitude. The intensity of electromagnetic energy; graphed as the distance from crest to trough of a wave.

Wave complexity. The varying wavelengths making up much of light energy. Reflected light made up of photons of a number of wavelengths is seen as unsaturated in color.

Wavelength. The frequency of electromagnetic energy; graphed as the distance from crest to crest of a wave.

Weber's law. $\Delta I / I = K$, where I is the magnitude of a reference stimulus and ΔI is the amount of change necessary to produce a *just-noticeable difference*.

Wechsler scales. See *WAIS* and *WISC*.

Wernicke's area. An area in the temporal lobe of the left hemisphere which, along with Broca's area, controls speech. The function of Wernicke's area is primarily sensory.

White matter. Areas of the central nervous system made up of the myelinated axons of neurons. Contrast with *gray matter*.

White noise. Noise composed of sound waves of all frequencies.

Whorfian hypothesis. The hypothesis of Benjamin Lee Whorf that thought is determined in part by language. See *linguistic determinism* and *linguistic relativity*.

Win-stay, lose-shift strategy. In problem solving, a strategy in which the individual continues to hold a particular hypothesis as long as it works and then switches to some other hypothesis.

WISC (Wechsler Intelligence Scale for Children). A test like the *WAIS*, developed by David Wechsler for children.

Withdrawal. A defensive response to stress in which the person is profoundly listless and indifferent and avoids contact with others.

Word-association test. A test, sometimes used for personality diagnosis, in which a person gives the first word that comes to mind in response to a series of stimulus words spoken by the examiner.

Work sample test. An aptitude test requiring the applicant to do a trial sequence of the work for which he or she desires training or employment.

X

x-axis (abscissa). The horizontal axis on a graph; usually represents the independent variable.

XYY males. Males having an extra Y chromosome in their genetic makeup. It remains unclear whether these tall, thin men have criminal tendencies, but many do have low IQs.

Y

y-axis (ordinate). The vertical axis on a graph; usually represents the dependent variable.

Yoked-control experiment. An experimental method in which the control participant receives the same treatment as the experimental participant on the same schedule. Usually, the two procedures are run at the same time, and the experimental participant's reactions control what is presented to the control participant.

Yoked control group. The control group in a yoked-control experiment.

Young-Helmholtz theory. A theory of color vision that assumes three types of receptors in the retina maximally responsive to red, green, and blue, respectively.

Z

Z-score. A number which expresses the distance of a particular score (X) above or below the mean (M) in units of standard deviation: $Z = (X - M)/S$.

Zeigarnik effect. The tendency to remember interrupted or unfinished tasks better than completed tasks.

Zero-sum-game. A two-person game in which one person's winnings are exactly the other's losses. Contrast with *non-zero-sum game*.

Zygote. A cell formed from the union of male and female gametes. In higher animals, the union of sperm and egg cells to form a fertilized egg which will grow to a new individual.

REFERENCES

Abelson, R. P. (1976) Script processing in attitude formation and decision-making. In J. S. Carroll and J. W. Payne (Eds.), *Cognition and social behavior*. Hillsdale, N.J.: Lawrence Erlbaum Associates.

Abelson, R. P. (1981) Scripts: The psychological status of the script concept. *American Psychologist*.

Abramson, L. Y., Garber, J., Edwards, N. B., and Seligman, M. E. P. (1978) Expectancy changes in depression and schizophrenia. *Journal of Abnormal Psychology, 87,* 102–109.

Achenbach, T., and Zigler, E. (1968) Cue-learning and problem-learning strategies in normal and retarded children. *Child Development, 39,* 827–848.

Agras, W. S., Barlow, D. H., Chapin, H. N., Abel, G. G., and Leitenberg, H. (1974) Behavior modification of anorexia nervosa. *Archives of General Psychiatry, 30,* 279–286.

Ainsworth, M. D. S., and Bell, S. M. (1973) Mother-infant interaction and the development of competence. In K. Connolly and J. Bruner (Eds.), *The growth of competence*. New York: Academic Press.

Allen, N. E., Hart, B., Buell, J. S., Harris, F. R., and Wolf, M. M. (1964) Effects of social reinforcement on isolate behavior of a nursery school child. *Child Development, 35,* 511–518.

Allison, J., Blatt, S. J., and Zimet, C. N. (1968) *The interpretation of psychological tests*. New York: Harper and Row.

Allport, G. W. (1935) Attitudes. In C. Murchison (Ed.), *A handbook of social psychology*. Worcester, Mass.: Clark University Press.

Allport, G. W. (1943) The ego in contemporary psychology. *Psychological Review, 50,* 451–478.

Allport, G. W. (1954) *The nature of prejudice*. Reading, Mass.: Addison-Wesley.

Allport G. W., and Odbert, A. S. (1936) Trait names, a psycholexical study. *Psychological Monographs, 47,* 1–171.

Amabile, T. M. (1979) Effects of external evaluation on artistic creativity. *Journal of Personality and Social Psychology, 37,* 221–233.

American Psychological Association. (1973) *Ethical principles in the conduct of research with human participants*. Washington, D.C.: American Psychological Association.

Argyle, M., and Dean, J. (1965) Eye-contact, distance and affiliation. *Sociometry, 28,* 289–304.

Arieti, S. (1976) *Creativity: The magic synthesis*. New York: Basic Books.

Aristotle. *Historia animalium,* Books 1–3. Loeb Classical Library. Cambridge, Mass.: Harvard University Press.

Arkes, H. R., and Garske, J. P. (1982) *Psychological theories of motivation*. Belmont, Calif.: Brooks/Cole.

Arkowitz, H., Lichtenstein, E., McGovern, K., and Hines, P. (1975) The behavioral assessment of social competence in males. *Behavior Therapy, 6,*3–13.

Armor, D. J., Polich, J. M., and Stambul, H. B. (1978) *Alcoholism and treatment*. Santa Monica, Calif.: Rand Corporation.

Aronfreed, J. (1968) *Conduct and conscience*. New York: Academic Press.

Aronson, E., and Carlsmith, J. M. (1963) Effect of the severity of threat on the devaluation of forbidden behavior. *Journal of Abnormal and Social Psychology, 66,* 584–588.

Aronson, E., and Mills, J. (1959) The effect of severity of initiation on liking for a group. *Journal of Abnormal and Social Psychology, 59,* 177–181.

Asch, S. E. (1956) Studies in independence and conformity: A minority of one against a unanimous majority. *Psychological Monographs, 70* (19).

Ashby, W. R., and Walker, C. C. (1968) Genius. In P. London and D. Rosenhan (Eds.), *Foundations of abnormal psychology*. New York: Holt, Rinehart and Winston.

Ayllon, T. (1963) Intensive treatment of psychotic behavior by stimulus satiation and food reinforcement. *Behavior Research and Therapy, 1,* 53–61.

Baggett, P. (1975) Memory for explicit and implicit information in picture stories. *Journal of Verbal Learning and Verbal Behavior, 14,* 538–548.

Bahrick, H. P., Bahrick, P. Q., and Willinger, R. P. (1975) Fifty years of memory for names and faces: A cross-sectional approach. *Journal of Experimental Psychology: General, 104,* 54–75.

Baldessarini, R. J. (1977) *Chemotherapy in psychiatry*. Cambridge, Mass.; Harvard University Press.

Bandura, A. (1977) *Social learning theory*. Englewood Cliffs, N.J.: Prentice-Hall.

Bandura, A., Grusec, J. E., and Menlove, F. L. (1966) Observational learning as a function of symbolization and incentive set. *Child Development, 37,* 499–506.

Barash, D. (1979) *The whisperings within: Evolution and the origin of human nature*. New York: Harper and Row.

Bard, P. (1934) On emotional expression after decortication with some remarks on certain theoretical views. *Psychological Review, 41,* 309–329, 424–449.

Barnlund, D. C. (1959) A comparative study of individual, majority, and group judgment. *Journal of Abnormal and Social Psychology, 58,* 55–60.

Barron, F. (1958) The psychology of imagination. *Scientific American, 199,* 150–166.

Barry, H., Child, I. L. and Bacon, M. K. (1959) Relation of child training to subsistence economy. *American Anthropologist, 61,* 51–63.

Bartlett, F. (1958) *Thinking*. New York: Basic Books.

Baumrind, D. (1975) The contribution of the family to the development of competence in children. *Schizophrenia Bulletin, 1*(14), 12–37.

Bayley, N. (1955). On the growth of intelligence. *American Psychologist, 10,* 805–818.

Bayley, N., and Schaefer, E. S. (1964) Correlations of maternal and child behaviors with the development of mental abilities: Data from the Berkeley Growth Study. *Mono-*

graphs of the Society for Research in Child Development, 29 (6). (Whole 97.)

Beach, F. A. (1970) Coital behavior in dogs: VI. Long-term effects of castration upon mating in the male. *Journal of Comparative and Physiological Psychology, 70,* 1–32.

Beck, A. T. (1976) *Cognitive therapy and the emotional disorders.* New York: International Universities Press.

Beck, A. T., Rush, A. J., Shaw, B. F., and Emery, G. (1979) *Cognitive therapy of depression.* New York: Guilford Press.

Beck, A. T., Ward, C. H., Mendelson, M., Mock, J. E., and Erbaugh, J. K. (1962) Reliability of psychiatric diagnosis: II. A study of consistency of clinical judgments and ratings. *American Journal of Psychiatry, 119,* 351–357.

Beck, R. C. (1983) *Motivation: Theories and principles.* Englewood Cliffs, N.J.: Prentice-Hall.

Becker, W. (1964) Consequences of different kinds of parental discipline. In M. L. Hoffman and L. Hoffman (Eds.), *Review of child development research,* Vol. 1. New York: Russell Sage Foundation.

Bee, H. L. (1974) The effect of maternal employment on the development of the child. In H. L. Bee (Ed.), *Social issues in developmental psychology.* New York: Harper and Row.

Bell, A., Weinberg, M., and Hammersmith, S. K. (1981) *Sexual preference.* Indianapolis: Indiana University Press (Alfred C. Kinsey Institute for Sex Research Publication).

Bem, D. J. (1972) Self-perception theory. In L. Berkowitz (Ed.), *Advances in experimental social psychology,* Vol. 6. New York: Academic Press.

Bem, D. J., and Lord, C. G. (1979) Template matching: A proposal for probing the ecological validity of experimental settings in social psychology. *Journal of Personality and Social Psychology, 37,* 833–846.

Bennett, I. (1960) *Delinquent and neurotic children.* New York: Basic Books.

Bergin, A. E., and Lambert, M. J. (1978) The evaluation of therapeutic outcomes. In S. L. Garfield and A. E. Bergin (Eds.), *Handbook of psychotherapy and behavior change.* (2nd ed.) New York: Wiley.

Berkeley, G. (1709) *An essay towards a new theory of vision.* Doublin. In G. Berkeley, *Works on vision.* (Edited by C. M. Turbayne.) Westport, Conn.; Greenwood Press, 1981.

Berkeley, M. A. (1978) Vision: Geniculocortical system. In R. B. Masterton (Ed.), *Handbook of behavioral neurobiology.* New York: Plenum Press.

Berko, J. (1958) The child's learning of English morphology. *Word, 14,* 150–177.

Berko, J., and Brown, R. W. (1960) Psycholinguistic research methods. In P. H. Mussen (Ed.), *Handbook of research methods in child development.* New York: Academic Press.

Berkowitz, L. (Ed.) (1966–1982) *Advances in experimental social psychology,* Vols. 1–15. New York: Academic Press.

Berkowitz, L., and Friedman, P. (1967) Some social class differences in helping behavior. *Journal of Personality and Social Psychology, 5,* 217–225.

Berlin, G., and Kay, P. (1969) *Basic color terms: Their universality and evolution.* Berkeley: University of California Press.

Berstein, I. L., and Sigmundi, R. A. (1980) Tumor anorexia: A learned food aversion? *Science, 209,* 416–418.

Bevan, W. (1982) A sermon of sorts in three plus parts. *American Psychologist, 37,* 1302–1322.

Biller, H. B. (1970) Father absence and the personality development of the male child. *Developmental Psychology, 2,* 181–201.

Billig, M. G., and Tajfel, H. (1973) Social categorization and similarity in intergroup behaviour. *European Journal of Psychology, 3,* 27–52.

Binet, A. (1903) *L'etude experimentale de l'intelligence.* Paris: Schleicher Frères.

Blake, R. R., and Mouton, J. S. (1979) Intergroup problem solving in organizations: From theory to practice. In W. Austin and S. Worchel (Eds.), *The social psychology of intergroup relations.* Monterey, Calif.: Brooks/Cole.

Blakemore, C., and Cooper, G. F. (1970) Development of the brain depends on the visual environment. *Nature, 228,* 447–478.

Bleuler, E. (1911) *Dementia praecox or the group of schizophrenias.* (English translation.) New York: International Universities Press, 1950.

Block, J. (1971) *Lives through time.* Berkeley, Calif.: Bancroft Books.

Block, J. (1977) Advancing the psychology of personality: Paradigmatic shift or improving the quality of research? In D. Magnusson and N. S. Endler (Eds.), *Personality at the crossroads: Current issues in interactional psychology.* Hillsdale, N.J.: Lawrence Erlbaum Associates.

Block, N. J., and Dworkin, G. (Eds.) (1976) *The IQ controversy.* New York: Pantheon.

Blommers, P., and Lindquist, E. F. (1960) *Elementary statistical methods in psychology and education.* Cambridge, Mass.: Riverside Press.

Bloom, L. M. (1970) *Language development: Form and structure in emerging grammars.* Cambridge, Mass.: M.I.T. Press.

Bockhoven, J. S. (1963) *Moral treatment in American psychiatry.* New York: Springer.

Boring, E. G. (1950) *History of experimental psychology.* New York: Appleton-Century-Crofts.

Boring, E. G., Langfeld, H. S., and Weld, H. P. (1948) *Foundations of psychology.* New York: Wiley.

Bornstein, M. H., Kessen, W., and Weiskopf, S. (1976) The categories of hue in infancy. *Science, 191,* 201–202.

Borus, J. F. (1976) The re-entry transition of the Vietnam veteran. In N. L. Goldman and D. R. Segal (Eds.), *The social psychology of military service.* Beverly Hills, Calif.: Sage Publications.

Bos, M. (1937) Experimental study of productive collaboration. *Acta Psychologia, 3,* 315–425.

Bouchard, T. J., Jr., and McGue, M. (1981) Familial studies of intelligence: A review. *Science, 212,* 1055–1059.

Bourne, P. G. (1970) *Men, stress, and Vietnam.* Boston: Little, Brown.

Bousfield, W. A. (1953) The occurrence of clustering in the free recall of randomly arranged associates. *Journal of General Psychology, 49,* 229–240.

Bower, G. H. (1970) Analysis of a mnemonic device. *American Scientist, 58,* 496–510.

Bower, G. H., and Clark, M. C. (1969) Narrative stories as mediators for serial learning. *Psychonomic Science, 14,* 181–182.

Bowlby, J. (1969) *Attachment and loss,* Vol. 1, *Attachment.* New York: Basic Books.

Bowlby, J. (1973) *Attachment and loss,* Vol. 2, *Separation: Anxiety and anger.* New York: Basic Books.

Brackbill, Y. (1958) Extinction of the smiling response in infants as a function of reinforcement schedule. *Child Development, 29,* 115–124.

Brainerd, C. J. (1978) *Piaget's theory of intelligence.* Englewood Cliffs, N.J.: Prentice-Hall.

Bransford, J. D., and Johnson, M. K. (1972) Contextual prerequisites for understanding: Some investigations of comprehension and recall. *Journal of Verbal Learning and Verbal Behavior, 11,* 717–720.

Brecher, E. M., and Editors of Consumer Reports. (1972) *Licit and illicit drugs.* Boston: Little, Brown.

Breggin, P. R. (1979) *Electroshock: Its brain-disabling effects.* New York: Springer.

Brehm, J. W. (1966) *A theory of psychological reactance.* New York: Academic Press.

Breland, K., and Breland, M. (1961) The misbehavior of organisms. *American Psychologist, 16,* 681–684.

Brener, J., and Kleinman, R. A. (1970) Learned control of decreases in systolic blood pressure. *Nature, 226,* 1063–1064.

Brenner, M. H. (1973) *Mental illness and the economy.* Cambridge, Mass.: Harvard University Press.

Brenner, M. H. (1981–1982) Industrialization and economic growth: Estimates of their effects on populations. In M. H. Brenner, A. Mooney, and T. J. Nagy (Eds.), *Assessing the contributions of the social sciences to health.* Washington, D.C., American Association for the Advancement of Science.

Breuer, J., and Freud, S. (1895) *Studies in hysteria.* New York: Basic Books, 1957.

Bridges, K. M. B. (1932) Emotional development in early infancy. *Child Development, 3,* 324–341.

Broadbent, D. E. (1957) A mechanical model for human attention and immediate memory. *Psychological Review, 64,* 205–215.

Brome, V. (1978) *Jung.* New York: Atheneum.

Bronfenbrenner, U., and Crouter, A. (1981) Work and family through time and space. Report prepared for the Panel on Work, Family and Community, Committee on Child Development Research and Public Policy, National Academy of Science, National Research Council.

Brophy, J. E., and Good, I. L. (1974) *Teacher-student relationships. Courses and consequences.* New York: Holt, Rinehart and Winston.

Brown, B. L., Strong, W. J., and Rencher, A. C. (1974) Fifty-four voices from two: The effects of simultaneous manipulations of rate, mean fundamental frequency and variance of fundamental frequency on ratings of personality from speech. *Journal of the Acoustical Society of America, 55,* 313–318.

Brown, E. L., and Deffenbacher, K. (1979) *Perception and the senses.* New York: Oxford University Press.

Brown, G. W., Birley, J. L., and Wing, J. K. (1972) Influence of family life on the course of schizophrenic disorders: A replication. *British Journal of Psychiatry, 121,* 241–258.

Brown, G. W., and Harris, T. (1978) *Social origins of depression: A study of psychiatric disorder in women.* New York: Free Press.

Brown, G. W., Harris, T., and Copeland, J. R. (1977) Depression and loss. *British Journal of Psychiatry, 130,* 1–18.

Brown, P. L., and Jenkins, H. M. (1968) Autoshaping of the pigeon's keypeck. *Journal of the Experimental Analysis of Behavior, 11,* 1–8.

Brown, R. W. (1959) *Words and things.* New York: Free Press.

Brown, R. W. (1973) *A first language: The early stages.* Cambridge, Mass.: Harvard University Press.

Brown, R. W., Cazden, C. B., and Bellugi, U. (1969) The child's grammar from I to III. *Symposia on child psychology,* Vol. 2. Minneapolis: University of Minnesota Press.

Brown, R. W., and McNeil, D. (1966) The "tip of the tongue" phenomenon. *Journal of Verbal Learning and Verbal Behavior, 5,* 325–337.

Bruner, J. S., and Kenney, H. J. (1966) On multiple ordering. In J. S. Brunner, R. R. Olver, and P. M. Greenfield (Eds.), *Studies in cognitive growth.* New York: Wiley.

Bruner, J. S., and Rodriguez, J. S. (1953) Some determinants of apparent size. *Journal of Abnormal Social Psychology, 48,* 585–592.

Bryan, J. H. (1975) Children's cooperation and helping behavior. In E. M. Hetherington (Ed.), *Review of child development research,* Vol. 5. Chicago: University of Chicago Press.

Bryan, T. H. (1974) Peer popularity of learning disabled children. *Journal of Learning Disabilities, 7,* 261–268.

Bryan, T. H., and Bryan, J. H. (1978) *Understanding learning disabilities.* (2nd ed.) Sherman Oaks, Calif.: Alfred Publishing Company.

Bryan, T. H., and McCrady, H. J. (1972) Use of a teacher rating scale. *Journal of Learning Disabilities, 5,* 199–206.

Buck, R. (1976) *Human motivation and emotion.* New York: Wiley.

Burt, C. (1955) The evidence for the concept of intelligence. *British Journal of Educational Psychology, 25,* 158–177.

Butcher, H. J. (1970) *Human intelligence: Its nature and assessment.* London: Metheun.

Butcher, J. N. (1978) Minnesota Multiphasic Personality Inventory. Reviews of computerized scoring and interpreting services. In O. K. Buros (Ed.), *The eighth mental measurements year book.* Highland Park, N.J.: Gryphon Press.

Butcher, J. N., and Gur, R. (1974) A Hebrew translation of the MMPI: Assessment of translation adequacy and preliminary validation. *Journal of Cross-Cultural Psychology, 5,* 220–227.

Byrne, D. (1977) Sexual imagery. In J. Money and H. Musaph (Eds.), *Handbook of sexology.* New York: Elsevier.

Campbell, A., Converse, P. E., and Rodgers, W. L. (1976) *The quality of American life: Perceptions, evaluations and satisfactions.* New York: Russell Sage Foundation.

Campbell, D. T. (1961) Conformity in psychology's theories of acquired behavioral dispositions. In I. A. Berg and B. M. Bass (Eds.), *Conformity and deviation.* New York: Harper and Row.

Cannon, W. B. (1927) The James-Lange theory of emotions: A critical examination and an alternative theory. *American Journal of Psychology, 39,* 106–124.

Cannon, W. B. (1934) Hunger and thirst. In C. Murchinson (Ed.), *Handbook of general experimental psychology.* Worcester, Mass.: Clark University Press.

Carey, G. L. (1958) Sex differences in problem-solving performance as a function of attitude differences. *Journal of Abnormal and Social Psychology, 56,* 256–260.

Carver, C. S. (1975) Physical aggression as a function of objective self-awareness and attitudes toward punishment. *Journal of Experimental Social Psychology, 11,* 510–519.

Cattell, R. B. (1950) *Personality: A systematic theoretical and factual study.* New York: McGraw-Hill.

Cattell, R. B. (1963) Theory of fluid and crystallized intelligence: A critical experiment. *Journal of Educational Psychology, 54,* 1–22.

Cattell, R. B. (1965) *The scientific analysis of personality.* Chicago: Aldine.

Cattell, R. B. (1973) Personality pinned down. *Psychology Today, 7,* 40–46.

Cavalli-Sforza, L. L., and Bodmer, W. F. (1971) *The genetics of human populations.* San Francisco: W. H. Freeman.

Charlesworth, W. R. (1976) Human intelligence as adaptation. In L. B. Resnick (Ed.), *The nature of intelligence.* Hillsdale, N.J.: Lawrence Erlbaum Associates.

Chomsky, N. (1957) *Syntactic structures.* The Hague: Mouton Publishers.

Ciminero, A. R. (1977) Behavioral assessment: An overview. In A. R. Ciminero, K. S. Calhoun, and H. E. Adams (Eds.), *Handbook of behavioral assessment.* New York: Wiley-Interscience.

Ciminero, A. R., Calhoun, K. S., and Adams, H. E. (Eds.) (1977) *Handbook of behavioral assessment.* New York: Wiley-Interscience.

Clark, H. H., and Clark, E. V. (1977) *Psychology and language.* New York: Harcourt Brace Jovanovich.

Clausen, J. A., and Williams, J. R. (1963) Sociological correlates of child behavior. *Yearbook of the National Society for the Study of Education, 62,* 62–107

Cleckley, H. J. (1976) *The mask of sanity.* (5th ed.) St. Louis, Mo.: C. V. Mosby.

Cleland, C. C. (1978) *Mental retardation: A developmental approach.* Englewood Cliffs, N.J.: Prentice-Hall.

Clements, R. J. (1963) *Michelangelo: A self-portrait.* Englewood Cliffs, N.J.: Prentice-Hall.

Coghill, C. E. (1929) *Anatomy and the problem of behavior.* New York: Macmillan.

Cohen, F., and Lazarus, R. S. (1979) Coping with the stresses of illness. In G. C. Stone, F. Cohen, and N. E. Adler (Eds.), *Health psychology.* San Francisco: Jossey-Bass.

Coleman, J. C. (1976) *Abnormal psychology and modern life.* (5th ed.) Glenview, Ill.: Scott, Foresman.

Coleman, J. C., Butcher, J. N., and Carson, R. C. (1980) *Abnormal psychology and modern life.* (6th ed.) Glenview, Ill.: Scott, Foresman.

Connolly, K. J., and Bruner, J. S. (Eds.) (1974) *The growth of competence.* New York: Academic Press.

Conrad, R. (1964) Acoustic confusions in immediate memory. *British Journal of Psychology, 55,* 75–84.

Cooper, C. L., and Payne, R. (Eds.) (1978) *Stress at work.* London: Wiley.

Cooper, J. (1980) Reducing fears and increasing assertiveness: The role of dissonance reduction. *Journal of Experimental Social Psychology, 16,* 199–213.

Cooper, R. M., and Zubek, J. P. (1958) Effects of enriched and restricted early environment on the learning ability of bright and dull rats.

Canadian Journal of Psychology, 12, 159–164.

Coren, S., Porac, C., and Ward, L. M. (1978) *Sensation and perception.* New York: Academic Press.

Corsini, R. J. (Ed.) (1979) *Current psychotherapies.* (2nd ed.) Itasca, Ill.: F. E. Peacock Publishers.

Cottrell, N. B. (1972) Social facilitation. In C. G. McClintock (Ed.), *Experimental social psychology.* New York: Holt, Rinehart and Winston.

Cottrell, N. B., Wack, D. L. Sekerak, G. J., and Rittle, R. H. (1968) Social facilitation of dominant responses by the presence of an audience and the mere presence of others. *Journal of Personality and Social Psychology, 9,* 245–250.

Cox, C. M. (1926) The early mental traits of three hundred geniuses. In L. M. Terman (Ed.), *Genetic studies of genius,* Vol. 2. Stanford, Calif.: Stanford University Press.

Cox, T. (1978) *Stress.* Baltimore: University Park Press.

Craik, F. I. M., and Tulving, E. (1975) Depth of processing and the retention of words in episodic memory. *Journal of Experimental Psychology: General, 104,* 268–294

Crome, L., and Stern, J. (1972) *Pathology of mental retardation.* (2nd ed.) London: Churchill Livingstone.

Cruikshank, W. (1967) *The brain-injured child in the home, the school, and the community.* Syracuse, N.Y.: Syracuse University Press.

Cutting, J. E., (1981) Coding theory adapted to gait perception. *Journal of Experimental Psychology: Human Perception and Performance, 7,* 71–87.

Damon, W. (1981) Exploring children's social cognition on two fronts. In J. H. Flavell and L. Ross (Eds.), *Social cognitive development.* Cambridge, England: Cambridge University Press.

Darley, J. M., and Gross, P. H. (1983) A hypothesis-confirming bias in labeling effects. *Journal of Personality and Social Psychology, 44,* 20–33.

Darley, J. M., and Latané, B. (1968) Bystander intervention in emergencies: Diffusion of responsibility. *Jounal of Personality and Social Psychology, 8,* 377–383.

Darwin, C. (1859) *On the origin of species.* New York: Macmillan, 1962.

Darwin, C. (1872) *The expression of the emotions in man and animals.* Chicago: Chicago University Press, 1965.

Dasen, P. R. (1975) Concrete operational development in three cultures. *Journal of Cross-Cultural Psychology, 6,* 156–172.

Dasen, P. R. (1977) Introduction. In P. R. Dasen (Ed.), *Piagetian psychology: Cross-cultural contributions.* New York: Gardner Press.

Davis, D. E. (1964) The physiological analysis of aggressive behavior. In E. Etkin (Ed.), *Social behavior and organization among vertebrates.* Chicago: University of Chicago Press.

Davis, P. G., McEwen, B. S., and Pfaff, D. W. (1979) Localized behavioral effects of tritiated estradiol implants in the ventromedial hypothalamus of female rats. *Endocrinology, 104,* 898–903.

Davison, G. C., and Neale, J. M. (1982) *Abnormal psychology.* (3rd ed.) New York: Wiley.

DeLamate, J., and MacCorquodale, P. (1979) *Premarital sexuality: Attitudes, relationships, and behavior.* Madison: University of Wisconsin Press.

Dennis, W. (1940) The effect of cradling practices upon the onset of walking in Hopi children. *Journal of Genetic Psychology, 56,* 77–86.

Dennis, W. (1973) *Children of the créche.* New York: Appleton-Century-Crofts.

Deutsch, M., and Brown, B. (1964) Social influences in Negro-white intelligence differences. *Journal of Social Issues, 20,* 20–35.

DeValois, R. L., Abramov, I., and Jacobs, G. H. (1966) Analysis of response patterns of LGN cells. *Journal of the Optical Society of America, 56,* 966–977.

de Villiers, J. G., and de Villiers, P. A. (1973) Development of the use of word order in comprehension. *Journal of Psycholinguistic Research, 2,* 331–341.

DeVries, R. (1969) Constancy of generic identity in the years three to six. *Monographs of the Society for Research in Child Development, 34* (3), Serial 127.

Dobzhansky, T. (1955) *Evolution, genetics, and man.* New York: Wiley.

Dobzhansky, T. (1964) *Heredity and the nature of man.* New York: Harcourt Brace Jovanovich.

Dohrenwend, B. S., and Dohrenwend, B. P. (1974) *Social status and psychological disorder: A causal inquiry.* New York: Wiley.

Doise, W., Mugny, G., and Perret-Clermont, A. N. (1975) Social interaction and the development of cognitive operations. *European Journal of Social Psychology, 5,* 367–383.

Doise, W., Mugny, G., and Perret-Clermont, A. N. (1976) Social interaction and cognitive development: Further evidence. *European Journal of Social Psychology, 6,* 245–247.

Dole, V., and Nyswander, M. (1966) Methadone maintenance: A report of two years' experience. In *Problems of drug dependence.* Washington, D.C.: National Academy of Science, National Research Council.

Dollard, J., and Miller, N. E. (1950) *Personality and psychotherapy: An analysis in terms of learning, thinking and culture.* New York: McGraw-Hill.

Donaldson, H. H. (1900) *The growth of the brain.* New York: Charles Scribner's Sons.

Donaldson, M., and Balfour, G. (1968) Less is more: A study of language comprehension in children. *British Journal of Psychology, 59,* 461–472.

DSM-III (1980) *Diagnostic and statistical manual of the American Psychiatric Association.* (3rd ed.) Washington, D.C.: American Psychiatric Association.

Dugdale, R. (1877) *The Jukes: A study in crime, pauperism, disease, and heredity.* New York: G. P. Putnam's Sons, 1910.

Duncker, K. (1945) On problem solving. *Psychological Monographs, 58,* 1–113. (Whole 270.)

Dunnette, M. D., Campbell, J., and Jaastad, K. (1963) The effect of group participation on brainstorming effectiveness for two industrial samples. *Journal of Applied Psychology, 47,* 30–37.

Dweck, C. S. (1975) The role of expectations and attributions in the alleviation of learned helplessness. *Journal of Personality and Social Psychology, 31,* 674–685.

Dweck, C. S., and Repucci, N. D. (1973) Learned helplessness and reinforcement responsibility in children. *Journal of Personality and Social Psychology, 25,* 109–116.

Ebbinghaus, H. (1885) *Memory: A contribution to experimental psychology.* (Translated by H. A. Ruger and C. E. Bussenius.) New York: Columbia University Press, 1913.

Edgerton, R. B. (1967) *The cloak of competence.* Berkeley: University of California Press.

Edgerton, R. B., and Bercovici, S. (1976) The cloak of competence: Years later. *American Journal of Mental Deficiency, 80,* 485–497.

Eells, K., Davis, A., Havighurst, R. J., Herrick, V. E., and Tyler, R. (1951) *Intelligence and cultural differences.* Chicago: University of Chicago Press.

Eibl-Eibesfeldt, I. (1970) *Ethology: The biology of behavior.* (2nd ed., 1975.) New York: Holt, Rinehart and Winston.

Eimas, P. D., and Corbit, J. (1973) Selective adaptation of linguistic feature detectors. *Cognitive Psychology, 4,* 99–109.

Eimas, P. D., Siqueland, E. R., Jusczyk, P., and Vigorito, J. (1971) Speech perception in infants. *Science, 171,* 303–306.

Elkind, D. (1973) Giant in the nursery—Jean Piaget. In *Annual editions, readings in human development 73–74.* Guilford, Conn.: Dushkin Publishing Group.

Ellis, A. (1962) *Reason and emotion in psychotherapy.* New York: Lyle Stuart.

Ellis, A. (1977) The basic clinical theory of rational-emotive therapy. In A. Ellis and R. Grieger (Eds.), *Handbook of rational-emotive therapy.* New York: Springer.

Endler, N. S., Boulter, L. R., and Osser, H. (Eds.) (1976) *Contemporary issues in developmental psychology.* (2nd ed.) New York: Holt, Rinehart and Winston.

Endsley, R. C., Garner, A. R., Odom, A. H., and Martin, M. J. (1975) Interrelationships among selected material behaviors and preschool children's verbal and non-verbal curiosity behavior. Paper presented to the Society for Research in Child Development, Denver.

Enoch, M. D., Trethowan, W. H., and Barker, J. C. (1967) *Some uncommon psychiatric syndromes.* Bristol, England: John Wright and Sons.

Enzle, M. E., Harvey, M. D., and Wright, E. F. (1980) Personalism and distinctiveness. *Journal of Personality and Social Psychology, 39,* 542–552.

Epstein, S. (1967) Toward a unified theory of anxiety. In B. A. Maher (Ed.), *Progress in experimental personality research,* Vol. 4. New York: Academic Press.

Epstein, S. (1977) Traits are alive and well. In D. Magnusson and N. S. Endler (Eds.), *Personality at the crossroads: Current issues in interactional psychology.* Hillsdale, N.J.: Lawrence Erlbaum Associates.

Ericsson, K. A., Chase, W. G., and Faloon, S. (1980) Acquisition of memory skill. *Science, 208,* 1181–1182.

Erikson, E. H. (1963) *Children and society.* (2nd ed.) New York: W. W. Norton.

Erikson, E. H. (1964) *Insight and responsibility.* New York: W. W. Norton.

Erikson, K. T. (1976) *Everything in its path.* New York: Simon and Schuster.

Erlenmeyer-Kimling, L., and Jarvik, L. F. (1963) Genetics and intelligence: A review. *Science, 142,* 1477–1478.

Escher, M. C. (1967) *The graphic work of M. C. Escher.* New York: Ballantine Books.

Estes, W. K. (1944) An experimental study of punishment. *Psychological Monographs, 57.* (Whole 263.)

Evans, J. R., Goldstein, M. J., and Rodnick, E. H. (1973) Premorbid adjustment, paranoid diagnosis and remission. *Archives of General Psychiatry, 28,* 666–672.

Evans, J. R., Rodnick, E. H., Goldstein, M. J., and Judd, L. L. (1972) Premorbid adjustment, phenothiazine treatment, and remission in acute schizophrenia. *Archives of General Psychiatry, 27,* 486–490.

Evans, R. I. (1973) *Jean Piaget: The man and his ideas.* New York: E. P. Dutton.

Eysenck, H. J. (1960) Learning theory and behavior therapy. In H. J. Eysenck (Ed.), *Behaviour therapy and the neuroses.* London: Pergamon Press.

Eysenck, H. J. (1961) The effects of psychotherapy. In H. J. Eysenck (Ed.), *Handbook of abnormal psychology.* New York: Basic Books.

Eysenck, H. J. (1964) Principles and methods of personality description, classification and diagnosis. *British Journal of Psychology, 55,* 284–294.

Eysenck, H. J., and Rachman, S. (1965) *The causes and cures of neurosis.* San Diego, Calif.: Robert R. Knapp.

Eysenck, H. J., Wakefield, J. A., Jr., and Friedman, A. F. (1983) Diagnosis and clinical assessment: The DSM-III. In M. R. Rosenzweig and L. W. Porter (Eds.), *Annual review of psychology,* Vol. 34. Palo Alto, Calif.: Annual Reviews.

Fantz, R. L. (1961) The origin of form perception. *Scientific American, 204,* 66–72.

Fazio, R. H., Zanna, M. P., and Cooper, J. (1977) Dissonance and self-perception: An integrative view of each theory's proper domain of application. *Journal of Experimental Social Psychology, 13,* 464–479.

Federal Register (1976) *41* (230), November.

Fein, G. (1978) Play revisited. In M. E. Lamb (Ed.), *Social and personality development.* New York: Holt, Rinehart and Winston.

Fein, G., and Clarke-Stewart, A. (1973) *Day care in context.* New York: Wiley.

Feldman, S. E., and Feldman, M. T. (1967) Transition of sex differences in cheating. *Psychological Reports, 20,* 957–958.

Festinger, L. (1954) A theory of social comparison processes. *Human Relations, 7,* 117–140.

Festinger, L. (1957) *A theory of cognitive dissonance.* Evanston, Ill.: Row and Peterson.

Field, P. M., and Raisman, G. (1973) Structural and functional investigations of a sexually dimorphic part of the rat preoptic area. In *Recent studies of hypothalamic function.* Symposium proceedings. Calgary, Alberta, May.

Field, T. M., Woodson, R., Greenberg, R., and Cohen, D. (1982) Discrimination and imitation of facial expressions by neonates. *Science, 218,* 179–181.

Figley, C. R. (Ed.) (1978) *Stress disorders among Vietnam veterans.* New York: Brunner/Mazel.

Fishbein, M., and Ajzen, I. (1974) Attitudes toward objects as predictors of single and multiple behavioral criteria. *Psychological Review, 81,* 59–74.

Fiske, S. T. (1981) Social cognition and affect. In J. H. Harvey (Ed.), *Cognition, social behavior, and the environment.* Hillsdale, N.J.: Lawrence Erlbaum Associates.

Flapan, D. (1968) *Children's understanding of social interaction.* New York: Teachers College Press.

Flavell, J. H. (1963) *The developmental psychology of Jean Piaget.* Princeton, N.J.: Van Nostrand.

Flavell, J. H. (1977) *Cognitive development.* Englewood Cliffs, N.J.: Prentice-Hall.

Ford, C. S., and Beach, F. A. (1951) *Patterns of sexual behavior.* New York: Harper and Row.

Fowler, J. W., and Peterson, P. L. (1981) Increasing reading persistence and altering attributional style of learned helpless children. *Journal of Educational Psychology, 73,* 251–260.

Fox, R., and McDaniel, C. (1982) The perception of biological motion by human infants. *Science, 218,* 486–487.

Franks, J. J., and Bransford, J. D. (1971) Abstraction of visual patterns. *Journal of Experimental Psychology, 90,* 65–74.

Freedman, B. (1974) The subjective experience of perceptual and cognitive disturbances in schizophrenia: A review of autobiographical accounts. *Archives of General Psychiatry, 30,* 333–340.

Freedman, D. G. (1964) Smiling in blind infants and the issue of innate vs. acquired. *Journal of Child Psychology and Psychiatry, 5,* 171–184.

Freedman, D. G., Loring, C. B., and Martin, R. M. (1967) Emotional behavior and personality development. In Y. Brackbill (Ed.), *Infancy and early childhood.* New York: Free Press.

Freedman, J. L. (1965) Long term behavioral effects of cognitive dissonance. *Journal of Experimental Social Psychology, 1,* 145–155.

Freeman, L. (1972) *The story of Anna O.* New York: Walker.

Freeman, S., Walker, M. R., Borden, R., and Latané, B. (1975) Diffusion of responsibility and restaurant tipping: Cheaper by the bunch. *Personality and Social Psychology Bulletin, 1,* 584–587.

Freud, S. (1885) *Cocaine papers.* (Edited by R. Byck.) New York: New American Library, 1974.

Freud, S. (1900) The interpretation of dreams. *The standard edition of the complete psychological works of Sigmund Freud,* Vols. 4, 5. London: Hogarth Press and the Institute of Psychoanalysis, 1953.

Freud, S. (1925) Some psychical consequences of the anatomical distinction between the sexes. In S. Strachey (Ed.), *The standard edition of the complete psychological works of Sigmund Freud,* Vol. 19. London: Hogarth Press and The Institute for Psychoanalysis.

Freud, S. (1955) Lines of advance in psychoanalytic psychotherapy. *The standard edition of the complete psychological works of Sigmund Freud,* Vol. 17, *On infantile neurosis and other works.* London: Hogarth Press.

Frisch, K. von (1950) *Bees: Their vision, chemical senses and language.* Ithaca, N.Y.: Cornell University Press.

Fuller, J. L. (1967) Experiential deprivation and later behavior. *Science, 158,* 1645–1652.

Fuller, J. L., and Thompson, W. R. (1978) *Foundations of behavior genetics.* St. Louis, Mo.: C. V. Mosby.

Gabrielli, W. F., Jr., and Mednick, S. A. (1980) Sinistrality and delinquency. *Journal of Abnormal Psychology, 89,* 654–661

Garber, J., and Hollon, S. D. (1980) Universal

versus personal helplessness in depression: Belief in uncontrollability or incompetence? *Journal of Abnormal Psychology, 89,* 56–66.

Gardner, E. J. (1975) *Principles of genetics.* (5th ed.) New York: Wiley.

Gardner, H. (1978) *Developmental psychology.* Boston: Little, Brown.

Gardner, R. A., and Gardner, B. T. (1975) Communication with a young chimpanzee: Washoe's vocabulary. In R. Chauvin (Ed.), *Edition du Centre National de la Recherche Scientifique.* Paris.

Garmezy, N. (1978) DSM-III: Never mind the psychologists. It is good for the children? *Clinical Psychologist, 31* (3-4), 1, 4–6.

Garner, D. M., Garfinkel, P. E., Schwartz, D., and Thompson, M. (1980) Cultural expectations of thinness in women. *Psychological Reports, 47*(2), 483–491.

Gazzaniga, M. S. (1967) The split brain in man. *Scientific American, 217,* 24–29.

Gazzaniga, M. S. (1970) *The bisected brain.* New York: Appleton-Century-Crofts.

Gazzaniga, M. S., Bogen, J. E., and Sperry, R. W. (1965) Observations on visual perception after disconnection of the cerebral hemispheres in man. *Brain, 88* (part 2), 231–236.

Gazzaniga, M. S., Steen, D., and Volpe, B. T. (1979) *Functional neuroscience.* New York: Harper and Row.

Gelman, R. (1969) Conservation acquisition: A problem of learning to attend to relevant attributes. *Journal of Experimental Child Psychology, 7,* 167–187.

Geppert, T. V. (1964) Management of nocturnal enuresis by conditioned response. In C. M. Frank (Ed.), *Conditioning techniques in clinical practice and research.* New York: Springer.

Gerard, H. B., and Connolley, E. S. (1972) Conformity. In C. G. McClinstock (Ed.), *Experimental social psychology.* New York: Holt, Rinehart and Winston.

Gerard, H. B., and Mathewson, G. C. (1966) The effects of severity of initiation on liking for a group: A replication. *Journal of Experimental Social Psychology, 2,* 278–287.

Geschwind, N. (1979) Specialization of the human brain. *Scientific American, 241,* 180–201.

Getzels, J. W., and Jackson, P. W. (1962) *Creativity and intelligence.* New York: Wiley.

Gewirtz, J. L. (1965) The course of infant smiling in four child-rearing environments in Israel. In B. M. Foss (Ed.), *Determinants of infant behavior,* Vol. 3. New York: Wiley.

Gibson, E. J., and Walk, R. D. (1960) The visual cliff. *Scientific American, 202,* 2-9.

Gilovich, T. (1981) Seeing the past in the present: The effect of associations to familiar events on judgments and decisions. *Journal of Personality and Social Psychology, 40,* 797–808.

Ginsburg, B. E. (1971) Developmental behav-

ioral genetics. In N. B. Talbot, J. Kagan, and L. Eisenberg (Eds.), *Behavioral science in pediatric medicine.* Philadelphia: Saunders.

Glanzer, M., and Cunitz, A. R. (1960) Two storage mechanisms in free recall. *Journal of Verbal Learning and Verbal Behavior, 5,* 351–360.

Glucksberg, S., and Danks, J. H. (1975) *Experimental psycholinguistics.* Hillsdale, N.J.: Lawrence Erlbaum Associates.

Glueck, S., and Glueck, E. (1950) *Unraveling juvenile delinquency.* New York: Commonwealth Fund.

Goddard, H. H. (1912) *The Kallikak family: A study in the heredity of feeble-mindedness.* New York: Macmillan.

Goddard, H. H. (1946) What is intelligence? *Journal of Social Psychology, 24,* 51–69.

Godwin, J. (1973) *The mating trade.* Garden City, N.J.: Doubleday.

Goertzel, V., and Goertzel, M. G. (1962) *Cradles of eminence.* Boston: Little, Brown.

Goldberger, L., and Breznitz, S. (Eds.) (1982) *Handbook of stress: Theoretical and clinical aspects.* New York: Free Press.

Goldfried, M. R., and Kent, R. N. (1972) Traditional versus behavioral personality assessment: A comparison of methodological and theoretical assumptions. *Psychological Bulletin, 77,* 409–420.

Goldsby, R. A. (1971) *Race and races.* New York: Macmillan.

Goldstein, E. B. (1980) *Sensation and perception.* Belmont, Calif.: Wadsworth.

Goodwin, D. W. (1979) Genetic determinants of alcoholism. In J. H. Mendelson and N. K. Mello (Eds.), *The diagnosis and treatment of alcoholism.* New York: McGraw-Hill.

Gorski, R. A. (1980) Sexual differentiation of the brain. In D. T. Krieger and J. C. Hughes (Eds.), *Neuroendocrinology.* Sunderland, Mass.: Sinauer Associates, Hospital Practice Book.

Gottesman, I. I. (1963) Genetic aspects of intelligent behavior. In N. R. Ellis (Ed.), *Handbook of mental deficiency.* New York: McGraw-Hill.

Gottesman, I. I., and Shields, J. (1972) *Schizophrenia and genetics.* New York: Academic Press.

Gottlieb, G. (1973) Neglected developmental variables in the study of species identification in birds. *Psychological Bulletin, 29,* 362–372.

Gottlieb, J., and Budoff, M. (1973) Social acceptability of retarded children in nongraded schools differing in architecture. *American Journal of Mental Deficiency, 78,* 15–19.

Gough, H. G. (1960) *Manual for the California Psychological Inventory.* (Rev. ed.) Palo Alto, Calif.: Consulting Psychologists Press.

Goy, R. W., and Goldfoot, D. A. (1973) Hormonal influences on sexually dimorphic behavior. In R. O. Green (Ed.), *Handbook of*

physiology, Section 7, Vol. 2, Part I. Washington, D.C.: American Physiological Society.

Graf, R., and Torrey, J. W. (1966) Perception of phrase structure in written language. *American Psychological Association Convention Proceedings.* Washington, D.C.: American Psychological Association.

Graham, C. A., and McGrew, W. C. (1980) Menstrual synchrony in female undergraduates living on a coeducational campus. *Psychoneuroendocrinology, 5,* 245–252.

Gray, C. R., and Gummerman, K. (1975) The enigmatic eidetic image: A critical examination of methods, data, and theories. *Psychological Bulletin, 82,* 383–407.

Greenblatt, M. (1978) The grieving spouse. *American Journal of Psychiatry, 135,* 43–47.

Greenfield, P. M. (1976) Cross-cultural research and Piagetian theory: Paradox and progress. In K. Riegel and J. Meacham (Eds.), *The developing individual in a changing world.* The Hague: Mouton Publishers.

Greenfield, P. M., and Smith, J. H. (1976) *The structure of communication in early language development.* New York: Academic Press.

Greenough, W. T., Carter, C. S., Steerman, C., and DeVoogd, T. J. (1977) Sex differences in dendritic patterns in hamster preoptic area. *Brain Research, 26,* 63–72.

Greenwald, A. G. (1980) The totalitarian ego: Fabrication and revision of personal history. *American Psychologist, 35,* 603–618.

Gregory, R. L. (1970) *The intelligent eye.* New York: McGraw-Hill.

Gregory, R. L. (1973) *Eye and brain: The psychology of seeing.* (3rd ed. 1977.) New York: World University Library.

Gregory, R. L., and Wallace, J. G. (1963) Recovery from early blindness: A case study. *Experimental Psychological Social Monograph (2).*

Gross, C. G. Rocha-Miranda, C. E., and Bender, D. B. (1972) Visual properties of neurons in inferotemporal cortex of the macaque. *Journal of Neurophysiology, 35,* 95–111.

Grossman, H. J. (Ed.) (1973) *Manual on terminology and classification in mental retardation.* Washington, D.C.: American Association on Mental Deficiency.

Groves, P., and Schlesinger, K. (1979) *Introduction to biological psychology.* Dubuque, Iowa: W. C. Brown.

Gruen, G. E., Ottinger, D. R., and Ollendick, T. H. (1974) Probability learning in retarded children with differing histories of success and failure in school. *American Journal of Mental Deficiency, 79,* 417–423.

Gurdon, J. B. (1968) Transplanted nuclei and cell differentiation. *Scientific American, 219* (6), 24–35.

Haber, R. N. (1969) Eidetic images. *Scientific American, 220,* 36–55.

Hachaya, M. (1955) *Hiroshima diary.* Chapel Hill: University of North Carolina Press.

Hainline, L. (1978) Developmental changes in visual scanning of face and nonface patterns by infants. *Journal of Experimental Child Psychology, 25,* 90–115.

Haith, M. M., Bergman, T., and Moore, M. J. (1977) Eye contact and face scanning in early infancy. *Science, 198,* 853–854.

Haldane, J. B. S. (1946) The interaction of nature and nurture. *Annals of Eugenics, 13,* 197–205.

Hall, C. S. (1951) The genetics of behavior. In S. S. Stevens (Ed.), *Handbook of experimental psychology.* New York: Wiley.

Hall, C. S., and Lindzey, G. (1978) *Theories of personality.* (3rd ed.) New York: Wiley.

Halverson, A. M. (1931) An experimental study of prehension in infants by means of systematic cinema records. *Genetic Psychology Monographs, 10,* 2–3.

Hamilton, D. L (1979) A cognitive attributional analysis of stereotyping. In L. Berkowitz (Ed.), *Advances in experimental social psychology,* Vol. 12. New York: Academic Press.

Hanson, J. (1981) Identical twin study full of surprises. *Report* (University of Minnesota), *1,* 10–11.

Harlow, H. F. (1962) The heterosexual affectional system in monkeys. *American Psychologist, 17,* 17–19.

Harlow, H. F. (1972) Love created—love destroyed—love regained. *Modeles animaux de comportement humain.* Edition du Centre National de la Recherche Scientifique, Paris, 198, 13–60.

Harlow, H. F., and Suomi, S. J. (1970) Nature of love—simplified. *American Psychologist, 25,* 161–168.

Harrell, T. W., and Harrell, M. S. (1945) Army general classification test scores for civilian occupations. *Educational and Psychological Measurement, 5,* 229–239.

Hart-Johns, M., and Johns, B. (1982) *Give your child a chance.* Reston, Va.: Reston Publishing Company.

Hartup, W. W. (1980) Two social worlds: Family relations and peer relations. In M. Rutter (Ed.), *Scientific foundations of developmental psychiatry.* London: Heinemann.

Hasher, L., and Zacks, R. G. (1979) Automatic and effortful processing in memory. *Journal of Experimental Psychology: General, 108,* 356–388.

Hathaway, S. R., and Monachesi, E. D. (1953) *Analyzing and predicting juvenile delinquency with the MMPI.* Minneapolis: University of Minnesota Press.

Hayes, J. H. (1978) *Cognitive psychology.* Homewood, Ill.: Dorsey.

Hayes, K. (1951) *The ape in our house.* New York: Harper and Row.

Hebb, D. O. (1949) *The organization of behavior: A neuropsychological theory.* New York: Wiley.

Hebb, D. O. (1972) *Textbook of psychology.* (3rd ed.) Philadelphia: Saunders.

Heider, E. R., and Oliver, D. (1972) The structure of the color space in naming and memory for two languages. *Cognitive Psychology, 3,* 337–354.

Heider, F. (1958) *The psychology of interpersonal relations.* New York: Wiley.

Heinicke, C. M., and Westheimer, I. *Brief separations.* New York: International Universities Press, 1965.

Held, R., and Bauer, J. A., Jr. (1967) Visually guided reaching in infant monkeys after restricted rearing. *Science, 155,* 718–720.

Held, R., and Hein, A. (1963) Movement-produced stimulation in the development of visually guided behavior. *Journal of Comparative and Physiological Psychology, 56,* 872–876.

Helson, H. (1948) Adaptation-level as a basis for a quantitative theory of frames of reference. *Psychological Review, 55,* 297–313.

Hess, E. H. (1958) "Imprinting" in animals. *Scientific American, 198,* 81–90.

Hess, E. H., and Polt, J. M. (1964) Pupil size in relation to mental activity during simple problem-solving. *Science, 140,* 1190–1192.

Hess, R. D., and Shipman, V. C. (1965) Early experience and the socialization of cognitive modes in children. *Child Development, 34,* 869–886.

Heston, L. L. (1966) Psychiatric disorders in foster home reared children of schizophrenic mothers. *British Journal of Psychiatry, 112,* 819–825.

Heston, L. L., and Denny, D. (1968) *Interactions between early life experience and biological factors in schizophrenia.* In D. Rosenthal and S. Kety (Eds.), *The transmission of schizophrenia.* Oxford: Pergamon Press.

Hetherington, E. M. (1972) The effects of father absence on personality development in adolescent daughters. *Developmental Psychology, 7,* 313–326.

Hetherington, E. M. (1979) Family interaction. In H. C. Quay and J. S. Werry (Eds.), *Psychopathological disorders of childhood.* (2nd ed.) New York: Wiley.

Higgins, E. T., Rholes, W. S., and Jones, C. R. (1977) Category accessibility and impression formation. *Journal of Experimental Social Psychology, 13,* 141–154.

Hill, J. P. (1964) Parental determinants of sex-typed behavior. Unpublished doctoral dissertation, Harvard University.

Hindley, C. B., Filliozat, A. M., Klackenberg, G., Nicolet-Meister, D., and Sand, E. A. (1966) Differences in walking in European longitudinal samples. *Human Biology, 38,* 364–379.

Hiroto, D. S. (1974) Locus of control and learned helplessness. *Journal of Experimental Psychology, 102,* 187–193.

Hirsch, J. (1970) Behavior-genetic analysis and its biosocial consequences. *Seminars in Psychiatry, 2,* 89–105.

Hirsch, J., and Knittle, J. L. (1970) Cellularity of obese and nonobese human adipose tissue. *Federation Proceedings, 29,* 1516–1521.

Hirst, E., Spelke, B. S., Reaves, C. C., Caharick, G., and Neisser, H. (1980) Dividing attention without alternation or automaticity. *Journal of Experimental Psychology: General, 109,* 187–193.

Hjelle, L. A., and Ziegler, D. J. (1981) *Personality theories: Basic assumptions, research, and applications.* (2nd ed.) New York: McGraw-Hill.

Hoffman, M. L. (1960) Power assertion by the parent and its impact on the child. *Child Development, 31,* 129–143.

Hoffman, M. L. (1970a) Conscience, personality, and socialization techniques. *Human Development, 13,* 90–126.

Hoffman, M. L. (1970b) Moral development. In P. H. Mussen (Ed.), *Carmichael's manual of child psychology,* Vol. 2. (3rd ed.) New York: Wiley.

Hoffman, M. L. (1981) Perspectives on the difference between understanding people and understanding things: The role of affect. In J. H. Flavell and L. Ross (Eds.), *Social cognitive development.* Cambridge, England: Cambridge University Press.

Hoffman, M. L., and Saltzstein, H. D. (1967) Parent discipline and the child's moral development. *Journal of Personality and Social Psychology, 5,* 45–57.

Hofstaetter, P. R. (1954) The changing composition of "intelligence": A study in technique. *Journal of Genetic Psychology, 85,* 159–164.

Hogan, R. (1976) *Personality theory: The personological tradition.* Englewood Cliffs, N.J.: Prentice-Hall.

Holden, C. (1980) Identical twins reared apart. *Science, 207,* 1323–1325, 1327–1328.

Hollingshead, A. B., and Redlich, F. (1958) *Social class and mental illness.* New York: Wiley.

Hollingworth, L. S. (1942) *Children above 180 IQ.* New York: Harcourt, Brace and World.

Holmes, T. H., and Rahe, R. H. (1967) The social readjustment rating scale. *Journal of Psychosomatic Research, 11,* 213–218.

Holt, R. R. (1971) *Assessing personality.* New York: Harcourt Brace Jovanovich.

Honzik, M. P., Macfarlane, J. W., and Allen, L. (1948) The stability of mental test performance between two and eighteen years. *Journal of Experimental Education, 18,* 309–324.

Hopson, J. L. (1979) Scent and human behavior: Olfaction or fiction? *Science News, 115,* 282–283.

Horn, C., and Smith, L. F. (1945) The Horn Art Aptitude Inventory. *Journal of Applied Psychology, 29.*

Horn, J. L., and Cattell, R. B. (1967) Age differences in fluid and crystallized intelligence. *Acta Psychologia, 26,* 107–129.

Horney, K. (1934) The overevaluation of love: Study of a common present-day feminine type. *Psychoanalytic Quarterly, 3,* 605–638.

Horowitz, M. J., and Solomon, G. F. (1978) Delayed stress response syndromes in Vietnam veterans. In C. R. Figley (Ed.), *Stress disorders among Vietnam veterans.* New York: Brunner/Mazel.

Hovland, C. I., Janis, I. L., and Kelley, H. H. (1953) *Communication and persuasion.* New Haven, Conn.: Yale University Press.

Hubel, D. H. (1963) The visual cortex of the brain. *Scientific American, 209,* 54–62.

Hubel, D. H., and Wiesel, T. N. (1959) Receptive fields of single neurons in the cat's striate cortex. *Journal of Physiology, 148,* 574–591.

Hubel, D. H., and Wiesel, T. N. (1963) Receptive fields of cells in striate cortex of very young, visually inexperienced kittens. *Journal of Neurophysiology, 26,* 994–1002.

Huff, D. (1954) *How to lie with statistics.* New York: W. W. Norton.

Hunt, E., and Love, T. (1972) How good can memory be? In A. W. Melton and E. Martin (Eds.), *Coding processes in human memory.* New York: Wiley.

Hunt, M. (1974) *Sexual behavior in the 1970s.* Chicago: Playboy Press.

Hurvich, L. M., and Jameson, D. (1957) An opponent-process theory of color vision. *Psychological Review, 64,* 384–404.

Hyde, J. S. (1982) *Understanding human sexuality.* (2nd ed.) New York: McGraw-Hill.

Inhelder, B. (1966) Cognitive development and its contribution to the diagnosis of some phenomena of mental deficiency. *Merrill-Palmer Quarterly, 12,* 299–319.

Irwin, D. M., and Ambron, S. R. (1973) Moral judgment and role-taking in children aged three to seven. Paper presented to the Society for Research in Child Development.

Itard, J. M. G. (1870) *The wild boy of Aveyron.* (Translated by G. Humphrey and M. Humphrey.) New York: Appleton-Century-Crofts, 1932.

Jackson, S. (1965) The growth of logical thinking in normal and subnormal children. *British Journal of Educational Psychology, 35,* 255–258.

Jakubezak, L. F., and Walters, R. H. (1959) Suggestibility as dependency behavior. *Journal of Abnormal and Social Psychology, 59,* 102–107.

James, W. (1890) *The principles of psychology,* Vols. 1 and 2. New York: Henry Holt.

James, W., and Lange, C. G. (1922) *The emotions.* (Edited by K. Dunlap.) Baltimore: Williams and Wilkins.

Janis, I. L. (1973) *Victims of group think.* Boston: Houghton Mifflin.

Janis, I. L., and Mann, L. (1977) Coping with decisional conflict. In I. L. Janis (Ed.), *Current trends in psychology.* Los Altos, Calif.: William Kaufman.

Jarvik, L. F., Eisdorfer, C., and Blum, J. E. (Eds.) (1973) *Intellectual functioning in adults.* New York: Springer.

Jenkins, J. G. and Dallenbach, K. M. (1924) Oblivescence during sleep and waking. *American Journal of Psychology, 35,* 605–612.

Jensen, A. R. (1969) How much can we boost IQ and scholastic achievement? *Harvard Educational Review, 39,* 1–123. Reprinted in *Environment, heredity and intelligence.* Cambridge, Mass.: Harvard Educational Review Reprint Series 2.

Jersild, A. T. (1960) *Child psychology.* (5th ed.) Englewood Cliffs, N.J.: Prentice-Hall.

Johnson, D. J., and Myklebust, H. (1967) *Learning and disabilities: Educational principles and practices.* New York: Grune and Stratton.

Johnson, D. L. (1981) Naturally acquired learned helplessness: The relationship of school failure to achievement behavior, attributions and self-concept. *Journal of Educational Psychology, 73,* 174–180.

Johnston, P. J., and Davidson, J. M. (1972) Intracerebral androgens and sexual behavior in the male rat. *Hormones and Behavior, 3,* 345–357.

Jones, E. E., and Davis, K. E. (1965) A theory of correspondent inferences: From acts to dispositions. In L. Berkowitz (Ed.), *Advances in experimental social psychology,* Vol. 2. New York: Academic Press.

Jones, E. E., and Nisbett, R. (1971) *The actor and the observer: Divergent impressions of the causes of behavior.* New York: General Learning Press.

Jones, E. E., and Pittman, T. S. (1982) Toward a general theory of strategic self presentation. In J. Suls (Ed.), *Psychological perspectives on the self.* Hillsdale, N.J.: Lawrence Erlbaum Associates.

Jones, L. (1981) Achievement test scores in mathematics and science. *Science, 213,* 412–416.

Jung, C. G. (1923) *Psychological types.* London: Routledge.

Kagan, J. (1971) The beneficiaries of change. Paper presented at Symposium on Crises on Our Conscience, October. Washington, D.C.: Joseph P. Kennedy, Jr. Foundation.

Kagan, J. (1972) Cross-cultural perspectives on early development. Paper presented to the Annual Meeting of the American Association for the Advancement of Science, Washington, D.C., December.

Kagan, J. (1983) Stress and coping in early development. In N. Garmezy and M. Rutter

(Eds.), *Stress, coping, and development in children.* New York: McGraw-Hill.

Kalish, H. I. (1980) *From behavioral science to behavior modification.* New York: McGraw-Hill.

Kanfer, F. H., and Phillips, J. S. (1970) *Learning foundations of behavior therapy.* New York: Wiley.

Kaplan, W., and Kimball, C. (1982) The risks and course of coronary artery disease: A biopsychosocial perspective. In T. Millon, C. Green, and R. Meagher (Eds.), *Handbook of clinical health psychology.* New York: Plenum Press.

Karlsson, J. L. (1974) Inheritance of schizophrenia. *Acta Psychiatrica Scandinavica,* Supplement 247.

Kasl, S. V., and Cobb, S. (1970) Blood pressure changes in men undergoing job loss: A preliminary report. *Psychosomatic Medicine, 33,* 19–38.

Kasl, S. V., and Cobb, S. (1980) The experience of losing a job: Some effects on cardiovascular functioning. *Psychotherapy and Psychosomatics, 34,* 88–109.

Kasl, S. V., and Cobb, S. (1982) Variability of stress effects among men experiencing job loss. In L. Goldberger and S. Breznitz (Eds.), *Handbook of stress.* New York: Free Press.

Katz, I. (1968) Factors influencing Negro performance in the desegregated school. In M. Deutsch, I. Katz, and A. R. Jensen (Eds.), *Social class, race, and psychological development.* New York: Holt, Rinehart and Winston.

Katz, P., and Zigler, E. (1967) Self-image disparity: A developmental approach. *Journal of Personality and Social Psychology, 5,* 186–195.

Katzell, R. A., and Guzzo, R. A. (1983) Psychological approaches to productivity improvement. *American Psychologist, 38,* 468–473.

Kazdin, A. E. (1977) *The token economy.* New York: Plenum Press.

Kazdin, A. E. (1978) *History of behavior modification: Experimental foundations of contemporary research.* Baltimore: University Park Press.

Keegan, J. (1976) *The face of battle.* New York: Viking Press.

Keenan, J. M., and Kintsch, W. (1974) The identification of explicitly and implicitly presented information. In W. Kintsch, *The representation of meaning in memory.* Hillside, N.J.: Lawrence Erlbaum Associates.

Keeney, T. J., Cannizzo, S. R., and Flavell, J. H. (1967) Spontaneous and induced verbal rehearsal in a recall task. *Child Development, 38,* 953–966.

Keiser, S. (1969) Superior intelligence: Its contribution of neurogenesis. *Journal of the American Psychoanalytic Association, 17,* 452–473.

Kelley, H. H. (1967) Attribution theory in social

psychology. In D. Levine (Ed.), *Nebraska Symposium on Motivation, 15,* 192–238.

Kelley, H. H. (1971) *Attribution in social interaction.* New York: General Learning Press.

Kelley, H. H., Thibaut, J. W., Radloff, R., and Mundy, D. (1962) The development of co-operation in the "Minimal social situation." *Psychological Monographs.* (Whole 538.)

Kellogg, W. N., and Kellogg, L. A. (1933) *The ape and the child.* New York: McGraw-Hill.

Kendall, P. C., Williams, L., Pechacek, T. F., Graham, L. E., Shisslak, C., and Horzoff, N. (1979) Cognitive-behavioral and patient education interventions in cardiac catheterization procedures. The Palo Alto Medical Psychology Project. *Journal of Consulting and Clinical Psychology, 47,* 49–58.

Keppel, G., and Underwood, B. J. (1962) Proactive inhibition in short-term retention of single items. *Journal of Verbal Learning and Verbal Behavior, 1,* 153–161.

Kety, S. S., Rosenthal, D., Schulsinger, F., and Wender, P. H. (1968) The types and prevalence of mental illness in the biological and adoptive families of adopted schizophrenics. *Journal of Psychiatric Research,* Supplement 1, 254–362.

Kety, S. S., Rosenthal, D., Wender, P. H., Schulsinger, F., and Jacobsen, B. (1975) Mental illness in the biological and adoptive families of adopted individuals who have become schizophrenic: A preliminary report based upon psychiatric interviews. In R. Fieve, D. Rosenthal, and H. Brill (Eds.), *Genetic research in psychiatry.* Baltimore: Johns Hopkins University Press.

Keys, A. B., Brozek, J., Henschel, A., Mickelson, O., and Taylor, H. L. (1950) *The biology of human starvation.* Minneapolis: University of Minnesota Press.

Kimble, G. A. (1978) *How to use (and misuse) statistics.* Englewood Cliffs, N.J.: Prentice-Hall.

Kimble, G. A. (1981) Biological and cognitive constraints on learning. In L. T. Benjamin, Jr. (Ed.), *The G. Stanley Hall Lectures,* Vol. 1. Washington, D.C.: American Psychological Association.

Kimble, G. A., and Perlmuter, L. C. (1970) The problem of volition. *Psychological Review, 77,* 361–384.

King, F. A., (Ed.) (1978) *Handbook of behavioral neurobiology.* New York: Plenum Press.

Kinsey, A. C., Pomeroy, W. B., and Martin, C. E. (1948) *Sexual behavior in the human male.* Philadelphia: Saunders.

Kinsey, A. C., Pomeroy, W. B., Martin, C. E., and Gebhard, P. H., (1953) *Sexual behavior in the human female.* Philadelphia: Saunders.

Kintsch, W. (1977) *Memory and cognition.* (2nd ed.) New York: Wiley.

Klatzky, R. L. (1975) *Human memory: Structures and processes.* San Francisco: W. H. Freeman.

Klaus, M. H., Jerauld, R., Kreger, N. C., McAlpine, W., Steffa, M., and Kennell, J. H. (1972) Maternal attachment: Importance of the first post-partum days. *New England Journal of Medicine, 286,* 460–463.

Klein, D. F. (1981) Anxiety reconceptualized. In D. F. Klein and J. Rabkin (Eds.), *Anxiety: New research and changing concepts.* New York: Raven Press.

Klerman, G. L. (1977) Better but not well: Social and ethical issues in the deinstitutionalization of the mentally ill. *Schizophrenia Bulletin, 3,* 617–631.

Klerman, G. L. (1983) The efficacy of psychotherapy as the basis for public policy. *American Psychologist, 38,* 929–934.

Klonoff, H. (1974) Marijuana and driving in real-life situations. *Science, 186,* 317–324.

Knittle, J. L. (1975) Early influences on development of adipose tissue. In G. A. Bray (Ed.), *Obesity in perspective.* Washington, D.C.: U.S. Government Printing Office.

Knox, R. E., and Safford, R. K. (1976) Group caution at the racetrack. *Journal of Experimental Social Psychology, 12,* 317–324.

Kohlberg, L. (1966) Sex differences in morality. In E. E. Maccoby (Ed.), *The development of sex differences.* Stanford, Calif.: Stanford University Press.

Kohlberg, L. (1969) Stage and sequence: The cognitive-developmental approach to socialization. In D. A. Goslin (Ed.), *Handbook of socialization theory and research.* Chicago: Rand McNally.

Kohlberg, L. (1971) Early education: A cognitive-developmental view. In P. S. Sears (Ed.), *Intellectual development.* New York: Wiley.

Kohlberg, L. (1976) Moral stages and moralization: The cognitive-developmental approach. In T. Lickona (Ed.), *Moral development and behavior: Theory, research, and social issues.* New York: Holt, Rinehart and Winston.

Köhler, W. (1925) *The mentality of apes.* New York: Harcourt, Brace and World.

Kohn, M. L. (1959) Social class and parental values. *American Journal of Sociology, 64,* 337–351.

Kohn, M. L. (1972) Class, family and schizophrenia: A reformulation. *Social Forces, 50,* 295–313.

Kohn, M. L. (1979) The effects of social class on parental values and practices. In D. Reiss and H. A. Hoffman (Eds.), *The American family: Dying or developing.* New York: Plenum Press.

Kolb, L. C. (1977) *Modern clinical psychiatry.* (9th ed.) Philadelphia: Saunders.

Konorski, J. (1948) *Conditioned reflexes and neuron organization.* New York: Cambridge University Press.

Kraepelin, E. (1904) *Lectures on clinical psychiatry.* London: Bailliere, Tindall and Cox.

Krasner, L. (1976) The operant approach in behavior modification. In J. T. Spence, R. C. Carson, and J. W. Thibaut (Eds.), *Behavioral approaches to therapy.* Morristown, N.J.: General Learning Press.

Krueger, W. C. F. (1929) The effect of overlearning on retention. *Journal of Experimental Psychology, 12,* 71–78.

Kugel, R. B., and Parsons, M. H. (1967) *Children of deprivation: Changing the course of familial retardation.* Washington, D.C.: Department of Health, Education and Welfare, Children's Bureau.

Kurtines, W., and Greif, E. B. (1974) The development of moral thought: Review and evaluation of Kohlberg's approach. *Psychological Bulletin, 81,* 453–470.

Laing, R. D. (1964) *The politics of experience.* New York: Ballantine Books.

Lamb, M. E. (1977a) The development of mother-infant and father-infant attachments in the second year of life. *Developmental Psychology, 13,* 637–648.

Lamb, M. E. (1977b) Father-infant interaction in the first year of life. *Child Development, 48,* 167–181.

Lamb, M. E. (Ed.) (1981) *The role of the father in child development.* (2nd ed.) New York: Wiley.

Lamb, M. E., Easterbrooks, M. A., and Holden, G. W. (1980) Reinforcement and punishment among preschoolers: Characteristics, effects, and correlates. *Child Development, 51,* 1230–1236.

Lamm, H., and Myers, D. G. (1978) Group-induced polarization of attitudes and behavior. In L. Berkowitz (Ed.), *Advances in experimental social psychology,* Vol. 11. New York: Academic Press.

Lane, H. (1976) *The wild boy of Aveyron.* Cambridge, Mass.: Harvard University Press.

Lang, P. J., and Melamed, B. E. (1969) Avoidance conditioning therapy of an infant with chronic ruminative vomiting: Case report. *Journal of Abnormal Psychology, 74,* 1–8.

Langhorne, J. E., and Loney, J. (1976) Childhood hyperkinesis: A return to the source. *Journal of Abnormal Psychology, 85,* 201–209.

LaPiere, R. T. (1934) Attitudes vs. actions. *Social Forces, 13,* 230–237.

Latané, B. (1981) The psychology of social impact. *American Psychologist, 36,* 343–356.

Latané, B., and Darley, J. M. (1970) *The unresponsive bystander: Why doesn't he help?* New York: Appleton-Century-Crofts.

Latané, B., and Harkins, S. (1976) Cross-modality matches suggest anticipated stage fright a multiplicative power function of audience size and status. *Perception and Psychophysics, 20,* 482–488.

Latané, B., Williams, K., and Harkins, S. (1979) Many hands make light the work: The cases and consequences of social loafing. *Journal* of Personality and Social Psychology, 37, 822–832.

Laughlin, H. P. (1967) The neuroses. Washington, D.C.: Butterworth.

Laurendeau, M., and Pinard, A. (1962) Causal thinking in the child. New York: International Universities Press.

Laurendeau-Bendavid, M. (1977) Culture, schooling, and cognitive development: A comparative study of children in French Canada and Rwanda. In P. R. Dasen (Ed.), Piagetian psychology: Cross-cultural contributions. New York: Gardner Press.

Lave, L. B. (1965) Factors affecting cooperation in the prisoner's dilemma. Behavioral Science, 10, 26–38.

Lazarus, R. S., and Cohen, J. B. (1977) Environmental stress. In I. Altman and J. F. Wohlwill (Eds.), Human behavior and environment, Vol. 2. New York: Plenum Press.

Lazarus, R. S., and Launier, R. (1978) Stress-related transactions between person and environment. In L. A. Pervin and M. Lewis (Eds.) Perspectives in interactional psychology. New York: Plenum Press.

Leahy, R. L. (1981) The development of the conception of economic inequality: I. Descriptions and comparisons of rich and poor people. Child Development, 52, 523–532.

Lee, E. S. (1951) Negro intelligence and selective migration. American Sociological Review 16, 227–233.

Leff, J. P. (1976) Schizophrenia and sensitivity to family environment. Schizophrenia Bulletin, 24, 566–574.

Lenneberg, E. (1967) Biological foundations of language. New York: Wiley.

Leon, G. R., Carroll, K., Chernyk, B., and Finn, S. (1982) Binge eating and associated habit patterns within college student and identified bulimic populations. Unpublished manuscript.

Leon, G. R., and Roth, L. (1977) Obesity: Psychological courses, correlations, and speculations. Psychological Bulletin, 84, 117–139.

Lepper, M. R. (1973) Dissonance, self-perception and honesty in children. Journal of Personality and Social Psychology, 25, 65–74.

Lepper, M. R., Greene, D., and Nisbett, R. E. (1973) Undermining children's intrinsic interest with extrinsic reward: A test of the overjustification hypothesis. Journal of Personality and Social Psychology, 28, 129–137.

Lerner, S. E., and Burns, R. S. (1978) Phencyclidine used among youth: History, epidemiology and acute and chronic intoxication. In R. C. Petersen and R. C. Stillman (Eds.), Phencyclidine (PCP) abuse: An appraisal. National Institute of Drug Abuse Research Monograph 21, Rockville, Md.

Lerner, T. W. (1971) Children with learning disabilities: Theories. diagnosis, and teaching strategies. Boston: Houghton Mifflin.

Lesser, G. S., Fifer, G., and Clark, D. H. (1965) Mental abilities of children from different social class and cultural groups. Monographs of the Society for Research in Child Development, 30 (Serial 102).

Levine, J. D., Gordon, N. C., and Fields, H. L. (1978) The mechanism of placebo analgesia. Lancet, 23, 654–657.

Levine, M. (1966) Hypothesis behavior by humans during discrimination learning. Journal of Experimental Psychology, 71, 331–338.

Lewin, K. (1936) A dynamic theory of personality. New York: McGraw-Hill.

Lewis, M. (1972) Parents and children. Sex role development. School Review, 80, 229–240.

Lewis, M. (1975) Early sex differences in the human: Studies of socioemotional development. Archives of Sexual Behavior, 4, 329–335.

Liberman, R. P. (1979) Social skills and rehabilitation for schizophrenics. NIMH Program Project Grant. Mental Health Clinical Research Center for the Study of Schizophrenia, Camarillo State Hospital and University of California at Los Angeles.

Liberman, R. P. (1982) Assessment of social skills. Schizophrenia Bulletin, 8, 62–98.

Lindzey, G., and Aronson, E. (1968) The handbook of social psychology, Vols. 1-5. (2nd ed.) Reading, Mass.: Addison-Wesley.

Little, L. (1968) Cultural variations in social schemata. Journal of Personality and Social Psychology, 10, 1–7.

Livesley, W. J., and Bromley, D. B. (1973) Person perception in childhood and adolescence. London: Wiley.

Lloyd, G. G., and Lishman, W. A. (1975) Effect of depression on the speed of recall of pleasant and unpleasant experiences. Psychological Medicine, 5, 173–180.

Locke, J. (1690) An essay concerning human understanding. London. (Edited by P. H. Nidditch.) New York: Oxford University Press, 1979.

Loehlin, J. C., Lindzey, G., and Spuhler, J. N. (1975) Race differences in intelligence. San Francisco: W. H. Freeman.

Loftus, E. F., and Loftus, G. R. (1980) On the permanence of stored information in the human brain. American Psychologist, 35, 409–420.

Loftus, E. F., and Palmer, J. C. (1974) Reconstruction of automobile destruction: An example of the interaction between language and memory. Journal of Verbal Learning and Verbal Behavior, 13, 585–589.

Loftus, G. R., and Loftus, E. F. (1976) Human memory: The processing of information. Hillsdale, N.J.: Lawrence Erlbaum Associates.

Loro, A. D., Jr., and Orleans, C. S. (1981) Binge eating in obesity: Preliminary findings and guidelines for behavioral analysis and treatment. Addictive Behaviors, 6, 155–166.

Lott, A. J., and Lott, B. E. (1974) The role of reward in the formation of positive interpersonal attitudes. In T. Huston (Ed.), Foundations of interpersonal attraction. New York: Academic Press.

Luchins, A. S. (1942) Mechanization in problem solving. Psychological Monographs, 54. (Whole 248.)

Ludwig, A. M., Brandsma, J. M., Wilbur, C. B., Bendfeldt, F., and Jameson, D. H. (1972) The objective study of a multiple personality. Archives of General Psychiatry, 26, 298–310.

Luria, A. R. (1957) The role of language in the formation of temporary connections. In B. Simon (Ed.), Psychology in the Soviet Union. Stanford, Calif.: Stanford University Press.

Luria, A. R. (1961) The role of speech in the regulation of normal and abnormal behavior. New York: Liveright.

Lynch, J. J. (1977) The broken heart. New York: Basic Books.

Maccoby, E. E., and Bee, H. L. (1965) Some speculations concerning the lag between perceiving and performing. Child Development. 36, 367–377.

Maccoby, E. E., and Jacklin, C. N. (1974) The psychology of sex differences. Stanford, Calif.: Stanford University Press.

MacMillan, D., and Meyers, C. E. (1980) Larry P: An educational interpretation. School Psychology Review, 9, 136–148.

MacNichol, E. F., Jr. (1964) Three-pigment color vision. Scientific American, 211, 48–56.

Maddi, S. R. (1976) Personality theories: A comparative analysis. (3rd ed.) Homewood, Ill.: Dorsey Press.

Maher, B. A. (1963) Intelligence and brain damage. In N. R. Ellis (Ed.), Handbook of mental deficiency. New York: McGraw-Hill.

Maher, W. B., and Maher, B. A. (1984) Psychopathology: I. From ancient times to the eighteenth century. In G. A. Kimble and K. Schlesinger (Eds.), Topics in the history of psychology. Hillsdale, N.J.: Lawrence Erlbaum Associates.

Mahoney, M. J., and Mahoney, K. (1976) Permanent weight control. New York: W. W. Norton.

Maier, S. F., and Seligman, M. E. P. (1976) Learned helplessness: Theory of evidence. Journal of Experimental Psychology: General, 105, 3–46.

Malleus maleficarium of Heinrich Kramer and James Sprenger (1487) New York: Dover Publications, 1971.

Marañón, G. (1924) Contributions à l'etude de l'action émotive l'adrenaline. In Revue francaise d'endocrinologie, 2, 301.

Marks, I. M. (1972) Flooding (implosion) and allied treatments. In W. S. Agras (Ed.), Behavior modifications: Principles and clinical applications. Boston: Little, Brown.

Marks, I. M. (1978) Living with fear. New York: McGraw-Hill.

Marks, J. (1925) Genius and disaster: Studies

in drugs and genius. New York: Adelphi Company.

Marks, L. E. (1975) On colored-hearing synesthesia: Cross modal translations of sensory dimensions. *Psychological Bulletin, 82,* 303–327.

Marshall, G. D., and Zimbardo, P. G. (1979) Affective consequences of inadequately explained physiological arousal. *Journal of Personality and Social Psychology, 37,* 970–988.

Martin, R. A., and Poland, E. Y. (1980) *Learning to change: A self-management approach to adjustment.* New York: McGraw-Hill.

Maslach, C. (1979) The emotional consequences of arousal without reason. In C. E. Izard (Ed.), *Emotions in personality and psychopathology.* New York: Plenum Press.

Maslach, C. (1979) Negative emotional biasing of unexplained arousal. *Journal of Personality and Social Psychology, 37,* 953–969.

Maslow, A. H. (1970) *Motivation and personality.* (2nd ed.) New York: Harper and Row.

Masserman, J. H. (1961) *Principles of dynamic psychiatry.* (2nd ed.) Philadelphia: Saunders.

Masters, W. H., and Johnson, V. E. (1966) *Human sexual response.* Boston: Little, Brown.

Matarazzo, J. D. (1980) Behavioral health and behavioral medicine: Frontiers for a new health psychology. *American Psychologist, 35,* 807–817.

Matarazzo, J. D. (1983) Education and training in health psychology: Boulder or bolder. *Health Psychology, 2,* 73–113.

Maurer, D., and Barrera, M. (1981) Infants' perception of natural and distorted arrangements of schematic faces. *Child Development, 52,* 196–202.

Maurer, D., and Salapatek, P. (1977) Developmental changes in the scanning of faces by young infants. *Child Development, 47,* 523–527.

May, P. R. A. (1968) *Treatment of schizophrenia.* New York: Science House.

May, P. R. A. (1974) Psychotherapy research in schizophrenia: Another review of a present reality. *Schizophrenia Bulletin, 9,* 126–132.

Maw, W. H., and Maw, E. W. (1977) Nature and assessment of human curiosity. In P. McReynolds (Ed.), *Advances in psychological assessment,* Vol. 4. San Francisco: Jossey-Bass.

McArthur, L. Z., and Post, D. L. (1977) Figural emphasis and person perception. *Journal of Experimental Social Psychology, 13,* 520–535.

McClearn, G. E. (1962) The inheritance of behavior. In L. Postman (Ed.), *Psychology in the making.* New York: Knopf.

McClintock, M. K. (1971) Menstrual synchrony and suppression. *Nature, 229,* 244–245.

McDougall, W. (1926) *An introduction to social psychology.* Boston: Bruce Humphries.

McGuire, W. J. (1964) Inducing resistance to persuasion. In L. Berkowitz (Ed.), *Advances in experimental social psychology,* Vol. 1. New York: Academic Press.

McKay, D. G. (1973) Aspects of the theory and comprehension of memory and attention. *Quarterly Journal of Experimental Psychology, 25,* 22–40.

McNeill, D. (1966) Developmental psycholinguistics. In F. Smith and G. A. Miller (Eds.), *The genesis of language.* Cambridge, Mass.: M.I.T. Press.

McNemar, Q. (1942) *The revision of the Standard-Binet Scale.* Boston: Houghton Mifflin.

Mead, M. (1935) *Sex and temperament in three primitive societies.* New York: Morrow.

Meadow, A., Parves, S. J., and Reese, H. (1959) Influence of brainstorming instructions and problem sequence on a creative problem solving task. *Journal of Applied Psychology, 43,* 413–416.

Meehl, P. E. (1954) *Clinical versus statistical prediction.* Minneapolis: University of Minnesota Press.

Meehl, P. E. (1959) A comparison of clinicians with five statistical methods of identifying psychotic MMPI profiles. *Journal of Counseling Psychology, 6,* 102–109.

Meehl, P. E. (1962) Schizotaxia, schizotypy, schizophrenia. *American Psychologist, 17,* 827–838.

Megargee, E. I. (1972) *The California psychological inventory handbook.* San Francisco: Jossey-Bass.

Mehrabian, A., and Diamond, S. G. (1971) Seating arrangement and conversation. *Sociometry, 34,* 281–289.

Meichenbaum, D. (1977) *Cognitive-behavior modification.* New York: Plenum Press.

Meichenbaum, D., and Cameron, R. (1983) Stress inoculation training. In D. Meichenbaum and M. E. Jarembo (Eds.), *Stress reduction and prevention.* New York: Plenum Press.

Mellor, C. S. (1970) First rank symptoms of schizophrenia. *British Journal of Psychiatry. 117,* 15–23.

Melzack, R., and Wall, P. D. (1965) Pain mechanisms: A new theory. *Science, 150,* 971–979.

Mendelson, J. H., and Mello, N. K. (Eds.) (1979) *The diagnosis and treatment of alcoholism.* New York: McGraw-Hill.

Menninger, K. (1968) *The crime of punishment.* New York: Viking Press.

Menyuk, P. (1971) *The acquisition and development of language.* Englewood Cliffs, N.J.: Prentice-Hall.

Mercer, J. R. (1975) Sociocultural factors in educational labeling. In M. J. Begab and S. A. Richardson (Eds.), *The mentally retarded and society: A social science perspective.* Baltimore: University Park Press.

Merton, R. K. (1948) The self-fulfilling prophecy. *Antioch Review, 8,* 193–210.

Messick, D. M., and McClintock, C. G. (1968) Motivational basis of choice in experimental games. *Journal of Experimental Social Psychology, 4,* 1–25.

Michael, R. (1965) *British Medical Bulletin, 21,* 87–90. [Cited in S. Rose (Ed.), *The conscious brain.* New York: Knopf, 1973.]

Michael, R. P. (1980) Hormones and sexual behavior in the female. In D. T. Krieger and J. C. Hughes (Eds.), *Neuroendocrinology.* Sunderland, Mass.: Sinauer Associates, Hospital Practice Book.

Miles, C. C. (1954) Gifted children. In L. Carmichael (Ed.), *Manual of child psychology.* (2nd ed.) New York: Wiley.

Milgram, S. (1965) Some conditions of obedience and disobedience to authority. *Human Relations, 18,* 57–75.

Miller, D. (1966) Worlds that fail. *Transaction. 2,* 36–41.

Miller, D. R., and Swanson, G. E. (1958) *The changing American parent: A study in the Detroit area.* New York: Wiley.

Miller, G. A. (1956) The magical number seven plus or minus two: Some limits on our capacity for processing information. *Psychological Review, 65,* 81–97.

Miller, G. A. (1965) Some preliminaries to psycholinguistics. *American Psychologist, 20,* 15–20.

Miller, G. A. (1981) *Language and speech.* San Francisco: W. H. Freeman.

Miller, N. E. (1978) Biofeedback and visceral learning. *Annual Review of Psychology, 29,* 373–404.

Miller, N. E., and Brucker, B. S. (1979) A learned visceral response apparently independent of skeletal ones in patients paralyzed by spinal lesions. In N. Birbaumer and H. D. Kimmel (Eds.), *Biofeedback and self-regulation.* Hillside, N.J.: Lawrence Erlbaum Associates.

Miller, N. E., and DiCara, L. (1967) Instrumental learning of heart rate changes in curarized rats: Shaping and specificity to discriminative stimulus. *Journal of Comparative and Physiological Psychology, 63,* 13–19.

Millon, T. (1982) On the nature of clinical health psychology. In T. Millon, C. Green, and R. Meagher (Eds.), *Handbook of clinical health psychology.* New York: Plenum Press.

Milunsky, A. (1977) *Know your genes.* Boston: Houghton Mifflin.

Mineka, S., and Suomi, S. J. (1978) Social separation in monkeys. *Psychological Bulletin, 85,* 1376–1400.

Mischel, W. (1968) *Personality and assessment.* New York: Wiley.

Mittler, P. (Ed.) (1977) *Research to practice in mental retardation,* Vol. I, *Care and intervention;* Vol. II, *Education and training;* Vol. III, *Biomedical aspects.* Baltimore: University Park Press.

Money, J., and Ehrhardt, A. A. (1972) *Man and*

woman, boy and girl. Baltimore: Johns Hopkins University Press.

Monroe, S. M. (1982) Assessment of life events: Retrospective vs. concurrent strategies. *Archives of General Psychiatry, 39,* 606–610.

Moore, L. T. (1924) *Isaac Newton.* New York: Charles Scribner's Sons.

Moore, T. W. (1975) Exclusive early mothering and its alternatives: The outcome to adolescence. *Scandinavian Journal of Psychology, 16,* 255–272.

Morgan, G., and Ricciuti, H. N. (1969) Infants' responses to strangers during the first year. In B. M. Foss (Ed.), *Determinants of infant behavior,* Vol. 4. New York: Wiley.

Moroney, M. J. (1951) *Facts from figures.* Middlesex, England: Penguin Books.

Morse, D. R., and Furst, M. L. (1981) *Women under stress.* New York: Van Nostrand Reinhold.

Morton, J. T. (1942) The distortion of syllogistic reasoning produced by personal convictions. Unpublished doctoral dissertation, Northwestern University.

Moscovici, S., and Zavalloni, M. (1969) The group as a polarizer of attitudes. *Journal of Personality and Social Psychology, 12,* 125–135.

Mosher, F. A., and Hornsby, J. R. (1966) On asking questions. In J. S. Bruner, R. R. Olver, and P. M. Greenfield (Eds.), *Studies in cognitive growth.* New York: Wiley.

Mosher, L. R. (1971) Madness in the community. *Attitude, 1,* 2–21.

Mosher, L. R., and Keith, S. J. (1980) Psychosocial treatment: Individual, group, family, and community support approaches. *Schizophrenia Bulletin, 6,* 10–41.

Moskowitz, B. A. (1978) The acquisition of language. *Scientific American, 239,* 92–108.

Moss, H. A. (1967) Sex, age, and state as determinants of mother-infant interaction. *Merrill-Palmer Quarterly, 13,* 19–36.

Mossler, D. G., Marvin, R. S., and Greenberg, M. T. (1976) Conceptual perspective taking in two- to six-year-old children. *Developmental Psychology, 12,* 85–86.

Mowrer, O. H. (1938) Enuresis: A method for its study and treatment. *American Journal of Orthopsychiatry, 8,* 436–459.

Mueller, E., and Vandell, D. (1979) Infant-infant interaction. In J. D. Osofsky (Ed.), *Handbook of infant development.* New York: Wiley.

Muenzinger, K. F. (1934) Motivation in learning: I. Electric shock for correct responses in the visual discrimination habit. *Journal of Comparative Psychology, 17,* 267–277.

Mugny, G., and Doise, W. (1976) Socio-cognitive conflict and structuration of individual and collective performances. *European Journal of Social Psychology, 8,* 181–192.

Mulder, M., and Stemerding, A. (1963) Threat, attraction to group and need for strong leadership: A laboratory experiment in natural setting. *Human Relations, 16,* 317–334.

Munroe, R. L., and Munroe, R. H. (1975) *Cross-cultural human development.* Monterey, Calif.: Brooks/Cole.

Murray, J. P., and Lonnborg, B. (1980) *Children and television: A primer for parents.* Boys Town, Nebr.: Boys Town Center.

Myers, D. G., and Lamm, H. (1976) The group polarization phenomenon. *Psychological Bulletin, 83,* 602–607.

Nash, J. (1970) *Developmental psychology: A psychobiological approach.* Englewood Cliffs, N.J.: Prentice-Hall.

Nay, W. R. (1977) Analogue measures. In A. R. Ciminero, K. S. Calhoun, and H. E. Adams (Eds.), *Handbook of behavioral assessment.* New York: Wiley-Interscience.

Neimark, E. D. (1975) Intellectual development during adolescence. In F. D. Horowitz (Ed.), *Review of research in child development,* Vol. 4. Chicago: University of Chicago Press.

Neimark, E. D., and Lewis, N. (1967) The development of logical problem-solving strategies. *Child Development, 38,* 107–117.

Nelson, K. (1973) Structure and strategy in learning to talk. *Monographs of the Society for Research in Child Development, 38* (Serial 149), 1–2.

Nelson, K. (1981) Social cognition in a script framework. In J. H. Flavell and L. Ross (Eds.), *Social cognitive development.* Cambridge, England: Cambridge University Press.

Nelson, K., and Gruendel, J. (1981) Generalized event representations: Basic building blocks of cognitive development. In M. E. Lamb and A. L. Brown (Eds.), *Advances in developmental psychology,* Vol. 1. Hillsdale, N.J.: Lawrence Erlbaum Associates.

New York State Department of Mental Hygiene. (1955) *Technical report.*

Nirje, B. (1969) The normalization principle and its human management implication. In R. B. Kugel and W. Wolfensberger (Eds.), *Changing patterns in residential care.* Washington, D.C.: President's Commission on Mental Retardation.

Nisbett, R. E., and Ross, L. (1980) *Human inference: Strategies and shortcomings of social judgment.* Englewood Cliffs, N.J.: Prentice-Hall.

Nisbett, R. E., and Wilson, T. D. (1977) Telling more than we can know: Verbal resorts on mental processes. *Psychological Review, 84,* 231–259.

Noble, C. E. (1952) The role of stimulus meaning (m) in serial verbal learning. *Journal of Experimental Psychology, 43,* 437–446.

Norman, D. A. (1976) *Memory and attention: An introduction to human information processing.* (2nd ed.) New York: Wiley.

Norman, W. T. (1963) Toward an adequate tax-onomy of personality attributes: Replicated factor structure in peer nomination personality ratings. *Journal of Abnormal and Social Psychology, 66,* 574–583.

Öhman, A., Frederickson, M., Hugdahl, K., and Rimmo, P. (1976) The premise of equipotentiality in human classical conditioning: Conditioned electrodermal responses to potentially phobic stimuli. *Journal of Experimental Psychology: General, 105,* 313–337.

Olds, J., and Milner, P. (1954) Positive reinforcement produced by electrical stimulation of septal area and other regions of the rat brain. *Journal of Comparative and Physiological Psychology, 47,* 419–427.

Opper, S. (1977) Concept development in Thai urban and rural children. In P. R. Dasen (Ed.), *Piagetian psychology: Cross-cultural contributions.* New York: Gardner Press.

Orne, M. T. (1962) On the social psychology of the psychological experiment: With particular reference to demand characteristics and their implications. *American Psychologist, 175,* 776–783.

Osgood, C. E., and Suci, G. J. (1955) Factor analysis of meaning. *Journal of Experimental Psychology, 50,* 325–338.

Overmier, J. B., and Seligman, M. E. P. (1967) Effects of inescapable shock upon subsequent escape and avoidance responding. *Journal of Comparative and Physiological Psychology, 63,* 28–33.

Paivio, A. (1971) *Imagery and verbal processes.* New York: Holt, Rinehart and Winston.

Parkes, C. M. (1964) Recent bereavement as a cause of mental illness. *British Journal of Psychiatry, 110,* 198–204.

Parkes, C. M. (1972) *Bereavement: Studies of grief in adult life.* New York: International Universities Press.

Passini, F. T., and Norman, W. T. (1966) A universal conception of personality structure? *Journal of Personality and Social Psychology, 4,* 44–49.

Patterson, G. R. (1980) Mothers: The unacknowledged victims. *Monographs of the Society for Research in Child Development, 45* (5, Serial 186), 1–64.

Paul, G. L. (1966) *Insight and desensitization in psychotherapy: An experiment in anxiety reduction.* Stanford, Calif.: Stanford University Press.

Paul, G. L., and Lentz, R. J. (1977) *Psychosocial treatment of chronic mental patients. Milieu versus social-learning programs.* Cambridge, Mass.: Harvard University Press.

Pavenstedt, E. (1965) A comparison of the child-rearing environment of upper-lower and very low-lower class families. *American Journal of Orthopsychiatry, 35,* 89–98.

Pavlov, I. P. (1927) *Conditioned reflexes: An*

investigation of physiological activity of the cerebral cortex. London: Oxford University Press.

Peele, T. L. (1977) Neuroanatomical basis for clinical neurology. New York: McGraw-Hill.

Peevers, B. H., and Secord, P. F. (1973) Developmental changes in attribution of descriptive concepts to persons. Journal of Personality and Social Psychology, 27, 120–128.

Penfield, W., and Rasmussen, T. (1950) The cerebral cortex of man. New York: Macmillan.

Penfield, W., and Roberts, L. (1959) Speech and brain mechanisms. Princeton, N.J.: Princeton University Press.

Penrose, L. S. (1963) The biology of mental defect. London: Sidgwick and Jackson.

Pert, C. B., Kuhar, M. J., and Snyder, S. H. (1976) Opiate receptor: Autoradiographic localization in rat brain. Proceedings of the National Academy of Sciences, 73, 3729–3733.

Pervin, L. A. (1980) Personality: Theory, assessment, and research. (3rd ed.) New York: Wiley.

Peskin, H. (1964) Ego autonomy at optimal and minimal levels of intellectual functioning. Unpublished manuscript, San Francisco State College.

Peterson, D. R., Becker, W. C., Hellmer, L. A., Shoemaker, D. J., and Quay, H. C. (1959) Parental attitudes and child adjustment. Child Development, 30, 119–130.

Peterson, L. R., and Peterson, M. J. (1959) Short-term retention of individual verbal items. Journal of Experimental Psychology, 58, 193–198.

Petri, H. L. (1981) Motivation: Theory and research. Belmont, Calif.: Wadsworth.

Phillips, D. A. (1978) Children's self image disparity: Effects of age, socioeconomic status, ethnicity, and gender. Unpublished master's thesis, Yale University.

Phillips, D. A. (1981) High achieving students with low academic self-concepts: Achievement motives and orientations. Unpublished doctoral dissertation, Yale University.

Phillips, D. A., and Zigler, E. (1980) Self-concept and its practical implications. In T. D. Yawkey (Ed.), The self-concept of the young child. Provo, Utah: Brigham Young University Press.

Phillips, J. R. (1973) Syntax and vocabulary of mother's speech to young children: Age and sex comparisons. Child Development, 44, 182–185.

Piaget, J. (1932) The moral judgment of the child. New York: Collier Books.

Piaget, J. (1952) Autobiography. In E. G. Boring (Ed.), A history of psychology in autobiography, Vol. 4. Worcester, Mass.: Clark University Press.

Piaget, J. (1962) Plays, dreams and imitation in childhood. New York: W. W. Norton.

Piaget, J. (1971) Foreword to E. Delessert, How the mouse was hit on the head and so discovered the world. New York: Doubleday.

Piaget, J. (1973) States of cognitive development. In R. I. Evans (Ed.), Jean Piaget: The man and his ideas. New York: E. P. Dutton.

Plutchik, R., and Ax, A. F. (1967) A critique of "Determinants of emotional state," by Schachter and Singer (1962). Psychophysiology, 4, 79–82.

Premack, D. (1976) Intelligence in ape and man. Hillsdale, N.J.: Lawrence Erlbaum Associates.

President's Commission on Mental Health. (1978) Report of the Commission, Vols. 1–4. Washington, D.C.: U.S. Government Printing Office.

President's Committee on Mental Retardation (1967) MR67. Washington, D.C.: U.S. Government Printing Office.

Price-Williams, D. R., Gordon, W., and Ramirez, M. (1969) Skill and conservation. Developmental Psychology, 1, 769.

Quattrone, G. A., and Jones, E. E. (1980) The perception of variability within in-groups and out-groups: Implications for the law of small numbers. Journal of Personality and Social Psychology, 38, 141–152.

Rabkin, J. G., and Struening, E. L. (1976) Life events, stress, and illness. Science, 194, 1013–1020.

Ray, O. S. (1978) Drugs, society, and human behavior. (2nd ed.) St. Louis, Mo.: C. V. Mosby.

Reed, E. W., and Reed, S. (1965) Mental retardation: A family study. Philadelphia: Saunders.

Resnick, L. B. (Ed.) (1976) The nature of intelligence. New York: Wiley.

Reuter, M. W., and Biller, H. B. (1973) Perceived paternal nurturance: Availability and personality adjustment among college mates. Journal of Consulting and Clinical Psychology, 40, 339–342.

Revusky, S., and Garcia, J. (1970) Learned associations over long delays. The Psychology of Learning and Motivation, 4, 1–85.

Rheingold, H. L., and Eckerman, C. O. (1970) The infant separates himself from his mother. Science, 168, 78–83.

Rheingold, H. L., and Eckerman, C. O. (1973) Fear of the stranger: A critical examination. In H. W. Reese (Ed.), Advances in child development and behavior, Vol. 8. New York: Academic Press.

Richards, P., Bernall, J. F., and Brackbill, Y. (1977) Early behavioral differences: Sex or circumcision? Unpublished manuscript, Cambridge University.

Riesen, A. H. (1947) The development of visual perception in man and chimpanzee. Science, 106, 107–108.

Riggs, L. A., Ratliff, F., Cornsweet, J. C., and Cornsweet, T. N. (1953) The disappearance of steadily fixated visual test objects. Journal of the Opthamology Society of America, 43, 495–501.

Riley, R. T., and Pettigrew, T. F. (1976) Dramatic events and attitude change. Journal of Personality and Social Psychology, 34, 1004–1015.

Robins, L. N. (1966) Deviant children grown up. Baltimore: Williams and Wilkins.

Rock, I. (1973) Orientation and form. New York: Academic Press.

Rodnick, E. H., and Goldstein, M. J. (1974) Premorbid adjustment and the recovery of mothering function in acute schizophrenic women. Journal of Abnormal Psychology, 83, 623–628.

Roe, A. (1951) A psychological study of physical scientists. Genetic Psychology Monographs, 43, 121–235.

Roethlisberger, F., and Dickson, W. (1939) Management and the worker. Cambridge, Mass.: Harvard University Press.

Rogers, C. R. (1961) On becoming a person. Boston: Houghton Mifflin.

Ropp, R. S. (1957) Drugs and the mind. New York: St. Martin's Press.

Rosch, E. (1973) On the internal structure of perceptual and semantic categories. In T. E. Moore (Ed.), Cognitive development and the acquisition of language. New York: Academic Press.

Rosch, E. (1977) Human categorization. In N. Warren (Ed.), Advances in cross-cultural psychology, Vol. 1. London: Academic Press.

Rosen, E., Fox, R. E., and Gregory, I. (1972) Abnormal psychology. (2nd ed.) Philadelphia: Saunders.

Rosen, J. C., and Wiens, A. M. (1979) Changes in medical problems and use of medical services following psychological intervention. American Psychologist, 34, 420–431.

Rosenberg, M. (1979) Concerning the self. New York: Basic Books.

Rosenblatt, J. S., and Aronson, L. R. (1958) The decline of sexual behavior in male cats after castration with special reference to the role of prior sexual experience. Behaviour, 12, 258–338.

Rosenblum, L. A. (1971) Infant attachment in monkeys. In H. R. Schaffer (Ed.), The origins of human social relations. New York: Academic Press.

Rosenman, R. H., and Friedman, M. (1983) Relationships of Type A behavior pattern to coronary heart disease. In H. Selye (Ed.), Selye's guide to stress research, Vol. 2. New York: Van Nostrand Reinhold.

Rosenthal, R., and Jacobson, L. (1968) Pygmalion in the classroom. New York: Holt, Rinehart and Winston.

Ross, J., and Lawrence, K. A. (1968) Some

observations on memory artifice. *Psychonomic Science, 13,* 107–108.

Ross, J. B., and McLaughlin, M. M. (Eds.) (1949) *A portable medieval reader.* New York: Viking.

Ross, L. (1977) The intuitive psychologist and his shortcomings: Distortions in the attribution process. In L. Berkowitz (Ed.), *Advances in experimental social psychology,* Vol. 10. New York: Academic Press.

Ross, L., Amabile, T. M., and Steinmetz, J. L. (1977) Social roles, social control, and biases in social-perception processes. *Journal of Personality and Social Psychology, 35,* 485–494.

Ross, L., Greene, D., and House, P. (1977) The "false consensus effect": An egocentric bias in social perception and attribution processes. *Journal of Experimental Social Psychology, 13,* 279–301.

Ross, M., and Sicoly, F. (1979) Egocentric biases in availability and attribution. *Journal of Personality and Social Psychology, 37,* 322–336.

Rothkopf, E. Z. (1971) Incidental memory for location of information in text. *Journal of Verbal Learning and Verbal Behavior, 10,* 608–613.

Rozin, P. (1968) Specific aversions and neophobia as a consequence of vitamin deficiency and/or poisoning in half-wild and domestic rats. *Journal of Comparative and Physiological Psychology, 66,* 82–88.

Rubin, D. C. (1982) On the retention function for autobiographical memories. *Journal of Verbal Learning and Verbal Behavior. 21,* 21–38.

Rubin, D. C., and Kozin, M. (1983) Vivid memories. Unpublished manuscript.

Rumbaugh, D. M., Glaserfeld, E. von, Warner, H., Pisani, P., and Gill, T. V. (1974) Lana (chimpanzee) learning a language: A progress report. *Brain and Language, 1,* 205–212.

Rudquist, E. A. (1966) Item and response characteristics in attitude and personality measurement. *Psychological Bulletin, 66,* 166–177.

Rushton, J. P. (1980) *Altruism, socialization, and society.* Englewood Cliffs, N.J.: Prentice-Hall.

Russell, M. J. (1976) Human olfactory communication. *Nature, 260,* 520–522.

Rutter, M. (1971) Parent-child separation: Psychological effects on the children. *Journal of Child Psychology and Psychiatry, 12,* 233–260.

Rutter, M. (1972) *Maternal deprivation reassessed.* (2nd ed., 1981.) Harmondsworth, Middlesex: Penguin.

Rutter, M. (1981a) Social/emotional consequences of day care for pre-school children. *American Journal of Orthopsychiatry, 51,* 4–28.

Rutter, M. (1981b) Stress, coping, and development: Some issues and some questions. *Journal of Child Psychology and Psychiatry, 22,* 323–356.

Salzman, C. (1978) Electroconvulsive therapy. In A. M. Nicholi, Jr. (Ed.), *The Harvard guide to modern psychiatry.* Cambridge, Mass.: The Belknap Press of Harvard University Press.

Sameroff, A. J. (1977) Concepts of humanity in primary prevention. In G. Albee and J. Rolf (Eds.), *Primary prevention of psychopatholgy,* Vol. 1. Burlington, Vt.: Waters.

Sameroff, A. J., and Zax, M. (1973) Neonatal characteristics of offspring of schizophrenic and neurotically-depressed mothers. *Journal of Nervous and Mental Diseases, 157,* 191–199.

Sattler, J. M. (1970) Racial "experimenter effects" in experimentation, testing, interviewing, and psychotherapy. *Psychological Bulletin, 73,* 137–160.

Savage-Rumbaugh, E. S., Rumbaugh, D. M., and Boysen, S. (1978) Symbolic communication between two chimpanzees. *Science, 201,* 641–644.

Scarr, S., and Kidd, K. (1983) Developmental behavior genetics. In M. M. Haith and J. J. Campos (Eds.) *Mussen handbook of child psychology,* Vol. 2, *Infancy and developmental psychobiology.* (4th ed.) New York: Wiley.

Scarr, S., and Weinberg, R. A. (1978) Attitudes, interests, and IQ. *Human Nature, 1,* 29–36.

Schachter, S. (1951) Deviation, rejection, and communication. *Journal of Abnormal and Social Psychology. 46,* 190–207.

Schachter, S., and Singer, J. E. (1962) Cognitive, social and physiological determinants of emotional states. *Psychological Review, 69,* 379–399.

Schaffer, H. R., and Emerson, P. E. (1964) The development of social attachments in infancy. *Monographs of the Society for Research in Child Development, 29* (3). (Whole 94.)

Schaie, K. W., and Strother, C. R. (1968) A cross-sequential study of age changes in cognitive behavior. *Psychological Bulletin, 70,* 671–680.

Schiff, M., Duytme, M., Dumarent, A., Stewart, J., Tomkiewicz, S., and Feingold, J. (1978) Intellectual status of working-class children adopted early into upper-middle-class families. *Science, 200,* 1503–1504.

Schiffman, H. R. (1982) *Sensation and perception: An integrated approach.* (2nd ed.) New York: Wiley.

Schiffman, S. S., and Erickson, R. P. (1980) The issue of primary tastes versus a taste continuum. *Neuroscience and Biobehavioral Reviews, 4,* 109–117.

Schulsinger, F. (1972) Psychopathy: Heredity and environment. In M. Roff, L. Robins, and M. Pollack (Eds.), *Life history research in psychopathology,* Vol. 2. Minneapolis: University of Minnesota Press, 102–119.

Schultz, D. (1976) *Theories of personality.* Monterey, Calif.: Brooks/Cole.

Schwartz, B. (1983) *Psychology of learning and behavior.* (2nd ed.) New York: W. W. Norton.

Searle, L. V. (1949) The organization of hereditary maze brightness and maze dullness. *Genetic Psychology Monographs, 39,* 279–325.

Sears, P. (1976) Does a high I.Q. mean happiness? Dr. Pauline Sears says yes. *People,* January 12, *5,* 55–57.

Segal, J., and Yahraes, H. (1978) *A child's journey.* New York: McGraw-Hill.

Seligman, M. E. P., and Hager, J. L. (1972) *Biological boundaries of learning.* New York: Appleton-Century-Crofts.

Seligman, M. E. P., and Maier, S. F. (1967) Failure to escape traumatic shock. *Journal of Experimental Psychology, 74,* 1–9.

Selye, H. (1976) *The stress of life.* (Rev. ed.) New York: McGraw-Hill.

Selye, H. (Ed.) (1980) *Selye's guide to stress research,* Vol. 1. New York: Van Nostrand Reinhold.

Seyfarth, R. M., Cheney, D. L., and Marler, P. (1980) Monkey responses to three different alarm calls: Evidence of predator classification and semantic communication. *Science, 210,* 801–803.

Shatz, M., and Gelman, R. (1973) The development of communication skills: Modifications in the speech of young children as a function of listener. *Monographs of the Society for Research in Child Development, 38* (Serial 152).

Shaver, K. G. (1981) *Principles of social psychology.* (2nd ed.) Boston: Little, Brown.

Shaw, M. E. (1932) A comparison of individuals and small groups in the rational solution of complex problems. *American Journal of Psychology, 44,* 491–504.

Sherman, J. E., and Liebeskind, J. C. (1980) An endorphinergic, centrifugal substrate of pain modulation: Recent findings, current concepts, and complexities. In J. J. Bonica (Ed.), *Pain.* New York: Raven Press.

Shipley, E. S., Smith, C. D., and Gleitman, L. R. (1969) A study in the acquisition of language: Free responses to commands. *Language, 45,* 322–342.

Shirley, M. M. (1931) *The first two years of life: A study of twenty-five babies,* Vol. 1. Minneapolis: University of Minnesota Press.

Shopsin, B. (Ed.) (1979) *Manic illness.* New York: Raven Press.

Shultz, T., and Zigler, E. (1970) Emotional concomitants of visual mastery in infants: The effects of stimulus movement on smiling and vocalizing. *Journal of Experimental Child Psychology, 10,* 309–402.

Sidowski, J. B. (1957) Reward and punishment in a minimal social situation. *Journal of Experimental Psychology, 54,* 318–326.

Sidowski, J. B., Wycoff, L. B. and Tabory, L. (1956) The influence of reinforcement and punishment in a minimal social situation.

Journal of Abnormal Social Psychology, 52, 115–119.

Siegel, R. K. (1978) Phencyclidine, criminal behavior, and the defense of diminished capacity. In R. C. Petersen and R. C. Stillman (Eds.), *Phencyclidine (PCP) abuse: An appraisal.* National Institute of Drug Abuse Research Monograph 21. Rockville, Md.

Simpson, G. G. (1958) The study of evolution: Methods and present status of theory. In A. Roe and G. G. Simpson (Eds.), *Behavior and evolution.* New Haven, Conn.: Yale University Press.

Singer, D. G., and Singer, J. L. (1977) *Partners in play.* New York: Harper and Row.

Sinnott, E. W., Dunn, L. C., and Dobzhansky, T. (1958) *Principles of genetics.* (5th ed.) New York: McGraw-Hill.

Skeels, H. M. (1966) Adult status of children with contrasting early life experiences: A follow-up study. *Monographs of the Society for Research in Child Development, 31* (3). (Whole 105.)

Skinner, B. F. (1938) *The behavior of organisms: An experimental analysis.* New York: Appleton-Century-Crofts.

Skinner, B. F. (1948) *Walden two.* New York: Macmillan.

Skinner, B. F. (1971) *Beyond freedom and dignity.* New York: Knopf.

Skinner, B. F. (1972) *Cumulative record.* (3rd ed.) New York: Appleton-Century-Crofts.

Skinner, B. F. (1974) *About behaviorism.* New York: Knopf.

Skinner, B. F. (1978) *Reflections on behaviorism and society.* Englewood Cliffs, N.J.: Prentice-Hall.

Slaby, R. G., and Frey, K. S. (1975) Development of gender constancy and selective attention to same sex models. *Child Development, 46,* 849–856.

Slater, E., and Cowie, V. (1971) *Genetics of mental disorders.* London: Oxford University Press.

Smart, M. S., and Smart, R. (1967) *Children: Development and relationships.* New York: Macmillan.

Smith, C. U. M. (1970) *The brain.* New York: G. P. Putnam's Sons.

Smith, J. R. (1981) A review of 120 years of the psychological literature on reactions to combat from the Civil War through the Vietnam War. Unpublished paper.

Smith, M. L., Glass, G. V., and Miller, T. I. (1980) *The benefits of psychotherapy.* Baltimore: Johns Hopkins University Press.

Smith, S. M., Brown, H. O., Thomas, J. E. P., and Goodman, L. S. (1947) The lack of cerebral effects of d-tubocurarine. *Anesthesiology, 8,* 1–14.

Smoke, K. L. (1932) An objective study of concept formation. *Psychological Monographs, 42.* (Whole 191.)

Snyder, M., and Jones, E. E. (1974) Attitude attribution where behavior is constrained. *Journal of Experimental Social Psychology, 10,* 585–600.

Snyder, M., and Swann, W. B. (1978a) Hypothesis-testing processes in social interaction. *Journal of Personality and Social Psychology, 36,* 1202–1212.

Snyder, M., and Swann, W. B. (1978b) Behavioral confirmation in social interaction: From social perception to social reality. *Journal of Experimental Social Psychology, 14,* 148–162.

Snyder, M., Tanko, E. D., and Berscheid, E. (1977) Social perception and interpersonal behavior: On the self-fulfilling nature of social stereotypes. *Journal of Personality and Social Psychology, 35,* 656–666.

Solomon, R. L., and Corbit, J. D. (1974) An opponent-process theory of motivation: I. Temporal dynamics of affect. *Psychological Review, 81,* 119–145.

Sontag, L. W., Baker, C. T., and Nelson, V. L. (1958) Mental growth and personality development: A longitudinal study. *Monographs of the Society for Research in Child Development, 23* (2). (Whole 68.)

Sorensen, R. C. (1973) *Adolescent sexuality in contemporary America.* New York: World Publishing.

Spearman, C. (1940) General "intelligence" objectively determined and measured, *American Journal of Psychology, 15,* 201–293.

Spencer-Booth, Y., and Hinde, R. A. (1971) Effects of brief separations from mothers during infancy on behavior of rhesus monkeys 6 to 24 months later. *Journal of Child Psychology and Psychiatry, 12,* 157–172.

Sperling, G. (1960) The information available in brief visual presentations. *Psychological Monographs, 74.* (Whole 498.)

Spitz, R. A. (1972) Hospitalism: An inquiry into the genesis of psychiatric conditions in early childhood. In U. Bronfenbrenner (Ed.), *Influences on human development.* Hillsdale, Ill.: Dryden Press.

Spitzer, R. L., Skodol, A. E., Gibbon, M., and Williams, J. B. W. (1981) *DSM-III case book.* Washington, D.C.: American Psychiatric Association.

Spuhler, J. N., and Lindzey, G. (1967) Racial differences in behavior. In J. Hirsch (Ed.), *Behavior-genetic analysis.* New York: McGraw-Hill.

Stampfl, T. G., and Levis, D. J. (1967) Essentials of implosive therapy: A learning-theory-based psychodynamic behavior therapy. *Journal of Abnormal Psychology, 72,* 496–503.

Stein, B. S., and Bransford, J. D. (1979) Constraints on effective elaboration: Effects of precision and subject generation. *Journal of Verbal Learning and Verbal Behavior, 18,* 769–777.

Sterba, R. (1951) A case of brief psychotherapy by Sigmund Freud. *Psychoanalytic Review, 38,* 75–80.

Sterling-Smith, R. S. (1976) *A special study of drivers most responsible in fatal accidents.* Summary for Management Report, Contract DOT HS 310-3-595.

Sternberg, R. J., Conway, B. E., Ketron, J. L., and Bernstein, M. (1981) People's conceptions of intelligence. *Journal of Personality and Social Psychology Attitudes and Social Cognition, 41,* 37–56.

Stevenson, H. W., Iscoe, I., and McConnell, C. A. (1955) A developmental study of transposition. *Journal of Experimental Psychology, 49,* 278–280.

Stoner, J. A. F. (1961) A comparison of individual and group decisions involving risk. Unpublished master's thesis, Sloan School of Management, M.I.T.

Storms, M. D. (1981) A theory of erotic orientation development. *Psychological Review, 88,* 340–353.

Stratton, G. M. (1897) Vision without inversion of the retinal image. *Psychological Review, 4,* 341–360, 463–481.

Strupp, H. H. (1971) *Psychotherapy and the modification of abnormal behavior.* New York: McGraw-Hill.

Strupp, H. H., Hadley, S. W., and Gomes-Schwartz, B. (1977) *Psychotherapy for better or worse. The problem of negative effects.* New York: Jason Aronson.

Stunkard, A. J. (1982) Obesity. In A. S. Bellak, M. Hersen, and A. E. Kazdin (Eds.), *International handbook of behavior modification and therapy.* New York: Plenum Press.

Suinn, R. M., and Bloom, L. J. (1978) Anxiety management training for pattern A behavior. *Journal of Behavioral Medicine, 1,* 25–35.

Sutherland, N.S. (1976) *Breakdown.* New York: Stein and Day.

Swann, W. B., and Reed, S. J. (1981) Self-verification processes: How we sustain our self-conceptions. *Journal of Experimental Social Psychology, 17,* 351–372.

Tagatz, G. E. (1976) *Child development and individually guided education.* Reading, Mass.: Addison-Wesley.

Tajfel, H., Flament, C., Billig, M., and Bundy, R. F. (1971) Social categorization and intergroup behaviour. *European Journal of Social Psychology, 1,* 149–177.

Tajfel, H., and Turner, J. C. (1979) An integrative theory of intergroup conflict. In W. G. Austin and S. Worchel (Eds.), *The social psychology of intergroup relations.* Monterey, Calif: Brooks/Cole.

Talbot, J. A. (1974) Stop the revolving door: A study of recidivism to a state hospital. *Psychiatric Quarterly, 48,* 159–167.

Taylor, D. W., Berry, P. C., and Block, C. H. (1958) Does group participation when using brainstorming facilitate or inhibit creative thinking? *Administrative Science Quarterly, 3,* 23–47.

Taylor, S. E., and Fiske, S. T. (1975) Point of view and perceptions of causality. *Journal of Personality and Social Psychology, 32,* 439–445.

Teger, A. I., and Pruitt, D. G. (1967) Components of group risk taking. *Journal of Experimental Social Psychology, 3,* 189–205.

Terman, L. M. (1917) The intelligence quotient of Francis Galton in childhood. *American Journal of Psychology, 28,* 208–215.

Terman, L. M. (1925) *Genetic studies of genius,* Vol. 1, *Mental and physical traits of a thousand gifted children.* Stanford, Calif.: Stanford University Press.

Terman, L. M., and Merrill, M. A. (1960) *Stanford-Binet intelligence scale: Manual for the third revision.* Boston: Houghton Mifflin.

Terman, L. M., and Merrill, M. A. (1973) *Stanford-Binet intelligence scale: Manual for the third revison.* Boston: Houghton Mifflin.

Terman, L. M., and Oden, M. (1947) *The gifted child grows up.* Stanford, Calif.: Stanford University Press.

Terman, L. M., and Oden, M. (1959) *The gifted group at mid-life.* Stanford, Calif.: Stanford University Press.

Terrace, H. S., Petitto, L. A., Sanders, R. J., and Bever, T. G. (1979) Can an ape create a sentence? *Science, 206,* 891–902.

Thibaut, J. W., and Riecken, H. (1955) Some determinants and consequences of the perception of social causality. *Journal of Personality, 24,* 113–133.

Thibaut, J. W., and Kelley, H. H. (1959) *The social psychology of groups.* New York: Wiley.

Thomas, A., and Chess, S. (1977) *Temperament and development.* New York: Brunner/Mazel.

Thomas, A., Chess, S., and Birch, H. G. (1968) *Temperament and behavior disorders in children.* New York: New York University Press.

Thompson, G., and Masterton, R. B. (1978) Brainstem auditory pathways involved in reflexive head orientation to sound. *Journal of Neurophysiology, 41,* 1183–1202.

Thoresen, C. E., Telch, M. J., and Eagleston, J. R. (1981) Altering type A behavior. *Psychosomatics, 8,* 472–482.

Thorndike, E. L. (1926) The measurement of intelligence. New York: Bureau of Publications, Teachers College, Columbia University.

Thurstone, L. L. (1938) Primary mental abilities. *Psychometric Monographs, 1.*

Thurstone, L. L. (1941) *The primary mental abilities test.* Chicago: Science Research Associates.

Tinbergen, N. (1952) The curious behavior of the stickleback. *Scientific American, 182,* 22–26.

Titchener, J. L., and Ross, W. D. (1974) Acute or chronic stress as determinants of behavior, character, and neurosis. In S. Arieti and E. E.

Brody (Eds.), *American handbook of psychiatry,* Vol. 3, *Adult clinical psychiatry.* New York: Basic Books.

Torrance, E. P. (1962) *Guiding creative talent.* Englewood Cliffs, N.J.: Prentice-Hall.

Triplett, N. (1897) The dynamogenic factors in pacemaking and competition. *American Journal of Psychology, 9,* 507–533.

Tryon, R. C. (1942) Individual differences. In F. A. Moss (Ed.), *Comparative psychology.* (Rev. ed.) Englewood Cliffs, N.J.: Prentice-Hall.

Tulving, E. (1972) Episodic and semantic memory. In E. Tulving and W. Donaldson (Eds.), *Organization of memory.* New York: Academic Press.

Tulving, E., and Thompson, D. M. (1973) Encoding specificity and retrieval processes in episodic memory. *Psychological Review,* 352–373.

Tyler, L. E. (1978) *Individuality: Human possibilities and personal choice in the psychological development of men and women.* San Francisco: Jossey-Bass.

Ulrich, R. E. (1967) Pain-aggression. In G. A. Kimble (Ed.), *Foundations of conditioning and learning.* New York: Appleton-Century-Crofts.

Underwood, B. J. (1957) Interference and forgetting. *Psychological Review, 64,* 49–60.

U.S. Office of Education. (1971) *Education of the gifted and talented,* Vol. 1. Report to the Congress of the United States by the U.S. Commissioner of Education. Washington, D.C.: U.S. Government Printing Office.

Valenta, J. G., and Rigby, M. K. (1968) Discrimination of the odor of stressed rats. *Science, 61,* 599–601.

Vandenberg, S. G. (Ed.) (1965) *Methods and goals in human behavior genetics.* New York: Academic Press.

Vandenberg, S. G. (1971a) The genetics of intelligence. In L. C. Deighton (Ed.), *Encyclopedia of education.* New York: Macmillan.

Vandenberg, S. G. (1971b) What do we know today about the inheritance of intelligence and how do we know it? In R. Cancro (Ed.), *Intelligence: Genetic and environmental influences.* New York: Grune and Stratton.

Vaughn, C. E., and Leff, J. P. (1976) The influence of family and social factors, on the course of psychiatric illness. *British Journal of Psychiatry, 129,* 125–137.

Vernon, P. E. (1975) *Intelligence: Heredity and environment.* San Francisco: W. H. Freeman.

Vierck, C. J., Jr. (1978) Somatosensory system. In R. B. Masterton (Ed.), *Handbook of behavioral neurobiology.* New York: Plenum Press.

Vincent, E. L., and Martin, P. C. (1961) *Human psychological development.* New York: Ronald Press.

Waber, D. P. (1977) Sex differences in mental abilities, hemispheric lateralization, and rate of physical growth at adolescence. *Developmental Psychology, 13,* 29–38.

Wade, T. C., and Baker, T. B. (1977) Opinions and use of psychological tests: A survey of clinical psychologists. *American Psychologists, 10,* 874–882.

Wallach, M. A., and Kogan, N. (1965a) A new look at the creativity-intelligence dimension. *Journal of Personality, 33,* 348–369.

Wallach, M. A., and Kogan, N. (1965b) *Modes of thinking in young children.* New York: Holt, Rinehart and Winston.

Wallach, M. A., and Wallach, L. (1976) *Teaching all children to read.* Chicago: University of Chicago Press.

Wallerstein, J. S., and Kelly, J. B. (1980) *Surviving the breakup: How children and parents cope with divorce.* New York: Basic Books.

Walter, B. (1946) *Theme and variations.* New York: Knopf.

Walters, G. C., and Grusec, J. E. (1977) *Punishment.* San Francisco: W. H. Freeman.

Watson, J. B. (1928) *Psychological care of infant and child.* New York: W. W. Norton.

Watson, J. B., and Morgan, J. J. B. (1917) Emotional reactions and psychological experimentation. *American Journal of Psychology, 28,* 163–179.

Watson, J. B., and Rayner, R. (1920) Conditioned emotional reactions. *Journal of Experimental Psychology, 3,* 1–14.

Waxler, C. Z., and Radke-Yarrow, M. (1975) An observational study of maternal models. *Developmental Psychology, 11,* 485–494.

Webb, E. J., and Campbell, D. T. (1981) *Nonreactive measures in the social sciences.* (2nd ed.) Boston: Houghton Mifflin.

Wechsler, D. (1975) Intelligence defined and undefined: A relativistic appraisal. *American Psychologist, 30,* 135–139.

Weiner, B. (1980) *Human motivation.* New York: Holt, Rinehart and Winston.

Weingartner, H., Aderfis, W., Eich, J. E., and Murphy, D. L. (1976) Encoding imagery specificity in alcohol state-dependent learning. *Journal of Experimental Psychology: Human Learning and Memory, 2,* 83–87.

Weintraub, W. (1974) Obsessive-compulsive and paranoid personalities. In J. R. Lion (Ed.), *Personality disorders: Diagnosis and management.* Baltimore: Williams and Wilkins.

Weir, M. (1964) Developmental changes in problem-solving strategies. *Psychological Review, 71,* 473–490.

Weiss, G., Minde, K., Werry, J. S., Douglas, V., and Nemeth, E. (1971) Studies of the hyperactive child: A five year follow-up. *Archives of General Psychiatry, 24,* 409–414.

Weitzman, L. J. (1981) The economics of divorce: Social and economic consequences of property, alimony and child support awards. *VCLA Law Review, 28* (6), 1181–1268.

Werner, H. (1957) *Comparative psychology of mental development.* (Rev. ed.) New York: International Universities Press.

Wertheimer, M. (1961) Psychomotor coordination of auditory and visual space at birth. *Science, 134,* 1692.

Whalen, C. K., and Henker, B. (1976) Psychostimulants and children: A review and analysis. *Psychological Bulletin, 83,* 1113–1130.

White, P. L. (1971) *Human infants: Experience and psychological development.* Englewood Cliffs, N.J.: Prentice-Hall.

White, R. W., and Watt, N. F. (1981) *The abnormal personality.* (5th ed.) New York: Wiley.

Whiting, J. W. M., and Mowrer, O. H. (1943) Habit progression and regression—a laboratory study of some factors related to human socialization. *Journal of Comparative Psychology, 36,* 229–253.

Whorf, B. L. (1940) Science and linguistics. *Technology Review, 49,* 229–248.

Whorf, B. L. (1956) *Language, thought, and reality.* New York: Wiley.

Wickens, D. D. (1972) Characteristics of word encoding. In A. Melton and E. Martin (Eds.), *Coding processes in human memory.* New York: Holt, Rinehart and Winston.

Willerman, L. (1978) *The psychology of individual and group differences.* San Francisco: W. H. Freeman.

Wilson, G. T. (1980) Behavior modification and the treatment of obesity. In A. J. Stunkard (Ed.), *Obesity.* Philadelphia: Saunders.

Witty, P. A. (1940) A genetic study of fifty gifted children. *Yearbook of the National Society for the Study of Education, 39,* 401–408.

Wohlwill, J. F. (1970) The place of structured experience in early cognitive development. *Interchange, 1,* 13–27.

Wolfe, J. B. (1936) Effectiveness of token-rewards for chimpanzees. *Comparative Psychology Monographs, 12* (60).

Wolfensberger, W. (1971) Will there always be an institution? *Mental Retardation, 9,* 14–38.

Wolpe, J. (1958) *Psychotherapy by reciprocal inhibition.* Stanford, Calif.: Stanford University Press.

Woodcock, L. (1976) Commencement address, June 5, Amherst College, Amherst, Mass.

Worchel, S., and Cooper, J. (1983) *Understanding social psychology.* (3rd. ed.) Homewood, Ill.: Dorsey Press.

Yalom, I. D. (1975) *The theory and practice of group psychotherapy.* (2nd ed.) New York: Basic Books.

Yando, R., Seitz, V., and Zigler, E. (1979) *Intellectual and personality characteristics of children: Social class and ethnic group differences.* Hillsdale, N.J.: Lawrence Erlbaum Associates.

Zajonc, R. B. (1965) Social facilitation. *Science, 149,* 269–274.

Zajonc, R. B., Heingartner, A., and Herman, E. M. (1969) Social enchancement and impairment of performance in the cockroach. *Journal of Personality and Social Psychology, 13,* 83–92.

Zanna, M. P., and Cooper, J. (1974) Dissonance and the pill: An attributional approach to studying the arousal properties of dissonance. *Journal of Personality and Social Psychology, 29,* 703–709.

Zigler, E., Abelson, W. D., and Seitz, V. (1973) Motivational factors in the performance of economically disadvantaged children on the Peabody Picture Vocabulary Test. *Child Development, 44,* 294–303.

Zigler, E., Abelson, W. D., Trickett, P., and Seitz, V. (1982) Is an intervention program necessary in order to improve economically disadvantaged children's IQ scores? *Child Development, 53,* 340–348.

Zigler, E., and Balla, D. (1983) On the definition and reclassification of mental retardation. Manuscript submitted for publication.

Zigler, E., and Cascione, R. (In press.) What the study of mental retardation tells us about the gifted. In *Proceedings of the Symposium on Intelligence.* San Juan, Puerto Rico: Inter American University Press.

Zigler, E., and Harter, S. (1969) Socialization of the mentally retarded. In D. A. Goslin (Ed.), *Handbook of socialization theory and research.* Chicago: Rand McNally.

Zigler, E., and Phillips, L. (1961) Psychiatric diagnosis and symptomatology. *Journal of Abnormal and Social Psychology, 63,* 69–75.

Zilboorg, G. A. (1941) *A history of medical psychology.* New York: W. W. Norton.

Photo Credits

Chapter 1 *Opener:* Arthur Tress/Photo Researchers. *Page 3:* The Bettmann Archive. *Page 4:* Hella Hammid/Rapho–Photo Researchers. *Page 12:* Alice Kandell/Photo Researchers. *Page 16:* Jim Anderson/Woodfin Camp. *Page 23:* (Top left) Dan Hardy/Anthro–Photo File; (top right) Ken Karp; (bottom left) Sepp Seitz/Woodfin Camp; (bottom right) Ellian Young/Photo Researchers.

Chapter 2 *Opener:* Suzanne Szasz/Photo Researchers. *Page 31:* Erika Stone. *Page 32:* The American Museum of Natural History. *Figure 2.8:* Arthur D. Bloom, M.D., University of Michigan Medical School. *Page 46:* Alice Kandell/Photo Researchers. *Page 49:* Ira Berger/Woodfin Camp. Page 51: Enrico Ferorelli/Wheeler Pictures. *Pages 53 and 55:* The American Museum of Natural History. *Page 58:* Victor Englebert/Photo Researchers. *Page 60:* Erika Stone. *Page 64:* Ted Thai/ Time Magazine.

Chapter 3 *Opener:* Charles Gatewood/Stock, Boston. *Page 71:* Culver Pictures. *Page 79:* Bohdan Hrynewych/Stock, Boston. *Page 82:* Sybil Schackman/Monkmeyer Press. *Page 84:* (Left) Mark N. Boulton/National Audubon Society–Photo Researchers; (right) Donald Paterson/Photo Researchers. *Figure 3.14:* Courtesy Dr. James Olds. *Page 88:* Lynn McLaren/Rapho–Photo Researchers. *Page 91:* Courtesy Dr. Walcott Sperry. *Figure 3.19:* From "The Split Brain in Man," by Michael Gazzaniga, in *Contemporary Psychology.*

Chapter 4 *Opener:* Marjorie Pickens. *Page 103:* New York Public Library Picture Collection. *Page 107:* OMIKRON/Photo Researchers. *Page 109:* Photo by John Foraste/Brown Bulletin. *Page 110:* Joel Gordon. *Page 113:* The Bettmann Archive. *Page 114:* UPI. *Page 118:* Manfred Kage/ Peter Arnold. *Page 119:* Wide World. *Page 121:* Jason Laure/Woodfin Camp. *Page 126:* George S. Zimbel/Monkmeyer Press.

Chapter 5 *Opener:* M. C. Escher, "Relativity," Collection Escher Foundation. Haays Gemetemuseum, The Hague. *Page 142:* Photo by Joe Wrinn. Courtesy Harvard University News Office. *Page 147:* Michael Stratford. *Figure 5.10:* Reproduced with permission of the Trustees of the Pierpont Morgan Library. *Page 150:* (Top) George W. Gardner/Stock, Boston; *Figure 5.12:* William Reaves/EPA-Documerica; *Figure 5.13:* American Meteorite Lab. *Page 151:* M. C. Escher, "Waterfall." Collection Haays Gemetemuseum, The Hague. *Page 155:* Kathy Bendo. *Page 156:* Georg Gerster/Rapho–Photo Researchers. *Figure 5.24:* Photos by Philip Clark, from R. L. Gregory, *The Intelligent Eye,* George Weidenfeld and Nicolson, Ltd., London. *Page 158:* The William Hood Dunwoody Fund, The Minneapolis Institute of Arts. *Page 162:* Courtesy Eleanor Gibson, Cornell University Department of Psychology. *Page 163:* William Vandervert, from *Scientific American,* April 1960 and July 1962. *Figure 5.29:* Courtesy Dr. Tiffany M. Field. *Page 166:* Courtesy Richard M. Held, Massachusetts Institute of Technology. *Figure 5.30:* Courtesy Dr. Allen Hein, Massachusetts Institute of Technology.

Chapter 6 *Opener:* Jim Anderson/Woodfin Camp. *Page 175:* Abigail Heyman/Archive Pictures. *Page 176:* Joel Gordon. *Page 183:* (Top) Courtesy Allan Paivio; (bottom) Courtesy Walter Kintsch, University of Colorado. *Page 184:* Pat Baggett. *Page 186:* Courtesy Elizabeth Loftus. *Page 187:* Raimondo Borea/Art Resource. *Page 190:* National Library of Medicine.

Chapter 7 *Opener:* Marc and Evelyn Bernheim/Woodfin Camp. *Figures 7.1 and 7.2:* Courtesy Dr. A. M. Liberman, Haskins Laboratory and University of Connecticut. *Page 215:* From Karl von Frisch, "Decoding the Language of the Bee," *Science, 185,* (August 23, 1974), 663–668. Copyright © 1974, by The American Association for the Advancement of Science. *Figure 7.8:* Courtesy Dr. Beatrice Gardner, Yerkes Primate Research Center of Emory University. *Pages 218 and 219:* Courtesy Duane Rumbaugh. *Page 220:* Susan Kuklen/Photo Researchers. *Page 222:* Courtesy Princeton University. *Page 224:* Suzanne Szasz. *Page 231:* Walter Chandoha. *Page 233:* Pro Pix/ Monkmeyer Press.

Chapter 8 *Opener:* Peter Angelo Simon/Photo Researchers. *Page 247:* Culver Pictures. *Page 250:* Suzanne Szasz. *Page 251:* Public Information Office, Teachers College. *Page 252:* Kathy Bendo. *Figure 8.7:* Harvey S. Zucker. *Figure 8.8:* Ken Karp. *Page 255:* Robert Goldstein/Photo Researchers. *Page 256:* Stella Kupferberg. *Page 260:* Elliot Erwitt/Magnum. *Page 266:* Yerkes Primate Research Center of Emory University. *Page 267:* Courtesy Dr. Robert Liberman.

Chapter 9 *Opener:* Leslie Wong/Archive Pictures. *Page 280:* Richard Kalvar/Magnum. *Page 283:* Susan Rosenberg/Photo Researchers. *Page 291:* Erika Stone. *Page 294:* UPI. *Page 295:*

Svenskt Pressfoto/Keystone Press Agency. *Page 297:* Nina Leon/Life Magazine, © Time, Inc. *Figure 9.6:* Courtesy Eckhard H. Hess, University of Chicago. *Page 299:* Michael Mauney/People Weekly, © 1978 Time, Inc. *Figures 9.8, 9.9, and 9.10:* Courtesy Dr. Harry F. Harlow, Regional Primate Research Center. *Page 301:* Courtesy Hallmark Cards. *Page 302:* (Top) Alex Webb/Magnum; (bottom) Anestis Diakipoulos/Stock, Boston.

Chapter 10 *Opener:* Costa Manos/Magnum. *Page 305:* Karsh, Ottawa/Woodfin Camp. *Page 312:* Courtesy Jerome Kagan. *Page 313:* Suzanne Szasz. *Page 314:* Gilles Peress/Magnum. *Page 317:* (Top) Costa Manos/Magnum; (bottom) Russell Abraham/Stock, Boston. *Page 318:* Peter Vandermark/Stock, Boston. *Page 320:* UPI. *Page 321:* Scott Goldsmith/Black Star.

Chapter 11 *Opener:* Suzanne Szasz. *Page 340:* Gerry Cranham/Rapho–Photo Researchers. *Figure 11.11:* Courtesy Ann and Will Branch and Elizabeth Katz. *Page 349:* Harvard University News Office. *Page 352:* Yaesde Braine/Black Star. *Page 355:* Irene Bayer/Monkmeyer Press. *Figure 11.14:* From Rita Devries, 1969, p. 89. *Page 357:* Erika Stone. *Page 360:* Burt Glinn/Magnum. *Page 362:* Lynn McLaren/Rapho–Photo Researchers. *Pages 365 and 367:* Suzanne Szasz.

Chapter 12 *Opener:* Hella Hammid/Photo Researchers. *Page 372:* Courtesy Duke University Archives. *Page 373:* Erika Stone/Peter Arnold. *Page 376:* (Left) UNC News Bureau; (bottom) Ken Karp. *Pages 381 and 386:* Suzanne Szasz. *Page 387:* Courtesy University of Virginia. *Page 389:* Marjorie Pickens. *Page 394:* The Advertising Council. *Page 397:* Erika Stone/Peter Arnold.

Chapter 13 *Opener:* Susan Lapides/Design Conceptions. *Page 406:* The Bettmann Archive. *Page 407:* Courtesy David Wechsler. *Page 409:* (Right) Sepp Seitz/Woodfin Camp; (bottom) Drawing by CEM; © 1974, by The New Yorker Magazine, Inc.. *Page 416:* Yale University Library. *Figure 13.9:* Reproduced courtesy Stoelting Company. *Figure 13.14:* Copyright © 1943, by the President and Fellows of Harvard College, 1971 by Henry A. Murphy. *Page 432:* Courtesy Dr. Henri Ellenberger, University of Montreal. *Figure 13.15:* Courtesy Department of Psychology, Duke University.

Chapter 14 *Opener:* Owen Franken/Stock, Boston. *Page 454:* Sybil Shelton/Peter Arnold. *Page 456:* Earl Dotter/Archive Pictures. *Page 459:* Sybil Shelton/Peter Arnold. *Page 460:* Bruce Roberts/Rapho–Photo Researchers. *Page 466:* (Top left) The Bettmann Archive; (top right) AIP Niels Bohr Library; (bottom left) Dan Budnik/Woodfin Camp; (bottom right) Culver Pictures. *Page 471:* (Top left) The New York Public Library at Lincoln Center; (top right) TIME-LIFE Picture Agency; (bottom left) Courtesy The Washington Post; (bottom right) UPI. *Page 476:* Hans Namuth/Photo Researchers.

Chapter 15 *Opener:* Chester Higgins, Jr./Photo Researchers. *Page 482:* Harvard University News Office. *Page 483:* Courtesy Professor Raymond Cattell, University of Illinois. *Page 486:* Barbara Rios/Photo Researchers. *Page 487:* Courtesy H. J. Eysenck, The Maudsley Hospital. *Page 490:* Max Haberstadt. *Page 491:* Frontispiece from *The Story of Anna O,* by Lucy Freeman. New York: Walker and Company, 1972. *Page 496:* National Library of Medicine. *Page 497:* Courtesy Alfred Adler Consultation Center. *Page 498:* The Bettmann Archive. *Page 499:* (Top) Photo by Jon Erikson; (bottom) Alex Harris/Archive Pictures. *Page 500:* (Top) Frostie/Woodfin Camp; (center) Marjorie Pickens; (bottom) Susan Lapides/Design Conceptions. *Page 501:* Hella Hammid/Photo Researchers. *Page 503:* Courtesy Albert Bandura. *Page 505:* Photo by Antony d'Gesu. Courtesy Carl Rogers.

Chapter 16 *Opener:* John Launois/Black Star. *Page 512:* Courtesy Stewart Sutherland, University of Sussex, England. *Page 513:* Culver Pictures. *Page 527:* Mimi Forsyth/Monkmeyer Press. *Page 529:* Gerald Martineau/The Washington Post. *Figure 16.1:* Courtesy Professor Arnold Ludwig. *Page 536:* Mary Ellen Mark/Archive Pictures. *Page 537:* David M. Grossman. *Page 541:* Raymond Depardon/Magnum. *Page 547:* Courtesy Dr. Paul Meehl, University of Minnesota.

Chapter 17 *Opener:* Joan Menschenfreund. *Page 552:* The University Museum, Philadelphia. *Page 553:* (Right) Courtesy Eliot H. Rodnick, University of California; (bottom) Roy Zalesky/Black Star. *Page 558:* Joel Gordon. *Page 562:* Plate 11 from *Berggasse 19: Sigmund Freud's Home and Offices, Vienna 1938, The Photographs of Edmund Engleman,* New York: Basic Books, Inc. Publishers, 1976. *Page 566:* Van Bucher/Photo Researchers. *Page 573:* Courtesy University of Wisconsin. *Page 574:* Courtesy Albert Ellis. *Page 580:* Courtesy Dr. Joseph Matarazzo, University of Oregon Medical School. *Page 582:* Owen Franken/Stock, Boston.

Chapter 18 *Opener:* Joseph Szabo. *Page 589:* Courtesy Professor Harold Kelley. *Page 598:* Marjorie Pickens. *Page 600:* Photo by Karen Zebulon.

Chapter 19 *Opener:* Marjorie Pickens. *Page 612:* Joseph Szabo. *Figure 19.3:* Wide World. *Page 615:* William Vandervert. *Page 616:* Gilless Peress/Magnum. *Page 632:* David S. Strickler/Monkmeyer Press.

Table of Contents Color Plates *Part One:* Erich Hartman/Magnum. *Part Two:* Dan McCoy/Black Star. *Part Three:* Charles Harbutt/Magnum. *Part Four:* Mel DiGiacoma/The Image Bank. *Part Five:* Martha Bates/Stock, Boston. *Part Six:* Joan Menschenfreund/International Stock Photo. *Part Seven:* Michael Salas/The Image Bank.

Author Index

Subject Index